International Handbook of Public Procurement

PUBLIC ADMINISTRATION AND PUBLIC POLICY

A Comprehensive Publication Program

1. *Public Administration as a Developing Discipline,* Robert T. Golembiewski
2. *Comparative National Policies on Health Care,* Milton I. Roemer, M.D.
3. *Exclusionary Injustice: The Problem of Illegally Obtained Evidence,* Steven R. Schlesinger
5. *Organization Development in Public Administration,* edited by Robert T. Golembiewski and William B. Eddy
7. *Approaches to Planned Change,* Robert T. Golembiewski
8. *Program Evaluation at HEW,* edited by James G. Abert
9. *The States and the Metropolis,* Patricia S. Florestano and Vincent L. Marando
11. *Changing Bureaucracies: Understanding the Organization before Selecting the Approach,* William A. Medina
12. *Handbook on Public Budgeting and Financial Management,* edited by Jack Rabin and Thomas D. Lynch
15. *Handbook on Public Personnel Administration and Labor Relations,* edited by Jack Rabin, Thomas Vocino, W. Bartley Hildreth, and Gerald J. Miller
19. *Handbook of Organization Management,* edited by William B. Eddy
22. *Politics and Administration: Woodrow Wilson and American Public Administration,* edited by Jack Rabin and James S. Bowman
23. *Making and Managing Policy: Formulation, Analysis, Evaluation,* edited by G. Ronald Gilbert
25. *Decision Making in the Public Sector,* edited by Lloyd G. Nigro
26. *Managing Administration,* edited by Jack Rabin, Samuel Humes, and Brian S. Morgan
27. *Public Personnel Update,* edited by Michael Cohen and Robert T. Golembiewski
28. *State and Local Government Administration,* edited by Jack Rabin and Don Dodd
29. *Public Administration: A Bibliographic Guide to the Literature,* Howard E. McCurdy
31. *Handbook of Information Resource Management,* edited by Jack Rabin and Edward M. Jackowski
32. *Public Administration in Developed Democracies: A Comparative Study,* edited by Donald C. Rowat
33. *The Politics of Terrorism: Third Edition,* edited by Michael Stohl
34. *Handbook on Human Services Administration,* edited by Jack Rabin and Marcia B. Steinhauer
36. *Ethics for Bureaucrats: An Essay on Law and Values, Second Edition,* John A. Rohr

37. *The Guide to the Foundations of Public Administration,* Daniel W. Martin
39. *Terrorism and Emergency Management: Policy and Administration,* William L. Waugh, Jr.
40. *Organizational Behavior and Public Management: Second Edition,* Michael L. Vasu, Debra W. Stewart, and G. David Garson
43. *Government Financial Management Theory,* Gerald J. Miller
46. *Handbook of Public Budgeting*, edited by Jack Rabin
49. *Handbook of Court Administration and Management*, edited by Steven W. Hays and Cole Blease Graham, Jr.
50. *Handbook of Comparative Public Budgeting and Financial Management*, edited by Thomas D. Lynch and Lawrence L. Martin
53. *Encyclopedia of Policy Studies: Second Edition,* edited by Stuart S. Nagel
54. *Handbook of Regulation and Administrative Law,* edited by David H. Rosenbloom and Richard D. Schwartz
55. *Handbook of Bureaucracy,* edited by Ali Farazmand
56. *Handbook of Public Sector Labor Relations*, edited by Jack Rabin, Thomas Vocino, W. Bartley Hildreth, and Gerald J. Miller
57. *Practical Public Management*, Robert T. Golembiewski
58. *Handbook of Public Personnel Administration*, edited by Jack Rabin, Thomas Vocino, W. Bartley Hildreth, and Gerald J. Miller
60. *Handbook of Debt Management*, edited by Gerald J. Miller
61. *Public Administration and Law: Second Edition*, David H. Rosenbloom and Rosemary O'Leary
62. *Handbook of Local Government Administration*, edited by John J. Gargan
63. *Handbook of Administrative Communication*, edited by James L. Garnett and Alexander Kouzmin
64. *Public Budgeting and Finance: Fourth Edition,* edited by Robert T. Golembiewski and Jack Rabin
67. *Handbook of Public Finance*, edited by Fred Thompson and Mark T. Green
68. *Organizational Behavior and Public Management: Third Edition,* Michael L. Vasu, Debra W. Stewart, and G. David Garson
69. *Handbook of Economic Development*, edited by Kuotsai Tom Liou
70. *Handbook of Health Administration and Policy*, edited by Anne Osborne Kilpatrick and James A. Johnson
72. *Handbook on Taxation*, edited by W. Bartley Hildreth and James A. Richardson
73. *Handbook of Comparative Public Administration in the Asia-Pacific Basin*, edited by Hoi-kwok Wong and Hon S. Chan
74. *Handbook of Global Environmental Policy and Administration,* edited by Dennis L. Soden and Brent S. Steel
75. *Handbook of State Government Administration,* edited by John J. Gargan
76. *Handbook of Global Legal Policy,* edited by Stuart S. Nagel
78. *Handbook of Global Economic Policy,* edited by Stuart S. Nagel
79. *Handbook of Strategic Management: Second Edition,* edited by Jack Rabin, Gerald J. Miller, and W. Bartley Hildreth
80. *Handbook of Global International Policy,* edited by Stuart S. Nagel
81. *Handbook of Organizational Consultation: Second Edition,* edited by Robert T. Golembiewski
82. *Handbook of Global Political Policy,* edited by Stuart S. Nagel
83. *Handbook of Global Technology Policy,* edited by Stuart S. Nagel
84. *Handbook of Criminal Justice Administration*, edited by M. A. DuPont-Morales, Michael K. Hooper, and Judy H. Schmidt
85. *Labor Relations in the Public Sector: Third Edition*, edited by Richard C. Kearney
86. *Handbook of Administrative Ethics: Second Edition,* edited by Terry L. Cooper
87. *Handbook of Organizational Behavior: Second Edition*, edited by Robert T. Golembiewski

88. *Handbook of Global Social Policy,* edited by Stuart S. Nagel and Amy Robb
89. *Public Administration: A Comparative Perspective, Sixth Edition,* Ferrel Heady
90. *Handbook of Public Quality Management*, edited by Ronald J. Stupak and Peter M. Leitner
91. *Handbook of Public Management Practice and Reform*, edited by Kuotsai Tom Liou
93. *Handbook of Crisis and Emergency Management*, edited by Ali Farazmand
94. *Handbook of Comparative and Development Public Administration: Second Edition,* edited by Ali Farazmand
95. *Financial Planning and Management in Public Organizations*, Alan Walter Steiss and Emeka O. Cyprian Nwagwu
96. *Handbook of International Health Care Systems,* edited by Khi V. Thai, Edward T. Wimberley, and Sharon M. McManus
97. *Handbook of Monetary Policy,* edited by Jack Rabin and Glenn L. Stevens
98. *Handbook of Fiscal Policy,* edited by Jack Rabin and Glenn L. Stevens
99. *Public Administration: An Interdisciplinary Critical Analysis,* edited by Eran Vigoda
100. *Ironies in Organizational Development: Second Edition, Revised and Expanded,* edited by Robert T. Golembiewski
101. *Science and Technology of Terrorism and Counterterrorism*, edited by Tushar K. Ghosh, Mark A. Prelas, Dabir S. Viswanath, and Sudarshan K. Loyalka
102. *Strategic Management for Public and Nonprofit Organizations*, Alan Walter Steiss
103. *Case Studies in Public Budgeting and Financial Management: Second Edition,* edited by Aman Khan and W. Bartley Hildreth
104. *Handbook of Conflict Management,* edited by William J. Pammer, Jr. and Jerri Killian
105. *Chaos Organization and Disaster Management,* Alan Kirschenbaum
106. *Handbook of Gay, Lesbian, Bisexual, and Transgender Administration and Policy,* edited by Wallace Swan
107. *Public Productivity Handbook: Second Edition,* edited by Marc Holzer
108. *Handbook of Developmental Policy Studies,* edited by Gedeon M. Mudacumura, Desta Mebratu and M. Shamsul Haque
109. *Bioterrorism in Medical and Healthcare Administration,* Laure Paquette
110. *International Public Policy and Management: Policy Learning Beyond Regional, Cultural, and Political Boundaries,* edited by David Levi-Faur and Eran Vigoda-Gadot
111. *Handbook of Public Information Systems, Second Edition,* edited by G. David Garson
112. *Handbook of Public Sector Economics,* edited by Donijo Robbins
113. *Handbook of Public Administration and Policy in the European Union,* edited by M. Peter van der Hoek
114. *Nonproliferation Issues for Weapons of Mass Destruction,* Mark A. Prelas and Michael S. Peck
115. *Common Ground, Common Future: Moral Agency in Public Administration, Professions, and Citizenship,* Charles Garofalo and Dean Geuras
116. *Handbook of Organization Theory and Management: The Philosophical Approach, Second Edition,* edited by Thomas D. Lynch and Peter L. Cruise
117. *International Development Governance,* edited by Ahmed Shafiqul Huque and Habib Zafarullah
118. *Sustainable Development Policy and Administration,* edited by Gedeon M. Mudacumura, Desta Mebratu, and M. Shamsul Haque
119. *Public Financial Management,* edited by Howard A. Frank
120. *Handbook of Juvenile Justice: Theory and Practice,* edited by Barbara Sims and Pamela Preston
121. *Emerging Infectious Diseases and the Threat to Occupational Health in the U.S. and Canada,* edited by William Charney
122. *Handbook of Technology Management in Public Administration,* edited by David Greisler and Ronald J. Stupak
123. *Handbook of Decision Making,* edited by Göktuğ Morçöl
124. *Handbook of Public Administration, Third Edition,* edited by Jack Rabin, W. Bartley Hildreth, and Gerald J. Miller

125. *Handbook of Public Policy Analysis,* edited by Frank Fischer, Gerald J. Miller, and Mara S. Sidney
126. *Elements of Effective Governance: Measurement, Accountability and Participation,* edited by Kathe Callahan
127. *American Public Service: Radical Reform and the Merit System,* edited by James S. Bowman and Jonathan P. West
128. *Handbook of Transportation Policy and Administration,* edited by Jeremy Plant
129. *The Art and Practice of Court Administration,* Alexander B. Aikman
130. *Handbook of Globalization, Governance, and Public Administration,* edited by Ali Farazmand and Jack Pinkowski
131. *Handbook of Globalization and the Environment,* edited by Khi V. Thai, Dianne Rahm, and Jerrell D. Coggburn
132. *Personnel Management in Government: Politics and Process, Sixth Edition,* Norma M. Riccucci and Katherine C. Naff
133. *Handbook of Police Administration,* edited by Jim Ruiz and Don Hummer
134. *Handbook of Research Methods in Public Administration, Second Edition,* edited by Kaifeng Yang and Gerald J. Miller
135. *Social and Economic Control of Alcohol: The 21st Amendment in the 21st Century,* edited by Carole L. Jurkiewicz and Murphy J. Painter
136. *Government Public Relations: A Reader,* edited by Mordecai Lee
137. *Handbook of Military Administration,* edited by Jeffrey A. Weber and Johan Eliasson
138. *Disaster Management Handbook,* edited by Jack Pinkowski
139. *Homeland Security Handbook,* edited by Jack Pinkowski
140. *Health Capital and Sustainable Socioeconomic Development,* edited by Patricia A. Cholewka and Mitra M. Motlagh
141. *Handbook of Administrative Reform: An International Perspective,* edited by Jerri Killian and Niklas Eklund
142. *Government Budget Forecasting: Theory and Practice,* edited by Jinping Sun and Thomas D. Lynch
143. *Handbook of Long-Term Care Administration and Policy,* edited by Cynthia Massie Mara and Laura Katz Olson
144. *Handbook of Employee Benefits and Administration,* edited by Christopher G. Reddick and Jerrell D. Coggburn
145. *Business Improvement Districts: Research, Theories, and Controversies,* edited by Göktuğ Morçöl, Lorlene Hoyt, Jack W. Meek, and Ulf Zimmermann
146. *International Handbook of Public Procurement,* edited by Khi V. Thai

Available Electronically

Principles and Practices of Public Administration, edited by Jack Rabin, Robert F. Munzenrider, and Sherrie M. Bartell

PublicADMINISTRATION*netBASE*

International Handbook of Public Procurement

Edited by

Khi V. Thai

Florida Atlantic University
Boca Raton, Florida, U.S.A.

CRC Press
Taylor & Francis Group
Boca Raton London New York

CRC Press is an imprint of the
Taylor & Francis Group, an **informa** business

Auerbach Publications
Taylor & Francis Group
6000 Broken Sound Parkway NW, Suite 300
Boca Raton, FL 33487-2742

Printed in the United States of America on acid-free paper
10 9 8 7 6 5 4 3 2 1

International Standard Book Number-13: 978-1-4200-5457-6 (Hardcover)

Library of Congress Cataloging-in-Publication Data

International handbook of public procurement / [edited by] Khi V. Thai.
p. cm. -- (Public administration and public policy ; 146)
Includes bibliographical references and index.
ISBN 978-1-4200-5457-6 (alk. paper)
1. Government purchasing--Handbooks, manuals, etc. 2. Government spending policy--Handbooks, manuals, etc. 3. Public contracts--Handbooks, manuals, etc. I. Thai, Khi V., 1941-

JF1525.P85I58 2009
352.5'3--dc22 2008011592

Visit the Taylor & Francis Web site at
http://www.taylorandfrancis.com

and the Auerbach Web site at
http://www.auerbach-publications.com

Dedication

To my wife, Xuan,

and my two children, Xuan-Thu and Edward

Contents

SECTION II: PROCUREMENT SYSTEMS

SECTION III: E-PROCUREMENT

Preface

This book is a response to the persistent suggestion of Dr. Jack Rabin, former executive editor of the Public Administration and Public Policy Series. I agreed to undertake this challenging project several months before Dr. Rabin's death in late 2006. It is challenging because its scope is extremely broad.

First, from the perspective of procurement organization, how can a book cover the procurement systems of all the countries in the world? Should it cover only national government procurement systems? Should it focus on only public procurement systems and practices in industrialized countries and ignore the same in developing countries? Should it also cover procurement systems of public international organizations such as the World Bank and its development bank group, the United Nations, the International Monetary Fund, etc., as these organizations have a pronounced influence on procurement practices in their client countries?

Second, substantially, public procurement has become a very complex function of government that handles a great proportion of public expenditures (which reach 70 percent of total government expenditure, according to numerous World Bank reports) and procurement expenditures (or "spends," a term found in numerous reports and publications). Indeed, public procurement is a system that consists of

- Procurement laws and regulations, procurement organizational structure (central procurement agencies, procurement offices in user departments)
- Procurement processes (from procurement authorization, appropriations to contract formation, contract administration, etc.)
- Procurement methods (invitation to bid or request for bids, request for proposals, request for quotations, etc.)
- Procurement techniques (life-cycle costing, evaluation, negotiations, etc.)
- Procurement professionalism and workforce

Third, the public procurement function of government is further complicated when public procurement, due to the size of its spending, becomes a policy tool that policy makers use to address social issues (helping minority/women-owned enterprises, and small and medium firms), economic development (local preferences), and environment protection (green procurement). These policy concerns have made procurement practices more complicated. Finally, the recent globalization movement has further complicated public procurement as procurement officials have to comply with not only national laws and regulations but also to international trade agreements.

Thus, despite its deceptive size, this handbook cannot cover the entire spectrum of international public procurement. In addition to the broad scope of public procurement, there are other constraints.

First, as we all know, public procurement has until recently been a neglected area of research. Consequently, getting a good number of submitted papers is always a major challenge. Fortunately, the international network that I have built via the International Public Procurement Conference and the International Research Study of Public Procurement workshops, including Professors Guy Callender (Curtin University of Technology, Australia), Christine Harland (University of Bath, England), Gustavo Piga (University of Rome Tor Vergata, Italy), and Jan Telgen (University of Twente, the Netherlands), has resulted in a good number of chapter proposals and full paper submissions. Second, chapters selected for this book had to be of a very high quality. A number of submitted chapters covering very meaningful issues failed to clear our rigorous review process.

Finally, I would like to thank the staff of Taylor & Francis for their attention to detail, the timeliness of their work, and their suggestions throughout the publication process. I am indebted to Rosalyn Carter, dean, College of Architecture and Urban and Public Affairs, Florida Atlantic University (FAU), for asking me to manage a new partnership project between FAU and the National Institute of Governmental Purchasing, Inc. (NIGP). In this partnership, I had a chance to work with Rick Grimm, chief executive officer, NIGP, to whom I am truly grateful for his belief that practitioner/academic partnership, and knowledge and innovation sharing elevate public procurement.

Khi V. Thai

Editor

Khi V. Thai is a professor at the School of Public Administration, Florida Atlantic University. Professor Thai has taught since 1978 (University of Maine, 1978–1990; and Florida Atlantic University, 1990–present). His expertise is in public budgeting, financial management, and public procurement. He served as a director of the School of Public Administration at Florida Atlantic University (1992–1996), and as a founder and former director of the Public Procurement Research Center at Florida Atlantic University (1999–2007). He organized a variety of training programs, particularly international training programs, and has provided technical assistance to governments in the United States and other countries in Africa and Latin America.

He is the editor of three academic journals (*Journal of Public Budgeting, Accounting & Financial Management*, *Journal of Public Procurement*, and *International Journal of Organization Theory and Behavior*); has served on editorial boards of eight academic journals; and has authored/coauthored and edited/coedited over 100 refereed journal articles, technical reports, book chapters, and journal symposiums and books. Seven of his twelve books are on public procurement, including *Introduction to Public Procurement* (2nd ed.) (2007), *Developing and Managing Requests for Proposals in the Public Sector* (2nd ed.) (2008), *Economics of Public Procurement* (2007), and *Advancing Public Procurement: Practices, Innovation and Knowledge Sharing* (2007).

Contributors

Edgar Agaba, MA, is an executive director and technical advisor of the Ugandan Public Procurement and Disposal of Public Assets Authority. He is a member of the Uganda Bar and has been involved with the World Bank and the Organisation for Economic Co-operation and Development in projects to strengthen procurement capacity in developing countries.

Alessandro Ancarani, PhD, is an associate professor of managerial engineering, in the economical, managerial, and valuation engineering section, in the Department of Civil and Environmental Engineering at the University of Catania, Italy. Ancarani's expertise is in public services sourcing, performance evaluation, service quality, facilities management services procurement, supplier evaluation, and E-public services. He was one of the founders of the managerial engineering program at the University of Catania, and he is the Italian representative in the management committee of the C18 Cost Action program in the European Commission. He is associate editor of the *Journal of Purchasing and Supply Management* and is a reviewer for several international journals; he has authored/coauthored and edited/coedited over 70 refereed journal articles, book chapters, conference proceedings, and books. Some of the books he has edited are *Sourcing Decision Management* (2005) and *Performance Evaluation in Public Services* (2003). He is member of the IPSERA executive committee.

Teresa Medina Arnáiz is an administrative law professor and public sector coordinator at the Institute of Public Administration, Burgos University, Spain. She has conducted training programs in data protection, procurement, and E-administration for local and regional governments in Spain. She has been a visiting researcher at Autonomous University of Bucaramanga, Colombia, at Sheffield (U.K.) and University of Paris II Pantheon-Assas (France). She is a member of the Alfa network funded by the European Commission and has participated in several research projects on administration, local government, and procurement. She has authored/coauthored several articles.

Sue Arrowsmith is a professor of public procurement law and director of the Public Procurement Research Group in the School of Law, University of Nottingham, adjunct professor at Copenhagen Business School, and a foundation professor of the Chartered Institute of Purchasing and Supply (CIPS). Her numerous procurement publications have been extensively cited by courts and legislators in North America, Asia, and Africa as well as Europe. Her authored books include *The Law of Public and Utilities Procurement* (Sweet & Maxwell, 2nd ed. 2005); (with Linarelli and Wallace) *Regulating Public Procurement; National and International Perspectives* (Kluwer, 2000); and *Government Procurement in the WTO* (Kluwer, 2003). In 1992, she launched the first international academic procurement journal, *Public Procurement Law Review,* and she launched the international, interdisciplinary series of academic/practitioner conferences "Public Procurement: Global Revolution" in 1996. In 2007, she was awarded the CIPS Swinbank Medal for thought innovation in purchasing and supply. She has taught university modules on international procurement since 1995 and presented papers in more than 30 countries. She has been a member since 1997 of the European Commission's Advisory Committee for the Opening Up of Public Procurement; is a member of the UNCITRAL Experts Group on Procurement; and has been a consultant and trainer for inter alia, the U.K. Office of Government Commerce, WTO, European Commission, OECD, European Central Bank, ILO, and Law Commission of England and Wales. She is project leader of the European Commission-funded Asia Link project for developing a global academic network on public procurement regulation.

Elmer Bakker, PhD, is a business analyst at Bath & North East Somerset Council in the United Kingdom, where he advises on procurement issues. Before this recent move, Elmer worked as a research officer at the Centre for Research in Strategic Purchasing and Supply (CR*i*SPS), School of Management, University of Bath. In this capacity he worked with many public and private sector organizations on procurement issues, the U.K. National Health Service Purchasing and Supply Agency, in particular. His research interests have focused on a variety of public procurement issues such as evidence-based procurement, the professionalization of procurement in the public sector, collaborative procurement, and E-procurement adoption. He has published several academic articles and book chapters and is a committee member of the U.K. Chartered Institute of Purchasing and Supply, West of England branch.

Benon Basheka is currently a lecturer and consultant at the Uganda Management Institute, where he coordinates short and long training programs in procurement and supply chain management. His expertise and research interest are in public procurement, logistics management, research methods, project management, higher education policy, and organizational behavior. He is a trainer for the Ugandan Public Procurement and Disposal of Public Assets Authority where he has provided training services in public procurement to both central and local government stakeholders. He has also provided consultancy services to a number of private and nonprofit and government organizations in the country.

Phoebe Bolton is an associate professor of law at the University of the Western Cape, South Africa. She has written extensively on the field of government contracts and government procurement and is the author of the recently published *The Law of Government Procurement in South Africa*. She is the recipient of numerous academic awards, including the Codesria prize for the best doctoral thesis in Africa in 2006, the Andrew Mellon Foundation fellowship, the Abe Bailey Travel Bursary, and most recently the DAAD scholarship for young academics and scientists. The latter award is enabling her to pursue research in Germany on government procurement and the protection of the environment.

Alistair Brandon-Jones, PhD, is a lecturer in operations and supply management at the University of Bath, United Kingdom. His current research interests are in E-procurement implementation, service quality, and supply strategy, and he is the U.K. lead member for the International Purchasing Survey. His teaching expertise is in the areas of operations management, service operations, design and innovation, and supply chain management. Alistair has published in the *International Journal of Operations & Production Management*, *Journal of Purchasing & Supply Management*, and *Journal of Public Procurement*, and has contributed to the fourth and fifth editions of *Operations Management* by Slack, Chambers, and Johnston.

Giuseppe Bruno is an associate professor of operational research, Department of Business and Managerial Engineering, University of Naples Federico II, Italy. His research interests lie mainly in the fields of location and transportation planning, network design, logistics, and multicriteria analysis. He is associated with many national and international research institutes (National Research Council [CNR], Naples, Italy; Centre de Recherche sur le Transports, Montreal, Canada). Currently, he is the chair of the Italian Operation Research Society for Campania. He has authored several books and published papers in national and international journals.

William A. Buehring is a senior consultant at the Decision and Information Sciences Division, Argonne National Laboratory, where he served as a member of the technical staff from 1977 to 2000. His expertise is in critical infrastructure analysis, decision analysis applications, and energy systems analysis. He has served as a senior staffer at the President's Commission on Critical Infrastructure Protection (1996–1997) and has recently been involved in critical infrastructure protection in support of the U.S. Department of Homeland Security. He has authored over 80 publications, including journal articles, book contributions, international guide books, reports, and conference papers.

Nigel Caldwell is a research fellow, Centre for Research in Strategic Purchasing and Supply, University of Bath, United Kingdom. He gained practical experience by working in the automotive industry. His research includes emergency ambulance services, PFI in hospital construction and in military aerospace, transformation of organizations into service-based business models because of their major products, ensuring continual innnovation in established relationships and the risks involved, and asset management support and creation and maintenance of contestable markets with the help of new technologies. He has authored/coauthored several refereed articles, is editor of *Procuring Complex Performance* (forthcoming), and serves on the editorial board of the *Journal of Purchasing and Supply Management*. His coauthored paper won the best paper prize at the inaugural International Public Procurement Conference in 2004, Florida.

Guy C. Callender is a professor and chair of leadership in strategic procurement, Curtin Business School, Curtin University of Technology, Perth, Australia. Callender has had careers in banking and finance, tertiary education, and the building industry before joining the University of Technology, Sydney (1991–2002), and Curtin University of Technology (2002–present). His expertise is in accounting, organizational behavior, and procurement. He is the principal of the Asia-Pacific Procurement Research Group at Curtin University of Technology. He is the editor of the *Journal of Contemporary Issues in Business and Government*, and serves on the editorial board of several journals. He is an active author of refereed journal articles, technical reports, books, book chapters, and monographs, and is a member of the Research Committee of the National Institute of Governmental Purchasing, Inc. In 2007, Guy was appointed a fellow of the Chartered Institute of Purchasing and Supply.

Charles H. Coates, Jr. served in the U.S. Army Corps of Engineers from 1957 to 1978 in a variety of staff, engineering, and command positions, and entered private consulting civil engineering practice in Baton Rouge, Louisiana, until retirement in 1997. He possesses a wide range of experience in the construction and design of roadways, waterways, wastewater, transportation, and other areas, including engineering management. His main interest is in forensic engineering.

Simon Croom, CIPS research fellow, is executive director and professor of supply chain management at the University of San Diego, California. His research interests include E-business, strategic management, and supply chain management.

Csaba Csáki is a lecturer at the University College Cork, Ireland, where he is also a PhD candidate. He worked for Bell Northern Research as a senior research analyst and development manager (1993–2000). He worked as a research fellow at the Budapest University of Technology and Economics, Hungary, from 2001 to 2007. His recent research interest covers decision methodologies and decision support systems, with a special focus on how the changing regulatory environment—mainly changes to the laws of public procurement—affects the decision-making practice of large organizations. He has organized various vocational training programs in Hungary. He is a regular reviewer for journals, a guest editor for an issue of the *Journal of Decision Systems*, a member of the International Research Study of Public Procurement workshops program and of the Decision Support Systems Working Group of the International Federation of Information Processing (IFIP WG 8.3). He regularly presents papers at major conferences in the areas of both decision support and public procurement.

Donald R. Deis is the Ennis and Virginia Joslin endowed chair in accounting and interim chair of the accounting and business law department, Texas A&M University, Corpus Christi. He has previously taught at Louisiana State University and at the University of Missouri, Columbia. He served as president of the government and nonprofit section of the American Accounting Association (2001–2002), as a member of the AICPA's Government Performance and Accountability Committee (2003–2007), and as a member of the PCAOB task force on audit firm quality standards (2006–2007). He is on the editorial board of five journals and has authored/coauthored more than 50 refereed articles. His research interests include privatization of government services, audit quality, and auditor independence.

Ken Dooley recently retired from full-time employment after 32 years as a lecturer and senior lecturer in operations research at the Central Queensland University (CQU). He is now involved in consulting for manufacturing companies and in various research and education activities at a number of other Australian universities including Queensland University of Technology, University of Western Australia, Swinburne University, and University of Wollongong. In the last five years with CQU he managed two major projects—developing, setting up, and implementing a major development and training program for Queensland Purchasing, and the accreditation of the CQU degree in purchasing and materials management with the Chartered Institute of Purchasing and Supply. Recent publications include papers presented at various national and international professional conferences.

Sandra Dorobek is a PhD candidate and a research assistant at the Institute for Law and Management of Public Procurement at the Bundeswehr University, Munich. She graduated in national economics at the Ludwig-Maximilians-University of Munich. Her research focus is on public supply chain management.

Emilio Esposito is chair of the managerial engineering degree council and full professor of business economics and organization at the Department of Business and Managerial Engineering, University of Naples Federico II, Italy. His current research includes technology evaluation, ICT adoption and diffusion, technological evolution in the ICT industry, competition and collaboration among firms, technological relationships between large and small firms, customer–supplier relationships, E-procurement, and E-government. He is the author of more than 150 papers and books. His research has been published in several journals (French, German, English, and Italian) including the *European Journal of Purchasing and Supply Management*, *International Journal of Globalisation and Small Business*, *International Journal of Logistics, Research and Applications*, *Internationales Gewerbearchiv*,

Enterprise & Innovation Management Journal, Revue Internationale PME, Small Business, Technological Forecasting and Social Change, and *Technovation*.

Michael Essig is a professor and chair for materials management and distribution as well as codirector of the Institute for Law and Management of Public Procurement at the Bundeswehr University, Munich. His main research interests are strategic supply management, supply networks, supply chain management, public procurement, and economic theory, especially new institutional economics. For his dissertation, he received the Hans Ovelgönne Scientific Award of the German Purchasing Association (BME). Michael Essig serves on the review board of the *Journal of Supply Chain Management*, the *Journal of Purchasing and Supply Management, Supply Chain Management: An International Journal*, and for the Research College of the Chartered Institute of Purchasing and Supply (CIPS). He is the coeditor of the leading German scientific logistics journal *Logistik Management*, a member of the scientific boards of the German Purchasing Association and of the European Defence Public Private Partnership Association, and a member of the scientific committee of the Austrian Ministry of Defence.

Flóra Felsö is a PhD candidate at the University of Amsterdam, the Netherlands. She has worked as a researcher at SEO Economic Research (1998–2008) where she has been involved in contract research in the field of competition and regulation. She has published book chapters on the law and economics of procurements, on disclosure limitation methods, and on the liberalization of postal services.

Cao Fuguo is a professor of law at Law School, Central University of Finance and Economics (CUFE), Beijing, China, and director, the International Research Center for Law and Economics, China Public Procurement Research Group, and the EU Asia-link Program on public procurement regulation at CUFE. He is an expert group member and a Chinese delegate to the working group with respect to the revision of the UNCITRAL Model Law on Government Procurement and also a World Bank expert with respect to Chinese procurement law reforms. He is a member of the expert group of the *Chinese Public Procurement Journal* and of the editorial board of the U.K.-based *Public Procurement Law Review*. Cao is an expert on Chinese bidding law, Chinese government procurement law, law and policy in private finance in infrastructure and utilities, international government procurement laws (such as WTO-GPA), corporate law, and government contract law. He has directed and has been directing about ten research projects awarded by international and domestic institutions with respect to different areas of government procurement law. His publications include *Government Procurement Regulation: International Standards and Practice* (1998), *Theory and Practice of Chinese Bidding Law* (2002), *Annotation to the Chinese Government Procurement Law* (2002), and *Corporate Governance and Minority Shareholder Protection* (2006). He has also published more than 30 articles in leading journals such as *China Jurisprudence, Legal Science*, and *Public Procurement Law Review*.

Péter Gelléri has a PhD in psychology and is a scientific advisor at Corvinus University of Budapest, Budapest, Hungary. He is the founder of an MA program in decision support, a cooperation among several EU universities (University College Cork, Université Pierre et Marie Curie Paris 6, and Corvinus University of Budapest), and is working for its realization. He is also the founder and head of the department of information and knowledge management, Budapest University of Technology and Economics (BUTE), Hungary (1991–2006). He was the founder and leader of a public procurement manager vocational education program (2003–2006); head of the UNODC working group "The Sociological Mass-Media Aspects of Anticorruption Efforts in Hungary" (2003); founder and director of the research center for financial informatics (BUTE, 1999–2005);

and vice head of the department of sociology (BUTE, 1985–1991). He has a series of technical patents (software and know-how) with applications mainly in the fields of public–private partnership and public procurement. He has been a cofounder and chief executing officer of a few university spin-off companies, with activities in the decision support systems development industry and consulting in the field of public procurement. His publications are mainly in the field of decision support systems. He is a member of the editorial board of the upcoming *Encyclopedia of Decision Making and Decision Support Technologies*.

Elizabeth Gibson has several years of management experience in the information technology industry, including responsible positions in engineering, project management, procurement, and international sourcing. As a consultant she has focused on business process reengineering, database development, and E-business. Elizabeth has served as an instructor for Portland Community College, the University of Phoenix, and the Northwest College of Construction.

Diane L. Gilbert is a procurement consultant. Her research interest is in the areas of public sector reform and governance.

Andreas Glas is a PhD candidate and a research assistant at the School of Business Administration at the Bundeswehr University, Munich. His research focus is on public procurement.

Francine Holloway is a senior contracts officer and the team leader for the office of technology team of the World Bank Group, where she is responsible for purchasing hardware and software and leading electronic commerce initiatives.

P. Fraser Johnson is an associate professor at the Richard Ivey School of Business, University of Western Ontario, Canada, where he teaches purchasing and supply, and logistics and operations. Before accepting a faculty position, Fraser worked in the automotive parts industry where he held a number of senior management positions in both finance and operations. Professor Johnson is an active researcher in the areas of purchasing and supply chain management and he is the author of several articles that have been published in a wide variety of journals and magazines. Fraser is a member of ISM's education resources committee, currently is an associate editor for the *Journal of Supply Chain Management*, and sits on the editorial advisory board for the *International Journal of Logistics Management* and the editorial review board for the *Journal of Purchasing and Supply Management.* Professor Johnson's textbook, *Purchasing and Supply Management* (with Michiel Leenders, Harold Fearon, and Anna Flynn), published by McGraw-Hill/Irwin, is now in its thirteenth edition. In recognition of his ongoing research in purchasing, Dr. Johnson was awarded the ISM's senior research fellowship in 1999.

David S. Jones is an associate professor, Department of Public Policy and Administration, Faculty of Business, Economics, and Policy Studies, University of Brunei. His research interests include public sector reform, public financial management, government procurement, and land policy and administration. Previously, he held various academic posts in Singapore and elsewhere. These include associate professor, Department of Political Science, National University of Singapore; adjunct professor, School of Economics, Singapore Management University; and local director in Singapore for the masters in public administration program conducted by the Australian National University. He has published numerous articles in international journals in his fields of expertise, and essays in edited collections, as well as a book on land reform in Ireland. He has also undertaken extensive consultancy work in recent years and conducted professional training programs in Southeast Asia in policy evaluation, public budgeting, and government procurement.

Ralph G. Kauffman is an associate professor emeritus, College of Business, University of Houston–Downtown, Texas, where he was a supply chain management program coordinator. He has also taught at the University of Texas at Dallas, LeTourneau University, Texas, and the Berufsakademie Mosbach in Bad Mergentheim, Germany. Also, he has guest lectured at the Fachhochschule fur Wirtschaft, Berlin and the University of Stuttgart, Germany, among other institutions. In addition to his academic experience, he has over 27 years of industrial procurement and supply experience. His research interests include supply management and the organizational choice process. He is the coeditor of the sixth and seventh editions of the *Supply Management Handbook* and has served on the editorial review board of the *Journal of Supply Chain Management*. He has published numerous articles in various procurement, supply management, and general management journals. Over a 12-year period ending in 2006, he chaired first the Institute for Supply Management (ISM) Manufacturing Business Survey Committee and then the ISM Non-Manufacturing Business Survey Committee. In 2002 he received the J. Shipman Gold Medal, the most distinguished award presented annually by the ISM.

Jeffrey M. Keisler is an associate professor in management science and information systems, College of Management, University of Massachusetts, Boston, where he has been since 2000. He previously had ten years consulting experience with General Motors, Argonne National Laboratory, and Strategic Decisions Group, and has been a consultant for government agencies including DOD, DOE, NRC, and EPA, as well as Global 1000 companies in pharmaceutical, energy, financial, and consumer products industries. He is an expert in decision analysis, with regard to procurement, project management, and portfolio resource allocation. He has published numerous reports and articles in journals such as *Interfaces*, *Decision Analysis*, and *Risk Analysis*.

Jason Klemow is an international consultant with over 15 years of professional experience focusing on collaborative technology, strategic planning, and project management. His expertise is in supplier relations management and E-procurement. He has authored/coauthored various journal articles with respect to business technology, international procurement, and project management. In addition, he has been a guest speaker for a variety of organizations including SAP ASUG, the Gartner Group, the Institute for Supply Management, and the Delphi Group.

Kai Krüger, dr. juris, is a senior professor at the law faculty, Bergen University, Norway. He is a member of the Norwegian Complaint Board for public procurement. He teaches contract law, intellectual property, and EU and EEA law on procurement in the EU Erasmus program. His publications are on the areas of contract law, sales of goods, consumer law, tort law, intellectual property law, and procurement law.

Stephen J. Larson is an assistant professor, School of Business, Eastern Illinois University, Charleston. He teaches financial markets, and his research interests are in stock market overreaction, international markets, and insurance issues.

Wendell C. Lawther is an associate professor of public administration at the University of Central Florida. He is currently the book review editor for the *Journal of Public Procurement*. His publications include *Capital Acquisitions: Decisions of Lasting Value* (with John Adler, 2007); *Privatizing*

Toll Roads: A Public–Private Partnership (2000); and an IBM Business of Government monograph, *Contracting for the 21st Century: A Partnership Model* (2002). He has also published numerous articles and book chapters dealing with public procurement, public–private partnerships, transportation policy, and human resource management.

Michiel R. Leenders is the Leenders Purchasing Management Association of Canada chair and professor emeritus, Richard Ivey School of Business, University of Western Ontario. He has written a large number of articles in a variety of magazines and journals. His supply management texts have been translated into ten different languages and include *Value-Driven Purchasing: The Key Steps in the Acquisition Process, Reverse Marketing, The New Buyer–Supplier Relationship*, and *Improving Purchasing Effectiveness through Supplier Development*. He has also coauthored nine editions of the case method texts *Learning with Cases, Writing Cases, and Teaching with Cases* and nine editions of *Purchasing and Supply Management*. Mike has taught and consulted extensively both in Canada and internationally. He received PMAC's fellowship award in 1975, was elected to the PMAC chair in 1993, received the *Financial Post* Leaders in Management Education Award in 1997, and the Hans Ovelgönne Purchasing Research Award in 2001. He is the director of the Ivey Purchasing Managers Index and a director of the ING Bank of Canada since its inception.

Knut Leipold is a senior procurement specialist at the World Bank. He works as an E-government procurement (E-GP) and IT procurement expert in the bank's procurement policy and services group (OPCPR). Knut has led the bank's efforts of providing support and advice in designing and implementing E-GP programs in numerous low- and middle-income countries. Knut chairs the E-GP working group of multilateral banks' Procurement Harmonization Initiative and is a member of the E-procurement working group of the European Commission and of the procurement expert group of UNCITRAL. He has developed E-GP guidance in line with the bank's procurement policy and has assessed several E-GP country systems for their use under bank-funded operations. He has authored/coauthored various journal articles and is a speaker at multiple international procurement conferences in America, Asia, and Europe. Before his more than seven-year assignment at the bank, Knut had worked as director in the public sector and as an E-government business development manager in the private sector for more than ten years.

Veiko Lember is a PhD candidate and a research fellow, Institute of Humanities and Social Sciences, Tallinn University of Technology, Estonia. His main interests are in public procurement, contracting and public management, and sports management. His most recent research project includes public procurement for innovation. He has provided consultancy for governments in Estonia as well local governments in Denmark, Finland, Sweden, and in other Baltic Sea countries. He has published several book chapters and journal articles.

Sabrina Leuger is a research assistant at the Institute for Law and Management of Public Procurement at the Bundeswehr University, Munich. Her research focus is on public procurement law.

Philip G. Lightfoot is a retired deputy assistant director, Department of Public Works and Engineering, City of Houston, Texas. His expertise in procurement, both public and private, spans a career that included executive and managerial procurement positions with the city of Houston, Texas, and with private corporations.

Robert E. Lloyd is director of the Regional Procurement Support Office in Fort Lauderdale and in his spare time contributes to the Public Procurement Research Center at Florida Atlantic University. He began his career as a buyer at the Defense Fuel Supply Center, Cameron Station, of the Defense Logistics Agency. He was a founding member of the acquisition policy office at the Navy's Military Sealift Command, director of the Acquisition Policy and Review Office of the U.S. Department of the Treasury in Washington, and served on the Civilian Agency Acquisition Council. Lloyd then returned to the Department of Defense as a procurement analyst for the now-defunct Defense Communications Agency, a senior procurement policy analyst at the Department of Housing and Urban Development. For the rest of his career he has been employed by the U.S. Department of State. He served on the interagency committee that drafted the commercial item acquisition portion of the Federal Acquisition Regulation. He has authored over 20 articles on public procurement and related topics published in professional journals and books.

João Nuno Veiga Malta is a senior procurement specialist at the World Bank. His expertise is in E-procurement and E-government. In 2002, he joined the Inter-American Development Bank as the program coordinator, Electronic Government Procurement in the Project Procurement Division. He led a variety of important initiatives and was also a member of several international working groups on E-procurement.

Lawrence L. Martin, PhD, is a professor of public affairs, public administration, and social work at the University of Central Florida in Orlando. Martin has published extensively in the areas of government procurement and contracting, particularly service contracting. He has authored/coauthored 20 books and major monographs and over 100 professional articles and book chapters. His works have been published by the National Institute of Governmental Purchasing, the National League of Cities, the International City/County Management Association, the Reason Foundation, and others. Many of Martin's publications have been translated into other languages including Chinese, French, Korean, Portuguese, Russian, and Mongolian. In 2007, Martin served as a consultant to the Mongolian Ministry of Social Welfare and Labor on the development of policies and procedures for the contracting out of government services.

Michele Mastroianni, PhD, is currently the system and network manager at the Second University of Naples. He has taught computer networks and database systems at the Faculty of Engineering of the University of Naples, Federico II. His research interests lie mainly in the fields of IT adoption and diffusion, technological evolution in the personal computer industry, performance analysis of computer system and networks, and IS planning and management. He has been involved in various organizational committees of national and international conferences. He has authored various papers published in national and international journals and conferences.

Darin Matthews, CPPO, CPM, is currently the chief procurement officer for Metro, the regional government of Portland. He has nearly 20 years of purchasing and supply management experience in state and local governments, as well as private industry, and has served on local purchasing boards in Oregon and on the NIGP board of directors since 2001. Darin serves on the governing board of the Universal Public Purchasing Certification Council and is an adjunct instructor at Florida Atlantic University. Darin speaks throughout North America on a variety of procurement topics, and his writings have been featured in *Government Procurement, Contract Management*, and the *Journal of Public Procurement*. He has authored book chapters for NIGP's *Logistics and Transportation*,

Warehousing and Inventory Control, and the *Encyclopedia of Public Administration and Public Policy*. He holds a graduate certificate in acquisition management.

Clifford McCue is an associate professor, and director of the Public Procurement Research Center, School of Public Administration, College of Architecture, Urban, and Public Affairs, Florida Atlantic University, Fort Lauderdale. He has published over 30 articles in the top journals in public administration, finance, budgeting, and public sector procurement. His articles have examined such critical policy issues as state and local government financial planning, evaluating organizational effectiveness, productivity, decision making and risk management, public employee behavior, and public procurement. In addition, he recently has authored four books: *Leadership and Management of the Procurement Function*; *Planning, Scheduling and Requirement Analysis*; *Local Government Budgeting: A Managerial Approach*; and *Immigration and Its Impact on American Cities*. Currently, McCue serves as a consultant for a host of international organizations and governments on public sector procurement.

M. Jae Moon is currently teaching at the Department of Public Administration of Korea University, Seoul. His teaching and research interests include public management, information technology, and comparative public administration.

Gary W. Moore, USAF, is an instructor at the School of Systems and Logistics, Air Force Institute of Technology, Wright–Patterson AFB, Ohio. His areas of expertise involve finance, acquisition, and risk management, and he has a master of science in acquisition management.

Sander Onderstal is an assistant professor of economics, University of Amsterdam, the Netherlands. His research interests include auctions, competition policy, and experimental economics. He has published on auctions in numerous journals such as *Economic Theory*, *International Economic Review*, and the *Journal of Political Economy*. Onderstal has advised several Dutch ministries and private parties on (procurement) auctions for welfare-to-work programs, gasoline stations, and frequencies for commercial radio stations and mobile telecommunications.

Joseph A. Pegnato is director, Office of Acquisition Management, U.S. General Accounting Office. His research interests include organization theory, federal procurement, and the applicability of entrepreneurial models in the public sector.

Armand Picou is an associate professor, Department of Economics and Finance, University of Arkansas. His teaching and research interests are in empirical time series, mergers and acquisitions, and anomalies.

Sharon Purchase is a senior lecturer at the University of Western Australia Business School, Perth, Australia. Her current research interests include buyer–seller relationships, business networks, and procurement. Her publications have appeared in *Industrial Marketing Management* and *International Marketing Review*.

Rupert G. Rhodd is an associate professor of economics in the College of Business at Florida Atlantic University. Rhodd has taught since 1986 (Iona College, New York, 1986–1988; and Florida Atlantic University, 1989–present). His expertise is in the areas of applied macroeconomics, economic modeling, and regional economics. His published research can be found in many journals including the *Journal of International Development*, *Journal of Policy Modeling*, *Atlantic Economic Journal*,

Quarterly Review of Economics and Finance, Journal of Third World Studies, Handbook of Economic Development, Applied Economics, Encyclopedia of Public Administration & Public Policy, and the *Indian Journal of Business & Economics.* Rhodd has also coauthored *Contemporary Issues in the Development of Caribbean Economies* (2007).

Kristi D. Caravella Robinson, a PhD candidate, serves as an assistant to the city manager for the city of Davie, Florida. Her areas of expertise include public budgeting and financial administration. Her research interest is in using communication strategies to enhance public administration and governance at the state and local levels.

A.S.M. Sajeev is a professor and chair of IT and computer science in the School of Mathematics, Statistics, and Computer Science, University of New England, Australia. His research interests are in the areas of software engineering and Web engineering.

Toru Sakane is a fellow, Japan Society for the Promotion of Science. He is a researcher at the Graduate School of Law and Politics, University of Tokyo, Japan. His main research interests are public procurement within the United Nations System, administrative and budgetary studies of the United Nations, international public administration, and also public procurement in Japan. He has authored a book (in Japanese), *Procurement Administration and the United Nations System* (2005), and several papers and journal articles.

Paul R. Schapper is an international development consultant with experience in more than 20 countries and was previously a professorial fellow, School of Business, Curtin University of Technology, and director-general of the Department of Industry and Technology in Western Australia. His research interests are public procurement, E-government, E-governance, and telecommunications for development. He is also on the editorial board of the *Journal of Digital Evidence* and has authored numerous publications.

Helmut Schneider is a professor and chairman of the information systems and decision sciences department, Louisiana State University. He has taught statistics at the Free University in Berlin from 1978 to 1983. He was a visiting professor to the University of North Carolina at Chapel Hill and the University of Arkansas in Fayetteville. He has published two books and over 50 articles in refereed journals and is a member of several professional organizations including the Association for Information Systems, the Information Systems Audit and Control Associations, the American Statistical Association, and the American Society for Quality. His research interests include operations management issues of the supply chain, risk analysis in information systems development, and risk analysis of traffic crashes.

Nigel Shipman was formerly head of the government procurement service in Hong Kong and has been a visiting lecturer at the Hong Kong Polytechnic University. He served as an advisor, Public Procurement and Disposal of Public Assets Authority, Uganda.

Keith F. Snider is an associate professor of public administration and management in the Graduate School of Public Administration and Policy at the Naval Postgraduate School, Monterey, California. His teaching and research interests lie in the areas of defense acquisition policy, defense project management, public organizations, and public administration theory and history. Since 2003, he has also served as principal investigator for a program of sponsored research on defense acquisition topics. In this capacity, he manages Department of Defense-sponsored research projects conducted at NPS and numerous other universities, in addition to conducting the annual Acquisition Research

Symposium in Monterey. Snider has also performed numerous research and technical assistance projects for several U.S. and international sponsors, including ministries of defense in Egypt, Chile, Bulgaria, Slovenia, and the Republic of Slovekia.

Corey T. Stutte is a planner for the Polk County Board of County Commissioners in Bartow, Florida. He is also a doctoral student in public affairs at the University of Central Florida in Orlando. His expertise is in public–private partnerships, governance, and planning.

Travis K. Taylor is an associate professor of economics, College of Business and Leadership, Christopher Newport University. He teaches courses in microeconomic theory, macroeconomic theory, international contracting, and defense economics. His research interests include international public procurement, contract theory, and industrial policy. He is an expert on the economics of offset contracts, and has contributed articles to journals such as the *Journal of Public Procurement*, *Journal of Policy Modeling*, and the *Journal of International Business & Economics*.

Kishor Vaidya is a research analyst with the Australian Government Department of Education, Employment, and Workplace Relations. Following the completion of his PhD from the University of New England (New South Wales, Australia), he has accepted the position of honorary research associate with the responsibility of supporting and guiding PhD students at the School of Science and Technology. His expertise is in adoption/performance measurement of interorganizational information system (IOIS), E-government/E-commerce applications particularly E-procurement, and public procurement. He has recently developed research interest in using IOIS for combating corruption in public procurement. He has published extensively in refereed journals and international conference proceedings and has worked with a number of Australian organizations including ANZ Bank, Qantas Airways, and the Australian Government Department of Finance and Administration.

Veiko Vaske has a BA in law, and is a member of the review commission at the Public Procurement Office of the Republic of Estonia, an independent body adjudicating public procurement disputes as the first instance of the judicial system. Vaske graduated from the Faculty of Law of the University of Tartu, Republic of Estonia, in 2003. Since then and until 2007 he served as a chief specialist at the public procurement unit of the Ministry of Finance of the Republic of Estonia where he was engaged in drafting public procurement law and implementing European public procurement legislation in Estonia. In May 2007 he was appointed to a 5-year incumbency at the review commission. He is also pursuing a master of public administration degree at the University of Tartu. His expertise and research interests are in public procurement law and European community law.

Mark F. Walkner is an administrative contracting officer for the Defense Contract Management Agency (Rockwell Collins) in Cedar Rapids, Iowa. He obtained a BS from Iowa State University and an MSc in acquisition and contract management from the Naval Postgraduate School. He served several tours of duty as an officer in the U.S. Marine Corps, including an assignment as contracting officer at the Marine Air Ground Task Force Training Command in Twentynine Palms, California. Most recently, he was deployed from his current position to serve as an administrative contracting officer in Afghanistan in support of army operations.

Edward D. White III is an associate professor of statistics, Department of Mathematics and Statistics, Air Force Institute of Technology, Wright–Patterson AFB, Ohio. His teaching and research interests are in design of experiments, linear and nonlinear regression, and statistical consulting, and he has a doctorate in statistics.

Chester G. Wilmot is an associate professor, civil and environmental engineering department at Louisiana State University Baton Rouge, Louisiana, and was a professor at Rand Afrikaans University, Johannesberg, South Africa. He served as a researcher for the Council for Scientific and Industrial Research in South Africa and was a partner in a transportation research consultancy there. He has published numerous monographs, research reports, and more than 25 articles in refereed journals. His research interests include hurricane evacuation demand estimation, traffic safety, data collection for transportation planning, and transferability of transportation planning data.

Chapter 1

International Public Procurement: Concepts and Practices

Khi V. Thai

CONTENTS

1.1 Introduction

Public procurement is continuing to evolve both conceptually and organizationally. That evolution accelerated during the 1990s as governments at all levels came under increasing pressures to "do more with less." Indeed, all governmental entities of rich and poor countries are struggling in the face of unrelenting budget constraints; government downsizing; public demand for increased transparency in public procurement; and greater concerns about efficiency, fairness, and equity. Additionally, public procurement professionals have faced a constantly changing environment typified by rapidly emerging technologies, increasing product choice, environment concerns, and the complexities of international and regional trading agreements. Further, policy makers have increasingly used public procurement as a tool to achieve socioeconomic goals.

In this environment, public procurement has become much more complex than ever before, and public procurement officials must deal with a broad range of issues. They have been walking on a tightrope in:

- Balancing the dynamic tension between (1) competing socioeconomic objectives, (2) national economic interests, and (3) global competition as required by regional and international trade agreements
- Satisfying the requirements of fairness, equity, and transparency
- Maintaining an overarching focus on maximizing competition
- Utilizing new technology to enhance procurement efficiency, including e-procurement and purchase cards

Procurement officials have to constantly weigh the trade-offs between conflicting procurement objectives, for example:

Quality and Cost Trade-off. Public procurement officials constantly face difficult choices between cost and quality. Should they pick Firm A, which proposes $25,000 for an item at a quality of 90 percent of the best item available in the market, or Firm B, which proposes $27,000 for a similar item at a quality of 97 percent of the best item available? Quality cannot be considered without regard to cost, just as cost cannot be considered without regard to quality.

Timeliness and Cost Trade-off. Assume that a public procurement official has two offers for an item. Firm A, a local firm, proposes $50,000 for a contract and will deliver the item within two days after receiving an order, and Firm B, located in another part of the state, proposes $45,000 for the same item, and it takes him or her two extra days as compared with Firm A. Which firm should receive the contract?

Risk and Cost Trade-off. Public procurement officials may decide to pay a higher price to a responsible firm than gamble on a firm that cannot affirm its responsibility. Likewise, public procurement officials may decide to pay a higher award price to a firm which based on an evaluation of his or her relative technical and business management strengths is more likely than a competitor to succeed in meeting the government's objectives. There may also be an inverse relationship between the goals of minimizing risk and maximizing competition. If minimizing technical risk were the only procurement goal, public procurement officials would tend to award only to firms who successfully performed the same or similar work on their previous contracts.

Socioeconomic Objectives and Cost Trade-off. Government entities often pay a premium, explicitly or implicitly, to accomplish socioeconomic goals. The Buy American Act authorizes government entities, under certain circumstances, to pay a higher price for domestic-made goods vis-à-vis foreign-made goods. On the other hand, socioeconomic programs, despite their cost, have arguably contributed to accomplishing other procurement goals. The small business program, despite its cost, has provided considerable work for small businesses and in doing so can be said to have been effective in creating new sources of supply, thus maximizing competition.

Competition and Cost Trade-off. The primary benefit of competition is its demonstrated success in reducing contract prices. On the other hand, this benefit of competition is subject to diminishing returns. And, the government incurs an additional cost for every offer it considers (e.g., the salary expenses of government workers who read the offer, technically evaluate it, apply price-related factors, and—if the offer has a reasonable prospect for award in negotiated acquisitions—discuss it with the offeror). This suggests that there is an optimum level of competition for any given acquisition. This is among the reasons that the Federal Acquisition Regulation now allows for "efficiency" in terms of narrowing the number of offerors in the competitive range with whom a contracting officer must negotiate prior to award.

In this chapter, a public procurement framework that depicts basic components of public procurement as a function of government will be presented. Then, implications of this framework will be briefly explored. Actually, this framework became a basis for the chapter selection of this book. As public procurement has been a neglected area of study and research (Thai, 2000), and as much attention has been focused on procurement laws and regulations as evidenced by the existence of such academic journals as *Public Procurement Law Review* (published by Sweet and Maxwell), and *Public Contract Law Journal* (published by the American Bar Association Section of Public Contract Law), searching a public procurement framework that reflects the scope of public procurement is a challenge.

In the remaining part of the chapter, more attention will be given to procurement integrity and corruption, a problem that has been recently addressed by such international organizations as the World Bank, the United Nations, the Organization for Economic Cooperation and Development (OECD), and major donor countries including the U.S. Agency for International Development (USAID) and the U.K. Department for International Development.

1.2 Public Procurement Framework

The United Nations viewed public procurement as an "overall process of acquiring goods, civil works and services which includes all functions from the identification of needs, selection and solicitation of sources, preparation and award of contract, and all phases of contract administration through the end of a services' contract or the useful life of an asset" (United Nations Development Programme, UNDP, 2007). Although procurement process is the heart of a sound procurement system (Harink, 1999), public procurement, according to Harink (1999, p. 15), "involves more than the procurement process alone" and it should not only consist of supporting, but also "important components" including strategy and policy of the organization, methods and procedures, personnel and organization, and information. In the last decade, several authors and organizations have suggested conceptual procurement models. The World Bank has developed a framework of procurement assessment under its "Country Procurement Assessment Review." This framework consists of four elements: legal framework, institutional framework and capacity, procurement operations and practice, and integrity of the procurement system. This framework provides basic guidelines or a procurement benchmarking tool for assessing the quality and performance of country procurement systems. Detailed areas covered under this framework include (1) legal framework, (2) institutional framework, (3) procurement execution capacity, (4) procurement procedures/tools, (5) control system, (6) anticorruption initiatives, (7) private sector participation, (8) contract management, and (9) system for addressing complaints (Araujo, 2004).

In the United States, the Government Accountability Office (2005) suggested a conceptual framework for assessing the procurement function that is based on four "cornerstones": organizational alignment and leadership, policies and processes, human capital, and knowledge and information management. Most recently, in 2006, the OECD developed a procurement assessment model, based on indicators from OECD-DAC (Development Assistance Committee)/World Bank Round Table, which was convened in the period 2003 to 2004 (OECD-DAC, 2006). The model consists of four "pillars" including legislative and regulatory framework, institutional framework and management capacity, procurement operations and market practices, and integrity and transparency of the public procurement system.

Analyzing the above models, this author revisited his previous model (Thai, 2001) and the revised model consists of (1) public procurement system and (2) a government framework and environment within which the procurement system is operated. The public procurement system can be operated effectively or ineffectively depending on its four pillars: procurement organization, procurement laws and regulations, procurement workforce, and procurement process and procedures.

1.3 Governmental Framework and Environment

1.3.1 Governmental Framework

The term "government" implies the organizational structure and leadership within a country. In this framework, public procurement is one of many government functions, and the procurement system can be prescribed in the national constitution (like in South Africa where the public procurement is provided in its constitution), or determined through procurement laws and regulations and through policy and budget decisions by legislators and the executive branch. It is important that the "public procurement system is mainstreamed and well integrated into the public sector governance system" (OECD-DAC, 2006, p. 20).

Organizationally, public procurement is dictated by the government system. In general, there are two major government systems: unitary and federal. In a unitary system, the central government exercises various levels of control over local governments in various countries, be it provincial or local governments. Local government procurement structure and process are dictated by the national government. For example, in Uganda, the central government regulates local governments' public procurement structure and process. An amended Local Governments Act was enacted in 2006 to provide for the replacement of tender boards of local governments with contract committees, and to regulate the procurement procedures of local governments.

At the other extreme, in the federal system, state and local governments enjoy a high level of autonomy. Each state and each local government are free to create their own procurement structure, methods, and processes. Thus, the public procurement system in the federal system is very fragmented; and there exists a great variation in procurement organizational structure, methods, and processes. The United States of America and Canada are an exemplar federal system. However, in many unitary type countries, too much centralization tends to hinder procurement efficiency.

Within a country, be it in the unitary system or the federal system, public procurement organizations at each level of government can be decentralized or centralized. A decentralized structure must be carried out within the context of a larger organization. In a survey of NIGP (1997) members conducted in 1997, 48 percent of the 700 responding chief procurement officers of local and state governments in the United States reported to the director of the finance department or equivalent; and 21 percent reported to the director of general services department.

In all cases, public procurement officials spanned the boundary between their internal clients and suppliers or contractors. Those who do it well pay particular attention to effective interpersonal relations and the active maintenance of a broad network of business contacts.

1.3.2 Cultural, Administrative, Economic, Legal, and Social Environment

As each country has its own culture and its cultural, administrative, economic, legal, and social traditions, adopting any preconceived procurement system is not effective and appropriate.

1.3.2.1 Economic or Market Conditions

Economic or market conditions have a great influence over the public procurement system's effort to maximize competition. Moreover, the market determines whether or not socioeconomic objectives of procurement are accomplished; whether or not a governmental entity can fulfill its needs; the timeliness of fulfillment; and the quality and costs of purchased goods, services, and capital assets. As there are different levels of economic growth among countries in the world, market conditions may be very favorable in industrialized countries, while they may be less favorable in developing countries. Economists classify three fundamental types of competition: pure, imperfect, and monopoly. At one end of the scale is pure (or perfect) competition. At the opposite end of the scale is monopoly. In between the two, we have a situation defined as imperfect competition, such as oligopoly.

Pure or perfect competition exists only under the following circumstances:

- Market contains a large number of buyers and sellers of approximately equal importance.
- Products traded are homogeneous (a buyer would not desire one particular seller's product over any other's).
- Buyers and sellers always have a full knowledge of the market.
- Buyers always act rationally and sellers are free to enter and to leave the market at will (Dobler and Burt, 1996, p. 297).
- Under this market condition, the supply and demand principle dictates the deal, and suppliers compete for business of a third party by the offer of the most favorable terms as to price, quality, promptness of delivery, or service.

But is it true that under a perfect competition market, "a buyer is able to achieve a solid value with little or no effort" as Fearon et al. (1993, p. 639) stated? Actually, in the competitive automobile market, for example, two buyers pay two different prices for the same type of cars, depending on their buying efforts and negotiation skills.

Imperfect competition occurs in the competitive area between pure or perfect competition and monopoly. Imperfect competition may occur in two forms. One is a market characterized by few sellers, commonly referred to as an oligopoly. The second form of imperfect competition may exist when many sellers produce many products. Most of the products sold in this type of marketplace may be distinguished by specific differences. Neither the buyers nor the sellers are able to dominate in such a marketplace, so they get together to achieve some sort of a deal. The key to generating value in this type of market is the ability of the parties to solve the problems themselves. To be successful, buyers must be aware of the marketplace in which they are working and be prepared to negotiate their best deals.

Monopoly is defined as (1) a situation where there is one seller and many buyers of a product that has no close substitution and where the seller has considerable over-price because of the lack of competition or (2) the exclusive right to carry on a particular activity. A monopoly exists when one company is able to dictate the prices, quality, and service. In practice, these categories are not mutually exclusive and may overlap. Even under a perfectly competitive condition like that in the United States, some supplies and services are required only by the government (particularly for weapons systems) and are not available in the market. This is a captive market which is limited in scope and competition.

Markets can be grouped into two types: stable and unstable markets. Generally, materials purchased in stable markets tend to be standard off the shelf supplies. In the long run, the supply and demand principle (perfect competition) will determine the prices for these items. In running their daily business, buyers should concern themselves with short-term market conditions. In the short term, prices for the standard shelf items may not fluctuate, but we may become aware of a decrease in some raw material price or a "price war" in some product area. We would like to obtain the benefits of such a decrease. The only way a buyer can have some protection against the short-term fluctuations is to develop contracts that have some sort of economic adjustment clause.

Unstable markets exhibit substantial short-run fluctuations. This market is typically dominated by raw materials such as oil, minerals, agricultural products, and animal by-products. The supply of these raw materials is frequently influenced by political forces, weather conditions, speculative financial actions, and other unpredictable reasons that are not governed by the laws of supply and demand. Normally, there are a large number of suppliers in this market and a large number of relatively small purchasers. This means that the actions of any one individual buyer or seller may have little effect on the price in the marketplace. The buyer should be aware of the timing of purchases and be sure to plan for fluctuations.

1.3.2.2 Legal Environment

Different from public procurement regulations and rules, the legal environment refers to a broad legal framework that governs all business activities, including research and development (regulations dealing with safety and health of new products), manufacturing (safety and health regulations at workplace and pollution control), finance (regulations dealing with disclosure of information), marketing (regulations dealing with deceptive advertising and disclosure of product characteristics), personnel (regulations dealing with equal opportunity for women and minorities), and contract law. Indeed, most aspects of contracts—public or private—such as contract requirements, disputes, and breach of contract are governed under the same contract law. In developing and particularly transitional countries, where legal systems are not comprehensive, government contracts may need detailed clauses defining basic principles.

As "contract administration includes all relationships between the Government and the contractor," (Cibinic, Jr. and Nash, Jr., 1995, p. 1) the legal rights and duties of the parties determine the proper course of action.

1.3.2.3 Political Environment

In a democracy many individuals, groups, and organizations in the private sector including trade associations, professional associations, and business firms or companies (commonly known as interest groups) are actively involved in all aspects of the public procurement system. Having various interests, objectives, and beliefs, interest groups are involved in the public procurement system in several ways such as lobbying legislative bodies to pass or alter procurement statutes, influencing implementation of these statutes, and influencing budget authorization and appropriation processes. Normally, a government program that is eventually adopted is a compromise among different views of interest groups, policy makers, and management. In this democratic environment, there are cases of a strong coalition of policy makers, bureaucrats, and interest groups in their effort to get their programs adopted.

However, the iron triangle shifts immediately after the procurement program authorization and appropriation stages move to the procurement stage. As failure or success in winning large defense contracts has a great impact on a company, specialized defense companies compete against each other for these contracts. Public procurement professionals have difficult choices as they face various political pressures and have to make sound economic decisions as well. For example, should they be concerned with maintaining future business competition by keeping some relatively weak companies in business, or should they let these small weak firms go out of business and leave a few specialized firms to compete for contracts? This issue is more common in developing countries where perfect competition hardly exists. Large firms are more willing to make a small profit margin or even to take business losses by offering especially favorable pricing simply to obtain the contract. After small and weak firms are out of business, the larger firms will enjoy an imperfect competitive market.

1.3.2.4 Social Environment

A free media, vibrant civil society, engaged local communities, and an independent citizenry are crucial components for good governance: they have a unique place with respect to holding procurement officials accountable for procurement transparency, fairness, and efficiency. Although procurement transparency can help to facilitate participation and oversight, more proactive engagement of society is also vital: (1) creating concrete opportunities for participation and oversight, for example, through participatory development of procurement regulations and policies, procurement budget allocations, civil society and media oversight over public procurement, monitoring of income and asset declarations, and other arrangements that empower legitimate social groups; (2) helping civil society organizations to build sufficient capacity effectively to take advantage of these opportunities; and (3) enabling the development of independent and competitive media that can investigate and report on procurement process, including corruption (World Bank, 2006).

1.3.2.5 International Trade Agreement

Markets become more and more globalized through regional and international trade agreements and treaties. According to Becq (2006, p. 3), public procurement is "an area where unification of laws is particularly advanced. Generally, standardization efforts are more pronounced with respects to the selection phase." There are various significant international instruments promoting standardization which affect different aspects of the procurement contract. Among the most important is the Vienna Convention on the International Sale of Goods which, unless specifically opted out, applies automatically to parties having their place of business in two member countries. In addition to the Government Procurement Agreement, the World Trade Organization's codes system includes other agreements which are relevant to procurement such as those on reshipment inspection, rules of origin, and technical barriers to trade.

Consequently, the public procurement system has to be adjusted and become more complicated; public procurement professionals face additional challenges including standard conditions, protest and arbitration procedures, and uniform rules of interpretation for various aspects of international transactions, communication, currency exchange rates and payment, customs regulations, lead time, transportation, foreign government regulations, trade agreements, and transportation. Thus, before embarking on a foreign purchasing program, public procurement professionals must carefully assess the total cost implications and compare them to domestic costs. Public procurement professionals are torn between free trade agreements and their countries' economic development/stabilization policies when they face a choice between selecting domestic or foreign firms.

1.4 Public Procurement System

In this author's public procurement framework, the public procurement system, operated in the environment described above, is built on four pillars: procurement laws and regulations, procurement workforce, procurement process and methods, and procurement organizational structure. This system is determined by the government and is influenced by its economic, cultural, legal, political, and social environment, as explained above. Conversely, the procurement system can influence its environment and the government framework.

1.4.1 Laws and Regulations

A sound public procurement system needs to have good procurement laws and regulations. In practice and theory, public procurement laws and regulations have been considered as one of the most important pillars of a sound procurement system, as evidenced in past research, publications, and practices.[1] Procurement laws and regulations lead to procurement efficiency or inefficiency. There was a debate about a procurement legal framework that hinders or helps procurement discretion.

Ideally, procurement laws and regulations should be clear, consistent, comprehensive, and flexible.

- Clarity, which requires the primary sources be carefully drafted to ensure that basic principles are clear but do not prevent the use of more efficient procedures or new technology. All procedural details should be included in implementing regulations consistent with the primary sources. Delegation of regulatory responsibilities at the central government, political subdivision, or agency levels should be clearly defined, as appropriate.
- Consistency, which can be achieved when procurement provisions contained in different sources are well coordinated (i.e., there is no overlap or conflict, the hierarchy of the sources is clear, new provisions are promptly incorporated, and outdated provisions are repealed).
- Comprehensiveness, which entails that all relevant aspects of the procurement process are addressed (there are no gaps in the regulatory framework which allow "personal" or "distorting" interpretation of aspects of the process).

- Flexibility, which requires that primary sources set forth only principles, basic features of the system, an outline of the procurement methods, and conditions for the use. Depending on local conditions, there may be several layers of regulatory authority, including agency issued codes or rules regulating aspects which are particular to the agency. Lower level sources should provide practical guidance to practitioners in carrying out their work and should be easily updated.

Public procurement laws and regulations clearly cover the whole scope of public procurement, all stages of the procurement processes, methods and procurement, ethics, and transparency. In addition, procurement laws and regulations have to be easy to be accessed by the public. Uniformity and universality of coverage contribute to predictability and savings in the operation of the procurement system, while access to the rules and regulations contribute to transparency thereby resulting in more economic procurement.

1.4.2 Public Procurement Organization

Section 1.3 discusses the public procurement system as a function of government in the government framework. In this section, public procurement organizational structure is addressed. In some countries there may be a central procurement office for the whole nation, such as Uganda, Kenya, etc. In other countries, public procurement organizational structure is very complicated. In the United States, at the federal level, although procurement regulations are applied to all federal agencies, the General Services Administration is a central procurement office for civilian agencies, except the Department of Defense that does have its dependent procurement office.

According to Choi and Hong (2002), managers in the private sector simultaneously face three different forms of structural complexity in supply networks: vertical, horizontal, and spatial. Vertical complexity refers to the number of hierarchical levels in the whole system (i.e., the number of tiers), horizontal complexity refers to the number of different entities in the same level of the supply network (e.g., number of suppliers in each tier), and spatial complexity refers to the average distance between operating locations. This statement is particularly true in government.

An essential element of the role of the public procurement department in a government entity is the placement of procurement authority. This is not to be confused with the location of procurement personnel. Centralization occurs when all of the rights, powers, duties, and authority relating to public procurement are vested in a central procurement officer. That central authority often delegates some of these powers to others, but the point remains that they stay with that central figure. Such delegations are normally carried out within a regulatory or policy framework by means of specific letters or memoranda to those receiving the delegated powers; they very precisely delineate the delegated contract approval authority in terms of dollar amounts and commodities as well as whether or not the assigned authority may be further delegated.

Decentralization occurs when procurement personnel from other functional areas can decide unilaterally on sources of supply or negotiate with suppliers directly (Dobler and Burt, 1996). Rarely is an agency fully centralized or fully decentralized; it is usually somewhere in between, often with very specific exceptions on a commodity basis such as contracting for specialized professional services (e.g., architectural and engineering, legal, medical services) arranged directly by the using departments. It should be noted that procurements of low dollar value goods and services by clients, procurement cards, blanket orders, or standing offers do not represent decentralization because the procurement system establishes those mechanisms and monitors their use. Indeed, the automation of these processes through tools such as electronic catalog ordering or applications using electronic data interchange really represents a kind of "virtual centralization." Procurement is able to achieve the benefits of enhanced control and better data for monitoring and planning through the provision of these kinds of end-user tools.

The Model Procurement Code (Article 2-201) provides guidance to address the need for a centralized purchasing structure through "Creation of the Office of the Chief Procurement Officer" (American Bar Association, 2000, p. 11). Delegation and control requirements are covered in subsequent articles of the same section.

When functioning properly, procurement centralization yields the following benefits:

- Minimizing duplication of procurements by central coordination
- Avoiding haphazard procurement practices and maximizing efficiency because procurement officials with professional training and expertise are more efficient than less skilled user departments' managers or operational managers whose procurement responsibility is secondary
- Saving operational managers' time so that they can focus on their core responsibilities
- Lowering overall transaction costs due to consolidation of orders
- Achieving volume discounts through the consolidation of procurements
- Reducing shipping and handling charges through the consolidation of shipments
- Receiving better prices and better services offered by suppliers because their sales, shipping, and invoicing expenses are reduced
- Resulting in more efficient inventory control because of agencywide knowledge of stock levels, material usage, lead times, and prices
- Facilitating procurement control and accountability

On the other hand, some potential disadvantages of centralized purchasing stem from any suboptimal relationships that may develop between the central procurement office and the clients it serves. Disadvantages might include:

- Lack of sensitivity to the unique priorities and operational realities of different user departments
- Insufficient engagement of the central procurement office in the operational planning process
- User departments' possibility of bypassing blanket agreements negotiated by purchasing because specific commodities are not included, thereby foregoing any advantage of consolidated procurements
- Overall increased processing time of requisitions
- Possible difficult procurement and project schedule coordination as the central procurement office has it own priorities and the project manager has his or her tight project completion time table

1.4.3 Public Procurement Workforce

A sound procurement system has to have a competent professional workforce equipped with defined skills and knowledge for specified procurement jobs (OECD-DAC, 2006). The procurement workforce "permeates virtually every effort within an agency, including successfully acquiring goods and services and executing and monitoring contracts" (Government Accountability Office, 2005, p. 31). Unfortunately, public procurement has been a neglected area of education. Not until 2007, was a college degree program in public procurement offered. Thus, public procurement personnel are mostly on-the-job training or from law schools. Moreover, countries such as the United States and Canada will face a major problem: the shortage of its procurement workforce due to retirement and job turnover, which could create an imbalance with regard to acquisition experience and skill sets. Thus, it is a challenging task for an agency to choose the right staff in the right numbers applying skills where needed to accomplish the mission effectively. Creating a procurement workforce with the right skills and capabilities can be a challenge, given changes to procurement processes, the introduction or expansion of alternative contracting approaches, and increased reliance on services provided by the private sector (Government Accountability Office, 2005).

Thus, governmental entities need to have a comprehensive training program, a comprehensive strategic workforce plan to profile the current staff, and projects staffing needs for the future, to hire, develop, and retain talent.

1.4.4 Public Procurement Process and Methods

Traditionally, public procurement has been perceived as belonging to the implementation phase of the budgetary process. In other words, public procurement professionals are responsible for executing the approved procurement budget. This is a very narrow view of the role of these individuals. In reality, for certain procurement types, particularly building and road construction projects, public procurement professionals can be valuable sources of information for sound decisions. For a better procurement plan, they need to know in advance, before the procurement budget is approved:

1. How many procurement projects will be conducted in the fiscal year?
2. How many procurement projects' budgets have to be spent in the fiscal year and will expire by the end of the fiscal year if they are not spent?
3. What projects are most critical for the agency's mission so that extra attention can be given to them?

Moreover, market knowledge on the part of public procurement officials will be critical to decisions on such alternatives as privatization or "make-or-buy." Finally, knowing how a procurement project is planned, authorized, and budgeted, public procurement professionals will be able to implement procurement projects effectively, efficiently, and economically.

In reality, procurement officials are involved in procurement only after agencies obtain procurement budget. The procurement process consists of many stages.

1.4.4.1 Procurement Planning

According to appropriation law, government agencies cannot spend until the budget is appropriated by the legislature and apportioned by the central budget office. But as procurement is a long and time-consuming process, contract planning should "begin as soon as the agency need is identified, preferably well in advance of the fiscal year in which contract award is necessary" (FAR 7.104a) by:

1. Forming a team consisting of all those who will be responsible for significant aspects of the procurement, such as contracting, fiscal, legal, and technical personnel
2. Coordinating with and securing the concurrence of user departments in all planning

3. Consulting requirements and logistics personnel who determine type, quality, quantity, and delivery requirements
4. Establishing standard acquisition plan formats, if desired, suitable to agency needs

The purpose of this planning is to ensure that the procurement agents meet the agency's needs in the most effective, economical, and timely manner. FAR also recommends that knowledge gained from prior acquisitions be used to further refine requirements and acquisition strategies.

1.4.4.2 Preparing and Processing Procurement Requests

Although the procurement planning should start well in advance of the fiscal year in which contract award is necessary, the real procurement action will not commence until the user agency prepares and forwards a procurement request (PR) to the central procurement office.

The purpose of a PR is to provide the procurement professional (or contract specialist or contracting officer, in the federal government) with the information and approvals necessary for initiating procurement. When preparing the PR, user departments should consult with the procurement staff. The more the user department consults with procurement professionals, the more precise the document will be. A procurement that starts with a defective PR is likely to be troublesome at some point in the process. For example, if a single source acquisition is initiated without justification and approvals, the action may later be protested and the entire process disrupted and delayed. Other consequences of a deficient PR might include:

- Need to cancel a solicitation because of improper approvals or lack of funds
- Failure to order an economic quantity
- Failure to include price-related evaluation factors in the solicitation

1.4.4.2.1 Conducting Market Research

Normally, the central procurement office researches markets even before developing new requirements documents for an acquisition by user agencies, before soliciting offers for acquisitions with an estimated value in excess of the simplified acquisition threshold, and before soliciting offers for acquisitions with an estimated value less than the simplified acquisition threshold when adequate information is not available and the circumstances justify its cost. The extent of market research and analysis will vary depending on the urgency, value, and complexity of the proposed acquisition.

1.4.4.3 Developing and Reviewing Requirements Documents

In preparing the requirements documents, agencies may select from existing requirements documents, modify or combine existing requirements documents, or create new requirements documents to meet agency needs. To demonstrate that an item has achieved commercial market acceptance, the criteria in the solicitation should reflect the minimum need of the agency; relate to an item's performance and intended use, not an offeror's capability; and include consideration of items supplied satisfactorily under recent or current contracts for the same or similar items.

Requirements documents include the specifications or statements of work and related elements of the PR. The procurement professional may accept requirements documents proposed by the requiring activities "as is" or recommend improvements.

1.4.4.3.1 Specifications

According to Thai (2007), a good specification contains the following elements:

- It identifies a minimum requirement.
- It allows for maximum competition (competitive bids).
- It identifies the test methods to be used to verify compliance with the requirement.
- It contributes to obtaining best value at the lowest possible cost using a fair, equitable, and transparent (easy for the public to see and understand) contract award process.

1.4.4.3.1.1 Types of Specifications—For the procurement of goods (rather than services), there are two main categories of purchase descriptions: detailed specifications and other purchase descriptions. Commercial standards, design specifications, material and method-of-manufacture specifications, and engineering drawings are types of detailed specifications. Performance specifications, brand name, brand name or equal specifications, samples, market grades, qualified products lists (QPL), and combination of methods are the types of specifications found in the category of other purchase descriptions.

Material and Method of Manufacture Specifications. This type of specification is used primarily by the armed forces and by the Department of Energy. Potential suppliers are told precisely what materials to use and how they are to be processed. The buying organization assumes full responsibility for the performance of the products acquired under this arrangement. Large buyers of paint would use these specifications to request manufacturers to add or to delete certain chemicals when producing paint for them. In the industrial sector, for reasons of health or safety, some firms dealing with chemical or with pharmaceutical products also use these specifications to describe their requirements.

Engineering Drawings. Descriptions by blueprints or drawings are recommended when precise shapes, dimensions, close tolerances, and a high degree of manufacturing perfection are needed. Drawings may be used alone, although normally they accompany other purchase descriptions. Machined parts, forging, castings, construction, and special mechanical parts and components are the types of requirements that would normally justify the use of drawings.

This is an expensive method of describing requirements, both from the point of view of preparing the information and from using it in the manufacturing process. The availability of the information in an electronic format and the capability of manufacturing systems to utilize the data should help reduce some of the costs while increasing the effectiveness of this method of describing and communicating requirements.

Performance Specifications. Performance specifications, also known as functional specifications, are probably the best method of describing requirements. Instead of describing an item in terms of its design characteristics, a purchaser using a performance specification describes what the item is expected to do. The purchaser is much less concerned about the material composition of the item and the way it is manufactured or assembled and much more concerned about its performance when put into use. With this approach to procurement, the manufacturer/producer/supplier is not directed to act in a certain way but rather is given an opportunity to use ingenuity and to innovate to provide (likely at a relatively lower cost) an item which will adequately perform a specific task. Although a high degree of precision and a lengthy text may be used to describe the required performance, suppliers are not told what material to use in fabricating the item nor told which manufacturing process to use in assembling it.

Brand Name Specifications. Brand name specifications identify, by name, model number, or other designations, a specific product manufactured by a specific corporation. One reason for manufacturers to brand a product is to sell that product at a relatively stable price, which is normally higher than that of nonbranded products of equal quality. End users usually have a greater comfort level with a brand name product. It should be pointed out, however, that there is normally a price to pay for this comfort. One example is a battery. Even though they know that the manufacturer of a very popular brand of batteries sells the same item as a no-name product at a lower cost, some users will still insist on obtaining the brand name product. The use of brand name specifications in purchasing goods simplifies the task of a purchaser. Inspection is also easier to perform because the brand is the quality ordered and expected of the product.

Brand Name or Equivalent Specifications. Brand name or equivalent specifications go beyond the traditional brand name specifications by demonstrating and emphasizing the idea that any brands or models substantially equivalent to the branded product(s) referred to in the bid invitation will be considered for contract award. The purchaser reserves the right of determining equivalency. Brand name or equal specifications must specify that the brands designated in the bid documents are for reference purposes only and must not be interpreted as a statement of preference.

Samples. The comparison and testing of samples can effectively substitute for a detailed specification in some instances. Generally, they are used when other methods of specifying a requirement are impractical. For example, it would be quite appropriate to use samples when specifying that a precise shade of blue is to be used as the color of the needed product. The alternative would be to attempt to describe, in words, the required color. Samples are often utilized when acquiring uniforms, badges, decals, footwear, bulletproof vests, and other items of this nature.

Combination. Many of the more complex products cannot be adequately described by a single type of specification. A combination of two or more types is therefore appropriate in such cases. For many requirements, the design–performance combination may be the best approach, with design requirements kept to a minimum while the performance characteristics are very detailed.

Performance Specifications. Performance specifications describe the deliverable in terms of desired operational characteristics. Where an item is purchased against a performance specification, the contractor accepts general responsibility for design, engineering, and achievement of the stated performance requirements. The contractor has general discretion and election as to detail but the work is subject to the government's reserved rights of final inspection and approval or rejection. This type of specifications tends to be more restrictive than the functional specifications, in terms of limiting alternatives which the government will consider and defining separate performance standards for each such alternative.

Design Specifications. Design specifications establish precise measurements, tolerances, materials in process and finished product tests, quality control, inspection requirements, and other specific details of the deliverable. The government assumes liability for the design and related omissions, errors, and deficiencies in the specification and drawings.

Standards. Standards establish engineering and technical limitations and applications of items, materials, processes, methods, designs, and engineering practices. Standards include any related criteria deemed essential to achieve the highest practical degree of uniformity in materials or products or interchangeability of parts. Standards supplement specifications and are generally incorporated by reference in the solicitation document.

Product Descriptions (PDs). PDs describe physical characteristics or functions required to meet the government's need. PDs are prepared when FED Specs or MIL Specs are inapplicable or do not fully cover the requirement.

Services. There are two primary types of descriptions of services: the statement of work and the performance work statement.

- *Statement of Work* (*SOW*). A SOW describes the contract work to be performed and incorporates any applicable specifications. The scope and elements of a SOW vary greatly depending on what is being procured. A SOW for a major system may be complex, quite long, and incorporate numerous specifications. A SOW for lawn-mowing service, however, can be fairly simple and short. The SOW may or may not incorporate any specifications regarding products or equipment used in providing the service.
- *Performance Work Statement* (*PWS*). In recent years, public procurement has seen an *increased* emphasis on promoting better contract results through performance-based service contracting/acquisition (PBSC or PBSA). The heart of such a contract is the PWS that defines the specific performance required of the contractor, including standards to be met and a surveillance plan for the government to use in monitoring the work.
- *Statement of Objectives* (*SOO*). The SOO approach has become a popular variation of PBSC. A SOO is a high-level description of the outcomes desired by the government. The contractor reads the SOO in the solicitation document and prepares a proposal that outlines how it will provide a solution to the stated problem. In essence, traditional roles are reversed, as the contractor writes the PWS and surveillance plan, for evaluation by the public procurement professional, who selects the best solution offered. This technique requires less work up front, but it also demands clear knowledge of the results needed and allows great flexibility to the contractor in performing the work.

1.4.4.4 Planning for Evaluation

Another important step in the procurement planning phase is creating an evaluation team and procedure and developing evaluation criteria. The goal of the procurement is to achieve the "best value" for the user agency in terms of performance, delivery time, and cost while ensuring that all firms submitting offers are treated in a fair and equitable manner. The discussion in this section deals primarily with solicitations for competitive proposals, rather than sealed bidding. The procedures are much simpler in sealed bidding, where there is a public bid opening, determination of lowest responsive, responsible bidder, and award on that basis.

1.4.4.4.1 Appointing an Evaluation Team

Who has the authority to appoint an evaluation team? This depends on each government entity's policy or common practices, and sometimes on the importance and the politics of the procurement project. The evaluation team normally consists of professional staff within the government entity. Occasionally, an elected official or a representative from the community can be appointed to the committee, but it is important that the committee include a representative from the central procurement office and the user agency.

1.4.4.4.2 Establishing Evaluation Criteria

The development of evaluation criteria that will appear in a solicitation issued to the private sector should take into consideration many factors, including the nature of the specific requirement, the ability of the user agency to define the requirement in a clear and concise manner, relevant evaluation criteria, and the organizational culture or environment of the user agency.

Although the user agency is ultimately responsible for the evaluation criteria and the vendor selection, the procurement professional must ensure that the integrity of the process is maintained. Typically, the user agency develops the criteria with some assistance and guidance from the procurement professional. However, in some cases the procurement professional may be requested by the client to play a more proactive role and to actually develop the evaluation criteria. The user agency and the procurement professional must recognize that every case is likely to be different, and the evaluation procedure must be tailored to the particular requirement.

1.4.4.4.3 Evaluation Plan

The evaluation team, with help as required from the procurement professional, should develop an evaluation plan before issuing the solicitation documents. The purpose of this plan is to clearly identify:

- Evaluation criteria
- Their respective weighting factors
- Scoring grid against which these evaluation criteria will be evaluated
- Scoring method
- Contractor selection method that will be used to determine which response best meets the requirement

The first step in developing the evaluation plan is to identify the parameters that will be used in the solicitation method to measure both the competence of each firm submitting an offer and the worthiness of their particular responses. Rating factors are then assigned to the evaluation. The rating factors should reflect the relative importance of the evaluation criteria. By reviewing the proposed weighting at this stage, the procurement professional can help the client ensure that the significant factors drive the choice of the recommended vendor. Again, the relative weighting of each component will change for each requirement. Finally, the plan must indicate the contractor selection method that will be used, such as a cost–technical trade-off, lowest priced technically acceptable method, or any other approach.

1.4.4.4.4 Evaluation Criteria: Points or Adjectives

The two most common ways of expressing the relative importance of evaluation criteria are by point scoring or using adjectival descriptions. These evaluation criteria are used to establish the relative merits of one proposal over another. Again, the procurement professional should work with the client to determine which values or attributes are most important to the organization and to the requirement. Various criteria are used to identify the government's needs in order of priority. Points may then be assigned to those elements, such as 50 points out of 100 for a particular factor, with the other factors adding up to 100. Alternatively, the solicitation may simply state that the technical factors are worth approximately twice as much as the management plan, etc.

Proposals are usually divided into several sections: technical, management, and corporate background are generally combined into one part of the proposal (often referred to as the "technical proposal"), and financial details (the price or cost proposal) are included separately, as they are typically evaluated by different panels or individuals. The solicitation documents must detail exactly what should be included in each section. Points or adjectives are typically assigned to only the technical, management, and corporate background criteria. Some examples of rated criteria include:

- Understanding of the project scope and objectives
- Proposed risk management approach
- Demonstration of expertise
- Qualifications of management team
- Firm's experience with similar projects
- Quality assurance approach
- Reporting and documentation arrangements
- After sales warranty or service
- Proposed level of effort
- Past performance record

1.4.4.4.5 Contractor Selection Methods

In considering which selection method to use, the procurement professional must again consider the actual requirement and with the client determine which method will achieve the "best value." Generally, "best value" is determined by the client's view of the relative importance of the technical component of the proposal in comparison to the price that the client is prepared to pay.

The most common selection methods are:

- Selection on the basis of the lowest priced technically acceptable proposal (sometimes referred to as the "binary" approach)
- Selection on the basis of the highest combined rating of technical merit and price
- Selection on the basis of the highest rated acceptable proposal within a stipulated maximum budget
- Cost–technical trade-off (subjective comparison of cost and technical areas to determine the best proposal)
- Variations of the above

1.4.4.4.6 Determining Solicitation Methods

For all levels of procurement, the procurement professional seeks competition in some form. Without competition, there is little certainty that the price is the best available. Thus, during this planning phase, management and procurement professionals need to select an appropriate method that maximizes competition.

Most state statutes and local procurement ordinance provisions establish the monetary limits that require "formal advertised" competitive sealed bidding. Most statutes or ordinances also require that informal competition, which consists of obtaining two or more oral or fax quotations, be sought for purchases less than a specific amount established by law.

There are several solicitation methods available in public procurement:

- Competitive sealed bidding: formal and informal
- Competitive sealed proposals
- Small purchases
- Sole source
- Emergency purchases

1.4.4.5 Contract Award

The last major activity of the contract formulation phase is contract award. This activity consists of determining responsibility, preparing awards, signing the contract, notifying and debriefing losing firms, and dealing with possible irregularities such as mistakes and protests. The procedures vary depending on whether the contract results from simplified acquisition, sealed bidding, or negotiation procedures.

1.4.4.5.1 Debriefing

Debriefing means informing unsuccessful offerors of the basis for the selection decision and contract award, as well as what was wrong with their proposals. Successful offerors may also request debriefings whenever award is on the basis of competitive proposals. The goal is to provide offerors with information that will help them submit better proposals in the future, through frank and open dialogue.

Procurement professionals should only offer a debriefing upon request. An offeror may request a pre-award debriefing by submitting a written request for debriefing to the procurement professional (for federal agencies, the FAR imposes a three-day time limit, but state and local rules may differ) after receipt of the notice of exclusion from the competition. In like manner, an offeror may request a post-award debriefing (within three days, according to FAR) after the date on which that offeror has received notification of contract award.

Under the simplified acquisition threshold, debriefing is granted, with a brief explanation of the basis for the contract award decision, only if the award is based in part on factors other than price.

1.4.4.5.2 Awarding to Only Responsible Offerors/Quoters

Awarding solely on the basis of lowest evaluated price can be false economy if there is a substantial risk of subsequent default, late deliveries, or performance that is otherwise unsatisfactory. Procurement professionals are therefore not required to award to a supplier solely because that supplier has submitted the lowest price. Rather, procurement professionals may award only to firms that have affirmatively demonstrated their responsibility and, when necessary, the responsibility of proposed subcontractors. (In practice, the procurement professional's signature on a contract constitutes a determination that the prospective contractor is responsible with respect to that contract.) For small business vendors competing for federal contracts, if the procurement professional determines that it is not responsible, the matter is referred to the small business administration for a final decision.

1.4.4.6 Preparation and Signing of Contract

When awarding through sealed bidding or competitive negotiations, documentation should be sufficient to allow accurate reconstruction of the procurement for immediate review and for future reference. Drawing on that documentation, the procurement professional prepares a contract for execution that establishes a legal and binding agreement (e.g., offer, acceptance, consideration, competent parties, lawful purpose, and certainty of terms).

1.4.4.7 Contract Administration

1.4.4.7.1 Notice to Proceed

After a contract is awarded, the project manager or contract administrator issues a notice to proceed that sets the contract administration in motion. Although most government entities do not require a formal contract administration plan, public procurement professionals are responsible for ensuring that the parties have complied with all terms and conditions of the contract. At minimum, the procurement professional should therefore track receipt of the deliverable acceptance (for the furnishing and delivery of standard commercial items), performance of the service, or payment under the contract.

Post-Award Start-Up Conferences

It is often useful to hold a post-award conference meeting attended by the personnel from both parties to the contract. The contract has now been executed and it is time to discuss contract performance expectations with the contract administration team. Attendees should include all of the members of the contract administration team and corresponding contractor counterparts. A post-award meeting can prove to be of considerable value in helping ensure that the contractor understands your expectations and performs accordingly, and, in general, providing the foundation for an effective contract effort. When it is determined, after a contract award, that the contractor does not or may not have a clear understanding of the scope of the contract, the technical requirements, or the rights and obligations of each party, it is essential that the agency initiates post-award orientation action to clarify any ambiguities and resolve any misunderstandings.

Contract Administration Team

Depending upon the complexity of the contract, some or all of the following personnel may become involved in contract administration activities:

- Contracting officer (procurement professional, manager/supervisor of purchasing)—the role changes from being an advisor during the foundation stage of the statement of work, to a decision maker during the bid process, to coordinator and team player with the contract management team
- Contracting personnel (procurement professionals)
- Technical project personnel/contract administrator (initiating department, end user)
- Financial auditors (serve as advisors)
- Legal counsel (serve as advisors)

During the contract administration phase, there may be some disputes that need to be resolved. How to deal with contract disputes is normally prescribed in procurement laws and regulations. To maintain procurement integrity, there is a need to establish and maintain a clear separation of duties between procurement personnel and the project staff.

1.5 Implications of the Public Procurement Framework

Viewed as a system within the government and environment, public procurement can be effective or ineffective because of the type of government and environment within which the system is operated, or because of the system itself. Indeed, in a country where no democratic government exists, how can its procurement system be transparent and integral? Therefore, "in order for procurement reforms to be successful, governmental structure needs to be reformed, and the environment has to be improved. In other words, stakeholders (private sector, civil society, and ultimate beneficiaries of procurement/end users) support the creation of a procurement market known for its integrity and ethical behaviors" (OECD-DAC, 2006, p. 45). This procurement framework stresses the needs of an effective governmental structure and leadership, and a sound cultural, economic, political, and social environment. "The welcoming and respectful attitude of the government and the quality of the debate and the contributions of all interested stakeholders are an important part of creating an environment where integrity and ethical behavior is expected and deviations are not tolerated" (OECD-DAC, 2006, p. 45). As discussed in the next section, corruption is widespread in public procurement. To prevent or to reduce corruption, a system for reporting fraudulent, corrupt, or unethical behavior that provides for confidentiality needs to be established outside the public procurement system.

A public procurement system may be ineffective in a sound procurement environment and an effective governmental structure and leadership because all or one of its "pillars" is not efficient. The procurement system may be ineffective because procurement laws and regulations may be too rigid and do not allow any flexibility for procurement personnel in coping with special circumstances, or may not clearly define responsibilities, accountabilities, and penalties for individuals and firms found to have engaged in fraudulent or corrupt practices. The procurement system may be ineffective because a procurement workforce may not be of the quality and quantity essential to good procurement administration. The procurement system may be ineffective because its procurement process has major flaws or because its procurement organization is too decentralized or too centralized. These pillars—procurement laws and regulations, procurement workforce, procurement process and methods, and procurement organization—are very important for a sound procurement system.

This framework is a good tool for periodic procurement assessments and reforms. It is important that procurement reform decisions be carefully made as the procurement reform process is costly, in terms of money and in terms of staff's time and work disruptions. But in practice, in quite a few cases, procurement reforms were made not because of perceived flaws in the systems, but because of political ploys.[2] At the same time, should the government conduct periodic procurement review or assessment or should it conduct this as a study when there is crisis?

1.6 Procurement Integrity and Corruption

Studies show that public procurement is most prone to corruption (Søreide, 2002; Kaufman, 2004). It was estimated that systemic corruption can add 20–25 percent to the costs of government procurement (UNDP, 2006) or roughly $200 billion per year (Kaufman, 2004). Globally, public procurement is estimated at about 15 percent of the world's GDP, but in some developing countries, it may account for as much as 70 percent (UNDP, 2006, p. 4).

The word "corruption" is a strange term for social scientists to use, in view of its normative implications. A number of alternate definitions of corruption have been advanced, and researchers and policy makers should check their implicit assumptions whenever the term is used. The definition currently most widely used is "the use of public office for private gain" (Gray and Kaufmann, 1998). However, in recent years, this definition becomes debatable as there have been major corruption cases in the private sector, such as Enron and Adelphia in the United States. Thus, in February 2006, the heads of the African Development Bank, Asian Development Bank (ADB), European Bank for Reconstruction and Development, European Investment Bank, Inter-American Development

Bank, International Monetary Fund, and World Bank agreed on the need to standardize their definition of corruption. They established a task force to develop a uniform framework for preventing and combating fraud and corruption. At their September 17, 2006 meeting, all institutions agreed in principle on standardized definitions of corrupt, coercive, collusive, and fraudulent practices as follows (Asian Development Bank, 2006, p. 2):

1. Corrupt practice is the offering, giving, receiving, or soliciting, directly or indirectly, anything of value to influence improperly the actions of another party.
2. Fraudulent practice is any act or omission, including a misrepresentation, that knowingly or recklessly misleads, or attempts to mislead, a party to obtain a financial or other benefit or to avoid an obligation.
3. Coercive practice is impairing or harming, or threatening to impair or harm, directly or indirectly, any party or the property of the party to influence improperly the actions of a party.
4. Collusive practice is an arrangement between two or more parties designed to achieve an improper purpose, including influencing improperly the actions of another party.

On August 1, 2006, the World Bank adopted the definitions of corrupt, coercive, collusive, and fraudulent practices agreed by the above task force. The World Bank also added the term "obstructive practice," which it defined as "deliberately destroying, falsifying, altering or concealing evidence material to an investigation; making false statements to investigators to materially impede an institution's investigation into allegations of a corrupt, fraudulent, coercive or collusive practice; threatening, harassing or intimidating any party to prevent it from disclosing its knowledge of matters relevant to an investigation or to pursuing the investigation; or acts intended to materially impede the exercise of the institution's contractual rights of access to information" (ADB, 2006, p. 1).

Corruption has been viewed as a "multi-headed dragon" (Camerer, 1999), or "hydra" (USAID, 2005, p. 1) to describe a multitude of corrupt aspects, which requires a multitude of research approaches. At least four research approaches can be identified in the present literature:

- *Institutional Approach*. This approach is focused on "bureaucracies" or governance. This approach is focused on "governance and anticorruption" including government structure, bureaucracy, laws and regulations, civil society organizations, and media. "Good governance" has been a focus of international organizations and donor countries in assisting developing countries including the World Bank (2006), United Nations Development Programme (1997), and USAID.
- *Corruption Assessing or Measurement Approach*. There have been a number of attempts to "measure" corruption including measuring the *prevalence* of corruption in particular contexts, the *level* of corruption, and the *impact* of corruption. Many organizations, including Transparency International and the World, have initiated corruption indexes (see Lanyi (2004) for a comprehensive overview of corruption measurement).
- *Public Expenditure Tracking Surveys* (PETS). This research approach was pioneered by Jakob Svensson (2003) in Uganda and is now being implemented in several countries. PETS track public expenditures down the chain from the central government, to the provincial government, to the district government, to the subdistrict governments all the way to delivery points (i.e., schools and clinics). If one level of government reports distributing more funds than the level below receives, it may be possible to pinpoint the leakage (by theft or diversion) of public funds (Lanyi, 2004). This approach, when it is used to track procurement expenditure, is

called "spend analysis," which has been used widely in the private sector. Spend analysis is a tool that provides companies knowledge about how much is being spent for what goods and services, who are the buyers, and who are the suppliers, thereby identifying opportunities to leverage buying, improve performance, and save money. One survey of 147 companies in 22 industries indicated that such an approach produced savings of more than $13 billion in 2000 (U.S. Government Accountability Office, 2004). According to the U.S. Government Accountability Office (2004), the U.S. Department of Agriculture's spend analysis of products and services purchased in the fiscal year 2000 led the department to negotiate an agreement for office supplies with one major vendor that has so far yielded savings of $1.8 million; and the U.S. Department of Veterans Affairs used an automated spend analysis of pharmaceutical procurement and a strategic approach to help save $394 million in 2003. In addition to the above benefits, spend analysis is a very useful tool to detect the leakage of procurement funds.

- *Sectoral Approach.* This approach complements the general system approach. This approach identifies and addresses governance vulnerabilities in specific sectors. USAID had a series of sectoral research on corruption covering education, energy, environment, health, justice, political parties, private sector, public finance, and agricultural sector (Blechinger, 2002; Chapman, 2002; Fink, 2002; Ruth, 2002; Schaeffer, 2002; Vian, 2002; Webster, 2002; Winbourne, 2002; Pepys, 2003). Many other researchers also used this sectoral research on corruption covering tax administration (Fieldstad, 2006), and customs (Yang, 2006). This sectoral approach is described comprehensively by Campos and Sanjay Pradhan (forthcoming).

Although there have been a lot of publications and research reports on corruption, research focus on public procurement has just recently emerged, covering general corruption in public procurement (Søreide, 2002), construction and engineering industry (Stansbury, 2003), and public works (Golden and Picci, 2006). The Asian Development Bank and the OECD-DAC (2006) provide a very comprehensive list of measures for curbing corruption in public procurement in the Asia-Pacific region. The literature on corruption provides a challenging set of ideas and research approaches concerning public procurement corruption studies.

Notes

1. Public procurement law courses have been offered by many universities' law schools; and at least two academic journals in procurement laws had been published long before the *Journal of Public Procurement.*
2. This author was involved in a procurement reform in a country because the chief procurement officer of the government misused the procurement budget. Basically, instead of conducting a comprehensive review, the policy makers should have taken a personal action against that officer.

References

American Bar Association 2000. *The 2000 Model Procurement Code for State and Local Governments.* Chicago, IL: American Bar Association.

Araujo, A. 2004. Procurement Capacity Building in Developing Countries. A PowerPoint Presentation at the International Public Procurement Conference, October 21–23, Fort Lauderdale, Florida, United States.

Asian Development Bank 2006. *Anticorruption Policy: Harmonized Definitions of Corrupt and Fraudulent Practices.* Manila, Philippines: ADB.

Becq, B. 2006. Procurement Reform and Capacity Building: Shortcuts and Tools to Facilitate the Implementation of Sound Public Sector Procurement Systems. Paper presented at the 2nd International Public Procurement Conference, September 21–23, Rome, Italy. Available at www.ippa.ws.

Blechinger, V. 2002. *Corruption and Political Parties.* Washington, DC: USAID. Available at www.usaid.gov. Retrieved December 27, 2006.

Camerer, L. 1999. Tackling the Multi-Headed Dragon: Evaluating Prospects for a Single Anti-Corruption Agency in South Africa. Paper presented at the 9th International Anti-Corruption Conference, September 24–October 15, 1999, in Durban, South Africa.

Campos, J.E. and Pradhan, S. (Eds.) (Forthcoming). *The Many Faces of Corruption: Tracking Vulnerabilities at the Sector Level.* Washington, DC: World Bank.

Chapman, D. 2002. *Corruption and the Education Sector.* Washington, DC: USAID. Available at www.usaid.gov. Retrieved December 27, 2006.

Choi, T.Y. and Hong, Y. 2002. Unveiling the structure of supply networks: Case studies in Honda, Acura, DaimlerChrysler. *Journal of Operations Management* 20(5): 469–493.

Cibinic, Jr., J. and Nash, Jr., R.C. 1995. *Administration of Government Contracts.* 3rd edn., Washington, DC: George Washington University, Government Contracts Program.

Dobler, D.W. and Burt, D.N. 1996. *Purchasing and Supply Management.* 6th edn., New York: McGraw Hill Companies, Inc.

Fearon, H.E., Dobler, D.W., and Killen, K.K. 1993. *The Purchasing Handbook.* 5th edn., New York: McGraw Hill Companies, Inc.

Fink, R. 2002. *Corruption and the Agricultural Sector.* Washington, DC: USAID. Available at www.usaid.gov. Retrieved December 27, 2006.

Fieldstad, O.-H. 2006. Corruption in tax administration: Lessons from institutional reforms in Uganda. In: S. Rose-Ackerman (Ed.), *International Handbook on the Economics of Corruption* (Chapter 17). Bergen, Norway: Chr. Michelsen Institute.

Golden, M. and Picci, L. 2006. Corruption and the management of public works in Italy. In: S. Rose-Ackerman (Ed.), *International Handbook on the Economics of Corruption* (Chapter 16). Bergen, Norway: Chr. Michelsen Institute.

Government Accountability Office 2004. *Best Practices: Using Spend Analysis to Help Agencies Take a More Strategic Approach to Procurement* (GAO-04-840). Washington, DC: GAO.

Government Accountability Office 2005. *Framework for Assessing the Acquisition Function at Federal Agencies* (GAO-05-218G). Washington, DC: Author.

Gray, C. and Kaufmann, D. 1998. Corruption and Development. *Finance & Development.*

Harink, J.H.A. 1999. *Excelling with E-Procurement: The Electronic Highway to Competitive Advantage.* Alphen aan den Rijin, Holland: Samson.

Kaufman, D. 2004. *The Costs of Corruption.* Available at http://www.worldbank.org/wbi/governance/index.html. Retrieved December 27, 2006.

Lanyi, A. 2004. Measuring the Economic Impact of Corruption: A Survey. College Park, MD: Center for Institutional Reform and the Informal Sector, University of Maryland.

NIGP 1997. *Electronic Procurement Opportunities, Process and Tools.* Herndon, VA: Author, pp. 15–16.

OECD-DAC 2006. *Methodology for Assessment of National Procurement Systems.* Paris, France: OECD.

Pepys, M.N. 2003. *Corruption in the Justice System.* Washington, DC: USAID. Available at www.usaid.gov. Retrieved December 27, 2006.

Ruth, M. 2002. *Corruption and the Energy Sector.* Washington, DC: USAID. Available at www.usaid.gov. Retrieved December 27, 2006.

Schaeffer, M. 2002. *Corruption and Public Finance.* Washington, DC: USAID. Available at www.usaid.gov. Retrieved December 27, 2006.

Søreide, T. 2002. *Corruption in Public Procurement: Causes, Consequences and Cures.* Bergen, Norway: Chr. Michelsen Institute (http://www.cmi.no).

Stansbury, N. 2003. *Anti-Corruption Initiative in the Construction and Engineering Industry: Introductory Report.* London: Transparency International (UK). Available at www.transparency.org. Retrieved December 27, 2006.

Svensson, J. 2003. Who Must Pay Bribes and How Much? Evidence from a Cross Section of Firms. *Quarterly Journal of Economics*. Vol. CXVIII (February), 207–230.

Thai, K.V. 2001. Public procurement re-examined. *Journal of Public Procurement* 1(1): 9–50.

Thai, K.V. 2007. *Introduction to Public Procurement*. 2nd edn., Herndon, VA: National Institute of Governmental Purchasing, Inc.

United Nations Development Programme (UNDP) 1997. *Corruption and Good Governance* (Discussion Paper 3). New York: Management Development and Governance Division, Bureau for Policy and Programme Support, United Nations Development Programme.

United Nations Development Programme (UNDP) 2006. *Capacity Development Practice Note*. Available at http://capacity.undp.org/index.cfm?module=Library&page=Document&DocumentID=5599.

United Nations Development Programme (UNDP) 2007. *Contract, Asset and Procurement Management User Guide*. Available at http://content.undp.org/go/userguide/cap/procurement/?lang=en#top.

U.S. Agency for International Development. (USAID) 2005. *Tools for Assessing Corruption & Integrity in Institutions: A Handbook*. Washington, DC: USAID. Available at www.usaid.gov. Retrieved December 27, 2006.

U.S. General Accounting Office 2004. *Best Practices: Using Spend Analysis to Help Agencies Take a More Strategic Approach to Procurement* (GAO-04-870). Washington, DC: US GAO.

Vian, T. 2002. *Corruption and the Health Sector*. Washington, DC: USAID. [Online]. Available at www.usaid.gov. Retrieved December 27, 2006.

Webster, R. 2002. *Corruption and the Private Sector*. Washington, DC: USAID. Available at www.usaid.gov. Retrieved December 27, 2006.

White, L.D. 1958. *The Republican Era: 1869–1901: A Study in Administrative History*. New York: MacMillan.

Winbourne, S. 2002. *Corruption and the Environment*. Washington, DC: USAID. [Online]. Available at www.usaid.gov. Retrieved December 27, 2006.

World Bank 2006. *Strengthening Bank Group Engagement on Governance and Anticorruption*. Washington, DC: Development Committee, Joint Ministerial Committee of the Boards of Governors of the Bank and the Fund on the Transfer of Real Resources to Developing Countries.

Yang, D. 2006. The economics of anti-corruption: Lessons from a widespread customs reform. In: S. Rose-Ackerman (Ed.), *International Handbook on the Economics of Corruption* (Chapter 18). Bergen, Norway: Chr. Michelsen Institute.

PUBLIC PROCUREMENT: A CONCEPTUAL FRAMEWORK

I

Chapter 2

Framework for Assessing the Acquisition Function at Federal Agencies

U.S. Government Accountability Office

CONTENTS

2.1 Introduction

Federal agencies have responsibility for a vast array of missions—assuring national defense, building and maintaining the nation's infrastructure, assessing and collecting tax revenue, advancing scientific knowledge, and promoting the health and well-being of the nation's citizens, among many others. To achieve these various missions, federal agencies use a variety of approaches and tools, including contracts, to acquire goods and services needed to fulfill or support the agencies' missions. Federal agencies award contracts worth over $300 billion annually. Acquiring these goods and services in an efficient, effective, and accountable manner is therefore essential. However, our work—as well as the work conducted by the inspectors general, other accountability organizations, and the agencies themselves—continues to identify systemic weaknesses in key areas, which often result in cost, schedule, and performance problems on individual procurements.

The U.S. Government Accountability Office (GAO) has developed this framework to provide senior acquisition executives, as well as GAO and other accountability organizations, an ability to assess at a high level the strengths and weaknesses of agencies' acquisition functions. This framework comprises four interrelated cornerstones that our chapter has shown to promote an efficient, effective, and accountable acquisition function: (1) organizational alignment and leadership, (2) policies and processes, (3) human capital, and (4) knowledge and information management. These four cornerstones are summarized below.

Cornerstone 1: Organizational alignment and leadership—Organizational alignment is the appropriate placement of the acquisition function in the agency, with stakeholders having clearly defined roles and responsibilities. There is no single, optimal way to organize an agency's acquisition function. Each agency must assess whether the current placement of its acquisition function is meeting its organizational needs. Committed leadership enables officials to make strategic decisions that achieve agencywide acquisition outcomes more effectively and efficiently.

Cornerstone 2: Policies and processes—Implementing strategic decisions to achieve desired agencywide outcomes requires clear and transparent policies and processes that are implemented consistently. Policies establish expectations about the management of the acquisition function. Processes are the means by which management functions will be performed and implemented in support of agency missions. Effective policies and processes govern the planning, award, administration, and oversight of acquisition efforts, with a focus on assuring that these efforts achieve intended results.

Cornerstone 3: Human capital—The value of an organization and its ability to satisfy customers depend heavily on its people. Successfully acquiring goods and services and executing and monitoring contracts to help the agency meet its missions require valuing and investing in the acquisition workforce. Agencies must think strategically about attracting, developing, and retaining talent, and creating a results-oriented culture within the acquisition workforce.

Cornerstone 4: Knowledge and information management—Effective knowledge and information management provides credible, reliable, and timely data to make acquisition decisions. Each stakeholder in the acquisition process—program and acquisition personnel who decide which goods and services to buy, project managers who receive the goods and services from contractors, commodity managers who maintain supplier relationships, contract administrators who oversee compliance with the contracts, and the finance department that pays for the goods and services—needs meaningful data to perform their respective roles and responsibilities.

The framework is built on a foundation of strong internal control. Agency management is responsible for establishing and maintaining effective internal control, which includes the plans, methods, and procedures used to meet missions, goals, and objectives. Internal control serves as the first line of defense in safeguarding assets and preventing and detecting errors and fraud. The five standards of internal control—control environment, risk assessment, control activities, information, and communications—support the framework's four interrelated cornerstones.

2.2 Using the Framework

The main sections in this chapter focus on the four interrelated cornerstones. To assist the user in applying the framework, each cornerstone is broken down into elements and critical success factors. Each element is integral to effective stewardship at an organization and depends on critical success factors. The presence of critical success factors, which focus on program results and mission accomplishment, can enhance the likelihood of consistently achieving desired acquisition outcomes. Conversely, the absence of these critical success factors can point to areas embodying high degrees of risk or those areas needing greater management attention.

To help users discover whether their organizations are employing critical success factors, we offer three indicators: questions to ask, situations to look for, and caution signs to be aware of.

2.3 Scope and Methodology

The purpose of this framework is to provide a systematic method for evaluating the acquisition function within federal agencies. The framework can be used to identify opportunities for improvements in acquisition processes as well as to highlight specific risks faced by each agency.

To develop the evaluation framework, we made use of the experience, knowledge, and expertise within GAO, the executive branch, state agencies, the private sector, and academia to develop key cornerstones that comprise an integrated acquisition function. The outline of the evaluation framework was then further refined in discussions with

- Federal officials from a procurement executive council working group set up to assist GAO in assessing the acquisition function
- Individuals with acquisition expertise from the private sector and academia
- Senior acquisition executives at a forum held at GAO in March 2004

To provide us with a broad understanding of the weaknesses, issues, and potential reforms of the acquisition function, we consulted studies and reports from organizations such as Rand Corporation, the National Academy of Public Administration, the Australian National Audit Office, the National Association of State Purchasing Officials, the PricewaterhouseCoopers Endowment for the Business of Government, the Corporate Executive Board's Procurement Strategy Council, the Center for Advanced Purchasing Studies, and audit reports from GAO and various federal agency inspector general offices.

We also consulted guides on acquisition, human capital, financial management, and information technology from the Department of Defense, Office of Management and Budget, Office of Personnel Management, Department of Veterans Affairs, Department of Energy, Department of Transportation, Department of Treasury, Joint Financial Management Improvement Program, and GAO.

To verify the accuracy of the information provided and improve the technical usefulness of the information reported, we asked acquisition, human capital, financial management, and information technology experts to review a draft of the evaluation framework. We incorporated their comments to create an exposure draft, which was distributed to obtain comments from interested parties of the federal, state and local acquisition community, acquisition experts from associations, academia, and professional organizations. We then incorporated these additional comments as appropriate in this book.

2.4 Cornerstone 1: Organizational Alignment and Leadership

In this section, we focus on two elements and five critical success factors that can be used to assess the placement of an agency's acquisition function and the effectiveness of its leadership.

Organizational alignment is the appropriate placement of the acquisition function in the organization, with stakeholders having clearly defined roles and responsibilities. For example, Congress requires certain civilian executive agencies to designate a chief acquisition officer to take primary responsibility for managing agency acquisitions. In establishing chief acquisition officers, Congress recognized that the person in charge of the agency's acquisition function must have a respected and well-defined role that is consistent with the role of acquisition in meeting the agency's missions. Executive leadership is key to obtaining and maintaining organizational support for executing the acquisition function. Executive leadership determines the relationship between the various functional departments and is key to strengthening the interaction between the agency's management and employees.

Although there is no single, optimal way to organize an agency's acquisition function, officials from leading companies tell us that effective organizational alignment enables them to implement a coordinated and strategically oriented approach to acquisition activities. Similarly, to move toward a more results-oriented government, agencies must ask themselves how they can use acquisitions strategically to help them achieve their goals.

2.4.1 Element: Aligning Acquisition with Agency's Missions and Needs

The end goal of organizational alignment is to ensure that the acquisition function enables the agency to meet its overall missions and needs. The acquisition function needs proper management support and visibility within the organization to meet that goal.

2.4.1.1 Critical Success Factor: Assuring Appropriate Placement of the Acquisition Function

In response to market and other pressures, leading companies have assessed the current placement of their acquisition function to determine if it is meeting organizational needs, including acquiring needed goods and services, supporting strategic decision making, and ultimately improving overall business performance. In many cases, these organizations cut across traditional boundaries that contributed to a fragmented approach of buying goods and services by restructuring their acquisition function and typically assigning it growing responsibility and authority. Similarly, each agency must assess the current placement of its acquisition function to determine if it is meeting the agency's needs.

Key Questions

- What percentage of the discretionary budget does the agency spend on the acquisition of goods and services?
- Where is the acquisition function currently placed in the agency? What are the roles and responsibilities of the acquisition function and acquisition personnel in the agency?
- Do agency leaders, management, and staff view the acquisition function as a strategic asset in achieving their missions or supporting the agency's operations at lowest possible cost?
- To what extent is the agency's acquisition spending managed or influenced by the agency's acquisition office?

Look For

- Acquisition function has been assigned the appropriate degree of responsibility and authority for strategic planning, management, and oversight of the agency's purchases of goods and services, and this responsibility is consistent with the significance of acquisition to the agency's missions.
- Agency leaders view the acquisition function as a strategic asset in support of core agency missions and business processes.
- Agency managers and staff view the acquisition function as a business partner rather than a support function.
- Acquisition of goods and services is viewed from an agencywide perspective.

Cautions

- Disconnects exist between where the acquisition function is placed in the agency's hierarchy and its role in achieving the agency's missions or supporting its operations.
- Lack of coordination across the acquisition function results in redundancy, inconsistency, and an inability to leverage resources to meet common or shared requirements.
- Staff views the acquisition function merely as an administrative support function rather than as a business partner.

2.4.1.2 Critical Success Factor: Organizing the Acquisition Function to Operate Strategically

How an agency organizes and manages its acquisition function affects its ability to operate strategically. Traditionally, the acquisition function has been fragmented among business units, as each was responsible for its own acquisition activities. We found that leading organizations transformed the acquisition function from one focused on supporting various business units to one that is strategically important to the bottom line of the whole company.

Key Questions

- Has the agency assessed the current structure of the acquisition function and related controls? If so, what were the results of the study?
- Has the agency experienced significant changes in its missions, budget, workforce, technology, or other internal or external factors? What changes, if any, did the agency make in response to such factors?
- Does the agency have mechanisms to anticipate, identify, and react to risks presented by changes in conditions that can affect agencywide or acquisition-related goals?
- Does the agency have metrics related to acquisition efficiency, effectiveness, and results that are included as part of overall performance plan and communicated regularly to senior leaders and management? Are these metrics linked to agency missions and goals?
- Does the agency use its strategic and annual performance plan to document the contribution that agency officials expect the acquisition function will make to the agency's missions, strategic goals, and annual goals?

Look For

- Acquisition function's mission is well defined, and its vision for the future, core values, goals, and strategies are consistent with and support the agency's overall missions.
- Current structure of the acquisition function has been assessed in response to changes, such as in the missions, operating environment, budget, workforce, or technology.
- Outcome-oriented performance measures are used to assess the success of the acquisition function. These measures should be designed to gauge the contribution that the acquisition function makes to support the agency's missions and goals.

Cautions

- Agency lacks a clear definition of the acquisition function's mission, vision, core values, goals, or strategies.
- Agency has not assessed the role of the acquisition function in response to significant changes.
- Agency lacks a mechanism for addressing risks that arise in response to changing conditions.
- Performance measures are not used to evaluate the usefulness of the acquisition function to support the agency's missions.

2.4.1.3 Critical Success Factor: Clearly Defining and Integrating Roles and Responsibilities

An acquisition function that is successful at effectively and efficiently meeting the agency's missions generally reflects a consistent, cross-functional, and multidisciplinary approach. This approach requires engagement by all relevant stakeholders, including representatives from program offices, contracting officials, financial managers, human capital officials, information technology officials, and other appropriate participants. An integrated approach helps agencies better define their needs and identify, select, and manage providers of goods and services.

Key Questions

- What are the roles and responsibilities of stakeholders in the agency's acquisition process?
- Does the agency empower stakeholders to coordinate, integrate, and ensure consistency among acquisition actions?
- How are stakeholders held accountable for their actions?

Look For

- Each stakeholder in the acquisition process has clearly defined roles and responsibilities.
- There is a shared understanding of each participant's role in acquisition activities.
- Key stakeholders are empowered to coordinate, integrate, and implement decisions about acquisitions.
- Acquisition managers support the agency's strategic-planning and decision-making needs at field and headquarters levels.

Cautions

- Acquisition function's role is unclear.
- Acquisition and other agency offices do not clearly communicate and cooperate.
- There is little integration of acquisition planning among the different agency entities with a role in acquisitions.
- Conflicts among stakeholders are left unresolved, thereby resulting in inefficient operations.
- Agency's acquisition office is frequently bypassed.

2.4.2 Element: Commitment from Leadership

Organizations recognized for their best practices cite leadership as the most critical factor in providing direction and vision and, if necessary, changing the organization's culture. Leaders have the responsibility to set the corporate agenda, define and communicate the organization's values and culture, and remove barriers that block organizational changes. Research has found that lack of senior leadership commitment is the cause of most reengineering failures.

Congress recognized the critical role that leaders play in providing direction and vision by requiring certain civilian agencies to designate a chief acquisition officer to take primary responsibility for managing acquisitions. The officer's responsibilities include evaluating the performance of acquisition programs, advising the agency head on business strategies, and directing acquisition policy for the agency, among others.

2.4.2.1 Critical Success Factor: Clear, Strong, and Ethical Executive Leadership

Powerful, visionary leaders can set the direction, culture, and perceptions of the agency. Clear, strong, and ethical executive leadership can enable staff across the agency to work in an integrated fashion toward common goals.

Key Questions

- Does the agency have a chief acquisition officer? Is the officer's primary responsibility managing acquisitions?
- Has senior leadership articulated a strategic, integrated, and agencywide vision for the acquisition function?
- Is senior leadership actively involved in pursuing changes, if appropriate, to how the agency acquires goods and services?
- Are managers at all levels held accountable for their contributions to the acquisition process?
- Does agency leadership promote integration and coordination among the agency's budgetary processes and human capital, acquisition, and financial management functions?
- Do agency leadership and management have a positive and supportive attitude toward internal control?
- Has agency management recently reviewed its key acquisition-related internal controls? If so, what were the results? Are all aspects of the acquisition program covered in the internal control review?
- Does agency management take a proactive stance to correct any deficiencies identified in its acquisition-related internal controls?
- Has the agency established policies, such as a code of conduct, communicating appropriate ethical standards? How does the agency ensure that it interacts with the contractor community in a fair, equitable, and ethical fashion?

Look For

- Agency has a chief acquisition officer dedicated to managing acquisitions in the agency.
- Senior leadership provides direction and vision, facilitates the development of common processes and approaches, and is involved in identifying and assessing risks associated with meeting acquisition objectives.
- Senior leadership promotes a strategic, integrated, and agencywide approach to acquisition, as appropriate.
- Improvement initiatives involve stakeholders from across the agency.
- Senior leadership and management set a positive and supportive attitude toward internal control.
- Senior leadership and management support monitoring to assess the quality of internal control performance and to ensure that issues are promptly resolved.
- Senior leadership and management have assessed risks the agency faces from external and internal sources in relation to acquisition objectives.
- Actions taken to address risks are effectively implemented.

Cautions

- There is no chief acquisition officer, or the officer has other significant responsibilities and may not have management of acquisition as his or her primary responsibility.
- Senior leadership has not defined a common direction or vision for the acquisition function.
- Senior leadership does not continually support efforts to develop common processes and approaches.
- Senior leadership does not adequately set and maintain the agency's ethical tone, provides little guidance for proper behavior, and fails to remove temptations for unethical behavior or provide discipline when appropriate.
- Senior leadership has not comprehensively identified risks and considered all significant interactions between the agency and other parties.
- Agency management does not have adequate resources and support to implement common process and approaches.
- Agency personnel do not understand the importance of developing and implementing good internal controls.

2.4.2.2 Critical Success Factor: Effective Communication and Continuous Improvement

Agency leadership needs to effectively communicate to employees the agency's missions, values, and guiding principles. Leaders use meaningful metrics to measure the effectiveness of the acquisition function and to provide the foundation for continuous improvement. Leading organizations use performance measurements to gain insight into and make judgments about (1) an organization's current performance level, (2) the critical processes that require focused management attention, (3) realistic goals for improvement, and (4) results over time.

Key Questions

- How does agency leadership communicate the agency's missions, values, and guiding principles, as well as its vision and expectations for the acquisition function, to agency personnel?
- Have agency personnel been asked for their views on the effectiveness of this communication?
- Does agency leadership facilitate and support clear lines of communication among all parties?
- Have stakeholders been asked for their views on the effectiveness of the existing acquisition process and areas needing improvement?
- What metrics does the agency use to demonstrate the impact and value of the acquisition function in supporting the agency's missions?
- What process does the agency use to develop these metrics?
- Are control activities an integral part of the agency's planning, implementation, review, and accountability activities to ensure results and stewardship of government resources?

- Does the agency or an independent organization continuously monitor control activities for their effectiveness at ensuring acquisition objectives are met?

Look For

- Agency leadership listens to its program units and other affected parties' needs and concerns and remains open to revising acquisition processes as appropriate.
- Revisions to processes reflect appropriate incorporation of affected parties' needs and concerns.
- Metrics used by agency leadership are targeted at demonstrating the impact and value of the acquisition function and provide useful feedback to identify areas for improvement.

Cautions

- There is inadequate communication from agency leadership regarding the effectiveness of the acquisition function and how it supports agency missions.
- There is no mechanism in place for stakeholders to provide suggestions for improvement to the acquisition process.
- Little change is made to acquisition processes based on the needs and concerns expressed by affected parties.
- Internal control monitoring does not occur in the course of normal operations, is not performed continually, and is not ingrained in the agency's operations.
- Agency has inadequate policies, procedures, techniques, and mechanisms in place to ensure effective implementation of management directives.
- Agency has not implemented a program to continuously measure and assess the acquisition function's performance in supporting the agency's missions or achieving acquisition goals.
- Performance measures are in place but are not consistently utilized or communicated.

2.4.3 Quick Recap: How Organizational Alignment and Leadership Can Enhance the Acquisition Function

- Where the acquisition function falls in the agency's hierarchy and how the function is perceived are in balance with the overall agency missions.
- Agency leadership views the acquisition function as a strategic asset.
- Staff views the acquisition function as a business partner rather than merely a support function.
- An integrated approach to acquisition—involving stakeholders from program, contracting, finance, and human capital offices—helps agencies better define their needs and identify, select, and manage providers of goods and services.
- Agency leadership enables an integrated and agencywide approach to acquisition.
- Effective communications and use of measurements allow leaders to actively assess and continuously improve performance.
- Agency leadership establishes and maintains an environment that fosters a positive and supportive attitude toward internal control and conscientious management.

2.5 Cornerstone 2: Policies and Processes

Policies and processes embody the basic principles that govern the way an agency performs the acquisition function. Ideally, policies and processes clearly define the roles and responsibilities of agency staff, empower people across the agency to work together effectively to procure desired goods and services, and establish expectations for stakeholders to strategically plan acquisitions and proactively manage the acquisition process. To be effective, policies and processes must be accompanied by controls and incentives to ensure that they are translated into practice. Major acquisitions require special attention to promote successful outcomes. Policies and processes that fail to address these objectives contribute to missed opportunities to achieve savings, reduce administrative burdens, and improve acquisition outcomes.

2.5.1 Element: Planning Strategically

Planning strategically requires attention to the larger context within which acquisitions occur. First, it requires identifying and managing relationships among the parties involved in the acquisition process. Second, sufficient attention should be given to analyzing aggregate agency needs and devising strategic acquisition plans to meet these needs. Acquisition planning should also take into consideration the effects of the appropriations process and other external factors on the timing and execution of major contracts.

2.5.1.1 Critical Success Factor: Partnering with Internal Organizations

Leading organizations have found that an acquisition function that successfully supports their missions generally employs a multidisciplinary approach. This approach requires engagement by all stakeholders, including contracting, finance, legal, and other appropriate participants to identify needs, assess alternatives, develop cost-effective acquisition approaches, and help ensure financial accountability.

Key Questions

- Do end users of the goods and services acquired work with the acquisition office to discuss requirements for meeting end-users' needs?
- Do stakeholders work together to develop a joint strategy for acquisitions?
- How receptive are stakeholders at evaluating different acquisition approaches and solutions and making trade-off decisions?
- How does the agency promote coordination among the stakeholders as an acquisition action moves through the various steps in the process?
- Do stakeholders work together to understand each other's needs?

Look For

- Agency has empowered stakeholders and holds them accountable for coordinating, integrating, and implementing effective acquisition decisions.
- Acquisition planning and strategy development support the agency's missions rather than focus on the needs of individual units.

- Stakeholders work on an ongoing basis to define key business and acquisition drivers and to understand each other's needs.
- Lessons learned are identified and shared among stakeholders.
- Agency has structures in place that require appropriate coordination among stakeholders developing and implementing acquisition strategies.

Cautions

- There are only limited mechanisms for coordinating acquisitions in the agency.
- Stakeholders do not clearly communicate their needs or work together to identify solutions.
- Lack of integration across the acquisition function results in redundancy, inconsistency, and an inability to leverage resources to meet the shared requirements.
- Acquisition and financial management executives do not partner to develop a shared vision.

2.5.1.2 Critical Success Factor: Assessing Internal Requirements and the Impact of External Events

Successful acquisition strategies require sufficient attention for analyzing agencywide needs. Acquisition planning should include market research to identify appropriate products and services, determination of the extent of competition in the market, assessment of core competencies and opportunities to compete commercial-type activities, and identification of contract approaches that best meet end-users' needs. Additionally, past acquisitions should be reviewed to identify trends and opportunities for consolidating similar acquisitions planned in the coming year to leverage buying power and reduce administrative burdens.

Acquisition planning should take into consideration the effects of the appropriations process on the timing and execution of major contracts. Additionally, agencies must be cognizant of congressional mandates, administration initiatives, socioeconomic policy objectives, governmentwide fiscal imbalances, and other factors external to agencies. Additionally, acquisition processes should be sufficiently flexible to address unforeseen external events and emergencies.

Key Questions

- Does the agency strategically assess its needs and develop acquisition approaches to help it meet those needs?
- Does the agency leverage purchasing volume by identifying agencywide acquisitions of goods and services?
- Does the agency systematically identify and analyze agencywide acquisitions planned in the next 12–24 months?
- Are needs identified in the budget request submission consistent with planned acquisition strategies?
- Does the agency track the types of acquisition methods used for acquiring goods and services to ensure it is employing the most appropriate contract type?

- Does the agency have a mechanism to review planned acquisitions and identify opportunities for suppliers from the small or disadvantaged business community? Has the agency achieved its goals in each of the socioeconomic acquisition categories?
- Has the agency determined the type or extent of work that is and should be performed in-house and which could be contracted out?
- Has the agency assessed its core competencies and identified opportunities to compete commercial-type activities?
- Do agency officials track new or pending legislation that might affect acquisition policies and processes, training, and workload?
- Have agency officials assessed whether their acquisition processes are capable of responding to unforeseen external events and emergencies?
- Do agency officials carefully consider how to meet competing demands on the acquisition system?

Look For

- Strategic acquisition plans are current and reflect anticipated budgetary resources.
- Agency considers recurring purchases and develops acquisition plans that best leverage these acquisitions.
- Agency appropriately selects among the contracting tools available, including commercial item acquisition, performance-based contracting, and government purchase cards to best meet end-user needs in a cost-effective manner.
- Adequate and relevant data is available and used to make strategic decisions about what work the agency should perform in-house, and to identify opportunities to compete work with the private sector.
- Agency identifies opportunities for small and disadvantaged businesses and consistently achieves socioeconomic goals.
- There is an awareness of current and pending legislation and its potential implications on the agency's acquisition policies, processes, and practices.
- Agency has assessed and incorporated changes, as appropriate, to enable its acquisition processes to better respond to unforeseen external events and emergencies.
- There is an awareness of the agency's long-term budgetary outlook.

Cautions

- Agency lacks a strategic acquisition plan.
- Acquisition planning is completed on a contract-by-contract basis rather than with consideration of agencywide needs.
- Agency lacks data on the types of contracts used on procurement actions.
- Frequent emergency or sole-source purchases are made to meet routine or recurring agency needs.
- Agency fails to achieve socioeconomic goals.
- Little knowledge exists of what work is contracted out and what work is performed in-house.
- Agency has not assessed its core competencies or identified opportunities to compete commercial-type activities.

- Agency makes frequent changes to acquisition plans due to unforeseen expenses or budgetary shortfalls.
- Agency is ill-equipped to purchase goods and services needed to respond to emergency situations.

2.5.2 Element: Effectively Managing the Acquisition Process

The role of the acquisition function does not end with the award of contracts. Acquisitions that help the agency meet its needs require continued involvement throughout contract implementation and closeout. In other words, agency processes need to ensure that contracted goods and services will be delivered according to the schedule, cost, quality, and quantity specified in the contract. Factors that can help an agency effectively manage its acquisition process include empowering cross-functional teams, managing and engaging external suppliers, providing effective monitoring and oversight, and implementing sound financial accountability measures.

2.5.2.1 Critical Success Factor: Empowering Cross-Functional Teams

Leading organizations make extensive use of cross-functional teams to make sure they have the right mix of knowledge, technical expertise, and credibility. This approach helps organizations better define their needs and identify, select, and manage providers of goods and services, which in turn helps ensure that users' needs are met at the lowest total costs to the organization. Teams may vary in size but generally include representatives from the organization's purchasing unit, internal users of goods and services, and the budget or finance office. Teams are responsible for analyzing spending data, identifying and prioritizing potential opportunities for a more detailed review, defining internal needs and requirements, and conducting market research.

Key Questions

- To what extent does the agency use cross-functional teams in performing acquisition activities? Are staff from field offices involved at any level? How?
- Do team members feel empowered to make decisions and are they invested in the project's outcome?
- Do the teams use a project plan to manage and control project implementation?
- Does the project plan include performance measurement baselines for schedule and cost, major milestones, and target dates and risks associated with the project?
- Do individuals outside the project team regularly review the status of cost, schedule, and performance goals?
- Are incentives in place to encourage teams to meet project goals?
- How are teams held accountable for meeting cost, schedule, and performance goals?
- Is there good communication among all stakeholders?

Look For

- Agency uses cross-functional teams to plan for and manage projects. These teams develop a project plan to implement projects effectively.
- Agency systematically monitors project performance and establishes controls and incentives for accountability.
- Open, honest, and clear communication is encouraged among all parties, including team members, program officials, and contractors.

Cautions

- Agency makes limited use of cross-functional teams.
- Project team members do not feel empowered to make decisions or invested in the project outcome.
- Teams fail to use key elements of good project management techniques, including monitoring project performance and establishing controls and incentives to meet project goals.

2.5.2.2 Critical Success Factor: Managing and Engaging Suppliers

Leading organizations have found that more cooperative business relationships with suppliers have improved their ability to respond to changing business conditions. Such relationships have led to lower costs, higher quality, and shorter product design and delivery times. Among the strategies employed by leading organizations are to establish commodity managers to oversee key goods and services and to establish an effective feedback system between the agency and its suppliers.

Agencies can develop effective supplier relationships within the context of the federal acquisition regulation by

- Establishing effective supplier relationship management as a core business strategy
- Employing rigorous supplier selection to create a strong supplier base
- Establishing commodity managers to more effectively manage key goods and services
- Establishing and maintaining an effective communication and feedback system with suppliers

Key Questions

- Does the agency have a process to identify key suppliers?
- Does the agency use a rigorous supplier selection process to create a strong supplier base?
- Has the agency established commodity managers for key goods and services?
- What is the role of the commodity manager?
- Has the agency embraced effective supplier relationships as a core business strategy?
- Does the agency train its acquisition workforce on how to manage supplier relationships?
- Has the agency established an effective communication and feedback system with its suppliers to continually assess and improve its own and its suppliers' performance?

- Does the agency foster an environment in which suppliers invest their intellectual capital, i.e., their ideas, into the venture?

Look For

- Agency uses stringent supplier selection criteria while maintaining an appropriate level of competition among suppliers.
- Agency has established commodity managers for key goods and services.
- Commodity managers are actively involved in defining requirements with internal clients, negotiating with potential providers of goods and services, and assisting in resolving performance or other issues after the contract is awarded.
- Agency has established an effective communication and feedback system with its suppliers, by
  - Designating an authoritative person as a single interface with key suppliers
  - Using integrated teams to facilitate sharing of information
  - Establishing an objective basis for providing feedback by setting performance measures and expectations in terms of quality, responsiveness, timeliness, and cost
  - Providing periodic "report cards" and meeting formally with key suppliers to discuss issues
  - Using surveys, supplier meetings, and formal agency–supplier councils or supplier advisory councils to assess existing customer–supplier working arrangements, identify problem areas, and report back to suppliers

Cautions

- Knowledge of its key suppliers is not shared across the agency.
- Agency does not take full advantage of the suppliers' intellectual capital, such as design or product ideas.
- Agency makes limited or no use of commodity managers to manage the acquisition of key goods and services.
- Commodity managers lack expertise, knowledge, or adequate training in the goods and services being procured.
- Agency is dependent on one or two suppliers for key goods or services.
- Agency continues to select the same suppliers without periodically assessing whether the goods and services offered are competitive in terms of price, quality, and performance.
- Acquisition workforce lacks the skills, knowledge, and expertise to manage supplier relationships effectively.

2.5.2.3 Critical Success Factor: Monitoring and Providing Oversight to Achieve Desired Outcomes

Over the past decade, the federal government has increasingly relied on contractors to help carry out its missions. Consequently, agencies require effective oversight processes and staff with the right skills and training to ensure that the contractors provide the needed goods and services. Earned value management is one method to monitor large-projects' progress toward cost, schedule, and performance goals.

Key Questions

- Does the agency track the types of acquisition methods used for acquiring goods and services to assess workload and training requirements?
- What tools, processes, and controls does the agency use to ensure effective oversight of contractor performance?
- What tools, processes, and controls does the agency use to ensure effective oversight of employees making purchases?
- What incentives does the acquisition workforce have to effectively monitor contractor performance?
- Does the agency clearly define the roles and responsibilities for those who perform contract management and oversight?
- What actions has the agency taken to ensure that it has adequate staff with the right skills, knowledge, and training to implement policies and processes and to oversee contractors?
- Do agency personnel or external parties with appropriate knowledge, skills, and responsibilities monitor internal control over the acquisition process on a continuous basis?
- Does the agency effectively use and require its contractors to use earned value management as an investment planning and control tool?

Look For

- Agency has undertaken a workforce-planning effort to ensure that individuals who award, manage, and monitor contracts have clearly defined roles and responsibilities and have the appropriate workload, skills, and training to perform their jobs effectively.
- Agency employs contract monitoring plans or risk-based strategies, and tracks contractor performance.
- Agency regularly reviews contract oversight processes, identifies areas needing improvement, and establishes and implements corrective action plans.
- Agency monitors the effectiveness of policies and processes, completes a cost benefit analysis when considering alternative policies and processes, and follows up on findings identified in monitoring efforts.
- Agency's suppliers have established earned value management systems, and the agency verifies that it and its suppliers effectively implement earned value management processes and procedures on all applicable programs.

Cautions

- Personnel responsible for contract management have skills and knowledge gaps that inhibit their ability to properly oversee the types of contracts used by the agency.
- Agency does not monitor whether its contracts meet cost, schedule, performance, and quality requirements.
- Significant percentage of contracts fail to meet cost, schedule, performance, and quality requirements.
- Agency does not assign clear roles and responsibilities for overseeing contracts.
- There are material weaknesses or reportable conditions related to acquisitions in the agency's performance and accountability report.
- Earned value data is unavailable or unreliable, and earned value management principles are not properly implemented.

2.5.2.4 Critical Success Factor: Enabling Financial Accountability

The need for organizations to deliver goods and services despite shrinking budgets requires agencies to spend their resources wisely. Throughout the acquisition process, financial information should be tracked and communicated in a way that enables effective evaluation and assessment of acquisition activities. When financial data is not useful, relevant, timely, or reliable, the acquisition function, as well as other functions across an organization, is at risk of inefficient or wasteful business practices.

Key Questions

- Does the acquisition workforce have access to and use timely contractual financial information to monitor and oversee individual acquisitions?
- Is the agency's financial management system integrated with its contract management system?
- Does the financial management system report frequently enough to provide reasonable assurance of accountability in acquisitions?
- Is financial data resulting from new contracts, task orders, and contract modifications clear and recorded properly?
- Does the agency measure how often erroneous or improper payments are made? Is a risk assessment process in place to address improper payments?

Look For

- Acquisition workforce has ready access to information on obligated and expended funds, with sufficient information to assure proper oversight and accounting at the contract level.
- Entries are made to the financial management system that updates the contract management and property accountability systems.
- Agency reports frequently enough—monthly or quarterly—to ensure accountability in the acquisition function.
- Adjustments to contract accounting records are clearly reported and accurate; such adjustments represent a low percentage of financial transactions.
- Erroneous and improper payments and cost overruns are tracked and are not a significant problem.
- Agency takes appropriate corrective action when the contractor is not meeting expectations for cost, schedule, or performance.

Cautions

- Acquisition and financial management staffs lack access to critical information, including fiscal year; appropriation/Treasury fund symbol; organization code; cost center; object classification; estimated amount; project code; program code; transaction date; action code; subject-to-funds-availability indicator; asset identifier code; contractor code/name; trading partner; trading partner code; award date; and amounts increased or decreased.
- Acquisition and financial management staff independently update the same types of data into independent financial and contract management systems.

- Financial management systems fail to provide transaction details to support account balances or identify the method of acquisition, lack evidence that the contractor's final invoice has been submitted and paid, or fail to perform other transaction-processing and routine-accounting activities adequately.
- Inadequate transaction processing, particularly improper payments, occurs frequently.
- Financial management systems fail to include the taxpayer identification number for contractor identification and income reporting and debt collection purposes.
- Agency receives a qualified, disclaimed, or adverse audit opinion, which may indicate poor accountability.
- Auditors note weaknesses in the agency's acquisition or financial management function in the agency's audit report.

2.5.3 Element: Promoting Successful Outcomes of Major Projects

The federal government spends billions of dollars each year on major physical capital investment projects and to research, develop, and produce large custom projects. Capital investments and custom projects are generally expensive, span multiple years, and are crucial to the agency's strategy. Capital investments, therefore, usually require more analysis, support, and review than projects that cost less, have shorter time frames, or have less agencywide impact. Particular attention must be given to these long-term, capital-intensive projects.

2.5.3.1 Critical Success Factor: Using Sound Capital Investment Strategies

Capital investment includes expenditures for water, power, and natural resource projects; construction and rehabilitation of postal service facilities and veterans' hospitals; major equipment; facilities for space and science programs; the air traffic control system; and information technology for the entire federal government.

To ensure an effective capital investment strategy, leading organizations

- Integrate organizational goals into the capital decision-making process.
- Evaluate, select, and control capital assets using an investment approach.
- Balance budgetary control and managerial flexibility when funding capital projects.

2.5.3.2 Integrating Organizational Goals into the Capital Decision-Making Process

Leading organizations begin capital decision making by defining the organization's mission in comprehensive terms and results-oriented goals and objectives. This process enables managers to identify resources needed to satisfy program requirements based on program goals.

Key Questions

- Are the agency's capital investments linked to and driven by its missions and long-term strategic goals?
- Has the agency that completed a comprehensive capital investment needs assessment?

- Does the agency thoroughly consider alternatives to capital investments?
- Does the agency perform an annual needs assessment on large capital investment projects lasting more than one year?
- Does the agency have an asset inventory? If so, does it contain assessments of the condition of the assets?
- Does the agency ensure it has the necessary resources available before beginning investments in capital projects?

Look For

- Capital and strategic plans are clearly linked.
- Agency has completed a comprehensive needs assessment that considers the overall missions and identifies the resources needed to fulfill immediate requirements and anticipated future needs.
- Gaps between current and needed capabilities have been identified.
- Agency tracks the use and performance of existing assets and facilities.
- Agency routinely evaluates alternatives, including noncapital options, and repair and renovation of existing assets, before choosing to purchase or construct a capital asset or facility.
- Agency annually assesses capital investment projects lasting more than one year to assess the continued viability, need, and size of the project.
- Agency has an asset inventory that includes condition assessments.
- Agency ensures it has adequate time, money, technology, and other resources in place before beginning major projects.

Cautions

- Capital investment decisions are made without strategic consideration of what assets the agency already has and what it needs or the resources needed to fulfill its long-term and short-term goals and objectives.
- There is little consideration of alternatives to satisfy agency needs.

2.5.3.3 *Evaluating and Selecting Capital Assets Using an Investment Approach*

An investment approach builds on an agency's assessment of where it should invest its resources for the greatest benefit over the long term. Projects that are expensive, span multiple years, and are crucial to the agency's strategy usually require more analysis, support, and review than projects that cost less, have shorter time frames, or have less agencywide impact.

Key Questions

- Does the agency develop a decision or investment package, such as a business case, to justify capital project requests?
- Does the agency have preestablished criteria and a relative ranking of investment proposals?
- Does the agency develop a long-term capital plan that defines capital asset decisions?

Look For

- Agency develops an investment package that includes common categories of information, such as links to organizational objectives; solutions to organizational needs; project resource estimates and schedules; and project costs, benefits, and risks.
- Agency requires appropriate levels of management review and approval, supported by proper financial, technical, and risk analyses.
- Processes for ranking and selecting projects are based on preestablished criteria, a relative ranking of investment proposals and trade-offs, and an understanding of potential project risks.
- Long-term capital plan guides implementation of organizational goals and objectives and helps decision makers establish priorities in the long run.

Cautions

- No framework exists to ensure appropriate levels of management review, analysis, and approval for capital investment projects before initiating projects.
- Projects are selected without using preestablished criteria and without consideration of project risks.
- Year-to-year changes are made in the absence of a long-term capital plan, without consideration of strategic decisions.

2.5.3.4 Balancing Budgetary Control and Managerial Flexibility

Leading organizations generally require that the total life cycle costs of a project be considered when making decisions to provide resources. In the federal environment, to mitigate the risks of unplanned changes in future budgets, agencies may budget for "useful segments" of capital projects.[1]

Key Questions

- Does the agency budget for useful segments of capital projects?
- Do managers have the necessary information to plan for capital investment projects? For example, does the agency have systems to estimate the full cost of a project?
- Are alternatives to full up-front funding considered when they may be in the best economic interest of the government?

Look For

- Agency budgets projects in useful segments.
- Information and data systems are in place to develop estimates of the full cost of a project or segment early in the life of the project.

- Agency considers innovative approaches to full up-front funding, such as outsourcing capital-intensive services and developing public/private partnerships, when these are in the best economic interest of the government.

Cautions

- Capital projects are not funded in useful segments, which leads to acquisitions that may not be fully analyzed or justified, cancellation of major projects, and loss of associated sunk costs.
- Agencies lack information to make strategic capital investment decisions.

2.5.3.5 Critical Success Factor: Employing Knowledge-Based Acquisition Approaches

The federal government spends billions annually to research, develop, and produce large custom projects, such as weapon systems, air traffic control systems, information technology, and space projects. Undesirable acquisition outcomes often occur, however, because agency officials proceed further into development or production without obtaining sufficient knowledge that the product will be able to meet established cost, schedule, performance, and quality targets.

The risk of undesirable acquisition outcomes can be significantly reduced. All product development efforts, whether for an automobile, airplane, missile, or satellite, go through a process of building knowledge. Ultimately, this process brings together and integrates the technology, components, and subsystems needed for the product to work and be reliably manufactured. GAO has identified three discrete points in the development process at which obtaining certain levels of knowledge promote successful outcomes. The attainment of each successive knowledge point builds on the preceding one. These knowledge points—technology maturity, design stability, and production process maturity—are defined in the following manner.

Knowledge point 1: A match between resources and needs occurs when the customer's requirements and the available resources—knowledge, time, and funding—correspond. Achieving a high level of technology maturity at the start of development is an important indicator of whether this match has been made.

Knowledge point 2: Design stability occurs when a program determines that a product's design is stable, that is, it will meet customer requirements and cost and schedule targets.

Knowledge point 3: Production process maturity occurs when it has been demonstrated that the product can be manufactured within cost, schedule, and quality targets and that the process is repeatable and sustainable.

Key Questions

- Is a knowledge-based approach used to develop new products?
- What techniques does the agency use to match end-users' requirements with the technology resources available and the program's ability to meet cost and schedule predictions?

- Does the agency have an established metric or benchmark, such as the percentage of engineering drawings complete or similar criteria, to demonstrate that the product's design is stable?
- Is there an established metric or benchmark, such as having 100 percent statistical control over key manufacturing processes, to demonstrate that the product can be reliably produced and with high quality?
- Do program managers quantify the extent to which development efforts fail to achieve established benchmarks and assess whether those shortcomings are critical and correctable during the next phase?
- Does the agency measure the extent to which new product development activities meet the baseline cost, schedule, or performance requirements of the activities?
- Does the agency use lessons learned from programs that did not meet their baseline requirements to improve the agency's acquisition processes?

Look For

- Agency embodies a knowledge-based approach to acquisition that is reinforced in its policies, implemented in its processes, reflected in individual acquisition decisions, and demonstrated through knowledge-based deliverables.
- At knowledge point 1 or an equivalent milestone, the agency regularly matches requirements and technology resources before beginning product development.
- At knowledge point 2 or an equivalent milestone, agency policy requires the developer to demonstrate that the design is able to meet requirements. To do so, the agency uses an established benchmark, such as the release of at least 90 percent of its engineering drawings, as its criteria.
- At knowledge point 3 or an equivalent milestone, agency policy requires the developer to demonstrate that the production process is mature and uses an established benchmark, such as 100 percent statistical control of key manufacturing processes, as its criteria.

Cautions

- Agency does not use a knowledge-based process for developing new products.
- Agency does not use the necessary controls, such as demonstrating knowledge-based deliverables, to gauge whether adequate knowledge has been attained before deciding to move a product to the next phase of development.

2.5.4 *Quick Recap: How Policies and Processes Can Enhance the Acquisition Function*

1. Effective partnering with internal organizations and awareness of external factors that could impact acquisitions are two keys to strategic acquisition planning.
2. Effectively managing the acquisition process leads to improved acquisition outcomes and involves
   a. Empowered agencywide teams
   b. Strategy for managing external suppliers

   c. Monitoring and oversight
   d. Steps to ensure financial accountability throughout the acquisition process
3. Major acquisition projects, including capital investment and large custom projects, require special attention to achieve desired outcomes.

2.6 Cornerstone 3: Human Capital

People are assets whose value can be enhanced through investment. Leading organizations understand that the success of an organization and its ability to satisfy customers is dependent on the contributions of its people. Human capital policies and practices should support an organization's overall missions and performance goals.

Human capital permeates virtually every effort within an agency, including successfully acquiring goods and services and executing and monitoring contracts. Effective human capital management ensures that an agency has the right staff in the right numbers applying skills where needed to accomplish the mission effectively. Creating an acquisition workforce with the right skills and capabilities can be a challenge, given changes to acquisition processes, the introduction or expansion of alternative contracting approaches, and increased reliance on services provided by the private sector. In addition, agencies are facing a growing number of employees eligible for retirement, which could create an imbalance with regard to acquisition experience and skill sets.

2.6.1 Element: Valuing and Investing in the Acquisition Workforce

Successful acquisition efforts depend on agency leadership and management valuing and investing in the acquisition workforce.

2.6.1.1 Critical Success Factor: Commitment to Human Capital Management

In leading organizations, senior leadership is committed to develop better ways to invest in human capital and is personally committed to implementing change.

Key Questions

- How does the agency's leadership demonstrate commitment to the acquisition workforce?
- What is the role of acquisition officials in developing the agency's human capital strategic plans?
- Does the agency have performance expectations for senior leaders and managers to foster collaboration within and across organizational boundaries and demonstrate a commitment to lead and facilitate change?
- How are senior leaders and managers held accountable for effectively managing the acquisition workforce?

Look For

- Acquisition officials play a significant role in developing the agency's overall human capital strategy and ensure that it reflects the goals of the acquisition function.

- Acquisition officials develop, implement, and evaluate human capital approaches designed to meet customer needs and improve overall business performance.
- Acquisition officials secure the support of managers at all levels for human capital approaches.
- Acquisition officials are held accountable for managing the acquisition workforce effectively.
- Acquisition employees are provided with resources for continuous learning efforts, competency-based appraisal systems, and retention and reward programs.

Cautions

- Agency leadership views people as costs rather than as assets.
- Agency leadership makes decisions about the workforce without considering how the decisions affect mission accomplishment.
- Agency leadership and management are not held accountable for managing the acquisition workforce.
- Business decisions proceed without considering the human capital needs they entail or human capital approaches necessary for success.

2.6.1.2 Critical Success Factor: Role of the Human Capital Function

The human capital function should incorporate a strategic approach for accomplishing the agency's missions and program goals. This requires the agency to elevate the role of human capital professionals from paperwork processors to trusted advisors and partners of senior leaders and acquisition managers. To accomplish this, agency leaders need to ensure that human capital professionals have the appropriate authority, competency, and experience.

Key Questions

- What are the roles and responsibilities of human capital officials with respect to the acquisition workforce?
- How do acquisition managers collaborate with human capital personnel to make hiring and staffing decisions?

Look For

- Human capital professionals partner with the agency's leaders and managers, including acquisition officials, to develop strategic and workforce plans.
- Human capital professionals use streamlined personnel processes and other means to meet customer needs, including hiring and retaining an acquisition workforce with the right skills.

Cautions

- Leaders view human capital management as a support or overhead function.
- Human capital management is largely process oriented and compliance focused.
- Acquisition and human capital officials do not coordinate with each other.

2.6.2 *Element: Strategic Human Capital Planning*

By focusing on recruiting, hiring, training, and professional development, strategic workforce planning outlines ways to help the agency fill gaps in knowledge, skills, and abilities.

2.6.2.1 *Critical Success Factor: Integration and Alignment*

Leading organizations take human capital into account when developing ways to accomplish their missions, program goals, and results. These organizations assess the effectiveness of the integration and alignment effort by how well human capital approaches help to achieve organizational goals.

Key Questions

- Does the agency have a strategic human capital plan that incorporates the needs of the acquisition function? If not, does the acquisition function have its own plan?
- Does the agency's strategic human capital plan address the use of contractors who provide commercial-type services to the agency?
- Does the agency's succession planning and management of its acquisition workforce receive active support from top leadership; link to strategic planning; identify people with critical skills; emphasize development assignments in addition to formal training; and address such human capital challenges as diversity, leadership capacity, and retention?
- Does the agency ensure that teams developing plans for the acquisition workforce consist of all stakeholders, such as customers or end users, contracting officers, representatives from budget and finance, legal counsel, and human capital personnel?
- How does the agency track the effectiveness of human capital strategies for its acquisition workforce?

Look For

- Comprehensive strategic workforce-planning efforts.
- Strategic workforce plan that reflects the needs of the acquisition function, including consideration of which functions to maintain in-house.
- Strategies for recruiting, retaining, and developing acquisition staff, including performance measures to evaluate the contribution these strategies make in supporting the agency's acquisition function and achieving its mission and goals.
- Knowledge and skills inventory is used to identify current and future weaknesses and needs in acquisition skills.

Cautions

- Agency does not fully recognize the link between its human capital approaches and organizational performance objectives.
- Agency adopts human capital approaches without considering how well they support organizational and acquisition goals and strategies or how these approaches may be interrelated.

2.6.2.2 Critical Success Factor: Data-Driven Human Capital Decisions

A fact-based, performance-oriented approach to human capital management is crucial in maximizing the value of human capital and in managing risk. Leading organizations use data to determine key performance objectives and goals, enabling them to evaluate the effectiveness of their human capital approaches.

Key Questions

- Who is included in the acquisition workforce?
- How does the agency track data on the acquisition workforce?
- How does the agency determine the appropriate size of its acquisition workforce?
- Is the mix of entry-level, mid-level, and top-level executives appropriate given the agency's missions and role of the acquisition function?
- What training and professional certifications have current acquisition employees attained?
- How does the agency track the workload of the acquisition staff?
- Does the agency have a skills inventory for the acquisition workforce? How is it used to make human capital decisions?
- How long does the recruitment process take?
- What has the attrition rate been for the acquisition workforce?
- Does the agency conduct exit interviews with departing acquisition workforce employees to determine why people are leaving? If so, how are lessons learned used?
- What is the acceptance rate of applicants offered positions?
- How are training and development programs and results evaluated, and how does the agency track, report, and use this information?

Look For

- Data on the agency's acquisition workforce are reflected in strategic workforce-planning documents. This includes size and shape of the workforce; skills inventory; attrition rates; projected retirement rates and eligibility; deployment of temporary employee/contract workers; dispersion of performance appraisal ratings; average period to fill vacancies; data on the use of incentives; employee feedback surveys; and feedback from exit interviews, grievances, or acceptance rates of job candidates.
- Data is available on staff development, including the number of people receiving training; money spent on training; and measures to determine the real impact on the agency's goals and objectives (such as increased productivity, enhanced customer satisfaction, increased quality, and reduced costs and errors).
- Agency uses data to evaluate and continuously improve the effectiveness of training and development programs.

Cautions

- Agency officials lack critical information with which to create a profile of the workforce or to evaluate the effectiveness of human capital approaches.

- Performance measures and goals for the agency's human capital programs, especially as they link to programmatic outcomes, have yet to be identified.
- Agency has little knowledge of what work is contracted out and what work is performed in-house.

2.6.3 Element: Acquiring, Developing, and Retaining Talent

Recent trends in hiring and retirements in the federal government will leave many agencies with workforce imbalances in terms of skills, knowledge, and experience. Without sufficient attention given to acquiring, developing, and retaining talent, federal agencies could lose a significant portion of their contracting knowledge base.

2.6.3.1 Critical Success Factor: Targeted Investments in People

Leading organizations realize that investing in and enhancing the value of their acquisition staff benefits both employers and employees alike. For example, investing in training for the acquisition workforce is critical to ensuring adequate oversight of the quality, cost, and timeliness of goods and services delivered by third parties.

Industry and government experts recognize that training is a critical tool in successfully introducing and implementing new ways of doing business as well as reacting to change. An agency's overall training strategy—including planning, developing, implementing, and continuous improvement of its programs—is an important factor in ensuring that the staff has the necessary skills, knowledge, and experience to meet agency missions. The success of investment in training can be measured with balanced indicators that are results oriented and client based, encompass employee feedback, and incorporate multiple dimensions of performance.

Key Questions

- What process does the agency follow to determine the appropriate level of spending on training, recruiting, and retention efforts?
- Does the agency have individual training plans established for all employees?
- Do employees have opportunities for continuous learning, such as attending meetings, seminars, and summits, to hear about best practices or otherwise stay up to date on issues in their fields?
- What are the training requirements for new and current acquisition staff and related positions?
- How is the staff trained regarding new practices in acquisition?
- Does the agency have a comprehensive training management system that can track the delivery of training? Does it identify and track the associated costs of specific training and development programs?
- Do managers consistently provide resources (funds, people, equipment, and time) to support training and development priorities for the acquisition staff?
- Does the agency actively work with colleges and universities to (1) market the opportunities available for acquisition professionals and (2) include a federal acquisition course that

will prepare students for careers in federal acquisition and help promote federal career possibilities?
- Are model career paths charted for acquisition staff?

Look For

- Agency demonstrates that it has prioritized the most important training initiatives; secured top-level commitment and provided resources; obtained and considered input on training and resource needs from management and staff; identified those needing training, and set training requirements; tailored training to meet the needs of the workforce; tracked training to ensure it reaches the right people at the right time; and measured the effectiveness of training.
- Agency targets investments in human capital to help it attract, develop, retain, and deploy talented, high-performing staff to accomplish its mission. These investments include training and professional development, recruiting bonuses, retention allowances, and skill-based pay.
- Goals, expectations, and criteria for investments in human capital development are clearly defined, transparent, consistently applied, and based on expected improvement in results.
- Agency investments are monitored and evaluated for effectiveness.

Cautions

- Training and other human capital expenditures are minimized rather than viewed as an investment.
- Funding decisions are made without clearly defined objectives or adequate consideration of how they will impact the workforce.
- Agency does not establish priorities, provide adequate funding, or track investments in human capital.

2.6.3.2 Critical Success Factor: Human Capital Approaches Tailored to Meet Organizational Needs

Existing laws, rules, and regulations provide the agency with flexibility to offer competitive incentives to attract skilled acquisition employees; to create performance incentives and training programs; and to build constructive labor–management relationships based on common goals. Such flexibility should enable agency officials to tailor their human capital approaches to their agency's specific needs and context.

When making decisions about the most appropriate approaches, the agency's acquisition officials should work with human capital professionals, managers, employees, and employee unions. Managers must be held accountable for applying these approaches in a fair and equitable manner across the agency.

Key Questions

- What human capital flexibilities have agency officials used over the past few years and with what results?

- What laws, regulations, or policies, if any, do agency officials view as limiting flexibility in human capital approaches?

Look For

- Agency has a human capital strategy for the acquisition workforce, and it is based on the agency's missions.
- Agency explores opportunities to increase its competitiveness as an employer and eliminate barriers for building an effective, skilled acquisition workforce and takes appropriate action.

Cautions

- Managers view improvements in the acquisition workforce as improbable.
- Managers fail to fully explore the range of tools and flexibilities available under existing laws and regulations.

2.6.4 Element: Creating Results-Oriented Organizational Cultures

Leading organizations foster a work environment in which people are empowered and motivated to contribute to continuous learning and mission accomplishment.

2.6.4.1 Critical Success Factor: Empowerment and Inclusiveness

Getting employees directly involved in the planning process helps to develop goals and objectives from a frontline perspective. Leading organizations commonly seek employee input on a periodic basis and explicitly address and use it to adjust their human capital approaches.

Key Questions

- Does the agency seek ideas from the acquisition workforce?
- Do employees feel a sense of ownership about policies and procedures?
- Do managers involve employees when planning and sharing acquisition performance information?
- Has the agency established a communication strategy to create shared expectations about the acquisition function and to report progress?

Look For

- Agency obtains employees' ideas, involves employees in planning and sharing acquisition performance information, and incorporates employee feedback into new policies and procedures.
- Employee unions or councils are involved in major workplace changes, such as competitive sourcing or redesigning work processes.

- Agency has established a communication strategy to create shared expectations and report progress.
- Alternative dispute resolution programs are used effectively to resolve workplace disputes.

Cautions

- Managers and staff rigidly adhere to standardized procedures.
- Relations between management and employees and their representatives appear adversarial.
- Substantial time and resources are consumed by reacting to workplace disputes and long-standing sources of conflict.

2.6.4.2 Critical Success Factor: Unit and Individual Performance Linked to Organizational Goals

Leading organizations find that effective performance management systems can transform their cultures to be more results oriented, customer focused, and collaborative in nature. These systems are used to achieve results, accelerate change, and facilitate discussions about individual and organizational performance throughout the year. An effective performance management system links organizational goals to individual performance for all acquisition-related employees and creates a "line of sight" between individual activities and organizational results.

Key Questions

- Has the agency recently assessed whether its performance management systems for the acquisition workforce adequately meet its needs?
- What efforts, if any, are underway to review or improve existing performance management systems?
- Does the agency's performance management system provide
  - Candid and constructive feedback to help individuals understand their contributions and help the organization achieve its goals
  - Objective information to reward top performers
  - Documentation and information to deal with poor performers

Look For

- Individual performance expectations are aligned with organizational and crosscutting goals.
- Performance information is routinely used to track and plan follow-up actions to address organizational priorities.
- Competencies are used that enable fuller assessments of performance.
- Pay is linked to individual and organizational performance.
- Meaningful distinctions in performance are made.

- Roles and responsibilities are defined and enable staff to maintain a consistent focus on programmatic priorities even during organizational transitions.

Cautions

- Agency has not aligned performance expectations with organizational goals.
- Agency does not use performance information to track progress at meeting organizational priorities.

2.6.5 Quick Recap: How Human Capital Can Enhance the Acquisition Function

- Agency leadership and managers value and invest in the acquisition workforce.
- Human capital professionals partner with acquisition managers to make staff development decisions.
- Acquisition managers take human capital approaches into account when developing ways to attain organizational goals.
- A strategic workforce plan profiles the current staff and projects staffing needs for the future.
- Agency invests in talented, high-performing staff.
- Agency fosters a work environment in which people are empowered and motivated to meet missions and goals.

2.7 Cornerstone 4: Knowledge and Information Management

Knowledge and information management refers to a variety of technologies and tools that help managers and staff make well-informed acquisition decisions. Such decisions have a direct impact on many levels—program and acquisition personnel who decide on the goods and services to buy; project managers who receive the goods and services from contractors; commodity managers who maintain supplier relationships; contract administrators who oversee compliance with the contracts; and the finance department that pays for the goods and services. They all need meaningful data to perform their respective roles and responsibilities.

2.7.1 Element: Identifying Data and Technology That Support Acquisition Management Decisions

Leading organizations gather and analyze data to identify opportunities to reduce costs, improve service levels, measure compliance with supplier agreements, and provide better management of service providers. Information systems help managers learn how much is being spent with which service provider and for what supplies or services. Additionally, data collected in support of meaningful metrics can assist agencies track achievements in comparison with plans, goals, and objectives. They can also allow agencies to analyze differences between actual performance and planned results. Generating meaningful data, however, requires good data stewardship.

2.7.1.1 Critical Success Factor: Tracking Acquisition Data

When buying goods and services, many leading organizations have implemented comprehensive systems that integrate contracting, financial, and other data to support management decision making and external reporting requirements. These data

- Track events throughout the life of a contract
- Monitor contractor performance and work progress
- Record and validate the receipt of goods and services
- Link to human capital systems to obtain information that monitors workload levels of contracting officers and contract specialists, and workforce training and education

The agency's financial systems support the preparation of auditable financial statements, track financial events, and help to ensure correct and timely payments for goods and services acquired. Financial data can, in conjunction with contracting and other data, enable strategic decision making by supporting an analysis of the agency's buying patterns. External data is obtained from commercial sources or other federal organizations. Examples include market research information and supplier financial status and performance.

Additionally, metrics, when designed to measure outcomes rather than inputs, can be used to evaluate and understand an organization's current performance level; identify critical processes that require focused management attention; obtain the knowledge needed to set realistic goals for improvement; and document results over time.

Key Questions

- What acquisition-related data does the agency collect? Is data kept current?
- Are the agency's financial (including budgetary), acquisition, operating, and management information systems integrated? Do the systems provide timely, accurate, and relevant information?
- Do stakeholders believe the agency's information systems meet their business needs?
- How does the agency make needed data available to stakeholders within the acquisition process, such as program officials, commodity managers, and contracting officers?
- How does the agency manage institutional knowledge and identify and share best practices?
- Has the agency established specific goals and metrics, and collected data in support of those metrics, to assess the performance of the acquisition function?

Look For

- Stakeholders generally agree that the agency's information systems provide credible, reliable, and timely information that they can use to make informed decisions.
- An effective agencywide system integrates financial, acquisition, operating, and management information and allows decision makers to access relevant information easily and perform ad hoc data analysis.
- Agency's contracting management information system tracks events throughout the life of a contract, such as:

- Contract award
- Period of performance
- Contract modifications
- Key milestones
- Contractor performance, including cost and schedule status
- Contract closeout
- Identification of outstanding acquisition requests
- Expected cost
- Types of goods and services acquired
- Receipt and acceptance of goods and services
- Trouble spots and progress in dealing with them

- Financial data, such as budgetary resources and funds availability, status of obligations and expenditures on individual contracts, outstanding purchase requests, and payments for the receipts of goods and services, are readily available to stakeholders.
- Knowledge and information management systems support strategic-planning and performance improvement by enabling
  - Real-time benchmarking
  - Sourcing and volume discount tracking
  - Complete vendor information
  - Contractors' past performance
  - "What-if" analysis and planning
- Data is available on the agency's overall "health," internal capabilities, and the external environment. Useful sources include
  - Agency financial statements
  - Customer and employee satisfaction surveys
  - Knowledge and skills inventories
  - Workforce training and education data
  - Retention and recruitment reports
  - Internal audit reports
- Metrics have been established and are used to assess the effectiveness of the acquisition function, and measurements taken are credible.
- Metrics established allow the agency to assess the acquisition function's progress in meeting financial, customer satisfaction, and business operation objectives, as well as day-to-day activities, such as compliance with applicable laws, regulations, and best practices.

Cautions

- Agency has not collected the full set of information or data to make effective and fact-based decisions.
- Incomplete data prevents the agency from maximizing information tools for strategic acquisition planning and analysis.
- Data is not current, reliable, complete, or accurate.
- Agency does not make needed data accessible to decision makers, leading them to rely on informal, ad hoc systems to make acquisition decisions.
- Decisions are not supported by demonstrable, underlying information.

- Lack of integration among systems hinders a user's ability to access acquisition-related information in a timely manner.
- Metrics established measure only inputs rather than outputs.
- Measurements taken in support of metrics are not credible, leading to disagreements over numbers and the value of the assessment process.

2.7.1.2 Critical Success Factor: Translating Financial Data into Meaningful Formats

New technology tools can generate volumes of data, but the data is meaningless unless they can be translated into relevant, understandable formats for acquisition officials. Financial information is meaningful for acquisition officials when it is relevant, timely, and reliable, and enables them to manage costs, measure performance, and make program funding decisions.

Key Questions

- Do finance executives work with acquisition executives and managers to determine their information needs?
- What types of financial data or reports are regularly provided to acquisition officials?
- To what extent do acquisition personnel use financial information to support acquisition decisions?

Look For

- Finance executives work with acquisition executives and managers on an ongoing basis to determine business and acquisition information needed to manage and oversee the agency's missions and objectives.
- Relevant financial information pertaining to acquisition is presented with suitable detail in an understandable format. Multiple levels of detail are available to provide complete and consistent obligation and expenditure information for an agency's overall contracting activities and for individual contracts.
- Financial management staff and officials receive feedback from acquisition staff and officials to ensure that the acquisition function's data and reporting needs are being met.

Cautions

- Financial information pertaining to acquisition is not of the proper scope, level of detail, timing, content, and presentation format to provide real value to users.
- Acquisition information received by financial management staff is not clear and understandable, impairing efficient processing of the information into management reports.

2.7.1.3 Critical Success Factor: Analyzing Goods and Services Spending

Leading organizations continually analyze their spending on goods and services to answer basic questions about how much is being spent and where dollars are going. This approach is called "spend analysis." When organizations complete these analyses, they often realize they are buying similar goods and services from numerous providers, often at greatly varying prices.

Key Questions

- Does the agency regularly conduct and make use of spend analyses for key goods and services?
- What process does the agency use to conduct a spend analysis?
- Does the agency include purchases made with purchase cards in its spend analysis?
- If spend analyses have been conducted, how were the results used?
- Does the agency use a standard taxonomy to uniquely identify the products and services being analyzed?

Look For

- Agency makes regular use of spend analysis techniques to support strategic-planning efforts.
- Agency knows how much it is spending using purchase cards and has considered this information in its spend analysis.
- Agency uses a variety of information, including financial data, to conduct a spend analysis. At a minimum, the agency's spend analysis identifies the following:
  - What types of goods and services are being acquired
  - How many suppliers for a specific good or service the agency is using
  - How much they are spending for that good or service, in total and with each supplier
  - Which units within the agency are purchasing the goods and services
  - What goods and services have been or could be purchased to meet socioeconomic supplier goals

Cautions

- Agency does not conduct or make regular use of spend analysis.
- Agency information and financial management systems are unable to provide credible, reliable, and timely data needed to conduct a spend analysis.
- Information is not maintained in a standardized format or is of poor quality, thus hampering efforts to use the data to more effectively manage goods and services spending.

2.7.2 Element: Safeguarding the Integrity of Operations and Data

Internal controls, such as structures, policies, and procedures, promote efficiency, reduce the risk of asset loss, and help ensure that financial and acquisition management systems issue reliable reports and that the organization is in compliance with laws and regulations. It is essential that acquisition management systems contain appropriate, cost-effective controls to safeguard assets, ensure accurate aggregation and reporting of information, and support the accomplishment of organizational objectives. Internal control actions and activities occur throughout an agency's operations and on an ongoing basis.

Management must balance safeguards with the need to make accessible, timely, and accurate data available to managers and others needing acquisition information.

There are two broad groupings of information systems controls that can help safeguard the integrity of operations and data: general controls and application controls. Assessing general and application controls is a technical analysis and requires the assistance of persons knowledgeable in computer systems evaluation.

2.7.2.1 Critical Success Factor: Ensuring Effective General and Application Controls

General control applies to all information systems and includes agencywide security program planning, management control over data center operations, system software, acquisition and maintenance, access security, and application system development and maintenance. Application control is designed to help ensure the completeness, accuracy, authorization, and validity of all transactions during application processing.

General and application controls over computer systems are interrelated. General control supports the functioning of application control, and both are needed to ensure complete and accurate information processing.

Key Questions

- When was the last information systems control review performed?
- What documentation exists of the reviews?
- What issues or problems did the reviews identify?
- How were the issues and problems addressed?
- What are the unresolved issues or problems?
- What is the impact of the unresolved issues and problems?
- What practices and procedures does the agency use to ensure that hardware and software are reliable, secure, and user-friendly?

Look For

- Evidence in general controls that the structure, policies, and procedures, which apply to all or a large segment of the agency's information systems, help to ensure proper operation, data integrity, and security.
- Evidence in application controls that the structure, policies, and procedures that apply to individual application systems, such as inventory or payroll, produce outputs that are complete, accurate, authorized, consistent, timely, relevant, and useful for its intended purpose.

Cautions

- Agency has not recently reviewed the internal controls governing its major systems.
- Agency has not addressed all identified major internal control issues or established corrective action plans.

2.7.2.2 Critical Success Factor: Data Stewardship

Data stewardship ensures that data captured and reported is accurate, accessible, timely, and usable for acquisition decision making and activity monitoring. Effective stewardship provides the structure, oversight, and assurance that data can be accurately translated into meaningful information about organizational activities. Taking the time to manage quality of data ultimately helps support the agency's acquisition management needs.

Key Question

- How does the agency ensure that data reflected in its knowledge and information management systems have the following properties:
  - Integrity of data
  - Synchronization of data collection
  - Reduced data redundancy
  - Accessibility of data
  - Transferability of data
  - Flexibility in the data management process

Look For

- Agency's internal controls provide reasonable assurance that data is accurate, complete, timely, and reliable.
- There is consistency among data definitions, sources, controls, and edit routines.
- Managers group data into logical categories and collect data according to commonly accepted reporting time frames.
- Data is redundant only when necessary. Inconsistencies are eliminated.
- Data is accessible to authorized users when needed.
- Data can be transferred to other systems for operational, analytical, and forecasting processes.

Cautions

- Data is unreliable, incomplete, or unsuitable for efficient and effective management decisions.
- Users have little or no confidence in the credibility of the data and outputs from information systems.
- Management does not periodically test the reliability of its data.

2.7.3 Quick Recap: How Knowledge and Information Management Can Enhance the Acquisition Function

- Acquisition personnel should track data on the contracting, financial, and external environment when developing an integrated acquisition information system.
- Data is relevant, timely, reliable, and presented with suitable detail in understandable formats.

- Spend analyses answer basic questions about how much is being spent and where the money is going.
- Hardware and software are safeguarded to ensure the integrity of operations and acquisition data.

Notes

1. The Office of Management and Budget has defined a "useful segment" as a component that (1) provides information that allows the agency to plan the capital project, develop the design, and assess the benefits, costs, and risks before proceeding to full acquisition (or canceling the acquisition) or (2) results in a useful asset for which the benefits exceed the costs even if no further funding is appropriated.

Chapter 3

Assessing Federal Procurement Reform: Has the Procurement Pendulum Stopped Swinging?

Joseph A. Pegnato

CONTENTS

3.1 Introduction

About $200 billion a year is funneled through the federal procurement system to buy everything from stealth fighters to paper clips. The federal procurement system more or less consists of hundreds of thousands of contracting officials in thousands of contracting organizations in every federal agency. An incessantly changing body of procurement regulations guides the work of these officials. Of all the federal government reforms attempted during the 1990s either by reinventing government initiatives, reform laws, or other administrative action, procurement reform of defense and civilian agency contracting has been widely praised as the most successful. These procurement reforms are viewed by many as permanent positive changes. In the manner of tilting at windmills, it is being argued here that political forces inherent in the American democratic system will undermine the permanence of these reforms. If the history of federal procurement is a guide, then no procurement reform is permanent.

3.2 Procurement Pendulum

Since the Revolutionary War, the federal procurement system has oscillated between two extremes. At one extreme the system can be characterized as consisting of very tight and burdensome controls. At the other extreme the system is in a relaxed regulatory condition. Forces such as the nation's wartime arms needs would lead to relaxed procurement rules so the nation could arm quickly. Opposite forces such as contractor profiteering and waste would lead to a tightening of procurement rules and controls. This pattern of oscillation is easily discerned throughout the history of federal procurement. For example, at the outset of the civil war, a loophole was created in the law requiring advertising on all government contracts to speed up the time to award contracts (Culver, 1984a, p. 7). But because of wartime profiteering, a joint Senate House commission, after the war, established a board to review every proposed contract award (House of Representatives, 1895, p. 30).

World War I reveals another example of oscillation. Three months after the United States entered World War I, advertising on all contracts was eliminated. Cost plus a percentage of cost contracts (now deemed illegal because they give contractors no incentive to control costs) were widely used (Culver, 1984b, p. 8). But because of contractor profiteering and influence peddling scandals, Congress passed an excess profits tax (ibid., p. 9). After the war normal procurement regulations were reapplied.

Yet another example of oscillation took place during World War II. The president signed the War Powers Act on December 18, 1941, just a few days after the attack on Pearl Harbor (Culver, 1984c, p. 11). This act authorized the president to allow any agency engaged in the war effort to enter into contracts without regard to public advertising or competitive bidding. After the war, Congress recognized the need to restore nonemergency competitive procurement procedures so that every prospective supplier would have an equal opportunity to win a contract. And again, during the Korean War, the ebb and flow of procurement regulation was evident. Following the invasion of 200,000 Chinese troops into Korea on November 26, 1950, Congress immediately passed the National Emergencies Act, which, among other things, rescinded the requirement for advertising before contract award (Culver, 1985, p. 14).

These examples help to show that the history of federal procurement consists of slow, but inexorable oscillation like a pendulum swinging between two poles. Very tight controls exist at one extreme of the swinging pendulum, very relaxed controls exist at the other extreme. The existence of this oscillating phenomenon has been confirmed by several histories of federal procurement (Commission on Government Procurement, 1972; Culver, 1984a,b,c, 1985; Nagle, 1992). Moreover, this is not the first time this phenomenon has been referred to as a pendulum: "Sure, right now, federal procurement has been moving in the direction of fewer rules and more leeway for government folks to use their judgment. But the pendulum will swing back. After awhile we'll go back to the way things were before procurement reform, and the regulations and distrust will return…" (Kelman, 1998a). It may help to understand this phenomenon by associating it with the natural tension in government between accountability and efficiency.

Out of a sense that the procurement pendulum had swung too far toward overregulation, two major procurement reform laws were passed during the 1990s: the Federal Acquisition Streamlining Act of 1994 and the Clinger–Cohen Act of 1996. Many observers suggest that these two laws have led to a revolution in the way the government buys products and services. Some of these changes include widespread use of credit cards, electronic contracting, increased purchase of commercial-off-the-shelf instead of "mil-spec" commodities, and relaxation or elimination of many rules. These changes were deemed necessary because of a broad consensus that government procurement was wasteful, fraught with red tape, inefficient, and unresponsive. Only trained procurement specialists were allowed to buy things. The process called for properly completed paper forms and multiple approvals. The typical nonprocurement federal worker was not trusted to buy a simple $4 stapler (Gore, 1996, p. 12). One infamous anecdote concerns the outrageous inflexibility of the procurement system. Procurement rules were preventing the military from quickly obtaining badly needed radios during the Gulf War. To get around the rules the Japanese government bought the radios and donated them to the U.S. Army (Acquisition Law Advisory Panel, 1993, p. 6).

This chapter attempts to provide answers to two questions. First, have these reforms been successful? (Although there are clear short-term successes, overall it is too soon to make a definitive judgment.) And second, are these reforms permanent or will the procurement pendulum swing back toward a less streamlined condition of burdensome regulations? (It will be argued that politics will ensure that the pendulum never stops oscillating.)

3.3 Procurement Reform Legislation

The two legislative pillars of procurement reform are the Federal Acquisition Streamlining Act of 1994 (Public Law 103–355) and the Clinger–Cohen Act of 1996 (Public Law 104–106). Many, but not all, of the 1990s reforms received their impetus from specific provisions of these two laws. Other procurement reforms were pursued through executive orders, widespread use of flexible contracting instruments, as well as several initiatives to downsize the procurement workforce.

The Federal Acquisition Streamlining Act of 1994 (Public Law 103–355), signed into law on August 21, 1994, included the following provisions:

- Simplified acquisition threshold was increased from $25,000 to $100,000. Because procurements below this threshold are exempt from many laws, they can be awarded quickly and easily.
- Preference for procurement of commercial-off-the-shelf products rather than products specifically designed to meet burdensome government specifications was established.
- Old paper-based procurement system would be converted to an electronic commerce system.

- Many regulatory restrictions on purchases under $2500 were eliminated.
- Use of contractor past performance data in awarding contracts was mandated.

On February 10, 1996, the president signed the Clinger–Cohen Act, the other major procurement reform bill. The Clinger–Cohen Act, a part of the National Defense Authorization Act for fiscal year 1996, consists of two separate provisions: Division D is the Federal Acquisition Reform Act and Division E is the Information Technology Management Reform Act. The key reforms contained in these two acts are listed here.

- Old competition standard of "full and open competition" was replaced by a less restrictive standard of "efficient competition."
- Regulations governing procurement of commercially available off-the-shelf items were further relaxed and simplified.
- Many restrictions on the conduct of former government officials were eliminated.
- The Brooks Act, which governed procurement of computers for over 30 years, was repealed. With the repeal of the Brooks Act, Congress eliminated centralized control of computer procurement by the General Services Administration (GSA), and eliminated the special protest jurisdiction of the GSA Board of Contract Appeals.
- New concept called modular contracting was introduced. Modular contracting of major information technology systems was defined as successive acquisitions of interoperable pieces of systems. This provision of the law was based on the theory that an incremental approach might eliminate the chaos associated with major computer buys.
- Use of electronic commerce in procurement was expanded.

3.4 Assessing Specific Procurement Reforms

The following discussion is not intended to be a point-by-point assessment of each enacted reform. Rather, this assessment will focus on, for practical reasons, easy to measure factors such as the number of purchase cards being used, the average time to award contracts, the number of protests, and other measures. Measuring these very visible factors over time may be one of the best ways to determine the positive or negative effects of current reforms on the federal procurement system. The following assessments are not intended to be thorough, empirical reviews. They are simply snapshots more in the style of brief case studies of specific procurement reforms. But these snapshots will provide useful views on reform impacts. In other words, these assessments are more along the lines of administrative case studies rather than scientific studies.

3.4.1 Purchase Cards

On October 13, 1994, the same day the president signed the Federal Acquisition Streamlining Act, he issued an executive order directing federal agencies to expand use of government purchase cards (Clinton, 1994). Less than a year later, over 100,000 purchase cards were in circulation. The fact that the Federal Acquisition Streamlining Act eliminated many regulatory restrictions under $2500 gave strong impetus to the card's growth. As a procurement approach, the purchase card eliminates most of the normal paperwork and decentralizes procurement authority into the hands of federal officials who actually identify needs for products and services instead of contracting officers.

Table 3.1 Purchase Card Growth

Fiscal Year	*Sales ($)*	*Transactions*	*Number of Cards*
1989	<100,000,000	Not available	Not available
1990	100,000,000	271,000	Not available
1991	100,000,000	600,000	Not available
1992	300,000,000	1,100,000	Not available
1993	472,143,417	1,562,190	Not available
1994	808,617,304	1,672,078	82,784
1995	1,591,773,703	4,248,496	130,350
1996	2,914,368,604	7,327,878	209,295
1997	4,945,523,006	11,408,158	264,505
1998	7,960,818,859	16,447,721	340,078
1999	10,187,006,498	20,631,398	517,591
2000	12,288,744,026	23,457,456	670,374

Sources: From Office of Federal Procurement Policy in *From Paper to Electronics: An Assessment of Current Electronic Commerce Activity in Procurement,* Washington, DC, 1998a; General Accounting Office (GAO) in *Acquisition Reform: Purchase Card Use Cuts Procurement Costs, Improves Efficiency* (NSIAD-96-138), Washington, DC, 1996; General Services Administration (GSA) in *Federal Procurement Report,* Washington, DC, 1993–2000.

Since becoming available governmentwide in 1989, use of the purchase card has grown rapidly. This exploding growth rate is depicted in Table 3.1. Figures for fiscal years before 1993 are estimates.

It is widely believed that use of the purchase card has led to large savings. The purchase card shifts the process of making simple purchases from the procurement office to the program office. Agencies are then better able to absorb cuts in administrative staff. The cost of making purchases using the purchase card are generally considered to be far less than the cost of writing formal, paper purchase orders. Costs associated with bulk purchasing such as storage, warehousing, and contracting staff are eliminated by card use. On the other hand, GAO found "no one precise dollar figure that could be used to reliably calculate savings for all government agencies" (GAO, 1996, p. 5).

Not only is the amount of savings unknown, but the costs of using the cards also are unknown. Gone are the savings accrued by bulk purchases made by centralized purchasing units. The price breaks available when large quantities are bought are not available for credit card orders of one unit of an item or even orders of very small quantities. Another unidentified cost is the time spent shopping by purchase cardholders. Oversight of purchase card activity to prevent misuse is rapidly becoming another large undefined cost.

In any case, it is clear that the purchase card will improve the speed with which individual buys are made. Although the cost and savings are not yet quantified, the purchase card program has added a powerful and flexible procurement instrument to the government's procurement tool-bag. It is probably a permanent reform. On the other hand, recent press reports of purchase card fraud could easily erode that permanence.

3.4.2 Electronic Commerce

Title IX of the Federal Acquisition Streamlining Act of 1994 mandated that the paper-based procurement system be replaced by an electronic system called FACNET for Federal Acquisition Computer Network. The conversion got off to a rocky start. FACNET turned out to be difficult to use, expensive to implement, unreliable, and not popular with small businesses. In a 1997 GAO survey of 24 federal agencies, senior procurement officials concluded that FACNET would not work because of the following reasons. Widespread public solicitation of offers was inappropriate. Transmitting essential contracting information through the network was not practical or feasible. Alternative purchasing methods were faster and more efficient (GAO, 1997, p. 3). For example, agencies can use credit cards or telephone solicitations more efficiently than FACNET. GAO also reported that agency use of FACNET declined from 1996 to 1997 (ibid., p. 8). The GAO report included the following comments by a senior procurement official from the National Aeronautics and Space Administration: "We continue to believe that there is no single electronic commerce solution. We advocate a strategy that recognizes the variety of users, situations, and transaction types and moves to match them with the appropriate EC technology" (ibid., p. 17).

Steven Kelman, the former administrator of the Office of Federal Procurement Policy, believes that FACNET "was a conceptually flawed concept. To use a widespread public system for small purchases turns out not to be a streamlined way of doing business…the idea of replacing a system that generally worked quite well…was not a good idea" (Dooley, 1997, p. 305). It is fitting then that Section 850 of the National Defense Authorization Act for fiscal year 1998 repeals the mandatory requirement to use FACNET as the only approved electronic commerce method. Agencies can now use other electronic commerce techniques such as the Internet. Although FACNET has been a bust, there has been progress in other areas.

In the mid 1990s, the GSA launched an electronic shopping mall called GSA Advantage. It provides the entire federal government with online access to over one million products and services. Orders can be placed electronically. GSA Advantage has become a very popular procurement vehicle. Electronic commerce initiatives received a big boost with the enactment of the Government Paperwork Elimination Act in 1998 and the Electronic Signatures in Global and National Commerce Act in 2000. These acts allow the use of electronic signatures in the creation of legal electronic contracts.

On September 22, 2000, the government launched a governmentwide Internet portal called FirstGov (www.firstgov.gov). The stated aim of FirstGov is to provide the public easier access to government services and benefits. It is an easy way for the public to access online hundreds of other government Web sites. Links are provided to a variety of sites that provide such services and benefits as, e.g., registering for the draft, applying for grants, applying for retirement benefits, buying savings bonds, and obtaining a passport. FirstGov also links to GSA Advantage.

Another electronic commerce innovation is something called a reverse auction. In an online reverse auction, a single buyer solicits bids from multiple suppliers. Those suppliers bid the price of a product down instead of up in the more traditional auction. In the last few years, several agencies have successfully used reverse auctioning to buy computers and electronic parts.

After a shaky beginning, electronic commerce as a procurement reform initiative is starting to show positive results. Clearly this initiative holds great potential to reform the procurement of goods and services in a radical and permanent way. On the other hand, the director of Defense Procurement recently suggested it is unlikely that the federal government could adopt a completely commercial model for electronic procurement because of such fundamental requirements as open competition, accountability, and audits. She sees the commercial model as less than a perfect fit (GSA, 2001, p. 6). So far there has probably been more promise than progress from electronic commerce. It has been sold, perhaps oversold, as the grand panacea of federal procurement. But paperless procurement is far from becoming a reality. For example, only 1 percent of eligible GSA procurement transactions were completed electronically. Why is this the case? Electronic commerce is harder than it looks. Unrealized reductions in manpower and operating costs are other barriers to more progress.

3.4.3 Commercial Buying Practices

Another key procurement reform designed to bring about revolutionary improvement is to replace standard government buying practices with commercial practices. Title VIII of the Federal Acquisition Streamlining Act of 1994 requires federal agencies to give preference to procurement of commercial items. The law also requires agencies to eliminate most of the standard government clauses in commercial item contracts. Moreover, Section 4201 of the Federal Acquisition Reform Act of 1996 eliminated the requirement for contractors to submit cost data on commercial contracts. Section 4202 of this act established special procedures for a commercial contracting experiment. Congress authorized a test program that allowed the use of simplified procedures in the procurement of commercial items. The test program could be used for procurements under $5 million. This experiment was intended to save both the government and industry time and money. But a 2001 assessment of this experimental authority revealed that no concrete benefits could be demonstrated (GAO, 2001a, p. 6).

According to Jacques Gansler, former under secretary of the Department of Defense (DOD), DOD has a long way to go before commercial contracting becomes a reality. In making his point, Gansler compared the 15-year cycle time for a major weapons systems to the five years it took Boeing to produce the 777 airliner (*The Government Contractor*, 1998, p. 79). Gansler also noted that Caterpillar Inc. delivers parts to its commercial customers in two days, but an army contract requires parts delivery in 20–30 days (ibid., p. 80). The following examples further support Gansler's contention. The DOD inspector general (IG) reported to a senate committee that DOD spent $75.60 for a screw that should have cost $0.57 and $714.00 for an electrical bell that should have cost $46.68 (Barr, 1998). The navy now is paying $800 a yard for material used to repair naval aircraft, but had been paying only $100 a yard before it being offered as a commercial item (GAO, 1998a, p. 25). The air force paid nearly $400,000 for an engine control unit after the procurement reforms took effect, but only $80,000 before the reforms were in place (ibid.). In a perverse way, one of the commercial buying reforms may be contributing to this problem: government-contracting officers now face a larger challenge in trying to obtain fair prices because vendors are no longer required to provide detailed cost data to the government on commercial items.

Given the millions of purchases made by DOD each year, it is relatively easy to find procurement anecdotes to support either argument that government buying is efficient or wasteful. But it is necessary to go beyond anecdotal analysis to draw more accurate conclusions about commercial contracting success. One study provides such a broader perspective. All purchases of commercial electronic parts made by one DOD supply center over an 18-month period during 1995–1996 were analyzed (Kelman, 1998b). On big dollar buys, federal contracting personnel paid 22.6 percent less than the commercial retail price, a far different picture than the anecdotes mentioned above.

On the other hand, the opposite conclusion was reached in a large study (676,999 items) comparing DOD's pre-reform buying practices to standard commercial practices. The research showed that DOD obtained lower prices using standard government procurement methods as compared to commercial buying (Besselman et al., 2000, p. 421). It is suggested by this study that adoption of commercial practices across the board would lead to the military paying more.

The largest commercial buying program outside of DOD is the very successful Federal Supply Schedule (FSS), managed by the GSA. Although this program predates the recent procurement reforms, the FSS has become much more popular due to recent GSA streamlining of the program. The number of FSS orders by agencies is skyrocketing. From fiscal year 1996 to 1999, FSS orders have grown from $4.3 to $11.4 billion, an increase of 165 percent (GSA, 1999, p. 33). The success of the FSS program provides clear evidence that commercial buying can be successful. What is not clear is whether the commercial reforms had anything to do with the success?

In sum the record is mixed with regard to commercial contracting reforms. The federal government probably still has a "long way to go."

3.4.4 Performance-Based Contracting

In performance-based contracting, a contractor is given a specific performance goal to meet instead of a set of detailed design specifications. For example, a contractor may be directed to perform aircraft maintenance so that 98 percent of flight schedules are met. The contractor is not instructed on how it should perform the work or what process to use, but is given direction only on what should be accomplished. Although performance-based contracting is a 1990s procurement reform, it is not one of the initiatives of the overarching procurement reform laws of the 1990s. Rather, it began as an executive branch policy. In 1991, the Office of Management and Budget (OMB) directed federal agencies to use performance-based contracting methods when acquiring services (OMB, 1991).

The most recent assessment of performance-based contracting was completed in 1998. The assessment covered 27 contracts awarded by 15 agencies using performance-based contracting methods. On average, contract prices on these 27 contracts decreased by 15 percent (Office of Federal Procurement Policy, 1998b, p. 2). Lower prices may have resulted from an increase in the level of competition. On average the number of firms submitting proposals on a given procurement increased from 5.3 to 7.3 suggesting a significant improvement in competition (ibid., p. 3). Agency satisfaction with contractor performance was measured on five factors: quality, quantity, timeliness, cost-effectiveness, and overall performance. Using a scale from one to five, agency satisfaction improved from 3.3 to 3.9, or more than 18 percent. On the downside, the average procurement lead time on these 27 performance-based contracts increased by 16 percent from 237 to 275 days.

A sample of 27 contracts is far too small to accurately assess the overall effects of performance-based contracting. As a reform it may have the potential to reduce government-contract expenditures. However, this benefit will be neutralized if it takes longer to award performance-based contracts. The adoption of performance-based contracting methods is progressing slowly. Apparently, agencies do not fully understand how to write such contracts.

3.4.5 Procurement Administrative Lead Times

The length of time needed to award federal contracts is often referred to as "procurement administrative lead time." Every recent procurement reform study describes the adverse impacts associated with excessively long procurement administrative lead times. For example, a 1982 Office of Federal

Procurement Policy study cited delays in the procurement of new systems as leading to cost growth and wasted resources (p. v). A 1983 study by the National Academy of Public Administration deplored the "steady increase in the time it takes to move procurement actions through the pipeline" (p. 32). The procurement of weapons system, according to the 1986 Packard Commission, takes too long (President's Blue Ribbon Commission on Defense Management, 1986, p. 13). To make the defense procurement process more efficient, the 1993 Section 800 Advisory Panel recommended streamlining and consolidating nearly 600 defense procurement laws (Acquisition Law Advisory Panel, 1993, pp. 9–10). The report of the National Performance Review issued in 1993 was critical of the federal procurement system for purchasing low quality items that are delivered too late (Gore, 1993, p. 26).

Reducing procurement administrative lead time is not a specific procurement reform initiative. On the other hand, reducing this time is an indirect goal of almost every reform. For example, reforms to raise the simplified acquisition threshold, increase the purchase of commercial-off-the-shelf products, move toward electronic commerce, and increase the use of purchase cards are all aimed at speeding up the procurement process. It would be expected that average procurement administrative lead time would have decreased because the reforms have been in place as a consequence of all the streamlining efforts. Have these lead times, in fact, decreased? Some preliminary data suggests that the reforms may have helped to produce just such a reduction. Procurement administrative lead times were reduced at five of six agencies studied by GAO since the reforms have been implemented (GAO, 1998b, pp. 13–14).

In 1995, Congress gave the Federal Aviation Administration flexibility to ignore government-wide procurement rules and authority to create its own streamlined rules. A 1998 study indicates that lead time has been reduced from 380 days to 174 days (Burman, 1998). Reforms at the commerce department have led to procurements being awarded in just 28 percent of the time of the traditional process on average (ibid.). According to a DOD IG report issued on November 23, 1998, lead times within inventory units had been reduced by 14 percent since mid-1995 (*Federal Contracts Report*, 1998c). Shrinking procurement lead time appears to be another important success of recent reforms.

3.4.6 Bid Protests

Bid protests can be very time consuming and costly to both government and contractors. Consequently, several provisions designed to reduce the number of protests were included in the various procurement reform bills. Sections 1014 and 1063 of the Federal Acquisition Streamlining Act of 1994 require that agencies provide more meaningful post-award contractor debriefings to better explain why vendors were not selected for contract awards. Demystifying the selection decision is thought to increase trust and reduce suspicion among the parties. Section 4104 of the Federal Acquisition Reform Act of 1996 gave losing vendors the right to debriefing before contract award. In another important reform, the bid protest forum established in the 1980s to adjudicate information technology contract protests was eliminated by Section 5101 of the Information Technology Management Reform Act of 1996. This forum, the General Services Board of Contract Appeals, was almost solely responsible for the huge jump in the number of protest filings that occurred during the 1980s and early 1990s.

Have these reforms led to fewer protests? The answer is clearly yes. Since fiscal year 1993, the last pre-reform year, the number of protests filed with GAO has declined steadily every fiscal year from 3377 in 1993 to 1220 in 2000 (GAO, 1998b, pp. 11–13; *Federal Contracts Report*, 2000). Although the number of protests may be decreasing, the number of successful protests has increased significantly. The number of protests won by the protester jumped from 12 to 21 percent over the same period, an increase of 75 percent.

Although there are fewer protests, it cannot be said with scientific certainty that the reduction was caused solely or primarily by the reforms. It may be that changing economic conditions or some other externality is a larger factor in the reduction. The most important factor responsible for the large reduction in the number of protests may very well be the large decrease in the number of federal contract awards. According to the Federal Procurement Data Center, the total number of contract awards dropped from 19,712,511 in fiscal year 1993 to 10,470,158 in fiscal year 1999 (GSA, 1993, p. 2, 1999, p. 2). GAO reported that the number of prime contracts awarded by DOD declined by 35 percent from 1988 to 1997 (GAO, 1998c, p. 2). The reduced number of contract awards suggests fewer contract protest opportunities. Over $200 billion was spent on contracts in fiscal year 1993; about the same was spent in fiscal year 1999. But when adjusted for inflation, the total dollars spent on contracting declined.

Another factor may be the recent spate of company mergers. Obviously when companies merge, fewer companies are bidding for government contracts. This reduced number of companies bidding suggests fewer potential protesters.

Moreover, agencies are using less contentious contracting methods such as GSA schedule contracts, indefinite quantity task order contracts, and other agencies' contracts. These alternatives have been made more widely available by recent reforms. These more flexible methods are generally not targets of contract protests. In the case of task order competitions under indefinite quantity contracts, such procurements can no longer be protested. This no-protest rule is contained in Section 1003 of the Federal Acquisition Streamlining Act. Moreover, because many of these multiple-award task order contracts have overly broad scopes of work, they are easy to use not only by the contracting agency, but also by other agencies. In other words, fewer contracts need be written leading to fewer protest opportunities.

Although the reduction in the number of protests may have been strongly influenced by such factors as contract mergers and fewer contract awards, recent procurement reforms have also contributed to this result. Here the reforms clearly have worked as designed.

3.4.7 Procurement Workforce Downsizing

Is procurement workforce downsizing a reform in the sense that electronic commerce and purchase cards are reforms? No, but there is a widely held view that successful procurement reform would lead to efficiencies and savings, enabling large-scale workforce reductions. Assessing downsizing, therefore, is an appropriate and necessary element of an assessment of the procurement reforms of the 1990s.

The Clinton administration, in September 1993, called for a 12 percent reduction in the federal civilian workforce to be achieved by the end of fiscal year 1999 (Gore, 1993, p. iii). The procurement workforce was a targeted workforce category in this planned reduction. The Federal Workforce Restructuring Act of 1994 (Public Law 103–226) also called for the federal government to reduce its workforce by 272,900 over the period from 1994 to 1999. From 1989 to 1999, the civilian procurement workforce was, in fact, reduced by nearly 47 percent (GAO, 2001a, p. 8). Over the same period the total civilian workforce reduction was 17 percent.

The National Defense Authorization acts for fiscal years 1996, 1997, 1998, and 1999 (Public Laws 104–106, 104–201, 105–85, and 105–261) required DOD to reduce its procurement personnel by at least 25 percent by fiscal year 2001. From 1991 to 1999, the DOD procurement workforce's actual reduction was 50 percent (*Federal Contracts Report*, 2001a, p. 370). Over the same period the total DOD civilian workforce reduction was 37 percent. The conclusion of the cold war played no small part in making these large reductions possible. Moreover, additional DOD reductions occurred in 2000 and 2001. In 1991, five percent of all contract specialists were eligible to retire; this figure is projected to climb to 35 percent by 2005 and 50 percent by 2009.

According to the DOD IG, at the same time that the workforce decreased by 50 percent over the period from 1990 to 1999, workload, measured by number of procurement actions (the most valid indicator of workload), increased by about 12 percent (Office of the Inspector General, 2000, p. i). Moreover, for those procurement actions over $100,000 (procurements exceeding $100,000 involve the greatest amount of work), the IG reported a 28 percent increase. Some of the adverse impacts associated with this workload imbalance, says the IG report, include more time to award contracts, increased program costs, insufficient staff to manage requirements, increased backlog of contracts to close out, and personnel retention difficulty (ibid.).

What does the IG have to say about the productivity and efficiency gains afforded by various procurement reforms, efficiencies that theoretically could offset any adverse impacts from staffing reductions? "These improvements helped offset the impact of acquisition workforce reductions… Nevertheless, concern is warranted because staffing reductions have clearly outpaced productivity increases and the acquisition workforce's capacity to handle its formidable workload" (ibid., p. ii). At his confirmation hearing, Pete Aldridge, President Bush's nominee for under secretary for Acquisition, testified: "I am concerned about the effects of the reductions on the acquisition workforce. As DOD continues to emphasize contracting out and competitive sourcing, the skills training and experience of the acquisition workforce will be critical in effectively managing these contracts" (Cahlink, 2001, p. 4).

A decade of downsizing at the National Aeronautics and Space Administration has left the workforce stretched to the limit. The Kennedy Space Center launch site was left with 35 percent fewer federal workers. According to the center's deputy director James Jennings, "Folks aren't going to be able to survive long under these current working conditions" (Dickey, 2001, p. 73). The loss of two Mars probes valued at $360 million in 1999 was blamed on deficient communications, but an overworked staff may have been partly responsible as well.

According to one former NASA official, contractor officials may have failed to alert higher-ups in the chain of command about being stretched too thin out of concern that such notification might jeopardize contractor funding. Is this an inherent weakness of overreliance on contractors who may be more inclined to send forward only "good news"? At a senate committee hearing on the space shuttle, a GAO official suggested that NASA's downsizing initiatives might have been based on overly optimistic assumptions (GAO, 2000, p. 1). For example, NASA believed it could reduce its workforce by consolidating several shuttle contracts into one large master contract. But after contract award, NASA could not identify any work savings.

GAO testified about the negative effects of downsizing on NASA's workforce. According to GAO, many critical areas such as solid rocket booster and shuttle range safety do not have sufficient backup. The workforce is stretched to the point where there is just one qualified person on many important tasks. The workforce may not be sufficient to support the planned shuttle flight rate. Signs of overwork and fatigue plague the workforce. Forfeited leave, overtime, and counseling visits are all on the rise; stress levels may have reached the point of creating an unhealthy workforce (ibid., pp. 2–4). GAO reported that NASA had terminated its downsizing program and was seeking to add hundreds of employees to the shuttle program workforce starting in fiscal year 2000.

According to Joseph Rothenberg, associate administrator for Space Flight at NASA, "Downsizing is over" (NASA says shuttle cuts, 2000). Rothenberg, in responding to criticism that NASA had been increasing the risk of a space shuttle accident by cutting budgets and personnel, admitted that NASA might have gone too far. A recent internal study concluded that NASA did not have enough inspectors to oversee the private contractor, United Space Alliance, a firm owned by Boeing Co. and Lockheed Martin Corp., operating the shuttle (ibid.). During the 1990s more than 4500 NASA scientists and engineers left the agency. Many of these federal workers were veteran overseers of the shuttle program. One former NASA official believes that NASA's contractors, to cut costs, were relying on inexperienced workers and were providing insufficient oversight (ibid.). According to Rothenberg, "... there is a minimum level of government involvement that should maintain a continuity of knowledge ... and that we were below that level and about to get worse" (ibid.).

An argument easily can be made that the NASA formula of contracting out, plus inexperienced contractor staff, plus a downsized government workforce equals serious quality problems and higher risk to equipment and personnel. It may be more than coincidence that recent NASA projects ended in failure.

The Department of Housing and Urban Development may be yet another agency adversely impacted by recent downsizing. As the department reduced its workforce, it added more program responsibility. The department's IG blamed the lack of adequate staff resources as the root cause of many material weaknesses (Gaffney, 2000).

Workforce downsizing has been made possible by the use of credit cards, multiple-award task order contracts, increased automation, and by shifting responsibility for some contractor oversight to contractors. Some cuts probably were necessary to eliminate pockets of overcapacity. But "doing more with less" is not an accurate characterization of what is going on in federal procurement offices. Cash buyouts, early outs, hiring freezes, and retirements are leading to a drastic reduction of the most experienced knowledgeable staff. This problem is part of what has been labeled a human capital crisis. According to GAO, as a consequence of the Federal Workforce Restructuring Act, some agencies have experienced increased work backlogs, skill imbalances, and loss of institutional knowledge (GAO, 2001b, p. 5).

Over a decade, downsizing has seriously reduced the ability of the contracting workforce to cope with rapidly changing technology and more complex missions. Although the workforce shrank, contracting for services jumped 24 percent during the 1990s. As of fiscal year 2000, spending for services accounts for 43 percent of all contracting expenses. It appears that one less-accountable workforce (private sector) is simply being substituted for another (federal sector). In other words, downsizing may be just an illusion. In recent testimony before a House committee, a GAO official stated: "It is becoming increasingly evident that agencies are at risk of not having enough of the right people with the right skills to manage service procurements. Consequently, a key question we face in government is whether we have today, or will have tomorrow, the ability to acquire and manage the procurement of increasingly sophisticated services the government needs" (GAO, 2001c, p. 1). Angela Styles, administrator of the Office of Federal Procurement Policy, recently stated: "We don't have the workforce in place to manage those contracts. There are some agencies that we believe could look at contracting-in" (Peckenpaugh, 2001a).

The 1990s downsizing was driven mostly by a cutting quota and very little by strategic planning to determine what skills were most needed. The net result was to reduce the capacity of agencies to fulfill their missions. For example, as the contracting workforce is reduced at the same time that the service contractor workforce is increased, there may not be adequate resources to monitor performance and hold contractors accountable. This should not be a surprise. Downsizing studies have shown that anticipated organizational benefits do not develop. Downsized organizations do not have lower overhead, less bureaucracy, smoother communications, faster decision making, and increased productivity (Cascio, 1993, p. 97).

An unintended consequence of contract workforce downsizing may be a reduction in number of contracts awarded to small businesses. There are indications that many small contracts have been bundled into fewer large contracts. Without the capacity or resources to manage such large contracts, small businesses are at a competitive disadvantage with larger firms. One DOD official implied that downsizing might have led to such bundling (Peckenpaugh, 2001b).

3.4.8 Procurement Reform Assessment Summary

Table 3.2 contains a brief summary of pluses and minuses of the various reforms discussed above. There are many notable procurement reform successes. The use of credit cards is exploding. This is improving the speed and flexibility of small purchases. An increase in the availability of flexible contracting instruments such as GSA schedule contracts, blanket purchase agreements, and multiple-award task order contracts has led to a drastic improvement in the ability of agencies to award

Table 3.2 Assessing Procurement Reform: A Summary

Specific Reform	*Legislative or Regulatory Basis*	*Pluses and Minuses*
Expand use of purchase cards	Executive Order 12931	Plus: Fast, decentralized buying Minus: Savings, if any, undetermined
Electronic commerce	Title IX of FASA, Section 850 of 1998 National Defense Act	Plus: Some progress and high potential Minus: Paperless procurement still a dream
Commercial buying	Title VIII of FASA, Sections 4201 and 4202 of FARA	Plus: Commercial buying is increasing Minus: Still a long way to go
Performance-based contracting	OMB directive	Plus: Prices reduced Minus: Full potential far off
Shrink procurement administrative lead time	Not tied to specific legislation, but indirectly tied to every reform	Plus: Lead times are decreasing Minus: Lead times still too long
Decrease bid protests	Sections 1014, 1063 of FASA, Section 4104 of FARA, and Section 5101 of ITMRA	Plus: Protests down Minus: Contractor protest rights reduced
Workforce downsizing	Public Laws 103–226, 104–105, 104–201, 105–85, and 105–261	Plus: Workforce declined Minus: Work backlogs, loss of institutional knowledge

Note: FASA, Federal Acquisition Streamlining Act; FARA, Federal Acquisition Reform Act; OMB, Office of Management and Budget; ITMRA, Information Technology Management Reform Act.

large dollar procurements more quickly. These flexible instruments are helping the government mirror the private sector by adopting commercial buying practices. There are many indications that the time to award major contracts has been reduced. And the number of bid protests has decreased significantly. On the other hand, not all of the reforms have produced intended positive results. For example, it is not clear if the use of credit cards is reducing actual savings. The first electronic commerce initiative, FACNET, proved to be a complete failure and was abandoned. Transition to a commercial practice world is proving to be difficult. It is too soon to judge whether performance-based contracting will be successful. Although the number of protests has declined, are the reasons for the decline cause for concern? In other words, are protest opportunities being reduced at the expense of small businesses? Are the legitimate protest rights of businesses being trampled on? Similarly, the increased use of flexible contracting instruments may be placing small businesses at a competitive disadvantage. The chairman of House Small Business Committee reported a decline in the number of prime contracts to small businesses after the reforms took effect (*Federal Contracts Report*, 2001b). Moreover, it is troubling that downsizing of the procurement workforce was undertaken before the effects of procurement streamlining could be realized.

Any attempt to accurately assess any reform in its early stages suffers from obvious weaknesses. Nevertheless, this snapshot of the pluses and minuses of procurement reform is an important short-run balance sheet assessment. Just as important to the state of procurement reform is the degree of permanence of these reforms.

3.4.9 Prospects for Permanent Reform Are Not Good

Many of the recent procurement reforms are clearly aimed at making the practice of federal procurement more like that of standard commercial practice, but the transition to a commercial world has not been smooth. But how far can government go in that direction? Many major differences between the public and the commercial world remain and probably will always remain.

One example is the federal annual appropriation process. This process places restrictions on expenditures and drives up prices by inhibiting long-term deals. To write long-term contracts, federal contracting officials generally write one-year contracts that include unfunded option years. Federal contractors clearly understand that annual options, which can only be exercised at the government's unilateral discretion, are far from long-term contracts available in the commercial world. Such restrictions do not exist in the commercial world.

Another difference concerns the government's requirement to rigidly adhere to broad scale equity in all its transactions. This principle leads to inefficiencies nonexistent in the commercial world. Giving every business an opportunity to bid on contracts or to protest contract awards is another example. A business can retain its subcontractors as long as it desires or until performance deteriorates; a government agency generally must re-compete its contracts every five years, good performance notwithstanding.

In the commercial world, buyers routinely consolidate contract requirements for administrative convenience and to achieve savings and efficiencies. The bundled contract has the effect of reducing the number of suppliers being managed by private sector buyers. But these benefits are not available to federal sector buyers. Contract bundling has a negative connotation in the government-contracting world. Because of concern that the practice of bundling contracts harms small businesses, Congress passed the Small Business Reauthorization Act of 1997. Federal buyers are required to demonstrate actual benefits before proceeding to consolidate or bundle contracts that would displace small businesses. Private sector administrative savings become public sector inequities; the private–public contrast is stark here.

Unlike the private sector the federal procurement system is used to implement socioeconomic goals. These nonprocurement goals reduce the efficiency of federal contracting, a problem nonexistent in the commercial world. The government-contracting environment is infamous for its excessive and expensive reporting requirements and monitoring by auditors, inspectors general, and others. Another important difference between government and private sectors contracting is the government's ability to unilaterally terminate its contracts at its convenience. Contractors have no recourse in the face of this very powerful governmental right; many refuse to do business because of this. No such one-sided right exists in the commercial world. All of these are large barriers that may prevent the government from making a permanent switch to contracting like the commercial world.

The view here is that any government reform based on free market business principles faces serious survival obstacles. Concerns about such reforms expressed by James Q. Wilson and J. Edward Kellough support this view. Whether business can serve as a model for exercising administrative power causes Wilson to be skeptical (1994, p. 670). Although he believes in the constructive power of markets, he does not believe that market principles can lead to permanent sweeping cultural changes in government agencies as is possible in private sector organizations (ibid., p. 672).

To keep these agencies, with awesome power to tax, regulate, and arrest, accountable and responsive, they are controlled by laws and regulations and exposed to reporters and committee investigators. The result, according to Wilson, is a risk avoidance culture not easily altered (ibid.). It is not enough for government agencies to be just efficient; they also must be accountable to a system of laws. Indeed, accountability is just as important as efficiency when measuring government's overall effectiveness. For example, the efficiencies afforded by contract bundling are only available if federal agencies ensure no harm to small businesses. Efficiency can be sought only by ensuring, at the same time, accountability with national policy on protection of small businesses.

According to J. Edward Kellough, improvements in government operations based on entrepreneurial market dynamics may be difficult to achieve or sustain (1998, p. 17). "Politics may not be so easily dismissed as the reinventors would have us believe," says Kellough (ibid., p. 15). He is concerned that equity or fair treatment of all people will be compromised to increase efficiency. Again, the contract bundling example is relevant here.

In short, because government is different from business in certain key aspects, the prospects for permanent reform are not very good.

3.4.10 Has the Procurement Pendulum Stopped Swinging? Can It Stop Swinging?

During a March 18, 1998, Senate committee hearing, Senator Charles Grassley stated, "after 15 years to the month, the sound we are hearing is of history repeating itself" (*Federal Contracts Report*, 1998a, p. 310). The sound he referred to was the strident criticism raised during that hearing on the matter of overpriced DOD spare parts. (In March 1983, 15 years earlier, overpriced DOD spare parts also were the subject of a Senate committee hearing.) On learning of possible overpriced spare parts, Senator Fred Thompson warned that flexibility granted by Congress in recent procurement reforms "may be short-lived" (Capaccio, 1997, p. 10). In fact, in June 1998, Senator John Warner introduced a bill designed to eliminate the problem of the Pentagon being overcharged for commercially available spare parts (*Federal Contracts Report*, 1998b, p. 724). Warner's bill would require vendors to submit cost data on commercial items. If enacted, this would have been a clear step backward; the recent reforms had just deleted the requirement to submit such cost data. The bill died.

The past is prologue; procurement scandals will recur. The administrative history of the federal government is replete with such scandals. This has been a permanent part of the history of the U.S. government and will be part of its future. Moreover, such scandals always tend to undermine preceding reforms.

But, as discussed earlier, many of the recent reforms are producing large improvements in the federal procurement system. Many procurement practitioners are hoping that some of the more successful reforms (e.g., credit cards and flexible GSA contracts) are permanent. Nevertheless, the pendulum will swing back toward a more regulatory environment. That is because this procurement process, largely a rational business process, is embedded in a political process. Kettl (2000, p. 21) suggests that "Any attempt to reform bureaucracy must take account of not just efficiency but rather of the constellation of political forces that will create rules under which the bureaucracy must operate". When inevitable procurement scandals occur, scandals that in no way represent the millions of scandal-free procurement transactions, it will make great political sense, to enact laws to "clean up these procurement messes." This is an easy way to please voters. Because accountability is such an important principle, government will spend much more to prevent corruption than the actual cost of such corruption by several factors. Business would take the opposite cost-effective tack.

An early indication of the pendulum swinging back is evident in recent GAO interest in DOD's use of the credit card. GAO has begun to identify instances of fraud and abuse and is calling for tighter internal controls. It is easy to project that the credit card, as a streamlined, flexible procurement reform, may become less streamlined.

Not everyone accepts the inevitability of the swinging procurement pendulum. Government reform enthusiasts argue that the pendulum metaphor does not apply here. "Procurement reform means real organizational change in a linear fashion," goes the argument. The problem with this argument is that it seems to apply to business environments not government environments. What is not adequately recognized is the power that political forces exert on the pendulum when it swings too far in either direction. The pendulum metaphor is appropriate because the executive branch does not operate independently of the other branches in our political system of government. Moreover, the scandal hungry media often forms an unhealthy and unwitting alliance with political interests to help keep the pendulum swinging. According to Shoop (1999), the media is interested in "sex, scandal, drama, or anything that can be expressed in simple, good-versus-evil terms." Shoop believes that the media has great influence over major policy decisions and how the government operates. Journalists package their reports under such labels as "The Fleecing of America" to underscore their arguments.

Procurement reform and government reinvention are ultimately only management reforms. These management reforms are being sought in a highly political environment and usually affect only the margins of such environments. Over time the political forces are so strong that even the successfully implemented procurement reforms will be influenced by or overcome by such forces.

This chapter has attempted to do two things: to assess the impact of recent procurement reforms and to assess their permanence. What can be said in brief summation of both issues?

Many of the procurement reforms have been successful. Paper purchase orders are being replaced with credit card orders. Contracts are being awarded more quickly. The number of bid protests has decreased. The government is slowly adopting commercial contracting practices. The proliferation of flexible procurement instruments such as GSA schedule contracts, blanket purchase agreements, and task order contracts is producing drastic improvement in the contract award process. On the other hand, electronic commerce initiatives have not worked well. It is not yet clear if the new contracting techniques are actually saving money. There is an open question as to whether benefits of reforms outweigh costs to small businesses in the form of lost opportunities. Changes made to reduce bid protests may be reducing legitimate protest rights of certain contractors. Many question whether it is really possible for government to conduct its business like business. And it may be too soon to try to accurately assess the broad impact of these reforms.

Perhaps the strongest argument against the permanence of these procurement reforms is contained in the history of procurement. From pre-revolutionary days this history can be characterized as a swinging pendulum. All reforms seem to have been just temporary. The procurement pendulum has always swung between two extreme poles. At one extreme the procurement system is being reformed generally to ease the purchase of war munitions. At the other extreme procurement system controls are tightened due to a scandal largely caused by reforms or previously relaxed rules. So far nothing seems to suggest that the current reform movement will have any more permanent success than all of the previous reforms.

Are these reforms permanent? The view here is they are not. That is because the federal procurement system is part of a political process. Political forces always have and always will cause this system to swing like a pendulum back and forth between highly regulated and unregulated environments notwithstanding the best intentions of reformers.

References

Acquisition Law Advisory Panel, U.S. Department of Defense. January 12, 1993. *Streamlining Defense Acquisition Laws: Report of the Acquisition Law Advisory Panel, 1993*. Newington, VA: U.S. Department of Defense.

Barr, S. March 23, 1998. Defense reform saves millions but helps reinvent overspending. *Washington Post*: A17.

Besselman, J., Arora, A., and Larkey, P. 2000. Buying in a businesslike fashion—and paying more? *Public Administration Review*, 60(5): 421–434.

Burman, A.V. 1998. Teamwork makes a difference. *Government Executive*, 30(4): 67.

Cahlink, G. April 30, 2001. Pentagon nominee aims to rejuvenate acquisition workforce. *GovExec.Com Daily Briefing*. Available at www.govexec.com.

Capaccio, T. December 1997. Senators call for GAO probe of parts costs. *Defense Week*, 7–11.

Cascio, W.F. 1993. Downsizing: What do we know? What have we learned? *Academy of Management Executive*, 7(1): 95–104.

Clinger–Cohen Act of 1996 (The National Defense Authorization Act for Fiscal Year 1996). (Public Law 104–106, 110 Stat. 186.) February 10, 1996. (This act contains two distinct acquisition reform provisions: Division D—Federal Acquisition Reform Act of 1996 and Division E—Information Technology Management Reform Act of 1996.)

Clinton, W.J. October 13, 1994. Executive order 12931, Federal procurement reform. *Federal Register*, 59(199): 52387–52388.

Commission on Government Procurement. 1972. *Report of the Commission on Government Procurement, Appendix G*. Washington, DC: Author.

Culver, C.M. May 1984a. Federal government procurement: An uncharted course through turbulent waters, Part 1—From colonial times to World War I. *Contract Management*, 24: 4–7, 32.

Culver, C.M. July 1984b. Federal government procurement—An uncharted course through turbulent waters, Part 2—World War I to World War II. *Contract Management*, 24: 7–10, 32.

Culver, C.M. September 1984c. Federal government procurement—An uncharted course through turbulent waters, Part 3—World War II. *Contract Management*, 24: 8–12.

Culver, C.M. January 1985. Federal government procurement: An uncharted course through turbulent waters, Part 5—Korea to Vietnam—The fifties. *Contract Management*, 25: 13–17.

Dickey, B. April 2001. The few, the tired. *Government Executive*, 32(5): 71–78.

Dooley, M.I. September 22, 1997. An interview with Steven Kelman. *Federal Contracts Report*, 68(1): 304–305.

Federal Acquisition Streamlining Act of 1994 (Public Law 103–355, 108 Stat. 3243), October 13, 1994.

Federal Contracts Report. 1998a. Gansler defends acquisition reform against IG reports of overpriced spare parts, 69(12): 310–311.

Federal Contracts Report. 1998b. Warner amendment to DOD bill closes loophole in commercial items acquisition, 69(25): 724–725.

Federal Contracts Report. December 1998c. DOD initiatives lower acquisition lead time 14 percent since 1995, IG Says, 70(22): 631.

Federal Contracts Report. October 31, 2000. GAO protests drop 13 percent in FY 2000, 74(16): 404.

Federal Contracts Report. April 10, 2001a. Acquisition workforce: DOD's acquisition workforce mirrors government's human capital crisis, IG says, 75(15): 370–371.

Federal Contracts Report. June 2001b. DOD acquisition reforms are hurting small businesses, House Panel told, 75(26): 664.

Federal Workforce Restructuring Act of 1994 (Public Law 103–226), March 30, 1994.

Gaffney, S. September 26, 2000. *Testimony before the Subcommittee on Housing and Transportation of the Senate Banking Committee*. Washington, DC: Inspector General, U.S. Department of Housing and Urban Development.

General Accounting Office (GAO). August 1996. *Acquisition Reform: Purchase Card Use Cuts Procurement Costs, Improves Efficiency* (NSIAD-96-138). Washington, DC: Author.

General Accounting Office (GAO). January 1997. *Acquisition Reform: Obstacles to Implementing the Federal Acquisition Computer Network* (NSIAD-97-26). Washington, DC: Author.

General Accounting Office (GAO). March 1998a. *Defense Acquisition: Improved Program Outcomes are Feasible* (NSIAD-98-123). Washington, DC: Author.

General Accounting Office (GAO). March 1998b. *Acquisition Reform: Implementation of Key Aspects of the Federal Acquisition Streamlining Act of 1994* (NSIAD-98-81). Washington, DC: Author.

General Accounting Office (GAO). August 1998c. *Defense Spending: Trends and Geographical Distribution of Prime Contract Awards and Compensation* (NSIAD-98-195). Washington, DC: Author.

General Accounting Office (GAO). March 2000. *Space Shuttle: Human Capital Challenges Require Management Attention* (GAO/T-NSIAD-00-133). Washington, DC: Author.

General Accounting Office (GAO). April 2001a. *Contract Management: Benefits of Simplified Acquisition Test Procedures Not Clearly Demonstrated* (GAO-01-517). Washington, DC: Author.

General Accounting Office (GAO). April 2001b. *Federal Employee Retirements* (GAO-01-509). Washington, DC: Author.

General Accounting Office (GAO). May 22, 2001c. *Contract Management: Trends and Challenges in Acquiring Services* (GAO-01-753T). Washington, DC: Author.

General Services Administration (GSA). 1993–2000. *Federal Procurement Report*. Washington, DC: Author.

General Services Administration (GSA). 1999. *Annual Report*. Washington, DC: Author.

General Services Administration (GSA). 2001. *GSA Launches On-line E-gov Inventory*. Washington, DC: Author. Available at www.gsa.gov.

Gore, A. September 7, 1993. *From Red Tape to Results: Creating a Government that Works Better & Costs Less* (Report of the National Performance Review). Washington, DC: National Performance Review.

Gore, A. September, 1996. *The Best Kept Secrets in Government* (Report of the National Performance Review). Washington, DC: National Performance Review.

House of Representatives. March 2, 1895. *House Report 2000*. 53rd Congress, 2nd Session. Washington, DC: Author.

Kellough, J.E. 1998. The reinventing government movement: A review and critique. *Public Administration Quarterly*, 22(1): 6–20.

Kelman, S. February 16, 1998a. Pendulum metaphor need not dictate our destinies. *Federal Computer Week*, 12(4): 21.

Kelman, S. August 24, 1998b. PhD proves DOD on right procurement track. *Federal Computer Week*, 12(29): 19.

Kettl, D.F. 2000. Public administration at the millennium: The state of the field. *Journal of Public Administration Research and Theory*, 10(1): 7–34.

Nagle, J.F. 1992. *A History of Government Contracting*. Washington, DC: The George Washington University.

National Academy of Public Administration. 1983, November. *Revitalizing Federal Management*. Washington, DC: Author.

National Defense Authorization Acts for Fiscal Years 1996, 1997, 1998, and 1999 (Public Laws 104–106, 104–201, 105–85, and 105–261).

Office of Federal Procurement Policy. February 26, 1982. *Proposal for a Uniform Federal Procurement System*. Washington, DC: Author.

Office of Federal Procurement Policy. March 1998a. *From Paper to Electronics: An Assessment of Current Electronic Commerce Activity in Procurement*. Washington, DC: Author.

Office of Federal Procurement Policy. May 1998b. *A Report on the Performance-Based Service Contracting Pilot Project*. Washington, DC: Author.

Office of Management and Budget (OMB). April 15, 1991. Service contracting. *Federal Register*, 56(72): 15113.

Office of the Inspector General, DOD. February 29, 2000. *DOD Acquisition Workforce Reduction Trends and Impacts* (Report No. D-2000-088). Washington, DC: Author.

Peckenpaugh, J. November 5, 2001a. OMB pushes some agencies to "contract in" key jobs. *GovExec.com Daily Briefing*. Available at www.govexec.com.

Peckenpaugh, J. June 21, 2001b. Small business committee blasts pentagon for contract bundling. *GovExec.com Daily Briefing* [Online]. Available at www.govexec.com.

President's Blue Ribbon Commission on Defense Management. February 28, 1986. *An Interim Report to the President*. Washington, DC: Author.

Shoop, T. 1999. Facts and details. *Government Executive*, 31(1): 16.

Small Business Reauthorization Act of 1997 (Public Law 105–135), December 2, 1997.

The Government Contractor. February 18, 1998. Gansler says DOD has long way to go in acquisition reform, 40(7): 79–80.

NASA says shuttle cuts have led to higher risk. March 10, 2000. *Washington Post*: A14.

Wilson, J.Q. December 1994. Reinventing public administration. *PS: Political Science and Politics*, 27(4): 667–673.

Chapter 4

Analytical Framework for the Management and Reform of Public Procurement

Paul R. Schapper, João Nuno Veiga Malta, and Diane L. Gilbert

CONTENTS

4.1 Introduction

The concepts of transparency and accountability are nowhere more significant in public administration than in procurement, which may account for more than a third of a government's annual outlays. Although these attributes are paramount with regard to good governance, they do not on their own distinguish procurement from many other activities of public process. However, there are many other elements that combine to make public procurement especially enigmatic, one of the least understood and most vulnerable areas of public administration.

Public procurement is inherently a politically sensitive activity, not least because it involves significant amounts of public money even within the context of a national economy. Pegnato (2003) estimated U.S. federal procurement at around $200 billion per annum, and Coggburn (2003) put the combined procurement for state and local governments at more than $1 trillion. Thai and Grimm (2000) estimated government's collective purchasing at around 20 percent of GDP, and for developing countries, Nicol (2003) put the figure at 15 percent of GDP. For Russia, federal procurement in 2004 was expected to amount to about 40 percent of the country's budget (Fradkov, 2004). The Organisation for Economic Co-Operation and Development (OECD) Development Assistance Committee (DAC) (2003) estimated the volume of global public sector procurement at 8 percent ($3.2 trillion) of the worldwide GDP of $40 trillion. Aspirations to depoliticize public procurement face major hurdles: decisions about its appropriation can involve financial hardships and job losses for various regional or sectional constituencies, thereby inviting intense political interest. Further, even just a few low-value performance failures can, it seems, be of greater political significance than pandemic inefficiency (Osborne and Gaebler, 1992; Dilulio, 1994).

Compounding the issues implied by its overtly political and business dimensions are widespread misunderstandings and even gross ignorance within the executive structures of governments as to what procurement actually entails (Coggburn, 2003; OECD/DAC, 2003). There is often little understanding of what skills are required and what risks are implied as well as what opportunities may be available (GAO, 2000). Failure of awareness and expertise at this level commonly represents a real risk to good governance, even creating the anomaly whereby public procurement may sometimes be characterized as transparent although not accountable (see Isaac (1997) on the Cave Creek disaster).

The significance of public procurement reform for developing countries is increasingly being appreciated by development agencies globally, recognizing that the social and economic costs (Schapper and Malta, 2004) of the weaknesses in public procurement governance are compounded by increases in sovereign risk that this represents for foreign investment (Jones, 2002). However, even amongst the reformists in this area there are common misunderstandings and a lack of consensus about this activity with, for example, many perceiving it as a regulatory problem and others as a mainstream management function.

These problems are by no means limited to developing countries (Nagle, 1992; Hunja, 2003). Even in those jurisdictions with stronger administrations the issues are poorly appreciated and are susceptible to systemic failure of accountability often because the agents of accountability themselves have at best a weak appreciation of the issues (Peachment, 1992). Cases have involved, for example, failures to understand when contractual relationships exist, or when the passing of information on the process constitutes breach of confidentiality (Finn, 1997). Even where these weaknesses are exposed, it will commonly be on an occasional and exceptional basis despite the problems sometimes being ongoing and endemic.

Although many of the issues have already been discussed in the literature, this chapter seeks to develop a model to suggest why traditional reform of public procurement as a narrow management concept is unlikely to succeed beyond delivering minimal governance benchmarks. The analysis shows that public procurement is subject not only to divergent political, managerial, and regulatory objectives but also to key performance measures associated with these divergent objectives that introduce conflicts between and even within government agencies themselves. However, the analysis is extended to suggest how the tensions embedded in the procurement environment may be vulnerable to emerging technologies that may be significant in reconciling the ideas about the management of this function. On the other hand, in circumstances where there is only superficial appreciation of the broader management issues and of their technological possibilities, the reform of public procurement remains exposed to ill-fitting management models and influences.

To develop this analysis it is first necessary to identify and understand the concepts, management, and political agendas that define and constrain the procurement environment itself.

4.2 Scoping the Procurement Environment

It is unlikely that an analytical framework for public procurement can be understood by digesting a procurement training manual. It is impossible to develop a comprehensive framework for the understanding, analysis, or management of public procurement independent of its political context. By its very magnitude, public procurement demands high quality public governance in terms of transparency and accountability as well as effective management that can deliver optimum risk management and value-for-money outcomes (NPR, 1993). It also demands coherence with other public policy environments, especially business policy because of its significance in the economy (Harland et al., 2000) even though these various operational elements often fail to come together into a coherent policy or politically sensitive management framework.

Within the management environment, control, risk mitigation, and transparency objectives are often the focus of centrally mandated regulatory compliance frameworks although management performance in terms of value outcomes is often pursued through devolved decision making and deregulation.

In what follows, we seek to develop each of these factors as a foundation for a framework within which they can be more meaningfully ordered, related, and understood. All of these elements make up the procurement environment and need to be accounted for in any useful framework if it is to reconcile the activities of procurement managers with the demands of their executives and the agendas of the politicians and the expectations of the business sector, the media, and the community.

4.2.1 Procurement Management Objectives

Many jurisdictions worldwide have, implicitly or explicitly, similar management objectives for public procurement (Thai, 2001; Jones, 2002; Qiao and Cummings, 2003). Common policies are widespread between jurisdictions, notwithstanding the great variances in methodologies and operational practice. For example, in a collective action by the forum for Asia-Pacific Economic Cooperation (APEC) countries, their government procurement experts group has developed a set of nonbinding principles that included transparency, value-for-money, open and effective competition, fair dealing, accountability, and due process (APEC, 1999). Individual member countries decide on the applicability of individual elements to them, taking into account the specific characteristics of their economies and the costs and benefits of adopting specific measures.

Such common policies are generally constructed from the following elemental objectives:

- *Public confidence*—underpinned by attributes of accountability, transparency, equity, and fair dealing in relation to procurement processes
- *Efficiency and effectiveness*—in the use of public monies to achieve value-for-money and efficiency of delivery of procurement outcomes

- *Policy compliance and consistency*—of both processes and outcomes of procurement in relation to other policy objectives and expectations of the public sector such as environmental issues, training and apprenticeships, international obligations, and especially business and regional employment impacts

These objectives are unsurprising and are consistent with generic public management. They simply say that the management of public procurement needs to be in accordance with community standards, and be effective, efficient, and consistent with the broader roles of government. However, although they seem simple, experience shows that translating them into operational reality involves issues and policies that are frequently in conflict, if not mutually incompatible.

Broadly, three approaches, sometimes in various degrees of combination, are employed to deliver these objectives. The following discussion includes each of these approaches, generally defined in terms of their focus on *regulation, management*, and *centralization* of public procurement.

4.2.2 Regulation and Compliance

In jurisdictions where the dominant political concern has been the principles of transparency, equity, and fair dealing (public confidence), management of public procurement through an extensive regulatory framework often constitutes the status quo. This framework reflects a traditional approach to public procurement—and for many other government functions perceived as basic processing—by relying heavily on regulation as the primary means of control of administrative process and implementation of policy. Regulations control the micromanagement steps throughout the procurement process.

A highly regulated procurement environment is designed to minimize discretion in circumstances considered to be at high risk from undue influence. A highly prescriptive approach may also seem appropriate in jurisdictions where officials have minimal procurement skills, and which are striving to ensure transparency or prevent or overcome corruption: the regulated approach is almost universal in, but not exclusive to, developing countries. An attempt to standardize procurement regulations is the *Model Law on Procurement of Goods, Construction and Services* developed by the United Nations Commission on International Trade Law (UNCITRAL, 1994) through its working group on the new international economic order.

A highly regulated management environment is also often a means of political risk minimization (Pegnato, 2003) in developed countries. In these cases, the focus is on compliance with the prescribed process as a means of elimination or avoidance of risk. Assessment of procurement management performance is defined in terms of compliance with the set rules. Examples of regulated environments are diverse and include Canada, the United States, Brazil, and Thailand. Many of the state and local entities in the United States also undertake their procurement in a regulated environment, under the provisions of the model procurement code (MCP) for state and local governments, developed by the American Bar Association (Rickard and Radwan, 2004).

The penalty for a highly prescribed framework is its lack of flexibility in managing agency needs, placing it in tension with performance and efficiency. The detailed codification of process is designed to eliminate scope for partiality in outcomes and protect governments from scandal and corruption (often with limited success), but in doing so also tends to eliminate all but the most mechanical aspects of this activity (Kelman, 1990; Pegnato, 2003). Regulated frameworks are procedurally costly and, although readily prescribed for simple procurement, are slow to adapt to changes that require the reengineering of process or the development of increasingly complex procurement associated with sophisticated supply chains. Microregulation of the process also has the unintended consequence of eroding the skill requirements of procurement officials, thereby undermining professionalism in this activity. Procurement training in this context consists of learning the rules. This lack of professionalism might, in turn, be expected to increase the need for further regulation of process as well as reduce value-for-money in procurement, which requires extensive management skills. This erodes accountability except in terms of compliance.

Significantly, the transparency goal of this regulatory model can also be self-defeating: the daunting volume of regulations acts to obfuscate transparency by making the processes difficult for stakeholders, such as businesses, to comprehend (MacManus, 1991).

4.2.3 Managerialism and Performance

Social and economic pressures at both domestic and global levels have required governments to seek better performance from their public sectors. Successive waves of management and financial reforms have, inter alia, focused on improving public procurement efficiency, effectiveness, and outcomes (Callender and Matthews, 2002). Many of these reform initiatives have featured managerialism and a general shift toward devolution and decentralization (McCue and Gianakis, 2001; Thai, 2001). Usually, this shift away from the center has been attributed to a need to respond more effectively to the sensitivities of the client or the community, or to engage more fully the capabilities of all of the human resources at the disposal of the organization or the public sector. The management of public procurement has been subjected to the same reform pressures. For example, this statement from the Australian government's procurement reforms (Purchasing Australia, 1995, p. 1):

> ...In seeking improvements to the accountability and administration of the procurement function, the Government expects departments and agencies to exploit fully procurement's potential to add value to program delivery, contain and reduce costs in real terms and contribute to the achievement of broader policy objectives, particularly for industry development.

The requirement for procurement to deliver higher performance in terms of improved value-for-money and fit-for-purpose outcomes has led to the development of more complex supply chains (e.g., through outsourcing and partnering arrangements) to deliver comprehensive service solutions, requiring more sophisticated relationships with suppliers. These more complex supply chains represent a move away from simple competitive markets and require a deeper understanding of industry structures and capabilities. These higher-value supply chains also require more extensive management skills to develop and maintain (NASPO, 1999; Martin, 2002). Some characteristics of this evolution are presented in Table 4.1.

To be able to manage these more complex relationships and outcomes, management of procurement has faced increasing pressure for devolution from centralized control to line agencies. Accompanying this devolution has sometimes been an assignment of greater flexibility, or varying degrees of deregulation within a broader governance framework and with more highly skilled managers. A lesser reliance on regulated prescription of the process of procurement has also given rise to the need for more coherent management tools and policies (which are not always provided) to manage stakeholder interests and risks.

Table 4.1 Changing Nature of Public Procurement

Simple processes→	Complex contracts and relationships
Largely goods→	Complete service solutions
Sourcing considerations→	Strategic business decisions
Low value, low risk→	High value, high risk
Back-office function→	Central to strategic management
Warehousing→	Just-in-time
Basic skills→	High-level skills

4.2.4 Efficiency of Process

The foregoing discussion has centered on public procurement management first for compliance and then for effectiveness in terms of best value-for-money and fit-for-purpose outcomes. These objectives traditionally have each led jurisdictions down quite different paths, the first defining procurement as a legal process, the second in terms of management.

Of further significance is the operational efficiency of the process as it relates both to government and to business. Efficiency of process is a concurrent consideration regardless of whether procurement is defined as a regulated process or managerial task. The efficiency equation is important in this discussion because it introduces complications to the tension between centralization and decentralization of management of the framework (see also discussion on centralization and delegation in Johnson et al. (2003)).

The efficiency of procurement processes and some of the approaches intended to deliver value-for-money outcomes are not neutral to the degree of centralization or devolution. Indeed, the sources of efficiency available to best-practice procurement are multiple. The efficiency and effectiveness of procurement are often sensitive to scale and coordination and involve both public administrative processes and industry structural and transactional issues. In this way, efficiency overlaps with the concept of value-for-money outcomes.

Even in highly competitive markets, price can be negotiable in terms of volume and time undertakings provided to suppliers, often at little or no risk to buyers. Thus, additional to the low credit risk represented by government, the level of supplier risk can almost always be decreased through agency demand aggregation, giving greater certainty and volume to suppliers with the associated savings available to be passed on. These benefits sometimes become evident through, for example, outsourcing service arrangements such as for IT networks and services. An example of enhanced coordination and aggregation in IT acquisitions is the opening up in early 2003 of the U.S. General Services Administration IT schedule to allow access by state and local governments, thereby expanding the potential customer base for federal IT contracts, with benefits for both buyers and suppliers.

These factors militate against optimum efficiency outcomes, consistent with complete devolution of contracting for many simple goods and services as well as for more complex services such as IT systems and networks and telecommunications arrangements. These considerations explain the hybrid management systems of some governments such as Singapore (McCue and Gianakis, 2001; Jones, 2002), although others employ consortia approaches (Aylseworth, 2003).

A second avenue for efficiency relates to the costs of transactions. Transaction costs are greater in the public sector because of the generally more demanding requirements of transparency. Also, the great majority of transactions are small purchases, typically a few hundred dollars or less, such that the cost of transaction processing becomes a large or even a dominant proportion of the purchase. The significance of transaction costs can be gauged by the cost of processing of a simple procurement commonly estimated at between \$75–\$100 (NASPO, 1997) and the reality that generally about 70 percent of public sector procurement transactions are less than \$500 (Schapper, 2000).

A third avenue for efficiency savings emerges through redefining the outcome requirements themselves and represents an overlap between efficiency and performance. This category of opportunity requires significant management data as well as strategic agency management with a strong interagency coordination of efficiency goals. Here, public administration challenges the existing and often traditional modes of business and administration and seeks new solutions. For example, an administration with 10,000 IT "seats" may seek to use this buying power to negotiate a better licensing deal for its desktop systems, or it may consider alternative solutions altogether such as outsourcing of all or part of the function, use of a shared service center, or a total reengineering of the relationship with its clients and stakeholders, such that much of the processing is done outside the organization as has occurred with e-tax in the taxation industry in Australia (ATO, 2004). The first option represents an example of aggregate buying although the latter ones are examples of more strategic approaches.

All of these issues and options are further complicated by the structure of public procurement which in most countries is dichotomized between low-value, high-volume procurement (such as office supplies) and high-value, low-volume procurement such as major capital works. Most *transactions* in every jurisdiction will be of low value and high volume, including most office supplies, for example, although most *expenditure* will be involved with high-value, low-volume exercises. Small transactions (for less than \$5000) will usually be undertaken though a simplified quoting system or even straight off a preexisting contract. For higher-value procurement (typically above \$25,000–\$100,000) a public bidding or tendering process is usually the standard methodology. These larger complex exercises require high levels of expertise relating to not only contract specification and risk management but also in the ongoing relationship and performance management.

4.2.5 Policy Coherence

Some jurisdictions develop procurement policy to address only the relatively narrow agenda of transparency, value, or process efficiency. A broader, more strategic policy suite is adopted by others who have recognized that this function can be developed to harmonize more effectively the elements of procurement with other government policies such as workforce training, environmental protection, and regionalization and business policies. This broader approach to procurement policy can also reflect a view that an inherent role of government is to recognize and exploit the potential for externalities.

It is in this extended policy environment that procurement may often appear to become politicized. An alternative model accepts that this broader holistic policy set that may seem to interfere with the scope of the procurement professional is in reality valid and even a preferred state of affairs. Political interference often may simply be a manifestation of legitimate political representation for the broad impacts of procurement beyond the relatively one dimensional value-for-money objective. Of course this is only a small step away from illegitimate interference which means that transparency becomes of even greater significance. To the extent that this presence has a legitimate role the challenge is not one of quarantining public procurement from politics, community, and business but one of incorporating these stakeholders in a way that good governance is preserved. Indeed it seems that there is substantial scope for harmonization between these seemingly opposing forces.

For example, the nexus between public procurement and business policy is especially evident and has been embraced by many, including Canada, Korea, and the United States, with explicit legislative preference given to domestic and small business suppliers to the government. The significance of this policy integration reflects the appreciation that governments, in the normal course of their activities and in addition to their business development programs, are major players in national and regional economies of many countries around the world.

The methodologies and policies they adopt for procurement for their service and construction inputs, as well as through their contractors, can therefore have significant influence over the prosperity or survival of many businesses or industries. For example, in some jurisdictions the public sector represents more than 50 percent of the IT market. Evidence also supports the contention that access to government work acts to improve small and medium enterprise (SME) capabilities, competitiveness, and potential to enter other markets, as well as boost the economies of remote communities (U.K. Procurement Policy Unit, 2001).

This alignment of public procurement with business policy can be reflected at numerous levels within the procurement cycle, without resorting to the use of expensive and anticompetitive price discrimination or breaching agreements such as the World Trade Organization's agreement on government procurement. For example, typically more than 85 percent of government procurement transactions are of low-value goods or services for which small local suppliers can have an inherent competitive advantage, or disadvantage, depending on how governments might go about aggregating these transactions into a higher-value supply chain.

At another level, the tendering or competitive bidding exercises by government are generally expensive and time consuming for business: for small businesses these costs can be prohibitive, effectively barring them from competing (MacManus, 1991) even though they might otherwise be highly competitive. For larger businesses and multinationals these costs can be readily absorbed. In this example, the procurement methodology adopted by government can be seen to be both anti-competitive as well as anti-small (generally local) business.

Similarly it is significant for SMEs that bidding documentation be standardized across government in order that industry does not have to undertake an ongoing and expensive learning process agency by agency. Inconsistent documentation creates uncertainty amongst suppliers as to what agencies are actually seeking, and often requires bidders to provide similar information repeatedly but in slightly different formats. One of the most persistent complaints by industry in some jurisdictions relates to the inconsistent application of policy and procedures between government agencies or even by different officials within the same agency. This creates confusion, reduces the potential for industry (especially SMEs) to improve its skill base, reduces transparency, undermines confidence, adds to cost, and is the root cause of why some otherwise competitive SMEs conclude that doing business with government is "too hard" (MacManus, 1991; Kovacic, 1992). Well-understood and transparent processes also provide a powerful audit mechanism by recruiting much of industry to engage in informal peer review of bid outcomes.

Thus the very structure, efficiency, and application of the bidding processes engaged by governments can be implicitly biased for or against otherwise competitive small and regional businesses. If these and other issues are not recognized and accounted for within the policy framework, or if the policy is simply laissez faire, it is unlikely that they will be competitively neutral to the business environment.

Therefore operational or process methodologies cannot be divorced from public policy if the holistic policy set is to be coherent, even though, to the procurement professional, political interest in these issues may seem unprofessional and even improper. These issues involving the harmonization of business policy and public procurement, significant as they are, become of even greater importance in the way government adopts technology into its supply chain management.

4.3 Reform and Public Procurement

The complexities of the foregoing discussion suggest why the reform of public procurement is frequently simplistic and cyclical. Public procurement and public administration, more generally, have been the focus of successive waves of management reform worldwide, stretching across the past 30 years. These reforms have included managerialism, outsourcing, corporatization, centralization, and devolution, and have been driven by an imperative to improve the performance and cost-effectiveness of the public service (Self, 1993). These reforms have frequently been confronted by apparent tensions between the basic qualities of public governance, such as accountability and transparency versus outcomes and performance (Hughes, 1994; Considine and Painter, 1997).

Operational failures of procurement governance are attributed by pro-regulators to weaknesses in the professionalism of practitioners rather than to any inherent weaknesses in the regulations as such, although pro-management advocates also attribute failure to professional weaknesses they identify the causes with the regulatory regime itself, which tends to reduce the role of management of everything other than mechanical compliance. In both cases the broader political context and policy roles are frequently not acknowledged at all.

Governments have responded to many of the issues with cyclical reforms of regulation and management and sometimes centralization to deliver the corresponding expectations of the day in terms of compliance and performance, respectively. Some reforms have revealed a lack of understanding of the basic elements of procurement. Well-planned public procurement, especially aggregated buying, can frequently outperform the spot and auction markets, yet some governments have devolved away this option (for example, the Australian government) although some others may be building unrealistic expectations around the new capacity for online auctions that potentially disaggregate buying and forgo returns to scale. The drivers of these responses have been such as to generate predictions that they condemn public procurement to never ending cycles of reform, as illustrated in Figure 4.1, that swing between rigid regulation of microprocesses through to the deferment to performance management (Kovacic, 1992; Shoop, 1994; Pegnato, 2003).

Requirements for greater performance produce a refocusing of procurement management away from accountability for compliance through rule-bound codified processes (McCue and Pitzer,

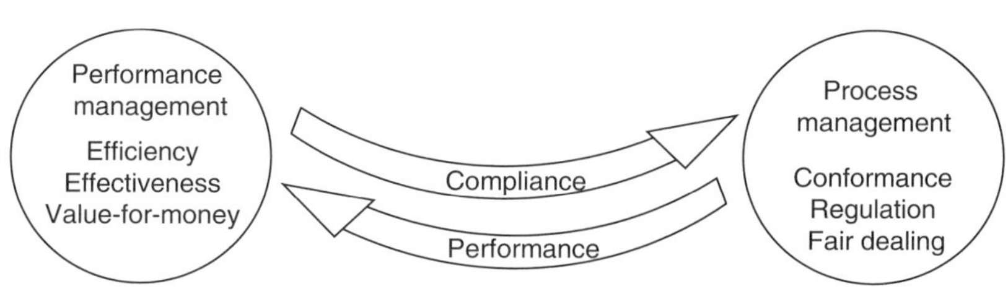

Figure 4.1 Compliance–performance reform cycle.

2000) toward accountability for outcomes. In turn, inevitable failures in due process produce a return to regulation for compliance. A degree of polarization can be observed worldwide between jurisdictions governed by compliance and those by value-for-money or performance.

Within a performance model for public procurement, the role of regulation is primarily to establish management principles and objectives rather than to micromanage the processes. In contrast to the UNCITRAL model law approach, the performance management approach advocated by the OECD/DAC (2003) describes procurement and its governance in terms of strategic mainstream management (see also Qiao and Cummings, 2003). Representing the management approach are the European Commission, United Kingdom (Thai, 2001), and Australia (Purchasing Australia, 1995).

This substantial political tension between compliance and performance and the relationships with centralization versus devolution lies at the heart of the debate around the reform of public procurement, as it has done over its history (Nagle, 1992). Piecemeal government reforms will often seem clumsy, but at least some of the responsibility for this lies with management itself. Management often exacerbates the problem by narrowly defining the scope of procurement such that it cannot be expected to encompass many higher level demands including often legitimate political agenda.

4.4 Analytical Framework for Public Procurement

The preceding discussion describes a procurement management environment which includes elements of law, finance and accounting, risk management and politics; and where practitioners from each of these professions at times claim this function as their province. This claim-staking is recognized explicitly in the various management frameworks that can be found worldwide for procurement governance and is indicative of the lack of consensus, including within reform agendas, about what government procurement entails or of its strategic significance.

This lack of consensus about the scope and nature of public procurement is often as prevalent and varied within organizations and even between procurement practitioners as it is between these professions. For organizations in which procurement is conceived of as a mid- to low-level backroom activity driven by compliance, process management will be the status quo, and relatively few agendas of performance or wider policy will be met, and reform becomes endemic. Alternatively, where organizations conceive of procurement in terms of organizational performance—usually in terms of indicators such as budget impact—broader policy expectations and compliance will be neglected. Frequently too, public sector organizations will be of a scale that does not seem to justify anything more than a clerical approach to this function.

Even where the impacts of these elements are acknowledged, there is often insufficient scope or incentive for management to coordinate or collaborate with other public sector agencies, or to develop the means and roles to reconcile transparency with substantial bodies of regulations as well as with efficiency and effectiveness objectives and related policy goals such as business development. These elements do not readily coexist and may even seem incompatible. For example, the commercial and operational realities of procurement efficiency and effectiveness generate management responses in opposing terms of both centralization and devolution.

Only where organizations or governments recognize the appropriate scope of public procurement, balancing the process and performance and strategic imperatives, can they develop the skills, incentives, performance measures, organizations, and management tools to deliver the full range of political and community expectations. These elements and their relationships are illustrated in the

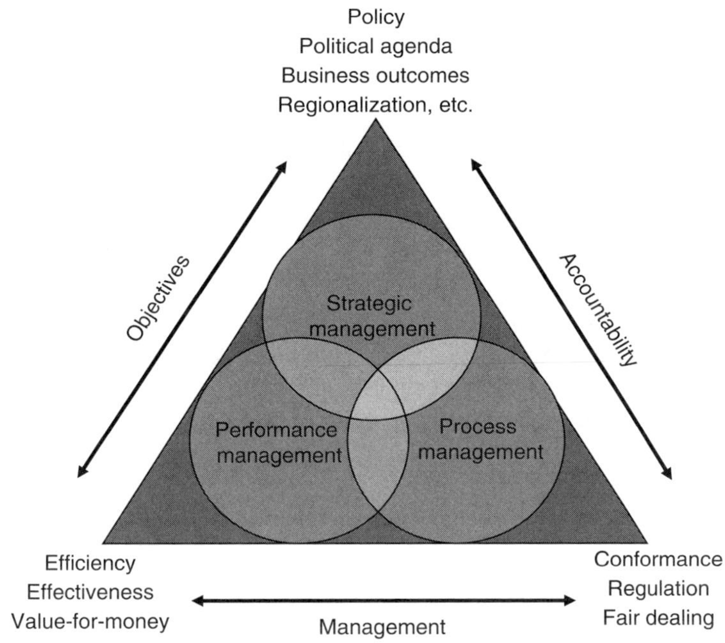

Figure 4.2 Procurement management framework.

model in Figure 4.2. In the absence of a comprehensive framework such as this, government reforms can be expected to remain piecemeal and cyclical.

Figure 4.2 shows that any public procurement exercise can be subject to competing goals of conformance management and performance management, and each of these may also be competing with broader strategic political goals of the government or reforms such as outsourcing and privatization which in turn may not coincide with the roles and related performance measures of each organization. Within this model, strategic management will be associated, inter alia, with broader reforms such as process reengineering, outsourcing, and restructuring as well as policy issues such as business and regional development, although process management will be associated with simple, off-the-shelf purchasing, and performance management with complex procurement, alliance contracting, and construction. This also suggests that the different regimes of process management, performance management, and strategic management are likely to be associated with the centralization–devolution conflict often evident in procurement reforms. In particular:

- Strategic management will be consistent with the centralization of contract design and documentation, specification and evaluation, and also the regulation of process. This will also be consistent with central agency roles.
- Performance management will be consistent with the de-centralization of contract specification, evaluation and regulation, but also with central aggregation of contracts to gain economics of scale. This will be consistent with the larger operational organizations including those responsible for public works.
- Process management will be consistent with the devolution of contract processes, mostly consistent with smaller organizations requiring simple purchases.

Managing public procurement would seem to demand an arbitrage between these various elements but this is rarely evident in practice. Procurement practitioners respond to the requirements of their own organization and will generally identify their role in terms of process management/simple procurement versus performance management/complex procurement versus strategic procurement and policy depending on whether they are in a small or a larg operational organization or a central policy agency. But this role identification cannot quarantine these managers from the inherent tensions that arise from the conflicts between centralization and decentralization, a consequence of these alternate roles. Efforts to strengthen or reform public procurement will often include centralization versus decentralization or devolution considerations but have rarely reconciled or even recognized the tensions between these basic constituents of the procurement environment, and instead have identified the need for change with the outcomes of these problems and in doing so have often preserved the underlying divergences.

Understanding these complex issues is often unappetizing both to executives and to politicians, making their reconciliation seem unachievable. The emergence of technology into this field is, however, beginning to reshape the possibilities.

4.4.1 Impact of Technology

The effects of technology on this environment should be assessed in terms of the three broad objectives already listed: transparency of process, efficiency, and policy coherence. The potential for technology to enhance governance and transparency has been noted by others for public administration generally (see, for example, Shadrach and Ekeanyanwu, 2003). E-commerce in government provides the opportunity for major enhancements to transparency, primarily through more effective audit, for the great volume of simple, low-value transactions. Technology can, at very low cost, transform procurement fraud control from a process that relies largely on chance to one based on audit sampling of 100 percent if required. Further, audits can be improved not just in terms of coverage but also through profiling that can readily be constructed of the buying activities and sourcing decisions for each procurement agent within any government agency.

The mechanism is different for high-value complex procurement exercises. Key transparency features here include enhanced public access to up-to-date policies, information on bidding programs, standardized documentation and lodgement of bids, progress of tender evaluation, and announcements of outcomes. Thus for high-value exercises, transparency is strengthened primarily through direct public disclosure of all stages of each procurement exercise, although for low-value procurement, transparency is strengthened primarily through greatly improved audit capabilities.

This enhanced transparency from the application of technology to this function delivers directly what volumes of regulations seek to do indirectly and often tenuously. Procurement regulation usually aims at ensuring transparency through due process by stipulation of procedural steps. The outcome of this is, as already noted, often a lack of transparency because of obfuscation by comprehensive rule sets. Technology bypasses much of this by delivering very low-cost audit paths and highly accessible activity records: transparency is delivered more directly. Much of the cumbersome volume of regulations is irrelevant to the technology other than as a one-off to guide systems development. The regulation versus performance issue becomes substantially circumvented.

In terms of efficiency the opportunities for technology to streamline procurement come through at many levels both for suppliers and for buyers in the payment cycle, financial management integration, approvals, reporting, etc. The degree of manual processing in simple procurement, which can be streamlined with a well-designed and functional government e-commerce system, can be appreciated through an understanding of all of the elements that make up typical supply chain processing, which includes search, requests for quotations, authorizations, financial reconciliations, and much more.

For complex procurement, the efficiency equation is more related to the quality and relevance of management information instead of manual processing. Performance in terms of value-for-money outcomes can be affected by improvements in management information facilitated by technology, but these benefits can only be fully realized where the application of technology is accompanied by adequate skill sets of procurement managers. Thus, efficiencies provided by online access to catalogs and prenegotiated contractual arrangements will be negated if the contractual arrangements themselves are inadequate.

Evidence supporting these conclusions has been reported by a recent survey carried out by the School of Business, Curtin University of Technology (2007), Perth, Western Australia, of electranic government procurement in 13 countries in Asia, South America, and Europe. This survey reported substantial increases in competition, greater efficiency, and greater transparency for government procurement following the introduction of e-GP. Also reported were improved management information, declines in supplier complaints, and reductions in prices paid by between 3–80 percent by government for low-value items.

Thus, the potential effects of technology on this environment are at three levels. First, by significantly enhancing the capacity for transparency for simple procurement, technology can help reconcile the tension between performance and conformance. Second, by reducing the cost of transactions for simple procurement, it can directly contribute to efficiency objectives of management. Third, it has the capacity to strengthen management information and thereby increase the effectiveness of more complex procurement, provided that the skill levels of management are in place. It can also significantly reconcile centralized policy determination with devolved management, as well as enhance the policy role itself.

4.4.2 Externalities

Most of this discussion has focussed on government as a buyer. Many of the transactional efficiencies to benefit government through the application of technology will also benefit businesses as suppliers to government and so intersect with business development policies of government. Also the greater access to documentation and more efficient information and document transmission, together with improved transparency, makes bidding for government work more attractive for business, and competition can be expected to increase. Indeed there is evidence that this is what happens: online availability of tender information has been attributed to increasing competition for government work in both developed and developing countries. OECD/DAC (2003) reported an analysis of individual procurement projects as showing that such methods that enhance competition and transparency can result in a reduction of contract costs by as much as 20–30 percent.

Beyond these microeconomic and management benefits of technology, there are externalities that have the potential to be important, especially for smaller and developing countries which do not have robust, broad-based private sectors to drive technology take-up. With government accounting for a significant proportion of the economy, the speed of take-up of technology by the broader economy will be influenced substantially by the rate of government adoption. The role of government in accelerating the technological enablement of economies has been observed by the OECD (2003). It is also for this reason that the e-commerce model and standards adopted by government carry significance much greater than the immediate applications intended for in government. A strategic approach to technology by government that harmonizes with its industry policies will enhance interoperability and connectivity throughout the economy in a shorter time horizon than might otherwise be expected with potentially significant gains in productivity and competitiveness. This effect once again reflects the need for synergy between procurement and broader policy agendas.

4.5 Discussion and Conclusion

The conduct of public procurement has reflected tensions between public expectations of high standards of governance, management requirements for performance, overt (and covert) political influence, and pressures from broader stakeholder interests such as business. However, there are no clearly agreed international best-practice models for the management of public procurement to address these issues, and government responses have varied accordingly. As discussed, at one extreme are highly prescriptive and regulated structures, although others are characterized by almost complete deregulation and devolved responsibilities where procurement is just another element of mainstream management. These disparities reflect fundamental differences in the understanding of procurement in different jurisdictions, often deriving from their historical circumstances and political constraints. In many jurisdictions these tensions remain in unstable equilibrium (NPR, 1993; Peters, 1996; Hunja, 2003; McCue et al., 2003).

The scope of procurement processes is rarely well defined. Differentiating between high-value and low-value acquisitions often fails to acknowledge that devolved decision making and deregulation are not entirely consistent with improved management outcomes.

These issues reveal quite different perceptions of what public procurement is for different organizations, agendas, and stakeholders. This also suggests that reconciliation between these competing forces is not simply difficult but improbable because it represents more than conflicting expectations about what procurement is all about—it also represents broader conflicting roles between, for example, central and operational organizations. However, the reform of much of this area becomes more viable when the reform process addresses the technological possibilities as a starting point.

The information-sharing capabilities of technology allow, inter alia, elements of centralization of process and devolution of procurement decision making to be combined more efficiently, thus alleviating the management, accountability, and objectives tensions illustrated in Figure 4.2. Here technology can efficiently combine centralized aggregated procurement and complex approaches to the market, and evaluation and contract management, with the information, buying techniques and any controls applicable to the resulting arrangements accessed simply by devolved buyers.

Should this potential of technology seem simple and attractive, the question arises as to why so few jurisdictions have availed themselves of the full potential of these applications. In reality, numerous governments have found the promises to be compelling but are often unprepared for the implied level of reform. E-commerce in government can lead to improved expenditure analysis and control, but requires a redesign of the purchasing cycle and associated management reform. It will not result in improvements by simply grafting technology onto existing manual processes (Schapper and Malta, 2004). Instead, the benefits of this application of technology require understanding of the politics and reform in management, policy, legislation, business acceptance, and sometimes infrastructure as well as technological functionality and connectivity. The need for awareness and management strategies to bring all these issues together has been identified by multilateral development banks as a key to reform (Multilateral Development Bank, 2004).

There have frequently been mistaken presumptions that because the potential of this technology is great then it is easy, or because results have not come easily the potential is not great. It is possible to allocate substantial resources to procurement systems and technologies without impacting significantly on the underlying issues, partly because of the lack of understanding of procurement itself, and partly through a lack of understanding of the scope and limitations of technology in addressing the issues. The complexity of the procurement management environment and its interaction with the skill set of procurement professionals, summarized in Figure 4.2, illustrates why reform does not come easily and reform with technology is not necessarily any easier than reform historically (MacManus, 2002; Pegnato, 2003).

The opportunities for genuine reform and a break in the cyclical reinvention of the procurement management framework require a holistic approach to each of these political and operational realities of public procurement and its strategic significance. Weaknesses at this level continue to be the greatest area of risk to the successful application of technology in the reform of this function.

References

Asia-Pacific Economic Cooperation. 1999. *Non-Binding Principles on Government Procurement* (Report by the Chair of the Government Procurement Experts Group). Available at www.epec.org.

Australian Taxation Office (ATO). 2004. The ATO's E-tax and On-line Lodgement. Available at http://www.ato.gov.au.

Callender, G. and Matthews, D. 2002. The economic context of government procurement: New challenges and new opportunities. *Journal of Public Procurement*, 2(1): 55–71.

Coggburn, J.D. 2003. Exploring differences in the American states' procurement practices. *Journal of Public Procurement*, 3(1): 3–28.

Considine M. and Painter, M. (Eds.). 1997. *Managerialism: The Great Debate*. Melbourne, Australia: Melbourne University Press.

Curtin University of Technology. 2007. *International Survey of E-procurement Systems*. World Bank Publication. Available at http://idbdocs.iadb.org/wsdocs/getdocument.aspx?docnum=1064452.

Dilulio, J.J. 1994. *Deregulating the Public Service: Can Government be Improved?* Washington, DC: The Brookings Institute.

Finn, J. July 2, 1997. Major Changes in Tendering Law—the Hughes Case. *Legal Briefing No. 33*. Available at http://www.ags.gov.au/publications/agspubs/legalpubs/legalbriefings/br33.htm.

Fradkov, M. May 13, 2004. State procurement to reach 40% of 2004 budget expenses. *The Russia Journal Daily*. Available at http://www.russiajournal.com.news/cnewswire.shtml?nw=43741.

General Accounting Office (GAO). 2000. *Space Shuttle: Human Capital Challenges Require Management Attention* (GAO/T 00-133). Washington, DC: Author.

Harland, C., Gibbs, J., and Sutton, R. 2000. Supply strategy for the public sector: Framing the issues. *Conference 2000 Proceedings*. London, Ontario, Canada: Richard Ivey School of Business, pp. 342–351.

Hughes, O.E. 1994. *Public Management & Administration: An Introduction*. London, United Kingdom: MacMillan.

Hunja, R. 2003. Obstacles to Public Procurement Reform in Developing Countries. A Paper Presented at the WTO-World Bank Regional Workshop on Procurement Reforms and Transparency in Public Procurement for Anglophone African Countries, Tanzania. Available at www.worldbank.org.

Isaac, A. 1997. The cave creek incident: A reasoned explanation. *The Australian Journal of Disaster and Trauma Studies*, 3. Available at www.massey.ac.nz/~trauma/issues/1997-3/contents.shtml-9k (retrieved September 23, 2004).

Johnson, P.F., Leenders, M.R., and McCue, C. 2003. A comparison of purchasing organizational roles and responsibilities in the public and private sectors. *Journal of Public Procurement*, 3(1): 57–74.

Jones, D.S. 2002. Procurement practices in the Singapore civil service: Balancing control and delegation. *Journal of Public Procurement*, 2(1): 29–53.

Kelman, S. 1990. *Procurement and Public Management: The Fear of Discretion and Quality of Government Performance*. Washington, DC: AEI Press.

Kovacic, W.E. 1992. Regulatory controls as barriers to entry in government procurement. *Policy Sciences*, 25(1): 29–42.

MacManus, S.A. 1991. Why businesses are reluctant to sell to government. *Public Administration Review*, 51(4): 328–344.

MacManus, S.A. 2002. Understanding the incremental nature of e-procurement implementation at the state and local levels. *Journal of Public Procurement*, 2(1): 5–28.

Martin, L.L. 2002. Performance based contracting for human services: Lessons for public procurement? *Journal of Public Procurement*, 2(1): 55–71.

McCue, C.P. and Gianakis, G.A. 2001. Public purchasing: Who's minding the store? *Journal of Public Procurement*, 1(1): 71–95.

McCue, C.P. and Pitzer, J.T. 2000. Centralized vs decentralized purchasing: Current trends in government procurement practices. *Journal of Public Budgeting, Accounting & Financial Management*, 12(3): 400–420.

McCue, C.P., Buffington, K.W., and Howell, A.D. 2003. The Fraud/Red Tape Dilemma in Public Procurement: A Study of U.S. State and Local Governments. Paper Presented at the International Research Study of Public Procurement Workshop, Budapest, Hungary, April 10–12.

Multilateral Development Bank resource paper. March 2004. Strategic Electronic Government Procurement—An Introduction for Executives. Available at http://idbdocs.iadb.org/wsdocs/getdocument.aspx?docnum=645439.

Nagle, F.J. 1992. *A History of Government Contracting*. Washington, DC: George Washington University.

National Association of State Procurement Officials (NASPO). 1997. *State and Local Government Purchasing: Principles and Practices*. Lexington, KY: Author.

National Association of State Procurement Officials (NASPO). 1999. *Survey of State and Local Government Purchasing Practices*. 5th edn., Lexington, KY: Author.

National Performance Review (NPR). 1993. *From Red Tape to Results: Creating a Government that Works Better and Costs Less*. Washington, DC: U.S. Government Printing Office.

Nicol, W. 2003. *Mainstreaming the Procurement Function into the Public Expenditure Policy and Effectiveness Dialogue* (OEDC/DAC). World Bank Roundtable, Paris, France, 22–23 January.

OECD/DAC. 2003. Mainstreaming the Procurement Function into the Public Expenditure Policy and Effectiveness Dialogue (OECD/DAC). World Bank Roundtable, Paris, 22–23 January. Available at www.oecd.org.

Organisation for Economic Co-Operation and Development (OECD). 2003. ICT and Economic Growth: Evidence from OECD Countries, Industries and Firms. Available at www.oecd.org.

Osborne, D. and Gaebler, T. 1992. *Reinventing Government: How the Entrepreneurial Spirit is Transforming the Public Sector*. New York: Plume.

Peachment, A. 1992. *The Executive State: WA Inc and the Constitution*. Perth, Australia: Constitutional Press.

Pegnato, J.A. 2003. Assessing federal procurement reform: Has the procurement pendulum stopped swinging? *Journal of Public Procurement*, 3(2): 145–175.

Peters, B.G. 1996. *The Future of Governing: Four Emerging Models*. Lawrence, KS: University of Kansas Press.

Procurement Policy Unit. 2001. *Procurement Policy Guidelines*. London, U.K.: Office of Government Commerce.

Purchasing Australia. 1995. *Transforming Procurement: Guidance on the Organisation and Management of Procurement*. Canberra, Australia: Australian Government Printing Service.

Qiao, Y. and Cummings, G. 2003. The use of qualifications-based selection in public procurement: A survey research. *The Journal of Public Procurement*, 3(2): 215–249.

Rickard, R. and Radwan, C.M. June 2004. Meet bid protests head-on. *Government Procurement*, 20–22.

Schapper, P.R. 2000. Electronic Business Solutions. Proceedings of the Institute of Chartered Accountants Congress, The Business Forum of the Millennium, held at the University of Western Australia, Perth, June 6–9.

Schapper, P.R. and Veiga Malta, J. 2004. Cómo Hacer para que el Estado Compre Mejor. *Gobierno Digital*, 3: 16–29.

Self, P. 1993. *Government by the Market? The Politics of Public Choice*. London, U.K.: MacMillan.

Shadrach, B. and Ekeanyanwu, L. 2003. Improving the Transparency, Quality and Effectiveness of Pro-poor Public Services Using the ICTs: An Attempt by Transparency International. Paper Presented at the 11th International Anti-Corruption Conference, Seoul, Korea, 25–28 May, 2003.

Shoop, T. 1994. Steven Kelman: Advocate of reform. *Government Executive*, 26(8): 68–72.

Thai, K.V. 2001. Public procurement re-examined. *Journal of Public Procurement*, 1(1): 9–50.

Thai, K.V. and Grimm, R. 2000. Government procurement: Past and current developments. *Journal of Public Budgeting, Accounting & Financial Management*, 12(2): 231–247.

United Nations Commission on International Trade Law (UNCITRAL). 1994. UNCITRAL Model Law on Procurement of Goods, Construction and Services. Available at http://www.uncitral.org/en-index.htm.

Chapter 5

EU Directives as Anticorruption Measures: Excluding Corruption-Convicted Tenderers from Public Procurement Contracts

Teresa Medina Arnáiz

CONTENTS

5.1 Introduction

Acts of corruption have been with us since time immemorial and are all too familiar throughout civilization since classical antiquity. The first documented cases of bribery date back to 3000 BC (Noonan, 1984), which provides us with a myriad of situations, contexts, and actors. It is a widespread phenomenon whose manifestations have changed over time and in different cultures; nonetheless, it has not allowed us to reach agreement on a single, commonly held definition (Amundsen, 2000). Consensus only exists in relation to its pernicious influence on the proper management of public institutions and the disruption of private markets.

The harmful effects of corruption are evident in economic life (Mauro, 1995; Tanzi and Davoodi, 1997), but they also have an impact at a social and political level (Méndez and Sepúlveda, 2006). In fact, in the preamble to one of the most important regulatory instruments in the fight against corruption, the United Nations Convention against Corruption refers to the destructive effects of corruption when it points out that it "is concerned about the seriousness of problems and threats posed by corruption to the stability and security of societies, undermining the institutions and values of democracy, ethical values and justice and jeopardizing sustainable development and the rule of law." As a result, although there are authors who try to water down the effects of corruption, Tanzi (1998) contends that it propagates its own harmful effects beyond the specific illegal acts of public bodies or businesses and damages society as a whole by threatening social equality and the social contract.

The attention that corruption has attracted, above all since the 1990s, is due to its wide-ranging nature that goes beyond a few isolated cases. It emerges in developing countries as much as in the developed ones (Tanzi, 1998). The globalization of economic exchange between countries has aided the transmission of corrupt models and the transfer of criminal profits. Similarly, techniques used to extend corruption are also exported, spreading out beyond national frontiers. Media accusations highlighting the corruption of high-ranking officials also contribute to increased public interest in this phenomenon and confirm that it is not exclusively a local problem. Instead, we find ourselves up against a range of corrupt patterns of behavior that replicate themselves in different corners of the world, even though they are at some distance from each other, thereby acquiring a global dimension.

The perception of corruption as having international implications (Rose-Ackerman, 1997; Stessens, 2001) has led to significant changes in the measures applied to combat it. Since the early years of programs and declarations, we have moved on to a more active method of fighting corruption and thus, alongside the specific activities of each state, initiatives to counter corruption have proliferated in different international organizations.[1] A broad range of mechanisms are available for this purpose. Codes of conduct, pacts of integrity and standards of transparency along with covenants, protocols, and recommendations all share one and the same aim: to call attention to the need to foster cooperation between states to put an end to corrupt practices. It is this line of action that the European Union (EU) is also following.

This chapter carries out an in-depth study of one of the measures adopted by the EU as part of its anticorruption policy. It examines mandatory exclusion from public procurement procedures in those circumstances in which tenderers have been convicted of acts of corruption in a final judicial sentence in the context of community directives on public procurement; directives that make it are binding upon the legislator in each member state to introduce mandatory exclusion from procurement into domestic legislation. The chapter therefore examines the way in which different member states implement this measure when they transpose the community Directives on public procurement into their national laws, and reveals the problems that arise when the latter exclusion is applied.

5.2 Corruption in Public Procurement

Aware that the problem of corruption also affects member states, the EU has developed a comprehensive anticorruption strategy in those sectors that are more prone to corrupt practices.[2] It has therefore intensified the fight through measures in those areas that, because they jeopardize greater amounts of public resources, might endanger the community objective of ensuring the effective operation of the internal market.[3]

This is one of the reasons why addressing corruption in public procurement is an important component of any effective anticorruption strategy, though it is not the only one. Of all the government activities, public procurement is the one most vulnerable to corruption, which is evident from the recurrent scandals related to the award of public contracts.[4] One of the causes of the spread of these practices is found in the turnover of procurement contracts in the public sector: procurement of goods, works, and other services by public bodies alone amounts on average to between 15 percent and 30 percent of gross domestic product (GDP) (Transparency International, 2006a), and, in the case of the EU, it represents 16.3 percent of community GDP.[5]

These percentages of total public expenditure earmarked for public procurement constitute an incentive for firms to position themselves more favorably relative to their competitors through the use of corrupt practices (Stapenhurst and Langseth, 1997). Such that, whenever criminal acts are present in the selection of the tenderer, the tender will not presumably be awarded to whoever offers the best conditions for price and quality, but to whoever is more skilled, in a word, at using corrupt channels and corrupt practices.

The result is a loss of competitiveness in the procurement process. In the absence of any real competition, the execution of public works, the procurement of goods, or the delivery of services become more costly for the public purse and brings to light a significant derailment of resources. According to Strombom (1998), the costs added to the contract can even reach 20 percent or 25 percent, but in some cases can climb as high as 50 percent of the total cost of the contract (Evenett and Hoekman, 2005). The reason for this extra cost is evident: the firms recoup from the contract costs the payments made as bribes to the government officials, technicians, or politicians who have a hand in the award of the contracts. The corrupt tendencies of these actors do not go unnoticed by European citizens. To the question "In (our country), do you think that the giving and taking of bribes, and abuse of positions of power for personal gain, are widespread among any of the following?", one out of two citizens considers that corruption exists among officials awarding public tenders and among officials issuing building permits; that is, ten points over the average in other sector (Table 5.1). So, EU citizens consider that bribes and the abuse of positions of power for personal gain are widespread among 39 percent of people working in the police service, 38 percent in customs service, and 37 percent among officials issuing business permits and inspectors in various services.[6]

Table 5.1 European Citizens Who Consider That Officials Awarding Public Tenders Are Likely to Be Corrupt

EU Member State	*Percentage of Respondents*
Denmark	31
Austria	34
United Kingdom	34
Latvia	37
Ireland	38
Estonia	39
Luxembourg	40
Finland	41
Spain	41
Portugal	41
Hungary	41
Slovakia	46
Sweden	47
EU 25[a]	50
Italy	51
Netherlands	52
Belgium	54
Poland	55
Greece	56
France	58
Slovenia	58
Malta	59
Lithuania	61
Germany	63
Cyprus	69
Czech Republic	73

Source: From Special Eurobarometer num. 245, March 2006. *Opinions on Organized, Cross-Border Crime and Corruption*. http://ec.europa.eu/public_opinion/archives/ebs/ebs_245_en.pdf (accessed July 24, 2007). With permission.

[a] The accession of Rumania and Bulgaria to the EU took place on January 1, 2007, which is why they are not included in the study.

5.3 Public Procurement and Measures to Limit Corruption in EU

5.3.1 Legal Framework

European regulations on public procurement respond to the dynamic of all-encompassing community policies on community freedoms, and, as pointed out earlier, come under the first EU pillar. Harmonization of the respective national legal systems in the field of public procurement forms part of the global EU policy to secure a single market,[7] and for that reason, since the 1970s, European institutions have been carrying forward the work of harmonizing the legislations of the different member states in this field. This legislative harmonization is brought about through the adoption of different community directives that, among their objectives, seek to assure the free circulation of goods, people, services, and capital in the terms set out by the European Community Treaty (EC Treaty).[8]

To ensure the full availability of these freedoms, the EU public procurement directives seek to guarantee competition across frontiers between the European firms. This competition is made possible through the establishment of objective selection procedures for contractors, which ensure the opening of public procurement markets to bidders from other member states and safeguard the different economic operators from discrimination because of their nationality (Arrowsmith, 2005; Trybus, 2006a). However, these objectives have not always been fully complied with because their application is resisted by some member states whose criteria are to continue to support their own nationals.[9] All too frequently, they neither incorporate nor rigorously apply the regulations on public procurement. This noncompliance on the part of some states when transposing the directive on public procurement into their national legal systems has been an ongoing issue ever since the first directive on this matter (Directive 70/32/EEC of December 17, 1969[10]) was adopted over more than 30 years ago.

Since the early 1990s up until the year 2004, the legislative package of the EU for the harmonization of public procurement rules has been composed of three directives referring to the three basic sectors: public service contracts (Directive 92/50/EEC), public supply contracts (Directive 93/36/EEC), and public works contracts (Directive 93/37/EEC), and additionally by Directive 93/38/EEC relating to contracts in the special sectors, which is to say, water, energy, transport, and telecommunications.[11]

However, based on the consultation procedure in its *Green Paper on Public Procurement*,[12] the Commission began to question those regulatory instruments. Hence, in its communication of March 11, 1998, entitled *Public Procurement in the European Union*,* [13] after presenting a diagnosis of the situation regarding public procurement in the European context, it proposed to adapt the community directives to the demands of a market in a constant state of flux. It was felt necessary to simplify and to modernize the procurement procedures that required more than a mere adjustment of the directives in force at that time.

As things stood, the legislative changes were not long in coming. Since 2004, a new regulatory framework on public procurement has existed in the EU whose deadline for transposition into national law ended on January 31, 2006.† Current community regulations on public procurement

* COM (98) 143, 11.03.1988.

† On February 1, 2006, "the morning after the deadline," only a minority of member states had formally implemented the new EU Directives (Austria, Denmark, Hungary, Lithuania, Malta, the Netherlands, Slovakia, and the United Kingdom) (Trybus, 2006b). For a general analysis of the new Directives, see Arrowsmith, 2004.

are enforced through two directives: Directive 2004/17/EC of the European Parliament and of the Council of March 31, 2004 coordinating the procurement procedures of entities operating in the water, energy, transport, and postal services sectors (Utilities Directive) and Directive 2004/18/EC of the European Parliament and of the Council of March 31, 2004 on the coordination of procedures for the award of public works contracts, public supply contracts, and public service contracts (Public Sector Directive).* [15]

The aforementioned directives, each having its own sphere of action, seek to ensure the conditions for real competition between European firms in the award of tenders by the contracting authorities, so that these acquire goods and services under the best possible terms—the primary objective (Arrowsmith, 2005). However, it also pursues the achievement of other objectives, secondary or noncommercial goals (Schooner, 2002), and the fact is that public procurement does not solely constitute a form of supply. It is also a powerful legal tool at the service of contracting authorities to meet other public ends, among which environmental protection, the promotion of social policies, and the fight against corruption are all worth highlighting. With respect to the fight against corruption, the community directives can contribute to the EU overall policy in the fight against corruption through two sets of measures—the first is of a general nature and refers to the legal framework and, the second, which one could say has more of a specific nature, is aimed at promoting probity among those economic operators who wish to become contractors (Bovis, 2006).

5.3.2 General and Specific Measures

A clear and comprehensive regulatory framework for the conduct of public procurement is a fundamental prerequisite for curbing corruption in public contracting (ADB/OECD, 2006). A legal framework that contemplates objective procedures for awards, based on the principles of publicity and transparency, and that provides for subsequent supervisory mechanisms over the awards through the incorporation of effective review procedures will contribute to restricting the space for corrupt practices, as it implies a barrier against corruption and other illicit uses of public resources.

This idea is underlined in Article 9 of the United Nations Convention against Corruption.† The UN Convention requires each state party to "take the necessary steps to establish appropriate systems of procurement, based on transparency, competition and objective criteria in decision-making, that are effective, inter alia, in preventing corruption." Its objective is to reduce the risks of corruption in public procurement through the establishment of the principles of transparency, competition, and objective criteria in decision making.

These principles are also found in the new EU rules on public procurement. The community directives establish five obligations referring to the preparation and the award of public contracts: advertising of the contracts that are above certain economic thresholds, transparency in the award procedures, equivalence of the technical specifications, approval of the suitability of the contractors, and objectivity in the criteria for making the award (Gimeno Feliú, 2006). These obligations

---

* OJ L 134, 30.04.2004.

† Only 14 of the 27 member states that make up the EU have ratified or accepted this important international instrument in the fight against corruption. The first to do so was one of the last to join the EU: Rumania in 2004, the latest were Denmark and Lithuania in December 2006. Retrieved March 9, 2007, from the UN Office on Drugs and Crime Web site:
http://www.unodc.org/unodc/crime_signatures_corruption.html (accessed July 25, 2007).

represent the concrete expression of the aforementioned community freedoms and are interlinked between each other such that the "obligation of transparency which is imposed on the public authority consists in ensuring, for the benefit of any potential tenderer, a degree of advertising sufficient to enable the public contracts market to be opened up to competition and the impartiality of procurement procedures to be reviewed."*

As a result, fair competition and equal treatment of bidders, which are highlighted in the directives, are important in the fight against corruption as measures of a general nature. However, although the regulatory aspects imply great progress in this battle, we cannot ignore that, on occasions, the rules are broken by procurement officials and policy makers. Thus, corruption in public procurement is often caused by those officials who disregard existing procurement rules (Søreide, 2002), and whenever this happens, the personal interest of whoever is taking the decisions in the contractual process waives aside the desired objectivity. Countering this requires the implementation of another type of more specific measure.

These more specific measures tend to limit corruption by promoting the probity of the actors involved in public procurement procedures and these include codes of conduct, conflict of interest regulations, incompatibility laws, rules on abstention designed for public officials, and politicians, as well other procedures that refer to the integrity of the candidates or tenderers. Among the measures of this type is the obligatory exclusion from tendering procedures of those tenderers who have been convicted of corruption in a final sentence against which no further appeal is possible.

5.4 Exclusion from Public Procurement Procedures: General Considerations

The 2004 directives on public procurement establish the conditions for participation in tendering procedures under the general heading of "criteria for qualitative selection." These criteria regulate the positive requirements to be met by candidates and tenderers to become contractors. At the same time, they empower the contracting authorities "to bar from award procedures contractors whose capabilities do not suffice for the execution of the contract" (Mardas and Triantafyllou, 1997). In other words, the contracting authorities decide who can and who cannot be a contractor by looking into the personal circumstances of the candidate or the tenderer, their economic and financial capacity, their technical knowledge, and their experience, and even their reliability, by laying down the circumstances under which certain actors may be excluded from the award procedures.

Generally speaking, exclusion is a disqualification that restricts an individual or a legal person from exercising certain activities. Applied to the field of public procurement, the exclusions may be configured as limitations of the right to participate freely in the public procurement procedures, such that they can be defined as administrative remedies utilized by governments to disqualify contractors from obtaining public contracts (Schooner, 2004; Williams, 2006).

These exclusions are laid down in Article 45 of Directive 2004/18/EC (Public Sector Directive) and in Article 54 (4) of Directive 2004/17/EC (Utilities Directive) "which, by cross-reference, applies the public sector requirement to some utilities" (Arrowsmith, 2005). The above-mentioned Article 45 provides for debarment because of various acts that can be grouped into three categories.

---

* Judgment of the European Court of Justice, Case C-458/03, *Parking Brixen* [2005] E.C.R. I-8612, Paragraph 49.

The first comprises those exclusions deriving from the commission of specific acts that constitute a crime; the second comprises the prohibitions deriving from the breach of certain legal obligations, such as those relating to late payment of social security contributions or nonpayment of taxes; and the third comprises those circumstances in which the personal situation of the candidate or tenderer is undesirable and is not deemed conducive to further the economic relations with them, for reasons such as bankruptcy, insolvency, winding-up, etc. (Bréchon-Moulènes, 2005; Piselli, 2000).

This classification by categories is not, however, an obstacle to finding a common objective shared by all: to prevent the contracting authorities from contracting people who due to their conduct are not held to be trustworthy. This protects the contracting authority from dishonest suppliers,* at the same time as it dissuades contractors from breaking the law.

5.4.1 Exclusions Deriving from a Criminal Conviction

Section 1 of Article 45 of Directive 2004/18/EC (Public Sector Directive) provides, in certain circumstances, for the mandatory exclusion from participation in a public contract of any candidate or tenderer who has been the subject of a conviction by final judgment for participation in a criminal organization, corruption, fraud to the detriment of the financial interests of the Communities, or money laundering:

> *Any candidate or tenderer who has been the subject of a conviction by final judgment of which the contracting authority is aware for one or more of the reasons listed below shall be excluded from participation in a public contract:*
>
> *(a) participation in a criminal organization, as defined in Article 2 (1) of Council Joint Action 98/733/JHA;*
> *(b) corruption, as defined in Article 3 of the Council Act of 26 May 1997 and Article 3 of Council Joint Action 98/742/JHA, respectively;*
> *(c) fraud within the meaning of Article 1 of the Convention relating to the protection of the financial interests of the European Communities;*
> *(d) money laundering, as defined in Article 1 of Council Directive 91/308/EEC of 10 June 1991 on prevention of the use of the financial system for the purpose of money laundering.*

Likewise, the Financial Regulation applicable to the general budget of the European Communities† also contemplates under Article 93 (e), the mandatory exclusion from participation in contractual procedures of those candidates or tenderers who have been the subject of a judgment that has the force of *res judicata* for fraud, corruption, involvement in a criminal organization, or any other illegal activity detrimental to the communities' financial interests.

These exclusions arising from a previous criminal conviction are part and parcel of the general preventive nature referred to earlier for all types of exclusions; although they are also of a punitive

* This is the expression used by the Committee of the Regions in its Opinion on the Proposal for a Directive of the European Parliament and of the Council on the coordination of procedures for the award of public supply contracts, public service contracts, and public works contracts (OJ C 144, 16.05.2001, p. 26).

† In the wording given by Council Regulation No. 1995/2006, of December 13, 2006, amending Regulation No. 1605/2002 on the Financial Regulation applicable to the general budget of the European Communities (OJ L 390, 30.12.2006).

nature in that they have an impact, aside from the criminal conviction itself,* in terms of a tarnished business reputation, as well as the implicit economic loss of ceasing further business with public authorities (Bourgoin, 1985; Hollard, 1989).

Owing to its combined effects, debarment "potentially represents a major step forward in curbing corruption" (Drew, 2005); however, some fine-tuning is needed before this measure is put into practice.

5.4.1.1 Mandatory Rule to Exclude Candidates or Tenderers Convicted of Corruption

The adoption of this measure is not entirely new in the community directives on public procurement as, ever since Directive 71/305/EEC,† the possibility of excluding those candidates or tenderers who had been convicted for a crime related to their professional conduct from public procurement procedures was considered.‡ Implicit among these types of offences are those related to different types of bribery or trafficking of influence that involve acts of corruption. However, it was not until the drafting Directive 2004/18/EC that the term corruption was included in contractual legislation and the obligation to exclude those economic operators convicted for acts of corruption from contractual procedures.

This duty is the main innovation of Article 45 (1) of Directive 2004/18/EC. In this article, a distinction is made between exclusion criteria on the basis of their severity, such that those viewed as grave, which are those contained in Article 45 (1), have to be written into national legislation to progress toward legislative harmonization in the fight against certain sorts of criminal conduct, whereas greater flexibility is allowed in relation to the provisions contained in the second section:

Article 45 (1) "Any candidate or tenderer who has been the subject of a conviction by final judgment of which the contracting authority is aware for one or more of the reasons listed below shall be excluded from participation in a public contract (…)"

Article 45 (2) "Any economic operator may be excluded from participation in a contract where that economic operator: (…)"

The voluntary nature of the exclusion contained in the second section of Article 45 implies, in practice, that its application is left very much in the hands of member states. They can choose not to apply those grounds of exclusion at all and opt for the widest possible participation in procedures for the award of public contracts or to incorporate them into national law with varying degrees of rigor according to legal, economic, or social considerations prevailing at national level. In this voluntary context, the member states have the power to make the grounds of exclusion less onerous

* The punitive nature of the exclusion is not due to it being considered a punishment, as the criminal systems of the member states may not include the exclusion from public tendering procedures as a punishment. In the Spanish legal system, debarment from tendering with the public authority is considered a crime for the criminal act defined in Article 262 of the Criminal Code: on the alteration of prices in public competitive tenders and contracts. Similarly, included within the catalog of additional sanctions for some administrative infringements are matters concerning subsidies, urban development, and the environment. Another example is found in the Polish system, where the exclusion from public procurement is expressly provided for in the list of additional sanctions available against legal persons under the Law on Collective Entities (as amended in 2005).

† Directive 71/305/EEC of July 26, 1971 concerning the coordination of procedures for the award of public works contracts (OJ L 185, 16.08.1971).

‡ This possibility was mentioned in the derogated Articles 29.1.c) of Directive 92/50/EEC (public service contracts), 20.1.c) of Directive 93/36/EEC (public supply contracts) and 24.1.c) of Directive 93/37/EEC (public works contracts).

or more flexible. The only limits placed on their freedom of choice are that they cannot include grounds for exclusion that are not foreseen in the Directives or that violate the general principles of transparency and equal treatment.* However, the obligatory nature of the grounds for exclusion in the first section implies that these disqualifications will have to be incorporated in the domestic legislation of the member states when the community directives are eventually transposed.

The same obligation, with regard to the transposition into domestic law of the grounds for exclusion due to corruption, is laid down in Article 54 (4) of Directive 2004/17/EC (Utilities Directive). Nevertheless, it should be pointed out that in this directive, this latter obligation is restricted because of the actors who have to apply such exclusions. It is only mandatory for the contracting entities that are public contracting authorities.

The reason for this restriction is to be found in the area in which this directive is applied. Directive 2004/17/EC applies to contracting authorities as well as to public undertakings and private firms that operate in the water, energy, transport, and postal services sectors on the basis of special or exclusive rights. These contracting entities are not obliged to apply the criteria for exclusion, given that such an obligation would necessarily presuppose that such entities would have to access information held on judicial records, which would pose serious problems concerning data protection.

5.4.1.2 Concept of Corruption as Defined by the Directives on Public Procurement

As has already been highlighted in previous sections, an ill-fated relationship exists between corruption and public procurement; however, the inclusion of the term corruption in directives on public procurement had to wait until the approval of Directive 2004/18/EC. The definition of corruption given in this directive, on the one hand, is intended to save it from the absence of a single unambiguous description that brings together the various criminal activities that tend to be labeled as corrupt. On the other hand, it is intended to avoid the lack of authority on the part of the EU to typify these offences. It should not be forgotten that legislative authority in criminal matters has not been transferred to community organs. Criminal law remains the exclusive authority of each state, which means that they are the only ones with the authority both to approve criminal legislation and to impose sanctions of that same nature; nevertheless, the prevention and fight against corruption has a predominant role around the third pillar of the EU (the areas of justice and home affairs [JHA]).

Article 29 of the Treaty of the European Union converts the fight against corruption into one of the conditions for the establishment of an area of liberty, security, and justice. One of the proposed mechanisms to achieve it is the "approximation, where necessary, of rules on criminal matters in the Member States." This approximation of criminal legislation has already been initiated through specific legal instruments of the third pillar such as the framework decisions, common actions, and agreements in the field of JHA.

It is for this reason that description of corruption established in Directive 2004/18/EC is expressed in reference to two European legal instruments that are incorporated in this area of intergovernmental cooperation; thus, corruption is defined as is, respectively, set forth in Article 3 of the Council Act of May 26, 1997† and in Article 3 (1) of Council Joint Action 98/742/JHA‡, although it should be noted that this latter regulation was derogated before the publication of Directive

* See, Judgment of the European Court of Justice Joined Cases C-226/04 and C-228/04, *La Cascina and Zilch* [2006] E.C.R. I-I-1347, Paragraphs 22 and 23.

† OJ C 195, 25.06.1997.

‡ OJ L 358, 31.12.1998.

2004/18/EC. It was derogated by Article 8 of the Council Framework Decision 2003/568/JHA of July 22, 2003 on combating corruption in the private sector.*

Article 3 of Council Act of May 26, 1997: the convention drawn up on the basis of Article K.3 (2) (c) of the Treaty on European Union on the fight against corruption involving officials of the European Communities or officials of member states of the EU define *active corruption* as

> (...) the deliberate action of whosoever promises or gives, directly or through an intermediary, an advantage of any kind whatsoever to an official for himself or for a third party for him to act or refrain from acting in accordance with his duty or in the exercise of his functions in breach of his official duties (...).

Article 3 (1) of Council Joint Action 98/742/JHA of December 22, 1998 on corruption in the private sector, defines active corruption as

> (...) the deliberate action of whosoever promises, offers or gives, directly or through an intermediary, an undue advantage of any kind whatsoever to a person, for himself or for a third party, in the course of the business activities of that person in order that the person should perform or refrain from performing an act, in breach of his duties, shall constitute active corruption in the private sector.

Once Directive 2004/18/EC made it obligatory to exclude from the tender procedures those tenderers or candidates convicted of active corruption, whether in the public or the private sector, national legislation must include those same grounds for disqualification in its legislation, given that "a directive shall be binding, as to the result to be achieved, upon each Member State to which it is addressed, but shall leave to the national authorities the choice of form and methods" (Article 249 EC Treaty). On that basis, Article 45 (1) of this directive should have been implemented by all EU member states before January 31, 2006 that was the deadline for its transposition into national law; however, not all the member states have met that obligation.†

An examination of member states legislations that have already transposed Article 45 (1) of Directive 2004/18/EC into national law offers us, the following panorama, with regard to the description of corruption (see Table 5.2): EU member states can be divided into three groups. A first group of countries (Cyprus, Denmark, Finland, Greece, Hungary, Italy, Lithuania, and Malta) refer to the same European legal instruments as the Community Directive to give us their definition of corruption, although in the case of Finland, this reference is also made to Council Framework Decision 2003/568/JHA; a second group (Austria, Bulgaria, France, Germany, Netherlands, Slovenia, and United Kingdom) is made up of those member states that refer us back to their own criminal regulations for the legal description of offences that are included under the heading of

* OJ L 192, 31.07.2003.

† On February 1, 2006, only a minority of member states had formally implemented the Directive 2004/18/EC (Austria, Denmark, Hungary, Lithuania, Malta, the Netherlands, Slovak Republic, and the United Kingdom). On March 30, 2007, Bulgaria, Cyprus, Czech Republic, France, Germany, Greece, Ireland, Italy, Latvia, Poland, Romania, and Slovenia were added to the list of member states that had implemented the Directive. On May 1, 2007, the new Public Procurement Act entered into effect in Estonia and the Finnish public procurement legislation just one month later (Trybus and Medina, 2007).

On January 1, 2008, Directive 2004/18/EC had been implemented in 23 of the 27 member states. The only expectations are Luxembourg, which has not yet approved its new Public Procurement Law, and Belgium, Portugal, and Spain where the national legislation that will incorporate the EU Directive has not yet entered into force even though it has been approved and published in the official Bulletin of State.

Table 5.2 Conditions for Exclusion on the Grounds of Corruption in Member States Legislations That Have Transposed Directive 2004/18/EC (September 2007)

Legislation	*Persons Subject to Exclusion*	*Certificates/Information to Be Submitted*
Europe Article 45.1 Directive 2004/18/EC	Any candidate or tenderer who has been the subject of a conviction in a final judgment of which the contracting authority is aware for (...) (b) corruption, as defined in Article 3 of the Council Act of May 26, 1997 and Article 3 of Council Joint Action 98/742/JHA	Extract from the judicial record Equivalent document Declaration under oath Solemn statement
Europe Article 93.1. (e) Regulation No. 1605/2002 (amended by Council Regulation No. 1995/2006) Financial Regulation applicable to the general budget of the EC	Candidates or tenderers that have been the subject of a judgment that has the force of *res judicata* for corruption	Candidates or tenderers shall certify that they are not in one of these situations. However, the contracting authority may refrain from requiring such certification for very low value contracts
Austria Paragraph 68 (1) BVergG 2006 Nr. 17/2006	The contracting authority will exclude those business managers from participation in tendering procedures if it is aware of a final judgment against them or—in the case of legal persons, companies subject to mercantile law, registered for-profit companies, or partnerships—against the physical persons in charge of the business of the latter entities and those affected by one of the following acts: bribery, fraud, unfair management, accepting gifts, abuse of subsidies (Articles 302, 307, 308, 310 StGB [Penal Code])	Natural persons Extract from the judicial record (criminal record certificate)
Bulgaria Articles 47, 48, and 49 Public Procurement Law amended SG No. 79 of September 26, 2006	The contracting authority shall exclude from participation in a public procurement award procedure a candidate or tenderer who: 1. has been convicted by an effective sentence, unless rehabilitated, for: (b) bribery under Art. 301–307 of the Penal Code	Extract from a court register Equivalent document by a judicial or administrative authority Declaration on oath Solemn declaration made before a judicial or administrative authority, a notary or a competent professional or trade body

Table 5.2 (continued) Conditions for Exclusion on the Grounds of Corruption in Member States Legislations That Have Transposed Directive 2004/18/EC (September 2007)

Legislation	*Persons Subject to Exclusion*	*Certificates/Information to Be Submitted*
Cyprus Article 51.1 Law No. 12 (I)/2006 of February 17, 2006	Any candidate or tenderer who has been the subject of a conviction by final judgment of which the contracting authority is aware for (…) (b) corruption, as defined in Article 3 of the Council Act of May 26, 1997 and Article 3 of Council Joint Action 98/742/JHA	Natural persons Equivalent document (criminal record certificate) Legal persons Equivalent document (letter issued by Cyprus Police)
Czech Republic Article 53.1. (a) Act No.137/2006 of March 14, 2006	Suppliers convicted in a final sentence of accepting bribes, bribery, indirect bribery, fraud, loan fraud including cases of preparation for and attempts of or conspiracy to commit such a crime, or if such sentences pronounced for such crimes have been expunged	Natural persons Extract from the judicial record (extract from the criminal register)
Denmark Governmental Order No. 937 of September 16, 2004	Any candidate or tenderer who has been the subject of a conviction by final judgment of which the contracting authority is aware for (…) (b) corruption, as defined in Article 3 of the Council Act of May 26, 1997 and Article 3 of Council Joint Action 98/742/JHA	Extract from the judicial record Equivalent document (certificate of criminal record)
Estonia §38 (1) Public Procurement Act 2007	Exclusion of the tenderer (…) 1) which is or which legal representative has been penalized for organizing the criminal group or belonging thereto or violation of the requirements of public procurement, commission of offences related to office and money laundering (…)	Punishment register notice Declaration on oath Autographic confirmation
Finland §53 Public Procurement Act 348/2007, of March 30, 2007	Exclusion of candidates and tenderers that have received sentences for certain crimes The crimes that involve obligatory exclusion are: (…) (b) corruption, as defined in Article 3 of the Convention of May 26, 1997, (…) on the fight against corruption involving officials of the European Communities or officials of Member States of the EU and Article 2.1 a) Council Framework Decision 2003/568/JHA on combating corruption in the private sector	Natural persons Extract from the criminal record Extract from business prohibition register Solemn statement Legal persons Extract from the criminal record

(continued)

Table 5.2 (continued) Conditions for Exclusion on the Grounds of Corruption in Member States Legislations That Have Transposed Directive 2004/18/EC (September 2007)

Legislation	*Persons Subject to Exclusion*	*Certificates/Information to Be Submitted*
France Article 43 Public Procurement Code 2006 Article 8(1) Ordinance 2005-649, June 6, 2005	Persons convicted in the last five years in a final judgment of: swindling, active corruption, trafficking of influence, active corruption of civil servants of the European Community, civil servants of member states of the EU, members of the institutions of the European Community; forgery (Articles 433-1 and 435-2 Penal Code)	Declaration of honor
Germany §8a Nr. 1 Public Procurement Order for Works Contracts VOB/A 2006 §7a Nr. 2 Public Procurement Order for Supply and Services Contracts VOL/A 2006 §11 Abs. 1 Public Procurement Order for Professional Services VOF 2006	Any candidate/tenderer will be excluded from participation in procurement procedures when the contracting authority has knowledge that a person, whose conduct has to be attributed to the firm, has been condemned in a final sentence for: e) §334 of the Penal Code (bribery/corruption) (…) also in connection with Article 2, Section 1 of the Convention on Combating Bribery of Foreign Public Officials in International Business Transactions (…)	Extract from the Central Federal Registry Equivalent document issued by an authorized jurisdictional or administrative body in the country of origin Declaration on oath made before an authorized jurisdictional or administrative body
Greece Article 43.1.b) Presidential Decree 60/2007, March 2007 (amended by Presidential Decree 118/2007)	Candidate or tenderer, who has been the subject of a conviction by final judgment of which the contracting authority is aware for one or more of the following reasons: b) corruption, as defined in Article 3 of the Council Act of 26 May 1997 and Article 3(1) of Council Joint Action 98/742/JHA	Extract of the judicial record Equivalent document issued by a judicial or administrative authority

Table 5.2 (continued) Conditions for Exclusion on the Grounds of Corruption in Member States Legislations That Have Transposed Directive 2004/18/EC (September 2007)

Legislation	*Persons Subject to Exclusion*	*Certificates/Information to Be Submitted*
Hungary Articles 60.1. (h) and 60.3 Act 129/2003 (amended by Act 172/2005)	Tenderers and subcontractors who commit crimes of bribery, bribery in international relations, provided they are the subject of a court judgment which has the force of *res judicata* In the case of tenderers established in other member state of the EU (...) corruption, as defined in Article 3 of the Council Act of May 26, 1997, and Article 3 (1) of Council Joint Action 742/98/JHA	Natural persons Equivalent document (certificate of clean record) Legal persons Extract from the judicial record Solemn statement
Ireland Article 53.1 (b) Public Sector Procurement Regulations-SI 329 of 2006	Any person who, to the knowledge of the authority, has been convicted of an offence involving corruption	Declaration on oath Solemn statement A contracting authority shall accept as sufficient evidence a copy of the relevant judicial record, or equivalent document
Italy Article 38 Legislative Decree No. 163 of April 12, 2006 (Code), and special anti-mafia provisions (Law 575/1965 of May 31)	Subjects who have been convicted in a final sentence on counts of corruption as defined by the community actions contained in Article 45 of Directive 2004/18/EC. Exclusion and disqualification will be effective if the sentence has been pronounced against the: Owner or manager if it is an individual firm Partner or manager if it is a collective firm Limited partner or manager if it is a limited partnership Administrators empowered to represent the company or the manager if it is another type of company or consortium Persons subject to criminal proceedings related to the mafia	Extract from the judicial record Equivalent document Solemn statement Declaration under oath that their company is not involved in any mafia activity

(continued)

Table 5.2 (continued) Conditions for Exclusion on the Grounds of Corruption in Member States Legislations That Have Transposed Directive 2004/18/EC (September 2007)

Legislation	*Persons Subject to Exclusion*	*Certificates/Information to Be Submitted*
Latvia Article 39 (1) and (3) Law on Public Procurement of April 6, 2006	Any candidate or bidder who has been found guilty in a court ruling of participating in corruption Requirements (...) may apply to the candidate or bidder, as well as to natural and legal persons, including persons with the right of representation and persons who have decision-making and supervisory rights with respect to the relevant candidate or bidder	Extract from the judicial record Equivalent document (Certificate on conviction) Declaration on oath
Lithuania Article 33 (1) Law on Public Procurement version December 22, 2005	Supplier has a spent or unexpunged conviction for the following criminal acts defined in Directive 2004/18/EC: (2) Corruption	Extract from the judicial record Equivalent document (certificate on conviction)
Malta Article 49.4. (b) Legal Notice 177/2005, S.L.174.04 (amended by Legal Notice 130/2006)	Any candidate or tenderer who has been the subject of a conviction by final judgment of which the contracting authority is aware for (b) corruption, as defined in Article 3 of the Council Act of May 26, 1997 and Article 3 of Council Joint Action 98/742/JHA	Natural persons Extract from the judicial record Legal persons Declaration on oath Solemn declaration
The Netherlands Article 45 (1) Decree on Procurement Rules for Government Tender (*BAO*) 2005/408	Any candidate or tenderer convicted by an irrevocable judgment for bribery, fraud, accepting gifts, forgery [Penal Code]	Equivalent document Certificate of good conduct for legal persons (VOG RP)
Poland Article 24.1 Public Procurement Law 2004 (amendment approved on April 7, 2006)	(4) Natural persons, who have been validly sentenced for bribery (5) Registered partnerships whose partner has been validly sentenced for bribery (6) Professional partnership whose partner or member of the management board has been validly sentenced for bribery	Extract from the judicial record (Regulation of the Prime Minister of May 19, 2006 on the types of documents that may be requested by the awarding authority)

Table 5.2 (continued) Conditions for Exclusion on the Grounds of Corruption in Member States Legislations That Have Transposed Directive 2004/18/EC (September 2007)

Legislation	*Persons Subject to Exclusion*	*Certificates/Information to Be Submitted*
	(7) Limited partnership and limited joint-stock partnership whose general partner has been validly sentenced for bribery (8) Legal persons whose active member of the managing body has been validly sentenced for bribery	
Romania Article 180 Government Emergency Ordinance No. 34/2006 regarding the award of the public procurement contracts, public works concession contracts, and services concession contracts, approved by Law 337/06	Any tenderer/candidate whereof it has information that, in the last five years, it was convicted by definitive court judgment, for participation in a criminal organization, for corruption, for fraud, or for money laundering	Extract from the judicial record Equivalent document Declaration on oath Solemn declaration made by the person concerned before a competent judicial or administrative authority, a notary or a competent professional or trade body
Slovakia Article 26.1 (a) Act No. 25/2006 Coll. on Public Procurement of December 14, 2005	A person may only participate in tendering for the public award of contracts if his personal status satisfies the conditions for participation: a) neither that person nor his statutory body nor any member of the statutory body has been lawfully convicted for the offence of corruption	Extract from the judicial record not older than three months
Slovenia Article 42 (1) Public Procurement Act of November 23, 2006	Candidates or tenderers and all their legal representatives who have been convicted of committing any of the following crimes specified in criminal law: accepting bribes in elections (applicable to physical persons), accepting nonauthorized gifts, accepting bribes (applicable to physical persons), attempted bribery, accepting gifts through illegal intermediation	Extract from the judicial record (certificate) Solemn declaration Affidavit

(continued)

Table 5.2 (continued) Conditions for Exclusion on the Grounds of Corruption in Member States Legislations That Have Transposed Directive 2004/18/EC (September 2007)

Legislation	*Persons Subject to Exclusion*	*Certificates/Information to Be Submitted*
United Kingdom Article 23 (1) Public Contract Regulations 2006 (SI 2006/5)	An economic operator in accordance with these regulations if the contracting authority has actual knowledge that the economic operator or its directors or any other person who has powers of representation, decision, or control of the economic operator has been convicted of any of the following offences: (b) corruption within the meaning of Section 1 of the Public Bodies Corrupt Practices Act 1889 or Section 1 of the Prevention of Corruption Act 1906	Declaration on oath

Sources: From National legislations and data taken from the European Commission. http://ec.europa.eu/internal_market/publicprocurement/2004_18/index_en.htm (accessed July 20, 2007). With permission.

corruption and which, for the most part, coincide with the different types of bribery, trafficking of influence, and fraud. In the third group of member states (Czech Republic, Estonia, Ireland, Latvia, Poland, Romania, and Slovakia), no reference is made to any regulations and the word corruption is used without offering us a working definition. Nevertheless, regardless of whether the definition of corruption is in reference to European regulations or national legislation, it remains clear that in this type of criminal act, the personal interest of whoever takes the decisions in the contractual procedure replaces a desirable objectivity, as they are taking advantage of their position to obtain some kind of benefit, for themselves or for a third part, in breach of their own duties and in disregard of the public interest.

5.4.1.3 Connection with a Judicial Conviction

The obligation laid down in Directive 2004/18/EC is that of prohibiting access to public contracts of those people convicted of corruption, but member states remain free to decide the conditions under which it is applied and its time limit.* Thus, we find ourselves up against the deprivation of a right that is tied to a criminal conviction, but one which does not have to receive equal treatment in all member states, as directives are legal instruments whose only concern is the result and not the means. It is for this reason that the exclusion might be due to a criminal conviction on various counts:

* In Article 46 (1) of the original proposal for a council directive, it was foreseen that the exclusion would be applicable to "*convictions secured in the five years prior to contract award procedure*" COM (2000) 275 final/2, 30.08.2000 (OJ C 29 E, 30.01.2001). This draft provision has disappeared from the wording of Article 45 (1), but is contemplated in national laws, such as in the French case. Article 8 of Ordinance 2005-649, of June 6, 2005, foresees the exclusion from contractual procedures of those people that have been the subject, over the last five years, of a definitive sentence for active corruption.

- It can be a penalty ordered by the court, either as an addition to the principal penalty or as an alternative penalty if it is ordered in place of one or more principal penalties.*
- It can be an additional penalty, automatically imposed as a consequence of the principal penalty, even if it is not ordered by the court.†
- It can be ordered in administrative or disciplinary proceedings arising as a result of a criminal conviction.

Because of these differences in nature, the exclusions pose specific problems with regard to their appreciation and application, not so much in relation to the citizens of each member state, but with regard to the exchange of effective information between the member states on the sentences handed down by their own courts.

Information relating to exclusions is not always included in national criminal records. Moreover, where information is available, it is not always of any legal consequence outside the territory of the member state in which the exclusion was enforced, as the lack of harmonization between national legislations constitutes a real obstacle to mutual recognition of these grounds for exclusion.‡ Nevertheless, if these inconveniences are overcome, Article 45 (1) of Directive 2004/18/EC, according to the European Commission, "is an instrument which entails the partial mutual recognition of convictions since it results in a conviction handed down in one Member State normally having as a consequence the exclusion from public procurement on a Union-wide basis."§

5.4.1.4 *Requirements of Final Judgment*

Directive 2004/18/EC has restricted exclusion from award procedures for corruption to conviction by final judgment. A judgment becomes final when it has not been appealed against in due time and manner, or because the appeals process has been exhausted. In some member states, appeals procedures against a judgment delivered by a court of first instance may have to pass through two other levels of the judicial system (appeals court and final court of appeal), and that a judgment is not considered final until all the avenues for appeal have been exhausted.

In these cases, if we wish to speak of a legally valid situation for exclusion, it is necessary to await the end of the lengthy appeals process; certainly the wait impinges on the effectiveness of the exclusion,

* For example, Article 131-39 of the French Criminal Code and Article 262 of the Spanish Criminal Code. Article 131-39 of the French Criminal Code states that: "Where a statute so provides against a legal person, a felony or misdemeanor may be punished by one or more of the following penalties: 5° disqualification from public tenders, either permanently or for a maximum period of five years." Article 262 of the Spanish Criminal Code: On the alteration of prices in competitive tenders and "(...) If it concerns competitive tendering or bidding called by the Public Authorities or public bodies, a special penalty of disqualification will be imposed on the agent and the legal person or firm that he represents that will apply, in all cases, to the right to enter into contractual relations with the Public Authorities for a period of three to five years."

† For example, Article 314-10 of the French Criminal Code "Natural persons convicted of any of the offences provided for under articles 314-1, 314-2, and 314-3 also incur the following additional penalties: 4° disqualification from public tenders for a maximum period of five years."

‡ White Paper on exchanges of information on convictions and the effect of such convictions in the European Union, COM (2005) 10 final, 25.01.2005, p. 6.

§ Communication from the Commission to the Council and the European Parliament "Disqualifications arising from criminal convictions in the European Union," COM (2006) 73 final, 21.02.2006, p. 6.

but there is no doubt that it guarantees the presumption of innocence, and has regard for one of the fundamental right laid down in the European Convention for the Protection of Human Rights and Fundamental Freedoms and the Charter of Fundamental Rights of the European Union.

Having said as much, in Italy, Article 38 of Legislative Decree No. 163 of April 12, 2006,* which transposes Article 45 of Directive 2004/18/EC into Italian law, provides for exclusion as a preventive measure applicable in procedures pending judicial decisions in cases related to the mafia, and therefore in the absence of a final sentence (Law no. 1423 of December 27, 1956 and Law no. 575 of May 31, 1965).

5.4.1.5 Eligibility of Candidates and Tenderers: Proof of No Convictions for Corruption

Another of the questions foreseen in Article 45 of Directive 2004/18/EC relates to the proof submitted by tenderers and candidates of no convictions for corruption. Likewise, the proof needed to apply the exclusion is directly related to the information required by the contracting authorities. The fact is that the success of Article 45 depends on contracting authorities being aware of corruption convictions (Drew, 2005).

For them to gain this knowledge, the directive provides for the possibility of accessing criminal record certificates or any other documents issued by a competent authority that allows them to verify the eligibility of tenderers.† However, Article 45 does not make any provisions with regard to questions of such importance for setting up these mechanisms for exclusion, such as the creation of a computerized system for the exchange of information on criminal convictions between member states or the publication of lists of companies excluded from contracts—blacklists (Jacobs and Anechiarico, 1992; White, 2000; Moran et al., 2004; Schooner, 2004; Olaya, 2005; White, 2005; Schultz and Søreide, 2006).

The Financial Regulation applicable to the general budget of the European Communities‡ attempts to overcome the absence of a system for exchanging information on the exclusions enforced by other member states through the creation of a community database, which lists candidates or tenderers named as litigants in one or more of the categories for exclusion included in the regulations:

Article 95 (1) "A central database shall be set up and operated by the Commission in compliance with Community rules on the protection of personal data. The database shall contain details of candidates and tenderers which are in one of the situations referred to in article 93 (...)."

Under this system, authorities are not obliged to consult the database before awarding a contract and regulation depends on a voluntary system. Nonetheless, despite its voluntary nature, this database should be just the first stage of an effective debarment system for the EU§ (Transparency International, 2006b).

---

* *Codice dei contratti pubblici relativi a lavori, servizi e forniture,* published in the Official Gazette of the Italian Republic No. 100, of May 2, 2006.

† http://ec.europa.eu/internal_market/publicprocurement/2004_18/index_en.htm (accessed July 25, 2007).

‡ Council Regulation No. 1995/2006 of December 13, 2006 amending Regulation No. 1605/2002 on the Financial Regulation applicable to the general budget of the European Communities (OJ L 390, 30.12.2006).

§ Many EU member states also have their own debarment systems. In Spain, for example, a list may be found of those firms prohibited by the ministry from participation in tendering procedures is posted on the Web site of the Ministry of Economy and Finance.
http://documentacion.meh.es/doc/C6/C3/Junta%20Consultiva/Prohibicion%20de%20contratar.pdf (accessed July 28, 2007).

5.4.1.6 *Criminal Liability of Legal Persons*

Tenderers may be natural persons or legal entities and the exclusions can apply to both legal and natural persons. The connection between exclusion and a judicial sentence leads us to question the effectiveness of this measure with respect to legal persons, because their criminal liability is not recognized in all the member states.*

In those member states in which the criminal liability of legal persons is not recognized—as is the case of Spain—it is argued that criminal guilt cannot be imputed to legal persons because they have no legal animus (Gosálbez Pequeño, 2000). When a criminal act is committed within a legal person or entity then those who are in effect responsible for the criminal acts in question are the physical persons within it. This does not mean that legal persons are not accountable for their acts: they are accountable under both civil and administrative law. Nevertheless, the traditional principle of *societas delinquere non potest* is still fully in force in the criminal law of certain member states, and this means accepting that legal persons will not be held liable under criminal law, and that physical persons will therefore be answerable for the criminal acts that they commit within these legal persons. This makes it possible to get around the impunity that would otherwise be associated with criminal actions perpetrated under the veil of a legal person by its members who are clearly identifiable as individuals.

For example, in Poland Article 24 of the Public Procurement Law automatically excludes legal persons from contractual procedures, in circumstances where a partner or manager of the entity has been convicted for bribery in connection with an award procedure, although the legal persons have not been themselves punished for bribery. The same situation occurs in Hungary, according to whose national criminal law, crimes can be committed only by physical persons; however, if for instance the director of a company is found guilty of bribery, the court may restrict the business activity of this company by virtue of Act 104/2001 on punitive actions applicable against legal persons.

5.4.1.7 *Exceptions to Exclusion*

Despite exclusion being obligatory in nature, member states will be able to decide on a derogation due to "overriding requirements in the general interest"† (Article 45 (1) Directive 2004/18/EC); however, this article does not offer a definition of what is to be understood as the general interest, which complicates its practical application.

The contracting authorities enjoy a great deal of discretion when assessing the grounds for exception due to the inexistence of any list of cases. Nevertheless, such cases must be limited to those that are justified and proportionate to the pursued objectives, because, like all exceptions, they are subject to a restrictive interpretation so that exceptions do not arise so frequently as to render this debarment ineffective at fighting corruption.‡

---

* Belgium, France, Ireland, the Netherlands, and the United Kingdom recognize the criminal liability of legal personas; on the other hand, Spain, Greece, Germany, and Hungary do not consider legal persons to be the active subjects of crimes.

† This exception is set forth in the Austrian legislation (paragraph 68 (1) *BVergG* 2006) and Dutch (Article 45.2 Decree on Procurement Rules for Government Tender, *BAO*) in which it says: "the contracting authority can deviate from [this] obligation…for compelling reasons in the public interest."

‡ On the principle of the restrictive interpretation of exceptions to the principles of procurement law, see Case C-84/03 *Commission* v *Spain* [2005] ECR I-139, Paragraph 48; Case C-26/03 *Stadt Halle and RPL Lochau* [2005] ECR I-1, Paragraph 46, and Case C-410/04 *ANAV* [2006] ECR I-3303, Paragraph 26.

On the basis of this restrictive interpretation, among the cases that give rise to exclusion it would appear that those referring to the protection of public health are highlighted.* The Committee of the Regions, in its opinion on directive proposals,† proposed the hypothetical situation of the provision of a unique, lifesaving medicine that could not be supplied by any other supplier than one that had been convicted of corruption, and posed the following question: What happens in a case where only a supplier who has been convicted of corruption can deliver certain goods? Faced with the existence of one single contractor with the capacity to respond to that supply, member states reserve the right not to exclude the candidate or tenderer convicted of corruption from the tender procedures given that the needs of the contracting authorities cannot be satisfied through any other economic operator. By doing so, they seek to strike a balance between the fight against corruption and a pragmatic vision of the general interest.

The possible scenarios do not end there. In line with Williams (2006) and Kramer (2005), others that could be included in this exception are the national security and pressing needs for the supply of certain goods. In these cases, it also seems clear that we are up against a case of the general interest that justifies the facultative nature of the way that the exclusion is applied in view of the values that it seeks to guarantee.

5.5 Conclusions

The fight against corruption is a priority of the EU's political action in the context of building an area of freedom, security, and justice. This is the reason why, ever since 1995, European institutions have been developing a comprehensive anticorruption strategy that involves activities in different public sectors. One of these sectors is that of public procurement, given that the volume of economic resources allocated to public sector contracts makes it a very tempting area for corrupt practices.

Directives 2004/17/EC and 2004/18/EC set out the criteria as defined by Community Law that regulate the selection of contractors in matters relating to public procurement. Since 2004, these directives, in addition to standardizing the procedures for awarding public contracts in all member states, seek to achieve other objectives among which may be found the fight against corruption. Obligatory exclusion from the tendering procedures of those tenderers or candidates that have been convicted of corruption in a judicial sentence with the force of *res judicata* may be found in this framework. This mandatory exclusion is binding on legislators from the different member states with respect to the obligation to include crimes of corruption in their legislation on contract law as a cause of disqualification from the tendering process; nevertheless, putting this measure into practice comes up against two obstacles.

The first refers to the difficulties of regulatory precision, insofar as there is no consensus to determine what activities we are to understand as conduct that is likely to be qualified as corrupt conduct. Member states that have transposed the directives into their domestic legal systems have set out definitions of corruption of different scope; thus, while a first group of countries (Cyprus, Denmark, Finland, Greece, Hungary, Italy, Lithuania, and Malta) refer to the same European instruments as Directive 2004/18/EC; others (Austria, Bulgaria, France, Germany, Netherlands, Slovenia, and United Kingdom) refer back to their own criminal laws, and a third group (Czech

* This exception on the basis of cases related to public health is also expressed in North-American legislation, in particular, the Department of Health and Human Services. Acquisition Regulation 309.405(a)(1)(i).

† (OJ C 144, 16.05.01, p. 26).

Republic, Estonia, Ireland, Latvia, Poland, Romania, and Slovakia), without reference to any regulations at all, use the word corruption without providing it with an operative concept.

The second obstacle is its actual working practice, its effectiveness at preventing and curbing such conduct. The aim of obligatory exclusion, which is to become an effective instrument in the fight against corruption, disappears when faced with such specific aspects as the contracting authorities' lack of information on sentences that involve convictions for corruption. This shortcoming complicates the practical application of the measure not only between the member states but also within the frontiers of each state.

A solution is sought to all these difficulties to which reference has been made through the creation of a communitywide database in which those candidates or tenderers appear who have been condemned for corruption in different member states. Despite its voluntary nature, as use of the system is not yet compulsory for the contracting authorities, this database should be just the first stage of an effective exclusion system for the EU.

Notes

1. The principal international legal instruments in the fight against corruption are: United Nations Convention against Corruption, adopted by the United Nations General Assembly by Resolution 58/4 of October 31, 2003; OECD Convention on Combating Bribery of Foreign Officials in International Business Transactions, signed on December 17, 1997; African Union Convention on Preventing and Combating Corruption, adopted on July 11, 2003; Inter-American Convention against Corruption, adopted on March 29, 1996; Criminal Law Convention on Corruption of the Council of Europe, adopted on January 27, 1999; and Civil Law Convention on Corruption of the Council of Europe, adopted on November 4, 1999.
2. According to the *2007 Corruption Perceptions Index*, published by the NGO Transparency International, 7 of the 27 member states—26 percent—receive a score of below 5 points, from a maximum of 10 given to the least-corrupt and 0 to the most-corrupt countries. These seven countries are as follows: Slovakia (4.9), Latvia (4.8), Lithuania (4.8), Greece (4.6), Poland (4.2), Bulgaria (4.1), and Romania (3.7).
3. Communication to the Council, the European Parliament, and the European Economic and Social Committee (1997, May 21). *On a Union Policy against Corruption*. COM (97)192, 21.05.97; Communication from the Commission to the Council, the European Parliament, and the European Economic and Social Committee (2003, May 28). *On a Comprehensive EU Policy against Corruption*. [Online]. Available at http://eur-lex.europa.eu/smartapi/cgi/sga_doc?smartapi!celexplus!prod!DocNumber&lg=en&type_doc=COMfinal&an_doc=2003&nu_doc=317.
4. European Parliament: Working Paper Measures to Prevent Corruption in EU Member States (Annex: Combating corruption in public procurement contracts). Legal Affairs Series JURI 101 EN 03-1998. Works by Rose-Ackerman (1999) and Della Porta and Vannucci (1999) provide examples on bribery in public procurement.
5. According to data from the European Commission, this would imply 1500 billion euros in 2002. http://europa.eu/publicprocurement/index_es.htm (accessed July 25, 2007). According to the OECD, the figure for the same year might be as much as $5.8 trillion (OECD, 2002).
6. Special Eurobarometer num. 245, *Opinions on Organized, Cross-Border Crime and Corruption,* March 2006, p. 16.
7. The Single European Act (which was signed in February 1986 and came into force on July 1, 1987) incorporated the concept of the Internal Market in the EC Treaty as "*an area without internal frontiers in which the free movement of goods, persons, services and capital is ensured.*" The importance of public procurement as a key element to achieve a single market was highlighted by the European Commission in the White Paper *Completing the Internal Market* (COM (85) 310 final, 14.06.1985), and it is referred to,

on numerous occasions, by the European Court of Justice: "the purpose of coordinating at Community level the procedures for the award of public contracts is to eliminate barriers to the freedom to provide services and goods and therefore to protect the interests of traders established in a Member State who wish to offer goods or services to contracting authorities established in another Member State" (Case C-380/98 University of Cambridge [2000] ECR I-8035, Paragraph 16, and Case C-237/99 *Commission vs. France* [2001] ECR I-939, Paragraph 41).

8. The Treaty of Rome, establishing the European Economic Community (EEC), signed in Rome on March 25, 1957.
9. Italy has more than three times the "average" number of infringement proceedings for incorrect transposition or incorrect application of internal market rules. Spain, France, Greece, Germany, Portugal, and Belgium are also well above the average (European Commission: *Internal Market Scoreboard: Best Result Ever.* IP/07/126, 01.02.2007).
   http://ec.europa.eu/internal_market/score/index_en.htm (accessed July 24, 2007).
10. Directive 70/32/EEC of December 17, 1969 on provision of goods to the State to local authorities and other official bodies (OJ L 13, 19.01.1970).
11. Council Directive 92/50/EEC of June 18, 1992, relating to the coordination of procedures for the award of public service contracts (OJ L 209, 24.07.1992); Council Directive 93/36/EEC of June 14, 1993 relating to the coordination of procedures for the award of public supply contracts (OJ L 199, 09.08.1993); Council Directive 93/37/EEC of June 14, 1993, concerning the coordination of procedures for the award of public works contracts (OJ L 199, 09.08.1993); and Council Directive 93/38/EEC of June 14, 1993, coordinating the procurement procedures of entities operating in the water, energy, transport and telecommunications sectors (OJ L 199, 09.08.1993).
12. European Commission: *Green Paper on Public Procurement in the European Union: Exploring the Way Forward*, 27.11.1996. Green papers are discussion papers published by the Commission on a specific policy area. They are primarily documents addressed to interested parties—organizations and individuals—who are invited to participate in a process of consultation and debate.
13. COM (98) 143, 11.03.1988.
14. OJ L 134, 30.04.2004.

References

Amundsen, I. 2000. *Corruption. Definitions and Concepts.* Bergen: Chr. Michelsen Institute.

Arrowsmith, S. 2004. An assessment of the new legislative package on public procurement. *Common Market Law Review* 41(5): 1277–1325.

Arrowsmith, S. 2005. *The Law of Public and Utilities Procurement.* 2nd edn. London: Sweet & Maxwell.

Asian Development Bank/OECD. 2006. *Curbing Corruption in Public Procurement in Asia and the Pacific.* Manila: Asian Development Bank. http://www.adb.org/Documents/Books/Public-Procurement-Asia-Pacific/public-procurement.pdf (accessed July 24, 2007).

Bourgoin, P. 1985. Les exclusions de marchés publics. *Revue Marchés Publics* (208): 27–31.

Bovis, C. 2006. *EC Public Procurement: Case Law and Regulation.* Oxford: Oxford University Press.

Bréchon-Moulènes, C. 2005. Conditions d'accès à la commande publique. In: *Droit des marchés publics.* Paris: Le Moniteur.

Della Porta, D. and Vannucci, A. 1999. *Corrupt Exchanges: Actors, Resources, and Mechanisms of Political Corruption.* New York: Aldine de Gruyter.

Drew, K. 2005. The challenges facing debarment and the European Union public procurement directive. In: *Fighting Corruption and Promoting Integrity in Public Procurement.* Paris: Organization for Economic Cooperation and Development (OECD).

Evenett, S.J. and Hoekman, B.M. 2005. Government procurement: Market access, transparency, and multilateral trade rules. *European Journal of Political Economy* 21(1): 163–183.

Gimeno Feliú, J.M. 2006. *La nueva contratación pública europea y su incidencia en la legislación española: la necesaria adopción de una nueva ley de contratos públicos y propuestas de reforma*. Cizur Menor (Navarra): Thomson-Civitas.

Gosálbez Pequeño, H. 2000. *El contratista de la Administración Pública*. Madrid: Marcial Pons-Cámara de Cuentas de Andalucía.

Hollard, V. 1989. *L'exclusion des marchés publics (Annexe au rapport sur le projet de réforme du Code penal)*. Paris: Chambre de Commerce et d'Industrie de Paris.

Jacobs, J.B. and Anechiarico, F. 1992. Blacklisting of public contractors as an anti-corruption and racketeering strategy. *Criminal Justice Ethics* 11(2): 64–76.

Kramer, R.E. 2005. Awarding contracts to suspended and debarred firms: Are stricter rules necessary? *Public Contract Law Journal* 34(3): 539–552.

Mardas, D. and Triantafyllou, D. 1997. Selection criteria and the award procedure in public procurement. *International Advances in Economic Research* 3(1): 91–112.

Mauro, P. 1995. Corruption and growth. *Quarterly Journal of Economics* 110(3): 681–712.

Méndez, F. and Sepúlveda, F. 2006. Corruption, growth and political regimes: Cross country evidence. *European Journal of Political Economy* 22(1): 82–98.

Moran, J., Pope, J., and Doig, A. 2004. Debarment as an Anti-Corruption Means—a review report—U4 Anti-Corruption Resource Centre.
http://www.u4.no/themes/debarment/debarmentreport.pdf (accessed July 28, 2007).

Noonan, J.T. 1984. *Bribes*. New York: Macmillan.

OECD. 2005. *Fighting Corruption and Promoting Integrity in Public Procurement*. Paris: Organization for Economic Cooperation and Development.

——. 2007. *Bribery in Public Procurement: Methods, Actors and Counter-Measures*. Paris: Organization for Economic Cooperation and Development.

Olaya, J. 2005. Blacklisting corrupt companies. In: *Global Corruption Report 2005*. Berlin: Transparency International.

Piselli, E. 2000. The scope for excluding providers who have committed criminal offences under the E.U. procurement directives. *Public Procurement Law Review* 6: 267–286.

Pope, J. 2000. Public procurement: Where the public and private sectors do business. In: *TI Sourcebook 2000. Confronting Corruption: The Elements of a National Integrity System*. Washington: Transparency International.

Rose-Ackerman, S. 1997. Corruption as an international policy problem: Overview and recommendations. In: K.A. Elliott (ed.), *Corruption and the Global Economy*. Washington: Institute for International Economics.

——. 1999. *Corruption and Government: Causes, Consequences, and Reform*. Cambridge: Cambridge University Press.

Schooner, S.L. 2002. Desiderata: Objectives for a system of Government Contract Law. *Public Procurement Law Review* 11(2): 103–110.
http://papers.ssrn.com/sol3/papers.cfm?abstract_id=304620 (accessed July 26, 2007).

——. 2004. The paper tiger stirs: Rethinking suspension and debarment. *Public Procurement Law Review* 5: 211–217.

Schultz, J. and Søreide, T. 2006. *Corruption in Emergency Procurement*, Issue 7. Bergen: U4 Anti-Corruption Resource Centre, Chr. Michelsen Institute.
http://www.u4.no/themes/ces/documents/U4_issue_7_2006_corruption_emergency_procurement.pdf (accessed July 28, 2007).

Søreide, T. 2002. *Corruption in Public Procurement: Causes, Consequences and Cures*. Bergen: Chr. Michelsen Institute.

Stapenhurst, F. and Langseth, P. 1997. The role of the public administration in fighting corruption. *The International Journal of Public Sector Management* 10(5): 311–330.

Stessens, G. 2001. The International Fight against Corruption. *International Review of Penal Law* 72(3–4): 891–937.

Strombom, D. 1998. Corruption in Procurement. *Economic Perspectives* 3(5): 22–26.

Tanzi, V. 1998. Corruption around the world: Causes, consequences, scope, and cures. *International Monetary Fund Staff Papers* 45(4): 559–594.

Tanzi, V. and Davoodi, H.R. 1997. *Corruption, Public Investment, and Growth.* International Monetary Fund Working Papers No 97/139.

Transparency International. 2005. *Global Corruption Report.* Berlin: Transparency International. http://www.transparency.org/publications/gcr/download_gcr/download_gcr_2005#download (accessed July 27, 2007).

——. 2006a. *Handbook for Curbing Corruption in Public Procurement.* Berlin: Transparency International.

——. 2006b. *Recommendations for the Development and Implementation of an Effective Debarment System in the EU.* Berlin: Transparency International. http://www.transparency.org/content/download/5661/32802/file/TI_EU_Debarment_Recommendations_06-03-28.pdf (accessed July 25, 2007).

Treisman, D. 2000. The causes of corruption: A cross-national study. *Journal of Public Economics* 76(3): 399–457.

Trybus, M. 2006a. Improving the efficiency of public procurement systems in the context of the European Union enlargement process. *Public Contract Law Journal* 35(3): 409–425.

——. 2006b. The Morning after the Deadline: The State of Implementation of the New EC Public Procurement Directives in the Member States on February 1, 2006. *Public Procurement Law Review* 15(3): NA82–NA90.

Trybus, M. and Medina, T. 2007. Unfinished Business: The State of Implementation of the New EC Public Procurement Directives in the Member States on February 1, 2007. *Public Procurement Law Review* 16(4): NA89–NA97.

White, S. 2000. *Procurement and Organised Crime: An EU Wide Study.* London: Institute of Advanced Legal Studies.

——. 2005. Exclusion of tenderers in the European Union: The only way forward against procurement fraud? In: *Fighting Corruption and Promoting Integrity in Public Procurement.* Paris: Organization for Economic Cooperation and Development (OECD).

Williams, S. 2006. The mandatory exclusions for corruption in the new EC Procurement Directives. *European Law Review* 31(5): 711–734.

Chapter 6

Public Procurement Reforms in Africa: A Tool for Effective Governance of the Public Sector and Poverty Reduction

Benon Basheka

CONTENTS

6.1 Introduction

Effective governance of the public sector is at the center of many pressing challenges confronting both developed and developing countries. Good governance entails a well-functioning public sector, which is thought to be responsive to the citizenry and to be reasonably efficient in the delivery of public services. A well-functioning public sector also involves the following: transparency and predictability of its decision-making processes and oversight mechanisms (checks and balances) to guard against arbitrariness and to ensure accountability in the use of public resources. However, these oversight mechanisms do not eliminate the flexibility and delegation needed to respond quickly to changing circumstances. In summary, they are accountable and result oriented (World Bank, 2000). Over time, the challenge for decision makers in Africa has been to structurally and institutionally transform the state and the government to become legitimate and relevant to the masses (Kalu, 2004). Good governance is measured around four key pillars: accountability, transparency, predictability, and participation, and has taken a center stage in any discussion on sustainable development in the developing world. None of the four pillars and their constituent components can stand alone without the other because the public sector operates like a system. A mistake or weakness in one part of the public sector is felt by other components of the public sector.

Africa operates in a global environment, exploiting the opportunities of globalization, and also being shaped by the demands and expectations of the global economy. Ensuring effective governance and poverty reduction are among the expectations. But surprisingly, the African continent was not until the 1990s responsive to the call for good governance. As a result of internal and external pressures, the public sector was forced to have a second look at the institutions and systems through which public services were being delivered. Africa as a continent has never been short of public sector challenges. It is a continent that is "ever" in the news for negative development issues such as poverty, political instability, corruption, and malfunctioning public sector institutions, and poor governance systems have almost become synonymous to Africa since 1970s. Africa was thus expected to devote its efforts toward reforming its systems to address their serious weaknesses—nontransparency, lack of accountability, excessive intervention, lack of delegation, and poor results—all contributing to arbitrariness, corruption, and poverty (World Bank, 2000).

What was really expected of the African public system by the mid-1980s was a well-functioning public administration. An effective and efficient administration is to be built on the fundamental principles and practices framed around transparency, accountability, and cost economy (Dibie, 2004), and with globalization, localization, and information revolution, citizens have been empowered to demand accountability from their governments for it is accountability that provides a mechanism for measuring governments' performance (Shah, 2005).

Since the late 1980s and early 1990s the debate on public sector management reforms and the promotion of good governance became the center of discussion among donor agencies, academics, and policy makers. Several reforms have taken place with mixed degrees of successes and failures. Public procurement reforms have occupied a center stage in broad public sector reforms in Africa since the late 1990s. The increasing number of players in public procurement, the pressures to cut costs in public sector operations, the increased demand for accountability and transparency from the tax payers, the increased link between public procurement and trade and investment, the influences of world class management philosophies, the changing roles of the public sector, and the overall desire for efficiency among others combined to generate a renewed interest in the area of public procurement. Public procurement systems were generally weak in a number of African countries. A weak public procurement system was a breeding ground for inefficiency in service delivery. This was because public procurement was and is still directly related to economic growth, development, poverty-reduction strategies, and overall service delivery. There is no sector of government that is not affected, directly or indirectly, positively or negatively, expectedly or unexpectedly, by public procurement. This is because each sector needs goods, services, and works of varying magnitude to effectively perform its function. Such goods have to be acquired through a procurement process. This implies that a problem in the functioning of the public procurement system will have wider implications for the entire public sector. The government work like a system, with different sub-systems, which are interconnected (but where different components work together for the common good of the broader system).

Procurement and its management is a core function of public financial management and service delivery (Harmonizing Donor Practices for Effective Aid Delivery, 1999). And effective and efficient public procurement systems are essential for the realization of the millennium development goals (MDGs) and promotion of sustainable development. Unfortunately, the procurement systems in many developing countries are particularly weak and serve to squander scarce domestic and foreign resources. Public procurement has always been a big part of developing countries' economies accounting for an estimated 9–13 percent of their gross domestic products (GDPs), and it is therefore an area that needs attention because resources are not being used properly (Witting, 1999). Thai (2004, p. 6), while quoting Calendar and Mathews (2000), notes that

> …The sheer magnitude of the public procurement dollar expenditure outlay has a dramatic impact on the economy, and, thus, needs to be well managed. Indeed in all countries in the world, estimates of the financial activities of government procurement managers are believed to be in the order of 10%–30% of the GNP…

Despite the huge financial expenditure of public resources on the acquisition process, it is only recently that the area started receiving attention. The field of public procurement has largely been a neglected area of academic education and research, but policy makers and public procurement professionals have paid great attention to procurement improvements and reforms (Thai, 2001). Efficient and effective public procurement systems significantly influence the provision of government services like the provision of roads, hospitals, healthcare, sanitation, telecommunication facilities, education, environmental protection, promotion of human rights, etc. It is because of its importance to the well-functioning public sector and good governance that those public procurement systems in Africa were subjected to a reform so as to create a well-functioning public procurement system. Table 6.1 summarizes the components of an effective public procurement system put forth by the African Development Bank.

Table 6.1 Components of an Effective Public Procurement System

Component	*Description or Function*
Legal framework	Based on a procurement law that defines responsibility of procuring agencies and suppliers.
Policy	Consistent, national policies and standards to be followed by all procuring agencies, including arbitration procedures.
Institutional setup	Defined structures for conducting procurement that minimize subjective decisions and politicization (including approval mechanisms, authorities, and composition of bid and evaluation committees).
Professional civil service	Procuring agencies staffed with procurement professionals, trained and recognized as such under civil service regulations.
Resources	Procurement agencies supported with adequate budget, standard documents, and operational manuals.
Fraud prevention	Clear laws applicable to procurement officials and suppliers that increase transparency and encourage inclusion of civil society.

Source: From African Development Bank, Governance and Regional Cooperation Division in *Understanding Public Procurement*. With permission.

6.2 Conceptual Framework

In this chapter, I provide a conceptual framework on how public procurement reforms in Africa can be effective ingredients in achieving good governance, thereby contributing to poverty reduction on the continent. The key concepts addressed in the chapter are public procurement reforms, effective public procurement systems, good governance, and poverty reduction. Africa is a continent currently experiencing high levels of poverty, which is an outcome not only of economic processes but also of interacting economic, social, and political forces. In particular, it is an outcome of the accountability and responsiveness of state institutions (WDR, 2000/2001). During the last two decades, the number of poor in Africa has doubled from 150 million to 300 million, more than 40 percent of the region's population. It is the only region that has remained behind on most of the MDGs (World Bank, 2005b). In the current World Bank report (2007, p. 3), poverty in Africa according to the World Bank has increasingly shown "an African face, and eradicating it has predominantly become an African challenge." Although the region currently accounts for only 10 percent of the world's population, it now accommodates 30 percent of the world's poor. Although the world has made remarkable progress in reducing extreme poverty over the last three decades, the trend in sub-Saharan Africa has been in the opposite direction, with poverty increasing from 36 percent of the population in 1970 to 50 percent in 2000. And as a result, one in two Africans (300 million people) is poor, spending less than $1 a day on basic necessities of life.

The African public sector has been grappling with poverty and provision of effective services. Tackling the poverty challenge is the responsibility of the public sector in collaboration with other stakeholders. However, the state will deliver more effectively to all citizens, and to poor people in particular if certain mechanisms are in place to man the running of government operations. For example, public institutions that implement policies should be efficiently instituted and they should be accountable and responsive to users, corruption and harassment should be curbed, the power of the state should be used to redistribute resources for actions benefiting poor people, legal systems that promote legal equity should essentially be accessible to poor people; central and local governments should create decentralized mechanisms for broad participation in the delivery of public services and minimize the scope for capture by local elites; governments should generate political support for public action against poverty by creating a climate favorable to pro-poor actions and coalitions, by facilitating the growth of poor people's associations, and by increasing the political capacity of poor people; and political regimes honor the rule of law, allow the expression of political voice, and encourage the participation of poor people in political process (WDR, 2000/2001).

Faced with such challenges, the functional and organizational structure of the public sector needs to be rationalized to improve resource allocation for programs that are priorities to the pressing needs of society. Beyond rationalizing the structure of the public system, there is a need to make public programs more efficient and accountable. All this requires effective governance, which is at the heart of a well-functioning public sector in both developed and developing countries. The public sector is that sector that is not private, it is that part of the economy that is comprised of all levels of government (central and local), and it excludes business and households. Governance is how those who have power use it in the management of public affairs. In terms of the public sector, the term "governance" is synonymous to "government." Governments are established for a purpose. Inherently, government or public sector is established to provide public services to citizens of a particular country. The sector is arranged under organizational units, each with specialized constitutional and administrative roles. To perform the specialized roles and responsibilities, such units require resources (financial, material, and human), and these resources have to be acquired through a process of procurement. The public sector has three branches, namely the legislative branch, often called the national assembly or parliament, the judiciary, which is the system of courts, and the executive that implements government policies.

In any country, there will always be goods and services that citizens expect from their governments. Such goods and services include national security or defense, medical and health provision, protection of their rights and their property, sanitation and provision of water, electricity provision, education, and transport services. Such services can be provided if there are effective public procurement systems. Poor public procurement management has serious impacts on the functioning of the public sector. Poor systems may, for example, lead to delays in the implementation of government programs and this could have adverse effects on society. A discussion of the contribution of public procurement to the functioning of the public sector has to be made in the context of the objectives of public procurement.

During the 1980s and 1990s, many countries were performing badly in achieving their public service objectives. The public procurement systems were not working properly. It was therefore held that effective public procurement systems could be created through public procurement reforms. A well-functioning procurement system is built on certain benchmarks, which revolves around four pillars—legislative and regulatory framework, institutional framework and management capacity, procurement operations and market practices, and integrity of procurement practices (Agaba and Shipman, 2006). Each of these pillars has certain indicators. Public procurement was conducted within the public sector, which had essentially broader social and economic goals to fulfill through offering efficient and effective services like health, education, transport, sanitation, etc. Efficient and effective service delivery would in turn contribute to good governance.

Figure 6.1 depicts the conceptual framework through which this chapter has been conceived. The primary core concepts are effective public procurement systems, good governance, poverty reduction, and public procurement reforms in Africa.

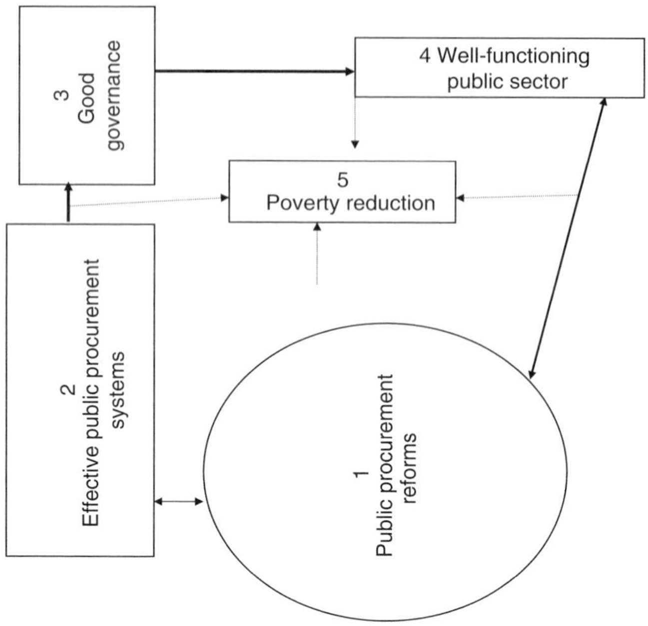

Figure 6.1 Effect of public procurement reforms on improved governance and poverty reduction.

As shown in Figure 6.1, the overall goal of the public sector in Africa is poverty reduction. Poverty reduction however depends on a well-functioning public sector, which offers public goods and services in an efficient and effective manner, and this is possible only if effective governance is in place. To have effective governance in the public sector, public procurement systems have to be efficient due to the critical role procurement plays in the functioning of organizations. Many countries in Africa had serious weaknesses in their public procurement systems and it was hoped that by reforming these systems and by incorporating a new system that was accountable and transparent, it would have far reaching impacts on improved governance.

6.3 Public Procurement Reform Environment in Africa

6.3.1 Definition of Public Procurement Reform

To reform public procurement is to have a second look at the existing public procurement systems (in response to problems arising from internal and external pressures), with a view of making systems more responsive to changing circumstances and meeting desired goals. Public procurement reforms can be defined as policy attempts at changing organizational, institutional, and legal structures that manage public procurement process (to improve the conduct of procurement), signaling a major shift from traditional systems and processes to new responsive systems and processes. The purpose of public procurement reform is to create responsive systems that encourage effective and efficient performance of the public sector. Such reform efforts would require all stakeholders to shift from traditional bureaucratic processes to more flexible processes that focus more on outputs and on realization of broad social and economic goals of government. Public procurement reform advocates for a procurement system that puts in place a management style of realization of government objectives through effective procurement governance. In this way, public procurement reform means inducing change and is a strategy for improving the performance of the public sector. This would essentially entail a strategy to "do more with less, concentrate on value for money procurement, encourage competition, instil transparency and accountability, have responsive legal regimes, and involve a number of stakeholders in procurement governance."

Public procurement reforms can be considered as the process of transforming government procurement from systems incapable of achieving government procurement objectives to those systems with a capacity to achieve the objectives of government procurement. It may also be looked at as the process of attempting to make the process of government acquisition more accountable and transparent to a range of stakeholders. It involves strengthening systems, processes, procedures, and people involved in the process of acquiring goods, services, and works needed by government departments and units to perform functions of delivering efficient and effective services. Public procurement reform may equally be the process of attempting to "fix" problems that have engulfed public procurement systems.

6.3.2 Nature of the Public Procurement Systems in Africa before the Reforms

On November 30, 1998, there was a conference on public procurement reform in Accra, Ghana, attended by over 30 representatives from African governments, and cosponsored by the African Development Bank, International Trade Centre, United Nations Development Programme, and the World Bank. Through the distribution of a questionnaire (whose questions were derived from the World Bank's *CPAR* [*Country Procurement Assessment Report*]) to participants at the conference, and through the four-day deliberations, the performance of public procurement systems on the continent came to the forefront. It was concluded that public procurement in Africa had serious weaknesses, and a summary of the weaknesses are listed in Table 6.2.

Table 6.2 Public Procurement Weaknesses in Africa before the Reforms

Public Procurement Aspect	*Distinguishing Features of Public Procurement Systems in Africa*
Public procurement legal framework	• Was unclear and not comprehensive • Several scattered laws governed procurement • Old laws that had been overtaken by events, i.e., public procurement was now much more complex
Information and transparency in public procurement	• Failure in individual procurement entities to predetermine and disclose in advance the award criteria was a common occurrence • Imposition of discretion by the concerned minister and senior government officials • Procurement rules were not followed in practice • Application of competitive and transparent methods of public procurement were not streamlined • Information on public procurement performance was generally lacking and where it did, it was difficult to find

(continued)

Table 6.2 (continued) Public Procurement Weaknesses in Africa before the Reforms

Public Procurement Aspect	*Distinguishing Features of Public Procurement Systems in Africa*
Rules of conduct and accountability	• Serious weaknesses in implementation of procurement rules • Lack of rules concerning conflict of interest in public procurement • Few countries had anticorruption provisions in place • Limited resources for policing corruption was noticeable in a number of countries
Preferential treatment of local bidders	• There were some degree of preferential treatment for national goods • Some nationals also received some preferential treatment but there were country differences
Institutional and administrative arrangements	• Involvement of central procurement authorities in operational activities (e.g., sitting on evaluation committees, serving as adjudicator bodies, procuring common use items, etc.) • Limited concentration by procurement central authorities on regulation • Prevalent conflicts of interest by officials working in central procurement units and procurement required standards of conduct
Human resource capacity	• Limited or lack of professional requirements for procurement personnel • Limited or complete lack of training programs in procurement-related areas • Conduct of procurement was by clerical staff • There was no minimum civil service rank for procurement personnel
General features of the procurement systems	• Adversarial/arm's length relationship with supplies • Limited consultation of the private sector

A consensus on a public procurement reform strategy emerged at the end of this conference:

(1) Building support for reform that required enabling legislation and regulations; organizations; well-trained and competent procurement officials; and informed, willing, and supportive business and professional sectors at both local and international levels.
(2) Obtaining political commitment to changes, or in other words, obtaining public support and government staff endorsement; prioritizing key procurement elements, such as transparency, anticorruption, etc.; promoting socioeconomic objectives; keeping parliament informed; and reassuring potential donors.

(3) Obtaining resources for reform needed for technical assistance to help prepare a business plan to describe and implement key objectives for reform. Potential sources of funds were identified as follows: the country's own resources (government and private sectors) and grants and loans from multilateral agencies such as the African Development Bank, the World Bank, or the United Nations Development Programme.

(4) Detailing a strategy for reform whose key elements are expected to build local capacity and transfer skills, designating a leader/champion for reform, integrating reform with a macroeconomic framework, monitoring and evaluating reform efforts, maximizing national expertise, obtaining media support to promote acceptance of the reform, communicating national commitment and progress, ensuring clear, understandable goals, and anticipating obstacles and barriers and quickly overcoming them.

(5) Communicating the strategy by determining a vision and establishing goals to fulfill the vision with regard to anticorruption measures, transparency enhancement, economy in purchasing, improved accountability of funds, sustainable human development, business opportunity, harmonization of procurement policies and procedures, changing organizational structures, accelerated economic growth (as percentage of gross national product [GNP]), clearer government communication to private sector participants of the system, more effective trade policies, and promotion of socioeconomic objectives.

(6) Marketing specific changes in the following areas to support reform: legal framework (conform where possible to the UNCITRAL [United Nations Commission for International Trade Law] model law on public procurement), procurement operations (create decentralized procurement entities with authority to do the actual buying operations following centralized policy), regulatory bodies (assure effective audit and review capability of contracting and expenditures), organizational structure (specific ministry and office structure unique to each country), procurement policy at center of government level (management office to formulate policy and regulations and measure the effectiveness of the public procurement system and its operation), and professional infrastructure (help establish and train a cadre of professional procurement officials) including a reference knowledge base of best practices.

6.3.3 Examples of Some Significant Reforms

Public procurement reforms among African countries are not significantly different, in terms of stages of reform, components of reform strategies, and implementation. In almost all African countries, the public procurement reforms have been preceded by assessments of the existing system, either by consultants or by external donor agencies particularly the World Bank through country procurement reports. Such studies made recommendations to governments based on which reforms of public procurement have been coined. In terms of components of reform, almost all African countries have created new procurement legislations that have put in place new institutional arrangements through which procurement is to be managed. In each country that has attempted to reform the public procurement system, a central authority to coordinate procurement activities has been put in place. Interestingly, weaknesses in public procurement systems in Africa were almost similar.

6.3.3.1 Uganda

In 2000, the implementation of public procurement reforms commenced with the cabinet endorsing the procurement reforms. This was against the background of a task force that had been commissioned to undertake a study (Government of Uganda, 1999) and make recommendations to the government on how to implement the reforms. The process followed promulgation of public (procurement) finance regulations under a statutory instrument in March 2000 and this came into effect in May 2001. This led to the use of contract committees in government ministries and departments except for security agencies and local governments. Ultimately the central tender board (CTB) was replaced with the creation of the procurement reform implementation unit (PRIU) and appointment of senior management personnel to the unit to prepare the transition from a CTB structure to an autonomous one, leading to the enactment of a law to replace the statutory instrument of 2002.

The Government of Uganda passed the Public Procurement and Disposal of Public Assets Act and Regulations of 2003, which established the Public Procurement and Disposal Authority (PPDA) with regulatory, political, capacity building, and information functions. In 2006, there were local government amendments where the central procurement regulations were harmonized with the local government procurement. In all cases, there was a new institutional arrangement with each factor having roles and responsibilities. Figure 6.2 illustrates the key stakeholders.

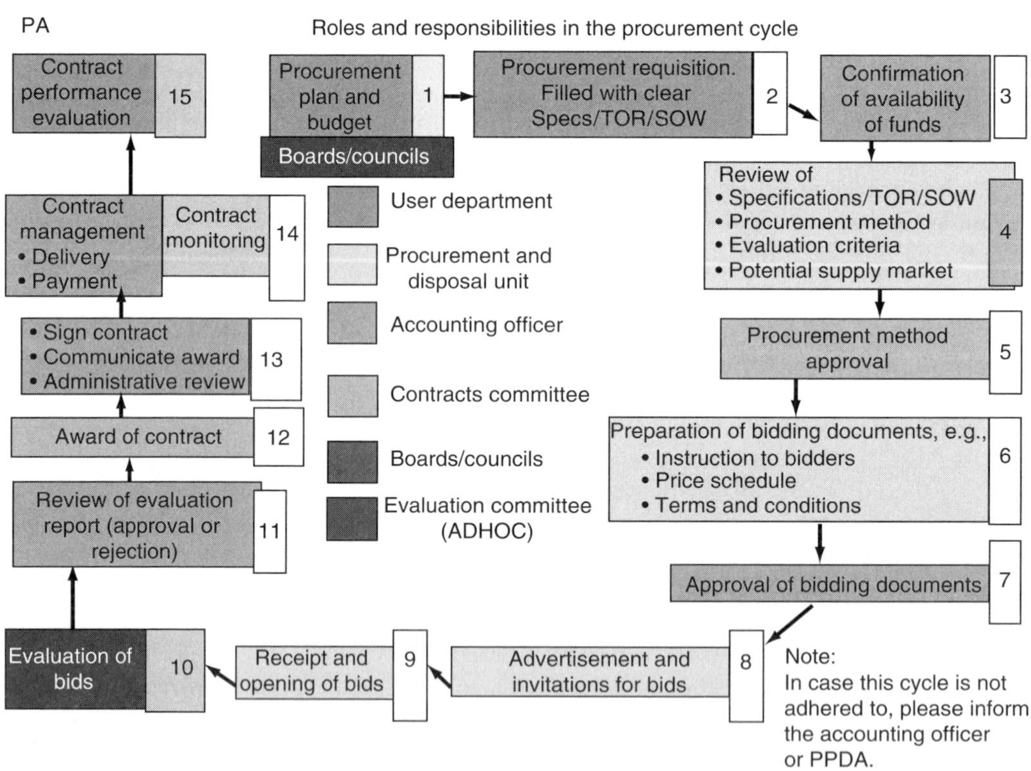

Figure 6.2 Chart of roles and responsibilities of key stakeholders in the new procurement institutional framework in Uganda.

6.3.3.2 Kenya

In Kenya, public procurement reforms were initiated in 1997, after the Government of Kenya and the World Bank carried out a countrywide procurement assessment review. It was noted that the procurement system was not based on a sound legal and regulatory framework and did not promote fair competition, thereby rendering it liable to serious abuse. The government subsequently issued the Public Procurement Regulations 2001, which established the public procurement directorate and the appeals board, at the treasury. To strengthen, streamline, and have a sound legal framework the government enacted the Public Procurement and Disposal Act 2005, and the regulations to implement this act were gazetted by the minister for finance. The act came into force on January 1, 2007.

In cooperation with the European Union, the Government of Kenya carried out an independent procurement review, in May 2005, and the main findings highlighted a series of weaknesses including abuse and mismanagement of contract variations, lack of effective checks and balances with respect to authorizing the different procurement and expenditure steps, lack of fair and transparent competition, inappropriate application of required procurement methods, incomplete evidence of full receipt of goods and services paid, embezzlement of funds under pretext of low value items, poor filing of procurement and related expenditure documentation, excessive delays in procurement process, inappropriate use of arbitrary compliance criteria to eliminate bidders, and poor linkage between procurement and other areas of finance management.

An elaborate program has been set out to tackle the above issues in a structured manner. Other reforms being undertaken includes the following:

- Development and implementation of an E-procurement strategy
- Capacity building assessment and enhancement
- Development of a modern framework contracts mechanism
- Development of certification of supplier's system
- Establishment of a strong public procurement oversight authority comprised of an advisory board and a review board
- Development and implementation of a monitoring and evaluation system
- Reforming the public health sector procurement system

6.3.3.3 Tanzania

In the United Republic of Tanzania, public procurement reforms were undertaken as in other African countries. The government's efforts to undertake public procurement reform in the Tanzanian mainland started in 1992 after the government commissioned a consultant to undertake a public procurement and supply management study, with the consultant's report identifying serious weaknesses, thereby creating an urgent need for reform. The major recommendations of the consultant hinged on three major aspects, namely (1) need to enact a new procurement law establishing principles, policies, and structure of public procurement, supported by detailed procurement regulations, (2) raise levels of authority, but at the same time institute effective control of commitments and payments, and (3) strengthen the CTB as a regulatory authority for all public procurement.

Arising out of the consultant's recommendations, the Public Procurement Act No. 3 of 2001 was passed to provide a legal framework within which public procurement was to be conducted. The act became effective on July 1, 2001 and it provided a comprehensive coverage of all regulatory aspects critical to public procurement in Tanzania. The new act was to be applicable to all procurements undertaken by public institutions except for financially independent parastatal organizations and defense procurement. The act also provided for the establishment of a public procurement appeals authority to settle procurement disputes before a judicial review process.

An institutional framework through which public procurement was organized and to be managed was put in place by the new act of 2001. The institutions involved in public procurement included procurement management units in ministries, government departments, district and urban authorities, tender boards, the CTB, government stores, medical stores department, government press/printer, Maji stores department, veterinary stores, and third-party procurement agents. Procurement from departments' government stores (government stores of ministry of works, Maji stores department, government press/printer, veterinary stores, and medical stores department) can only be made if prices offered by these institutions are lower than or equal to market prices.

6.3.3.4 Nigeria

Another example of an African country that has reformed its public procurement systems is Nigeria. The Nigerian government commissioned the World Bank in collaboration with some Nigerian private sector specialists to undertake studies of its financial systems and general procurement-related activities. This was intended to assist the government with a process of enthroning efficiency, accountability, integrity, and transparency in government procurement and financial management systems. At the end of the exercise, two reports, namely the *Country Report on the Financial Systems* and the *CPAR* were published. The comprehensive review of the country's public procurement system covered the existing legal framework, organizational responsibilities and capabilities within government, present procedures and practices, the reliability of government accounting systems, and the effectiveness of budgeting systems in directing resources for intended purposes. Comparisons were made in each of these areas on how practices in Nigeria differ from established international best practice.

The countrywide procurement assessment , which was conducted on national procurement systems, identified six major weaknesses in the existing procurement systems, which in effect were not substantially different from what was happening in other African countries. The major weaknesses identified in Nigeria were

(1) Lack of a modern law on public procurement and a permanent overseeing body to provide guidance and monitor purchasing entities.

(2) Gaps and deficiencies in the Finance (Control and Management) Act of 1958, and of financial regulations that set basic rules for managing public expenditure leading to faulty implementation of existing regulations on procurement (e.g., lack of permanent arrangements for control and surveillance), which creates opportunities for bribery and corruption.

(3) Inflation and lack of regular adjustments on thresholds of approving limits of tender boards, and constant erosion of their authority resulting in abuses, prominent among which is splitting of contracts.

(4) Proliferation of tender boards perceived by the private sector as sources of delays and nontransparency. In addition, these tender boards appeared to have limited mandates with powers to decide contracts resting de facto with the permanent secretary and the minister/commissioner.
(5) Cumbersome customs systems and procedures causing major delay in clearing goods, and hence a source of corruption.
(6) Execution of procurement by staff who substantially lack relevant training.

To address the weaknesses that had been identified, the *CPAR* made numerous recommendations that can be grouped under six core areas, forming the basis of procurement reforms:

(1) Need for a procurement law based on the UNCITRAL model
(2) Need to establish a central procurement unit (public procurement commission, PPC) to serve as the regulatory and overseeing body on public sector procurements, as in other countries
(3) Need to revise key areas of financial regulations to make them more transparent (reflecting a direct link between public procurement and financial management)
(4) Need to streamline tender boards and strengthen their functional authority, including powers to award contracts
(5) Need to rebuild procurement and financial management capacity in the public sector
(6) Need to comprehensively review businesses related to export, import, and transit regulations, procedures, and practices.

As expected, given the experience in other countries that had reformed their procurement systems, the Government of Nigeria accepted the *CPAR* in its entirety with the exception of the registration of contractors and the involvement of political office holders such as ministers and commissioners in the award of contracts in excess of 50 million Naira, which the report was against. This led to the issue of a landmark circular, New Policy Guidelines for Procurement and Award of Contracts in Government Ministries/Parastatals, No. F.15775, dated June 27, 2000. The circular outlined in great detail the procedures and levels of approvals for the award of contracts to meet best international practice.

In all African countries, there is a noticeable attempt to institute a new procurement law and the establishment of a central procurement unit to coordinate the conduct of public procurement reforms. There are several other countries that have reformed their public procurement systems in Africa, for example, South Africa, Ghana, Egypt, and Guinea, among others. In essence, all public organizations were reforming their systems to move from the old procurement framework to the new public procurement system. The status of public procurement would be elevated from a clerical function to one that is strategic. The shift is summarized in Table 6.3.

6.4 Drivers of Public Procurement Reforms in Africa

Public procurement systems in Africa were generally weak and characterized by corruption and nontransparent mechanisms. Hunja (2003, p. 5) describes public procurement systems that existed before reforms were instituted in many developing countries as

> public procurement was not previously viewed as having s a strategic impact on the management of public resource. It was treated largely as a process-oriented 'back

Table 6.3 Public Procurement Elevation from Clerical to Strategic Function

Old Public Procurement	*New Public Procurement*
Clerical function	Strategic function
Cost center	Profit center
Reactive function	Proactive function
Passive-vertical administrative function	Integrative-initiative set of leadership roles
National in outlook	Global in outlook
Suppliers taken as adversaries	Suppliers taken as partners
Short-term focus relationships	Long-term relationship
Nonvalue adding activity	Value adding activity
Unprofessional activity	Professional activity
Fused under other functions	Growing into a separate management function
Manually oriented	Computer oriented
Goods based	Service based
Construction based	Other sectors
Procurement not taught in many institutions	Academic discipline

> office' support function, often implemented by non-professional staff of the buying agencies. Consequently, little effort was expended to ensure that policies and rules and the institutional framework governing the procurement systems were maintained in a manner that ensured public funds were used in the most efficient and economic way and that the system delivered the based value for money.

And it is this kind of situation that was the source of problems to governments as described earlier; a well-founded public procurement system is essential for the effective functioning of government systems in any part of the world and more so in Africa.

Public procurement consumes a substantial amount of public money. Public procurement accounts for a high proportion of government expenditures in a number of African countries. In Malawi, it was estimated in 2005 that public procurement constituted 40 percent of the total expenditure, while in Uganda, it was at 70 percent (Development Assistance Committee, OECD, 2005).

Public bodies are established to accomplish certain tasks and in an attempt to accomplish tasks they acquire resources in varying magnitudes from outside their operations through a process of procurement. This procurement of public sectors, herein referred to as public procurement, utilizes taxpayer's money and aims at fulfiling certain objectives. And as Thai (2001) argues, procurement, though an important function of any government for it has to satisfy requirements for goods, works, systems, and services in a timely manner, has been a neglected area of academic education and research. In a similar attempt, Arrowsmith et al. (2000, p. 12) maintain that "government procurement in a very general sense of making arrangements for the acquisition of public needs, can probably be identified in any country."

As far as core areas of the public sector with potential to improve the effectiveness of the public sector was concerned, public procurement was singled out. It was seen as an area having significant potential for the realization of good governance and efficient public sector organizations, thereby contributing to poverty reduction. It was and is still an area that consumes substantial amount of resources in any country's economy. Any dollar spent well on public procurement makes a significant contribution to the realization of the broad social and economic goals of governments. In Africa, procurement as a core function of public financial management was envisioned to have had a direct impact on effective service delivery (Harmonizing Donor Practices for Effective Aid Delivery, 1999).

Effective and efficient public procurement systems are essential for the realization of MDGs and the promotion of sustainable development, but unfortunately, procurement systems in many developing countries are particularly weak and serve to squander scarce domestic and foreign resources (Development Assistance Committee, OECD, 2005). Public procurement is a business process within a political system and it is inherently a politically sensitive activity, not least because it involves significant amounts of money (Schapper et al., 2006). It remains a big part of the developing countries' economy accounting for an estimated 9–13 percent of the developing nations' GDP, and it is therefore an area that needs attention because resources are not being used properly (Witting, 1999, p. 2). The field of public procurement has largely been a neglected area of academic education and research, but policy makers and public procurement professionals have paid considerable attention to procurement improvements and reforms (Thai, 2001).

Specifically, there were two drivers of public procurement reforms in Africa. The first were endogenous (internal) drivers. Internally, the failure of public procurement systems to deliver expected social and economic objectives precipitated a reform of the systems. The internal drivers were a result of weaknesses in public procurement systems. The second were the exogenous (external) drivers for public procurement reforms. Externally, the demands for accountability and transparency by development partners and the bandwagon effect combined with internal drivers to enable many African countries embark on reforming their public procurement systems. Kernaghan et al. (2000) argued that environmental forces stimulating reform in public organizations could be grouped into external and domestic forces. External forces like globalization, and the technological revolution, combine with domestic forces like financial constraint, public demand for quality service, the changing political culture, demographic change, and the legal of earlier reforms to compel public organizations reform their systems (ibid., p. 15).

In the African context, the following forces were drivers of public procurement reforms.

6.4.1 Driver 1: To Improve the Governance of the Public Sector

In response to the call for governments to have effective governance structures, there was a desire to reform the public procurement systems. Governance was at the heart of expectations of many countries in the developing world and Africa was in a desperate situation because of the challenges it was facing. In an attempt to address the governance crisis that the African public sector was experiencing, public procurement reform had to be undertaken. This was in itself an outcome of both internal and external pressures. Internally, citizens were demanding effective and efficient services from public sectors, and externally the donor community was equally demanding accountability and transparency for their funds. Given the expenditure of many African countries on public procurement is estimated at more than 10 percent of the total GNP, its effective management was seen as a key element in improving governance systems. Because procurement cuts across a number of social sectors, which are critical for improved governance, it has received the attention for reform in many African governments. The intention was to improve procurement governance, which in turn would lead to improved governance of the public sector. The desired public procurement system should be as follows:

- Accountable with clear lines of responsibility for procurement
- Characterized by transparency in procurement decision making
- Guided by procurement professionalism
- Responsive to the needs of citizens
- Recognize the integrated role and contribution of all functional aspects of the organization

6.4.2 Driver 2: To Respond to Global Forces and to Improve the Participation Rates of Private Sector in Public Procurement

The late 1980s and early 1990s saw a significant increase in the influence and the associated effects of globalization. During this period, there was a general belief that public sector should open its operations to market forces if they were to benefit from the opportunities created by global dynamics and at the same time it was the only way of addressing the poor performance of the public sector. In essence, this meant that all public sector activities were to be subjected to forces of demand and supply thereby increasing participation by private sector. As an area that had a direct impact on the strategic and tactical operations of the private sector, and owing to the fact that the old procurement systems were not responsive to the market forces, African countries had to increase the participation rates of the private sector through procurement reform. Specific legal and institutional reforms were to be initiated if the situation was to be reversed.

6.4.3 Driver 3: To Improve on Transparency Thereby Minimizing Corruption in Public Procurement Systems

The principle of transparency in the conduct of public affairs has been a long-cherished principle of effective management. Its absence has always contributed to weaknesses in government operations. Specific approaches and strategies therefore are demanded to introduce transparency in processes, systems, procedures, and operations of any government function. There is no area of public management that needs these more than the area of public procurement. Realizing that this cardinal principle was lacking in the old procurement systems, many African countries, with certainly a direct influence from the donors, had to embark on a public procurement reform strategy.

In African governments, corruption, in its various ramifications, was starting to eat away the virtues of African public services (although its prevalence is on the increase even against reforms). The procurement systems in turn were characterized by lack of transparency and there was generally no value for money in public procurements. There was thus a need to reform the public procurement systems to make them much more transparent thereby increasing the chances of value for money. It was anticipated that transparency would help in creating a well-functioning public procurement system. In the context of procurement, transparency was used to mean the ability of all relevant participants to know and understand the actual means and processes by which contracts were awarded and managed. Transparency in public procurement was to be characterized by the following:

- Well-defined regulations and procedures open to public and other stakeholders' scrutiny
- Effective processes for sharing information across divisions and projects
- Clear, standardized tender documents containing complete information
- Equal opportunity for qualified suppliers in the bidding process

6.4.4 Driver 4: To Improve Accountability of the Procurement Systems

The role of accountability (managerial, administrative, political, and financial) to the performance of the public sector and improved service delivery cannot be overemphasized. It is a cardinal principle of sound public sector performance. Managerial/administrative accountability is the way in which managerial decisions of the public sector exercise powers and authority entrusted to them. It is the accountability that offers an obligation for managers or administrators to answer for the performance of the roles and responsibilities assigned to them, taking into account the existing legal and institutional framework, and also the resources assigned to them. Unlike political accountability that is exercised by elected officials, managerial or administrative accountability is exercised by public servants who essentially do not go through an election but are allocated a full budget for the implementation of government program and thus must show how best they have utilized such resources.

Political accountability revolves around the mandate citizens give their elected officials at various levels. Citizens use the power of their votes to keep leaders in their office or remove them from office depending on how accountable they have been. In addition to administrative and political accountability, there is financial accountability that focuses on accurate and timely reporting on financial resource utilization through professional audits, conducted by a professional group of auditors. This ensures value for money in the operations of government functions. Public servants who misuse public resources are to be punished and the information from financial accountability can be used to mobilize more resources and also in the allocation of public resources.

In the public procurement systems that characterized most African governments before reforms, there was general lack of managerial and administrative accountability in public procurement, political accountability, as well as procurement financial accountability. Public procurement was generally not conducted in an accountable manner and thus when confronted with challenges of diminishing resources, most governments had to reform their systems to create a strong accountable public procurement system. An accountable system is characterized by the following:

- Power of prior approval as this regulates the behavior of public servants by requiring them to go through a clear procedure intended to enable them to get clearance to conduct any public procurement expenditure. This is a strong mechanism, when followed by detection of public procurement fraud.
- Responsibility or accountability which essentially means a public servant's ability to provide answers for the public procurement decision taken at any stage of the public procurement process.

Public procurement audit and inspection is essential in improving accountability. There should be a mechanism for reviewing and systematically assessing the performance of a department or procuring and disposing entity with a view of ensuring compliance to set procurement rules and procedures.

6.4.5 Driver 5: To Improve the Coordination of Public Procurement System

An effective public procurement system is one that has a strong and well-organized structure of relationships and distribution of roles. Such a structure is concerned with elements as the definition and allocation of specific tasks—for example, "who does what;" the grouping of related tasks into manageable functions, divisions, departments, sections, or other units; the creation of systems that facilitates the coordination between functions or other units; the distribution of formal authority across the organization and within the functions or units comprising the organization; and the allocation of responsibility within the organization and to constituent functional groups (Lysons, 2000).

Public procurement systems in many African governments were fragmented in various institutional frameworks and this made coordination a difficult task. Procurement coordination was a serious challenge that many public procurement practitioners were experiencing. At a time when resources were dwindling, the task became a complete disaster. Public procurement reforms were therefore intended to have a harmonized central public procurement system and as such could facilitate the coordination of the procurement function in government departments thereby leading to improvements in the operations.

6.4.6 Driver 6: To Improve Public Procurement Professionalism

Public procurement has been a major activity of many governments in both developed and developing countries. In Africa, the acquisition of public goods, services, and works for government operations has traditionally occupied a central position in government operations.

In the context of Uganda, it was recognized before the actual start of public procurement reforms that the country lacked a serious cadre of public procurement professionals. But at the same time such a cadre was essential for the realization of effective procurement governance. The desire to reform public procurement systems was therefore partly to create such a cadre of professional staff.

6.4.7 Driver 7: To Improve Service Delivery and Reduce Poverty

Africa has been amazing in terms of poverty and development. According to the World Bank (2005), during the last two decades, the number of poor in Africa has doubled from 150 million to 300 million, more than 40 percent of the region's population. It is the only region that has remained behind on most of the MDGs (p. ii). Poverty in Africa has been showing an African face and the solutions to address it have been argued to take an African face. This has made many African policy makers, with the direct influence from funding agencies, to scratch their heads for ways of reversing this trend. For the last ten years, public procurement has been singled out as a solution to the drastic poverty levels. Given the total expenditure on public procurement compared to the national budgets, the reform of public procurement systems in Africa could not be delayed anymore.

6.5 Challenges of Public Procurement Reform in Africa

Reforming any system is not an easy task. There are forces for and against and they come from different directions—the political, economic, social, and technological environments. Public

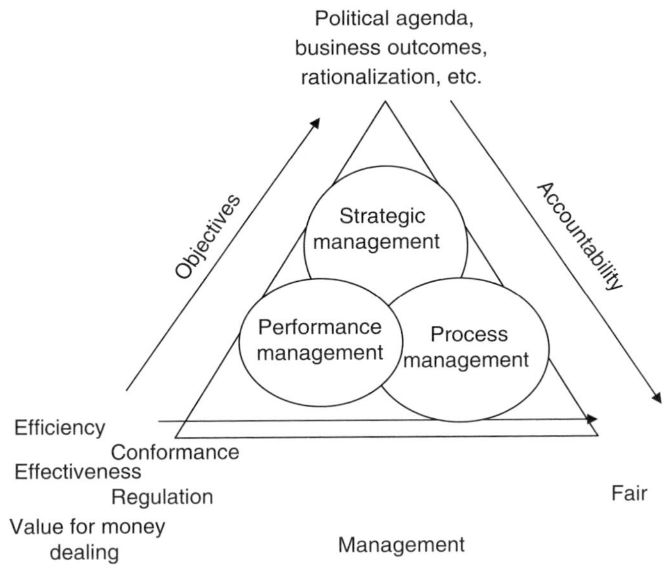

Figure 6.3 Scope and nature of public procurement model. (From Schapper, P.R., Malta, J.N.V., and Gilbert, D.L., *J. Public Procurement*, 6, 15–17, 2006.)

procurement has competing broader social and economic objectives. The objectives of procurement from the broader policy perspective have to be measured against certain performance indicators within the processes, procedures, and systems of public procurement. Hunja (2003) has argued that success in achieving comprehensive procurement reforms has proven more difficult. Thus, although many countries have implemented fundamental changes to procurement systems, there is little evidence of these efforts achieving full-fledged, fundamental reforms. The lack of political will at the highest levels of government has been singled out as the greatest culprit in preventing successful reforms. Relatedly, Schapper et al. (2006) have noted that the dilemma of public procurement reform is the the lack of consensus about the scope and nature of public procurement (Figure 6.3), which is often as prevalent and varied within organizations and even between procurement practitioners as it is between these professions. It is only where governments or organizations recognize the appropriate scope of public procurement, balancing the process, performance, and strategic imperatives, that they can develop the skills, incentives, performance measures, organizations, and managerial tools to deliver the full range of political/community expectation measures. Managing public procurement would seem to demand an arbitrage between various elements but this is rarely evident in practice (Schapper et al., 2006).

Major challenges that African countries have experienced in reforming their public procurement systems include the following.

6.5.1 Corruption and Declining Ethical Conduct of Public Sector Personnel

Corruption in African countries has increasingly put on an "African face." Defined as the abuse of public office for private gain or simply the misuse of public resources for personal profiteering, public procurement and corruption are commonplace in most of the African public sector acquisition processes. Procurement reforms were undertaken, partly to increase transparency and accountability of the public procurement systems. Viewed as bureaucratic and a breeding ground for corruption, the old procurement systems were expected to be turned around into sound public procurement systems that emphasized ethical and professional management. But even in a system with the highest degree of ethical conduct, corruption can emerge.

In all African countries, strong legal and institutional frameworks have been put in place with a hope of addressing corruption. But the systems are largely redundant because of the failure of the political leaders to punish public officials who have glaringly misused public money. The general lack of political will and commitment to fight corruption has encouraged other public officials to engage in the same practice. The ethics infrastructure with its core principles have been either missing or weak in the African public systems—political commitment, enforceable codes of conduct, professionalism, ethics coordinating bodies, supportive public service conditions, effective legal framework, efficient accountability mechanisms, and a vibrant civil society have been in an inactive state in many African countries. Their absence has led to illegal activities or illicit behavior characterized by the following list of corrupt practices (Schiavo-Campo and Sundaram, 2000):

- Design or selection of uneconomical projects because of opportunities for financial kickbacks and political patronage
- Illicit provision of undervalued foreign exchange
- Procurement fraud, including collusion, overcharging, or the selection of contractors, suppliers, and consultants on criteria other than the lowest price and best quality service
- Illicit payments of speed money to government officials to facilitate access to goods, services, or information to which the public is not entitled, or to deny the public access to goods and services to which it is legally entitled
- Illicit payments to prevent the application of rules and regulations in a fair and consistent manner, particularly in areas concerning public safety, law enforcement, or revenue collection
- Payment to government officials to foster or sustain monopolistic or oligopolistic access to markets in the absence of a compelling economic rationale for such restrictions
- Misappropriation of confidential information for personal gain such as using knowledge about public transportation routings to invest in real estate that is likely to appreciate
- Deliberate disclosure of false or misleading information on the financial status of corporations that would prevent potential investors from accurately valuing their worth, such as the failure to disclose large contingent liabilities or the undervaluing of assets in enterprises slated for privatization
- Theft or embezzlement of public property or monies
- Sale of official posts, positions or promotions, nepotism, or other actions that undermine the creation of a professional, meritocratic civil service
- Extortion and abuse of public office, such as using the threat of a tax audit or legal sanctions to extract personal favors
- Obstruction of justice and interference in the duties of agencies tasked with detecting, investigating, and prosecuting illicit behavior

All the above features of corrupt behavior threaten public procurement reforms. For countries that have made serious strides, these malpractices hinder progress.

6.5.2 Poverty and Organizational Issues

The second major challenge that continues to affect the successful implementation of public procurement reforms in Africa is poverty- and organizational-related issues. First, most African countries, particularly the sub-Saharan nations, are poor and many factors have been identified as contributing to this situation (Dibie, 2004). Reversing this trend requires flexible organizational coherence. In Africa, although some countries have adopted such flexible organizational structures, there are others that have deviated from their expectations and have instead become instruments of corruption, mismanagement, and bureaucratic–authoritarian leadership (Szeftel, 1983).

Global forces and expectations affect the public sector like any other organization. For example, because of competition, there is a growing demand for flexible organizational systems to obtain transparency, accountability, and cost economy. There is a need for an innovative approach to public administration and by extension to public procurement. But while reforming public procurement in Africa has received some momentum, the organizational structures have largely remained rigid. Poor organizational structures of ministries are often a major cause of inefficient implementation of government policies (Schiavo-Campo and Sundaram, 2000).

In Africa, the fundamental challenge to public procurement reform has been lack of interest and neglect by public sector operational managers who have left procurement to the specialists. And in an environment where good governance through accountable, transparent, and value for money emphasis is at the core value of public performance, such managers distancing themselves from the process has hampered the reformation of public procurement system. Sometimes, this neglect could be attributed to public procurement professionals themselves who do not want such managers to interfere in their work. Efficient systems are created through a close collaboration of the functions of the public sector. Procurement has a direct relationship with finance, human resources, etc. In any system where cooperation between these are lacking, public procurement reforms have not achieved the desired expectations.

6.5.3 Inadequate Procurement Capacity

Reforming public sector procurement operations demands the availability of a strong capacity of professionals. However, African governments were seriously missing out on this key principle. Good procurement training, as argued by Walker (2003, p. 7), involves training both government officials and private employees. Government staff and those involved in the business need to know about basic procurement theory to apply it to the specifics, and training for government officials should not be limited to those in central government but also to all other parts of government institutions.

6.5.4 Poor Monitoring and Evaluation Mechanisms

Building a strong public procurement system requires a deliberate strategy to monitor and evaluate the progress of reforms. Effective monitoring and evaluation systems provide timely, accurate, and reliable information upon which decision making can be effected. In many African countries, monitoring and evaluating the progress of procurement reforms have either been weak or lacking. This has, in turn, affected the public procurement systems. Writing from the Ugandan context, Agaba and Shipman (2006) observed that the country's public procurement reform efforts were being affected by inadequate monitoring and evolution mechanisms and in particular by the lack of comprehensive statistics on the value of goods and services procured and on the procurement process. The absence of such vital information affects the performance of the public procurement reform strategy.

6.5.5 Inadequate Resources

During the 1998 public procurement reform conference in Africa, it was agreed among the participating countries that one of the critical strategies for implementing public procurement reforms was to obtain resources for reform. The resources were needed for technical assistance to help prepare a business plan to describe and implement key objectives of the reforms. The conference identified potential sources of funding as the country's own resources, multilateral agencies. However, many public procurement reform efforts have largely depended on donor assistance and the national governments have not provided adequate resources. The oversight institutions and central procurement units that have been put in place are overstretched in terms of roles and obligations, but lack the adequate financial resources to implement the reform strategies. There is a strong financial base for procurement training, procurement audits and investigations, and general awareness of the various stakeholders on the benefits of the new reforms.

6.6 Strategies for Successful Public Procurement Reform

What strategies then can be put in place to improve public sector procurement reforms so as to have good governance and reduce poverty in Africa? It is a well-acknowledged fact that efficient and effective public procurement systems contribute to good governance, which is a critical component of a well-functioning public sector and poverty-reduction strategies in Africa. But how will the African governments achieve this long-term objective amid the challenges experienced during the past years of procurement reform? Is there a need for a comprehensive package of strategies that can be adopted to achieve this long-term goal? How sure can the African governments be that once the proposed strategies are implemented, the long-term objectives will be realized? Providing answers to all these questions is not an easy task. However, for any government to achieve the objectives of a reform undertaking, certain strategies have to be carefully selected and coordinated.

The overall strategy of improving public procurement reforms rotates around instilling the principles of good governance in the public sector. Improved accountability, transparency, legislative frameworks, and addressing corruption are among the much-needed strategies for improving public sector performance through procurement reforms. Implementing public procurement reforms have to be seriously planned and require coordinated processes. Amid the poverty and development challenges that the continent is experiencing, uncoordinated public procurement will not yield many benefits. Political commitment and will is critical.

A well-functioning public sector should balance the policy, efficiency, and process objectives of public procurement. But as the authors of the above framework argue, the conduct of public procurement has reflected tensions between public expectations of high standards of governance, management requirements for performance, overt (covert) political influence, and pressures from broader stakeholder interests such as business. However, there are no internationally accepted standards of best practice for the management of public procurement to address these issues. It has been apparent that each country has tried its own approach although there are common strategies that have cut across.

Walker (2003) identified a six-step model, which provides requirements for successful public procurement reforms. For any change to take pace, the following should be available:

(1) Support from the highest political levels
(2) Publicity about the advantages of the new system
(3) Cooperation between the public and the private sectors
(4) Good procurement training
(5) Good procurement legislation
(6) Establishment of a central public procurement office/division or board

The stages do not need to follow a systematic logical order. In Africa, the reforms of public sector have followed a "bandwagon approach" where nearly all countries have followed the same stages in reforming their public procurement systems albeit at different periods and with mixed results. Agaba and Shipman (2006) have provided such a framework that seems to have been applied to many African countries. Citing the example of Uganda the procurement reform process has followed the following stages:

- Recognition of the need for reform
- Study of possible procurement models and identification of blueprint for reform
- Enactment of the procurement law
- Establishment of a regulatory institution
- Publication of regulations, guidelines, and standard bidding documentation
- Capacity building
- Compliance assessment, procurement audits, and the hearing of appeals

The African continent and its public sector have similarities and diversities. The same applies to the challenges such countries have faced in their attempts to reform the public procurement systems. There have been some common challenges as well as those that are unique to individual countries depending on a host of political, economic, social, environmental, and social cultural divergences. Strong leadership and strategic planning are critical components for the success of procurement reforms. The leaders must be driven by a never-ending quest for improvements and innovation. In this environment, leaders are expected to have analytical, and diagnostic competencies and skills, to enable them scan the environment to exploit the opportunities but also to address the threats. The involvement of various stakeholtders in the public procurement reform is equally essential. The following strategies could be helpful in ensuring a successful public procurement reform project.

Firstly, public procurement reform in Africa requires the right leadership. In today's dynamic world, leaders to challenge the status quo, to create visions for the future, and to inspire organizational members to want to achieve the visions are critical (Robbins, 2001). Without the support of top leadership either at organizational or political level, the procurement reforms will not achieve the good governance objectives. The leadership needs to have a clear understanding of change management, and strategies of building partnerships and consensus among all stakeholders. By itself, this requires a comprehensive package of skills to scan the environment in which the procurement reforms are taking place, to acknowledge diversity in the reform process, and to drum up support for a comprehensive procurement reform strategy. Such leaders require strong team building and conflict handling, negotiation, and people-working skills.

Secondly, public procurement reform in Africa will achieve the objectives of good governance and poverty reduction if there is a deliberate strategy of investing in human resources. This is possible through training all stakeholders who have a direct or indirect role in public procurement management. For example, all public officials at both the central and local government levels should be targeted, as well as the consultants, suppliers, and contractors who offer their services to public enterprises, and all these require close collaboration with training institutions in both the public and private sectors.

The trainings to various stakeholders should offer technical skills and improve trainees' competencies, but at the same time should change their attitudes. The high level staff as well as those in the operational and tactical levels of public life have to be targeted. In addition to procurement skills, competencies, and focusing on attitudes, the human resource capacity can be improved through offering modern management philosophies and technological approaches to solve public sector problems. Issues that affect policy in public organizations should find their way on such trainings.

Thirdly, ethics and integrity of public officials are critical components of successful public procurement reform strategy. Successful procurement reforms in Africa and their implementation depend on procurement staff and public officials who have a minimum code of moral behavior when conducting public affairs. Ethics, the ability to differentiate between what is right from what is wrong while conducting public affairs (public procurement), is particularly important because of the temptations public procurement official are exposed to during the entire process of acquiring goods, services, and works for government. A public procurement professional with high moral standing contributes to the effectiveness of the procurement process leading to the realization of good governance principles.

Fourthly, mechanisms that encourage citizen voice have to be strengthened. Good governance thrives in a publicly accountable system that not only allows citizens to demand accountability from their leaders and public servants but also for leaders and public servants to listen to their voice on critical aspects that affect them. As public procurement cuts across a wide range of public services, citizens are likely to voice their voices on any aspect of the public acquisition and they should be given uninterrupted opportunity for the reforms to be implemented successfully.

6.7 Conclusion

During the last two decades or so, many African governments have failed to achieve the provision of effective and efficient services. The greatest culprit has been the weak institutional arrangements through which public services are offered. As a result of this, the standards of living among the majority of Africans have been miserable. As seen above, Africa is one of the poorest continents in the world and far behind other continents in the realization of MDGs. The late 1990s saw a major attempt to reform the public procurement systems so as to have effective governance structures, which would eventually contribute to poverty reduction. Some progress has been made but a lot remains to be done. Public procurement takes place in an environment surrounded by other systems, namely economic, political, social, and legal systems. A change in any of these systems provides both opportunities and challenges for public procurement reforms. In any attempt to reform the public procurement system, understanding each of these systems is critical. Africa has its unique public sector environment, which must be understood, before the universal principles can be applied.

References

African Development Bank, Governance and Regional Cooperation Division. *Understanding Public Procurement*, Governance Brief, Issue 3. Available at http://www.adb.org/documents/periodicals/gb/GovernanceBrief03.pdf.

Agaba, E. and Shipman, N. 2006. Public procurement reform in developing countries: The Ugandan experience. In G. Piga and K.V. Thai (Eds.), *Advancing Public Procurement: Practices, Innovation and Knowledge-Sharing*. Boca Raton, FL: PrAcademics Press.

Arrowsmith, S., Linarelli, J., and Wallace, D. 2000. *Regulating Public Procurement: National and International Perspectives*. The Hague, the Netherlands: Kluwer Law International.

Calender, G. and Mathews, D. 2000. Government Purchasing: An evolving profession? *Journal of public budgeting, Accounting and Financial Management* 12(2): 272–290.

Dibie, R. 2004. Public sector management policies in sub-Saharan Africa. In A.K. Kalu (Ed.), *Agenda Setting and Public Policy in Africa*. London, United Kingdom: Ashgate Publishing Limited.

Development Assistance Committee, OECD. 2005. *Harmonising Donor Practices for Effective Aid Delivery (Vol. 3): Strengthening Procurement Capacities in Developing Countries*. Paris, France: OECD.

Hunja, R.R. 2003. Obstacles to public procurement reform in developing countries. In S. Arrowsmith and M. Trybus (Eds.), *Public Procurement: The Continuing Revolution*. The Hague, the Netherlands: Kluwer Law International.

Kalu, A.K. 2004. Introduction: The role of ideas, theory and models of public policy in Africa. In A.K. Kalu (Ed.), *Agenda Setting and Public Policy in Africa*. England: Ashgate.

Kernaghan, K., Marson, B., and Borins, S. 2000. *The New Public Organisation*. Canada: Institute of Public Administration.

Lysons, K. 2000. *Purchasing and Supply Chain Management* (5th ed.). Financial Times, Prentice Hall, Pearson Education Ltd, England.

Robbins, S.P. 2001. *Organisational Behavior* (9th ed.). New Delhi, India: Prentice Hall of India.

Schapper, P.R., Malta, J.N.V., and Gilbert, D.L. 2006. An analytical framework for the management and reform of public procurement. *Journal of Public Procurement* 6(1 and 2): 15–17.

Schiavo-Campo, S. and Sundaram, P. 2000. *To Serve and to Preserve: Improving Public Administration in a Competitive World*, p. 619. Available at http://www.adb.org.

Shah, A. (Ed.). 2005. *Public Sector Governance and Accountability Series: Public Services Delivery*. Washington, DC: The World Bank.

Szeftel, M. 1983. Corruption and the spoil system in Zambia. In M. Clarke (Ed.), *Corruption, Causes, Consequences and Control*. New York: St. Martin's Press.

Thai, K.V. 2001. Public procurement re-examined. *Journal of Public Procurement* 1(1): 9–50.

Thai, K.V. 2004. *Introduction to Public Procurement* (1st ed.). NIGP Inc.

Walker, C. 2003. Setting up a public procurement system: the six step method. In S. Arrowsmith and M. Trybus (Eds.), Public Procurement: The Continuing Revolution (pp. 3–12). Dordrecht, The Netherlands, Kluwer Law International.

Witting, W.A. 1999. Building value through procurement: A focus on Africa. A paper presented to the 9th International Anti-Corruption Conference. Available at www.legacy.transparency.org.

World Bank. 2000. *Reforming Public Institutions and Strengthening Governance: A World Bank Strategy*. Public Sector Group: Poverty and Economic Management Network, Washington, DC: The World Bank.

World Bank. 2007. *Challenges of African Growth: Opportunities, Constraints and Strategic Directions*. Washington, DC: The World Bank.

World Development Report (WDR). 2000/2001. Attacking Poverty, World Bank, Washington, DC. Available online at http://web.worldbank.org/.

Chapter 7

Simulation Approach to In-House versus Contracted-Out Cost Comparisons

Donald R. Deis, Helmut Schneider, Chester G. Wilmot, and Charles H. Coates, Jr.

CONTENTS

7.1 Introduction

Turning to private sector companies to provide goods and services to the public is commonplace. Although, a wide variety of services are contracted out, or privatized, the merits of doing so remains in dispute. In general, contracting out by governments generates interest in how the quality and the cost of the service or product are affected. Although quality is understandably difficult to measure and compare, cost analysis is usually considered to be a straightforward process. The costs are what they are, it would seem. For a variety of reasons, however, that is not the case. Certainly, the price paid to contractors is known, but the costs to contract and to monitor the contractor are hidden. Moreover, most government accounting systems are not designed to provide product or service costs. Rather, the accounting system's main purpose is to keep track of line item budgets to ensure that the government stays within budget. So neither the full cost of public sector nor private sector provision is readily known. If a government stops providing the service when it contracts out, the situation is complicated further. That is, the case for state transportation agencies that commonly use consultant firms for a majority of the services and products they provide. The Louisiana Department of Transportation and Development (hereafter referred to as the "department" or "LaDOTD"), like many state Departments of Transportation (DOTs), currently uses both consultants and in-house staff in designing state transportation facilities. The relative cost of doing so, however, is unknown. Is it less or more expensive to use consultants rather than in-house staff to provide these services? The answer to this question is the prime objective of this study.

Past studies in other states strongly suggest that consultants are more expensive than in-house staff in providing the design services needed by the DOTs (Wilmot, 1995). These studies also reveal the difficulty in comparing public sector costs to those in the private sector. This is particularly true for indirect costs. The public sector, for example, incurs costs of advertising for contract bids, consultant supervision, and general administration. Meanwhile, the private sector has taxation, marketing, and compliance costs. Moreover, costs incurred for office rental, utilities, senior administrative staff, and insurance are incurred differentially across private and public organizations. Moreover, as stated before, contracting out sometimes means that the government no longer performs that service, which complicates cost comparisons.

In this study, three simulation approaches were used to compare consultant and government agency costs. Given the real-world problems just identified, simulation approaches such as the one used here appear to be a fruitful methodology to conduct cost comparisons. The remainder of this study is organized as follows: the next section reviews other DOT cost comparison studies, the third section describes the cost comparison approaches used for this study followed by an explanation of the computation overhead cost rates. The fifth section presents the results from an analysis of samples of projects taken and is followed by conclusions.

7.2 Literature Review

Whether costs of in-house engineering work are lower than consulting engineering work is not a new question. Several state transportation agencies have commissioned studies to address this issue.

The studies listed below were performed by independent consultants (Burke et al., 1987; Ernst & Whinney, 1987; Ward et al., 1987; Ashley et al., 1992), by government agencies (Bezruki et al., 1990; Laffoon et al., 1993), and by professional engineering groups (Fanning, 1992).

7.2.1 The University of California, Berkeley, Study

The objective of this study was to compare the cost to the California Department of Transportation (CALTRANS) of employing in-house versus consulting engineering services staff for conducting designs for the department (Ashley et al., 1992). The analysis was conducted using 204 in-house projects and 32 consultant projects. The study collected actual costs incurred by CALTRANS to complete the designs for the in-house and consultant projects. The ratio of engineering design costs to completed construction costs was used as a measure of relative design cost. The ratio of average engineering design costs to final construction costs was 15.46 percent for the consultant project group and 17.76 percent for the in-house project group. The difference was not statistically significant. The projects were bundled and compared as groups rather than paired. Thus, differences in design project complexity, size, and type were not considered in the study.

7.2.2 Texas State Department of Highways and Public Transportation

The Texas State Department of Highways and Public Transportation (SDHPT) commissioned three studies to answer the questions of how the cost and quality of preconstruction engineering services provided by consulting engineers compare with those provided by in-house staff. All three studies concluded that the cost of engineering services is lower when using in-house staff instead of consultants (Burke et al., 1987; Ernst & Whinney, 1987; Ward et al., 1987).

7.2.3 Ernst & Whinney

Ernst & Whinney (1987), the accounting firm, compared the costs of ten pairs of project (each consisting of one consultant project and one similar in-house project). Three measures of design cost were used: the ratio of design costs over construction costs, design costs per plan sheet, and design cost per roadway mile. These three ratios were used to control for variations in the type of projects. The study found that in-house work costs less than consultant work. Because the sample was small, statistical tests were not performed.

7.2.4 Center for Transportation Research

The Center for Transportation Research (CTR) at the University of Texas at Austin examined accounting methods, global cost comparisons, and quality issues (Ward et al., 1987). CTR concluded that consultant overhead and indirect costs (as paid by SDHPT) were about 45 percent higher than similar overhead and indirect costs incurred by the department. In the study, overhead was expressed as the ratio of indirect costs to direct labor cost. In-house overhead rates ranged from 194 to 212 percent compared to 286 to 307 percent for consultant services. In addition, the study indicated that consultant salary rates were 5 to 22 percent higher than in-house rates. Similar to the Berkeley study for CALTRANS, a "global" approach was used in that results were developed for the entire group of projects instead of for project pairs. The study concludes that the in-house preconstruction engineering services may be delivered for less cost than those of consultants' services.

7.2.5 Texas Transportation Institute

The study by the Texas Transportation Institute (TTI) at Texas A&M University compared 18 pairs of projects (Burke et al., 1987). The percentage of engineering costs to total construction costs was lower for in-house projects in 15 of the 18 pairs. The study relied extensively on interviews with various SDHPT officials to determine an overhead rate for in-house projects. Consequently, some overhead cost items may have been left out or estimated with error.

7.2.6 Legislative Audit Bureau of Wisconsin

A large increase in the use of engineering consultants between 1982 and 1989 led the state of Wisconsin to commission a study on the cost-effectiveness and impact on quality of contracting out design services. The legislative audit bureau of the state of Wisconsin conducted the study (Bezruki et al., 1990). The ratio of design costs to total construction costs was the measure used for project comparison. Though the number of projects involved in the comparisons was not given, it is implied to be large given the history of consultant use. The study concludes that the use of consultants is no more costly than if the state had used in-house staff. Two reasons for this finding were offered. First, projects given to consultants were less complex, and second, in-house projects were not managed efficiently.

7.2.7 Study for the Missouri Highway and Transportation Department

Laffoon et al. (1993) compared preliminary engineering (PE) design costs for projects performed in-house with projects performed by consultants. Three methods of comparison were used. In Method 1, the total in-house PE design costs to total construction costs for a 19 year period were computed and compared to the total consulting PE design costs to total construction costs for the same time period. In Method 2, two samples of bridge and roadway design projects were selected for in-house and consultant projects, respectively. The ratios of PE costs to total construction awards were compared for the in-house and the consultant jobs. Method 3 compared the salary and associated costs for identical projects done both in-house and by consultants. The results of Method 1 showed that in-house PE was on the average 7.34 percent of construction awards versus 9.62 percent for consultants. Methods 2 and 3 support these findings that in-house design work is more cost-effective than consultant design work.

7.2.8 Professional Services Management Journal

Fanning (1992) reported a scale of economy effect from outsourcing. Using data collected by Federal Highways Administration (FHWA) from all 50 states for the period 1979–1989, he showed that states that contract out less than 20 percent of their engineering design work have the highest design costs in relation to construction spending. States that contract out between 50 and 70 percent of their engineering design work have achieved the lowest ratios of design to construction spending. Specifically, states that contracted out less than 10 percent of their design work had an average ratio of design cost to construction cost of 0.21 while states that contracted out between 50 and 70 percent of their design work had an average ratio of only 0.11. No relationship to topography, size of highway system, size of construction program, or any other characteristic of the state, except proportion of engineering work conducted by consultants, could be established to explain the relationship.

Table 7.1 Summary of Past Study Findings

Study	*Cost*
Ward et al., 1987	Consultants more expensive
Burke et al., 1987	Consultants more expensive
Ernst & Whinney, 1987	Consultants generally more expensive
Fanning, 1992	Consultants cheaper than in-house staff
Bezruki et al., 1990	No difference in cost
Ashley et al., 1992	No difference in cost
Laffoon et al., 1993	Consultants 31 percent more expensive. In survey of ten states, eight said consultants more expensive and two said costs were the same

The majority of the work in the field of engineering design cost comparisons between in-house and consultants has concentrated on samples of projects and used available accounting data to determine cost differences. This has usually taken the form of direct cost comparisons and overhead rate examinations. Table 7.1 summarizes the aforementioned studies. As shown in the table, most studies have found consultants to be more expensive than their in-house counterparts. While direct project charges have generally been taken straight from accounting databases, overhead rates have been more critically examined with regard to their composition. Although in-house versus consultant costs have been compared on many criteria, the ratio of design costs to construction costs is the most popular approach.

7.3 Cost Comparison Methodology

In general, previous studies have shown that it is difficult to measure design costs accurately. To add to these difficulties, the type of projects and their complexity and size also affect any cost comparison. Some of the ways in which past studies attempted to establish more equitable conditions include:

- Using the ratio of design cost over construction cost to eliminate the effect of the size of the project
- Pairing of projects to eliminate the effects of type of project
- Sampling to establish similar mixes of projects among those designed by in-house staff and consultants and to ensure that the results are representative

Two interrelated problems can limit the usefulness of the approaches typically used to conduct the cost analysis. First, although the ratio of design cost over construction cost takes into account the influence that project size has on design cost, it does not capture the impact of important factors such as the number of plan changes, unique environmental conditions where the facility is to be constructed, and design complexity. A measure that is capable of canceling out these additional factors is the ratio of design costs by in-house staff divided by the design cost by consultants for similar projects. Finding similar projects, however, is difficult because it is commonplace to entirely outsource particular types of projects (e.g., waterway bridge designs) and retain others entirely in-house (e.g., interstate overpasses). Hence, pairing projects or drawing samples with a similar mix of projects is not possible.

A simulation approach was adopted by this study to overcome the lack of available comparable projects conducted by the public sector and a private sector counterpart. Three approaches were used to simulate the costs to either the public or private sector. The three approaches are as follows: (1) simulate consultant cost for projects done in-house; (2) simulate in-house costs for projects done by consultants; and (3) simulate the cost of one "typical" hour of engineering design for each. Each approach is explained in turn.

In the first approach shown in Figure 7.1, only projects designed in-house are considered. The in-house design costs are determined from accounting records. Estimates of the consultant design costs of the same projects are simulated by using a formula to estimate consultant design hours for bidding purposes and then applying consultant labor and overhead rates as determined by average rates determined through audits of consultant records by the auditing division of the department. Comparisons are then made between the actual in-house costs and estimated consultant design costs by simulation of each project.

The design hours used in Approach 1 may be questioned on two counts. First, it is generally acknowledged by in-house staff that the record of in-house time may not be accurate. However, if there is a consistent bias to either underreport or overreport design time, the method used to incorporate "nonproject" related time within the overhead will cause the overhead rate to be either inflated or deflated to compensate for the effect. Thus, although in-house recorded hours may be inaccurate, in-house total design costs should be accurate.

The second concern with the methodology of Approach 1 is more serious because there is no way in which it can be controlled. The concern centers on the fact that consultant design hours had to be specially estimated for these projects by in-house staff, and there is no guarantee that the design hours estimated were not consciously or unconsciously deflated to put in-house design times in a more favorable light. For this reason, the results of Approach 1 cannot be considered in isolation, and Approaches 2 and 3 were compiled to eliminate any bias introduced with Approach 1.

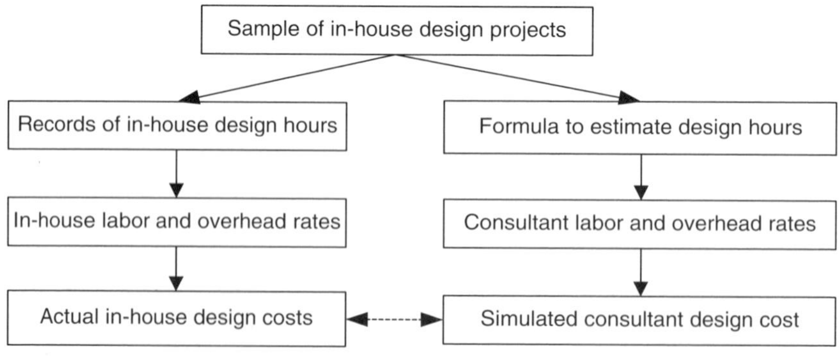

Figure 7.1 Methodology of Approach 1—simulation of consultant costs.

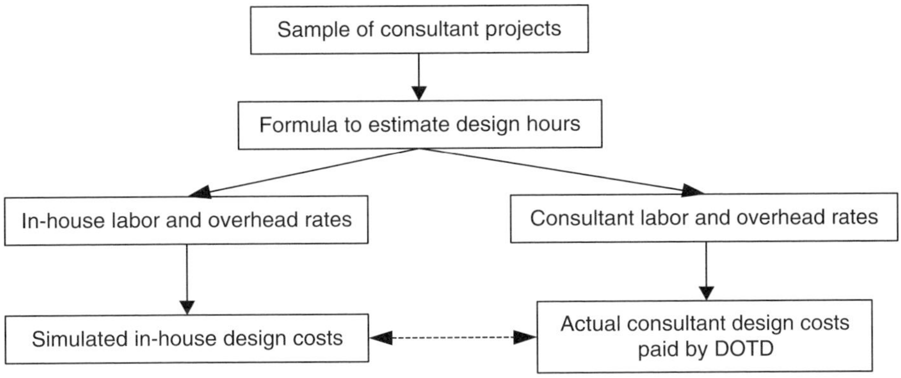

Figure 7.2 Methodology of Approach 2—simulate in-house costs.

Approach 2 is described in Figure 7.2. In this approach, all the projects in the sample that were designed by consultants in the past are considered. However, contrary to Approach 1, the same design hours are used to estimate both in-house and consultant design costs. The design hours were extracted from the records of awarded consultant design contracts.

Approach 3 was developed to not depend on estimates of design hours for any particular project. Rather, for consultant projects, it considers the average mix of staff used on 35 randomly selected consultant projects and applies labor and overhead rates to determine the average cost of one design hour. For in-house projects, the recorded total cost and total time for 20 randomly selected projects are used together with overhead costs to estimate the average cost of one in-house design hour. The method is illustrated in Figure 7.3.

7.3.1 Description of Project Sample

A sample of twenty preliminary or final designs from fourteen in-house projects and seventeen preliminary or final designs from nine consulting projects were selected. The projects chosen closely

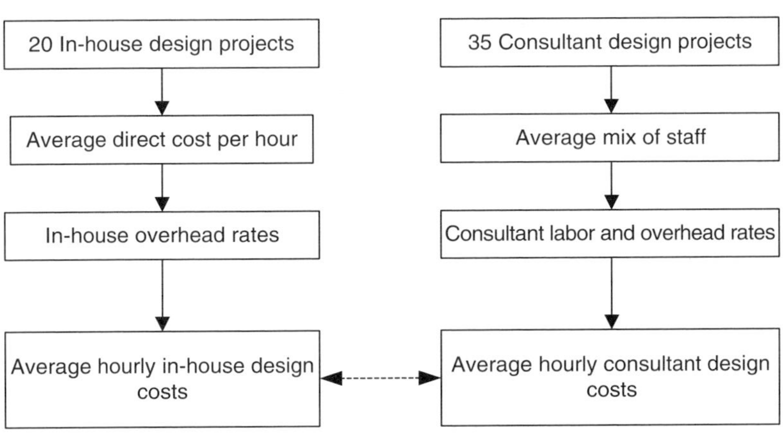

Figure 7.3 Methodology of Approach 3—simulated hourly cost.

resemble a population of 73 projects with respect to bid estimate, engineering cost, and ratio of engineering cost to consultant cost. In addition, the projects also canvas all kinds of work done including river crossings, railroad overpasses, two-lane rural roads, intersections, and four-lane rural roads. Only projects designed within the last five years were considered to avoid extensive adjustments of costs for time elapsed.

To generate the total cost of design projects, LaDOTD overhead is calculated at several levels of the organization and allocated step-by-step to finally reach the individual sections that work directly on the project. Step 1 is to determine the LaDOTD-wide support services' overhead rate and to assign this to each section in the department. Step 2 is to identify upper management supervision within the Directorate of Engineering and Program and Project Development and assign the cost to each section that it supervises. Step 3 is to determine supervision, clerical, and other indirect charges incurred in each section and add this to the cost estimates of the previous two steps to form actual indirect cost estimates for each section. An overhead rate is established by dividing total indirect costs for each section by the direct costs of that section. The end result is a single composite overhead rate for each section working directly on design projects that incorporates on LaDOTD-wide support services, upper level management, and the section's own indirect costs. Tables 7.2 through 7.4 show the overhead computation for three sections: (1) consultant contract services, (2) in-house road design, and (3) in-house bridge design, respectively.

LaDOTD conducts audits of consultant records as part of LaDOTD's oversight of consultant contracts. The 158 percent average overhead rate was found for 104 audits of projects completed by 37 consulting firms. The contracts also include a 13 percent profit factor. In addition, departmental supervision of the consultant contracts was found to add 15 percent to road design projects and 25 percent to bridge design projects. Table 7.5 illustrates how these additional factors affect the consultant overhead rate. Table 7.6 compares in-house road design and bridge design overhead rates to average and effective consultant overhead rates.

Two factors contribute to in-house overhead rates being higher than the average consultant overhead rate. First, LaDOTD's fringe benefit rate is nearly 58 percent compared to around 33 percent for consultants. Second, LaDOTD has a lower percent of labor time charged to projects.

Table 7.2 Overhead Rate for Consultant Contract Services Section

Description	*Amount ($)*
Section-specific indirect costs	217,056
Applied Overhead	
Allocated in-house supervision costs	10,175
Insurance	25,489
Other support services	46,847
Total nonproject charges and overhead	299,567
Divided by project charges	91,151
Section blended overhead rate	329 percent

Table 7.3 Overhead Rate for Road Design Section

Description	*Amount ($)*
Section-specific indirect costs	1,210,774
Applied Overhead	
Allocated in-house supervision overhead costs	77,869
Insurance	179,953
Other support services	330,748
Total nonproject charges and overhead	1,799,344
Divided by project charges	965,198
Section blended overhead rate	186 percent

Table 7.4 Overhead Rates for Bridge Design Section

Description	*Amount ($)*
Section-specific indirect costs	1,408,574
Applied Overhead	
Allocated in-house supervision costs	85,337
Insurance	196,525
Other support services	361,207
Total nonproject charges and overhead	2,051,643
Divided by project charges	967,786
Section blended overhead rate	212 percent

Table 7.5 Effective Consultant Overhead Rates

Description	*Bridge Projects (Percent)*	*Road Projects (Percent)*
Average consultant overhead rate	158	158
Net Effect of Other Factors on Overhead		
Thirteen percent profit factor	34	34
LaDOTD supervision Fifteen percent road design section Twenty-five percent bridge design section	73	44
Effective consultant overhead rates	265	236

Table 7.6 Comparison of Overhead Rates

Description	Overhead Rates (Percent)
Road design section	186
Bridge design section	212
Average consultant overhead rate	158
Effective Consultant Overhead Rate	
Road projects	236
Bridge projects	265

Consultants average 63 percent of labor costs charged to projects, while LaDOTD road and bridge design sections were substantially lower at 52 and 48 percent, respectively.

7.3.2 Salary Rate Comparisons

Although LaDOTD has higher fringe benefit rates, the base salary rates are lower than those of consultants. This is demonstrated in Table 7.7. As shown in Table 7.8, salary rates with fringe benefits are nearly the same for three skilled positions (preprofessional, engineer, and principal); higher for consultants in two areas (technician and supervisor); and higher for in-house at another area (drafting). This suggests that, overall, total in-house labor costs are very similar to those of consultants on an hourly basis.

7.4 Analysis of Projects

To compare the cost of providing preconstruction engineering services by in-house staff or by consultants, two sets of project samples were analyzed using three separate analysis approaches. In each

Table 7.7 Comparison of Base Salary Rates

Position Description	Average Hourly In-House Base Salary Rate ($)	Average Hourly Consultant Base Salary Rate ($)	Consultant/In-House Hourly Rate over (Percent)
Drafting	10.55	11.47	8.7
Technician	12.64	15.45	22.2
Preprofessional	13.94	16.35	17.3
Engineer	22.32	26.14	17.1
Supervisor	24.17	32.23	33.4
Principal	34.53	40.18	16.4

Table 7.8 Comparison of Salary Rates with Fringe Benefits

Position Description	*Average Hourly In-House Salary Rate with Benefits ($)*	*Average Hourly Consultant Salary Rate with Benefits ($)*	*Consultant/In-House Hourly Rate over/ (under) (Percent)*
Drafting	16.61	15.30	(7.9)
Technician	19.90	20.61	3.6
Preprofessional	21.94	21.81	(0.6)
Engineer	35.13	34.87	(0.8)
Supervisor	38.05	42.99	13.0
Principal	54.35	53.60	(1.4)

analysis, the costs of an actual sample of projects by one provider are compared with the estimated costs of the alternative provider. The following sections consider several cost features of the sampled projects. The additional costs incurred by LaDOTD in letting contracts to consultants are discussed. Costs related to the sample of in-house projects are discussed and analyzed. As applicable, the in-house and consultant overhead rates developed in this study are applied in the analysis of projects. In the first analytical approach, the actual in-house costs are compared with estimated costs as if the project had been offered to consultants. The second analysis compares the costs of the sample of consulting projects to the estimated costs that would have occurred had the project been done in-house. The third analysis considers the average cost of one design hour for in-house and consultant staff. A summation (or summary) of the findings of the three approaches is included at the end of this section of the report.

7.4.1 Approach 1: Analysis of In-House Projects

Actual costs for 20 designs from 14 in-house projects were compared to the costs that would have been paid to consultants had LaDOTD contracted out the engineering design. Five preliminary plans and fifteen final plans were included in the sample. The sample has three types of waterway crossings (large, medium, and small), two- and four-lane rural highways, a railroad overpass, intersection improvements, and interstate rehabilitation. Because two of the projects include both bridge and road design, there are actually 22 comparisons made between in-house actual costs and simulated consultant costs. Nine bridge designs and thirteen road designs are included in the sample.

Cost comparisons and direct labor hour comparisons were made for the bridge and road sections. The in-house costs and hours are actual amounts charged to the projects. The consultant costs and hours are simulated by LaDOTD engineers according to the formula-based process used by LaDOTD to let contracts to consultants. It is important to realize, therefore, that the comparison being made is between actual in-house costs (and hours) to estimated consultant costs (and hours) that LaDOTD would have paid rather than costs (and hours) consultants might have incurred.

The audit division of LaDOTD periodically conducts man-hour studies to determine how the number of hours estimated by the formula compares to the actual hours incurred by consultants. Discussion with the audit manager in charge of these man-hour studies revealed that variances between estimated hours and actual hours were relatively small and did not suggest there was a systematic bias in the formula. Cost comparisons for both bridge and road projects appear in Table 7.9. The costs include labor, supervision, overhead, and direct costs for in-house and consultant projects.

In all cases, the in-house costs were less than costs that would have been paid to consultants. On average, in-house costs for bridge design were just under 76 percent of the simulated consultant costs. Among road projects, in-house costs were about 65 percent of those that would have been paid to consultants under the formula. Because of the large variation in project cost, a weighted average was used. The differences, in both cases, are statistically significant at the 0.1 percent level.

Table 7.9 In-House Project Cost Compared to Simulated Consultant Costs

Plan Type		*Bridge Design*			*Road Design*		
Prelim	*Final*	*Consultant*	*In-House*	*Percent*	*Consultant*	*In-House*	*Percent*
	X	286,538	245,881	86			
	X	387,191	206,798	53			
	X	91,933	101,596	111	126,035	80,930	64
	X	165,992	172,682	104	124,198	117,041	94
	X	60,744	33,031	54			
	X	98,356	80,310	82			
	X	343,768	249,413	73			
	X	142,240	133,744	94			
	X				284,666	240,524	84
X					57,352	13,567	24
	X				55,420	20,967	38
X					62,412	26,905	43
	X				74,437	21,677	29
	X	91,575	40,368	44			
	X				271,589	226,127	83
X					104,560	38,913	37
	X				99,689	37,087	37
X					146,177	83,951	57
	X				133,397	99,552	75

The major conclusion of the cost comparison shown in Table 7.9 is that in-house costs are significantly lower for both bridge and road projects. This result can be attributed to differences in the price of labor, indirect costs, or some combination thereof.

7.4.2 Approach 2: Analysis of Consultant Projects

A sample of nine bridge or road projects representing seventeen preliminary or final designs by consultants was drawn for analysis. For each project, actual consultant costs were compared to simulated in-house costs using consultant labor hour amounts and current LaDOTD average salary rates for the same time period. This analysis results in significant differences in both bridge and road design as shown in Table 7.10.

Simulated in-house costs average 83 percent of consultant costs for bridge design and about 81 percent for road design. Again, because of the large variation in project costs, the weighted average was used. Both of these differences are statistically significant at the 5 percent level.

7.4.3 Approach 3: Comparison of Average Design Hour Costs

The final approach focuses on effective hourly rates that consider the mix (or use) of staff. Table 7.11 shows the mix of staff for 35 randomly selected consultant projects. Based on this sample, a percentage mix of staff was computed for consultants.

Using the average of the consultant staff mix in Table 7.11, the cost per hour of a representative consultant project can be computed. A similar computation can be done for in-house projects. Although the percentage of staff mix cannot be computed for in-house projects, an average hourly cost can be obtained by dividing total in-house direct cost of the projects by the total number of

Table 7.10 Consultant Project Cost Comparison

Plan Type			*Consulting*		*In-House*		*In-House/ Consulting (Percent)*	
Prelim	*Final*	*Letting Cost ($)*	*Bridge ($)*	*Road ($)*	*Bridge ($)*	*Road ($)*	*Bridge*	*Road*
X	X	2,495,987	80,721	134,289	66,757	134,510	83	100
X	X	1,526,216	63,467	142,484	53,001	118,317	84	83
X	X	9,138,060	0	378,067	0	301,634		80
X	X	993,616	0	80,805	0	55,008		68
	X	3,167,176	0	96,808	0	62,091		64
X	X	1,665,692	86,940	66,103	62,230	56,163	72	85
X	X	1,074,508	25,252	63,433	21,777	56,910	86	90
X	X	1,851,295	27,928	72,025	21,605	61,583	77	86
X	X	5,491,587	22,100	119,097	9,581	88,501	43	74

Table 7.11 Mix of Staff for Consultant Projects

Type	*Hours*	*Type (Percent)*
Draftsman	13,689	30
Technician	11,773	26
Preprofessional	8,934	19
Engineer	7,963	17
Supervisor	3,090	7
Principal	370	1
Total	45,819	100

hours used for the projects. This average of $15.03 is considered the direct payroll cost per design hour at the LaDOTD. Table 7.12 shows the computations of the respective hourly salary rates. Adding the costs of overhead, profit, and consultant contract initiation and supervision provides a further comparison of in-house and consultant costs.

The upper section of rows in Table 7.12 gives the average salary rates for LaDOTD and consultants. The middle section of rows provides the overheads. The percentage of total payroll is then computed without and with the cost of LaDOTD supervision. The bottom section of rows shows

Table 7.12 Estimated Cost per Project Hour

	LaDOTD		*Consultant*	
Type	*Road*	*Bridge*	*Road*	*Bridge*
Draftsman			$11.47	$11.47
Technician			$15.45	$15.45
Preprofessional			$16.35	$16.35
Engineer			$26.14	$26.14
Supervisor			$32.23	$32.23
Principal			$40.18	$40.18
Overhead (percent)	186	212	143	143
Profit (percent)	0	0	13	13
Total percent payroll overhead	186	212	175	175
Contract (percent) (Sections 18, 24, 25)			5	6
Supervision (percent) (Sections 24, 25)			10	19
Total percent payroll additive including contract	186	212	188	193

Table 7.12 (continued) Estimated Cost per Project Hour

Type	LaDOTD		Consultant	
	Road	Bridge	Road	Bridge
Total percent payroll additive including contract and supervision	186	212	216	244
Direct payroll ($)	15.03	15.03	17.63	17.63
Direct payroll + overhead ($)	43.06	46.90	48.47	48.47
LaDOTD/consult (percent) without contract and supervision			89	97
Direct payroll + overhead + contract ($)	43.06	46.90	50.75	51.60
LaDOTD/consult (percent) with contract			85	91
Direct payroll + overhead + contract and supervision ($)	43.06	46.90	55.65	60.71
LaDOTD/consult (percent) with contract and supervision			77	77

the effect of the overheads on cost per hour. The average payroll cost per hour is $15.03 for the LaDOTD and $17.63 for consultants. Adding overhead, the average cost ranges from $43.07 to $47.04 at the LaDOTD and $48.47 for the consultants. This means that the cost per hour for in-house design is 89 percent that of consultants in road design and 97 percent in bridge design sections, respectively. However, adding LaDOTD contract initiation and supervision for projects results in 77 percent of consultant costs for both roads and bridges. Table 7.12 also shows clearly the main causes for the cost differences; namely, the LaDOTD has a lower base salary rate, and the overall salary additives for consultant projects including LaDOTD supervision are higher than LaDOTD overhead.

An overhead rate of 143 percent is used for consultants because this is the value that was established by the department from a statewide survey. This is different from the 158 percent overhead rate for consultants derived from the 37 audits conducted by the department. The 143 percent is the official value used by the department and is, therefore, used here. However, the difference between the statewide average and audited values is not large and would not influence the findings in Table 7.12 significantly.

Table 7.13 summarizes the results of the three different approaches for comparing costs. Approach 1 comprises the analysis of actual in-house projects with simulated consultant costs, Approach 2 analyzes actual consultant projects with simulated in-house costs, and Approach 3 compares hypothetical hourly rates based on the mix of staff used by each. For bridge design, all three approaches give about the same result, namely, that in-house designs are about 80 percent of the cost of consultant designs. For road design, Approaches 2 and 3 give the same result. However, Approach 1 leads to a lower percentage for road design. Taken together, the results suggest that a collective interpretation could be that in-house designs are in the order of 80 percent of the cost of consultant designs.

Table 7.13 Comparison of Approaches

Approach	Sample	In-House/Consultant (Percent)	
		Road Design Average	Bridge Design Average
1	In-house projects—simulate consultant costs	65	76
2	Consulting projects—simulate in-house costs	81	83
3	Cost per design hour including mix of staff	77	77

The cost comparisons listed in Tables 7.9 and 7.10 show that there is substantial variation in the percentage of in-house cost over consultant cost. Figure 7.4 shows the percent of in-house over consultant cost plotted as a function of design cost divided by construction cost. The graph shows that as projects become more complex (i.e., the higher the percentages of design to construction cost), the consultant design costs become increasingly competitive with those of in-house designs.

7.5 Policy Factors

The objective of this study was to compare the cost of providing preconstruction engineering services by in-house staff or consultants. In this section, factors other than cost are discussed that should be considered in deciding on an appropriate level of involvement of consultants.

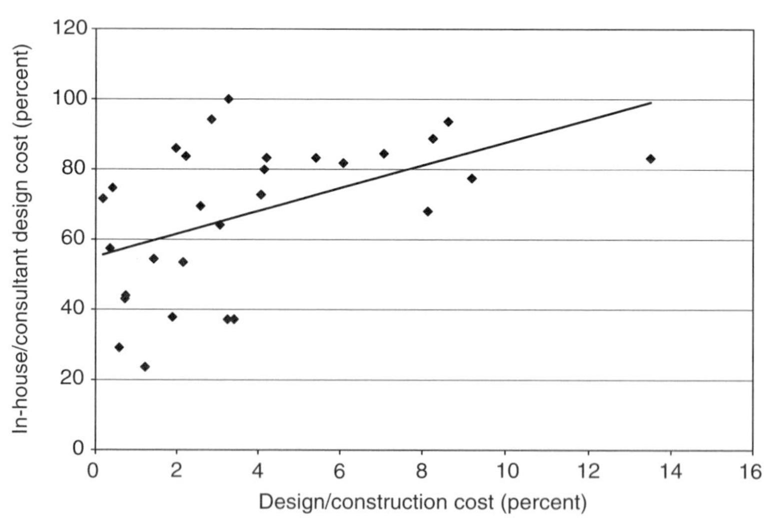

Figure 7.4 Percent in-house/consultant cost by construction cost.

The Transportation Research Board sponsored a study in 1984 of the use of contract services in state DOTs (Cook, 1985). The study included a survey among all state DOTs to establish current practice. Two-thirds of the respondents indicated that they do not use, or only occasionally use, cost as a factor in deciding whether to contract design work out to consultants or not. One of the common reasons quoted for using consultants is the need to accommodate fluctuating demand for services. The implicit assumption is that consultants can more easily accommodate fluctuating demand than a state department because of their more flexible hiring and firing policy. Closely associated with the issue of using consultants during periods of peak demand is the matter of meeting demands in a timely manner. Consultants have a larger reservoir of manpower resources to draw upon and can be contractually induced to meet important deadlines. Consultants are also sensitive to meeting deadlines because their appointment to future projects depends in part on being able to deliver services on time.

Few state DOTs can afford to retain specialized design expertise on their staff for complex designs that arise infrequently. Such specialized expertise could involve the design of large bridges or complex freeway interchanges. In such cases, it is more cost-efficient to make use of consultants to provide such expertise. Allied to this issue is the matter of proficiency through experience. For example, if consultants are regularly used to perform certain types of designs, they are more likely to become more proficient in producing such designs. Similarly, in-house staff may, through custom, perform most of the designs of another type and, therefore, become more proficient in that area. Identifying such areas of distinct capabilities is an issue that administrators of the program should be mindful of in providing the most efficient delivery of designs for the department.

Qualifications-based selection of consultants not only serves to ensure quality of consultant design work, but it also serves to reduce the degree of departmental supervision needed. The LaDOTD uses a rating system to evaluate the performance of its consultants, and this is used to identify those consultants who, in the opinion of the LaDOTD coordinators serving as contact persons between the consultants and the department, are the most efficient in performing their design tasks. In some states, consultants are handling the majority of the state's design activities. Can in-house staff retain the necessary design skills and experience to effectively check, evaluate, and approve designs without personal design experience? Indications are that a department can quickly lose (through resignations and transfers) the experience necessary to effectively supervise design activities in the department if there is not an ongoing design service being performed in the department (Lay, personal communication, 1997, October). Another factor is that in-house staff deserves the opportunity to develop their careers in the department in a meaningful way. Having no or little previous design experience adversely affects the ability of in-house staff to gain new experience for a career. If engineers are to be retained, career development opportunities must be maintained in the department.

7.6 Conclusions

The objectives of this study were (1) to identify and compare the cost of providing preconstruction engineering services to LaDOTD when these services are provided by in-house staff or by consultants and (2) to list other factors that are relevant to establishing an optimum balance between the use of in-house staff and consultants in providing preconstruction engineering services. The cost of providing road and bridge designs to LaDOTD is, on the average, lower when provided by in-house staff than by consultants. The best estimate of the average cost for in-house designs is that it is 81 percent the cost of consultant designs for road projects and 83 percent the cost of consultant designs for bridge projects.

The factors other than design cost that are relevant to establishing an optimum balance between in-house and consultant design work include the need to accommodate fluctuating design demand, being able to meet deadlines, having access to specialized expertise, having flexibility in workforce size, supporting the state's consulting industry, maintaining a core of consultants who are experienced in departmental requirements and standards, maintaining in-house capability to effectively supervise consultants, and maintaining an environment in the department which adequately serves the training and career development needs of in-house staff.

Acknowledgments

The authors are grateful to the Louisiana Transportation Research Center, its director Joe Baker, and the Louisiana Department of Transportation and Development for financial support, advice, and help in data collection. The contents of this report reflect the views of the authors, who are responsible for the facts and accuracy of the data presented herein. The contents do not necessarily reflect the official views or policies of the Louisiana Department of Transportation and Development. This report does not constitute a standard specification or regulation.

References

Ashley, D.B., Ibbs, C.W., Ballard, G., Staneff, S.T., and Ho, K.C. 1992. *A Cost Comparison of Contracting Out for Engineering Services by CALTRANS versus In-House Engineering.* Berkeley, CA: University of California, Berkeley.

Bezruki, D., Sausen, L., and Sommerfeld, R. 1990. *Use of Engineering Consultants* (Report 90–9). Madison, WI: Wisconsin Legislative Audit Bureau.

Burke, D., Cavazos, R., Garcia-Diaz, A., and Tenah, K. 1987. *Utilization of Consultants by SDHPT* (Research Report 1100–1F). College Station, TX: Texas Transportation Institute, Texas A&M University.

Cook, K.E. 1985, November–December. Use of Contract Services by State DOT, *Transportation Research News* (Transportation Research Board).

Ernst & Whinney. 1987. *Utilization of Consulting Engineers for Highway Project Development.* Austin, TX: Texas Department of Highways and Public Transportation.

Fanning, W.T. 1992. *Contracting Out Engineering Services Is Cost Effective: U.S. Government Data Shows Contracting Out Saves Money,* Marietta, GA: Professional Services Management Journal.

Laffoon, A., Martin, F., Gupta, S., Spencer, G., Sfreddo, R., Sommerer, J., Hudson, R., Smith, J., Harris, J., Denkler, C., Kaiser, A., and Bell, M. 1993. *Review of Design Costs—MHTD Designed Projects vs. Consultant Designed Projects.* Columbia, MO: Missouri Highway and Transportation Department.

Ward, W.V., Lee, C.E., and Bradley, C.M. 1987. *Utilization of Consultants by the State Department of Highways and Public Transportation* (Research Report 1101–1F). Austin, TX: Center for Transportation Research, University of Texas.

Wilmot, C.G. 1995. *Investigation into the Cost-Effectiveness of Using Consultants versus In-House Staff in Providing Professional Engineering Services for Louisiana's Department of Transportation and Development* (Louisiana Transportation Research Technical Assistance Report No.3). Baton Rouge, LA: Louisiana Transportation Research Center.

Chapter 8

Public Procurement Organization: A Comparison of Purchasing's Organizational Roles and Responsibilities in the Public and Private Sectors

P. Fraser Johnson, Michiel R. Leenders, and Clifford McCue

CONTENTS

8.1 Introduction

The mission of the supply function, whether in the public or private sectors, is to manage the delivery of goods and services through the supply chain in a cost-effective manner. However, it is well recognized that there are a number of unique aspects in public sector procurement. For example, public procurement is characterized by high levels of public disclosure and a heavy reliance on the bid process compared to private sector organizations (Osborne and Plastrik, 1997). Notwithstanding these differences, there are also many commonalities between public and private sector groups. Benchmarking by the Center for Advanced Purchasing Studies (CAPS) found a common trend toward using automated purchasing systems to process transactions and track purchasing activities and an increased use of multi-year contracts (Center for Advanced Purchasing Studies, 1999).

One area of substantial research interest in the public and private sectors has been an examination of organizational issues in the supply area. The first large-scale North American research effort concerning private sector supply organizations was by Fearon (1988), who surveyed 297 large U.S. firms. Since that time, other work by Cavinato (1991), Pooley and Dunn (1994), Telgen et al. (1997), Johnson et al. (1998a,b), Harland et al. (2000), and Leenders and Johnson (2000) have examined a range of organizational factors in private sector organizations. Fearon's original 1988 survey was replicated in 1995, providing the basis for a longitudinal examination of the trends and changes in large North American supply organizations (Fearon and Leenders, 1995).

Despite the interest in organizational issues in supply, absent from the literature is research that identifies organizational similarities and differences between public and private sector organizations. Moreover, existing research (e.g., Muller, 1991) has failed to identify meaningful differences between the two groups. Consequently, the purpose of this research is to compare large private and public sector North American purchasing organizations. In doing so, the following research questions will be addressed:

1. What differences exist between large public and private sector purchasing organizations with respect to organizational structure and supply chain responsibilities?
2. To what extent does the use of team-based purchasing activities differ between private and public sector organizations?
3. What differences exist between the chief purchasing officer's background in the public and private sectors?
4. How does purchasing's involvement in major organizational activities differ between the private and public sectors?

By developing an understanding of these issues, this research will clarify how purchasing's organizational roles and responsibilities differ between private and public sector organizations.

8.2 Previous Research

A number of research efforts have investigated organizational issues in public sector organizations. The 1999 CAPS benchmarking study collected data from 40 state and county governmental organizations. It found high levels of centralization within public sector supply organizations, with 57.5 percent of respondents describing their organizations as centralized, while 37.5 percent used a hybrid structure (Center for Advanced Purchasing Studies, 1999). This research also provided findings with respect to chief purchasing officer (CPO) reporting and supply chain responsibilities. Purchasing reported to administration in 25 percent of the respondents, to finance in 17.5 percent, and others in 55 percent. The most common supply chain responsibilities were scrap and surplus disposal (58 percent of respondents), fixed asset management (33 percent), building construction (25 percent), receiving and warehousing (25 percent), and consultants and professional services (15 percent).

Although centralized purchasing structures have been common in state and local governments, there has been a recent trend toward decentralization as a result of efforts to improve responsiveness, eliminate bureaucratic obstacles, improve interdepartmental coordination, and empower service delivery managers (Thai, 2001). McCue and Gianakis (2001) found that considerable decentralization of core purchasing functions was occurring and that frontline personnel were engaged in considerable boundary spanning activities.

Muller (1991) surveyed NAPM members in the U.S. state and local governments, and in manufacturing, institutional, services, retail, and food sectors regarding purchasing duties in 13 areas. The results showed relatively little differences in the responsibilities of the respondents across sectors, with the exception of three areas: inventory management, material flow, and special considerations for enhancing purchasing performance. Public sector purchasers were less involved in these three areas, compared to purchasers in the private sector.

Whereas Muller (1991) argued in favor of the similarities in public and private sector purchasing responsibilities, Harland et al. (2000) identified the features that differentiate the private and public sectors: the nature of the particular public sector being considered; the nature of the interorganizational network; the nature of the public service being provided; factors relating the recipients of the service; the nature of the supply market; the extent of availability of private sector alternatives; the nature of accountability; regulation, government, and investment cycles; and influential government themes. The framework presented by Harland et al. (2000) suggested that the macroenvironment and the sector context contributed to differentiation between private and public sector purchasing organizations.

Private and public sector organizations react differently to scarcity of resources. In the private sector, declining industries are characterized by increased competition and shakeout (Harrigan, 1980), although public sector organizations react to cutbacks by increasing interorganizational cooperation through increased centralization to avoid duplication (Ludwig, 1993). The creation of purchasing consortia represents one organizational response in the public sector. Johnson (1999) used case studies to examine how and why public sector organizations implement purchasing consortia and proposed a life cycle model of consortia evolution. This research found that although price and cost reductions were the primary motivation for the creation of consortia, other factors, namely opportunities to reduce staff, product and service standardization, improved supplier management capabilities, specialization of staff, customer service, higher profile of consortium members, expanded role of purchasing, and transition of products through volume categories, were responsible for public sector purchasing organizations adopting consortia.

Johnson (1999) also found high levels of organizational change in the public sector purchasing organizations studied, including a strong interest in participating in consortia buying activities. Although other research has established that private sector organizations participate in purchasing consortia (Hendrick, 1997), it was expected that the public sector organizations in our study would indicate higher levels of consortia purchasing activities compared to the private sector group.

8.3 Research Method

In 1995, CAPS undertook its second major research project investigating purchasing's organizational roles and responsibilities (Fearon and Leenders, 1995). This research collected data from 308 large private sector North American companies using a mail questionnaire, with a 51 percent response rate. Overall, 21 different industry groups were represented with 78 percent of the respondents from manufacturing industries and only 22 percent from service industries. The research instrument collected data relating to firm size, background and information related to the CPO, size of the purchasing organization, supply chain responsibilities, participation in various forms of purchasing teaming activities, and involvement in major organizational activities.

Five years later, research sponsored by Florida Atlantic University and the National Institute of Governmental Purchasing Research Center (FAU-NIGP) replicated the CAPS survey, collecting data from 267 governmental purchasing groups in cities and counties in the United States. The response rate for the FAU-NIGP survey was 33 percent.

The data from the CAPS and FAU-NIGP surveys was used in this research to address the four research questions. Respondents in both groups were asked to identify their organization's total revenues. Recognizing that the two groups differed with respect to the total revenues, the respondent groups were purposely selected for the analysis. The FAU-NIGP group consisted of respondents that had revenues ranging from under $1 million to greater than $300 million. For this group, respondents with revenues in the top three categories ($100 million to $200 million; $200 million to $300 million; and, greater than $300 million) were selected for use in the analysis, representing 117 organizations. From the CAPS group, respondents in the two lowest sales categories (under $500 million; and, $500 million to $1 billion) were selected, representing 97 organizations.

8.4 Findings

As established in the research questions, data analysis involved examining differences between the two groups in the following areas: organizational structure, supply chain responsibilities, characteristics of the CPO and reporting line, use of team-based purchasing activities, and purchasing's involvement in major organizational activities. Results indicate differences in several key areas.

8.4.1 Organizational Structure

Consistent with the findings of the CAPS benchmarking studies, one-half of the public sector purchasing organizations were centralized (51 percent), while virtually none were decentralized (2 percent). Approximately one-half of the respondents (47 percent) in the FAU-NIGP group had adopted a hybrid mode of organizational structure. Overall, 98 percent of the public sector organizations had some form of centralization (e.g., centralized or hybrid modes). This finding contrasts sharply with the data from the firms in the CAPS study, which reported hybrid structure in 51 percent of the firms surveyed and centralization in 27 percent of the respondents. The level of decentralization was low in the FAU-NIGP group (2 percent), compared to 22 percent in the CAPS group. Table 8.1 summarizes the data from the two respondent groups.

Differences with respect to the degree of centralization represent an interesting finding. In the private sector, the magnitude of the spend as a percentage of total costs and the need to manage common suppliers across business units represent arguments in favor of centralized purchasing organizational structures. For example, purchased goods and services at private sector manufacturing organizations may represent 60–70 percent of the cost of sales (Heberling et al., 1992), with a significant portion related to direct materials and services. The sheer magnitude of dollars spent focuses the management's attention on the purchasing function and establishes a need for a centralized group to oversee key supply activities. Similarly, leveraging purchases across business units, or creating purchasing clout, to gain price discounts, is a common purchasing

Table 8.1 Organization Structure

Organization Structure	*CAPS*		*NIGP*	
	N	*Percent*	*N*	*Percent*
Centralized	26	27	60	51
Hybrid	49	51	55	47
Decentralized	21	22	2	2
Total	96	100	117	100

practice. Meanwhile, purchased goods and services for public organizations represent a much smaller portion of the total budget, and purchases mostly relate to indirect spending. Furthermore, substantial diversity across user groups within public sector organizations can exist. For example, requirements for municipal offices, police, and public recreation departments are much different, and would, therefore, argue in favor of decentralization to address unique user needs. Clearly, more research is required to understand the reasons for the differences in these findings. A case-based methodology may be required to capture accurately the nature of the differences and the reasons why they occur.

Although the majority of public sector firms favored centralization, an interesting finding was that the two groups reported similar levels of hybrid organizational structures. Because the hybrid organizational mode can potentially offer the advantages of both centralization and decentralization, it would appear that a significant number of public sector organizations are attracted to the opportunity to decentralize some elements of their procurement activities. A major issue facing public procurement organizations is the challenge of providing improved service. Decentralization of some activities, through the adoption of the hybrid organizational mode, is considered one means of addressing this challenge (Thai, 2001).

8.4.2 Supply Chain Responsibilities

Significant differences were also found in supply chain responsibilities. Respondents were asked to indicate which activities were organizationally part of purchasing. Table 8.2 shows the differences between the two groups. Pearson chi-square tests were used to evaluate the differences between the two groups.

The CAPS group had greater responsibility in the areas of inbound traffic, material planning and control, and outbound traffic ($p < .05$). There was also some evidence that the CAPS group had greater responsibility in the area of receiving ($p < .10$). This finding supports the research by Muller (1991), who also found differences in material flow between public and private sector groups.

The differences related to inbound and outbound transportation may be related to the types of products acquired. The private sector organizations in the CAPS study would purchase significant amounts of direct materials. Such companies carefully control the flow of materials in the supply chain through techniques such as just-in-time delivery systems. In addition, the CAPS firms were large organizations—potentially larger than many of their suppliers. Consequently, these companies may have developed capabilities to dominate the flow of goods in the supply chain through development of logistics and transportation capabilities.

Table 8.2 Supply Chain Responsibilities

Responsibility	*CAPS*		*NIGP*	
	N	*Percent*	*N*	*Percent*
Scrap and surplus disposal***	56	57	100	86
Material and purchasing research	57	59	79	68
Inbound traffic***	50	52	15	13
Inventory control	43	44	41	35
Stores and warehousing	40	41	41	35
Material planning and control***	41	42	27	23
Outbound traffic***	36	37	10	9
Receiving*	36	37	30	26
Quality assurance	21	22	29	25
In-plant materials movement	18	19	24	21
Other	24	25	26	22

* $p < .10$, ** $p < .05$, *** $p < .01$.

In contrast, the public sector firms in the study would acquire mainly indirect materials. In such situations the specifier may arrange delivery. Furthermore, most governmental organizations do not have delivery fleets and rely on suppliers to provide such services. As a practical matter, it is also easier for purchasers to specify delivery terms FOB (free on board) destination to facilitate comparison of bids among suppliers.

A surprising finding was that the FAU-NIGP group indicated higher levels of involvement in scrap and surplus disposal (86 percent) compared to the CAPS group (57 percent). Although the need for efficient and responsible disposal was important to both groups, these results do not reflect Muller's (1991) findings, even though his research was completed almost a decade earlier.

It is common for private sector firms to establish relationships with suppliers to handle scrap and surplus material and equipment, and frequently, it is the responsibility of the purchasing function to manage such relationships (Johnson, 1998). Whereas the high level of purchasing involvement in scrap and surplus disposal in public sector organizations may be caused by procedural requirements, the emphasis on the tendering process for the sale and disposal of scrap and surplus equipment and materials may require the involvement of the supply function in such activities.

It may also be possible that the level of centralization influenced responses related to supply chain responsibilities. The higher level of centralization in the public sector firms may account for its control over scrap and surplus disposal, whereas many private sector firms may delegate this responsibility to individual business units or plants. Additional research is required to gain an understanding for the differences between the two groups.

Although the FAU-NIGP group also indicated a slightly greater involvement in material and purchasing research (68 versus 59 percent), these differences were not found to be statistically significant. Meanwhile, the respondents indicated similar levels of involvement in the other four areas: inventory control, stores and warehousing, quality, and in-plant materials movement.

8.4.3 Chief Purchasing Officer

The CPOs were asked to indicate their level of education (high school, college undergraduate, or postgraduate). The respondents from both groups were well educated, with 88 percent of the CAPS group and 93 percent of the FAU-NIGP group indicating completion of a university degree at some level. However, one interesting difference was the significantly higher percentage of CPOs in the FAU-NIGP group (47 percent) that indicated a postgraduate degree (master or PhD degree) compared to the CAPS group (25 percent). Table 8.3 summarizes the reported educational levels of the two groups. Although the research could not explain why the differences exist, one possible explanation is that education may be an important criterion used to hire senior purchasing staff in the public sector. Once again, additional research is needed to determine the reasons for the differences.

There were also several important differences between the groups with respect to CPO and reporting line. Table 8.4 summarizes differences between CPO characteristics and Table 8.5 shows differences in reporting line.

CPOs from the FAU-NIGP group had spent significantly fewer years at their employer (13.4 versus 17.4 years) but had been in their current job for a longer period (8.5 versus 7.2 years). Although the differences between the two groups were not statistically significant, it would still appear that public sector CPOs spent longer periods in their position compared to CPOs in the private sector. There are a number of possible explanations for this finding. CPOs in the public sector may have spent less time working in other functional areas, compared to their counterparts in the private sector. Alternatively, public sector CPOs may progress faster to senior management ranks.

It may also be possible that public sector organizations are more likely to hire from outside and the career progression of public sector CPOs involves movement to larger organizations to take advantage of increased job responsibilities and remuneration. The evidence suggests that a significantly greater percentage of public sector firms recruit CPOs from outside the organization, with 47 percent

Table 8.3 CPO Education

	CAPS		*NIGP*	
Education	*N*	*Percent*	*N*	*Percent*
High school	12	12	8	7
College undergraduate	61	63	54	46
College graduate	24	25	55	47
Total	97	100	117	100

Table 8.4 Chief Purchasing Officer

	CAPS	*NIGP*
Number of years in present position	7.2	8.5
Number of years with present employer**	17.4	13.4
Hired as CPO (percentage)**	29	47

** $p < .01$.

Table 8.5 Reporting Line

CAPS			*NIGP*		
	N	*Percent*		*N*	*Percent*
President/CEO	10	10	City/county manager	32	27
Executive VP	8	8	Assistant city/county manager	7	6
Senior VP/group VP	14	14	Director of administration	10	9
Administrative VP	6	6	Finance director	47	40
Financial VP	14	14	Director general services	8	7
Operations VP	22	23	Other	13	11
Logistics VP	10	10			
Engineering VP	1	1			
Other	12	12			
Total	97	100	Total	117	100

of the respondents hired as head of the purchasing department, compared to only 29 percent in the private sector group. Public sector organizations may be more willing to look outside for talent, or are required to consider external candidates for vacant positions through a process of publicly posting open positions. Additional research is also required to understand why CPO tenure is longer in public organizations and why such a large percentage of CPOs are recruited from outside the organization.

Approximately 40 percent of the public sector CPOs reported to the finance director, while only 14 percent of CPOs in private sector groups did so. This finding suggests a stronger emphasis on cost and budget control, although the private sector companies indicated a much broader range of reporting lines. The most common reporting line for the CAPS group was to operations VP, for nearly one-quarter of the cases.

The second most common reporting line for CPOs in the FAU-NIGP group was to the city/county manager in 27 percent of the cases. Although caution should be used in drawing direct comparisons, CPOs in the CAPS group reported to the CEO, executive VP, and senior VP/group VP positions in 32 percent of the cases.

8.4.4 Team-Based Purchasing Activities

Each respondent was asked to rate the levels of involvement of the procurement function in nine areas of team-based purchasing techniques (1 = none and 5 = extensive). Table 8.6 presents the data related to team-based purchasing activities.

The data indicates that the CAPS group reported statistically significantly ($p < .05$) higher levels of use for four of the nine forms of team-based purchasing activities (supplier councils, cross-functional teams, teams involving suppliers, and co-location of purchasing with end users). Meanwhile, the FAU-NIGP group indicated higher levels of involvement in teams involving customers and consortia buying.

Table 8.6 Teaming

Form of Team	CAPS		FAU-NIGP	
	Mean	*Std. Dev.*	*Mean*	*Std. Dev.*
Purchasing councils	2.61	1.19	2.35	1.23
Supplier councils**	2.21	1.08	1.78	0.92
Commodity teams	2.69	1.33	2.51	1.28
Cross-functional teams**	3.33	1.16	2.80	1.19
Teams involving suppliers**	2.71	1.08	1.84	0.92
Teams involving customers**	2.25	1.04	2.90	1.22
Teams involving suppliers and customers	1.93	1.04	2.09	1.38
Co-location of purchasing with users**	2.38	1.27	1.73	1.01
Consortia buying**	1.43	0.82	3.22	1.10

** $p < .01$.

The manufacturing orientation of the CAPS group may account for these differences. Such organizations have more extensive new product development activities, and therefore have a greater need to use cross-functional teams and supplier teams. The emphasis of public purchasers on the bid process may also affect supplier-teaming opportunities.

One interesting finding, however, was that the FAU-NIGP group indicated greater involvement in teams involving customers. This may reflect differences in the definitions of the term "customer" between the two groups. Public sector purchasers define customers as specifiers, whereas the CAPS research defined customers as external to the organization.

That the FAU-NIGP group was found to have greater involvement in consortia buying was not a great surprise. This finding supports previous research that public sector organizations have a strong motivation to use cooperative purchasing techniques (Johnson, 1999).

It is worth recognizing that the reported scores for team-based purchasing activities were low for both groups. On a five-point scale, the highest score for the FAU-NIGP group was 3.22 for consortia buying and 3.33 for cross-functional teams for the CAPS group.

8.4.5 Involvement in Major Organizational Activities

Respondents were asked to rate purchasing's level of involvement in a list of major organizational activities on a five-point scale (1 = none and 5 = extensive). Statistically significant differences between the two groups were found in eight of the eleven areas of involvement in major organizational activities (see Table 8.7).

The data indicated statistically higher ($p < .01$ or $p < .05$) levels of involvement of the private sector group in five areas (technology planning, marketing planning, environment planning, financial/cash flow planning, and international countertrade/offset planning). For new product development, risk management/hedging, and outsourcing, the differences were not as pronounced ($p < .10$).

Table 8.7 Involvement in Major Organizational Activities

	CAPS		FAU-NIGP	
Activity	*Mean*	*Std. Dev.*	*Mean*	*Std. Dev.*
Corporate strategic planning	2.77	1.09	2.69	1.01
Technology planning***	2.28	1.01	2.77	0.91
Capital project/investment planning	2.65	1.22	2.50	1.04
Marketing planning**	2.13	1.00	1.85	0.96
New product development*	2.78	1.20	2.51	1.09
Information systems planning	2.75	1.05	2.60	0.89
Environmental planning**	2.18	1.02	1.89	0.93
Financial/cash flow planning***	2.61	1.15	1.73	0.93
Risk management/hedging*	2.25	1.12	1.98	1.00
Outsourcing*	3.25	1.30	2.94	1.08
International countertrade/offset planning***	2.02	1.22	1.13	0.33

* $p < .10$, ** $p < .05$, *** $p < .01$.

Although some areas have little relevance to public sector organizations, such as new product development and countertrade, the results indicate an overall lower level of involvement of public sector supply organizations in major organizational activities, compared to the public sector organizations. In many of these areas, opportunities exist for public sector purchasing organizations to play an active role in the planning process, such as financial/cash flow planning, risk management and hedging, and environmental planning. More research is required to understand the nature and causes of the differences between the two groups.

The only area where the public sector group indicated higher levels of involvement was in technology planning ($p < .01$). It is possible, however, that the five-year time lag between the two studies and the prominence of Y2K planning at the time the FAU-NIGP data was collected accounts for this difference.

It is also worthy to highlight the relatively low scores from both groups in the area of involvement in major organizational activities. On a five-point scale, only outsourcing exceeded a mean of 3.0 in the CAPS group, while the FAU-NIGP group had a mean of 2.94 for this activity. Most other scores for both groups were in a disappointing low range. Although the literature argues that organizations can use their supply chain to create competitive advantage, these results suggest that opportunities exist to involve the supply function in organizational strategy.

8.5 Conclusion

This research presents a basis for understanding the different organizational approaches to supply in the public and private sectors and provides insights regarding the roles and contributions made by the supply organization. Furthermore, it also offers useful benchmarking information that can be used to question preexisting approaches to purchasing's roles and responsibilities for private and public sector organizations.

Results from this research provide valuable information regarding the specific commonalities and differences between the two groups, and the findings can be useful for both public and private sector purchasers and executives. The research offers useful insights concerning the career path, reporting line options, and important activities involving purchasers in both sectors. Furthermore, the findings can be beneficial in establishing training and educational programs for purchasers.

The results indicated that public and private sector supply organizations differ in several important areas. Each of the five areas examined—organizational structure, supply chain responsibilities, the CPO and reporting line, teaming, and involvement in major organizational activities—demonstrated significant areas of difference. Although some research has argued that purchasing roles and responsibilities in the public and private sectors are more alike than dissimilar, our findings indicate that significant differences exist.

8.6 Limitations and Opportunities for Future Research

This research is limited by the characteristics of the respondents. The CAPS sample included a large percentage of manufacturing firms, while the FAU-NIGP sample consisted solely of respondents from city and county governments. For both groups, the samples were North American based. The sample of NIGP members from city and county governments may bias the results and may not necessarily reflect broader trends in public purchasing organizations. It would also be helpful to increase the percentage of private sector service organizations in future research. Meanwhile, an opportunity still exists to compare large private sector firms with large governmental purchasing organizations, such as state and federal government agencies. Collecting data from international organizations would enhance the richness of the results by providing an opportunity to compare North American and European based organizations, for example.

The five-year time span between the two samples places limitations on the generalizability of the results. Consequently, the nature of this research should be regarded as exploratory. Nonetheless, there are a number of important research questions raised by this research. Although the data indicates differences between the groups with respect to organizational structure, supply chain responsibilities, the CPO and reporting line, teaming, and involvement in major organizational activities, why such differences exist is unexplained. For example: Why are public sector procurement organizations more likely to operate in the centralized mode? Is the career path for CPOs in the private sector different from those in the public sector, and why did a higher percentage of public sector CPOs have post-graduate degrees? Why are public sector purchasing organization firms more likely to report to finance when such reporting relationships are much less common in the private sector? In an era where both public and private sector organizations are being challenged to deliver more value, an understanding of different organizational approaches can help identify potential opportunities.

References

Cavinato, J.L. 1991. Evolving procurement organizations: Logistics implications. *Journal of Business Logistics, 13*(1), 27–45.

Center for Advanced Purchasing Studies 1999. *Purchasing Performance Benchmarks for State/County Governments.* Tempe, AZ.

Fearon, H.E. 1988. *Purchasing Organizational Relationships.* Tempe, AZ: Center for Advanced Purchasing Studies.

Fearon, H.E. and Leenders, M.R. 1995. *Purchasing's Organizational Roles and Responsibilities.* Tempe, AZ: Center for Advanced Purchasing Studies.

Harland, C., Gibbs, J., and Sutton, R. 2000. Supply strategy for the public sector: Framing the issues. In *Conference 2000 Proceedings* (pp. 342–351). London, Ontario, Canada: Richard Ivey School of Business.

Harrigan, K.R. 1980. Strategy formulation in declining industries. *Academy of Management Review, 5*(4), 599–604.

Heberling, M.E., Carter, J.R., and Hoagland, J.H. 1992. An investigation of purchases by American businesses and governments. *International Journal of Purchasing and Materials Management, 28*(4), 39–45.

Hendrick, T.E. 1997. *Purchasing Consortiums: Horizontal Alliances among Firms Buying Common Goods and Services.* Tempe, AZ: Center for Advanced Purchasing Studies.

Johnson, P.F. 1998. Managing value in reverse logistics systems. *Logistics and Transportation Review, 34*(3), 217–227.

Johnson, P.F. 1999. The pattern of evolution in public sector purchasing consortia. *International Journal of Logistics: Research and Applications, 2*(1), 57–73.

Johnson, P.F., Leenders, M.R., and Fearon, H.E. 1998a. Evolving roles and responsibilities of purchasing organizations. *International Journal of Purchasing and Materials Management, 34*(1), 2–11.

Johnson, P.F., Leenders, M.R., and Fearon, H.E. 1998b. The influence of organizational factors on purchasing activities. *International Journal of Purchasing and Materials Management, 34*(3), 2–11.

Leenders, M.R. and Johnson, P.F. 2000. *Major Structural Changes in Supply Organizations.* Tempe, AZ: Center for Advanced Purchasing Studies.

Ludwig, D.C. 1993. Adapting to a declining environment: Lessons from a religious order. *Organizational Science, 4*(1), 41–56.

McCue, C.P. and Gianakis, G.A. 2001. Public purchasing: Who's minding the store? *Journal of Public Procurement, 1*(1), 71–95.

Muller, E.W. 1991. An analysis of the purchasing manager's position in private, public and nonprofit settings. *International Journal of Purchasing and Materials Management, 27*(4), 16–23.

Osborne, D. and Plastrik, P. 1997. *Banishing Bureaucracy: The Five Strategies for Reinventing Government.* New York: Addison-Wesley.

Pooley, J. and Dunn, S.C. 1994. A longitudinal study of purchasing positions: 1960–1989. *Journal of Business Logistics, 15*(1), 193–213.

Telgen, J., Zomer, G., and de Boer, L. 1997. The efficiency and effectiveness of government purchasing in the Netherlands. *IPSERA Conference Proceedings*, Naples, Italy: T8/2 1–8.

Thai, K.V. 2001. Public procurement reexamined. *Journal of Public Procurement, 1*(1), 9–50.

Chapter 9

Service Sourcing

Alessandro Ancarani

CONTENTS

9.1 Purchasing of Services in Public Organizations

The government sector is, to a large degree, a service sector, where a high proportion of the external sourcing concerns services. In Europe, it is estimated that around 50 percent of the total external sourcing in local government is contracts for services, such as construction work, maintenance work, public transport, garbage collection, social services and consultants, network services, etc.

Purchasing of services in public sector is becoming an increasingly important issue, thanks to an emerging service industry context, the deregulation of public service sectors, and a general trend of increased outsourcing in both the private and the public sectors. Support services such as cleaning, catering, and security are in a high degree contracted out, but outsourcing is also applied to other kind of services, namely in public services which the public organizations must provide to the citizens, increasingly through external suppliers.

The keyword in the current international approach to public procurement is value, which involves making taxpayers' money go further in meeting user requirements. Value can be further broken down to three popular ideas of public procurement goals: economy, efficiency, and effectiveness. Economy is concerned with minimizing the cost of resources acquired or used, having regard for the quality of inputs. Efficiency is concerned with the relationship between the outputs of services and the resources used, while effectiveness is concerned with the achievement of targets, not only in terms of quantity but also quality (Stainer and Stainer, 1998). The means by which value is to be achieved is a source of much debate. Economy efficiency through competition can reduce cost and improve quality (Domberger and Jensen, 1997). However, this is mainly because of increased attention paid to quality through monitoring, explicit inspections, and emphasis on standards. Erridge et al. (1999) argue that competition creates lengthy tendering procedures, which increases transaction costs, while the arms length relationship limits the ability of buyers and sellers to forecast accurately the risks and eventualities in the contract.

Several procedures characterize government decision-making, thus, focusing purchasers more on the public's perception of their adherence to procedure, rather than on value for money achieved (Mechling, 1995; de Boer and Telgen, 1998; Pettijohn and Qiao, 2000).

A conceptual framework for public sector service procurement needs a more detailed characterization of market behaviors than that outlined in the traditional "markets v. hierarchies v. networks" framework (Ouchi, 1980; Powell, 1990). This framework needs to incorporate two important and widespread trends in public procurement in recent years: the move to more collaborative working in public sector organizations (both joined-up working within the public sector and closer working with organizations in other sectors) and the move to more complex forms of coordination in the procurement process, with larger numbers of players involved in both the commissioning and providing roles. The combination of these two factors produces the opportunity for a range of different market relationships from those traditionally considered in the make-or-buy decision.

Traditional contracting-out involves a single commissioner of a service placing contracts with a range of providers for its services and is based on an explicit specification of the service and performance criteria that are predetermined. The need to predetermine a specification for what are, typically, complex services in a dynamically changing environment and then to manage subsequent (typically frequent) contract variations has made public agencies vulnerable to all the opportunistic behaviors which are associated with "transactional contracting" (Williamson, 1975; Walsh, 1995).

In most countries, there is a general increase of outsourcing of technical services, social services, and administrative functions in government (at different levels), because of competition and privatization policies (Baily et al., 1994; Deakin and Walsh, 1996; Kirkpatrick and Lucio, 1996). Outsourcing results in a concentration on and increased importance of supplier management. The structure of public service offered is determined primarily by politics and cannot be changed quickly as such change is embedded in the social system expenditure traditions and other ideological influences (Essig and Batran, 2005).

The development has not been undisputed. Different kinds of problems have been identified in contracting out of public services. According to Kirkpatrick and Lucio (1996), there are new problems and contradictions that are emerging as a consequence of managing public services through contracts. The administrative costs involved in specification and monitoring of services are one of the main issues of discussion (Audit Commission, 1993). A general need of skills in management of contract relationships has also become apparent. In particular, skills in contract management, networking, organizational understanding, negotiating, and building relationships for multi-organizational teams are required (Clarke and Stewart, 1988).

It is generally emphasized that the service purchasing process is more complex and less standardized than the purchasing of goods. Some aspects have been outlined, such as the increased need for written specifications of the content of purchase, because of the invisibility of the product. Taking references and judging the qualities of the contractor are also considered to be more important for the same reason (Graw and Maples, 1994). The high degree of personnel involved is suggested to imply that specific attention has to be given to laws and regulations for taxation, social security, health and safety, etc. The issue of make-or-buy is seen as more significant in purchasing of services (Van Weele, 2005). Finally, the ensuring of good communication with the contractor and the end users is considered to be of crucial importance to deal with variation and unforeseen events in service delivery.

Also, the environment has an important impact on the decisions made by organizations. The public scrutiny associated with the money spent by public organizations is a type of environmental factor that impacts the way in which purchasing departments are involved (Schiele and McCue, 2006).

Such different issues have to be taken into account when dealing with the wide range of services that the public organization can buy either for internal use or for providing services to the citizens.

9.2 Services' Characteristics

9.2.1 Differences between Goods and Services

Services have some peculiar features, which can be assumed to have implications for the organization of the purchasing function. There are four commonly cited features that make services differ from goods: intangibility, heterogeneity, perishability, and inseparability (Shostack, 1977; Berry, 1980). Several other authors claim that (Berry and Parasuraman, 1991; Grönroos, 1990; Normann, 1992)

- Services are intangible and not possible to transport or buffer.
- Production and consumption are occurring at the same time, often involving the customer.
- There are difficulties in specifying and measuring the output and quality of services, including problems with delayed effects.
- Services are performed in multiunit organizations, with dispersed locations.
- There is a high degree of personnel resources involved in service production.

Some authors (Grönroos, 1978; Cherubini, 1981) suggested considering goods and services as a continuum that can be represented along an axis with pure goods and pure services at the two extremes, while goods with both tangible and service content should be represented in the middle (Figure 9.1).

Zeithaml (1981) considered the intangibility of services as the critical goods–services distinction from which all other differences arise (Figure 9.2). The intangibility of services is critical as Shostack (1977) argued that the greater the weight of intangible elements in a market entity, the greater the divergence from product marketing in terms of priorities and approach. The intangibility of services will result in purchasers having difficulty assessing service quality in that they are unable to handle or see the service, only experience it (Parasuraman et al., 1985; Zeithaml and Bitner, 1996).

Although services are heterogeneous (Gadde and Hàkansson, 1993), the context could generally be stated as uncertain and complex, with a large input from human actors. There is, because of

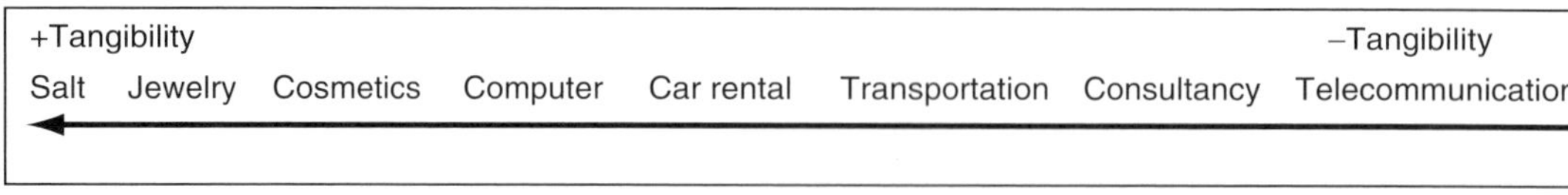

Figure 9.1 Classification of goods according to their tangibility. (Modified from Grönroos, C., *Eur. J. Market.*, 12, 588, 1978.)

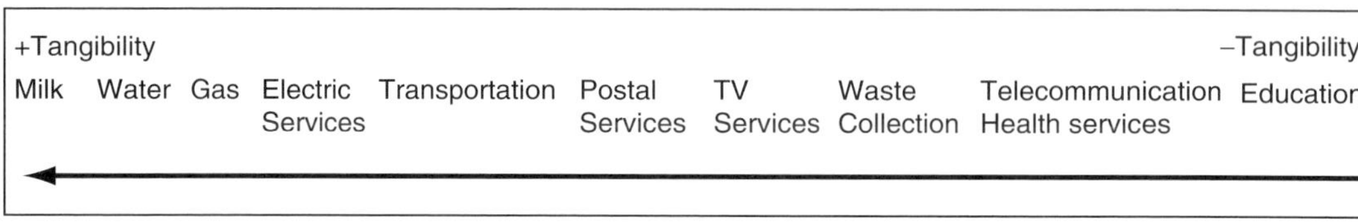

Figure 9.2 Public services classification in terms of tangibility. (Modified from Zeithaml, V.A., *Marketing of Services*, American Marketing Association, Chicago, 1981.)

the invisibility, a specification and evidence problem regarding performance. The dispersed nature of services makes control difficult for a central purchasing department. Findings from American studies also indicate that the major part of services is purchased by the user departments and not by the purchasing department (Fearon and Bales, 1995).

The final distinctive feature of a service is its inseparability, i.e., as buyers experience the delivery of services, it is inevitable that they are part of the delivery process. The participation of the buyer in the delivery process means that the buyer can have a direct effect on the outcome of the service delivered. This inseparability of service production and consumption forces the buyers and sellers into intimate contact (Grönroos, 1978). The interaction that occurs during the service encounter becomes the basis of organizational relationships (Czepiel, 1990; Berry, 1995). Specifically, through interpersonal relationships customers are acquired, long-term customer relationships built, thus ensuring customer satisfaction (Payne, 1995). The distinct service characteristics in comparison to those of goods explain why it is more appropriate to purchase services through a relational stance with long-term relationships in mind.

9.2.2 Differences between Public and Private Services

Within the last decades, an extensive literature has developed on the characteristics that distinguish public or collective services from private or individual services. Exclusion and jointness of use or consumption are two essential defining characteristics to distinguish between private and public services.

Exclusion has long been identified as a necessary characteristic for services to be supplied under market conditions. Exclusion occurs when potential users can be denied services unless they meet the terms and conditions of the vendor. If both agree, services are supplied at a price. The buyer acquires the service and the seller acquires the value specified. Where exclusion is infeasible, anyone can derive benefits from the service as long as nature or the efforts of others supply it.

Another attribute of services pertains to jointness of use or consumption. No jointness of consumption exists when consumption by one person precludes its use or consumption by another person. In this case, consumption is completely subtractable. A service having no jointness of consumption and with which exclusion is feasible is defined as a purely private service.

Jointness of consumption, on the other hand, implies that the use or enjoyment of a service by one person does not foreclose its use or enjoyment by others; despite its use by one person, it remains available for use by others in undiminished quantity and quality. Few, if any, joint consumption services are perfectly non-subtractable. At certain thresholds of supply, one person's use of a service subtracts in part from its use and enjoyment by others. Each further increase in use impairs the use of the service for each other person in the community of users. Such services are then subject to degradation or erosion in their quality unless supply is modified to meet the new demand.

Both exclusion and jointness of consumption are characteristics that vary in degree, rather than being all-or-none characteristics. The two extreme cases of jointness of consumption—complete subtractability and complete non-subtractability—give logical clarity in distinguishing purely private from purely public services.

Exclusion and jointness of consumption are independent attributes. Both characteristics can be arrayed in relation to one another. The jointness characteristic can be arrayed into two classes: alternative uses which are highly subtractable and joint uses which are non-subtractable. Exclusion can also be arrayed into two classes, in which exclusion is either feasible or infeasible. Exclusion is technically infeasible where no practical technique exists for either packaging a service or controlling access by a potential user. Exclusion may also be economically infeasible where the costs of exclusion are too high.

Market arrangements can be used to deliver either private services or services where exclusion is feasible. In the case of toll services, a price is charged for access or use but the service is enjoyed in common. The value of the service depends both on the quality of the service produced and on the way it is used by others.

In the case of a common pool resource, exclusion may be infeasible in the sense that many users cannot be denied access. But, use by any one user precludes use of some fixed quantity of a service by other users.

Because public services are difficult to package or unitize they are also more difficult to measure. Performance measurement depends on estimates in which indicators or proxy measures are used as estimates of performance. By utilizing multiple indicators, weak measures of performance can be developed even though direct measures of output are not feasible.

9.2.3 Services Bought by Public Organizations

The broad range of services rendered by governmental agencies may cover all different types of services. Most governmental services, however, are of the public service, toll service, or common pool resource types.

Where a service is characterized by jointness of consumption and non-exclusion, a user is generally unable to exercise an option and has little choice whether to consume or not. The quality of a service is available under existing terms and conditions, and one's preference will not materially affect the quality of such a service. Furthermore, individuals may be forced to consume public services that have a negative value for them. Streets, for example, may become congested thoroughfares restricting the convenience of local residents and shoppers who are required to cope with the traffic whether they like it or not.

The public sector has some specific characteristics, which also have to be considered in analyzing the purchasing of public services. One important feature is the highly regulated context, with detailed procedures prescribed for purchasing (e.g., the European Commission Directives on public procurement). Another important feature is the demand for public accountability and openness to media (Baily et al., 1994). An American characterization of purchasing in the public sector is that it is like buying in a fishbowl (Kolchin, 1990), because purchasing is restricted by regulations and exposed to scrutiny of the public.

According to the characteristics of services and the conditions of purchasing in the public sector, transaction cost theory (Williamson, 1975) predicts that a situational context with a high degree of uncertainty involves high transaction costs, and accordingly services should be managed by hierarchy instead of by contract. But as Stinchcombe (1990) notes, there are obviously a lot of contracts running under these conditions. He argues that contracts can simulate hierarchies by having authoritative systems, incentive systems, administered pricing systems, procedures for resolving conflicts, and established standard operating procedures. Williamson (1985) refers in his later work to these kinds of contracts as relational contracting, a term coined by MacNeil (1978). Relational contracting is characterized by an atmosphere of common culture and norms, and by using the entire relationship as a reference point for evaluation, instead of a particular contract.

The classification of services bought by public organizations has to take into account that under the heading "purchasing services in public organizations" two main typologies of services should be considered:

- Internal support/ancillary services such as maintenance, catering, gardening, security, that some authors generally grouped under the term facilities management services whereas others call business services, including ICT and logistic services
- Public services, which the public organizations must provide to the citizens

The number of service offerings is highly diverse. Also, the character of services will differ: long term or short term, simple or highly complex, comprise standardized or customized solutions (Axelsson and Wynstra, 2002). Furthermore, the importance of a service is relative, namely depending on the specific business circumstances (Fitzsimmons et al., 1998).

With reference to business services, an interesting classification (Doty and Glick, 1994) identifies four types of services (Wynstra et al., 2006):

- Component services: passed on to the end-customer unaltered and can add value to the buying organization's offering; the customer may have specific requests/fears regarding the sourcing of this service; the supplier has to have detailed knowledge of the offering and of the way the final customer uses that offering
- Semi-manufactured services: altered to some extent before being passed on to the final; they should be ready to be added to the offering
- Instrumental services: tools to produce the buying organization's own offerings and its processes; it is important to know how the service provision fits with the existing production methods and procedures
- Consumption services: are part of the buying organization operations without becoming part of the offering to the final customer; they generally consist of services involving substantive administrative efforts

Actually, the one and the same service can belong to different categories depending on how it is used by the customer. For example, cleaning for railways organizations can be a consumption service with reference to offices, a component service with reference to stations, although it can be both with reference to trains.

With reference to the public services to be provided to the citizens, they can be divided into two main categories, as follows:

- Network services (such as telecommunications, water and gas supply, public transportation, etc.)
- Human services (such as health services, education, elderly care, social housing, etc.)

In general terms, to procure the services, several steps should be followed:

- Prequalification of main providers: a service does exist when it is provided as it cannot be tested or inspected beforehand to ensure it conforms to the specification of the buyer; the preliminary assessment and prequalification will strongly focus on the organization, processes, expertise, and capabilities of the service provider.
- Secure supplier capacity and capabilities—because services can only be produced at the same moment as they are consumed—in terms of manpower, equipment and other resources are available beforehand to ensure delivery at the moment the service is needed.
- Check upon key personnel: the quality of the services to be provided is directly related to the expertise, experience, and quality of the service provider's employees.
- Defining and managing expectations: because often both the customer and supplier are involved in the production process of the service, it should be agreed who will be responsible for what part of the result.
- Contractual arrangements: for services it is almost impossible to include clauses that can deal with all possible misunderstandings.
- Performance-based contract: a performance-based contract should be preferred over a best effort agreement; rather that making the effort of the provider the core of the agreement, it is preferable to focus on the performance or result that should be derived from these efforts; this could require a thorough discussion of what needs to be delivered in terms of outcome.

Compared to buying goods, it is more difficult to determine the total costs that are related to buying a specific service. It is also much more difficult to decide on clear specifications and scope of work. The fact that a service provider has done well on one occasion and location does not necessarily mean he or she will also perform well in another situation. In comparing supplier offerings, the objective comparison of the service providers is a difficult task. One of the problems related to buying services is to forecast future supplier performance based on past performance. Another problem is to have trust in a continuous, reliable performance level (Graw and Maples, 1994). This discussion illustrates why purchasing services in public organizations is such a highly sensitive and political matter.

9.3 Procurement of Internal Services in Public Organizations

In recent years, organizations in public sectors have placed more attention on cost reduction and flexibility, concentrating on core competences and outsourcing noncore activities. However, the relevance of these activities for the organization's performance requires an accurate analysis of what it is outsourced and how (Walker et al., 2001; Kakabadse and Kakabadse, 2005).

Outsourcing can be defined as the contracting-out of services that were previously performed in-house. Outsourcing is a supply strategy often chosen as a means of increasing organizational efficiency and effectiveness (Steane and Walker, 2000). Although some short-term benefits for organizations can be achieved through outsourcing, there is a growing recognition that there may be longer-term costs not fully assessed by them (Bettis et al., 1992). Outsourcing can impact on the size, structure, and competitiveness of purchaser and vendor sectors. Outsourcing also has an effect on employment levels, patterns, and conditions (Postner, 1990). Social issues may be affected in respect of growth in earnings inequality because the contracts offered little scope to compete other than by worsening employees' terms and conditions of employment (Patterson and Pinch, 1995). Moreover, there are political effects at local and national level as one conclusion that might be drawn from this trend is that the public sector has managed effectively to transfer low-paid jobs into the private sector (Cully et al., 1999; Sachdev, 2001). Risks of outsourcing include losing in-house expertise and knowledge (Boston, 1996), unintentional loss of control, and reductions in quality (Lei and Hitt, 1995).

There is an increasing awareness in management literature that the decision to outsource is a complex one with uncertain outcomes (Hui and Tsang, 2004). Knight and Harland (1999) argued that in the public sector there should be some sector level monitoring and, if necessary, proactive interventions to guide and regulate local decision making as the cumulative effect of locally taken outsourcing decisions can be to create a supply market structure that is detrimental to the purchasers and suppliers in the long term.

In the local authorities, the sourcing strategy and the make-or-buy decisions are dealt with in a complex interaction between politicians and officers representing different interests. The discussions on make-or-buy center around the controversial issue of whether to maintain in-house staffing or reduce it. This is an extremely delicate and conflict-loaded issue in many local authorities, which confirms that the issues of make-or-buy are an essential part of contracting-out services, as is pointed out by Van Weele (2005).

With respect to service provision, various sourcing strategies are available (Atkin and Brooks, 2002). These options may be considered as follows:

- In-house: where a service is provided by a dedicated resource directly employed by the organization; monitoring and control of performance is normally conducted under the terms of conventional employer/employee relationships, although internal service-level agreements may be employed as regulating mechanisms
- Outsourcing: where a service is commissioned from an external supply organization, usually under the terms of a formal contractual arrangement based on terms and conditions derived from a service-level agreement; there may be several of these contractual relationships operating in parallel for a range of services from a variety of suppliers
- Public–private partnership (PPP): where a partnership or strategic alliance has been formed between the organization and service provider based on a sharing of the responsibility for the delivery and performance of the service, including the sharing of the benefits arising from any efficiency gains and cost savings
- Bundled services management (TFM): where a whole range of services are bundled together and externalized to a single supplier, which becomes totally responsible for the delivery, monitoring, control, and attainment of performance objectives that relate to operational benefit

When the ownership of the firm is considered, both public and private organizations can be entrusted with the service provision (Figure 9.3).

There are two different strategy elements involved in the purchasing process (see Figure 9.3). One is the sourcing strategy with the general decisions of make-or-buy. The other is the

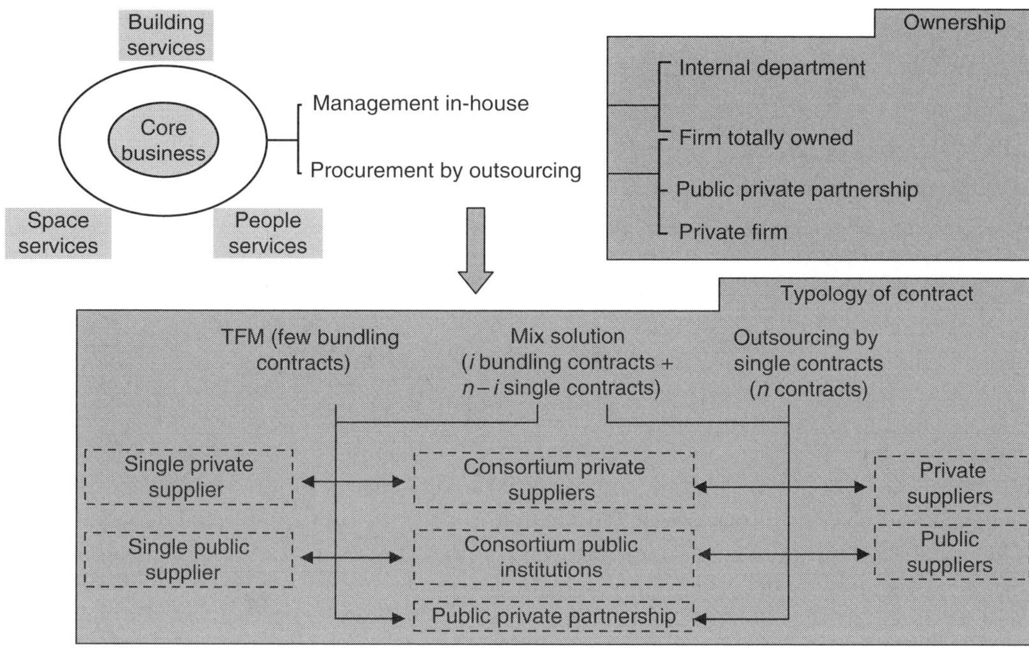

Figure 9.3 Sourcing strategies for procuring services in public organizations. (From Ancarani, A. and Capaldo, G., *J. Purchasing Supply Manag.*, 11, 232, 2005.)

service-specific contract strategy of how to combine different services, activities, and functions into contracts to benefit from or to stimulate competition, or to create efficient administration of the contracts. This is often labeled as bundling contract.

The strategy of packaging the contract seems to be handled by the managers of the service department. In large cities, it is handled by specialized units, corporate strategy departments, or commercial units. The main considerations are how to divide contracts to enhance competition or to bundle contracts to reach synergy or larger volumes. Only the largest cities have contract volumes that can be divided, and have resources to handle the administration of many different contracts. An important competence for this function is to have a good knowledge of the market situation and the market structure.

Taken to its logical extreme, the starting point for outsourcing options could consist merely of one service being outsourced, while all the remaining services are retained in-house. A progression can then follow, whereby eventually all services could be outsourced under individual contracts (n contracts). The next stage would be to group some of the contracts together and place that group of services with one contractor (few contracts for i bundled services and $n - i$ individual contracts), a concept known as bundling. Next, several bundles could be let to the same supplier. Inherent in such a scheme is that bundling contracts tend to collect together groups of operational services separately from those of management services (Ancarani and Capaldo, 2005).

The solution to have only a few services can have potential benefits for public sector organizations but there are also potential risks (Brackertz and Kenley, 2002). In fact, to outsource services to different suppliers through several specific single contracts allows high levels of specialization to be achieved for the supplied services as well as the risk of possible inefficiencies to be reduced. Moreover, by widening the range of services supplied by the same actor, improved performance can be achieved due to a holistic vision of clients and their present and potential requirements. Against this, resorting to a single supplier for TFM makes the dependency of the public sector organization on the supplier greater, resulting in higher vulnerability (Atkin and Brooks, 2002). As a result, when choosing TFM, the public organization should carefully consider the following issues:

- Existence of firms guaranteeing an effective services integration
- Extent to which the potential suppliers are knowledgeable about the specific needs of the customer as well as the local context
- Ability of the public organization in planning and controlling integrated services rather than single ones

According to Venkatesan (1992), a detailed understanding is required of both the needs of the users and the conditions of production, because these two dimensions are mixed together and are interdependent. He argues that it is not necessary to keep all production in-house if there are competent contractors. The most important thing is to keep the competence to specify and control the performance specifications. If this competence gets lost, it can be very difficult to rebuild it again.

The service specifications contain information about quantities and norms of quality. The quantities are mostly based on detailed information about surface areas, length of streets, number of real estate properties, number of trees that need maintenance, etc.

Concerning the norms of quality, there are different opinions about whether to write strictly detailed contract specifications, with descriptions of input resources and the exact activities that have to be performed, or to specify the services in a functional way, by describing the desired output and outcome. The most common solutions seems to be a combination of different ways to explain the essence of the service.

The specification task is handled mainly by service specialists at the service departments. The service specialist is also the main contact person in the relationship with the contractors. In some authorities, consultants are employed to deal with the service specification and the contract design. In-house units are also consulted.

The important competence for this activity is deep knowledge of the characteristics of the service, interpretation of the local policy and the government budget, and the ability to communicate this to the contractor. The most common formal competence for the officers in this position turned out to be an engineering exam combined with several years of experience in the service, as a manager or a construction engineer.

The importance of service knowledge is in accordance with what Venkatesan (1992) defines as the need of the architectural knowledge. He describes it as the intimately detailed and specialized power of translation required to capture customer requirements and reproduce them in the language of subsystem performance specifications. It is based on many detailed understandings of the linkages between user requirements, system parameters, and component specifications.

Many buyers increasingly try to make arrangements through a performance-based agreement. The results or the performance to be delivered by the suppliers are stated in quantitative terms, usually in the form of a limited number of key performance indicators. Where the supplier meets the agreed service levels, he will receive full payment. When he is unable to meet these targeted service levels, he will be paid less. Of course, when arranging for this type of agreement, the buyer and supplier should agree on the precise definition of the key performance indicators. The buyer should be able to report regularly on the supplier's performance. These reports should then be discussed to see where both parties could make improvements to realize a better result. An advantage of using a performance-based agreement in the relationship with a service provider is that both parties need to become very specific about the results that should be gained from the provider's services. Furthermore, both parties should be explicit about who within the customer company is going to benefit from the service and in what way (lower cost, faster response, less process interruptions, etc.). Apart from the results, the performance-based agreement will outline the resources that will be used by both the buyer and the supplier to be able to fulfill the service requirements. In doing so, the service-level agreement helps both parties to be explicit about the expectations both parties have from the relationship.

Preparing a detailed service-level agreement usually takes a lot of time and effort. In some case, circumstances may be such that these time and effort are not available. In general, services may be specified in terms of (Axelsson and Wynstra, 2002)

- Inputs used by the service provider: the agreement focuses on describing the resources that will be used by the provider to deliver the service required; no agreements on the actual performance to be delivered by the people involved are made.
- Throughput or process necessary to provide the service required: the buyer meets with the supplier and, based upon a general works description, agrees with the supplier on the range of activities that will be performed.
- Output or results required by the customer through the supplier's service activities: the buyer provides a description of the final result to be gained from the supplier's intervention. The functionality of the service is stressed rather than the activity itself.
- Outcome of the service: when the value rather than the functionality of the service is stressed; in buying services arriving at a proper description of what the outcome of the service needs to be requires a lot of effort and time.

The key suggestions for contracting in an effective way for a business service provision in a public organization could be summarized as follows (Van Weele, 2005):

- Specify performance or outcome to be delivered from service.
- Agree on the activities to be conducted.
- Describe when and where the service needs to be provided.
- Describe who will benefit from the service and in what way.
- Discuss and agree on dispute resolution procedure.
- Check supplier reputation, expertise, and qualifications, including key personnel available during the service period.
- Analyze supplier service process and quality system.
- Assess "cultural fit" between buying company and service provider.
- Pursue performance-based contract, which outlines key performance indicators and detailed work-plan and time schedule.
- Agree on what financial, human, technical, and information resources will be made available by the buyer.
- Allow for detailed inspection and quality procedures.

9.4 Procurement of Public Services

The public sector has sought to solve the tensions between more market-based provision and more "public value-added" from the provision of public services (Moore, 1995) considering that the public economy can be a mixed economy with substantial private participation in the delivery of public services.

Until a few years ago, the most important alternative for delivering public services, applied all over the world, was constituted either by public utilities or by public service agencies. The services were funded through the public budgets, infrastructures and plants were acquired as public properties, monopolies were protected against competition, and the main decisions were defined by means of administrative procedures.

Since the late 1970s, public organizations have been urged to concentrate on the core activities, divesting themselves of other activities. Prahalad and Hamel (1990) sought to achieve business focus through defining and protecting core practices. A plethora of terms emerged to cover essentially the same activity (that of using suppliers for activities that were originally conducted in-house): outsourcing, subcontracting, contracting-out, and externalization.

Taking into account the different typologies of organization that could be entrusted with a public service provision (see Figure 9.3), a public organization to supply a public service has several options:

- Product the service through its own production unit: it is the typical in-house provision.
- Contract with a private supplier: the decisions about the quantity or quality of public services have to be translated into specifications used to secure bids from potential suppliers, state the terms and conditions for contractual arrangements, and establish standards for assessing performance; the public organization receives information about costs and production possibilities from potential suppliers, negotiates and contracts with suppliers, receives service complaints from users, and monitors suppliers' performance in delivering services.
- Establish standards of service: each potential user can choose what provider should supply service; multiple suppliers may be franchised or anyone wishing to do business under the terms and conditions specified by the public organization for such a service may do so; the limited degree of jointness can be taken care of by applying common standards to all users and suppliers.
- Collect taxes: a voucher has to be make available to each potential user so that it can decide among alternative suppliers and service packages.
- Contract with a different unit of government: many local authorities acting as buyer contract with other municipalities, or some other unit of government, to supply a wide range of public services.
- Supply some components of a service through its own production unit, but to rely upon other organizations to arrange for other components of a service: any given public organization may rely upon the joint production efforts of several different providers in supplying and delivering a particular bundle of services that are subject to joint consumption, as well as it may act in cooperation with others that are willing to contribute supplemental funds to procure a particular level of services.

Since the 1980s, the public sector has followed a government policy oriented toward contractual relations. It has been suggested that a contract state has emerged whereby an increasing proportion of public services are organized around market relations and commercial contracts between purchasers and providers. Under this model, local authorities would cease to provide or manage public services directly and instead become largely residual bodies that coordinate and monitor services through a range of contracts.

Characteristics of this model include a clear division between clients and contractors, with service provision regulated by a legally enforceable contract. Contracts should specify in detail the nature and level of services required, and provide remedial mechanisms for poor performance. Such a separation between buyer and supplier, as well as the use of competitive bidding, requires

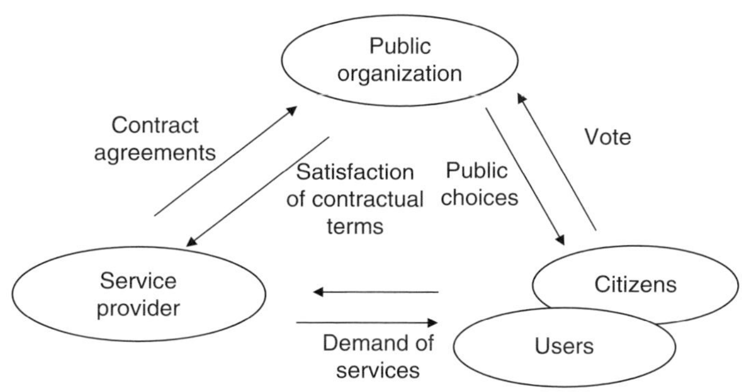

Figure 9.4 Triangulation among citizens/users, public buyer, and service provider.

that the service could be clearly specified in a form that can be used as a part of the contract and against which performance can be monitored both by buyers and end users. Thus, a sort of triangulation has been defined among the buyer (who owns the assets), the supplier (a public, private, or PPP organization) to which the service provision is contracted out, and the customers (end users) (Figure 9.4).

The underlying foundation of the trend toward competition and outsourcing is that they would result in improved outcomes such as greater efficiency, higher quality of service, clearer focus on customers, and better value for money (Larbi, 1998). Actually, the contracting-out of services blurred the boundaries between public and private sectors and PPPs are set to reduce this distinction still further. More recently, the debate as to the form and funding of public services has emerged as the central issue in politics all over the world.

Contracting out fundamentally changed the process of providing many public services, regardless of who provided it. Irrespective of whether work was awarded internally or externally, the management restructuring required by tendering created potentially market-inclined pressures within public organizations. In-house providers were instructed to operate as if they were independent contractors, maintaining their own accounts, to generate a return on their assets, and providing or purchasing their own support services (finance, payroll, personnel, etc.).

This approach is far from being straightforward. Firstly, there is the principal-agent problem, where the agent may have different objectives and may also have better information on what is going on than the principal (sometimes referred to as asymmetric information). Secondly, market arrangements need to be closely monitored; otherwise the supplier will seek to take advantage of the client through "opportunism." This sort of exploitation is particularly evident where there are a small number of firms supplying these services. Thirdly, critics have argued that the claims of citizenship are being subordinated to a consumer culture inimical to public service. Issues of accountability are also raised.

To facilitate the benefits that the use of forces of supply and demand in the market can offer, many regulatory frameworks have been issued in several countries. The private sector, while not working to the same ethos as the public sector, has been deemed to be more efficient because of the market's pull and tug against quantity, price, and quality (Baily et al., 1998). In particular, with reference to the competition among domestic and foreign firms, since the 1970s, public procurement in the European Union (EU) has been governed by directives designed to prohibit hidden protectionism in the form of buy national public purchasing regimes.

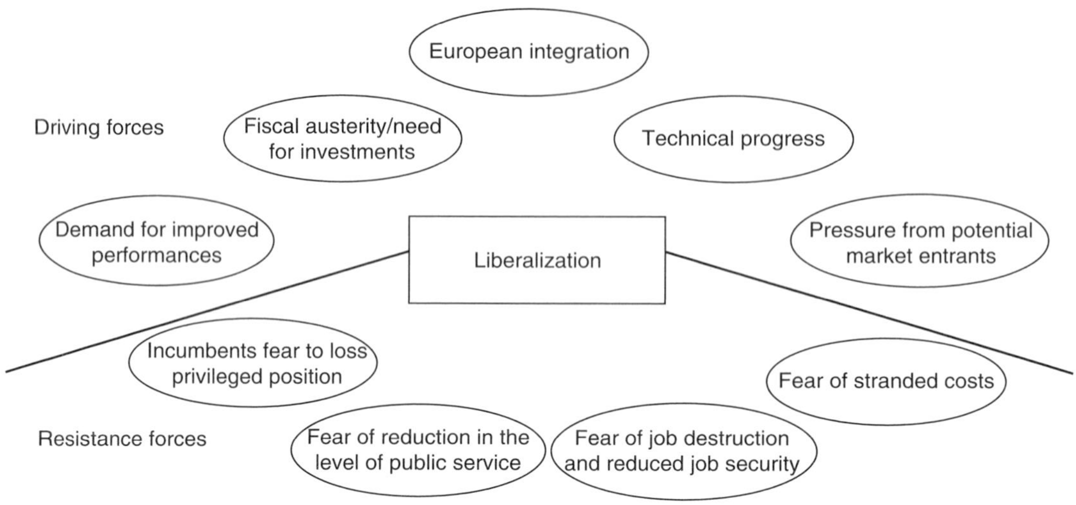

Figure 9.5 Main forces acting in liberalization process. (From European Commission, 1999.)

Notwithstanding several resistances (Figure 9.5), due to the public opinion pressure, in recent years outsourcing or buying-in of services from sources external to public bodies has emerged as a key policy option in several countries seeking to reform and improve the public service sector, and it is increasingly being recommended.

Conventionally, this has taken the form of using private contractors to operate public assets. Increasingly, government agencies are contracting to purchase services and are leaving the design, build, and ownership of the physical assets to the partner who delivers the service in what is known as services' contracting-out in the form of either privatization, or PPP, or public commercialization (Ancarani, 2003).

In spite of many critiques of the move to externalization of services by the late 1990s there was a much greater understanding than ever before that the market had a major potential role in supplementing—even sometimes replacing—the role of public sector in-house provision. With this understanding, however, came the realization that the public sector had traditionally misunderstood the range of possible relationships between actors in the market (Kettl, 1993; Boyne, 1998). With the dawning appreciation that market relationships were socially constructed in the procurement process, not simply a product of market conditions, the need became clear for a more proactive role by public sector organizations in market management and greater attention to developing mutually rewarding relationships with external contractors, whether they were in the public, private, or voluntary sectors (Erridge and Greer, 2002).

9.5 Strategic Approach to Services Procurement

Over the last decade, there have been a number of important drivers of change in public sector procurement, which reflect new strategic directions, new policies, and new practices in public service provision. Although these trends at least partly mirror similar developments in the private sector, the way they have played out in the public sector has had a number of distinctive aspects. The first key driver of these different procurement approaches is the nature of the organizational relationships in the procurement process (Bovaird, 2006). In the traditional model, it was adversarial, with the principal trying to find ways of procuring services from the agent on beneficial terms by means of contract mechanisms, which would curb any opportunistic behavior on the part of the agent and reduce the agent's inherent advantage that could stem from asymmetric access to information (Williamson, 1975). In the new approaches to procurement, the emphasis has switched dramatically to collaborative behavior whereby each party expects to reap benefits from helping to make the joint working more successful (Lorange and Roos, 1992; Dror and Hamel, 1998)—the creation of collaborative advantage (Huxham, 1993; Kanter, 1994). A recent survey suggested that half of U.K. local authorities now use partnerships as an approach to supplier relationships and a further 9 percent intend to introduce them in the future (Birch, 2001).

A second key driver of these different procurement approaches is the growth in the number of interfaces between service commissioners and service providers in the procurement process. This growth is partly due to the rapid fragmentation of public service commissioners and providers into a larger number of organizations. This is something that has been observed in most services and in most European countries (Mukherjee and Wilkins, 1999; Rosenau, 2004; Skelcher, 2005) and is partly due to the unbundling of services in the last two decades (Drucker, 1992; Hagel and Singer, 1999). The result has been greater challenges of coordination in the procurement decision and therefore the need for more systematic procurement procedures (Byatt, 2002; Erridge, 2003).

Usually, partnership purchasing is said to be superior because it leads to long-term collaboration based on trust between buyer and supplier. Bensaou (1999), however, found no performance differences among the different types of relationships. No one type of relationship, not even the strategic partnership, is inherently superior to the others. Each type of relationship can be well or poorly managed. Supply-chain management failure is the result of a mismatched relational design or a poorly managed appropriate design. Bensaou (1999) found, for instance, that successful strategic partnerships exhibit a high level of mutual trust, early supplier involvement in design, extensive cooperation, and a high level of information exchange. To be successful, organizations need to match the optimal type of relationship to the various product, market, and supplier conditions.

Within the public sector, however, there are conflicting developments (Parker and Hartley, 1997). For example, on the one hand, the regulatory directives and the compulsive competitive tendering legislation for government services are the driving bodies toward competitive supply arrangements. Tenders are based on the principle of arm's length relationships with little information sharing, contrary to the body of academic thinking which favors partnership agreements. On the other hand, most governments seek to promote relationships with suppliers combining competition and cooperation. For instance, the U.K. government's 1995 white paper on procurement emphasizes that relationships with suppliers need to combine competition and collaboration (Treasury, 1995). This reflects a recent change in the U.K. legislation whereby compulsory competitive tendering has been replaced by an emphasis on creating value through partnerships (Boyett et al., 1996; Hoxley, 2000; Lian and Laing, 2004). However, it is recognized that a number of conditions are required for partnerships sourcing in the public sector, not all of which are consistent with the partnership paradigm. These include competition to select the partner followed by periodic re-competition and a clear definition of the contractual responsibilities of both partners. Also, specific and measurable contract milestones for improved performance are necessary (Parker and Hartley, 1997).

The use of competition in the procurement of public services is now well established and central to the notion of the reinvention of government being pursued by many governments today. A central tenet of this approach is to require the providers of most public services to be chosen by competitive tendering (Smyth, 1997).

The regulatory procurement rules make it difficult for public purchasers to use collaborative approaches, even when the supply environment dictates that that this type of approach is appropriate. The process of change from arm's length relationships to partnerships is a difficult task for any organization to achieve. But it is even more difficult in public sector organizations, where profit-maximization has not been central to organizational behavior, and where past practices have been the basis for current operational decisions (Boyett et al., 1996). As government departments operate within a framework of public accountability and cost-effectiveness, considerable emphasis is placed on the fair treatment of suppliers, compliance, competitive tendering, and procedures for ensuring propriety and regularity, hindering the development of collaborative procurement arrangements (Erridge and Greer, 2002).

Because of the trend of strategic partnerships in the private sector, and because of the regulatory legislation prohibiting, or at least hindening, this type of procurement strategy within the public sector, organizations within the public sector put more emphasis on selection procedures, indicating the criteria for the selection in order to create a genuine competitive tendering situation.

However, the public sector has only relatively recently defined and applied a set of management techniques to evaluate and monitor their suppliers, such as formal evaluation systems and supplier certification programs. A certified supplier represents a vendor who, after extensive investigation of its manufacturing operations, production capabilities, personnel, and technology, is certified to provide materials and components without routine testing of each receipt. Because the public sector is increasingly operating in an environment defined by marketing principles and directed by business forces, these management practices are increasingly applied. But this is not an easy process because often the relevant skills and expertise needed to bring about these changes are absent within the public sector.

9.6 Supplier Selection, Regulation, and Control

The procedures for supplier selection are highly regulated everywhere (e.g., the EC Directives for public procurement are applied in all countries in Europe). They contain detailed prescriptions of tendering procedures regarding, for instance, how to advertise, how to handle incoming bids, and the choice of supplier, which has to be clearly motivated according to predetermined criteria. The tendering activities in the local authorities are performed by the contract managers or by special commercial units. An important competence is a thorough knowledge of the legislation.

The commercial regulation in the contract concerns the choice of contract period, procedures of payment, rules for dealing with unforseen contingencies sanction clauses, and arrangements for dealing with disputes. The contract period seems to vary between different types of service, and also, to some degree, between different countries.

The legal and commercial conditions of contracts are mainly designed by a support function from the authorities. The function is more developed in larger authorities, with a larger volume of contracts to handle. In smaller authorities, one solution is to delegate the commercial aspects to the controller function or to the legal department of the authority. Other solutions are to consult central purchasing departments or other service departments with expertise of contractual issues. A third alternative is to use external consultants or to get advice from other authorities or from general associations of local authorities.

Monitoring is a major problem in the management of contracts for public services because of the difficulties of specifying services in a way that is measurable. There is a special problem of how to organize the monitoring, because often the service is performed at many different locations.

The organization of monitoring depends on whether the service delivery is regulated by the written details of the contract or by a general evaluation of the performance. Finally, there is a problematic time dimension in the monitoring of maintenance services or network services. The results of a mistreatment of plants, assets, conduits, etc. will perhaps not show up until several years later, and the lack of proper maintenance of streets, sewers, or facilities will end up causing larger problems in the long run.

The cost of monitoring is considered as one of the main issues of contracting-out. A survey by the Audit Commission in 48 English authorities showed that the monitoring costs were about 50–60 percent of the costs of the client/purchasing function and about 1–6 percent of the total annual turnover in these services (Audit Commission, 1993). According to the analysis by the Audit Commission, the costs depend on the monitoring approach of the authority, the degree of uncertainty in the service, and the possibilities of involving the customer in the monitoring.

Different ways of organizing the monitoring function and different ways of assigning resources to it can be defined. At one extreme there is a reliance on the service users (e.g., in garbage collection, where you can be quite sure to hear from the customer if the garbage has not been collected as usual). Most authorities have or could easily develop some sort of systematic complaints procedure and different kinds of user survey for evaluation purposes. At the other end of the scale, there are strictly organized inspections several times a week.

Even if it is important to specify the contract in detail, the reference point for the evaluation of performance should be the relationship and not the details of the contract. This is also argued by MacNeil (1978), who suggests that in long-term relationships characterized by high uncertainty, it is more relevant to evaluate the performance according to the entire relationship as a reference point. This means that there can be a certain acceptance of errors, as long as they are corrected and the supplier relationship as a whole is judged as valuable and important. Special competences required for monitoring include good knowledge about what is agreed upon in the contract and a good knowledge of the service and its potential problems.

An aspect of the delivery control regards the procedures for payments and the connection to the approval of work. The purchasing officer authorizes the payment according to work reports from the monitoring officer or signed reports from the contractor. The conditions for the work are often discussed at regular meetings with the representatives of the contractor. These meetings function as an arena of early problem solving, adjustments of the specifications, and planning for the coming period.

In the control of service delivery, there is also a management control dimension. This includes economic reporting to the politicians in the service committees. This reporting has increased because of a general need to control the economy, but also because of the need to control contract expenditure.

9.7 Collaborative Relationships in the New Procurement Environment

Whereas the traditional in-house provision model involves no external parties, and the traditional contracting-out model is one of the atomistic competitions between many uncoordinated providers, which provide services to the commissioning principal, each of the new variants involves a significant degree of coordination, either of the commissioners or the providers, or of both. What has made for the largest changes, however, is where this coordination has moved further to positive collaboration. It is possible to distinguish three types of market relationship where these collaborative relationships have become important: (1) relational contracting, (2) partnership procurement, and (3) distributed commissioning.

Relational contracting, as a conceptual approach, derives from a number of theoretical sources—transaction cost minimization in economics (Walsh, 1995), economies of scope in collaborative networks (Piore and Sabel, 1984), strategic alliances (Lorange and Roos, 1992) and collaborative advantage (Huxham, 1993) in strategic management, and relationship marketing (Christopher et al., 2002).

Relational contracting first appeared as a major force in the U.K. public sector in the national health system (NHS) internal market (Le Grand and Bartlett, 1993) and in social services (Kirkpatrick et al., 2001) in the late 1980s and early 1990s. Since then, it has become the new conventional wisdom in public service contracting.

Nevertheless, it has still not become the dominant practice. Perhaps it is because the critical lesson at the heart of relational contracting—that partners who work together closely and learn to trust each other's contribution can be much more imaginative in the way they jointly seek to solve problems—demands both an open-minded approach to sharing and a willingness to innovate (Coulson, 1998). Neither of these are, as yet, common characteristics in public agencies (Allen, 2002). The former often falls foul of the political determination—evident both in national ministries and in individual local authorities—to maintain control over decision making rather than sharing responsibilities (Klijn and Teisman, 2004). In addition, the latter is often sacrificed to safety-first procedures because of the penalties attached to failure in public life (Perri et al., 2002). Because public sector service purchasers in such relationships are inherently monopsonistics, some analysts are suspicious of the long-term risks to private firms from entering into such long-term partnerships, and argue that the results of such partnerships can be lower payoffs for the final service user (Parker and Hartley, 1997).

Distributed commissioning involves a public sector purchaser in the task of enabling many smaller agencies, often geographically defined to determine for themselves the priorities between public services that will be provided for them.

Recent trends toward market-based approaches in public sector procurement have given a new impulse to the use of market management and marketing approaches and techniques, using marketing in the sense of the creation and maintenance of beneficial exchanges (Andreason and Kotler, 2003). Whereas in the compulsory competitive tendering (CCT) approach, marketing was conceived in largely operational terms, involving such activities as promotion and sales, and oriented primarily toward the end user, marketing is now much more often seen as an approach to multi-stakeholder co-planning, codesign, and comanagement of public services—in other words, as a set of collaborative relationships linking stakeholders in the pursuit of their mutual interests.

This change has been driven by factors both internal and external to the new partnerships. Whereas in-house provision can often function relatively straightforward by means of bureaucratic decision making, joint working requires increased sensitivity to the requirements of each partner and increased clarity about the aims and priorities of the partnership. In a context of relationship contracting, this can be partly handled simply by deepening the interactions between partners. However, in the contexts of partnership procurement and distributed commissioning, where arrangements are much more complex, an increased level of explicitness in how relationships will be conducted is likely to be required. This is likely to require that strategies for working together are formulated and agreed more formally than before, in order that all partners are kept fully informed and in line with partnership strategy and policy.

The issue of strategic collaboration in a context of distributed commissioning is a particularly thorny one. At the strategic level, there is a need for clear guidelines, to be agreed between the purchaser and the commissioning agencies because the commissioning agencies will have access to the purchaser's budget.

These guidelines normally set out the limits of the commissioner's discretion and any minimum standards to be imposed by the purchaser. At the service delivery level, agreements have to be reached on key issues such as pricing and concession policies and the range of access channels to be made available. Each of these issues can lead to disputes as to whether commissioning has genuinely been devolved or whether the purchaser is simply deflecting the flak for poor quality services or inappropriate strategic decisions in the local area to another agency.

9.8 Theories Pursuing Emergent Market Practice

Clearly, the emerging world of public sector procurement is now much more complex. This is not necessarily a problem—the dangers of fragmentation in service provision and agency structure that are created by these new market relationships are potentially offset by the concomitant possibilities of more imaginative and creative solutions to the wicked problems facing the public sector (Rittel and Weber, 1973). However, the result of these contrasting forces will depend greatly on the willingness and the capacity of public sector organizations to manage these new markets.

This willingness is clearly still a moot point, for example, even after several years of Best Value in the United Kingdom, many local authorities are reluctant to go much further along the outsourcing route, and many of those local authorities that express a willingness in theory have done little in practice (Martin and Bovaird, 2005). The capacity issue is partly a technical one and relates to skills available in public sector organizations, but it also relates to the power of the tools available.

Current practices in partnership and distributed procurement have been partly driven by changes in the conceptual frameworks used in marketing and market management in recent years, particularly the concepts of relationship marketing and strategic collaboration, but in practice these developments are in turn challenging current theoretical and conceptual frameworks.

The limitations of the traditional provider-centric models of services are shown up when the potential role of users within service systems is considered. Normann (1984) suggests that in service management systems the client appears twice, once as a customer of the service and then again as part of the service delivery system. Sometimes, service professionals do the service for the customer in which case Normann suggests that their role embodies a relieving logic.

However, services are often provided in a different way, one in which the service professional has an enabling role, and the client actually performs the service task per se. In this sense, the client becomes a coproducer of the service. Normann (1984) predicted that enabling relationships would become more prominent in the future and that relievers would experience tougher competition from service agencies, which emphasize the enabling role.

This tendency has been understood for some time—the concept of coproduction was originally mooted in the late 1970s (Zeleny, 1978; Lovelock and Young, 1979; Parks et al., 1981; Normann, 1984; Percy, 1984) and by the late 1990s it had already become well established in some parts of the private and public sectors. As a result, there had already been a partial changeover to the relieving logic of service provision. However, this has not occurred without major battles with some professional groups who have tended to assume that if the client gains the status of coproducer then the role and status of the professional will necessarily be diminished. As so often happens, there has been a predominance of provider-centric behavior in many contexts, however dominant is the rhetoric of user orientation. However, the issue is not simply one of managing new bilateral relationships. There are usually multiple relationships between service clients in the public sector and other stakeholders. Often, for example, service clients may coproduce welfare increases with service professionals. At the same time, the service client may coproduce welfare with others in their communities. Once service clients and community activists become engaged in the codesign and comanagement of services alongside professional staff, the networks created may behave as complex adaptive systems, which behave in ways that the professional and commercial providers cannot easily control and indeed may not fully understand (Stacey, 1996). The theories of relationship-building in relationship marketing and strategic collaboration are usually based on relatively linear cause-and-effect models, whereas relationship-building in multipurpose, multiagency, multilevel partnerships may be much more self-organized and less amenable to linear social engineering interventions.

The recognition that procurement decisions in the public sector involve the understanding of behaviors within complex adaptive systems is an important counterweight to the belief in linear procurement models, such as those which were embodied within CCT in the 1980s and most of the following decade. It means that procurement now has to be seen as a social rather than just a technical process. Furthermore, successful procurement requires knowledge of the initial conditions, the relationships between the players, and the psychological effects of procurement decisions on their behaviors. Indeed, given how common user coproduction has become in public services, the motivational effects of procurement decisions, in terms of mobilizing the resources of users, their careers and significant others, and their communities, may be much more important in public service improvement than any potential efficiency gains through purely technical or organizational reconfigurations.

References

Allen, E. 2002. *Managing Strategic Service Delivery Partnerships: From Governance to Delivery*, New Local Government Network, London.

Ancarani, A. 2003. The impact of public firms commercialisation on purchasing management. *Journal of Public Procurement*, 3(3), 357–369.

Ancarani, A. and Capaldo, G. 2005. Supporting decision making process in facility management services procurement: A methodological approach. *Journal of Purchasing and Supply Management*, 11(5–6), 232–241.

Andreason, A.A. and Kotler, P. 2003. *Strategic Marketing for Nonprofit Organizations*, 6th edn., Prentice Hall/Pearson Education International, Upper Saddle River, NJ.

Atkin, B. and Brooks, A. 2002. *Total Facilities Management*, Blackwell, Oxford.

Audit Commission, 1993. *The Client Role for Contracted Services*, Audit Guide, Audit Commission, London.

Axelsson, B. and Wynstra, F. 2002. *Buying Business Services*, Wiley, Chichester.

Baily, P., Farmer, D., Jessop, D., and Jones, D. 1994. *Purchasing Principles & Management*, 7th edn., Chartered Institute of Purchasing & Supply, Pitman Publishing, London.

Baily, P., Farmer, D., Jessop, D., and Jones, D. 1998. *Purchasing Principles & Management*, Prentice Hall, Harlow, UK.

Bensaou, M. 1999. Portfolios of buyer–seller relationships. *Sloan Management Review* (Summer), 35–44.

Berry, L.L. 1980. Services marketing is different. *Business*, 30, 24–29.

Berry, L.L. 1995. Relationship marketing of services-growing interest, emerging perspectives. *Journal of the Academy of Marketing Science*, 23, 236–245.

Berry, L.L. and Parasuraman, A. 1991. *Marketing Services: Competing through Quality*, Free Press, New York.

Bettis, R., Bradley, S., and Hamel, G. 1992. Outsourcing and industrial decline. *Academy of Management Executive*, 6(1), 7–22.

Birch, D. 2001. *Local Authority Procurement: A Research Report*, Department for Transport, Local Government and the Regions, London.

Bovaird, T. 2006. Developing new forms of partnership with the "market" in the procurement of public services. *Public Administration*, 84(1), 81–102.

Boston, J. 1996. The use of contracting in the public sector—recent New Zealand experience. *Australian Journal of Public Administration*, 55(3), 105–110.

Boyett, I., Robinson, P., Brown, A., and Finlay, D. 1996. Supplier–purchaser relationships within a quasi-market: The case of British Rail and British Steel Track Products. *European Journal of Purchasing and Supply Management*, 2, 145–151.

Boyne, G.A. 1998. Competitive tendering in local government: A review of theory and evidence. *Public Administration*, 76(4), 695–712.

Brackertz, N. and Kenley, R. 2002. A service delivery approach to measuring facility performance in local government. *Facilities*, 20(3/4), 127–135.

Byatt, I. 2002. *Delivering Better Services for Citizens: A Review of Local Government Procurement in England*, Department for Transport, Local Government and the Regions/the Local Government Association, London.

Cherubini, S. 1981. *Il marketing dei servizi*, Franco Angeli, Milano.

Christopher, M., Payne, A., and Ballantyne, D. 2002. *Relationship Marketing: Creating Stakeholder Value*, Butterworth-Heinemann, Oxford.

Clarke, M. and Stewart, J. 1988. *The Enabling Council*, Local Government Training Board, Luton.

Coulson, A. (ed.), 1998. *Trust and Contracts: Relationships in Local Government, Health and Public Services*, Policy Press, Bristol.

Cully, M., O'Reilly, A., Woodland, S., and Dix, G. 1999. *Britain at Work*, Routledge, London.

Czepiel, J.A. 1990. Service encounters and service relationships: Implications for research. *Journal of Business Research*, 20, 13–21.

de Boer, L. and Telgen, J. 1998. Purchasing practice in Dutch municipalities, *International Journal of Purchasing & Materials Management*, 34(2), 31–36.

Deakin, N. and Walsh, K. 1996. The enabling state: The role of markets and contracts. *Public Administration*, 74(Spring), 33–48.

Domberger, S. and Jensen, P. 1997. Contracting out by the public sector: Theory, evidence, prospects, *Oxford Review of Economic Policy*, 13(4), 67–78.

Doty, D.H. and Glick, W.H. 1994. Typologies as a unique form of theory building: Toward improved understanding and modelling, *Academy of Management Review*, 19(2), 230.

Dror, Y. and Hamel, G. 1998. *Alliance Advantage*, Harvard Business School Press, Cambridge, MA.

Drucker, P.F. 1992. Sell the mailroom: Unbundling in the 1990s, In: P.F. Drucker (ed.), *Managing for the Future: The 1990s, and beyond*, Butterworth-Heinemann, Oxford, pp. 220–223.

Erridge, A. 2003. Contracting for public services: Competition and partnership, In: T. Bovaird and E. Loeffler (eds.), *Public Management and Governance*, Routledge, London, pp. 89–99.

Erridge, A. and Greer, J. 2002. Partnerships and public procurement: Building social capital through supply relations. *Public Administration*, 80(3), 503–522.

Erridge, A., Fee, R., and McIlroy, J. 1999. An assessment of competitive tendering using transaction cost analysis. *Public Money and Management*, 19(3), 37–42.

Essig, M. and Batran, A. 2005. Public–private partnership—Development of long-term relationships in public procurement in Germany. *Journal of Purchasing and Supply Management*, 11, 221–231.

European Commission, Directorate-General for economic and financial affairs, 1999. *European Economy: Liberalization of Network Industries*, n. 4, Belgium.

Fearon, H. and Bales, W. 1995. *Purchasing of Non-Traditional Goods and Services*, Center for Advanced Purchasing Studies (CAPS), Tempe, AZ.

Fitzsimmons, J.A., Noh, J., and Thies, E. 1998. Purchasing business services. *Journal of Business and Industrial Marketing*, 13(4/5), 370–380.

Gadde, L.E. and Håkansson, H. 1993. *Professional Purchasing*, Routledge, London.

Graw, L. and Maples, M. 1994. *Service Purchasing: What Every Buyer Should Know?* Van Nostrand Reinhold, New York.

Grönroos, C. 1978. A service-orientated approach to marketing of services. *European Journal of Marketing*, 12, 588–601.

Grönroos, C. 1990. *Service Management and Marketing: Managing the Moments of Truth in Service Competition*. Lexington (MA), Lexington Books.

Hagel, J. and Singer, M. 1999. Unbundling the corporation. *Harvard Business Review*, March–April, 133–141.

Hoxley, M. 2000. Measuring U.K. construction professional service quality: The what, how, when and who. *International Journal of Quality and Reliability Management*, 17(4/5), 511–526.

Hui, E.Y.Y. and Tsang, A.H.C. 2004. Sourcing strategies of facility management. *Journal of Quality in Maintenance Engineering*, 10(2), 85–92.

Huxham, C. 1993. Collaborative capability: An intra-organisational perspective on collaborative advantage. *Public Money and Management*, 13(3), 21–28.

Kakabadse, A. and Kakabadse, N. 2005. Outsourcing: Current and future trends. *Thunderbird International Businsess Review*, 47(2), 183–204.

Kanter, R.M. 1994. Collaborative advantage: The art of alliances. *Harvard Business Review*, July–August, 96–108.

Kettl, D.F. 1993. *Sharing Power*, The Brookings Institute, Washington, D.C.

Kirkpatrick, I. and Lucio, M. 1996. The contract state and the future of public management. *Public Administration*, 74(Spring), 1–8.

Kirkpatrick, I., Kitchener, M., and Whipp, R. 2001. Out of sight-out of mind: Assessing the impact of markets for children's residential care. *Public Administration*, 79(1), 49–71.

Klijn, E.-H. and Teisman, G.R. 2004. Public–private partnerships, the right form at the wrong moment? An analysis of institutional and strategic obstacles, In: A. Ghobadian, D. Gallear, N. O'Regan, and H. Viney (eds.), *Public–Private Partnerships: Policy and Experience*, Palgrave Macmillan, Basingstoke.

Knight, L. and Harland, C. 1999. Outsourcing: A national and sector level perspective on policy and practice. In: *Proceedings of the Eighth IPSERA Conference*, Belfast, Dublin.

Kolchin, M. 1990. *Purchasing in the Industrial, Institutional, Governmental, and Retail Sectors: A Comparative Study*, Center for Advanced Purchasing Studies (CAPS), Tempe, AZ.

Larbi, G.A. 1998. Contracting-out in public health and water services in Ghana. *International Journal of Public Sector Management*, 11(2/3), 154–163.

Le Grand, J. and Bartlett, W. 1993. Quasi-markets and social policy: The way forward? In: J. Le Grand and W. Bartlett (eds.), *Quasi-Markets and Social Policy*, Macmillan, Basingstoke.

Lei, D. and Hitt, M. 1995. Strategic restructuring and outsourcing: The effect of mergers and acquisitions and LBOs on building firm skills and capabilities. *Journal of Management*, 21(5), 835–859.

Lian, P.C.S. and Laing, A.W. 2004. Public sector purchasing of health services: A comparison with private sector purchasing. *Journal of Purchasing & Supply Management*, 10, 247–256.

Lorange, P. and Roos, J. 1992. *Strategic Alliances: Formation, Implementation and Evolution*, Blackwell, Oxford.

Lovelock, C. and Young, R.F. 1979. Look to customers to increase productivity, *Harvard Business Review*, 57 (May–June), 168–178.

MacNeil, I. 1978. Contracts: Adjustment of long-term economic relations under classical, neo-classical, and relational contract law. *Northwestern University Law Review*, 72(6), 854–905.

Martin, S. and Bovaird, T. 2005. *Service Improvement in Local Government*, Office of the Deputy Prime Minister, London.

Mechling, J. 1995. *Information Technology and Government Procurement: Priorities for Reform*, John F. Kennedy School of Government, Harvard University, Cambridge, MA.

Moore, M. 1995. *Creating Public Value: Strategic Management in Government*, Harvard University Press, Cambridge, MA.

Mukherjee, R. and Wilkins, J.K. 1999. Unbundling bureaucracy through agency creation, Paper presented at the *IPAC National Conference*, 30 August, New Brunswick, Canada.

Normann, R. 1984. *Service Management*, John Wiley, Chichester.

Normann, R. 1992. *Service Management*, Liber Ekonomi, Stockolm.

Ouchi, W.G. 1980. Markets, bureaucracies and clans. *Administrative Science Quarterly*, 25(1), 129–141.

Parasuraman, A., Zeithaml, V.A., and Berry, L.L. 1985. A conceptual model of service quality and its implications for future research. *Journal of Marketing*, 49, 41–50.

Parker, D. and Hartley, K., 1997. The economics of partnership sourcing versus adversarial competition: A critique. *European Journal of Purchasing and Supply Management*, 3(2), 115–125.

Parks, R.B., Baker, P.C., Kiser, L., Oakerson, R., Ostrom, V., Percy, S.L., Vandivort, M.B., Whitaker, G.P., and Wilson, R. 1981. Consumers as co-producers of public services: Some economic and institutional considerations. *Policy Studies Journal*, 9(7), 1001–1011.

Patterson, A. and Pinch, P. 1995. Hollowing out the local state: Compulsory competitive tendering and the restructuring of British public sector service. *Environment and Planning*, A27, 1437–1461.

Payne, A. 1995. *Advances in Relationship Marketing*, Kogan Page, London.

Percy, S. 1984. Citizen participation in the co-production of urban services. *Urban Affairs Quarterly*, 19(4), 431–446.

Perri 6, Leat, D., Seltzer, K., and Stoker, G. 2002, *Towards Holistic Governance: The New Reform Agenda*, Palgrave, Houndmills.

Pettijohn, C. and Qiao, Y. 2000. Procuring technology: Issues faced by public sector organizations. *Journal of Public Budgeting, Accounting & Financial Management*, 12(1), 441–461.

Piore, M. and Sabel, C. 1984. *The Second Industrial Order: Possibilities for Prosperity*, Basic Books, New York.

Postner, H. 1990. The contracting-out problem in service sector analysis: Choice of statistical unit. *Review of Income and Wealth*, 36(2), 177–186.

Powell, W.W. 1990. Neither market nor hierarchy: Network forms of organisation. *Research in Organisational Behaviour*, 12, 295–336.

Prahalad, C.K. and Hamel, G. 1990. The core competencies of the corporation. *Harvard Business Review*, May–June, 79–90.

Rittel, H.W.J. and Weber, W.W. 1973. Dilemmas in a general theory of planning, *Policy Sciences*, 4, 155–169.

Rosenau, J. 2004. Strong demand, huge supply: Governance in an emerging epoch, In: I. Bache and M. Filinders (eds.), *Multi-Level Governance*, Oxford University Press, Oxford.

Sachdev, S. 2001. Contracting culture-from CCT to PPPs: The private provision of public services and its impact on employment relations. *Report UNISON*. http://www.unison.org.uk/acrobat/12080.pdf.

Schiele, J.J. and McCue, C.P. 2006. Professional service acquisition in public sector procurement. A conceptual model of meaningful involvement. *International Journal of Operations & Production Management*, 23(3), 300–325.

Shostack, G.L. 1977. Breaking free from product marketing. *Journal of Marketing*, 41, 73–80.

Skelcher, C. 2005. Jurisdictional integrity, polycentrism and the design of democratic governance. *Governance*, 18(1), 89–110.

Smyth, J.D. 1997. Competition as a meant of procuring public services. *International Journal of Public Sector Management*, 10(1/2), 21–46.

Stacey, R. 1996. *Complexity and Creativity in Organisations*, Berrett Koehler, San Francisco, CA.

Stainer, A. and Stainer, L. 1998. Strategic change in public services: A productivity and performance perspective. *Strategic Change*, 7, 111–119.

Steane, P.D. and Walker, D.H.T. 2000. Competitive tendering and contracting public sector services in Australia—A facility management issue, *Facilities*, 18(5/6), 245–255.

Stinchcombe, A.L. 1990. *Information and Organizations*, University of California Press, Berkeley, CA.

Treasury, 1995. *Setting New Standards: A Strategy for Government Procurement*, Cm2840, London, HMSO.

Van Weele, A.J. 2005. *Purchasing and Supply Chain Management*, 4th edn., Thomson Learning, London.

Venkatesan, A.L. 1992. Sourcing: To make or not to make. *Harvard Business Review*, November–December, 98–107.

Walker, H., Knight, L., and Harland, C. 2001. Imbalanced supply markets: A sector level perspective on the case of outsourced services. In: *Proceedings of the Tenth IPSERA Conference*, Jonkoping, Sweden.

Walsh, K. 1995. *Public Services and Market Mechanisms: Competition, Contracting and New Public Management*, Macmillan Press, Basingstoke.

Williamson, O.E. 1975. *Markets and Hierarchies: Analysis and Anti-Trust Implications*, Free Press, New York.

Williamson, O.E. 1985. *The Economic Institutions of Capitalism*, Free Press, New York.

Wynstra, F., Axelsson, B., and Van deer Valk, W. 2006. An application-based classification to understand buyer–supplier interaction in business services. *International Journal of Service Industry Management*, 17(5), 474–496.

Zeithaml, V.A. 1981. How consumer evaluation process differ between goods and services. In: Donnelly, J. and George, W. (eds.), *Marketing of Services*, American Marketing Association, Chicago, IL.

Zeithaml, V.A. and Bitner, M.J. 1996. *Service Marketing*, McGraw-Hill, New York.

Zeleny, M. 1978. *Towards Self-Service Society*, Columbia University Press, New York.

Chapter 10

How Many Vendors Does It Take to Screw Down a Price? A Primer on Competition in Procurement

Jeffrey M. Keisler and William A. Buehring

CONTENTS

10.1 Introduction

In the mid to late 1990s, the Department of Energy (DOE) undertook a "privatization" initiative for the Hanford site waste cleanup. The DOE had a large amount of hazardous and nuclear waste to process, and had planned to have a vendor or vendors develop new technologies such as vitrification (glass bricks) or grouting (embedding waste in a stone-like substance). After proving their technology on a trial basis, vendor(s) would then build capacity to process all the waste. DOE planned to ultimately pay for waste processed on a per-unit basis. For practical purposes, the minimum rate of processing was determined by the fact that the fixed existing amount of waste had to be processed within a given time based on agreements DOE had signed.

There was a debate within DOE about how to structure the cottage industry that this initiative would create. DOE's traditional approach was to build a facility and have an operations and management (O&M) contractor operate it on a cost-plus type basis. To minimize costs in this regime, the DOE would build a single facility rather than duplicate its efforts. There was a lot of pressure for adopting this viewpoint to minimize startup costs. But how well would this work under privatization?

One of the main reasons for the privatization initiative was the belief that competitive forces of private industry would lead to substantially reduced costs on a task that in the best case was forecast to cost tens of billions of dollars. Based on past experiences, however, some DOE staff were concerned that merely choosing a single lowest bid would lead to a situation where the vendor would then find a pretext and raise its price enough to eliminate the savings.

While developing its request for proposals (RFP) for the first phase of the cleanup, technology development, and proof of concept, DOE had to make a decision about how many vendors to support. After the first phase, it would be difficult to add new vendors, and it could be problematic to remove vendors.

At that point in time, we conducted a study to inform DOE's debate about the necessary number of vendors. Making the assumption that renegotiation would inevitably occur, we wanted to understand the implications of the initial conditions that DOE would create for the industry—number of contractors and their capacities and cost structures. Specifically, we wanted to understand the prices that the industry could support and therefore, what DOE could expect to pay. A related issue was how much profits vendors could expect to earn, and this was important to understand because there was uncertainty over whether the whole prospect would be attractive enough to solicit a sufficient number of bids.

Our intent was to provide qualitative insights to inform the broad debate about whether to have one vendor or many, rather than to develop a precise decision and forecasting model. The numbers we use, although disguised, were meant to approximate the situation faced by DOE. This study influenced DOE's decision (DOE Privatization Working Group, 1998) to contract with two vendors rather than one. Although an even higher number of vendors might have been preferable, in the political environment at that time, where the DOE had no choice but to meet short-term cost reduction goals, even starting with two vendors was a relative victory. For well-documented reasons (e.g., Welch, 2000), the privatization initiative never came to full fruition. Our findings, however, were not specific to this situation and we present and analyze them here in more general form to provide valuable background to other government agencies.

10.2 Theoretical Background

10.2.1 Government Agencies and Competitive Bidding

As budgets decrease, government agencies are under increasing pressure to reduce costs without compromising their missions. An important mechanism for cost-cutting is procurement practices that facilitate competition among vendors, so that government agencies benefit from efficiencies inherent in private enterprise. Often, the government is the only customer for certain products or services; that is, a natural market for such products does not exist. In such cases, the government must create a market structure by defining rules by which firms must play.

The challenge is to define rules that create enough competition to be cost-effective without deterring entrants; give and take is necessary between government and potential vendors. A model has been designed to examine some tools that the government can use in establishing this market. This study provides general insights and specific process recommendations (e.g., questions to ask, factors to quantify) for decision makers. The goal is to transmit some lessons learned from previous modeling efforts for the benefit of future procurement managers.

In this study, it is assumed that the government (or another monopsonistic buyer) wishes to procure a fixed quantity of a good over a fixed time. The ability to establish and maintain a sufficient level of competition among vendors is one of the major uncertainties that affects the cost of service procurements, and one of the least understood. For example, it is unclear to policy makers whether one or two vendors, or even more, are needed to ensure price competition. Through economic theory and, in particular, industrial organization, methods have been developed to describe and predict the competitive environment for an industry.

The situation considered in this study is a fairly typical government procurement problem. The good being procured is not a commodity for which a competitive market price has been established. Rather, the government, as the primary customer, must agree on a price with its vendors. Economies of scale are assumed to be present, which means that (1) barriers to entry exist and (2) least-cost solution in the absence of transaction costs is to have a regulated monopoly, that is, a single company providing the good for a standardized rate of profit. In addition, it is assumed that the government is obligated to purchase an exogenously determined quantity of the good. Thus, at the time of initial bids, a monopsony is in place so that competitive prices might be anticipated, and in some cases it may be optimal to simply bid out the whole contract all at once (e.g., Engel et al., 2002). Other recent research, however, suggests that up-front bidding processes are ripe for intentional or unintentional exploitation, for example, Athey and Levin (2001) show that bidders can exploit inside information on values involved.

Once a vendor signs the contract, however, simple bilateral negotiation takes place between a monopsonist and a monopolist, with no clear equilibrium price. Because the government must purchase a fixed quantity, its prospects for obtaining a pre-signing equilibrium price are low; the vendor can be expected to raise the price, renegotiating on the basis of some unforeseen contingency, to a new equilibrium. If significant transaction costs are involved in writing a contract precisely enough to preclude such contingencies, the opportunistic vendor can take advantage of the situation. Furthermore, in the same type of complex situation even up-front bids made in good faith have the potential to be inefficient (Hong and Shum, 2002).

This study explores the circumstances under which excess vendor profits caused by asymmetric power offset the greater cost-efficiency of a single-vendor solution, as, for example, Ewerhart and Fieseler (2003) suggest. Put another way, this study examines the optimal excess capacity to build to establish competition. The answer depends on several quantifiable characteristics (described later). The intent is that insights and lessons learned from this model can be applied to similar future procurement transactions.

Accordingly, we modeled an ongoing competitive bidding process. Numerous scenarios were defined in terms of the set of vendors, their fixed and variable cost structures, their capacities, and the allocation rule by which market share is determined on the basis of the prices bid. For each scenario, the model computes the Nash equilibrium (Nash, 1950), that is, a set of prices bid by each vendor, so that no vendor can improve its position by raising or lowering its price. When the Nash equilibrium exists, a unique set of bids hold up if all firms try to maximize profit. Other models may suggest different equilibria based on different assumptions about vendor behavior (e.g., price leader/follower models).

Realistic predictions for what will happen when the government attempts competitive procurement are hard to obtain. For this study, a number of stylized scenarios have been analyzed to explore specific questions (one issue per scenario). The findings are then summarized as general insights and specific estimates of cost savings under defined competitive conditions for sample scenarios. The primary finding is that cost reduction attainable through wise management of the competitive environment can be of the same order as the total cost of the project.

It is difficult to quantify the competitive situation that would be best for a given agency. Simulation of the competitive environment makes it possible to explicitly compute the premium the government agency would pay over the vendor's actual costs. The simulation also takes into account how much power (i.e., ability to create a situation to one's liking) the situation gives to the government and various vendors.

10.2.2 Level of Competition

Understanding how to create and maintain competition (in the context assumed here) could allow agencies to lower costs. These benefits include the following:

- If prices were to be set below those determined through a competitive process, there would be a constant threat that prices would be raised under any pretext. In fact, prices would probably be raised once the agency's dollar limit was discovered.
- If prices were set above those of a competitive equilibrium, the government agency would pay less if it allowed competition to set prices.
- If a government agency understands what a sufficient level of competition is, it can establish and maintain adequate and consistent competition for the duration of a program.
- If competition adequately determines prices, an adverse change in a vendor's situation could lead to renegotiation of a price that would be competitive, while still fairly addressing changes in circumstances. Without sufficient competition, on the other hand, renegotiation is more a threat than a matter of fairness.
- If an agency understood the effect of competition on its own costs, it would better understand whether vendor profits are reasonable. Some vendor profitability, but not too much, is good for the government because it keeps multiple competitors in business. Bids that appear to provide insufficient profitability could be attempts to force out competitors.

This section describes the characteristics that, when present, make competitive procurement an attractive option for government agencies.

10.2.3 Cutting Costs

Experience with procurement shows that appropriate competition often cuts costs, but it does not explain how costs are lowered. Procurement refers to a situation in which a single purchaser (usually a government agency) buys a product or service for its own use; it is assumed in this study to require the development of dedicated facilities. Significant differences exist between government-agency-style procurement of management services and classic, military-style procurement of weapons.

Examined in this study are the development and provision on a long-term basis of an essentially continuous flow of product with significant fixed and variable costs. A number of technical solutions to the government's procurement problem are possible. With this type of economic structure, common in large-scale procurement scenarios, the government may benefit from establishing competition.

10.2.4 Feasibility and Benefits

In theory, competition is sometimes, but not always, feasible and beneficial in procurement. Basically, the procurement process consists of two stages: bidding and postcontract. The potential for competition in the bidding stage is great, whereas vendors often attempt to raise prices during the latter stage. Once work begins, the chances of keeping a tight competitive lid on prices can decrease because the government agency may be unable to switch vendors in the middle of a project. Second sourcing can help resolve this problem.

Deciding whether competition is worthwhile and should be encouraged depends on several factors: constraints, goals, and specific details of the situation; feasibility of creating competition; costs of maintaining competition (and excess vendors and capacity); and benefit in terms of reduced prices (or at least prices that are not raised) from competition. Table 10.1 provides an incomplete list of such factors. It is a matter of judgment where any specific situation lies on the spectrum for each factor and whether the net effect of these factors strengthens competition.

10.2.5 Data on the Benefits of Competition

Limited data is available on the benefits of competition in procurement. Data may be limited because of the long lag time between the start of a procurement test and the incorporation of its results into data sets. Because empirical information is limited (billions of dollars are needed to run a reasonable test), many researchers use the same data. Although it is worthwhile to consider the data, it is also necessary to assess how well this data apply to any specific procurement situation. The lack of data makes it necessary to rely, to some extent, on theoretical models and to evaluate the reasonableness of their implications for procurement.

10.2.6 Summary of Theoretical and Empirical Literature

Decisions about the level of competition necessarily must be made under uncertain conditions. The data, however, seems to support dual sourcing and bids by private contractors.

Theoretical arguments (not detailed here) also tend to support competition for cases that do not fall clearly into either pure competition or pure government control. The existence of such techniques as lowballing (and the expectation of barriers to entry after contracting) favors ongoing competition after initial contracts are awarded. The presence of economies of scale and the potential for implicit collusion make it less attractive to try to establish ongoing competition; however, laws are in place to prevent explicit collusion. In practice, some mixed set of variations on basic competitive themes (e.g., multiple sourcing, competitive bidding) may be needed to capture benefits of competition while avoiding complicating factors (see Table 10.2).

Table 10.1 Factors Affecting Competitive Procurement

Panel 1. Factors Relating to Benefits of Market Solution		
Factor	*Benefit of Multiple Sourcing Is High If Factor Is*	*Benefit of Single Contractor Is High If Factor Is*
Capacity	High	Low
Economies of scale	Low	High
Potential price sensitivity	High	Low
Length of commitment	Short	Long
Barriers to late entry/reentry	High	Low
Learning potential	Significant	Insignificant
Ability of buyer to walk away from a particular seller	Unclear	Unclear
Opportunity cost	Low	High
Buyer's knowledge of costs	No	Yes
Panel 2. Factors Relating to Risk of Collusion		
Factor	*Collusion Is Likely If Factor Is*	*Collusion Is Unlikely If Factor Is*
Complexity of technology	Low	High
Complexity of price format	Low	High
Number of big players	Few	Many
Ease of communication between players	Easy	Hard
Frequency of purchase	Infrequent	Frequent
Panel 3. Factors for Private Contractor versus Government Control		
Factor	*Private Contractor Favored If Factor Is*	*Government Control Favored If Factor Is*
Severity of impact of failure	Low	High
Externalities	Low	High
Collective interests	Low	High
Distributional goals	Low	High
Process affects preferences	No	Yes
Equity among bidders	Yes	No

Table 10.2 Data on the Benefits of Competitive Procurement

Study	*Topic*	*Data*
Uttley and Harper, 1993	Privatization of local services. Investigation of the effect of introducing a competitor to government.	With competition, private provider outbid government 80 percent of the time, with an average savings of 20 percent. The primary source of savings was technology, with secondary savings because people work more hours for less pay.
Hilke, 1992	Analysis of Department of Defense concludes that privatization value is limited. Savings come from allocative efficiency (e.g., prices determine what gets made) and production efficiency (e.g., better management/ technology).	Private providers won 65 percent of competitions, and the government won 35 percent, with average savings of 35 percent in both cases. Increasing competition is difficult because dollar benefits are delayed. Postcontractual opportunism occurs to a modest extent. Cost savings estimated at $10,000 per employee.
Pilling, 1989	Existing data is of poor quality, so analyzes military procurement for items costing less than $10,000 each.	Second sourcing prevents prices from being raised, but does little to reduce prices. One in 17 initial producers wins in later competition, which implies that second sourcing does not force much learning for the primary source. Runner-up price in the first period should be a contract to develop design for the second period.
Bajari and Ye, 2001	Firms collude in bidding and furthermore it is hard to detect such collusion when cost drivers are complex.	Seal-coating of roads for cities. Several pairs of firms appear to have nonindependent bids, although they do not bid against each other often.
Carrick, 1988	The author analyzes the Navy Commercial Activity program, focusing on how often government bids beat private contractors (mostly small-scale items).	Government does better than chance would predict; on average, it is no less or more efficient than private contractors. Efficiency is realized, however, only when competition is opened.
Anton and Yao, 1990	Empirical models and data are flawed. The authors offer methodology that compares predicted cost curve without competition to actual cost curve.	The median savings from competition were 37 percent (ranging from 0 to 60 percent). "Winner-take-all" awards do better than split awards (can be implemented after a learning period). The number of bidders is not significant in predicting savings. The initial savings were 24–40 percent, which represents a small improvement in the learning curve. Savings result from reduced margins and costs. Suggests competition when capacity utilization is less than 80 percent.

(*continued*)

Table 10.2 (continued) Data on the Benefits of Competitive Procurement

Study	*Topic*	*Data*
Morgan, 1992	Competition is necessary for savings in privatization.	Negative examples from Oklahoma sewage are given, but without statistics.
Poole and Fixler, 1987	The authors study local garbage pickup, municipal building maintenance, etc. by analyzing 1970s National Science Foundation data.	Providing services in-house costs 37–96 percent more than providing services from an outside source.

10.3 Model

In this section, two examples are used to demonstrate a model developed to assist in understanding the effect of price competition in procurement. The next section shows results from a number of possible situations.

10.3.1 Base Case Assumptions

The first example, base case, operates under the following illustrative assumptions that, for the purpose of estimating the relative benefit of competition, have similar characteristics to the actual numbers faced by DOE:

- Government agency requires 100 units of a product.
- Vendors set their price to maximize their profit.
- Government agency has two vendors with identical fixed and variable costs. (This strong assumption can later be relaxed.)
- Each vendor builds a plant that can fulfill 60 percent of the government's needs.
- Fixed cost to each vendor for building a plant is $1 million.
- Vendor's per-unit variable cost of production is $71,500. The base case assumes that variable costs per unit are constant. A more complex assumption could have been added (i.e., operating costs consist of both variable and fixed components or that production costs behave in some other nonlinear way).
- Each vendor proposes to charge a fixed price per unit.
- Each vendor's costs are known to all vendors. This assumption keeps the model simple. Vendors use their best estimates about each others' and their own costs and bid to maximize their expected profit.
- Vendors cannot drop out; that is, they must accept any amount of production work they are awarded by the buyer up to their capacity. Although this assumption is not reasonable in most cases, it is included because it significantly simplifies the construction of the competition model. A more complex model could be developed in which this assumption does not hold. For present purposes, when this assumption is critical, it is not used in drawing conclusions.
- Buyer allocates shares of the total production volume S to vendors on the basis of their proposed price P. Specifically, the base case assumes that each vendor receives a share S_i based on its bid price P_i, the bid of the other vendor, and a price sensitivity parameter g (typically multiplied by –1 when used as an exponent here) according to the logit function:

$$S_1 = \frac{P_1^{-g}}{\left(P_1^{-g} + P_2^{-g}\right)} \tag{10.1}$$

Similarly,

$$S_2 = \frac{P_2^{-g}}{\left(P_1^{-g} + P_2^{-g}\right)}$$

And if there are n vendors, the general equation for computing vendor i's share based on its bid price and the other vendors' bid prices is

$$S_i = \frac{(P_i)^{-g}}{\sum_{j=1\ldots n}(P_j)^{-g}}$$

For example, if two vendors offer prices of \$85,800/unit and \$114,450/unit (numbers fabricated), Equation 10.1 predicts the first vendor's share for $g = 2$ would be

$$85{,}800^{-2}/(85{,}800^{-2} + 114{,}450^{-2}) = 64 \text{ percent}$$

The logit function is used to describe the behavior of markets, such as energy markets (Baughman and Joskow, 1974), where price is an important, but not the only, determinant of share. It is often used to estimate the probability that a single consumer will choose one product in cases having multiple attributes of unknown value. By using actual aggregate government (or consumer) purchase data, the logit function is applied in the reverse direction to estimate the trade-off values that government agencies place on different product attributes (McFadden, 1975, 1976; Beggs and Strong, 1982). Particular services have multiple attributes, and some are specified (i.e., cost per unit in some dimensions). For each micro-level decision (e.g., government offers a small fraction of the total 100 units in each contract), it is reasonable to predict the probability that one vendor will be preferred over another by using the logit function, and therefore the aggregate share achieved by each vendor would be given by Equation 10.1. This assumption about how the buyer allocates market share is for convenience. The actual rule may or may not be under the buyer's control and depends on much more detailed price and value factors than could be specified in the future.

In this case, the parameter g (or gamma) represents the sensitivity of a vendor's share (allocated by the buyer) to the price it proposes to charge. The higher g is, the more important price is in determining share. Specifically, when n identical vendors start with the same price, the percent increase in a vendor's volume for a 1 percent drop in price is $g\,(n - 1)/n$. For example, consider two vendors who initially bid \$286,000/unit for a total of 100 units, and $g = 3$. If one vendor were to reduce its price by 1 percent to \$283,140/unit, the buyer would increase the work awarded to that vendor by 1.5 percent, from 50 to 50.75 units.

The desire to maintain competition, as well as differential capabilities of vendors and friction in shifting of production between plants, may make pure price competition unlikely, so g is set at a moderate level of price sensitivity (2.5) in the base case. In empirical work on energy choice, cross-price elasticities range from 2 to 3. The range of what is reasonable could vary significantly on the basis of what is done to improve the government's flexibility in switching allocations of share based on price.

A policy in which share does not depend on bid price would correspond to $g = 0$. A policy in which the low bidder always produces and sells to the government as much as it can buy would correspond to an infinite value of g.

The actual sensitivity of share to price is determined by factors such as uncertainty, switching costs, diseconomies of scale, political pressures, and the need to ensure continuing competition over time. The combination of these factors determines, for example, whether government should establish a winner-take-all market because of its production economies of scale.

The competition model determines the prices that vendors charge the government in a one-period model (i.e., prices and shares are set once and assumed to stay constant for the duration of the program). To determine costs from competition, the model starts vendors at prices equal to their marginal costs. For each set of prices, the model computes a vendor's profits. The profit Pr for each vendor is defined as

$$\mathrm{Pr} = (P - V) \times Q - F \tag{10.2}$$

where

P is price charged to the buyer per unit
V is variable cost per unit
Q is quantity produced (output)
F is fixed cost for building a plant

The model then simulates a cycle in which the first vendor raises prices to the point of maximum profit. This is where additional price increases would reduce profit by more than a threshold level because the effect of decreasing market share more than offsets the effect of increasing revenue per unit. The second vendor also adjusts prices to the profit maximizing level, assuming the first vendor's prices remain unchanged. This cycle continues until neither vendor acting on price alone can improve its profit.

This set of prices is called an "equilibrium." In this case, an equilibrium unit price calculated by the model is \$356,700 for both vendors; although if vendors had different cost structures, they would probably charge different prices in equilibrium. Each vendor receives 50 percent of the total production order. Again, if the vendors had different cost structures, they would probably receive different shares.

10.3.2 Equilibrium Prices and Their Relevance

The market equilibrium price expresses the level of competition to the world, and this concept is critical in understanding the benefits of competition. A market is in equilibrium when the set of prices and corresponding volumes is such that no single firm can improve its expected profit by either raising or lowering its price. The competition model computes the market equilibrium, prices, and market share by simulation. Mathematically, equilibrium occurs when the derivative of profit with respect to price is zero for each firm:

$$\begin{aligned} \mathrm{dPr}_i/\mathrm{d}P_i &= \partial \mathrm{Pr}_i/\partial P_i + (\partial \mathrm{pr}_i/\partial Q_i)\,(\partial Q_i/\partial P_i) \\ &= Q_i + (P_i - V_i)(\partial Q_i/\partial P_i) = 0 \end{aligned} \tag{10.3}$$

When Equation 10.1 is used to compute share and the price is expressed in dollars per unit share, then equilibrium can be computed analytically, through a bulky equation, by setting the total derivative of profit with respect to price equal to zero for each vendor. Equilibrium is important for the following reasons:

- Equilibrium arises when vendors act in their own self-interest. For this reason, equilibria are self-regulating in contrast to mandated price schemes.
- For economic analysis in a private business-driven system, equilibrium analysis is the only way to estimate (or influence) prices. In general, controls on prices that conflict with equilibrium prices are artificially imposed and impinge on free enterprise, which tends to reduce efficiency.
- Because the conditions for what constitutes equilibrium are precisely defined, equilibria (if they exist) can be estimated with precision if data is complete. This fact allows a quantitative simulation of the effect of changes to the plan, rather than mere speculation about whether those changes would lower procurement costs.

Returning to the base case, in an equilibrium, the vendors' total revenues are about $17,835,000 each (50 × $356,700), and their total costs are $4,575,000 each ([50 × $71,500] + $1 million). The difference between revenues and costs is profit, which, in this case, is $13,260,000 per vendor.

To test whether the outcome predicted for the base case is an equilibrium, consider the following experiment: if the first vendor raised its price to $372,000/unit to try to increase profit, the buyer would purchase fewer units (i.e., 47.4 units), and the vendor's profit would drop to $13,250,000 in spite of its increased price. Conversely, if the first vendor lowered its price to $343,400/unit to try to take more of the second vendor's share, its share would rise only to 52.4 units, which is not enough to offset its lost revenues, as the new profit would be $13,255,000. The same applies for the second vendor.

Interestingly, these equilibrium prices are far above vendor costs. Although the total cost incurred by vendors ([fixed costs + variable costs] × units produced) is only $9,150,000, the buyer pays $35,670,000 for the product. The vendors' profit is $26,520,000. Even an inefficient cost-plus contractor would probably cost government less. The problem is that this case does not have sufficient real competition to control prices.

A simple algebraic formula is not available to determine an equilibrium in all cases. However, economics textbooks give the general characteristics of an equilibrium when the relationship between price and share is well behaved (e.g., share decreases smoothly as price increases, going asymptotically to zero as price increases and to one as price decreases, with no points of inflection in between). Specifically, the first-order partial derivatives of profit with respect to all controllable variables are zero for all firms, and the second-order partial derivatives (the Hessian) are all negative.

In our example, the government agency could set a cap below the prices (e.g., $228,900/unit) referred to above, which would result in a total cost to that agency of $22,890,000. Vendors would still profit enough to accept the proposal. For efficiency, it could select a single supplier at such a price. Common economic advice for dealing with monopolies is to impose an up-front charge in return for granting a monopoly, where the charge is large enough to make up for the later excess profits expected to accrue to the monopolist.

The problem is that government agencies often lack flexibility in the quantity needed. If the agency sets a price cap and the vendors raise prices to that cap, there is no real competition. If competition were sufficiently intense, the market would self-regulate, and the competitively determined prices would be below the agency's price cap.

10.3.3 Base Case Plus Intense Competition

In this second case, all factors are identical to those in the base case, except that a third vendor, with a cost structure and capacity similar to the first two (fixed costs of $1 million, variable costs of $71,500/unit, and 60 percent capacity), is added. The simulated bidding process now leads to an equilibrium price of $178,100 for the three vendors. Each vendor receives one-third of the total volume to be produced and sustains lower (though still substantial) profits of $2,575,000. The total costs incurred by vendors are somewhat higher ($10,157,400) because a third plant has been built. Total payments by the government agency, however, are reduced by 50 percent (i.e., $17,800,000).

In this case, the threat of being undercut by the other vendors keeps each vendor from raising its prices. Therefore, adding a third vendor saves the government about $18 million. Also, the presence of both additional capacity and vendors increases the buyer's power (e.g., its ability to shop around) compared with that of the vendor.

These two cases illustrate an important lesson. Rather than simply focusing on understanding vendor costs, which would be appropriate for cost-plus type contracting, it is also important for the government agency to recognize the competitive environment in which contracts are signed and prices are set. Regardless of what the buyer wants to pay, the vendors will charge what the buyer will bear unless the vendors keep each other in check.

10.4 Sensitivity Analysis

This section contains variations on the base case example to approximate systematically the impact of other factors on government-agency costs. For each factor (number of vendors, total capacity, price sensitivity, and cost structure), an equilibrium resulting from each of a range of possible values is computed, and the results are tabulated. The results of scenarios are summarized as follows: how the situation varies from the base case; what are the new government costs and other outputs; and what lessons should be drawn from the result.

10.4.1 Government Payments and the Number of Vendors

Starting with the base case, the number of vendors varied from one to five; all other factors remained constant. It was determined that government costs would drop by 60 percent, particularly when four vendors were bidding. Using five vendors drives profits to near zero. Using more than five vendors makes the market unprofitable and therefore unsustainable (Table 10.3). Therefore, when share is only moderately sensitive to price ($g = 2.5$), the difference between two and three competing vendors is critical for government agencies.

10.4.2 Effect of Vendor Capacities on Government Payments

Vendor capacity is only a factor under certain conditions, but it has a surprisingly large impact on the buyer's power relative to the vendors' power. Therefore, it also greatly affects price.

The base case is modified, setting $g = 3$, to intensify the effect. The capacities of the two vendors vary from 40 to 110 percent. The effect of a redundant vendor is not apparent in this case, but it is evident in cases with three vendors. The cost to the buyer drops slightly when there is a redundant vendor but does not drop when there are two vendors, at least with the base case level of price sensitivity and symmetric vendors. However, when one vendor is even slightly capacity constrained,

Table 10.3 Predicted Government Payments Compared with the Number of Vendors

No. of Vendors	*Government Payments ($)*	*Total Vendor Cost ($)*	*Average Vendor Profit ($)*
1	Upper limit	8,154,000	Upper limit
2	35,600,000	9,156,000	13,233,200
3	17,800,000	10,157,400	2,575,100
4	15,000,000	11,158,800	1,073,000
5	14,300,000	12,160,200	429,200

the buyer's cost increases by 20 percent. When both are capacity constrained, there is no equilibrium. Table 10.4 shows the relation of predicted payments to vendor capacity.

A vendor is capacity constrained when the share it would receive in equilibrium based on its costs alone is greater than its capacity. In this case, the vendor cannot produce the volume demanded at the prices that would arise in an unconstrained equilibrium. Therefore, the vendor can raise prices above the unconstrained equilibrium price without decreasing its actual production volume.

In general, the capacity-constrained vendor contributes almost nothing to the competitive environment. For example,

- If a bidder cannot be completely excluded because the total capacity of other bidders is less than 100 percent, the high-cost vendor is guaranteed a share.
- The vendor with low costs may charge the highest price if it is capacity constrained; alternatively, the vendor with highest fixed costs may have the largest per-unit profit margin if it is capacity constrained.

Although this effect appears in part because of the way in which the model estimates vendor cost structures as a function of capacity (it assumes significant decreases in variable costs for larger capacity plants), the major impact on buyer costs is from capacity constraints.

The primary lesson in this case is that an effective competitive environment exists only when vendors have excess capacity; under these conditions, vendors would like a greater share (without reducing price), while government agencies could afford to offer a lower share, which favors the agencies' power in determining price. When capacity is constrained, the agency would like to purchase more products than the vendor can provide, which means the vendor has more power.

In an extreme case (not discussed here), at least one vendor's capacity would be entirely redundant (i.e., the capacity of other vendors would total more than 100 percent of the buyer's needs).

Table10.4 Relation of Predicted Payments to Vendor Capacity

Vendor Capacities (Percent)	*Government Payments ($)*	*Total Vendor Cost ($)*	*Average Vendor Profit ($)*
48, 48	Upper limit	9,012,900	Upper limit
40, 80	42,920,000	9,155,900	16,811,300
60, 60	21,460,000	9,155,900	6,151,600
80, 80	20,030,000	9,012,900	5,436,300

When vendors have markedly different costs, this situation is particularly advantageous for government agencies because it might be desirable to eliminate a high-cost player. The base case does not indicate any benefit from maintaining a large excess capacity.

10.4.3 Effect of Buyer's Sensitivity and Price on Payments

The price sensitivity parameter g varied in the base case from two (low but nonzero price sensitivity) to complete (infinite) price sensitivity. This variable becomes very important. As sensitivity varies, the buyer's costs range from the maximum possible (the buyer's total budget) to minimum possible (the vendor's marginal costs). Most of this change occurs within a fairly small range of price sensitivity (Table 10.5).

When relatively few vendors compete, it is important to impose sufficient competitive pressure in the way share is allocated as a function of price:

- Below a certain level of price sensitivity (e.g., $g = 2$), no equilibrium is present. Prices are unstable and spiral out of control. Each time the two vendors offer the same price, they benefit by raising prices because the penalty in terms of lost shares is minimal.
- An important implication of this finding is that a simple 60/40-type rule, in which the low bidder receives a 60 percent share and the high bidder receives a 40 percent share, in some cases, translates to a price sensitivity that is completely ineffective in inducing competition.
- Although it is not illustrated in Table 10.5, the more vendors, the less price sensitivity is required for an equilibrium to exist; for example, when three vendors are bidding, $g = 2$ is sufficient to reduce payments to the same level as for $g = 3$ in the two-vendor case.

10.4.4 Effect of Proportion of Fixed-to-Variable Costs on Pricing

Vendor cost structures (assuming lower variable costs are associated with higher fixed costs) range from all fixed to all variable. Assumptions about the cost-capacity relationship are modified to ensure that each vendor incurs approximately the same total cost in each case. Starting with the base case, and not changing any other assumptions, vendor capacity is set at 80 percent each rather than 60 percent, so that fixed costs are higher and variable costs are lower.

Table 10.5 Predicted Buyer Payments Compared with Price Sensitivity

Buyer Price Sensitivity	*Buyer Payments ($)*	*Total Vendor Cost ($)*	*Average Vendor Profit ($)*
Low ($g <= 2$)	Upper limit	9,155,900	Upper limit
Mild (2.5)	35,765,400	9,155,900	13,233,200
Moderate (3)	21,459,200	9,155,900	6,151,600
High (5)	11,874,100	9,155,900	1,359,100
Complete	7,153,100	9,155,900	1,000,000

Table 10.6 Payments versus Vendor Fixed and Variable Costs (g = 2.5)

Fixed and Variable Costs per Unit ($)	*Buyer Payments ($)*	*Total Vendor Cost ($)*	*Average Vendor Profit ($)*
Fixed: 0 Variable: 90,129	27,181,700	9,155,900	9,012,900
Fixed: 1,000,000 Variable: 71,531	21,459,200	9,012,900	6,223,200
Fixed: 1,251,800 Variable: 66,524	20,028,600	9,012,900	5,507,900
Fixed: 1,430,600 Variable: 61,516	18,598,000	9,155,900	4,721,000
Fixed: 9,155,900 Variable: 0	0	9,155,900	4,578,000

In the first variation, the price drops from $27,181/unit to $21,459/unit, so the buyer's costs drop to $5.7 million. Although the vendor's total costs are nearly unchanged, the profit per vendor drops to $2.8 million.

Table 10.6 illustrates an important point: relatively low variable costs and high fixed costs lead to increased price competition in an ongoing market. One interpretation of this point is that any technology development that reduces variable cost for any vendor is good for the buyer, even vendor proprietary technology.

In this model, fixed costs do not affect bids unless vendors are forced out (and have the option of exiting the market). In reality, fixed costs affect bids whenever a vendor is assumed to lose money—vendors' prices include a sufficient cushion over the marginal cost to cover their fixed costs; otherwise, they do not want the contract.

The effect of asymmetric vendor costs can be explained as follows. When one vendor has lower costs, these costs are partially passed on to the buyer as savings; however, the benefit to the buyer is greatest when at least two vendors have low costs because price is largely driven by the second lowest cost producer. Reductions in cost to any vendor should be good for the buyer, but it is better if these reductions are more evenly spread among vendors.

10.5 Conclusion

10.5.1 Limitations

The exact relationship between payments and competitive conditions, in practice, depends on many considerations. Costs cannot be known with certainty, and the cost structures of vendors are more complex than the one in this model. In addition, substitute products may be available for both buyer and seller.

This model describes ongoing competition in a market rather than initial bidding for a market. If variable costs are held constant, fixed costs are actually irrelevant to the results, except for situations in which at least one bidder operates at a loss. These situations are unstable. (A vendor would continue to operate at a loss, however, when the government agrees to lease back a production facility, so that some rent is paid each period as long as it operates.) In bidding situations, vendors will not bid at prices for which they anticipate a loss.

The cost structures assumed in the model may be conservative. Over time, vendors have incentives to cut costs to gain share or profit margin. The process assumed in this model is also not entirely realistic because of the following reasons:

- When the payments are exorbitant, the buyer would likely impose a price cap, which vendors would accept as long as they could still make a profit.
- The spiraling of prices that occurs in this model does not occur in real time, but is meant to represent what happens in the mind of a strategically thinking bidder.

However, what is true in simple cases (in terms of general factors that affect prices and the order of magnitude of their effects) also tends to be true (within reasonable bounds) in complex cases: savings are comparable, even if they are harder to identify because of all the other factors contributing to prices.

10.5.2 Key Lessons

The following list represents the key lessons learned about how price competition affects government agencies:

- Increased competition tends to accompany increased total costs to vendors because of the fixed costs of additional production facilities. A happy medium is present where vendor costs, and vendor margins, are reasonably low.
- The different factors that can influence the level of competition have diminishing marginal effects on price, individually and collectively.
- For the case examined here, increasing the number of vendors has a significant effect up to four vendors. It is even possible that costs could be lowered by subsidizing extra vendors.
- Increasing price sensitivity has a strong effect, until moderately high levels are reached; with two vendors, the cutoff occurs approximately when a 1 percent increase in price leads to a 3.5 percent decrease in the amount a vendor sells. The cutoff would be lower if more vendors participated or if other factors increased competition.
- The ratio of fixed-to-variable costs is significant, but not as much so as the number of vendors and the buyer's price sensitivity. These depend, of course, on the ranges of possible values for each factor.
- Capacity must be high enough to support competition, that is, some slack must exist, but more slack is not better after a point. Excess capacity is necessary, but not sufficient, for competition.

10.5.3 Recommendations

To save money in the long term, the government agency as a buyer must make farsighted decisions regarding competition at the time it commits to establish a private market to meet its demand. Suggested actions for government buyers facing a situation similar to that in this study include the following:

- Government buyers should ensure that vendors have some excess capacity (it does not take much excess to allow competition). Depending on the cost, the buyers should consider contracting for capacity where a redundant plant exists.
- If a fixed quantity of product is needed over a fixed period, an important relationship occurs between the schedule for production and the maintenance of competition. Hastening the schedule reduces the overall capacity as a percentage of the buyer's annual needs, which could eliminate competitive pressures. On the other hand, if capacity is expensive (i.e., it would be impossible to build excess capacity and remain within budget), the schedule could be relaxed, which would increase a plant's capacity as a percentage of the buyer's annual needs. Technology improvements that cut costs could also increase vendor capacities, which would give the buyer a competitive balance.
- Under competitive pressures similar to those in the model, government buyers should attempt to have four vendors (having fewer than four vendors results in conditions that are worse [three vendors] to catastrophic [one vendor]). If few vendors are available, the government should be extremely vigilant in enforcing a high sensitivity of vendor share to bid price. It may pay for the buyer to subsidize the entry of an extra vendor (possibly from a favored class, e.g., domestic vendors) to maintain competition (Rothkopf et al., 2003). The margin for error in the number of vendors is small.
- The buyer should prefer products with relatively low variable costs, even if this preference leads to higher fixed costs (although this advice must be balanced by the cost in terms of financing and flexibility compared with lower up-front costs). The buyer may be able to lower variable costs for vendors by developing new technology for distribution to all vendors (e.g., developments at national laboratories). This method is most effective when it leads to more evenly distributed vendor costs, rather than when it helps one vendor achieve significantly lower costs.
- Government buyers should develop systems that increase their ability to be price-sensitive (e.g., make it easy to compare bids, avoid getting locked into a price or a particular vendor's technology or location). In particular, rules in which the low bidder gets 60 percent of production and the high bidder gets 40 percent do not provide sufficient price sensitivity to ensure ongoing competition.
- Buyers should be realistic about what can and what cannot be controlled. For example, it is desirable to keep vendor costs low, but it is more important to keep buyer costs low. It is desirable to keep vendor margins reasonable, but buyers should not be concerned if vendors make a reasonable profit; it may be necessary to keep competition alive. Also, it may be impossible to simultaneously minimize vendor profit and buyer cost. The only reason for a buyer to try to manage vendor profit is to minimize buyer cost. This idea implies that micromanaging vendor costs, as they relate to bids, could be self-defeating.
- Buyers should be aware of ways in which vendors might try to damage the competitive environment. For example, beware of bids that seem so low they would force another vendor out of business or of attempts to limit capacity. (On the other hand, if the threat of entry is maintained, such bids may be fortuitous for the buyer.) Buyers who anticipate such tactics may be able to preclude them through contract terms.
- Buyers should identify ways in which vendors may worry about the competitive environment being turned excessively against them and ensure that this action will not happen, especially if it is a prohibitive concern. Otherwise, attractive potential vendors will not want to bid.

Procurement of government services occurs in an artificial market, even if the market is competitive. Government buyers who use competitive procurement processes can save large sums of money or incur very high costs, depending on their actions at the time the rules of competition and the structure of the artificial market are established. In fact, recent findings about waste in government procurement are bringing calls for reform and increased competitiveness (Office of Procurement Policy Advisory Panel, 2006). This study examines issues that affect the ability of buyers to achieve their desired outcomes. The modeling approach can be used to estimate the magnitude of the impact of different factors and to predict the costs associated with a contemplated competitive procurement process.

Acknowledgments

This document is derived from work done for the Tank Waste Remediation System (TWRS) Contractor Support Team, under the direction of Robert Broderson and Jerry Straalsund of Pacific Northwest National Laboratory (PNNL). The authors wish to thank Gale Boyd of Argonne National Laboratory, Robert Drake of Los Alamos National Laboratory, and Mark Weimer of PNNL, as well as Drs. Broderson and Straalsund, for their insights and support in the preparation of this material. Design and publishing support was provided by ANL's Information and Publishing Division.

References

Anton, J.J. and Yao, D. 1990. Measuring the effectiveness of competition in defense procurement: A survey of the empirical literature. *Journal of Policy Analysis and Management*, 9(1): 60–79.

Athey, S. and Levin, J. 2001. Information and competition in U.S. forest service timber auctions. *Journal of Public Economics*, 109(2): 375–417.

Bajari, P. and Ye, L. 2001. *Competition versus Collusion in Procurement Auctions: Identification and Testing,* Working Paper: Stan Ec 01001. Stanford, CA: Stanford Economics Department.

Baughman, M.L. and Joskow, P. 1974. *Interfuel Substitution in the Consumption of Energy in the United States, MIT-EL74-002.* Cambridge, MA: Massachusetts Institute of Technology, Energy Laboratory.

Beggs, J. and Strong, S. 1982. Cake slicing and revealed government preferences. *Bell Journal of Economics*, 13(2): 534–540.

Carrick, P.M. 1988. New evidence on government efficiency. *Journal of Policy Analysis and Management*, 7(3): 518–528.

Department of Energy (DOE) Privatization Working Group. 1998. *Harnessing the Market: The Opportunities and Challenges of Privatization. Report to the secretary of Energy, DOE/S-0120.* Washington, DC: Author.

Engel, E., Fischer, R., and Galetovic, A. 2002. *Competition in or for the Field: Which Is Better?* Center Discussion Paper No. 844. New Haven, CT: Yale University Economic Growth Center.

Ewerhart, C. and Fieseler, K. 2003. Procurement auctions and unit-price contracts. *Rand Journal of Economics*, 34(3): 568–580.

Hilke, J.C. 1992. *Competition in Government-Financed Services.* New York: Quorum Books.

Hong, H. and Shum, S. 2002. Increasing competition and the winner's curse: Evidence from procurement. *Review of Economic Studies*, 69: 871–898.

McFadden, D. 1975. The revealed preferences of a government bureaucracy: Theory. *Bell Journal of Economics*, 6(2): 401–416.

McFadden, D. 1976. The revealed preferences of a government bureaucracy: Empirical evidence. *Bell Journal of Economics*, 7(1): 55–72.

Morgan, D.R. 1992. The pitfalls of privatization: Contracting without competition. *American Review of Public Administration*, 22(4): 251–269.

Nash, J.F. 1950. Equilibrium points in N-person games. *Proceedings of the National Academy of Sciences, USA*, 36: 48–49.

Office of Procurement Policy Advisory Panel. 2006. Report of the Advisory Panel to the Office of Procurement Policy and the United States Congress (Draft). Available at http://acquisition.gov/comp/aap/documents/DraftFinalReport.pdf.

Pilling, D.L. 1989. *Competition in Defense Procurement*. Washington, DC: The Brookings Institution.

Poole, R.W., Jr. and Fixler, P., Jr. 1987. Privatization of public-sector services in practice: Experience and potential. *Journal of Policy Analysis and Management*, 6(4): 612–625.

Rothkopf, M.H., Harstad, R.M., and Fu, Y. 2003. Is subsidizing inefficient bidders actually costly? *Management Science*, 49(1): 71–84.

Uttley, M. and Harper, N. 1993. The political economy of competitive tendering. In: T. Clarke and C. Pitelis (Eds.), *The Political Economy of Privatization*. London, United Kingdom: Routledge, pp. 145–158.

Welch, C. May 1, 2000. Skyrocketing costs may delay nuclear cleanup at Hanford. *Seattle Times*. Available at http://seattletimes.nwsource.com/news/local/html98/hanf01m_20000501.html (downloaded on February 27, 2002).

PROCUREMENT SYSTEMS

II

Chapter 11

Public Procurement in the United Nations System

Toru Sakane

CONTENTS

11.1 Introduction

Although the United Nations System* (hereinafter, the UN System) is not a country, it is the largest group of international organizations and surely a group of public entities composed of member states, whose functions are essential for the international society. There is, actually, a public procurement system in the UN System too. This procurement system is out of the WTO GPA (Government Procurement Agreement) and the UNCITRAL Model Law. This chapter analyzes such a unique and important procurement system.

In the UN System, public procurement is essential for both operation and administrative budgetary management. When we observe procurement operations of the UN System, it may not be a common notion but it is not an exaggeration to say, "public procurement can save lives." In the case of humanitarian operations and PKOs, many people's lives often depend extensively on the success of international constructive engagements that try to alleviate, stabilize or normalize such serious situations. They can only succeed not only through procuring finance, human resources, and authority but also through procuring necessary goods and services. Not limited to these two areas, the importance of procurement can be observed in various areas of activities such as development and technical assistance, and also in the internal management of the organizations. Therefore, although procurement does not draw much attention compared to forums such as the Security Council and the General Assembly and their activities, procurement operations, in fact, significantly support activities and management of UN System organizations.

This chapter consists of three sections. The first section (Section 11.2) is an overview of the UN System procurement. Here, basic statistical information and its implications are analyzed, and interagency coordination and cooperation mechanisms are observed. Through these analyses, we know that a high portion of actual procurements is done by each organization. The UN System is actually independent and decentralized organizationally in terms of procurement. Therefore, procurement operation at the individual organizational level is important.

The second and third sections (Sections 11.3 and 11.4) focus on organizational and operational issues on procurement of individual organizations, based on the understandings and findings outlined in the overview. Organizations are not analyzed individually because there are numerous organizations in the UN System and procurement amount varies widely. Instead, some critical points are raised at the beginning of the second and third sections. These points are analyzed based on the research findings of procurement activities of individual organizations. As such, cross-organizational analysis becomes possible.

Finally, the last section summarizes the significance, basic structure, difficulties confronted, efforts to tackle them, and future challenges of the UN System procurement.

Considering the scarcity of comprehensive academic research on this theme, this chapter was written based mainly on the reviews and analyses of the official documents. In addition, to acquire current information on implementation issues, interviews were conducted at various UN System organizations in New York, Geneva, Copenhagen, and Rome. This chapter therefore bases itself partly on these interviews. Some inputs were also taken from the author's prior work on this subject (Sakane, 2005a,b).

* The United Nations System consists of the United Nations, its affiliated organizations (such as UNICEF and WFP), and specialized agencies (such as WHO and FAO). (See http://www.un.org/aboutun/chart.html.) In this chapter, the World Bank Group had been excluded from the focus of this analysis because it is virtually quite independent from UN and other UN system organizations. Furthermore, there is a significant difference in the type of procurement activities conducted between the World Bank Group and the other organizations. The World Bank Group normally lends money to the recipient countries and they in turn implement the actual procurement.

Though not limited, due attention shall be paid to UN, WFP, and UNICEF.* These three occupy more than half of the total UN System's procurement volume. Procurement of these organizations has typical features of the UN System procurement, especially compared to national procurement. That is, these organizations conduct their activities in various places far away from their headquarters. They conduct various emergency operations and thus timely procurement is vital. This is why it is important to focus on these organizations. Also, in national procurement systems such as in the United States, emergency procurement is getting more attention and its importance is being recognized (Drabkin and Thai, 2007).

11.2 Overview

11.2.1 Basic Information and Its Implications

As shown in Table 11.1, the total amount of procurement in the UN System was approximately $8.3 billion in 2005. Although the procurement amount is quite small compared to national procurement, it is nevertheless substantial for these international organizations.

Procurement in the UN System consists of approximately $4.5 billion of goods and $3.7 billion of services in 2005. A huge amount of procurement is conducted for emergency humanitarian assistance and PKO operations. The main contents of procurement are listed in Figure 11.1.

As procurement has close relations especially with budgetary management, financial resource information (summation of regular and extra budget) was added to Table 11.1 and it was compared to the procurement amount to estimate the comparative budgetary importance that the procurement has. From this statistics, it has become clear that the procurement amount is equivalent to about 40 percent of the total financial resources of the entire UN System organizations. Although there are other financial resources used for procurement, a considerable portion of the budget is spent on procurement. Here, the importance of procurement is apparent in terms of not only individual project and program implementation but also fundamental administrative and budgetary management for UN System organizations.

According to statistical data from IAPSO (Inter-Agency Procurement Service Office), the procurement amount has increased from $2.9 billion in 1996 to $8.3 billion in 2005. The main reasons behind this are the increases in large-scale PKOs as well as the increase in humanitarian and reconstruction activities, especially in some African conflict-ridden countries, Iraq, Afghanistan, and Kosovo.

As shown in Table 11.1, it is clear that the amount of procurement differs widely among UN organizations. The major procurement organizations are WFP, UN, UNDP (containing IAPSO), and UNICEF. These organizations have a common characteristic in their main operational style. That is, all these organizations perform their main activities not only in their headquarters, but also in their field offices located in the developing countries. Such activities include not only managing conferences but also directly assisting people in need of help. Figure 11.1 summarizes the importance of procurement for the operations done by major UN System organizations.

Despite the fact that almost all headquarters of these organizations are located in developed countries, procurement in developing countries occupies quite a high percentage (about 43 percent in 2005). The decentralization measures from headquarters to regional and field offices is the significant reason

* In addition, two procurement specialized organizations, IAPSO and UNOPS, are partly focused upon. UNDP is also one of the main procurement organizations. IAPSO is a part of UNDP, and UNOPS was historically also a part of UNDP though it is an independent entity now.

Table 11.1 Procurement in the UN System and Its Relations with Financial Resources in 2005

Organizations	*Procurement of Goods (Millions $)*	*Procurement of Services (Millions $)*	*Procurement Total (Millions $)*	*Procurement by Each Organization (Percent)*	*Procurement in Developing Countries (Percent)*	*Total Financial Resources (Millions $)*	*Comparison with Procurement Volume (Percent)*
WFP (World Food Programme)	860.5	1320.0	2180.4	26.2	33.9	3104.4	70.2
UN (United Nations)	800.9	896.7	1697.6	20.4	35.5	2728.3	62.2
UNDP (United Nations Development Programme)	710.2	626.3	1336.5	16.0	N/A	4573.5	29.2
UNICEF (United Nations Children's Fund)	1135.1	N/A	1135.1	13.6	45.1	2191.1	51.8
UNOPS (United Nations Office for Project Services)	110.6	608.9	719.4	8.6	74.3	N/A	N/A
WHO (World Health Organization)	349.5	6.2	355.7	4.3	27.0	1706.3	20.8
UNFPA (United Nations Population Fund)	179.9	73.6	253.5	3.0	48.6	523.3	48.4
Other organizations	406.7	245.7	652.5	7.8	1.2	6212.2	10.5
Total	4553.4	3777.2	8330.5	100.0	43.1	21039.1	39.6

Sources: From IAPSO, *Annual Statistical Report 2005*. pp. 6, 7, 12. Available at http://www.iapso.org/pdf/ASR_2004.pdf, 2006a; UN, Budgetary and Financial Situation of Organizations of the United Nations System: Note by the Secretary-General Transmitting the Statistical Report of theUnited Nations System Chief Executives Board for Coordination (A/59/315), Table 3, 2006a.

Notes: IAPSO is a part of UNDP. PHAO (Pan American Health Organization) and ITC (International Trade Centre) are parts of WHO and UN, respectively. The other organizations are: FAO, UNRWA, UNHCR, IAEA, ILO, UNIDO, WIPO, ITU, WMO, WTO, UPU, ICAO, UNESCO, UNAIDS, IMO, UNODC, UNFCCC, and IOM. Numbers were rounded off to one decimal place. So, there can be slight deviations.

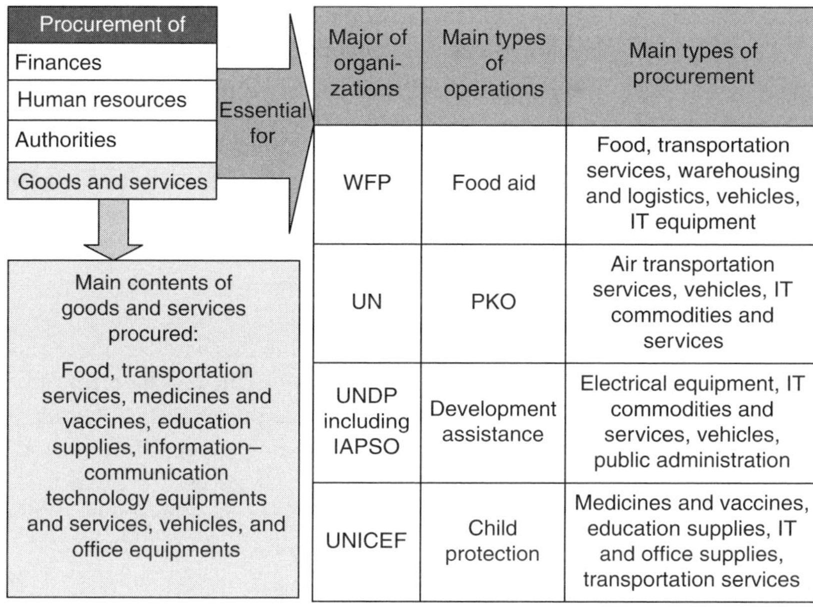

Figure 11.1 Major organizations in the UN system and importance of procurement for their operations. (Adapted from IAPSO, *United Nations System General Business Guide* (20th ed.), pp. 6, 12, 17, 28, 50, 65, 114–120, 2006b. Available at http://www.iapso.org/pdf/gbg_master.pdf. and several interviews listed at the end of this chapter.)

for this figure. This tendency is elaborated in Section 11.3. The percentage of procurement in the developing countries differs very much depending on the organization (Table 11.1).

In addition to the findings of the basic statistical information stated above, one of the most important characteristics of the UN System procurement is that the basic structure of the UN System's procurement operation is independent and decentralized. From Table 11.1 and the above analysis, it is apparent that there is no central procurement implementation agency. Furthermore, the UN System does not have any actual strong central strategic procurement policy-making body. Therefore, a detailed individual organizational level procurement analysis is required.

11.2.2 Interagency Cooperation Mechanisms

Before analyzing individual UN organization's procurement, some of the major interagency procurement mechanisms need to be analyzed. An important interagency procurement mechanism in the UN System is IAPWG (Inter-Agency Procurement Working Group), which is a procurement specialist forum. IAPWG is an informal consultation body composed of the head of procurement section of UN System organizations established in 1976 by UNDP. IAPWG's mandate is to coordinate the organizations' procurement management and its activities. The meeting is held once a year at various places with seminar session for the host country suppliers.

IAPWG has dealt with various procurement matters including the Common Procurement Guideline issued in 1996 (analyzed in detail later), procurement coordination of common-user item, collective price arrangement and its standardization negotiation, diversification of procurement sources, procurement promotion from developing countries, harmonization of procurement procedures, and promotion of business opportunity (UNDP, 1995). UNGM (UN Global Marketplace) is a very important achievement example that provides supply source information to UN System organizations (http://www.ungm.org).* The role of the secretariat of IAPWG has been performed by IAPSO since 1978. As IAPWG itself is just a forum, the actual implementation is designated to IAPSO and other UN System organizations. IAPSO is a part of UNDP and it holds both procurement coordination and procurement service functions of UNDP.

Location-based common procurement mechanisms are also worth mentioning. It is notable to mention that though there are many organizations within the UN System, most of these headquarters are located in either New York or Geneva. In Geneva, the Joint Purchase Service located within the UN office at Geneva has been active for a long time. According to the procurement official in charge, this common procurement mechanism is important to realize the economy of scale. Through this scheme, various goods and services are procured jointly including paper, furniture, and information technology services. In New York, the Task Force on Common Services, Procurement Service Working Group was established based on the initiative of the UN Secretary General in 1997 (JIU, 2004). However, the task force is no longer active (Interviews at UNFPA and UN, 2006).

In addition to these coordination mechanisms, there are two procurement service agencies, IAPSO and UNOPS. They are the important means for other UN System organizations to be able to request procurement implementation on their behalf when they wish. IAPSO procures automotive products, antituberculosis medicines, technical and IT equipment, and freight and transportation services (IAPSO, 2006b). UNOPS (UN Office for Project Service), formerly named PED (Project Execution Division), was established by UNDP in 1973 to strengthen project implementation ability of UNDP. After various discussions, its status was stabilized in 1995 as an independent agency to provide procurement and project management services to UN System organizations and to other entities including governments (Dijkzeul, 2000). According to the statistics provided by UNOPS, the most major procurement categories in 2006 are construction and engineering services. It also procures office IT equipments, motor vehicles, machinery, transport and logistics service, security service, elections, peacekeeping, and mine action services.

These two organizations are very unique because both are self-financing entities. Both procurement offices are located in Copenhagen. However, procurement service amount of these two organizations is not so big within the total UN System. In 2005, IAPSO procured about $193 million or only 2.32 percent of the total UN System procurement; and UNOPS procured about $719 million or 8.64 percent (IAPSO, 2006a).

Although interagency procurement mechanisms such as IAPWG, location-based common procurement mechanisms, and procurement service agencies are important, they are neither a strong central procurement policy-making body nor an integrated procurement implementation body. Common procurement measures† are developed more functionally and partially than systematically. It is difficult to have sufficient UN Systemwide common procurement coordination because of independency of each organization. The realization of effective interagency procurement coordination and cooperation has been a long-term basic agenda and also a major challenge.

---

* All URLs listed in this chapter were checked for their accessibility on February 27, 2007.

† In addition to location-based type such as in Geneva and agency type such as IAPSO, lead agency type is the third common procurement method. For example, WFP is the lead agency for some interagency humanitarian transportation service procurement. For details, see http://www.unjlc.org/about/.

11.3 Organizational Issues

As has already been analyzed, though some interagency mechanisms are institutionalized, procurement organizational structure in the UN System is basically independent and decentralized. There is neither a central procurement implementation agency nor a strong central strategic procurement policy-making body. Therefore, organizational issues at each organization level need to be analyzed. In the UN System, many major organizations have operational fields away from the headquarters. So, as regards procurement functions, observations are needed not only on headquarters level but also on regional and field levels. Decentralization and increase of field and regional procurement are further analyzed. Also, oversight and staff matters are examined as very critical organizational issues.

11.3.1 Status and Location of Procurement Function

As regards the status of the procurement function, many organizations have a central procurement section although their structure varies depending on each organization. For example, UN has a central procurement function called procurement division within the Department of Management in New York. In many organizations, such a central procurement function often lies within management or financial department, though independent status and location can be observed such as in the case of UNICEF.

However, not all organizations take on a central procurement arrangement. WFP is an unique example. In WFP, operation and administration are separated into different two departments. Food procurement and transportation procurement are implemented within the operational department. On the other hand, procurement of other goods and services is implemented within the management department (Interviews at WFP). According to JIU (Joint Inspection Unit), ITU also takes on product-based decentralization of procurement activities. ITU has four separate units engaged in procurement, each reporting to a different head of department. These four are in-house administration goods, ICT products, development projects, and TELECOM exhibition activities (JIU, 2004).

Geographical location of procurement agencies is more important in the case of the UN System than in the case of national procurement administration because the UN System conducts activities all over the world and the operation often needs to be done swiftly. From the following analysis, geographical locations and various aspects including prompt supply, availability of goods and services, location costs, and geographical equity consideration of procurement are found to be important factors in selecting a geographical location.

Interestingly, the procurement section of some organizations is not located within its headquarters. Notable examples are UNICEF's Supply Division, UNDP's IAPSO, and UNFPA's Procurement Service Section. Quite interestingly, these three organizations' procurement sections are all located in Copenhagen, although their headquarters are located in New York.* Copenhagen is one of the biggest procurement bases for the UN System.

Then, why is Copenhagen so prosperous in procurement function? We can see several reasons from the relocation of UNICEF UNIPAC (UNICEF Packing and Assembly Centre), the predecessor of Supply Division, in 1962 from New York. At that time, UNICEF tried to find an appropriate location in Europe. Copenhagen was selected because of its logistical convenience, availability of transportation services from international cargo companies, of goods like penicillin for tuberculosis, and of stable workload, and a generous offer of land from the government of Denmark (UNICEF, 1992).

---

* UNOPS's Division of Procurement Services has been also located in Copenhagen since 1997, while its headquarters was in New York. In 2006, UNOPS moved its headquarters to Copenhagen.

It is apparent that IAPSO's relocation to Copenhagen has not only operational and economic consideration but also political consideration. As explained in UNDP's official document, the relocation of IAPSO in 1989 from Geneva to Copenhagen was "in direct response to a request for measures to achieve more equitable geographical distribution of procurement through increased utilization of supply sources from underutilized major donor countries, in particular the Nordic countries and the Netherlands" (UNDP, 1995). In return for such a generous contribution to these organizations, Demark got not only more procurement supply opportunity but also more employment opportunity.

Locations of regional level procurement function are logistical. Notable cases are organizations conducting field activities. Various regions and countries are often far from the headquarters of UNICEF, UN, WFP, and UNOPS. Unlike the case of IAPSO in Copenhagen, the geographical locations vary widely depending on each organization.

UNICEF established regional supply centers in Ankara and Pretoria in 1998. The Ankara center was created to procure supplies including educational kits for the Oil-for-Food Programme (OFFP). The Pretoria center was set up to source suppliers of bed nets and insecticides as part of the Roll Back Malaria initiative. Both centers quickly expanded to provide a wider range of supplies to UNICEF offices (UNICEF, 2003a).

The UN's logistic base in Brindisi is a special organizational arrangement for PKO procurement as well as logistics and storage. Brindisi is a military port in the southeast coast of Italy. The location was selected based on the Italian government's generous offer of land for the UN. The commodities procured for PKO are stocked there and this enables their prompt initial deployment. It also stocks used procurement equipments from prior missions (UN, 2000). WFP also has a humanitarian response depot called UNHRD in Brindisi (http://www.unhrd.org).

In the case of UNOPS, the Middle East is the ideal geographical area. UNOPS established its procurement base in Dubai in the summer of 2005. There are major UN operation countries like Iraq, Afghanistan, and Pakistan in and around the Middle East. Also, the Middle East is a convenient location for covering both Asia and Africa at the same time. It takes less than five hours to fly to all the major operational areas. Although business environment and security are sometimes unstable in the Middle East, Dubai is relatively very stable. Therefore, UNOPS regards it as a permanent supply base (Interview at UNOPS).

From the above analyses, it becomes clear that central procurement section in the headquarters level and functional location procurement base in regional and local levels are the main characteristics in the UN System.

11.3.2 Decentralization Measures and Procurement in Developing Countries

Procurement decentralization is an important and challenging matter. Many UN System organizations have delegated authority to their country offices to undertake procurement up to a certain financial limit or threshold, from $5,000 up to $100,000. Local procurement by peacekeeping missions is authorized up to $200,000 for larger missions. As developing countries become more self-reliant in managing their own technical cooperation, there is an increase in national execution of projects and programs, including procurement of necessary goods and services (IAPSO, 2006b). As is the case of WFP, delegation of authority tends to increase in emergency situations to satisfy the needs swiftly. In the national procurement system, provision of special contracting authorities is also regarded as one of the important tools for satisfying the needs of emergency procurement. As for the case of the U.S. federal government, see Drabkin and Thai (2007).

Procurement in developing countries and countries in transition are quite high in the UN System. In the recent decade, it occupied around 35 to 45 percent of the total procurement amount.

This percentage varies by a large margin depending on each organization. As shown in the Table 11.1, there are wide differences even among organizations with field activities (IAPSO, 2006b).

Due to the procurement decentralization and procurement in developing countries, organizations can expect a reduction in transportation cost and delivery time compared to international procurement. Also, local goods and services sometimes tend to be more suitable than the internationally procured ones, once the matter of quality is overcome. For example, in the case of WFP, local or regional procurement sometimes fits more the eating habits of the recipients, as in the case where wheat and maize are procured for many African peoples rather than rice. It also helps the development of related industry in the developing countries except for emergency situations (WFP, 1998 and Interview at WFP Food Procurement Service).

To implement such decentralization measures, development of market is essential. For example, the pharmaceutical industry and other health-related industries are growing in developing countries especially in India, South Africa, Thailand, Turkey, Indonesia, and so on. The automotive industry is still concentrating on developed countries but there is a possibility to grow more in the developing countries in the future. Local procurement has advantages in training, after-sales service, guarantee, and acquisition of spare parts (Interview at UNICEF and UNICEF, 2003b). This is an important reason why UNICEF could increase its procurement in developing countries except for emergency situations.

To promote procurement decentralization, computerization of internal processing is a very efficient measure. Also, long-term agreements (LTA) are established at the headquarters level to ease the burden of procurement operation at the field level. Without them, successful decentralization with enough headquarters assistance and control would not be realized.

However, some care should be taken on procurement decentralization and local or regional procurement. In addition to suppliers' implementation capacity, organizations must be very prudent in making sure of the contractors' goodwill. The organization should scrutinize the suppliers' credentials before signing a major contract. This should be done especially in the field, where there are many unreliable "would-be traders" who only have small capital, low storage capacity, and are unfamiliar with trade customs (WFP, 1996). More importantly, the organization must be very careful in preventing corruption and misconducts. Therefore, the headquarters' control and monitoring mechanisms are important. The next section deals with such oversights.

11.3.3 Oversight and Control

In addition to daily operational control mechanisms such as review by contract committees, and governing board discussions, there are several oversight and control mechanisms in UN System organizations. They are very important for preventing procurement corruption and keeping procurement integrity.

First of all, there is the internal oversight body. In the case of UN, OIOS (Office of Internal Oversight Service) was established in 1994 through the strong support of the U.S. government. On the first summary report of OIOS issued in 1995, OIOS focused on "procurement" as one of the three priority areas for oversight in addition to "peacekeeping" and "humanitarian and related activities" (UN, 1995). Since then, OIOS has constantly kept monitoring the UN procurement. Other organizations have similar internal oversight sections.

There are not only internal oversights, but also two external oversight bodies in the UN System. One is called JIU. JIU was established in 1968 by the General Assembly. Eleven inspectors serve in their personal capacity and are appointed for a term of five years, renewable once.* In 2004, JIU (2004) issued the first most comprehensive JIU work on the UN System procurement.

* The inspectors can investigate organizations in all matters. (http://www.unsystem.org/jiu/en/about.htm.)

The other external oversight body is the Board of Auditors. It was established by the General Assembly in 1946 to carry out external audit of the accounts of UN and its funds and programs. The Board of Auditors reports findings and provides recommendations to the General Assembly.* For example, in 2002, the Board of Auditors issued an audit report about UNDP. In this report, lead-time reduction, formal evaluation of supplier performance, and proper control of purchase cards were examined and recommended (UN, 2002). However, unlike OIOS and JIU, the Board of Auditors' activities are not so transparent.

In addition, the activities of ad hoc examination groups are significant. For example, Independent Inquiry Committee into the UN OFFP (so-called Volker commission), headed by Paul Volker, former Chairman of the U.S. Federal Reserve, has issued reports containing very detailed inspection results and reform proposals. As for the procurement aspect, conflict of interest and financial disclosure rule revisions were strongly recommended among other issues (The Volker Commission, 2005).

Consultants also sometimes play an important role. Deloitte has issued the report focusing on internal control measures in November 2005. The report is very elaborate and the recommendations cover various aspects including governance, management and staff development, procurement and financial management systems, strategic and operational management, and rotation policy (Deloitte, 2005). Procurement expert association outside of the UN System is involved in related oversight work. For example, although not exclusively focused on control matter, the NIGP (National Institute of Governmental Purchasing) report is worth mentioning. In 2005, NIGP assessed the procurement processes of UN Procurement Service and presented 47 recommendations including vendor registration and sourcing, systems and internet infrastructure, procurement cards, acquisition planning, policies and procedures, organization and staffing, and professional development (NIGP, 2005).

What is important is to what extent the recommendations are really considered, examined, and incorporated into the actual procurement reform if such recommendations are desirable. Systematic follow-up of these recommendations is necessary. The political powers hold the key for actual implementation. The final reform decision lies in the hands of the member states.

Even though there are several concrete efforts made by oversight bodies stated above, transparency is still a challenging agenda in the UN System. As analyzed later on, international open competition is not fully implemented. Instead of advertisement, especially in the case of below $100,000, often invitation to bid/proposal is sent only to some suppliers in the rosters. Such limited international competition (LIC) is quite widely used. However, in recent times, UN is keen on transparency after criticisms of the OFFP scandals and on PKO procurement mismanagements. Disclosures of tender information, and income declaration of procurement officers are some examples. Some of the future challenges are to release more bidding information, have an independent bid protest system, implement whistle-blower protection policy, and strengthen the Vendor Review Committee† (UN, 2006b).

11.3.4 Staff Matters

It is critical for the UN System procurement management to "procure" and secure competent procurement staffs. Many UN System procurement officers were previously employed in private

* The General Assembly appoints three members, each of whom shall be the auditor general (or officer holding the equivalent title) of a member state. (http://www.unsystem.org/auditors.)

† In addition, material management, especially procured humanitarian relief material tracking, is important for the various UN System organizations to keep transparency and accountability. In this respect, PHAO's supply management system (SUMA) is a notable effort (Tomasini and Van Wassenhove, 2004).

companies. Once employed, due to the needs of specialty, many procurement officers transfer laterally. In other words, the officer transfers to another post within his or her procurement section or to the other organization's procurement section. Shortage of procurement staff is a deep concern (Interviews at UN 2002 and 2006, WHO, UNHCR and WFP). Without enough human resource, efficient and transparent procurement cannot be secured. In this respect, the situation is getting better in UN because importance of procurement staff has been recognized by member countries.*

Regarding staff training, despite the recognition of its importance among procurement officials, the resource spent is not enough. For example, UN had a budget of only about $300 per person for training in 2005 (Interviews at UN 2006). The situation seems quite similar in the UN System as a whole. In 2002, total investment in procurement training amounted to only 0.01 percent of aggregate procurement expenditure with the majority of organizations allocating no resources for that purpose (JIU, 2004).

From the JIU report, it is also apparent that the number of total staff, procurement amount per staff, labor costs, and training budget, all vary immensely between organizations. Therefore, interagency cooperation on training and related staff matters is essential (JIU, 2004). The Common Procurement Certification Scheme had just been consolidated in early 2006. It is expected to contribute toward the UN Systemwide capacity building and also smoother lateral transfer of the procurement officers (Interview at IAPSO 2006).

IAPSO's role is important in supplying training to UN System organizations. IAPSO provides various types of training courses (http://www.iapso.org/training/index.asp). They are held not only in Copenhagen but also in various other places. In addition to internal training provision conducted by each organization, off-site training courses like that of IAPSO are possible options for UN System organizations once the problem of training cost scarcity is resolved.

11.4 Operational Issues

As for operational issues, the main focus is on international competition arrangement and its actual implementations. Competitive biddings and proposals are the fundamental methods. Here, we can observe one special feature of UN System procurement operation. Additionally, LTA is an important operational method. At the end, E-procurement and socioeconomic and political objectives are discussed as matters that are still challenging.

11.4.1 Procurement Procedures

There are no strict systemwide procurement regulations. To support and regulate the daily detailed procurement operation, each organization has its own internal rules that are often incorporated within the financial regulations and the financial rules, supplemented by the procurement manual. However, there is the Common Guideline for Procurement in the UN System (IAPSO, 2006b). Though the guideline is not a binding legal rule, it is very helpful to understand the common basic procurement procedures. The guideline was created by IAPWG in 1996. Its purpose is to communicate basic principles for procurement by the organizations and within the UN System, to guide procurement activities, and to facilitate harmonization of procurement procedure among UN System organizations. The core content is summarized as follows.

* Establishment of more procurement staff posts realized. For details, see UN (2006c).

The guideline defines the objectives of the procurement activities as the timely acquisition of goods, works, and services while addressing the objectives of the UN organizations concerned; fairness, integrity, and transparency through competition; economy and effectiveness; and best value for money.

As regards the participation of the suppliers, the guideline stresses the basic principle of equal treatment regardless of the country of origin. It also demands from suppliers the eligibility requirements including the legal capacity, technical competence, and financial strength. Each organization maintains rosters of eligible suppliers. Solicitation documents addressed by procurement organizations shall contain all information necessary to prepare a suitable offer. There are three types of solicitation documents (invitation to bid, request for proposal, and request for quotation) that are widely used at national procurement procedures as well.

Procuring entities, as a general rule, use competition to procure goods and services. Such competition may be undertaken on an informal or formal basis and be either open or limited. As many suppliers as is practicable will be given the opportunity to offer the required goods, works, or services.

The guideline also defines submission, receipt, opening, and evaluation of offers as key procedures before procurement contracts. Ethical behavior and relationships with suppliers is mentioned but not in detail. To take statistics is required especially with regard to details of geographical distribution of contracts.

This is the essence of the guideline and basic procedures used in the UN System. However, the guideline neither explains in detail nor mentions some important procurement operational methods such as LTA and E-procurement. These issues are discussed here.

11.4.2 Limited International Competition

As introduced in the previous section, competitive procurement is the most recommended principle. However, we must be careful of the manner and degree of competitiveness. Here, we can see one of the special features of the UN System procurement method.

The Common Guideline for Procurement sets the types of procurement methods as follows: open international competition (OIC), LIC, local competition, and direct contracting. Among them, OIC is the most basic method that contains the important procurement principles such as fairness and transparency. OIC is initiated by advertisements through the official home pages, special procurement circulation magazines,* and international publications.

However, when LIC is used, solicitation is basically addressed to short-listed qualified suppliers selected in a nondiscriminatory manner by the organization from rosters, prequalifications, expressions of interest, and other sources. LIC is appropriate where OIC is unsuitable for economical and efficient procurement because of the value, urgent demand, or limited availability of the required goods and services (IAPSO, 2006b).

Through several interviews and information found in the official documents and home pages of UN System organizations, it is clear that the main feature of UN System procurement implementation would be LIC. Each UN System organization manages its roster of suppliers, solicits companies from the registered potential suppliers, and conducts bidding among them. Although some organizations, such as UNDP and IAPSO, advertise procurement opportunities through their home pages, such advertisement is limited to expensive cases (normally more than $100,000). Some organizations even do not advertise their bidding information in their home page. Normally, the procurement rules do not implement OIC strictly.

* "Development Business" (http://www.devbusiness.com) is the most famous.

Let us take a look at UNICEF as an example of LIC. According to the UNICEF Supply Manual, invitation to bid and request for proposal are defined as written solicitation sent to a number of suppliers sufficient to obtain preferably at least three valid and acceptable bids/proposals. On the contrary, uninvited bids/proposals are not to be accepted. To be registered as a potential supplier, the supplier must be prequalified through assessment of its financial viability and its capability to meet quality, delivery, price, and after-sales requirements (UNICEF, 2003b). Therefore, the rule itself does not impose formal OIC and actual operation is said to be LIC.

Such an LIC-based operation could be regarded as a critical fault against the basic principle of the procurement theory. However, there seem to exist practical reasons. Such arrangement enables procurement officers to ease the burden of financial and quality check tasks each time. Especially in the case of very high volume of medicines and vaccines that UNICEF purchases, quality assurance is a very important aspect (Interview at UNICEF).

It is also true that LIC contributes toward swift procurement, contract, and delivery. The UN System has many emergency activities. Therefore, this point is important. In addition, unlike national procurement, in the case of breach of contract, remedies for UN System organizations are often more difficult.

Considering the merits given above and considering the unreliability and costliness of contract enforcement, such LIC arrangement has some operational advantages compared to national procurement. However, the degree of necessity and actual LIC feasibility need to be tested further.

11.4.3 Long-Term Agreement

LTA is quite a widely used method in the UN System.* LTA is generally used for goods and services as the organizations have repetitive needs. If an LTA is signed, the organization has the right to purchase from the supplier at a fixed price for a certain period, normally for one or a few years but not to exceed approximately five years at the longest. LTA has strong possibility for the organization to reduce cost through realizing the economy of scale and omitting bidding procedures each time. Also, the supplier can have more opportunity for further orders.

Let us take a look at the example of UN. LTA is referred to as system contracts in UN. System contracts have advantages of the volume discount potential and setting up a mechanism for drawing requirements without repeating the bidding exercise for each requisition. However, on such contracts, greater vigilance in monitoring vendor performance and carrying out effective contract administration are needed (UN, 1996). According to the UN procurement official, this type of contract is thought to be very useful in transportation service, vehicle spare service, and office equipments.

LTA can better support the field offices. In the case of UNICEF, Supply Division Headquarters often signs LTA with suppliers detailing the price and delivery term. Because of this, country offices can very easily implement procurement through LTA. Such an arrangement is called direct ordering arrangement (UNICEF, 1992). It was first introduced around 1993 and has expanded since then. As a result, it succeeded in reducing the delivery time on average from four months to six weeks. Additionally, there has been a positive effect in reducing the purchasing price and the burden of the procurement officers (UNICEF, 1994).

LTA can help other organizations too. It is becoming more and more common among UN System organizations to use other organizations' LTA. By combining the needs across several

---

* Interestingly, similar mechanisms to LTA can be found in national procurement system too, although it is not such a major tool. Prepositioned contracts capable of meeting emergency needs are its example in the case of the United States. For details, see Drabkin and Thai (2007).

organizations, more economy of scale can be pursued. For other organizations, it is very convenient and cost saving to utilize an established LTA rather than to create a new LTA through a bidding process (Interviews at UNHCR and UNOPS). Just as in the case of UNICEF and IAPSO, procurement through LTA for other organizations can sometimes be conducted more smoothly through the provision of catalogs for organizations and customers.

11.4.4 E-procurement

Many UN System organizations have not been advanced in E-procurement. The entire bidding process through the use of computers is still a very uncommon practice. Also, bidding through e-mail is normally allowed only for low-value procurements.

IAPSO developed one of the most significant E-procurement systems in UN System organizations. In 2000, IAPSO created the web-based procurement system called UNWebBuy. In May 2002, a new and enhanced version of UNWebBuy was launched. For example, an improved shopping cart and quotation system was introduced that enables eligible clients to receive a comprehensive and firm quotation in a matter of seconds. However, this system has not been widely introduced in other UN System organizations except for WHO (UNDP, 2002; Interview at WHO and IAPSO 2006; and http://www.unwebbuy.org).

At many organizations, there are obstacles that need to be overcome to promote E-procurement. First, organizations are not necessarily keen on E-procurement, partly because of the governing body's reluctance. Some governments among developing countries feel that if the procedures are conducted mainly through E-procurement, the vendors of these countries are disadvantaged because of the technology gap or so-called digital divide. Some developed countries are concerned that they must incur more costs for the preparation of E-procurement. Second, it is essential to check data convertibility and compatibility to the existing ERP system, especially when specialized E-procurement system like UNWebBuy is considered its introduction. ERP companies' cooperation is necessary for this to happen. Third, security problem must be overcome (Interviews at UN 2002, 2003 and 2006; and at IAPSO 2003 and 2006).

In addition to the above points, there are several constraints. The JIU report contends the following points: staff resistance at many levels, interagency's lack of ICT compatibility, field office compatibility and lack of in-house awareness, and lack of senior management commitment (JIU, 2004). In fact, establishing an interorganizational E-procurement infrastructure is a very difficult task in the UN System.

11.4.5 Socioeconomic and Political Objectives

There are various socioeconomic and political objectives in the UN System for which public procurement is regarded as a tool. However, the most eminent and stressed objective is the importance of growth in economy of developing countries through the increase of procurement from companies located in these countries. Procurement statistics are normally required to contain its amount and percentage from developing countries.

Even preferential treatment on bidding results for suppliers in the developing countries is demanded intermittently. For example, at UN in the late 1990s, the demand of preferential treatment to developing countries and countries in economic transition became stronger (UN, 1999). However, the secretary general virtually rejected that demand, citing the rule of awarding contracts based on "lowest acceptable bid" written in the financial regulations (UN, 1998). Not limited to such a demand, procurement operations are often influenced by several political objectives from member countries.* The main challenge is to keep a balance between these objectives and essential procurement values such as efficiency, transparency, and maximizing operational goals.

There are various types of preferential treatments that are common in national procurement but not so in UN System organizations. Small business, small disadvantaged business, women-owned small business, indigenous enterprise, and NGOs do not normally receive preferential treatments. Although some organizations like UNHCR and WFP give importance to environment (IAPSO, 2006b), environmentally friendly procurement seems not a strong requirement yet.

11.5 Conclusion

Public procurement operated by UN System organizations is not a well-known agenda compared to national procurement systems. Despite this, it is an important and challenging theme. Though the total procurement amount is small compared to many national procurements, the welfare and even lives of people who have been suffering from war, conflicts, violence, threats, natural disasters, hunger, and poverty, partly depend on the success of procurement operations conducted by UN System organizations. Procurement is the essential part of the implementation of various missions for these international organizations. In addition, as shown in the overview, total procurement volume is equivalent to approximately 40 percent of total financial resources in the UN System. Therefore, procurement is also important from the viewpoint of budgetary and administrative management.

The basic structure of the UN System procurement is independent and decentralized. The UN System has neither any strong central procurement policy-making body nor any central procurement implementation organization. Even though there are several notable procurement interagency mechanisms such as IAPWG, location-based common procurement, and procurement service agencies, both procurement policy making and procurement implementation are the responsibility of each organization. Therefore, this chapter also focused on the procurement measures and actual implementation of the individual organizational level.

In fact, procurement operation is not easy especially in the UN System because its organizations are faced with various difficulties. Although the organizations are confronted with enormous needs, financial resources available for the UN System are very limited compared to national governments. Therefore, the organizations must procure efficiently. The entire operation depends on the support of member states. Therefore, the organizations must maintain proper oversight and control functions to prevent corruption and mismanagement. The UN System lacks a strong central procurement authority. Therefore, it is imperative for the organizations to conduct various interagency procurement cooperation. Headquarters of the organizations are often far from the operational regions and fields. Therefore, the organizations must overcome the problems of distance. There are many emergency operations. Therefore, the organizations must procure and deliver swiftly.

Through various analyses in this chapter, it is clear that UN System organizations are making several concrete efforts to tackle such difficulties. Some measures are the same as the cases of national procurement systems. They include interagency cooperation, central procurement system on

* For example, WFP (2006) states: "Donor or recipient countries' conditions and restrictions on origin, destination, quality, packing and marking often limit the flexibility of the purchase and impact on this procurement planning." Regarding this, GM (genetically modified) food aid is a good example. WFP does not procure GM food without the consent of both donor and recipient countries. See WFP (2003).

headquarters level, several organizational oversight measures, and international competition. However, the following issues are said to be quite specific with regard to the UN System procurement compared to the national procurement practices.

In terms of organizational aspects, functional location is eminent. At the headquarters level, procurement sections of some organizations are not located within their headquarters but in Copenhagen where there are several operational merits and strong political support from the government of Denmark. The locations at the regional level are quite functional too. The location of procurement bases and regional supply offices varies widely depending on each organizational need and operational area. Furthermore, decentralization measures have been on the rise and procurement amount in developing countries is quite high. Reductions in both transportation cost and delivery time can be expected.

As for operational aspects, one of the main features of procurement implementation is LIC. LIC is a widely used method and it has some operational feasibility in the UN System especially from the viewpoint of swiftness, cost-effective proceeding, and secure transactions. LTA is also a very widely used method. Compared to the normal one-time OIC, LTA is beneficial in terms of swiftness and in obtaining cost reduction by realizing the economy of scale and by omitting bidding procedures each time.

Despite such organizational and operational efforts, there are still many future challenges. Some important examples are strengthening staff training with sufficient resource, effective interagency cooperation, promotion of E-procurement, implementing measures toward increasing demand of procurement in developing countries, and the incorporation of socioeconomic and political objectives.

Further research is needed from various perspectives on this theme. There is an abundance of possibilities that public procurement studies can contribute to enhancement of the UN System procurement both organizationally and operationally. At the same time, there are various features that are quite specific in the UN System procurement. Therefore, the analysis of the UN System procurement can be regarded as one of the additional interesting research objectives for public procurement studies both theoretically and practically.

Acknowledgments

The author would like to sincerely thank the procurement officials and officers in charge of procurement in UN System organizations for their kind cooperation and accepting my interviews. Furthermore, deep appreciations are addressed to Japan Society for the Promotion of Science, and to the Twenty-first Century Center of Excellence (COE) Program at the University of Tokyo, Graduate School of Law and Politics, for the funding on this research project.

References

Deloitte. 2005. Assessment of Internal Controls in the United Nations Secretariat Procurement Operations (Final Report). pp. 6, 7, 39–49. http://www.un.org/reports/procurement/UNPSReport.pdf.

D. Dijkzeul. 2000. *Reforming for Results in the UN System: A Study of UNOPS*. St. Martin's Press, New York, pp. 19–42, 71–73.

D. Drabkin and K.V. Thai. 2007. Emergency contracting in the US Federal Government. *Journal of Public Procurement*, Vol. 7, No. 1, pp. 84–103.

IAPSO. 2006a. *Annual Statistical Report 2005*. pp. 6, 7, 12. http://www.iapso.org/pdf/ASR_2004.pdf.

IAPSO. 2006b. *United Nations System General Business Guide* (20th ed.). pp. 6, 12, 17, 28, 50, 65, 114–120. http://www.iapso.org/pdf/gbg_master.pdf.

JIU. 2004. Procurement Practices within the United Nations System (prepared by Inspector Muhammad Yussuf) (JIU/REP/2004/9). paras. 4, 10, 26, 34, 35–36, 50, 65–66. http://www.unsystem.org/JIU/data/reports/2004/en2004_9.pdf.

NIGP. 2005. (Stefan Rollwage and William D. Brady). Assessment of UNPS Procurement Processes (Final Draft) (NIGP report). pp. 45–49.

T. Sakane. 2005a. *Procurement Administration and the United Nations System* (the Research Book Series of the Pubic Administration Research Society of the University of Tokyo, Vol. 1) (in Japanese). Twenty-first Century Center of Excellence (COE)—Invention of Policy Systems in Advanced Countries, the University of Tokyo, pp. 60–156.

T. Sakane. 2005b. An analysis of procurement administration in the United Nations system (in Japanese), *Kokka Gakkai Zassi* (*The Journal of the Association of Political and Social Sciences*), Vol. 118, No. 7–8, pp. 93–159.

R.M. Tomasini and L.N. Van Wassenhove. 2004. Pan-American health organization's humanitarian supply management system: De-politicization of the humanitarian supply chain by creating accountability. *Journal of Public Procurement*, Vol. 4, No. 3, pp. 437–449.

UN. 1995. Report of the Secretary-General on the Activities of the Office of Internal Oversight Services: Note by the Secretary-General (A/50/459).

UN. 1996. Procurement Reform: Fourth Report of the Advisory Committee on Administrative and Budgetary Questions (A/51/7/Add.3). para. 10.

UN. 1998. Procurement Reform: Report of the Secretary-General: Corrigendum (A/53/271/Corr.1). paras. 17–20.

UN. 1999. Procurement Reform: Resolution/Adopted by the General Assembly (A/RES/54/14). para. 26.

UN. 2000. Measures Taken to Improve Procurement Activities in the Field: Report of the Secretary-General (A/54/866). paras. 7–8.

UN. 2002. United Nations Development Programme: Financial Report and Audited Financial Statements for the Biennium Ended 31 December 2001 and Report of the Board of Auditors: Corrigendum (A/57/5/Add.1). paras. 155–167.

UN. 2006a. Budgetary and Financial Situation of Organizations of the United Nations System: Note by the Secretary-General Transmitting the Statistical Report of the United Nations System Chief Executives Board for Coordination (A/59/315). Table 3.

UN. 2006b. Investing in the United Nations: For a Stronger Organization Worldwide. Detailed Report: Report of the Secretary-General. Addendum: Corrigendum (A/60/846/Add.5/Corr.1). paras. 12–13, 17, 28–29.

UN. 2006c. Procurement Reform: Draft Resolution/Submitted by the Chairman Following Informal Consultations (A/C.5/61/L.23). paras. 38–43.

UNDP. 1995. Activities of the Inter-Agency Procurement Services Office. Report of the Administrator: United Nations Development Programme (DP/1996/7). paras. 5, 12–15, 16–18, 19–22. http://www.ods.un.org. (The following UNDP, UNICEF, and UN documents with document numbers are also available from this URL.)

UNDP. 2002. Report of the Inter-Agency Procurement Services Office for the Biennium 2000–2001 (DP/2002/31). paras. 17–20.

UNICEF. 1992. *UNIPAC 30 Years 1962–1992*. pp. 1, 21, 27, 35.

UNICEF. 1994. *Supply Division Annual Report 1994*. pp. 8, 41.

UNICEF. 2003a. Review of the UNICEF Supply Function in the Context of the Medium-Term Strategic Plan (E/ICEF/2003/7). para. 43.

UNICEF. 2003b. *UNICEF Book G: The Supply Manual* (Chapter7) (2003 last revision). Section2–2.1, Section4–3.0 and Section4–7.10.

Volker Commission (The Independent Inquiry Committee into the United Nations Oil-for-Food Programme). 2005, 7 September. The Management of the United Nations Oil-for-Food Programme (Volume I—The Report of the Committee). pp. 63–65. http://www.iic-offp.org/Mgmt_Report.htm.

WFP. 1996. *Food Procurement User Guide.* 4.5.
WFP. 1998. Local Purchases of Food and Non-Food Items (WFP/EB.A/98/8-B). para. 22. http://www.wfp.org/eb/docs/1998/wfp000184~1.pdf.
WFP. 2003. WFP Policy on Donations of Foods Derived from Biotechnology (WFP/EB.A/2003/5-B/Rev.1). p. 5. http://www.wfp.org/eb/docs/2003/wfp016888~3.pdf.
WFP. 2006. WFP Food Procurement January–December 2005. p. 2.

Quoted Interviews

UN, Department of Management, Procurement Division, Logistics & Transportation Section Chief, on 25 September 2002 and on 12 March 2003, at the Procurement Division HQ in New York.
IAPSO (UNDP), ICT & E-Commerce Manager, on 3 March 2003, at the HQ in Copenhagen.
UNICEF, Supply Division Communication Officer, on 5 March 2003, at the Supply Division HQ in Copenhagen.
UNHCR, Supply Management Service, Procurement and Contracts Section Chief, and Procurement Unit Senior Supply Officer, on 7–8 February 2006, at the HQ Annex in Geneva. WHO, Contracting and Procurement Services Coordinator, on 9–10 February 2006, at the HQ in Geneva.
IAPSO (UNDP), Director, Deputy Director, and E-procurement Manager, on 14 February 2006, at the HQ in Copenhagen.
UNOPS, Division of Procurement Services Chief, on 15 February 2006, at the HQ in Copenhagen.
UNFPA, Division of Management Services, Procurement and Facilities Management Branch, Procurement Specialist, on 1 March 2006, at the HQ in New York.
UN, Department of Management, Procurement Division, Support Services Section Chief, on 3 March 2006, at the Procurement Division HQ in New York.
WFP, Operations Department Food Procurement Service Senior Procurement Officer, Management Services Division Good and Services Procurement Branch Chief, and Ocean Transport Service Transport and Procurement Division Senior Shipping Officer, on 25–26 September 2006, at the HQ in Rome.

Chapter 12

EC Regime on Public Procurement*

Sue Arrowsmith

CONTENTS

* This chapter was completed and submitted for publication in August 2007.

12.1 Introduction

Many governments have traditionally followed protectionist practices in public procurement—such as reserving contracts for national suppliers—that can have a significant impact on trade. The aim of the European Community (EC) procurement regime is to eliminate such practices to open up public procurement to trade between the EC member states. The EC's system is of interest for several reasons.

First, although many trade regimes now deal with public procurement (Nwogwugwu, 2005), the EC's is one of the oldest and certainly the most comprehensive, and its experience is valuable for other trade regimes. This is not to say that its value is necessarily mainly as a model for other regimes—as Schwartz (2002) has pointed out, the value of comparative study in procurement often lies in learning of mistakes to be avoided. Further, the value of the EC's experience is limited by different economic and political circumstances that prevail in different regions, and the unique nature of the EC enterprise itself. Nevertheless, other regimes can benefit from studying the EC's experience. For example, studies of the EC shed light on the economic impact of regulation (See the studies cited near the end of this section).

Second, several non-EC states are affected by the EC rules, either because the same rules apply under trade agreements with EC (notably with Norway, Iceland, and Liechtenstein under the Economic Area Agreement) (Bock, 1993), because they aspire to membership of the EC (e.g., Turkey: Alyanak, 2007), or because they are expected to follow at least the basic principles of EC procurement law under trade agreements.

Third, the EC's regime has influenced the design of other regimes notably the World Trade Organization's (WTO) Agreement on Government Procurement (GPA) (which is itself used as the basis or model for other agreements). This is both because it was one of the first available models and because the EC was an influential participant in the GPA. The EC regime's influence is seen, in particular, in the GPA's rules on award procedures and challenge procedures. The likely increasing importance of the GPA—particularly in light of the possible accession of China, which is committed to make an offer of GPA accession in 2007—magnifies its importance in this respect.

Fourth, the EC system is of obvious interest to those wishing to supply the public procurement markets of EC member states, including under access granted under the GPA. Knowledge of the EC regime is also important for governments wishing to access the EC market in future. For both groups, it is important to note that the extent and nature of contracts that the EC is willing to open up to trade, including under the GPA, is substantially influenced (as with the other GPA parties) by the coverage rules of its internal regime, and is much better understood with knowledge of that regime. For example, many of its exclusions under the annexes listing its commitments under the GPA refer to the exclusions that exist under its internal directives.

Finally, whilst the EC's objective is to open up procurement for trade reasons, the regime is interesting not only from the perspective of trade. This is because the EC legislation is the product of pooled experience of a number of states that have considered how to regulate particular issues—including new issues, such as electronic auctions—in a manner that is acceptable to all of them. This experience is interesting for other countries looking to regulate the same phenomenon, even when this is for other reasons, such as to ensure "value for money"—with the caveat that in drawing on EC experience it is essential to keep in mind that the EC's reasons for regulation (opening up trade) differ from those of most national regimes.

This chapter outlines the EC system in a way that is intended to be accessible to those without prior knowledge of EC law. The regime is complex and what is offered here is merely an overview; for a more detailed practitioners' review readers are referred to Trepte (2007), and for an in-depth analysis of the law and policy to the author's own treatise (Arrowsmith, 2005).

The EC (before 1993 called the European Economic Community [EEC]) was established in 1957 to promote economic cooperation and peace in Europe. The EC, together with the European Atomic Energy Community (Euratom), constitutes one element—or "pillar"—of the broader European Union (EU), (the first pillar). (The second and third pillars, which have limited relevance for procurement, are concerned with a common foreign and security policy and with justice and home affairs, respectively.) Currently, the EC has 27 member states, namely Belgium, France, Germany, Italy, Luxembourg, and the Netherlands (the founding members); Denmark, Ireland, and the United Kingdom (members from 1973); Greece (1981) Spain, and Portugal (1986); Austria, Finland, and Sweden (1995); Cyprus, the Czech Republic, Estonia, Hungary, Latvia, Lithuania, Malta, Poland, the Slovak Republic, and Slovenia (2004); and Bulgaria and Romania (2007). The main objective of the EC has been to create a common market in Europe by removing barriers to trade in goods and for free movement of business, labor, and capital. Its basic constitutional document is the EC Treaty, which has been amended and reshaped many times since 1957. The treaty places obligations on member states concerned with creating a single market and also confers on the EC powers to legislate further. This legislative power is exercised mainly through the Council of Ministers, composed of ministerial-level representatives of all member states, and the elected European parliament. The administrative arm of the EC, responsible for proposing and enforcing legislation is the Commission of the European Communities (the commission). Responsibility for interpreting EC law lies with the European Court of Justice (ECJ).

The reason that the EC regulates public procurement is to further its policy of creating a free market. This policy is based on the theory of comparative advantage. A state enjoys a comparative advantage in producing particular goods or services when it produces these relatively efficiently in comparison with other states. The theory of comparative advantage states that under free trade a country tends to specialize in producing those goods and services in which it enjoys a comparative advantage and trades them for others, and that this trade leads to an increase in economic welfare. This theory and its qualifications are well explained for lay readers by Sykes (1998). Public procurement practices that do not allow for free competition from other states distort the natural patterns of trade and thus may be detrimental to economic welfare (as summarized by Trionfetti, 2003). Such practices arise both because governments deliberately favor national or local industry and for other reasons, such as inertia in seeking out new sources of supply. Removing trade barriers in public markets can make an important contribution to economic growth both because of the size of these markets (estimated as 16.3 percent of the EC's GDP: Commission of the European Communities, 2004a) and their nature, which gives significant scope for economies of scale through restructuring. (On the projected benefits see the Atkins study [W.S. Atkins Management Consultants, 1988]; and on the actual benefits and factors affecting this see Commission of the European Communities, 1997 [also summarized in Bohan and Redonnet, 1997; Gordon et al., 1998] and Commission of the European Communities, 2004a; and also Uttley and Hartley, 1994; Cox and Furlong, 1996, 1997; McDonald and Winkelman, 1996; de Boer and Telgen, 1997; Martin and Hartley, 1997; Martin et al., 1999; Milne and Osler, 2000; Nielsen and Hansen, 2001; Madsen, 2002.)

The rules created to implement this internal market policy in procurement derive mainly from two sources: the EC Treaty, which applies in principle to all contracts, and the procurement directives, which regulate procedures for awarding certain larger contracts. In this chapter, we first consider the EC Treaty's basic obligations not to discriminate, which are important for all contracts (Section 12.2). We then introduce the public procurement directives (Section 12.3) and set out their coverage (Sections 12.4 and 12.5) and main procedural requirements (Section 12.6). Next we consider how far contracts outside the directives are also subject to procedural rules under the treaty's regime of positive obligations (Section 12.7). We then consider how the EC regime deals with some specific issues, namely defense procurement, electronic procurement, collateral policies, and enforcement (Sections 12.8 through 12.11). There then follows a section on the position of non-EC suppliers (Section 12.12) and, finally, a brief critical review.

12.2 Impact of the EC Treaty on Procurement

As mentioned, the first main source of obligations is the EC Treaty itself (Arrowsmith, 2005, Chapter 4). The treaty does not expressly mention public procurement in the internal market. However, it contains certain general provisions, the free movement provisions, that (inter alia) prohibit states from discriminating against the firms, products, and services of other EC member states. From the outset these were assumed to apply to discrimination in public procurement, and this has been confirmed by the ECJ, as we will discuss later in this section. In this, the EC Treaty differs from the WTO Agreements on trade in goods and services (the General Agreement on Tariffs and Trade (GATT) and General Agreement on Trade in Services (GATS)), which exclude government procurement from their core obligations not to discriminate against the industry of other states (Dischendorfer, 2000; Arrowsmith, 2003, Chapter 6).

The EC obligation not to discriminate also differs from similar obligations on public procurement in other trade agreements, including the GPA, in another important respect. This is that it applies in principle to all public procurement. In contrast to the GPA, for example, member states do not negotiate to include (or exclude) specific entities, specific types of contract, or specific industries from the obligation not to discriminate: all types of contracts and all public bodies are included for all member states. Member states also may not negotiate special exemptions for specific types of programs, such as programs to support small businesses, which are important under the GPA (Arrowsmith, 2003, Chapter 13) and some other trade regimes; policies of this kind are permitted only insofar as allowed for all member states under the general principles of EC law (see Section 12.10). A different approach has been adopted under the GPA and other agreements because of the difficulty of achieving adequate coverage at all using a common approach for all states. However, within the EC, states were prepared in the early days of the EC to accept a broad obligation not to discriminate in public procurement, and to abolish during the first few years of the EEC their existing discriminatory practices. The same approach has been required of all new member states. This does not, of course, mean that all states immediately complied with the obligation that they had accepted, as will become apparent from the discussion below.

The most important specific provisions of the EC Treaty for public procurement are Article 28 EC on free movement of goods (formerly Article 30) and Article 49 EC on freedom to provide services (formerly Article 59).

Article 28 prohibits, in effect, all restrictions on imports from other member states, including measures such as import quotas and discriminatory technical regulations, as well as discrimination in procurement. It covers, first, any measures that discriminate directly between domestic and imported products, such as a policy of buying only domestic products for government, or price preference for such products. For example, in the *Storebaelt* case, the ECJ stated that a requirement for using Danish material in a contract for constructing a bridge in Denmark violated Article 28 EC. Another example is the *Du Pont de Nemours* case. In this case the ECJ ruled that an Italian law requiring public authorities to reserve 30 percent of certain supplies for firms with establishments and fixed plant in the underdeveloped Mezzorgiorno region of Italy to reduce regional inequalities violated Article 28. Article 28 also covers measures that apply equally to domestic and imported products (indistinctly applicable measures) but have the *effect* of favoring domestic products as against imports. We can note that the ECJ has assumed that Article 28 and the other provisions discussed below apply not merely to general measures on public procurement, such as legislation requiring price preferences to domestic products, but also to decisions relating to individual contracts (e.g., recently, in the *Telaustria* case).

Article 49, on freedom to provide services, is concerned to open the market for firms of one member state who wish to provide services, including construction services, in another member state, while based in their home state. It covers both those who wish to base themselves temporarily abroad and those who propose to carry out services in other states while remaining at home. This provision prevents public bodies from discriminating, directly or indirectly, against firms from other states in relation to public services contracts. Obviously, it again prohibits practices such as reserving contracts for national firms only, and also covers measures that favor national firms further down the supply chain. An example is Case C–360/89, *Commission v. Italy*, in which the ECJ held contrary to Article 49 two provisions in Italian legislation. One required public works contractors to reserve a proportion of works for subcontractors with a registered office in the region of the works; this discriminated against firms established outside Italy in affording opportunities to undertake the contract work. The other was a provision stating that in choosing who should be invited to tender for certain works contracts preference should be given to firms whose main activity was in the region of the works: this indirectly favored firms established in Italy, which were more likely than firms from other member states to have their main activities in the region of the works.

There are, however, exceptions to the above principles: discriminatory measures can be justified when they promote legitimate interests of member states that override the interest in promoting free trade.

First, they can be justified under certain exceptions stated in the EC Treaty. For Article 28, Article 30 provides exceptions on grounds of "public morality, public policy or public security; the protection of health and life of humans, animals or plants; the protection of national treasures possessing artistic, historic or archaeological value; or the protection of industrial and commercial property." Similar exceptions for Article 49 apply under Articles 46 and 55 EC. In practice, the most important exception for public procurement is that for public security. This might be relied on, for example, to justify making defense purchases from national industry to ensure the survival of a national capability (see Section 12.8).

Discriminatory procurement can also be justified on the basis of various public interest grounds that are not stated in the treaty but have been recognized by the ECJ. These include, for example, environmental protection and improvement of working conditions. An interesting illustration of how this might be relevant in public procurement is provided by the *Preussen Elektra* case. This case concerned German legislation that required electricity suppliers to purchase electricity produced from renewable sources within their area of supply, at prices above economic value, to encourage production of electricity from renewable sources. The ECJ ruled that although this prevented purchasers from procuring electricity from suppliers in other member states it was justified on environmental grounds (and also on health grounds). The use of a measure that discriminated directly against suppliers in other member states was apparently justified by the practical problems of verifying the source of electricity with suppliers from other areas. These public interest grounds, which are open ended and may be added to further by the ECJ, could potentially be invoked to justify implementing a range of social policies in public procurement, such as policies to promote gender equality, as discussed in Section 12.10. However, the ECJ has consistently ruled that purely economic interests can never be used to justify restrictions on trade, and it is clear that supporting jobs or employment in uncompetitive industries or developing infant industries cannot be used as a justification: this is contrary to the very purpose of the free movement rules. We have also seen above that in the *Du Pont de Nemours* case procurement measures to support regional development were held contrary to the treaty: the ECJ ruled that these could not be justified. (However, the ECJ does expressly provide for support for underdeveloped regions through other means, namely the award of state aid (e.g., subsidies), that are subject to tight control to prevent abuse.)

In addition to controlling measures that discriminate against other member states, the EC Treaty also imposes some control over even nondiscriminatory measures that restrict access to markets: that is, it prohibits some measures that prevent firms or products from other EC states from accessing a state's market, even if those restrictions affect domestic firms equally. This is a very complex question and the position of nondiscriminatory measures in public procurement has not yet been clearly established (Arrowsmith and Kunzlik, forthcoming, Chapter 2). Thus, a few brief remarks must suffice.

First, what is clear is that measures concerning the characteristics of products sold are caught by Article 28 even when not discriminatory. Thus, all general technical regulations—for example, on the health standards to be met by products in the market—are considered hindrances to trade that must be justified (e.g., under Article 30 by the need to protect public health). This principle has also been applied in public procurement. Thus, the ECJ has held that contract specifications concerning goods contravene Article 28 EC even when they affect domestic and nondomestic suppliers equally, where they exclude access to government markets of products that fulfill the government's functional requirements. Thus, in the *UNIX* case, the ECJ held that it violated Article 28 EC to refer to UNIX (a de facto industry standard) as the required operating system for connecting computers in a contract for a weather station, because other systems could equally meet the functional requirements for the contract—that is, were equivalent in functional terms.

What is not clear, on the other hand, is how far nondiscriminatory restrictions are caught in public procurement that are not concerned with products themselves—for example, restrictions concerning the suppliers themselves, such as requirements for a certain number of years experience, or requirements that suppliers should have fair recruitment policies. If such measures are caught even when (as is often the case) they have the same effect on domestic and nondomestic suppliers, such measures will have to be justified under treaty exceptions or on grounds of public interest if they are to be allowed. This would have the effect that almost every procurement decision by a member state would, if challenged, have to be justified before the ECJ. This seems impractical and undesirable, especially if (as mentioned above) even individual contract decisions are subject to the treaty. Thus, it seems unlikely that the ECJ would take this approach. However, the matter remains to be clarified.

These rules are binding on member states and enforceable against them and their procuring entities, in accordance with the rules set out in Section 12.11 on remedies. Member states have an obligation to repeal any laws or other measures that contravene the treaty—for example, national laws that provide for price preferences for domestic products. However, even if member states fail to do this the EC rules will still apply and be enforceable: they will override any national measures that are inconsistent with them.

It should also be mentioned that, as well as the free movement rules, Articles 87–89 EC are significant in public procurement. These articles control subsidies to industry, referred to in the EC as state aid, because such subsidies may give an industry an advantage over its competitors in other member states. In particular, any public procurement contracts awarded to national firms that involve excessive remuneration (beyond a commercial market price) may constitute unlawful state aid contrary to the EC Treaty: such contracts involve indirect financial support for national industry (the *BAI* case; Priess and von Merveldt, forthcoming).

12.3 Procurement Directives

12.3.1 Introduction to the Directives

As noted earlier, for a long time the EC Treaty was considered to impose only negative obligations in public procurement, prohibiting discrimination, and certain other restrictions on access to markets. However, negative obligations alone are not sufficient to open up procurement markets. One reason is the difficulty of proving discrimination. Many contracts are likely to be awarded to national firms because they are the most competitive suppliers, including because of market advantages such as proximity, language skills, etc., and it may be difficult for a competitive foreign supplier to show that discrimination, rather than other factors, have lead to awards to national suppliers. In addition, trade barriers arise also for reasons other than deliberate discrimination. To deal with these issues the EC has adopted directives on public procurement that regulate the procedures for awarding major contracts and also provide for the means to enforce these procedures. These require public bodies (and some private bodies, as discussed in Section 12.5.2) to award contracts using procedures that are transparent. The purpose of the transparency rules is to ensure that member states cannot hide discrimination, and also to require them to take positive steps to improve access to contracts for firms from other member states, such as by advertising contracts.

These directives are a form of secondary legislation adopted by the EC under the EC Treaty, based on the power found in Articles 47, 55, and 95 EC Treaty to legislate for an internal market. Each member state must adopt legislation that places on its purchasers a legal requirement to follow the directives' procedures, for example, to advertise their contracts, and that sets up a system of legal remedies for suppliers (see Section 12.11). For some states, such as the United Kingdom, that did not previously regulate procurement through legal instruments but mainly through guidance, this meant introducing significant legislation on procurement for the first time. For others, such as France, the process required integration with, and amendment of, existing procurement codes. Generally, member states are given a period of at least a year to implement directives after they enter into force. With the latest directives adopted in 2004 a period of 21 months was generally allowed.

In practice, especially in the early years, many member states did not implement the directives in a timely manner. From the mid-1980s, however, the Commission became much more active in enforcing the EC procurement rules and took many member states before the ECJ for failing to implement them or implementing them only in part or incorrectly. Implementation rates have now greatly improved. However, even the most recent directives of 2004 have not been implemented in a timely manner by all member states—although, unlike in earlier years, member states have generally made good faith efforts to enact the relevant legislation (Trybus and Medina, forthcoming).

The fact that a directive is not implemented does not mean that purchasing entities need not follow its rules. Under the principle of direct effect in EC law, once the time limit for implementing has expired a directive must be followed and can be enforced even when it has not been implemented whenever its provisions are clear, precise, and unconditional. This is the case with the rules on awarding procurement contracts (e.g., the *Walter Tögel* case). Although the Commission has referred to non-implementation of the directives as a reason for its policies' limited success (Commission of the European Communities, 1996), the Commission's own study (Commission of the European Communities, 1997) has shown no correlation between observance of the rules by procuring entities and implementation through national legislation—in particular, some states that had not implemented the directives had high compliance rates.

The first procurement directives were adopted in the 1970s to regulate works and supply contracts of public bodies, whether central, provincial, or local. Since then they have been extended and amended many times (Arrowsmith, 2005, Chapter 3). At present, the rules on contract award procedures are contained in two directives adopted in 2004, which were required to be implemented by January 2006 (although, as noted above, not all states have yet implemented them). These are as follows:

(1) Directive 2004/18/EC (Public Sector Directive). This regulates most major contracts awarded by public bodies. It replaced three previous directives that dealt separately (although in an almost identical manner) with works contracts (Works Directive 93/37), supply contracts (Supply Directive 93/36), and services contracts (Services Directive 92/50).
(2) Directive 2004/17 (Utilities Directive). This regulates procurement in four specific areas of activity, namely water, energy, transport, and postal services—for example, procurement of water pumps by state-owned water companies. It replaces the previous directive governing utilities (Directive 93/38).

These follow the same basic approach as the original directives, though with some amendments. They also contain provisions on new issues, such as electronic procurement.

Before considering the directives' detailed rules, it is appropriate to highlight some of their important characteristics and their general approach.

First, the directives are concerned only with creating an internal market in public procurement—they are based solely on treaty provisions concerned with the internal market, as noted above. They are not, on the other hand, intended to provide a general system for implementing objectives found in national procurement systems, such as ensuring best value for taxpayers' money, preventing corruption, balancing financial and social considerations in procurement, or ensuring accountability. Of course, the directives are concerned with value for money to the limited extent that removing trade barriers is one way of obtaining better value for goods and services. For some states they may also incidentally result in improvements to the procurement system that will enhance value for money in other respects—for example, the advertising requirements that are designed to improve access for foreign suppliers may also result in better information for local suppliers. However, it is the author's view that beyond their effect in opening markets it is not the directives' objective of ensuring that public purchasers obtain value for money (Arrowsmith, 2005, Chapter 3). This, like most other aspects of procurement policy, remains a matter for member states.

It is necessary to appreciate this to understand the approach taken by the directives to various issues, and to appreciate the limits of the guidance that they offer for regulating procurement. This is why, for example, they apply only to contracts above certain financial thresholds: they are not confined to these contracts because formal competition is not appropriate for smaller contracts. To obtain value for money or prevent corruption, many member states indeed have their own competition requirements at much lower thresholds. Rather, the directives are limited to high-value contracts because the legislature decided to regulate only those contracts sufficiently large to be of interest to firms in other member states. Similarly, the provisions on framework agreements do not contain significant limits or guidance on the types of products or services for which different types of framework agreements can or should be used (see Section 12.6.6), even though these are often included in national procurement laws. This is explained by the fact that the EC directives do not set out the circumstances in which it is appropriate to use frameworks for effective purchasing, but merely to ensure that if states choose to use them they do so in a transparent manner to prevent discrimination. Thus, anyone looking for guidance on how to regulate low-value contracts or when to use framework agreements should not conclude from the absence of provisions in the directives that regulation is not appropriate, but should appreciate that the directives have no concern with these matters. The UNCITRAL (United Nations Commission for International Trade Law) Model Law on Procurement of Goods, Construction, and Services, on the other hand, does contain guidance on many issues that are not covered in the directives (including procedures for low-value purchases). Even though the latter instrument is, like the directives, not entirely exhaustive (because it accepts that states may want to regulate some matters in different ways according to their circumstances) it is more comprehensive in its general approach and coverage, because it does seek to guide states on how to obtain value for money in all its aspects, and to meet other objectives such as preventing corruption.

A related point is that the directives do not lay down an exhaustive set of procurement rules, but leave room for member states' own rules, provided that these are consistent with the directives (*Beentjes* and *CEI/Bellini* cases). States may, for example, adopt stricter rules than those in the directives. For example, as explained in Section 12.6.2, the Public Sector Directive allows entities to use either open procedures, in which all firms may tender, or restricted procedures, in which only a limited number of those who respond to an advertisement are permitted to tender. However, states may take the view that for value for money reasons their entities should generally use only open procedures, and may provide for this in their procurement laws. Similarly, for value for money reasons, states may decide that their own entities should not have access to some of the purchasing techniques allowed under the directives, such as framework agreements, or should be allowed to use them only in limited cases, such as for standard products (Recital 16 to the Public Sector Directive). That said, it needs to be recognized—as argued in detail elsewhere—that the scope of discretion left to member states has substantially diminished in recent years (Arrowsmith, 2006). This is due in part to the fact that the content of the explicit directives has become more detailed over the years (see, e.g., Section 12.9 on electronic procurement), in part to the ECJ's strict interpretation (see, e.g., Section 12.10 on collateral policies), and in part to the development of general principles that apply even when the directives contain no explicit rules on a subject (see Section 12.4.1 and 12.6.1). Although in theory the directives still retain their character as a framework within which member states implement their own procurement policies, the actual freedom to choose how to implement those policies is increasingly limited.

It is also important to note that (as with the treaty) the directives' coverage is the same for all member states, and it is not possible to negotiate for state-specific derogations.

12.4 Coverage: The Public Sector Directive

12.4.1 Which Procuring Entities Are Covered?

So far as covered entities are concerned, the Public Sector Directive applies to all entities classified as contracting authorities, namely all of the following (Article 1(9)):

- State—this covers, inter alia, government departments and ministers
- Local and regional authorities—for example, municipal authorities and—in federal states—state governments
- Associations formed by the above bodies
- Bodies governed by public law

The concept of a body governed by public law is a "catch-all" provision designed to bring within the directive procuring entities that are potentially subject to governmental influence to favor national industry. The concept is defined in Article 1(9) to cover a body that has legal personality *and either* (1) is financed for the most part by a contracting authority, (2) is subject to management supervision by a contracting authority, or (3) has a board more than half of whose members are appointed by a contracting authority, *and is* "established for the specific purpose of meeting needs in the general interest, not having an industrial or commercial character …."

This last condition basically excludes from the definition certain entities that supply goods on a market—for example, a local authority company setup to operate a theme park along commercial lines might be excluded. However, it does not exclude all state-owned companies: the ECJ has indicated that it applies, in effect, only when they are operating according to strict economic considerations (Arrowsmith, 2005, Chapter 6). It should also be noted that some state companies (e.g., those supplying water or electricity) are now regulated by the Utilities Directive, as discussed in Section 12.5.

In the United Kingdom, the concept of a body governed by public covers, for example, hospitals, publicly funded schools, and most universities. Annex III of the directive sets out a list of specific named bodies considered to be within this category in various member states, but Article 1(9) makes clear that this is for illustrative purposes only: a body is covered only if it falls within the definition (a body that is listed but does not fall within the definition is outside the rules), and is always covered if it falls within the definition, even if not listed. In line with the principle of the common coverage of the directives for all member states, the ECJ has emphasized that the concept of body governed by public law has a common meaning for all, and thus does not necessarily correspond with the definition of "public" or "administrative" bodies in states' domestic law. The relevant definition is the one in the directives themselves, not the definition of public/administrative body in domestic law (*SIEPSA* case). All the different elements of the definition have been elaborated more precisely in many cases of the ECJ (Arrowsmith, 2005, Chapter 6; Papangeli, 2000).

In addition to regulating contracting authorities as defined in the beginning of this section, the directive imposes some obligations on private bodies, because of the risk that their purchasing may be influenced by government and the importance of the contracts concerned. Thus, the rules of the directive must be applied to certain types of works and services contracts that are subsidized by more than 50 percent by contracting authorities (Article 8). The contracts covered are those connected with activities covered by Group 502 of the NACE nomenclature on public works (general civil engineering) and building work for hospitals, sports recreation and leisure facilities, school and university buildings, and administrative buildings. For example, in the United Kingdom, the rules would apply to works contracts of this kind when paid for with funds awarded from the national lottery, even though the purchaser is a private entity. Very limited rules also apply to private bodies holding public works concessions.

12.4.2 Which Contracts Are Covered?

12.4.2.1 Type of Contracts Covered

The directive applies very broadly to all types of procurement contracts—it applies in principle to works contracts, supply contracts, and services contracts, where these are "in writing" and "for pecuniary interest" (Article 1(2)).

However, the directive does not apply fully to all services contracts: these are divided (under Articles 20–21) into priority services, which are subject to the directive's full rules as outlined in Section 12.4.2.2, and non-priority services, which are subject only to very limited rules (on technical specifications, award notices, and statistics). Priority services are listed in Annex IIA—they include some manual services such as vehicle maintenance and refuse collection, as well as various professional services such as accountancy, IT services, and consultancy. They have been selected on the basis of potential scope for cross-border trade, potential savings, and availability of information on the service.

12.4.2.2 Exclusions

Although coverage is generally broad, some contracts are excluded altogether. The main exclusions are as follows:

(1) Concessions. Services concession contracts are excluded (Article 17). These are contracts in which the contractor is remunerated by exploiting the service (Article 1(4))—for example, a contract to build and operate a leisure center where remuneration comes from charging users. Works concessions are subject to only very limited rules, namely to advertise the contract in the EU's *Official Journal* (Article 58(1)), and to give at least 52 days (as a general rule) for firms to respond (Article 59).
(2) Certain contracts awarded to another contracting authority (see Section 12.4.2.4).
(3) Certain contracts for hard defense equipment (Article 10) and other contracts affected by various concerns relating to secrecy or security (Article 14). These are discussed in Section 12.8 on defense.
(4) Contracts governed by different procedural rules connected with joint projects with non-member states, those by international bodies (e.g., the United Nations or World Bank), and those made pursuant to international agreements on the stationing of troops (Article 15).

(5) Contracts for certain services. Apart from the fact that non-priority services are subject only to limited rules, some services contracts are excluded altogether, each for different reasons. These are arbitration or conciliation services, certain financial services, and certain research and development services (Article 16).
(6) Utility contracts. Contracts awarded by contracting authorities connected with the activities regulated under the Utilities Directive are excluded—these are subject to that directive instead (Article 12). Contracts connected with telecommunications activities (which were previously regulated by the Utilities Directive but are now excluded from regulation altogether) are also excluded.

Authorities are also permitted to dispense with some of the usual rules, where necessary in certain cases and, to the extent necessary, in awarding contracts for the design and construction of public housing schemes (Article 34).

12.4.2.3 Financial Thresholds

The directive applies only to contracts above certain financial values (thresholds). As noted in Section 12.3, this is because the legislator decided to regulate only contracts large enough to interest firms from other member states. We have already mentioned that in many states competition is required at lower thresholds, to promote objectives such as value for money and integrity. The rules on thresholds are set out in Articles 7–9.

The thresholds are stated in euros. They are revised every two years to align them with the thresholds in the GPA (which are set out in SDR, not euros, and are themselves adjusted every two years to take account of movement of the euro and other currencies). The thresholds have already been revised since 2004: the current threshold figures are set out in Commission Regulation (EC) No 2083/2005. For countries not in the euro-zone, the euro thresholds are converted into national currencies when the euro rates are established, and that conversion value (which is based on the exchange rate in the previous two years) is applied for the next two years.

In principle, the relevant value for determining the threshold is the value of each contract. However, it is well known that purchasers sometimes split contracts into smaller amounts, to bring them below regulatory thresholds, and this phenomenon has also been seen in the EC regime. To address it, the Public Sector Directive includes two sets of provisions. First, the directive (like the GPA) prohibits purchasers from splitting up purchases with the intention of bringing the value of contracts below the threshold to avoid the directives (Article 9(3)). However, this is difficult to prove. Second, the directive also includes an additional set of provisions that are more stringent than those in other trade agreements, such as the GPA. These require a purchaser to add together the value of purchases made under a number of similar contracts: the directive will apply if the value of these added together exceeds the threshold (aggregation rules). These rules on aggregation help prevent purchasers from evading the rules, because they remove the need to prove that contracts were artificially split. Further, they have the practical effect of ensuring that the directives are not rendered inoperative by inefficient purchasing, and provide an incentive for authorities to award work in a single package that might attract cross-border competition. These rules do not actually prohibit authorities splitting up work and awarding it in smaller amounts, but discourage them from doing so because they will have to apply the procedures in the directives to a number of small contracts. One effect is to discourage authorities from splitting up work to encourage participation by small and medium-sized enterprises (SMEs), although encouraging SME participation is an objective not only of the procurement policy of many member states but also of the EC's own industrial policy.

The aggregation rules are complex and their precise application uncertain (Brown, 1993)—features of the rules that limit their successful application (Commission of the European Communities, 1997). Their broad principles are as follows:

- For supplies and services, purchasers must aggregate all purchases of a particular product or service over a year (see Article 9(7)). There is an exemption for small lots, provided that the total value of exempt lots is not more than 20 percent of the value of all the lots (see Article 9(5)). This exemption can help facilitate participation of SMEs.
- For works contracts, the only rule is that where a single work is divided into several lots the value of all lots must be added together. A work is defined as the outcome of building or civil engineering works taken as a whole that is sufficient of itself to fulfill an economic or technical function. For example, separate contracts relating to a sports stadium (one for the main building, one for a retractable roof, etc.) would have to be aggregated. Again, an exemption applies for small lots.

12.4.2.4 Contracts Awarded to Other Contracting Authorities

In principle, contracts awarded to another public body are covered by the directives—thus a public body can only perform work for another if it wins that work in a competition under the directives (the *Teckal* case). However, there are certain exceptions to this.

(1) For services that are provided by another contracting authority with an exclusive right to provide them, or an exclusive right necessary for their provision (Article 18). This covers, for example, a rule requiring public bodies to buy services (such as accounting services) from a centralized service provider.
(2) For contracts awarded to central purchasing bodies. Central purchasers are bodies set up to provide supplies or services to a range of public bodies. The directive allows authorities to buy from another contracting authority—a central purchasing body—without following the directive, in the case of supplies and services (Articles 1(10) and 11), provided that the central purchasing body has followed the directive in making its own purchases (as is required, because it is itself a contracting authority). In such a case, it is considered unnecessary to apply the directive to those purchases for a second time.
(3) *Teckal* principle. In this case, the ECJ stated that the directives (and treaty) do not apply to agreements made with another legal entity under certain conditions, which are considered to be "in-house" arrangements rather than contracts with a "separate" person—for example, contracts made with certain 100 percent owned subsidiary companies of a local authority.

Arrangements are in-house only when made with a separate entity over which the purchaser has the same control as its own departments, and where the awardee carries out the essential part of its activities for the purchasing entity (i.e., does not generally sell its goods or services in the marketplace). If any private firm has an interest in the awardee then the first condition cannot be met (the *Stadt Halle* case) and, further, even companies that are 100 percent owned are sometimes not treated as in-house departments, because of limited control by the parent authority (the *Carbotermo* case). However, the exception can in principle be used where control of the supplying entity is shared by several entities—for example, where several local authorities set up a joint company to provide refuse collection service to all the authorities (the *Carbotermo* case). The ECJ has made it clear that the in-house rule cannot be relied upon when an authority sets up a separate entity with the intention of privatizing it once it has been given the work under the in-house rule—this is simply a device to get round the directives (the *Mödling* case).

12.5 Coverage: The Utilities Directive

12.5.1 Which Sectors Are Covered?

The Utilities Directive regulates procurement by entities operating in four sectors, namely water, energy, and transport (since 1990, under Directive 90/531) and postal services (added in 2004). Previously, the directive also regulated bodies providing telecommunications services, but this sector was omitted from the 2004 directive as a result of liberalization of the sector.

For the most part, contracts relating to these sectors of activity were not regulated until the 1990 directive, even when carried out by public bodies. The reason given by the EC for initially excluding these sectors was that the activities were carried on in some states by public bodies, such as local authorities or state-owned companies, and in others by the private sector (though often under monopoly licenses). It was considered unfair to regulate these activities only in the former case, but member states were not ready to accept regulation of private bodies. In reality, there was probably also a lack of political will to regulate these sensitive sectors.

However, it was eventually decided to regulate these sectors by covering both public bodies and certain private bodies (see Section 12.5.2). Private bodies were covered where it was considered that they were inclined to discriminate because of (1) their dependency on public authorities for licenses combined with (2) the fact that they did not operate in competitive markets that would force them to purchase in a competitive manner. Supplies and works contracts were first regulated by the 1990 directive, as noted above, and the regime was extended to services in 1993 (Directive 93/38). Some other utilities, and other sectors of industry in which public companies operate, were not selected for regulation (e.g., the airlines) because it was considered that these services were provided in sufficiently competitive markets to ensure competitive purchasing without regulation.

Because of their initial exclusion from the directives, the utilities sectors were once referred to as the excluded sectors, and the terminology "excluded sectors" is sometimes used even though these sectors have been within the EC regime for more than a decade.

More specifically, the Utilities Directive covers contracts related to the following activities:

(1) *Water sector*: Article 4. The directive covers mainly the following: contracts relating to the provision or operation of a fixed network for supplying drinking water to the public, contracts relating to the supply of water to fixed networks, and contracts relating to the disposal or treatment of sewage. Contracts actually to purchase water are excluded: it was felt that water needs to be procured from close to its source and there would be no competition for its supply.

(2) *Energy sector*: Article 3. The directive covers contracts relating to provision or operation of a fixed network for the supply of electricity, gas, or heat to the public (i.e., generation of electricity, and the supply of electricity to homes and industry) and contracts relating to exploitation of a geographical area for the purpose of exploration for, or extraction of, oil, gas, and solid fuels. However, the main states involved in oil and gas extraction enjoy an exemption (see Section 12.5.3). There is an exemption for contracts for the purchase of energy and of fuel for the production of energy (e.g., contracts for purchasing coal for use in power stations); as with purchases of water, it was considered that the absence of a cross-border competitive market for the supply of this fuel would make the directive's application pointless.

(3) *Transport sector*: Article 5. The directive covers contracts relating to the provision of air terminal facilities, and the provision of port and similar facilities (e.g., construction of new runways and airport terminal buildings). The activity of transportation is not included—for example, purchases of airplanes and uniforms by air carriers such as British Airways are not regulated. The directive also covers contracts relating to the operation of transport networks in the field of transport by railway, automated systems, tramway, trolleybus, bus, and cable. For example, companies running underground and overground railway services must generally follow the directive in purchasing rolling stock, uniforms, etc.

(4) *Postal services sector*: Article 6. The directive also covers postal services, namely the clearance, sorting, routing, and delivery of postal items. It also covers various other services (e.g., transmission of registered electronic mail) when provided by an entity that also provides the above services as defined in the new directive; these were included because it is feared that entities might use their special position in respect of postal services to gain a competitive advantage in providing other services (e.g., because of the special access they have to postal customers). Member states do not have to apply the directive to postal services until January 1, 2009.

Apart from the standard procurement of central and provincial/local government for governmental purposes, it can be noted that all the procurements that the EC has opened up to its trading partners under the GPA, as set out in its Annex III to the GPA, are procurements covered by its Utilities Directive. In principle, the EC has covered procurement by state companies in the above areas, except for activities connected with the distribution of gas or heat, those connected with fuel exploration or extraction, and some of the transport activities (including non-urban transport). (The position with postal services, which is new under the directive, is also a bit more complex.) However, GPA parties do not all have access to all these utilities markets; for other parties that have not offered comparable concessions, the EC has made specific exceptions to this GPA coverage (e.g., the EC does not apply the GPA to Japan in the areas of urban transport and electricity, since Japan has not made reciprocal concessions in these areas).

12.5.2 Which Procuring Entities Are Covered?

The Utilities Directive covers a broader group of entities than the Public Sector Directive. Article 2(1) provides that it covers three groups of entities:

(1) *Contracting authorities*. Entities that are contracting authorities under the Public Sector Directive (see Section 12.4). These entities' contracts relating to utility activities are, in general, excluded from that directive and governed instead by the Utilities Directive. For example, if a local authority is responsible for water supply and sewage treatment for its area, its contracts relating to this activity (e.g., to build a sewage treatment plant) are governed by the Utilities Directive.

(2) *Public undertakings*. The directive applies to public undertakings, defined as undertakings over which public authorities may exercise, directly or indirectly, a dominant influence, by virtue their ownership, financial participation in the entity, or the rules which govern it (Article 2(1)(b)). A dominant influence is presumed when contracting authorities hold the majority of the subscribed capital, where they control the majority of the votes attached to the shares, or where they can appoint more than half the members of its administrative, managerial, or supervisory body. However, it is not limited to these cases (e.g., a lesser shareholding may in practice result in a dominant influence).

(3) *Entities with special or exclusive rights.* The third category of regulated entities comprises those which operate on the basis of special or exclusive rights. The directive defines "special or exclusive rights" as "rights granted by a competent authority of a Member State by way of any legislative, regulatory or administrative provision the effect of which is to limit the exercise of [the utility activities] to one or more entities, and which substantially affects the ability of other entities to carry out such activity" (Article 2(3)). This covers, for example, an entity with a monopoly license to supply water to homes in a particular area, even if that entity is governed by ordinary company law with 100 percent of its shares in private ownership.

The EC decided to regulate these entities because, as mentioned in Section 12.5.1, they are considered liable to engage in discriminatory purchasing. This is because of susceptibility to government pressure (e.g., because of the government's power to grant licenses), combined with the fact that they often do not operate in competitive markets in providing their services, so that there are no commercial incentives to resist this pressure.

A private entity is not covered by the directive, however, merely because it requires a license from government to carry out its activities. The directive does not cover the case in which licenses are awarded to any applicant who can satisfy objective conditions, provided that the licensing system is objective, proportional, and nondiscriminatory (Recital 25 to the directive): when anyone who meets the conditions can obtain a license in a transparent process there is no room for covert pressure from government. Further, the fact that other firms can obtain licenses tends to result in competitive pressures from license-holders that will induce them to procure commercially.

It is unusual for a domestic procurement regime to regulate private entities: in many regimes even state companies are not regulated. The EC's decision to regulate these companies is based specifically on the purpose of the rules as being to prevent discrimination and on the premise that these entities are susceptible to discriminatory behavior.

Other countries have not been so willing to submit their private companies to regulation under trade agreements, perhaps because they do not share the view that such companies are subject to real pressure to discriminate or perhaps because of the political difficulty of bringing them under trade agreements. Thus, although the EC was prepared to commit to open up the purchasing of these private purchasers to suppliers from GPA parties under the GPA, it did not do so, because other GPA parties were not willing to bring their own private entities within the GPA's regulatory regime. Under the GPA, the EC has thus undertaken to open up only the markets of utilities that are contracting authorities or public undertakings under the directive.

12.5.3 Exclusion for Entities Operating in Competitive Markets

We have already mentioned in Section 12.5.2 that when utilities supply their services in competitive markets, there may be no need to regulate their procurement to prevent discrimination, because competitive pressure will make them procure in a commercial manner. The previous directives on utilities (90/531 and 93/38) included several exemptions for utilities operating in competitive markets in specific sectors, namely bus transport, telecommunications, and (a limited exemption only) oil and gas, in which competitive markets existed in some state when the original utilities rules were adopted. The new 2004 directive, in Article 30, introduced a more general exemption for entities in competitive markets that applies to all the sectors covered by the directive.

This provides that the directive does not apply to an activity when, in the member state in which the activity is performed, that activity "is directly exposed to competition on markets to which access is not restricted." The criteria for deciding whether this condition is met are elaborated in other provisions of Article 30. The exemption only applies when the Commission takes a positive formal decision that the conditions for an exemption exist (or fails to make a decision when an application is made). Detailed procedures for making exemption decisions are set out in Commission Decision 2005/15/EC of January 7, 2005 (Williams, 2005). Some exemptions have already been granted for electricity generators in some member states (e.g., Commission Decision 2006/11/EC).

12.5.4 Which Contracts Are Covered?

The rules on contracts covered are very similar to those of the Public Sector Directive so far as concerns covered contracts. The most important differences are higher threshold values for supply and services contracts, and a number of additional exemptions. The main ones are for the following: contracts for activities involving the physical use of a network or geographic area outside the EC (Article 20), certain contracts for acquiring goods, works, or services for hire or resale (Article 19), certain contracts for companies in the same undertaking (effectively, a broader exemption for in-house transactions than applies under the *Teckal* principle discussed in Section 12.4.2.4) (Article 23), and certain contracts connected with joint ventures (Article 23).

12.6 Obligations under the EC Procurement Directives

As we have noted in Section 12.3.1, the directives lay down transparent award procedures that regulated purchasers must follow in awarding covered contracts. The procedures applied under the Public Sector Directive are stricter than those applied under the Utilities Directive; it was considered that the commercial nature of utilities and the complexity of their projects require greater flexibility.

The following account focuses on the Public Sector Directive, with the main differences for utilities being noted at the end.

12.6.1 General Principles: Nondiscrimination, Equal Treatment, and Transparency

First, in addition to laying down detailed procedural rules, the directives set out three general principles. They are now set out in Article 2 of the Public Sector Directive and Article 10 of the Utilities Directive, but even before this, the principles were held by the ECJ to be implied into the directives. They are as follows:

(1) Nondiscrimination (on grounds of nationality).
(2) Equal treatment. This means that entities must not treat suppliers who are in a comparable position differently, unless there is a justification for this (*Fabricom* case). This applies to domestic suppliers, as well as suppliers from other member states.
(3) Transparency.

The EC has used these general principles both to interpret the directives and to add obligations that are not stated expressly, that is, to supplement the explicit obligations in the directives. For example, in the *Universale-Bau* case, the ECJ ruled that the transparency principle requires entities to disclose to tenderers a detailed methodology they have drawn up for selecting firms to tender, even though the directive does not state this (but does state other disclosure requirements). The use of these principles, and their very general nature, creates a great deal of uncertainty for procuring entities. It also gives the ECJ significant potential to develop rules on matters that the directives do not address. For example, the directive does not deal expressly with late tenders, but the ECJ could develop EC-level rules on this through the principle of equal treatment (e.g., to determine that late tenders can never be accepted, or can be accepted only in circumstances specified by the court) (Arrowsmith, 2006). The development of the principles is as yet in an early stage, however, and it remains to be seen how exactly they will be applied.

12.6.2 Permitted Award Procedures (Procurement Methods)

So far as the more explicit obligations are concerned, under the Public Sector Directive contracting authorities must use one of the five types of award procedures, as set out below. As elaborated, two of these procedures, open and restricted, are available for any procurement, although the others, which are considered less transparent, are available only in special cases. Because the directives apply only to major contracts, there are no procedures designed for low-value purchases: for example, there is no equivalent to the "request for quotations" procedure found in the UNCITRAL Model Law on Procurement of Goods, Construction, and Services.

12.6.2.1 Open Procedure

As a general rule, authorities must use either the open procedure or the restricted procedure (Article 28). They may choose the open procedure for any contract. This is a formal tendering (bidding) procedure, under which the authority must establish clear specifications as the basis for submission of bids, must advertise the contract in the EU's *Official Journal*, must allow any interested firm to submit a bid (although it may reject bids received from those considered not to be qualified [responsible]), and must evaluate the bids, as received, without entering into significant negotiations.

With all competitive procedures the directive provides minimum time limits for the key phases to ensure suppliers (especially, those from other member states) have sufficient time to respond. With all procedures there is a general obligation to allow sufficient time, along with specified minimum periods (which are themselves, however, subject to various extensions and reductions—for example, reductions where electronic specifications are available). With open procedures, firms must generally be given at least 52 days to tender (Article 38(2)) from the date of dispatch of the contract notice.

12.6.2.2 Restricted Procedure

An authority may also choose the restricted procedure for any contract (Article 28). Like the open procedure, this is a formal tendering (bidding) procedure that must be advertised in the EU's *Official Journal*. The key difference from the open procedure is that the authority can select only a limited number to bid from those who express interest. It may either invite all those interested whom it considers qualified (responsible), or may limit numbers by issuing invitations to tender only to a pre-stated number of firms (at least five, and in all cases sufficient to ensure genuine competition (Article 44(3)). In choosing whom to invite, the entity may only consider certain criteria listed in the directive, namely technical and financial criteria and certain other limited criteria (see Section 12.6.4 on qualification). It must also indicate in the advertisement which criteria it will use (Article 44(3)). Apart from this, the same rules generally apply to open and restricted procedures, including the requirement to establish clear specifications and evaluate the bids as received and without significant negotiations. Firms must generally be given 37 days to respond after dispatch of the contract notice (Article 38(3)(a)) and 40 days to bid (Article 38(3)(b)), although an accelerated version of the procedure (with periods of 10 and 15 days) is available for cases of urgency.

There is scope for confusion between this EC procedure and the procedure called "restricted tendering" under the UNCITRAL model law. Despite the similarity in names, the two are in fact very different. Although the EC's restricted procedure requires the authority to advertise the contract widely and choose participants from those who respond, using objective and predisclosed criteria, the UNCITRAL restricted tendering procedure does not require an advertisement or contain detailed rules on selection, but simply allows the procuring entity to approach known suppliers. Unlike the EC procedure, it is available only in limited cases, and not for all contracts.

12.6.2.3 Competitive Dialogue

Competitive dialogue is a new procedure, introduced in 2004 to provide more flexibility in awarding complex contracts, especially for major infrastructure projects, such as contracts for building and operating prisons and hospitals. Open and restricted procedures are often unsuitable for various reasons, including the limited scope for dialogue with suppliers. The main rules on the new procedure are found in Article 29 and Article 1(11). It is available, in brief, for procurements in which the entity is unable to define the technical, financial, or legal aspects of the project. For example, it might be used when an entity cannot draw up a specification for a bespoke information technology system, because it does not know what sorts of functions are feasible or how easily it can be integrated with other systems.

The procedure involves the following: (1) advertisement of the contract in the *Official Journal*; (2) selection of a limited number of suppliers to participate, with the same rules as for restricted procedures (Article 44), except that three rather than five may be sufficient (Article 44(3)); (3) a dialogue phase, in which the entity may discuss with invited suppliers their proposed solution, including to reduce the number of suppliers involved (they may conduct this phase through discussions alone or through initial rounds of tendering); and (4) a final tender stage, in which the suppliers remaining in the competition submit final tenders (which may involve each submitting a proposal based on its own solution). The procuring entity must choose the winner based on these tenders. There is much uncertainty over how far, if at all, the details of the contract may be adjusted or completed after choosing the winner (e.g., whether the finer details of the winning design may be filled in at this stage, or must be included in the final tender) (Arrowsmith, 2005, Chapter 10; Verschuur, 2006).

12.6.2.4 Negotiated Procedure with a Contract Notice

The negotiated procedure with a notice is a competitive procedure, but less structured than those described above. The authority must advertise the contract in the EU's *Official Journal* as with the other procedures and select firms to participate using the same rules as competitive dialogue. It may then proceed to choose the winning supplier simply through negotiations. The choice must be made using the same award criteria as other procedures (see Section 12.6.5 on award criteria), but the directives do not otherwise regulate the process for choosing the best offer.

Authorities can use the procedure also only in specific cases (Article 28) that are considered essential for member states to engage in effective purchasing, namely (1) where specifications cannot be drawn up with sufficient precision for formal tendering under the open or restricted procedures; (2) for works carried out purely for research, experiment, or development, for example, for the development of a prototype construction technique; and (3) in exceptional cases where overall pricing is not possible, either because of the nature of the works, supplier, or services, or because of the risks of performance (Article 30).

12.6.2.5 Negotiated Procedure without a Notice

This procedure allows the authority simply to negotiate with a selected supplier to choose the best offer, without advertisement or competition. It is available for cases specified in Article 31, which are very similar to the grounds for using limited tendering under the GPA. They are, briefly, as follows:

(1) For goods to be manufactured purely for research, experiment, study, or development—that is, for the purchase of a prototype (as noted above, with works the directive requires an advertisement for acquiring prototype works, a difference from goods that seems anomalous)
(2) Where the works, goods, or services can be provided only by one particular provider for technical or artistic reasons (e.g., a unique picture by a famous artist), or for reasons connected with exclusive rights (e.g., intellectual property rights)
(3) Where strictly necessary for reasons of extreme urgency, which were unforeseeable and cannot be attributed to the authority
(4) In certain cases where extra work is awarded to an existing contracting partner (certain unforeseen works or services which are additional to an existing contract; certain limited repetition of works or services under an existing contract, where the original contract notice mentioned that additional work might be awarded; and for certain goods that are a partial replacement for or addition to existing goods or installations)
(5) Where an open or restricted procedure was held but no tenders received, or all tenders were either irregular (e.g., do not comply with the specification or where there has been collusion between bidders), or unacceptable in accordance with relevant national provisions (e.g., are from unqualified firms, or exceed the budget)
(6) For services where the contract is negotiated with firms who were successful in a design contest under the directive (e.g., a contest to design a public building)
(7) For goods purchased on a commodity market (e.g., for metals, tea, and cocoa), allowing entities to buy directly from the market rather than through middlemen who have themselves bought through a market and added a mark up
(8) (For supplies only) For purchases under particularly advantageous conditions from firms that are winding up, or in circumstances of insolvency/bankruptcy (or where an arrangement is made with creditors)

12.6.3 Rules on Advertising Contracts

We have seen that, with limited exceptions, contracts must be advertised by an advertisement in the EU's *Official Journal* (a contract notice). The key information from the notice is published in all EC languages, in the Tenders Electronic Daily database (TED), available as CD-ROM on subscription or free on the Internet. The Commission has developed search tools that are available on the commission's SIMAP website (http://simap.eu.int). This also links to national websites offering advertisements for contracts below the thresholds. Notices must describe contracts using the Common Procurement Vocabulary (CPV), which was given formal status as a Community nomenclature by Regulation (EC) No 2195/02. The CPV is available at http://simap.eu.int. These publication and information initiatives are designed to improve access to contracts for EC firms, but also benefit suppliers outside the EC, who can also access this information.

12.6.4 Qualification (Responsibility)

Authorities may wish to exclude firms from contracts for various reasons. In this case, it may be said they are not qualified (broadly equivalent to responsibility in U.S. procurement). The directives limit the grounds and procedures for exclusion to ensure transparency and to remove unreasonable barriers to participation. These rules apply to all award procedures.

Four main categories for exclusion are listed in the directive:

(1) Absence of financial and economic standing (Article 47). This is not defined but refers to whether firms have adequate financial resources to perform.
(2) Absence of technical or professional ability (Article 48).
(3) Enrolment on relevant trade/professional registers and possession of licenses in the state in which the firm is established (Article 46). Relevant member state registers are listed in Annex IX. Special provision is made for states (such as the United Kingdom) where none exist.
(4) Various grounds that the ECJ in *La Cascina* case characterized as concerned with professional honesty, solvency, and reliability (Article 45). These are where the provider is bankrupt, subject to a winding up order or similar; has been convicted of an offence or been guilty of grave misconduct relating to the business; has failed to pay tax or social security contributions; or has been guilty of serious misrepresentation in supplying information.

In the first two cases, information required from firms must be set out in the contract notice or tender invitation and any specific minimum requirements (such as certain years of experience) must be specified in the notice. Any minimum requirements must be related to and proportionate to the subject matter of the contract.

As well as controlling the grounds for exclusion, the directive also contains various rules, on the evidence that entities may require, to avoid unduly burdening contractors.

In general, authorities can exclude firms only on these grounds (*Beentjes* and *La Cascina* cases). However, in the *Fabricom* case, the ECJ accepted that there is an implied power to exclude to give effect to the equal treatment principle; in this case, it stated that entities may exclude firms to avoid a conflict of interest (in this case, the exclusion concerned the supplier's participation in preparing specifications for the contract), even though the directive does not expressly provide for exclusion on this ground.

It was the practice of many authorities before the directives to award contracts only to those firms registered on the authority's approved lists (sometimes referred to as qualification lists). However, the ECJ ruled in Case C–71/92, *Commission v. Spain* that the directives' rules on qualification now preclude this (although it is allowed under the Utilities Directive; see Section 12.6.9). However, authorities can maintain lists that are optional for suppliers, in that they merely indicate that suppliers are qualified for a particular contract, to save time and effort for suppliers in qualifying separately for lots of contracts.

Because the directives are not concerned with value for money, in general they do not require purchasers to exclude firms on any of these grounds; they merely regulate the position where authorities decide to exclude. However, there is one exception—the 2004 directive introduced a new provision (Article 45) that requires exclusion of contractors convicted of participation in a criminal organization, corruption, fraud, and money laundering (Williams, 2006). This was included to support the EU's own policies of combating these crimes. (See also Section 12.10).

12.6.5 Contract Award Criteria

Once tenders have been received, the contract must be awarded on one of two bases: lowest price or most economically advantageous tender (Article 53). (Generally authorities can choose either basis, but for competitive dialogue only the latter.) The latter allows consideration of nonprice as well as price criteria. Article 53(1)(a) lists various permitted criteria, such as price, quality, running costs, after sales service, and delivery date, but states that the list is not exhaustive.

An important limit on the permitted criteria, however, is that they must be linked to the subject matter of the contract. This means, in particular, that authorities cannot take account of social or environmental considerations unconnected with contract performance (see Section 12.10).

To ensure transparency, the authority must disclose in the advertisement or contract documents the criteria to be used and their relative weighting. This weighting may be expressed as a range with an appropriate maximum spread (e.g., 70 percent for price and 30 percent quality or, using a range, perhaps 70–80 percent for price and 20–30 percent for quality, deciding later on the more precise weighting). There is an exception when "in the opinion of the [procuring entity] weighting is not possible for demonstrable reasons." However, even here it must indicate the criteria in order of importance.

The directive also contains explicit provisions on abnormally low offers—offers that, because of their favorable terms, raise a suspicion that the supplier will not be able to perform according to the terms offered. The directive prohibits an authority from rejecting such an offer without first seeking a written explanation and allows rejection only if there is no good reason for the favorable terms (Article 55). This is to prevent authorities rejecting bids that appear low but actually reflect cost advantages (e.g., lower labor costs in the supplier's home state). Thus, the provision reflects the purpose of the directive in opening markets to trade. It is not, on the other hand, designed to safeguard authorities' financial interests by preventing them from accepting risky bids.

12.6.6 Framework Agreements

Framework agreements are arrangements for repeat purchases (e.g., of computers or repair services), used, in particular, when entities do not know the timing or quantity of their requirements. They involve advertising the requirement and obtaining tenders, selecting a limited number of suppliers (or even a single supplier) as framework suppliers, and then placing orders with one of these suppliers (or the single chosen supplier) on a periodic basis, as the need arises. This process avoids the need for a wholly new tendering procedure for every new order (which, because of the aggregation rules discussed in Section 12.4.2.3, would have to be conducted under the directive even for small orders). The Utilities Directive has always contained express provisions on frameworks, but the old Works, Supply and Services Directives did not. However, it was possible to operate them without contravening the directives' obligations and they were in fact used in many member states (Arrowsmith, 1999). The 2004 directive included new provisions to provide expressly for these arrangements.

Article 1(5) defines a framework agreement as "an agreement between one or more contracting authorities and one or more economic operators, the purpose of which is to establish the terms governing contracts to be awarded during a given period, in particular, with regard to price and, where appropriate, the quantity envisaged."

Article 32(1) expressly authorizes frameworks and regulates their use. They do not constitute a special kind of award procedure, but rather are a specific variation of the directives' normal procedures (open procedure, restricted procedure, etc.). The directive is merely concerned to ensure that if member states use these procedures they do so in a fair and transparent manner. The directive does not, on the other hand, require member states to use them, or limit the kind of products or services for which they may be used. These matters for member states to determine, based on their own judgments of how best to obtain value for money in procurement.

In using frameworks, entities must follow the directive's usual rules for all phases up to the award (Article 32(2)). For multi-supplier frameworks, Article 32(4) generally requires the entity to select at least three frameworks suppliers. It then provides that for each order the winner may be selected in one of two ways:

(1) Without a new competition. Often the authority selects the best tenderer from the prices etc. in the original tenders submitted, based on the usual award criteria. It is not clear whether the directive's usual award criteria apply. According to the Commission (Commission of the European Communities, 2005a) they do not, but it is necessary only to comply with the directive's principles when selecting the supplier. Thus, for example, it may be possible to rotate the work between suppliers to ensure security of supply. What is clear, however, is that the decision must have some justification that needs to be documented in case of legal challenge.
(2) Through a reopening of competition, under a mini-tender procedure (in writing, to a specified time limit that is sufficiently long for tenders, and confidential). All framework operators capable of meeting the requirement must be invited to participate in the mini-tender (Article 32(4)). This mini-tender process may be used to supplement original tenders by adapting them to the particular requirement. For example, with a framework for management consultancy, the initial framework may involve tenders on matters such as hourly rate, whilst the mini-tender can be used to obtain proposals for the specific project (such as the supplier's proposals and timescales for addressing it). Mini-tenders can also be used to solicit changes to the terms of the original tender (e.g., changes to prices in markets where prices are very volatile). A grey area is whether price always needs to be included in the initial tenders and used as a basis for selecting the framework suppliers, or whether it is possible ever to have frameworks in which price is examined only at the mini-tender stage.

An important limitation is that authorities may not add new suppliers during the framework's life (Article 32(2)). Thus, if competitive new suppliers enter the market or become interested in contracts they can only be considered if a new framework is advertised and awarded.

The directive includes various controls over the use of frameworks, including a requirement that frameworks must not exceed four years, save in exceptional cases duly justified, and that entities may not use framework agreements improperly or in such a way as to restrict or distort competition.

12.6.7 Rules on Specifications

We have seen in Section 12.2 on the treaty that it outlaws all specifications, even those that are not discriminatory, which exclude products or services that meet an authority's functional requirements. For major contracts these are supplemented by additional rules in Article 23 of the directive. These, first, require entities to define requirements in one of two ways (or through a mixture of the two):

(1) By reference to certain specified European-level standards (such as national standards that give effect to European standards) or international standards (such as those of the ISO), or, where these do not exist, certain national-level standards (Article 23(3)). The reference must be accompanied by the words "or equivalent" and functional equivalents must be accepted (as required by the treaty). The burden of proving equivalence is on tenderers (Article 23(4)).
(2) By using performance or functional requirements as a means of description.

Thus, when the listed specifications, such as European standards, exist, authorities have a choice of using either these or performance or functional requirements to describe their requirements. When the listed specifications do not exist, authorities must use performance or functional specifications; the reason is that such specifications are often more transparent than detailed ad hoc specifications or nonlisted standards (that may not be easily accessible). However, drafting performance or functional requirements may, in practice, be burdensome in some cases.

Article 23(8) additionally prohibits purchasers from using technical specifications that refer to goods of a specific make or source, or to a particular process, or to trademarks, patents, types, origin, or means of production, where this has the effect of favoring or eliminating certain firms or products. Article 23(2) of the new directive also states that technical specifications "shall afford equal access for tenderers and not have the effect of creating unjustified obstacles to the opening up of public procurement to competition."

There is also another piece of legislation, Council Decision 87/95 (the IT Standards Decision), which imposes some obligations relating to standards and specifications in contracts for the supply of equipment relating to information technology (IT), which pre-dates the directives.

12.6.8 Information Obligations

Other key obligations are concerned with provision of information to interested parties to enhance monitoring and enforcement. The main obligations are as follows (subject in some cases to exceptions, e.g., for confidentiality): to inform firms on request why they have been rejected (Article 41(2)), to inform participants automatically (without a request) of decisions taken on contract awards (Article 41(1)), to give suppliers' reasons for any decision not to award a contract or to recommence the procedure (Article 41(1)), to send to the *Official Journal* a notice for publication giving details of the award (Article 35(4)), to keep a written report of procedures, which may be requested by the Commission (Article 43): and to supply the Commission of the European Communities with various statistics about contracts awarded (Articles 75–76), to provide information about the operation of the directives and GPA.

12.6.9 Procedures under the Utilities Directive

As noted in the introductory part of Section 12.6, the Utilities Directive provides for more flexible procedural rules than the Public Sector Directive. The main differences are as follows:

(1) Except in specified cases the Public Sector Directive requires use of the open or restricted procedure, but utilities may choose the negotiated procedure with a notice, as well as the open or restricted procedure, for any contract.
(2) Public sector rules require every contract to be advertised through a contract notice, but the utilities rules allow, in addition, the following:
   (a) Advertisement through a periodic indicative notice (PIN). This is an optional notice that gives advance notice of general requirements for the year, and can be used to advertise specific contracts where the specific contract is referred to in the PIN.
   (b) Advertisement by advertising a qualification system—that is, a list on which firms interested in particular types of contracts can register. Individual contracts can be awarded simply by inviting firms on the list, without further advertisement.
(3) Utilities, unlike bodies operating under the Public Sector Directive, may restrict participation in their contracts to suppliers who have registered on a qualification system, provided it is conducted under certain rules (e.g., it is regularly advertised and access is permitted at any time).

(4) Utilities have an additional exemption from competition, where there is a particularly advantageous opportunity that is available only for a very short time and the price is considerably lower than the market price.
(5) Utilities may use any objective rules and criteria for selecting suppliers to tender, rather than being confined to a list of specific criteria (financial, technical, etc.). However, it is not at all clear what these mean or how far the available criteria really differ (Arrowsmith and Maund, forthcoming). The rules on evidence for exclusions are also more flexible.
(6) Utilities have more flexibility in setting time limits for award procedures.
(7) Utilities that are not contracting authorities are not obliged to exclude firms convicted of corruption etc. (though they may do so).

12.7 Regulation of Contracts Outside the Directives

It is important to note that the ECJ has also recently brought under closer regulation those contracts that are outside the directive. For many years the treaty was regarded as imposing only "negative" obligations not to restrict access to contracts. However, in 1998 in the *Telaustria* case, the ECJ interpreted the treaty itself as involving "positive" obligations that are similar to some of those in the directives: according to the ECJ, the treaty implies a requirement to be transparent in contract awards to support the treaty's obligation not to discriminate. The ECJ stated expressly that this transparency obligation includes a requirement to advertise contracts. However, it is not clear what else, if anything, this treaty obligation of transparency requires. It is also unclear whether significant positive obligations apply to all contracts: the *Telaustria* case itself concerned a service concession contract, which is a type excluded for political reasons from the directives despite its clear importance for trade; and it is not yet clear how far the same rules apply also to contracts that were excluded from the directives because of their limited trade impact, notably those below the thresholds and non-priority services contracts. The Commission has endorsed a broad interpretation of both the content and scope of the *Telaustria* case obligation (Commission of the European Communities, 2006a). However, this is controversial and Germany has contested the commission's views before the ECJ in a case that was ongoing at the time of writing (Case T–258/06 *Germany v. Commission*). The *Telaustria* case has also been much criticized because of the uncertainty it creates and because it involves judicial development of the law in a manner that undermines the legislator's decision not to require transparency for certain types of contracts (Braun, 2000; Hordijk and Meulenbelt, 2005). One effect of the development may be to motivate member states to agree new secondary legislation to regulate areas currently outside the directives, and to secure control of the regime (Arrowsmith, 2006). In this respect, the Commission has already announced plans for regulating concessions (Commission of the European Communities, 2005b), although it has not yet published detailed legislative proposals.

12.8 Defense Contracts

Defense procurement is a sensitive area for member states, both because of the security concerns involved and because for some states defense contracts support many jobs. On the other hand, the potential benefits of open markets, both financial and military (e.g., through standardization of equipment) are considerable (Hartley, 1998; Commission of the European Communities, 2004b).

Some progress has been made toward a liberalization regime, but in practice open markets are a significant way off. Space precludes a full summary but the following are the key points to note.

First, the treaty and the directives apply in principle to defense procurement.

Second, there are, however, significant exceptions to this principle. With regard to the treaty, this, first, contains a specific exception for procurement of hard defense equipment (tanks, missiles, etc.) in Article 296(1)(b) (and see Council Decision of 15 April 1958). In 1999 in C–414/97, *Commission v. Spain*, the ECJ ruled that the exemption applies only when a measure is excluded by member states for security reasons; thus, it cannot be used simply to protect industry from foreign competition. How far the ECJ will leave the question of whether there is a security justification to member states themselves is not clear (Georgopoulos, 2005; Trybus, 2005; Commission of the European Communities, 2006b). In addition, for defense procurement that does not fall under Article 296 (e.g., purchases of army uniforms or tents) member states may derogate from the treaty on grounds of public security, as outlined earlier (e.g., to justify purchasing from national suppliers to maintain capability). Case C–252/01, *Commission v. Belgium* on the security exceptions in the directives (see later in this same paragraph below) seems to suggest that member states will enjoy a wide discretion in applying security exemptions. Finally, Article 297 EC gives an exemption from the treaty in case of serious internal disturbances affecting the maintenance of law and order, serious international tension constituting a threat of war, or the carrying out of obligations that a state has accepted for the purpose of maintaining peace and international security. With regard to the directives, hard defense contracts excluded from the treaty under the above provisions are clearly also outside the Public Sector Directive (Article 10). With regard to hard defense contracts that are not outside the treaty, one view is that Article 10 excludes only contracts that are themselves excluded from the treaty on security grounds (Trybus, 2005); another is that it excludes all hard defense procurement (Arrowsmith, 2005). In a recent communication, the Commission has suggested adopting a separate new directive to regulate hard defense procurement that is not outside the treaty (Commission of the European Communities, 2005c). In addition, the current Public Sector Directive does not apply to the following: (1) contracts declared secret, (2) contracts accompanied by special security measures, and (3) when the protection of the essential interests of that member state so requires (Article 14 Public Sector Directive). We noted at the beginning of this section that *Commission v. Belgium* suggests states enjoy a wide discretion in applying these exemptions.

Alongside the application of the above general EC regime on defense procurement, some further developments are taking place that have important implications for liberalization. Most notably, in July 2004 the Council of the European Union established a European Defence Agency (Council Joint Action 2004/551/CFSP; Georgopoulos, 2006). This agency has issued a nonbinding *Code of Conduct on Defence Procurement of the EU Member States Participating in the European Defense Agency*, which came into effect on July 2006, for awarding hard defense contracts (which is optional, but accepted by the vast majority of member states). The Code states that it applies only to hard defense contracts that are not covered by the treaty. However, if a member state sees fit to advertise a contract under the Code, it is hard to see how it can claim an exemption from advertising and other obligations under the treaty for security reasons. It remains to be seen how this initiative will be coordinated with the Commission's efforts to develop a binding regime for hard defense procurement through a new directive.

12.9 Electronic Procurement

One of the main reasons for reforming the directives in 2004 was to adapt them to electronic commerce. The EC had already adopted two directives for promoting E-commerce in general (public and private), namely Directive 2000/31 (Pearce and Platten, 2000) that removed various obstacles to E-commerce (such as by requiring states to recognize contracts concluded electronically), and Directive 1999/93 that created an EC framework for electronic signatures. The 2004 directives sought to ensure that the EC's framework applying specifically to public markets did not hinder E-commerce, and also to encourage its use. At the same time, they regulated its use in public markets to ensure that it does not operate as a trade barrier. In 2004, the Commission published an action plan on E-procurement (Commission of the European Communities, 2004c), and it has also issued an explanatory document on the rules on E-procurement (Commission of the European Communities, 2005d). As noted, the EC had previously developed an electronic database for advertising.

The rules on electronic procurement cover the following:

(1) Storing and communicating information (Articles 42 and 71 of the new Public Sector Directive and Articles 48 and 64 of the new Utilities Directive). These provisions clarify that entities may use electronic means for all communications, and may require suppliers to use such means. The rules also state that any reference to written or in writing means "any expression consisting of words or figures which can be read, reproduced and subsequently communicated" (Article 1(12) of the Public Sector Directive and Article 1(11) of the Utilities Directive), ensuring that where the directive requires actions (such as notifications to and by suppliers) to be in writing, electronic means such as e-mail will suffice. In addition, Articles 42 and 71 restrict the precise way in which the electronic means are used, to prevent the means used from excluding certain suppliers (e.g., requiring means of communication to be generally available and nondiscriminatory) and to ensure suppliers have confidence in the system, including by ensuring integrity and confidentiality of data. (For critique, see Bickerstaff, 2004.)

(2) Reduced time limits in procedures involving electronic communications. The new directives also encourage use of electronic means by reducing the minimum timescales for phases of the award procedure when electronic means are used in the procurement, to take advantage of the fact that this is a speedier method of communication. For example, the usual timescales are reduced when the purchaser provides electronic access to specifications.

(3) Electronic auctions. Another set of new provisions concerns electronic reverse auctions. Probably, it was possible to conduct some types of auctions under the old directives (Arrowsmith, 2002a), and a number of countries, such as the United Kingdom, did so. The new directives now contain explicit rules on electronic auctions to give legal certainty over their use, and also to regulate their operation (Article 1(7) Public Sector Directive and Article 1(6) Utilities Directive [definition], and Article 54 of the Public Sector Directive and Article 56 of the Utilities Directive [procedural rules]; Arrowsmith, 2005, Chapter 18).

(4) Dynamic purchasing systems. The new directives also include something called a "dynamic purchasing system" (Article 33 of the Public Sector Directive and Article 15 of the Utilities Directive), available for standardized purchases. They are essentially lists of registered suppliers that submit the terms on which they are willing to supply products or services. Entities using these systems must advertise them in the *Official Journal*. Anyone submitting a compliant tender must be allowed to register on the system. However, the procedure for placing orders is cumbersome—for each order an entity must on each occasion place a new notice in the *Official Journal* to give notice of the system to those not yet registered, give 15 days for registration before calling for tenders for the order, and then invite tenders from all registered suppliers—and these systems are hardly used in practice (ibid.).

12.10 Collateral or Horizontal Policies

One of the most controversial issues under the EC procurement regime is the extent to which EC law limits member states' powers to use procurement to promote policy goals that are not connected with the goods, works, or services (e.g., to promote the economic development of ethnic minorities). Such policies have sometimes been referred to (including by this author) as secondary policies or, in the United States, as collateral policies. However, the term "horizontal" policies is preferable, because it eliminates any suggestion that such policies are somehow unusual or inappropriate or, at least, that they are less important than the acquisition of the goods, works, or services themselves (Arrowsmith and Kunzlik, forthcoming). This is a complex area, and only a brief overview is possible.

Member states are constrained in their policies, first, under the EC Treaty. As we have seen, policies that are discriminatory are permitted only if justified. We have also seen that policies designed merely to support national industry for economic reasons cannot generally be justified, and nor can regional development policies. However, many environmental or social policies (such as promotion of equal opportunities) will in principle be capable of justification. This was the case, for example, with a policy promoting renewable energy in the *Preussen Elektra* case, discussed in Section 12.2. One difficult area, however, is small business development, which is a policy in many member states and of the EC itself: is it justified to divide contracts into smaller amounts, for example, to encourage access of small companies, or to set aside contracts or provide for price preferences for such companies? Such policies are arguably discriminatory in tending to favor local firms, even if not confined to these firms. In Case C–360/89, *Commission v. Italy*, the ECJ seemed to suggest that policies for promoting small businesses can never be justified as they are economic in nature. However, it is possibly too broad to reject all policies of an economic nature, including those with objectives that are entirely consistent with, or even supported by, the EC Treaty, and arguably small business policies are capable of justification. Case C–360/89 itself can probably be considered as turning on the fact that the particular preferences involved did not pass the proportionality test (they were not open to small firms outside the region of the works, and thus were more restrictive of trade than was necessary to promote the objective of assisting small firms). However, even if such policies are justifiable in principle, it is not clear that the ECJ will accept restrictive policies, such as set asides, under the proportionality test.

Another controversial issue concerns policies that go beyond the contract being awarded (e.g., policies excluding firms that do not comply in their business generally with standards set by the procuring entity on environmental practice). The Commission of the European Communities appears to consider that, in view of their restrictive effects on access to markets, such policies cannot be justified. The Commission also considers that it is not generally possible to justify policies concerning the way in which products are produced in other states (e.g., that products supplied under the contract should be products produced without pollution, or by workers who are paid fair wages) (Commission of the European Communities, 2001a). Such policies have become increasingly important with greater outsourcing to developing countries, such as China and India. However, there is no case law to confirm the Commission's view, which has been criticized as unduly narrow (Arrowsmith and Maund, forthcoming).

Another grey area is the extent to which nondiscriminatory horizontal policies are caught. As discussed in Section 12.2, it is not clear how far nondiscriminatory measures fall within the Treaty at all. If they do, the treaty will have a significant effect on horizontal policies, particularly if the ECJ also accepts the Commission's view that policies going beyond the contract or concerning the production of supplies abroad cannot generally be justified. This will mean that policies of this kind (e.g., to purchase only fair trade products) will effectively be precluded, even when they affect domestic and foreign suppliers equally.

Even when horizontal policies are permitted under the treaty, they may be affected by the directives.

In particular, even if the treaty itself permits policies that go beyond the contract, the directives probably rule policies of this kind out for major contracts.

First, as mentioned in Section 12.6.5, award criteria must be linked to the subject matter of the contract. This rules out preferences at the award stages that relate to matters such as the nature of the contractor (e.g., the fact that it is a small business) or its activities unrelated to the contract. This point is illustrated by the *EVN and Wienstrom* case. In this case, the award of the contract was to be made on the basis of the most economically advantageous tender using two criteria. One was price, weighted at 55 percent. The other was the amount of energy that the tenderer could supply in excess of 22.5 GW h per annum from renewable energy sources, weighted at 45 percent. The amount of energy estimated to be needed under the contract was 22.5 GW h. It was a condition of qualification that all tenderers should be able to supply at least 22.5 GW h from renewable sources over the next two years, or have supplied that amount over the last two years. Thus, the award criterion gave preference to tenderers who could supply from renewable sources more than the amount needed under the contract, which the ECJ considered was directed at increasing the overall supply of renewable energy, for environmental reasons. The ECJ held that the criterion was unlawful as it was not limited to the contract's own requirements to supply energy from renewable sources (which would have been acceptable).

Second, the directives state expressly (Article 26 of the Public Sector Directive and Article 38 of the Utilities Directive) that authorities may lay down special conditions on social or environmental matters relating to the performance of a contract, implying that contract conditions not relating to performance are not permitted. Thus, although a procuring entity can, for example, include a contract term requiring the contractor to employ disabled persons on the contract work, it cannot include a term imposing broader obligations, such as a requirement to recruit more disabled persons in the business as a whole.

Third, as noted above, a procuring entity can in general only exclude firms from participating for limited reasons, relating mainly to inability to perform. Thus, it is not generally possible to exclude firms because they do not comply with policies set for government contractors (such as fair recruitment policies), or to reserve contracts specifically for particular groups (such as small businesses). There is, however, an exception that allows exclusion for criminal convictions and grave misconduct (see Section 12.6.4). This enables states to use procurement as an additional sanction to support norms contained in general regulatory legislation on social issues and the environment (Piselli, 2000)—for example, they may exclude firms that have not complied with applicable national rules on wages and working conditions, or with legislation on pollution (and the concept of grave misconduct probably permits exclusion even without an actual conviction in serious cases). The other main exception is a provision introduced in 2004 that allows set asides for workshops for the disabled, provided that those contracts are open to workshops in all member states (Article 19 of the Public Sector Directive and Article 28 of the Utilities Directive).

Overall, however, the directives leave little scope for social or environmental policies that are unrelated to the way in which the contractor will carry out the contract.

As well as the directives' restrictions on policies going beyond the contract, there are some restrictions on measures that do relate to the contract. First, it appears that when a purchaser includes special conditions on environmental and social matters, it may not exclude contractors who accept the conditions, even if the purchaser thinks that the contractor will not comply in practice; thus, the only redress will be a later remedy for breach of contract if the condition is not met (*Beentjes* case), which weakens the ability to implement such conditions effectively. Second, although purchasers clearly may include contract conditions concerning the contract workforce, such as requirements to employ disabled persons on the contract work, it is not entirely clear whether they may include such workforce issues as award criteria in comparing tenders: the ECJ appeared to endorse this in the *Nord Pas de Calais* case, but the Commission has suggested that this is limited to the (rare) case in which economic aspects of tenders are equal (Commission of the European Communities, 2001a), as was the case in *Nord Pas de Calais* itself.

The restrictive approach to horizontal policies promoted by the Commission and to some extent endorsed by the ECJ has been criticized by many writers, as giving undue weight to trade considerations as against other policies of member states and the EC itself (e.g., Arrowsmith, 2005, Chapter 19; Arrowsmith and Maund, forthcoming; McCrudden, forthcoming). The new directives have broadened the possibilities to a limited extent, notably in including the new provision on workshops for the disabled. However, despite many other proposals for broadening the directives in this respect, especially from the European Parliament, the new directives largely confirmed the preexisting position (Arnould, 2004).

In addition to the question of how far member states retain the discretion to implement horizontal policies in procurement, the question has arisen as to whether the EC should harness the collective procurement power of member states to support EC policies, by *requiring* states to implement certain horizontal policies through their procurement. A first step in this direction was taken with the 2004 directives. These introduced a new provision that requires all EC contracting authorities to exclude from contracts firms convicted of certain offences, namely corruption, money laundering, fraud, and participation in criminal organizations, to support EC policies for combating these activities (Article 45 of the Public Sector Directive and Article 54 of the Utilities Directive; Williams, 2006).

Finally, as in other areas of procurement, EC member states—and the EC collectively—may be constrained in the area of horizontal policies by the GPA (Arrowsmith, 2003, Chapter 13). The scope of the GPA in this respect is not clear. The application of the GPA to horizontal issues was raised in the context of a complaint under the GPA against the United States (the *Burma/Massachusetts* case), which concerned a Massachusetts law limiting access to procurement for firms doing business with Myanmar. However, the issues raised were not resolved within the GPA context because the U.S. Supreme Court held that the law in question was unconstitutional. The scope of the GPA seems unlikely to be tested in this context by the EC policies for the same reasons—most policies that might violate the GPA already appear to be ruled out by the EC's own internal regime.

12.11 Remedies and Enforcement

There are two main mechanisms provided by EC law for enforcing its procurement rules. Member states may also, of course, provide for their own additional mechanisms.

The first mechanism provided by EC law is through the Commission of the European Communities (Delsaux, 2004). The commission has a general responsibility for ensuring that member states comply with EC law. If it learns of measures that violate the procurement rules—whether general laws or practices, or individual procurement decisions—the Commission may take up the matter with the member state concerned to seek a solution. As a last resort, it may bring proceedings before the ECJ under Article 226 of the EC Treaty. If the ECJ finds that a violation has occurred, it declares that a violation exists, and the member state then comes under an obligation under Article 228 EC to take the necessary measures to comply with the judgment. If the member state does not do so, the Commission may bring it before the court again, and penalty payments can then be imposed under Article 228(2) EC. Violations may come to the Commission's attention through complaints by suppliers, trade bodies, etc., complaints by other member states, or the Commission's own monitoring. Other member states may also proceed in the ECJ against other member states, but in practice they do not do this, but leave it to the Commission. The procedure is inter-governmental in nature: proceedings are always brought against the relevant member state, and not against individual purchasers.

The second main enforcement mechanism provided is a system of remedies for suppliers (which can be used at the same time as a complaint to the Commission, and even when proceedings are ongoing in the ECJ). All the EC procurement rules are enforceable by affected parties, including suppliers, in the national courts of the state that has violated the rules, in accordance with general principles of the EC Treaty. These require member states to provide remedies for enforcing EC law that are (1) effective and (2) no less favorable than those available in that member state for breaches of similar domestic rules. However, in the mid-1980s when the Commission of the European Communities reviewed EC procurement policy, it found that most member states did not provide effective remedies. Believing that these were key to the success of its policy, the EC adopted specific legislation on remedies for contracts covered by the directives, namely Directive 89/665/EEC (Public Sector Remedies Directive) and Directive 92/13/EEC (Utilities Remedies Directive). The approach adopted to supplier remedies is similar to that of the GPA rules on challenge procedures: the precise remedies system is left to each member state, but the legislation lays down minimum standards for all systems. In 2006, the Commission published a proposal for strengthening the system (Commission of the European Communities, 2006c).

The main standards applicable at present include the following:

(1) A requirement for effective and rapid review.
(2) Requirements for review before a judicial body, or one that is independent.
(3) Obligation to make certain specified remedies available to the review body, set out in Article 2 of each directive. These are as follows:
   (a) Interim relief, to suspend (or secure the suspension of) the process. In principle, the criteria for awarding are left to the national courts, and Article 2(4) states that member states may refuse relief if the adverse consequences (including for the public interest) are considered to exceed the benefits. The Commission's 2006 proposal suggests a new requirement for automatic suspension for five working days.
   (b) Damages. Based on general EC law principles, it is generally accepted that the damages remedy must provide compensation for profits lost, and (unlike the GPA and some other systems) cannot be limited to bid costs. The Utilities Remedies Directive Article 2(7) also provides that a supplier may automatically recover the costs of preparing a bid or participating in a procedure provided the supplier can demonstrate a real chance of winning the contract. This is not instead of recovery of lost profits, but an alternative.
   (c) Power to set aside, or ensure the set-aside of, unlawful decisions.

By way of exception, under the Utilities Remedies Directive, states have an option to impose other penalties—especially financial penalties—to ensure compliance, rather than requiring interim measures and set asides. This takes account of the sensitivity in some states of direct interference in procedures of utilities, especially private utilities.

States may provide that after the conclusion of a contract remedies are limited to damages (Article 2(6)). This appears to allow a state to prevent a challenge (other than damages) by concluding a contract with the successful firm before announcing the award, but the ECJ has precluded this by its decision in the *Alcatel* case. This case concerned the Austrian system, in which challenges to concluded contracts were prohibited, and the contract was concluded at the moment the winning bidder was informed of its success, with no obligation to inform other bidders before this. The court ruled that such a system violated the directive's general obligation to provide effective remedies. According to the Commission, the *Alcatel* case decision means that states that prohibit the setting-aside of a concluded contract must provide for a reasonable delay between notifying the award decision and concluding the contract, to allow time for a legal challenge. In its 2006 proposal, the Commission suggests including an express requirement in the Remedies Directives for a ten-day delay.

The *Alcatel* case is a significant development that will lead to much greater uniformity in member states' remedy systems. Although it concerned an award decision in a competitive procedure, it also has much broader implications. For example, the principle that there must be an effective remedy to challenge any decision may require provision for ensuring an effective challenge to a decision to dispense with competition. The Commission has proposed such a system in its 2006 proposal—it suggests that a notice should be published in the *Official Journal* before any contract is concluded without a competition.

If a national review body is not clear as to the meaning of the EC law that it must apply, it may request an interpretation from the ECJ under a procedure set out in Article 234 EC.

Finally, there was set up in January 2003 a public procurement network (PPN) involving experts (mainly officials involved in procurement policy) from the 27 EC member states, Turkey and EEA/EFTA members (Norway, Iceland, Switzerland, and Liechtenstein). One of its two main purposes is to resolve complaints by foreign firms about award procedures in other countries, on an informal basis, to avoid formal proceedings. Suppliers can take their complaints to their country's PPN representative who will seek an informal resolution with the country concerned. (The other purpose of the network is to exchange information on best practice.) The PPN is not officially an EC organization but its work is supported by the Commission of European Communities, which attends as an observer. It works closely with the commission's own "SOLVIT" network, which is a network for complaints concerning the single market as a whole. If formal legal proceedings commence, the PPN ceases to pursue the complaint.

12.12 Access to EC Markets for Suppliers and Products Outside the EC

It needs to be emphasized that the EC regime described in this chapter so far confers rights only on EC suppliers. Neither the treaty nor the directives guarantee access to EC public procurement markets for non-EC suppliers, and the remedies they provide need to be given only to EC suppliers (although a foreign company can often easily set up an EC subsidiary that will then benefit from these rules).

The EC has, however, concluded trade agreements with most of its main trading partner that guarantee access to all or part of the EC's procurement market for suppliers from those states (Schnitzer, 2005). One of the most important is the WTO's GPA, already referred to in Section 12.1 (Arrowsmith, 2003). This is a plurilateral agreement of the WTO, which means it is optional for WTO members, but current parties include the EC's major trading partners, including Japan, the United States, and Canada. This agreement gives suppliers from these countries access to many of the markets covered by the directives, and in accordance with the same kind of rules, requiring non-discrimination, transparent procedures, and supplier remedies. However, the GPA does not give access to the whole of the market covered by the Treaty and directives—it provides access to just parts of the market (although substantial parts), which varies for different trading partners, according to the extent to which those partners have opened up their own markets to EC suppliers.

In practice, it can be pointed out that many member states also in any case allow access to their markets by non-EC suppliers, even though not required to do so by EC law. It is also relevant to note that the rules laid down to promote the internal single market also have the practical effect of improving access to non-EC suppliers (e.g., non-EC suppliers can in practice make use of the contract information provided in different languages through the EU's *Official Journal*).

12.13 Critical Perspective

We have seen that the EC has addressed the problem of discriminatory public procurement by imposing on all its member states identical and detailed transparency rules. This approach has, however, been the subject of criticism (Fernández Martín, 1996; Arrowsmith, 2002b).

First, the EC regime limits governments' freedom to implement national procurement policies, such as value for money, in the manner most suitable to the particular member state. As well as being used to tackle discrimination, transparency can also, of course, play an important role in supporting value for money and other national objectives and to this extent the EC's requirements support, rather than conflict with, national policies. Nevertheless, a degree of conflict may exist, because some member states may conclude that value for money is not best served by transparency but by allowing for a degree of discretion. For example, limits on post-tender negotiations in standard procurements may prevent abuse to favor particular firms. The EC limits negotiations for this reason, to prevent governments favoring national firms, and member states may prefer to limit such negotiations for similar reasons, such as to prevent corruption. However, other states may take the view that in their own circumstances the benefits of negotiations (e.g., in enabling firms to adjust their offers to the purchaser's priorities or to avoid collusive tendering) outweigh the cost. For these states, EC requirements conflict with legitimate national objectives. The degree of conflict depends on the degree to which particular national systems choose to rely on transparency for their own national goals—which in turn depends on many factors, such as the skills of procurement personnel, or the prevalence of corruption—and also the value assigned to different procurement goals. We have also seen in Section 12.10 that the EC's transparency regime affects the ability of states to pursue horizontal policies. To this extent, the EC regime clearly imposes a cost on member states.

A second important point is that it is difficult to adjust detailed supranational rules to new circumstances, because of the difficulties of securing agreement. This is amply shown by the fact that it took nearly four years to adopt the 2004 directives, which introduced urgently needed measures to adapt the directives to developments such as electronic commerce and the growth of privately financed infrastructure projects. This limits member states' ability to act effectively to obtain value for money. Further, new issues continue to arise. One current problem, for example, is that the Utilities Directive constrains utilities' power to pursue the kind of corporate social responsibility agenda followed by other private companies—a constraint that may affect competitive advantage (Arrowsmith and Maund, forthcoming). Another is a global shortage of certain materials and products caused by expanded production in countries such as China—this has resulted in buyers competing for suppliers in some areas, rather than the reverse, and it is not clear that the current directives provide the means for entities to dispense with competition in this case.

These costs of the current approach must be considered in the context of the benefits achieved, which we have seen are quite limited. Further, the very value of this approach for achieving the benefits of open markets is questionable for several reasons. First, provided that some discretion remains, which is inevitable, there is always scope for hidden discrimination when this is deliberate, rather than simply the product of inertia. Detailed transparency rules are also difficult to apply; they require changes to existing practices, which can generate hostility from interested parties; and they often involve uncertainties that deter enforcement actions. They may be counterproductive, generating reduced transparency where they hinder effective procurement: for example, entities forbidden to hold post-tender discussions that they feel will lead to improved value for money, may simply respond by negotiating in secret with the best bidder, rather than openly with all bidders, as they would if negotiations were permitted. In the area of remedies, research has shown that entities are the subject of vexatious litigation and may reach compromise agreements that involve promising future contracts to the complainant, contrary to the very objective of the rules (Pachnou, 2005).

Thus, some commentators have suggested that a different approach should be considered. Fernández Martín (1996) has suggested that the regime should focus only on limited types of contracts where the greatest benefits are to be realized—very large infrastructure contracts and limited product sectors that are of real cross-border interest. The present author has argued for a different approach to regulation that does not rely on detailed procedural rules at all. There are several options (Arrowsmith, 2002b). One is to adjust the detailed rules to increase flexibility—perhaps by allowing public bodies in general the flexibility currently provided only under the Utilities Directive. Another, even more flexible, approach is to require member states to comply both with the treaty requirements and with a transparency principle as a means of securing compliance with the treaty, but not to lay down the details of transparency requirements at EC level. Such a principle-based system would, however, need to come with a modified enforcement regime that would include a more proactive enforcement mechanism to assess both member states' laws and their actual application (e.g., through a system of national audit authorities, or a panel of independent attesters). Such a principle-based system could replace the current system of detailed regulations, but in the short term, at least, the directives could be retained as an alternative. An even more radical option is to abandon the requirement for transparency and to allow entities to focus solely on compliance with the treaty principles in whatever way they choose. For example, member states might show compliance by demonstrating that purchasing performance or import penetration matches that of comparable private sector bodies. Such approaches can be supported by the principle of effectiveness, which was identified as one of the five key governance principles in the Commission's 2001 White Paper on European governance (Commission of the European Communities, 2001b), which entails that policies should be implemented in a proportionate manner and decisions taken at the most appropriate level. This requires the Community to consider whether to give local discretion in the implementing policy, particularly in circumstances involving different local conditions.

In the short term, however, a change in approach seems unlikely, and is also precluded by the GPA.

References

Books, Articles, etc.

Alyanak, S. 2007. The public procurement system of Turkey in comparison to European Community procurement legislation. *Public Contract Law Journal* 36: 203–228.

Arnould, J. 2004. Secondary policies in public procurement: The innovations of the new directives. *Public Procurement Law Review* 13: 187–197.

Arrowsmith, S. 1999. Framework purchasing and qualification lists under the European Procurement Directives. *Public Procurement Law Review* 8: 115–146, 168–186.

Arrowsmith, S. 2002a. Electronic reverse auctions under the EC Public Procurement Rules: Current possibilities and future prospects. *Public Procurement Law Review* 11: 299–230.

Arrowsmith, S. 2002b. The EC Procurement Directives, national procurement policies and better governance: The case for a new approach. *European Law Review* 27: 3–24.

Arrowsmith, S. 2003. *Government Procurement in the World Trade Organisation*. The Hague, the Netherlands: Kluwer Law International.

Arrowsmith, S. 2005. *The Law of Public and Utilities Procurement*, 2nd ed., London, United Kingdom: Sweet and Maxwell.

Arrowsmith, S. 2006. The past and future evolution of EC Procurement Law: From framework to common Code? *Public Contracts Law Journal* 35: 337–384.

Arrowsmith, S. and Maund, C. Forthcoming 2008. CSR in the utilities sector and the implications of EC procurement policy: A framework for debate. Chapter 11 in S. Arrowsmith and P. Kunzlik (Eds.), *Social and Environmental Policies in EC Public Procurement: New Directives and New Directions*, Chapter 1. Cambridge, United Kingdom: Cambridge University Press.

Arrowsmith, S. and Kunzlik, P. (Eds.). Forthcoming 2008. *Social and Environmental Policies in EC Public Procurement: New Directives and New Directions*. Cambridge, United Kingdom: Cambridge University Press.

Bickerstaff, R. 2004. The new directives' rules on e-communication mechanisms in Public and Utilities Procurement. *Public Procurement Law Review* 13: 277–284.

Bock, C. 1993. The EEA agreement: Rules on Public Procurement. *Public Procurement Law Review* 2: 136–157.

Bohan, N. and Redonnet, D. 1997. EU procurement legislation: Does the emperor have clothes? An examination of the new empirical evidence. *Public Procurement Law Review* 6: 141–173.

Braun, P. 2000. A matter of principle(s): The treatment of contracts falling outside the scope of the European Public Procurement Directives. *Public Procurement Law Review* 9: 39–48.

Brown, A. 1993. Getting to grips with aggregation under the E.C. Public Procurement Rules. *Public Procurement Law Review* 2: 69–81.

Cox, A. and Furlong, P. 1996. The jury is still out for Utilities Procurement: The impact of the EU Procurement Directives on the location of utility contract awards in the twelve member states. *Public Procurement Law Review* 5: 57–66.

Cox, A. and Furlong, P. 1997. Cross-border trade and contract awards; the intellectual myopia at the heart of the EU Procurement Rules. *European Journal of Purchasing and Supply Management* 3: 9–20.

de Boer, L. and Telgen, J. 1997. Experience with the EC Directives on Public Procurement: A survey of Dutch municipalities. *Public Procurement Law Review* 6: 121–127.

Delsaux, A. 2004. The role of the Commission in enforcing EC Public Procurement Rules. *Public Procurement Law Review* 13: 130–152.

Dischendorfer, M. 2000. The existence and development of multilateral rules on Government Procurement under the framework of the WTO. *Public Procurement Law Review* 9: 1–38.

Fernández Martín, J. 1996. *The EC Public Procurement Rules: A Critical Analysis*. Oxford, United Kingdom: Clarendon Press.

Gordon, H., Rimmer, S., and Arrowsmith, S. 1998. The economic impact of the European regime on Public Procurement: Lessons for the WTO. *The World Economy* 21: 159–187.

Georgopoulos, A. 2005. Defence Procurement and EU Law. *European Law Review* 30: 559–572.

Georgopoulos, A. 2006. The European Defence Agency's code of conduct for armament acquisitions: A case of paramnesia? *Public Procurement Law Review* 15: 51–61.

Hartley, K. 1998. Defence Procurement, the single market and the European Armaments Agency. In: S. Arrowsmith and A. Davies (Eds.), *Public Procurement: Global Revolution*, Chapter 1. London, United Kingdom: Kluwer Law International.

Hordijk, E. and Meulenbelt, M. 2005. A bridge too far: Why the European Commission's attempts to construct an obligation to tender outside the scope of the Public Procurement Directives should be dismissed. *Public Procurement Law Review* 14: 123–130.

Madsen, P. 2002. Re-opening the debate on the lack of impact of EU tenders on the openness of public procurement. *Public Procurement Law Review* 11: 265–281.

Martin, S. and Hartley, K. 1997. Public procurement in the European Union: Issues and policies. *Public Procurement Law Review* 6: 92–113.

Martin, S., Hartley, K., and Cox, A. 1999. Public Procurement Directives in the European Union: A study of local authority purchasing. *Public Administration* 77: 387–406.

McCrudden, C. 2007. *Buying Social Justice.* Oxford University Press. Oxford.

McDonald, F. and Winkelman, T. 1996. Public Procurement Rules in the European Union and the prospects for efficient supply: the cases of the UK and Germany. In: A. Cox (Ed.), *Innovations in Procurement Management*, Chapter 16. Lincolnshire, United Kingdom: Earlsgate Press.

Milne R. and Osler, D. 2000. Regulating Public Procurement in the single market: Past, present and future. In: L. Macgregor, T. Prosser, and C. Villiers (Eds.), *Regulation and Markets Beyond 2000*, Chapter 13. Aldershot, United Kingdom: Ashgate/Dartmouth.

Nielsen, J. and Hansen, L. 2001. The EU Public Procurement regime—Does it work? *Intereconomics: Review of International Trade and Development* 36: 255–263.

Nwogwugwu, E. 2005. Towards the harmonisation of international procurement policies and practices. *Public Procurement Law Review* 14: 131–152.

Pachnou, D. 2005. Bidders' use of mechanisms to enforce EC Procurement Law. *Public Procurement Law Review* 14: 35–64.

Papangeli, E. 2000. The application of the E.U.'s Works, Supplies and Services Directives to commercial entities. *Public Procurement Law Review* 9: 201–225.

Pearce, G. and Platten, N. 2000. Promoting the Information Society: The EU Directive on electronic commerce. *European Law Journal* 6: 363–378.

Piselli, E. 2000. The scope for excluding providers who have committed criminal offences under the EU Procurement Directives. *Public Procurement Law Review* 9: 267–286.

Priess, H. and von Merveldt, G. Forthcoming 2008. The impact of the EC state aid rules on horizontal policies in public procurement. Chapter 5 in S. Arrowsmith and P. Kunzlik (Eds.), *Social and Environmental Policies in EC Public Procurement: New Directives and New Directions.* Cambridge, United Kingdom: Cambridge University Press.

Schnitzer, S. 2005. The external sphere of Public Procurement Law: Bi-regional trade relations from the perspective of the European Community. *Public Procurement Law Review* 14: 63–90.

Schwartz, J. 2002. Learning from the United States' procurement law experience: On "law transfer" and its limitations. *Public Procurement Law Review* 11: 115–125.

Sykes, A. 1998. Comparative advantage and the normative economics of international trade policy. *Journal of International Economic Law* 34: 49–82.

Trepte, P. 2007. *Public Procurement in the EU: A Practitioners Guide*, 2nd ed. Oxford, United Kingdom: Oxford University Press.

Trionfetti, F. 2003. Home biased government procurement and international trade. In: S. Arrowsmith and M. Trybus (Eds.), *Public Procurement: The Continuing Revolution*, Chapter 1. The Hague/London: Kluwer Law International.

Trybus, M. 2005. *European Union Law and Defence Integration.* Oxford, United Kingdom: Hart Publishing.

Trybus, M. and Medina, T. Forthcoming. Unfinished business: The state of implementation of the New EC Public Procurement Directives in the member states on February 1, 2007. *Public Procurement Law Review* 16.

Uttley, M. and Hartley, K. 1994. The single European market and public procurement policy: The case of the United Kingdom. *Public Procurement Law Review* 3: 114–125.

Verschuur, S. 2006. Competitive dialogue and the scope for discussion after tenders and before selecting the preferred bidder: What is fine-tuning etc.? *Public Procurement Law Review* 15: 327–331.

Williams, R. 2005. Commission decision on which utilities are exposed to competition. *Public Procurement Law Review* 14: NA69–NA71.

Williams, S. 2006. The mandatory exclusions for corruption in the new EC Procurement Directives. *European Law Review* 31: 711–734.

Legislation and Administrative Decisions

Council Decision of April 15, 1958. The list is set out in Answer to Written Question 574/85. 1985. O J C287/9.

87/95: Council Decision of December 22, 1986, on standardization in the field of information technology and telecommunications. 1987. O J L36/81 ("IT Standards Decision").

Directive 1999/93/EC of the European Parliament and of the Council of December 13, 1999, on a Community framework for electronic signatures. 2000. O J L13/12.

Directive 2000/31/EC of the European Parliament and of the Council of June 8, 2000, on certain legal aspects of information society services, in particular electronic commerce, in the Internal Market. 2000. O J L178/1.

Regulation (EC) No 2195/02 of the European Parliament and of the Council on the Common Procurement Vocabulary (CPV) of November 5, 2002. 2002. O J L340/1 (as amended).

Directive 2004/17/EC of the European Parliament and of the Council of March 31, 2004, coordinating the procurement procedures of entities operating in the water, energy, transport and postal services sectors. 2004. O J L134/1.

Directive 2004/18/EC of the European Parliament and of the Council of March 31, 2004, on the coordination of procedures for the award of public works contracts, public supply contracts and public service contracts. 2004. O J L134/114.

European Defence Agency (Council Joint Action 2004/551/CFSP) of July 12, 2004, on the establishment of the European Defence Agency. 2004. O J L245/17. Up to date information can be found on the agency's website at www.eda.eu.int.

Commission Decision 2005/15/EC of January 7, 2005 on the detailed rules for the application of the procedure provided for in Article 30 of Directive 2004/17/EC of the European Parliament and of the Council coordinating the procurement procedures of entities operating in the water, energy, transport, and postal services sectors. 2005. O J L7/7.

2006/211/EC: Commission Decision of March 8, 2006, establishing that Article 30(1) of Directive 2004/17/EC of the European Parliament and of the Council coordinating the procurement procedures of entities operating in the water, energy, transport, and postal services sectors applies to electricity generation in England, Scotland, and Wales. 2006. O J L76/6.

Government Documents

W.S. Atkins Management Consultants. 1988. *The Cost of Non-Europe in Public Procurement*, vol. 5A, Luxembourg: Official Publications of the EC.

Commission of the European Communities. 1996. Green Paper, *Public Procurement in the European Union: Exploring the Way Forward*, COM 583 final.

Commission of the European Communities. 1997. *The Single Market Review*, subseries III, vol. 2, Public Procurement.

Commission of the European Communities. 2001a. *Commission Interpretative Communication on the Community Law Applicable to Public Procurement and the Possibilities for Integrating Social Considerations into Public Procurement*, COM (2001) 566 final.

Commission of the European Communities. 2001b. *European Governance: A White Paper*, COM (2001) 428 final.

Commission of the European Communities. 2004a. *A Report on the Functioning of Public Procurement Markets in the EU: Benefits from the Application of EU Directives and Challenges for the Future.*

Commission of the European Communities. 2004b. *Green Paper on Defence Procurement*, COM (2004) 608 final.

Commission of the European Communities. 2004c. *Communication from the Commission to the Council, the European Parliament, the European Economic and Social Committee and the Committee of the Regions, Action Plan for the Implementation of the Legal Framework for Electronic Procurement*, COM (2004) 841 final.

Commission of the European Communities. 2005a. *Explanatory Note—Framework Agreements—Classic Directive*, available at http://europa.eu.

Commission of the European Communities. 2005b. *Communication from the Commission to the European Parliament, the Council, the European Economic and Social Committee and the Committee of the Regions on Public-Private Partnerships and Community Law on Public Procurement and Concessions*, November 15, 2005, COM (2005) 569 final.

Commission of the European Communities. 2005c. *Communication from the Commission to the Council and the European Parliament on the Results of the Consultation Launched by the Green Paper on Defence Procurement and on the Future Commission Initiatives*, COM (2005) 626 final.

Commission of the European Communities. 2005d. *Explanatory Document on the Requirements for Electronic Public Procurement—Commission Staff Working Document*, available at http://europa.eu.

Commission of the European Communities. 2006a. *Commission Communication on the Community Law Applicable to Contract Awards Not or Not Fully Subject to the Provision of the Public Procurement Directives*, available at http://europa.eu.

Commission of the European Communities. 2006b. *Commission of the European Communities, Interpretative Communication on the Application of Article 296 of the Treaty in the Field of Defense Procurement*, COM (2006) 779 final.

Commission of the European Communities. 2006c. *Proposal for a Directive of the European Parliament and of the Council Amending Council Directives 89/665/EEC and 92/13/EEC with Regard to Improving the Effectiveness of Review Procedures Concerning the Award of Public Contracts*, COM (2006) 195 final.

Legal Authorities (in Chronological Order by Date of Proceedings)

C-27/86, *Construction et Entreprises Industrielles SA (CEI) v. Association Intercommunale pour les Autoroutes des Arden*nes ("*CEI/Bellini*"). 1987. E.C.R. 3347.

C-31/87, *Gebroeders Beentjes BV v. Netherlands* ("*Beentjes*"). 1988. E.C.R. 4635.

C-21/88, *Du Pont de Nemours Italiana SpA v. Unita Sanitaria Locale No. 2 Di Carrara* ("*Du Pont de Nemours*"). 1990. E.C.R. I-889.

C-360/89, *Commission v. Italy*. 1992. E.C.R. I-3401.

C-243/89, *Commission v. Denmark* ("*Storebaelt*"). 1993. E.C.R. I-3353.

C-71/92, *Commission v. Spain*. 1993. E.C.R. I-5923.

C-359/93, *Commission v. Netherla*nds ("*UNIX*"). 1995. E.C.R. I-157.

C-76/97, *Tögel (Walter) v. Niederoesterreichische Gebietskrankenkasse* ("*Walter Tögel*"). 1998. E.C.R. I-5357.

C-81/98, *Alcatel Austria AG v. Bundesministerium fur Wissenschaft und Verkehr* ("*Alcatel*"). 1999. E.C.R. I-7671.

C-107/98, *Teckal Srl v. Comune di Viano* ("*Teckal*"). 1999. E.C.R. I-8121.

C-225/98, *Commission v. France* ("*Nord Pas de Calais*"). 2000. E.C.R. I-7445.

C-324/98, *Telaustria Verlags GmbH v. Telekom Austria AG* ("*Telaustria*"). 2000. E.C.R. I-10745.

C-379/98, *Preussen Elektra AG v. Schleswag AG* ("*Preussen Elektra*"). 2001. E.C.R. I-2099.

C-470/99, *Universale-Bau AG v. Entsorgungsbetriebe Siemmering GmbH* ("*Universale-Bau*"). 2002. E.C.R. I-11617.

C-283/00, *Commission v. Spain* ("*SIEPSA*"). 2003. E.C.R. I-11697.

C-252/01, *Commission v. Belgium*. 2003. E.C.R. I-11859.

C-448/01, *EVN AG, Wienstrom GmbH v. Republik Österreich* ("*EVN and Wienstrom*"). 2003. E.C.R. I-14527.

C-21/03, *Fabricom SA v. Belgium* ("*Fabricom*"). 2005. E.C.R. I-1559.
C-26/03, *Stadt Halle v. RPL Lochau* ("*Stadt Halle*"). 2005. E.C.R. I-1.
C-29/04, *Commission v. Austria* ("*Mödling*"). 2005. E.C.R. I-9705.
C-226/04, *La Cascina Sarl v. Ministero della Difesa* ("*La Cascina*"). 2006. E.C.R. I-1347.
C-340/04, *Carbotermo SpA v. Comune di Busto Arsizio* ("*Carbotermo*"). 2006. E.C.R. I-4137.
T-14/96, *Bretagne Angleterre Irlande v. Commission* ("*BAI*"). 1999. E.C.R. II-139.

WTO Disputes

United States—Measures Affecting Government Procurement—Constitution of the Panel Established at the Request of the European Communities and Japan (October 21, 1998, WT/DS88/4, WT/DS95/4) ("*Burma/Massachusetts*").

Chapter 13

U.S. Federal Government Procurement: Organizational Structure, Process, and Current Issues

Kristi D. Caravella Robinson

CONTENTS

13.1 Introduction

Although it would be impossible to consider every aspect of the federal procurement system in the United States in a single chapter, this chapter highlights some of the key aspects of this system: the use of procurement as various types of policy, the structure of procurement organizations, the procurement process, and some of the techniques that procurement organizations have at their disposal. One common aspect of public procurement throughout nations is that it is an essential function of any government because it involves the purchasing of all goods, services, and capital assets to be provided for public consumption.[1] Without public procurement, a government could not operate or provide services. In addition, a large portion of public procurement involves the purchasing of defense weapons and supplies; without these goods, which are not available in many markets, a nation would not be able to defend itself and protect its citizens.

Although many procurement systems throughout the world have similar functions, the U.S. procurement system has many aspects that are unique and make it a worthy example to study. For example, the system of checks and balances that is made possible by a federalist system, the overriding influence of the executive branch, the various, resulting organizational structures assumed by federal procurement agencies, and a workforce that is highly tuned into the competitive, global market make the U.S. federal procurement system special. This chapter highlights these unique characteristics and considers their influence on the organizational structure of federal procurement agencies. Further analysis of these characteristics can provide fruitful grounds for comparing procurement systems' successes and failures around the world.

In the United States, "the first significant procurement, made in 1794, was for a group of six large frigates for the new U.S. Navy."[2] In 2006, according to the National Institute of Government Purchasing (NIGP), the total procurement in the United States was more than $200 billion, or 10 percent of the total U.S. budget. This figure has decreased since 2004 when the total U.S. annual procurement budget was close to $400 billion. In recent years in the United States, defense procurement, or major systems acquisition, has taken a larger chunk of the total federal government procurement pie. Overall, the U.S. procurement system is still an evolving function, moving from a clerical and police-like role to one of the professional, strategic consultants operating in a purchasing system.

In the United States, as in many other countries, there are both similarities and differences between governmental (public) and commercial (private) purchasing. While in areas of continuity of supply, avoidance of waste, and maintenance of quality standards government and commercial procurement tend to be the same, the two differ greatly in areas of the range of goods and services provided and the types of goods and services provided.[3] In addition, government procurement works in a different environment than commercial procurement does; the public procurement environment is dictated by public oversight and demands for transparency and openness, but yet, it often involves areas of purchasing that involve national security, national defense, and disaster management, which require a certain amount of secrecy. This often creates a conflict in the goals of the government procurement process. Also, because government procurement must give equitable and fair treatment to all suppliers due to regulations, there is likely to be more red tape than in the private sector, causing delays in the achievement of public procurement goals.

Despite these differences in environment and goals, both U.S. government and commercial procurement organizations operate in the same global market system.[4] One might say that these differences enable private sector purchasers an unfair advantage in the marketplace. To better compete with private purchasers, U.S. federal procurement has become more strategic in its purchasing behaviors, often adopting methods deemed successful, and used, by its private competitors. By evolving from a clerical gatekeeper to a strategic player, the U.S. federal government has become a more effective and efficient purchaser, or a smart buyer.[5] Examination of the changes in the U.S. procurement workforce can be useful to nations with a less-developed procurement system as well as other federalist nations.

13.2 Overview

This chapter provides an analysis of the public procurement systems in the United States. First, the concept of public procurement as a policy tool is explored. Because of the size and significance of the procurement process, political pressures arise within and from outside the various stages of contracting.[6] These include bureaucratic politics, congressional (elective) politics, and interest group politics. Therefore, the U.S. federal government procurement system often functions as a policy tool. Public procurement is truly a game of managing conflicting interests to achieve a common goal; it is very political in nature. Buyers want to buy high-quality goods and services at the lowest price (best price for a reasonable quality from a reliable supplier). Sellers want to sell easily produced goods at as high a price as possible; users want high-quality, easy-to-use products; and elected officials want completion of highly visible programs to help reelection. Government procurement might reflect any one of these interests depending on the political direction of the country. In essence, public procurement, or governmental purchasing in the United States, is the pursuit of the common goal that satisfies all the requirements to help get all stakeholders to where they want to be—not an easy or apolitical task. Specifically, U.S. procurement often is used as social, economic, and political policy; these areas are discussed and examples are provided.

Next, the distinctive regulations that govern the U.S. procurement process are surveyed at the federal, state, local, and organizational levels. Federal regulations are predominately aimed at maintaining a centralized structure that enforces uniform standards. In principle, the president is responsible for implementing procurement statutes, authorizing procurement appropriations, and appointing or influencing the appointment of many procurement officers.[7] In practice, state, local, and organizational regulations equally influence the procurement process. In other words, the U.S. procurement system is one that is highly regulated under a myriad of federal, state, common (case), and local laws intended to dictate behaviors of those actors in the procurement process. In this chapter, a history of relevant federal regulation is provided with consideration of a trend toward centralization or decentralization of procurement policy. Often, a by-product of decentralized procurement policy, corruption, is considered. Specifically, recent charges of contract corruption in defense procurement are provided. In addition, a comprehensive analysis of U.S. procurement organizational structure is provided through discussions of the constitutional framework, executive branch, and structure and workforce. Finally, a brief description of the procurement process and techniques is provided.

13.3 Public Procurement as a Policy Tool

Thai (2001) describes two types of goals in the procurement system: nonprocurement goals and procurement goals.[8] Procurement goals are primarily associated with quality, reduction of financial and technical risks, and protection over competition and integrity in the system. Nonprocurement goals usually involve the economic, social, and political goals within the system. Although it is important for any government to consider the economic, social, and political effects of procurement, the administration must realize that procurement is a political, complex process of conflicting interests, and if it is used too often to bring benefits or advantages to one group over another, the system will be seen as unfair and inequitable. In addition, the public might lose confidence in the system. For example, one type of nonprocurement goal aimed at inducing social benefits might be offering contracts to businesses owned by minorities or women. This might help the group and even the economy for a short time, but the action brings a certain bias to the procurement system.

Over the years, the use of the federal procurement system as a social, political, and economic policy has been debated in the courts as well. For example, in 1979, President Carter's use of the Federal Property and Administrative Services Act of 1949 (the Procurement Act) was challenged in federal court on two grounds; first, the suit asserted that no statute empowered the president to use the federal procurement system to encourage adherence to the wage–price guidelines, and second, the suit claimed that by denying federal contracts to noncompliant parties, the president's program effectively constituted a scheme of mandatory controls and should be prohibited.[9] Although the Procurement Act in its exact interpretation was aimed solely at increasing the economy and efficiency of the procurement process, the Carter administration was able to convince the courts that the "immediate effect of the Order (Executive Order 12092) would be to hold down expenditures and the long run effects would be to reduce inflation throughout the economy, leading to lower government costs than would otherwise have been incurred."[10] In *AFL-CIO v. Kahn*, the U.S. Court of Appeals for the District of Columbia Circuit held that this use of the procurement system was a valid exercise of presidential authority.[11]

In general, social and political goals are a little harder to justify than economic goals when it comes to using public procurement as a policy tool because economic goals are intended at the national level and are more quantifiable, and, therefore, involve less bias or preference toward certain segments of the population.[12] In this way, the function of public procurement can be understood as an attempt to spread the wealth of government through social programs and political spending. For example, in 1971, President Nixon attempted to control inflation by imposing the first mandatory peacetime wage and price controls in U.S. history.[13] To provide U.S. government procurement officers a single point of reference, socioeconomic rules also are implemented in the Federal Acquisition Regulation (FAR). FAR sets forth the rules and processes for implementing these socioeconomic programs. In addition, federal agencies may supplement FAR to provide additional rules and processes for socioeconomic programs specific to the agency.

13.3.1 Procurement as Social Policy

Within the procurement process, the government seeks to meet the needs of many special interest groups. Often, U.S. procurement legislation is aimed at satisfying the needs of these special interest groups; in this way, procurement policy is used as a social policy. Some of these special interest groups include small vendors, local vendors, and minority vendors. In addition, advocacy groups for such issues as the environment and homosexuals (domestic partner preferences) often look to government to lend greater, often, preferential treatment to businesses that uphold their values and ideals (i.e., companies that "go green," or are environmentally safe) and provide goods to the government. As noted, the major deficiency of providing special treatment to particular interest groups is that the government will be seen as unfair in its procurement, and the entire system loses credibility.

13.3.2 Procurement as Economic Policy

On the other hand, procurement as an economic policy can compensate for unfairness and inequities in the private sector, which tends to be dominated by large vendors, global vendors, and nonminority vendors. Federal purchases are today one of the most important national economic factors.[14] By offering economic incentives to particular vendors who perform according to a government request, the government can achieve multiple benefits. For example, by providing an economic incentive to vendors who use American supplies and produce their goods or services in the states, the government not only obtains its goods but also boosts the local economy by keeping supplies and labor in the country.

13.3.3 Procurement as Political Policy

It should be understood that the origin of all procurement policy is political. Procurement as political policy can be found in the concept of trade-offs. A trade-off is when one political gain is achieved by sacrificing something in its place. A common trade-off in public procurement occurs between quality and cost. Procurement officials and policy makers, alike, are involved in these trade-off decisions. There is a constant tension between procurement officials and policy makers with regard to searching for the optimal quality (procurement officials) that can be obtained with the amount of money appropriated (policy makers) for purchase of the good or service. U.S. policy makers are known to make trade-offs for funding particular projects in their district; as a result, procurement officials are often faced with the dilemma of continuing to provide necessary, quality goods despite abrupt shortages in funding. To continue providing the good or service, the procurement official often attempts to reduce the cost of the unfunded good by purchasing a good or service with a lower level of quality or cost.

In addition, procurement as a political policy can be seen as corruption, political or administrative corruption, or both. For example, if a politician sits on a request for proposals (RFP) board and the project is in his or her district, this can be seen as corruption in the form of indirect and direct favoritism. This type of corruption limits the effectiveness of the larger checks and balance system that governs the procurement process.

13.4 Federal Procurement Regulations

In the United States, the procurement process fluctuates between environmental periods of regulation and deregulation dictated by the federal government. Usually operating between two extremes, the federal procurement system is either characterized as consisting of very tight and burdensome controls or as a system with relaxed regulatory condition. While forces like "wartime arms needs often lead to relaxed procurement rules so the nation could arm quickly," other forces such as "contractor profiteering and waste lead to a tightening of procurement rules and controls."[15] The federal constitution supersedes all other laws with regard to procurement. A period of regulation is characterized by many rules for procedures and processes and little discretion for procurement officials in the process. A period of deregulation is characterized by rules that are aimed at injecting more power and control to the procurement office and its officials. In addition to setting standards of conduct, federal procurement regulations are used to state executive policies; to establish procurement organizational structure, roles, and responsibilities; and to prescribe procurement phases and processes.

After experiencing a difficult period with contracting during the two major world wars, the United States enacted two major pieces of legislation, the Armed Services Procurement Act of 1949 (ASPA) and the Federal Property and Administrative Services Act of 1949 (FPASA), to deal with the use of contracts to accomplish government programs. These acts were designed to make a complex contract process easier for both federal agencies (purchasers) and sellers.[16] Up until the 1990s,

ASPA and FPASA plus two other major pieces of federal legislation established procurement rules.[17] The Competition in Contracting Act of 1984 established rules for choosing suppliers based on the policy of full and open competition (procurements should be widely advertised, open to all, and evaluated strictly on criteria announced in advance). The Truth in Negotiations Act of 1962 established rules for disclosure by bidders of cost information, which government could use to negotiate prices that also served as a basis for audits and legal action against firms failing to disclose accurate, current, and complete cost data. Under the pre-1990 system, rules were predominately aimed at "what process must be followed in making a decision," or "decision rules."[18] A centralized system with uniform procedures guided procurement.

During the 1990s, the procurement system entered a period of deregulation often associated with the administration of Vice President Al Gore and his policy of "reinventing government."[19] Periods of deregulation usually are associated with less red tape (procedural or decision rules) and more efficiency. Both the Federal Acquisition Streamlining Act (1994) and the Federal Acquisition Reform Act (1995) were aimed at simplifying the procurement process by easing procedures for buying commercial goods, encouraging consideration of past performance in selecting contractors, authorizing two-phase design-build selection procedures, and raising the dollar limit for discretionary purchasing.[20] In addition, the Government Performance and Results Act of 1993 and the Clinger–Cohen Act of 1996 reinforced the federal message about performance expectations in programs and acquisitions in light of decentralized procurement. These acts require that agencies maintain accurate performance measures and reporting mechanisms. All these initiatives decentralized the procurement process at the executive agency level, but also put in place a centralized, uniform structure for federal procurement.

When the procurement process is deregulated, there is more risk (of corruption) involved for the government. The U.S. procurement system is inundated with players. From bidders to contractors and subcontractors, and from policy makers to procurement officials, the system relies on the trustworthiness and ethics of these players. Although there are regulations in place that make false statements or claims against the government including actions within "their scope as related to inflated or false payment requests from vendors, and purposely inflated claims filed under a contract" punishable by civil or criminal penalty, it is the personal ethics of the procurement official that must prevail when unethical propositions are made.[21] Even with additional safeguards of organizational regulations and rules that reflect broader procurement laws and regulations, procurement organizations experience corruption. Vigorous regulations and systems of checks and balances also have proven futile; the public procurement system is prone to corruption.[22]

Since the United States entered into war with Iraq, charges of corruption in the defense procurement system have been rampant.[23] U.S. state representatives have publicly attacked the federal government's contracting in Iraq in various areas such as accelerated discretionary spending, widespread contract mismanagement, and direct waste and fraud.[24] One of the top five U.S. defense contracting companies, Lockheed Martin, and the nation's fastest growing defense contracting company, Halliburton, Inc., have been criticized for their close ties to members of the executive branch as well.[25] A report by the Committee on Government Oversight states that federal spending on Halliburton contracts increased over 600 percent between 2000 and 2005.[26] Another report by the Government Accountability Office found no direct violations of procurement regulations in the government's dealings with defense contractors for the Iraq War, questionable situations are illuminated in the report and it states that further reports on contracts awarded using other than full and open competition must be provided to ensure more transparency and accountability in the award of new Iraq reconstruction contracts.[27]

13.5 Procurement Organizations

The structure of procurement organizations in the Unites states can be understood by examining the procurement structure as established in the constitutional framework of the legislative, executive, and judiciary branches, the procurement structure as regulated by the executive branch, either toward centralization or decentralization of procurement policy, and the procurement structure promoted by a strategic procurement workforce. Each of these unique aspects—a tri-part system of checks and balances, a dominating executive branch, and a strategic workforce—is considered in light of its influence on organizational structure in this section.

13.5.1 Procurement Organization Structure in the Constitutional Framework: Legislative, Executive, and Judiciary Branches

There are two main types of government structures: unitary and federal. While unitary systems maintain a central government that exercises absolute control over local governments, federal systems maintain a central government, but state and local governments under the system have much more autonomy than in unitary governments.[28] In the United States, each state in the union has its own constitution, civil service system, elected legislative body, budget, and judiciary system, more or less maintaining a great degree of independence from each other. Also, many local governments (city or county level) maintain similar, separate structures as those enjoyed at the state level. This federalist structure of government has great effect on the structure of procurement organizations. Each government entity, whether it is federal, state, or local, has a "distinctive procurement organizational structure, depending on its size, procurement needs, and environment."[29] It can be said that the three branches of government—executive, legislative, and judiciary—act as a system of checks and balances for the procurement process. In a federalist system, each branch of government (executive, legislative, and judiciary) exists at each level (federal, state, and local) of government creating an extensive web of checks and balances over the procurement system.

Although there is some difference in each state, the functions of the executive, legislative, and judiciary branches can be summarized. The executive branch is responsible for implementing statutes and authorizing appropriations for procurement. The federal government maintains volumes of procedures for procurement in the *Federal Acquisition Regulation (FAR) manual* and other detailed manuals. In addition, the executive branch recommends programs and funding levels for procurement organizations. The legislative branch primarily influences the procurement system through "laws, budget appropriations, and by its oversight powers."[30] The laws passed by the legislative branch often reflect the time and amount of funds a procurement organization can spend and also provide guidance for compliance with higher laws. Finally, the judiciary branch investigates and examines all legal cases that involve procurement practices, like terms and conditions of contracts, and disputes that cannot be settled at the organizational level. In essence, this complex system made up of the various levels and branches of government often leads to an organizational structure that is centralized, but yet, highly fragmented.

13.5.2 Procurement Organization Structure as Dictated by the Executive Branch

The federal procurement administrative structure utilizes a centralized structure to maintain uniform standards and controls and a decentralized structure allowing for flexibility to meet the unique requirements of over 60 federal agencies.[31] For example, the Office of Management and Budget recommends programs and funding levels for programs, including procurements; monitors programs and adjusts funding levels, if necessary; provides procurement policy guidance through the Office of Federal Procurement Policy (OFPP); and reviews proposed regulations for compliance with policy guidance.[32]

The Office of Federal Procurement Policy, a part of the U.S. Office of Management and Budget, among other responsibilities, provides leadership in the establishment, development, and maintenance of FARs; coordinates the development of governmentwide procurement systems standards; and provides direction in the development of procurement systems of executive agencies. The Federal Acquisition Regulatory Council assists in the direction and coordination of federal procurement policy and regulatory activities. In addition, there are three Acquisition Regulatory Councils: the Defense Acquisition Regulatory Council, the Civilian Agency Acquisition Council, and the Federal Acquisition Regulatory Council. Chaired by the Secretary of Defense and comprised of representatives from the Departments of Air Force, Army, Navy, the Defense Logistics Agency, and the National Aeronautics and Space Administration, the Defense Acquisition Regulatory Council is primarily responsible for Defense Acquisition Regulations. The Civilian Agency Acquisition Council, chaired by the Administrator of the General Service Administration, and comprised of representatives from 13 civilian agencies, is primarily responsible for civilian acquisition regulations. The Federal Acquisition Regulatory Council consists of the administrators of General Service Administration (GSA), National Aeronautics and Space Administration (NASA) and OFPP, and the Secretary of Defense. When one council develops a proposed amendment to FAR, the amendment is referred to the other council for review and concurrence. Before its issuance, the FAR amendment is reviewed by the OFPP administrator and is jointly signed by all members of the Federal Acquisition Regulatory Council. The existence of the three acquisition regulatory councils makes the procurement structure of the federal government further fragmented.[33]

Boards of Contract Appeals (BCA) resolve contract disputes between contract officers and contractors. Several of the large agencies have their own BCA. Agencies that do not have a BCA use the BCA of another agency, when needed, as is the case for the Department of State, which uses the GSA board. Executive agency heads (whether the secretary, attorney general, administrators, chairperson, other chief official of an executive agency, or their authorized representatives) establish supplementary acquisition regulations and other internal policies and procedures, which are responsible for fulfilling agency procurement needs, and carry out the FAR.[34]

These are only a portion of the influential agencies, boards, and actors involved in the procurement system. Each agency will have a different organizational structure depending on the relative importance of procurement to the agency's mission. In some executive agencies, such as the GSA and the Department of Defense where the procurement function is very important, a separate procurement office is created. In other executive agencies that do not consider procurement to be a prominent function, procurement is normally placed within a unit that is responsible for other functions. Overall, these differing organizational structures result in a fragmented procurement system that is bound to a centralized executive office.

13.5.3 Centralization versus Decentralization

Owing to the highly political and, often, conflicting nature of the environment in which public procurement occurs, the U.S. federal procurement process itself has developed with conflicting goals as well. This conflict can be seen with regard to trends toward both centralization and decentralization of the process initiated by the federal government.[35] As in most governments, U.S.

government purchasing is neither completely centralized nor completely decentralized. Some of the main reasons a procurement process must have a decentralized nature are to "provide more responsive support to end users, eliminate bureaucratic obstacles to program accomplishment, improve inter-departmental coordination, and empower service delivery managers to procure what they need without impediment by a centralized organization"; in short, decentralization provides flexibility to the process.[36] One major disadvantage to a decentralized procurement process is that it opens up the doors to bribes and corruption.

On the other hand, a centralized procurement process ensures uniformity and accountability of government contracts, procurement personnel, and the procurement process overall.[37] The amount of centralization for a particular procurement agency depends on the size of the agency; the geographic disbursement of the entity; legislative, executive, or judiciary branch influence; public participation; and business community influence. The major drawbacks to a centralized procurement process are the added amount of paperwork, red tape (bureaucracy), and formal procedures that become part of a centralized system. In addition, the cost of enforcing regulations on a highly centralized, but extremely fragmented procurement process is quite high.[38]

The best way to determine whether a decentralized or centralized procurement organization is appropriate is to examine the actual goals the government would like to achieve. In essence, there is no one-best method for procurement organizations because each government has different needs. At the federal level, a trend toward decentralization for small projects and centralization for large projects has developed in the United States. In an agency where many small projects are considered, there is more discretion needed to keep the flow of procurement, therefore, necessitating a decentralized structure of regulation. More importantly, the procurement structure adopted by the executive branch (federal level) tends to influence the structure of other procurement organizations, especially in terms of transparency and efficiency.

Transparency is the ability for those outside the procurement system to see inside the system, or the openness of the system to those not in it. The structure of the procurement agency affects the amount of transparency in the system. Transparency is necessary in government procurement process for several reasons. One of these reasons is that the system is governed by detailed procedural guidance dictated by public oversight for ethics and compliance.[39] This is done with regard to concerns for equity in public decisions and ethics in procedures. In addition, the public's opinion of government's equity in expenditures is enhanced by transparency in the process of procurement, which is accomplished, to a certain extent, through centralization of the process. Also, because "public agencies are not in commercial competition with one another... buyers (can) share information freely and work cooperatively toward process improvement."[40] Transparency in the procurement system, therefore, operates to make information-sharing and cooperative process possible. U.S. procurement officials use several techniques to ensure transparency:

- Make deals fairly and in good faith.
- Maintain impartiality and avoid preferential treatment.
- Avoid any appearance of conflict of interest.
- Maintain public trust without compromise.
- Maintain clear, documented files on all procurement acts.

Efficiency also is affected by the structure of the procurement system. Efficiency in U.S. public procurement is, more or less, dictated by procurement laws and regulations at the various levels of government (federal, state, and local) and policy-related legislation that determines spending levels.

In addition, each agency is likely to have its own rules and procedures for procurement. The hierarchy of law is first, federal; second, state; and third, county, city and its authorities, if they do not deviate from the higher laws. These various levels of procurement regulations are independent of each other and tend to create red tape (i.e., excessive steps that must be complied with to make a purchase) and inefficiency. To avoid conflict and inefficiency, it is important that procurement officials maintain a clear knowledge of these differing regulations.

13.5.4 Procurement Organization Structure and Workforce

Public procurement organizations in the United States have become more strategic in their approaches to purchasing for competing in the global and local market. Strategic behavior such as optimizing savings, maximizing competitive bidding, integration of supply strategies, and life cycle maintenance describes this new professional approach to public procurement.[41] In the past, public procurement operated as a purely "clerical gatekeeper" and engaged in "housekeeping activity of minor national significance."[42] In the United States, the procurement field, in its early days, lacked procurement professionals. The role of the clerical gatekeeper was of monitoring fraud in the system and searching for the lowest bid. The clerical gatekeeper played no role in the strategic plans and goals of government. There has been a shift from hiring clerical gatekeepers to strategic planners in the U.S. procurement workforce. The Clinger–Cohen Act (1996) also required OFPP to establish, through the Federal Acquisition Institute (FAI) established in 1976, a consistent set of data elements for tracking education and training as well as career information within each civilian agency acquisition workforce. Through the FAI, the federal government has been able to analyze and improve its acquisition workforce of nearly 130,000 employees nationwide.[43]

Today, strategic procurement is more necessary than ever for a procurement organization to maximize the achievement of goals as any "short-term disruption of supply may affect government operations adversely."[44] Public procurement organizations of the past adhered to the clerical gatekeeper role, which mostly functioned to maintain efficiency and transparency. But as the procurement environment continues to change, the functions of procurement organizations are changing as well. An important theme of government over the past decade has been to empower personnel, bureaus, and agencies to acquire things using their own rules, regulations, and practices.[45] For example, now that fixed-firm pricing has become a thing of the past and the bargaining process has been accepted into the mainstream of the procurement process, negotiation techniques increasingly have become an important strategy for public procurement organizations. Overall, the growth of expertise in this area has enabled public procurement to become more strategic. Also, because the expertise of procurement officials has been increased in areas such as planning and service functions, these officials have been able to provide services such as demand analysis, market analysis, supplier analysis, and general procurement research that have proved critical to the achievement of public procurement organizational goals in today's market.

Another crucial consideration in U.S. procurement organizations that can make them more strategic has been the placement of the central procurement officer (CPO). The CPO is commonly placed in a position that reports to the finance director. All other department leaders report to a chief executive officer (CEO) who then reports to the CPO and the finance director. The result of this placement ensures that the CPO still has a "degree of independence and effectiveness" within the entity.[46] In addition, the CEO is responsible not only for managing each department in the entity but also for ensuring that each department has the information necessary to conduct its tasks and comply with legislation, regulation, and policies.[47]

13.6 Public Procurement Process and Techniques

The U.S. procurement process consists of the following phases:

- Procurement authorization and appropriations
- Procurement planning
- Contract formulation
- Contract administration
- Evaluation and feedback

Within this process, such techniques as RFPs (request for proposals), RFBs (request for bids), price analysis, cost analysis, negotiation technique, sole source, emergency, and ADR (alternative dispute resolution) are used to solicit goods and services. This section summarizes key aspects of the procurement process and some of the techniques used at various stages of the process.

First, the three main factors that determine the type of procurement process the government will use are the law, the dollar amount (cost), and the complexity of the purchase. For example, if the purchase is small, an informal technique like quotes can be used. But for large, complex purchases, formal techniques such as the RFPs and RFBs are necessary to determine responsive and responsible bidders, or aspects of vendors other than cost alone. The use of an RFP or RFB is dictated by procurement laws. In addition, the government does not want to spend more funds on the process than on the purchase as this would be a fruitless effort. So, if the expenditure amount is low, efforts are made to keep the process simple. U.S. procurement organizations have experimented with petty cash, field orders, delegated purchase orders, and procurement E-cards for small expenditure purchases. Often, the size and the complexity of the procurement purchase are the major determining factors in the adoption of a "do it all structure" (small government entities) and a "fragmented" (federal) organizational structure.[48]

During the procurement authorization and appropriations stage, the legislature and interest groups debate over amounts to be allotted for specific procurements.[49] The process begins with the federal budget process.[50] "Program authorizations and budget authority are made available to the agencies which can be used by means of contracts with private suppliers of products or services."[51] To use these funds, the requirements of the federal contracting process must be met by the agency or program.

The procurement planning phase is characterized by research and strategic planning for the procurement; both long- and short-term costs are considered and calculated. Procurement officials engage in price analysis and cost analysis. Great strides, including Web portals, have been made to engage federal agencies in information-sharing as it relates to achieving procurement goals through analysis of prices and costs. In addition, life cycle costing (LCC) is a technique that considers the total cost of ownership of a commodity or building, in contrast to traditional purchasing approaches that rely only on the initial acquisition cost.[52] The rationale behind LCC is that although the initial cost of a product may be greater than a competing product, the total cost of ownership may be less for the more expensive item because it is less expensive to operate or maintain the item over its life. Engaging in LCC can save the government money in the long run. After the procurement planning phase is completed, the government enters into the contract formulation phase during which several aspects are considered such as the type of bidding it will in engage in and the type of contract that is required.

Usually, the procurement processes of U.S. government agencies employ either competitive procedures or sole-sourcing. Competitive bidding involves the solicitation of multiple bids; in sole-sourcing, agencies bypass the solicitation of competitive bids and instead designate a single vendor as a sole-supplier.[53] For military departments until 1940 and for civilian agencies until 1942, by far the dominant mode of entering into a contract had long been advertisement for bids and award to the lowest, responsible bidder.[54] This procedure is called competitive bidding although it often fails to encourage competition.[55] The principal alternative is negotiation. Under wartime statutory authorizations, it is currently by far the most prevalent procedure for obtaining military procurement contracts. Negotiation differs from competitive bidding in that negotiation may entail some bargaining and in that it does not necessarily involve award to the lowest bidder.[56] In practice, a contract entered into through competitive bidding is likely to state an exact price per unit or in total. A negotiated contract, in practice, is likely to involve a promise by the government to pay all costs incurred by the contractor, plus a fixed fee. Currently, many of the current defense contracts entered into by the U.S. federal government for the war in Iraq are negotiated rather than competitive.[57]

The basis of any contract is that it is an agreement binding two parties for the performance of a particular service or provision of a product for a specified price, usually within a specified time.[58] There are many items procured by federal personnel in petty amounts by means of simple, over-the-counter operations. Often, these small purchases involve oral contracts, or an informal contract.[59] An informal contract involves a document containing the agency's invitation for bids, the bid made by one of the bidders, and (if he or she is awarded the contract) the agency's acceptance of the offer. A formal contract is preceded by separate documents for, respectively, the invitation and the bids.[60] These are the various contracts that can be entered into during the contract formulation phase. As noted, the use of an RFP or RFB is dictated by procurement laws and compliance guidelines, which specifically refer to the various types of contracts (oral, informal, or formal).

Once the government enters into a contract with a seller, the contract is not finished; the contract must be managed for its lifetime. This is considered the contract management phase of the process. Government contractual relationships may be more like treaties than contracts in that often no real separation between the government and vendor ever occurs.[61] Management of long-term contracts can be costly and time consuming for federal agencies. For example, "change order requests" originated around the time of the American Civil War.[62] These allow the contracting officer to issue change orders to a contractor whose work is in progress on plans or specifications; usually the purpose of the change order is to maintain state-of-the-art standards on government equipment and services as long-term projects progress. Although necessary, change order requests can be used to increase allowable costs for a particular good or service and decrease performance demands, therefore causing the government to spend more time and money than it initially intended on projects.[63] Resolution of disputes is also part of the contract administration phase. Alternative dispute resolution (ADR) is one technique where the purchaser and seller would attempt to resolve a contract dispute with a mediator that is used to avoid lengthy court battles. The final phase of the procurement process involves evaluation and feedback. Feedback is important in preventing future complications during the procurement process. Evaluation ensures accountability and transparency in the system.

13.7 Conclusion

This chapter has summarized the use of procurement as various types of policy, the structure of procurement organizations, the procurement process and techniques, and the development of a strategic purchasing workforce. As noted, the U.S. federal procurement system is still evolving and continues to make use of new technologies to better the system. For example, the current Bush administration has undertaken a number of E-government initiatives. These initiatives are designed to provide greater access to citizens in terms of the provision of government services, eliminate redundancy in purchasing, and achieve economies of scale where appropriate (procurement as social and economic policy). There are 24 such initiatives underway at the moment, one of which involves government procurement. The government procurement initiative is called the Integrated Acquisition Environment (IAE). The vision for IAE is to create a single Web-based portal for government acquisition, a portal to be used by government personnel as well as private sector companies in their transactions with the U.S. government. In addition, the U.S. government hopes this E-initiative will continue to bring efficiency and transparency to the federal procurement system.[64]

In summary, according to a recent report by the U.S. Government Accountability Office, the federal government procurement system at all levels will continue to be affected by its abilities to manage timely and accurate data, enable users to generate their own reports from this data, and to provide easier user access to data.[65] It is no doubt that the U.S. procurement system is a major player in the global market, even slight changes in its purchasing preferences can disrupt the flow of goods and services to countries near and far. But the U.S. federal procurement system only has so much power as it now competes with other major private sector players (including transnational companies) in the global market. If the U.S. federal procurement system is to continue as a major player in equalizing competition in purchasing, information-sharing will play a pivotal role in this equation. It may indeed be the unique characteristics discussed in this chapter that have enabled both successes and failures in the U.S. federal procurement system.

Notes

1. Khi Thai, Public procurement re-examined, *Journal of Public Procurement,* 1 2001, 9–50.
2. Thai, 2001, 14.
3. Khi Thai, *Introduction to Public Procurement*, Herndon, VA: National Institute of Governmental Purchasing, Inc., 2004.
4. The global market is often dominated by private sector interests.
5. Donald F. Kettl, *Sharing Power: Public Governance and Private Markets*, Washington: The Brookings Institution, 1993.
6. Phillip J. Cooper, Government contracts in public administration: The role and environment of the contracting officer, *Public Administration Review,* 40(5), September–October, 1980, 459–468.
7. Khi Thai, *Introduction to Public Procurement*, Boca Raton, FL: Florida Atlantic University Press, 2007, p. 47.
8. Thai, 2001, 27.
9. Harvard Law Review Association, Using federal procurement to fight inflation: *AFL-CIO v. Kahn, Harvard Law Review,* 93(4), February, 1980, 793–803.
10. Harvard Law Review Association, 794–795.
11. For a full discussion of *AFL-CIO v. Kahn* case see: Harvard Law Review Association, Using federal procurement to fight inflation: *AFL-CIO v. Kahn, Harvard Law Review,* 93(4), February, 1980, 793–803.
12. The theory that economic benefits are better subject to quantification than political or social benefits has been challenged.
13. Harvard Law Review Association, 793.
14. Arthur S. Miller, Administrative discretion in the award of federal contracts, *Michigan Law Review,* 53(6), April, 1955, 781–812.
15. Joseph A. Pegnato, Assessing federal procurement reform: Has the procurement pendulum stopped swinging? *Journal of Public Procurement,* 3(2), 2003, 145–175.
16. Cooper, 462.

17. Steven Kelman, Remaking federal procurement, *Visions of Governance in the 21st Century,* Harvard University, John F. Kennedy School of Government, January, 2003.
18. Kelman, 2003, 4.
19. Kelman, 2003.
20. The FAR document was established to codify uniform policies for acquisition of supplies and services by executive agencies. It is issued and maintained jointly, pursuant to the Office of Federal Procurement Policy (OFPP) Reauthorization Act, under the statutory authorities granted to the Secretary of Defense, Administrator of General Services and the Administrator, National Aeronautics and Space Administration.
21. General Services Administration, *Ethics Legal Council,* http://www.gsa.gov/Portal/gsa/ep/contentView.do?contentType=GSA_BASIC&contentId=12355&noc=T, May 9, 2007. Also in U.S. General Services Administration, *Federal Acquisitions Regulations* (Washington, DC, Department of Defense (DoD), GSA, and the National Aeronautics and Space Administration (NASA), 2005). (http://acquisition.gov/far/).
22. Thai, 2007, 46.
23. Griff Witte, Iraq contractor's work is further criticized: 13 of 14 projects found wanting by audit, *Washington Post,* Friday, September 29, 2006, p. A15.
24. For a full discussion of defense procurement fraud before 2000 see: Jonathan M. Karpoff, D. Scott Lee, and Valaria P. Vendrzyk, Defense procurement fraud, penalties, and contractor influence, *The Journal of Political Economy,* 107(4), August, 1999, 809–842.
25. U.S. House of Representatives, Committee on Government Oversight, *Dollars, Not Sense: Government Contracting under the Bush Administration,* Washington, DC, Henry A. Waxman, Chairman, Committee on Government Oversight, 2006.
26. *Dollars, Not Sense: Government Contracting under the Bush Administration.*
27. General Accounting Office, Rebuilding Iraq: Fiscal year 2003 contract award and management challenges, *Journal of Public Procurement,* 5(1), 2005, 95–132.
28. Thai, 2004, 47.
29. Thai, 2007, 60.
30. Thai, 2004, 55.
31. Thai, 2004, 55.
32. U.S. Office of Management and Budget, *Office of Federal Procurement Policy Act, 41 U.S.C. 401,* Washington, DC, Office of Federal Procurement Policy, 1974. (http://www.whitehouse.gov/omb/procurement/mission.html).
33. http://www.whitehouse.gov/omb/procurement/mission.html.
34. http://www.whitehouse.gov/omb/procurement/mission.html.
35. Gerasimos Gianakis and XiaoHu Wang, Decentralization of the purchasing function in municipal government: A national survey, *Journal of Budgeting, Accounting, and Financial Management,* 12 Fall, 2000, 421–440.
36. Thai, 2001, 12.
37. Gianakis and Wang, 2000.
38. Thai, 2001.
39. Thai, 2004.
40. Thai, 2004, 9.
41. Thai, 2004.
42. Thai, 2004, 46; Also, John J. Grossbaum, Procedural fairness in public contracts: The procurement regulations, *Virginia Law Review,* 57(2), March, 1971, 174.
43. Federal Acquisition Institute, *Office of Federal Procurement Policy Act (41 U.S.C. 405(d),* Washington, DC, Office of Federal Procurement Policy, 1974. (http://www.fai.gov/). Also in Federal Acquisition Institute, *Annual Report on the Federal Acquisition Workforce, FY 2005,* Fort Belvoir, VA, General Services Administration, 2005. (http://www.fai.gov/pdfs/FAWF2005.pdf).
44. Thai, 2004, 9.

45. Steven A. Daniels, An assessment of today's federal procurement system, *Office of Federal Procurement Policy Lecture Series,* August 15, 2002.
46. Thai, 2004, 8.
47. Thai, 2007, 34.
48. Thai, 2004, 88.
49. The intertwined nature of the legislature within the larger U.S. federal government system has been touched upon briefly throughout this chapter.
50. For a comprehensive review of the federal budgetary process see: Aaron Wildavsky, *The Politics of the Budgetary Process,* 4th Edn., Boston: Little, Brown, and Company, 1984.
51. Cooper, 462.
52. Charles K. Coe, Life cycle costing by state governments, *Public Administration Review,* 41(5), September–October 1981, 564–569.
53. Shane M. Greenstein, Sole-sourcing versus competitive bidding: US government agencies' procedural choices for mainframe computer procurement, *The Journal of Industrial Economics*, 43(2), June 1995, 125–140.
54. Clem C. Linnenberg, Jr., Policies & procedures in federal civilian procurement, *The Accounting Review*, 18(1), January 1943, 16–26.
55. Linnenberg, Jr., 16.
56. Linnenberg, Jr., 17.
57. Embry-Riddle Aeronautical University for the Florida Defense Alliance. *Florida Defense Contracts Monitor*, Embry-Riddle University: Florida, October 1–31, 2006.
58. Cooper, 462.
59. Linnenberg, Jr., 17.
60. Linnenberg, Jr., 17.
61. Cooper, 463.
62. Cooper, 465.
63. Cooper, 466.
64. Integrated Acquisition Environment, *The President's Management Agenda, FY 2002* (Washington, DC, Office of Management and Budget, 2002). (http://www.whitehouse.gov/omb/budget/fy2002/mgmt.pdf).
65. U.S. Government Accountability Office, *Improvements Needed to the Federal Procurement Data System—Next Generation,* Washington, DC, Office of Management and Budget, 2005.

Chapter 14

Public Procurement in Germany

Michael Essig, Sandra Dorobek, Andreas Glas, and Sabrina Leuger

CONTENTS

14.1 Public Procurement in the Context of Public Duties and Responsibilities

The function of public procurement is to ensure government acquire required goods and services that enable public performance in all areas of public duties and responsibilities. In general, public procurement includes all activities directed to achieve control over necessary but not self-produced goods and services.* In principle, public procurement can be used as a political instrument. Some selected aspects are, for instance, governmental aids for regions lacking in infrastructure or for small- and medium-sized enterprises, aid for handicapped persons or the pursuit of ecological objectives.† The decision on which public duties expenditures to spend‡ is not based on efficient business decisions; it is rather the result of political processes.§ Public duties and responsibilities are derived from the public interest as far as variety and volume are concerned, which again is in a permanent change apparently manifesting itself in the results of elections, acclamations, and numerous public–private negotiations.** Public interest determines political objectives. For these political objectives politicians are willing to spend money, which ideally, also creates an additional social benefit.†† To perform these public duties derived from a political decision-making process, different value-adding activities are necessary. *Public value-adding* takes place.‡‡ For instance, the state builds and maintains schools, universities, hospitals, foster homes, museums, recycling systems, airports, complex infrastructure, etc. The scope of procurement ranges accordingly from standard goods, like office equipment or simple services, to the procurement of sophisticated goods, such as a satellite-based highway-toll system or modern military weapons. Both, a warplane as much as a simple pen, provide a basis for the fulfillment of public duties. Hence, there is basically no difference between both needs.§§ Not only physical products but also services like consulting services and maintenance, repair or cleaning work, for instance, are requested. The German government can satisfy its demand for goods and services by three different means. Either (1) the respective goods are produced by the government, (2) needed goods are purchased by sovereign force,*** or (3) the demand is satisfied by contracts under private law.††† The most frequent case is satisfaction of demand by contracts on the market. Moreover, the satisfaction of the public administration's demand is only comparable to other private commercial subjects if the procurement is a financial one, based on contracts under private law and not accomplished by sovereign force.‡‡‡ Even if the state as a sovereign institution has the possibility to procure necessary goods by dispossession, in this chapter we concentrate on public procurement processes performed on the market.

---

* Arnold (1997), p. 3.

† Fante (2004), p. 31 et seq.

‡ Reasons for public activities: public goods, external effects, absence of property rights, imperfect competition, and natural monopolies; Nowotny (1999), p. 33ff.; Schleth (1987), p. 8ff; Spelthahn (1994), p. 42 et seq.; and Kirmer (1995), p. 42 et seq.

§ Naschold et al. (1996), p. 56.

** Eichhorn (2001), p. 410; Naschold et al. (1996), p. 56; and Grimm (2001), p. 773.

†† Hunziker (1999), p. 152 et seq. and Thom and Ritz (2003), p. 441.

‡‡ For public service value activities in the German healthcare system see for instance the survey realized by Accenture (2006).

§§ Kunert (2003), p. 94.

*** Legal base for dispossession Art. 14 (3) GG, special regulations among others in German building laws, aviation law, general railway act.

††† Rittner (1988), p. 29 et seq.

‡‡‡ For further information concerning sovereign force and dispossession among others Wachendorff and Hartle (1989), column 103.

After having integrated public procurement in the German political system, we will demonstrate its importance and potential in Section 14.2. Section 14.3 presents public buyers in Germany. Subsequently, Section 14.4 describes the current public procurement process as well as the referring legal guidelines. The chapter concludes with a summarizing overview of the results worked out.

14.2 Importance and Potential of Public Procurement in Germany

Due to the total volume of more than €260 billion spent for procurement activities of the public sector, public procurement processes have an exorbitant economic and political impact.* More than 20 percent of all available budget funds are expended for public procurement activities.† The total volume relates to 11.3 percent of the German gross domestic product (GDP).‡ In comparison, the average GDP of the member states of the European Union amounts to 16 percent; this corresponds to €1500 billion. The amount of public contracts varies between 11 and 20 percent depending on the member state.§ Assuming a procurement volume in Germany in the amount of €260 billion, marginal percentaged savings would have an enormous impact. Saved means could be used alternatively for important projects (e.g., projects in infrastructure or spendings for development aid), for financing necessary reforms in Germany (e.g., German tax law), or to increase payments of social benefits. These potential savings are of course only exemplary calculations without considering external effects (Figure 14.1). Nevertheless, this calculation demonstrates the potentials of a more efficient and effective public procurement.

14.2.1 Public Buyers

German antitrust law defines the notion of public buyers. They have to comply with the regulations of the German public procurement law that has been influenced by international and European law during the last years. When exceeding certain quantity thresholds, German law refers to European procurement law. Therefore, it has to be distinguished between the national and the European notion of public buyers depending on the public procurement volume.** When applying national procurement law, the notion of the "institutional public buyer" (institutioneller Auftraggeber) is used. This results in a restriction of public procurement law for public institutions and public authorities, namely regional and local authorities (Gebietskörperschaften und Kommunen), the federal state (Bund), the states (Laender),†† public entities, and also entities of private law when they

---

* BMWi/BME (2006), p. 8.

† Budget funds in 2006: €1054 billion, Federal Statistical Office Germany (2007a).

‡ German GDP in 2006: €2302 billion, Federal Statistical Office Germany (2007b); the volume of public procurement activities varies between 10 and 15 percent annually; Heil (2006), p. 17.

§ European Commission (2007), see URL: http://ec.europa.eu/internal_market/publicprocurement/index_de.htm.

** At the moment the limit for work contracts is fixed at €5,278,000; for performances in the potable water, energy, and public transportation sector at €422,000; for contracts of supreme federal authorities at €137,000; in all other cases at €211,000; see Vergaberechtsverordnung §2.

†† The Federal Republic of Germany is politically and administratively split up into 16 federal states or "Laender."

Volume of public procurement activities in Germany: €260 billion

Increase in efficiency in percent	Savings in € billion	Possible use
0.5	1.3	Infrastructure Construction of the first magnetic levitation train in Germany (transrapid) (cost ca. €1.6 billion)
1.0	2.6	Reform of the german tax law Abolition of three different taxes (tax deficit ca. €2.55 billion)
1.5	3.9	Infrastructure Abolition of autobahn tolls (annually costs ca. €3 billion)
2.0	5.2	Development assistance Duplication of the budget funds of the Federal Ministry for Economic Cooperation and Development (costs ca. €4 billion)

Figure 14.1 Possible savings and use of increases in efficiency of 0.5 up to 2.0 percent. (Adapted from Federal Statistical Office Germany, Einahmen und Ausgaben des Staates in der Abgrenzung des ESVG 95, 2007a, http://www.destatis.de/basis/d/vgr/vgrtab11.php, Stand: 03.02.2007 and own calculation.)

receive public means of at least 50 percent for public contracts.* The European public procurement law uses the notion of "functional public buyer" (funktionaler Auftraggeber) which includes more entities of private law that are influenced by the state.† Corresponding to the European Court of Justice this is the case when (1) the composition and the tasks of the entity are regulated by law, (2) the entity's members are appointed by the public authority, (3) the entity's duties and responsibilities are guaranteed by the public authority, and (4) the entity's contracts are paid by the authority, even if the entity is not a formal component of the state.‡ For conducting basic public functions, complex organizations have been established. In total, there are more than 30,000 different public buyers in Germany; as already mentioned they have to comply with national and European public procurement law.§ The focus is not on the supranational level although Germany's quota amounts to 19.5 percent of the budgetary fund of the European Union and 10 percent of the budgetary fund of the United Nations for the procurement of their institutions.**

The executive branch (including public administration with its institutions, authorities, and agencies) is of particular importance for public procurement.†† In the German federal state system, the executive branch is located at three different levels: (1) the federal level, (2) the regional level of the 16 Laender (federal states), for example, Baden-Württemberg or Bavaria, and (3) the local level including cities and municipalities. The local authorities obtain the biggest part of public procurement,

* §98 of German Law against restraints on competition (Gesetz gegen Wettbewerbsbeschränkungen, GWB).
† Matthey (2001), p. 63.
‡ Judgement of the European Court of Justice (EuGH), Rs. 31/87, Beentjes, Slg 1988, 4635, 4655.
§ Federal Ministry of Interior and Federal Ministry of Economy and Technology (2004), p. 3.
** Own calculations using data of the Institute of German Economy Cologne (2006), p. 72 and Federal Ministry for Economic Cooperation and Development (2007).
†† Legislature and judiciary are not the matter of the subject; for further information see Gornas and Beyer (2007), p. 1.

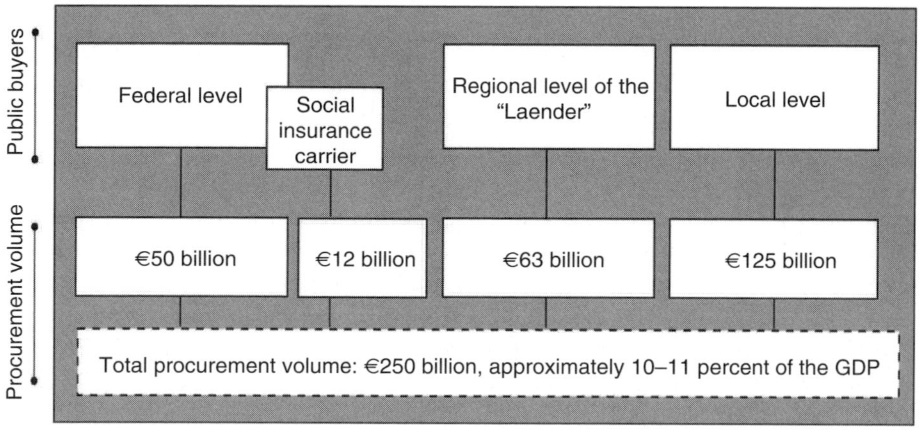

Figure 14.2 Public procurement volume in Germany. (From Federal Ministry of Interior (BMI) and Federal Ministry of Economy and Technology, Beschluss der Bundesregierung zur Optimierung öffentlicher Beschaffung, in: Bekanntmachung des Beschlusses der Bundesregierung zur Optimierung öffentlicher Beschaffung, p. 3, 2004, BMI IT2 (KBSt)-195107/1#22, BMWA I B 3-26 05 00/21, dated February 27, 2004, Berlin.)

spending more than €125 billion, that means more than 50 percent of the total public procurement volume. They are followed by the Laender with €63 billion which corresponds to a proportion of 25 percent of the total public procurement volume. The state itself spends more than €50 billion, that means 20 percent of the public procurement volume. The social insurance carriers in Germany (they are organized on a federal level) spend more than €12 billion for public procurement activities which amounts to 5 percent of the total public procurement volume (see Figure 14.2).*

14.2.1.1 Public Buyers at the Federal Level

The procurement of needed goods at the federal level takes place either by ad hoc established federal procurement authorities or by the respective public consumer itself.† The federal procurement authorities specialized in public procurement activities exonerate other administration entities so that those can concentrate on their core business. Furthermore, due to centralizing procurement processes, economies of scale can be reached, for instance by bundling demand and reducing transaction costs utilizing the learning experience curve.

The Federal Office of Defense Technology and Procurement (BWB)‡ is the largest public buyer at the federal level obtaining a procurement volume of €3.5 billion.§ It is the responsibility of the BWB to meet the material needs of the federal armed forces with modern equipment. At the same time financial aspects have to be considered, as the federal armed forces need different items worth €2 million. Key responsibilities are, therefore, development, tests, and procurement of defense material.**

* Federal Ministry of Interior and Federal Ministry of Economy and Technology (2004), p. 3.

† Bundesverwaltungsamt (2007), URL see further reading.

‡ Exact name: Bundesamt für Wehrtechnik und Beschaffung (BWB).

§ Figures for 2004, BWB (2006), p. 4.

** Over 12 other bureaus and departments are associated with the business domain of the Federal Office of Defense Technology and Procurement (BWB) among others the German Liaison Agency of the Armament Sector USA/Canada, BWB (2006), p. 10.

This includes highly complex weapon systems as armored vehicles, airplanes, and ships as well as soldiers' equipment like uniforms. As the central procurement authority of the federal armed forces, the BWB is an important public contracting authority with enormous purchasing expertise.*

The second largest federal procurement authority is the Procurement Agency of the Federal Ministry of the Interior (BeschA)† with a procurement volume of €611 billion while procuring goods for 26 federal organizations (e.g., federal police, federal offices and agencies, or international active organizations such as the German Federal Agency for Technical Relief). The spectrum of the procured objects differs from office equipments, consultations, research and development to vehicles, boats, police helicopters, and medication for humanitarian activities.‡

Other than the BWB and the BeschA, the Federal Customs Authority (BABZV)§ is quite a good example for bundling demand as well as procurement know-how. The BABZV is above all responsible for the supply of customs authorities and offices (the supply can differ from office equipment to police helicopters). Secondly, due to the complexity of the public procurement law, the BABZV assumes the procurement processes for other federal resorts, for example, the federal fiscal authority. If the necessary supply is not procured by a procurement authority mentioned above, the federal public buyer has to implement the procurement activities on its own. As a result, procurement activities at the federal level can be realized by the above-mentioned procurement methods and also a combination of both is common.**

14.2.1.2 Public Buyers at the State Level

The procurement process at the state level works similarly to the above-mentioned federal level: on the one hand, procurement activities are accomplished by procurement authorities at the level of the state, for example, the Logistical Center of Baden-Württemberg (LZBW). The LZBW, a public enterprise based on contracts of private law, is responsible for buying necessary goods and services for the police, judiciary system, and other administrative entities for Baden-Württemberg, which is one of the 16 states of Germany. It bundles the demand with the purpose of reducing process and production costs, for example, by using modern E-procurement technologies and to provide transparency by applying a multitude of controlling methods.†† In addition to Baden-Württemberg, the services of the LZBW are available to the rest of the 16 states (Laender). Of course, there are numerous examples in the other states (Laender), such as the GMSH in the state of Schleswig-Holstein.‡‡ If the procurement activities of the LZBW are not used, the respective states can act as a public buyer themselves.

14.2.1.3 Public Buyers at the Local Level

Procurement processes at the local level take place in the ad hoc established procurement offices depending on the size of the city or local authority. In bigger cities, such as Munich, multiple procurement offices can be found, each one specialized in certain areas to satisfy public demand. At the

* BWB (2006), p. 7.

† Exact name: Beschaffungsamt des Bundesministeriums des Inneren (BeschA).

‡ Procurement Agency of the Federal Ministry of the Interior (2005), URL see further reading.

§ Exact name: Beschaffungsamt der Bundeszollverwaltung (BABVZ).

** Bundesverwaltungsamt (2007), URL see further reading.

†† Logistikzentrum Baden-Württemberg (2005), URL see further reading, pp. 4–9.

‡‡ Exact name: Gebäudemanagement Schleswig-Holstein, see URL www.gmsh.de.

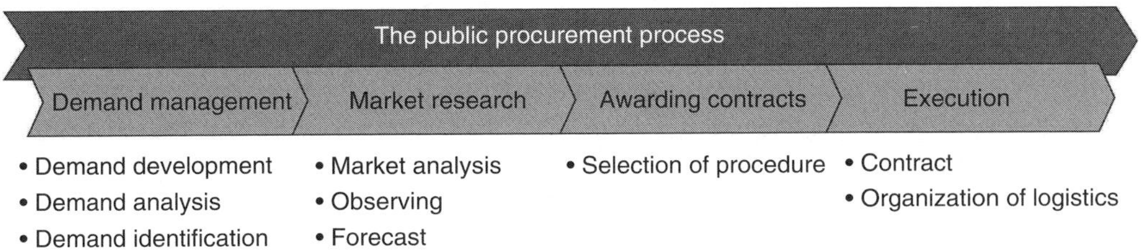

Figure 14.3 The public procurement process. (From Bundesverband für Materialwirtschaft, Einkauf und Logistik e.V. (BME) and Booz et al., Chancen und Entwicklungen im Public Procurement, p. 14, 2000, Berlin.)

local level, procurement cooperations become more and more important.* Generally, creating public cooperation is possible whenever bundling the demand does not affect competition on the market.† In addition, it has to facilitate the competitiveness of small- and medium-sized public authorities.‡

14.2.1.4 Public Procurement Process

For a better understanding of public procurement it is favorable to take up a process perception. Therefore, a reasonable point of view is an elementary basic procurement process without any upstream parallel or downstream subprocesses, like controlling or supplier management, so the basic workflow and the different regulations of public procurement law can be explained easily. The public procurement process used begins with the identification and specification of needs and ends with the payment and is composed of four subprocesses: (1) demand management, (2) market research, (3) awarding contracts, and (4) execution (see Figure 14.3).§

The public procurement process is fundamentally regulated by the public procurement law. Public procurement law subsumes a multitude of national and international laws and regulations as well as a variety of regional rules and agreements.** The German public procurement law is outstanding in every phase of the procurement procedure with the aim to assure an economic application of public resources, to avoid misapplication and corruption, and also to prevent private enterprises from facing the concentration of power of public procurement activities.†† In particular, there are basic public procurement law principles which have to be respected. The most important ones are efficiency, competition, transparency, the principle of nondiscrimination, and the consideration of medium-sized businesses. Before we dwell on the particularities of the specific subprocesses, these basic principles will be presented in detail.

---

* Judgement of the Federal Court of Justice (BGH, dated November 12, 2002—KZR 11/01 = BGHZ 152, 347et seq.).

† Schindler (2004), p. 124.

‡ §3 para. 1 German Law against restraints on competition (GWB).

§ Bundesverband Materialwirtschaft, Einkauf und Logistik e.V./Booz, Allen and Hamilton (2000), p. 14.

** Among others German Law against restraints on competition (GWB), order of public contracts (VgV), Federal Budgetary Regulations (BHO), 16 budgetary regulations for the 16 different federal states or "Laender" (LHO), and further regulations concerning specific goods: Verdingungsordnung für Bauleistungen (VOB), Verdingungsordnung für Leistungen (VOL), Verdingungsordnung für freiberufliche Leistungen (VOF).

†† Fabry et al. (2007), p. 13.

14.3 Basic Principles of the German Public Procurement Law

To secure the best application of public resources, administrative actions should comply with the principle of efficiency. This principle is unaffected by the contract value.* The term "efficiency" and the instructions based on it are specified in the Federal Budgetary Regulations,† in the corresponding administrative regulations,‡ and in an instruction paper of the Federal Ministry of Finance.§ According to this instruction paper, the principle of efficiency shows a tendency toward the most favorable relation between the intended purpose and the applied resources (proportion of price and performance). Efficiency includes two characteristics: the principle of economy (achievement of a certain objective with a minimum of resources) and the principle of productiveness (achievement of a maximum of outcome with certain resources). These correspond with the managerial minimum and maximum principle of efficient application of resources. Although the price is an integral criterion, it is not the only decisive factor.** In every case, all relevant circumstances and individual aspects have to be considered. Particularly quality, value, aesthetics, expediency, service, short delivery time, and the time of performance can be crucial.†† Basically, buyers have a certain scope for judgment evaluation within legal regulations; thus commercial–economic decisions and actions are possible within the public procurement law. Economic feasibility studies are the most important instruments for the implementation and control of this principle.‡‡ Microeconomic (e.g., present value method, comparative cost method, or comparisons of bids) as well as macroeconomic (e.g., cost–benefit analysis) studies have to be conducted during the entire procurement process, both in planning, change, execution, and at the end as a performance review of public procurement activities.§§

In addition, public buyers have to award contracts using transparent procedures regardless of the kind of required good.*** The objective of the principle of competition is to create a framework of necessary competitive terms and conditions with the aim to apply public means in an economic way. Furthermore, the German public procurement law is claiming for transparency in the procurement procedures to reach the best level of price–performance ratio and to prevent corruption and waste of public funds.

The principle of transparency aims to guarantee a maximum of information to a broad community of bidders and tenderers, as well as transparent and comprehensible procurement procedures. In the moment of the bid proposal all bidders necessarily have the same chances. The imperative of transparency is specified by numerous publicity regulations.

The extensive neutrality of treatment of all bidders assures the equality of opportunities and avoids influence in the public procurement process by personal, individual, social, or local preferences.††† Special regulations of the principle of equal treatment can be found in German constitutional and public procurement law as well as in European law.‡‡‡

---

* §7 BHO and §97 para. 5 GWB.

† §7 BHO.

‡ Administrative regulation defining the Federal Budgetary Regulation (BHO), 13.02.2001, VV-BHO, §7.

§ Order of the Federal Ministry of Finance, 31.08.1995 (II A 3-H 1005–23/95)—Instruction paper "Introduction in economic studies."

** Bechtold (2006), §97 Rn. 39.

†† Hopf (2002), p. 194.

‡‡ §7 para. 2 BHO, No. 2 VV of §7 BHO.

§§ Hopf (2002), p. 40.

*** §97 para. 1 German Law against restraints on competition (GWB).

††† §97 para. 2 German Law against restraints on competition (GWB).

‡‡‡ Art. 12 Contract of the European Union, Art. 3 Basic Constitutional Law (Grundgesetz), §97 para. 2 GWB, §§7 No. 1 para. 1 VOL/A, §§4 para. 2, 12 and 13 VOF, §55 para. 2 BHO, §2 No. 2 VOL/A.

To respect interests of small- and medium-sized enterprises, public procurement law in Germany is moreover ruled by the principle of splitting the order into lots.* This means that complex services must be divided into different lots to give small- and medium-sized enterprises the opportunity to bid according to their service capacities.

14.3.1 Public Procurement Process: Demand Management

The demand management marks the beginning of public procurement processes. The focus is on the exact identification and specification of needs in terms of quantity and function-specific quality. The starting point of our consideration is the political level where the decision is made about what type of public duties and responsibilities should be realized. As mentioned in the introduction, this decision is based on public interest expressed by elections and then results in further decisions of the competent procurement authority concerning type, amount, and quality of the necessary goods.

Demand Development: Normally, the demand occurs by reason of a lack of goods, services, or specific abilities needed by the public consumer. Placing orders is also used as a means to reach political goals, for example, economic aims.†

Demand Analysis: The preliminary task of demand management at this point is to identify the economic amounts and specific requirements concerning quality; if necessary the request of demand has to be corrected. This means that the perceived demand is to be compared with the actual demand. Due to different reasons, such as information deficits, environmental influences, or influences from suppliers or personal preferences, they hardly ever correspond. When determining the right amount (quantitative demand analysis), it has to be examined, in case of nondurable goods, to what extent the requested demand matches the expected consumption, and in the case of durable goods, if the capacity utilization is guaranteed. Furthermore, special attention has to be paid to goods or services that are time-critical. Because this is a matter of principle, economies of scale can be realized through bundling. When deciding on the quality of the needed demand, it is profitable, as the respective public consumer is able to determine the needed quality, to build up communication between consumer and the specific procurement authority.

Demand Identification: A characteristic of effective demand management is the rational identification of the needed goods and services considering utility and cost–benefit ratio. The final goal is to avoid expenditures due to wrongly evaluated amounts.

14.3.2 Public Procurement Process: Market Research

Public buyers as well as public consumers have to be informed about the market structure to avoid dependence from private suppliers and to identify the best supplier regarding the value for money.‡ This requirement can only be achieved by an intensive and professional market analysis. Recently, the technical possibilities have improved enormously: now there are electronic marketplaces for broad research concerning the local, national, and international markets.§ Market research includes

* §97 para. 3 GWB.

† Antweiler (2003): The placing of contracts seeks a wide set of objectives, for instance social intention. For example, awarding contracts can depend on the social behavior of the bidder, for example, the payment of adequate wages above the negotiated standard wage to his employees.

‡ Regarding problems with asymmetric information, Akerlof (1970) and Picot et al. (2005).

§ See chapter on electronic procurement for further details.

systematical research, collection, and preparation of all current and prospective information connected with the market. It includes elements of analysis, observation, and forecast of the markets. This information helps to increase transparency and creates a base for further buying decisions. The *market analysis* puts the focus on the basic structure of markets, for example, suppliers, turnovers, market shares, products, and technology. By *observing the market*, the development of specific market shares and supplier structures can be identified. Changes in market structures or of the demand behavior can be determined. The data collected by these methods can be useful for deductions and forecasts of the prospective development of the buying market, for example, changes in prices or oversupplies can be identified precociously. Information can be obtained by field research, for example, supplier interviews, or by secondary research, for example, by the evaluation of journals or through online research.*

14.3.3 Public Procurement Process: Awarding Contracts

After having specified the needed demand and having analyzed the market structure, the demand has to be covered by awarding contracts. Within the dichotomy of German public procurement law depending on the procurement volume, there are four different procurement procedures which are divided into formal and nonformal procedures. Having defined the scope, we will briefly illustrate the details of the procedures as well as marking the specialties of electronic procurement.

14.3.3.1 Formal Procedures: Open and Restricted

As a general rule, public buyers have to tender their orders relating to the demand. The *open procedure*† addresses an undetermined number of bidders. In contrast, the *restricted procedure*‡ is only applicable under certain conditions; for example, (1) if only a certain number of enterprises are able to deal with the requirements of the order, or (2) if the effort of performing open procedure is in disparity to the goods and services needed, or (3) if the open procedure has no success or cannot be performed because of reasons of secrecy or urgency.§ The restricted procedure addresses only a restricted number of bidders.

14.3.3.2 Informal Procedures: Negotiated Procedure and Competitive Dialogue

In contrast to the procedures mentioned above, the negotiated procedure does not require strict procedural rules. The public buyer can negotiate directly with the relevant suppliers.** This procedure as an exception is only valid if open or restricted procedures are not possible.††

Competitive Dialogue: Due to the strict hierarchy of the public procurement law, the public buyer is generally not allowed to negotiate with the suppliers. Since 2005,§§ however, the so-called

* For example, Meffert (2000), pp. 152–163.
† §3 No.1 para. 1 VOB/A, VOL/A.
‡ §3 No. 1 para. 2 VOB/A, VOL/A.
§ Jestaedt et al. (1999), p. 94, also §3 No. 3 para. 1 VOB/A, VOL/A.
** Hopf (2002), pp. 17, 21.
†† §3 No. 4 VOB/A, VOL/A.
§§ German Law for Acceleration of Public Private Partnership Projects and Improvement of the Legal Framework of Public Private Partnerships, 01.09.2005, BGBl. I, p. 2676.

procedure of competitive dialogue has been in place, which is applied to especially complex orders with difficult technical challenges or legal and financial conditions.* This procedure combines elements of the open and negotiated procedure and allows a flexible dialogue between public buyer and supplier.† Therefore, the public buyer has the option to develop solutions together with the supplier by conducting negotiations and working out concepts. Firstly, the public buyer has to announce the problem and a solution is worked out subsequently together with a multitude of suppliers (tenderers). Based on these negotiations and solution proposals, the public buyer compiles the bidding documents and invites to tender. Introducing the competitive dialogue yields the economic idea of partnership into German public procurement law.

14.3.3.3 Procedural Details

At the beginning of the open procedure, all the information and the announcements are published in newspapers, official bulletins, or journals,‡ depending on the order value the announcement has to be published in the official bulletin of the European Union. Using the method of restricted or negotiated procedure, the public buyer has to collect information about the circle of bidders when he lacks knowledge about the market structure.§ If necessary and appropriate, he can announce public participation competition (Teilnahmewettbewerb), which allows suppliers to send requests for participation. After announcing and having performed the participation competition in case of a restricted or negotiated procedure, the bidding documents including the invitatii ad offerendum are sent to the suppliers/bidders. These documents contain the bid conditions, the service specifications, and the terms and conditions.** Also, the valuation criteria have to be published in the announcement, at the latest in the bidding documents. The bidders' offers have to be sent to the public buyer within due time. This period of time must be chosen adequately. First of all, offers which do not fulfill specific criteria concerning form and content are excluded.†† Secondly, criteria such as personal and functional ability are examined. Technical qualification, service capability, and trustworthiness have to be especially considered:‡‡ the bidder has to guarantee the needed know-how, experience, and skills to perform the awarded order properly. Furthermore, the bidder's enterprise has to ensure adequate staffing, technology, and finance situation, so that the contractual duties can be fulfilled. Finally, the bidder is trustworthy, if—considering his former business activities—he is able to guarantee proper business management and fulfill his legal duties,§§ for example, tax payments.*** After that the offers are examined regarding their price–performance ratio. In the following evaluation, the remaining offers are analyzed applying the above-mentioned principle of efficiency.††† After this analysis—which must be performed in a certain and adequate time by the public buyer—the offer that fulfills the

---

* 6 a VgV, §101 para. 1, para. 5 GWB.

† European Commission, Explanations to the Competitive Dialogue, p. 1.

‡ §§17 No. 1(1), para. 2(1) VOB/A, VOL/A.

§ §§3 No. 1 para. 4 VOL/A, 4 VOL/A.

** The goods and services have to be described in a definite and sufficient way, so that all bidders can understand the description equally to achieve comparable offers.

†† §25 No. 1 VOL/A.

‡‡ §97 para. 4 GWB.

§§ Daub and Eberstein (1998), §25 Rn. 33–35.

*** Bechtold (2006), §97 Rn. 23.

††† Kunert (2003), p. 97.

requirements best is awarded. The award represents the conclusion of the contract under private law between the public buyer and the bidder/supplier. Then, the unsuccessful bidders have to be informed so that they have the possibility to request a revision.* Also, criteria which have nothing to do with procurement per se but have political implication can be applied but only if they are based on federal or regional law.† Consequently, German public procurement law can be exploited to reach political aims, for example, avoiding job reductions or environment protection. This was also confirmed by the European Court of Justice in 2002.‡

14.3.3.4 Electronic Procurement

The described procedures (see Figure 14.4) can also be conducted electronically via modern information and communication systems. The public buyer can allow offers to be sent not only via mail but also via e-mail.§ In this case, the public buyer has to point out in the announcement and in the bidding documents that electronic offers are possible.** When admitting electronic offers it has to be guaranteed that the content is not disclosed to the public buyer before the set time period expires. At the federal level an electronic marketplace, called "e-Vergabe" (www.evergabe-online.de), was implemented. This platform allows all potential bidders to see the current tenders of the federal authorities; furthermore, electronic tools for submitting their offers are provided. Electronic marketplaces also exist at the regional and local level, for example, the platform of the German procurement network, the "Deutsche Vergabe- und Beschaffungsnetz" (www.dvbn.de) as well as electronic tools.

14.3.4 Public Procurement Process: Procurement Execution

The services agreed on in the contract are accompanied by several operative procurement and logistic activities both of bidder and public buyer. This means finally that the supplier/bidder has to guarantee that the correct quantity will be delivered at the right time at the right place in the quality agreed upon. The public buyer has to pay. This simplified illustration cannot ignore the fact that already the act of buying office materials causes multiple operative processes like a multitude of commissions, storing, and transportation processes. The complexity is much higher when dealing with difficult orders, for example, in the defense sector. Research and development orders, prototypes, complex schooling, and maintenance contracts require multiple repetitive processes, intensive cooperation of both contracting parties, and certainly an intensive controlling of all activities. The contracting parties are liable for defects in the performance according to contract law and to the general terms and conditions.

14.4 Conclusion

Figure 14.5 presents the current public procurement system in Germany. Considering today's procurement practice in the private sector based on several approaches for supplier partnerships in the

* §13 VgV.
† §97 para. 4 Hs. 2 GWB.
‡ European Court of Justice, Judgement 17.09.2002, NZBau 2002, p. 618.
§ §15 VgV.
** §21 No. 3 para. 1 VOL/A and §17 para. 1 VOL/A.

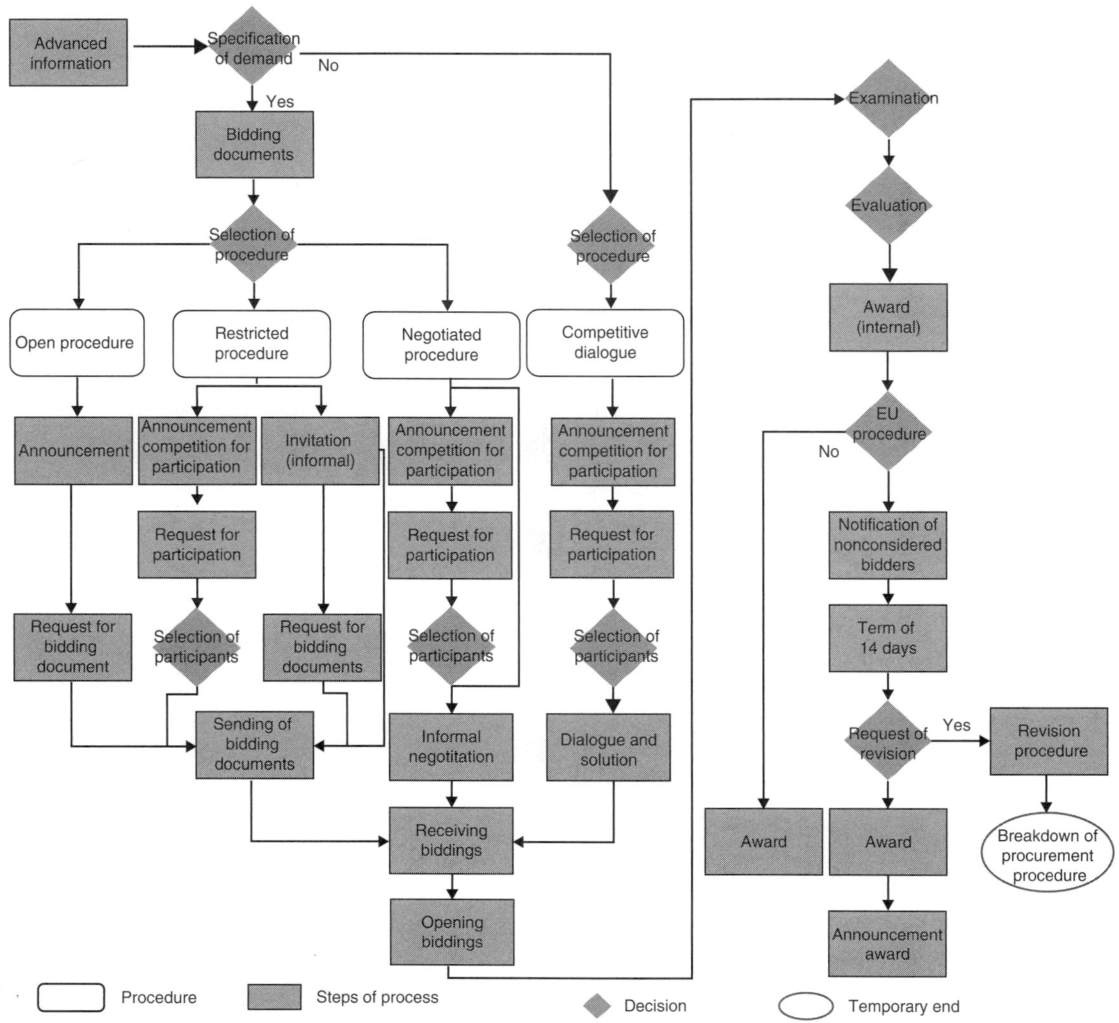

Figure 14.4 Procurement procedure. (Adapted from Procurement Agency of the Federal Ministry of the Interior/Beschaffungsamt des Bundesministeriums des Innern, 2006, Vergaberecht—Einblicke, Bonn März.)

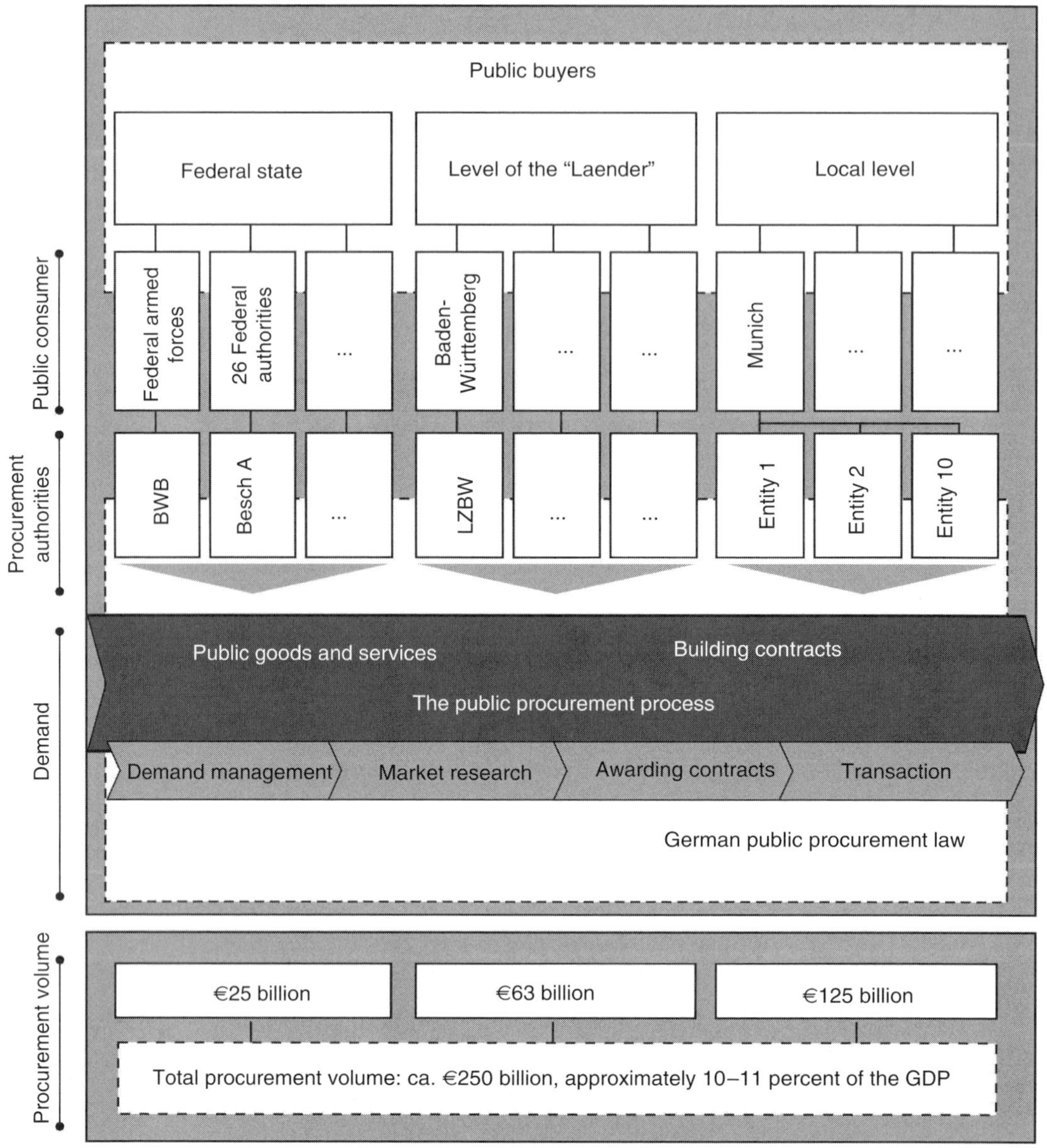

Figure 14.5 Public procurement in Germany.

network context, procurement of entire systems or solution sourcing,* multifaceted implications for public procurement are more than obvious. Various activities during the entire procurement process have enormous prospective importance.† The question remains open to which extent private sector experience can be transferred to the public procurement processes while at the same time complying the legal public procurement regulations.

* Präuer (2004).

† Essig and Batran (2006), Essig (2005, 2006).

References

Accenture 2006, Public Service Value im Gesundheitswesen: Wer bietet wirklichen Bürgernutzen?

Akerlof, G.A. 1970, The market for "lemons", in: *Quarterly Journal of Economics*, Vol. 84, pp. 488–500.

Antweiler, P. 2003, Instrumentalisierung staatlicher Auftragsvergabe für politische Zwecke, Schriftenreihe arbeitsrechtliche Forschungsergebnisse, Bd. 39, Hamburg.

Arnold, U. 1997, Beschaffungsmanagement, 2. überarbeitete Auflage Stuttgart.

Bechtold, R. 2006: Kommentar zum GWB, München.

Bundesverband für Materialwirtschaft, Einkauf und Logistik e.V. (BME) and Booz et al., 2000, Chancen und Entwicklungen im Public Procurement, Berlin.

Bundesverwaltungsamt 2007, Beschaffungsbehörden, http://www.bund.de/nn_176712/DE/WuW/A-Z/A-wie-Ausschreibungen/Ausschreibungen/Beschaffungsbehoerden/Beschaffungsbehoerden-knoten.html_nnn=true, dated April 3, 2007.

Daub, W. and Eberstein, H. 1998, Kommentar zur VOL/A.

Eichhorn, P. 2001, Öffentliche BWL als eine Spezielle BWL, in: WiSt, X, 8, S. 409–416.

Essig, M. 2005, Zur Anwendbarkeit der logistischen Führungskonzeption auf den öffentlichen Sektor: Vorüberlegungen für ein Public Supply Chain Management, in: Lasch, R. und Janker, C.G., Logistik Management: Innovative Logistikkonzepte, Wiesbaden 2005, S. 93–109.

Essig, M. 2006, Ansatzpunkte für eine konzeptionelle Re-Orientierung der Militärökonomie aus logistischer und beschaffungswirtschaftlicher Sicht, in: Kuhn, E., Potentiale und Effekte der Militärökonomie—Fähigkeiten für Europa, Fürstenfeldbruck 2006, S. 93–100.

Essig, M. and Batran, A. 2006, Konzeptionelle Grundlagen des Public Supply Chain Management, in: Zeitschrift für öffentliche und gemeinwirtschaftliche Unternehmen, 29, 2, S. 117–146.

Fabry, B., Meininger, F., and Kayser, K. 2007, Vergaberecht in der Unternehmenspraxis, Wiesbaden.

Fante, J. 2004, Die Instrumentalisierung des öffentlichen Sektors zur Durchsetzung politischer Ziele, Aachen.

Federal Ministry for Economic Cooperation and Development/Bundesministerium für wirtschaftliche Zusammenarbeit und Entwicklung (BMZ) 2007, United Nations, http://ec.europa.eu/internal_market/publicprocurement/index_de.htm, dated March 29, 2007.

Federal Ministry of Interior (BMI) and Federal Ministry of Economy and Technology 2004, Beschluss der Bundesregierung zur Optimierung öffentlicher Beschaffung, in: Bekanntmachung des Beschlusses der Bundesregierung zur Optimierung öffentlicher Beschaffung, BMI IT2 (KBSt)-195107/1#22, BMWA I B 3-26 05 00/21, dated February 27, 2004, Berlin.

Federal Office of Defense Technology and Procurement/Bundesamt für Wehrtechnik und Beschaffung (BWB) 2006, Auftraggeber Bundeswehr, Organisation, Auftragsvergabe, Vertragsgestaltung, Köln.

Federal Statistical Office Germany 2007a, Einahmen und Ausgaben des Staates in der Abgrenzung des ESVG 95, http://www.destatis.de/basis/d/vgr/vgrtab11.php, Stand: 03.02.2007.

Federal Statistical Office Germany 2007b, Bruttoinlandsprodukt 2006 für Deutschland, http://www.destatis.de/presse/deutsch/pk/2007/bip2006i.pdf, dated March 28, 2007.

Gornas, J. and Beyer, W. 2007, Betriebswirtschaft in de öffentlichen Verwaltung, Köln.

Grimm, D. 2001, Staatsaufgaben—eine Bilanz, in: Grimm, D., Staatsaufgaben, Baden-Baden, S. 771–785.

Heil, I. 2006, Deutschland in Zahlen 2006, Köln.

Hopf, H. 2002, Vergabemanagement bei öffentlichen Aufträgen, Bund-Länder-Gemeinden, Heidelberg.

Hunziker, A.W. 1999, Prozessorganisation in der öffentlichen Verwaltung: New Public Management und Business Reengineering in der schweizerischen Bundesverwaltung, Bern, Stuttgart, Wien.

Institute of German Economy Cologne/Institut der deutschen Wirtschaft Köln 2006, Deutschland in Zahlen, Köln.

Jestaedt, T., Kemper, K., Marx, F., and Prieß, H.-J. 1999, Das Recht der Auftragsvergabe, Kriftel.

Kirmer, P. 1995, Der Begriff der öffentlichen Aufgaben in der Rechtsprechung des Bundesverfassungsgerichts, München.

Kunert, O. 2003, Vergaberecht und öffentliches Recht, München.

Logistikzentrum Baden-Württemberg 2005, Das Logistikzentrum stellt sich vor, http://www.initiative-papier.de/cms/download/LZBW_Kruck.pdf, dated April 2, 2007.

Matthey, P. 2001, Das Recht der Auftragsvergabe in den Sektoren, Unter besonderer Berücksichtigung der deutschen Elektrizitätswirtschaft, Baden-Baden.

Meffert, H. 2000, Marketing, 9. Auflage, Wiesbaden.

Naschold, F., Budäus, D., Jann, W., Mezger, E., Oppen, M., Picot, A., Reichard, C., Schanze, E., and Simon, N. 1996, Leistungstiefe im öffentlichen Sektor: Erfahrungen, Konzepte, Methoden, Berlin.

Nowotny, E. 1999, Der öffentliche Sektor—Einführung in die Finanzwissenschaft, 4. Auflage, Berlin, Heidelberg u.a.

Picot, A., Dietl, H., and Franck, E. 2005, Organisation, eine ökonomische Perspektive, Stuttgart.

Präuer, A. 2004, Solutions sourcing, Strategien und Strukturen interorganisaler Wertschöpfungssysteme, Wiesbaden.

Procurement Agency of the Federal Ministry of the Interior/Beschaffungsamt des Bundesinnenministeriums (BeschA) 2005, http://www.bescha.bund.de, dated April 2, 2007.

Procurement Agency of the Federal Ministry of the Interior/Beschaffungsamt des Bundesministeriums des Innern 2006, Vergaberecht—Einblicke, Bonn März.

Rittner, F. 1988, Rechtsgrundlage und Rechtsgrundsätze des öffentlichen Auftragswesens—eine systematische Analyse, Tangstedt, Hamburg.

Schindler, S. 2004, Die wettbewerbsrechtliche Zulässigkeit kommunaler Einkaufsgemeinschaften, in: KommJur 4/2004, S. 121–160.

Schleth, J.P. 1987, Die Theorie des natürlichen Monopols—Eine preis- und wettbewerbstheoretische Analyse und ihre Bedeutung für den Telekommunikationssektor der Bundesrepublik Deutschland, Dissertation an der Justus-Liebig-Universität Gießen, Gießen.

Spelthahn, S. 1994, Privatisierung natürlicher Monopole—Theorie und internationale Praxis am Beispiel Wasser und Abwasser, Wiesbaden.

Thom, N. and Ritz, A. 2003, Möglichkeiten der Wertschöpfungssteigerung durch Public Private Partnership, in Bach, N., Buchholz, W. und Eichler, B. (Hrsg., 2003), Geschäftsmodelle für Wertschöpfungnetzwerke, Wiesbaden, S. 435–457.

Wachendorff, P. and Hartle, J. 1989, Beschaffungswesen öffentlicher Verwaltungen, in: Chmielewiecz, K. and Eichhorn, P., Handwörterbuch öffentlicher Verwaltungen, Stuttgart, Sp. 102–112.

Chapter 15

China's Government Procurement Policy and Institutional Framework: History, Structure, and Operation

Cao Fuguo[1]

CONTENTS

15.1 Introduction

Liberalization of Chinese procurement markets, beginning with bidding reform, can be traced back to the outset of China's economic reforms in early 1980s. In 1999 and 2002, China enacted two primary laws governing government procurement, the Bidding Law (BL) and Government Procurement Law (GPL).[2] The two laws were supplemented by various implementing measures issued by different government agencies. Therefore, the current Chinese GP framework consists of two laws with their respective implementing rules. The dual-law system has posed the issues of coordination and compatibility, which requires a review and new measures (legislative or authorative interpretations) to address. Recent developments[3] provide internal and external dynamics for the improvement of the Chinese government procurement system and more interactive to international government procurement regimes.

This chapter will provide an overview and analysis of the policy and institutional framework of the GP system in China.

15.2 Historical and Recent Developments

15.2.1 BL and Its Implementing Regulations

The BL was the logical outcome of the many earlier experiments of regulatory reforms for introducing the bidding mechanism into public sector, notably the public works sector.[4] Its enactment provided a higher-level legal framework for bidding in China and made significant improvements to the earlier bidding mechanism.[5] Notable improvements were made to

- Objectives and principles, emphasizing quality, efficiency, importance of transparency, and equal treatment, in contrast with the previous regulations
- Approach to compulsory coverage, which is now similar to that in most modern public procurement laws[6]
- Publication of procurement notices
- Qualification and specifications, with greater emphasis on nondiscrimination
- Procedures, which is a more streamlined bid-opening system (for more detail see Section 15.5)
- Revolution of the evaluation and award system with abolishment of the base price system and adoption of internationally accepted criteria making the bidding mechanism a real market-based system
- Strengthened administrative measures for enforcement (see Section 15.7.2.3)
- Procedures with stricter rules on negotiation in the bidding process. Under the BL no negotiation is allowed both before and after the award of contract[7]

However, the BL still suffers from serious flaws, for example, the divergent administrative system is unfortunately maintained and an adequate remedies system also remains lacking. Some secondary legislation at both central and local levels has followed the passing of the BL,[8] and some efforts have been made to correct the flaws. For example, an interministerial committee has been established to serve as a mechanism for the coordination of policies among different ministries. Local governments have also been urged to make their implementing rules.[9] Web-based media have been set up by SDPC and designated as the official electronic means for publishing procurement notices.[10]

15.2.2 Government Procurement Reform and Legislation

15.2.2.1 Government Procurement Reform and Regulation before the GPL

The beginnings of GP reform came in Shanghai in 1996.[11] In 1998, the reform took momentum and the following years saw a surge of policies, regulations, and new offices responsible for the management of government procurement at both central and local government levels.[12] At the central level, MOF issued a series of departmental provisions in 1999 and following years.[13] These provisions addressed many issues typical of a GP regulatory system and laid out the framework and basis for future government procurement legislation at National People's Congress (NPC). Besides, MOF also set up a new office for this reform and envisaged an organizational model of centralized procurement to conduct all centralized procurement under its authority.[14] However, the proposed model soon caused concerns among other agencies, especially the one traditionally responsible for supplies to the State Council, the State Council Administration for Logistic Affairs (SCALA). The State Council later overruled MOF's plan to set up a centralized purchasing agency under its authority and authorized SCALA to conduct procurement on behalf of the central government. However, the issue of a centralized procurement institution continued to loom over the GP draft legislation and later its implementation.

In sharp contrast to the failed initiative at central level, local-level finance departments managed a landslide success in setting up centralized purchasing functions under their respective authorities. According to a survey, an overwhelming majority of centralized procuring entities were set up under finance departments.[15] The local reform and legislation in some provinces and cities seemed even more active. Shanghai and Shenzhen issued their provisions on GP earlier than the provisional measures of MOF. Following their example, almost all provincial governments issued their regulations and established new offices for GP in the following two years.[16] Meanwhile, Web-based networks for publishing GP notices at both central and local levels were also established.

15.2.2.2 GPL and Its Implementing Measures

In early 1999, when the BL was about to be enacted, the NPC initiated a new legislative move on GP, which was prepared by the NPC itself.[17] On June 29, 2002, the new GPL was promulgated effective on January 1, 2003. The new GPL was not very mature as it provided only a legal framework for China's future GP reform.

The law is general and many aspects of the GPL demand further implementing rules, a task that was generally delegated to the State Council.[18] Right after the enactment of the GPL, the State Council issued a notice briefly outlining the implementation plan at central level, mainly concerned with institutional issues (hereafter referred to as implementation plan),[19] as well as the centralized procurement catalogue (CPCatalogue), which was an annually updated list of goods, works, and services covered by the GPL.

However, more extensive implementing rules were not enacted until 2004 when the Ministry of Finance (MOF), rather than the State Council, issued three ministerial measures.[20] Meanwhile, a few attempts were also made to implement the secondary policies enacted in the GPL. New forms of government procurement methods and regulations, such as E-procurement and procurement under framework agreements, are being explored.

15.2.3 Recent Developments in Works Procurement and a New Test for the BL and GPL

15.2.3.1 Project Legal Person System

A system gradually introduced over recent years is the project legal person (PLP) system (*xiang mu fa ren zhi*). The system was designed to increase accountability in construction projects and constituted a significant improvement over the old regime where, after completion of the project, the legal entity responsible for undertaking the works was dissolved. A PLP must now, therefore, be designated by the contracting entity to be held accountable for all construction-related aspects of the project.[21]

The PLP can take the form of a commercial entity[22] or a nonprofit entity,[23] and usually acts as a consultant to the contracting entity and manager of the construction project. Although some regulations require a selection of the PLP by bidding "when the conditions permit,"[24] it is observed that this requirement is very loose and could easily be bypassed.

However, new practices and policies are emerging and a breakthrough has been achieved in the procurement of Olympic construction projects. According to the provisions governing the selection of PLPs for the construction and operation of Olympic projects, all PLPs are to be selected through international bidding.[25] The policy later is expanded to other municipal infrastructure projects,[26] and seems to be evolving in other sectors, for example, in selecting PLPs for the provision of housing or roads.[27]

15.2.3.2 Works Procurement: The Project Agent System

Another evolving procurement system in the works sector is the so-called project agent system (PAS) (*dai jian zhi*). The Chinese-coined term refers to a designated agent, rather than a PLP, who carries out the works project, then transfers the project to the investor once construction is complete. The agent can be a dedicated government agency in charge of government construction works[28] or a commercial consultant, with either the role of a primary construction contractor or only a management consultant to the project sponsor. Policies to encourage the use of the PAS system have appeared at both central and local levels,[29] and the system is still evolving.

15.2.3.3 Concession Regulation in Utilities and Municipal Infrastructure Sectors

The development of private sector participation has been gaining momentum following series of recent policy initiatives at the central level,[30] and along with this development came the third wave of Chinese procurement reform and regulation—the regulatory framework governing the procurement of privately financed infrastructure projects (PFIP) and the distinctive legislative development of concession regulation in urban infrastructure and utilities sectors. Currently, Beijing Municipality is taking the lead in promulgating the first concession regulation on its municipal infrastructure and a number of other local governments have enacted concession regulations on municipal utilities.[31] A new legal framework for private finance in urban infrastructure and utilities seems to be taking shape in China and current regulations as a whole could provide models for future national regulations.[32]

15.2.3.4 Implications of New Developments

The above developments indicate that works procurement system is still evolving in China. The increasing number of complexities in procurement have also created a strain on the current policy, legal and institutional framework. A number of observations can be made in this regard. First, there is a tendency to rely on external expertise or finance for works projects, rather than the traditional self-sufficient model. Second, some governments choose to set up specialized government agencies to conduct government works procurement and a centralized government works procurement function is taking shape. When works procurement is performed by a specialized government agency, the separation of the roles of users from purchasers can help the government build core purchasing expertise and thus provide better quality works projects. Third, while some of the developments in essence fall under the concept of GP for the purposes of the GPL, the various terms coined throughout these developments have led to a situation where works procurement has effectively been excluded from the scope of what is referred to in China as "government procurement."

These developments have also created a new test for the BL. Although the BL is arguably perceived as a law governing the procurement of construction works and related goods and services, it is unclear whether it also applies to the selection of PLPs and concessionaires. This lack of clarity has been the source of much frustration for regulators and practitioners in their efforts to balance strict procedural requirements and commercial flexibility for complex projects involving works.

The developments also present challenges for the application of the GPL. By concept under the Chinese GPL, some of these arrangements, especially the PAS, are government procurement in essence and as such should be subject to provisions of the GPL. However, the tradition of works procurement administration and the coined term of PAS itself indicate that the new system has nothing to do with government procurement.

15.3 Policy Objectives

15.3.1 BL: Economy and Quality

15.3.1.1 Primary Objectives

The primary purpose of the earlier bidding regulations was to reform the administration of government investment and finance to reduce corruption and the inefficiencies created by the noncompetitive allocation of projects by government agencies. Therefore, the primary objectives found in modern procurement systems, such as value for money, were not a major concern in earlier bidding regulations.[33] The BL significantly improved the old BMs by embracing the objectives of economy and quality of procurement in Article 1. It further revolutionized the award criteria by abolishing the base price criteria and adopting the market-based ones found in modern procurement regimes. These improvements, among others, have greatly enhanced the ability of procuring entities to meet the new objectives provided for in the BL.

15.3.1.2 Secondary Objectives

Except for in a few cases where the bidding regulations implement a buy national policy by first using competition to test whether a domestic source of supply of a certain product exists,[34] the Chinese BL and related regulations provide no explicit secondary policies. However, the BL does leave many policy issues for the procuring entities to stipulate in the bidding document; therefore, it is likely that secondary policies are implemented in the real procurement field through the qualification process, technical specifications, or during the award stage. Besides, secondary policies may also be implemented where procurement is excluded from coverage.[35]

15.3.2 Government Procurement Law

15.3.2.1 Primary Objectives

Under the GPL, the declared primary policy was "to increase the effectiveness of government procurement funding," and "promote the construction of a clean government." The purpose of the reforms was closely related to the functions and authority of MOF, either as a means of budgetary reform or of expenditure reform. It is interesting to note that the first departmental provision on government procurement by MOF referred to the Budget Law as its legal basis and a new office for procurement policy was set up within the budget department of the ministry. However during the later reorganization of MOF, the office was moved to the Department of Treasury, which seemed to indicate that MOF began to take the reform more as means of public expenditure control than its budgetary perspective.

15.3.2.2 Secondary Objectives

15.3.2.2.1 Buy National Policy

The GPL implements a buy national policy in Article 10 which provides that the government shall procure domestic goods, works, and services except where

1. Goods, works, or services to be procured are not available within the territory of People's Republic of China or though available, cannot be acquired on reasonable commercial terms and conditions.
2. Items to be procured are for use abroad.
3. Otherwise provided by laws and administrative regulations.

The GPL leaves the definition of the term "domestic goods, works, and services" to be specified by the State Council. However, this policy has proved to be difficult to implement due to the general and vague nature of the wording. Draftsmen of the implementing rules also met with technical difficulties concerning the definition of "domestic goods, works, and service" and were also subject to a number of domestic pressures.[36] The implementing tender measure requires that the eligible supplier in a bidding process be a domestic supplier[37] supplying domestic products, except otherwise provided by law and administrative regulation (Article 8). However, this rule unfortunately helps little to technically clarify the situation.

15.3.2.2.2 Other Social and Economic Policies

Other secondary policies can also be implemented through Article 9, which provides that

> Government procurement shall be conducted in such a manner as to facilitate achievement of the economic and social development policy goals of the State, including but not limited to environmental protection, assistance of underdeveloped or ethnic minority regions, and promotion of small- and medium-sized enterprises.

Later, implementing measures were enacted requiring purchasers at all levels give priority to energy-conserving products[38] and the procurement of WELAN product and product for purposes relating to national security and the promotion of the indigenous information and communications technology (ICT) sector.[39] In recent years, with a national campaign to bolster innovation in China, great emphasis is now placed on "indigenous" innovation, where government procurement is planned to play an important role, a role which is outlined in a State Council notice[40] and an MOF white paper (the Innovation Opinions).[41]

15.4 Legislative Framework: Scope and Coverage

The drafting stages of procurement legislation in China were marked by intense institutional rivalry between the MOF and what was then the SPC. Hence, a basic understanding of the legislative history of procurement legislation is crucial in comprehending the somewhat gray nature of the divergent legal framework, which to some degree is overlapping and conflicting.[42]

The result of the regulatory battles has been a tacit agreement establishing institutional fences around the terms "bidding" and "government procurement," with regulatory jurisdiction of each term falling under the exclusive competence of the proponent of the law in question. Although both sides recognize that bidding and government procurement are not mutually exclusive, the distinction between the two terms represents a way of agreeing to disagree, and remains in place to date.

15.4.1 BL: Works and Related Goods and Services

As a result of the institutional rivalry, the term government procurement was dropped in the coverage of the final drafts of the BL. However, a new article appeared that was sweeping in its scope of application—Article 2, which states that the law would apply to "bidding activities within the territory of China." Although the intention behind Article 2 was to ensure that the BL could be applied to all government procurement (not just works procurement) where bidding was concerned, the problems associated with such a scope of application are clear. The law would have to be applied to all entities, private or public, when a bidding mechanism was used, thereby imposing unnecessary regulatory burdens on private purchasers.

To complicate matters even further, bidding was not defined under the BL; the only guidelines to serve as a working definition of bidding being the two prescribed bidding procedures in the BL—open and selective bidding. Such a definition has been adopted for practical reasons; however, the flaws of such a definition are apparent: not only are other types of bidding such as two-stage or negotiated bidding excluded, but also the BL only applies to those bidding activities that are already following its prescriptions.

Despite the attempts to broaden the scope of the BL's application, its compulsory coverage was limited to works procurement, elaborated in Article 3, which requires inter alia that (1) works involving the public interests or public security and (2) works invested or financed by the state are to be procured through bidding. This requirement also extends to works-related procurement of goods and services. In addition to meeting the criteria set out in Article 3, the procurement value must also exceed certain thresholds, which are dealt with later in this section.

In contrast with Article 2, Article 3 exhibits the features of a typical coverage provision under modern public procurement law. While Subparagraph (2) of Article 3 defines its coverage by reference to the source of procurement funding, Subparagraph (1) defines its coverage by a different method, namely whether or not "public interests or public security" are concerned. Though the two definitions overlap to some degree, it is this definition that brings the most procurement under the regulatory framework, be it undertaken or financed by public or private entities.

15.4.1.1 Public Interest or Public Security Test

To clarify "public interest or public security" within the meaning of Article 3, the SPC issued an implementing regulation in 2000[43] specifying that works projects in the following sectors were deemed to involve public interest or security: energy, transportation, telecommunications and post, hydraulics, municipal facilities, ecology, environment, and "other infrastructure projects." Utilities projects concerning public interest or security include municipal engineering, science, education and culture, sports and tourism, sanitation and social welfare, commercial housing, and "other public utilities" projects. Any works projects in the above areas are, therefore, deemed to concern public interest and security, regardless of the source of funding.

15.4.1.2 Source of Funding Test

The BL provides in Subsections (2) and (3) of Article 3 that "projects invested wholly or partly by state-owned funds or projects funded wholly or partly through state finance" and "projects funded through loans or grant from international organisation or foreign governments" shall be subject to compulsory bidding.

State-owned funds generally refer to state fiscal funds including budgetary and extra-budgetary funds. The implementing provision stipulates that projects invested by state-owned funds include projects that are financed through[44] (a) budgetary funds of any level of government; (b) various government special construction funds; or (c) funds owned by state-owned enterprises or public institutions and actually controlled by state-asset investors.

The implementing provision further specifies that the scope of projects funded through state finance include projects that are financed through[45] (a) issuing of state bonds, (b) foreign loans or security by the state, (c) state policy loans, (d) financing arrangement by state-authorized investment entity, or (e) financing arrangement under state concession.

15.4.1.3 Thresholds

The thresholds for the value of each individual contract are provided in an implementing provision.[46] Thresholds will be deemed to be exceeded if (a) for individual construction contracts, the estimated contract value is RMB 2,000,000; (b) for individual supply contracts for key equipment and material etc., the estimated contract value is RMB 1,000,000; (c) for individual service contracts for survey, design and supervision, etc., the estimated contract value is RMB 500,000; or (d) if each individual contract value is below the threshold under (a), (b), and (c), the total investment value is above RMB 30,000,000.

15.4.1.4 Exemptions

Contracts falling within the compulsory scope of coverage but below the thresholds are exempted. It is also provided in Article 66 that procurement involving special circumstances may be exempted from the bidding obligation according to relevant regulations. The article also provides for a non-exhaustive list of such special circumstances such as national security, state secrets, emergency rescue, or the use of poverty relief funds as remuneration for poor regions or rural laborers.

It is noteworthy that an implementing regulation has effectively added more procurement to this list.[47] Such exemptions include circumstances where (a) construction projects require special confidentiality arrangements; (b) the survey or design of a construction project requires the use of a specific patent or know-how, or there is a specific requirement for an architectural or artistic model; (c) the number of contractors, suppliers, or service providers is fewer than three and effective competition is unattainable; or (d) other circumstances make bidding inapplicable.

Moreover, Article 67 of the BL provides that procurement entities will be exempted from compulsory coverage under the BL, if the foreign or international loan/grant providers require application of their own procurement rules.

15.4.2 GPL: Goods and Services

Procurement activities must meet the following three conditions to fall under the coverage of the Chinese GPL:[48]

1. Procurement must be conducted by state organs, public institutions, social organizations at all levels. It is apparently intended that state-owned companies are not subject to the GPL.
2. Procurement must be of goods, works, and services listed in the CPCatalogue or above the officially specified threshold.
3. Procurement must be conducted with fiscal funds.

A number of intricacies in the GPL, however, make the determination of coverage far from a straightforward exercise. The first is the position of works procurement, which is by no means clear. The second is the reference to thresholds and the CPCatalogue, while the third relates to the definition of fiscal funds. These issues are dealt with in the following sections.

15.4.2.1 CPCatalogue and Thresholds

The CPCatalogue lists products, services, and works that must be procured through a centralized agency, be it the central purchasing agency or a department of central purchasing agency. In the pre-GPL stages, only the procurement of listed items was regulated to make reform more manageable[49] in view of the lacking capacity of finance departments to conduct procurement. Even though the scope of products covered by the CPCatalogue is enlarged on an annual basis, it still remains relatively small.[50]

Under the GPL, the CPCatalogue is still used but the law also makes use of thresholds, which serve as an additional determinant for whether or not the procurement in question is covered.[51] It could be observed therefore that the CPCatalogue is now more concerned with allocating centralized purchasing power between the different central purchasing agencies.[52]

Another function of the CPCatalogue is to establish thresholds for the purpose of defining the coverage of the GPL. Under the GPL, procurement outside the CPCatalogue is caught only when it exceeds RMB 500,000 for central government procurement of goods and service and RMB 600,000 for works, as is provided in the currently published CPCatalogue.[53] A different threshold is provided for in the CPCatalogue for triggering open bidding procedures, which, at central level, is RMB 1,200,000 for goods and service and RMB 2,000,000 for works.[54]

The CPCatalogue is updated annually by the State Council at central level and by the provincial government at local level. The content of the CPCatalogue is interesting to note; it provides a window for observing how comprehensively services and works procurement are covered in reality. At the central level, the listed works in the CPCatalogue only covers building works for public use, e.g., office buildings. Listed services only cover vehicle repair, insurance and oil filling, printing service, conference service, computer software, the development and maintenance of information management systems, and other services of special nature. Many professional services like consultancy, audit, and legal service are not covered by the CPCatalogue. However, at the local level, the list covers a much wider scope of services and works procurement. A large number of economic and social infrastructure works are included in the list and professional services such as consultancy and design are also included.[55] The difference at central and local levels may be related to the fact that local governments are in a better position to coordinate their different departments than the central government.

15.4.2.2 Issue of Fiscal Funds

Procurement is only caught by the GPL when fiscal funds are used. Therefore, it is important to further define the nature of fiscal fund. A notice issued later by MOF makes it clear that fiscal funds include budgetary and extra-budgetary funds.[56] While budgetary funds consist of government appropriations in various forms, extra-budgetary funds are revenues generated on administrative service charge and government-sponsored foundations. These extra-budgetary funds also include the special purpose funds appropriated from higher-level government.[57] Procurements with a combination of both fiscal funds and other sources of funding fall under the coverage of the GPL.[58]

15.4.2.3 Excluded Procurement

Article 85 excludes from the coverage of the GPL urgent procurements such as those warranted by natural disaster and force majeure, and those procurements involving state security and secrecy. Still another article excludes military procurement, in general, and authorizes the Central Military Commission to enact its own procurement regulations (Article 86).

15.4.2.4 Coordination Effort

Despite the provision in Article 4 of the GPL, which states that "Whereas works is procured through bidding method the Bidding Law shall apply," the position of works procurement under the GPL is by no means as clear as it seems to be. One ambiguity is related to the question of the extent to which the BL shall apply to government works procurement. A restrictive explanation would be that only the bidding procedure under the BL applies to government works procurement and many other important aspects of the GPL will prevail over the BL, for example, the buy national policy, the bid challenge system, and the supervisory authority provided in the GPL. A more expanded explanation would be that the BL as a whole applies to government works procurement. In other words, government works procurement is excluded from the coverage of the GPL. The problem of ambiguity seems to result from the overlapping coverage of the two laws, a problem which in essence is rooted in the allocation of regulatory powers among ministries. Until a reallocation of regulatory powers is effected, there will continue to be a gray regulatory zone marked by careful bureaucratic maneuvering and occasional regulatory battles. The GPL implementation rules issued by the MOF (Tendering Measures) recently seem to concede to National Development and Reform Commission (NDRC) and MOFCOM by confining the coverage to goods and services and excluding the procurement of imported machinery and electrical equipment through bidding.[59]

Another inconsistency concerning coverage is found in the different treatment of state-owned enterprises (SOEs) under the two laws. Given the fact that public works in China are ordinarily undertaken either by establishing an independent agency or by entrusting the project to an entity, usually taking the form of an SOE, it is safe to say that the majority of procuring entities under the BL are SOEs. However, the GPL clearly does not bring SOEs within its coverage. This applies regardless of whether these SOEs are using budgetary funds to conduct their procurement or their own funds, whether these SOEs are operating in a competitive sector or a monopolistic sector, or whether or not these SOEs are utilities operators.

The question of SOEs has become a contentious topic domestically, and with China launching negotiations on GPA accession this year, the issue will almost certainly be revisited. If and how SOEs should be brought under modern procurement law will require careful consideration by China's policymakers.

15.5 Legislative Framework: Procurement Procedures

15.5.1 Procedures under the BL

In contrast with the three procedures in the previous bidding regulations, only two procedures, namely open bidding and selective bidding, are adopted in the BL with the negotiated procedure being omitted. The two adopted procedures are similar except that under the selective procedure no public procurement notice is required and bidders are invited directly. Bidding procedures have also been made much more rigid and no negotiation is allowed at any stage of the procurement process.

The consequences of this omission are serious. While the broad coverage of the BL meant that it needed more flexible procurement arrangements, the two bidding procedures adopted are rigid, leaving no room for negotiation. A practical but unduly liberal way to allow for negotiations in procurements that require flexibility is to provide more exemptions from bidding requirements altogether. Thus Article 66, the only article dealing with such exemptions, provides that in "special circumstances," a procuring entity may be exempted from the obligation to procure by bidding according to relevant state regulations. However, three problems exist with this provision.

First, what constitutes these special circumstances? There are surely more than three circumstances of this kind that are provided in this article. Additional exemptions were supplemented by an implementing provision of SDPC.[60] However, more exceptions should be made to enable procurement to be effective.

Second, who has the authority to decide whether such conditions are met? This is also dealt with by the above SDPC provision. Although this provision requires procuring entities to justify the circumstances of non-applicability in the feasibility report presented to SDPC or other competent departments for approval, it is up to the competent departments to verify this justification.

Third, when these circumstances are met and bidding requirements are subject to an exemption, no other procedures are provided through which the procurement can be conducted. Thus, the excluded procurement is completely unregulated. Therefore, future legislation should ideally provide some more flexible procurement procedures to meet the realities of the need for flexible procurement.

One possible way to rectify the situation is adoption of the two-stage bidding procedure, which is recommended in both the World Bank guidelines and the UNCITRAL Model Law.[61] Interviews with procurement professionals reveals that this procedure is sometimes followed in practice when complex procurement is involved. Another alternative would be to allow the use of negotiation in the context of a selective procedure as permitted under Article XIV of the GPA or the newly adopted procedure of competitive dialogue under the EU system.

15.5.2 Procedures under the GPL

The GPL provides a lengthy menu of methods for government procurement: open tendering, selective tendering, competitive negotiation, single source procurement, request for quotation, and other methods authorized by the state supervisory authority for government procurement. It promotes open tendering as the preferred procurement method,[62] provides conditions for the use for each procurement procedure, and requires prior approval from supervising authorities.[63]

15.5.3 BM for Goods and Services

As discussed in earlier section,[64] the bidding measure (BM) was issued as an implementing regulation of the GPL. However, Article 2 of the BL is clear that it applies to all bidding activities,[65] which must be taken to include those covered by the GPL. Meanwhile, Article 4 of the GPL can not be understood to exclude the BL from coverage of goods or services through bidding since the article does not provide that the procurement of goods and services through bidding shall not be subject to the BL. Therefore, there is no ambiguity here that the BL is the primary law that governs government procurement of goods and services by bidding procedures and any secondary laws governing bidding shall not deviate from the principle and provisions of the BL. In any case, the BM must be understood to implement not only the GPL but also the BL.

Also, the GPL requires that all government procurement of goods, works, and services be subject to the GPL. However, this requirement should be construed together with other relevant articles especially those relating to procurement through bidding. When read together with the BL (Article 2), the GPL only contains a few provisions on bidding procedures and, moreover, these articles are designed with utmost care to avoid conflict with the BL by limiting their application to only goods and services. The scope of the BM seems to support this observation. First, its scope of application is deliberately confined to a smaller coverage—goods and services procured through bidding (Article 2). Second, procurement of imported mechanical and electrical equipment through bidding (Article 86), the authority of which is conferred upon a different ministry (MOFCOM),[66] is also excluded. Therefore, the BM, a secondary law supposedly to implement the GPL, also implements the bidding procedures provisions, which are mostly contained in the BL.

15.5.4 Methods of Bidding and Their Application

The BL provides for two bidding methods. By definition, open bidding refers to a procurement procedure where "the procuring entity invites, through bid notice, unspecified legal persons or other organizations to submit bids" and selective tendering refers to bidding procedures under which "the procuring entity invites, through a invitation letter, specified legal persons or other organizations to submit bids"(Article 10 of the BL).

The BL further requires in Article 17 that procuring entities using the selective method send the invitation letter to three or more specified bidders with the capacity to perform the proposed project and good financial standing. A strong argument can be made for an open prequalification procedure in the selective bidding procedure, but uncertainty remains as to how the specified bidders are chosen and whether a public notice needs to be published.

The GPL follows the BL in providing the same two bidding methods and makes some improvements to the selective bidding procedures by requiring that procuring entities randomly choose three or more bidders from those qualified (Article 34). The BM further elaborates on the procedural requirements in the GPL by providing a definition of selective bidding, and further requires in Article 15 that procuring entities publish a prequalification notice in designated media and randomly choose three or more bidders from the qualified potential bidders.

Both the BL and the GPL require open bidding as the preferred method for government procurement when the procurement is above a certain threshold and clearly prohibit the evasion of open bidding through disaggregation (Article 4 of the BL, Article 28 of the GPL). The BM repeats these provisions (Article 5). The selective bidding method can only be used when (a) the procurement is special and can only be procured from limited sources and (b) the cost of the procurement through open bidding would be disproportionate to the overall value of the procurement, a concept which can be found in some of the international government procurement regimes.[67]

15.5.4.1 Solicitation Procedure

15.5.4.1.1 Solicitation and the Prequalification Notice

The BL simply requires the publication of a solicitation notice when using the open bidding method. The notice should be published in the media designated by the state (Article 16). A similar requirement exists in the BM (Article 14). Requirements are stricter when using selective bidding under the GPL, which requires a prequalification procedure.

15.5.4.1.2 Qualification

A common doctrine followed by both the BL and the GPL regarding the qualification of potential bidders or suppliers is the prohibition of discriminatory or preferential treatment among potential bidders or suppliers based on "unreasonable" terms (Article 18 of the BL and Article 22 of the GPL).The GPL outlines general qualification criteria for suppliers, which includes considerations such as the supplier's commercial reputation, financial and accounting system, professional expertise, possession of equipment required to perform the contract, a clean tax, and social security record as well as a clean legal record for the preceding three years (Article 22).

15.5.4.1.3 Solicitation Document

The BM provides that procuring entities may consult experts or suppliers for advice on the solicitation document "where necessary" (Article 22). Although this may be based on the need to specify in further detail aspects of the solicitation document, for example, technical specifications, safeguards should also be put in place to avoid conflicts of interest, especially where certain suppliers may gain an advantage by participating in the consultation process. To this end, it is advisable that the consultation process be an open one, and the eventual solicitation document shall be subject to the test of the general principle of equal treatment for all suppliers and nondiscrimination regarding technical specification.

Another provision in the BM concerns the form of the solicitation document. Although electronic forms of procurement are emerging as an increasingly important regulatory issue in GP regimes around the world, most GP regimes, including the one established by the BL and the GPL, assume that the transaction is based on paper documents. The BM recognizes the validity of the electronic solicitation documents for the first time in the history of GP. Article 19 provides that procuring entities shall prepare paper solicitation documents, but may also issue electronic solicitation documents through the designated Web media with the paper and electronic versions being identical and having the same legal effect.

One particular issue concerns the procuring entity's right to amend the solicitation document and to extend the deadline for submission of tender. To ensure transparency and fairness, the BL requires the procuring entity to notify any clarification and amendments to all recipients of the solicitation document in writing at least 15 days before the deadline for submission of tender (Article 23). The requirement for such a minimum period is intended to ensure that bidders have sufficient time to respond to the clarifications and amendments.

There has been some criticism that the 15-day rule is too rigid in limiting the procuring entity's ability to amend the solicitation document; however, Article 28 of the BM foresees the possible need for amendments before the deadline by providing that "the procuring entity may take into consideration particular circumstances and extend the deadline for the submission of tenders as long as all the recipients of the solicitation document are notified in writing of the change and a notice of amendment to that effect is published in the designated media at least 3 days prior to the deadline." This article thus, on one hand, creates the possibility to amend the document even after the 15-day deadline has passed. On the other hand, the term particular circumstances may leave considerable space for abuse of discretion.[68]

15.5.4.2 Termination

One of the practical issues of the bidding process concerns the termination of the bidding activities. Article 24 of the BM makes it clear that procuring entities shall not terminate the bidding process once the bid notice, bid invitation letter, or solicitation document has been issued. Termination of the bidding process is only justified in the following cases (Article 36 GPL):

1. There are fewer than three suppliers who meet the qualification or who are responsive to substantive elements in the solicitation document.
2. There arises unlawful conduct that prejudices the fairness of the procurement.
3. Bid price exceeds the budget level for the procurement involved and the procuring entity is not competent to pay.
4. Procurement is canceled due to significant change.

When the termination is based on one of the first three cases, the procuring entity is under an obligation to reopen the bidding process, unless it is justifiable that another procurement procedure is more applicable.

15.5.4.3 Award Criteria

Under the BL (Article 41), the successful tender shall either be

1. Bid with the lowest price subject to satisfying all substantive requirements provided in the solicitation document (hereafter referred to as the lowest bid price). This method should generally be used in the procurement of standard or commoditized goods and common services (Article 51 BM)
2. Bid satisfying all comprehensive evaluation criteria provided in the solicitation document to the greatest degree (hereafter referred to as the most advantageous method)

For the most advantageous method, the BM provides two variants: the comprehensive evaluation method and the performance/price ratio method. The comprehensive evaluation method (Article 52) allows for comprehensive factors specified in the bidding document to be taken into consideration in the bid evaluation; such factors include price, technology, financial situation, reputation, experience, after-sales service, and the degree of responsiveness to the bidding document, and are quantified and weighted. Price must be accorded a weight of 30–60 percent for goods and 10–30 percent for services. The successful bid shall be the one with the highest evaluated scores subject to satisfying all substantive requirements. Under the performance/price ratio method, the non-price or performance factors are evaluated and the score is then compared to the price. The successful bid is the one with the highest ratio between the scores of the performance factors and the bid price (Article 53).

The BL prohibits a bid price that is lower than the product cost (Article 41), while the BM employs the term "abnormally lowest price." When the lowest bid price is considered to be "obviously unreasonable" or lower than the cost and, thus, may affect the quality of the goods to be delivered and dishonor a guarantee of good performance, the Tender Evaluation Committee (TEC) shall require the bidder in question to submit an written explanation within a designated period with supporting documents (Article 54). Otherwise, the TEC may reject the tender.

15.5.5 Competitive Negotiation

Under Article 30 of the GPL, government purchasers may use competitive negotiation to conduct procurement for goods and services when one of the following conditions is met:

1. When bidding proceedings have been engaged in but no bids or no responsive bids were submitted or[69] reopening of the bidding proceedings is unlikely to result in a procurement contract
2. When it is not feasible to formulate detailed specifications or identify specific requirements due to technical complexity
3. When there is an urgent need for procurement and engaging in bidding proceedings would therefore be impracticable
4. When the total value of the procurement cannot be determined in advance

When the negotiation stage has been completed, best and final offers are required. Because there has not been much experience in China in applying competitive negotiations in GP and the above provision was designed on the base of a comparative study of international GP regimes,[70] there still remains much ambiguity in the application of this article. For a better understanding, it should be read together with relevant articles in other jurisdictions.

15.5.6 Sole Source Procurement

It is provided in Article 31 of the GPL that a procuring entity may use sole source procurement when

1. Procurement can only be made from the sole source supplier.
2. It is not feasible to procure from other suppliers due to an unexpected emergency.
3. Consistency or compatibility of services require procurement of additional services from the same supplier, provided that the total value of the additional procurement does not exceed 10 percent of the value of the original contract.

It is further provided in Article 39 that "when sole source procurement is applied, the procuring entities and suppliers shall follow the principles provided for under this Law. The award shall be based on good quality and reasonable price."

15.5.7 Request for Quotation

It is provided in Article 32 of the GPL that requests for quotation may be employed for the procurements of goods with uniform standards and specifications, sufficient off-shelf supplies, and with a small scope of price fluctuation. Article 40 also lays out the basic procedure to be followed for the application of request for quotation.

15.5.8 New Methods and Technologies in Government Procurement

In addition to the named procurement methods, it is provided in Article 26 of the GPL that a procuring entity may employ other methods approved by the competent authority. These include the supply agreement arrangement and new electronic procurement methods, e.g., electronic reverse auctions (ERA). Much room is left for future regulation on the emerging policy issues with respect to the design and application of these methods.

15.5.8.1 Supply Agreement and Designated Spot Procurement

Framework agreements (also known as supply arrangements and indefinite-delivery/indefinite-quantity contracts) can be defined as agreements for securing the repeat supply of a product or service over a period, and which involve a call for initial tenders against set terms and conditions, the selection of one or more suppliers on the basis of the tenders, and the subsequent placing of periodic orders with the suppliers chosen as particular requirements arise.

In the Chinese context, similar arrangements can be found under different labels: supply agreement and designated spot procurement, or designated spot procurement through agreement. An early legal definition defines supply agreements as arrangements where finance departments, through centralized open tendering, determine the product, price, service, and duration of a supply agreement and notify the agreement to the procuring entities for their use.[71] This definition reflects the situation in earlier days, when finance departments were more involved in the operational aspects.

A more recent definition can be found in the draft Measure on Supply Agreement by MOF, which defines supply agreements as arrangements where the successful bidders, price, and service terms for bid products are centrally determined through open bidding and laid down in the form of an agreement under which the procuring entities may discretionally choose to procure among the successful bidders and their bid products (Article 3 of the draft). Designated spot procurement and designated spot procurement through agreement are for all practical purposes the same arrangement as the supply agreement.[72]

At the central level, there are basically no dedicated rules governing the use of supply agreements. The position of the supply agreement is not clear under the GPL in terms of whether or not it falls under one of the main five procurement methods, or whether it constitutes one of the other methods, the use of which must be authorized by the MOF. The working understanding among procuring entities is that they are simply a variant of the prescribed bidding methods and hence no MOF authorization is required. However, careful consideration of the nature of the supply agreement and of international best practice would suggest that the supply agreement is a distinct method that requires further regulation.

Currently, it is provided in the Bidding Measure (Article 85) that the supply agreements be reached through open bidding in the first instance, and through other methods only exceptionally and subject to the approval of the competent finance departments.

15.5.8.2 New Technology and Electronic Procurement

Information technology has been reshaping the contracting world and is gradually being embraced in the world of law. The Chinese Contract Law, in broad language, recognizes the validity of contracts consummated in the form of electronic data messages, but does not address a wide range of related issues. The E-Signature Law[73] fills some of the gaps by providing legal definitions of the terms "electronic data message" and "electronic signature," the requirements applicable to the communication and enforceability of electronic data messages, the legal effect and certification of electronic signatures, and the consequences of violating the E-Signature Law. These laws generally also govern the world of government procurement through the Internet.

With the advancement of new IT and the encouragement of E-government, many local governments have been exploring electronic means to conduct business and regulate government procurement through the Internet. One such regulation can be found as early as 1999, when Nanning Municipality, the capital of Guangxi Autonomous Region and a forerunner of Chinese government procurement reform, enacted a regulation governing Internet-based government procurement bidding activities.[74] What the regulation describes as "Internet-based government procurement bidding" is actually a process of procurement where the government publishes the bidding notice through the Internet, receives bids through e-mails, decides the successful bid, and publishes the successful bid and its bid price on the Internet.[75] Many other local governments followed later and enacted their own regulations on Internet-based government procurement bidding.[76] Such Internet-based procurement is actually similar to ERA found in other jurisdictions.

However, there are currently no national laws specifically governing E-procurement. The position of ERA is also not clear under the GPL as to whether it constitutes an electronic means of the traditional open bidding method or a separate new method, which falls under the category of other methods. Procuring entities that are applying or regulating E-procurement tend to place them under the traditional open bidding method, so that they do not need to have the authorization from MOF. However, there are substantive policy issues regarding the practice of E-procurement and the regulation thereof which may require future national regulation.

15.6 Enforcement and Remedies

15.6.1 Bidding Law

Under the BL, the status quo of the decentralized supervision responsibility was maintained among various departments and local authorities in line with the structure of the administrative system. No formal challenge system is provided and remedies to cover loss or damage to the aggrieved suppliers are limited.

15.6.1.1 Article 65 of the BL and the Implementing Measure

Under Article 65 of the BL, a bidder or any other interested person has the right to challenge the decision of the procuring entity or to complain to the relevant administrative supervision department, if he believes there has been a violation. However, neither effective challenge and review procedures nor remedies for loss or damage for the aggrieved suppliers are provided. The legislators of the BL took the view that bidders could rely on strict administrative sanctions to readdress any breach. The gap was filled to some degree by an implementing measure, the Bid Complaint Measure, issued four years later dealing with procedural issues for handling complaints.[77]

The Bid Complaint Measure confirms that the authority of agencies handling complaints in relation to bidding activities in construction projects is derived from a notice issued by the State Council office.[78] It further clarifies that for complaints in relation to bidding activities for key national construction projects (including industrial projects), the competent authority handling the complaint is the NDRC. However, where other regulatory authorities have accepted a complaint, they are required to notify NDRC and NDRC will then not accept the case (Article 4 of the Bid Complaint Measure).

15.6.1.1.1 Eligible Complainants

The Bid Complaint Measure (Article 3) reiterates the provision in Article 65 of the BL. It further clarifies the meaning of the "other interested persons" and refers them as "legal persons, other organizations and individuals other than the bidders that are directly or indirectly related to the interest of a bidding project or bidding activity."

15.6.1.1.2 Scope of Permissible Complaints

A complaint can be made in relation to any phase of the bidding activities including bid invitation, submission of bids, opening of bids, evaluation of bids, determination of the successful bid, and conclusion of the contract (Article 2).

15.6.1.1.3 Available Remedies

A complainant's preferred remedy will usually be the rectification of the breach by the procuring entity. Procurement remedies in many legal systems include damages, annulment of an unlawful act or decision, or annulment of a contract, although this may cause serious disruption of procurement and may deserve special consideration.

As discussed above, the BL relies heavily on administrative sanctions for enforcement. However, it does provide some limited remedies for an aggrieved bidder to redress its grievance. The most important one is the requirement of correction of the unlawful acts and where these unlawful acts lead to an award decision, the annulment of the award, in which case a new successful bidder may be chosen from the other bidders, or alternatively a new bidding procedure must be reopened.[79] While these measures might serve as effective remedies for the aggrieved bidder, they rely heavily on the effectiveness of the administrative review body. It is doubtful whether, without a formal challenge procedure, the bidder's right to this remedy can be effectively guaranteed.

Another problem with the BL is that there is no provision for recovery of damages for loss caused by the unlawful acts of the procuring entity.

One particular legal void relating to remedies is that concerning the unlawful conclusion of a contract. While "annulment of award" is listed as a possibility, the term implies that this remedy is only available up to the conclusion of the contract.[80] In the event that unlawful acts are only disclosed and addressed after the contract is already in force, the BL makes no provision.

15.6.1.2 Procedural Issues

The Bid Complaint Measure provides detailed rules governing the handling of the complaint. A complaint shall be filed to the competent authority within ten days after the complainant learns or should have learned that his rights are infringed.[81] On receiving the complaint, the competent supervisory authority shall conduct a review and make a decision within five days on whether it accepts the complaint or not according to the conditions laid out in Articles 11 and 12.[82] If the competent authority eventually accepts the complaint, it shall review the records and documents, and investigate and verify the violation. For grave violations that involve complex circumstances and a wide range of sectors, the competent authority may conduct joint investigations with other supervisory authorities.[83] While handling the case, the competent authority shall hear the respondent's presentation and defense and may summon parties involved to cross-examine the evidence when necessary.[84]

The competent authority should make a decision within 30 working days after it accepts the complaint and notify all parties involved (Article 21).

Some articles are also designed to address the possibility of false or malicious complaints. They impose a general obligation on the complainant not to file false or malicious complaint and interfere with the normal operation of bidding activities.[85] A violation of such obligations may be subject to administrative penalties such as warnings and fine.[86]

15.6.2 GPL: Emergence of a Challenge System

15.6.2.1 Introduction

The GPL is distinctive in establishing a bid challenge and complaint system. Under this system, the aggrieved bidders may make enquires (*xun wen*) when they consider the procurement irregular (Article 51). A supplier who believes its legitimate interests have been infringed may file a challenge (*zhi yi*) to the procuring entity for redress (Article 52). When the supplier who initiates the challenge is not satisfied with the reply concerning its challenge from the procuring entity or there is simply no timely reply, the supplier may submit a complaint (*tou su*) to the competent government finance department within 15 working days of the expiry of the challenge period (Article 55). The competent financial department then acts as an administrative adjudicator to settle the dispute between the procuring entity and the complainant (Article 56) through an administrative decision.

If the complainant supplier is still not satisfied with the administrative decision or the decision is not made in a timely manner, it has the right to apply for administrative review of the decision or to file an administrative suit to the courts (Article 58).

15.6.2.1.1 Eligible Complainants

Under the GPL, the complainant can arguably be any supplier who considers its legitimate rights infringed due to the procurement documents, process, or award decision (Article 52). The GP Complaint Measure (see Note 21) provides a narrower definition limiting the possibility to complain to suppliers who have participated in the procurement involved (Article 10).

Other articles provide for a detailed list of unlawful conducts that are subject to administrative or even criminal penalties (Articles 71, 72, and 73) and this list is supplemented by the bidding measure. An aggrieved supplier may be able to bring a challenge to any of the unlawful conducts listed. For example, a supplier may file a challenge to the procuring entity or a complaint to the finance department claiming the loss of contract opportunity if the open bidding procedure is circumvented.

15.6.2.1.2 Scope of Permissible Complaints

The GPL contains a general provision that misconduct of procurement relating to the procurement document, process, or award decision (Article 52) may be challenged by the aggrieved supplier. However, this provision is so broad that it needs to be interpreted and tested. One test can be found in Articles 71 and 72, which provide a list of misconducts that are subject to administrative or criminal penalties, supplemented again by the GP Complaint Measures.[87] In principle, all the conducts listed in these articles can be challenged by the aggrieved supplier.

Another test can be found in Article 73 of the GPL (and is repeated in Article 71 of the Bidding Measure and Article 19 of the GP Complaint Measures), which provides that those listed unlawful conducts shall be dealt with either through cancellation of the procurement, annulment of the contract or damages, if they are found to have affected or might have affected the outcome of the procurement. Therefore, the aggrieved supplier may challenge at minimum those listed conducts that directly affect or have directly affected the outcome of the procurement.

Still another test can be found in Article 10 of the GP Complaint Measures, which requires the complainant to be a supplier "involved in the procurement activities." The wording is slightly problematic as it excludes suppliers who have never learned of the procurement due to unpublicized tender information.

15.6.2.1.3 Available Remedies

The GPL and relevant implementing rules provide administrative and criminal penalties for the conducts listed in Articles 71 and 72 of the implementing rules. These include an order of correction within a time limit, warnings, fines, criminal liability, confiscation of unlawful gains, etc, as the case may be. In addition, the GPL and the BM also prescribe remedies to the procurement process when the listed conducts are found to have or might have affected the outcome of the procurement based on three circumstances (Article 71 BM):

1. When the successful tender has not been decided, terminate the procurement activity.[88]
2. When the successful tender has been decided but the contract not yet performed, annul the contract and choose the successful tender from among other qualified candidates.[89]

3. When the contract has been performed and the purchaser or supplier suffers loss, the liable party shall pay compensation to the other party.

The GP Complaint Measures (Article 19) takes a different approach. First, the circumstances that the different remedies are accorded to are based on the general definition of the challengeable conducts found in Article 52 of the GPL, not on the approach of listed conduct adopted in both the GPL (Articles 71 and 72) and the BM (Articles 68 and 69). For example, it is provided in Article 19 of the GP Complaint Measures that when finance departments find that the bidding documents and procurement process (might) have affected the outcome of the procurement, or that the decision process of the successful tender was unlawful, it should handle the case according to the particular circumstances provided. It is also noteworthy that the implementing article makes it clear that unlawful conduct in the award decision process does have an effect on the outcome of the procurement and therefore should be handled accordingly.

Second, the various circumstances and their corresponding remedies in the GP Complaint Measures differ from those found in the primary law and the BM:

1. When the contract has not been signed, declare the whole or certain parts of the procurement unlawful, as the case may be, and order reopening of the procurement.
2. When the contract has been signed but not yet performed, annul the contract and order reopening of the procurement.
3. When the contract has been performed, declare the procurement unlawful and when the unlawful conduct of procurement has incurred loss to the procuring entity or the complainant, the liable party shall pay compensation for such loss.

What is striking is that the remedy available for circumstance 2 is different from that provided in the primary law, which annuls the contract but strangely seeks to preserve the whole procurement process. The new provision in the implementing rule may be well founded but the consequences of its conflict with the primary law remains to be seen since the GP Complaint Measures is a regulation issued by MOF for implementing the GPL and only secondary to the GPL which is passed by the NPC.

Third, the GP Complaint Measures separately provides for the remedies available for the case of preferential and discriminatory provisions in the procurement document (Article 18), which states that "when the financial department after review finds that the preferential and discriminatory provisions contained in the procurement document have incurred or might have incurred damage to the complainant or other suppliers concerned, it shall remedy the procurement process in the following three ways, as the case may be:"

1. When the procurement has not been completed, order revision of the procurement document and conduct the procurement based on the revised procurement document.[90]
2. When the procurement has been completed but contract not yet signed, declare the procurement unlawful, and order reopening of the procurement.
3. When the procurement has been completed and contract signed, declare the procurement unlawful, and the respondent (presumably the procuring entity) shall pay compensation to the complainant for the incurred loss.

First, it is not clear why there is a need for such a provision at all in the GP Complaint Measures, because the issue is covered in both the primary law and the BM, and remedies are also available. Second, the remedies provided in the GP Complaint Measures are not consistent with either the primary law or its corresponding provision (Article 19 specifying the circumstances and the remedies available). Especially noteworthy is the provision in 3 above that seems to honor the contract even when the contract has not been performed, which is a big deviation from the primary law, the BM, and its corresponding provisions in the GP Complaint Measures. This article is either an example of poor drafting,[91] or if it is justified for application in particular cases, it must not be read as falling under Article 73 of the GPL, but only as dealing with preferential or discriminatory cases without the effect of affecting the outcome of the procurement. It is much more likely that the former is the case.

One outstanding feature of the GPL is its adoption of an interim measure.[92] The GPL provides that the supervising department may notify the procuring entity at its own discretion to suspend the procurement pending the review. While using its discretion, the law requires the administrative review department to judge the merits of the complaint and other particularities and decide whether to grant this interim relief. Though the law does not specify these particularities, it could be argued that they include urgency of the procurement, public interest, and the interests of other bidders. The GP Complaint Measures repeats the provision in the primary law and further requires that the respondent, upon the receipt of the notice, should suspend the procurement instantly and shall not proceed with the procurement before the statutory period for suspension expires or the financial department issues the notice to resume (Article 22 of the GP Complaint Measures).

15.6.2.2 Procedural Issues

The GP Complaint Measures provides detailed rules governing the handling of complaints. When the financial department concerned receives the complaint, it shall conduct a preliminary review on the admissibility and jurisdiction of the complaint to decide whether it accepts the complaint or not according to the conditions laid out in Article 11. If it decides to accept the complaint, the financial department shall send copies of the complaint to the respondent (the procuring entity) and other suppliers involved within the following three working days (Article 12). The respondent and other suppliers involved are required to submit written explanations and relevant supporting documents within five working days (Article 13).

As a principle, the finance departments only review the records and documents. However, it may initiate an investigation to collect evidence or summon the parties involved to cross-examine the evidence when necessary (Article 14). Unless the complaint is withdrawn or dismissed, the finance department shall make a decision within 30 working days after it accepts the complaint (Article 56 of the GPL) and notifies all parties involved (Article 20). The decision shall be in written form with a printed seal and contain the decision itself, the supporting evidence and legal basis, a notice to the complainant of his right to a second review by a higher administrative authority, and his right to suit (Article 21). The GP Complaint Measures also requires the finance departments to publish the result of complaint cases handled (Article 23). GP Complaint Measures also contains an article addressing the concerns of false or malicious complaints. The supplier who submits false or malicious complaint would be blacklisted and subject to administrative penalties (Article 26).

15.7 Institutional Framework

15.7.1 NDRC and the BL

As is discussed earlier, the BL maintains the status quo, which leaves the State Council to provide for detailed rules concerning the allocation of authority. The State Council Opinions[93] seems to be based on a compromise between the NDRC and other ministries. On the one hand, it recognizes the key role played by the NDRC in formulating bidding policy and, on the other hand, it allows line ministries to supervise bidding activities in line with their administrative functions. Under the Opinions, NDRC is the delegated authority to guide and supervise key national works (for instance the Three Gorges Dam) procurement, play a leading role in preparing overall policy, implementing regulations, and determine the scope of coverage, thresholds, and exemptions for compulsory bidding projects, though this must be done in consultation with relevant ministries and approved by the State Council. NDRC also designates official media to publish bid notices. Other agencies are in turn allowed to formulate specific implementing measures in accordance with the BL and other relevant regulations and policies.

A later implementing regulation endorsed NDRC's supervisory role in relation to its traditional function of approval for construction projects. Under this regulation, NDRC is responsible for determining the bidding mode (whether to conduct the bidding itself or through a bidding agent) and for decisions relating to the scope of compulsory bidding projects, after which the line ministry will take over the task of supervision. Throughout the project, NDRC retains overall authority and reserves the right to suspend execution of the project and withhold funding as the case may be.

15.7.2 MOF and the GPL

15.7.2.1 Separation of Supervision from Procurement Functions

To separate supervision and procurement functions, the GPL makes it clear that regulatory agencies, i.e. MOF at central level,[94] shall not set up a centralized procurement agency or be involved in procurement activities (Article 60). This requirement is reiterated in a State Council notice implementing the GPL at central level,[95] which establishes the principle of "reasonable separation of functions and mutual balance" (*he li fen gong, hu xiang zhi heng*), which is similar to the Western notion of separation of powers and checks and balances),[96] for the relationships between the regulatory department and the CPA.

However, the current wording in the primary legislation concerning the allocation of powers leaves substantial space for interpretation. The GPL charges "finance departments at all levels with supervising government procurement and conduct their duties in accordance with law," while also providing that "other departments concerned at various levels shall fulfil their duties of supervision regarding government procurement."[97] Hence, although the GPL establishes the finance departments as the competent regulatory authority, it does not encroach upon the authority of other departments regarding government procurement, especially those whose authority was conferred by the BL.[98]

The result is that each regulator has interpreted the law in its own favor. Therefore, it is advisable that the lines of authority in the two laws are more precisely delineated. The implementation plan seems to be following such a more precise approach defining the scope of the duties for MOF and reiterating the regulatory power already conferred on the ministries sponsoring the BL.

15.7.2.2 Regulatory Power of the Finance Departments

There is a general provision in the GPL establishing the MOF and finance departments as the competent authorities to regulate government procurement activity (Article 13). However, the case is not as clear-cut as it may seem. The term "competent regulatory authorities" should be checked against the various substantive provisions in both the GPL and other regulations that define the newly emerging authorities, especially the implementation plan. To summarize, the regulatory duties conferred upon the financial departments include the following:

1. Government procurement policy and rules. The GPL does not confer any authority on the financial departments to draft new government procurement policy and rules. The GPL makes it clear in Article 87 that "the specific steps and measures to implement this law

shall be provided by the State Council." Therefore unless authorized by the State Council, MOF does not have the power to issue implementing rules on government procurement. However, such authorization can be found in a legal document approved by the State Council implementation plan regarding the functions of MOF on government procurement, though the authorization is only limited to the rules regarding government procurement by central government agencies.[99] It is also noteworthy that the authorities over government procurement activities through bidding are placed with the other authorities by another State Council Opinions, which was confirmed in the State Council implementation plan.

2. Preparation of government procurement plan. This is not provided by the GPL but by the implementation plan.
3. Approval of departmental budgets in accordance with the relevant authority and procedures (Article 33 of GPL).
4. Preparation of the CPCatalogue and the thresholds (for coverage of the GPL and application of open bidding), and submitting to the State Council for the approval.[100]
5. Publication of information.[101]
6. Approval of new procurement methods by MOF (Article 26).
7. Approval of procurement methods and procedures other than open bidding.
8. Supervision of procurement activities and operation of the CPAs. The measures provided in the GPL for such supervision include checks on the activities of the CPAs (Articles 59 and 65), specifying the qualifications of government procurement professionals in the CPAs (Article 62), review of the CPA's procurement prices and effectiveness of cost-saving, reviewing service quality and supplier reputation, and regular publication of such reviews (Article 66). In addition, the implementation plan extend MOF's function of qualification of procurement professionals to training of government procurement managers.
9. Regulating contracts. MOF is delegated the authority to provide for the compulsory articles to be included the government procurement contracts in consultation with other relevant departments (Article 45).
10. Handling bid complaint and review (Articles 55–58).
11. Others functions. In addition to those provided for in the GPL, the financial departments are also conferred with other functions including the management of appropriation of fund for centralized purchase, registration of the bidding agencies, statistics and publicity of government procurement information, etc.[102]

15.7.2.3 Interministerial Coordination Mechanism

Implementation of parallel procurement systems requires great coordination efforts. In 2005, the NDRC released Measures[103] establishing such a coordination mechanism. The NDRC-led mechanism is comprised of 11 relevant authorities that either play a direct administrative role in bidding supervision or a general role of administrative supervision or regulatory affairs. Interministerial conferences are regularly held and attended by director-general level representatives from each ministry, supported by a working-level group of coordinators representing each ministry and an office, which deals with the daily operation of the mechanism. Consensus is reached based on the principle of "collective consultation and unanimity" of the ministries and codified in the form of meeting minutes. The mandate of the mechanism is mainly to

1. Analyze the development of national bidding markets and review the implementation of the BL, administrative regulations, and ministerial provisions, and discuss work plans and strategies involving multi-sector bidding activities
2. Resolve contradictions and inconsistencies over administrative supervision of bidding activities
3. Exchange of information regarding bidding
4. Strengthen consistency among relevant departments in formulating bidding regulations and model documents
5. Strengthen communication among relevant departments and local governments in handling bid complaints and enforcement

The mechanism is encouraging and its functioning seems effective as far as BL-related activity is concerned. However, it seems to be of little help in harmonizing inconsistencies between the parallel development of the GPL and the BL, since the Measure clearly excludes from the mandate any bidding activities relating to procurement of goods and services (Article 4). MOF is part of the mechanism, but plays a very passive role.

15.7.3 Centralized Purchasing Function

15.7.3.1 Commercial Bidding Agencies under the BL

Under the BL, a procuring entity may choose to conduct the procurement itself or authorize a bidding agency to conduct the proposed procurement. However, if a procuring entity cannot demonstrate that it has sufficient skills to conduct the procurement, it can be obliged to engage a commercial bidding agency. There is, however, little regulation regarding the appointment of these bidding agencies. In reality, a large amount of procurement is outsourced and there is heavy reliance on the use of commercial bidding agencies to conduct procurement. However, a centralized in-house procurement function is being developed in the form of the Project Agent System (see Section 15.2.2.3.2).

15.7.3.2 Purchasing Functions under the GPL

When procurement reform was initiated, a centralized procurement system was preferred and as a part of common practice, a CPCatalogue was established to define the scope of centralized procurement. The GPL confirms this practice. It requires that government procurement be conducted in a combination of centralized and decentralized fashion and the scope of centralized procurement be defined by the CPCatalogue established by central and provincial government, respectively.[104] When the procurement is covered by the CPCatalogue, a purchaser must engage a central procurement agency, a nonprofit making public institution specially set up to conduct the centralized procurement defined by the CPCatalogue.[105] The law also provides that governments above the provincial level have the freedom to establish a central agency at their own will,[106] but such agencies may not be established by the supervisory authority of government procurement,[107] the finance department. This reflects concern among legislators of a conflict of interest in the event that the supervisory authority gets involved in the procurement process.

15.8 Conclusion

Like in many other jurisdictions, China has been experimenting GP reforms for the past decades. The reforms are fundamental, comprehensive, and consecutive but may not be consistent with each other. As China's GP framework is relatively young, some teething problems can be expected in implementation. Central laws are not always coherent and consistently applied and the existing remedies framework appears to have fallen short of addressing the growing number of complaints of economic operators. In many cases, this may be attributed to lack of procurement skills and facilities among procuring entities; in other cases to outright corruption.

On the policy level, coverage is relatively limited, both in terms of goods and services and entities covered. The extent of GP reaches far beyond these items, and if the benefits of effective GP are to be maximized, the scope of the current legislation should be broadened significantly.

More important, however, is the lack of an overall conceptual framework and the need for strong leadership on GP policy. Developing a strategy that integrates the role of GP and outlines its goals within the wider reform efforts of the Chinese government is crucial in this regard. Moreover, while various government agencies have made efforts to develop GP policy, a lack of effective coordination has resulted in fragmentation of the legislative and regulatory framework, as well as the emergence of separate regulators whose competences are not clearly delineated. The new arrangements for the coordination of policy and practice will therefore be critical.

It is therefore submitted that China will need to develop a clear policy objective that describes the role of GP in China's economic development and reform, is endorsed by the highest levels of government, and is applicable at all levels. China will also need to have one or more competent authorities with powers to coordinate national policy on government procurement, promote best practice, lead on consolidating relevant legislation, arrange for or undertake its enforcement. Procurement practice should continue to be devolved to the ministries, regional and local government accountable for expenditure, but within national policy and with an option to take advantage of central purchasing skills and facilities. Moreover, there is also a pressing need for a more comprehensive and coherent legal framework. The currently proposed State Council secondary legislations may provide a good opportunity toward this goal. But in the long run, the reform of the primary laws is a must. Future reforms also need to address the issue of modernizing procurement techniques, for example, to introduce more flexibility for the award of complex contracts and to facilitate the use of electronic means of communication and procurement systems.

Notes

1. The author is professor of law and codirector of government procurement and public construction at the Central University of Finance and Economics and senior researcher at School of Government Peking University. The author is indebted to the invaluable comments by John Collins and Peter Trepte. All errors are mine.
2. For a brief review of the development, see Cao Fuguo, China's government procurement regulation: From the BL to the GPL, in Sue Arrowsmith and Martin Tybus (eds.), *Public Procurement: Global Revolution*, Kluwer Law International, 2003.
3. For example, new secondary State Council Regulations for the GPL and for the BL are currently being undertaken by the MOF the NDRC, respectively; a new regulatory framework governing the procurement of privately financed infrastructure and utilities is emerging in China (see general, Cao Fuguo, Regulating procurement of privately financed infrastructure in China: A review of current regulations and the emerging regulatory issues, *Public Procurement Law Review*, 3, 2007). On the international level, China committed to starting negotiations for joining the World Trade Organization's (WTO) Government Procurement Agreement (GPA) by December 2007. (See general, Cao Fuguo *China development: A critical review of the rules implementing the Chinese Government Procurement Law and China's new initiative for GPA, Public Procurement Law Review*, 4, 2006 and Liuzzi, John. Opening up the Chinese Government Procurement Market. International Trade Update, May 2006. Available at http://www.ita.doc.gov/press/publications/newsletters/ita_0506/gpa_0506.asp).

4. For a brief review of the evolution of the bidding system in China, see Cao Fuguo, *China's government procurement regulation: From the Bidding Law to the Government Procurement Law*, in Sue Arrowsmith and Martin Tybus (eds.), *Public Procurement: Global Revolution*, Kluwer Law International, 2003.
5. The BL legislation program was initiated by the eighth NPC in June 1994 and its preparation allocated to the (then) State Planning Commission (later State Planning and Development Commission [SDPC] and later NDRC). In 1999, the BL was enacted and took effect on January 1, 2001.
6. See discussion in Section 15.4.1.
7. In Article 43 of the BL of China it provides that "Before the determination of the winning bidder, the procuring entity shall not undertake negotiation with the bidders on such substantive contents of the bid as bid price, bid solution etc." In Article 46, it provides, among others, that "the procuring entity shall not conclude any other agreement contrary to the substantive content of the contract," which could be understood that no substantive negotiation on the award is made.
8. These include the State Council Provision on the Division of Supervision Responsibility among Ministries (2000), Temporary Provision on Thresholds of Compulsory Coverage (2000) by SDPC Order No. 3, Temporary Provision on Publish of Bidding Notice (2000) by SDPC Order No. 4, Temporary Provision on Self-Conducting Bidding Business (2000) by SDPC Order No. 5, and the Temporary Provision on the Bid Evaluation Committee and Method of Evaluation (2001) jointly issued by seven ministries. The Measure on Handling the Complaints of Bidding for Construction Projects by NDRC, Ministry of Construction, Ministry of Railway, Ministry of Communications, Ministry of Information Industry, Ministry of Water Resource, and General Administration of Civil Aviation, issued and effective on August 1, 2004.
9. Notice on Furthering Implementation of BL by SDPC (2001), Circular on the Draft of Implementation Rules of the BL by Local Government (2001) by SDPC.
10. Temporary Provision on the Publish of Bidding Notice by SDPC Order No. 4 (2000).
11. *China Finance & Economy* newspaper, April 20, 1998.
12. Survey of government Procurement in 2000, in the third circular of the Department of Treasury, April 20, 2000.
13. These include the Provisional Measures on Government Procurement Management (1999), the Provisional Measures on Supervision of Government Procurement Contract (1999) and the Provisional Measures on Bidding Management in Government Procurement (1999), the Management Measures on the Advertisement of Government Procurement Notice (2000), the Provisional Measures on the Operational Procedure of Government Procurement (2000), and the Provisional Measures on the Management of Direct Appropriation of Government Procurement Fund (2000).
14. This model has firstly been embodied in the failed State Council Regulation and then elaborated in a booklet edited by senior officials of MOF. This booklet was published and widely circulated as a propaganda to promote the reform. J. Lou (ed.), *Government Procurement*, China Finance & Economics Press, 1998.
15. Survey of government Procurement in 2000, in the third circular of the Department of Treasury, April 20, 2000.
16. Ibid.
17. This program was initiated in March 1999 by NPC and was authorized to its Financial & Economy Committee for preparation. In April 9, 1999, the drafting group was set up including senior officers of the committee, senior officials from government departments, and a few academics.
18. Article 87 of the GPL provides that "Detailed procedures and measures for the implementation of this law shall be promulgated by the State Council."
19. Notice of the State Council Office on Issuing the Implementation Plan to Completely Promote the Government Procurement System across the Central State Organs, No. 53 (2002) of the State Council Office.
20. The Measure on the Administration of the Publication of Government Procurement Information, MOF Order No. 19 of MOF, published on August 21, 2004, effective on September 11, 2004.

(Hereafter referred to as the Publicity Measure); The Measure on the Administration of Tendering in Government Procurement of Goods and Services, MOF Order No. 18, published on August 21, 2004, effective on September 11, 2004. (Hereafter referred to as the Tendering Measure.) The Measure for Handling the Complaints of Government Procurement Suppliers, MOF Order No. 20, published on August 21, 2004, effective on September 11, 2004. (Hereafter referred to as the GP Complaint Measures.) The Measure on Qualification of Government Procurement Agent Organization, MOF Order No. 31, published on December 28, 2005, effective on March 1, 2006. (Hereafter referred to as the Qualification Measure.)

21. The Temporary Provision on the Implementation of Project Legal Person Responsible System in Construction Projects (April 1996) by SDPC. Article 2: Business-featured medium to large-scale infrastructure construction projects of SOE must set up a PLP in construction phase. Article 3: Implement Project Legal Person Responsible System. The PLP should take full responsibility in the whole process of project design, financing, construction, producing, loan paying off, and capital increment.
22. The Temporary Provision on the Implementation of Project Legal Person Responsible System in Construction Projects (April 1996) by SDPC. Article 2: According to the Company Law, the PLP could build limited liability company (including only state-owned corporation) and incorporated company.
23. The Temporary Provision on the Implementation of Project Legal Person Responsible System in Construction Projects (January 04, 2000) by State Administration of Radio Film and Television (SARFT). Article 5: In the construction projects of government-sponsored institutions, which are directly subordinate to SARFT, the institution legal person is the PLP.
24. Article 3: The Temporary Provision on Implementing Bidding in National Medium to Large-Scale Infrastructure Construction Projects (August 18, 1997) by SDPC, has been announced invalidation by the List of Abolished Bidding Regulations and Regulatory Documents issued by NDRC on August 30, 2004.
25. The Measure on the Management of Bidding for Olympic Game Construction Project Legal Person (July 28, 2002) by Committee on Organization of the 29th Olympic Game.
26. The Notice on Transmitting the Regulation Trial of the Bidding Process for Beijing Government Project Legal Person (Beijing Municipal Government Office 42/2002) by Beijing Municipal Government Office. Article 2: this regulation is applicable in the bidding of following projects: A. The infrastructure construction project with a concession. B. The construction project of arena and other relevant facilities for 2008 Olympic Game. C. Other projects decided by Beijing Municipal Government.
27. The Notice on the Publish of the Management Measure of Bidding for Business-Featured Road Construction Project Legal Person in Guangzhou (August 10, 2005) by Guangzhou Municipal Government.

    Article 2: this measure is applicable in all the biddings for business-featured road construction PLP in Guangzhou, exclusive of the biddings directly organized by the state or province government; Article 3: the investors of business-featured road construction projects must be selected by bidding system. After approving the construction project, the investment body should clarify the road corporation legal person.

    The Notice on the Publish of the Implementation Measure of Bidding for Economic House Construction Project Legal Person in Zhengzhou (March 27, 2006) by Zhengzhou Municipal Government.
28. For example, the Agency for Works Affairs of Shenzhen Government, and the Construction Center for nonprofit government works of Hebei Province.
29. The Decision of State Council for Investment System Reform requires local governments to implement the PAS in municipal projects as soon as possible.
30. For example, the Notice on Publishing the Opinions on Promoting and Guiding Private Investment, issued by the then National Planning Commission on December 11, 2001. Some Opinions on Some Policy Measure to Increase the Development of Service Sectors in the 15th Five Year Period, issued by the then National Planning Commission in January 2002; Opinion on Promoting the Marketisation of Urban Public Utilities, issued by Ministry of Construction on December 27, 2003; Measures on Urban Public Utilities Concession, issued by MOC in 2004; State Council Decision Regarding the

Investment System Reform, issued by the State Council in July 2004; the Opinions on Encouraging, Supporting and Guiding the Development of Non-state Sector Economies, issued by State Council in 2005.

31. See Cao Fuguo, The Emerging Legal Framework of Private Finance in Infrastructure in China: A Preliminary Review of the Beijing Concession Regulation, in 2006 15 P.P.L.R.
32. See Cao Fuguo, Regulating procurement of privately-financed infrastructure in China: a review of the recent legislative initiatives and the emerging regulatory framework, paper firstly presented at the International Conference of Public Procurement Global Revolution III, June, 2006, Nottingham University and later published in *Public Procurement Law Review*, 3, 2007.
33. For example, the award criteria, based on set base prices, undermined the objectives of economy and effectiveness. Even though the procurer was able to negotiate with the successful bidder before conclusion of the contract (a general practice at the time), this deviated from the principle of using market-based bidding mechanisms and increased the opportunity for corruption.
34. See Temporary Provisions on Domestic Bidding Management in Applying for Import of Mechanical and Electrical Equipment (1986) by the Office of State Economic and Trade (1986). See also comment by Tian Jingbin, Public procurement in China: The way forward, *Public Procurement Law Review* 10, 208, 2001.
35. For the excluded procurement, see general discussion in Section 15.4.1.4.
36. A test of this policy is found in the "buy Microsoft" case in Beijing Municipality at the turn of 2004. Following Shanghai and Tianjin, Beijing Municipal Government awarded a large contract to Microsoft Company. The case caused an outcry from domestic suppliers, some outspoken senior government officers, academics, and the general public for the alleged violation of not only the open bidding procedure but also the "buy national" provision in the GPL as well. The domestic pressure to enact an implementing rule on software procurement is getting increasingly high. However, the pressure from the U.S. government to suspend the implementing rules is also high and ever increasing. The proposed implementing rule has not yet been issued at the time of writing.
37. A domestically registered wholly foreign-owned enterprise is a domestic supplier for the purpose of the Chinese law.
38. Notice from the MOF and the NDRC on the issuance of Implementation of Government Energy Conservation Procurement, *Treasury* [*2004*] 185, December 17, 2004.
39. In 2004, the Chinese government issued a regulation imposing WAPI as the national WLAN standard, effectively excluding all WLAN products supporting Wi-Fi, the internationally recognized WLAN standard, from the Chinese domestic market. Following pressure by foreign companies and governments, the measure was temporarily shelved and reappeared in 2006, applying only to government procurement.
40. State Council Opinions on Some Policies to Implement the National Medium and Long Term Outline for the Development and Planning of Science and Technology (2006–2020), No. 6 of the State Council Office (2006).
41. Some opinions on Promoting Independent Innovation through Government Procurement, No. 47 of Treasury (2006), June 13, 2006.
42. Simply put, the BL was the SPC's brainchild while the GPL was a creation of the MOF.
43. The Regulation on Bidding Scope and Scale Standards of Construction Project (May 1, 2000) by SDPC.
44. Article 4 of the Regulation on Bidding Scope and Scale Standards of Construction Project (May 1, 2000) by SDPC.
45. Article 5, Ibid.
46. Article 7, Ibid.
47. Research on the Feasibility of Construction Projects: Temporary Provision on Adding Bidding Contents and Approving Bidding Issues by SDPC extends the exception scope of BL, which includes the project with special confidential requirements; the construction project applying specific patents or techniques in reconnaissance and design phase, or the project with special requirements in architectural

sculpt; the project with less than three suppliers that can not generate effective competition; the project unsuitable for bidding due to other reasons.

48. Article 2 of the GPL.
49. The catalogue is a practical mechanism to strike a balance between the lack of capacity in financial departments to conduct procurement on one hand, and the ambition to have more regulated procurement on the other.
50. One should be careful not to be misled by the official government procurement figures, which understate the real scale of government procurement in China.
51. The employment of the two regulatory tools, the catalogue and the thresholds, to define the concept of government procurement under the GPL is unique in the Chinese GPL. The earlier understanding of the concept of government procurement (a synonym of centralized procurement) lingers on and fits in well with the new conception of the GPL. It also seems to reflect a compromise between a narrow scope of regulation reflected in the catalog system and a more ambitious effort to regulate wider government procurement.
52. Under the GPL, two kinds of centralized purchasing mechanisms are employed. One is the Central State Organ Centralized Purchasing Agency (CPA), which conducts all centralized procurement of a general nature at the central level. However, if the procurement is of a special nature associated with the function of a department, the department can also establish their own centralized purchasing agency. Therefore, one main function of the catalogue is to distinguish between procurement of a general and special nature.
53. The Notice on the Publish of Governmental Procurement List and Standards of Central Government Budgetary Unit (14/2006) by State Council Office.
54. Ibid.
55. The Centralized Government Procurement Catalogue and Threshold of Liaoning Province in 2003, issued by the Office of Liaoning Provincial Government; The Centralized Government Procurement Catalogue and Threshold of Shanghai Municipality in 2006, issued by the financial departments of Shanghai Municipality.
56. Notice on the Implementation Issues of Government Procurement by Central Government Unit, No. 56 [2003], issued by MOF. According to Article 3 of the Implementation Issues of Government Procurement by Central Government Unit issued by MOF on September 1, 2004, financial resource includes budgetary capital, governmental capital, extra-budgetary capital, and self-financed capital by central government unit.
57. The Centralized Government Procurement Catalogue and Threshold of Tianjin Municipality in 2005–2006, issued by the financial departments of Shanghai Municipality.
58. Notice on the Implementation Issues of Government Procurement by Central Government Unit, No. 56 [2003], issued by MOF.
59. The Implementing Measure on International Tendering of Imported Machinery and Electrical Equipment, No. 13 of MOFCOM Order, published on November 1, 2004 and effective on December 1, 2004.
60. See Article 5 in the Temporary Provisions on Supplementing Bidding Related Issues to the Feasibility Report of Works Construction Project (June 18, 2001) by SDPC. See discussion in Section 15.4.1.4.
61. This procedure allows flexibility in the first stage of bidding while formal bidding is required in the second stage, and may serve as a good substitute for the less structured procedure that involves simple negotiations.
62. Article 26 of the GPL of PRC.
63. Articles 27, 29, 30, 31, and 32 of the GPL of PRC.
64. Section 15.2.2.2, see also Note 21.
65. The term of bidding activities arguably refers only to open bidding and selective bidding specified by the BL.
66. The Measure on Implementation of International Bidding of Machinery and Electronic Equipment, Ministry of Commerce order No. 13, 2004.

67. For example, Article 20 of UNCITRAL Model Law on Procurement of Goods, Construction, and Services.
68. Article 30 of the UNCITRAL Model Law provides an example of such circumstances: (a) when it is necessary to afford suppliers or contractors reasonable time to take the clarification or modification made by the procuring entity, or the minutes of the meeting of suppliers or contractors, into account in their tenders; or (b) if it is not possible for one or more suppliers or contractors to submit their tenders by the deadline owing to any circumstance beyond their control.
69. A comparable article can be found in Section 1(a) of Article 30 of EC Directive on Public contract and in Article 19(1)(d) of the UNCITRAL Model Law on government procurement. It is noteworthy that under the Model Law, insufficient bids or rejection of all bids do not necessarily justify the use of competitive negotiation. A competitive negotiation procedure is only justified when no or an insufficient number of bids are received "and when, in the judgment of the procuring entity, engaging in new bidding proceedings would be unlikely to result in a procurement contract." The wording of Subparagraph (1) of Article 30 of the GPL, which using the term or rather than and seems to be the result of poor drafting.
70. For Section (ii) of GPL Article 30 see Section 1(c) of Article 30 of EC Directive on Public contract and in Article 19(1)(a) of the UNCITRAL Model Law on government procurement. For Section (iii), see Article 19(2)(a) of the UNCITRAL Model Law on government procurement. See Section 1(b) of EC Directive on Public contract for GPL Section (iv).
71. Provisional Measure on Government Procurement of Computer through Supply Agreement of Nanjing Municipality.
72. Supply agreements were originally used and operated by MOF at central level. With the enactment of the GPL, the operation of the arrangement was shifted to the centralized purchasing agency (CPA) as it is considered a procurement activity, which the GPL prohibits MOF from being involved in. Designated spot procurement can be originally found in the Management Measure for Government Procurement in Shanghai Municipality (1999). Some procuring entities run both supply agreements and the designated spot procurement with the former arrangement mainly for procurement of goods, while the latter for certain services. Recognizing that they are basically the same arrangement, some regulators simply combined the two terms and coined a new words for them, the designated spot procurement through agreement. For example, it is provided that designated spot procurement through agreement refers to such an arrangement where designated suppliers and the product brand, product specification and type, price, duration for supply, and service commitments to be provided by the suppliers are decided through open bidding and laid out in an agreement, and purchasers can discretionally choose the supplier and its products within the valid period for supply. See for instance the Provisional Measure on the Administration of the Designated Spot Supply Agreement for Fujian Provincial Government.
73. The Electronic Signature Law of the People's Republic of China (E-Signature Law) issued by the Standing Committee of the tenth NPC, August 28, 2004, effective April 1, 2005.
74. Provisional Measure on the Administration of Government Procurement through Bidding on Internet of Nanjing Municipality Guangxi Autonomous Region, issued on June 18, 1999.
75. Article 2 of Provisional Measure on the Administration of Government Procurement through Bidding on Internet of Nanjing Municipality Guangxi Autonomous Region, issued on June 18, 1999.
76. For example, Provisional Measure on the Administration of Government Procurement through Bidding on Internet of Zhejiang Provincial Government, effective on September 1, 2000; Provisional Measure on the Administration of Government Procurement through Bidding on Internet of Hefei Municipality, effective on March 13, 2001; Provisional Measure on the Administration of Government Procurement through Bidding on Internet of Zhuhai Municipality, effective on June 27, 2002; Provisional Measure on the Administration of Internet-based Government Procurement of Shenzhen Municipality, effective on October 15, 2003; Provisional Measure on the Administration of Government Procurement through Bidding on Internet of Shanghai Municipality, effective in December, 2004.

77. The Measure on Handling the Complaints of Bidding for Construction Projects by NDRC, Ministry of Construction, Ministry of Railway, Ministry of Communications, Ministry of Information Industry, Ministry of Water Resource, and General Administration of Civil Aviation, issued and effective on August 1, 2004. (Hereafter referred to as Bid Complaint Measure.)
78. The Notice on the Publish of the Opinions on Responsibility Division of Administrative Supervision on Bidding Activities by Relevant Departments in State Council (34/2000) by State Council Office.
79. Article 64 of the BL of China.
80. Under the BL and applicable contract law, the award decision does not constitute the conclusion of a contract. To be concluded, a contract has to be singed by both parties within 30 days after the award notice is issued.
81. Article 9.
82. Article 11.
83. Article 14.
84. Article 16.
85. Article 8.
86. Article 26.
87. This includes situations where (i) open bidding is avoided through splitting of the contract or other means (Article 71 of GPL and Article 68 of the Bidding Measure); (ii) the procurement standard is presumptuously raised (Article 71 of GPL); (iii) government procurement business is authorized to ineligible government procurement agent organizations (Article 71 of GPL); (iv) suppliers are treated discriminatorily based on unreasonable terms (Article 71 of GPL) and (is further added in Article 68 of the Bidding Measure) suppliers are restricted or excluded based on unreasonable requirements; (v) the bidding document designates specified supplier or contains other content that is preferential to or exclusive of potential suppliers; (vi) negotiation is conducted with bidders in the bidding process (Article 71 of GPL); (vii) the contract is not signed based on the bidding documents and the tender, or a separate agreement is signed with the successful bidder that deviates from the substantive content of the contract (Article 68 of the Bidding Measure); (viii) the procuring entity refuses to sign the contract with the successful bidder after the issuance of the successful tender notice (Article 71 of the GPL) unreasonably (added in Article 68 of the Bidding Measure); (ix) the procuring entity maliciously colludes with supplier or procurement agency (Article 72 of GPL and Article 69 of the Bidding Measure); (x) the procuring entity accepts bribes or other illegitimate interests (Article 72 of GPL and Article 69 of the Bidding Measure); (xi) the procuring entity discloses the base price (Article of GPL) or the name and number of the potential bidder who buys the bidding document or other information which could prejudice fair competition before the opening of tender (added in Article 69 of the Bidding Measure); (xii) compulsory information is not published on the media designated by the financial departments (Article 68 of the Bidding Measure) or the published bidding information restrict or excludes potential suppliers based on unreasonable terms, or the published information is false (Publicity Measure); (xiii) the formation of the evaluation committee is not in conformity with the Bidding Measure (Article 68 of the Bidding Measure); successful bidder is not chosen based on the recommended list of candidates and without justification, or successful bidder is chosen from outside of the recommended list of candidates (Article 68 of the Bidding Measure); (xiv) copies of the authorization agreement for tendering, bidding document, tender evaluation report, procurement contract are not filed with the financial departments (Article 68 of the Bidding Measure); (xv) the procuring entity refuses to accept supervision and checks implemented according to law (Article 71 of GPL and Article 68 of the Bidding Measure) or presents false information in the process of supervision and checks implemented according to law. (Article 72 of GPL and Article 69 of the Bidding Measure.)
88. In which case a new procurement shall be conducted (Article 37 of the GPL).
89. It is indicated that the procurement itself is valid and not cancelled.
90. It is not clear whether this refers to a new procurement process or the continuation of the previous process.
91. And a simple and direct copy from a local government measure on handling complaint. See Article 12 of the Provisional Measure on Handling Supplier Compliant of Gansu Province.

92. Article 57 of the GPL of PRC.
93. The Opinions on Responsibility Division of Administrative Supervision on Bidding Activities by Relevant Departments in State Council (March 4, 2000) by State Commission Office for Public Sector Reform.
94. At local level, the Department of Finance, which is provided in Article 13 of the GPL.
95. Notice of the State Council Office on Issuing the Implementation Plan to Completely Promote the Government Procurement System across the Central State Organs, No. 53 (2002) of the State Council Office (hereinafter referred to as the implementation plan).
96. For example, the separation of the purchaser as the user from the CPA.
97. These departments include, for example, other departments that are charged with duties of administrative supervision over government procurement conferred by law and administrative regulations, the supervision role of audit organ of the government, the supervision rule of discipline organ of the government over public servants.
98. Whereas the procurement is conducted through bidding method, the supervision of the bidding activities shall be in accordance with the State Council Notice on Opinions of the Allocation of the Departmental Administrative Supervisory Duties regarding Bidding Activities (No. 34 (2000) of the State Council Office), Notice of the State Council Office on Issuing the Implementation Plan to Completely Promote the Government Procurement System across the Central State Organs, No. 53(2002) of the State Council Office.
99. Notice of the State Council Office on Issuing the Implementation Plan to Completely Promote the Government Procurement System across the Central State Organs, No. 53 (2002) of the State Council Office.
100. It is noteworthy that the GPL confers the authority to decide and publish CPCatalogue and the relevant thresholds with the State Council. The implementation plan reserves the right of decision for State Council but delegate the preparation work to MOF. It is also noteworthy that the implementation plan qualifies such a delegation—it does not include the preparation of threshold for works procurement through opening bidding. Also, according to Article 7, only MOF and the Department of Finance at provincial level have authority to prepare the CPCatalogue and determine the GP thresholds.
101. The GPL provides for the government procurement regulatory departments to designate media to publish government procurement information (Article 11) and by definition, the regulatory departments could be at various levels of government (Article 13). However, the Publicity Measure qualifies the provisions in the GPL and only provides for the financial departments at central and provincial level with authority to designate such media and regulate content of information to be published (Article 6), among others (see discussion in Section 15.5.2).
102. Notice of the State Council Office on Issuing the Implementation Plan to Completely Promote the Government Procurement System across the Central State Organs, No. 53(2002) of the State Council Office.
103. Article 2, the Interim Measure on the Inter-Ministries Coordinative Mechanism over Bidding Activities, issued by NDRC, Ministry of Supervision, Ministry of Finance, Ministry of Construction, Ministry of Railway, Ministry of Communications, Ministry of Information Industry, Ministry of Water Resource, Ministry of Commerce, General Administration of Civil Aviation, and Legislative Affairs Office of the State Council on July 14, 2005.
104. Article 7 of the Government Procurement Law of PRC.
105. Article 16 of the Government Procurement Law of PRC.
106. Article 16 of the Government Procurement Law of PRC.
107. Article 61 of the Government Procurement Law of PRC.

Chapter 16

Overview of the Government Procurement System in South Africa*

Phoebe Bolton

CONTENTS

* For a detailed and in-depth analysis of the legal regulation of government procurement in South Africa, see Bolton, P. *The Law of Government Procurement in South Africa* (LexisNexis Butterworths, South Africa, 2007).

16.1 Introduction

In 2004, government procurement in South Africa was estimated to amount to approximately 14 percent of gross domestic product.[1] As is the case in most countries therefore government procurement is of huge economic significance. The aim of this chapter is to provide readers with an overview of the most significant features of the South African government procurement system. First, attention is given to the organization of procurement and the law that applies to government procurement in South Africa. Next, the focus is on the constitutional framework of government procurement. Thereafter, attention is given to the way in which legislation gives effect to the constitutional principles governing procurement. Special attention is also given to the constitutionally prescribed use of procurement as a policy tool in South Africa. Lastly, the focus is on the availability of remedies to parties aggrieved by government procurement decisions.

16.2 Organization of Procurement

Before the constitutionalization of government procurement in South Africa,[2] the State Tender Board Act[3] governed procurement at national and provincial government levels and at local government level various provincial ordinances were in place to govern the procurement of goods and services. From an organizational point of view, organs of state were required to conduct procurement only via the State Tender Board, and they had no authority to make ad hoc procurement decisions. The regulations to the State Tender Board Act have, however, been amended.[4] The regulations now allow accounting officers to procure goods and services either through the State Tender Board or alternatively in terms of recently enacted legislation, which allows for the establishment of supply chain management (SCM) policies and units within government departments that comply with national legislative frameworks.[5] The aim is for all organs of state to have SCM policies and units in place and for accounting officers/authorities to be responsible and accountable for procurement-related functions. There is, in other words, a move toward the granting of more autonomy to organs of state in the procurement of goods and services within the framework of national legislation. The dual system (procurement through the state tender board or recently enacted legislation) is intended to be available until such time that the State Tender Board Act is repealed. At provincial government level, the different tender board acts will also eventually be repealed and the various provincial tender boards will be dismantled. In most provinces, this phased process has already commenced.

The National Treasury, as part of its role of managing and overseeing government expenditure, exercises overall responsibility for public procurement policy at all three levels of government (national, provincial, and local).[6] The Specialist Functions Division of the National Treasury, in particular, is responsible for issuing practice notes, guidelines, and circulars on procurement policy.

These range from, inter alia, general conditions of contract and standardized bidding documents, appointment of consultants, codes of conduct for SCM practitioners, and threshold values for the invitation of price quotations and competitive bids.[7] Where appropriate, Provincial Treasuries may issue complementary guidelines within the parameters set by the National Treasury provided that they do not jeopardize national objectives. A Provincial Treasury must also submit to the National Treasury such SCM information as the National Treasury may require. At local government level, the Municipal Council is the highest authority within a municipality or municipal entity and it is vested with significant powers of approval and oversight. In light hereof, councilors are prohibited from being members of municipal bid committees or any other committees evaluating or approving bids, quotations, contracts, or other bids. Councilors are also prohibited from attending meetings as observers. Accounting officers, in turn, are fully responsible and accountable for expenditures relating to SCM and they must implement the SCM policy adopted by council. Consultants or advisors may be used to assist in the execution of the SCM function. Structures are further in place for the training of SCM practitioners.[8]

It is common for organs of state in South Africa to conclude procurement contracts with other organs of state. At local government level, in particular, it is possible for a municipality to make use of another organ of state (i.e., a municipal entity, another municipality, or a national or provincial organ of state) for the delivery of a municipal service.[9] The National Treasury further facilitates the arrangement of transversal term contracts for the procurement of goods or services required by more than one government department. Such arrangements, however, only take place if they are cost-effective and in the national interest. National departments and provincial departments may, through their relevant treasury, choose to join in or participate in the transversal contracts facilitated by the National Treasury. Upon doing so, no similar contracts may be arranged by any of the participating departments during the tenure of the contract.[10]

16.3 Applicable Law

16.3.1 Public Law and Private Law

As is the position in other common-law countries,[11] the law that applies to the entire process of government procurement in South Africa is, in principle, the private law of contract—the same law that governs the dealings between private parties.[12] This does not, however, mean that the private law of contract is never customized or supplemented in its application to organs of state. Special public law rules exist to take account of the distinct needs and responsibilities of organs of state. Principles of both the law of contract (private law) and administrative law (public law) influence government procurement in South Africa. It is particularly administrative law that applies to government procurement, defining the scope of the government's powers, the way in which such powers should be exercised, and the consequences that flow from the misuse of powers. In short, organs of state must act within the limits of their constitutional and statutory powers; organs of state may not fetter the discretion afforded to them, and persons affected by administrative decisions must be given an opportunity to be heard. In South Africa, these rules are generally regulated by the Promotion of Administrative Justice Act (Paja).[13]

16.3.2 Paja and Administrative Action

Paja is the national legislation that gives effect to Section 33 of the constitution, which provides that

(1) Everyone has the right to administrative action that is lawful, reasonable, and procedurally fair
(2) Everyone whose rights have been adversely affected by administrative action has the right to be given written reasons
(3) National legislation must be enacted to give effect to these rights, and must
  (a) Provide for the review of administrative action by a court or, where appropriate, an independent and impartial tribunal
  (b) Impose a duty on the state to give effect to the rights in subsections (1) and (2)
  (c) Promote an efficient administration

In brief, Paja deals with general administrative law and lays down rules and principles that apply to and bind all levels of government in South Africa (national, provincial, and local). It applies to organs of state when "(i) exercising a power in terms of the constitution or a provincial constitution or (ii) exercising a public power or performing a public function in terms of any legislation."[14] It further applies to "a natural or juristic person, other than an organ of state, when exercising a public power or performing a public function in terms of an empowering provision, which adversely affects the rights of any person and which has a direct, external legal effect."[15] Paja deals with the power of the courts to scrutinize the lawfulness, reasonableness, procedural fairness, and the right to written reasons for administrative action. It also provides for remedies that are available if these requirements are not adhered to. It further provides for procedures and methods aimed at encouraging good decision making by organs of state, thereby aiming to reduce the need for judicial review.

The right to just administrative action in Section 33 of the constitution is of paramount importance in South African administrative law. Where previously, the courts had an intrinsic or common-law power to review administrative action, the review power of the courts is today subject to the constitution and Paja. The prerequisite for recourse to judicial review under Paja, however, is administrative action: only if the action or decision complained of amounts to administrative action can recourse be had to judicial review.[16]

16.3.3 Government Procurement and Administrative Action

The courts have held that the conduct of the government procurement process, the evaluation of tenders, and the award of a contract to a successful tenderer are all forms of administrative action within the meaning of Section 33 of the constitution and Paja.[17] An unsuccessful tenderer also has *locus standi* to challenge government procurement decisions by means of an application for judicial review.[18] An unsuccessful tenderer can challenge government procurement decisions on the grounds of lawfulness, reasonableness, and procedural fairness. An unsuccessful tenderer can also challenge government procurement decisions on the basis of the reasons given for such decisions.

16.3.4 Other Legislative Provisions

Aside from Paja, there are also various express legislative provisions regulating the way in which specific powers must be exercised. Of particular importance to the subject of government procurement is the constitution; the most important provisions being Section 217, which, inter alia, provides for a procurement system that is fair, equitable, transparent, competitive, and cost-effective, and the use of procurement as a policy tool; Section 9, which provides for the right to equality; and Section 33, which, as noted in Section 16.3.2, deals with just administrative action. Of particular significance also is the Promotion of Access to Information Act (PAIA),[19] which gives "effect to the constitutional right of access to any information held by the State and any information that is held by another person and that is required for the exercise or protection of any rights; and to provide for matters connected therewith."[20] There is also the Prevention and Combating of Corrupt Activities Act (Corruption Act)[21] that applies to all three levels of government. The Corruption Act creates offences in respect of corrupt activities relating to contracts, and offences in respect of corrupt activities relating to the procuring and withdrawal of tenders.

Parliament has furthermore established a legislative regime for the procurement procedures and decisions of organs of state to reflect the constitutional status of government procurement in South Africa. The relevant legislation can be referred to as primary or dedicated legislation, the most important of which include the Preferential Procurement Policy Framework Act (Procurement Act)[22] and the regulations thereto[23] which make provision for the use of procurement as a tool to correct the imbalances caused by South Africa's history of discriminatory policies and practices.[24] At national and provincial government levels, the Public Finance Management Act (PFMA)[25] regulates financial management in the national and provincial governments. At local government level, the Local Government: Municipal Systems Act (Municipal Systems Act)[26] enables municipalities to, inter alia, provide for municipal services by way of service delivery agreements, the selection of service providers then having to be done through specified selection and prequalification processes; and the Local Government: Municipal Finance Management Act (MFMA),[27] inter alia, aims "[t]o secure sound and sustainable management of the financial affairs of municipalities and other institutions in the local sphere of government."[28] The different legislation further empower the National Treasury to issue guidelines and instructions or practice notes on various issues relating to procurement with the aim to ensure uniform minimum norms and standards within government.

16.3.5 Summary

In South Africa, the government procurement system is extensively regulated. Government procurement procedures are, in addition to being subjected to the private law of contract, also subjected to public law rules, in particular the law of judicial review. Thus, aggrieved parties in the government procurement process can approach a court of law under the private law of contract or opt for the judicial review of the procurement decisions and procedures of organs of state. In certain circumstances, aggrieved parties may also have recourse to the (private) law of delict.[29] Government procurement has further been afforded constitutional status.[30] This means that parties aggrieved by government procurement procedures are also constitutionally protected. A number of statutes, that is, primary or dedicated legislation and secondary or general legislation, also impact on government procurement in South Africa.

16.4 Constitutional Framework

16.4.1 Procurement Clause: Section 217

The procurement clause in the constitution is Section 217; it is headed "Procurement" and provides as follows:

(1) When an organ of state in the national, provincial, or local sphere of government, or any other institution identified in national legislation, contracts for goods or services, it must do so in accordance with a system that is fair, equitable, transparent, competitive, and cost-effective

(2) Subsection (1) does not prevent the organs of state or institutions referred to in that subsection from implementing a procurement policy providing for
   (a) Categories of preference in the allocation of contracts
   (b) The protection or advancement of persons, or categories of persons, disadvantaged by unfair discrimination
(3) National legislation must prescribe a framework within which the policy referred to in subsection (2) must be implemented

Five principles are therefore laid down in the constitution that apply to the mechanisms and procedures employed by organs of state when they contract for goods or services. They must comply with the notions of fairness, equity, transparency, competitiveness, and cost-effectiveness. Provision is also made for the use of procurement as a means to address past discriminatory policies and practices in South Africa. In what follows, brief attention is given to (1) the nature of the principles in Section 217(1), (2) the problem of corruption and the significance of the inclusion of principles in Section 217, (3) the use of procurement as a policy tool, and (4) the scope of application of Section 217.

16.4.2 Nature of the Principles in Section 217(1)

Section 217(1) of the constitution specifically refers to a system of procurement; organs of state must contract for goods or services in accordance with a system that is fair, equitable, transparent, competitive, and cost-effective. The word "system" generally refers to a set of elements that form a cooperative body or interrelated network.[31] In this sense, the words "fair, equitable, transparent, competitive, and cost-effective" in Section 217(1) should be understood as a set of elements forming an interrelated network. They should, in other words, not be viewed in isolation, they are at all times interconnected and interrelated. This is particularly noteworthy with the principles of competitiveness and cost-effectiveness. In emergencies, for example, it may not be cost-effective for an organ of state to make use of competition—the time and costs involved in using competitive procedures may defeat the purpose of using competition and defeat the attainment of value for money. Where, on the other hand, competitive procedures are used, this should give rise to cost-effectiveness. The principles of competitiveness and cost-effectiveness are therefore at all times interconnected and interrelated. Cost-effectiveness may either restrict or reinforce the use of competition. The use of competition in and of itself does not guarantee the attainment of value for money.

The principles of fairness and equity are also particularly interconnected and interrelated. The idea of fairness or equal treatment in the procurement process should be understood in light of South Africa's history of unfair discriminatory policies and practices. Before the abolishment of apartheid in 1994, the majority of state contracts were awarded to large and usually white-owned businesses.[32] To address past discriminatory policies and practices, the right to equality in Section 9 of the constitution has been held by the constitutional court to refer to a "substantive" conception of equality as opposed to a "formal" conception of equality.[33] The actual social and economic circumstances of individuals and groups should, in other words, be taken into account when reading Section 9 of the constitution. It cannot be presumed that everyone in South Africa is equal. The actual social and economic disparities among people cannot be ignored.[34] The right to equality thus allows organs of state in certain defined circumstances to treat contractors differently. Affording preference in the award of government contracts is not an infringement of the right to equality. This, in turn, links up with the principle of equity in Section 217(1).

The notion of equity plays a significant role in South Africa and is reflected in a number of provisions in the constitution.[35] The relevant constitutional provisions that make reference to the notion of equity are generally aimed at the equaling of disparate groups in South Africa. Equity is a measure that compares one group with another, for example, black with white or rich with poor. Instead of treating all groups exactly the same, groups who face different levels of resources and development are required to receive different treatment.[36] When reference is therefore made in the constitution to, for present purposes, the contracting for goods or services in accordance with a system that is equitable, it means that account should be taken of the different levels of resources and development of different groups in South Africa. The reference to "equitable" does not mean "equal shares" or "equal opportunities," but rather that procurement should be aimed at improving the position of vulnerable groups in South Africa. Procurement should be used as a means to address past inequalities and unfair discriminatory policies and practices.

The principle of transparency is of course tied to and supports all the other principles in Section 217(1). It enables interested and affected parties to check up on government procurement procedures to ensure compliance with the notions of fairness, equity, competitiveness, and cost-effectiveness. In the end, all the principles in Section 217(1) always apply when organs of state contract. The weight attached to each principle will however be determined by the circumstances of a particular case. The principles are not the equivalent of rules. Unlike rules that eliminate one another when in competition, principles when in competition can be balanced and afforded weight in the given circumstances.[37] Thus, for a court to determine whether or not an organ of state has complied with the principles in Section 217(1), it must take account of all the facts and circumstances of the particular case and on that basis determine overall compliance with Section 217(1).

16.4.3 Principles and Corruption

Corruption is commonly regarded as immoral and improper in terms of good procurement practice because it diminishes the confidence that honest contractors and the public at large have in the government. In the procurement context, corruption gives rise to the slackening of competition and impacts negatively on the government's ability to obtain the best value for money. Corruption also defeats the attainment of other objectives, for example, the use of procurement as a policy tool and the fair treatment of contractors. The inclusion of the principles in Section 217(1) is therefore, in addition to ensuring the prudent use of government resources, also aimed at preventing corruption and safeguarding the integrity of the procurement process. If organs of state contract for goods or services in a manner that is fair, equitable, competitive, cost-effective, and most importantly, transparent, there is no doubt that there will be a notable decline in the occurrence of corruption. The principle of transparency, in particular, supports the other principles because, as noted in Section 16.4.2, it enables interested and affected parties to scrutinize government procurement procedures, that is, whether the procedures employed are fair, equitable, competitive, and cost-effective.

16.4.4 Use of Procurement as a Policy Tool

Section 217(2) of the constitution does not prevent organs of state from using procurement as a means to effect socioeconomic change. Procurement may, in other words, be used as a tool of development and transformation. This gives expression to the right to equality in South African law, because, as noted in Section 16.4.2, this right has been held by the constitutional court to refer to a substantive conception of equality as opposed to a formal conception of equality. Organs of state are allowed to treat contractors differently in certain defined circumstances: they are allowed to afford preference to certain contractors in the award of contracts. Organs of state do not, however, in terms of Section 217(2) of the constitution, appear to be under an obligation to implement preferential procurement policies. Section 217(2) simply states that organs of state are not prevented from using procurement as a policy tool.[38] This should not be cause for alarm. The constitution is meant to govern the country in the long term and the use of procurement as a policy tool is a temporary measure to address past discriminatory policies and practices in South Africa. The obligatory use of procurement as a policy tool should be left to legislation—this is examined in Section 16.6.

16.4.5 Scope of Application of Section 217

Section 217 of the constitution applies to all organs of state, that is, organs of state in the national, provincial, and local spheres of government and any other institution identified in national legislation.[39] Bodies or entities that perform public powers or functions also fall within the scope of Section 217.[40] The actual conclusion of a contract furthermore falls within the ambit of Section 217 including negotiations leading up to the conclusion of a contract.[41] Organs of state must also comply with Section 217 when they contract for their own purposes and when they contract for goods or services on their behalf. Organs of state at local government level, however, need not comply with Section 217 when they specifically contract with other organs of state for the delivery of municipal services. The reason for this is because all organs of state are entities exercising powers on behalf of the state. When a municipality contracts with another organ of state for the delivery of a municipal service, the service will still be provided by the state. There is, accordingly, no need for there to be compliance with Section 217. The principle of transparency, however, should, as a general rule, always be complied with. The public has a right to government contracting procedures that are open and transparent irrespective of whether a municipality contracts with a private party or another organ of state. Where an organ of state in the local government sphere does not specifically contract with another organ of state for the delivery of a municipal service, or contracts for goods or services in general, Section 217 must be complied with.

The word "procurement" in the South African context should, furthermore, be understood as referring to the acquisition of goods or services and the sale and letting of assets. The whole rationale for prescribing a system that complies with principles such as fairness, equity, transparency, and in particular, competitiveness and cost-effectiveness would be defeated if the principles were to apply only to instances when an organ of state contracts for the acquisition of goods or services. The public has a right to procurement procedures that comply with the principles mentioned whenever organs of state contract, whether for the acquisition of goods or services or the sale and letting of assets. Before 1994, the state also, as noted in Section 16.4.2, contracted with large and usually white-owned businesses. The aim today is to use the procurement power of the state as a means to remedy past injustices. If the word "procurement" was to refer only to instances when the state acquires goods or services, contracts that entail the sale and letting of assets will still end up in the hands of large and usually white-owned businesses. Thus, even though Section 217 of the constitution is headed "Procurement," the term should be given a wide interpretation and be read as referring to instances when an organ of state contracts for the acquisition of goods or services and when it contracts for the sale and letting of assets.[42]

16.5 Legislation and Section 217

Having looked at the constitutional framework of government procurement in South Africa, it is important to see how legislation gives effect to Section 217 of the constitution. Space does not permit a detailed examination of the way in which all the different legislation seek to give effect to

Section 217.[43] The focus is instead on the dedicated legislation, in particular the PFMA, the MFMA, and the Municipal Systems Act. Brief attention is also given to the way in which Paja and PAIA give effect to Section 217. The way in which the Procurement Act and regulations give effect to the constitutionally prescribed use of procurement as a policy tool is not examined here. It is, instead, examined in Section 16.6. As noted in Section 16.4.2, all the principles in Section 217(1) are interconnected and interrelated. In this section, the principles of competitiveness and cost-effectiveness, and fairness and transparency are grouped together for the purpose of showing how legislation seeks to give effect to them. The way in which legislation seeks to give effect to the principle of equity is dealt with in Section 16.6.

16.5.1 Competitiveness and Cost-Effectiveness

On the whole, the dedicated legislation (PFMA, MFMA, and Municipal Systems Act) that structures cost-effectiveness has much to commend it. Provision is generally made for the attainment of cost-effectiveness throughout the procurement process. It is particularly in the context of municipal service delivery by an external provider and the conclusion of public–private partnership (PPP) agreements that strict rules are in place. In principle, organs of state may use external providers for the delivery of municipal services and conclude PPPs only if doing so will give rise to value for money.[44] Legislation also emphasizes that the time and costs involved in using a certain type of competition (e.g., petty cash purchases, the use of quotations, or competitive bidding) should be proportional to the size or value of the goods or services needed. The higher the value of contracts, the more formal procurement procedures should be.[45] The factors to take account of in evaluation and selection procedures are further determined by the nature of the contract. Where an organ of state sells or lets assets, price is generally the most important criterion. Where an organ of state acquires goods or services, the capability or ability of a contractor and the payment of taxes, levies, and charges are important. It is also especially in the context of municipal service delivery that the capacity and potential future capacity for the delivery of the service by an internal mechanism as opposed to an external provider are important. Organs of state further have discretion to determine the weight to be given to different factors when procuring goods or services, for example, price; the nature, quality, and reliability of the product or service to be rendered; the experience and track record of a contractor; the technical knowledge and capacity of a contractor; the financial and economic standing of a contractor; etc. The courts may, as a general rule, interfere in the weight given to relevant factors only if the organ of state disclosed to contractors the weight it would attach to factors, but failed to apply such weighting, or legislation specifies the weight to be given to factors.[46] Case law also illustrates that even though the use of procurement as a tool for upliftment is important in South African law, the attainment of value for money remains the most important factor when organs of state contract. As the use of procurement as a policy tool is important, it does not outweigh the attainment of the best value for money.[47]

On the whole, the dedicated legislation that structures competitiveness has much to commend it. Organs of state are not obliged to use tender procedures as appears to be the case under the 1993 constitution.[48] The choice of procurement method is, however, considerably structured by legislation. As noted in the beginning of this section, the higher the value of contracts, the more formal procurement procedures should be. It is mainly in the context of competitive bidding that a number of rules and guidelines are laid down, many of which aim to ensure that organs of state attract the biggest pool of competitors. Provision is generally made for uniformity in bid documentation, sufficient advertising, enough time for the preparation and submission of tenders, and the drafting of specifications in an unbiased manner to allow all potential bidders to offer their goods or services.[49] The drafting of specifications in an unbiased manner in particular serves as a safeguard against the advertising of custom-made contracts that defeats competition and the fair treatment of all who participate.

16.5.2 Fairness and Transparency

At all three levels of government, the dedicated legislation (PFMA, MFMA, and Municipal Systems Act) prescribes the use of fair and transparent procurement procedures. Provision is generally made for the pre-disclosure of tender evaluation and adjudication criteria, the publication of contract opportunities, the publication of contract awards, and the disclosure of conflicts of interest. Provision is also made for transparency in the conclusion of municipal PPPs and the delivery of municipal services by external providers. Strict rules further apply to the negotiation or variation of contracts.[50] As a general rule, when an organ of state calls for tenders and selects a preferred tenderer, the parties are prohibited from negotiating the terms of the contract to be concluded. Negotiations are allowed only if the preferred tenderer will remain the most favored tenderer in accordance with the tender criteria, and the contract will not be significantly different from the contract initially advertised.[51] More or less similar rules also apply to the variation of a contract after its conclusion—changes made may not result in a contract that is materially different from the contract initially advertised.

There are constitutional provisions other than Section 217(1) that reflect the principles of fairness and transparency, that is, Sections 32, 33(1), and 33(2). These sections respectively make provision for the right of access to information, procedural fairness, and the furnishing of reasons. All these rights are, to a certain extent, given content by PAIA and Paja, in other words, the general or secondary legislation that finds application to government procurement decisions and procedures in South Africa.[52] These two statutes therefore, in addition to the dedicated legislation (PFMA, MFMA, and Municipal Systems Act), reflect the principles of fairness and transparency. Paja, in particular, provides indirect protection for tenderers in respect of the changes made to tender specifications by organs of state, their acceptance of alternative or qualified tenders, the amendment and withdrawal of tenders by tenderers, and the need for the provision of sufficient information by organs of state to enable tenderers to submit responsive tenders.[53] Tenderers also have the right to reasons for the non-award of a tender, or the cancellation or discontinuation of a tender process. PAIA, on the other hand, ensures that tenderers are able to request access to relevant information and documentation to ensure that their rights have not been infringed. The onus is on an organ of state to show that it is entitled to refuse access to the requested information or documentation. Case law further illustrates that the courts view the right of access to information, procedural fairness, and the right to reasons in the government procurement process to be of great significance.[54]

16.6 Procurement as a Policy Tool[55]

Government procurement is not only business, that is, the acquisition of goods and services on the best possible terms, but also has broader social, political, and economic implications. Throughout history governments have used their procurement power to promote social, industrial, and environmental policies.[56] The use of government procurement as a policy tool is of particular significance for South Africa. Because of past apartheid policies and practices, many groups in South Africa were denied the award of government contracts. Most contracts were, as noted in Section 16.4.2, awarded to large and usually white-owned businesses, and price was generally the overriding criterion for the award of contracts. This has changed with the enactment of the 1993 and 1996 constitutions. Even though price is still a very important criterion in the award of contracts, it is no longer the only or decisive criterion. It is particularly the notion of empowerment that plays a significant role in the award of contracts.

The dedicated legislation that has been enacted to give effect to the constitutionally prescribed use of procurement as a policy tool in South Africa is the Procurement Act and the regulations thereto.[57] On the whole, the act and regulations give effect to the use of procurement as a policy instrument. Case law also illustrates the effective enforcement of the Procurement Act and regulations by the courts.[58] The act and regulations create a framework for the implementation of procurement policies. Organs of state are obligated to implement a procurement policy and use the framework provided therefore in the act; they have no discretion in this regard. This can be commended. True reform of the South African government procurement system can take place only if organs of state have little (if any) discretion on whether or not to implement a preferential procurement policy.

The Procurement Act and regulations proceed on the assumption that contracts are awarded by way of competitive tender procedures and a points system is created for the award of contracts. Contractors are awarded points out of 100 and they are awarded points for price and preference. The points system is dual-scale in that more preference points are awarded for higher value contracts and less preference points for lower value contracts. For contracts between R30,000 and R500,000, for example, the 80/20 point system applies. In terms of it, 80 points are awarded for price and a contractor may be awarded a maximum of 20 points for being a historically disadvantaged individual (HDI) or subcontracting with an HDI or attaining certain specific goals. For contracts above R500,000, the 90/10 point system applies. In terms of it, 90 points are awarded for price and a contractor may be awarded a maximum of 10 points for being an HDI or subcontracting with an HDI or attaining certain specific goals. An HDI, in turn, is defined as a South African citizen, who before 1994 had no franchise in national elections; or who is a female; or who has a disability. Persons who acquired citizenship after 1994 are not regarded as HDIs. Specific goals, on the other hand, include inter alia the promotion of South African-owned enterprises; the promotion of small, medium, and microenterprises (SMMEs); the creation of new jobs; the promotion of enterprises in a specific region, municipality, or rural area; and the upliftment of communities.

In light of the above, it is clear that even though the use of procurement as a policy tool is of huge significance in South African law, the attainment of value for money remains the most important criterion when procuring goods or services. A maximum number of 10 and 20 points are specified for the allocation of preference points; organs of state have no discretion to award more than the specified maxim. Contractors that belong to designated or target groups further do not have a right to preferential treatment. Contracts are awarded depending on the score of a contractor out of 100, preference counting only for a maximum of 10 or 20 points (out of 100) depending on the value of the contract. Thus, all the principles in Section 217(1) of the constitution find application when organs of state contract for goods or services and the principle of equity is only one of those principles. All the principles must be afforded weight in a given set of circumstances to ensure overall compliance with Section 217. The Procurement Act and regulations also make provision for penalties. The use of false information by a contractor to obtain preference points may result in the termination of its contract; the recovery of all costs, losses, and damages incurred by the organ of state; and debarment from future government contract awards.[59]

Overall it can be said that the use of procurement as a policy tool in South Africa is justified. It does not amount to an infringement of the right to equality, because as noted in Section 16.4.2, the constitutional court has held that Section 9 of the constitution reflects a substantive conception of equality and not a formal conception of equality. The preference points system created by the act and regulations also emphasize the importance of price; and contractors are not awarded contracts simply because they fall within a specific target group. There are of course time and cost-premiums involved in using procurement as a policy tool,[60] but this should be regarded as an integral part of South Africa's growth and transformation.

16.7 Availability of Remedies

Government procurement in South Africa is, as noted in Section 16.3, regulated by the constitution; the dedicated legislation enacted to give effect to Section 217; the common law, that is, the law of contract and the law of delict; and the general rules of constitutional and administrative law. The mere existence of rules or laws to regulate procurement, however, is not enough. To ensure compliance with different rules, and most importantly, the principles in Section 217(1) of the constitution, it is important for measures to be in place to ensure the application and enforcement of the rules and principles. It is important for aggrieved parties to have recourse to practical and effective dispute resolution mechanisms to enable them to enforce compliance with their rights. It is also important for aggrieved parties to be afforded adequate remedies where their rights are found to have been unjustifiably infringed. In considering the availability of dispute resolution mechanisms and remedies in the South African government procurement system, a distinction will be drawn between public law remedies and private law remedies.

16.7.1 Public Law Remedies

Public law remedies find application primarily during the pre-contractual stage of the procurement process, that is, the stage before the actual award of a tender and the conclusion of a contract. During this stage, there is, in South African law, no contract and thus the nonavailability of contractual remedies.[61] Remedies are instead available under Paja and other legislation. In exceptional circumstances, public law remedies are also available during the contractual and post-contractual stage of the procurement process.

Insofar as dispute resolution is concerned, the dedicated legislation (PFMA, MFMA, and Municipal Systems Act) generally encourages aggrieved parties to use internal remedies for the resolution of disputes and to use court proceedings as a last resort.[62] In light of the time and costs that generally accompany litigation in a court of law, this can be commended. Aggrieved parties are also able to have recourse to nonjudicial bodies to enforce compliance with their rights, that is, the public protector, the auditor-general, and the national prosecuting authority. In those instances when recourse is had to a court of law for the judicial review of procurement decisions, the remedies available under Paja (e.g., setting aside, directions to give reasons, declaratory orders, interdicts, and cost orders) generally ensure the enforcement of Section 217, especially the principles in Section 217(1). The requirements to be met for claiming compensation under Paja are, however, controversial. It is my view that expecting an aggrieved tenderer to prove all the elements of a delict (wrongfulness, fault, causation, and loss) to successfully claim compensation under Paja is unduly onerous. In most instances, it would make more sense for an aggrieved tenderer to institute a claim in delict rather than claim compensation under Paja.[63] In some instances, however, a claim for compensation under Paja may be appropriate. A private contractor should, for example, be entitled to compensation where the contract it is a party to is terminated in the public interest because it amounts to a fetter of discretion, or where the contract is declared invalid because it was concluded without the necessary power or authority.[64]

Legislation (other than Paja) further provides that an organ of state is allowed to reject or disregard the tender of a contractor for the nonpayment of taxes.[65] From a cost-effectiveness point of view, it can safely be assumed that a contractor that is unable or unwilling to pay its taxes is unlikely to render satisfactory performance under a contract and is likely to cost an organ of state more in the long run. Contractors who do not pay their taxes also have an unfair competitive advantage over contractors who do pay their taxes because they are able to submit lower tenders. Thus, in addition to the rejection or disregard of tenders for the nonpayment of taxes serving as revenue collecting measures, they also ensure compliance with the principles of competitiveness, fairness, and cost-effectiveness. They further ensure that organs of state are not perceived by the general public as giving support to those who fail to pay their taxes, which, in turn, enhances the integrity of the government procurement process.

Legislation also provides that a contractor may be debarred from government contract awards on the ground of unsatisfactory contractual performance in the past, and on the ground of fraud or corruption.[66] From a cost-effectiveness point of view, a failure on the part of a contractor to render satisfactory performance under a previous government contract leads to the logical assumption that the contractor is unlikely to render satisfactory contractual performance in future. The debarment of contractors on the ground of unsatisfactory contractual performance thus ensures that organs of state only conduct business with responsible and reliable contractors, which, in turn, ensures the efficient use of taxpayers' money. As noted in Section 16.4.3, corruption is very harmful to the procurement process because it lessens the confidence that honest contractors and the public at large have in the government. Corruption leads to the slackening of competition for government contracts and impacts negatively on the government's ability to obtain the best possible value for money. Corruption also impacts negatively on the attainment of other objectives in the procurement process, for example, policy promotion and the fair treatment of contractors. It is, therefore, not strange for legislation in South Africa to make provision for the debarment of contractors from government contract awards on the ground of fraud or corruption.[67]

During the contractual and postcontractual stage of the procurement process, two remedies are available to organs of state in terms of legislation: termination of the contract and financial penalties.[68] A contract may be terminated on the ground of corruption, insolvency, or default. Termination on the ground of corruption, in particular, requires an organ of state to take account of a number of factors, an examination of which illustrates that value for money is, and remains, a very important consideration. In principle, a contract should not be terminated on the ground of corruption if doing so will result in noncompliance with the principle of cost-effectiveness.[69] The prescribed financial penalties, on the other hand, save organs of state the time and effort of resorting to the often cumbersome rules available under the law of contract for the payment of damages. Effect is therefore also given to the principle of cost-effectiveness.

16.7.2 Private Law Remedies

Private law remedies find application primarily during the contractual and postcontractual stage of the procurement process. In exceptional circumstances, private law remedies are also available during the pre-contractual stage. Remedies are available under the law of contract and the law of delict. The constitution provides that when a court, tribunal, or forum interprets any legislation, the common law or customary law, it must promote the spirit, purport, and objects of the Bill of Rights.[70] The constitution also provides that "[t]he Constitutional Court, Supreme Court of Appeal and High Courts have the inherent power to…develop the common law, taking into account the interests of justice."[71] The remedies available under the law of contract and the law of delict must therefore be used to give effect to the constitution, and for present purposes, this means the enforcement of Section 217 of the constitution and the principles in Section 217(1).

Insofar as dispute resolution during the contractual and postcontractual stage is concerned, the dedicated legislation generally ensures that effect is given to the principle of cost-effectiveness. The contracting parties are encouraged to resolve disputes amicably, that is, by means of negotiation, failing which mediation and, as a last resort, litigation in a court of law.[72] This can be commended: litigation in a court of law is, as noted in Section 16.7.1, generally time-consuming and costly and defeats the attainment of value for money. The remedies available under the law of contract (interdicts, specific performance, cancellation, and damages) and the law of delict (damages) further enable the contracting parties to enforce their rights under the contract, which, in turn, ensures the enforcement of Section 217 and the principles in Section 217(1) of the constitution. Case law also illustrates the judiciary's commitment to enforce the rights of contracting parties.[73] In particular, delictual liability may arise on the following grounds: (1) fraud on the part of public officials,[74] (2) misleading statements made by an organ of state during the tender process resulting in the conclusion of a more onerous contract than anticipated,[75] and (3) the wrongful interference by a third party (an unsuccessful tenderer) in the contractual relationship between the successful tenderer and the organ of state.[76] Delictual damages could, furthermore, take the form of bid preparation costs and out-of-pocket expenses,[77] loss of profits,[78] and the loss of a chance to bid for or win a tender.

16.8 Conclusion

In South Africa, government procurement procedures are, in addition to being subjected to the private law of contract, also subjected to public law rules, in particular the law of judicial review. Aggrieved parties can approach a court of law under the private law of contract or opt for the judicial review of the procurement decisions and procedures of organs of state. Government procurement has furthermore been constitutionalized. In this sense, the government procurement system in South Africa is unique. Not only has the procurement procedures and decisions of organs of state been constitutionalized, but also the procurement clause in the constitution (Section 217) captures the most essential elements of a good procurement system. The principles of value for money (competitiveness and cost-effectiveness) and fairness and transparency, in particular, are internationally regarded as the cornerstone of good procurement practice. The principles in Section 217(1) serve to prevent manipulation by organs of state in the award of contracts and give power to the courts to review government procurement procedures and decisions. The principles are flexible in the sense that they are broad in nature, but at the same time, they ensure that organs of state are bound by the most critical elements that ensure good procurement practices. The principles will further be part of South Africa's government procurement system for a long period of time. The most essential elements of a good procurement system will therefore bind organs of state whenever they contract for goods or services. This, in turn, obliges organs of state to always take serious account of the principles in Section 217(1) and ensure compliance therewith.

Overall, the legal regime in South Africa generally gives effect to the principles in Section 217(1) of the constitution and the use of procurement as a policy tool. All three levels of government employ a more or less similar structure to ensure compliance with Section 217. Case law also illustrates the judiciary's commitment to enforce compliance with Section 217. The legal regime generally seeks to ensure that organs of state contract for goods or services in accordance with a system which is fair, equitable, transparent, competitive, and cost-effective. The legal regime also seeks to ensure that organs of state use procurement as an empowerment tool, that is, as a tool of development and upliftment.

Notes

1. Mkhize, ZL (MEC for Finance and Economic Development) Supply Chain Management Conference: Transforming Government Procurement System (22-23 November 2004, Durban) 11.
2. Firstly in Section 187 of the Constitution of the Republic of South Africa 200 of 1993 and currently in Section 217 of the Constitution of the Republic of South Africa 108 of 1996.
3. 86 of 1968.
4. State Tender Board Act, 1968 (Act 86 of 1968): Amendment to Regulations of the State Tender Board Act in terms of Section 13, Government Gazette No. 25766, December 5, 2003.
5. For more discussion on the legislation, see Sections 16.3.4 and 16.5.
6. See generally www.treasury.gov.za.
7. Ibid.
8. National Treasury: Policy Strategy to Guide Uniformity in Government Procurement Reform Processes in Government (April 7, 2003).
9. See Section 16.4.5.
10. National Treasury: Policy Strategy to Guide Uniformity in Government Procurement Reform Processes in Government (April 7, 2003).
11. For example, the United Kingdom, Canada, Australia, and New Zealand.
12. This is in contrast with civil law countries, most notably France, where a separate body of law (*contrats administratifs*) regulates many of the contracts concluded by organs of state. See Brown, LN and Bell, JS (with the assistance of Jean-Michel Galabert) *French Administrative Law* (Clarendon Press, Oxford, 5ed 1998) Chapter 8.
13. 3 of 2000.
14. Section 1(a) of Paja.
15. Section 1(b) of Paja.
16. "Administrative action" is defined in Section 1 of Paja. Currie, I and Klaaren, J (*The Promotion of Administrative Justice Act Benchbook* (Siber Ink, 2001) para 2.4) simplify the definition as follows: "[a]dministrative action is: (1) a decision or a proposed decision; (2) of an administrative nature; (3) that is made in terms of an empowering provision; (4) that is not specifically excluded; (5) that is made by an organ of state or by a private person exercising public power; (6) that adversely affects rights and (7) that has a direct external legal effect."
17. See, inter alia, *Transnet Ltd. v. Goodman Brothers (Pty) Ltd.* 2001 (1) SA 853 (SCA); *Grinaker LTA Ltd. and Another v. Tender Board (Mpumalanga) and Others* 2002 3 All SA 336 (T); *Logbro Properties CC v. Bedderson NO and Others* 2003 (2) SA 460 (SCA).
18. *National & Overseas Modular Construction (Pty) Ltd. v. Tender Board, Free State Provincial Government* 1999 (1) SA 701 (O).
19. 2 of 2000.
20. Section 32 of the Constitution.
21. 12 of 2004.
22. 5 of 2000.
23. Preferential Procurement Regulations, Government Gazette No. 22549, August 10, 2001.
24. The Procurement Act and Regulations are currently in the process of being repealed. The aim is to bring them more in line with the Broad-Based Black Economic Empowerment Act 53 of 2003 (BBBEEA), the aim of which is, inter alia, "[t]o establish a legislative framework for the promotion of black economic empowerment [BEE]" in South Africa. At the time of completion of this chapter (May 8, 2008), the revised act had not been finalized and the new regulations were still in draft form (National Treasury "Supply Chain Management: Alignment of Preferential Procurement with the Aims of the BBBEEA and its Related Strategy," April 18, 2007; Preferential Procurement Policy Framework Act, 2000 [Act No. 5 of 2000]: Draft Preferential Procurement Regulations, Government Gazette No. 26863, October 4, 2004). The focus of this chapter is thus on the Procurement Act of 2000 and the promulgated regulations of 2001.

25. 1 of 1999 (as amended by Act 29 of 1999).
26. 32 of 2000 (as amended by Act 44 of 2003).
27. 56 of 2003.
28. See the preamble to the act.
29. See Section 16.7.2.
30. Section 217.
31. *Compact Oxford English Dictionary*; Collins *English Dictionary: Complete and Unabridged* (6ed 2003) 1637; *Oxford English Dictionary*.
32. Gounden, SM 'The Impact of the Affirmative Procurement Policy on Affirmable Business Enterprises in the South African Construction Industry' (unpublished PhD thesis, University of Natal, 2000) 3.11.
33. *Bato Star Fishing (Pty) Ltd. v. The Minister of Environmental Affairs and Others* 2004 (4) SA 490 (CC); *National Coalition for Gay and Lesbian Equality and Another v. Minister of Justice and Others* 1998 (12) BCLR 1517 (CC); *President of the Republic of South Africa and Another v. Hugo* 1997 (6) BCLR 708 (CC); *Harksen v. Lane NO and Others* 1997 (11) BCLR 1489 (CC).
34. Albertyn, C and Kentridge, J. 1994. *South African Journal on Human Rights* 10(2): 149; *Brink v. Kitshoff NO* 1996 (4) SA 197 (CC) para 40. See also the preamble to the 1996 Constitution.
35. See Sections 25(3), 25(5), 25(7), 155(4), 195(1)(d), 214, 236, and, of course, 217(1).
36. On the notion of equity in South African law, see Du Plessis. 1998. *Stellenbosch Law Review* 3: 239, 244; Steytler, N. 2003. *Law, Democracy and Development* 7(2): 227, 229.
37. See Dworkin, R *Taking Rights Seriously* (London Duckworth, 1977) 22–29.
38. This is in contrast with the use of the word "equitable" in Section 217(1) of the Constitution. Section 217(1) provides that organs of state must contract for goods or services in accordance with a system that is equitable.
39. Section 217(1) of the Constitution.
40. See Section 239 of the Constitution. An organ of state is defined as "(a) any department of state or administration in the national, provincial or local sphere of government; or (b) any other functionary or institution (i) exercising a power or performing a function in terms of the Constitution or a provincial constitution; or (ii) exercising a public power or performing a public function in terms of any legislation, but does not include a court or a judicial officer."
41. See *Transnet Ltd. v. Goodman Brothers (Pty) Ltd.* 2001 (1) SA 853 (SCA) 862A-B. Olivier J.A. noted that "[i]t may well be that the words 'contracts for goods and services' [in s 217(1) of the Constitution] must be given a wide meaning, similar to 'negotiates for' etc."
42. For more detailed discussion on the scope of application of Section 217, see Bolton, P *The Law of Government Procurement in South Africa* (LexisNexis Butterworths, South Africa, 2007) 63–70.
43. For a detailed and in-depth examination, see Bolton, P *The Law of Government Procurement in South Africa* (LexisNexis Butterworths, South Africa, 2007).
44. The Municipal Systems Act provides that a municipality has a choice whether to deliver a municipal service through an internal mechanism or an external provider, but a number of factors must be considered in deciding on the mechanism to be employed. Some of these include the direct and indirect costs and benefits involved in making use of an internal mechanism as opposed to an external provider, and the capacity and potential future capacity for the delivery of the service by an internal mechanism as opposed to an external provider. The conclusion of a PPP must further (in terms of the MFMA PPP Regulations) provide value for money, be affordable, and transfer appropriate technical, operational, and financial risks to the private party. A municipality must carry out a feasibility study before the conclusion of a PPP. The feasibility study must include an assessment of, inter alia, the number of municipal officials that would become redundant as a result of the PPP agreement, the costs involved in staff retrenchments or the retention of redundant staff, any assets that would become obsolete, and any revenue that would be foregone by the municipality. The assessment must also show the full costs to the municipality if the PPP agreement is not concluded compared to the full costs to the municipality if the PPP agreement is concluded.
45. See generally the PFMA SCM Regulations and the MFMA SCM Regulations.

46. *Bato Star Fishing (Pty) Ltd. v. The Minister of Environmental Affairs and Others* 2004 (4) SA 490 (CC) para 48.
47. See, in particular, *Cash Paymaster Services (Pty) Ltd. v. Eastern Cape Province and Others* 1999 (1) SA 324 (Ck) 349E-G. See also the concurring judgment of Ebrahim A.J. 359A-360B.
48. Section 187 made reference to "tender boards" and a "tendering system."
49. See the PFMA SCM Regulations and the MFMA SCM Regulations.
50. For detailed discussion, see Bolton, P. *The Law of Government Procurement in South Africa* (LexisNexis Butterworths, South Africa, 2007) 199–207.
51. See *Roy Ramdaw Incorporated v. Amajuba District Municipality and Others* 2003 JDR 0180 (N) (held that under the circumstances, the negotiations conducted with the successful tenderer were not improper; the negotiations surrounding the conclusion of the contract took place in good faith); *Coolcat Restaurante BK h/a Die Kafeteria, UOVS v. Vrystaatse Regering* 1999 (2) SA 635 (O) (held that the tender board was entitled to negotiate with the sole remaining tenderer for a lower price; after all the other tenderers had been eliminated for noncompliance with the tender requirements there was no danger of prejudice to the other competing tenderers).
52. See Section 16.3.4.
53. See Section 3(2)(*b*)(i) of Paja which provides that an administrator must give "adequate notice of the nature and purpose of the proposed administrative action."
54. See, inter alia, *SA Metal & Machinery Co (Pty) Ltd. v. Transnet Ltd.* 2003 1 All SA 335 (W)—confirmed on appeal in *Transnet Ltd. and Another v. SA Metal Machinery Co (Pty) Ltd.* 2006 (4) BCLR 473 (SCA); *Logbro Properties CC v. Bedderson NO and Others* 2003 (2) SA 460 (SCA); *Putco Limited v. Minister of Transport for the Republic of South Africa and Others* [2006] JOL 17250 (W); *Lepogo Construction (Pty) Ltd. v. City of Tshwane Metropolitan Municipality* 2005 JOL 15778 (T); *Golden Reward 156 CC v. The Provincial Tender Board of the Eastern Cape and Others* [2004] JDR 0409 (Ck); *Sha-Bash Quarry Services (Pty) Ltd. t/a Mandlethu Civils & Mechanical Engineering Contractors v. Minister of Roads & Public Works, EC and Others* 2005 JOL 15509 (Ck).
55. For a more detailed and in-depth examination, see Bolton, P. *The Law of Government Procurement in South Africa* (LexisNexis Butterworths, South Africa, 2007) Chapter 10.
56. See, in particular, Arrowsmith, S. 1995. *Law Quarterly Review* 111: 235.
57. As noted in footnote 24, the act and regulations are currently (May 8, 2008) in the process of being repealed with the aim of bringing them more in line with the BBBEEA.
58. See, inter alia, *Manong & Associates v. Director General: Department of Public Works and Others* 2005 (10) BCLR 1017 (C); *Cash Paymaster Services (Pty) Ltd. v. Eastern Cape Province and Others* 1999 (1) SA 324 (Ck); *Grinaker LTA Ltd. and Another v. Tender Board (Mpumalanga) and Others* 2002 3 All SA 336 (T); *RHI Joint Venture v. Minister of Roads and Public Works and Others* 2003 (5) BCLR 544 (Ck); *Shearwater Construction v. City Tshwane Metropolitan Municipality and Others* 2006 JOL 16809 (T); *Black Top Surfaces (Pty) Ltd. v. Member of the Executive Council of Public Works & Roads Limpopo Province and Others* 2006 JOL 17099 (T).
59. On the debarment of contractors in South African law, see Section 16.7.1.
60. Costs may flow from, inter alia, the following: longer tender periods to secure participation by the relevant groups (target groups), the training of emerging businesses, and the administrative costs associated with the enforcement of policies.
61. This is in contrast with the position in other countries, for example, Canada, where contract law governs the stage before the actual award of a contract. See Hogg, PW and Monahan, PJ *Liability of the Crown* (Carswell, 3ed 2000) 216-219; Seddon, N *Government Contracts: Federal, State and Local* (The Federation Press, New South Wales, 3ed 2004) Chapter 7.
62. See, in particular, the PFMA SCM Regulations and the MFMA SCM Regulations.
63. It must be pointed out, however, that the Supreme Court of Appeal and the Constitutional Court have thus far generally been cautious in awarding delictual (or constitutional) damages to tenderers as a result of a tender award being invalidated because of a failure to comply with all administrative law requirements. See *Olitzki Property Holdings v. State Tender Board and Another* 2001 (3) SA 1247 (SCA); *Steenkamp*

NO v. Provincial Tender Board, Eastern Cape 2007 (3) SA 121 (CC). Compare *Transnet Ltd. v. Sechaba Photoscan (Pty) Ltd.* 2005 (1) SA 299 (SCA).

64. For more detailed discussion, see Bolton, P. *The Law of Government Procurement in South Africa* (LexisNexis Butterworths, South Africa, 2007) Chapter 11.
65. See the PFMA SCM Regulations and the MFMA SCM Regulations.
66. See the PFMA SCM Regulations, the MFMA SCM Regulations, and the Corruption Act.
67. For more detailed discussion, see Bolton, P. *The Law of Government Procurement in South Africa* (LexisNexis Butterworths, South Africa, 2007) 388–402.
68. See the PFMA SCM Regulations, the MFMA SCM Regulations, and the Corruption Act. See also the General Conditions of Contract for National and Provincial Government and the General Conditions of Contract for Local Government.
69. See Section 28(3)(a)(i)(aa) of the Corruption Act.
70. Section 39(2).
71. Section 173.
72. See, in particular, the General Conditions of Contract for National and Provincial Government, the General Conditions of Contract for Local Government, and the MFMA SCM Regulations.
73. See, inter alia, *Mr. Walsh t/a Wondaland Instant Lawn v. City of Tshwane Metropolitan Municipality* 2006 JDR 0155 (T).
74. *Minister of Finance v. Gore NO* 2006 SC 97 (RSA).
75. *Rainbow Construction (Pty) Ltd. and Others v. Government of the Republic of South Africa* 2002 JOL 9414 (T).
76. *GNH Office Automation CC and Another v. Provincial Tender Board and Others* 1996 (9) BCLR 1144 (Tk).
77. See, however, *Steenkamp NO v. Provincial Tender Board EC* 2006 JOL 16187 (SCA) where the court held that an unsuccessful tenderer, even if initially successful, is unable to claim out-of-pocket expenses incurred subsequent to and in reliance on the award of a tender. See also the majority judgment of Moseneke D.C.J. in *Steenkamp NO v. Provincial Tender Board, Eastern Cape* 2007 (3) SA 121 (CC).
78. *Transnet Limited v. Sechaba Photoscan (Pty) Ltd.* 2005 (1) SA 299 (SCA); *CCII Systems (Pty) Ltd. v. Minister of Defence and Others* 2006 JOL 17448 (T).

Chapter 17

Public Procurement in Cambodia

David S. Jones

CONTENTS

17.1 Introduction

With the enactment of a new constitution in 1993, Cambodia embarked upon a gradual process of recovery after many years of turbulence and civil war. The priorities were to create a modern democratic system of government and administration within the traditions of the country, and a market economy that could spur the development of private business and alleviate unemployment, deprivation, and chronic poverty.

The path of recovery has involved, among other things, reforming the system of public procurement, with the help of technical assistance from international financial and donor institutions, and placing the procurement legal and procedural framework on a footing comparable with that in other countries. This was and continues to be a key factor in creating properly resourced and well-managed development programs entailing public services, business support, rural development schemes, and infrastructure projects. However, further substantial reforms of public procurement are necessary. In addition, practices in public procurement are often inconsistent with the legal and procedural stipulations, requiring changes in behavior and mindset among officials responsible for managing procurement and awarding contracts.

After considering the system of government and administration, this chapter will examine the features of public procurement in Cambodia, as stipulated in the laws and regulations governing it, including the methods of procurement, the registration of suppliers and contractors, and other important elements of the procurement process. It will also consider the organizational basis of procurement, highlighting the functions and powers of public bodies involved in one way or another in the procurement process. The chapter will then consider the shortcomings of public procurement in Cambodia, highlighting the limitations of the legal and procedural framework, and the informal practices which have proliferated often independently of it. Attention will be focused on the most deleterious consequences of this: curtailment of competition, widespread corruption, and lack of transparency and accountability. A further shortcoming considered is the dearth of procurement knowledge and skills among public officials in Cambodia. In light of these shortcomings, the conclusion will identify in what ways the public procurement system can be reformed in Cambodia, so as to ensure fair competition, integrity, transparency, and accountability, as well as improved levels of competence in procurement management.

17.2 System of Government and Administration in Cambodia

Cambodia is a constitutional monarchy, whose system of government, according to the constitution, is based upon democratic principles. Formal power resides in the King, but executive power is exercised by the prime minister and council of ministers who are responsible to an elected bi-cameral legislature, comprising the National Assembly and the Senate, the latter being a revising chamber, which on legislative matters can be overridden by the National Assembly (Hughes, 2003; Europa World, 2005).

There are several layers of law making in Cambodia. At the highest level are basic or sovereign laws (Kram) passed by the legislature and assented to by the King. The council of ministers as the cabinet of the King, may issue royal decrees (Kret), and in its own right may issue subdecrees (Anukret) on the recommendation of ministers. Both these expand the provisions of basic laws. Ministers themselves may issue implementing rules and regulations or IRRs (Prakas) for laws, decrees, and subdecrees, and also ministerial instructions and guidelines (Sarachor).

The government bureaucracy consists of 25 line ministries, together with several state-owned enterprises and nonprofit public institutions such as educational and cultural institutions. The political head of the line ministry is the minister (or senior minister) under whom there is one or more state secretaries and one or more state undersecretaries, all being political appointees as well (Europa World, 2005). The Ministry of the Interior is responsible for the effective functioning of a now well-established system of local or subnational government. This consists of two layers. At the higher layer are 20 provincial and 4 municipal authorities subject to central government control. They are headed by a provincial governor or a municipal mayor, who is appointed by the central government (similar to a prefect). Provincial and municipal authorities are dependent on the central government for their staffing and budgets. At the lower level are the smaller commune and sangkat (urban commune) elected councils, numbering 1621, which are involved in local development projects, but like provincial and municipal authorities depend almost entirely for funding on financial transfers from the central government (plus financial aid from donor agencies) and administrative personnel (Westcott, 2002; Smoke, 2005; White and Smoke, 2005).

In 2005, Cambodian budget expenditure was 3521 billion Riels (KHR) (=$880 million), which consisted of current expenditure (including transfers) amounting to KHR2073 billion ($518 million), and capital expenditure totaling KHR1412 billion ($274 million). Seventy-eight percent of capital spending was externally financed from international financial and donor institutions in the form of loans and grants. Total budget spending in 2005 was a modest 13.4 percent of GDP (compared to the average for the previous five years of 16 percent, and dropping from a high point of 18.1 percent in 2002), while a deficit of only 2.8 percent of GDP was incurred (compared to the average for the previous five years of 5.4 percent, decreasing from a peak of 7.4 percent in 2002) (IMF, 2006b; MEF, 2007).[1]

No figures are available on the amount spent on procurement within both the current and capital budget. However, nonwage operating expenditure (which excludes transfers) within the current budget was KHR783 billion ($195.3 million) comprising 38 percent of total current expenditure. Much of this would comprise procurement of supplies, low value or small-scale equipment, and services. Most of the capital budget would involve procurement in one form or another: chiefly public works projects, build–operate–transfer (BOT) concessions (which are explained below in Section 17.3.2), and the purchase of vehicles, IT systems, and other high value assets (IMF, 2006b; MEF, 2007).

17.3 Features of Public Procurement in Cambodia

17.3.1 Legal Framework

The legal framework governing public procurement comprises three subdecrees and a list of IRRs and other ministerial directives. It should be noted that, as yet, despite being proposed by the World Bank, no basic law governs public procurement in Cambodia, which would consolidate and harmonize the disparate set of legal instruments which now exist. The main subdecree is that of 1995 which was followed by the subdecree of 1998 governing BOT projects and two subdecrees of 2002 on financial management of commune/sangkat councils which specify their procurement powers. The three main IRRs, which were passed in 1995, 1998, and 2005, relate to the 1995 subdecree, while an important directive was issued in 2002 covering guidelines for commune/sangkat procurement.

17.3.2 Methods of Public Procurement

In Cambodia, procurement includes supplies, services, and public works. Often large public works are undertaken as BOT contracts, in which a franchise (commonly called a concession) is given to the contractor who built the facility, or to a subsidiary, to manage and to operate the resultant infrastructure facility as well. The concession is subsumed under the same contract. The concession granting "sole management rights over the infrastructure project," may extend up to 30 years. At the expiry of the term, the facility is transferred to the government, unless the concession is renewed (RGC, 1998).[2] BOT concessions are an important aspect of the public private initiative (PPI) program, whereby the Cambodian government engages in partnerships with the private sector to pursue its development aims. Although the concessionaire receives full payment from the government for building the facility, it is required to pay the government a royalty (which may be a portion of the revenue received from any fees and charges it levies on end users of the facility) (RGC, 1998).

Five methods of procurement are used in Cambodia. These are domestic shopping (sometimes called domestic canvassing), international shopping, domestic competitive bidding, international competitive bidding, and direct negotiation.

According to article 5 of the 1995 subdecree, competitive bidding is adopted if it is in the "general interest" and when "a sufficient number of suppliers or companies is able to deliver the goods and carry out the requested works" (RGC, 1995). For procurements from KHR50 million ($12,500) to KHR200 million ($50,000), domestic competitive bidding is compulsory, providing "local production and construction capacities are sufficient, when the procurement value will not attract foreign bidders, or when it is highly improbable that foreign bidders will be interested" (RGC, 1995; ADB-OECD, 2005).[3] The domestic tender, as the name implies, is confined to Cambodian firms, but allows a greater degree of competition than shopping.

International competitive bidding may likewise be adopted for procurements valued at KHR50 million ($12,500) and above, providing the procurement is "important for which foreign bidders can offer a wide choice of technical proposals so that the best offer can be selected" (RGC, 1995). For procurements valued at KHR200 million ($50,000) and above, international bidding is mandatory unless it can be shown that there was an overriding reason for direct contracting, as discussed below (ADB-OECD, 2005). Given the emphasis on competitive bidding in the 1995 and 1998 subdecrees and the low thresholds for it as laid down in the IRRs, Cambodia has, in theory, as noted by the WTO, a "relatively open" system of public procurement (ADB-OECD, 2005). However, as will be discussed below in Section 17.4.2, the formal commitment to competition does not always tally with what happens in practice.

Low value and simple procurements are often undertaken through the shopping method, involving soliciting three or more suppliers to submit quotations. Although competition is limited to suppliers who are solicited, shopping does allow some degree of price comparison, and together with a proper evaluation of the quality of the goods offered, may ensure value for money and quick delivery (ADB-OECD, 2005).

If international shopping is undertaken, quotations shall be solicited from at least three suppliers from two different countries. The international shopping method, rather than international competitive bidding, is to be followed "when the market value is insufficient to allow a large international tender, or when there is a limited number of foreign suppliers for the goods or works required, or when the urgency (of the procurement) is such that it does not permit an international tender" (RGC, 1995). International shopping may be adopted up to a procurement value of KHR200 million ($50,000) (ADB-OECD, 2005). National shopping may be used when the desired goods are ordinarily available from three or more suppliers in Cambodia itself (a Cambodian-owned company or a Cambodian registered subsidiary of a foreign-owned company). These may include low value everyday supplies, spare parts, light materials, and small items of equipment (RGC, 1995). This is permitted up to a procurement value of KHR20 million ($5000).

Notwithstanding, direct purchasing and contracting (single sourcing) is permitted, without competitive bidding in certain circumstances, which are stated in article 7 of the 1995 subdecree.

These include low value procurements of not more than KHR20 million ($5000), and the purchase of goods where there is only one available supplier, or which are to be used for repairing or upgrading existing goods. Direct contracting may also apply to goods which are the same as but additional to those already supplied in a contract awarded through the bidding or shopping process, when "it is improbable that a cheaper price will be obtained in a new call for tender" (RGC, 1995). It may be similarly adopted in the procurement of works that are a "normal extension" of an ongoing project. Further conditions in which direct contracting is allowed are urgent needs for the goods to be procured, the failure of two rounds of competitive bidding to produce a suitable outcome, lack of sufficient number of bidders or lack of suitable bidders, and the purchase of goods from another public institution (e.g., a state-owned enterprise) (RGC, 1995; WB, 2004a).[4]

BOT projects, as stipulated in the 1998 subdecree, "shall be conducted strictly through international or national (open or closed) bidding process" regardless of value. However, article 9 of the subdecree does allow important exceptions from this requirement, to enable "negotiation" (direct contracting) to be undertaken instead. These include an outcome in which "the bidding process was not successful," and also the necessity for a "special concessionaire," or a "qualified concessionaire," arising from "special criteria for the infrastructure project" (RGC, 1998). The choice of the procurement method depends on a "consensus" between the line minister whose ministry covers the sector in which the project falls, the Minister for Economy and Finance, and the Council for the Development of Cambodia (CDC) (which will be discussed below in Section 17.3.4) (RGC, 1998).

As indicated by the significant amount of financial assistance received by Cambodia from international financial or donor institutions and foreign governments, many high value procurements are funded by these sources. According to the 1995 subdecree, most of the procurements so funded are undertaken "in accordance with the procedures laid down by institution or contracting government" (RGC, 1995). The main sources of external funding in the case of Cambodia are the Asian Development Bank and the World Bank. Their procurement guidelines normally specify international competitive bidding, accompanied by, among other things, pre- or postqualification of bidders and two-stage bidding for turnkey, complex, and specialized projects. Several other methods of procurement are accepted by the Asian Development Bank and the World Bank. One is limited international bidding, that allows bids to be invited from a list of suppliers "broad enough to ensure competitive prices" (WB, 2004b; ADB, 2006). This is applicable when the number of suitable suppliers is limited. Another is national competitive bidding, which may be adopted if the tender is unlikely to attract foreign competition, or if the goods and works are available locally at prices lower than the international market. For low value procurements, shopping based on the invitation to submit a quotation is also acceptable. In a specific and narrow range of circumstances, direct contracting is permitted but this should be, in the view of these institutions, the exception rather than the norm (WB, 2004b; ADB, 2006).

17.3.3 Other Features of the Public Procurement Process

Several other features of public procurement may be mentioned. As in other countries, to bid for a supply or public works contract in Cambodia requires a company to be registered with the Department of Public Procurement. The registration specifies the type of works the company can undertake, or goods and services it can provide, and the scope and value of the contract it can be awarded. The registration is undertaken by the Department (for public works contracts, in conjunction with the Ministry of Public Works). The registration is considered as obviating the need for prequalification as mentioned below (WB, 2004a; ADB-OECD, 2006).

The use of prequalification tests is not widespread, except for consultancy services and externally financed procurements and projects when such a test is insisted on by the donor institution or government. This means that in many high value procurements, contracts are awarded to companies without a rigorous assessment of their financial standing, capability, and track record. Postqualification tests are not normally undertaken either. Here there is an obvious need for reform because procurement registration is no substitute for pre- or postqualification especially in high value and complex tenders (WB, 2004a).

It should be noted that a contractor can novate a contract to a third party. For BOT contracts, no specific circumstances are cited to allow novation, except that 30 percent of the construction of the facility must be completed, and the transfer of the concession must be approved by the government. The original concessionaire as well as the third party remain jointly liable for the successful completion of the construction and subsequent operation of the facility (RGC, 1998).

According to the World Bank's procurement assessment report of Cambodia in 2004, the time taken in procuring goods, services, and public works varies considerably. In the hiring of consultancy services, the process from advertising a request for proposals to the signing of the contract may range from 2.5 to 5.5 months. In the supply of goods, the length of time from the issue of bidding documents to the signing of the contract depends on how openly competitive and international the procurement is. In the case of international competitive bidding, the period averages 5.5 months within a four to seven month range, while for national competitive bidding it is three months within a range of 2–3.5 months. The time intervals for shopping procurements are much shorter, ranging between one and two months, depending on whether overseas suppliers are sought. In hiring public works contractors under competitive tender, the time taken averages 3.5 months when the bidding is confined to domestic companies, and eight months (within a three to twelve month range) when overseas firms are allowed to tender (WB, 2004a).

17.3.4 Organization of Public Procurement

Limited responsibility for procurement is given to line ministries, state-owned enterprises, and other public institutions, and at the subnational level, to provincial and municipal authorities, and commune/sangkat councils, allowing them to undertake their own purchasing up to certain value thresholds. State-owned enterprises and the ministries of health, and education, youth, and sport, may do this up to a procurement value of KHR1 billion ($250,000), other line ministries up to KHR500 million ($125,000), and provincial and municipal authorities up to KHR300 million ($75,000). However, within these thresholds, final approval or "no objection" confirmation must be obtained from the Ministry of Economy and Finance before the contract can be awarded (RGC, 1995; ADB-OECD, 2005).

In line ministries, state-owned enterprises, and public institutions, the management of purchasing and contract awards is centralized in a procurement unit. However, in each of these organizations, a special committee exists to evaluate bids and quotations and recommend who should be awarded the contract. This is known as the prequalification, evaluation, and awards committee. One of the undersecretaries of a line ministry (who are the third highest officials in the ministry), or the second highest official in each state-owned enterprise and public institution, exercises overall management supervision of procurement activities (RGC, 1995; WB, 2004a; ADB-OECD, 2005).

Above the thresholds stated, procurement is the responsibility of the Ministry of Economy and Finance, which decides the method of procurement, evaluates proposals, and makes the selection. This task falls to the minister, assisted by one or more of the state sectaries and undersecretaries. However, the procurement units in line ministries, state-owned enterprises, and public institutions may still draw up the specifications and manage technical and practical matters relating to the procurement (RGC, 1995). In addition, all contracts at or above KHR1.3 billion ($325,000) must be referred to and approved by the council of ministers (WB, 2004a).

Procurements financed by international financial and donor institutions and foreign governments often have to follow the donor's own purchasing and hiring guidelines, and, with the exception of BOT contracts, are monitored by the Department of Investment and Cooperation within the Ministry of Economy and Finance. As with high value procurements that are domestically financed, the relevant line ministry handles the day-to-day work but the key decisions in the process are outside its remit, such as the approval of specifications, evaluation of bids, assessment of suitability of tenderers, and award of contract. These involve the Department of Investment and Cooperation in tandem with the sponsoring institution. The latter would normally vet the method of procurement chosen and the contract award, exercising a veto where necessary (WB, 2004a).

In the case of BOT projects of KHR20 billion ($5 million) or less, the key decisions in the procurement process, such as the evaluation of bids and selection of contractor, are made jointly by the minister for the relevant line ministry, the Minister for Economy and Finance and the CDC, with the additional approval of the prime minister required for projects between KHR20 and KHR40 billion ($5–10 million), and of the council of ministers for those at or above KHR40 billion ($10 million). The CDC, it should be noted, was set up under the Law on Foreign Investment of 1994 as the highest decision-making level of the government concerned with private and public sector investment. It is chaired by the prime minister and includes other senior ministers in the government (RGC, 1998; CDC, 2007). The central role played by the prime minister, the Minister for Economy and Finance, and other ministers, either as individual officials in their own right or within the CDC or council of ministers, prompted the World Bank in its procurement assessment report of 2004, to state that "(BOT) contracts appear to be chosen, negotiated and signed at high levels in RGC (Royal Government of Cambodia) with little involvement of the sector ministry" (WB, 2004a).

Procurement powers have also been vested in subnational entities, viz. provincial or municipal authorities and at a lower level in local commune/sangkat councils, as part of the policy to promote decentralization. Each provincial or municipal government under the direction of a governor or mayor may purchase goods and services and manage the procurement process but the value of the purchase remains small and officially cannot exceed KHR300 million ($7455). In addition, each commune/sangkat council is given a block grant from the commune fund managed by the central government (which can be topped up by a small amount of local revenue mainly from land charges) (Vanna, 2001; Wong and Guggenheim, 2005). The block grant can be spent by the council on procurements and public works necessary to local poverty alleviation and employment creation schemes (Peterson and Muzzini, 2005; UNDP, 2005).[5] Of course, the value and range of such procurements, as with provincial and municipal authorities, remains limited, stemming from the lack of well-trained procurement personnel, limited local availability of suitable suppliers and contractors, and a significant risk of corruption among local officials.

Commune/sangkat councils are also responsible for procurements of small-scale local or rural-based infrastructure projects sponsored by the World Bank, Asian Development Bank, NGOs, and other donor agencies. However, the projects must be evaluated and approved by a central body known as the social development fund of the Kingdom of Cambodia, which also controls the disbursements of donated funds. The projects include improving irrigation systems, equipping commune health centers, sinking water wells, and constructing bridges, culverts, and local drainage and sewerage systems (Vanna, 2001; Peterson and Muzzini, 2005; IMF, 2006a). Commune/sangkat councils may be allowed to draft specifications, manage the routine aspects of the procurement process, and, in some cases, choose the contractor. But the social development fund can reject the method of the procurement to be adopted, and assist in the drafting of specifications. In addition, it must vet the financial status and technical capacity of the contractor chosen, with the power to veto the choice of contractor made by the commune/sangkat council. In practice, the fund exercises substantial influence in nearly all the key steps in the procurement process, and in effect determines who the contractor or supplier should be. As a measure of its influence, in 2000, it compelled the commune/sangkat authorities (which were then still unelected bodies) to abandon the frequent practice of direct contracting for externally financed projects, having identified irregularities in the procurement process, and to adopt instead the domestic shopping method which involved a greater degree of competition.

The social development fund in exercising these responsibilities is not subject to interference from the Ministry of Economy and Finance (WB, 2005b). However, the fund board, which consists of 11 members, is largely composed of members of the leading political parties, as is the executive committee, though according to the statute by which the fund was established, a broad range of stakeholders in community development programs should be included (WB, 2005b). This suggests that political cronyism may play a part in awarding procurement contracts.

Despite the involvement of ministries, state-owned enterprises, public institutions, and subnational authorities in procurement, an essentially centralized structure of purchasing and contracting exists in the Cambodian public sector, as shown by the value limits imposed on the purchasing role of these agencies, and the central role of the social development fund of the Kingdom of Cambodia, Ministry of Economy and Finance, the CDC, and the council of ministers in high value purchases and infrastructure projects.

A central procurement authority exists in the form of the Department of Public Procurement in the Ministry of Economy and Finance, mentioned above, which was set up in 1995 under the procurement subdecree. Its official brief is to register suppliers and contractors and oversee and monitor procurements in accordance with the legal and procedural framework. However, in reality, the powers it possesses are quite limited and it cannot be considered as equivalent to the central procurement authorities in other countries, as will be discussed below in Section 17.4.5.

17.4 Shortcomings of Public Procurement in Cambodia

17.4.1 Shortcomings in the Legal Framework, Noncompliance, and Fragmentation

The legal and procedural framework governing procurement in Cambodia is not sufficiently far reaching, a fact highlighted by the IMF in a report on Cambodia in July 2006 (IMF, 2006b). Important aspects of the procurement process are still not covered and these can be illustrated in the following examples.

As mentioned above in Section 17.3.3, neither pre- nor postqualification tests (with the exception of consultancy services) are stipulated in any of the procurement subdecrees and IRRs. Thus, apart from the limited information provided by the registration grade and category, there is no means of determining whether a supplier or contractor has the financial standing, management capability, technical expertise, and relevant experience to undertake a major technically complex project at the bid price submitted. In the absence of such tests, there is every risk of a successful bidder defaulting on the contract and abandoning the project.

Nor is there any provision in the 1995 procurement and 1998 BOT subdecrees and in the IRRs for a two-stage bidding process, under which unpriced broad technical proposals, such as concept design, are first submitted, which are then followed in the second stage by the submission of detailed technical proposals and price bids by a short list of bidders. This saves firms who will not succeed, from the need to prepare complete technical specifications and detailed cost breakdowns in advance. Two-stage bidding is appropriate in the case of turnkey projects, contracts for large complex plants or works, and major computer and communications systems contracts, and will become increasingly relevant to Cambodia as more of such contracts become necessary.

Similarly, there is no mention in the procurement and BOT subdecrees and the IRRs of pre-bid conferences, whereby the contracting authority meets the would-be suppliers and contractors together, before bids are submitted. The purpose of the meeting is to enable the contracting authority to explain specifications, provide clarifications, and answer queries, and to arrange on-site visits for public works projects. This again is useful in the case of technically complex procurements, as with two-stage bidding, and reduces the risk of the failure of the tender to produce suitable bids, so avoiding the need for direct contracting (ADB-OECD, 2006). Where an international tender is called, there is equally no provision to enable the bid validity period to be extended and to specify when that would be allowable. Given the frequent failure to quickly and widely disseminate information on an intended procurement in Cambodia (as discussed below in Section 17.4.4), extending the bid validity period may be necessary to ensure genuine competition especially in international tenders (WB, 2004a).

Another shortcoming of the legal framework governing procurement is the absence of provisions covering bid challenge and complaints procedures in the 1995 and 1998 subdecrees and the IRRs. Thus, if a company which has failed to win a contract believes that unfair and irregular practices were followed, there exists no formal channel for a bid challenge and to secure proper redress. Complaints are received and dealt with on an ad hoc basis, but feedback from the private sector suggests that the outcomes are rarely satisfactory, except in the case of donor-sponsored projects (WB, 2004a). A further failing in the procurement laws and regulations is the failure to allow price adjustments for supply, service, and public works contracts extending for more than 18 months, which may be needed in the event of a rising rate of inflation. Added to this is the lack of clarity in the legal framework in delineating the different roles of government agencies in the procurement process (IDA-IFC, 2005).[6]

To make matters worse, the formal rules governing procurement according to the IMF are "weakly enforced" and are often flouted by contracting authorities, taking advantage of the leeway which they have been allowed in following their own practices and the lack of effective procurement oversight by the National Audit Authority, and the Department of Public Procurement, as discussed below in Section 17.4.5 (IMF, 2006b). The same tendency has been evident in donor-sponsored purchasing and infrastructure projects, in which the procurement rules and procedures of the sponsoring institution have frequently been disregarded, as revealed in the World Bank's fiduciary review in 2005 (WB, 2005a).

The upshot of the gaps in the legal and procedural framework, and the ability of contracting authorities to adopt their own procurement practices, has been fragmentation and inconsistency of purchasing and hiring practices. Consequently, these may vary from one contract to another and from one contracting authority to another at both the central government and subnational levels. The fragmentation has been compounded by inconsistencies in procurement methods and procedures prescribed by the several laws and regulations relating to procurement (WB, 2004a).

17.4.2 Limited Competition

Despite provisions in the procurement and BOT subdecrees and IRRs stipulating competition in procurement, they are not necessarily observed by the procurement officials, who often decide for themselves when competitive bidding should be adopted. With limited auditing mechanisms and weak enforcement of the laws and regulations, there is thus insufficient control and accountability to curtail this tendency. Added to this are the provisions permitting direct contracting and single sourcing in the circumstances stated above in Section 17.3.2. These provisions, on the face of it, are sensible enough as reasons to waive competition, but the terms in which they are couched are not sufficiently well defined, and so, according to the World Bank's procurement assessment report on Cambodia, depend on "judgment in their application." Procurement officials have made the most of their resultant discretion to ensure they are "applied more widely than intended" at the expense of competitive bidding, resulting in the "arbitrary creation of situations justifying direct contracting" (WB, 2004a; ADB-OECD, 2006). The Cambodian government in a self-assessment report on procurement and corruption in 2005 has acknowledged as much, referring to "numerous incidents" of direct contracting that affect "much public procurement," with the most noticeable examples being BOT contracts (ADB-OECD, 2005).

Further undermining competition is the "poor information infrastructure" in Cambodia that prevents information on intended procurements from being widely disseminated. The official gazette is the main channel for advertising bidding opportunities but it is not always used for this purpose, while copies are difficult to obtain. In addition, it does not provide detailed and up-to-date announcements of new procurement regulations and procedures. Matters are made worse by the lack of online advertising. Thus, would-be suppliers and contractors may often remain unaware of an intended procurement. This has allowed many contracts to be awarded through direct negotiation.

In a hard-hitting assessment, the International Monetary Fund and the International Development Association in 2003 described the procurement of services in Cambodia in the following terms:

> Closed, opaque and non-competitive bid transactions that lack performance indicators or regulatory oversight have been a common feature of Cambodia's procurement of private providers of public services to date at the cost of revenue opportunities for the government and efficient and sustainable service provision for the consumers (IDA-IMF, 2003).[7]

Despite strongly urging the Cambodian government to adopt fully competitive bidding, the IMF in three reports in the following year noted that direct contracting and negotiation was still far too prevalent (IMF, 2004a,b,c).

The eschewal of competitive bidding has been particularly noticeable in major public works programs including BOT projects (WB, 2004a, c). For example, the World Bank report in 2004 on investment opportunities in Cambodia noted that major public works contracts in transport, telecommunications, water supply, electricity, and waste management involved direct private negotiations between the CDC and other senior officials in government on the one hand, and the contractor on the other, without any recognizable bidding process (WB, 2004c). Of particular importance were recent directly negotiated contracts with power producers, and a directly negotiated contract awarded to a French–Malaysian joint venture in 2004 to operate Cambodia's two international airports. Such projects, according to the World Bank, were, therefore not commissioned on a least cost basis and were undertaken by contractors who had not necessarily met the technical criteria to ensure proper and reliable delivery (WB, 2004c). This tendency has been more than encouraged, as mentioned above in Section 17.3.2, by the vague wording of article 9 of the 1998 BOT subdecree relating to competitive tendering. Wide discretion may be exercised in determining if the bidding process was "unsuccessful," when a "special concessionaire" or a "qualified concessionaire" is needed, and whether the project involves "special criteria" which allows procurement officials to resort to direct contracting (RGC, 1998).

High value procurements of equipment have also been based on direct contracting. The IMF in 2004, in its consultation report on Cambodia, drew attention to the absence of competitive bidding in the procurement of capital goods (IMF, 2004b). For example, according to the World Bank, the purchase of a container scanner at the country's leading seaport was based on a direct award without a competitive tender (WB, 2004c). Even in high value purchases the World Bank has sponsored, there has been a lack of competitive bidding, according to its fiduciary review of Cambodia in 2005 (WB, 2005a).

17.4.3 Corruption

In reports from international bodies dealing with Cambodia, corruption is cited time and again as being all-pervasive in government administration, including public procurement. All the main forms of corruption, viz. bribery, embezzlement, nepotism and cronyism, collusion, and fraud, have been and continue to be commonplace. The World Bank's control of corruption governance indicator provides evidence of how widespread corruption is. According to the indicator, Cambodia's percentile ranking for control of corruption was 24.9 in 2000, dropping to a mere 8.9 in 2005 (number of jurisdictions surveyed was 211). Using the same indicator, Cambodia's point score for control of corruption within the range of −2.5 to +2.5 was −0.79 in 2000 (compared to the regional average for East Asia of −0.29). The point score decreased to −1.12 by 2005 (compared to the regional average of −0.13) (WB, 2007). The World Bank data is supported by that of Transparency International (TI). In its corruption perception index, Cambodia's percentile rank in 2006 was only 6, with a score of 2.1 out of 10 (number of jurisdictions surveyed was 163) (TI, 2007).[8] Cambodia now ranks within the 10 percent of countries of the world considered to be most corrupt. The extent of its corruption noticeably exceeds the average in East Asia as a whole, and has increased since 2000.

All this ties in with a finding from an IMF survey in 2005 of businesses in Cambodia, which revealed that 80 percent of the sample declared the need to pay a bribe when dealing with public agencies including winning a contract to supply goods and services, and a contract for a public works or BOT project. Seventy-one percent indicated such payments are "frequent" (IDA-IFC, 2005). The prevalence of corruption was alluded to in a statement in 2002 by the IMF representative in Phnom Penh, Robert Hagemann, who noted that in Cambodia "anticorruption agencies need to focus on public procurement, which gives rise to some of the most egregious abuses." He further remarked that "public works and construction are widely perceived to be the sectors most riddled by corruption, followed by the defense sector" (IMF, 2002). A recent joint report by the Asian Development Bank and the OECD, has referred to "numerous incidents of often-undeclared conflicts of interest" in the procurement process (ADB-OECD, 2006). This was corroborated by the World Bank's fiduciary review of Cambodia in 2005 (WB, 2005a). The joint report recognized too that the opportunities to engage in direct contracting has inevitably given rise to bribery and cronyism (ADB-OECD, 2006). What is more, the World Bank's fiduciary review drew attention to evidence of both collusion among contractors including "similarities in bid prices, different bids under the same format and including the same mistakes, different contractors using the same bank accounts" and also of fraudulent practices "through the provision of falsified bid securities and other documents" (WB, 2005a).

Corruption has been all too apparent even in donor-funded projects implemented by the Cambodian government and subnational agencies. In the fiduciary review of Cambodia in 2005, referred to above, the World Bank uncovered plenty of evidence of collusion and fraud by contractors, and also of conflicts of interest involving procurement officials, as well as partisan bid evaluations, that suggested bribery, cronyism, and nepotism (WB, 2005a). Furthermore, in 2006, in a survey of projects it had sponsored in Cambodia, the World Bank found misprocurement due to corruption by Cambodian officials, in 43 contracts covering 5 projects. The total value of the contracts was $11.9 million. Three of the projects involving land management, rural infrastructure, and water supply and sanitation have been suspended by the Ministry of Economy and Finance, pending a rectification of the malpractices identified. They will be eventually handed over to an international procurement agent at which point implementation will be resumed (WB, 2006). Corruption has also affected projects funded on a bilateral basis. For example, the South Korean government withdrew its commitment to fund a road transport project because it perceived that contractors had been selected on a fraudulent basis (WB, 2004c).

Several reasons may be given to explain the prevalence of corruption in Cambodia's public procurement. One is the inadequate legal framework and internal guidelines to combat corrupt practices. It is true that corruption is prohibited under the 1995 procurement subdecree and the civil service code. In addition, public servants who solicit or take bribes may be removed or suspended, and selected bidders are required to formally declare that they have not bribed a procurement official or another company submitting a bid (ADB-OECD, 2006). But these are token measures which have limited scope and are "weakly enforced." They are further undermined by the absence of strong accountability mechanisms such as that provided by an effective state audit institution and anticorruption agency (ADB-OECD, 2006). This is coupled to the lack of rigorous sanctions against those who have engaged in corrupt dealings. For example, there is no legal mandate to suspend a company temporarily or permanently from further government contracts when it has engaged in bribery or collusion in its attempts to win a contract. Likewise, procurement officials are not required to declare conflicts of interest.

Further increasing the chances of corruption is the absence of a rotation arrangement among members of prequalification, evaluation, and awards committees, and the lack of multitiered reviews involving different committees and personnel. Furthermore, no comprehensive ethical code to which public servants are bound currently exists nor a training program for procurement officials that emphasizes ethical responsibility.

At the very heart of the corruption problem in Cambodia is the low remuneration of public servants, a culture of corruption in which unethical practices are accepted as a matter of course, and related to this the absence of, as yet, a comprehensive anticorruption law.

17.4.4 Lack of Transparency

Closely linked to noncompliance with the legal and procedural framework, the limited amount of competition, and widespread corruption, is the lack of transparency in the procurement process. In particular, it is commonly accepted that in Cambodia (as in other countries), corruption and the absence of transparency go hand in hand (though this begs the question whether the lack of transparency gives rise to corruption, or vice versa) (IMF, 2004b; WB, 2004a). Lack of transparency has been emphasized repeatedly in the IMF, World Bank, OECD, Asian Development Bank, and UNDP reports on Cambodia as being at the heart of procurement failings in Cambodia. Indeed, it has been only too evident from the difficulties encountered in their own attempts to find out what procurement practices are actually followed.

The nontransparent practices in public procurement in Cambodia are reflected in the fact that the business community often does not know the method of procurement and the evaluation criteria which are to be or have been adopted in a particular purchase or public works contract, or that even a procurement is to be undertaken at all. In fact, in a self-assessment of procurement by the Cambodian government, it was stated there were "no strict rules for publishing of tenders or invitation to bidders" (ADB-OECD, 2005). Equally, would-be suppliers and contractors are frequently kept in the dark about the bidding or quotation procedures they must follow and the documents and information to be submitted, as well as the full range of specifications to be met relating to a purchase or public works contract. Neither are reasons for a selection nor the contents of a contract, once it has been awarded, divulged for the benefit of the public and the business community. Also there is no way of knowing if the terms of a contract have been adhered to during the contract period (ADB-OECD, 2005; IMF, 2006b). Compounding the problem is the failure to keep regular written records of the procurement process, including a register of bids received and minutes of meetings of prequalification, evaluation, and awards committees (ADB-OECD, 2005).

Such lack of disclosure is especially apparent in BOT concessions. According to the World Bank report in 2004 on investment in Cambodia, "few if any concession agreements or negotiated contracts have been made public for review, publication, or public scrutiny" (WB, 2004c). Similarly, there is hardly any disclosure on whether there has been compliance to the detailed provisions of these contracts during the period of the concession (IMF, 2006c).

17.4.5 Weakness of Overseeing and Watchdog Mechanisms

The failings in the system of public procurement in Cambodia can be linked to the absence of strong overseeing and watchdog mechanisms to ensure proper accountability. As mentioned above in Section 17.3.4, official responsibility to monitor procurements and ensure compliance to laws and regulations, as well as to review laws and procedures, is vested in the Department of Public Procurement. However, its formal role bears little relation to what it actually is able to do. The department often finds it has no real authority to enforce compliance to official rules and procedures in respect to procurements which officially come under its purview (most which are domestically funded). It has no involvement in monitoring procurements of goods and services, and public works, sponsored by international financial and donor institutions. Nor does it have any power to monitor procurement in local development schemes implemented by the commune/sangkat councils. Furthermore, the department has no major say in reviewing procurement laws and policies and has little responsibility for procurement training (WB, 2004a). The question arises whether the weakness of the Department of Public Procurement is caused by or alternatively results in the ability of the contracting authorities to adopt their own in-house procurement practices outside the official rules and procedures.

Another watchdog institution is the National Audit Authority, which was set up in 2001 under the Law on Audit enacted in 2000. As specified in articles 5–9, it is responsible for auditing the financial accounts, and "the functions and on-going operations" of the entire range of public organizations, including their compliance to procurement laws and regulations, together with the mandate to evaluate the performance of supply and public works contractors (RGC, 2000). Several international financial institutions in their reports on Cambodia in 2005 commented on the effectiveness of the National Audit Authority observing that it is "gradually assuming and discharging its mandated responsibilities" and is "gradually gaining capacity," but pointing to a pressing need to strengthen its capacity (ADB-OECD, 2005; IDA-IFC, 2005). According to the U4: Anti-Corruption Resource Center (UARC) in Germany, the National Audit Authority, "is not yet able to fulfill its auditing functions according to international standards." The center stated that the main problems are "the lack of know-how and expertise [and] a deficit in capacity" (ARC, 2005).[9]

To reflect the growing importance of the National Audit Authority as a check on the performance of the public sector, it was decided by the Cambodian government in 2004 that the authority would review the contracts in BOT and other infrastructure projects. The IMF has noted that this included evaluating the performance of contractors to "verify compliance with the terms of the contract" but expressed doubts whether it was equal to the task in view of its limited expertise and resources (IMF, 2004b).

Further adding to the lack of effective accountability is the fact that no specialist anticorruption body has yet been established to investigate corrupt dealings and take action against the offending parties. As mentioned below in Section 17.5, the clear intention is to set up such a body under a proposed anticorruption law, but its establishment must await the enactment of this law, which may not happen for another year or two.

17.4.6 Deficiencies in Procurement Knowledge and Skills

Public procurement in Cambodia is further undermined by the limited knowledge and skills of procurement personnel. The deficiency is evident in a number of ways. Most pressing is lack of knowledge of the official procurement rules and procedures. In the World Bank survey of procurement personnel in Cambodia, which was carried out in 2004, only 25 percent of respondents were able to recall the most important rules and guidelines governing procurement, with 25 percent also admitting that they had less than a full understanding of them (WB, 2004a; ADB-OECD, 2006). The competence of officials in tender management especially in drafting specifications, drawing up contracts, and making selections is equally poor. Skills too are often lacking in project management for major public works procurements. The paucity of adequately skilled procurement personnel is part of the wider problem of the low caliber of personnel in the Cambodian public service at both the management and operational levels, and is linked not only to the lack of sufficient training but also to "low rates of remuneration compared to those offered by the growing private sector" (WB, 2004a). This means that the public service loses out in attracting talented recruits.

17.5 Challenge of Further Reform

In view of the shortcomings identified in Cambodia's public procurement system, a number of reforms are necessary. These have been and continue to be advocated by international financial and donor institutions such as the World Bank, the Asian Development Bank, and the IMF.

The IMF has urged the Cambodian government to develop an "enhanced legal and regulatory framework, including the development of a new procurement law" (IMF, 2006b). The end product, it is hoped, would be a wide-ranging sovereign law or Kram governing public procurement, with accompanying implementing regulations, that comprehensively and precisely define the methods, procedures, and selection criteria under which procurement would be undertaken (WB, 2005a; IMF, 2006a).

Such a comprehensive law would provide, in particular, an opportunity to rectify the omissions in the present legal framework, for example, through the incorporation of provisions for two-stage bidding, pre- and postqualification, pre-bid conferences, bid challenge and grievance remedy procedures, and price adjustments in period contracts. Unclear provisions and terms in the present legal framework could be clarified too, such as the circumstances under which direct contracting is permissible (with a view to restricting the opportunities for such), the "monitoring role" of the Department of Public Procurement and state undersecretaries, and the sometimes overlapping procurement responsibilities of various public agencies and bodies. A new law could also provide a better legal framework for enhancing competition, not only by restricting direct contracting, but also by lowering the stipulated thresholds for international bidding and allowing registration to occur in conjunction with bid submission and extensions of the bid validity period. A further advantage arising from a new law would be the consolidation of all the existing subdecrees relating to procurement, with its provisions applied across all ministries, state-owned enterprises, other public institutions, and subnational authorities, ensuring a much greater degree of standardization of procurement practices than currently exists (WB, 2005a; IMF, 2006a,b).

Progress has been made in creating a far-reaching sovereign law for combating corruption. A draft law was submitted to the legislature in 2004. It spells out different types of offences relating to corruption, and various types of conflicts of interest, provides for rules of evidence in corruption cases that come before the courts, and requires senior public officials (both appointed and elected) to declare their assets and debts in writing on entry into and exit from office, and at least once a year when holding office. The law stipulates penalties for corrupt public officials which range from imprisonment for one month to fifteen years, depending on the amount of illicit benefit obtained, together with a fine which is twice the amount of the benefit measured in monetary terms. The law further establishes an anticorruption agency, the Supreme Council against Corruption, mentioned below (Rendak and Eastman, 2006). However, the process of enactment of the anticorruption law has been stalled by the necessity to bring other laws, decrees, and subdecrees in line with it. Mindful of the delay in enactment, IMF has urged the "fast track passing of the comprehensive anti-corruption law" (IMF, 2006a).

Linked to reforming the legal framework are necessary institutional reforms for the purpose of enforcing accountability. This entails strengthening the role of the Department of Public Procurement, as the central procurement authority, in monitoring how procurements are undertaken, so it can take to task and sanction agencies and officials, as well contractors and suppliers, who fail to adhere to procurement laws and regulations. To ensure further accountability is the continued development of the National Audit Authority by strengthening its powers of investigation and providing it with the necessary auditing expertise. This would enable it to scrutinize accounts and assess compliance to procurement procedures so that it can uncover waste, corruption, and noncompliance.

Added to this is the necessity to put into operation "an independent and effective body to fight corruption," which can "ensure the strictest and total enforcement of the law sparing no one from its provisions, however highly placed" (IMF, 2006a). The draft anticorruption law, once it has been enacted, will go someway to meet this necessity, because it proposes, as mentioned above, the establishment of such an authority in the form of Supreme Council against Corruption. This body will have an independent budget and will be able draw on resources from external donors. Within its competence will be the ability to draft further measures to combat corruption. It would be empowered to undertake wide-ranging investigations into alleged corruption, and in the process summon officials and others to appear before it. However, it will not have the power to prosecute, which will remain with the Department of Public Prosecution (Rendak and Eastman, 2006).

Institutional reform of public procurement in Cambodia could also entail greater delegation of procurement functions to line ministries, state-owned enterprises, and other public institutions, and subnational entities. The limited delegation that has occurred has been regarded as enabling procurements to be more responsive to end-user needs (both the agencies delivering public services and the recipient communities). For this reason, international financial and donor institutions have pressed for a greater degree of delegation so as to more fully realize its benefits, and to avoid the drawbacks of over-centralized procurement, especially the failure to meet end-user needs and to allow community participation in procurement decisions (IMF, 2004b, 2006a; WB, 2004a; ADB-OECD, 2006). This could be achieved by raising the value thresholds below which line ministries, state-owned enterprises, and other public institutions, and subnational entities can undertake their own procurements, provided their staff are given training to upgrade their procurement knowledge and skills, as discussed below.

However, on the IMF's own admission, the legal and institutional changes indicated above, so as to be effective, still depend on "behavioral changes" and the creation of a "culture of service" (IMF, 2006b). To reform procurement practices will require a change of mindset among leaders, officials, and companies alike, in which procurement rules are taken seriously at all levels and their violations are not tolerated. In all probability, this will only be achieved gradually, especially because irregular and informal procurement practices at variance with legally stipulated rules and acceptable standards have now become ingrained in the Cambodian bureaucracy and business sector. Likewise, the institutional reforms will depend on the independence of monitoring, auditing, and anticorruption bodies, their ability to remain free from corruption themselves, and their commitment to undertake the responsibilities vested in them without compromises to powerful interests. In this regard, the draft anticorruption law does not specify that those appointed to the proposed Supreme Council against Corruption should meet relevant professional standards which may create opportunities to undermine its independence of government leaders and powerful political factions (Rendak and Eastman, 2006).

A further area where new initiatives are necessary is the training of officials involved in procurement. The reports of international financial and donor institutions have consistently pointed to the need to upgrade their knowledge and skills. Sixty percent of respondents in the World Bank survey of public procurement personnel in Cambodia, referred to above in Section 17.4.6, indicated that they received "no or hardly any training." According to feedback given to the Asian Development Bank and OECD by the Cambodian government, procurement personnel receive on average only two days training per year (ADB-OECD, 2005). However, the implementation of a comprehensive training program for procurement officials depends on a number of factors. These include a commitment of government leaders and the senior hierarchy of the Cambodian public service to such a program, the availability of funds to finance it, the acquisition of experienced training staff with the necessary expertise, and the strengthening of the Department of Public Procurement, as the central procurement authority, with overall responsibility for training. It is imperative that in addition to teaching the core competencies of procurement, such a program imparts common practices and standards to facilitate harmonization, and inculcates ethical responsibilities with respect to bribery, embezzlement, nepotism and cronyism, and conflicts of interest.

Notes

1. "MEF" refers to the Ministry of Economy and Finance, Cambodia; "IMF" refers to the International Monetary Fund.
2. "RGC" refers to the Royal Government of Cambodia.
3. "ADB-OECD" refers to the Asian Development Bank and the Organisation of Economic Co-Operation and Development.
4. "WB" refers to the World Bank.
5. "UNDP" refers to the United Nations Development Program.
6. "IDA-IFC" refers to the International Development Association and International Finance Corporation.
7. "IDA-IMF" refers to the International Development Association and International Monetary Fund.
8. "TI" refers to Transparency International.
9. "UARC" refers to the U4: Anti-Corruption Resource Center, Eschborn, Germany.

References

Asian Development Bank. 2006. *ADB: Procurement Guidelines.* Manila: Author. Available at http://www.adb.org/Documents/Guidelines/Procurement (downloaded on February 23, 2007).

Asian Development Bank and Organisation of Economic Co-Operation and Development. 2005. *Anti-Corruption Policies in Asia and the Pacific: Thematic Review on Provisions and Practices to Curb Corruption in Public Procurement: Self Assessment Report—Cambodia.* Manila: Author.

Asian Development Bank and Organisation of Economic Co-Operation and Development. 2006. *Curbing Corruption in Public Procurement in Asia and the Pacific: Progress and Challenges in 25 Countries.* Manila: Author.

Council for the Development of Cambodia. 2007. *Who We Are.* Phnom Penh: Author. Available at http://www.cambodiainvestment.gov.kh (downloaded on February 4, 2007).

Europa World. 2005. *The Europa World Year Book,* vol. 1. London: Routledge.

Hughes, C. 2003. *The Political Economy of Cambodia's Transition, 1991–2001.* London: Routledge Curzon.

International Development Association and International Finance Corporation. 2005. *Country Assistance Strategy for the Kingdom of Cambodia.* Washington, DC: Author.

International Development Association and International Monetary Fund. 2003. *Cambodia: Poverty Reduction Strategy Paper: Joint Staff Assessment.* Washington, DC: Author.

International Monetary Fund. 2002. *Post-Consultative Group Meeting Between the Royal Government of Cambodia and the Donor Community: Statement by Robert P. Hagemann, IMF Resident Representative in Cambodia.* Washington, DC: Author.

International Monetary Fund. 2004a. *Cambodia: Ex Post Assessment of Longer Term Program Engagement.* Country Report No. 04/324, Washington, DC: Author.

International Monetary Fund. 2004b. *Cambodia: 2004 Article IV Consultation—Staff Report, Public Information Notice and Press Release on the Executive Board Discussions; and Statement by the Executive Director.* Country Report No. 04/328, Washington, DC: Author.

International Monetary Fund. 2004c. *Cambodia: Poverty Reduction Strategy Paper Progress Report.* Country Report No. 04/333, Washington, DC: Author.

International Monetary Fund. 2006a. *Cambodia: Poverty Reduction Strategy Paper.* Country Report No. 06/266, Washington, DC: Author.

International Monetary Fund. 2006b. *Cambodia: Selected Issues and Statistical Appendix.* Country Report No. 06/265, Washington, DC: Author.

Ministry of Economy and Finance, Cambodia. 2007. *Statistics: Macro-Economic Framework 2005–2006.* Phnom Penh: Author. Available at http://www.mef.gov.kh/statistics/ (downloaded on February 23, 2007).

Peterson, G. and Muzzini, E. 2005. Decentralizing basic infrastructure service. In World Bank (Ed.), *East Asia Decentralizes: Making Local Government Work* (pp. 209–236). Washington: World Bank.

Rendak, N. and Eastman, D. 2006. Legal and judicial reform: Recent developments and prospects (pp. 99–109). In D. Coe et al. (Eds.), *Cambodia: Rebuilding for a Challenging Future.* Washington: International Monetary Fund.

Royal Government of Cambodia. 1995. *Anukret of July 31st Governing Public Procurement,* no. 60. Phnom Penh: Author.

Royal Government of Cambodia. 1998. *Anukret on Build–Operate–Transfer (BOT) Contract.* Phnom Penh: Author.

Royal Government of Cambodia. 2000. *Law on Audit of the Kingdom of Cambodia.* Phnom Penh: Author.

Smoke, P. 2005. The rules of the inter-governmental game in East Asia: Decentralization frameworks and processes. In World Bank (Ed.), *East Asia Decentralizes: Making Local Government Work* (pp. 25–51). Washington: World Bank.

Transparency International. 2007. *Corrupt Perceptions Index.* Berlin, Germany. Available at http://www.transparency.org (downloaded on January 19, 2007).

U4: Anti-Corruption Resource Center. 2005. *Support to an Independent National Audit Authority, Cambodia*. Eschborn, Germany: GTZ. Available at http://www.u4.no/projects/ (downloaded on February 21, 2007).

United Nations Development Program. 2005. *Investing in Cambodia's Future: United Nations Development Program Annual Report, 2004*. New York: Author.

Vanna, N. 2001. *Post-conflict Rehabilitation Experiences of the Social Fund for the Kingdom of Cambodia*. Manila: Asian Development Bank.

Westcott, C. 2002. *Key Governance Issues in Cambodia, Lao PDR, Thailand and Viet Nam*. Manila: Asian Development Bank.

White, R. and Smoke, P. 2005. East Asia decentralizes. In World Bank (Ed.), *East Asia Decentralizes: Making Local Government Work* (pp. 2–23). Washington: World Bank.

Wong, S. and Guggenheim, S. 2005. Community driven development: Decentralization's accountability challenge. In World Bank (Ed.), *East Asia Decentralizes: Making Local Government Work* (pp. 254–267). Washington: World Bank.

World Bank. 2004a. *Cambodia: Country Procurement Assessment Report*. Report No. 29950 KH, Bangkok: Author.

World Bank. 2004b. *Guidelines: Procurement under IBRD and IDA Credits*. Washington, DC: Author. Available at http://siteresources.worldbank.org/ intprocurement (downloaded on January 19, 2007).

World Bank. 2004c. *Cambodia: Seizing the Opportunity: Investment Climate. Assessment and Reform Strategy for Cambodia*. Report No. 27925-KH, Washington, DC: Author.

World Bank. 2005a. *Cambodia: Fiduciary Review*. Washington, DC: Author.

World Bank. 2005b. *Implementation Completion Report on a Credit in the Amount of US$25 Million Equivalent to the Kingdom of Cambodia for a Social Fund II Project*. Washington, DC: Author.

World Bank. 2006. *Cambodia: The Fight against Corruption*. Washington, DC: Author.

World Bank. 2007. *Governance Indicators: 1996–2007*. Washington, DC: Author. Available at http://www.worldbank.org/wbi/governance/govdata (downloaded on January 19, 2007).

Chapter 18

Procurement Systems in Uganda

Edgar Agaba and Nigel Shipman

CONTENTS

18.1 Political, Social, and Economic Background

The frontiers of many African countries do not reflect the limits of natural regions nor separate ethnic groups, but were shaped in detail by the chances of conquest and compromise between colonial powers. This is true of Uganda, which was created as a political entity in 1894 with the establishment of a British Protectorate, bringing together in an artificial union approximately 32 different indigenous ethnic and language groups. The main ethnic division occurs at central Uganda's Lake Kyoga between the Bantu-speaking south and the northern Sudanic and Nilotic language speakers (Ofcansky, 1996, p. 72). Another consequence of the establishment of artificial frontiers was to divide in separate colonies people who belonged to the same ethnic group or clan and they were soon to be further separated by the introduction of new foreign languages and cultures (Mutibwa, 1992, p. 3). It has been claimed that ethnic diversity has thwarted all government plans for national integration (Ofcansky, 1996, p. 73).

Since becoming an independent state in 1962, Uganda has had a turbulent history, especially during the brutal rule of Idi Amin (1971–1979), when many of the intellectual and business elite were killed or fled abroad and the economy was destroyed. During the 1970s, gross domestic product (GDP) declined by approximately 25 percent and exports by 60 percent, and there was an annual inflation rate of more than 70 percent (Ofcansky, 1996, p. 95). By 1986, when President Yoweri Kaguta Museveni's National Resistance Movement (NRM) came to power, "the whole of Uganda was in the last extremes of disintegration, and the odds against its survival, let alone recovery, had to remain heavy" (Davidson, 1992, p. 311). For most of the period of NRM rule, Uganda has been a no-party state, where candidates stood as individuals and political parties were not allowed to contest elections. This system was defended as a means of combating tribalism. It was argued that multiparty politics were unsuited to societies at Uganda's stage of development, as they "tend to have vertical polarizations based mainly on tribe and ethnicity… people support someone because he belongs to their group, not because he puts forward the right policies" (Museveni, 1997, p. 187). However, some critics have claimed that this system operated little differently from a one-party system (Meredith, 2005, p. 405). A multiparty system was restored late in 2005, though as in many other parts of Africa, political divisions continue to be based largely on ethnicity and personal patronage rather than different economic and social programs.

With per capita gross national income of $280 in 2005, Uganda ranks 144th among the 177 countries covered in the 2005 Human Development Index (World Bank, 2007, p. 3). The average Ugandan has to live on 77 cents a day. Although GDP increased by 5.6 percent in 2003–2004 and 2004–2005 (International Monetary Fund, 2006), this growth was offset by one of the highest population growth rates in the world. As U.S. Agency for International Aid (USAID) has observed, "Uganda's 3.4% population growth rate continues to erode economic gains, deepen poverty, and negatively affect other achievements in the social sectors" (USAID, 2005). Uganda's poverty is reflected in other indices, including life expectancy at birth of around 49 years, and infant and child (under five) mortality rates of around 88 and 152, respectively, per 1000 live births in 2005 (World Bank, 2007, p. 9).

18.2 Importance of Public Procurement Reform

It has been estimated that about 31 percent of local government revenue and 35 percent of central government revenue are expended by way of public procurement (Government of Uganda, 2006). Much of this expenditure is applied to key development projects in education, health, and transport infrastructures. Thus, any failure to achieve value for money in the procurement system will impact adversely on development goals, particularly in view of the shortage of resources.

Public procurement reform in Uganda and elsewhere in Africa was based on an attempt to achieve better value in this major area of government expenditure and to reduce corruption in government activities, recognizing that the procedures leading to the award of government contracts and contract management were major areas where corruption took place and that the failure to combat such corruption effectively was adding to the cost of development projects and leading to a poor standard of purchased facilities. Transparency International, a leading civil society anti-corruption organization, has argued that good public procurement is an important instrument for good governance and thereby contributes to the government's legitimacy and credibility. On the other hand, bad public procurement that facilitates corruption may increase poverty and inequality by diverting funds away from social needs, engender bad choices, encourage competition in bribery rather than in quality or price, and create a market-entry cost or nontariff barrier for those companies that do not wish or cannot afford to bribe their way in (Transparency International, 2006, p. 28).

International development agencies and developed country donors contribute to roughly half of Uganda's national budget and consequently have exerted substantial influence on all areas of governance (USAID, 2005). Uganda's dependence on foreign donor support for its budgeted programs is remarkably high when compared to a developing country's average of 15 percent (Easterly, 2006, p. 45). Unfortunately, there has been found to be little correlation between the amount of foreign aid provided and the pace of development: over the period 1950–2001, countries with below-average foreign aid had comparable growth rates as those receiving above-average aid (ibid., p. 39). Much of the aid is given in support of good governance programs, which include procurement reform. The procurement reform program was carried through by the government of Uganda and its public officials, but the international and foreign government donor agencies exerted pressure and contributed expertise.

In most developed countries, public procurement takes place within a framework of international obligations, such as the World Trade Organization's Agreement on Government Procurement or the Procurement Directives made under regional agreements such as the European Union or the North America Free Trade Agreement. Public procurement in most developing countries does not have to meet these international requirements. Consequently, the pressure to reform may not have been as strong. However, in recent years, the impetus for reform has increased, partly in consequence of requirements set by the World Bank and other donor organizations as conditions for providing development aid, but principally because the inefficiencies of the unreformed systems had become self-evident. Most donors consider that a well-functioning procurement system is an essential requirement if their funds are to be used effectively to promote development. Where such a system is not provided by the host country, donors may insist on using their own procedures. There has been a trend in recent years for using national systems where these are suitable, through multidonor budget support programs (Abeillé, 2003). As most developing countries prefer the flexibility that comes with receiving development aid through budget support, they have an incentive to reform their public procurement and financial management systems.

18.3 Features of the Unreformed System

The features of the Ugandan public procurement system before the inception of the reform program in the late 1990s were typical of many developing African countries that were at one time British colonies or protectorates. Many newly independent African countries retained the procurement system of their former colonial masters until it was no longer able to cope with requirements.

The procurement reform program was thus concerned with an overdue abolition of the colonial procurement system and its replacement by a system better suited to the needs of a modern developing country.

In the unreformed system in Uganda, procurement was centralized, with contracts above a threshold value of $1000 being awarded by a Central Tender Board in the Ministry of Finance, on the basis of regulations that had been approved in 1977. There were separate tender boards for the police and military. Procurement of many items on behalf of ministries was undertaken by the Government Central Purchasing Corporation. The corporation had been set up by statute in 1990, replacing a central purchasing organization within the civil service. Although these arrangements offered the advantages of consolidated purchasing and central control, the Central Tender Board was unable to keep pace with the expansion of government activities and their attendant procurement requirements. There was a consequential backlog of tender submissions and the procurement process became protracted. The public procurement system was regarded as a key obstacle to effective service delivery and development.

A study of the changes that were needed in the procurement system (Task Force on Public Procurement Reform, 1999) reported that

- Guidance for the current procurement system was scattered among various outdated regulations and procedures.
- Little action was taken to ensure that the procurement process complied with established regulations and procedures.
- There were no clear lines of public accountability in the procurement process and little transparency.
- There was little institutional coordination.
- Operating through cash budgets and with inadequate financial planning, the government was an unreliable business partner and suppliers frequently suffered delays in receiving payment for goods and services supplied; consequently, bidders sought to offset these risks by higher prices.
- System suffered from various forms of malpractice and unethical conduct, including a high incidence of vested interests, interference and insider dealings, and occasional cases of retrospective approval of contract awards.
- There was a lack of professional knowledge and expertise in the purchasing and contracting functions at all levels.

18.4 Stages in the Procurement Reform Process in Uganda

Some writers have observed that public procurement reform is most likely to succeed when it proceeds through various stages of progression (Walker, 2003, pp. 3–12). The procurement reform process in Uganda went through the following stages of progression, though some of these stages proceeded concurrently and others are part of a continuing process of change management.

18.4.1 Stage One: Recognition of Need for Reform

By the late 1990s, the failure of the existing procurement system to cope with the expansion in government procurement requirements and to deliver value for money had become generally accepted among government and donor partners. In December 1997, a National Public Procurement Forum was held to bring together key decision makers to discuss procurement reform. The Minister of Finance then established a task force on public procurement reform, which began its work in May 1998 and reported in January 1999. In advocating the need for procurement reform, the task force considered the desired outcomes to be as follows:

- Transparency, characterized by well-defined regulations and procedures open to public scrutiny; clear, standardized tender documents containing complete information; and equal opportunity for all in the bidding process
- More effective means for fighting waste and corruption and improving financial accountability
- Integration of the public procurement system with national budgeting procedures
- More attractive investment climate by lowering risk
- Greater competitive pressure to satisfy customer needs
- Streamlined procurement process through greater use of electronic commerce

Foremost among these desired outcomes was a substantial reduction in corruption. The inspector general of government, who acts both as the ombudsman against inefficiencies and abuse of power and as the chief protagonist against corruption in the public sector, had claimed that

> There is still a lot of corruption in our public procurement system. Most of this corruption is not known because it is done in utmost secrecy. It is, however, manifested in wrong computation of costs by evaluation teams, shoddy commodities and goods, poor performance of construction works, failure to complete performance of contracts on time or not at all, etc. (Task Force on Public Procurement Reform, 1999, p. 14)

18.4.2 Stage Two: Study of Possible Procurement Models and Identification of Blueprint for Reform

Among the principal recommendations in the report of the task force was the replacement of the Public Finance (Tender Board) Regulations 1977 by a legal framework that would decentralize responsibility to each procuring entity while defining the procurement procedures to be followed, giving preference to competitive methods. The World Bank supported these local reform initiatives by undertaking a comprehensive study of the development needs of the procurement system in a *Country Procurement Assessment Report*, which was published in 2001 and revised in 2004.

18.4.3 Stage Three: Enactment of Procurement Law

Some countries have preferred to regulate government procurement through administrative instructions, such as those made under Public Finance Regulations, rather than by a comprehensive procurement law. This was the traditional position in the United Kingdom until it developed procurement law, partly to meet its obligations as a member state of the European Union. Consequently, former British colonies did not have a public procurement law upon gaining independence. The drawbacks of prescribing procurement procedures through administrative instructions are as follows:

1. Because the administrative instructions are essentially directed at civil servants, the business community may not be fully aware of the rules governing public procurement.
2. Regulations only apply to the civil service, so that other parts of the public sector need to formulate their own rules. This plethora of procurement rules in different public sector bodies may add to the confusion among suppliers.
3. Law is a more powerful instrument than administrative instructions for influencing behavior, particularly in some African countries where control over the public service is lax.

As the practice of regulating public procurement through administrative instructions rather than a public procurement law is a leftover from British colonial practice and does not represent a suitable model, several African countries have promulgated a public procurement law in recent years as a key part of the procurement reform program. In Uganda, the Public Procurement and Disposal of Public Assets Act passed into law in 2003. The act requires all public procurement and disposal to be conducted in accordance with the principles of transparency, accountability, and fairness, and in a manner that maximizes competition and achieves value for money. The law provides for delineation of roles and separation of powers among the following:

- User departments, which initiate the procurement process and evaluate bids
- Procurement and disposal units, comprising procurement professionals who manage the procurement process
- Contracts committees, comprising public servants who approve each stage of the procurement or disposal process and decide on the best evaluated bidder and contract award
- Accounting officer, a senior official in the ministry or agency who is responsible for ensuring the proper functioning of the system

The law sets out detailed procedural rules, whose provisions include the advertising and public display of bid opportunities, notices of best evaluated bidder, and contract award. The required procedures are supported by an enforcement system that allows dissatisfied suppliers to seek administrative review and provides for suspension of providers for offences and disciplinary measures to be taken against public officers who commit malpractices.

18.4.4 Stage Four: Establishment of a Regulatory Institution

If the procurement law is to work effectively, there is need for a mechanism to familiarize practitioners with its requirements and to provide for monitoring and enforcement. Establishment of a suitable regulatory mechanism is particularly important in Africa, where many laws are laxly enforced. This mechanism can be provided through existing structures, provided that responsibilities are made clear and there is capacity to take on this work. On the other hand, it is desirable that there should be effective coordination between the various strands of the procurement reform program and this may be easier to bring about when these strands are brought under a dedicated institution. In Uganda, the act established an autonomous regulatory body, the Public Procurement and Disposal of Public Assets Authority (PPDA). The main functions of the PPDA are as follows:

- Training and capacity building
- Provision of advice on the law and consideration of applications for deviations in particular procurement cases
- Compliance monitoring and assessment
- Procurement audits and investigation of alleged malpractices
- Hearing of applications for administrative review of alleged breaches of the law or alleged impropriety in contract award

18.4.5 Stage Five: Publication of Regulations, Guidelines, and Standard Bidding Documentation

Although the act describes the key principles and features of the new procurement system, this legislation needs to be supported by more detailed prescriptions if standardization is to be achieved. An early task of the PPDA was to devise regulations, guidelines, forms, codes of conduct, and standard bidding documentation that would determine how the law should be implemented and assist the procuring and disposing entities and providers of services, goods, and works to carry out processes according to the law and good practice.

18.4.6 Stage Six: Capacity Building

If the procurement law is to be carried out effectively, there is need to promote understanding of its requirements and to ensure that procuring entities have the equipment and other necessary resources. One department of the PPDA is dedicated to capacity building, by developing training modules, conducting training programs directly or through other agencies, and promoting professional development. Training modules have been prepared on various aspects of the law, and good practice, most procurement practitioners, and some other stakeholders, including suppliers, have been made familiar with the procedures to be followed and the purposes they serve. To address the need for greater professionalism, higher education institutions have been encouraged to develop programs in purchasing. Proposals have been prepared to establish a national professional body that would set standards and regulate professional conduct. Recognizing that many local government authorities in Uganda do not have essential modern office equipment, such as computers with Internet connectivity, the European Union in 2006 agreed to sponsor a program of retooling in selected local government districts.

18.4.7 Stage Seven: Monitoring and Enforcement

In a decentralized procurement system, the regulator needs an effective system for monitoring actual practices in procurement and for enforcing the law. A requirement on procuring entities to report regularly on the contracts they have made enables the regulator to identify possible malpractices in the procurement process and to compile statistical data on key indicators, such as the choice of procurement method. The law requires each procuring entity in central government to submit monthly reports on contracts placed, contract amendments, and contracts completed, together with a total value of micro-procurements (contracts below or around $1100). In addition, each entity is obliged to prepare a procurement plan, detailing the timeframe for each procurement in relation to the budget allocation. As well as constituting an important mechanism for ensuring the timely commencement of action that may avoid unnecessary emergency procurements, such plans also assist the process of monitoring.

There are four main mechanisms for enforcement, each of which provides further support for the monitoring process:

1. **Compliance checks.** These consist of visits to an entity to assess whether the required structure of contracts committees and procurement and disposal units is in place and whether these bodies are carrying out their functions in accordance with the law. Compliance checks may identify problems within a certain type of procurement or within a particular entity that warrant further investigation. This is done through a formal process that is

designed to rate each entity according to whether it has in place the key structures and is following the required procedures. The following indicators cover the key requisites of many procurement systems:

Compliance Area	*Compliance Indicators*
Procurement structures	Existence of properly constituted contracts committee and Procurement Unit performing their requisite roles
Procurement planning	Existence of a suitably prepared procurement plan that is linked to the approved budget and is used as a basis for procurements
Reporting	Required reports and statistical data are submitted in the standard format regularly and on time to the procurement regulator
Record keeping	Records covering all stages of the procurement process are maintained and made available for inspection
Evaluation procedures	Evaluation committees are properly constituted, use an appropriate methodology, and record their decisions with suitable justification
Notification	Notices of bid opportunities, of best evaluated bidder (if applicable), and of contract award are properly displayed

2. **Procurement audits**. Procurement audits are a specialized part of the audit process within government. Based on the value and critical importance of their procurements and on the degree of risk that their handling of cases has presented, procurement entities are selected for a detailed review of a sample of their procurement contracts. These audits are designed to establish whether the procurement function has been carried out correctly, in accordance with the law and generally accepted standards of good practice. The PPDA carries out some procurement audits using its own staff and commissions external auditing firms to carry out others. This arrangement enables the size of the PPDA to be kept at a reasonably low level, builds up capacity within the private sector to undertake procurement audits, and utilizes a broader range of expertise and opinion. However, no matter whether the actual audit is carried out by internal staff or by an external firm, responsibility for the proper conduct of the audit rests with the PPDA. The audit report provides an assessment of each procurement case according to a standard format to facilitate comparisons. It brings out the main organizational weaknesses that affect all of the entity's procurements, for example, lack of procurement plans, poor maintenance of records, as well as detailing the faults in each procurement case in the sample, with the degree of risk assessed. Each procurement audit report contains an action plan for remedying the defects that have been identified.
3. **Investigations**. These provide a detailed examination of particular procurement or disposal cases that have given rise to public controversy, have been the subject of complaints, or where malpractice is suspected. They are carried out as the need arises.
4. **Administrative review**. It is the bidders who are most likely to be aware of the faults and malpractices in the procurement system. Accordingly, establishment of a mechanism for review of a proposed contract award with the participation of bidders is a powerful tool for enforcing compliance, particularly if accompanied by suitable remedies. In order that bidders have an opportunity to file a protest before a binding contract has been signed, procuring entities in Uganda are required to post a notice of best-evaluated bidder for a stipulated period before they may proceed to contract award. Otherwise, bidders may not have a

reasonable opportunity to lodge a challenge before a binding contract is in place. Bidders in Uganda have a statutory right to seek administrative review, initially from the accounting officer of the entity concerned and thereafter from the PPDA, when they consider that an award of contract has been made unfairly. The number of such appeals increases once bidders find that they provide an effective means of redress.

18.4.8 Stage Eight: Harmonization of the Central and Local Government Procurement Systems

In many countries where both central government and local government authorities engage in procurement, the reform process is likely to commence at the central government level. However, as local governments account for a substantial proportion of total government expenditure (about 34 percent in Uganda) and as some of the worst abuses take place at the local government level, the reform process would be seriously deficient if it did not cover local government procurement. The importance of applying the procurement reforms to the local government system in Uganda was made clear by a recent survey of perceptions of corruption, which singled out district tender boards for the extent to which they abuse their powers. A key factor was seen to be the presence of local politicians on tender boards, as one participant in the survey remarked

> The District Tender Board charges prospective tenderers highly, thus leading to poor quality of services when unqualified firms win tenders and also try to accommodate bribes earlier given in their profit margin. (Inspectorate of Government, 2003)

Moreover, as many local politicians are involved in businesses in their district, there were instances of tender boards awarding contracts to one of their members. To prevent such abuses, the Local Governments Act was amended in 2006 to replace district tender boards by contracts committees whose members would be public servants and which would function similarly to their counterparts in central government with the support of procurement and disposal units staffed by professionals. Supporting regulations were issued in the same year. Thus, while local government procurement is governed by separate legislation from that which applies to central government procurement, common principles and practices apply.

18.5 Present Public Procurement System in Uganda

By 2007, the law governing central government procurement had been in place for four years. At the central government level, the requirements of the Public Procurement and Disposal of Public Assets Act 2003 and the associated regulations had been widely promulgated to staff in the ministries and government agencies that carry out procurement and to other stakeholders, including the companies that regularly bid for government contracts. The PPDA had developed a Web site, www.ppda.go.ug, that served to promulgate the law, guidelines, and standard bidding documents, and which also contained useful information about PPDA activities, including an executive summary of reports of procurement audits and investigations. The training sessions had also sought to explain the benefits that flow from a procurement system that is transparent and accountable and under which contracts are awarded on the basis of fair competition. The supply of qualified procurement professionals who possess the equipment and other resources to do their job had gradually improved. The monthly reports submitted by each entity to the PPDA provided a good basis for monitoring performance and detecting irregularities. Some of this information had been compiled into statistical data, enabling better understanding of the categories of main purchases and the most frequently used procurement methods. The compliance checks, investigations, and procurement audits served as a further tool for monitoring and evaluation and provided a basis for enforcement action to be taken. In addition, bidders had come to recognize the benefits to be gained from challenging malpractices that may have disadvantaged their bid, by lodging complaints for the PPDA to investigate or by making formal application for administrative review. Through these means, malpractices were brought out into the open and sometimes corrected. Procuring agencies had been obliged to adopt various good practices, for example, the 2007–2008 Budget Call Circular stated that cash releases would not be given to ministries and government agencies that had not prepared procurement plans on the basis of budget allocations. The public procurement reform program had thus reached a stage of maturity, when it was capable of being tested against the desired outcomes that had been set at the outset of the program and against international standards.

A framework for evaluating a developing country's public procurement system has been devised by the Development Assistance Committee of the Organization for Economic Cooperation and Development (OECD), together with the World Bank, at a series of roundtable conferences for developing countries and bilateral and multilateral donors (Organization for Economic Cooperation and Development, 2006, pp. 9–46). The aim has been to develop an integrated set of tools and good practices to improve procurement systems and the outcomes they produce. Various benchmarks establish whether the elements of a well-functioning public procurement system are in place.

The benchmarks are based on four pillars, each of which contains a number of baseline indicators, which are in turn supported by detailed sub-indicators. The pillars and baseline indicators are as follows:

1. Pillar I: Legislative and regulatory framework
   (a) Public procurement legislative and regulatory framework achieves the agreed standards and complies with applicable obligations.
   (b) Existence of implementing regulations and documentation.
2. Pillar II: Institutional framework and management capacity
   (a) Public procurement system is mainstreamed and well integrated into the public sector governance system.
   (b) Country has a functional normative/regulatory body.
   (c) Existence of institutional development capacity.
3. Pillar III: Procurement operations and market practices
   (a) Country's procurement operations and practices are efficient.
   (b) Functionality of the public procurement market.
   (c) Existence of contract administration and dispute resolution provisions.
4. Pillar IV: Integrity and transparency of the public procurement system
   (a) Country has effective control and audit systems.
   (b) Efficiency of appeals mechanism.
   (c) Degree of access to information.
   (d) Country has ethics and anticorruption measures in place.

Each of these indicators is defined against a desirable good practice standard that can be used to determine the degree of achievement.

When measured against the outcomes envisaged by the 1998–1999 Task Force and the criteria set out by the OECD, the procurement reforms in Uganda have been partially successful, though important shortfalls remain. Among the desired outcomes set by the 1999 Task Force, the system can be considered to have been made more transparent, at least insofar as the stipulated practices have been made known through an easily accessible law and standard bidding documents. There is also better integration of procurement with the national budget. However, there is no evidence that Uganda has been made a more attractive place for local and international companies to do business. Companies continue to complain about the deterrents to business, in particular that governments are slow payers, difficult to work with, or have their own favored suppliers for contract award, and where corruption plays a part in decisions.

When set against the international standard promulgated by the OECD, the first two pillars, providing for a legislative and regulatory framework and an institutional framework and management capacity, are largely in place at the central government level and are being extended to the local government procurement system. The model that has been adopted, providing for decentralized procurement practice supported by central regulation, can provide operational flexibility within a national standard of good practice. Tanzania and Kenya have recently enacted procurement and disposal laws that are on similar lines to the PPDA Act. The efficacy of the regulatory system in Uganda has been attested by the World Bank, whose program document for the Fifth Poverty Reduction Support Credit notes that Uganda has become one of the most advanced countries in the region in terms of implementing procurement reforms so that, at the central government level, all the ingredients for making the procurement system more efficient, economic, transparent and accountable are now in place (International Development Association, 2005, p. 15). However, there are some remaining weaknesses in respect of the third and fourth pillars. Putting in place a sound legal framework and regulatory body are the easiest part of the procurement reform process in African countries. Bringing practice into compliance with the law and ensuring that the practitioners carry out the procurement process with integrity are the more formidable challenges, yet unless desired outcomes are obtained in these areas, the procurement reform program cannot be considered to be a success.

There are many factors that make corruption in Uganda institutionalized and particularly difficult to eradicate. Many politicians and public servants, although better remunerated than the mass of the population, feel that their official salary is insufficient to maintain the lifestyle they expect and to meet necessary expenses, such as school fees.* There is the widespread practice in the public service of supplementing one's official salary by other means, including private business activities. The acceptance of a bribe in return for performing a service for a bidder is seen by some as an acceptable way of supplementing salary and this is facilitated by the traditional custom of providing gifts in appreciation of services received. In 2006, a survey sponsored by USAID (Government of Uganda, 2006) into the perceptions of corruption in public procurement found that bribery was institutionalized, with the going rate of bribe to public officials being around 7–9 percent of the contract value, leading to losses of between $64 and $85 million in the financial year 2004–2005, in addition to the costs arising from the failure to meet stipulated standards in construction, goods, and services, as contractors try to recover their outlay in corruption payments by delivering substandard work. In consequence of corruption and other factors, the procuring entities frequently

* Although there are free schools in Uganda at the primary level and free education is being extended to the secondary level, most schools that are considered to provide a good standard of education are fee-paying. $170–200 a term would be a typical fee for a secondary school of moderate standard. School fees and other expenses thus take a substantial bite out of a medium to senior executive level public servant's salary of $500–1000 a month.

fail to obtain good value for money in their procurements. A 2005 report that was sponsored by the national chapter of Transparency International found that public procurement tendering was the most abused channel for political corruption. Comparing primary schools built by the government with a similar school built by World Vision, a nongovernment organization (NGO), the report found that government schools were more poorly constructed and considerably more expensive than were similar projects by NGOs (Center for Basic Research, 2005, p. 38).

Corruption not only adds to the cost of winning a government contract in Uganda, but it also prevents procurement operations from being carried out in accordance with the law. There are widespread departures from the practices prescribed by law: for example, despite the law prescribing open bidding as the preferred method of procurement, direct procurement to a single provider without going through a competitive process accounted for around a quarter of procurements by value in 2005–2006. A substantial number of departures from the law have been revealed by the procurement audit reports: out of the 935 cases in 21 ministries and government agencies covered by procurement audits by the end of 2006, some 51 percent were assessed as high risk in terms of offering value for money and a further 23 percent were assessed as medium risk, leaving only 26 percent assessed as presenting low risk or having been carried out satisfactorily. Among the key malpractices identified were the following: inadequate procurement planning, leading to an excessive use of direct procurements and failure to align procurement with the budgetary process; poor record-keeping, leading to many procurement documents being untraceable (or indicating that procurements took place with stipulated procedures being undocumented or that the procedures did not take place); and abuse of process, for example, contracts having been awarded to a company other than the best evaluated bidder, retrospective approvals for contracts, inconsistencies in tender evaluation, and interference in the contract award process by unauthorized parties.

A key test of the prevalence of corruption in public procurement is whether the system is able to manage high-value projects, where there are huge potential profits and consequently much greater scope for bribery. In Hong Kong, where corruption has been effectively controlled, large-scale projects have been managed effectively. The new airport at Chek Lap Kok that was completed in 1998 was one of the world's largest infrastructure projects, involving expenditure of $20 billion on land reclamation, a major highway and rail network, and construction of the world's longest combined rail and road suspension bridge (1377 m). In a review of the project, a mission of Transparency International found that the vast project had been implemented largely within budget and with minimal corruption (Rooke and Wiehen, 1999). The main factors in the success of the project were the following:

- Strict anticorruption laws and strong enforcement
- Clear rules for procurement of services and supplies, monitoring of contract performance, enforcement of accountability, and dispute resolution
- Favorable working environment, including good salary levels, strong professionalism, and high morale

By contrast, there have been several cases in Uganda where large projects have collapsed on account of failures in the procurement system. High-value contracts are particularly vulnerable to political interference. The $550 million Bujagali Dam hydroelectric project collapsed in 2002 when the World Bank suspended funding after a former energy minister admitted to having accepted a $10,000 bribe from a construction company that had been awarded the contract without going through a fully competitive bidding process (Inspectorate of Government, 2006). In 2006, the evaluation of tenders for supply of a population data bank and national identity card system was halted when the inspector general of government intervened to investigate corruption allegations. In her report published in August 2006 (Inspectorate of Government, 2006), she found that the procurement process had been carried out improperly; that the evaluation of proposals was flawed; and that a government minister had exerted undue influence on the Evaluation Committee to pass firms that had not met the set criteria, either during the prequalification or detailed evaluation stage, and that he was fronting or lobbying for one of the bidders.

Even where irregular and illegal practices have been discovered through procurement audits or other investigations, there has been inadequate follow-up to ensure that those responsible are punished and that the practices do not recur. The act only empowers the PPDA to make recommendations on disciplinary action and even when such recommendations are acted upon, they are subject to public service disciplinary procedures. Although the inspector general of government has more extensive powers, including powers of prosecution, action has not always been taken against prominent persons who have been criticized in investigation reports. For example, the minister who was severely criticized for his role in the population data bank procurement was still a government minister in 2007.

At the local government level, there is continued interference in the procurement process on the part of local politicians, who find that exerting influence over tenders is a useful means of recovering election expenses. Since the establishment of contracts committees under the Local Governments (Amendment) Act of 2006, local politicians are prohibited from direct involvement in the procurement process, but there have been examples of this rule being ignored. Kampala City Council has been criticized for showing favoritism and abuse of the procurement process over contracts for the management of markets and disposal of land, on which there were conflicting positions from the technical and political arms of the city council, and in the course of the dispute the financial records on the markets disappeared (Mwanje and Izama, 2007). A report submitted in January 2006 by a Commission of Inquiry found widespread abuse of office by city officials, corruption, influence peddling, and abuse of procurement regulations (Ministry of Local Government Commission of Inquiry, 2006).

Procurement is of course merely a means to an end, the acquisition of a suitable product on reasonable terms that is delivered within time constraints. In many government procurement systems, there is tension between the procurement rules, which may require a prolonged time for the procurement process and the perceived need to obtain a product or service quickly. An example of the damaging effect of such tension can be seen in the procurements required for the Commonwealth Heads of Government Meeting, held in Kampala in November 2007. This was considered by the Government of Uganda to be a very important event and it sought to have several major projects completed in time to be ready for the meeting. Although proper planning might have allowed the procurement process to commence in sufficient time by the normal rules, some of the necessary funds were released late and it was argued that only direct procurement on a noncompetitive basis would ensure timely project completion. The PPDA had sought to retain an element of competition in the procurement process, while allowing for a shortened bidding period. Consequently, the PPDA was seen by some ministries as an obstacle to the timely completion of an important project. This has led to pressure for the procurement law to be amended to provide for wider exemptions from the stipulated procurement process.

18.6 Conclusion

Uganda has made great strides toward establishing a procurement system that is transparent, accountable, and delivers value for money. The law embodies these principles and prescribes detailed tendering procedures that would provide for all bidders to be treated fairly. However, there have been many departures from these procedures in current operations and delivery of the system has fallen short of expectations. The making of the procurement law has not changed long-established practices. This may in part be attributed to Uganda's political legacy. It has been observed that the African nation-state, being a creation of the colonialists, failed to achieve legitimacy in the eyes of most of its citizens (Davidson, 1992, p. 12). Many Ugandans' loyalty is to the family, the village, and the tribe and they do not identify their own interests with those of the state. The inability of the state to serve as a focus for loyalty and national pride limits the extent to which law may be used as an effective instrument for regulating behavior. This has implications for the control of corruption in public procurement and elsewhere, as many people who would condemn theft from a neighbor and demand severe punishment if the culprit was caught do not regard theft from the state as morally wrong. Such attitudes are not unique to African countries, but are more prevalent there than in the West or, especially, in China and Japan, where there are strong cultural traditions that subordinate the interests of the individual to those of the state (Pye, 1996, p. 16). The success of the public procurement reform program may ultimately depend on whether there occurs a change in attitude among ordinary Ugandans concerning the individual's responsibility as a citizen, together with understanding that overpriced and poorly constructed government facilities impact adversely upon their well-being.

References

Abeillé, B. 2003. Overview of Procurement Reforms in Africa. Paper presented at the Joint World Trade Organisation/World Bank Regional Workshop on Procurement Reforms. Available at http://www.wto.org/english/tratop_e/gproc_e/wkshop_tanz_jan03/wkshop_tanz_jan03_e.htm.

Center for Basic Research. 2005. *The Impact of Political Corruption on Resource Allocation and Service Delivery in Local Governments in Uganda*. Kampala Uganda: Transparency Uganda.

Davidson, B. 1992. *The Black Man's Burden: Africa and the Curse of the Nation-State*. New York: Three Rivers Press.

Easterly, W. 2006. *The White Man's Burden*. New York: The Penguin Press.

Government of Uganda. 2006. *National Public Procurement Integrity Baseline Survey 2006*. Kampala Uganda: Inspectorate of Government.

Inspectorate of Government. 2003. *Final Report: Second National Integrity Survey*, Vol. 1, p. 66. Available at http://www.igg.go.ug/pdfs/Final_Integrity_Report.pdf.

Inspectorate of Government. 2006. *Executive Summary of the Report of the Investigation on the Procurement of the Vendor for the National Population Databank & Identification Solution*. Available at http://www.igg.go.ug/docs/population_Dbank.doc.

International Development Association. 2005. *Program Document for a Proposed Grant of SDR77.7 Million (Equivalent to US$112.5 Million) and a Proposed Credit of SDR 15.5 Million (Equivalent to US$22.5 Million) to the Republic of Uganda for the Fifth Poverty Reduction Support Operation (PRSC5)*. Available at http://www-wds.worldbank.org/external/default/WDSContentServer/WDSP/IB/2005/12/22/000160016_20051222110436/Rendered/PDF/34382.pdf.

International Monetary Fund. 2006. *IMF Executive Board Completes Final Review of Uganda's PRGF Arrangement and Approves 16-month Policy Support Instrument*. Press Release No. 06/14, January 24. Available at http://www.imf.org/external/np/sec/pr/2006/pr0614.htm.

Meredith, M. 2005. *The State of Africa*. London, United Kingdom: The Free Press.

Ministry of Local Government Commission of Inquiry. 2006. *The Report of the Commission of Inquiry into the Sale, Lease and Purchase of Land by Kampala City Council*. Kampala, Uganda: Ministry of Local Government.

Museveni, Y.K. 1997. *Sowing the Mustard Seed: The Struggle for Freedom and Democracy in Uganda*. Oxford, United Kingdom: Macmillan.

Mutibwa, P. 1992. *Uganda since Independence: A Story of Unfulfilled Hopes*. London, United Kingdom: Hurst & Company.

Mwanje, R. and Izama, A. 2007. On whose behalf is KCC running Kampala? *Daily Monitor*, February 14. Available at http://www.monitor.co.ug/inspol/inspol02141.php.

Ofcansky, T.P. 1996. *Uganda: Tarnished Pearl of Africa*. Boulder, CO: Westview Press.

Organization for Economic Cooperation and Development. 2006. *Methodology for Assessment of National Procurement Systems, Version 4*. Available at http://www.oecd.org/dataoecd/1/36/37390076.pdf.

Pye, L.W. 1996. The state and the individual: An overall interpretation. In: B. Hook (Ed.), *The Individual and the State in China*. Oxford, United Kingdom: Oxford University Press.

Rooke, P. and Wiehen, M.H. 1999. *Hong Kong: The Airport Core Project and the Absence of Corruption*. Available at www. transparency.org.

Task Force on Public Procurement Reform. 1999. *Improving Public Procurement in Uganda*. Kampala Uganda: Government of Uganda.

Transparency International. 2006. *Handbook for Curbing Corruption in Public Procurement*. Available at http://www.transparency.org/regional_pages/asia_pacific#infocus.

USAID. 2005. *Budget Justification to the Congress: Fiscal Year 2006*. Available at http://www.usaid.gov/policy/budget/cbj2006/afr/ug.html.

Walker, C. 2003. Setting up a public procurement system: The six step method. In: S. Arrowsmith and M. Trybus (Eds.), *Public Procurement: The Continuing Revolution*. Dordretch, the Netherlands: Kluwer Law International.

World Bank. 2007. *The World Bank in Uganda: Country Brief 2005–2006*. Available at http://web.worldbank.org/.

Chapter 19

Public Procurement in Post-Transitional Context: The Case of Estonia*

Veiko Lember and Veiko Vaske

CONTENTS

* The study was supported by the Estonian target financing grant no. SF0140094s08 and by the Estonian Science Foundation grant no. 7441.

19.1 Introduction

Estonia is representing one of the countries that have undergone a rapid change in public procurement system in the past two decades. After regaining independence in 1991, the whole public administration had to be changed from the totalitarian Soviet system to the modern European one. The reform has been complicated due to the absence of regulated public procurement per se in the Soviet type plan economy and therefore the system had to be built up from scratches. Although today Estonia can be described as post-transitional country with an annual economic growth of over 10 percent and a membership status of the European Union (EU) since 2004, the procurement system is still in the ending phase of transition. In 2007, the Estonian parliament, the Riigikogu, adopted a new version of Public Procurement Act, which assumingly marks the end of the harmonization era with the EU regulation.

Among other Central and Eastern European (CEE) countries, Estonia has been referred to as a successful public procurement system reformer, a judgment that is made in comparison with different developing and transitioning countries (Hunja, 2002). According to the Global Competitiveness Report 2001–2002, Estonia's public procurement system is perceived by business community as above the average in all categories characterizing public procurement systems in developing countries (cited in Evenett and Hoekman, 2005). In fact, assessing the connection between procurement and innovation, Estonia is placed above the average of the OECD countries (Evenett and Hoekman, 2005). The Estonian electronic Public Procurement Register has been recommended as a role model to other countries as being an excellent example of a model solution for the dissemination of procurement information (SIGMA, 2003).

These are only episodic examples. If one were to look for more empirical evidence on the public procurement reform in Estonia or in any other CEE countries, then one must agree with Evenett and Hoekman (2005, p. 21) that "it is not much of an exaggeration to argue that the literature on procurement reform in developing countries is in an embryonic state." The few available case studies on Estonia (e.g., Lamvol, 2002; SIGMA, 2003; Raudla, 2007) have pointed to the problems with legal framework such as presence of formalistic and bureaucratic obstacles, unclear monitoring mechanisms, vague definition of contracting authorities, and conflicts with constitutional norms as well as to problems with implementation such as abnormally high use of least competitive tendering processes and balancing the goals of transparency and cost effectiveness. Although some of the problems have been solved over the course of time, there is an obvious need to analyze more carefully the actual situation of the public procurement system in Estonia after adopting the latest principles of the EU legislation.

After providing an overview of the main regulative principles of the Estonian public procurement system by presenting the new Public Procurement Act that was adopted in 2007, this chapter identifies the main aspects and features of the Estonian public procurement model covering areas of procurement budget and methods, transparency in procurement, procurement organization, and personnel, political, economic, and social goals associating with public procurement; and then analyzes some of the main challenges that Estonia as a post-transitioning country faces in developing its public procurement system. The approach deserves interest due to the opportunity to analyze the main features and dynamics characterizing a CEE public procurement system in the light of the latest EU public procurement reform ideas and the ending phase of a transition era. The chapter starts with an overview of the general background influencing the Estonian public procurement system.

19.1.1 Transitional Context, Liberal Economic Policy, and Public Procurement

Hunja (2002) distinguishes between four groups of countries reforming public procurement systems. The first group is formed by the CEE countries including Estonia, which are transforming their economies from socialist to market-based systems. The second group is formed by middle-income countries (e.g., Argentina and India). The developing countries and the developed countries form the third group and the fourth group, respectively. So far, two aspects have received the main attention when the relative success of the CEE countries is analyzed. It has been claimed that the success is based on the fact that the public procurement systems were built up from scratch and that there was a strong external pressure from international donors like EU and WTO for implementing the reform (Hunja, 2002; Evenett and Hoekman, 2005).

After the collapse of the communist regimes, the CEE societies were eager to copy everything coming from West (Drechsler, 1995). A simple dichotomous viewpoint prevailed in Estonia, promoted by the so-called Washington consensus and international donors like IMF—everything associating with (neo)-liberalism and capitalism was unconditionally perceived as something good, whereas socialism and the very meaning of government was taken as something bad. Estonia is well known for its liberal economic reforms for more than a decade now. A radical tax reform, strict state budget policy, and massive privatization of state-owned enterprises in 1990s are the best examples illustrating the prevalence of the liberal agenda. Hence, it should not be surprising that, for example, United Nations Commission on International Trade Law (UNCITRAL) as a "Western product" helping modernize post-Soviet government found such a good reception in CEE countries compared to, for example, many developing countries.[1]

In accordance with the overall government downsizing movement, all the economic and administrative reform plans have emphasized the need to extend the use of contracting tool to purchase services and goods from the private sector. However, all the public administration reform initiatives have been limited with the adoption of legal or strategic documents, whereas not enough attention has been given to what happens after a law or policy program is approved (Verheijen, 1998).

19.2 Legal Environment

The current legal environment of public procurement in Estonia has been modeled for the most part by EU public procurement directives that are based primarily on the WTO Government Procurement Agreement. The basis of Estonian national procurement law is one main legal act—the Public Procurement Act, the previous version of which was adopted in year 2000 and largely amended in 2003. In January 2007, the Estonian parliament, the Riigikogu, adopted a new Public Procurement Act that came into force as of May 1, 2007 (Riigikogu, 2007).

The history of legal regulation of public procurement in the Republic of Estonia began already before World War II, during the first period of independence of Estonia before Soviet occupation and annexation. A State Procurement Act was adopted in 1936 as well as a more specific implementing government decree (Ploom, 1996). After Estonia had regained independence in 1991, the parliament adopted a modern Public Procurement Act in May 1995 (Riigikogu, 1995). The act followed all modern public procurement principles and established, for example, a dual-stage tendering procedure, which was fairly similar to the competitive dialogue provided by the EU procurement directive 2004/18/EC not until several years later.

In 2000, a new version of the act was adopted to start harmonizing the regulation with EU law as Estonia was proceeding toward EU membership (Riigikogu, 2000). A large-scale amending law was passed toward the end of 2003 to finalize the harmonization process (Riigikogu, 2003).

Transposition of EU procurement law into Estonian national regulation simultaneously entailed some significant drawbacks. For example, the European Commission directives at that time did not allow public contracting authorities to enter into framework agreements that put the authorities in some fields under pressure to cut down the long-term projects and find ways to deal with strict budget regulations.

Already in March 2004, the EU Council and the European Parliament approved a new set of procurement directives, which were finally transposed into Estonian national law at the beginning of 2007 (Riigikogu, 2007). As the fundamental features of Estonian national public procurement law result from EU and international regulations, the following description will concentrate on the peculiarities deviating from the base regulation.[2]

19.2.1 Range of Application

The range of persons and authorities subject to the law is slightly more extensive than the European law would require. The most remarkable difference is that the circle covers additionally all foundations under the control of public sector or where the state has been one of the founders (Riigikogu, 2007, §10). The material scope of application does not differ from EU regulations.

The temporal or functional range of application of Estonian procurement law is rather extensive. The law regulates not just the publication requirements but also the procedures to be followed before awarding a contract. It also stipulates rules for altering the terms of public contracts, engagement of new subcontractors during the execution of the contract, and requires the contracting authority to submit a report to the public procurement register once the contract has expired (Riigikogu, 2007, §69, 31, 37).

19.2.2 National Thresholds and Procedures

The Estonian procurement law traditionally provides national subthresholds for contracting authorities to increase transparency and control of public expenditures. Because of the small size of the market, most public contracts are relatively low-valued and hence application of international (WTO and EU) thresholds only would leave most public expenditures outside the scope of the regulation. In the law of 2007, the threshold values were €30,000 for goods and service contracts and €190,000 for construction works and concessions (Riigikogu, 2007, §15). From 2008 onward, these thresholds were lifted to €40,000 and €250,000, respectively, still remaining approximately 4–20 times lower than the EU thresholds. Practically, contracting authorities have to follow the EU procedures like they were fixed above the EU thresholds, except the following main differences:

1. Freedom of choice between all procedures with prior publication of a contract notice (open, restricted, and negotiated procedure with prior publication of a contract notice and the competitive dialogue) (Riigikogu, 2007, §25–27). This regulation is analogous to the regulation in the EU sectors directive 2004/17/EC coordinating the procurement procedures of entities operating in the water, energy, transport, and postal services sectors (European Parliament, 2004a).

2. Shortened minimum time limits for publication of contract notices. As European law does not require the contract notices of below-international-threshold value to be published in the EU *Official Journal* (European Parliament, 2004a,b), such notices are only published nationally, combined with substantially shorter deadlines for publication (Riigikogu, 2007, §35).

The obligations of contracting authorities are limited to complying with general public procurement principles except for the obligation to publish a contract award notice for all contracts above €10,000 (Riigikogu, 2007, §37).

19.2.2.1 Transparency and Public Procurement Register

Although in most European countries, public procurement procedures are generally performed in camera, in Estonia, openness and transparency have been the cornerstones of procurement rules (Ministry of Finance, 2006). The most remarkable expression of openness is the open procedure of opening tenders. According to Estonian law, contracting authorities have to allow all bidders to participate in the opening operation and reveal, for example, the prices of all opened tenders (Riigikogu, 2007). Although it has raised questions about its effect on real competition, no material changes were introduced in the new law in 2007.

In addition to the obligation to invite bidders to the opening of tenders, a copy of written protocol of this operation including basic data about all the tenders must be sent to all bidders within three working days as of the date of the procedure (Riigikogu, 2007, §54). Similarly, all candidates and bidders shall receive a written motivated decision on each operation within the tendering procedure that might have a legal effect on his rights in the procedure such as qualification of bidders or candidates, suitability checkup of tenders, and selection of the best tender (Riigikogu, 2007). According to the law of 2007, nevertheless, the contracting authority may deviate from this obligation and send all the respective documents together within three days after the successful tender has been selected, provided the choice has been notified in advance (Riigikogu, 2007).

An issue tightly connected to transparency is the requirement that the terms of a public contract must be exactly those that were stated in the contract notice and contract documents on one side and the tender on the other side, being null and void in other cases. Pursuant to the law of 2007, the obligations of the contracting authority have become even more rigorous: the contracting authority must also specify all contract terms in the contract documents. All contract negotiations are excluded in case of open and restricted procedures (Riigikogu, 2007, §58).

One of the main instruments for ensuring transparency of public procurement is the State Public Procurement Register.[3] The register is the exclusive medium for publishing all public contract notices above national thresholds and procurement reports (extended contract award notices) already from €10,000 (Riigikogu, 2007, §37). All contracting authorities and entities are obliged to publish all respective notices in the register. The notices are submitted by filling in online forms on the Internet and no paper is used in this process. Users of the Web environment are fully responsible for the correctness of the data submitted. All the information in the Register is publicly accessible via the Internet and reliable as any other official documents.

The law of 2007 yet expanded the amount of information to be submitted to the register. From May 2007 onward, not only information about the contracts concluded but also information on contracts executed or otherwise terminated must be submitted, including any agreed changes to the terms of the contract, any involved subcontractors that were not enlisted in the tender, and any breaches or deviations in execution (Riigikogu, 2007, §37).

Additional functionalities of the register include forwarding the notices to be published to the Office for Official Publications of the European Communities to fulfill the obligation deriving from EU directives and various possibilities to compile public procurement data and statistics. Basic procurement statistics, gathered from the register, is published quarterly on the Web site of the Ministry of Finance (see http://www.fin.ee/?id=76329).

19.2.2.2 Subcontracting Rules

One of the most important innovations in the new Public Procurement Act of 2007 is the regulation on subcontracting that lays several obligations on the contracting authorities. According to the new act, the contracting authority shall, firstly, demand the bidder to indicate the predicted amount of subcontracting to be used in execution of the contract as well as the names of the supposed subcontractors and the nature of their performance (Riigikogu, 2007, §31). Secondly, the bidder has to confirm that all his subcontractors correspond to the general requirements for participation such as proper payment of taxes and absence of bankruptcy proceedings (Riigikogu, 2007, §38). Thirdly, the bidder has to confirm the same for each subcontractor it wishes to involve additionally during the execution phase of the contract (Riigikogu, 2007).

At the same time, the contracting authority has a right to limit the use of subcontracting and demand that the bidder itself perform at least an essential part of the contract. Such limitations have to be necessary to guarantee the quality or verifiability of the performance and comply with the customs of trade of the specific industry (Ministry of Finance, 2006).

19.2.2.3 Review and Supervision

A mechanism that is set up to ensure fair competition and lawfulness of procurement decisions is the review and supervisory system, implemented by the Public Procurement Office, a subunit within the Ministry of Finance, yet independent in its function. Until 2007 the jurisdiction of the office used to be a mixture of state surveillance and course of justice. Regarding the state surveillance capacity, the office has a right to inspect observance of procurement law by any contracting authorities or entities in Estonia, call for any documents concerning procurement procedures and any relevant information (Public Procurement Office, 2006). As a result of an ascertained breach of law, the office may declare an ongoing procurement procedure void if the deviation forecloses restoration of a lawful and fair competition, for example, if the contracting authority has not predefined the criteria for selecting the successful tender and the tenders have already been opened or if negotiations have taken place in an open tendering procedure (Riigikogu, 2007). The office has also a right to impose financial penalties on procurement officers responsible for the lawfulness of the procurements (Riigikogu, 2007, §111).[4]

On the other hand, the Public Procurement Office acted until 2007 as an independent review body, resolving protests submitted by bidders against contracting authorities and entities regarding violations of the Procurement Law in drafting the contract notice or the contract documents or any decisions made in a certain procurement procedure (Public Procurement Office, 2006). The law also obliges the office to give advice to the players in the public procurement market (Ministry of Finance, 2006).

The functions of the Public Procurement Office certainly enabled it to play an important role as a procurement competence and knowledge accumulation center. At the same time, blending different functions of so diverse nature can cause problems in fulfilling all of them. OECD SIGMA Public Procurement Review already pointed out 2003 that there is a risk of a conflict of interests (SIGMA, 2003). The risk becomes obvious in point of the nature of the administration of justice as a review body, which requires impartiality and objectivity vis-à-vis the case pending and the parties to the proceedings, in relation to the other aforementioned functions that require expressing clear predefined positions. Arguably, this conflict also caused formalism in the office's advisory activities as any positions taken might have had an effect of a preliminary ruling in a pending case.

It was also argued that the Public Procurement Office acting as a review body did not fulfill the requirements set by the EU procurement remedies directives. The regulation of appeals is said to have been in contradiction with the directives because "where a contractor seeks judicial review after the PPO's decision to deny a protest, the statute only authorizes a complaint against the decisions made by the contracting authority and not of any defects in PPO's decision" (Lamvol, 2002, p. 87). Similarly the office as such did not meet the criteria set for an independent review body in the directives as members of the body should be appointed and leave office under the same conditions and at least president of the body should have the same legal and professional qualifications as members of the judiciary (Riigikogu, 2007).

Partly in response to these critics, the new Public Procurement Act of 2007 established a separate public procurement review commission that is independent of the Public Procurement Office and acts in reality as a special court of first instance (Riigikogu, 2007, §119). Members of the commission have to meet the same educational and reliability criteria as judges and shall be appointed to office by the government of the republic for a five-year term (Riigikogu, 2007).

19.2.2.4 Budget Laws

Other main relevant legal acts concerning public procurement in Estonia are the base acts for budget regulation and the Administrative Cooperation Act. The State Budget Act and the Rural Municipality and City Budgets Act set explicit limitations on most contracting authorities regarding their future obligations and, thus complicate procurement planning, especially in co-effect with the aforementioned restrictions on framework agreements.

The State Budget Act states that a state authority may enter into contracts to purchase goods or to contract for services, including construction work, out of the budgets of future budgetary years provided that the volume of contractual payments in any of the future budgetary years does not exceed 50 percent of the amount of the corresponding item of expenditure prescribed for the authority for the current budgetary year (Riigikogu, 2004, §31). Only the government of the republic on the proposal of the Minister of Finance may grant permission for entry into contracts exceeding that limit (ibid.).

The regulation on local authorities is somewhat more liberal as the law prescribes a maximum limit on the total amount of future obligations. The Rural Municipality and the City Budgets Act stipulate that a municipality may assume debt obligations provided that all financial obligations shall not exceed 60 percent of proposed budget revenue for that budgetary year, from which allocations from the state budget, intended for a specific purpose, have been deducted. The total amount of repayable debt obligations must not exceed, in any coming budgetary year, 20 percent of the proposed budget revenue for the budgetary year during which the loans or financial leases are taken and debt instruments are issued, net of allocations from state budget.

19.2.2.5 Contracts under Public Law

One specific legal issue associated with public procurement in Estonia is the order of entering into contracts under the public law, i.e., contracts for the act of delegation of public (administrative) law functions. Pursuant to the Administrative Cooperation Act contracts under public law have to be awarded according to the Public Procurement Act. Although it has been argued that in some cases public procurement procedures are not the most appropriate methods for concluding contracts under public law as it may bring along unnecessary expense of money and time, the legislator has retained the position that public interest concerning the quality of public services outweighs the consideration of expediency (Aedmaa and Parrest, 2004).

19.3 Public Procurement Statistics and Methods

19.3.1 Gross Public Procurement Value

In this section, the key statistical figures characterizing the Estonian public procurement market is provided. To understand the Estonian situation, the section starts with a short overview of the Estonian macroeconomic indicators.

The gross domestic product of Estonia was approximately EEK147 billion (€9.4 billion) in 2004 and EEK173 billion (€11 billion) in 2005, growing by roughly 10 percent. An estimated 10 percent annual economic growth is likely for the year 2006 as well. The public sector expenditures were approximately EEK55 billion in 2004 and EEK64 billion in 2005 (Bank of Estonia, 2007). The gross value of public procurement declared in the Public Procurement Register was EEK10.7 billion in 2004 and EEK13.6 billion in 2005, making up approximately 7.3 and 7.9 percent of GDP, respectively (Public Procurement Office, 2006). The statistical data of the first three-quarters of 2006 shows a possible increase in the total value again at EEK12.8 billion with the last quarter to be added yet (Ministry of Finance, 2007).

The statistics utility of the Public Procurement Register indicates even larger numbers: EEK25.9 billion for 2004, EEK15.9 billion for 2005, and EEK22.3 billion for 2006 as declared by March 1, 2007. Especially, the data for 2004 should be revised carefully: the declared EEK25.9 billion included 48 long-term healthcare service contracts declared by the Estonian Sick Fund with a total value of EEK14.3 billion and hence the real costs of these contracts should be partitioned between several consecutive years (Public Procurement Register, 2007). However, this data raises the estimated percentage of GDP allocated through public procurement up to approximately 8 percent in 2004, 9 percent in 2005, and clearly more than 10 percent in 2006.

The number of contracts awarded to international bidders has grown constantly over the recent years (Public Procurement Office, 2006). In 2002, 14 contracts were entered into with international bidders; then in 2005 the respective figure increased to 327. This clearly indicates the effect the harmonization process with the EU public procurement directives had on the Estonian context. In 2005, the value of registered public tenders exceeding the EU thresholds was EEK3.9 billion (€249 million), representing 42 percent of the total value of registered public procurement in Estonia. However, it has to be noted here that this covered only 3.6 percent of the total number of registered public tenders, which indicates to the small size of the market and a modest influence the Estonian public procurement market has on EU and the rest of the world. The value of tenders won by international bidders represented 10 percent of the total value of the registered public procurement in Estonia.

The statistical data collected from the Public Procurement Register should be treated with reasonable criticism, as it does not reveal full data about contracts below the national thresholds. Taking the small size of most Estonian municipalities into account, a relatively large amount of purchases might remain uncovered by the official statistics.[5] Another problem is, as illustrated above, the fact that just the total value of contracts is declared although the real expenditures may split between several years. Nevertheless, this should not be a problem in longer perspective.

19.3.2 Procurement Methods and Objects

An interesting issue that can be outlined on the basis of the data collected from the Public Procurement Register is the use of different procurement methods or types of procedures. The open procedure has been the most popular method throughout the years of 2002–2005, growing from 62 to 70 percent of the total procurement volume by declared value but falling from 45 to 31 percent of the total procurements declared by number. The second most popular method in 2002 was the negotiated procedure without prior publication of a contract notice, i.e., the direct award, in short, making up over 25 percent of the volume and outright 52 percent of the procurements declared by number. However, the percentage of direct award by procurement volume has decreased steadily to some 7 percent in both volume and number in 2005 and 2006. The main reason for that is the changing legal environment—until the end of 2003 there existed a certain intermediate threshold between the national and EU thresholds, the contracts falling below this value being legal to be awarded directly. Since 2004, the national thresholds were raised to approximately the same level and since then most of these low-value contracts have been declared as being awarded through simplified procedure, i.e., just following the general principles of procurement law, obligatory below the national thresholds. The fact that the average value of the contracts awarded through a negotiated procedure without earlier publication of a contract notice was about EEK0.85 million in 2002 and EEK4.2 million in 2006 also supports this speculation.

The other types of procedures are used rather seldom, the negotiated procedure with prior publication of a contract notice making up less than 10 percent of the volume and only 1–3 percent of the number of procurements. The restricted procedure is used only in 10–15 cases per year in Estonia—probably due to the clause in the Public Procurement Act that the use of the restricted procedure has to be economically justified. Another important factor might be the relatively small number of economic operators in the market that precludes the necessity to restrict the number of bidders.

Surprisingly, the two-stage procedures are relatively often used for goods and service contracts, although in theory they should be more appropriate for complex construction works contracts where it is rational to restrict the circle of participants in the qualification stage.

Out of the total public procurement volume since 2002 through 2006, construction works formed roughly one-half, goods amounted to nearly 30 percent and services from 20 to 24 percent. As a matter of fact, the public expenditures on services probably exceed the expenditures on goods if we add the aforementioned long-term healthcare service contracts concluded in 2004. (Public Procurement Office, 2006; Public Procurement Register, 2007).

19.4 Procurement Organization and Personnel

Dimitri et al. (2006) distinguish between three different procurement setups—fully centralized, fully decentralized, and hybrid models. The Estonian public procurement model can be described as decentralized model with some minor hybrid aspects. The role of the central bodies responsible for procurement issues—the Ministry of Finance and Public Procurement Office—is limited to regulation, monitoring, and complaints review. The actual procurement decisions and implementations are fully decentralized which in practice means that every minister decides on and is responsible for ministry's and its subunits' procurement matters. The same holds for local governments.

In most cases, the ministries have delegated the procurement duties to their departments and agencies (i.e., boards, inspections, centers, and independent legal bodies).[6] The procedures for implementing actual procurement vary substantially between ministries and their agencies. For example, although the Ministry of Foreign Affairs carries out all procurement at the ministerial level, the actual implementation is delegated to ministerial departments and there is no special unit created for procurement issues (State Audit Office, 2004). In the Ministry of Agriculture, most of the procurement is carried out by its agencies, which have elaborated their own procurement processes, but in some cases (e.g., high-value tenders), the agencies have to get approval for certain procurement activities from the ministry (State Audit Office, 2004). In some ministerial agencies, smaller (regional) structural units are authorized to carry out procurement tasks independently without coordinating it with governing body, in others the smaller units have to get approval from the head of agency or agency's legal unit (ibid.).

Although the statutes of ministries and agencies specify the responsible unit for procurement issues, these units usually have only advisory functions and organize mostly tenders for supporting goods and services (e.g., office supply, maintenance, etc.). Most of the procurement preparation and implementation work is done by officials later responsible for exploiting procured goods or services. In those cases where the value of tender is expected to exceed the national thresholds, special commissions are created for procurement implementation and bid evaluations (State Audit Office, 2004). The commissions consist of senior officials, procurement specialist(s) (if there is any), and specialists responsible for exploiting the purchased good or services. There is no common strategy developed for organizing the work of these commissions, the responsibilities are allocated and work is organized on ad hoc basis. Although the Public Procurement Act does not include any implications for such commissions, it is a widely employed practice in Estonia (State Audit Office, 2004).

19.4.1 Centralization in Estonian Public Procurement System

There have been some attempts to introduce centralized public procurement in Estonia to increase transparency and to take more advantage from economies of scale. So far, the centralized initiatives have failed and the current situation can be described as only facilitating voluntary consolidation. In 2001, the Estonian government established Public Procurement Centre (*Riigihangete Keskus*) and State Info–Communication Foundation (*Riigi Infosüsteemide Sihtasutus*) to carry out consolidated procurement in areas of cars, IT goods and services, and office supplies (Raudla, 2007). The first consolidated tenders indicated to several problems the Estonian context had, such as the small size of the Estonian market and problems with considering the variety of needs organizations have.[7] After two years of existence, the organizations were reorganized and consolidated procurement was never made mandatory. As of today, the Public Procurement Act does not include any implication for compulsory consolidated procurement, although voluntary consolidation is allowed. This possibility is mainly used by local governments, especially when sourcing for infrastructural solutions. In addition, the government has established some central agencies, which among other duties carry out public procurement for all public institutions. The examples include state-owned private legal body, the State Real Estate Company (*Riigi Kinnisvara Aktsiaselts*), which was founded in 2001 and governmental agency the Estonian Informatics Centre (*Riigi Infosüsteemide Arenduskeskus*), founded in 2003. In the former case, the central government institutions as well as local governments can use the service of the State Real Estate Company to build, reconstruct, or maintain public real estate. In the latter case, the public organizations can authorize the Estonian Informatics Centre to carry out procurement of IT goods and services.[8] The creation of the organizations is not a part of a larger procurement policy, but stem from decisions made within a specific policy field. Using the assistance of these central bodies is not compulsory and depends on the vision of public authorities. As of today, there are no signs indicating on massive usage of the services of these central agencies by public organizations.[9]

Estonia, having a very strong reputation of being among the international leaders of introducing E-governance and having an exceptional electronic public procurement register, has not developed central public platforms for E-procurement.[10] As the EU has been developing a special policy for unified E-procurement platforms for many years (European Commission, 2007), the Estonian government has taken a passive role and has decided to wait for the EU solutions. It is expected that in Estonia, the first changes in E-procurement platforms should happen in 2008.

19.4.2 Procurement Personnel

Owing to the decentralized nature of the public procurement system and relatively small sizes of public organizations there is no unified group of procurement professionals developed in the Estonian public service. There is no professional certification system elaborated for procurement professionals; moreover, most of the tenders are carried out by officials whose main duties do not lie in the area of public procurement (State Audit Office, 2004).

Training of procurement personnel is not centrally coordinated at the Ministry of Finance nor the Public Procurement Office, the former occasionally organizes courses to introduce new legal principles of public procurement. The Public Procurement Act of 2007 tries to address this question by adding to the Public Procurement Office a responsibility to counsel public organizations on procurement matters (Riigikogu, 2007, §104). Although the law does not go into more details, it is expected that this brings along more systematic training in the public procurement field (Ministry of Finance, 2006). Owing to the need to adopt the principles of the new EU procurement directives, the cabinet named procurement as one of the top priorities for public service training in 2005 and 2006 (State Chancellery, 2006b). This initiative resulted with elaboration of the EU sponsored series of courses for introducing the new Public Procurement Act.[11] In 2007, private consultancy market offered five different public procurement courses, all of them concentrating on legal issues of public procurement (State Chancellery, 2007a). Universities and other schools do not offer special programs on procurement, there are only a few special courses in the curricula dedicated to procurement issues.[12]

19.5 Social, Economic, and Political Goals

By becoming a member of the EU and adopting the main principles of the EU procurement policy, it is clear that at least formally Estonia aims at achieving the same goals as EU—nondiscriminative and transparent procedures in line with "modern purchasing techniques, an efficient and independent enforcement and remedies system, competent contracting authorities and competitive bidders" (Trybus, 2006: 410). In addition to the above-mentioned goals, public procurement is seen as a powerful vehicle for achieving wider purposes, namely social, economic, and political goals. Positive discrimination and promoting environment-friendly goods and services are one of the principles that can be found in the EU legislation (European Parliament, 2004a, b). In the context of wider economic goals, public procurement is increasingly seen as an important instrument for promoting innovation and economic growth (e.g., Nyiri et al., 2007).

At the time of this writing, the government has no clear vision where the public procurement system should strive to. The loads of unanswered questions raised during the latest debates in the parliament (Riigikogu, 2006a) and the acknowledgments of head of the Commission of Economic Affairs of the Parliament that there is no understanding what should be the proper role for the Public Procurement Office in the future (Opmann, 2007) are just some examples illustrating the current state of affairs.

As stated in the Public Procurement Act, the main goal of the public procurement system in Estonia is achieving the best value in using public funds. However, in Estonia, public procurement is not seen as a vehicle for achieving social goals and one can find only indirect implications for facilitating wider economic goals through procurement. Although one cannot ignore the indirect influence of public procurement on society and economy, there are no policies elaborated at any level to directly connect government procurement with social and economic goals. This has not even been an issue for policy makers during the past ten years (Raudla, 2007).[13] For example, neither the previous nor the 2007 Public Procurement Act includes the institution of reserved contracts to award contracts for disabled persons or small and medium enterprises (SMEs). The new act adopted in 2007 states that contracting authorities, when possible, should prefer environment-friendly bidders (Riigikogu, 2007, §3).

Compared to the EU and international experience, the Estonian national thresholds are relatively low, which in itself can be regarded as a policy favoring the participation of SMEs and therefore promoting innovation. But it has been demonstrated that due to various factors, low thresholds have not had this effect. For example, even if in 2000 the national thresholds for goods and services was lowered to EEK50,000 (€3,196) and to EEK500,000 (€31,960) for construction works, the effect was nullified by overusing the least competitive sourcing mechanisms that prevailed during the same period (Raudla, 2007). It can be speculated, of course, that decentralized model *per se* favors SMEs as the value of individual tenders are always smaller than in the case of consolidated tenders and therefore more opportunities are created for SMEs, but whether this kind of unintentional policy is of any good remains to be tested.

Politically, the current public procurement model fits nicely to the overall idea of neoliberalism that has marked the main reform initiatives in Estonia. The government has only the functions of regulating and overseeing, the actual purchasing transactions are treated as typical market transactions where central interference is seen inappropriate, not to mention linking government's purchasing with wider economic policy. Further, the statistical evidence demonstrating a rapid increase in awarding contracts to international bidders coincides with the overall purposes of the liberal economic policy that Estonia has followed. Therefore, it can be concluded that in spite of the modest social and macroeconomic dimensions in the current public procurement framework, the political goals have been more or less achieved.

19.6 Challenges of the Estonian Public Procurement System

The new law adopted in 2007 incorporates the latest changes in the EU public procurement law into the Estonian legislation and addresses many issues poorly regulated in the previous acts. As this regulation is very recent, no experience on application can be reported yet. Nevertheless, one can point to many problems stemming from the current regulation and organizational framework. Two important questions stand out here deserving a closer look. First, is the decentralized public procurement model the best possible choice for a transitioning country? Second, whether the government should take more active role in training of procurement personnel?

On the basis of the Estonian example, one can come up with several negative side effects of fully decentralized procurement model. These include lack of coordination and cooperation, unexploited economies of scale, and episodic and ineffective supervision. The resistance to cooperate and coordinate when procuring goods and services that need detailed specification and high level of competence is one of the factors driving up the number of complaints filed in by bidders. In 2005, 51 percent of the reviewed complaints fell into the categories of IT, building and reconstruction, and healthcare equipment procurement.[14] The need for higher level coordination is well illustrated by the fact that in 2005, in case of contested IT tenders, no contractor had turned to the Estonian Information Center for advice, which is an organization that is made responsible, inter alia, for counseling, and for organizing for public IT procurement.

An unexploited economy of scale is a problem that was tried to solve by creating central purchasing agencies in 2001. Although the agencies were dissolved the problems remained acute. It is estimated that in 2003 only 7.4 percent of central government maintenance budget was allocated through compulsory tender procedures (State Audit Office, 2005). This became possible as every central agency and subunits contracted for maintenance services separately and the values were below the national thresholds. This example clearly demonstrates that the government has not taken advantage of its potential bargaining power it had in case of consolidated procurement.

The State Audit Office (2004), which has no sanctioning power over auditees, has many times implied that even in cases where the law requires application of the official tender procedures, the public authorities may simply ignore the requirement without any consequences following. In 2005, the Public Procurement Office managed to audit altogether 78 contracting organizations (Public Procurement Office, 2006), which makes only a fraction of all public organizations in Estonia. At the same time, it has been demonstrated that, for example, the central ministries, with much more developed auditing mechanisms than local governments, do not have proper and systematic procurement auditing procedures in place (State Audit Office, 2004). Dimitri et al. (2006) suggest that E-platforms can serve as powerful tools for increasing monitoring capacity in decentralized model of public procurement. If, generally, the role of the international donors like EU has been regarded as positive for the development of the transitional countries, then in this context, public E-procurement stands out as a topic that seems to be having an opposite effect, however, as Estonia has decided not to introduce central E-procurement platform before EU has managed to develop its own platform. In addition to the monitoring issue, the missing E-procurement platform has not let Estonia minimize transaction costs for the public contractors as well as for private bidders (European Commission, 2007).[15]

The lack of unified group of procurement professionals and vague training system has created the situation where after ten years of introducing the first version of Public Procurement Act, a large number of public officials are not fully informed about public procurement issues. On the local governmental level, 50 percent of officials have admitted that they need training in procurement issues (State Chancellery, 2006a). As nearly half of the civil servants at the local as well as the central government level have work experience less than five years in their offices and the general staff turnover rate is 13 percent per year (State Chancellery, 2007b), the need for systematic training should become more evident.

The lack of proper know-how on procurement is also emphasized by the State Audit Office (2005). When analyzing technical specifications in maintenance contracts of the government organizations, the State Audit Office referred to significant difference in services regulated by law and services not regulated by law. In the former cases, the contracts were well specified, and in the latter cases, the contracts were mostly vaguely specified and without any reference to expected results. Similarly, especially if the expected value of sourcing is lower than the national thresholds, then the Estonian public organizations are reluctant to take ex post calculations or comparative bids as a basis for justifying "make or buy" decisions (State Audit Office, 2005). It can be claimed that one of the reasons causing these problems in the Estonian public administration is insufficient knowledge regarding overall purchasing logic.[16]

Opposing to this evidence, the 2007 Public Procurement Act assumes the procurement personnel's capacity to be very high. As indicated earlier, from 2007 onward, all contract terms in cases of open and restricted procedures must already be specified in detail in the tender documents and no subsequent negotiations are allowed, which makes it quite possible that several smaller contracting authorities will find this provision problematic due to the administrative capacity to compile all contract terms overall might be insufficient.

Uncoordinated, unsystematic, and market-based training system raises many questions in the light of modernization of procurement procedures. With the new procurement methods like competitive dialogue and dynamic auctioning, the public officials are given more discretional power, which means that the officials do not only need to follow the official procedures and rules but they also actually need to understand the logic of procurement. Trybus (2006) has pointed that besides criminal law, the training of procurement personnel is the main tool to overcome problems with corruption. The existing training programs are overwhelmingly biased toward legal aspects, which alone falls short securing economic use of public resources. On one side the bias is understandable as the officials need to be informed about the changes in regulation. This is especially helpful for overcoming a typical feature of transitional context—constantly changing laws—which impedes the development of good practices in public administration. On the other side, this bias means that the strategic and management issues of procurement are covered only indirectly. Hence, the challenge Estonia faces is how to secure implementation of flexible and innovative procurement procedures when a significant number of procurement officials lack the state-of-the-art know-how.

19.7 Conclusion

The Estonian public procurement market has been forced to cope with a condition of constant change. The driving force behind most of the changes has been the then still only expected perspective of joining the EU. This process has had its pros and cons as, for example, the transposition of an internationally approved package of rules, which fosters Estonia's competitiveness on the one hand and the unnecessary restrictions on framework agreements on the other. However, Estonia has managed to elaborate a modern legal environment for public procurement, an outstanding electronic system for publication and statistics and is about to take the next step forward into the electronic procurement era soon. It seems that the relative success is based on the liberal economic policy, which eagerly followed the advice of different international donors, and influence of the joining process with EU, which forced the government to adapt the EU principles into the Estonian legal framework.

In spite of the fact that Estonia with other CEE countries is seen as a successful reformer of public procurement system, the article revealed that many challenges are yet to be faced. There are many issues the current regulation does not address or does it indirectly. The main challenges include the questions how to take more advantage from economies of scale, how to elaborate a coherent training system, and whether public procurement should used be to promote wider social and economic goals. The Estonian case suggests that decentralized public procurement system has many problems and more centralized system could be beneficial when economies of scale and bargaining power are important. Nevertheless, one should be precautious when suggesting radical implementation of more centralized system for a post-transitioning country like Estonia. Estonia has had some negative experience with central procurement model and there are still many processes whose effects remain to be tested in the near future like implementation of modern procurement methods and the EU-wide E-procurement platform. On the basis of Estonian example, it should be noticed that E-procurement and other modern purchasing methods will have less significant impact without increasing internal capacity of procurement personnel. In addition, more competent staff would give the public more confidence that less rigid procurement rules may actually increase the national welfare and not those involved in particular transactions. Well-trained procurement officials can be taken as the most important precondition if a society expects public procurement to influence the growth of innovative entrepreneurship. Hence, the current problems indicate that the approach where the government's role is limited only with regulation and protest review should be redirected toward of more active one with coherent policy.

Notes

1. First version of the Estonian Public Procurement Act adopted in 1995 was based on the UNCITRAL model (Lamvol, 2002). UNCITRAL refers to the United Nations Commission on International Trade Law (see http://www.uncitral.org).
2. For the international regulation see European Parliament (2004a, b), The United Nations Commission on International Trade Law (http://www.uncitral.org) and WTO Government Procurement Agreement (http://www.wto.org/english/docs_e/legal_e/gpr-94_01_e.htm).
3. For more information, see the Register's Web site https://riigihanked.riik.ee.
4. Criminal conviction is also possible in case of more serious violations of procurement law but can naturally be judged by a court, not the Public Procurement Office.
5. As of January 1, 2007 the total number of persons inhabiting Estonia is 1.37 million. There are altogether 227 local governments in Estonia, of which 66 percent are with less than 3000 residents.
6. See Tavits and Annus (2006) for an overview of the public agencies in Estonia.
7. Centralized procurement of fuel was abolished due to the fact that it would have forced the potential suppliers to violate Competition Act (Raudla, 2007).
8. For example, in 2006, Pärnu County government authorized the Estonian Informatics Center to carry out the tender process for fixed Internet connection in sparsely populated rural areas of Pärnu County (for more information on this specific case, see http://www.ria.ee/27426; for general IT procurement issues see http://www.ria.ee).
9. As of today, 99 objects have been assigned to the State Real Estate Company by central government and 31 objects by local governments (State Real Estate Company, 2007). Two factors explain this relatively small number of contracts. First, it has been claimed that the price of using the services of the State Real Estate Company is not competitive (Postimees, 2005). Secondly, according to the Estonian law, the contracts agreed with State Real Estate Company are considered as a part of local governments' debt burden, which has prevented using the State Real Estate Company services.
10. Several examples can be outlined here. For instance, Estonia was the first country to implement overall E-voting system for parliamentary elections; by February 2006, electronic ID cards had been issued to 61 percent of the population; in 2007, 85 percent of tax declarations is expected to be submitted online; 95 percent of banking operations are carried out electronically. For these and additional facts see Estonian Informatics Center http://www.ria.ee/27525.
11. Program involved also certification of 15 trainers for future public procurement training courses (see Ministry of Finance http://www.fin.ee/?id=76690).
12. For example, University of Tartu offers a course "Government Procurement" at the Faculty of Law and "Public Procurement and Public Property" at the Department of Public Administration. For more information, see http://www.ut.ee.
13. When preparing the new Public Procurement Act in 2006 the members of the Estonian parliament, Riigikogu, were aware and had some discussion of the possible social and economic impacts of public procurement, but no direct steps were taken to introduce the principles in the law (Riigikogu, 2006b).
14. Calculations are based on the data provided by Public Procurement Office (2006).
15. It has to be mentioned here that E-platforms may not always bring along decreased (transaction) costs. For example, the government of New Zealand dropped plans regarding to development of central E-procurement platform after the trial period (see European Commission http://ec.europa.eu/idabc/en/document/1909/359).
16. See Lember (2006) for an in-depth example of implementation problems of contracting out of public services in Estonia. Similar deficits have been identified in other CEE countries (e.g., Nemec, 2001).

References

Aedmaa, A. and Parrest, N. 2004. *Public Contract* (Haldusleping), Riigikantselei. Available at http://www.riigikantselei.ee/failid/Haldusleping.pdf (accessed February 22, 2007).

Bank of Estonia. 2007. Annual indicators of Estonian economy. Available at http://www.eestipank.info/dynamic/itp2/itp_report_2a.jsp?reference=503&className=EPSTAT2&lang=en (accessed January 30, 2007).

Dimitri, N., Dina, F., and Piga, G. 2006. When should procurement be centralized? In: N. Dimitri, G. Piga, and G. Spagnolo (Eds.), *Handbook of Public Procurement*, Cambridge: Cambridge University Press, pp. 47–81.

Drechsler, W. 1995. Estonia in transition. *World Affairs*, 157(3): 111–117.

European Commission. 2007. eProcurement. Available at http://ec.europa.eu/idabc/eprocurement (accessed January 31, 2007).

European Parliament and Council of Europe. 2004a. Directive 2004/17/EC of the European Parliament and of the Council of 31 March 2004 coordinating the procurement procedures of entities operating in the water, energy, transport and postal services sectors. *Official Journal* L 134.

European Parliament and Council of Europe. 2004b. Directive 2004/18/EC of the European Parliament and of the Council of 31 March 2004 on the coordination of procedures for the award of public works contracts, public supply contracts and public service contracts. *Official Journal* L 134.

Hunja, R.R. 2002. Obstacles to public procurement reform. In: S. Arrowsmith and M. Trybus (Eds.), *Developing Countries Public Procurement: The Continuing Revolution*, The Hague: Kluwer Law International, pp. 13–22.

Lamvol, A. 2002. From transition to cohesion: The reform of public procurement in Estonia. *Public Procurement Law Review*, 11: 74–97.

Lember, V. 2006. On importance of ex ante analysis in implementing contracting out: Lessons from the Estonian emergency medical service. In: W. Dunn, K. Staranova, and S. Pushkarev (Eds.), *Implementation – the Missing Link in Public Administration Reform in Central and Eastern Europe*, Bratislava, Estonia: NISPAcee, pp. 111–124.

Ministry of Finance. 2006. *Explanatory Report on the Draft Public Procurement Act*. Available at http://eoigus.just.ee/?act=6&subact=1&OTSIDOC_W=114425 (accessed February 22, 2007).

Ministry of Finance. 2007. *Statistics of the Public Procurement Register*. Available at http://www.fin.ee/?id=76329 (accessed February 22, 2007).

Nemec, J. 2001. Competitive contracting: Problems and potential in the public sector reform process in CEE. In: G. Wright (Ed.), *Government, Market and the Civic Sector: The Search for a Productive Partnership*, Bratislava, Estonia: NISPAcee, pp. 63–89.

Nyiri, L., Osimo, D., Özcivelek, R., Centeno, C., and Cabrera, M. 2007. *Public Procurement for the Promotion of R&D and Innovation in ICT*. Luxembourg: Office for Official Publications of the European Communities.

Opmann, M. 2007. *Shorthand Notes of the Estonian Parliament*, the Riigikogu, 24.01.2007. Available at http://web.riigikogu.ee/ems/stenograms/2007/01/t07012403-05.html (accessed January 31, 2007).

Ploom, E. 1996. Peculiarities in the development of a public procurement system in the Republic of Estonia. *Juridica Interanational*, 2: 45–53.

Postimees. 2005. *The State Real Estate Company Can Be Dissolved* (*Riigi kinnisvara haldav aktsiaselts võib kaduda*). Available at http://www.postimees.ee/200905/esileht/siseuudised/177423.php (accessed February 19, 2007).

Public Procurement Office. 2006. *Yearbook 2002–2005*. Available at http://www.rha.gov.ee/?id=1342 (accessed February 22, 2007).

Public Procurement Register 2007. *Statistical Reports*. Available at http://riigihanked.riik.ee/index.jsp?page=RHRStatReport.jsp (accessed February 28, 2007).

Raudla, R. 2007. Law and economics analysis on the Estonian Public Procurement Act. In: G. Piga and K.V. Thai (Eds.), *Advancing Public Procurement. Practices, Innovation and Knowledge-Sharing,* Boca Raton, FL: PrAcademics Press, pp. 202–238.

Riigikogu (The Estonian Parliament). 1995. Public Procurement Act.

Riigikogu (The Estonian Parliament). 2000. Public Procurement Act. RTI, 07.11.2000, 84, 534.

Riigikogu (The Estonian Parliament). 2003. *Public Procurement Act Amendment Act. RTI* 17.12.2003, 78, 521.

Riigikogu (The Estonian Parliament). 2004. State Budget Act.

Riigikogu (The Estonian Parliament). 2005. Public Procurement Act Amendment Act. RTI 1995, 54, 883.

Riigikogu (The Estonian Parliament) 2006a. Shorthand notes of the Estonian Parliament 22.03.2006. Available http://web.riigikogu.ee/ems/stenograms/2006/03/t06032209-13.html (accessed January 31, 2007).

Riigikogu (The Estonian Parliament). 2006b. Report of the Committee of Economic Affairs 01.06.2006. Available at http://web.riigikogu.ee/ems/saros-bin/mgetdoc?itemid=062210002&login=proov&password=&system=ems&server=ragne11 (accessed January 30, 2007).

Riigikogu (The Estonian Parliament). 2007. Public Procurement Act. RTI, 21.02.2007, 15, 76.

SIGMA. 2003. Acceeding countries. Central and Eastern Europe. Estonia. *Public Procurement Review,* 8. Available at http://www.sigmaweb.org/dataoecd/11/32/34992314.pdf (accessed November 22, 2006).

State Audit Office. 2004. Internal Audit and Monitoring System of Public Procurement. Audit Report nr 2–5/04/117 (*Riigihangete korraldusele rakendatav sisekontrollisüsteem ja järelevalve nr 2–5/04/117*). Available at http://www.riigikontroll.ee (accessed November 27, 2006).

State Audit Office. 2005. Procurement of Maintenance Services. Audit Report nr 2–6/05/6 (*Hooldusteenuste hanked. Kontrolliaruanne nr 2–6/05/6*). Available at http://www.riigikontroll.ee (accessed November 27, 2006).

State Chancellery. 2005. Public Service Training Priorities for 2005 (*Avaliku teenistuse koolitusprioriteedid 2005. aastal*). Available at http://www.riigikantselei.ee/?id=3054 (accessed January 30, 2007).

State Chancellery. 2006a. *Study on the Long-term Training of Local Government Officials* (*Kohalike omavalitsuste ametnike pikaajalise koolitusvajaduse uuring*). Geomeedia: Tallinn-Tartu.

State Chancellery. 2006b. Public Service Training Priorities for 2006 (*Avaliku teenistuse koolitusprioriteedid*). Available at http://www.riigikantselei.ee/?id=2957 (accessed January 30, 2007).

State Chancellery. 2007a. On-line Training Database for Civil Servants. Available at http://www.riik.ee/koolitus/koolitaja (accessed January 30, 2007).

State Chancellery. 2007b. Aggregated Statistics on Public Service Personnel in 2005. Available at http://www.riigikantselei.ee/index.php?id=6596 (accessed January 30, 2007).

State Real Estate Company. 2007. Contracts Signed (Sõlmitud lepingud). Available at http://www.rkas.ee/?id=3985 (accessed February 19, 2007).

Tavits, M. and Annus, T. 2006. Agencification in Estonia. *Public Administration and Development,* 26: 3–14.

Trybus, M. 2006. Improving the efficiency of public procurement systems in the context of the European Union enlargement process. *Public Contract Law Journal,* 35: 409–425.

Verheijen, T. 1998. Public management in Central and Eastern Europe: The nature of the problem. In: T. Verheijen and D. Coombes (Eds.), *Innovations in Public Management: Perspectives from East and West Europe,* Cheltenham, England: Edward Elgar, pp. 207–219.

Chapter 20

Procurement Process in the Public Sector: An International Perspective

Nigel Caldwell and Elmer Bakker

CONTENTS

20.1 Introduction

This chapter describes the purchasing process in public sector organizations; the public procurement process. The objective is to explore the main activities carried out through the procurement process and demonstrate how these procurement activities support or hinder policy level decisions. To this end we use one of the most respected examples of a staged procurement process (Van Weele, 2005), which like most accounts of the purchasing process focuses on the firm, and how it fulfills its own processes. We then populate that staged process or framework with examples from public procurement practices across the world. These examples are drawn from a major international research program on public procurement (Harland et al., 2004).

Twenty-first century public procurement faces a new challenge where both the problems it is asked to tackle are complex societal ones (e.g., in much of the Western world providing a fertile environment for small, sustainable local businesses, buying care for rapidly changing age demographics in innovative ways (Caldwell et al., 2007) as well as promoting competitive markets (Caldwell et al., 2005)), and that these problems (and their current solutions such as public–private partnerships) are services that were once seen as the sole preserve of either the public or private sectors (Lucyshyn, 2007). "A further feature of these issues is that they cut across the traditional jurisdictions of organizations and cross the boundaries between the public and private sector" (Koppenjan and Erik-Hans, 2004:1).

In an increasingly "networked society" twenty-first century procurement involves more and more actors, both institutional and individual. In this chapter, our focus is on how public procurement processes impact suppliers and markets. This focus results in us analyzing practices in terms of how they translate for suppliers, effectively assessing how public procurement processes make the public sector perform as an "intelligent" customer.

In spite of the distinction between the public and private sectors, the purchasing process is still similar in that there are a set of core and common phases that organizations go through. However, the decision-making process is different in terms of the outcomes or factors that are taken into consideration, although the activities performed are similar. Both public and private sector procurements start with a buying need—a demand for certain resources—which, as with any exchange relationship, forms the basis for supplier relationships (Robinson et al., 1967; Emerson, 1976; Pfeffer and Salancik, 1978). The purchasing process constitutes the activities, both formal and informal, that have to be performed to provide this problem a solution.

There are a variety of academic descriptions of the purchasing process (e.g., Robinson et al., 1967; Ford, 1980; Johnston and Lewin, 1996; Van Weele, 2005). The common approach is to portray the purchasing process as divided into a number of different stages. This chapter adopts Van Weele's approach, which specifies six distinct activities—specification, supplier selection, contracting, ordering, expediting, and follow-up/evaluation (see Figure 20.1). This combination of precision and a broad-brush approach makes this six stage approach effective as a framing device for mapping out the contingent approaches of the many forms of public procurement.

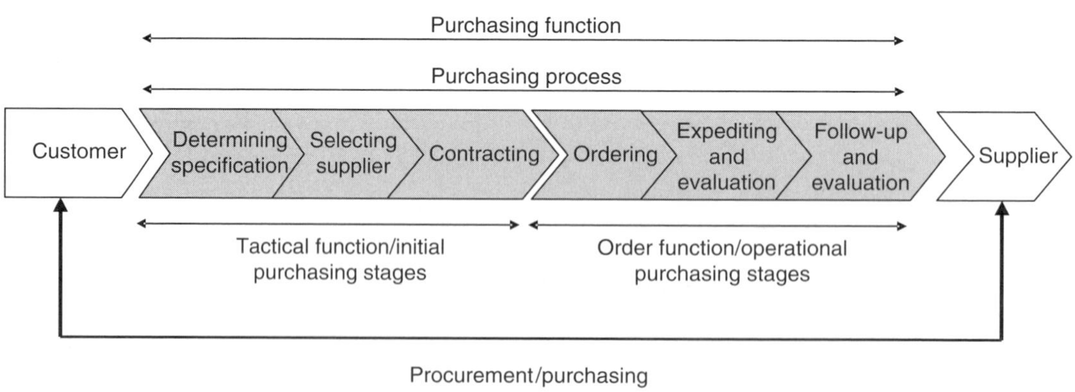

Figure 20.1 The procurement process. (Adapted from Van Weele, A.J., *Purchasing and Supply Chain Management, Analysis, Planning and Practice*, Thompson Learning, London, 2005, p. 13.)

In practice, of course, the six distinct phases can become blurred, or are combined or given different names. For example, a large U.K. metropolitan council describes their "contract cycle" as project scoping and contract preparation (specification phase), contract letting (selection and contracting phase), contract management (ordering and expediting and evaluation), and contract review (follow-up and evaluation). "Procurement" and "purchasing" are often used interchangeably but are known to refer to the same set of activities (Van Weele, 2005; Knight et al., 2007). In practice, however, our experience is that procurement is often used for public sector "buying," whereas purchasing is mainly identified with the private sector. Although the original model by Van Weele sees procurement as wider than purchasing, including the management of the relationship between customer and supplier, this chapter treats procurement and purchasing as synonymous, acknowledging that the management of the relationship is a core element, regardless of level of public procurement, for example, national, regional, state, city level, etc.

20.2 Determining Specifications

Before procurement can enter into negotiations and contracting, or build supply relations, the organization needs to know what it really requires. Assessing this need occurs in the specification phase. Traditionally, procurement addressed technical specifications, describing the technical properties and characteristics of the product or service required (often based on a need to replace a certain product). An example is specifying lease cars by brand and engine capacity, etc. Another way of specifying is functionally, which is related to a current drive toward using more "outcome-focused" approaches. Thus, new approaches to specifying describe the functionality and outcome for the user; broadly what does a product or service have to do, including any constraints (e.g., to fit in with legacy IT systems). An example is specifying that one needs "fast possible transportation from A to B." The use of functional specifications leaves more alternatives open and can be a first step toward enabling the adoption of innovative solutions. Functional specifications can in certain instances be used on their own, when looking for innovative solutions, taking advantage of suppliers' knowledge and expertise. On the other hand, functional specifications do tend to be followed by setting the technical specifications at some point (e.g., to take into account technical or compatibility constraints).

The introduction gave an example from U.K. local government of public procurement taking specifications explicitly into account in their purchasing process. This attention to specifications is also found in other countries, for example, in Singapore (Jones, 2007) and Belgium (Baeyens and Martel, 2007). In these countries there is national level attention to specifications on a policy level. In Singapore, ministries and statutory boards now have autonomy to determine most aspects of specifications, but it is forbidden by statute to discuss specifications in advance with potential suppliers. In Belgium, military procurement has found it difficult to write technical specifications for complex long-term capital intensive products. Products such as tanks and planes are specified at the beginning of a life cycle that will see many changes before a piece of military hardware comes into service. In this case, suppliers depart from certain "basic" specifications, yet are involved after the contract award in influencing these specifications.

Determining the specifications is an important phase in the procurement process, as it will be harder to justify the awarding of a contract when it is difficult to write the specifications. This is especially relevant in the light of EU legislation (discussed in Section 20.3) requiring a transparent process and selection. One solution is clearly early engagement with potential suppliers (Erridge and Nondi, 1994), but procurement rules designed to ensure accountability and competition mitigate against public entities making such early links. Exceptions are likely to be part of a specific process where such accountability rules can be wavered in particular cases, for example, as found in small-scale hospital construction projects in the United Kingdom (Caldwell et al., 2005).

The examples above suggest that specifications are easier to achieve for simple buying needs, for example, "re-buy" situations (Robinson et al., 1967), or when procurement is highly rule driven. However, specifications become problematic when an innovative solution is required, where there are complex systems, extended life cycles or "new task" buying needs (ibid.). It is a common criticism of the public sector that specifications are too precise and detailed. For example, the U.S. military specification for hot chocolate is 20 pages long (Gansler, 1989:191–192).

Other countries are more flexible and allow experimentation, such as Australia (Callender and Schapper, 2007) and the United States (McCue et al., 2007). Australian public procurement and U.S. state and local governments feature an increasing focus on outcomes, whereas in Belgium the rigidity of public procurement comes from a focus on inputs (e.g., detailed specifications). There appears to be a direct correlation between the amount of formal attention and processes paid to specifications and a focus on inputs rather than an outcome-oriented environment. Making wider socioeconomic goals part of the responsibility of procurement, as increasingly happens in some Anglo-Saxon countries (such as helping small businesses, helping ethnic businesses, sustainability), means specifications are becoming increasingly intangible and determining them is becoming more complex. Furthermore, abstract policies such as the need for sustainability can make it more difficult to set the specifications, which will make the supplier selection phase more difficult, or can even affect the selection phase by excluding certain suppliers. In other words, whether led by policy or not, the way specifications are set can expand or contract the potential supply market.

20.3 Selecting Suppliers

After having determined their need, public sector organizations enter the supplier selection phase. Scanning the supply market for available solutions and eventually selecting the supplier that is going to fulfill the buying need are the main tasks in this phase. In reality, determining the specifications and undertaking market scanning and supplier selection often happen at a similar time, as suppliers may have been involved in the process through requests for cost estimates or technical specifications, or specifications can be written—consciously or unconsciously—with particular suppliers in mind. The latter is not deemed "good" public procurement practice, which sets an expectation that all suppliers will be treated equally. Yet, this especially tends to happen when it concerns a "re-buy" situation (Robinson et al., 1967), or is triggered when organizations have long-term relationships with certain suppliers. From its earliest appearances in the wider management literature, good procurement practice has been engaged with how to prevent suppliers (in connivance with employees, particularly in the early literature, engineers) from effectively cowriting specifications such that their business appears the most suitable (Strauss, 1962; Pingry, 1974). However, the other side of the coin is that maintaining a detachment from suppliers often prevents public sector organizations developing long-term relationships or partnerships, a topic which has received a lot of attention and has been pursued in the private sector (e.g., Lamming, 1993). Setting specifications can determine which supply market, or even which specific suppliers can be considered for selection, which means the selection phase is highly influenced by the specification phase.

Selection criteria can be divided into "order-qualifying criteria"—the minimum requirements needed to be met for consideration—and "order-winning criteria"—other criteria (sometimes additional offerings by suppliers such as free training) based on which the deal can be won (Hill, 1993).

In many purchases multiple criteria will be used to help choose a supplier, weightings can be applied to the criteria to prioritize and assess what is most important. Awarding weightings is of course subjective and can depend on context (e.g., significant budget cuts will usually be followed by a price focus), but as long as this subjectivity is recognized and if used appropriately, weightings can be helpful to trigger discussions and help assess which requirements are really necessary.

Which suppliers are selected as an outcome of the decision-making process can be influenced through public organizations by how specifications are set, or more specifically through including policy and wider socioeconomic objectives. A leading example can be found in South Africa where "Black Economic Empowerment" is pursued as part of a national policy (Van Vuuren and Badenhorst-Weiss, 2007). In South Africa, public procurement is being used to support a supplier selection process that enables a specific sector of the supply base—the economically disadvantaged black majority—to both compete for and win public contracts. Another example is the United Nations (UN), where suppliers must confirm they do not use child labor to qualify for selection (Van Gronden et al., 2007). Here, the subject of supplier selection also starts to link up with organizational choices on ethical codes of conduct in purchasing and supply. In many instances, public procurement requires detailed documentation from suppliers at the selection stage. This can make the selection process an expensive undertaking for the supplying organizations and is a relatively greater disadvantage for smaller businesses and the voluntary sector, which have lower levels of human and financial resources. From the perspective of these suppliers, too many failed bids incur disproportionate costs, and these bidding costs will have to be regained in other bids or contracts.

As mentioned above, countries in the European Union are also influenced by EU public procurement directives and regulations when the procurement represents a value above a certain threshold. These rules apply to purchases made on local, regional—state or county—and on a central government level. The EU guidelines differentiate between the categories "supplies," "services," and "works" for which there are different threshold levels. Contracts with a value above a threshold level set by EU procurement rules must be advertised in the supplement to the *Official Journal of the European Union* (OJEU) before being notified elsewhere, widening the potential supply market. Such transparency means, at least in theory, that the market has opened up to "foreign" competitors, yet local suppliers who sometimes have to be seen to bid for the sake of being awarded other businesses have a higher risk of failed bids due to this increased competition. One innovative solution to reduce tender costs for suppliers used in the United States (McCue et al., 2007) is to move to a system in which suppliers only have to demonstrate conformance to certain standards once, instead of repeatedly, tender by tender. Collaborative procurement initiatives undertaken in Finland (Kivisto et al., 2007), Canada, the United States, the United Kingdom, and Australia (Aylesworth, 2007) also have reduced bidding costs as a by-product, as suppliers only have to prove they conform to the required standards once for the consortium, instead of individually to each municipality.

Next to policy, the selection phase is also influenced by legislation. This can be subnational (e.g., state, federal), national, or international legislation and is affected by how countries structure their governance and public procurement. For example, in the Federal Republic of Germany, although individual states are independent states, public sector organizations operate generally under federal (or state) law; however, for volumes over €200,000 they also operate under German national law. In addition to the EU rules on publishing tenders over certain limits, a more open, international marketplace for potential suppliers to governments is also created through free trade agreements between particular nations. The potential advantage of such competition is that it can bring new ideas and innovations, or create such pressure for suppliers in the home country to innovate, to remain an appropriate alternative for the buying organization. Although the creation of a larger market through EC rules may generate diversity in supply sources, it is also likely to result in uncertainty in the supply market. For example, the local supply markets could be affected, as only larger suppliers can be eligible as they have the capacity to match highly aggregated procurement demands. Additionally, selecting foreign suppliers, for example, could come with higher risks of poorer quality or ethical standards in the supplying country. Such side effects could include lower standards of animal welfare in the case of imported meat or impacts on the environment in the supplying country that would not be permitted in the importing nation, or even the use of child labor. Furthermore, it will be more difficult to gain insight into the other tiers that make up the supply chain and whether these suppliers to the suppliers conform to certain standards. Therefore, public procurement has to be aware of how such selection discussions impact other governmental agendas or priorities (e.g., the sustainability agenda).

A final feature of the selection process is the influence of organizational structure and the role procurement plays within the public entity. In Germany, local budgets and local decision making are used to support local small businesses. Dutch and English hospital systems are similarly decentralized (Harland et al., 2007; Telgen and van Vliet, 2007); in both countries it is common for purchasing decisions to be taken within individual hospital departments. The sections responsible for such buying can however be relatively small and are sometimes seen as a clerical or administrative function; procurement is not seen as a core activity and clinicians have significant power over buying decisions, resulting in what is referred to as "clinical preference" (Cox et al., 2005). The result is that decisions are taken without professional purchasing involvement and at a system level this leads to the use of many suppliers and much duplication by individuals performing similar activities. Although, as in the Netherlands, the fragmentation favors smaller, local suppliers, it also results in a lack of standard specifications and higher prices for buyers and leads to situations in which for the same product, suppliers can receive different specifications. It can also lead to a varied and wide supply base, which—from a system or network perspective—could become very difficult and expensive to manage and coordinate. The current approach by the German government is to introduce E-procurement to tackle this and related issues such as high transaction costs (Essig and Schaefer, 2007). However, a note of caution is necessary: in the information systems world it is a truism that if you automate flawed systems, they will be flawed once they are computer based. A first step in the process of automating procurement processes—such as going to E-procurement—must be to review and improve basic processes. This was what Australian jurisdictions discovered where a similar E-strategy was pursued; a fundamental reform of processes was necessary before transaction savings could be achieved (Tonkin, 2007).

Finally, the trend toward more horizontal collaboration (e.g., consortiums) in public witnessed in countries such as Finland, the Netherlands, the United Kingdom, the United States, and Germany (Bakker et al., 2006) affects those who become involved in the selection of suppliers. Collaborative buying arrangements can mean existing relationships with local suppliers are interrupted. Often, smaller local-type companies do not have the capacity to cope with a greater geographical scope of clients or increased volumes. This in its turn could influence selection criteria, interfere with a potential agenda to help small businesses, and could mean EU thresholds are reached involving Europeanwide advertising and so on.

20.4 Contracting Award Stage

In a recent book, Broussueau and Glachant (2005:3) note that contracts are viewed differently by economists and lawyers. For the former, a contract is an agreement under which two parties make reciprocal commitments in terms of their behavior—a bilateral coordination arrangement. Since the early 1990s, there has been a shift toward a relational rather than contractual basis for relationships in the private sector (Sako, 1992; Dyer and Singh, 1998). "Trust" and abstract concepts such as "mutuality" retain a high visibility in the academic literature but nevertheless public procurement is still firmly contract based. "Although scholars have lamented the shortcomings of contracts for governing exchange (e.g., Macaulay, 1963; MacNeil, 1980), there has been no decrease in the use of contracts or in the length or complexity of the rather formidable contracts that circulate in many industries" (Wuyts and Geyskens, 2005:113).

Public procurement contracting deals with the same issue of whether to "make or buy" familiar to manufacturing organizations, except in this service context, the decision is whether to provide the service (make) or to contract with an external provider (buy). Brown and Potoski (2004) use transaction cost and public sector network theories to compare the costs public managers face in delivering services directly or via contract. Their study was based on a survey of refuse collection managers, and comes with the caveat that it is easier to contract for the transparent activity of emptying dustbins, than for intangible services such as elements of social care and healthcare (Coulson, 1998). Brown and Potoski conclude that direct service provision incurs higher management costs but that contracting involves more monitoring costs. Various authors have cited the need to maintain in-house capacity to manage contracted-out provision (Bettis et al., 1992; Harland et al., 2005). If the current trend in public procurement continues to shift away from direct provision to contracting for, and monitoring of, external performance, then new measures of procurement outcomes are needed.

Value for money in public procurement is gaining a higher profile (Heinrich, 2002). There is some consensus in Anglo-Saxon countries that selecting the "most economically advantageous" rather than lowest priced bids and outcome/performance-based contracting are two different techniques for delivering better value for money. In contrast to traditional price-based contracting, performance-based contract specifications, for example, potentially offer different risk allocations. Contracting for outcomes rather than relying on specifications gives suppliers flexibility and wider scope to bring their expertise and capacity for innovation. The success of outcome-based contracting in part depends on how public procurement is organized. In some countries (e.g., Belgium and Germany), comprehensive, formal procurement rules are seen as necessary and desirable to prevent abuses that could slip through more ambiguous criteria. But such normative approaches to procurement activity make it more difficult to use qualitative criteria and functional performance descriptions (the basis of outcome contracting) which are more prone to relative and subjective judgments and therefore harder to police.

Balanced against the appeal of contracting for outcomes rather than solutions the buyer has specified in detail, is the potential risk when applied to the management of public activities more complex than, for example, refuse collection. The introduction referred to the twenty-first century public procurement challenge as being able to respond to complex societal demands within the context of a shifting boundary of what is and is not deemed the public or private sector. In major public/private partnerships, governments are increasingly contracting with the private sector to build, run, maintain, and update large facilities ranging from hospitals, transport infrastructure, prisons, computer systems to major military installations and related equipment. Academics such as Lonsdale (2005) see these new demands on public procurement and the new contractual uncertainties in the form of how to obtain value for money from suppliers and subcontractors in large-scale, long-term (e.g., 20–30 years) contracts as potentially shifting power from the public sector to the private.

Finally, the contracting process can also be affected by the estimated value of the contract. In Germany, for example, we have seen earlier that the value of a contract can determine that both federal and national legislations apply. Similarly, for the European Union, different thresholds for different categories of procurement (supplies, works, and services) affect the purchasing process and the types of contracts to be used (national, international, chosen contract duration to make the tender process worthwhile, etc.). In U.S. federal government procurement, a combination of different values and different purchases are used in a matrix that identifies solicitation provisions and contract clauses for specific types of purchases (Thai and Drabkin, 2007).

20.5 Ordering

It is all too easy to dismiss the ordering stage as the mere clerical or computer-driven calling off of goods or services from the selected supplier. Viewed in this light, ordering is a mundane and repetitive part of the procurement process. Yet, particularly in public procurement, the nature of the public sector ordering process impacts directly upon the supply base, and therefore, indirectly, on procurement outcomes. What may seem the mundane activity of ordering can reflect tensions between efficiency and policy; for example, at a local government level, local politicians (whose priority is among others, reelection) may favor local businesses over nonlocal suppliers. Similarly, in the public healthcare sector and other sectors, professional preferences (e.g., in healthcare, physician choice is based on noneconomic grounds) can mean that instead of using contracts, so-called "maverick" ordering takes place, where suppliers are used who are not validated by procurement procedures. Such maverick activity means demand appears highly variable to suppliers and procurement cannot take full advantage of economies of scale. These two factors undermine reaching full potential efficiency, affecting the ability to fulfill other policy objectives such as sustainability.

The U.S. federal government has recognized the importance of ordering patterns (Thai and Drabkin, 2007); they are aware that public procurement can create sporadic and lumpy demand patterns, with disastrous effects for suppliers (i.e., feast, where there are too many orders to meet without employing relatively expensive interim resources, or famine where months pass without a reasonable distribution of the annual order value). The U.S. federal government has hence improved procurement practices to allow sufficient time to complete the competitive procurement process and avoid the problem of having a huge proportion of contract awards being made in the closing period of the fiscal year, a problem common across public sector procurement the world over.

Many governments are leading the way in asking the public sector to use E-procurement and other innovations as a means of trying to reduce the transaction costs involved in ordering from many suppliers. For example, in the Gauteng province of South Africa, order transaction cost reduction initiatives include the use of SAP software and the use of purchasing cards. The distribution of purchasing cards (and therefore the authority to purchase on behalf of the organization) to nonpurchasing staff raises responsibility issues in public procurement. When purchasing cards were introduced in Australia many examples of misuse were found soon after the introduction; problems quickly solved through rigorous audit (Tonkin, 2007). In the United States, the federal government was very forward-looking in being positive on the value of cards. Federal investigation of purchasing card use includes an example where the purchase of a horse on a purchasing card, in a bar, was investigated and found to be perfectly reasonable. In that remote location only the bar had the facility to handle such a high value card transaction and the use of horses as part of delivering public service was common (illustrating once again the diversity of public sector procurement practices).

The impact of ordering and the need for public procurement to understand the impact of public ordering patterns comes through clearly in the take-up of framework style agreements. In essence, framework agreements are agreements with a (or multiple) supplier(s) to deliver a certain product or service X against a pre-agreed price Q. These agreements are often based on expected demand (based on the previous use of that product or service by multiple public sector organizations), but without commitment to, or guaranteeing, volumes. It is up to the individual local public organizations to use the contract or—as happens—find their own deal, using the framework contract as benchmark and starting point for further negotiations. Thus, in the fragmented U.K. National Health Service (NHS), take-up of nationally negotiated agreements is voluntary and varies. Claims of the success of such agreements caution is always needed and disillusionment by suppliers could lead to unwillingness to devote energy to bidding in a possible next round. For example, the Canadian department of Public Works and Government Services (PWGSC) discovered a framework agreement on fire cylinders in which the supplier given the national standing order found they achieved zero business (Read, 2007).

A core ordering issue where public procurement decision making can have a profound economic and social impact is what size of orders should be let, or more formally what level of aggregation of contracts should occur. Findings from Gauteng province suggest that disaggregating contracts makes public sector business much more attractive to smaller suppliers, and avoids placing small and emerging businesses under the financial risks inherent in larger contracts. In the German system, disaggregating contracts is seen to support large numbers of smaller suppliers through low volume contracts. Letting small size contracts is also used as a means of helping smaller suppliers, where contracts under certain thresholds do not need to pass stringent national laws and regulations, lowering costs for smaller suppliers. The Belgian system examines suppliers for compliance at an early stage, for example, suppliers have to be up to date with worker social security payments before an order can be placed. This is an example of how ordering can be matched to the achievement of wider goals. Sometimes IT systems can help restrict choice and assist in containing "maverick buying" by only allowing ordering from a preferred or selected suppliers list or electronic catalog. Internationally, there appears some link between public procurement being more advanced, and how seriously the impact of ordering processes is viewed and reviewed by public sector actors. The more proactive nations' public procurement systems perceive the impact of their own ordering process as contributing to being a good, ethical customer.

Finally, we should note that the growth of schemes that engage the private sector much more in provision, delivery, and financing of previously purely public sector activities noted above will bring fundamental changes to the nature of ordering, shifting responsibility (and possibly volume in significant industries such as construction) to the private sector.

20.6 Expediting and Supplier Evaluation

Van Weele's (2005) procurement process framework couples expediting with evaluating suppliers, demonstrating the strong link between performance and actual delivery. In many manufacturing organizations expediting is related only to the physical delivery of products. By combining expediting with supplier management and postcontract award management, the framework by Van Weele takes a wider view. In this wider view of expediting, procurement's role is assessing the achievement of purchasing objectives.

Postcontract management of suppliers raises a further issue, as it reflects a tension between audit and performance, that is, is it enough that procurement outcomes were satisfactory or should superlative performance be the goal? The attention this issue receives varies between countries, between public sectors and organizations within countries, and even between product/service categories within organizations. It can, for example, depend on how much political attention a certain service area in healthcare receives, or it can be made part of a standard procedure. An example of the latter can be found at the U.S. federal level, where government has to provide written performance evaluation to the supplier during delivery of the contract. Further, in the United States, the use of past performance data on suppliers is mandatory in the contact award process. With the establishment of collaborative procurement initiatives, expediting is likely to receive increased attention; timely delivery becomes a crucial element of the value experience of the customers of collaborative initiatives.

Evaluating suppliers in the public arena highlights the tension between fulfilling operational procurement requirements, for example, delivery, quality and price, and the more strategic or policy dimensions such as capability building. Operational purchasing by nature is price focused whereas the emerging role of public procurement in socioeconomic change is linked to value for money, which is often not compatible with lowest price and has broader objectives. The concept of value rather than price in public procurement also shifts the time focus to the longer term achievement of systemwide goals rather than discrete operational performance. The more complex the outcome required, for example, economic rejuvenation of a run-down area through procuring resources locally, the more likely there will be tensions between operational and strategic or policy requirements. Such tensions can only be resolved through transparent links between performance measurement, performance management, and wider system goals. Procurement officials are often most comfortable and arguably most successful with lowest cost objectives, typically achieving savings against budget; in part a reflection of how simple the measurement of cost metric can be. In evidence from a U.S. state public procurement case (McCue et al., 2007), this tension was obvious and highlighted the difficulties of various performance evaluations required by different stakeholders. The general public's expectations of public procurement may not match public sector aspirations; the Dutch public expressed satisfaction with their hospital public procurement, despite its shortcomings (fragmentation, duplication, and failure to deliver advantages through economies of scale). Trends to involve the public as stakeholders in public procurement decision making will accentuate this tension. Different stakeholders may hold incompatible views on what is important (e.g., cost or value) and on the timescales evaluation should report on. For example, buy-local initiatives, such as those in Austria and Germany, transfer cost around the public system, the national public budget picking up the cost of the local initiative.

Finally, central to performance measurement is how it is linked to the application of incentives and sanctions. In Singapore, the government rates failing suppliers using an escalating penalty points system; as the number of penalty points escalates so does the likelihood of the contract being canceled. Whatever sanctions or incentives are being used, the key and absolute prerequisite to performance measurement is the availability of data. There are many examples especially in devolved systems such as U.K. and Dutch hospitals, in which the public sector lacks the kind of aggregated supply data that is critical to driving a coherent performance process. Without this data, high-profile incidents are likely to emerge that drive specific reactions to one supplier or perhaps a product category, rather than achieving overall policy. That public procurement can be subject to high-profile interventions, for example, events that mean existing resource decisions are changed overnight, exhibits not only how reactive (and therefore to some extent unplanned) public procurement interventions can be but also how public procurement can be a key enabler.

20.7 Procurement Follow-Up and Evaluation

In this step of the Van Weele (2005) framework of the procurement process we are concerned with how public procurement policy makers and procurement officials follow up and evaluate activities, that is, with a view to improving them. This means our focus here is on the impact the procurement process has upon process improvement and learning, not on system level features such as transparency, probity, and openness.

With the pressures on public sector spending, it is not surprising that the most concrete claims for improvement relate to cost savings. This, however, poses a problem for procurement, as if the role and added value of procurement can only be communicated in terms of cost savings; procurement will thus be viewed as such and will not be seen in the light of its potential role in wider system objectives. For example, although Singapore's price-led purchasing might not necessarily always achieve best value in financial terms when compared to other countries, if the actual policies are examined in the wider context of other public policies, it appears that it is critical in supporting the wider public sector goal of making Singapore an international business center through its reputation for probity and accessibility to foreign suppliers.

When "value for money" is perceived as a key objective, evaluations can run into conflicts with accounting and control systems, which tend to revolve around monetary value alone. In the U.K. NHS, the Purchasing and Supply Agency increasingly aims to contribute to patient care but is constrained by a measurement system that measures the agency on "savings and financial benchmarks." Silo-budgeting is a common problem, where budgets are allocated by department and yet the relevant activity crosscuts such artificial boundaries, leading to protecting one's own turf. Silo-budgeting in, or even between, sectors can constrain the uptake of innovations, and can make it difficult to measure the added value of a purchase. This silo effect is especially significant where the purchase leads to benefits (e.g., if patients do not need to be referred to a hospital specialist or when demands on social services are reduced) to another part of the system (i.e., a "different silo").

The role of public procurement should be both achieving internal objectives and in being a good customer to do business with. For public organizations, measures of performance beyond cost and price can increase understanding and awareness of how procurement processes impact on suppliers. Consistency in procurement processes is vital to suppliers' costs of doing business, yet can also benefit the buying organization. An example of the potential for mutual benefit from the public sector being a better customer is the purchasing of CT scanners in the U.K. NHS. This happens in a fragmented manner through individual hospitals with different formats of specifications flooding the suppliers with requests for tenders toward the end of the financial year. As the supply market is limited (globally there are only four major CT scanner suppliers), some turn down such requests as they are too busy, leaving the buying organization with gaps in the information used to assess requirements. In addition, as the customer specifications are diverse, suppliers have to provide similar data in different ways, which is clearly not the most efficient way of working for suppliers. There is little scope for learning and improvement in this market. Examples of good practice do exist though. The United Nations Development Programme, Inter-Agency Procurement Services Office (UNDP IAPSO) in cooperation with relevant trade promotion bodies of developing countries conduct supplier seminars and a help desk is available on how to do business with the UN system (Van Gronden et al., 2007).

Another potential measure that emerges from certain procurement initiatives is that of take-up of such programs. In collaborative procurement initiatives, for example, the take-up of contracts can be measured; in Wales, local authorities' uptake of certain collaborative contract categories increased approximately 50 percent in 2006–2007 compared to 2005–2006. The take-up of such contracts can be quantified with the help of E-procurement technologies, or using suppliers' E-catalog information. In Australia, E-commerce initiatives have been viewed with some skepticism. Overall, the lack of detail on take-up could suggest that certain initiatives are somewhat user-led and maybe biased in performance monitoring. For example, Harland (2004) notes the threats cost-cutting programs pose to sustaining local communities, small businesses, and innovation (Harland, 2004).

Where statistics appear to have been used to great effect is where reliable procurement figures are recorded and evaluated in the context of diversity. In the United States and in Canada procurement information is recorded, and more significantly, published, on small business and minority take-up. It should be noted that North American transparency on this issue is far ahead of European performance. In the United States, a 1997 federal act increased the federal goal for the small business share of procurement dollars from 20 to 23 percent (Clark and Moutray, 2004). David Drabkin of the U.S. General Services Administration was able to report in 2004 that 21 percent was being achieved. Such performance data and target setting are essential to drive standards up, and the absence of such formal targets and reporting against such targets in European examples in an international public procurement study (Harland et al., 2004) tells a story.

Many of the measures discussed so far may relate more to the purchaser than the supplier. Anecdotal evidence suggests given freedom to comment without censure, suppliers to the public sector will nearly always complain that public sector demand is not managed. Orders are placed when programs are announced or when new budget year funds are allocated, regardless of the capacity of the market (see, e.g., the earlier example on CT scanners in the U.K. NHS). Such "lumpy" demand patterns create feast and famine conditions for suppliers where there is either too much or too little work; market forces mean that when capacity is tight, prices paid by the public sector will rise. Managing demand to avoid suppliers facing feast or famine swings in demand is a public sector performance measurement that could be used in certain sectors where capacity can easily be exceeded in the short term, for example, construction. In addition, a wider metric of how good a customer a public entity is, something like an index of ease of doing business with from the suppliers' perspective, seems justified by the increasing engagement of public procurement with wider objectives than cost. A further area where public procurement needs more advanced metrics is introducing or supporting innovation (see Phillips et al., 2007).

20.8 Conclusions

A central tenet of this chapter has been the purchasing process in a variety of international contexts and the link in each phase between the activities in that phase and higher system level and policy objectives. In the specification process, we noted contradictions between "narrow" specifications and achieving wider political or socioeconomic outcomes. In the selection phase the inclusion of criteria other than price and the effects of policy, legislation, and organizational structure on selecting suppliers were discussed. The main issue of conflicting objectives between process and outcomes was also discussed in the contracting phase and we demonstrated that the "clerical or automated" ordering phase was impacting on policy objectives at the operational level. What happens in the ordering phase is indicative of how much effort the public sector puts into being a good customer to do business with. The evaluation phase highlighted the importance of availability of data for successful performance measurement and incentives and sanctions were discussed as potential "motivators" to achieving wider socioeconomic objectives. The last phase, procurement follow-up and evaluation, examined the issue of procurement evaluation and the barriers measurement systems and metrics can be to achieving broader, nonprice-based procurement objectives.

The standard staged model of the procurement process portrays a simple cumulative linearity to decision making, which in reality is not the case. However, viewing the process as a set of sequential stages does give insight into the different activities and how throughout the process policy objectives play a role and have to be taken into account. This chapter has used international examples to highlight the contradictory forces driven by diverse objectives present in public procurement.

For public procurement professionals there is a greater need to understand, account for, and accommodate to users', recipients', politicians', and national policy objectives and interests. In particular, the chapter has focused on the need for public procurement to be a "smart" or intelligent customer in the light of public spending impacts on suppliers and markets, a perspective largely absent in portrayals of the private sector purchasing process.

References

Aylesworth, M.M. 2007. Consortia purchasing for higher education in Canada, US, UK and Australia. In: Knight, L.A., Harland, C.M., Telgen, J., Callender, G., Thai, K.V., and McKen, K.E. (Eds). *Public Procurement: International Cases and Commentary.* Routledge, Oxford, U.K., pp. 176–189.

Baeyens, B. and Martel, M. 2007. Budget and organization reform in Belgium: Impact on public procurement. In: Knight, L.A., Harland, C.M., Telgen, J., Callender, G., Thai, K.V., and McKen, K.E. (Eds). *Public Procurement: International Cases and Commentary.* Routledge, Oxford, U.K., pp. 72–88.

Bakker, E., Walker, H., and Harland, C. 2006. Organising for collaborative procurement: An initial conceptual framework. In: Piga, G. and Thai, K.V. (Eds). *Advancing Public Procurement.* PrAcademics Press, Boca Raton, FL, pp. 14–44.

Bettis, R., Bradley, S., and Hamel, G. 1992. Outsourcing and industrial decline. *Academy of Management Executive*, 6(1), 7–22.

Broussueau, E. and Glachant, J.-M. 2005. The economics of contracts and the renewal of economics. In: Brousseau, E. and Glachant, J.M. (Eds). *The Economics of Contracts: Theories and Applications*, Cambridge University Press, U.K., pp. 3–30.

Brown, T.L. and Potoski, M. 2004. Assessing the management costs of delivering services under alternative institutional arrangements, *Journal of Public Procurement*, 4(3), 375–396.

Caldwell, N.D., Walker, H., Harland, C., Knight, L., Zheng, J., and Wakeley, T. 2005. Promoting competitive markets: The role of public procurement, *Journal of Purchasing and Supply*, 11(5–6), September–November, 242–251.

Caldwell, N.D., Phillips, W., Johnsen, T., and Lewis, M. 2007. Procurement ethics and telecare innovation in UK healthcare. In: Piga, G. and Thai, K.V. (Eds). *Advancing Public Procurement.* PrAcademics Press, pp. 139–155.

Callender, G. and Schapper, P. 2007. Public procurement reform in Australia: A federal-state evaluation. In: Knight, L.A., Harland, C.M., Telgen, J., Callender, G., Thai, K.V., and McKen, K.E. (Eds). *Public Procurement: International Cases and Commentary.* Routledge, Oxford, U.K., pp. 25–41.

Clark, M. and Moutray, C. 2004. The future of small businesses in the US federal government marketplace. *Journal of Public Procurement*, 4(3), 450–470.

Coulson, A. (Ed.). 1998. *Trust and Contracts : Relationships in Local Government, Health and Public Services.* The Policy Press, Bristol, U.K.

Cox, A., Chicksand, D., and Ireland, P. 2005. Sub-optimality in NHS sourcing in the UK: Demand-side constraints on supply-side improvement. *Public Administration*, 83(2), 367–392.

Dyer, J.H. and Singh, H. 1998. The relational view: Cooperative strategy and sources of interorganizational competitive advantage, *Academy of Management Review*, 23(4), 660–679.

Emerson, R.M. 1976. Social exchange theory. *Annual Review of Sociology* 2, 335–362.

Erridge, A. and Nondi, R. 1994. Public procurement, competition and partnership. *European Journal of Purchasing and Supply Management*, 1(3), 169–179.

Essig, M. and Schaefer, B. 2007. Public procurement in Germany: General remarks and the case of a purchasing cooperative for energy sourcing at the German Aerospace Center. In: Knight, L.A., Harland, C.M., Telgen, J., Callender, G., Thai, K.V., and McKen, K.E. (Eds). *Public Procurement: International Cases and Commentary.* Routledge, Oxford, U.K., pp. 104–116.

Ford, D. 1980. The development of buyer–seller relationships in industrial markets. *European Journal of Marketing*, 14(5–6), 339–353.

Gansler, J.S. 1989. *Affording Defense*. Cambridge: MIT Press.

Harland, C., Rudd, A., Knight, L., Forrest, S., and Bakker, E. 2007. Procurement in the English National Health Service. In: Knight, L.A., Harland, C.M., Telgen, J., Callender, G., Thai, K.V., and McKen, K.E. (Eds). *Public Procurement: International Cases and Commentary*. Routledge, Oxford, U.K., pp. 42–59.

Harland, C.M. 2004. How much will savings cost us? *The Guardian*, Public Report, September 2004. pp. 30.

Harland, C.M., Knight, L.A., Caldwell, N.D., and Telgen, J., 2004. *Government Reform and Public Procurement—Executive Report of the First Workshop*, International Research Study on Public Procurement. Bath, U.K.: Centre for Research in Strategic Purchasing and Supply, University of Bath School of Management.

Harland, C.M., Knight, L.A., Lamming, R.C., and Walker, H.L. 2005. Outsourcing: Assessing the risks and benefits for organisations, sectors and nations, *International Journal of Operations and Production Management*, 25(9), 831–850.

Heinrich, C.J. 2002. Outcomes-based performance management in the public sector: Implications for government accountability and effectiveness, *Public Administration Review*, 62(6), November–December, 712–725.

Hill, T. 1993. *Manufacturing Strategy*. MacMillan, Basingstoke, U.K.

Johnston, W.J. and Lewin, J.E., 1996. Organizational buying behaviour: Toward an integrative framework. *Journal of Business Research*. 35, 1–15.

Jones, D.S. 2007. The features and recent reforms of government procurement in Singapore. In: Knight, L.A., Harland, C.M., Telgen, J., Callender, G., Thai, K.V., and McKen, K.E. (Eds). *Public Procurement: International Cases and Commentary*. Routledge, Oxford, U.K., pp. 117–137.

Kivisto, T., Virolainen, V., and Tella, E. 2007. Consortia purchasing and logistics in Kuopio area (Finland)—lessons learned from a 4-year project. In: Knight, L.A., Harland, C.M., Telgen, J., Callender, G., Thai, K.V., and McKen, K.E. (Eds). *Public Procurement: International Cases and Commentary*. Routledge, Oxford, U.K., pp. 190–201.

Knight, L., Harland, C., Telgen, J., and Caldwell, N. 2007. Public procurement: An introduction. In: Knight, L.A., Harland, C.M., Telgen, J., Callender, G., Thai, K.V., and McKen, K.E. (Eds). *Public Procurement: International Cases and Commentary*. Routledge, Oxford, U.K., pp. 1–15.

Koppenjan, J. and Erik-Hans, K. 2004. *Managing Uncertainties in Networks*. Routledge, London, U.K.

Lamming, R.C. 1993. *Beyond Partnership: Strategies for Lean Supply*, Prentice Hall, Basingstoke, U.K.

Lonsdale, C. 2005. Contractual uncertainty, power and public contracting. *Journal of Public Policy*, 25(2), 219–240.

Lucyshyn, W. 2007. Market-based government: Lessons from five cases. In: Piga, G. and Thai, K.V. (Eds). *Advancing Public Procurement*. PrAcademics Press, pp. 116–138.

Macaulay, S. 1963. Non-contractual relations in business: A preliminary study. *American Sociological Review*, 28(1), 55–67.

MacNeil, I.R. 1980. *The New Social Contract: An Inquiry into Modern Contractual Relations*. New Haven, CT: Yale University Press.

McCue, C., Buffington, K., and Howell, A.D. 2007. The fraud/red tape dilemma in public procurement: A study of U.S. state and local governments. In: Knight, L.A., Harland, C.M., Telgen, J., Callender, G., Thai, K.V., and McKen, K.E. (Eds). *Public Procurement: International Cases and Commentary*. Routledge, Oxford, U.K., pp. 247–263.

Pfeffer, J. and G.R. Salancik, 1978. *The External Control of Organisations, a Resource Dependence Perspective*. Harper and Row Publishers, New York.

Phillips, W.E., Knight, L., Caldwell, N.D., and Warrington, J. 2007. Policy through procurement—the introduction of digital signal process (DSP) hearing aids into the English NHS, *Health Policy*, 80(1), 77–85.

Pingry, J.R. 1974. The engineer and purchasing agent compared, *Journal of Purchasing*, 11(April), 33–45.

Read, J.J.D. 2007. A new era: How to improve procurement services to clients in Canada. In: Knight, L.A., Harland, C.M., Telgen, J., Callender, G., Thai, K.V., and McKen, K.E. (Eds). *Public Procurement: International Cases and Commentary.* Routledge, Oxford, U.K., pp. 264–277.

Robinson, P.C., Faris, C.W., and Wind, Y. 1967. *Industrial Buying and Creative Marketing.* Allyn and Bacon, Boston, MA.

Sako, M. 1992. Prices, quality and trust: Inter-firm relations in Britain and Japan. Cambridge Studies in Management, Cambridge University Press, Cambridge.

Strauss, G. 1962. Tactics of lateral relationship, *Administrative Science Quarterly*, 7(2), 161–186.

Telgen, J. and van Vliet, H. 2007. Purchasing consequences of Dutch health care organisation and financing. In: Knight, L.A., Harland, C.M., Telgen, J., Callender, G., Thai, K.V., and McKen, K.E. (Eds). *Public Procurement: International Cases and Commentary.* Routledge, Oxford, U.K., pp. 60–71.

Thai, K. and Drabkin, D. 2007. U.S. federal government procurement: Structure, process and current issues. In: Knight, L.A., Harland, C.M., Telgen, J., Callender, G., Thai, K.V., and McKen, K.E. (Eds). *Public Procurement: International Cases and Commentary.* Routledge, Oxford, U.K., pp. 89–103.

Tonkin, C. 2007. e-Procurement: A cross jurisdictional comparison. In: Knight, L.A., Harland, C.M., Telgen, J., Callender, G., Thai, K.V., and McKen, K.E. (Eds). *Public Procurement: International Cases and Commentary.* Routledge, Oxford, U.K., pp. 216–246.

Van Gronden, J., Bloch, K., Ramm, N., Ejlskov Jensen, K., Harland, C., and Walker, H. 2007. Procurement in the United Nations System. In: Knight, L.A., Harland, C.M., Telgen, J., Callender, G., Thai, K.V., and McKen, K.E. (Eds). *Public Procurement: International Cases and Commentary.* Routledge, Oxford, U.K., pp. 160–175.

Van Vuuren, K. and Badenhorst-Weiss, J.A. 2007. South African provincial government reform: Using a shared services model to transform "back-office" support. In: Knight, L.A., Harland, C.M., Telgen, J., Callender, G., Thai, K.V., and McKen, K.E. (Eds). *Public Procurement: International Cases and Commentary.* Routledge, Oxford, U.K., pp. 278–301.

Van Weele, A.J., 2005. *Purchasing and Supply Chain Management, Analysis, Planning and Practice.* London: Thompson Learning.

Wuyts, S. and Geyskens, I. 2005. The formation of buyer–supplier relationships: Detailed contract drafting and close partner selection. *Journal of Marketing*, 69(October), 103–117.

E-PROCUREMENT III

Chapter 21

Key Issues in E-Procurement: Procurement Implementation and Operation in the Public Sector

Simon Croom and Alistair Brandon-Jones

CONTENTS

21.1 Introduction

Electronic procurement systems represent an important development for the purchasing process (Neef, 2001), offering benefits to the organization through purchase process efficiency gains and price reductions (Croom, 2000; Essig and Arnold, 2001; de Boer et al., 2002), enhanced collaborative relationships (Holland, 1995; Dyer, 2000; Tang et al., 2001), and significant opportunity for improving internal services and statutes of the purchasing function (Croom, 2000; Stanley and Wisner, 2001; Osmonbekov et al., 2002; Croom and Johnston, 2003).

Probably because of the combined influence of the relative newness of E-procurement adoption, the perennial issue of research publication lead times and the limited opportunities to date for longitudinal research, much of the existing E-procurement research has concentrated on motivations and expectations relating to E-procurement implementation. In this chapter, we set out to address the need for experience-based research into the operational issues of E-procurement by examining not just the implementation process, but also the experiences from public sector E-procurement operation in both local authorities and national civil government departments. An important question that helped shape this research was: what are the actual benefits being achieved from E-procurement? Our research was conceived initially as an exploratory study and conducted over 18 months across a range of U.K. public sector bodies.

This chapter is structured into four sections. In the first section, we examine the current E-procurement and E-business literature to review current understanding of the E-procurement effect and to provide a framework for defining what we call transactional structures. The second section briefly describes our research methodology. The third section sets out the seven key lessons from E-procurement implementation across the U.K. public sector. The final section responds to one of our key findings to propose some potential for future research.

21.2 E-Business Phenomenon

What we now call E-business arose through the proliferation of the Internet as a platform for inter-organizational systems (IOS) in the late 1990s and has had a particularly significant impact on supply chains and networks. This is not a surprise for Evans and Wurster's (2000) thesis that the rise of the Internet has changed the economics of information, giving rise to new forms of affiliation between organizations, of relationship between organizations, and of transaction between organizations. Giving specific attention to the implications for supply chain management, Tan (2001) identified potential for improvements in supply chain management arising from adoption of E-business systems in four areas:

(1) Cost performance (from improved productivity and lower input prices)
(2) Customer service (service quality)

(3) Process capability (quality consistency)
(4) Productivity and dependability (from increased control of material flows along the supply chain)

E-procurement is the generic term applied to the use of integrated database systems and wide area (commonly Web-based) network communication systems in part or all of the purchasing process. The procurement process encompasses the initial need for identification and specification by users through the search, sourcing, and negotiation stages of contracts and order placement, and includes mechanisms that register receipt, trigger payment, and support postsupply evaluation.

As Neef (2001) notes, electronic procurement represents a significant and important development in the employment of E-business in supply chain management and in the rest of this chapter we will concentrate on the procurement elements of upstream E-business.

21.3 Existing E-Procurement Research

The following review of the body of literature to date identifies five main themes in E-procurement research relating to the following:

- Cost-efficiency benefits
- Impact of E-procurement systems on the form and nature of supplier governance
- System implementation
- Information technology (IT) infrastructure issues
- Organizational and relational issues

Each of these issues will now be examined.

21.3.1 Cost Efficiencies

One of the key themes in the existing literature on E-procurement has been concerned with the economies of information (Evans and Wurster, 2000), in particular, the realization of cost improvements achieved as a result of transactional and process efficiencies. These efficiencies arise through greater opportunity for lower prices from suppliers; from the reduction in process activity needed to complete the total requisition-to-payment process; and through the increased speed of the procurement process and better decision making as a result of improved management information (Min and Galle, 1999; Croom, 2000; Emiliani, 2000; Zsidisin and Ellram, 2001; de Boer et al., 2002; Wyld, 2002). The lure of cost efficiencies has been a major catalyst for the adoption of E-procurement (Croom, 2000) and it has been widely contended in this body of literature that E-procurement implementation will have considerable implications for the design of the procurement process. However, it was contended by Lancioni et al. (2000) that the precise nature of these process changes was empirically unclear.

Recently, Yen and Ng (2003) carried out a case study investigation of electronic commerce implementation providing a useful comparison of pre- and post-E-commerce procurement process performances. They support the claims from prior literature that such changes deliver process efficiencies. In addition to the three categories of efficiency improvement mentioned above, they highlighted four additional sources of cost benefit:

- Reduction in costs arising as a result of digitizing catalogs
- Reducing errors in order transmission

- Reductions in inventory
- Reductions in suppliers' marketing costs

Consequently, improved economies of management information are considered to be a major catalyst for reducing purchase prices through greater transparency of market prices and lower search costs. This observation is supported in the practitioner and general management literature, where there is a plethora of anecdotal case evidence to support the view that electronic procurement is a far more efficient and reliable method for the requisition-to-payment process than preceding manual and semi-automated processes (e.g., *Electronic Commerce News*, 2003; Hayward, 2003; Moore, 2003; Parker, 2003; Trommer, 2003; Wheatley, 2003).

21.3.2 Forms of Transactional Structure

Galliers (1999, pp. 229–230) states that

> with the advent of inter-organizational systems, and e-commerce in particular, it is clear that questions of alignment go beyond what we have come to know as the Business-IT alignment issue (e.g., Baets, 1992). It is no longer simply a case of internal alignment alone. Such issues now include alignment with collaborating companies' business and IT strategies (Finnegan et al., 1998) and customer requirements (cf., recent heightened interest in customer relationship management).

In other words, an organization's deployment of E-business has a significant impact on suppliers' IT and information system (IS) strategies and on the forms of governance, or transactional, structure employed in the supply chain.

How E-procurement may impact supply transactions has been discussed by Holland (1995) and Croom (2001a), both noting that the literature posits two opposing schools of thought. On one side is the view that E-procurement and associated E-business systems will increase the tendency toward arms' length, market forms of transaction because the barriers to entry in electronic transactions are low (Malone et al., 1987, 1989). Indeed, Malone et al. (1987) argued that the electronic brokerage effects of systems such as E-procurement reduce search costs. Consequently, their view implies that E-procurement adoption would result in a movement away from close, hierarchical relationships to more short-term, market relationships. Barratt and Rosdahl (2002) temper Malone et al.'s position slightly by claiming that ease of search and transparency acts as an advantage to the buyer, but may be a disadvantage for the seller. This may, of course, still influence a move toward market-based relationships under E-procurement purely through the attraction to buyers of greater economies in the search process.

In contrast to this view, others have argued that the proprietary nature of certain IOS may in fact serve to tie in customers and suppliers to virtual hierarchies or virtual integration (Johnston and Lawrence, 1988; Johnston and Vitale, 1988; Konsynski and McFarlan, 1990). This would be particularly important for E-procurement systems that involve complex data exchange (such as links to customer's production or sales schedules). For example, Brousseau (1990) reviewed 26 IOS networks, finding that most were used to reduce production or distribution costs and served to reinforce already existing hierarchical relationships among firms. Evans and Wurster (2000) claimed that the low infrastructure and transaction costs of Internet-based systems not only allowed organizations to exploit the increased opportunities for complex information exchange with multiple partners, but also recognized the value to be gained through closer, hierarchical relationships between regular trading partners (affiliation). Amit and Zott (2001) likewise discussed the importance of close relationships (lock-in) between trading partners as a key source of advantage to both buyer and seller.

21.3.3 Classifying the Forms of E-Procurement Transactional Structures

It has been widely recognized in the industrial marketing and purchasing literature that organizations will typically have a range of transactional relationships with their supply base. For example, the Robinson et al. (1967) buyclass framework distinguished between relationships on the basis of the frequency and variability of the purchased contract. It is our view that it is thus more appropriate to utilize some form of classification of E-procurement governance structures. Thus, in Figure 21.1, we illustrate five contrasting exchange types employed within E-procurement transactions.

21.3.3.1 Public Web

Via the public web (Internet) buyers have the opportunity to identify potential suppliers via standard search engines (such as google.com, yahoo.com) or specialist trading search engines (such as kellys.co.uk). Online search and comparison of list prices are typically used for specialist or low-value purchases. Depending on the nature of the supplier's Web site facility, orders may be placed online, via e-mail or through the more traditional route of telephone, fax, or mail.

21.3.3.2 Exchange

The term "exchange" here refers to trading sites such as the eBay B2C (business to consumer) E-commerce auction site and the B2B (business to business) auction service providers, FreeMarkets and Synerdeal. These sites allow buyers or sellers to bid for contracts—which in eBay's case simply involves bidding for products offered for sale by private as well as commercial sellers, while B2B exchanges provide reverse auction facilities. Online reverse auctions have been extremely successful

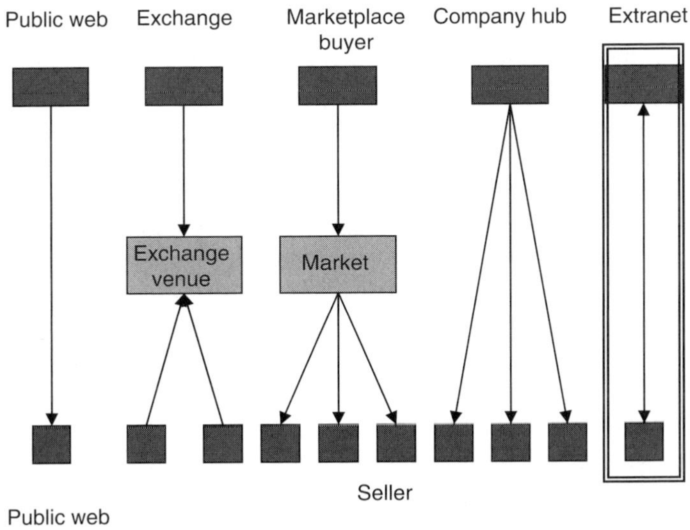

Figure 21.1 Classifying E-procurement transaction structures.

in reducing purchase prices—our experience has been that typical price savings achieved are around 16 percent and such auctions have been used for products as varied as foodstuffs, engineered components, and utilities supplies.

21.3.3.3 Marketplace

A marketplace is in essence a multisupplier/multiproducts catalog often hosted and maintained by a third party providing access to users via Internet or LAN connection.

21.3.3.4 Company Hub

A company hub is often also called a "buy-side" solution. It is similar to a marketplace because the buyer (rather than a third party) hosts and maintains a multisupplier/multiproduct catalog.

21.3.3.5 Extranet

An extranet is a secure, often security protected, Internet link between buyer and seller. Such extranets are used primarily for shared and collaborative data, such as delivery scheduling and product design data. Pre-Internet, electronic data interchange (EDI) links represent a type of extranet connection that is dedicated to an individual customer. Although there remain concerns for the security of transmission over the World Wide Web, extranets represent an effective means of communication between close trading partners.

21.3.4 System Implementation

There have been few detailed empirical studies of E-procurement implementation in the public sector, although in the United States McManus (2002) identified expectations of cost and process efficiencies as the primary motivation for public sector implementation. However, she observed that as experience with E-procurement systems has grown, so has considerable debate about some of the fundamental principles behind public sector procurement, including lowest bid wins. In a second, case-based study, of Taiwanese military procurement (Liao et al., 2003), the main challenge for E-procurement implementation was found to be the cultural resistance to changes in established procurement processes and practices.

Heijboer (2003) has proposed a framework for the operational implementation or rollout of E-procurement across the supply base. In his paper, he proposed an analytical model based on the return on investment (ROI) and payback resulting from the E-procurement rollout on a commodity-by-commodity basis. His model proposes that organizations should determine their rollout of E-procurement by aiming for quick wins (or by harvesting the low hanging fruit).

21.3.5 IT Infrastructure

Issues concerning ISs development and adoption are central to the E-procurement issue. Rajkumar (2001) identified systems integration as a critical success factor for E-procurement implementation, both with the customer's information infrastructure and with its links to suppliers. In an earlier study, Croom (2001b) surveyed the adoption pattern of IOS. Table 21.1 sets out the frequency of adoption of the main forms of Web-based and Web-related ISs used to support part or much of the procurement process found in this earlier study.

Table 21.1 Incidence of E-Procurement System Adoption

System	*Incidence (Percent)*
E-mail	85.9
Web sites	83.5
Funds transfer	83.1
Electronic data interchange	73.5
Microsoft Outlook	69.9
Lotus Notes	39.8
Knowledge sharing	63.9
E-procurement	38.6
Intranet	36.5
Middleware	37.3
Extranet	36.5
Portals	34.9
Global positioning systems	22.9

Source: From Croom, S. in *Supply Chain Management in the E-Business Era*, University of Warwick, Coventry, United Kingdom, 2001b. With permission.

It was not surprising that e-mail, Web sites, funds transfer, and EDI dominated the list. E-mail and Web sites are dominant and ubiquitous systems, while major banks provide support for electronic funds transfer that provides a secure, low cost means of payment. EDI, on the other hand, is only cost-effective for high-volume transaction and communication between common trading hierarchies. Often, EDI is deployed for the management of, direct, supply chains, that is, for components and materials used in the manufacturing process, or products for sale in retailing. The cost per unit is then relatively low, the benefits of high-speed transmission and the sunk cost of investment are all factors that are seen as likely to sustain EDI, or at least integrate it into an Internet-EDI structure for the management of specific high-frequency exchange supply chains.

In terms of knowledge management, nearly two-thirds of respondents employed knowledge sharing systems, which included Microsoft Outlook, Lotus Notes, and other systems. Using an existing and, to some degree, standardized package such as Outlook within organizations enabled greater communication and coordination in areas of innovation, product development, customer strategies, sourcing, specifying and supply management, and training and development coordination.

The use of middleware (i.e., software used to integrate two systems) recognized the challenge of integrating systems, typically with legacy finance systems. At the time of this study, 37.3 percent of respondents were addressing the challenges of integrating various elements of procurement systems. Less than 40 percent of respondents deployed total E-procurement systems such as Ariba, Peoplesoft, or SAP's enterprise buying module.

A recent commercial report by IDC (2003) demonstrated that there remained a slow uptake of E-procurement systems, emphasizing that system infrastructure-related issues such as software integration (including discussion of XML-related opportunities) were inhibiting implementation.

21.3.6 Organizational and Relationship Issues

The adoption of E-procurement can impact internal and external relational linkages. Internally, the motivation of buyers to use the Internet as a resource for various elements of the purchasing process was investigated by Kennedy and Deeter-Schmelz (2001), who concluded that organizational characteristics and organizational influences were significant motivators to the use of E-procurement. In other words, training and relative influence of the purchasing function are key factors influencing the uptake of Internet-enabled purchasing tools. Also focusing on internal relational linkages, Croom and Johnston (2003) argued that in the context of indirect (MRO-maintenance, repair, and operating) purchases, reduction in maverick or noncompliant buying by users is critical to the achievement of cost and efficiency gains from electronic procurement, contesting that internal customer satisfaction should be a key concern for E-procurement implementation.

Externally, Carr and Smeltzer (2002) found that increased use of IT between buyer and supplier did not improve levels of trust between buyer and seller, although Ellram and Zsidisin (2002) found that close buyer–supplier relationships had a strong positive impact on the adoption of E-procurement. E-procurement per se could not be considered to deliver improved levels of trust, but it has been found that E-procurement transactions are more likely to be established first between close trading partners in high-trust relationships (Malone et al., 1989).

Because longitudinal research is required to fully explore how buyer–seller relationships develop under E-procurement (e.g., by adopting an evolutionary approach similar to that of the IMP Group; Ford et al., 2003), relatively little literature exists on this topic—although Archer and Yuan (2000) and Croom (2001a) both support the view that increased use of E-procurement and IOS will enhance opportunities to build closer and more effective customer–supplier relationships over time.

21.4 Research Objectives and Methodology

We have seen that the existing E-procurement literature has identified a number of key themes concerning efficiency benefits, governance, systems implementation, IT infrastructure, and relational influences. In this research, we aimed to contribute to the literature through an exploratory study in two ways: by exploring these themes and by allowing for some inductive analysis of the characteristics of E-procurement system implementation and their operational consequences. To meet our objectives for an exploratory study, our research design used both semistructured and open questions, thereby allowing respondents to discuss at length their experiences, perceptions, and reflections of a range of electronic procurement implementation projects. The research project was funded by a public sector organization wishing to construct guidelines relating to the main lessons learnt from implementation in the U.K. public sector as a mechanism for diffusing practice across the sector.

The research participants consisted of adopters of E-procurement, namely seven central government departments, six local authorities, and two agencies, whose main role was to offer consultancy and systems support to the public sector.

Initial telephone interviews were semistructured and typically lasted for one hour. Following the completion of the initial round of interviews, a summary analysis of the findings and pertinent issues was circulated to all participants as the basis for a second round of face-to-face interviews. In the second round of interviews, we utilized semistructured interviews, in which open questions and participant-identified critical incidents were used as the mechanism for identifying the key successes and barriers in each project examined.

All interviews were taped and transcribed verbatim. Coding of all interviews was undertaken by both researchers independently and then cross-compared for final coding.

Across our responding sample, experience of electronic procurement varied. At one extreme, the two agency bodies had both developed their own E-procurement systems and had over ten year's active involvement with E-procurement. At the other extreme, three bodies had less than twelve months active operational experience. Of the remaining ten participating bodies, the modal length of experience was three years. (It should be noted that the U.K. public sector is further supported by a central government department, the Office of Government Commerce [OGC], which has been established to support and direct E-procurement and procurement system developments across the whole of civil government in England and Wales. The OGC provides a significant resource in terms of development projects, research knowledge, and expertise accessible by all of the respondents.)

In the next section of this chapter, we present the key findings relating to the experiences of our sample respondents from their involvement with E-procurement implementation.

21.5 Findings

Our analysis identified seven key issues arising from the experiences of E-procurement implementation:

21.5.1 External Price Efficiencies

The main routes for achieving clear, accountable cost savings on purchases were through three main mechanisms:

(1) *Consolidation of purchase specifications.* Through reduction in the variety of alternatives available for users to select, the opportunity to negotiate discounted prices had been a significant benefit. For example, one respondent cited the reduction in the range of writing pens purchased by their department from 47 to 3, reducing the average price per pen from 60p (approximately €1) to 45p (approximately €0.75). This had also reduced the total quantity of pens purchased per annum because of the combined effect of various reductions on minimum order quantities.

(2) *Reducing the number of suppliers.* Improved management information had enabled consolidation of supply to fewer providers and increased user awareness of the approved suppliers for each purchased item.

(3) *Improved compliance with existing contracts.* All the public sector organizations involved in our study reported that compliance with existing contracts had been one of the major difficulties they had encountered before E-procurement implementation. E-procurement adoption had significantly improved compliance because of the ease of access for users to contracted supplies. Only one of the respondents had made participation in the E-procurement system a mandatory requirement for suppliers, but all respondents found that greater accessibility and ease of use were significant catalysts in encouraging users to conform to process.

21.5.2 Internal Cost Efficiencies

Although savings in terms of purchase expenditure were relatively easy to identify through invoice and budget data, respondents reported significant difficulties in clearly identifying process savings. Although the E-procurement literature discussed earlier identifies process efficiencies per transaction as a significant benefit of E-procurement adoption, only one of our participants had been able to validate such savings. One of the agency respondents had commissioned external consultants to conduct a cost analysis of the E-procurement ordering process. The study estimated the cost per order under E-procurement to be £17 (approximately €30), approximately one-third of the pre-E-procurement cost of £60 (approximately €110). However, this cost estimate was considered to be applicable only to a narrow range of standard, high-volume, single-source purchases. A number of respondents used the term "elusive" to describe the realization of internal cost benefits. One statement that typified a widely held view was that "...we know it's a lot better, but how do you capitalise a saving of just 5% of a person's time; there may be hundreds of people each saving less than 30 minutes a day."

(1) *Implementation rollout.* Although there was diversity in how long our respondents had been using E-procurement as noted above, we identified only two approaches to the rollout of E-procurement externally (i.e., across the supply base). The most common methodology involved limiting rollout to the organization's top five suppliers. A second cluster of organizations had undertaken a total supply-base rollout. There was no evidence that the approach adopted was related to the length of time the respondent organization had been involved with E-procurement. The underpinning logic was primarily related to the overall strategy of the adopter, but the following statements do illustrate the contrasting logic employed:

> we decided to focus our efforts on the high volume, low value purchases in order to concentrate on achieving the process savings, since that was the basis on which our implementation proposal was made.
>
> we needed to demonstrate that we could take control over purchasing and supply, so we were adamant that we should roll this out to all of our suppliers...which involved making e-capability a mandatory requirement for all suppliers.

(2) *Problem of the tail of the Pareto distribution of the supply base.* Related to the issue of rollout, one of the key concerns expressed by four respondents but not considered by the remainder, was the challenge of incorporating suppliers with whom they had low expenditures into the E-procurement system. A key determinant in the approach to "C" category suppliers was the marginal cost of adding an additional supplier to the procurement system. One of the central issues in this was the nature of the database employed. We found cases where even large, national suppliers were unable to readily provide compatible data files for uploading onto some E-procurement catalog databases. The emergence of common XML standards for database integration was believed to be a potential solution to this problem, but we did not encounter any evidence that this had been realized.

(3) *Finance systems integration.* Finance systems integration was an important determinant of system selection (when purchasing proprietary E-procurement systems) or system design (if the E-procurement system was to be developed internally). This also had a direct impact on the level of process savings and the nature of the system rollout. All of the large central

government departments involved in our study stated that their choice of E-procurement provider had been determined by their current or intended choice of finance system provider. Integration between purchasing and finance systems was seen as the most critical constraint for the selection of system. A breakdown of the systems adopted is provided in Table 21.2.

(4) *IT infrastructure.* The reliability and capability of the organization's infrastructure (particularly network connectivity) impacted directly on the operational performance of the E-procurement system. In many cases, the links to suppliers were not directly over Internet but via existing EDI connections, automated fax, or mail printout. Details of the infrastructural characteristics are also summarized in Table 21.2. (It should be noted that the agencies between them also provided all six local authority respondents' systems.)

(5) *Project management.* All of the participants in our study had established project teams to manage the development and implementation process. The team structures reflect two stereotypes: open structures incorporating finance, IT, HR, and other operational representatives, and closed structures driven by the IT function (Clark and Fujimoto, 1991). Our initial conclusions are that the open protocol served to overcome preexisting political barriers, while the closed protocol was most often employed in small-scale implementation where internal political barriers were not perceived to be significant. Not surprisingly, we found that all of the large, central government departments employed an open protocol because the issue of internal functional power was seen to be a major issue to be addressed in the E-procurement program.

Table 21.2 E-Procurement and Finance System Characteristics

Department	*System*	*Finance/ERP Punch-Out Process*	*Link to Suppliers*
Infrastructure 1	Oracle 11I	Oracle integrated	E-mail, fax, and mail
Treasury 1	Proprietary	In progress	EDI. Moving to Web-enabled
Security 1	Proprietary	In progress	EDI
Security 2	SAP/SAP EBP	Payment via BACS	EDI with six suppliers
Infrastructure 2	SAP R/3/SAP EBP v2.0c	SAP integrated	E-mail, fax, and mail
Infrastructure 3	Not confirmed	Only for logistics operations: electronic payment	E-mail, fax, and mail
Agency 1	Proprietary		E-mail, fax, and mail
Agency 2	Proprietary	Via procurement card and XML	E-mail, fax, and mail
Treasury 2	Oracle 11I	Oracle integrated	E-mail, fax, and mail

Note: ERP, Enterprise resource planning; EDI, Electronic data interchange; SAP, Systems applications and products; EBP, Enterprise buyer professional; and XML, Extensible markup language.

21.6 Conclusion

In our review of the literature, we identified seven issues relating to experiences from E-procurement adoption. In issues 1 and 2, significant motivation for E-procurement adoption was considered to be the economic benefit. The possibility of lower prices arising through greater informational economies from the use of E-procurement was discussed by many, including Malone et al. (1989), Evans and Wurster (2000), and Croom (2000). In our study, we found that an important mechanism for realizing lower prices was through encouragement for users to comply with existing contracts. Principally, this allowed purchasers to provide a more accurate forecast of contract volume requirements to their suppliers, with the concomitant price benefits arising from economies of volume. However, in terms of process cost reductions, these were far more difficult to identify. Only one of the respondents had validated process cost savings at the time of the study and this supported the claims in the literature of a saving of approximately two-thirds on process costs (Croom, 2000).

In issues 3 and 4, we detailed the rollout experiences. This aspect of E-procurement has been examined by Heijboer (2003) who recommended a commodity-based strategy. However, our study respondents adopted a mixed commodity/supplier rollout strategy. Such a strategy recognized the importance of establishing the purchaser–supplier connectivity and communications in any rollout program. This supplier-oriented approach was further emphasized when examination of supply-base rollout identified some concerns for integrating low-value suppliers in their E-procurement program.

Issues 5 and 6, concerning system selection and integration (as illustrated in Table 21.2), were dominated by E-procurement/finance system integration issues. The ability to punch out procurement order data into financial control systems is regarded as a critical requirement for the success of an E-procurement system and thus close integration with finance systems was identified as an important criterion.

Finally, in issue 7, we examined organizational commitment and support required for E-procurement. One of the key characteristics in achieving organizational support was found to be the structure of the implementation project team—we distinguished between the inclusive, open project team protocol and a more narrow, closed protocol, using Clark and Fujimoto's (1991) terminology. An inclusive project team structure was found to allow far greater involvement by the system stakeholders and thus had the consequent benefit of directly addressing any user resistance to E-procurement.

21.7 Future Research

Our research into E-procurement is ongoing. The study reported has to date attempted to explore the main characteristics of E-procurement adoption and the implementation process. Further research is now being carried out in the U.K. public sector into user compliance and E-procurement performance to validate the prognoses of early commentators. We still feel that E-procurement represents an opportunity for revolution in procurement, but E-procurement per se does not carry a cast iron, copper-bottomed guarantee of success. To enrich the debate, we feel that one avenue for future research should be to investigate E-procurement failures as a way of furthering our understanding of critical factors for E-procurement performance. A second opportunity for research is to develop means for classification of the different forms of E-procurement, allowing for greater analytical comparisons between alternative forms of electronic purchasing and supply.

References

Amit, R. and Zott, C. 2001. Value creation in e-business. *Strategic Management Journal*, 22: 493–520.

Archer, N. and Yuan, Y. 2000. Managing business-to-business relationships throughout the e-commerce procurement life cycle. *Internet Research: Electronic Networking Applications and Policy*, 10(5): 385–395.

Barratt, M. and Rosdahl, K. 2002. Exploring business-to-business marketsites. *European Journal of Purchasing and Supply Management*, 8: 111–122.

Brousseau, E. 1990. Information Technologies and Inter-Firm Relationships: The Spread of Inter-Organizational Telematics Systems and Its Impact on Economic Structure. Paper presented at the International Telecommunications Society, March 18–21. Venice, Italy.

Carr, A.S. and Smeltzer, L.R. 2002. The relationship between information technology use and buyer–supplier relationships: An exploratory analysis of the buying firm's perspective. *IEEE Transactions on Engineering Management*, 49(3): 293–304.

Clark, K.B. and Fujimoto, T. 1991. *Product Development Performance. Strategy, Organisation, and Management in the World Auto Industry*. Boston, MA: Harvard Business School Press.

Croom, S. 2000. The impact of web-based procurement on the management of operating resources supply. *The Journal of Supply Chain Management*, 36(1): 4–13.

Croom, S. 2001a. Restructuring supply chains through information channel innovation. *International Journal of Operations and Production Management*, 21(4): 504–515.

Croom, S. 2001b. *Supply Chain Management in the E-Business Era*. Coventry, United Kingdom: University of Warwick.

Croom, S. and Johnston, R. 2003. E-service: Enhancing internal customer service through e-procurement. *International Journal of Service Industries Management*, 14(5): 539–555.

de Boer, L., Harink, J., and Heijboer, G. 2002. A conceptual model for assessing the impact of electronic procurement. *European Journal of Purchasing and Supply Management*, 8(1): 25–33.

Dyer, C. 2000. B2B exchange: The next step in an evolving marketplace. *DSN Retailing Today*, 39(20): 13.

Electronic Commerce News. 2003. Realizing rapid results using e-sourcing tools, 8(13): 1.

Ellram, L.M. and Zsidisin, G.A. 2002. Factors that drive purchasing and supply management's use of information technology. *IEEE Transactions on Engineering Management*, 49(3): 269–281.

Emiliani, M.L. 2000. Business-to-business online auctions: Key issues for purchasing process improvement. *Supply Chain Management: An International Journal*, 5(4): 176–186.

Essig, M. and Arnold, U. 2001. Electronic procurement in supply chain management: An information economics-based analysis of electronic markets. *Journal of Supply Chain Management*, 37(4): 43–49.

Evans, P. and Wurster, T.S. 2000. *Blown to Bits. How the New Economics of Information Transforms Strategy*. Boston, MA: Harvard Business School Press.

Ford, D., Gadde, L.-E., Hakansson, H., and Snehota, I. 2003. *Managing Business Relationships*, 2nd ed. Chichester, United Kingdom: John Wiley & Sons.

Galliers, R.D. 1999. Towards the integration of e-business, knowledge management and policy considerations within an information systems strategy framework. *Journal of Strategic Information Systems*, 8(3): 229–234.

Hayward, C. 2003. Three-year glitch. *Financial Management*, July/August: 30.

Heijboer, G. 2003. Determining the optimal rollout strategy. In: G. Heijboer (Ed.), PhD Thesis: *Quantitative Analysis of Strategic and Tactical Purchasing Decisions: Electronic Purchasing*. Twente, the Netherlands: Twente University Press, pp. 162–189.

Holland, C.P. 1995. Co-operative supply chain management: The impact of inter-organizational information systems. *Journal of Strategic Information Systems*, 4(2): 117–133.

IDC. 2003. *Easing into the Tub: Results of the 2002 Procurement Manager Survey*. Available at www.idc.com.

Johnston, H.R. and Vitale, M.R. 1988. Creating competitive advantage with inter-organizational systems. *MIS Quarterly*, 12(2): 153–166.

Johnston, R. and Lawrence, P.R. 1988. Beyond vertical integration: The rise of value-adding partnership. *Harvard Business Review*, July/August: 94–101.

Kennedy, K.N. and Deeter-Schmelz, D.R. 2001. Descriptive and predictive analyses of industrial buyer's use of online information for purchasing. *Journal of Personal Selling & Sales Management*, 21(4): 279–290.

Konsynski, B.R. and McFarlan, F.W. 1990. Information partnerships: Shared data, shared scale. *Harvard Business Review*, September/October: 114–120.

Lancioni, R., Smith, M.F., and Olivia, T.A. 2000. The role of the internet in supply chain management. *Industrial Marketing Management*, 29: 45–56.

Liao, S.-H., Cheng, C.-H., Liao, W.-B., and Chen, I.-L. 2003. A web-based architecture for implementing electronic procurement in military organisations. *Technovation*, 23(6): 521–532.

Malone, T., Yates, J., and Benjamin, R. 1987. Electronic markets and electronic hierarchies: Effects of information technology on market structure and corporate strategies. *Communications of the ACM*, 30(6): 484–497.

Malone, T., Yates, J., and Benjamin, R. 1989. The logic of electronic markets. *Harvard Business Review*, May/June: 166–171.

McManus, S.A. 2002. Understanding the incremental nature of e-procurement implementation at the state and local levels. *Journal of Public Procurement*, 2(1): 5–28.

Min, H. and Galle, W.P. 1999. Electronic commerce usage in business-to-business purchasing. *International Journal of Operations and Production Management*, 19(9): 909–921.

Moore, J. 2003. Manufacturers struggle with e-procurement, but still see gains. *Chemical Engineering Progress*, 99(9): 23.

Neef, D. 2001. *E-procurement: From Strategy to Implementation*. Upper Saddle River, NJ: Prentice-Hall/Financial Times.

Osmonbekov, T., Bello, D.C., and Gilliland, D.I. 2002. Adoption of electronic commerce tools in business procurement: Enhancing buying center structure and process. *Journal of Business and Industrial Marketing*, 17(2): 151–166.

Parker, R. 2003. BA makes online sourcing mandatory to save £300 m. *Supply Management*, 8(17): 9.

Rajkumar, T.M. 2001. E-procurement: Business and technical issues. *Information Systems Management*, 18(4): 52–60.

Robinson, P.J., Faris, C.W., and Wind, Y. 1967. *Industrial Buying and Creative Marketing*. Boston, MA: Allyn & Bacon.

Stanley, L.L. and Wisner, J.D. 2001. Service quality along the supply chain: Implications for purchasing. *Journal of Operations Management*, 19(3): 287–306.

Tan, K.C. 2001. A framework of supply chain management literature. *European Journal of Purchasing and Supply Management*, 7(4): 39–48.

Tang, J.E., Shee, D., and Tang, T. 2001. The supply–demand interaction in electronic commerce: A classification by type of relationship and dominance. *Journal of Service Technology and Management*, 2(3–4): 289–312.

Trommer, D. 2003. Learning the ABC's—Having succeeded in transforming its procurement processes for indirect materials, will Ametek now consider doing the same for direct electronic component materials? *EBN*, November 10: 25.

Wheatley, M. 2003. How to know if e-procurement is right for you; while some companies have achieved price reductions through online sourcing, the focus of e-procurement initiatives today is process efficiency. Here's how to decide if, what and how you should buy electronically. *CIO*, 16(17): 1.

Wyld, D.C. 2002. The electric company: How the supply chain is being reinvented through the rapid application of e-procurement processes in the business-to-business arena. *Management Research News*, 21(12): 22–23.

Yen, B.P.-C. and Ng, E.O.S. 2003. The impact of electronic commerce on procurement. *Journal of Organizational Computing and Electronic Commerce*, 13(3 and 4): 167–189.

Zsidisin, G.A. and Ellram, L.M. 2001. Activities relating to purchasing and supply management involvement in supplier alliances. *International Journal of Physical Distribution and Logistics Management*, 31(9): 629–646.

Chapter 22

Factors Influencing E-Procurement Usage

Ken Dooley and Sharon Purchase

CONTENTS

22.1 Introduction

E-procurement is the use of online technology to assist with the procurement function. It is considered an operational imperative in today's competitive environment, a growth area and one of the key issues purchasing and supply executives need to face now and in the near future (Carter et al., 2000; Davila et al., 2003). Although forecasts on the use of E-procurement have been downgraded with the burst of the Internet bubble in 2001 (Davila et al., 2003), experts are still predicting growth (Halal, 2003) with statistics showing an increased growth in the use of E-procurement for 2004. For example, a recent survey indicated that E-procurement of direct goods is now exceeding that of indirect goods (Bartels et al., 2003). Still even with these observed results and predictions of further growth, some research results are indicating that usage of E-procurement and the growth in this usage has not been as great as expected. Such confusion may be causing some type of inertia within the adoption process even though significant benefits can be obtained (Anonymous, 2002).

Significant operational benefits, such as the following, can be gained: lower transaction costs, lower staffing requirements, shorter procurement cycles, reduced inventory levels, higher degree of transparency, and increased communication and collaboration between supplier and buyer organizations (Carter et al., 2000; Rajkumar, 2001; Osmonbekov et al., 2002; Turban et al., 2002; Davila et al., 2003; Min and Galle, 2003). Yet, for all the benefits outlined there are many organizations that are taking a "wait and see" approach to the implementation of E-procurement technologies (Gottschalk and Abrahamsen, 2002; Davila et al., 2003). As Bartels et al. (2003, p. 6) point out: "While the data provides evidence that progress is being made in terms of online adoption and usage, those averages disguise a more complex picture in which certain segments of companies vary vastly in results. Large service sector firms are making the most progress and seeing the best results, while other segments—small manufacturers in particular—are lagging in online purchasing and tool usage." With such differing adoption practices between different industries, research conducted within specialized industry segments helps develop an understanding for that particular segment.

Debate exists as to whether such a wait and see approach is necessarily bad for an organization (MacManus, 2002). Research into government organizations has highlighted a number of factors that may influence this approach: inflexibility of organizational structures, lack of financial investment, lack of skills and training, and unsuitability to traditional government practices (MacManus, 2002). Yet, there is still a desire by government organizations to adopt E-commerce technologies. Understanding the factors that positively influence adoption of E-procurement technologies will help organizations develop strategies that assist implementation. This research investigates some of the factors that positively influence Australian semigovernment organizations' adoption of E-procurement.

There is also a debate as to what E-procurement entails (Vaidya et al., 2006). Confusion concerning the differences between E-purchasing and E-procurement has led to suggestions that the two terms are used interchangeably (MacManus, 2002). The approach taken in this research was to use an all-encompassing definition, and to define E-procurement to include all forms of use of electronic infrastructure that connects two organizations in the purchasing process (de Boer et al., 2002; Min and Galle, 2003). A broad perspective has also been taken in other research and ensures that respondents are not confused over intricate and minor differences in definitions when responding to self-administered questionnaires. Therefore, the definition of E-procurement provided to the respondents is as follows: "Electronic tendering, or auctioning and procurement of goods and services over the Internet. This may be via portals, extranets, E-auctions, private platforms, marketplaces, and/or electronic data interchange (EDI)." Such a broad definition is similar to that used by the World Bank and covers a wide range of information and communication technologies used by organizations to conduct relationships with suppliers when acquiring goods and services.

Therefore, the research focus is the following research question: What factors positively influence the buyers' intentions to implement E-procurement?

In particular, the research is focused on Australian semigovernment organizations where there is an emphasis in adopting newer technologies. The semigovernment organizations surveyed in this research included Australian state government departments that have become autonomous financial entities. Examples include railway infrastructure and transport, electricity supply, building services, airport corporations, department of primary industry service providers, and specialized healthcare providers.

22.1.1 Government and Semigovernment Usage of E-Procurement

There is particular concern that government and semigovernment organizations have not progressed to use E-procurement at anywhere near the levels forecast. The U.K. government publications are typical of the hype surrounding the use of E-commerce where it is seen as an important aspect in making government efficient (Foley, 2000). For example, the 1998 competitiveness white paper outlines "building sound foundations for e-commerce, improving understanding, increasing access, enhancing trust, promoting government as an exemplar, developing monitoring of e-commerce, and co-ordinating activities for e-commerce within government" (Foley, 2000, p. 1).

Similarly, the forecasts were upbeat in terms of the benefits government could obtain. E-commerce technologies provide effective and efficient ways in which corporate buyers can gather information rapidly about available products and services, evaluate and negotiate with suppliers, implement order fulfillment over communications links, and access post-sales services (Foley, 2000). Such benefits are similar to those outlined for private organizations although some researchers have highlighted that the requirements of government procurement differ from those of private enterprises (MacManus, 2002). She highlights that public sector procurement practices require departments to use a large number of suppliers to encourage competition and include minority business owners who may not have electronic access. Such requirements will change how they develop relationships with their suppliers and consequently how they develop strategies for electronic integration.

Given the variety of different E-procurement modes that organizations use, the most common task currently undertaken is that of purchasing through online catalogs (MacManus, 2002). Data gathered in this research project also substantiates such findings with 57 percent of respondents using online catalogs. Yet, online auctions and E-tendering is a low 12.6 and 23 percent, respectively. Therefore, different models and uses of E-procurement are being used across differing government departments, thus indicating that E-procurement is still in an early adoption stage with differing models being used to suit varied circumstances.

22.1.2 Factors Influencing Usage of E-Procurement

Exploratory studies have indicated that many organizations are pursuing electronic means to conduct business, that there are a number of factors influencing the adoption of electronic commerce, and that these may be summarized as E-procurement, E-sourcing, and E-collaboration (see, for example, Bartezzaghi and Ronchi, 2003). However, because the growth in the usage of E-procurement has not met expectations, most recent research has been investigating the barriers to E-procurement usage (Kheng and Al Hawamdeh, 2002; More and McGrath, 2002) rather than factors that positively influence adoption (Min and Galle, 2003).

As an example, although EDI has existed for a number of years, the number of organizations using EDI has been limited, due to the high cost of implementing an EDI system. The use of EDI is generally restricted to large manufacturing organizations and their major suppliers within a close geographical distance (Osmonbekov et al., 2002; Turban et al., 2002). The Internet effectively removed these restrictions allowing organizations to be networked together at a low cost, and it offers greater flexibility as the requirement for private networks are eliminated (Attaran, 2001). With the opening up of connectivity, however, a lowering in the security of data also occurred, and concern over security is a factor limiting the implementation of E-commerce systems (Carter et al., 2000; Croom, 2000). Nonetheless, more recent evidence indicates security concerns are becoming less of an issue (at least for the more aggressive adopters) and hence concerns about security are not restricting the use of business to business (B2B) E-commerce systems (Davila et al., 2003).

Another factor limiting the usage is the readiness of supplier firms to participate (Bartels et al., 2003). Buyers have indicated that they are willing to use E-procurement, but they perceive that their suppliers are not able to participate. Buyers then have the choice of either limiting the extent of their E-procurement processes (reducing the benefits obtained) or finding new suppliers who are willing to conduct transactions electronically.

22.1.3 Positive Factors Influencing E-Procurement

This research focused on investigating factors that positively influence the purchasing organization to become involved in the use of E-procurement rather than considering factors that inhibit the organizational adoption. A considerable number of studies have been conducted to determine what influences a firm to become involved in E-procurement (Croom, 2001; Kennedy and Deeter-Schmelz, 2001; Ellram and Zsidisin, 2002; Davila et al., 2003; Min and Galle, 2003; Croom and Brandon-Jones, 2005; Joo and Kim, 2004). From this research, a list of positive influencing factors was developed; the factors are discussed in more detail below.

22.1.4 Supplier Participation and Intentions

Some suppliers apply pressure on their customers to become involved in the use E-commerce to reduce costs, improve communications, and gain operational efficiencies (Kennedy and Deeter-Schmelz, 2001). Many buyers have indicated that they are not pleased with the online capabilities of their suppliers. An institute of supply management (ISM)/Forrester survey found that 36.6 percent of manufacturers rated their suppliers' online capabilities as very bad or poor (Olsztynski, 2003). Yet, for the procurement process to occur electronically both the supplier and the buyer need to be connected (often via the Internet). Some suppliers provide encouragements that can be either financial or nonfinancial. Examples of financial encouragements are lower prices or increased discounts for products ordered electronically or the option to reduce inventories. Nonfinancial incentives include training sessions, customized Web fronts, and better services (Croom, 2001; Deeter-Schmelz et al., 2001). Overall, previous research has highlighted that supplier support has a positive influence on the adoption of E-commerce (Deeter-Schmelz et al., 2001). Supplier strategies and willingness to take on new technologies such as E-procurement have been shown to have a positive effect on the utilization of the new technologies by the buying partner. Therefore, hypothesis H1 is as follows: Supplier participation and intentions have a positive relationship with electronic procurement intentions (EPI).

22.1.5 External Organizational Pressures

Suppliers can also exert pressure on their customers to use their systems and vice versa (Min and William, 1999; Joo and Kim, 2004). The use of power in such cases occurs when there is a relative power imbalance within the dyad. To fully gain from the benefits of E-procurement, suppliers need to have as many of their customers as possible using their electronic ordering systems. Powerful suppliers may indicate to their buyers that they must use their system or they will cease supplying them. Of course, the reverse can also occur where powerful buyers insist that their suppliers conduct transactions electronically or they will cease buying from that particular supplier. Supplier pressure to use new technology may have a positive effect on purchase intentions if the customer relies/depends on the supplier. Alternatively, it may have a negative effect if the buyer resists this pressure and purchases similar products from elsewhere. Owing to the coercive nature of supplier pressure, the researchers consider it still wise to postulate that such pressure will have an effect on the buyer's intention to use E-procurement. Therefore, overall, hypothesis H2 is as follows: Supplier pressure to use new technologies has a positive relationship with EPI.

22.1.6 Internal Organizational Support

The continuous drive toward organizational efficiency and lowering the cost to conduct business is also driving the adoption of E-procurement (Lancioni et al., 2003). Organizations are applying internal forces to boost adoption hoping to gain from the benefits E-procurement is purported to give (Croom and Brandon-Jones, 2005). Therefore, internal organizational support for adoption of such systems is vital if they are going to be implemented successfully. Previous research has highlighted a number of internal factors influencing adoption: staffing levels, training in new technologies, encouragement from management and other departments (in particular information systems) (Osmonbekov et al., 2002), sufficient financial and resource backing (Joo and Kim, 2004), and adequate budget allocations to ensure all the requirements are met. It is proposed that internal organizational support will have a positive influence on EPI. Therefore, hypothesis H3 is as follows: Internal organizational support has a positive relationship with EPI.

22.1.7 Network Connectivity/Integration

Suppliers' systems also need to be integrated and compatible with their buyers' systems if the transaction process is to be automatic thus gaining the full benefits available (Rajkumar, 2001; Croom and Brandon-Jones, 2005). Integration of electronic networks that are reliable and have sufficient capacity allows easy transfer of information. Research has shown that network connectivity has an impact on the performance of an E-procurement system (Croom and Brandon-Jones, 2005). Therefore, it can be expected that reliable and secure connectivity would increase an organization's intentions to use E-procurement. The extent of integration with major supplier's electronic networks will influence buyer organization adoption. It is proposed that electronic networks that are highly integrated between buyers and their major suppliers will positively influence the buyer organization's intention to use electronic purchasing technologies. Therefore, hypothesis H4 is as follows: Extent of electronic integration has a positive relationship with EPI.

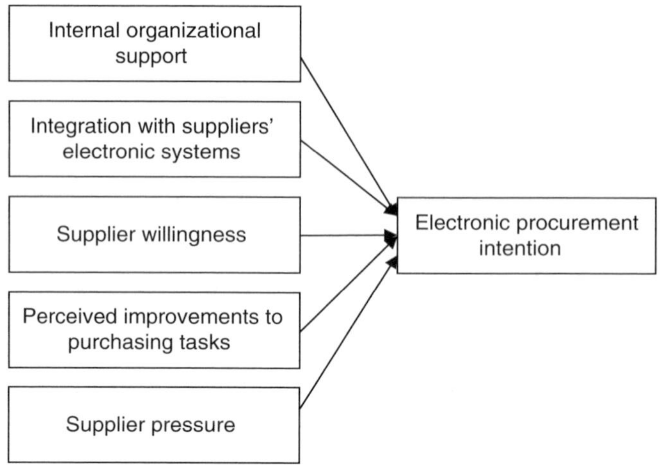

Figure 22.1 Model of EPI.

22.1.8 *Task Improvements/Convenience*

E-procurement has been shown in many cases to improve the task of the purchasing professional (Rajkumar, 2001; Olsen and Boyer, 2003). In particular, the amount of time spent on administrative tasks is reduced allowing supply personnel to concentrate on more strategic issues (Rajkumar, 2001). If individual purchasing professionals perceive that using such technologies will make their tasks easier, then their intention to purchase electronically will be increased. Therefore, hypothesis H5 is as follows: Perceived improvements to purchasing tasks undertaken have a positive relationship with EPI.

On the basis of the above hypotheses, a conceptual model was developed to illustrate how the main constructs are to be tested. This model is depicted in Figure 22.1.

22.2 Methods

The hypotheses were tested, using survey data gathered from purchasing professionals, through the multivariate technique of multiple regression analysis. This section outlines the research method undertaken to test the hypotheses.

22.2.1 *Sample*

Purchasing professionals within Australian semigovernment departments were the targeted respondents. To reach these respondents, members of the Australian Institute of Purchasing and Materials Management (AIPMM) and all purchasing professionals within the Queensland state government (Queensland Purchasing e-mailing list) were sent an e-mail inviting them to complete the survey at a specified Web site. Members of AIPMM are purchasing professionals representing government, semigovernment, and private organizations; however, only the government and semigovernment responses were used for this research. Purchasing professionals from the Queensland Purchasing list are all government employees. Because of privacy considerations, Queensland Purchasing and APIMM did not directly release their e-mailing lists to the researchers and the exact number of participants on the e-mailing lists is unknown. Estimates of the numbers who were sent the e-mail inviting responses would be 2500 for the AIPMM, a significant proportion (say 50 percent) of whom would be government and semigovernment, and 450 for the Queensland government all of whom would be government or semigovernment. A reminder e-mail was sent three weeks after the first e-mail, requesting those who had not completed the survey to do so. Web-based surveys have the advantage of targeting respondents who are used to using electronic tools, particularly the Internet, in their normal working environment. Research has also shown that Internet respondents are less likely to complete questionnaires using other distribution methods (Swoboda et al., 1997). From the e-mails sent, 211 surveys were completed, of which 199 were usable.

22.2.2 Questionnaire Development and Variables

A questionnaire was developed after a review of the literature related to E-purchasing and E-procurement and discussions with academics and the head of Queensland Purchasing. Items were anchored using a 7-point Likert scale (1—very strongly disagree to 7—very strongly agree). Item statements used to measure the independent variables are found in Table 22.1.

Table 22.1 Results of the Exploratory Factor Analysis

Variable	*Item*	*Factor Loadings*	*Cronbach Alpha*
Internal organizational support Eigenvalue = 3.74 Percent variance = 17.8	Sufficient staffing levels	0.84	0.87
	IS/IT department positive influences behavior	0.81	
	Sufficient budget allocation	0.79	
	Sufficient staff training	0.77	
	Management pressure to use systems	0.69	
	IS/IT determines choice of systems	0.55	
Electronic integration with suppliers Eigenvalue = 1.98 Percent variance = 9.4	Suppliers access our site for information	0.74	0.7
	We access suppliers sites for information	0.69	
	Electronically integrated with suppliers	0.67	

(continued)

Table 22.1 (continued) Results of the Exploratory Factor Analysis

Variable	*Item*	*Factor Loadings*	*Cronbach Alpha*
Suppliers willingness Eigenvalue = 2.26 Percent variance = 10.7	Suppliers plan to use E-procurement for one to five years	0.88	0.82
	Suppliers plan to use E-procurement for next 12 months	0.86	
	Suppliers willing to participate	0.59	
Perceived improvements to purchasing tasks Eigenvalue = 3.74 Percent variance = 16.7	Make job easier	0.85	0.85
	Online catalogs make job easier	0.82	
	Reduced time spent with sales people	0.79	
	Questions answered more effectively	0.70	
	More information on products and services available	0.66	
	Comfortable using electronic tools	0.59	
Supplier pressure Eigenvalue = 2.37 Percent variance = 11.3	Major suppliers exerted pressure on infrastructure development	0.89	0.85
	Major suppliers exerted pressure to initiate E-procurement practices	0.87	
	Major suppliers exerted pressure on behavior	0.80	

There were two items measuring the dependent variable, intentions, both asked statements relating to the respondent's intentions of increasing their use of the Internet in more of their purchasing activities within (1) less than 12 months and (2) greater than 12 months. The items were summed to form the dependent variable: intentions to use E-procurement. The mean for the dependent item was 3.96, standard deviation 0.95, and had a Cronbach alpha of 0.875, indicating acceptable reliability.

Content validity was addressed by using prior items wherever possible and by carrying out reviews on the instrument. Before the questionnaire was finalized, it was pretested on a sample of ten respondents who gave feedback on the interpretation of the questions and provided feedback on items that were unclear. Exploratory factor analysis allowed the researchers to determine construct validity of the independent variables (Hair et al., 1998). Calculations of Cronbach alpha confirmed the reliability of all variables as they were 0.7 or greater (Hair et al., 1998).

22.3 Results

This section outlines the data analysis undertaken and the results. All respondents had used the Internet in some form for purchasing activities although not necessarily for transaction purposes. Details of Internet usage was elicited using a number of specific questions on past experience such as how long they have been using the Internet/EDI and E-procurement within their work environment. Even though the respondents were in semigovernment organizations, the majority classified their operations as manufacturing type operations (49.7 percent), followed by service industry (39.1 percent) and primary industry (11.1 percent). Manufacturing type of industries would include construction of railroad vehicles, construction of new government facilities, and primary industry departments supplying product such as seed to farmers.

Respondent's purchasing experience ranged from less than 1 year to greater than 30 years with an average of 16.4 years. Of those who responded, 65 percent indicated that they had transacted online with the average time of usage being three years. This indicates that 35 percent did not consider that their organization was using E-procurement as defined. Also, the usage of E-procurement was less than one year for 17.8 percent of respondents, one to two years for 32.5 percent, and two to four years for 34 percent. Only 10 percent have been using E-procurement for more than four years. With respect to size of organization, 40 percent of respondents indicated that their organization had a budget over $30 million, while 50 percent had a budget of between $10 million and $30 million.

22.3.1 Factor Analysis

Factor analysis was carried out on the independent variables using principal component analysis with varimax rotation. All variables consisted of multi-item measures and the results of the factor analysis are given in Table 22.1. Two items were removed from the analysis owing to large cross loadings on more than one factor, improving the unidimensionality of the factors. All factors have eigenvalues greater then one and items have factor loadings of 0.55 or greater.

Overall, the factor analysis explained 65.9 percent of the variance, and reliability coefficients ranging from 0.7 to 0.87 and are considered acceptable (Hair et al., 1998). The independent variables aligned with those hypothesized from the literature and allowed the researchers to test all hypotheses generated.

22.3.2 Model Analysis

Overall model evaluation and testing of the proposed hypotheses was conducted using stepwise linear multiple regression analysis. Results are given in Table 22.2 with the overall model significant.

As indicated in Table 22.2, the relationship between supplier pressure and intention to use E-procurement was not significant and was not included in the model analysis. The final model, excluding supplier pressure, was highly significant with an R^2 of 0.462, $p < .001$, and F-test of 43.5. Given the sample size and specified significance level, the R^2 was great enough to ensure acceptable power level (Hair et al., 1998). Variance inflation factors are all above 1 indicating that multicollinearity is not a problem (Hair et al., 1998).

The results partially support the proposed model in that four of the five independent variables significantly influence the buyer organization's intentions to use E-procurement practices.

Table 22.2 Results of the Multiple Regression Analysis

Variable	*R^2 Change*	*β*	*F Change*
Supplier willingness	0.203	0.423	50.07*
Perceived improvements to purchasing tasks	0.124	0.356	36.15*
Internal organizational support	0.101	0.304	34.25*
Electronic integration with suppliers	0.045	0.213	16.66*
Supplier pressure	Not significant hence not included in the model	−0.02	

* $p < .001$.

Hypotheses H1, H3, H4, and H5 are all supported, while hypothesis H2 is not supported. Hypothesis H2 may not have been supported as coercive pressure can also be a disincentive as indicated earlier.

Major supplier willingness and future participation had the strongest influence on intentions to use E-procurement, with an R^2 of 0.203. Such a result should not be unexpected in that E-procurement practices need to be used by both buyers and suppliers if the benefits of using electronic systems are to be achieved. Internal organizational support and perceived improvements and convenience in purchasing activities also had an influence on intentions.

22.4 Discussion

The research indicates that major suppliers' willingness and future intentions to transact online are a driving force that influences the buyers' intentions to use E-procurement. This result has also been found in research conducted within the United States that found supplier support directly affected Internet purchase intentions (Deeter-Schmelz et al., 2001). The extent of supplier support varied, with the influence in this research being much stronger (0.423) and explaining a greater extent of the variance than the previous Deeter-Schmelz et al. (2001) study (0.16). The implication of this result is that either supplier's intentions have a greater effect in Australia, or as time and experience have grown so has the realization that supplier intentions and willingness are critical to the adoption of E-procurement. Therefore, if suppliers wish to encourage their buyers to initiate E-procurement practices, they should indicate to their buyers the extent of their future intentions in this area. Therefore, E-procurement is not an issue that can be addressed through internal processes only, but one that has consequences to the dyad or supplier–buyer relationship.

Internal organizational support also has an important effect on intentions to use the Internet for purchasing transactions. The organization must supply the purchasing or supply department with adequate resources if they are going to undergo the change processes required to implement E-procurement systems. Adequate resources in training, staffing levels, and systems support will be necessary if the intentions to further use the Internet for transactions are to be realized.

Note, however, that one implication of the results obtained here is that although organizational support is important, it is not as important as suppliers' intentions. Therefore, managers who wish their purchasing/supply departments to use this technology for efficiency and cost benefits must also approach their major suppliers and determine their intentions, preferring those suppliers who are expressing intentions to implement E-procurement.

Perceived improvements to purchasing tasks also have a positive effect on future EPI, although this research indicated that it does not have as strong an effect as previous research has indicated. Research by Deeter-Schmelz et al. (2001) showed that this variable had by far the strongest influence on Internet purchase intentions (0.55) unlike research that indicated it had a lesser effect (0.356). Such a difference could be due to the time difference of the data collection. Late 2000 and early 2001 saw the decline in optimism on what the Internet and its utilization could actually achieve. The data for this research was collected in late 2003, when the shake-up of Internet companies and consequent solutions had lowered the level of optimism throughout the business community.

Electronic integration with suppliers, although significant, did not have a large effect (0.21) and explained only 4.5 percent of the variance. Such a low result could be due to the level of knowledge and technical ability of the respondents. The low result could also be due to the fact that newer technologies, such as Web services, are perceived to overcome these issues.

Overall, the model highlights that online transaction intention is an issue that needs to be addressed by both sides of the purchasing process: buyers and suppliers. As with the development of purchasing relationships in general, unless E-procurement is seen as a tool to assist in the development of relationships by ensuring that both sides of the relationship have the willingness and future intentions to go down the path of electronic transactions—it will not work.

22.5 Conclusion

Major factors influencing the use of E-procurement in the semigovernment organizations were elicited in this study. The existence of these factors may be used by supplier organizations or by buyer organizations to facilitate the uptake of E-procurement.

It needs to be stressed that the respondents to this survey were purchasing professionals in semigovernment organizations, and applying generalizations to private industry organizations may be difficult. Future research needs to extend this study to other types of organizations to allow generalization of these results to the wider business community.

These results reinforce the view that there has been a change in attitude toward the use of electronic systems in the procurement process, and it is suggested that this is due to the overall drop in business expectations after the burst of the Internet bubble. Such changes in attitude and expectations are to be expected given the turbulent marketplace created by the rapid developments occurring in the information industry. To keep track of changes in attitudes to electronic commerce initiatives, future research needs to be conducted regularly to evaluate the extent and direction of those changes.

Acknowledgments

The assistance of the executive and staff of the Australian Institute of Purchasing and Materials Management is greatly appreciated, as is the contribution from the University of Western Australia research grants. Also the technical support of Dr. Robert Ho (Central Queensland University) has been of significant benefit in the analysis of the data. The authors would also like to thank the editor and reviewers for their helpful comments on earlier versions of this book.

References

Anonymous 2002. Electronic procurement—momentum needed. *Work Study*, 52(1). Available at http://docserver.emeraldinsight.vom/deliver/cw/mcb/00438022.

Attaran, M. 2001. The coming of age of online procurement. *Industrial Management and Data Systems*, 101(3): 177–174.

Bartels, A., Hudson, R., and Pohlmann, T. 2003. ISM/Forrester report on technology in supply management. *TechStrategy*: 1–9.

Bartezzaghi, E. and Ronchi, S. 2003. Internet supporting the procurement process: Lessons from four case studies. *Integrated Manufacturing Systems*, 14(8): 632–641.

Carter, P., Carter, J., Monczka, R., Slaight, T., and Swan, A. 2000. The future of purchasing and supply: A ten-year forecast. *The Journal of Supply Chain Management*, 36(1): 14–26.

Croom, S. 2000. The impact of web-based procurement on the management of operating resources supply. *The Journal of Supply Chain Management*, 36(1): 4–13.

Croom, S. 2001. Restructuring the supply chains through information channel innovation. *International Journal of Operations and Production Management*, 21(4): 504–511.

Croom, S. and Brandon-Jones, A. 2005. Key issues in E-procurement: Procurement implementation and operation in the public sector, *Journal of Public Procurement*, 5(3): 267–288.

Davila, A., Gupta, M., and Palmer, R. 2003. Moving procurement systems to the Internet: The adoption and use of e-procurement technology models. *European Management Journal*, 21(1): 11–23.

de Boer, L., Harinnk, J., and Heijboer, G. 2002. A conceptual model for assessing the impact of e-procurement. *European Journal of Purchasing and Supply Management*, 8: 25–33.

Deeter-Schmelz, D.R., Bizzari, A., Graham, R., and Howdyshell, C. 2001. Business-to-business online purchasing: Supplier's impact on buyer's adoption and usage intent. *The Journal of Supply Chain Management*, 37(1): 4–10.

Ellram, L. and Zsidisin, G. 2002 Factors that drive purchasing and supply management's use of information technology. *IEEE Transactions on Engineering Management*, 49(3): 269–281.

Foley, P. 2000. Internet editorial: e-commerce and the UK government. *European Business Review*, 12(3). Available at http://titania.emeraldinsight.com/vl=7453599/cl=55/nw=1/rpsv/cgi-bin/linker?ini=emerald&reqidx=/cw/mcb/0955534x/v12n3/s8001/p1l.

Gottschalk, P. and Abrahamsen, A.F. 2002. Plans to use electronic marketplaces: The case of B2B procurement markets in Norway. *Industrial Management and Data Systems*, 102(6): 325–331.

Hair, J., Anderson, R., Tatham, R., and Black, W. 1998. *Multivariate Data Analysis*. Upper Saddle River, NJ: Pearson Publishing.

Halal, W.E. 2003. E-commerce forecasts: A return of the dot.com boom? *On the Horizon*, 11(1): 23–25.

Joo, Y. and Kim, Y. 2004. Determinants of corporate adoption of e-marketplace: An innovation theory perspective. *Journal of Purchasing and Supply Management*, 10: 89–101.

Kennedy, K.D. and Deeter-Schmelz, R. 2001. Descriptive and predictive analyses of industrial buyers use of online information for purchasing. *The Journal of Personal Selling and Sales Management*, 21(4): 279–290.

Kheng, C.B. and Al Hawamdeh, S. 2002.The adoption of electronic procurement in Singapore. *Electronic Commerce Research*, 2: 61–73.

Lancioni, R., Schau, H., and Smith, M. 2003. Internet impacts on supply chain management. *Industrial Marketing Management*, 32: 173–175.

MacManus, S. 2002. Understanding the incremental nature of e-procurement implementation at the state and local levels. *Journal of Public Procurement*, 2(1): 5–28.

Min, H.G. and William, P. 1999. Electronic commerce usage in business-to-business purchasing. *International Journal of Operations and Production Management*, 19(9): 909–916.

Min, H. and Galle, W. 2003. E-purchasing: Profiles of adopters and nonadopters. *Industrial Marketing Management*, 32: 227–233.

More, E. and McGrath, M. 2002. An Australian case in e-health communication and change. *Journal of Management Development*, 21(8): 621–632.

Olsen, J. and Boyer, K. 2003. Factors influencing the utilization of Internet purchasing in small organization. *Journal of Operations Management*, 21: 225–245.

Olsztynski, J. 2003. Two studies track upsurge in industrial Internet buying. *Supply House Times*, 46(4): 20.

Osmonbekov, T., Bello, D., and Gilliland, D. 2002. Adoption of electronic commerce tools in business procurement: Enhanced buying center structure and processes. *Journal of Business and Industrial Marketing*, 17(2/3): 151–166.

Rajkumar, T. 2001. E-procurement: Business and Technical Issues. *Information Systems Management*, 18(4): 1–9.

Swoboda, W., Muhlberger, N., Weitkunat, R., and Schneeweiss, S. 1997. Internet survey by direct mailing: An innovative way of collecting data. *Social Science Computer Review*, 15(3): 242–255.

Turban, E., King, D., Lee, J., Warkentin, M., and Chung, H. 2002. *Electronic Commerce 2002: A Managerial Perspective*. New York: Pearson.

Vaidya, K., Sajeev, A., and Callender, G. 2006. Critical factors that influence E-procurement implementation success in the public sector, *Journal of Public Procurement*, 6(1/2): 70–100.

Chapter 23

Facilitators of Public E-Procurement: Lessons Learned from the U.K., U.S., and Australian Initiatives

Kishor Vaidya, Guy C. Callender, and A.S.M. Sajeev

CONTENTS

23.1 Introduction

This chapter presents the results of a literature survey developed to support a proposed model of the facilitators likely to impact the success of E-procurement initiatives in the public sector. It identifies a number of relevant variables for facilitator and presents a proposition for future research. It also analyzes the relative importance of different facilitators and observes that organization and management factors are the most important category for success of E-procurement initiatives. If E-procurement initiatives in the public sector are to assist the development of E-procurement across the information economy, there should be wider discussion and agreement on what constitutes the relevant facilitators and how the achievement of success can be assessed. It should be noted that we have used the term facilitators to denote the "critical success factors" (CSFs) and we have used the terms interchangeably.

Governments aspire to use public procurement as a lever of economic, technological, or social reform. This is evident from a recent study conducted by the International Research Study of Public Procurement (IRSPP). The IRSPP study also provides evidence of growing interest in modernizing public procurement, which accounts for significant proportions of countries' total expenditure (Harland et al., 2005). In fact, a number of public sector agencies worldwide are modernizing public procurement through electronic procurement (E-procurement) as a priority E-government agenda and have implemented or are in the process of implementing buy-side E-procurement systems. However, the scholarly evaluation of E-procurement initiatives, especially in relation to the use of CSFs in E-procurement, is very limited (Birks et al., 2001; DOF, 2001; CGEC, 2002; ECOM, 2002). A review of E-procurement literature, primarily from the last five years, shows a lack of core constructs around facilitators. The reason for this might be that implementation of E-procurement initiatives in the public sector is still in the early stages. Tonkin (2003) argues there was little history of extensive use of E-procurement in the public sector and, therefore, the academic literature covering early public sector adoption of E-procurement is limited. This chapter will assess the facilitators that are likely to influence the success of E-procurement initiatives in the public sector. The main overall objectives are to gain an exploratory understanding of E-procurement issues in the public sector; to develop a conceptual framework that aids in identification of facilitators for adopting and implementing E-procurement in the public sector; and to stimulate debate about the E-procurement facilitators and the associated measures for success.

Through a survey of the E-procurement literature, this chapter identifies 11 factors: end-user uptake and training, supplier adoption, compliance with best practices for business case/project management, systems integration, security and authentication, reengineering the process, top management support, performance measurement, change management, E-procurement implementation strategy, and technological standards. The following sections discuss the background, requirements, and the barriers to E-procurement implementation in the public sector. Following the methodological approach, each facilitator is discussed in detail and a research model is presented. Finally, an analysis of the relative importance of the facilitators is presented and the chapter concludes with a discussion on the differences and similarities of E-procurement projects compared with traditional IT projects in the public sector.

23.2 Brief History of Procurement

Callender (2003) briefly summarized the history of procurement practice tracing back over 2800 years and citing interesting examples from 215 BC to modern-day Web-based procurement practices. Some of these include the procurement practices of Roman armies in Spain in 215 BC, supplier management principles adopted by King Gustavus of Sweden in the sixteenth century, elements of procurement suggested by Adam Smith in the seventeenth century, some procurement policies of the British Navy in the eighteenth century, recognition of procurement as part of new concepts such as the "supply chain" in 1982, and the "value chain" in 1990. An important contribution was then made by Ellram and Carr in 1994 when they classified the procurement literature in three categories focusing on strategy: the role of strategy on procurement, the role of procurement on strategy, and strategic procurement. It appears that this emphasis on strategy is still the dominant paradigm in today's public procurement practice. Thus, if the emphasis shifts from tactical to a strategic role, as argued by Narasimhan and Carter (1998), the procurement "must shift its focus from efficiency to effectiveness." As concluded by Callender (2003), "the purchase requisition of yesterday has not entirely disappeared, but ... e-commerce or e-business, electronic ordering will free the procurement professional to focus on the strategic issues" (p. 8).

23.3 Public Procurement

Callender and Matthews (2003) regard procurement and the supply chain as consisting of a number of bodies of knowledge. They provide examples to show how various disciplines such as information science, accounting and finance, economics and law, sociology and marketing, organizational behavior, and even psychology are related to procurement and supply chain as shown in Table 23.1.

Public procurement has to satisfy requirements for goods, works, systems, and services in a timely and cost-effective manner (Thai, 2001) which demonstrates the achievement of "value for money" (DOF, 2001). Furthermore, it has to meet the basic principles of good governance: transparency, accountability, and integrity (Callender and Schapper, 2003; Wittig, 2003). However, public procurement tends to have been a neglected area of academic education and research, although governmental entities, policy makers, and public procurement professionals have paid a great deal of attention to procurement improvements and reforms (Thai, 2001).

Conventional wisdom suggests that government procurement differs from private procurement. Public sector procurement is large and complex, accounting for between 20 and 30 percent of gross domestic product (Thai and Grimm, 2000) and traditionally attempts to meet many social and political objectives (Tether, 1977). Governments procure goods and services using a complex contractual system designed to protect the public interest (Rasheed, 2004) and demonstrate an accountability and transparency of operation. Although private sector procurement is practiced under the sponsorship of each individual firm's governance policies, public sector procurement must operate within a range of regulations and policies established to accomplish desirable social (Tether, 1977) as well as economic (OCIO, 2000), financial, and public audit requirements.

Table 23.1 Related Disciplines of Procurement and Supply

Disciplines Related to Procurement and Supply Chain	*Representative Examples*
Information science	E-commerce, E-business, inventory management, communications and information management, E-marketplace etc.
Accounting and finance	Activity-based costing, financial modeling, net present value techniques to evaluate contracting opportunities and measure whole-of-life costs
Economics and law	Evaluation of procurement policies and contracts (terms and conditions, etc.) management
Sociology and marketing	Organizational and markets management, management of customer service, and B2B relationships
Organization behavior and psychology	Change management, supplier performance management, and buyer–supplier relationship management

Source: Adapted from Callender and Matthews. In: P.J.A. Nagel (Ed.), *Supply Chain Management, A Procurement Perspective*, Australian Institute of Purchasing and Materials Management Limited, 2003.

A core difference between public and private sector procurements is the relationship between the buyer and the supplier in each entity. In the public sector, the buyer may attempt to include as many sellers as possible to broaden competition and maximize opportunities for value for money. However, in the private sector, buyers may seek to use a small number of suppliers based on trusted relationships to minimize operating risks (OCIO, 2000). Governments are also obliged to disclose purchasing and contracting information to the public, including details about the outcome of government contracting decisions. Although government procurement policies and legislation have been established to limit discrimination in government procurement, it is unclear how successful they have been (Rasheed, 2004).

Thai (2001) views the public procurement system from three perspectives: the nested structure of systems within systems, organizational structures within organizational structures, and many independent procurement systems. MacManus (2002) notes the need to reexamine the four key principles that have guided public procurement over the past few decades, namely lowest price; demonstrable separation of buyer and seller; fixed term, fixed price contracts; and accountability and transparency. These diverging views and established principles may need to be examined as public procurement becomes E-enabled.

23.4 Public E-Procurement and Its Implementation

What is E-procurement? Confusion exists in defining the term E-procurement (Vaidya et al., 2003). Although the terms "E-procurement" and "E-purchasing" have been used synonymously in many jurisdictions in an attempt to prove their involvement in the E-commerce revolution (MacManus, 2002), the term "purchasing" has a narrower scope. Public electronic procurement refers to the "use of the Internet-based Inter-organizational Information System, which automates and integrates any part of the procurement process in order to improve the efficiency and quality in public procurement, and to promote transparency and accountability in the wider public sector" (Vaidya, 2007). There are various forms of E-procurement that concentrate on one or many stages of the procurement process such as E-tendering, E-marketplace, E-auction/reverse auction, and E-catalog/purchasing. However, E-procurement can be viewed more broadly as an end-to-end solution that integrates and streamlines many procurement processes throughout the organization. Although the term "end-to-end E-procurement" is popular, industry and academic analysts indicate that this ideal model is rarely achieved (DOIR, 2001) and E-procurement implementations generally involve a mixture of different models (S&A, 2003).

Although such end-to-end solutions offer robust and usually rich functionality, they are designed specifically to excel in just one or a few applications and thus pose various challenges (Cuthbert et al., 2003). Nevertheless, this chapter will refer to the end-to-end E-procurement system to avoid confusion but will not consider general e-mail, electronic fax, voice communications, or non-Internet/Web-based approaches, which are regarded as partial traditional E-procurement solutions. As one of the core enablers of an E-business supply chain, E-procurement is conceptualized as an innovation in public procurement.

Over the last 40 years, although private and public sector organizations have been utilizing information technology (IT) systems to streamline and automate their purchasing and other processes, it is only in the past decade that E-procurement systems have attracted attention. Although there is debate about how recently E-procurement has emerged (Dai and Kauffman, 2001; Koorn et al., 2001), there is no doubt that the use of the Internet in E-procurement provides several advantages over earlier interorganizational tools. For example, electronic data interchange has been providing automated purchasing transactions between buyers and their suppliers since it was launched in the 1960s. Enterprise resource planning (ERP) followed in the 1970s, and then came the commercial use of the Internet in the 1980s. It was only in the 1990s that the World Wide Web—the multimedia capability of the Internet—became widely enabled and provided the essential resource for the automation of procurement (OGC, 2002).

Some of the commonly used tools in the public sector are E-tendering, E-RFQ, E-auctions, E-catalogs, and E-invoicing. Regardless of the various shapes and sizes of E-procurement systems in the market, it has been argued that the basic procurement process is the same across the public sectors and can be addressed with straightforward technology to automate standard processes (NePP, 2005). However, this chapter has more of a conceptual approach to implementation of an innovation and, therefore, does not focus on the precise technical description of these E-procurement tools. The fundamental problem motivating this study is the need to understand the facilitators underlying the implementation of E-procurement initiatives in the public sector.

23.5 Methodology and a Survey of E-Procurement Facilitators

This section examines the literature for a number of E-procurement initiatives to investigate whether a general set of facilitators for E-procurement existed. This literature has been used for preliminary investigation into the CSF approach and for finding barriers and implementation outcomes of E-procurement initiatives for the purpose of this study. Although academic chapters stimulate and provide theoretical understanding, the focus of this study has been to use the practitioner materials (mainly government reports) to capture the practitioners' perceptions of E-procurement practices.

An extensive survey of the available E-procurement literature uncovered assessment and evaluation reports of eight E-procurement initiatives and five specialized research studies on E-procurement that provided some answers to the research question. These 13 reports were located through a Google search of the keywords "facilitators" or "critical/key issues/factors," and "E-procurement" or its equivalent such as "online procurement" or "Internet/Web-based procurement." From this nontraditional literature survey, 11 factors emerged as critical to the successful initiative of E-procurement implementations. These 11 factors were obtained after analysis and grouping of related subfactors and are inclusive of all the subfactors identified in the survey. Table 23.2 presents the process of surveying facilitators of E-procurement.

The publicly available assessment/evaluation reports of the following major E-procurement initiatives in the United Kingdom, the United States, Australia, and the European Union (2000–2003) were reviewed, including the specialized literature on E-procurement (DOF, 2001; CGEC, 2002; ECOM, 2002; WB, 2003):

- Electronic public procurement pilot projects (EPPPP) in the European Union (PLS-Ramboll, 2000)
- General Services Commission (GSC), United States (DOIR, 2001)
- University of California (UOC), United States (KPMG, 2001)
- Enhanced Comm-Pass Initiative (ECI), Commonwealth of Massachusetts, United States (OSD, 2001)
- ePilot Project (EPP), United Kingdom (OGC, 2002)
- Department of Premier and Cabinet (DOPC), Australia (S&A, 2003)
- Electronic Commerce for Procurement (EC4P), Australia (AGV, 2003)
- Government Electronic Marketplace (GEM), Australia (AOT Consulting, 2003)

The facilitators are rated according to the number of citations present in the specialized literature and the assessment/evaluation reports of the initiatives mentioned above.

23.6 Barriers to a Successful E-Procurement Implementation

Although various governments are encouraging public sector agencies to adopt E-procurement, its development and implementation does not appear to have been smooth and the rate of E-procurement implementation success has been less than spectacular. This is supported by Steinberg's (2003, p. 1) claim that "Government E-procurement projects have been notoriously unsuccessful." Furthermore, engaging suppliers in the process—especially smaller organizations—is also proving to be difficult given the level of investment expected in terms of providing catalog information to buyers, and marketplaces using different technologies, platforms, and business languages (OGC, 2002).

Difficulties seem to stem from the tension between buy local policies designed to promote a local economy, and the efficiencies to be achieved through volume purchasing from large suppliers (AGV, 2003). Although a number of public sector agencies are actively pursuing E-procurement, evidence from business press reveals that many of the efforts are not meeting original expectations. In fact, the implementation rate of public procurement systems has been slow and many government agencies tend to overstate the degree to which they are involved in E-procurement (MacManus, 2002). Despite the benefits that can be achieved from a successful E-procurement implementation in the public sector, the business press has reported a number of failures of E-procurement initiatives

Table 23.2 Survey of E-Procurement Facilitators

Facilitators (Number of Citations)	*S&A (2003)*	*AGV (2003)*	*WB (2003)*	*PLS-Ramboll (2000)*	*ECOM (2002)*	*KPMG (2001)*	*OGC (2002)*	*DOF (2001)*	*CGEC (2002)*	*OSD (2001)*	*Buy-IT (2002)*	*AOT (2003)*	*DOIR (2001)*
End-user uptake and training (11)	x	x	x	x	x		x	x	x	x	x	x	
Supplier adoption (10)	x	x	x		x		x	x		x	x	x	x
System integration (9)	x		x	x		x	x		x	x		x	x
Business case/PM (9)		x		x		x	x	x	x	x		x	x
Reengineering the process (8)	x	x	x			x	x		x	x	x		
Security and authentication (8)	x	x	x	x			x	x		x		x	
Top management support (7)	x	x	x				x		x		x	x	
Change management (7)	x	x	x				x	x	x				x
Performance measurement (7)				x			x	x	x	x		x	x
E-procurement implementation strategy (6)	x	x		x	x			x					x
Technical standards (7)	x		x	x		x	x	x				x	

in a number of public sector agencies in the United States, the United Kingdom, and New Zealand in recent years. As observed by Heywood (2002), E-procurement will result in large investments of time and money, without absolute certainty that its full potential will be achieved every time.

These views are supported by a number of cases reported in the business press. The U.S. government's General Services Administration had been criticized following embarrassing revelations that it was unreliable and error-prone (KableNet, 2002), while the British government decided not to extend its pilot E-tendering system across Whitehall (KableNet, 2002). In a similar vein, Bell (2003), Doesburg (2003), and Gifford (2003) report that the New Zealand government's GoProcure E-procurement system has proved more complex to develop than expected, while the U.K. Ministry of Defence had not achieved expected savings three years after its E-procurement service first started running (KableNet, 2003). According to Garson (2004), the state of South Carolina abandoned its E-procurement system in June 2002 and pilot projects were shut down in 2002 in Massachusetts, Indiana, and Michigan. The Virginia state auditor reported only 1.5 percent of the state's business was transacted through its state-of-the-art $14.9 million system (Garson, 2004).

There is, however, a view that the rumors of E-procurement's demise have been greatly exaggerated (Harris, 2002). For example, Davila et al. (2003), using a survey of 168 U.S. public and private sector organizations, indicate that E-procurement technologies will become an important part of supply chain management and that the rate of adoption will accelerate as the adopters share their experiences of success factors and perceptions of low risk. Similarly, Barua et al. (2001) identified E-procurement as the element of E-business most contributory toward the E-business operational excellence of large corporations.

Such success and failure stories imply that there is a need for a much better understanding of facilitators with regards to the E-procurement implementations and use in the public sector. Tonkin (2003, p. 13) provides a succinct summary of this sector's relationship with E-procurement: "The public sector cannot afford to uncritically follow the latest fads and fashions; it can, however, form a strong base of self-knowledge, confidence and with an eye to the future become an innovator in this field."

23.7 E-Procurement Facilitators and Propositions

Because the observations reported in this chapter are limited to evaluation/assessment reports of eight major E-procurement initiatives and five specialized literature on E-procurement, it is necessary to be very cautious in the presentation of results. Hence, the findings of this study will be presented in the form of propositions, rather than hypotheses, to be refined by interviews and confirmed by case studies. The resulting hypotheses will then have to be tested by means of a survey research.

23.7.1 End-User Uptake and Training

As E-procurement includes new technologies and changes in traditional procurement approaches, the need to train staff in procurement practices and the use of E-procurement tools are critical to the success of an E-procurement initiative (WB, 2003). End users can realize the immediate benefits of the E-procurement system once they understand the operational functionalities (CGEC, 2002). This means that training should be given a high priority, alongside the need for public sector agencies to identify the skills required by all those engaged in procurement (ECOM, 2002).

As technology alone does not ensure successful adoption, the success of a public sector E-procurement initiative depends on users and buyers making use of the new process and system. The solution must attract end users to view E-procurement as the preferred means by which to purchase goods and services (KPMG, 2001). The success of the project also depends on communication to the users (Birks et al., 2001). According to the CGEC (2002), the two major obstacles to increasing support among users are their level of technological awareness and acceptance, and their willingness to change long-established internal business processes. As the implementation process develops, periodic user satisfaction surveys may identify the possible need for additional training (OSD, 2001).

Proposition 1: The high level of end-user uptake and training is positively associated with the organization and management implementation perspective of an E-procurement initiative.

23.7.2 Supplier Adoption

E-procurement implementation success is closely related to early supplier involvement. It is important to demonstrate the proposed solution to the suppliers and discuss any necessary changes, issues, and concerns such as various options in developing and maintaining supplier catalogs (Birks et al., 2001). According to the OSD (2001), providing opportunities for suppliers to offer their feedback will allow the public procurement department to monitor areas for improvement and adjust practices accordingly. Because many suppliers may be unwilling to conduct business electronically with public sector agencies because they are unclear about the benefits to be gained, they might see E-procurement as a means by which public sector agencies will simply attempt to force down prices (ECOM, 2002). Suppliers, therefore, should be educated on the E-procurement benefits that can be provided to them through a process of consultation as early as possible in the project. The degree to which the success of an E-procurement initiative can be realized may well be related to the level of E-readiness of suppliers, and appropriate communication with suppliers is therefore important (AOT Consulting, 2003).

Proposition 2: The high level of supplier adoption is positively associated with the organization and management implementation perspectives of an E-procurement initiative.

23.7.3 Compliance with Best Practice for Business Case/Project Management

E-procurement initiatives only deliver the planned benefits if the users and buyers make changes to the way they work, which requires championing the project and senior management sponsorship. Specifically important, but also challenging, is ensuring “buy in” (Birks et al., 2001). Birks et al. (2001) suggest that the business case processes for E-procurement should include identifying drivers, understanding the starting point, benefits, approaches, affordability, risks, and benefit realization. To ensure achievement of the E-procurement objectives, the implementation project should proceed, as far as possible, in alignment with the business case.

Proposition 3: The high level of compliance with best practice/project management is positively associated with the organization and management implementation perspective of an E-procurement initiative.

23.7.4 System Integration

It is important to determine the level of integration required between the E-procurement solution and existing information systems (KPMG, 2001). The CIPFA report reasoned that if integration issues are complex, it is more likely that underlying business processes within an organization should be changed or adapted (ECOM, 2002). It is also critical to link the E-procurement system to the financial management system to facilitate the process of online payment to suppliers (WB, 2003). Purchase transactions carried out through an electronic ordering transaction support system have to be reflected in an agency's financial management systems and communicated to suppliers for fulfillment (DOF, 2001).

Proposition 4: The high degree of system integration is positively associated with the systems and technology implementation perspective of an E-procurement initiative.

23.7.5 Security and Authentication

Because of the sensitivity of the government data and the legal nature of orders and payments, security of data is critical in E-procurement systems. The system must have mechanisms for identifying and authenticating the user who places an order so that the supplier knows it is safe to fulfill the order. In an E-procurement environment, Birks et al. (2001) relate the security requirements at the E-tendering stage to authentication, arguing that E-purchasing systems and processes need protection because they involve a financial transaction and may be vulnerable to fraud. Stenning & Associates (2003) highlight the need for transactions between different systems to be exchanged in secure ways with absolute assurances regarding the identities of the buyers and suppliers. To encourage buyers and suppliers to engage in E-procurement, it is critical that both parties have complete confidence and trust in the underlying security infrastructure.

Proposition 5: The high degree of security and authentication is positively associated with the systems and technology implementation perspective of an E-procurement initiative.

23.7.6 Reengineering the Process

E-procurement should be viewed as an enabling mechanism to make the process of procurement more efficient in terms of cost, time, and achievement of value for money (ECOM, 2002). Where existing procurement practices and procedures may contradict the goals and objectives of the new initiative, the implementation of E-procurement will require the reengineering of existing purchasing processes (KPMG, 2001). Birks et al. (2001) suggest that roles and responsibilities might change substantially with the introduction of a new process, requiring staff to adapt to the new requirements.

According to the Stenning & Associates report (2003), as a significant proportion of the benefits to be gained from implementing E-procurement initiatives are related to the changes made through process reengineering rather than the implementation of the E-procurement initiatives themselves, existing processes for dealing with procurement will have to be revised. Birks et al. (2001) suggest that the process of reengineering should not only address process but also supplier relationships and all the internal groups affected by procurement.

Proposition 6: The high degree of reengineering of the process is positively associated with the practices and processes implementation perspective of an E-procurement initiative.

23.7.7 Performance Measurement

The continuous measurement of the key benefits is regarded as vital to the successful delivery of the business case. Measurement drives behavior and is a key to making the change a success (Birks et al., 2001). Establishing goals and baselines is very important. According to CGEC (2002), a general lack of measurement capability ensures management has only limited tools for assessing organizational progress. It is important to define key performance indicators (KPIs) early in the process to enable successful benefits tracking and distil the business case into measurable KPIs. These KPIs should then be monitored throughout the project.

Proposition 7: The greater level of use of the performance measures is positively associated with the practices and processes implementation perspective of an E-procurement initiative.

23.7.8 Top Management Support

There is little doubt that senior management leadership is critical to the success of an E-procurement implementation (AGV, 2003). The top management team (steering committee) must involve the project manager, any consultants working with the committee, and agency staff to develop an implementation strategy (ECOM, 2002). In this regard, considerable attention and support have to be provided by senior management to ensure that the procurement reform has been well understood in the agency (S&A, 2003). Furthermore, the executive management team is responsible for setting the vision and goals, bringing about collective commitment for change in process and organizational structures, and formulating the policies and strategies necessary to put an E-procurement initiative in place (WB, 2003).

Proposition 8: The high level of top management support is positively associated with the organization and management implementation perspective of an E-procurement initiative.

23.7.9 Change Management Program

Changes required to support business processes are directly related to the speed of adoption of E-procurement, with change management issues seemingly more substantial as stakeholder needs increase (CGEC, 2002). The Office of Government Commerce (OGC) (2002) recommends that increasing change in underlying processes requires more learning and effort on the part of users. Consequently, the OGC suggests more attention should be paid to change management issues, citing three ways to achieve successful change management for E-procurement: consultation, communication, and issue resolution (OGC, 2002). The World Bank report cautions that although change management may be the least expensive aspect of an E-procurement project, a lack of it can be a leading cause of project failure (WB, 2003).

Proposition 9a: The high degree of change management program is positively associated with the organization and management implementation perspective of an E-procurement initiative.

Proposition 9b: The high degree of change management program is positively associated with the practices and processes implementation perspective of an E-procurement initiative.

23.7.10 E-Procurement Implementation Strategy

The creation of documented and executable strategies prior to the deployment of the E-procurement solution is an important CSF. This notion is further supported by the OSD report (2001) findings that as the procurement strategy is intended to provide savings enabled by the technology, E-procurement should be procurement driven as well as technology driven. Therefore, a clearly defined E-procurement strategy not only emphasizes the importance of E-procurement in the public sector but takes into consideration major institutional changes from the procurement process perspective as well as from the organizational perspective (WB, 2003). Another report notes that the E-procurement strategy should be based on the introduction of sound procurement practices while taking into account the differences in requirements of the public and private sectors (DOF, 2001).

Proposition 10a: The greater level execution of E-procurement implementation strategy is positively associated with the organization and management implementation perspective of an E-procurement initiative.

Proposition 10b: The greater level execution of E-procurement implementation strategy is positively associated with the practices and processes implementation perspective of an E-procurement initiative.

23.7.11 Communication Standards

E-procurement requires various buyer–supplier systems to exchange information and electronic documents. This requires common standards. It seems that there is agreement emerging on the adoption of eXtensible Markup Language (XML) as the basis for standards (S&A, 2003). The XML standard defines the content in communication and in the selection of general data formats (KPMG, 2001). In defining E-procurement requirements, Birks et al. (2001) claim a key concern is the standard for formatting electronic catalogs. The World Bank (2003) suggests that developing an E-procurement system in an open environment allows it to link to other systems for interoperability and simplifies upgrading the system. According to the DOF (2001), successful introduction and adoption of E-procurement in the public sector also depend on the ease with which procurement-related data can be exchanged both within the agencies and between their supply bases.

Proposition 11: The high level of communication standards is positively associated with the systems and technology implementation perspective of an E-procurement initiative.

Table 23.3 presents some attributes for each CSF as discussed above. A review of the literature indicates that there is no research directly related to the topic of E-procurement facilitators. Thus, the

Table 23.3 CSF Item Attributes

CSF (Variable)	*Item Attributes*	*Literature Support*
End-user uptake and training	User involvement, user support/ communication, user training	KPMG (2001), OGC (2002), AGV (2003), CGEC (2002), and WB (2003)
Supplier adoption	Supplier E-readiness, supplier adoption strategy and communication plan, supplier education and benefits demonstration, compliance to best practices with content and catalog management	OSD (2001), Birks et al. (2001), S&A (2003), ECOM (2002), and Subramaniam and Shaw (2002)
Business case and project management	Identification of business drivers, business process assessment and requirement, return on investment (ROI), total cost of ownership (TCO), risks identification and management, pilot projects	Birks et al. (2001), AGV (2003), and AOT (2003)
System integration	Information matching, sending and receiving of real-time information to other information systems, electronic commerce with suppliers	DOF (2001), Birks et al. (2001), S&A (2003), and Subramaniam and Shaw (2002)

Table 23.3 (continued) CSF Item Attributes

CSF (Variable)	*Item Attributes*	*Literature Support*
Security and authentication	Infrastructure authentication and authorization, confidentiality and integrity, security requirements	DOF (2001), DOIR (2001), and PLS-Ramboll (2000)
Reengineering the process	Transparency improvement, automated invoice payment and reconciliation, compliance with purchasing procedures and standard	OGC (2002), OSD (2001), WB (2003), and KPMG (2001)
Performance measurement	Goals and targets, KPIs, baseline measurement, progress monitoring	CGEC (2002), DOF (2001), OSD (2001), and AOT (2003)
Top management support	Management sponsor, involvement of the steering committee, investment in organizational change	S&A (2003), AGV (2003), OGC (2002), CGEC (2002), and AOT (2003)
Change management	Identification and management of key stakeholders, E-procurement impact assessment, potential barriers to implementation, organizational resistance	Birks et al. (2001), DOF (2001), OGC (2002), OSD (2001), and WB (2003)
E-procurement implementation strategy	Sound procurement practices, opportunities for aggregation, a consistent approach to procurement, relationships with industry and small businesses	DOF (2001), DOIR 2001, ECOM (2002), and PLS-Ramboll (2000)
Technology standards	Technical standards, content standards, process and procedural standards, compliance with the standards frameworks, interoperability	DOF (2001), S&A (2003), WB (2003), AOT (2003), KPMG (2001), and Koorn et al. (2001)

proposed CSF model will be used as the basis for future research with the ultimate goal of validating the propositions and developing and testing hypotheses from the propositions. The research model (Figure 23.1) is a representation of the CSF model and permits the development of propositions to answer the research question. Based on the parameters defined by the literature review discussed in this chapter, the model presents performance measures for each category of implementation factor.

23.8 E-Procurement Implementation Perspectives and Outcomes

E-procurement solutions are seen as a way to address many public sector procurement requirements. It has become apparent that the more the procurement process is supported by Internet technology, the easier it will become to develop and implement E-procurement, though system

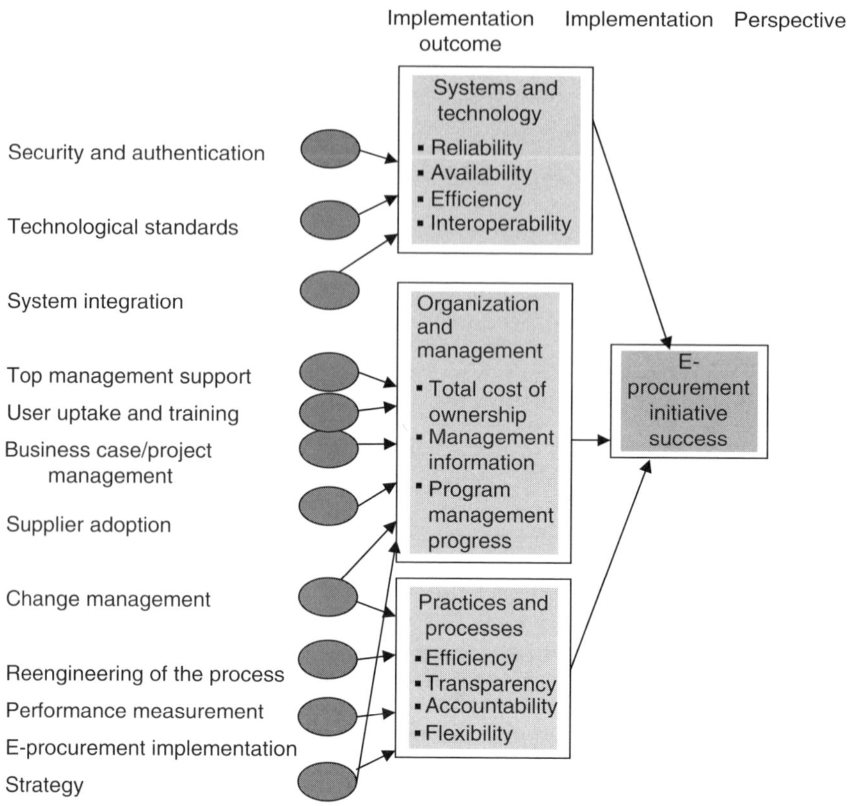

Figure 23.1 A research model of E-procurement CSFs.

security and reliability is essential. The E-procurement infrastructure and procedures can facilitate the achievement of the principles including transparency and accountability requirements of the public offices while enhancing efficiency, effectiveness, and flexibility in the procurement process (DOFA, 2002). E-procurement has the potential to promote operating efficiency in public sector procurement and provide significant cost savings (OCIO, 2000). One of the logical advantages of electronic transaction management is that it frees procurement staff for procurement evaluation and contract management roles. Furthermore, management information can be extracted from the E-procurement system using standard reporting software (OGC, 2002). The transparent management information provided by E-procurement also permits the monitoring of compliance with service level agreements and measurement of many other elements of supplier performance (OSD, 2001).

The implementation of E-procurement initiatives should be seen as an effort to enhance the procurement goals, which normally include quality; timeliness; cost; minimizing business, financial, and technical risks; maximizing competition; and maintaining integrity (Thai, 2001). In a similar vein, CGEC (2002) has identified cost, quality, program management progress measures (on-time, on-budget, and issue management), process performance factors, and return on investment as the most relevant measurements. There remains, however, the challenge of controlling the range of variables required to reap the benefits of E-procurement implementation. It should be remembered that because an E-procurement initiative is expensive, demanding upon staff, and time consuming, it may take several years for public sector agencies to fully reap the strategic and operational benefits of E-procurement.

23.9 Analysis of the Relative Importance of CSFs

Analysis of the CSFs through the use of citation frequency as a measure of their importance revealed that among the eleven facilitators, no one single factor was overly predominant. To further understand the relative importance, the facilitators were split into two categories: human factors and technology factors. Human factors are those issues dependent on human behavior and expertise while technology factors are those issues dependent on construction and deployment technologies. Human factors consist of end-user uptake and training, supplier adoption, business case and project management, and top management support. Technology factors consist of system integration and security and authentication. Change management, E-procurement implementation strategy, process reengineering, performance measurement, and technology standards are factors that involve aspects of both categories.

Although this type of analysis is subjective, the prominence of human factors in the success of E-procurement implementations is apparent. This suggests that where there is a conflict between human and technological issues, the returns on E-procurement initiatives may be higher if more attention is paid to the human issue.

23.10 Conclusions

This chapter surveyed a number of specialized reports on E-procurement initiatives in the U.K., U.S., and Australian public sectors readily available to practitioners and decision makers. The survey was a conceptual model showing a number of unique factors regarded as instrumental in the success of public sector E-procurement implementation. For example, it was found that E-procurement projects have a greater reach and scope than traditional IT development projects. Security and controls, and standards and interfaces emerged as more important requirements than those in other IT projects. Key differences in the approach to the development of E-procurement projects were also noted during the study. Interestingly, the security, legal, and legislative issues did not emerge as facilitators, although factors such as top management support and performance measurement were found to be critical projects.

As the management of E-procurement projects includes the involvement of a significant number of internal and external stakeholders (including buyers, end users, suppliers, service providers, consultants, an individual seller, and sponsors), the importance of stakeholder involvement cannot be underestimated. This conclusion is drawn from the findings of this study that user uptake and training turned out to be the most important factors followed by supplier adoption. These insights are consistent with Subramaniam and Shaw's (2002) view that E-procurement systems are different from traditional IT systems in many ways and there is a need to develop new concepts that help information systems researchers better evaluate E-commerce impacts. It became apparent from the literature survey that public sector E-procurement initiatives must also focus on interoperability, transparency, and accountability issues.

Although the introduction of E-procurement has created a lot of enthusiasm in the press, this study indicates that many public sector agencies are still at an early stage of implementation. Evidence in relation to the implementation of E-procurement initiatives indicates that this transition is turning out to be a major challenge for many public sector agencies at a time when governments worldwide are focusing on E-procurement as part of their E-government agenda. Once the facilitators are selected, it is critical to identify the measures of their success. Given the assertion that the human factors play a more important role than technological factors in the successful implementation of E-procurement initiatives, the findings of this study may assist senior procurement professionals and E-procurement project managers in the public sector to establish a system of progress assessment and decision making with regard to their E-procurement initiatives. As one of the aims of the chapter was to stimulate debate and generate feedback, the model presented is not a prescriptive CSF model. Nevertheless, this study also provides input to new theory development by proposing a "starting point" for future research. A focus on reliable facilitators can help reduce the time required for E-procurement implementation and result in economic benefits for an organization in line with its strategic and operational objectives.

Although the use of in-depth case studies of E-procurement initiatives in the public sector would have suited the research purpose of this study, time and financial restrictions limited the study to multiple case studies by literature survey to identify major cases to develop a set of facilitators. As such, it is essential that the research continues to further validate the observations of this study. In the next phase of this study, semistructured interviews on public sector E-procurement project managers will be carried out to capture the perspectives of interviewees. The results of this enquiry will be used to refine the CSF model and variables relating to each implementation factor and thus develop further hypotheses. The hypotheses for future research will also stem from multiple case studies, which will be tested by means of survey questionnaires distributed to public sector agencies. The surveys will help to evaluate the extent and criticality of the facilitators, the implementation factors, and associated variables. It would be useful to identify the specific performance measures for each CSF in terms of quantifiable indicators.

References

Auditor General Victoria (AGV) 2003. *Electronic Procurement in the Victorian Government*. Melbourne, Australia: Government of Victoria (AGV).

AOT Consulting 2003. *Review of the GEM Purchasing E-Procurement Business System*. Perth, Australia: AOT. Consulting (AOT).

Barua, A., Konana, P., Whinston, A., and Yin, F. 2001. Managing e-business transformation: Opportunities and value assessment. *Sloan Management Review,* 43(1): 36–44.

Bell, S. 2003. Going, Going...Govt e-Procurement Tool Shrinks Further. *Computerworld*. Available at www.computerworld.com. (Retrieved October 20, 2003.)

Birks, C., Bond, S., and Radford, M. 2001. *Guide to e-Procurement in the Public Sector: Cutting through the Hype*. London, U.K.: Office of Government Commerce, HMSO.

Callender, G. 2003. A short history of procurement. In: P.J.A. Nagel (Ed.), *Supply Chain Management, A Procurement Perspective*, Australian Institute of Purchasing and Materials Management Limited.

Callender, G. and Matthews, D. 2003. Professionalism, procurement and the supply chain. In: P.J.A. Nagel (Ed.), *Supply Chain Management, A Procurement Perspective*, Australian Institute of Purchasing and Materials Management Limited.

Callender, G. and Schapper, P. 2003. Public procurement reform in Australia: A federal-state evaluation. International research study of public procurement. In: *Proceedings of International Research Study of Public Procurement*, 10–12 April, Budapest, Hungary, pp. 48–61.

Consortium for Global Electronic Commerce (CGEC) 2002. *Measuring and Improving Value of E-procurement Initiatives*. Madison, WI: University of Wisconsin-Madison, Consortium for Global Electronic Commerce.

Cuthbert, C., Hamzic, D., and Archer, N. 2003. Barriers to SME e-Procurement Solutions in Canada (Working Chapter No. 7). Hamilton, Canada: McMaster eBusiness Research Centre, DeGroote School of Business, McMaster University.

Dai, Q. and Kauffman, R.J. 2001. Business Models for Internet-Based E-Procurement Systems and B2B Electronic Markets: An Exploratory Assessment. Thirty-Fourth Annual Hawaii International Conference on Systems Sciences, January 3–6, Maui, HI.

Davila, A., Gupta, M., and Palmer, R. 2003. Moving procurement systems to the Internet: The adoption and the use of e-procurement technology model. *European Management Journal*, 21(1): 11–23.

Department of Finance (DOF) 2001. *Strategy for the Implementation of e-Procurement in the Irish Public Sector*. Dublin, Ireland: Author.

Department of Finance and Administration (DOFA) 2002. *Commonwealth Procurement Guidelines and Best Practice Guidance*. Canberra, Australia: Author.

Department of Information Resources (DOIR) 2001. *Assessment of the General Services Commission's Electronic Procurement Project*. Austin, TX: Author.

Doesburg, A. 2003. Goodbye GoProcure. Available at http://computerworld.co.nz. (Retrieved October 1, 2003.)

ECOM Group 2002. *e-Procurement in the UK Public Sector: A Guide to Developments and Best Practices* (A CIPFA e-Government Forum Report). London, U.K.: Author.

Garson, G.D. 2004. *The Promise of Digital Government*. Hershey, PA: Idea Group Inc.

Gifford, A. 2003. *GoProcure Project Shrinking*. Available at www.nzherald.co.nz. (Retrieved October 10, 2003.)

Harland, C., Callender, G., Knight, L., Telgen, J., Thai, K., and Walker, H. 2005. Public Procurement as a Lever of Government Reform: International Research Evidence. International Research Study of Public Procurement (IRSPP).

Harris, S. 2002. The e-Buy dilemma. *Governing*. Available at www.governing.com/3eprocure.htm. (Retrieved October 1, 2003.)

Heywood, J.B. 2002. *e-Procurement: Managing Successful e-Procurement Implementation*. Harlow, NJ: Financial Times—Prentice Hall.

KableNet 2002. US Suffers e-Procurement Setback. Available at www.kablenet.com. (Retrieved October 1, 2003.)

KableNet 2003. Absent without e-Savings. Available at www.kablenet.com. (Retrieved October 1, 2003.)

Koorn, R., Smith, D., and Mueller, C. 2001. *e-Procurement and Online Marketplaces*. Amsterdam, The Netherlands: Compact.

KPMG 2001. *University of California Office of the President System-Wide E-Procurement Assessment and Strategy Recommendation*. Berkeley, CA: KPMG Consulting.

MacManus, S.A. 2002. Understanding the incremental nature of e-procurement implementation at the state and local levels. *Journal of Public Procurement*, 2(1): 5–28.

Narasimhan, R. and Carter, J.R. 1998. Linking business unit and material sourcing strategies, *Journal of Business Logistics*, 19(2): 155–171.

Office of the Chief Information Officer (OCIO) 2000. *E-Procurement: Working Group Report of Findings*. Miami, FL: Miami-Dade County.

Office of Government Commerce (OGC) 2002. *A Guide to E-Procurement for the Public Sector, Office of Government Commerce*, London. Available at www.ogc.gov.uk. (OGC). (Retrieved October 1, 2003.)

Operational Services Division (OSD) 2001. *Critical Success Factors and Metrics: Enhanced Comm-Pass Initiative*. Boston, MA: Commonwealth of Massachusetts.

Rasheed, H.S. 2004. Capital access barriers to public procurement performance: The moderating effects of ethnicity, gender and education. *Journal of Developmental Entrepreneurship*, 9(2): 22–43.

PLS-Ramboll 2000. *Analysis of Electronic Public Procurement Pilot Projects in the European Union*. Available at http://simap.eu.int/EN/pub/src/main4.htm. (Retrieved October 1, 2003.)

Stenning & Associates Pty Ltd (S&A) 2003. *Final Report: Evaluation and Review of the E-Procurement Pilot Project*, Version 1.2, Hobart, Australia.

Steinberg, R. 2003. *Strategies for Successful Government E-Procurement*. Available at http://www4.gartner.com/research/spotlight/asset_55997_895.jsp. (Retrieved October 5, 2003.)

Subramaniam, C. and Shaw, M. 2002. A study of the value of B2B e-commerce: The case of web-based procurement. *International Journal of Electronic Commerce*, 6(6): 19–40.

Tether, I. 1977. *Government Procurement and Operations*. Cambridge, MA: Ballinger Publishing Company.

Thai, K.V. 2001. Public procurement re-examined. *Journal of Public Procurement*, 1(1): 9–50.

Thai, K. and Grimm, R. 2000. Government procurement: Past and current developments. *Journal of Public Budgeting, Accounting and Financial Management*, 12(2): 231–247.

Tonkin, C. 2003, November 18. *e-Procurement in the Public Sector: Story, Myth and Legend*. Available at http://www.policyinstitute.tcd.ie/working_chapters/PIWPO7%20-%20Tonkin.pdf. (Retrieved January 5, 2004.)

Vaidya, K. 2007. *Electronic Procurement in the Australian Public Sector: The Organizational Assimilation Process and its Impact on Public Procurement Performance*. Unpublished PhD thesis submitted to the University of New England, New South Wales, Australia.

Vaidya, K., Yu, P., Soar, J., and Turner, T. 2003. Measuring the performance of e-procurement implementations in the Australian public sector. In: N. Cerpa and P. Bro (Eds.), *Building Society through e-Commerce: e-Government, e-Business and e-Learning*, Talca, Chile: University of Talca, pp. 47–61.

Wittig, W.A. 2003. *Public Procurement and the Development Agenda*. Geneva, Switzerland: International Trade Centre.

World Bank (WB) 2003. *Electronic Government Procurement (e-GP): World Bank Draft Strategy*. Washington, DC: Author.

Chapter 24

Evaluation of Public E-Procurement Services Accessibility: A Multicriteria Approach

Giuseppe Bruno, Emilio Esposito, and Michele Mastroianni

CONTENTS

24.1 Introduction

A wide range of literature has shown how information and communications technology (ICT) is driving profound social, economic, and administrative changes that are currently under way (Kautz and Pries-Heje, 1996; OECD, 1997; Lengrand and Chatrie, 1999). Because of its all-pervading character, ICT is deeply influencing and transforming every sector of the society (Burkhardt and Brass, 1990; Adams et al., 1992; Davis, 1993; Igbaria, 1993; Keil et al., 1995; Taylor and Todd, 1995; Agarwal and Prasad, 1997; Commission of the European Communities, 2000). In universities and research centers, small and medium firms, national and local government bodies, hospitals, schools, and families, ICT is spreading at a pace unprecedented in the history of technology (Halal, 1993; Agarwal et al., 1998; Baskerville and Pries-Heje, 1998; Hauptman et al., 1998; Esposito and Mastroianni, 2002).

In this context, the public sector appears to be more and more involved in the realization of user (citizen)-orientated information systems (Commission of the European Communities, 2000; EITO, 2002). Moreover, many industrial countries are developing relevant initiatives to improve public E-procurement services. At the beginning of 2000, the federal government of the United States launched an online reverse tender pilot project for the navy, army, air force, and U.S. postal service (O'Hara, 2000). Thanks to this activity, the navy saved about $38.8 million during the first step of the project (Hardy, 2003). Nowadays, many U.S. federal government agencies, such as the U.S. Department of State, currently use E-procurement systems (U.S. Department of State, 2004).

In general, three main factors are pushing the public sector to ICT:

- Stimulating organizational change
- Improving efficiency, effectiveness, and cost reduction (E-administration)
- Improving the relationship between citizens and the public sector (E-democracy), in terms of transparency of the administrative action and of participation (Bertelsmann Foundation, 2002)

In these circumstances, the problem of accessibility of ICT service Web sites is becoming crucial. The Okinawa Charter points out that accessibility to public services through Web sites must also be possible for users who suffer from any type of disability, be it physical or cultural. A cultural disadvantage is certainly the case of a low level of education, which can be tackled by publishing documents written in a simple and direct language instead of using bureaucratic terminology that is often incomprehensible. Another category of cultural disability is insufficient familiarity with the tools of information technology; for this reason Web sites have to be designed in such a way that noncomputer science users can easily access them.

In this chapter, the focus is on the problem of accessibility of public E-procurement services. In particular, the chapter shows some results of multidisciplinary research whose aim is to identify and test a support model for the improvement of accessibility of E-procurement systems. The specific goal is to identify a methodology to evaluate E-procurement service accessibility considering both the Web site performances (technical aspect) and user perceptions (perceptive aspect). The output of the model should provide useful suggestions for Web site designers to improve the accessibility of services.

This chapter is organized in eight parts. In Section 24.2, the conceptual framework is discussed and in Section 24.3, the methodology is illustrated. Section 24.4 focuses on the indexes introduced for the measurement of the Web sites' accessibility (Web site analysis). Section 24.5 is dedicated to the user analysis. In Section 24.6, the model to evaluate the accessibility of public E-procurement services is illustrated. In Section 24.7, five italian public E-procurement services are evaluated. Finally, in Section 24.8, the discussion and some indications on possible further developments of research are illustrated.

24.2 Conceptual Framework

The definition of E-procurement in literature is not unequivocal. Van Weele (1994) defines E-procurement as the use of Internet technology in the process of providing goods and services. In a review of methods supporting supplier selection, de Boer et al. (2002) analyzes E-procurement systems considering their main function. Bruno et al. (2004) classify E-procurement systems focusing on three variables: their main function, the impact on costs, and organizational aspects (Table 24.1).

In the process of evaluation of E-procurement systems, it is necessary to consider that the system is essentially based on a Web site. Consequently, it is useful to look at a preliminary synthetic analysis of methodologies and variables currently used in the evaluation of Web sites.

In the 1990s, various studies and research were developed to analyze Web sites (first approach). Most studies focus on aspects concerning the evaluation of Web site quality and generally use indicators that are largely estimated in a subjective manner (Nielsen, 1993; RUR, 2001). Moreover, almost all these studies evaluate Web site quality using either the criterion of accessibility or usability.

Table 24.1 Classification of E-Procurement Systems

Type of E-Procurement System	*Main Function of the System*	*Impact on Direct/ Indirect Costs of Purchase*	*Impact on the Organizational Aspects*
E-MRO	Acquisition of services of maintenance, repairs, and operations	Low/elevated	Extended to the entire organization
Web-based ERP	Integration of the process of purchase in the ERP of the agency	Low/limited to the operative phase	Extended to the entire organization
E-sourcing	Singling out of the providers through Internet technologies	Low/limited to the tactical phase	Limited to the purchasing department
E-tendering	Sending requests for information and prices to providers and the collection of offers via Internet	Low/limited to the tactical phase	Limited to the purchasing department
E-reverse auctioning	Online auctions	Relevant/low	Limited to the purchasing department
E-informing	Gathering or distribution of information relative to the process of provisioning through Internet	Low/limited to the operative phase	Limited to the purchasing department

Source: From Bruno, G., Esposito, E., Mastroianni, M., and Vellutino, D. in Proceedings IPSERA Conference, April 4–7, Catania, Italy, 2004. With permission.

The most important reference for the definition of accessibility is to be found in the WAI (Web Accessibility Initiative) guidelines, proposed by the W3C consortium, which represent the main platform of the technical rules for improving accessibility (The W3C Consortium, 1999). They regulate the accessibility of the Web site through a series of recommendations, authoring tools, and user agents. A checklist document is connected to each recommendation, which indicates priorities for setting up accessible sites. The W3C checklist considers 14 items that concern, above all, the writing of the code to favor the accessibility of users with physical disabilities (color-blind and visually impaired people). The checklist only generically considers the comprehensibility of the written message that represents a relevant and highlighted aspect of the Okinawa agreement (G8 Member States, 2000). The WAI guidelines have also been taken up by many nations, including the United Kingdom (guidelines for U.K. government Web sites) and Italy. For Italy, the authority represents the references for computer science in the public sector's Document No. 3/2001. As far as usability is concerned, Guidelines 924-11 for the ISO standardization define usability as the effectiveness, efficiency, and satisfaction with which specified users can reach specific aims in particular environments.

In the mid-1990s, Ratner et al. (1996) demonstrated that accessibility and usability are weakly correlated to each other; consequently, it is not possible to evaluate a Web site by measuring only one of these aspects.

At the end of 1990s, models that take into consideration a wide range of variables including accessibility, usability, and other parameters were proposed (recent approach). Such models, finalized at benchmarking research activities and Web site ranking, introduce a set of variables (mostly qualitative) based on the content, the scope of the Web site, and the type of users (Nielsen, 1994, 2000). The indicators are grouped together in thematic indexes that synthesize complex concepts, such as accessibility, usability, communication, functionality, availability of services, etc. Unfortunately, even if such models are well finalized at benchmarking, they are not equally efficient in individualizing the critical aspects and the type of intervention needed to improve Web site performance.

As far as the first approach is concerned, our hypothesis is in-line with that of Ratner et al. (1996), in that the two concepts of accessibility and usability are complementary and not independent of each other; therefore, it is not possible to separate them. The logical consequence of this hypothesis is that it is not possible to individualize an indicator (or a set of indicators) that is able to measure either accessibility or usability. In line with this consideration, our approach is that evaluation of a public E-procurement Web site should be based on a set of indicators that represent both concepts. For this reason, in the following sections we use the word accessibility to mean both concepts (accessibility and usability). Regarding the second approach, we underline the necessity to use quantitative indexes (instead of qualitative ones) grouped in such a way that it is possible to individualize the critical aspects, the professional skill involved, and the type of intervention needed to improve the Web site performance.

Starting from these considerations, this chapter introduces a quantitative methodology to evaluate the accessibility of public E-procurement Web sites. The proposed methodology allows the individualization of professional skills that could result in improved accessibility.

24.3 Methodology

Even if the factors affecting the accessibility of E-procurement Web sites in the public sector are various and different, they can be grouped according to the following aspects (G8 Member States, 2000; Nielsen, 2000):

- Information and services must be accessible to users with every kind of disability, social and cultural.
- Navigation in the system should be the simplest and most comfortable possible, in such a way that users are stimulated to use it.
- The public manager should be able to coordinate and evaluate the work of all the various professionals and consultants involved in the construction of the Web site (e.g., the Webmaster, graphic designers, communicators, system administrators, etc.)

On the basis of these factors, we assume that the main objective of an E-procurement service is to allow access to the widest number of users possible. From this point of view, it is crucial to analyze the problem of evaluating the accessibility of E-procurement services considering both the Web site performance (technical aspects) and the user point of view (perceptive aspect) (Mastroianni and Vellutino, 2002; Esposito et al., 2003; Bruno et al., 2004, 2005). For this purpose, we use the well-known analytic hierarchy process (AHP) methodology (Saaty, 1980, 1994). AHP is a general theory of measurement that depends on the values and judgments of individual and groups. More precisely, judgments are brought together according to a multilevel hierarchic structure to derive priorities. The major advantage of the hierarchical structure is that it allows for a detailed, structured, and systematic decomposition of the overall problem into its fundamental components and interdependencies, with a large degree of flexibility.

AHP has found its widest applications in multicriteria decision making, planning and resource allocation, and many other fields (Byun, 2001; Ngai, 2003; Sarkis and Talluri, 2004). The methodology is articulated into three fundamental steps (Figure 24.1):

1. *Structuring of the problem into a hierarchy*: In general, hierarchies concern the distribution of a property (the goal) among the elements being compared, to judge which one influences or is influenced more. In our study, the goal is to analyze the Web site accessibility and, then, this phase consists of individuating the hierarchy of attributes and indexes to measure Web site technical characteristics (Figure 24.2).
2. *Comparative judgment*: The aim is to measure the relative importance of the elements (attributes, indexes) to the overall goal. The question to ask when comparing two elements is

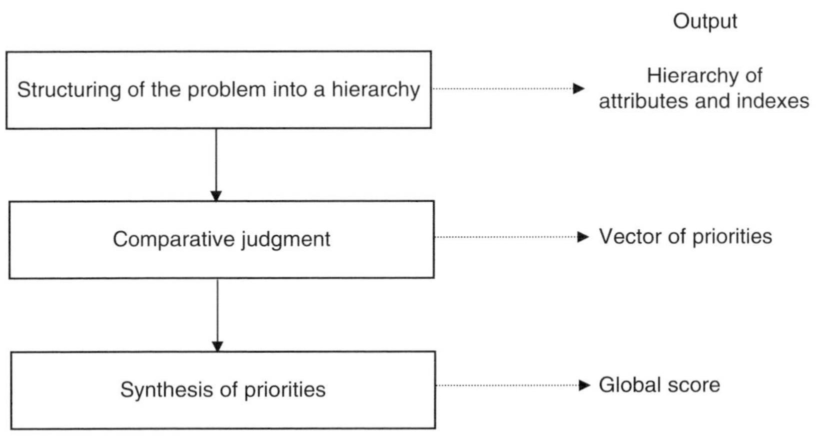

Figure 24.1 Steps of the AHP.

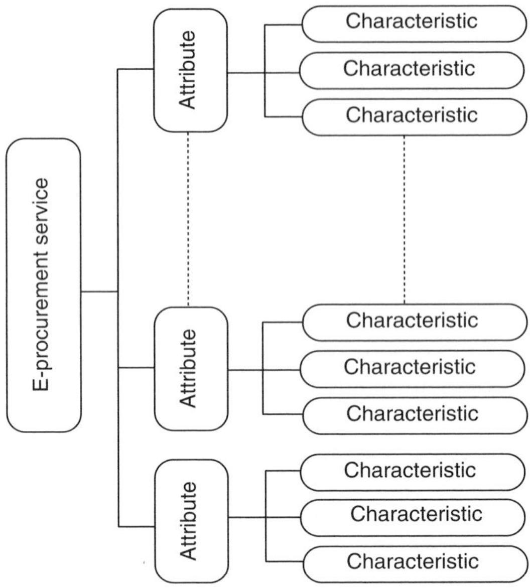

Figure 24.2 E-procurement Web site as a three levels hierarchical system.

"how much important is one of the two elements with respect to the goal of the problem?" In our study, the objective is the user and the aim is to investigate on his perceptions; in practice, the output of this phase is a priority vector associated to the set of elements.

3. *Synthesis of priorities*: The objective of this phase is to derive a total or global ratio scale score for each alternative starting from the measured scores and the calculated priorities of each element. In our study, it represents a model to evaluate the accessibility of public E-procurement services.

In the following, a detailed description of how each phase has been performed in our research is provided.

24.4 Structuring the Problem into a Hierarchy

The analysis of the Web site starts from the consideration that such a Web is a hierarchical system articulated on three levels. The first level represents the E-procurement service that is divided into a set of attributes (second level). Each attribute is defined through a set of characteristics (third level).

More precisely, four attributes have been identified: textual language, visual language, digitalization, and digital communication. Each attribute is associated to a specific skill that is able to modify the characteristics of the related attribute (Table 24.2). In this way, the model, together with the evaluation of each attribute, indicates the skill that can improve accessibility. For instance, low values of indexes relative to the visual language attribute indicate that an improvement in graphic quality is required and that the intervention of a designer or of a graphic expert is needed.

In turn, each attribute has been associated with two or three characteristics. In total, 11 characteristics have been defined: syntax comprehensibility, lexicon comprehensibility, legibility, positioning,

Table 24.2 Attributes and Associated Profession Skills

Attribute	*Associated Skill*
Textual language	Text writer
Visual language	Designer/graphics expert
Digitalization	Computer science professional (system or network)
Digital communication	Web designer

color contrast, connection speed, page download speed, broken links, reachability, navigability, and navigation help (Figure 24.3). The set of characteristics can be measured using quantitative indexes and computed using automatic or semiautomatic tools.

The proposed attributes and characteristics can be enlarged to take into account other factors and aspects affecting the general evaluation of an E-procurement system. For instance, indexes of quality and efficiency of the E-procurement service (such as security, costs, organization and management, etc.) could be also considered.

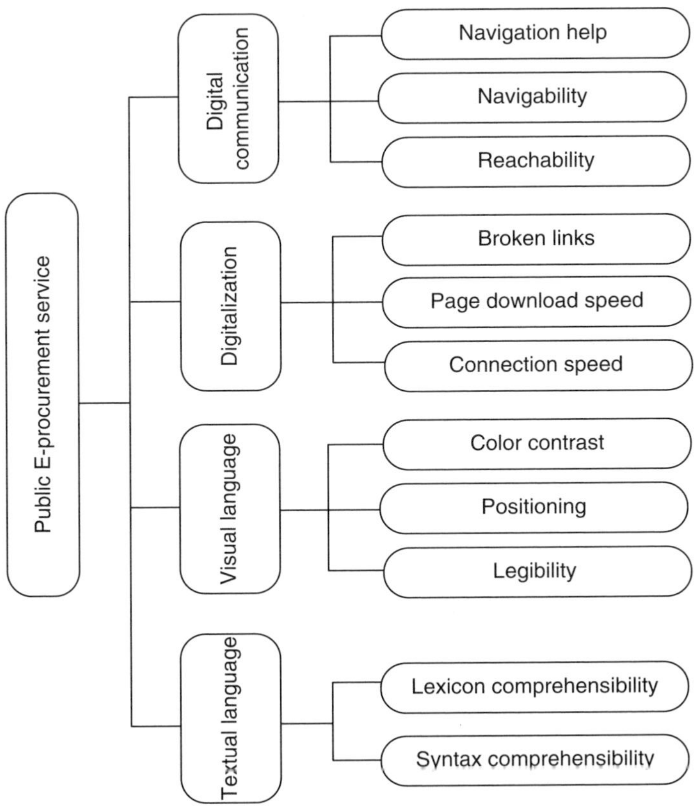

Figure 24.3 Attributes and characteristics for the evaluation of an E-procurement Web site accessibility.

The addition of further attributes does not influence the general architecture or functionality of the proposed hierarchical model. In its current state, the choice of attributes comes from the objective of measuring the accessibility of the Web service.

The set of characteristics can be measured using quantitative indexes and computed using automatic or semiautomatic tools. In this way, the model, together with the evaluation of each attribute, indicates the skill that can improve accessibility. For instance, low values of indexes relative to visual language attribute indicate that an improvement of the graphic quality is required and, then, the intervention of a designer or of a graphic expert is needed.

According to the hierarchical model, the indexes are divided into four groups: indexes relative to the textual language attribute, indexes relative to the visual language attribute, indexes relative to the digitalization attribute, and indexes relative to the digital communication attribute.

For each index, we also calculate an acceptable minimum value. These values are calculated in relation to an average user (for indexes relative to the textual language and visual language attributes) and to ICT generally available on the market (for indexes relative to the digitalization and digital communication attributes).

24.4.1 Textual Language Indexes

The indexes relative to the textual language attribute measure characteristics of the textual content with reference to ease of comprehension. To ensure accessibility to the services offered by the site, the language used should meet the needs of a large number of users, who are different from a social and cultural point of view. For this purpose, two indexes of textual comprehensibility have been used: syntax comprehensibility and lexicon comprehensibility.

Flesch (1951) and Gunning (1973) have demonstrated that a text is more or less comprehensible if some quantitative characteristics, objectively measurable and testable, reflect some criteria drawn from the use of formulas. On these bases, an index (Flesch index) has been proposed to measure the comprehensibility of a document written in American English, with a score system from 0 to 100. Starting from analogous considerations, the so-called Gulpease index has been developed for the Italian language (Lucisano and Piemontese, 1988). Considering a text sample of at least 100 words the syntax comprehensibility index (SCI) or Gulpease index is calculated using the following formula:

$$\mathrm{SCI} = 89 - (\mathrm{Lp}/10) + (3 \times \mathrm{Fr})$$

where

Lp is the number of letters × 100 (the number of words)
Fr is the number of phrases × 100 (the number of words)

The value of such an index may vary from 0 (hardest to read) to 100 (easiest to read). The score may be translated into school grades: a minimum value of 80, for example, indicates that the text proves to be comprehensible for a user with an elementary/junior school level of education, 60 for the Italian scuola media (ages from 10 to 13), and 40 for the high school.

The index of lexicon comprehensibility represents an index of the presence of commonly used words in the text. It is evaluated as the percentage of the presence in the text of words of basic vocabulary, which is defined in the lexicon of frequency in Italian (De Mauro et al., 1993). The lexicon comprehensibility index (LCI), which varies between 0 and 100, is constructed using the following formula:

$$\text{LCI} = (\text{Npl}/\text{Np}) \times 100$$

where
Np is the number of words in the text
Npl is the number of words in the text contained in basic vocabulary

The higher the index, the more comprehensible the text.

If we assume that the average user of a public E-procurement Web site is educated to at least high school level, the minimum acceptable value for both the SCI and the LCI is equal to 40.

24.4.2 Visual Language Indexes

The indexes relative to visual language measure the visible legibility of messages, referring to the screen layout of the site (position of objects on the screen, font and size of characters, and color contrast). Three indexes proposed by Bernard have been used to measure the recurrence of the equal elements in all the pages and the readability of the characters (Bernard, 2001; Bernard et al., 2002).

The index of legibility measures the average value of text legibility, as speed of reading (characters/second) of a sample text in terms of font and size. Bernard (2002) has measured the speed of reading and has set out these values in a table. The values can vary from 0 to 4. For example, the index value is 2.72 characters/second for the schoolbook 12 and 3.97 characters/second for the Tahoma 12. As a minimum value of reference for the index of legibility, a value that corresponds to a reading speed of 50 percent of the maximum (therefore equal to 2.0) is used.

The index of positioning measures the percentage of correct positioning of objects, text, and the functions of interaction in the area of the page on the basis of a standard layout (Bernard, 2002). According to such a layout, an ideal position on the screen is assigned to each object in such a way as to assure a more rapid and simpler access to the system functions. The minimum acceptable value of the index of positioning is 50.0, which corresponds to 50 percent of the objects positioned correctly compared to the standard layout.

The index of color contrast is calculated through numerical representation of the background and foreground color in Web pages. In HTML language, the color is identified using an additional representation called RGB (Red-Green-Blue) with three values, which represent the intensity of each fundamental color (Foley et al., 1990). The index is then calculated as the Euclidean distance between the two colors of background and foreground. Even if such a measurement is not necessarily representative of a great contrast, it has been chosen for the simplicity of the calculation. Alternative indexes could be the distance in the representation CIO XYZ (Cowan and MacIntyre, 1992) or in the system HSV (Foley et al., 1990). The index varies between 0 and 442. In line with WAI W3C recommendations (The W3C Consortium, 2000), the minimum acceptable value is 290.

24.4.3 Digitalization Indexes

The indexes relative to digitalization measure the technical performance of the Web site. Three indexes have also been used in this case. The index of connection speed measures the speed of connection of the site in bytes/seconds; it is calculated as the inverse of the average time of ping, measured by 13 public Italian trace route servers included in the list of www.traceroute.org. Therefore, the index is calculated as follows:

$$\text{Connection speed} = 32 \times 13/\sum_{i=1,13} (\text{Tping}_i)$$

where Tping_i indicates the average time of the ping relative to the trace route i. The minimum value of reference is defined as a user with a V90 56.000 bits/second modem and is therefore equal to 500.

The index of downloading speed measures the speed of page downloading calculated by dividing the average size in bytes by pages for the value of 7.000 (=56.000 bits/second, the maximum theoretical speed obtainable by a modem for domestic use). A special Web analysis program has been used to calculate the average size.

$$\text{Downloading speed} = \text{average size of the pages}/7.000$$

where the average size of a page is measured in bytes. The value 0.20 has been chosen as a minimum reference value and corresponds to a download speed of a page every five seconds.

The index relative to the unconnected links represents the percentage of links that are not connected with respect to the number of total links present in the site. The two values are calculated using a Web site analysis tool.

Given the specific nature of the sites analyzed, the absence of a document can affect whether companies purchase or not and therefore 95.0, which corresponds to a maximum of 5 percent of documents not available, is used as a minimum value.

24.4.4 Digital Communication Indexes

The indexes relative to digital communication measure the quality and level of interaction between users and the service provider. Three indexes have been used for this purpose.

The index of reachability calculates the average position of the site according to three different search engines: two international (Google and Altavista) and one Italian (Virgilio). Using the full name of the service as the search key and analyzing the first 100 results evaluate the position. For coherence with the other indexes (all growing with the goodwill of the service), the complement to 100 of the average position has been used.

$$\text{Reachability} = 100 - (\text{position}_{\text{Google}} + \text{position}_{\text{Altavista}} + \text{position}_{\text{Virgilio}})/3$$

The value 50.0 is used as a minimum value of reference for the index of reachability. This represents the average of the site presence in the first two pages of all the search engines chosen.

According to Bernard (2001, 2002), we propose to evaluate the index of navigability as a percentage of the links present in the first two levels of the structure, with respect to the total. The two values are calculated using a special program of Web analysis of Web sites.

$$\text{Navigability} = 100 \times A/B$$

where

A is the number of links present in the first two levels of the structure
B is the total number of links

The value 50.0 is used as a minimum value of reference for the index of navigability. This indicates that at least 50 percent of the site pages are reachable from the home page by no more than two clicks of the mouse. The index of the presence of help and support for navigation indicates the presence of support tools for site navigation such as internal search engines, online help, site maps, etc. The value 2 is used as a minimum value of reference for this index (for a site to be acceptable it must offer the user at least two different types of navigation support). In Table 24.3, the complete list of the attributes and relative indexes is shown with the indication of the unit of measurement, scale of measurement, and tools necessary for their calculation.

Table 24.3 Attributes and Indexes of Evaluation

Attributes	*Characteristics*	*Unit of Measurement/Scale/Tools*
Textual language	Syntax comprehensibility	Unidimensional value/[0,100]/ computation formula
	Lexicon comprehensibility	Unidimensional value/[0,100]/ dictionary of the basic Italian lexicon
Visual language	Legibility	Characters/seconds/[0,4]/table of character legibility
	Positioning	Unidimensional value/[0,100]/diagram of objects positioning
	Color contrast	Unidimensional/[0,442]/RGB color representation
Digital communication	Connection speed	Bytes/seconds/[0,1 million]/ping command
	Page download speed	Pages/seconds/[0,50]/utility
	Broken links	Unidimensional value/[0,100]/utility
Digitalization	Reachability	Unidimensional/[0,100]/public access search engine
	Navigability	Unidimensional value/[0,100]/utility
	Presence of help and support for navigation	Unidimensional/[0,3]/direct observation

24.5 Comparative Judgment

The core of the AHP is the use of relative comparisons that is elements are compared in pairs through relative measurement scales. The output is a matrix of pairwise comparison, $A = a_{ij}$ where a_{ij} express a relative significance of the element i and j according to the scale illustrated in Table 24.4 (Saaty, 1980). The pairwise comparison approach represents a simple and intuitive way of expressing judgments on the relative importance of the different constituents of the hierarchy.

Table 24.4 Pairwise Comparisons and Scores

Score	*Pairwise Comparison*
1	A_i and A_j equally important
3	A_i slightly more important than A_j
5	A_i strongly more important than A_j
7	A_i very strongly more important than A_j
9	A_i absolutely more important than A_j

Table 24.5 Attributes and Characteristics Weights

Attribute	*Weight*	*Characteristic*	*Weight*
Textual language	0.3266	Syntax comprehensibility	0.32
		Lexicon comprehensibility	0.68
Visual language	0.0863	Legibility	0.25
		Positioning	0.44
		Color contrast	0.31
Digital communication	0.0896	Connection speed	0.38
		Page download speed	0.38
		Broken links	0.25
Digitalization	0.4975	Reachability	0.88
		Navigability	0.1
		Presence of help and support for navigation	0.02

It can be proven mathematically that, given a matrix of pairwise comparison, $A = a_{ij}$, the principal eigenvector provides the only correct way to derive the vector of the priorities *wi*. For the detailed description of the method, which is beyond the scope of this chapter, see Saaty (1980).

In our research, to test and to verify the consistency of the methodology, a first cluster of ten potential users of E-procurement systems was selected. The members of the clusters were chosen on the basis of common characteristics (age, culture, computer science ability, etc.) to assure homogeneity of the cluster. To each member of the cluster, a series of questions were asked to compare the relative importance of one attribute to another attribute according to the scale suggested by Saaty (1980). These pairwise comparisons are summarized in ten pairwise comparison matrices.

The vector of priorities, according to the AHP methodology, was computed as the eigenvector of the pairwise comparison matrix. In this case, as we derived a pairwise comparison matrix for each member of the cluster, we obtained ten different vectors. To aggregate the results and to provide a unique priority vector, a geometric mean of the obtained values was computed (Saaty, 1980).

The optimal dimension and characteristic of the cluster should be better investigated together with the methods to aggregate individual judgments. In Table 24.5, the final values of the weights, which represent the output of this step, are shown.

24.6 Synthesis of Priorities

Once indexes have been measured (first step) and weighted (second step), diverse methodologies can be used to establish a composite or global priority of each alternative. One of the possible techniques consists in the construction of a multi-attribute function *F* of the indexes and of the priorities. In our context, *F* represents a synthetic indicator of the accessibility of the E-procurement service.

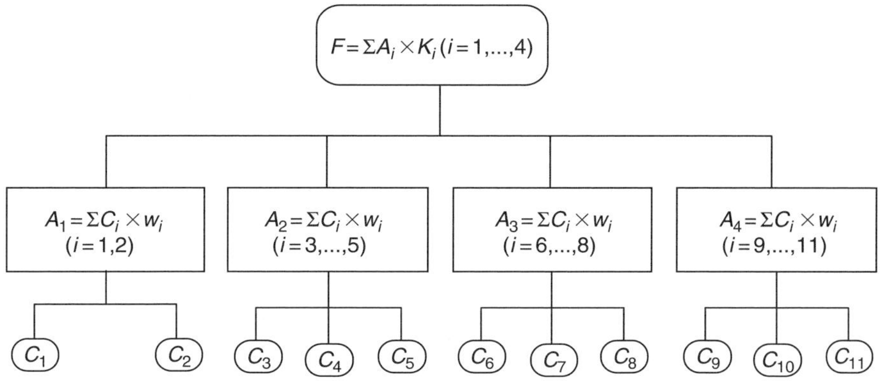

Figure 24.4 Tree of evaluation.

In our study, we used an additive synthesis to build a tree of evaluation as illustrated in Figure 24.4, where

A_i $(i = 1,\ldots,4)$ are the values of the four attributes in the hierarchy model
c_i $(i = 1,\ldots,11)$ are the values of the eleven characteristics presented in the model
w_i $(i = 1,\ldots,11)$ are the values of the eleven priorities calculated with the AHP method
k_i $(i = 1,\ldots,4)$ are the values of the four priorities associated to each attribute

The tree of evaluation is a powerful tool to analyze the accessibility of E-procurement service. In fact, the first level, *F*, allows for a comparison among different service and synthesizes the accessibility of the service. The second level, A_i, individualizes possible attributes to improve and the professional skills involved. The third level indicates what kind of intervention must be realized, that is, the specific characteristic to increase.

24.7 Results

The proposed methodology has been tested to evaluate the accessibility of five Italian public E-procurement services:

1. Ministry of finances' online purchasing (Consip)
2. Piemonte region
3. Province of Florence
4. Lombardia and Liguria regions, which use the applicative supplied by Biztop
5. Trambus (Rome public transport)

The Consip site is conceptually subdivided into two parts. The first, reserved for providers, presents the procedures for purchasing goods and services. The second is reserved for the public sector managers of purchasing departments and offers a catalog of available goods and services. Each user, once registered by the site, can participate in the tender using his username, PIN, and digital signature. The evaluation of the Web site service has been performed only from the point of view of the final user (the public sector managers).

The site of E-procurement of the Piemonte region and province of Florence together with Biztop and Trambus are based on a system of auction online. The firms, previously identified through registration in a specific register, participate by presenting their respective offers through online transactions.

Thanks to the first step of the proposed procedure, the selected eleven characteristics of the five E-procurement Web sites have been measured (technical analysis). Table 24.6 synthesizes the results. The second step analysis has allowed to weight how user perceives the eleven characteristics and the four attributes (perceptive analysis). In Table 24.5, the results of this second step are shown.

Finally, on the base of the technical and perceptive analysis, for each case study, the tree of evaluation has been built. In this way, a hierarchical evaluation of the accessibility of the public E-procurement service is possible. The results of this final step are illustrated in Figures 24.5 through 24.9.

The five trees of evaluation highlight that the Piemonte region E-procurement service is the best; by contrast Biztop is the worst. This latter may improve its service by increasing the digital communication attribute. For this purpose, a Web designer must be involved, with the aim to improve reachability and navigability characteristics. Moreover, the five E-procurement services

Table 24.6 Five Italian E-Procurement Web Site Performances

Indicators	*Consip*	*Piemonte*	*Florence*	*Biztop*	*Trambus*	*Minimum Acceptable Value*
Indexes of textual language						
Syntax comprehensibility	40	49	39	41	55	40.0
Lexicon comprehensibility	82.3	80.9	89.9	87.9	83.8	40.0
Indexes of visual language						
Legibility	2.9	3.6	3.7	2.9	2.9	2.0
Positioning	80	77	66	57	71	50
Color contrast	277	442	369	414	365	290
Indexes of digitalization						
Connection speed	769	1111	1171	205	1026	500
Page downloading speed	0.11	0.65	0.64	0.32	0.78	0.20
Broken links	100.0	95.8	100.0	97.4	98.3	95.0
Indexes of digital communication						
Reachability	63.3	99.3	67.7	19.3	100.0	50.0
Navigability	9.1	81.7	49.0	21.6	17.9	50.0
Help	1	1	1	1	0	1

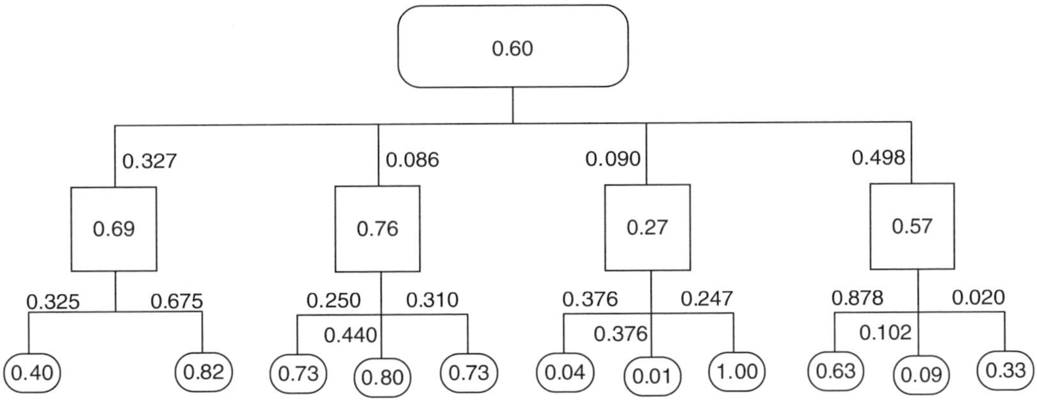

Figure 24.5 Consip.

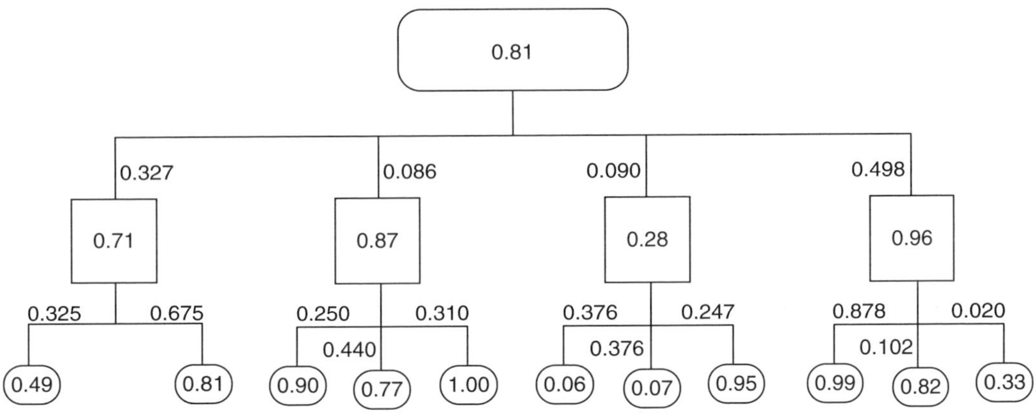

Figure 24.6 Piemonte region.

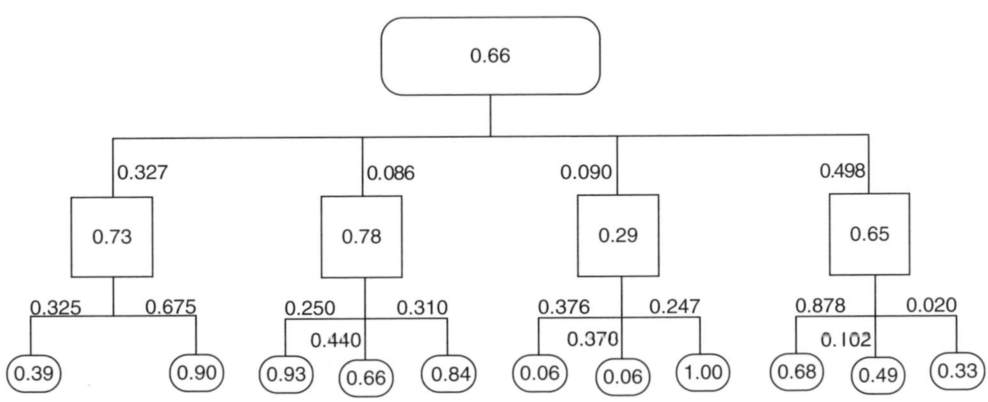

Figure 24.7 Province of Florence.

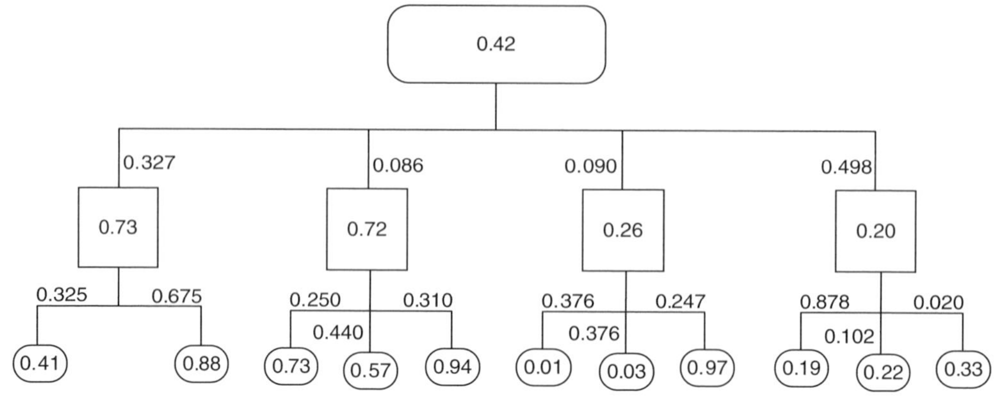

Figure 24.8 Biztop.

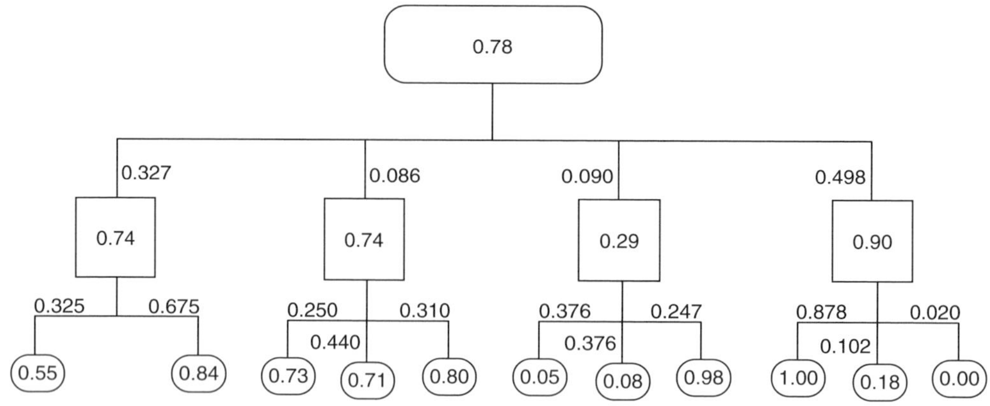

Figure 24.9 Trambus.

present a high value of textual language and visual language attributes, that is, texts are easy to understand and the layout is clear; whereas, they are characterized by a low level of digital communication, that is, the services are very slow to use. This means that a computer science professional may improve the service performance increasing the connection speed and the page download speed. The technical analysis also allows the analysis of the specific Web site.

As far as the Consip site, Table 24.6 shows that four indexes are below the reference minimum (color contrast, page downloading speed, navigability, and navigation help). The SCI is equal to the minimum, while the other indexes have satisfactory or high values. This indicates that the site has a combination of colors that does not make reading easy, the pages are generally very slow to download, and the site has a complicated structure that makes navigation difficult. There is also not enough user support and the text published is not simple to read. On the other hand, the page layout is easy to understand and the connection speed is good. Three different types of action with different levels of priority are needed to improve the accessibility of the site. The highest priority action is to improve the digital communication index. A Web designer (see Table 24.2) needs to be employed to restructure the architecture of the information and the site instruments. A second action could be to improve the visual language and digitalization attributes, using a graphic designer and an ICT technician to tune up the site performance. A third course of action with the lowest priority could be to improve the textual language attribute, by employing an editor to rewrite the texts used to make them easier for users to understand.

The Piemonte region site shows that the navigation help index is lower than the minimum of reference. The other indexes show values that are satisfactory or high. This shows that the site does not have sufficient user support and that the user cannot easily reach a certain number of pages. On the other hand, the page layout is easy to understand and the connection speed is excellent. Also in this case, the hierarchical structure of the model allows us to identify possible ways to improve site accessibility. The higher priority action must be to improve the digital communication index. A Web designer is needed to create user support tools for the site.

Regarding the Biztop site, the reachability, navigability, and navigation help indexes, together with the connection speed index, are lower than the minimum of reference. This means that, although the text used is easily understandable, the site has a complicated structure, is difficult to navigate, does not have enough user support, and that the speed of the Internet connection is scarce. The technical analysis suggests two different actions to improve site accessibility. The first priority action should be to improve the digital communication index. A Web designer (see Table 24.2) should be employed to restructure the architecture of the information and the site instruments. The second priority action should be to improve the digitalization index by employing an ICT technician to improve Internet performance.

Concerning the province of Florence site, Table 24.6 shows that two indexes are near the reference minimum (syntax comprehensibility and navigability). The other indexes have satisfactory or high values. The technical analysis shows that the site is easy to read, in terms of textual and visual comprehensibility, the pages are generally fast to download, and the site has a structure that makes navigation no difficult. Two actions could furthermore improve the site accessibility. A Web designer and a text writer could improve both the navigability and the syntax comprehensibility.

For the Trambus site, the navigability and navigation help indexes are lower than the minimum of reference. The other indexes are satisfactory or high. This indicates that the site has a complicated structure and is difficult to navigate. Moreover, it does not have enough user support. On the other hand, the text used is easily understandable and the speed of the Internet connection is significant. The technical analysis suggests that a Web designer (see Table 24.2) should be involved to restructure the architecture of the information and the site instruments.

Finally, we must underline an element common to the three sites and that is a clear lack of support for users. Users only have one kind of help and there is no internal search engine or site map. This lack has also been found in other Italian E-procurement analyzed using the same model and is in sharp contrast to an approach that focuses strongly on these characteristic found in leading E-commerce sites (e.g., eBay and Amazon).

24.8 Discussion

This chapter has highlighted how one of the primary goals in the design of Web site services is to promote accessibility. In particular way, this aspect involves public services and, hence, public E-procurement Web site systems. For this reason, the introduction of a methodology, to evaluate the accessibility of a given E-procurement service, appears crucial and represents a fundamental aspect in the appraisal of the E-procurement services effectiveness.

In particular, this chapter shows some results of a multidisciplinary research whose aim is to identify and test a support model for the improvement of accessibility of public E-procurement services. The specific goal is to specify a group of attributes and characteristics that can be measured using quantitative indicators, which allow for the comparison of E-procurement service. On the basis of these considerations, a model based on a hierarchical system (the tree of evaluation) articulated on three levels has been introduced. The first level represents the accessibility of the E-procurement service that is divided into a set of attributes (second level). Each attribute is defined through a set of characteristics (third level).

According to this approach, four attributes have been singled out:

1. Textual language refers to the textual content of the Web site with reference to the comprehensibility.
2. Visual language is understood as visual message legibility with reference to the layout of the site (position of objects on the screen, type of character, and color contrast).
3. Digitalization measures the technical performance of the Web site.
4. Digital communication deals with the quality and degree of interaction.

To evaluate these four attributes, eleven characteristics have been introduced: syntax comprehensibility, lexicon comprehensibility, legibility, positioning, color contrast, connection speed, page download speed, broken links, reachability, navigability, and navigation help.

To build the tree of evaluation, a three steps procedure has been proposed:

1. The Web site characteristics have been measured. For this purpose, a set of indicators measuring Web site technical characteristics have been introduced.
2. Thanks to a structured questionnaire, users have been interviewed and priorities measured.
3. The tree of evaluation has been built on the base of measured Web site characteristics (first step) and users priorities (second step).

The tree of evaluation represents a powerful tool to improve the accessibility of E-procurement services. The first level allows for a comparison among different service and synthesizes the accessibility of the service. The second level individualizes possible attributes to improve and the professional skills involved. The third level indicates what kind of intervention must be realized.

The proposed approach has been used, as part of the process of exemplification, to evaluate and compare the characteristics of five Italian public E-procurement services. The experimental results have highlighted the diverse peculiarity of the five analyzed services.

Finally, it should be stressed that accessibility could be considered a preliminary aspect for the evaluation of the effectiveness of a public E-procurement service. For this reason, the proposed approach should represent a first step in the building process of a more complex model for the evaluation of the global effectiveness of a public E-procurement service.

References

Adams, D., Nelson, R.R., and Todd, P. 1992. Perceived usefulness, ease of use, and usage of information technology: A replication. *MIS Quarterly*, 16(2): 227–248.

Agarwal, R. and Prasad, J. 1997. The role of innovation characteristics and perceived voluntariness in the acceptance of information technology. *Decision Science*, 28(3): 557–582.

Agarwal, R., Ahuja, M., Carter, P.E., and Gans, M. 1998. Early and late adopters of IT innovations: Extensions to innovation diffusion theory. Unpublished paper.

Baskerville, R. and Pries-Heje, J. 1998. Information technology diffusion: Building positive barriers. *European Journal of Information Systems*, 7: 17–28.

Bernard, M., Lida, B., Riley, S., Hackler, T., and Janzen, K. 2002. A comparison of popular online fonts: Which size and type is best? *Usability News*, 4(2). Available at http://psychology.wichita.edu/surl/usabilitynews/41/onlinetext.htm.

Bernard, M.L. 2001. Developing schemas for the location of common web objects. *Usability News*, 4(1). Available at http://psychology.wichita.edu/surl/usabilitynews/3W/Web_object.

Bernard, M.L. 2002. Examining user expectations for the location of common e-commerce web objects. *Usability News*, 4(1). Available at http://psychology.wichita.edu/surl/usabilitynews/41/web_object-ecom.htm.

Bertelsmann Foundation. 2002. *E-Government—Connecting Efficient Administration and Responsive Democracy*. Available at www.begix.de.

Bruno, G., Esposito, E., Mastroianni, M., and Vellutino, D. 2004. A Multi-Criteria Approach to Evaluate E-Procurement Web Sites. In Proceedings IPSERA Conference, April 4–7, Catania, Italy.

Bruno, G., Esposito, E., Mastroianni, M., and Vellutino, D. 2005. Analysis of public e-procurement web site accessibility. *Journal of Public Procurement*, 5(3): 344–366.

Burkhardt, M.E. and Brass, D.J. 1990. Changing patterns or patterns of change: The effects of change in technology on social network structure and power. *Administrative Science Quarterly*, 35: 104–127.

Byun, D.H. 2001. The AHP approach for selecting an automobile purchase model. *Information & Management*, 38: 289–297.

Commission of the European Communities. 2000. *eEurope*. Available at http://europa.eu.int/ information_society/eeurope/2002/action_plan/index_en.htm.

Cowan, W.B. and MacIntyre, B. 1992. A practical approach to calculating luminance contrast on a CRT. *ACM Transactions on Graphics*, 11(4): 366–347.

Davis, F.D. 1993. User acceptance of information technology: System characteristics, user perceptions and behavioral impacts. *International Journal of Man–Machine Studies*, 38: 475–487.

de Boer, L., Harink, J., and Heijboer, G. 2002. A conceptual model for assessing the impact of electronic procurement. *European Journal of Purchasing & Supply Management*, 8: 25–33.

De Mauro, T., Mancini, F., Vedovelli, M., and Voghera, M. 1993. *Lessico diFfrequenza Dell'Italiano Parlato*. Milan, Italy: ETASLIBRI.

EITO. 2002. *European Information Technology Observer 2002*. Frankfurt, Germany: Millennium Edition.

Esposito, E. and Mastroianni, M. 2002. Information technology and personal computers: The relational life cycle. *Technovation*, 22(1): 41–50.

Esposito, E., Mastroianni, M., and Vellutino, D. 2003. Evaluation of E-Marketplaces: A Model Proposed for Systems Operating in and for the Public Sector. In Proceedings IPSERA Conference, April 14–16, Budapest, Hungary.

Flesch, R. 1951. *How to Test Readability*. New York: Harper & Row.

Foley, J.D., van Dam, A., Feiner, S.K., and Hughes, J.F. 1990. *Computer Graphics: Principles and Practice*, 2nd ed.. New York: Addison-Wesley Publishing Company.

G8 Member States. 2000. Okinawa Document on the International Information Society. Paper Presented at the G8 World-Wide Summit of Kyushu-Okinawa, July 23, Okinawa, Japan.

Gunning, R. 1973. *The Technique of Clear Writing*. New York: McGraw-Hill.

Halal, W.E. 1993. The information technology revolution. Computer hardware, software, and services into the 21st century. *Technological Forecasting and Social Change*, 44(1): 69–86.

Hardy, M. 2003. Reverse auctions save navy millions. *Federal Computer Week*. Available at http://fcw.com/fcw/articles/2003/0428/pol-auctions-04-28-03.asp.

Hauptman, O., Tomczyk, M.S., and Kiggundu, M. 1998. The emerging role of telecommunication: Extrapolation of novel applications around the word. *Technological Forecasting and Social Change*, 57(1): 1–6.

Igbaria, M. 1993. User acceptance of microcomputer technology: An empirical test. *Omega*, 1(21): 73–90.

Kautz, K. and Pries-Heje, J. (Eds.). 1996. *Diffusion and Adoption of Information Technology*. London, United Kingdom: Chapman and Hall.
Keil, M., Beranek, P.M., and Konsynski, B.R. 1995. Usefulness and ease of use: Field study evidence regarding task consideration. *Decision Support System*, 13: 75–91.
Lengrand, L. and Chatrie, I. 1999. *Business Network and the Knowledge-Driven Economy*. Luxemburg: European Community.
Lucisano, P. and Piemontese, M.E. 1988. Gulpease: Una formula per la predizione delle difficoltà dei testi nella lingua italiana. *Scuola e Città*, 49(3): 110–124.
Mastroianni, M. and Vellutino, D. 2002. DA.MA: A Model for Automatic Evaluation of Public Sector Web Sites. Paper presented at the 2nd European Conference on E-Government, October 1–2, St Catherine's College, Oxford, United Kingdom.
Ngai, E.W.T. 2003. Selection of web sites for online advertising using the AHP. *Information & Management*, 40: 233–242.
Nielsen, J. 1993. *Usability Engineering*. Boston, MA: Academic Press.
Nielsen, J. 1994. *Usability Inspection Methods*. New York: John Wiley & Sons.
Nielsen, J. 2000. *Designing Web Usability*. New York: MacMillan Computer Publishing.
O'Hara, C. 2000. Feds buy in to reverse auction. *Federal Computer Week*, August 14. Available at http://www.fcw.com/fcw/articles/2000/0814/pol-reverse-08-14-00.asp.
Organisation for Economic Cooperation and Development (OECD). 1997. *Information Technology Outlook 1997*. Paris, France: Author.
Ratner, J., Grose, E.M., and Forsythe, C. 1996. Characterisation of and assessment of HTML style guide. *Conference on Human Factors in Computer Systems*, 2: 115–116.
RUR. 2001. *Le Città Digitali in Italia—Rapporto 1999–2000*. Milano, Italy: Franco Angeli.
Saaty, T.L. 1980. *The Analytic Hierarchy Process*. Mc-Graw-Hill, New York.
Saaty, T.L. 1994. Fundamentals of Decision Making in Economic, Political, Social and Technological Environment with the Analytic Hierarchy Process. RWS Publications, Pittsburgh, PA.
Sarkis, J. and Talluri, S. 2004. Evaluating and selecting e-commerce software and communication systems for a supply chain. *European Journal of Operational Research*, 159(2): 318–329.
Taylor, S. and Todd, P. 1995. Understanding information technology usage: A test of competing models. *Information Systems Research*, 6(2): 144–259.
The W3C Consortium. 1999. *Web Content Accessibility Guidelines 1.0. W3C Recommendation*. Available at http://www.w3.org/TR/1999/WAI-WEBCONTENT-19990505/.
The W3C Consortium. 2000. *Techniques for Accessibility Evaluation and Repair Tools*, W3C Working Draft. Available at http://www.w3.org/TR/AERT.
U.S. Department of State. 2004. *Electronic Commerce at the State Department*. Available at http://www.statebuy.state. gov/eleccom.htm.
Van Weele, A. 1994. *Purchasing Management: Analysis, Planning and Practice*. London, United Kingdom: Chapman & Hall.

Chapter 25

World Bank E-Procurement for the Selection of Consultants: Challenges and Lessons Learned

Knut Leipold, Jason Klemow, Francine Holloway, and Kishor Vaidya

CONTENTS

25.1 Introduction

The World Bank Group (World Bank) is transforming its former, highly manual process of selecting consulting services into a robust E-procurement solution as part of its procurement simplification and modernization agenda. The World Bank engages consultants and service providers for technical or managerial advisory services in all sectors from socioeconomic and environmental projects to reforms of state and financial sectors, privatization, information technology, and infrastructure. To that end, the World Bank needs to manage the selection of providers and the resulting contracts with thousands of businesses throughout the world. To ease this process and improve efficiency, the World Bank has implemented a new electronic procurement solution for the selection of consultants, with the goals of fostering consistency of practice worldwide, increasing transparency and competition, and minimizing processing time and effort.

In this chapter, electronic procurement (E-procurement) is conceptualized as a subset of E-commerce. Although E-commerce is simply a transaction conducted electronically, E-procurement is the automation of many procurement processes via electronic systems, especially the Internet. The World Bank definition of E-procurement is broad in that it accommodates the "use of information and communication technology (especially the Internet) by governments in conducting their procurement relationships with suppliers for the acquisition of goods, works, and consultancy services required by the public sector" (World Bank, 2003). However, the focus of this chapter is on the acquisition of consultancy services rather than the acquisition of goods and works.

This chapter explores the relevant issues surrounding the implementation of an E-procurement solution for the selection of consultants. Following the overview and background of selection of consultants, the chapter presents a case study (project) and discusses the system functionalities and benefits of the solution. Using critical success factors (CSFs) as identified by Vaidya et al. (2004), the authors explain the challenges encountered by the World Bank during the implementation of the solution, and suggest a research model for future research in this area.

25.2 Overview and Background

25.2.1 Philosophy behind "Selection of Consultants"

The term consultants includes a wide variety of private and public entities, including consulting firms, engineering firms, construction managers, management firms, procurement agents, inspection agents, auditors, United Nations (UN) agencies, and other multinational organizations, investment and merchant banks, universities, research institutions, government agencies, nongovernmental organizations (NGOs), and individuals (World Bank, 2004). These consultants help in a wide range of activities—such as policy advice; institutional reforms; management; engineering services; construction supervision; financial services; procurement services; social and environmental studies; and identification, preparation, and implementation of projects to complement borrowers' capabilities in these areas.

Although the specific rules and procedures to be followed for employing consultants depend on the circumstances of the particular case, five main considerations guide the bank's policy on the selection process (World Bank, 2004):

- Need for high-quality services
- Need for economy and efficiency
- Need to give all qualified consultants an opportunity to compete in providing the services financed by the bank
- Need for transparency in the selection process
- World Bank's interest in encouraging the development and use of national consultants in its developing member countries

25.2.2 Methods of Selection of Consultants

The method of selection should seek to develop mutual confidence and trust. Depending upon the various situations, different methods of selection of consultants have been suggested (FIDIC, 2003; World Bank, 2004):

- Quality and cost-based selection (QCBS): This method is based on the quality of the proposals and the cost of the services to be provided, and is appropriate when the scope of work of the assignment can be precisely defined and where the staff time as well as the other inputs and costs required of the consultants can be estimated with reasonable precision. QCBS is appropriate for assignments such as feasibility studies and designs where the nature of the investment is clear and well defined, known technical solutions are being considered, and the evaluation of the impacts from the project is not uncertain or too difficult to estimate.
- Quality-based selection (QBS): This method can be suitable for complex or highly specialized assignments for which it is difficult to define precise terms of reference and the required

input from the consultants. The fees paid to a consultant are invariably a small fraction of the total project life-cycle cost and yet the consultant's work is key to project success. For these reasons, it has been recommended that the preferred selection method for consulting services be the QBS method.

- Selection under a fixed budget (SFB): This method is appropriate only when the assignment is simple and can be precisely defined and when the budget is fixed.
- Least cost selection (LCS): This method is only appropriate for selecting consultants for assignments of a standard or routine nature.
- Selection based on the consultants' qualifications (CQS): This method may be used for small assignments for which the need for preparing and evaluating competitive proposals is not justified.
- Single-source selection (SSS): This method does not provide the benefits of competition in regard to quality and cost, lacks transparency in selection, and could encourage unacceptable practices. Therefore, SSS should be used only in exceptional cases.

However, QCBS is the preferred policy method as it uses a competitive process among short-listed firms that takes into account the quality of the proposal and the cost of the services in the selection of the successful firm (World Bank, 2004). However, in practice, it is not the most frequently used method. The World Bank's E-procurement for the selection of consultants solution supports all of the selection methods, plus the ability to select individual consultants, not associated with firms.

25.2.3 Complexity of Consultants Selection

Selecting the project consultant is one of the most important decisions an owner or client makes in the life of the project. The success of any project often depends on obtaining the most able, experienced, and dependable expertise available at an appropriate cost. The impact of selecting the consultants on the overall success of the project should never be underestimated. A consultant, be it an organization or an individual, can make substantial contributions to sustainable development, by undertaking work that is performed less effectively by government entities, and by increasing the industry's maturity and effectiveness (FIDIC, 2003). The best project results are achieved when there is a true professional relationship of trust between the client and the consultant who is expected to make sound, objective decisions.

However, selection of proper consultant is not an easy process. Corcoran and McLean (1998) argue that selection of consultants requires the purchaser to assess a supplier's ability to deliver consultancy, which is an intangible product. Furthermore, the consultancy cannot be realistically tested before purchase and the level of associated complexity becomes obvious because of the buyer's limited experience with purchasing such a service (Corcoran and McLean, 1998). The main problem in purchasing consultancy services appears to relate to the purchaser's difficulty in judging what is being offered (Lunsford and Fussell, 1993). Besides these problems, the multifaceted nature of the consultancy services (Gummesson, 1991) and the potential impact of the consultancy services on the reputation of the organization (Dunning, 1989) also contribute to making the purchase of the consultancy services to be riskier (Lunsford and Fussell, 1993). To combat these complexities, Corcoran and McLean (1998) suggest that purchasers and suppliers need to be aware of two aspects. First, they need to be aware of the issues purchasers are concerned about when assessing a consultant. Second, both purchasers and suppliers need to be aware of their style of interaction and its impact on purchase decision.

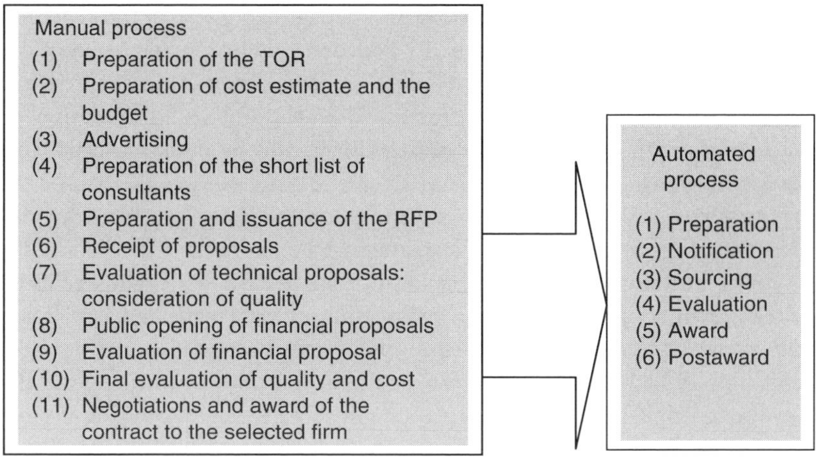

Figure 25.1 Manual versus automated process for the selection of consultants. (Adapted from World Bank/The International Bank for Reconstruction and Development, *Guidelines: Selection and Employment of Consultants by World Bank Borrowers*, World Bank, Washington, DC, May 2004.)

25.2.4 Process of Selection of Consultants: Manual versus Automated

The World Bank's E-procurement solution for the selection of consultants is seen as a way to address some of these concerns and suggestions. The transparent nature of the Internet truly makes evaluation and award stages of the selection process effective. The E-procurement infrastructure and procedures can facilitate the achievement of the principles of efficiency, transparency, service quality, and compliance in the consultant selection process required by the public sector procurement regulations. Furthermore, E-procurement has the potential to promote operating efficiency in public sector procurement and provide significant cost savings (Miami-Dade County, 2000).

On the basis of the QCBS method of consultant selection, Figure 25.1 depicts the various stages of the manual process—the E-procurement solution for the selection of consultants has the capability to automate these stages of the manual process and the resulting automated process is more effective in terms of speed and cycle time.

25.3 World Bank's E-Procurement Solution for the Selection of Consultants

25.3.1 The Project

The World Bank's E procurement solution consists of a Web based application that integrates E-commerce, procurement workflow, and document management in a single solution. The proposed E-procurement solution for the selection of consultants was intended to manage complex procurements in a decentralized, international environment, increasing transparency, enhancing compliance efforts, and improving institutional memory (as data is systematically collected during the process).

The new solution is expected to help the World Bank manage every step of the procurement process and to interact directly with consulting firms in a secured environment. In addition, consulting firms could monitor the procurement process online to view opportunities, express interest, obtain bidding documents, and start the bidding process. The solution would be designed to interface with the bank's legacy system to provide real-time information on bank projects, trust funds, and transaction systems.

The project team responsible for the new solution used an iterative approach to formulate the overall vision and develop requirements. The team first benchmarked the World Bank's current methodologies "as-is state" by documenting business processes and identifying technology capabilities. Next, the team defined the "future state" by creating process maps and storyboards, as well as determining the preferred technical architecture. This exercise resulted in the development of the technical specification, which was the basis for a competitive request for proposal (RFP) process, resulting in an award to Appian Corporation, a private software developer company, for its procurement product. In parallel to the application build-out, the project team formulated a communication plan to educate users on the new systems, as well as upcoming changes and key dates. For each stakeholder group, the team chose the best communication vehicle and coordinated timing, along with defining the key message and the desired outcome.

25.3.2 System Functionalities and Benefits

E-procurement for the selection of consultants is a Web-based solution that supports task teams of the World Bank in the selection of consultants for operations financed by trust funds or the bank's own budget. The Appian procurement software product consists of a core process engine, process design tools, document management, business rules, process reporting, community-based knowledge management, and other collaborative tools. The bank found that this set of technology was much more configurable and adaptable to the complex nature of procurement services than traditional online transaction-based E-procurement. The solution streamlines three selection scenarios: (1) selection and engagement of consulting firms, (2) selection and appointment of individual consultants, and (3) extension and amendments of contracts and appointments. The E-procurement solution offers interfaces to the bank's SAP enterprise resource planning (ERP) system to pull appropriate project data, available trust funds, budget, and existing contract data for each selection. The system also uses the bank's workflow system that provides for online reviews of process documentation and approvals. Lastly, E-procurement provides an interface to the bank's central document archiving system to store important data correctly and safely.

25.3.3 Process Description

Figure 25.2 provides a general overview of the system, the automated procurement process, its main users, and interfaces with other applications of the World Bank.

As discussed earlier, the automated selection processes can be divided into six stages: (1) preparation, (2) notification, (3) sourcing, (4) evaluation, (5) award, and (6) postaward and then automated with the help of an E-procurement solution. These automated stages can be described as follows:

- Preparation: In the preparation stage, the leader or member of a project task team enters all the requested data into the system. On the basis of the wizard approach (questions asked by the system), the system helps determine the appropriate procurement method (e.g., QCBS, direct selection, etc.).

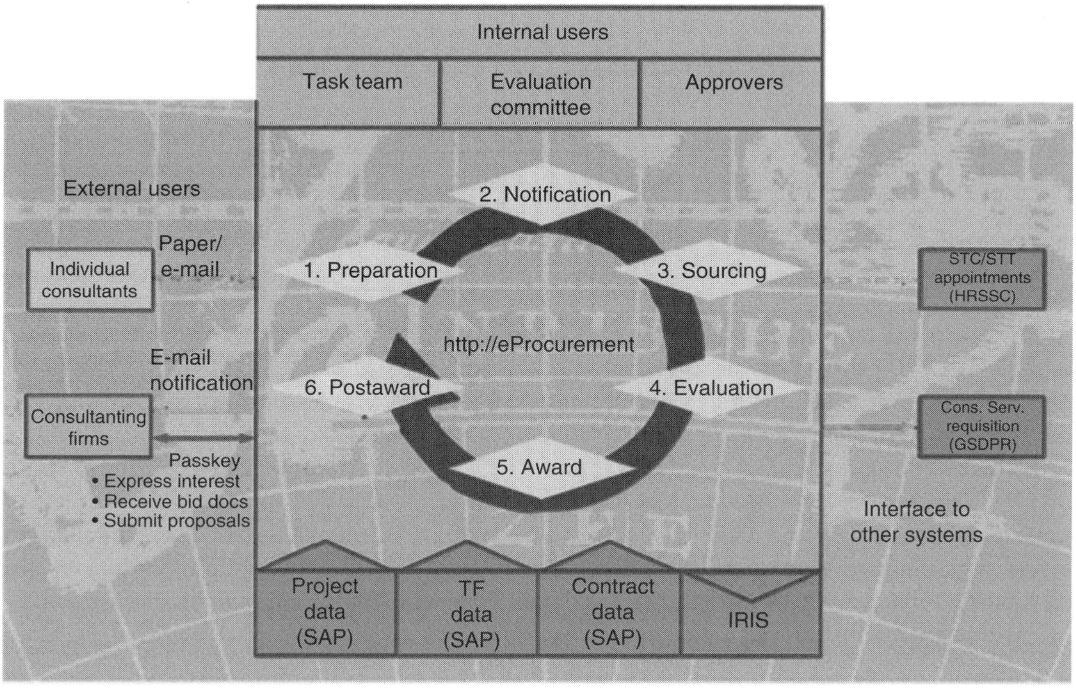

Figure 25.2 General overview of the E-procurement solution for the selection of consultants. (Adapted from World Bank/The International Bank for Reconstruction and Development, *Guidelines: Selection and Employment of Consultants by World Bank Borrowers*, World Bank, Washington, DC, May 2004.)

- Notification: The purpose of this stage is to create an online advertisement where firms can express interest online. The system is designed to publish notification to several advertisement channels to enable maximum exposure of new procurement opportunities.
- Sourcing: At this stage, the standard RFP is created, cleared, and issued to qualified firms. Firms can download the RFP documents, request clarifications online, and submit their proposals. Firms' proposal submissions are sealed until the formal opening.
- Evaluation: E-procurement provides the functionality of the online review and scoring of the proposals by an evaluation team, which is then combined with the financial score, based on predefined formulas. Each of these process steps is self-documented, forming the draft and final evaluation reports.
- Award: Once the evaluation is completed, a recommendation for award is requested and cleared, and if needed, a negotiation session with the firm can be conducted. Once finalized, the system automatically notifies all firms of the results and the E-procurement solution interfaces into the bank's back-office system to complete the contracting and payment processes.
- Postaward: This phase is used to rate the attached performance of the firm. This information can be reviewed when considering the firm for a future selection.

25.3.4 Benefits

The main benefits of E-procurement for the selection of consultants include

- Increased transparency of the procurement process, resulting in accurate audit trails
- Simplification of the selection process by providing online guidance throughout the process and assembling all relevant information and documents in an electronic format
- Automated compliance with the procurement guidelines
- Improved quality of institutional memory

Although it is too early to provide evidence on potential savings in transaction costs, it will be interesting to do a future study on the impact of the E-procurement solution on cost and time savings.

The use of E-procurement for the selection of consultants offers a win–win situation for all parties involved. Task teams are guided through the selection process and can view trust fund agreements rules and ensure compliance; they can also receive authorizations and share information online. Managers can track and monitor the selection process because E-procurement is linked to the bank's internal ERP and archiving system. Donors benefit from a Web-based tool that ensures compliance and increases transparency of consultant selection under trust funds. Consultants can view business opportunities, express interest, obtain documents, submit proposals, and communicate with the bank in a secure, online environment.

25.4 E-Procurement Solution for the Selection of Consultants: Critical Success Factors

25.4.1 Critical Success Factors

The approach of the CSFs has been used in this chapter because it represents the areas or functions where events and actions must occur to ensure successful competitive performance for an organization (Butler and Fitzgerald, 1999). The concept of CSF became popular in the field of management information systems in the 1970s, when researchers at the Massachusetts Institute of technology (MIT) investigated the importance of identifying CSFs to the design of information systems, and named their approach the CSF method (Cheng and Ngai, 1994).

For all information technology projects of this size and complexity, the World Bank follows an approval process including the creation of several documents such as a business plan, detailed project plan, and the aforementioned technical specification document. Specific, CSFs for the project can be derived from these documents and are summarized based on 11 CSFs as proposed by Vaidya et al. (2004) and as outlined in Table 25.1.

25.4.2 Challenges

This section describes the challenges experienced by the World Bank project team in terms of the E-procurement CSFs identified by Vaidya et al. (2004).

25.4.2.1 End-User Uptake and Training

To ensure the ultimate success of the E-procurement project, the World Bank formed focus groups involving all stakeholders. The focus groups helped with initial software selection, confirmed each

Table 25.1 E-Procurement CSFs

CSFs (Variable)	*Item Attributes*
End-users uptake and training	User involvement, user support/communication, user training
Supplier adoption	Supplier E-readiness, supplier adoption strategy and communication plan, suppliers' education and benefits demonstration, compliance to best practices with content and catalog management
Business case and project management	Identification of business drivers, business process assessment and requirement, return on investment (ROI), total cost of ownership (TCO), risks identification and management, pilot projects
System integration	Information matching, sending and receiving of real-time information to other information systems, electronic commerce with suppliers
Security and authentication	Infrastructure authentication and authorization, confidentiality and integrity, security requirements
Reengineering the process	Transparency improvement, automated invoice payment and reconciliation, compliance with purchasing procedures and standard
Performance measurement	Goals and targets, key performance indicators, baseline measurement, progress monitoring
Top management support	Management sponsor, involvement of the steering committee, investment in organizational change
Change management	Identification and management of key stakeholders E-procurement impact assessment, potential barriers to implementation, organizational resistance
E-procurement implementation strategy	Sound procurement practices, opportunities for aggregation, a consistent approach to procurement relationships with industry and small businesses
Technology standards	Technical standards, content standards, process and procedural standards, compliance with the standards frameworks, interoperability

Source: From Vaidya, K., Sajeev A.S.M., and Callender, G., Paper presented at the 13th Annual International Purchasing & Supply Education & Research Association (IPSERA) Conference, April 4–7, Catania, Italy, December 2004. With permission.

step in the development life cycle, and provided feedback. These focus groups were essential in creating and refining the user interfaces, from the first storyboards through production launch. Focus group attendees also helped determine appropriate training resulting in the bank creating a series of online training videos, of 10–15 minutes duration, which staff can access before and during any procurement. In addition, demonstrations and hands-on clinics are offered throughout the year.

25.4.3 Supplier Adoption

At the heart of the new solution is an online communication portal between the World Bank and external consulting firms. Key supplier bottlenecks were identified and targeted for online communication, including advertising opportunities linked to the ability for firms to express interest online, the downloading of bid documents, answering questions within a discussion list, and proposal submission. Although all interactions were recorded within the solution and accessible by firms at any time, communication was accomplished using e-mail. E-mail notifications were sent to the firm's primary and secondary contacts to inform them of any changes to the selection process with a hyperlink to enable the firm to quickly return to the solution. Other key interactions were identified outside of the selection process for future extensions, including vendor registration, which is tied to online invoicing, and the ability to check payment status.

25.4.3.1 Business Case/Project Management

The business objective for the new, electronic RFP was to build a more efficient process that fostered consistency of practice and compliance worldwide. Additional goals included increasing transparency in the process and minimizing processing tasks within a decentralized procurement environment. Much discussion took place on using a total solution approach versus a smaller implementation with incremental improvements. In the end, it was determined that the solution would need to complete an end-to-end procurement to be successful, hence a "total solution approach."

25.4.3.2 System Integration

To access real-time information from the World Bank's SAP R/3 system, the project team pioneered the use of basic Web Services at the bank with the use of XML over an HTTP link into the appropriate process steps. These services ranged from exchange rate conversions within the financial proposal templates to real-time procurement auditing. For example, the system monitors trust fund provisions that the SAP R/3 system maintains in a database. Trust funds are monies that donors provide to the World Bank that are earmarked exclusively to support specific operations. In addition, a similar interface was created to enable all documentation collected during the selection process to be archived into the bank's document management system. The use of Web services enabled the bank to manage the selection process within the E-procurement solution, without the need to duplicate or replicate data from other systems. Web services also helped to validate the services for future projects.

25.4.3.3 Security and Authentication

Before the launch of the E-procurement project, the World Bank adopted a set of security and authentication standards. The standards defined three types of users: self-identified external users, named external users, and the bank staff. E-procurement utilized the first standard, self-identified external users, for the registration process whereby firms expressed interest and submitted proposals. This standard enabled firms to create and administrate their own user IDs and passwords, with the added benefit of a lower, overall license cost to the bank for an expected, high-turnover group. Once a firm self-registers, it can manage all communications over a secure, encrypted network.

25.4.3.4 Reengineering the Process

The bank's new E-procurement solution automates the procurement process and increases information sharing between the World Bank and external firms. It combines business process management functionality with a portal framework. The business process management function both automates multiple, rule-based business processes and manages digital content that is stored, distributed, and archived. The portal framework lets all procurement parties access an easy-to-use interface, securely collaborate and share data seamlessly across different applications. This combination helps the World Bank increase efficiency and transparency and achieves best practice status in E-procurement.

To achieve the desired results, the project team examined each paper-based form used in the procurement process to determine if the form needed to be ported to the Web. In many cases, the paper form was simply converted into system templates to provide a standard and familiar format for information submission. Standardized formats simplified the sourcing process internally. If it was deemed that a document could not or should not be reengineered, a process step was provided for end users to upload the appropriate documents. For example, a firm's technical proposal was considered to be a document that firms would want to continue to create offline and upload for submission.

In addition to process forms, the project team also reviewed business rules. Many policies and procedures are required based on the decentralization of information and decisions. As E-procurement captured documentation and decision making in real time in a centralized location, several of these procedures were eliminated. For example, the team realized that attaching all paperwork to the requisition, including copies of e-mail approvals, was redundant as the E-procurement solution self-documented the entire process.

25.4.4 Performance Management

Two sets of performance measurements were tracked, the first set on the project and the second set on the original goals. On the first set, success will be determined by whether or not the system is accepted throughout all the different bank units, and the number of procurement selections within the system versus the number of selections done outside the system is one of the key measurements. Once a critical mass of selections was completed, a mandatory usage date will be determined. For the original goals, a second set of measurements will evaluate competitiveness, transparency, and compliance.

25.4.4.1 Top-Level Management Support

As with all projects, top-level management support was critical to the success of the World Bank's E-procurement project. To this end, the project started as a result of a request made by executive management and was sponsored by four key areas: operations procurement, trust funds, human resources, and corporate procurement. Having four units involved enabled the break down of many organizational barriers and across, as well as up and down the organizational hierarchy. This was very important as the system's end users are part of a matrix organizational structure based on project type and geographic location. Therefore, communication lines needed to occur from multiple sources to ensure maximum coverage. In addition, although top management support for the project was provided from multiple sources, messages on changes, benefits, and project status for each source needed to be created and provided for distribution down the different channels.

25.4.4.2 Change Management

The World Bank hires consultants and service providers to provide technical or managerial services in all sectors, ranging from socioeconomic and environmental projects to reforms of state and financial sectors, privatization, information technology, and infrastructure. With the bank's decentralization process, project managers are responsible for selecting these consultants and the project team, as one step within their projects. The automation of the previous manual process resulted in numerous business process changes for these managers and other stakeholders. For this reason, the project team tried to minimize the impact to end users with the goal of increasing acceptance.

Much care was taken to match the software application's terminology to the bank's terminology and user interface standards. Communications were personalized for each set of stakeholders to highlight the benefits. During every demonstration and presentation, all comments and requests were recorded and then entered into the Web-based tracking system. The end result was an excellent knowledge base of frequently asked questions, future communication plans, and future releases—complete with original justifications and the original source. In some cases, future release ideas were fleshed out with full requirements documents that were also stored. The knowledge base will enable a quicker implementation of any idea if later approved.

25.4.4.3 Procurement Implementation Strategy

As the project team reengineered paper-based forms into Web-based forms, the system became more intuitive and easier to use. These pages were reviewed and revised throughout the implementation to increase usability, reduce navigation training, and match other system and bank interface standards. Another aspect of the implementation strategy was the project teams' use of just-in-timing communication and learning approach. The communications element raised awareness of the efforts throughout the bank and included providing demonstrations and project updates during regular scheduled meetings and conferences. By being proactive and reaching out to meet with stakeholders during their meetings, the project was well received. The just-in-time learning portion included creating techniques to train end users as needed. These techniques included creating a series of online help, short training videos for each of the primary processes, walk-in computer clinics, and at your desk one-on-one help by appointment.

25.4.5 Technical Standards

Using a competitive procurement process, the bank licensed a customizable E-procurement solution that combines business process management functionality with a portal framework. The new system would allow program managers and procurement officers to manage and monitor every step of the procurement process and interact directly with bidders, project managers, and evaluation team members, regardless of location. As part of the competitive procurement process, the bank limited software solutions to those that would meet the bank's future technology standards stack: J2EE and an IBM WebSphere application server with an Oracle database.

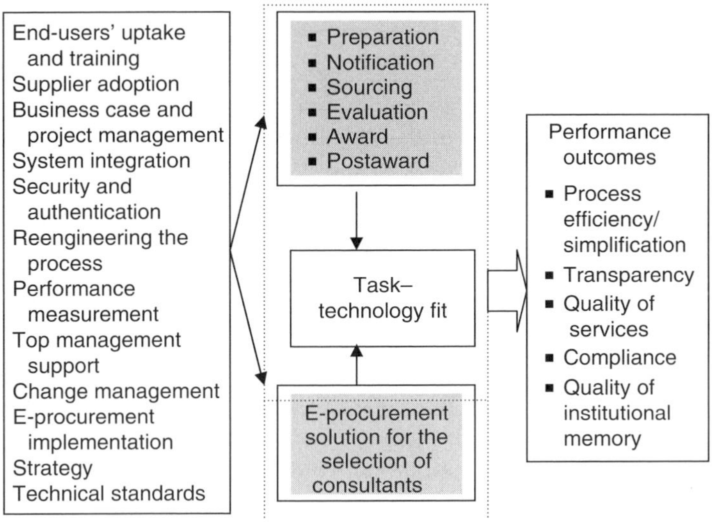

Figure 25.3 Research model.

25.5 E-Procurement for the Selection of Consultants: A Research Model and Future Study

It will be interesting to examine the impact of each CSF on the E-procurement for the selection of consultants process (tasks) and also on the E-procurement solution for the selection of consultants (technology). Thus, the fit between tasks and technology can be explained with the help of task–technology fit theory, which defines task–technology fit as the "degree to which a technology assists an individual in performing his/her portfolio of tasks" (Goodhue, 1998). The theory has been further extended to refer "to the congruence between technology and task, that is, the extent the particular task can be performed effectively and efficiently with a particular technology" (Mathieson and Keil, 1998). It will also be interesting to assess the intensity of the performance outcomes (benefits) of the E-procurement solution for the selection of consultants in relation to the process (tasks), and our future research efforts will be directed to this end.

In the next phase of our research, propositions will be developed based on the research model presented in Figure 25.3 and the model/propositions will be tested with the operational data extracted from the E-procurement solution itself and other organizational records.

25.6 Lessons Learned and Recommendations

The E-procurement system was deployed in July 2004 and the World Bank is monitoring the system's usage and processes to ensure that all transactions proceed smoothly. In conjunction with the budget processes, the bank is also considering expanding the application's breadth and depth. Options include adding vendor management functions to automate the approval and monitoring of the overall supplier base, or using newly available communications capabilities to handle invoice and payment functions on the Web.

Table 25.2 Lessons Learned

CSFs (Variable)	*Lessons Learned*
End-users uptake and training	Multiple training methods must be offered including online demonstration and laboratories—even for the most intuitive and easy-to-use system
Supplier (consulting firms) adoption	Provide for manual processing to enable participation by firms that lack sufficient electronic capabilities
Business case and project management	Budget allocations are always a constraint when measured against desired features and functionality
System integration	Not all planned integration points were achievable due to limitations in the ERP system. For example, the requisition request for consulting services was modified from the standard SAP requisition. Reengineering the requisition request was deemed out-of-scope for the initial release
Security and authentication	Provide for multilevel security, authentication, secure communication, workflow, and document control
Reengineering the process	Some exceptions to policies were acceptable and varied due to the decentralized decision-making process. However, these exceptions were not officially documented, resulting in a final system review of hard and soft stops. The project was also challenged by changing policies throughout the implementation process
Performance measurement	Performance management goals and measurements should be used within the communication plan and continually referenced during the project implementation
Top management support	Communication plans need to start early in the process to provide top management information on the project, status, and implementation plans
Change management	Change management for each stakeholder needs to be determined and communicated via the appropriate channels
E-procurement implementation strategy	Change requests increase as users begin to demo the system
Technology standards	Sticking with the bank's standard stack enabled quicker integrations to the bank's infrastructure and reduced the learning curve for system administrators and technical support staff

It is likely the World Bank will use the system to handle additional types of procurement, such as printing and graphics. Because all procurement processes are mapped and separated into autonomous steps, adding new procurement types into the workflow is as simple as designing the proper RFP templates.

Table 25.2 offers "lessons learned" for the design and implementation of an E-procurement system resulting from the implementation and rollout of the World Bank's E-procurement for the selection of consultants solution, with regard to the respective CSFs as proposed by Vaidya et al. (2004).

25.7 Conclusions

In view of increased transparency, compliance, and simplification in selecting suitable consultants for the World Bank, the utilization of an E-procurement solution is conducive to the selection process. The experience with the E-procurement solution for the selection of consultants has confirmed that the successful design and implementation of any such solution depends not only on the technological but also mainly on the human component. Although technology is available on the market and can be used to build sophisticated and fully automated procurement solutions, it is about the ability of the human beings involved in the development and use of the solution that determines success. To this end, expectations from all parties involved (i.e., top management, project management team, software developer, and end users including the buy side and the sell side) should be based on common and realistic understanding. For example, end users are often confronted with the rollout of several applications simultaneously. In this case, there were at least two more major applications—client connection and operations portal.

Knowing and understanding the specific situation of the end users helped immensely to formulate an appropriate communications strategy to raise the awareness of the benefits of the E-procurement solution and define a roadmap to roll it out successfully under realistic conditions. In this way, the frequent use of the E-procurement solution will result from the end-users' buy-in rather than from making it mandatory.

References

Butler, T. and Fitzgerald, B. 1999. Unpacking the systems development process: An empirical application of the CSF concept in a research context. *The Journal of Strategic Information Systems*, 8(4): 351–371.

Cheng, T.C.E. and Ngai, E.W.T. 1994. Management support systems for service quality management: A research direction. *International Journal of Quality & Reliability Management*, 11(8): 44–56.

Corcoran, J. and McLean, F. 1998. The selection of management consultants: How are governments dealing with this difficult decision? An exploratory study. *International Journal of Public Sector Management*, 11(1): 37.

Dunning, J.H. 1989. *Transnational Corporations and the Growth of Services: Some Conceptual and Theoretical Issues* (Series A, UNCTC Current Studies). New York: United Nations.

FIDIC. 2003. *FIDIC Guidelines for the Selection of Consultants (Test ed.)*. (International Federation of Consulting Engineers). Available at http://www1.fidic.org/resources/selection/fidic_cons_sel_1.pdf (retrieved on August 1, 2004).

Goodhue, D.L. 1998. Development and measurement of validity of a task-technology fit instrument for user evaluations of information systems. *Decision Sciences*, 29(1): 105–138.

Gummesson, E. 1991. *Qualitative Methods in Management Research* (revised ed.). Newbury Park and Beverly Hills, CA: Sage Publications.

Lunsford, D.A. and Fussell, B.C. 1993. Marketing business services in central Europe: The challenge. A report of expert opinion. *Journal of Services Marketing*, 7(1): 13–21.

Mathieson, K. and Keil, M. 1998. Beyond the interface: Ease of use and task-technology fit. *Information and Management,* 34(4): 221–230.

Miami-Dade County. December 2000. *E-Procurement: Working Group Report of Findings*. Miami, FL: Office of the Chief Information Officer of Miami-Dade County.

Vaidya, K., Sajeev, A.S.M., and Callender, G. 2004, December. e-Procurement initiatives in the public sector: An investigation into the critical success. Paper presented at the 13th Annual International Purchasing & Supply Education & Research Association (IPSERA) Conference, April 4–7, Catania, Italy.

World Bank. 2003. *Electronic Government Procurement (e-GP)* (Draft Strategy). Washington, DC: The World Bank.

World Bank/The International Bank for Reconstruction and Development. May 2004. *Guidelines: Selection and Employment of Consultants by World Bank Borrowers*. Washington, DC: Author.

Chapter 26

E-Procurement Management in State Governments: Diffusion of E-Procurement Practices and Its Determinants

M. Jae Moon

CONTENTS

26.1 Introduction

Information technology (IT) has helped solve many administrative problems in the public sector, and electronic procurement (E-procurement) has been introduced as a way to achieve better, more cost-effective procurement systems.[1] E-procurement is defined as a comprehensive process in which governments use IT systems to establish agreements for the acquisition of products or services (contracting) or to purchase products or services in exchange for payment (purchasing).[2] E-procurement employs various elements, including electronic ordering, Internet bidding, purchasing cards, reverse auctions, and integrated automatic procurement systems.

It has been argued that public organizations tend to be late adopters of new technologies and are perpetually behind the technology–diffusion curve. This view implies that incrementalism is inherent in the public sector, as Lindblom's (1959) "muddling through" process indicates. Similarly, governments, with their long-standing decision patterns, are risk averse and have unique accountability systems, along with the hierarchical and formal structures in which they exacerbate this tendency. MacManus's (2003) recent study also confirms that the diffusion of E-procurement at the state and local levels has been slow and incremental, and argues that many traditional procurement principles should be reconsidered.

Although state governments, as large purchasers, have frequently used IT to streamline procurement procedures and reduce overhead costs, few studies (Neef, 2001; Newcombe, 2001, 2002; MacManus, 2003) have looked at the nature of E-procurement and its diffusion in the public sector. In fact, IT applications in general are neither well explored nor rigorously analyzed in the current body of literature. For example, one study (Northrop, 1999) suggested that only 3–4 percent of articles published in major journals in the field of public administration address IT-related issues in government affairs. And despite being one of the key financial and managerial activities in the public sector, public procurement itself has not been well studied (Thai, 2001). Consequently, there has been little research on E-procurement, despite its growing significance.

Responding to this lack of research, the current chapter examines the diffusion of E-procurement among state governments and suggests potential stimuli for the wider adoption of E-procurement tools. The chapter first looks at the evolution of E-procurement tools at the state level and several research hypotheses (from a diffusion perspective) are then proposed. Next is a survey of current trends in the adoption of individual E-procurement tools. The proposed hypotheses are then tested based on E-procurement data and other state statistics. Finally, the findings and policy implications are discussed.

26.2 Evolution of E-Procurement

Just as IT applications are seen as the salvation of the private sector, electronic government (E-government) is touted as the deliverance of the public sector. A study by Hart-Teeter (2000) showed that both public and private managers have positive attitudes toward the prospects of E-government, despite some security and privacy concerns. To foster E-government, many public managers have pursued E-procurement, both to become "smart buyers" and from a belief that E-procurement enhances the overall quality of procurement management and leads to a more accountable procurement system.

Procurement is a significant governmental action. Public procurement is equal to about one-fifth of the nation's GDP (Thai and Grimm, 2000). One study estimates that federal and state governments spend about $1 trillion purchasing goods and services from the private sector. The federal government alone spent about $550 billion in 2000 (Neef, 2001). The majority of procurement transactions were valued at relatively small dollar amounts. This high volume of low-cost transactions represents a great opportunity for implementing E-procurement methods since processing IT-based transactions is much easier, faster, and cheaper than traditional paper-based procurement. In particular, by introducing various IT elements into procurement practices, governments have fundamentally changed paper-based procedures and other forms of conventional management. For example, the Federal Acquisition Streamlining Act of 1994 required the federal government to develop a more expedient procurement-management process based on electronic data interchange (EDI) (Schriener and Angelo, 1995). Since the mid-1990s, governments have begun to actively adopt various E-procurement tools, such as Web-based proposal requests and Internet bidding, digital signatures for procurement documents, reverse auctions, electronic ordering, automated procurement systems, purchasing cards, etc.

Proponents of E-procurement argue that it helps governments save money and provides a more accountable, more effective, and faster way to manage procurement. Neef (2001) suggested that the potential benefits of E-procurement are the following: (1) lowered transaction costs, (2) faster ordering, (3) wider vendor choices, (4) standardized, more efficient procurement processes, (5) greater control over procurement spending (less maverick buying) and better employee compliance, (6) more accessible Internet alternatives for buyers, (7) less paperwork and fewer repetitious administrative procedures, and (8) reengineered procurement workflows.

Despite the encouraging rhetoric, some argue that the diffusion of public E-procurement is slow and incremental because of the distinctive nature of the public sector with its political and legal complexities (MacManus, 2002). To implement effective E-procurement, governments must cope with various technical, legal, and managerial challenges, including technical complexity, the financial burden involved in the initial investment, security issues, and relationships with vendors.

26.3 Determining Factors for the Diffusion of E-Procurement among State Governments

There is abundant literature studying innovation adoption and diffusion (Rogers, 1995). As a result, much of the IT literature in public administration has also focused on the adoption of various technological tools (e.g., Web portals, PCs, mainframes, GIS, etc.) in the public sector. In his seminal study of the diffusion of innovations, Rogers examines five categories of factors contributing to innovation diffusion, including the perceived attributes of an innovation, the type of innovation decision, communication channels, the social system, and the extent of the change agent's promotion efforts. Surveying various diffusion models in policy studies, Berry and Berry (1999) present organizational determinants (e.g., motivation, size, resources, etc.) of the adoption of policy innovations. In their extensive study of "the process of technological innovation," Tornatzky and Fleischer (1990) also highlight organizational factors such as organizational structures (i.e., formalization, centralization, boundary-spanning structures), process factors (communication), as well as size and slack resources.

Applying a diffusion perspective, some scholars have attempted to examine the diffusion of E-procurement (MacManus, 2002) and procurement reforms (Coggburn, 2003). While MacManus calculates the implementation rate of public E-procurement systems and consequently offered a cautious and incremental perspective on their diffusion, Coggburn conducts an exploratory study to understand the political, socioeconomic, demographic, and geographic factors affecting the adoption of procurement reforms. Both studies provide insights into the diffusion of procurement innovations (E-procurement and procurement managerial reforms). As part of this continuing research effort, we propose several research hypotheses regarding the adoption of E-procurement as related to state demographic and managerial characteristics.

26.3.1 State Government Size

Many studies (Tornatzky and Fleischer, 1990; Bugler and Bretschneider, 1993; Brudney and Selden, 1995; Norris and Kraemer, 1996; Moon, 2002) have found that organizational factors are critical variables that explain the variance in the adoption of innovations. In particular, many (Bugler and Bretschneider, 1993; Brudney and Selden, 1995; Norris and Kraemer, 1996; Moon, 2002) agree that government size is one of the primary organizational determinants of IT adoption. As has been widely noted, size is closely associated with the magnitude, financial capacity, and service demand of the government. A larger state government is more likely to adopt an innovation than a smaller one because the larger government is often under greater pressure to find alternative ways of providing public services. The larger government may also have more resources to pursue such alternatives. This leads to the following hypothesis: A larger and better-funded state government is more likely to adopt E-procurement than a smaller one.

26.3.2 Authority over Procurement Policy

The implementation of E-procurement requires substantial managerial coordination between the procurement office and other state agencies. When a central state procurement office exercises a high level of authority over procurement policy, it may be much easier for the state government to initiate a procurement innovation. Strong leadership will more readily build a policy consensus among different offices and agencies. This leads to the following hypothesis: A high level of policy authority in the central procurement office is positively associated with the adoption of E-procurement.

26.3.3 Professionalism of State Procurement

It has been argued that an organization with a high level of professionalism is more receptive to changes and tends to value managerial characteristics such as efficiency and effectiveness. This is because professionalism often injects professional norms and values into a bureaucratic culture. Studying IT adoption by small city governments, Brudney and Selden (1995, p. 76) propose that "a professional administrative atmosphere is more conducive to the efficient and effective delivery of government goods and services and is more congenial to computer technology implementation and use." They propose that governments with "greater levels of professionalism are more likely to adopt computer technology and to use the technology more extensively" (p. 77).

In his study of innovative procurement practices, Coggburn (2003) also proposes a positive relationship between legislative professionalism and reformed procurement practices. Similarly, a state where procurement professionalism is more valued tends to pursue innovative procurement practices such as E-procurement. This characterization leads to the following hypothesis: State governments with greater levels of procurement professionalism are more likely to adopt E-procurement.

26.3.4 Culture of Innovation within a State

Although the literature explores various organizational determinants of IT adoption, it does not address carefully the effect of an innovative managerial culture on the adoption of IT and the development of E-procurement. It is reasonable to assume that a primary predictor for the adoption of any particular innovation is the attitude or decision taken previously on similar or relevant innovations; however, this has, surprisingly, not been thoroughly researched.

Some governments may be more receptive to managerial innovations and new practices than others. In particular, governments that more actively implement various managerial innovations might enjoy a strong culture of innovation, and, thus, are also likely to adopt E-procurement initiatives more easily and with less administrative resistance. For example, Coggburn (2003) finds that there is a close association between managing-for-result performance and innovative procurement practices in state governments. This leads to the following hypothesis: A state government with a more innovative managerial culture is more likely to adopt E-procurement.

26.4 Data Collection and Measurements

The descriptive statistics and regression analysis that follow are based on the procurement data collected by the National Association of State Procurement Officers (NASPO) in 1998 and 2001[3] and then updated by the author.[4] NASPO 1999, 2001, and the author's follow-up surveys were responded to by 47,[5] 43,[6] and 38[7] states, respectively. The surveys were designed to collect information on a wide range of topics, including procurement authority, bidding practices, ethics codes, environmental issues, the use of technology, and utility deregulation. The 2001 NASPO survey is updated with the follow-up survey for the analysis. This study also uses some government statistics (e.g., population and per capita income) from Horner's (2003) *Almanac of the 50 States*; the data for innovative managerial cultures are from the *2001 State Grade Report of the Government Performance Project (GPP)* conducted jointly by the Maxwell School at Syracuse University and *Governing* magazine.

This study examines nine primary elements of E-procurement drawn from four broad areas, including the dissemination of Web-based procurement information (RFPs and grant announcements), E-procurement practices (electronic ordering, reverse auctions, Internet bidding), E-procurement systems (purchasing cards and automated procurement systems), and E-procurement institutional infrastructure (the use of digital signatures and the establishment of statutes for Internet bidding). The diffusion of these elements is examined based on descriptive statistics. For the regression analysis, the dependent variable represents the degree to which a state government adopts E-procurement-related elements, which is based on the number of tools that each state adopts.

State size is measured by the state population in 2000; the state economy is measured by the per capita income in 2001. Represented by a 3-point scale variable, procurement authority is measured by the degree to which the policy authority of a central government over all state agencies increased, remained the same, or decreased during the last two years: 2 represents an increase in authority, 1 indicates no change, and 0 indicates a decrease in authority.

The procurement professionalism of state governments is determined by the following two elements (NASPO, 2001a): (1) whether state governments "place special weight on professional purchasing certification in procurement job description" (ibid., p. 84) and (2) whether state governments emphasize the managerial role in procurement by putting a specific statement about the managerial role for central procurement in statutes, rules or regulations, or administrative procedures.

To measure the receptivity to innovation within the managerial culture of a state, we used grade information from the government performance project (GPP). The GPP (2001) research team grades states on financial management, human resource management, IT, capital management, and managing-for-results. The managerial innovation–orientation of each state is measured by the 2001 GPP grade for managing-for-results. In his study of procurement reforms, Coggburn (2003) uses the 1999 GPP grade for managing-for-results as an independent variable. We use the 2001 GPP data because it is more relevant to 2001 E-procurement data.

Geographic location is also included as a control variable. Berry and Berry (1999) argue that there is often a regional effect on the diffusion pattern of certain policy innovations. Coggburn's (2003) study also includes location variables to examine any possible geographic effect. Based on the U.S. Census Bureau's regional classification, the location variable is one of four binary variables for four different regions: northeast, midwest, west, and south.

26.5 Analysis

To understand the trends in the use of specific E-procurement tools, this study examined the diffusion of specific-state E-procurement practices (Web-based information dissemination, electronic ordering, Internet bidding, reverse auctions), E-procurement systems (purchasing cards and automated procurement systems), and E-procurement institutional infrastructure (the use of digital signatures for procurement documents and the establishment of statutes for Internet bidding). This trend is summarized in Table 26.1.

26.5.1 Adoption of Web Technology

Public agencies have adopted Web technology widely in recent years. Agencies post a wealth of information on their Web sites, including their missions, functions, contacts, public relations material, and answers to frequently asked questions (FAQs). According to the 2001 combined survey data, the central procurement offices for all respondent states have their own Web pages; 43 states post information for the solicitation of bids on the Web, and 42 post contract-award information. Although all state governments used e-mail systems to communicate with vendors and internal buyers, their computer systems are not well integrated with other communication systems. For example, only 15 states (out of 43 responding) had integrated fax systems that linked a fax machine to the computer system of the central procurement office. Only eight states (Arizona, Arkansas, California, Iowa, Nebraska, South Carolina, South Dakota, and Virginia) received incoming faxes via this system. This indicates that communication systems at state procurement offices are fairly well equipped, but not well integrated.

26.5.2 Automated Procurement Systems

Automated procurement systems equipped with both ordering and contracting modules enable the state to make procurement decisions at the user level by providing vendors' information and catalogs on the Web. An automated system often decentralizes procurement management, making the

Table 26.1 Changes in State E-Procurement Practices between 1998 (NASPO Survey Only) and 2001 (NASPO and e-Mail Survey Combined)

Types of State E-Procurement Practices	*Yes in 1998*[a]		*Yes in 2001*[b]	
	Number	*Percent*	*Number*	*Percent*
Posting solicitation/bid on the Web	39	83.0	43	91.5
Posting contract-award information on the Web	35	74.5	42	89.4
Automated procurement system	N/A	N/A	42	89.4
Purchasing cards	32	68.1	40	85.1
Electronic ordering	21	44.7	32	68.1
Practicing Internet bidding	N/A	N/A	13	27.7
Governing Internet bidding procedures	N/A	N/A	10	21.3
Accepting digital signature for procurement documents	4	0.09	7	14.9
Reverse auction	N/A	N/A	5	10.6
Total	47		47	

Source: From GAO Analysis.

[a] Forty-seven state governments responded to the 1998 NASPO survey.

[b] Forty-seven state governments are included. The data from 2001 NASPO survey and 2001 follow-up e-mail survey is combined.

procurement organization flatter and less hierarchical. The system also saves time and reduces total costs by providing comprehensive views of procurement decisions and multiple procurement choices. Automated procurement systems offer functions ranging from simply providing vendors' performance information and order forms to such sophisticated services as lead-time analysis and asset-management support.

In the 2001 survey, 42 states responded that their central procurement offices have automated procurement systems, but few states responded that they are equipped with a full range of capabilities such as automatic purging, selection of vendors, vendor-performance screens, lead-time analysis, and asset management. For example, only 16 states have the capacity for lead-time analysis and have integrated their systems with an E-commerce system, whereas 18 states incorporate the EDI element in their procurement system.

26.5.3 Purchasing Cards

Purchasing cards, initially designed by a card company for the federal government, have become an alternative payment tool to reduce administrative costs while enhancing procurement accountability (NASPO, 2001b). A recent NASPO (2001b) report listed the benefits of purchasing cards, including reduced administrative costs, increased productivity, enhanced vendor flexibility, improved reporting, empowered employees, and greater convenience. Many E-procurement systems use purchasing cards, in particular, for small but frequent large-volume purchases. Many states have begun using purchasing cards to reduce processing costs and to enhance the quality of record keeping.

In the 2001 survey, 40 of 47 states responded that they use purchasing cards in procurement management. To prevent abuse of the cards, most of these states have limits for single purchases (often \$1000 or \$2500), daily purchases, and cycle purchases. Thirty-nine state governments use purchasing cards for statewide contracts and fleet management. Seventeen state governments responded that they post purchasing-card transactions to their accounting systems.

26.5.4 Electronic Ordering

Electronic ordering—filling purchase orders electronically—has been adopted by many states over the last three years. In the 2001 survey, 32 states responded that their E-procurement systems included electronic ordering, up from 21 state governments in the 1999 survey. The management of electronic ordering systems and procurement portal sites is often initiated, developed, and maintained by private businesses.

26.5.5 Internet-Based Bidding and Reverse Auctions

Internet-based bidding, that is, using E-commerce through online auctions, has become a common practice in the private sector. The private sector also uses reverse auctions, in which products are to be purchased at specific prices and vendors compete to offer the best prices. Despite their rising popularity in the private sector, these auctions have not been widely used by state governments. Only 10 states[8] have developed procedures or statutes governing Internet bidding, and 13 states[9] responded that their central procurement office had conducted electronic bidding. Only five states (Minnesota, Missouri, Pennsylvania, Virginia, and Wisconsin) currently conduct reverse auctions for procurement.

26.5.6 Adoption of Digital Signatures

Digital signatures provide a means of signing electronic documents that use public-key encryption for authentication. They aid procurement and E-commerce by facilitating online financial and documentary transactions. Thirty-one states had enacted digital-signature laws to facilitate online financial transactions. In eight states (Illinois, Kentucky, Louisiana, Minnesota, New Mexico, South Carolina, South Dakota, and Tennessee), procurement-management offices used digital signatures to route and approve documents internally. Only seven states (Idaho, Maine, Minnesota, Pennsylvania, Tennessee, Texas, and Washington) accepted vendors' digital signatures as legally binding on procurement documents.

This descriptive analysis suggests that simple E-procurement practices (Web-based information dissemination and electronic ordering) and basic E-procurement tools (procurement cards, automated procurement systems) have been widely and rapidly adopted by state governments in recent years. However, these tools seem to be still at the experimental stage and are not equipped with full capacities. For example, automated procurement systems are widely used, but many critical functions such as lead-time analysis, an EDI element, and asset management are not fully integrated into many state systems. State governments have been slower to invest in the more advanced practices of E-procurement (Internet bidding and reverse auctions) and institutional infrastructure (the application of digital signatures and the establishment of statutes for Internet bidding).

In addition to the descriptive examination of the adoption of specific E-procurement tools, we also conducted an exploratory analysis to examine the effects of various state characteristics such as size, economy, procurement administration, professionalism, managerial innovation–orientation, and geographic location on the adoption of state E-procurement. The extensiveness of E-procurement adoption by a state is represented by the summative number of the different aspects of adopted E-procurement tools. The results of an ordinary least square (OLS) regression analysis supported some of the proposed hypotheses (see Table 26.2). The model is statistically significant and explains about one-third of the variance of the dependent variable. The statistical results indicate that managerial innovation–orientation, increasing policy authority of the central procurement office, and size are positively associated with the extensiveness of procurement adoption. The results also support the hypothesis that government size is a key factor for the adoption of innovative E-procurement tools, since size acts as a proxy variable for the amount of service demanded, the magnitude of political pressure, and resource capacity.

Table 26.2 Regression Analysis of Adoption of E-Procurement in State Governments (*N* = 41)

Independent Variables	*Beta*	*Standardized Beta*	*Sig.*
(Constant)	2.925		0.173
Size			
Population of 2000	0.072[a]	0.276	0.078
Per capita income of 2000	0.000	–0.094	0.613
Procurement policy			
Procurement authority	0.776[b]	0.325	0.036
Professionalism			
Managerial role	–1.737[b]	–0.361	0.015
Procurement professionalism	–0.384	–0.108	0.487
Managerial innovation–orientation			
Managing-for-result grade	1.254[c]	0.535	0.001
Geographic factors			
Northeast	0.967	0.226	0.224
South	0.783	0.205	0.267
West	0.553	0.149	0.395
Adjusted R^2: 0.31			
F-value: 3.09 < 0.009			

[a] Statistically significant at the 10 percent level.
[b] Statistically significant at the 5 percent level.
[c] Statistically significant at the 1 percent level.

Managerial innovation–orientation, measured by the grade for managing-for-results, is positively associated with the adoption of E-procurement. This means that the state government's overall managerial attitude toward results and effectiveness-oriented reform affects the adoption of E-procurement, which is a subset of overall management reform. The results also support the hypothesis that a central procurement office with a high level of authority over procurement policy is positively associated with the adoption of E-procurement tools. This suggests that strong central control over procurement policy facilitates the adoption of E-procurement because it can enforce consensus and implementation.

However, per capita income, procurement professionalism, and geographic location do not seem to be related to the adoption of E-procurement. Interestingly, the relationship between the stated management role in procurement and the adoption of E-procurement is both negatively associated and statistically significant. Perhaps simple statements in statutes, regulations, or administrative procedures about the role of management do not necessarily ensure that managerial values are positively interjected into decision making. It may also be true that the role of management as written into statutes or procurement administrative procedures reflects a lack of managerial values in practice. This suggests that in the adoption of innovative practices, the actual practice of managerial values (related to the managerial innovation–orientation) is far more important than any nominal appreciation of management roles written into statutes.

26.6 Conclusions

The supporters of E-procurement in state government believe that it will overcome many of the problems of traditional paper-based procurement and that its innovations will lead to better, more efficient, and more effective procurement management. Working from this belief, many state governments have implemented E-procurement initiatives to improve their procurement management, some even attempting to pursue market integration through horizontal and vertical E-procurement. Relatively simple E-procurement tools have diffused widely and rapidly among state governments in the past years, including (1) posting both the solicitation of bids and contract-award information on the Web, (2) electronic ordering, (3) automated procurement systems, and (4) purchasing cards. Other tools, more technically complex and requiring a more specific legal framework, have been less widely adopted (MacManus, 2002). Some examples include (1) the use of legally binding digital signatures on procurement documents, (2) Internet-based bidding, and (3) reverse auctions.

This shows a distinct difference in the diffusion rates of simple E-procurement practices (Web applications and electronic ordering) and advanced E-procurement practices (Internet bidding and reverse auctions). Some E-procurement tools, like automated procurement systems, are widely adopted, but they are often rudimentary and not fully equipped with the necessary analytical tools and procurement functions. Many state governments unprepared for the full-scale implementation of E-procurement are slowly enacting statutes regulating Internet bidding and digital signatures. Overall, state E-procurement systems appear to be still in the experimental stages, and utilization of the systems has not yet delivered significant cost- or time-saving benefits. As MacManus (2002) noted, E-procurement diffuses slowly, and despite compelling rhetoric, it may be even slower to realize its potential.

Regression analysis suggests that a larger and more managerially innovative state government is more likely to be active in adopting various E-procurement tools, as is one that centralizes authority over its procurement policy. Implementing E-procurement requires strong policy leadership and a managerial willingness to innovate, both of which are continuing challenges for many states.

A promising alternative rather than an instant panacea, E-procurement offers state governments both opportunities and challenges. Procurement officers will experience new responsibilities in a rapidly changing environment (McCue and Gianakis, 2001; Bartle and Korosec, 2003). State governments will also have to meet various managerial and technical challenges actively and strategically when implementing E-procurement. In particular, to pursue sustainable E-procurement management, they should enhance appropriate technical and managerial capacities for procurement officers, improve the technical quality of the systems, and establish cooperative intersectorial and intergovernmental relationships among central procurement offices, state agencies, local governments, vendors, and application service providers. Governments should also address security and fraud issues, such as public employees' abusing or fraudulently using purchasing cards.

It is worth noting that the adoption of E-procurement tools does not necessarily ensure their effective or extensive utilization. In other words, governments that have adopted the tools may not use them for their daily procurement activities or experience positive outcomes. As Daly and Buehner (2003) found, the real challenges for state governments regarding E-procurement may not be technical, but organizational and managerial. As state governments grapple with these complexities, we should continue to try to understand actual E-procurement practices and their effectiveness.

Acknowledgment

This research was supported by a research grant from the PricewaterhouseCoopers Endowment for the Business of Government. The author has benefited from the constructive comments of anonymous reviewers and the editor.

Notes

1. One study shows that the government spends about 5.5 ¢ to administer each procurement dollar, whereas private counterparts spend 1 ¢ on the same task (JTFIT, 1996).
2. Definitions of related terms are available at the Web site of the National Electronic Commerce Coordinating Council. http://www.ec3.org/InfoCenter/02_WorkGroups/2000_Workgroups/eprocurement/definitions.htm.
3. The NASPO surveys are summarized in NASPO (1998, 2001a).
4. It should be noted that the results of this study are based on data collected from mail and e-mail surveys of senior state procurement officers, and not from a thorough investigation of the E-procurement practices of each state. Although I believe that state procurement officers are a reliable source of information regarding state E-procurement, there is a possibility that some of the information provided by the respondents is incorrect; this may be attributable to a misunderstanding of complicated technical terms or to a social desirability effect.
5. Nonresponding states: Alaska, Kentucky, and New Hampshire.
6. Nonresponding states: Alabama, Delaware, Florida, Maryland, New Hampshire, Oregon, and Wisconsin.
7. Nonresponding states: Florida, Georgia, Illinois, Indiana, Maryland, Montana, Nebraska, New Hampshire, New Jersey, New York, Oklahoma, Texas, Vermont, Virginia, and West Virginia.

8. California, Connecticut, Kentucky, Louisiana, Massachusetts, Michigan, Minnesota, Mississippi, Ohio, Pennsylvania, South Carolina, Utah, and Wyoming.
9. California, Connecticut, Kentucky, Louisiana, Massachusetts, Mississippi, Ohio, Pennsylvania, South Carolina, Utah, and Wyoming.

References

Bartle, J. and Korosec, R. 2003. A review of state procurement and contracting. *Journal of Public Procurement*, 3(2): 192–214.

Berry, R.S. and Berry, W. 1999. Innovation and diffusion models in policy research. In P. Sabatier (Ed.), *Theories of the Policy Process*. Boulder, CO: Westview. pp. 169–200.

Brudney, J. and Selden, S. 1995. The adoption of innovation by smaller local governments: The case of computer technology. *American Review of Public Administration*, 25(1): 71–86.

Bugler, D. and Bretschneider, S. 1993. Technology push or program pull: Interest in new information technologies within public organizations. In B. Bozeman (Ed.), *Public Management: The State of the Art*. San Francisco, CA: Jossey-Bass. pp. 275–293.

Coggburn, J. 2003. Exploring differences in the American states' procurement practices. *Journal of Public Procurement*, 3(1): 3–28.

Daly, J.L. and Buehner, M. 2003. P-card utilization in municipal government: Advantage and concerns. *Journal of Public Procurement*, 3(1): 75–94.

Government Performance Project. 2001. *State Grade Report 2001*. Available at http://www.maxwell.syr.edu/gpp/grade/state_2001/index.asp?id=2 (Accessed on June 7, 2003).

Hart-Teeter, Inc. 2000. *E-government: The Next Revolution*. Washington, D.C.: Council for Excellence in Government.

Horner, L. (Ed.) 2003. *Almanac of the 50 States: Basic Data Profiles with Comparative Tables*. Palo Alto, CA: Information Publications, Inc.

Joint Task Force on Information Technology of the National Association of State Purchasing Officers and the National Association of State Information Resource Executives. 1996. Buying Smart: State Procurement Saves Millions. (White Paper). Available at http://www.naspo.org/whitepapers/buyingsmart.cfm. (Accessed on October 13, 2001).

Lindblom, C. 1959. The science of muddling through. *Public Administration Review*, 29(1): 79–88.

MacManus, S. 2002. Understanding the incremental nature of e-procurement implementation at the state and local levels. *Journal of Public Procurement*, 2(1): 5–28.

McCue, C. and Gianakis, G. 2001. Public purchasing: Who's minding the store? *Journal of Public Procurement*, 1(1): 71–95.

Moon, M.J. 2002. The evolution of e-government among municipalities: Rhetoric or reality. *Public Administration Review*, 62(4): 424–433.

National Association of State Procurement Officials. 1998. *NASPO Survey of State and Local Government Purchasing Practices*. Lexington, KY: Author.

National Association of State Procurement Officials. 2001a. *NASPO Survey of State and Local Government Purchasing Practices*. Lexington, KY: Author.

National Association of State Procurement Officials. 2001b. *NASPO State and Local Government Purchasing Principles and Practices*. Lexington, KY: Author.

Newcombe, T. 2001. E-procurement rising? *Government Technology*. Available at http://www.govtech.net/megazine/story.phtml?id=2530000000002753.0. (Accessed on October 2, 2002).

Newcombe, T. 2002. Can ERP save e-procurement? *Government Technology*. Available at http://www.govtech.net/megazine/story.phtml?id=2530000000002753.0. (Accessed on October 2002).

Norris, D.F. and Kraemer, K.L. 1996. Mainframe and PC computing in American cities: Myths and realities. *Public Administration Review*, 56(6): 568–576.

Northrop, A. 1999. The challenge of teaching information technology in public administration graduate programs. In D. Garson (Ed.), *Information and Computer Applications in Public Administration: Issues and Trend*. Hershey, PA: Idea Group Publishing. pp. 7–22.

Neef, D. 2001. *e-Procurement: From Strategy to Implementation*. Upper Saddle River, NJ: Prentice Hall.

Rogers, E. 1995. *Diffusion of Innovations* (4th ed.). New York: The Free Press.

Schriener, J. and Angelo, W. October 2, 1995. Procurement going paperless. *ENR*: 13.

Thai, K.V. 2001. Public procurement re-examined. *Journal of Public Procurement*, 1(1): 9–50.

Thai, K.V. and Grimm, R. 2000. Government procurement: Past and current developments. *Journal of Public Budgeting, Accounting and Financial Management*, 12(2): 231–247.

Tornatzky, L.G. and Fleischer, M. 1990. *The Process of Technological Innovation*. Lexington, MA: Lexington Books.

PUBLIC PROCUREMENT METHODS AND PRACTICES

IV

Chapter 27

Best Practices: Using Spend Analysis to Help Agencies Take a More Strategic Approach to Procurement

U.S. Government Accountability Office

CONTENTS

27.1 Introduction

Taking a strategic approach to procurement involves a range of activities—from using "spend analysis" to develop a better picture of what an agency is spending on goods and services, to taking an enterprisewide approach for procuring goods and services, and to developing new ways of doing business. Our prior work has shown that such an approach could help agencies leverage their buying power, reduce costs, and better manage suppliers of goods and services, as leading private sector companies have discovered on adopting these activities. One survey of 147 companies in 22 industries indicated that such an approach produced savings of more than $13 billion in 2000.[1]

Spend analysis is a tool that provides companies knowledge about how much is being spent for what goods and services, who are the buyers, and who are the suppliers, thereby identifying opportunities to leverage buying, save money, and improve performance. To obtain these answers, companies use a number of practices involving automating, extracting, supplementing, organizing, and analyzing procurement data. Companies establish automated systems to extract and compile internal financial data covering everything they buy; supplement that data with information from external sources; organize this data into complete and consistent categories of products, services, and suppliers; and have the data continually analyzed. Companies then leverage this data to institute a series of structural, process, and role changes aimed at moving away from a fragmented procurement process to a more efficient and effective corporate process in which managers make decisions on a companywide basis.

We have already issued several reports examining the benefits of using a strategic approach to procurement and spend analysis at the Department of Defense (Government Accountability Office [GAO] 2002a; 2003a,b). Recognizing the potential that similar use might offer in civilian areas of government purchasing, on the initiative of the comptroller general, we reviewed the activities of five federal agencies—the departments of agriculture, health and human services (HHS), justice, transportation, and veterans affairs—whose goods and services spending totaled almost $37.2 billion in 2003.[2] Specifically, we assessed (1) if these agencies are using spend analysis to obtain knowledge to improve procurement of goods and services and (2) how these agencies' spend analysis practices compare to leading companies' best practices, including whether agencies have in place the supporting structure, processes, and roles to effectively use the results of spend analysis. We are addressing this report to you because of your jurisdiction over the efficiency, economy, and effectiveness of all agencies and departments of the government.

27.2 Scope and Methodology

To conduct this work, we obtained information from the five agencies about how they used spend analysis in support of a more cost-effective approach to procurement. We interviewed senior procurement management officials at departmental headquarters to obtain information and views about any agencywide spend analysis efforts and how such efforts compared to leading companies' best practices identified in our recent work (GAO, 2002a, 2003a). We reviewed internal memorandums and other documents related to ongoing or proposed agency procurement reforms that leveraged buying power, cut costs, and achieved other performance benefits. For background on the agencies' contract and purchase card spending on goods and services, we used summary fiscal year 2003 federal procurement data system (FPDS) data from the General Services Administration (GSA).[3] Because we used FPDS data for information purposes and not to support our findings, we did not verify the data.[4] We also did not verify the accuracy of any strategic procurement cost savings reported to us by the agencies. We conducted our work in accordance with generally accepted government auditing standards between December 2003 and June 2004.

27.3 Background

Our past work studying how leading private sector companies have reengineered their approach to procurement offers federal agencies both valuable insights and a general framework that could serve to guide their efforts.[5] Although each of the companies we studied is a leader in its respective market, each was also not immune to market or stockholder pressures to improve performance or to challenges from senior corporate leadership to improve the manner in which the company acquired goods and services. In turn, these companies adopted a strategic approach to leverage their buying power, reduce costs, better manage their suppliers, and improve the quality of goods and services acquired.

As shown in Table 27.1, we identified broad principles and practices that were critical to carrying out the companies' strategic approach successfully. Taking a strategic approach involves a range

Table 27.1 Broad Principles and Practices of Leading Companies' Strategic Approaches

Commitment...Secure Up-Front Commitment from Top Leaders
Recognize and communicate the urgency to change procurement spending practices Provide clear and strong executive leadership, including goals and targets
Knowledge...Obtain Improved Knowledge on Procurement Spending
Develop information system—i.e., a spend analysis system—to identify how much is being spent with which supplier for what goods or services Analyze the data to identify opportunities to reduce costs, improve service levels, and provide better management of suppliers
Change...Create Supporting Structure, Processes, and Roles
Create or identify organizations responsible for coordinating or managing purchases Establish proactive business relationships among end users, purchasing units, and other stakeholders Implement more integrated team-based sourcing processes Create commodity/service experts
Support...Enable Success Through Sustained Leadership, Communication, and Metrics
Obtain sustained support from senior leadership to facilitate change Establish clear lines of communication among all affected parties Demonstrate value and credibility of new processes through the use of metrics

Source: GAO analysis.

of activities from developing a better picture of what the company is spending on procurement to taking an enterprisewide approach to procuring goods and services and developing new ways of doing business.

Pursuing such an approach in the private sector clearly pays off. Studies have reported significant cost savings for some companies of 10 to 20 percent of their total procurement costs. And the leading commercial companies we studied reported savings and anticipated savings in the billions of dollars.

Conducting a spend analysis to obtain improved knowledge on procurement spending is a critical component of an effective strategic approach. A spend analysis permits company executives to review how much their company has spent each year, what was bought, from whom it was bought, and who was purchasing it. The analysis identifies where numerous suppliers are providing similar goods and services—often at varying prices—and where purchasing costs can be reduced and performance improved by better leveraging buying power and reducing the number of suppliers to meet the company's needs.

Spend analysis is an important driver of strategic planning and execution, and it allows for the creation of lower-cost consolidated contracts at the local, regional, or global level. At the same time, as part of a strategic procurement effort, spend analysis allows companies to monitor trends in small and minority-owned business supplier participation to address the proper balance between small and minority business utilization and equally important corporate financial saving goals for strategic sourcing.

Setting up a spend analysis program can be challenging, according to our prior research. Companies have had problems accumulating sufficient data from internal financial systems that do not capture all of what a company buys or are being used by different parts of the company but are not connected. Because simplified data may not exist or be available, companies have frequently been unsure who their buyers are and have had to contend with databases that include listings of items and suppliers that in reality are identical to each other but which are all stored under different names. Companies have also found that existing databases have not captured anywhere nearly enough details on the goods and services for which vendors are being paid.

Despite the challenges, companies that developed formal, centralized spend analysis programs have found that they have been able to conduct effective and ongoing spend analysis through the use of five key processes, involving automating, extracting, supplementing, organizing, and analyzing data.

Spend Analysis: Key Processes

1. **Automation**: Data automatically compiled.
2. **Extraction**: Essential data culled from accounts payable and other internal systems.
3. **Supplemental information**: Additional data sought from other internal and external sources.
4. **Organization**: Review data to ensure accuracy and completeness; organize data into logical, comprehensive commodity and supplier categories.
5. **Analysis and strategic goals**: Using standard reporting and analytical tools, data analyzed on a continual basis to support decisions on strategic-sourcing and procurement management in areas such as cost cutting, streamlining operations, and reducing the number of suppliers. Scope generally covers an organization's entire spending.

Source: GAO Analysis.

Building the foundation for a thorough spend analysis involves creating an automated information system for compiling spending data. The system routinely extracts vendor payment and related procurement data from financial and other information systems within the company. The data is then automatically compiled into a central data warehouse or a spreadsheet application, which is continually updated. Most of the automated spend analysis systems currently in use were developed in-house, although some companies have hired third-party companies for expertise and technology.

The data is primarily extracted from vendor accounts payable financial systems and reviewed for completeness. Accounts payable data can be voluminous and very detailed. Companies process large numbers of vendor invoices for payment each year, and each of those must be examined by their spend analysis systems. When necessary, the accounts payable data is supplemented with other sources, such as purchase card data obtained from external bankcard vendors' systems or other information, such as suppliers' financial status and performance information. Companies must obtain as much information as possible from both internal and external sources to gain a complete understanding of their spending.

For spend analysis to be effective, data files must be accurate, complete, and consistent. The data is subjected to an extensive review for accuracy and consistency, and steps are taken to standardize the data in the same format, which involves the creation of uniform purchasing codes. The data is typically organized into comprehensive categories of suppliers and commodities that cover all of the organization's purchases.[6]

In tandem with building a spend analysis foundation, commodity managers or cross-functional commodity teams are established to access and analyze the information on an ongoing basis, using standard reporting and analytical tools.[7] Each team is responsible for one or more commodities, which may also include responsibility for a number of subcategories. Once the spending data has been organized and reviewed, companies use the data as the foundation for a variety of ongoing strategic decisions and efforts.

Our past work also shows how federal agencies, in particular DOD, might apply these private sector best practices to obtain lower prices from suppliers and improve procurement effectiveness. For example, we noted that although DOD's spending on service contracts approaches $100 billion annually, its management of services procurement has been inefficient and ineffective (GAO, 2002a; 2003a,b). To achieve the potential for billions of dollars in savings, we recommended that DOD takes a more strategic approach to service contracting that includes adopting the spend analysis best practices of leading companies. In response, in 2004 the agency started developing a spend analysis system that will pull purchasing data from disparate databases for analysis by newly organized DOD-wide commodity teams. DOD expects that users of this spend analysis system will be able to identify procurement trends, buying patterns, and opportunities for strategic sourcing, which will result in cost savings and quality improvements.

The government purchase card program offers yet another arena for the use of spend analysis. Through the purchase card program, agency personnel can acquire the routine goods and services they need directly from vendors as long as the purchase is $2500 or less. From 1994 to 2003, the use of such cards exploded from $1 billion to $16 billion, but we found that agencies generally were not taking advantage of opportunities to negotiate discounts with major vendors (GAO, 2004a,b). We therefore recommended several actions—including conducting spend analysis using available data and gathering additional information where feasible—that would ultimately help agencies to achieve $300 million annually in potential savings.

27.4 Agencies Have Begun Analyzing Spending Trends to Improve Knowledge and Procurement

Three of the five agencies we reviewed—Veterans Affairs, HHS, and Agriculture—have each conducted spend analyses, either by using their own resources or by hiring consultants to do the work. Each agency is beginning to use spend analysis to obtain knowledge and to plan and carry out changes in agencywide procurement processes intended to leverage buying power, eliminate redundant and duplicative acquisition activity, and reduce purchasing costs for goods and services. The departments of justice and transportation have not begun to collect the data needed for using spend analysis nor taken steps that would be part of a strategic approach to procurement.

For several years, Veterans Affairs has had significant success using spend analysis on an ongoing basis to take a more strategic approach to pharmaceutical procurement. Reflecting national trends, Veterans Affairs' pharmacy procurement costs have risen significantly in recent years, consuming an increasing percentage of the department's healthcare budget. The $2.1 billion the agency spent on such items in 2000 were primarily for prescription drugs and their dispensing, but also included some supplies and over-the-counter drugs. To mitigate this increase in pharmacy procurement costs, the agency created a pharmacy benefits management strategic health group in 1995 that analyzes pharmaceutical spending trends across all medical facilities and employs various procurement arrangements for purchasing prescription drugs at substantial discounts (GAO, 2001, 2002b). According to the agency, the pharmaceutical procurement standardization program led to savings of $394 million in fiscal year 2003 alone.

Department of Veterans Affairs

Agency Profile

Mission highlights: To restore the capability of those who suffered harm during their military service; to ensure a smooth transition as veterans return to civilian life in their communities. Operates a healthcare system to provide about 3.8 million veterans healthcare through 163 hospitals and more than 800 outpatient clinics nationwide.

Organizations: Veterans Health Administration, Veterans Benefits Administration, and National Cemetery Administration.

Spending: In fiscal year 2003, contract spending on goods and services totaled $8.5 billion. Purchase card spending accounted for another $5 billion, which includes about $3.1 billion under the agency's prime vendor program.

Sources: GAO and FPDS.

Veterans Affairs has also made progress in the areas of medical and prosthetics supplies and equipment. In fiscal year 2001, the agency purchased about $500 million in medical–surgical supplies and $1.1 billion in medical equipment and prosthetics. For example, Veterans Affairs created a national prosthetics spend database that extracts procurement data from all medical facilities' systems and organizes data on purchased items into commodity categories, such as wheelchairs and aids for the blind. The agency's prosthetics strategic health group also formed a number of commodity teams with stakeholders from across the medical facilities and healthcare regions to use spend analysis to identify commonly used items that can be purchased at substantial discounts under a national contract.[8] The prosthetics group also uses spend analysis to monitor medical facility compliance with the national contracts and to ensure potential savings are realized. As of

June 2004, the group's spend analysis and strategic-sourcing efforts have resulted in 23 national contracts and accumulated more than $57 million in cost avoidance.

The agency is just beginning to develop a spend analysis tool for medical and surgical supplies and high-technology medical equipment. Specifically, it is working with a contractor to create uniform medical-product names for an agencywide spend analysis system. When the system is fully operational in fiscal year 2006, it will automatically extract medical supplies and equipment procurement data into a central data warehouse, organized by common categories of products. Until this system is fully operational, the agency decided to form several cross-functional commodity teams to pursue new national contracts on 45 categories of high-technology, high-cost medical equipment and supplies (such as magnetic resonance imaging and ultrasound equipment).

Department of Health and Human Services

Agency Profile

Mission highlights: The Department of Health and Human Services (HHS) is the U.S. government's principal agency for protecting the health and welfare of all Americans.

Organizations: National Institutes of Health, Administration for Children and Families, Food and Drug Administration, Centers for Medicare and Medicaid Services, Centers for Disease Control and Prevention, and Indian Health Service, to name a few.

Spending: In fiscal year 2003, contract spending for goods and services totaled $6.7 billion; purchase card spending accounted for another $392 million.

Sources: GAO and FPDS.

Since 2003, HHS has been obtaining spend analysis and procurement consolidation advice from outside consultants to help reduce the department's operating costs and redirect the savings to programs. Like other agencies, procurement activities in HHS were operating under a decentralized environment of independent, transaction-oriented buying processes, with limited visibility over the agency's total procurement spending.

For example, HHS has conducted a spend analysis of commonly contracted products. In its first phase, $100 million in yearly spending for thousands of office-related products such as custodial supplies, office supplies, office furniture, office equipment (such as photocopiers and facsimile machines), and peripheral information technology (IT) products (such as computer monitors and scanners) was analyzed to identify opportunities for significant savings to purchase card buyers through agencywide discount agreements.[9] Between May and July 2004, HHS awarded the first agreements to three vendors for the office supplies, custodial products, and peripheral items.[10] HHS estimates the potential savings from these discount agreements range from 7 to 54 percent and could yield at least $9.5 million in annual savings for the department on just the office supplies, office equipment, and IT peripherals. Later this year, the agency will work with its consultant to do a new round of spend analysis to identify potential categories and savings opportunities in the next phase of the strategic-sourcing initiative for products.

In a second initiative, HHS procurement headquarters hired a consultant in August 2003 to support a newly organized agencywide group of 100 senior procurement and other key managers to work on consolidation of services acquisitions.[11] One of the contractor's key tasks was to conduct a spend analysis of almost $4.9 billion in fiscal year 2002 HHS contract actions to identify high-volume or high-dollar common services for consolidation. Twenty-four categories—such as security guards and patrol services and office administrative services—were subsequently identified for possible consolidation (totaling almost $1.7 billion in value).

The consultant's plan included steps to organize and segment HHS contract workload and spend data into categories of services and suppliers. This step was intended to help the services acquisition consolidation working group identify opportunities across divisions to reduce the number of suppliers where competition for new agencywide contracts is practical. However, according to the working group's project officer, in view of small business and contract-bundling requirements and the long lead times needed to obtain division consensus on new contract arrangements, the working group decided instead to pursue alternative consolidation strategies in the near term.

As a result, HHS headquarters' officials expect the working group to finalize criteria and a timeline for selecting existing division service contracts that would be listed in an HHS-wide database that other division purchasers might use before initiating their own new, stand-alone contracts. Potential contract categories include temporary services, IT services, focus groups, and conference management and support.

Department of Agriculture

Agency Profile

Mission highlights: To support agriculture production by ensuring a safe, affordable, and accessible food supply; caring for agricultural, forest, and range lands; supporting sound development of rural communities; expanding global markets for agricultural and forest products and services; and working to reduce hunger in America and throughout the world.

Organizations: Forest Service, Food and Nutrition Service, Farm Service, Rural Housing Service, and Rural Development Service, to name a few.

Spending: In fiscal year 2003, contract spending on goods and services totaled $4.3 billion. Purchase card spending accounted for another $572 million.

Sources: GAO and FPDS.

Agriculture is currently using the results of a consultant's October 2001 spend analysis as updated with more recent spending data to obtain favorable prices on small purchase card buys through agencywide discount agreements with major vendors. The contractor analyzed almost $2.1 billion in fiscal year 2000 spending data from across the agency, organizing the agency's spending in terms of commodities and suppliers to identify high-volume, high-dollar areas that could yield significant savings and other benefits and also identifying 24 commodities for the agency's more detailed review.[12]

In 2003, Agriculture's procurement management division began to use this spend analysis, competitively awarding an agencywide discount agreement with a national office supply vendor that yielded savings of $1.8 million to the agency's purchase card holders—a price 10 percent less than the vendor's federal supply schedule contract prices.[13] To receive the discounts, registered agency purchasers must use the national office supply vendor's electronic catalog and ordering system.

Building on this experience, Agriculture recently began to use the consultant's spend analysis to improve its purchase card buying power in additional commodity areas. A temporary "electronic marketplace" subcommittee was organized in January 2004, including representatives from across the agency. According to the co-chair, this subcommittee is using the consultant's spend analysis and updating it with more recent data on spending with major vendors to help negotiate more favorable prices based on the agency's dollar volume. By October, the subcommittee plans to implement at least three agencywide discount agreements comparable to the 2003 agreement.

In the future, Agriculture plans to provide automated and repeatable spend analysis, data-mining, and reporting capabilities that identify opportunities for savings through negotiated volume discounts. These will be available through electronic catalogs as part of a redesign and modernization of its agencywide acquisition system, an effort that will be complete in about two years.[14] Agriculture began this effort upon recognizing that the current multisystem environment does not provide an integrated, streamlined, or consistent approach to procurement and does not effectively support the agencywide goal for electronic commerce between agency purchasers and suppliers.

To develop its spend analysis capabilities, Agriculture will create a centrally maintained data warehouse to be shared by agency procurement and financial management organizations. This warehouse will extract and capture all Agriculture procurement data, to be supplemented with business intelligence and organizational data from internal and external financial and corporate sources.[15] Once the warehouse is in place, it will allow for comprehensive spend analysis and reporting on procurement in real time, on issues such as the opportunities to be pursued for agencywide discount agreements with major suppliers for specific commodities and the extent of small business utilization.

The departments of justice and transportation have not used spend analyses yet to focus management attention on changing the way they purchase goods and services to foster a more strategic approach. One of the obstacles to using spend analysis cited by both was the lack of comprehensive, detailed, and reliable spending data. Nevertheless, future use of spend analysis could become an important tool in their efforts to streamline their administrative functions or improve procurement performance.

27.4.1 Department of Justice

Spend analysis could be useful in assisting the Department of Justice to implement its November 2001 strategic plan, which established streamlining, eliminating, or consolidating duplicative functions as key elements of supporting the agency's new counterterrorism mission. In February 2004, high-level discussions were begun to plan crosscutting initiatives to eliminate duplication and cut overall agency operating costs, so that funding can then be redirected to other critical tasks. The agency also formed a core group of financial and management executives responsible for overseeing the streamlining and efficiency initiatives.

Officials told us that it is too early to say if the new core group's efforts would include analysis of Justice's spending trends or considering broad-based structure, process, and role changes to support a more strategic approach to procurement, although some agency officials are familiar with the concepts. Officials said that some Justice components had made incremental progress in consolidating and leveraging certain categories of spending, such as litigation support services, jail detention space services, and prison system medical supplies. Officials also told us that the agency will similarly look into pursuing a comprehensive approach to buying Web-based training services, jail guard services, and employee household relocation services.

Department of Justice *Agency Profile*	Department of Transportation *Agency Profile*
Mission highlights: Enforcing laws in the public interest and protecting the public from terrorist and criminal activity.	**Mission highlights**: To ensure a fast, safe, accessible, and convenient transportation system that meets vital national interests and enhances the quality of life of the American people, today and into the future.
Organizations: Federal Bureau of Investigations, Office of Justice Programs, Federal Bureau of Prisons, Drug Enforcement Administration, U.S. Marshal Service, and Bureau of Alcohol, Tobacco, Firearms, and Explosives.	**Organizations**: Federal Aviation Administration, Federal Highway Administration, Federal Transit Administration.
Spending: In fiscal year 2003, contract spending on goods and services totaled $4 billion. Purchase card spending accounted for another $588 million.	**Spending**: In fiscal year 2003, contract spending on goods and services totaled $6.7 billion. Purchase card spending accounted for another $442 million.

Sources: GAO, FPDS, and Federal Aviation Administration.

In the near term, Justice officials questioned the agency's ability to analyze spending trends effectively, even though the officials agreed that such an analysis could benefit the agency. Lack of a single acquisition and financial management system makes it difficult to collect accurate and complete spending data and identify opportunities for coordinated purchasing, the officials said. Although the agency is trying to establish a single system, it is not likely to be in place until 2009.[16]

Before the single system can be put in place, we discussed with these officials the prospects for using existing contract and purchase card data that the agency feeds into the FPDS, in the same way that Agriculture and HHS have used such data to support their spend analysis efforts. Justice officials expressed interest in potentially using FPDS data for this purpose. According to the procurement executive, for financial audit purposes, Justice has been analyzing purchase card data and had already obtained better insight into what goods and services were being bought across the agency and opportunities to leverage buying power in return for lower prices from vendors.[17] Given that Justice has almost $5 billion in annual procurements, agency officials acknowledged that their streamlining and efficiency efforts could be substantially aided by the expanded use of spend analysis to consider taking a more strategic approach to procurement.

In commenting on a draft of this report, the agency reports that it is working to identify additional opportunities for purchase card savings through current discount agreements and has begun analyzing FPDS data to identify savings opportunities. We commend the agency for expanding purchase card spending analyses, which is also responsive to previous recommendations aimed at achieving agency savings through the purchase card program (GAO, 2004a). Moreover, by taking the promising first step to analyze FPDS data on contract spending for goods and services—which accounted for another $4 billion in 2003—we believe that Justice will be able to identify many more opportunities for leveraging buying power and achieve even more significant savings in the future.

27.4.2 Department of Transportation

Transportation's senior procurement officials told us that they plan to use spend analysis to support ongoing implementation of strategic procurement practices across the agency. According to these officials, such support should be facilitated by the favorable experience. Transportation has already gained from similar crosscutting strategic procurement planning to modernize information systems and standardize computer equipment as part of a fiscal year 2007 office relocation of agency headquarters. Under the agency's chief information officers' council, commodity councils are being formed to help the agency move to a common operating environment and leverage buying power for IT goods and services.[18]

According to these officials, the agency currently has no spend analysis capability, but a first step was taken this year through the agency's procurement performance management program that could help drive the adoption of a more strategic approach to buying goods and services.[19] A general analysis was conducted of fiscal year 2003 FPDS data for $1.6 billion in agency contracts, sorted by the categories of research and development, other services, and products.[20] A more in-depth agencywide analysis has yet to be achieved, however. Officials told us more detailed analysis of spending trends—for example, by high-dollar, high-volume commodity and vendor categories—was inhibited by workload constraints and their concerns about the accuracy of FPDS data and the lack of more specific product and service information. Nevertheless, they indicated that in the future, spend analysis could become an important tool in the agency's procurement performance management program. Specifically, in commenting on a draft of this report, the senior procurement executive indicated that agency leadership supports additional funding in fiscal year 2005 to enhance spend analysis capabilities. He also told us the agency is evaluating software options for a future agencywide spend analysis system as part of the ongoing financial information system modernization.

27.5 Agencies Have Not Adopted Full Range of Spend Analysis Best Practices and Lack Some Supporting Structure, Processes, and Roles

Veterans Affairs, HHS, and Agriculture have made good progress using spend analysis to improve their procurements, and they have adopted some elements of a strategic approach. Like the private sector's experience which indicates that implementing spend analysis can be challenging and take time, these three agencies have not had a lot of time to adopt the full range of private sector best practices with regard to automating, extracting, supplementing, organizing, and analyzing data that covers all of their procurement spending. Also, to one degree or another, they have not created the type of supporting structure, processes, and roles leading companies institute to make the best use of the knowledge gained and foster a more strategic approach to buying goods and services. The extent to which agencies can do both will determine their success in achieving substantial savings and performance improvements. Private sector experience suggests that agencies that start with effective spend analysis programs will be better able to institute the changes needed to move into a more coordinated, leveraged purchasing environment.

Veterans Affairs has earned a world-class reputation for highly cost-effective pharmaceutical procurement practices, which include spend analysis as well as supporting structure, processes, and roles (see Table A27.1). Its progress in making similar improvements in its procurements of other medical supplies and equipment has been slower, however, and its efforts related to clinical care or facilities support services are in their very early stages.

A March 2004 inspector general's audit report, for example, noted that the agency's efforts to reform medical supplies and equipment purchasing practices since 2002 have not yet translated into significant national contracting results and medical purchasing cost savings. The audit recommended increasing efforts to pursue aggressively more national contracts that, if implemented, could achieve about $82 million per year in savings.

A spend analysis tool that would examine Veterans Affairs' medical supplies and equipment spending trends will not, in fact, be ready before 2006, when best practices—such as automated compilation of purchase data, extracted from facilities' procurement and vendor payment systems and supplemented and organized—will be put in place for use by established commodity teams.

The agency is also beginning to focus on taking a more strategic approach to acquiring services for veterans' medical facilities from contract providers. In May 2004, the secretary announced that Veterans Affairs must more effectively purchase contract healthcare services for veterans (such as skilled nursing and laboratory services) by leveraging its purchasing power as a national healthcare system. The secretary directed that a national clinical-contracting strategy be drafted by November 2004 that would identify high-value, competitively priced purchasing options for obtaining medical services from contract providers throughout the country. In addition, in commenting on a draft of this report, the agency stated its intent to pursue national contracts for nonclinical services as well. Facilities now contract locally for a wide variety of support services, such as facilities maintenance, housekeeping, and food service.[21] According to the agency, both efforts will use spend analysis as appropriate. However, we believe it will be difficult for the agency to accomplish this objective because the new spend analysis tool, expected in 2006, will only capture data on medical supplies and equipment spending trends.

HHS asked its division heads to begin planning for departmentwide consolidation of procurement activities in April 2003. Although headquarters' managers had worked with consultants to conduct spend analyses to improve their knowledge of overlapping and duplicative procurement spending, they had no plan to develop an automated tool to repeat the process and only a small number of consolidated procurement actions were expected to result (see Table A27.2).

In June 2004, however, HHS procurement managers told us that an agencywide working group was going to propose obtaining commercial software to develop an automated spend analysis system to compile the necessary data and generate standardized reports. As a result, they believe that HHS' spend analysis efforts could make use of an automation tool in the future to enable the process to be repeated consistently, obtain data from HHS sources such as financial management systems, and analyze data on a continual basis. The proposal was intended to augment ongoing plans for an HHS-wide standard electronic procurement system to be phased in over the next year or so. According to these officials, details on the proposed system's spend analysis capabilities are forthcoming, pending approval and funding to implement it.

Agriculture's current spend analysis efforts are also not automated, include no financial management data such as vendor accounts payable systems, and do not analyze data on a continual basis (see Table A27.3). The agency does have plans to have an agencywide spend analysis system in place by 2006, but the system will be a centralized tool shared by component organizations that may or may not choose to chart their own strategic procurement paths.

A temporary subcommittee in the meantime is reviewing some agencywide spending data to identify a few categories of high-dollar purchase card vendors for use in negotiating discount agreements. However, a senior procurement policy official told us that a large-scale strategic approach to buying goods and services may be neither feasible nor advisable, given the agency's highly diverse missions and decentralized operations. When it comes to changing the buying culture across the agency, the agency wants to use spend analysis to create attractively priced discount agreements with a few vendors that agency purchasers will be encouraged, not mandated, to use. Although he indicated that Agriculture may establish a few agencywide commodity councils in the future to pursue more areas for consolidated buying, he did not anticipate creating new structure, processes, and roles within the agency.

Aside from their spend analysis activities, the three agencies have not consistently created the type of supporting structure, processes, and roles leading companies institute to foster a more strategic approach to buying goods and services. Although Veterans Affairs has used the best practice of establishing commodity teams that coordinate buying strategies for pharmaceutical, prosthetics, and more recently high-cost, high-technology medical equipment and supply items, the same practice has not been used to coordinate buying strategies for services. Outside of forming single, cross-agency working groups to leverage a few categories of supplies commonly bought by purchase cardholders, Agriculture and HHS have not fully embraced viewing procurement as an agencywide process for streamlining acquisitions, saving money, and increasing the quality of purchased goods and services when compared to the current decentralized environment of independent, stand-alone contract actions. Agriculture and HHS have not adopted the best practice of using cross-functional commodity teams to establish a network of technical experts to support volume and technical leveraging of agency spending.

27.6 Conclusions

When the government faces enormous fiscal pressures and a growing budget deficit, agencies' transformation of their business processes is more important than ever if the agencies are to get the most from every dollar spent. Leading companies that have successfully used spend analysis as a foundation for their procurement activities set an example for how the federal government can more effectively leverage its buying power.

Federal agencies such as the departments of veterans affairs, HHS, and agriculture can achieve significant benefits using spend analysis best practices to support a more strategic approach to buying goods and services. Like leading companies, agencies that establish an effective spend analysis program can then achieve a total-spending perspective across the agency; make the business case for collaboration in joint purchasing rather than fragmented purchasing; create supporting structure, processes, and roles to assign accountability and exercise oversight; identify potentially hundreds of millions of dollars in procurement savings opportunities by leveraging buying power; and identify opportunities to achieve other procurement process efficiencies such as reducing duplication in purchasing, supporting small and minority-owned business utilization, and improving supplier performance. In contrast, agencies such as the departments of justice and transportation, which have yet to make extensive use of spend analysis, may well miss out on the opportunity to achieve savings to the same extent possible as other agencies.

27.7 Recommendations for Executive Action

To help ensure that the varying spend analysis efforts by Veterans Affairs, HHS, and Agriculture go further in emulating the best practices of leading companies and that these agencies have the supporting structure, processes, and roles in place to effectively use the results of spend analysis, we are making the following three recommendations:

To identify, track, and evaluate what clinical care and support services are being purchased by veterans' medical facilities, the secretary of Veterans Affairs should direct procurement headquarters' officials to expand the planned development by 2006 of an automated medical supplies and equipment spend analysis system also to capture spending data on services. Such expansion should support automating, extracting, organizing, supplementing, and analyzing spending trends for clinical care and support services in the same way that improvements aimed at medical supplies and equipment are being made. The agency's new spend analysis system needs to include healthcare-related services' procurement data to improve decision makers' knowledge and help them identify opportunities for leveraged buying, including the planned development of a national strategy to contract for services.

To address agency leadership's direction to eliminate redundant management activities, the secretary of HHS should direct headquarters' procurement officials to identify additional steps needed to adopt a more strategic approach to acquiring goods and services. HHS headquarters' procurement officials should also be directed to consider using current financial and procurement management information systems to extract the type of spending data on an automated and repeatable basis that the agency needs to identify opportunities to leverage its buying power, reduce costs, and provide better management and oversight of key suppliers. Such data would include what categories of goods and services are being acquired; how many suppliers are being used for specific categories; and how much HHS is spending on specific categories, in total and with each supplier. Their assessment should also address the creation of supporting structures, processes, and roles as necessary, such as the establishment of cross-functional commodity teams, to help obtain the necessary buy-ins across the agency's divisions, eliminate duplication of effort, and improve the coordination and volume discounting of high-dollar, high-volume categories of goods, services, and suppliers on an ongoing basis.

While waiting until 2006 for the planned agencywide spend analysis system to come online, the secretary of Agriculture should assess whether the agency's temporary electronic marketplace subcommittee provides sufficient structure, processes, and roles for analyzing spending trends on an ongoing basis and supporting a more strategic approach to acquiring goods and services. Agriculture's assessment should address expanding the subcommittee's current narrow focus on leveraging the agency's almost $600 million in purchase card buying power, to also yield discounts applicable to larger contract actions across the range of goods and services being acquired and whether the establishment of cross-functional commodity teams would help obtain the necessary buy-in across the agency's diverse mission organizations and improve the coordination and acquisition of high-dollar, high-volume categories across a wide range of goods and services.

In light of the significant potential for savings and performance improvements that the two agencies not using spend analysis could achieve, we recommend that the attorney general of the United States and the secretary of Transportation direct officials responsible for procurement and financial management and other appropriate stakeholders to step up the process of gaining knowledge of their spending to take a strategic approach to procurement, adopting the type of best practices employed by leading companies. Specifically, we are making the following two recommendations:

Justice and Transportation should assess using current financial or procurement information systems such as FPDS and purchase card data on an automated and repeatable basis to extract the type of spending data that the agencies need to identify opportunities to leverage the agencies' buying power, reduce costs, and provide better management and oversight of suppliers. Such data would include what categories of goods and services are being acquired; how many suppliers are being used for specific categories; and how much the agency is spending on specific categories, in total and with each supplier.

Once an initial spend analysis can be completed to arm the agencies with the knowledge of such opportunities, Justice and Transportation should assess whether their current procurement structure, processes, and roles are adequate to support a more strategic approach to acquiring goods and services, for example, whether cross-functional commodity teams would provide more effective, coordinated management of high-dollar, high-volume categories of goods, services, and suppliers on an ongoing basis.

Appendix

GAO Analyses of Agencies' Spend Analysis Practices

We obtained information about agencywide spend analysis efforts through interviews with Veterans Affairs, HHS, and Agriculture procurement headquarters' officials and documents they provided to us. We reviewed this information and also discussed with agency officials how their efforts compared to leading companies' best practices identified in our recent work (GAO, 2002a, 2003a).

In analyzing agencies' practices, we compared their efforts with the five key processes that companies adopt that enable them to conduct effective and ongoing spend analysis, which are:

- Automation—data automatically compiled.
- Extraction—essential data culled from accounts payable and other internal systems.
- Supplemental information—additional data sought from other internal and external sources.
- Organization—review data to ensure accuracy and completeness; organize data into logical, comprehensive commodity and supplier categories.
- Analysis and strategic goals—using standard reporting and analytical tools, data analyzed on a continual basis to support decisions on strategic-sourcing and procurement management in areas such as cost cutting, streamlining operations, and reducing the number of suppliers. Scope generally covers an organization's entire spending.

Tables A27.1 through A27.3 summarize our analysis of agencies' spend analysis practices.

Table A27.1 Veterans Affairs Spend Analysis Practices

Spend Analysis Process	*Agency Practice*
Automation	Automated compilation of pharmaceutical and prosthetic and sensory aid purchase data into two central databases, which are updated continuously. Automated compilation of medical supply and equipment purchase data but not clinical care and support services into a central database will be available in 2006.
Extraction	Pharmaceutical and prosthetics spend analysis covers all veterans' medical facilities purchases. Facilities' pharmaceutical purchase and vendor payment data are extracted from centralized commercial distributors' online ordering and delivery systems. Prosthetics data extracted from multiple medical facilities' procurement and vendor payment systems. In 2006, standardized medical supply and equipment data will be extracted from facilities' procurement and vendor payment systems. None will be extracted on facilities' purchases for clinical care and support services.
Supplemental information	Veterans Affairs obtains pharmaceutical sales and payment data from centralized commercial distributors' online ordering and delivery systems. The agency's chief logistics office analyzes weekly summaries of bankcard vendor's transactions with the agency. The agency recently required purchase card program managers to consolidate quarterly reviews from the cardholders and analyze purchases.

(continued)

Table A27.1 (continued) Veterans Affairs Spend Analysis Practices

Spend Analysis Process	*Agency Practice*
Organization	Pharmaceutical and prosthetics spend analysis databases fall into logical comprehensive categories of commodities and suppliers. Veterans Affairs is organizing and standardizing procurement data on medical supplies and equipment purchases; a spend analysis database is planned for completion in 2006. In 2004, a naming standard will be developed for each high-technology/high-cost medical product given a national contract. To track compliance with contracted products, a standard name will have to be used when buying. Veterans Affairs will not organize facilities' clinical care and support services' procurement data into logical, comprehensive categories of commodities and suppliers.
Analysis and strategic goals	Commodity teams are continually analyzing pharmaceutical and prosthetics spending data to make decisions in contracting and procurement management. In 2003, Veterans Affairs saved $394 million through discounted pharmaceutical national contracts. As of June 2004, prosthetics contract savings were more than $57 million. By 2006, standard reporting and analytical tools will be in place for medical supplies and equipment purchases, which new commodity teams will use to help reduce the number of suppliers, cut costs, streamline operations, and address the agency's small business goals. Veterans Affairs' spend analysis system plan does not include purchased clinical care and support services, however.

Source: GAO analysis of agency information.

Table A27.2 HHS Spend Analysis Practices

Spend Analysis Process	*Agency Practice*
Automation	HHS furnishes services' procurement data to one consultant and products procurement data to a second. Although both use commercially available automation tools to compile data for more rapid spend analyses, these are one-time or periodic requirements. No automation tool is available to allow HHS to consistently repeat the spend analysis process, but the agency may consider obtaining such a system.
Extraction	HHS wants its acquisition consolidation initiative to cover as many of its services buys as possible, and provided its spend analysis consultant service contract data from one 2002 database. (Contracts for $25,000 or less were not included.) For its product-focused strategic-sourcing initiative, HHS provided a consultant with data from 2002 on office supplies, office equipment, office furniture; peripheral IT equipment, and custodial supplies. Furnished data was extracted from two contract databases, actions for $25,000 or less, and for more than $25,000. This year, the HHS consultant will receive 2003 purchase data for all other products, extracted from the same two databases, as well as data from HHS financial management sources, such as accounts payable systems.

Table A27.2 (continued) HHS Spend Analysis Practices

Spend Analysis Process	*Agency Practice*
Supplemental information	To identify the top-selling office product suppliers, HHS provided the consultant data from the agency's bankcard vendor on all purchase card transactions, as well as other information from prospective commodity suppliers on estimated sales to agency purchasers. This enhances awareness of the volume and scope of HHS purchasing. This year, the HHS consultant will receive 2003 purchase card data as well. HHS sought no additional spend analysis data for the services acquisition consolidation.
Organization	In 2003, both consultants cleansed and validated data that HHS furnished based on their spend analysis experience and supply market knowledge. The consultants used the federal product and service classification to organize categories of commodities and suppliers. This helped them identify and rank high-dollar, high-volume opportunities to target for office product strategic-sourcing and services acquisition consolidation. In 2004, the consultant will analyze new data involving small and larger purchase card and contract buys. The data will be organized into logical, comprehensive categories of products and supplies to identify and rank top categories to target for additional strategic sourcing.
Analysis and strategic goals	HHS is not analyzing data on a continual basis. The agency had two consultants analyze data in 2003 and will have one consultant do a second round of product-focused spend analysis in 2004. HHS is using that analysis to support strategic-sourcing decisions for national discount agreements with a few major suppliers for office supplies, office equipment, office furniture, IT peripherals, and custodial supplies. HHS will use the consultant's spend analysis of services acquisitions to plan areas where existing contracts can be used by agency division purchasers to leverage buying power and reduce the need for new stand-alone contracts. As of June 2004, HHS is continuing its planning and anticipates shared implementation of at least some of the existing contracts in 2005.

Source: GAO analysis of agency information.

Table A27.3 Agriculture Spend Analysis Practices

Spend Analysis Process	*Agency Practice*
Automation	In 2001, Agriculture furnished 2000 data to a spend analysis consultant, who used commercially available automation tools to compile the data to expedite the analysis to fulfill a one-time requirement. Agriculture plans to create an automated spend analysis tool to extract data from the single acquisition system to begin in October 2006. The data is expected to be compiled into a new shared data warehouse that will extract components' procurement data as the new system goes online. The warehouse is expected to contain business intelligence and data-mining capability so that the spend analysis process can be repeated at the agency or component levels.

(continued)

Table A27.3 (continued) Agriculture Spend Analysis Practices

Spend Analysis Process	*Agency Practice*
Extraction	Agriculture wanted the 2001 spend analysis to cover all products and services' procurements other than the nonprocurement-related agricultural commodity purchases. To accomplish this, the agency extracted data from three databases—contract actions for $25,000 or less; contract actions of more than $25,000; and the purchase card management system. Spend analysis did not include financial management data such as accounts payable systems.
Supplemental information	Agriculture's purchase card management system obtains data from the bankcard vendor on all purchase card transactions with agency cardholders. The agency furnished 2000 purchase card data for the 2001 spend analysis. In 2004, Agriculture obtained up-to-date purchase card data on agency transactions with high-dollar, high-volume vendors from its bankcard vendor to supplement the 2001 spend analysis.
Organization	Agriculture's spend analysis consultant cleansed and validated 2001 data the agency furnished, based on its spend analysis experience and supply market knowledge. The consultant used federal product and service classification to organize agency spending into 15 categories encompassing 52 more detailed subcategories. IT, for example, included telecom equipment, IT equipment, office technology, and IT/telecom services. The spend analysis consultant also proposed a feasibility classification strategy that could be used for more detailed opportunity analyses of high-potential subcategories.
Analysis and strategic goals	Agriculture is not analyzing data on a continual basis. Following the completion of the initial spend analysis in October 2001, Agriculture used the results to support decisions for an agencywide office supply discount agreement with a major supplier. An agreement was awarded in 2003 so that Agriculture purchase cardholders could use the supplier's Web-based catalog to obtain small purchases of a wide range of office supplies at reduced prices. In 2004, agriculture created a temporary subcommittee of procurement managers to review the 2001 spend analysis report and more recent purchase card data where available. The agency will identify a few more high-dollar, high-volume product subcategories where purchase card buying power can be leveraged through discount agreements with major suppliers.

Source: GAO analysis of agency information.

Notes

1. A.T. Kearney, Inc. 2002. *Assessment of Excellence in Procurement*. Chicago, IL: Author.
2. Fiscal year 2003 data for contract actions (about $30.2 billion) and purchase card spending (about $7 billion), Federal Procurement Data System and the Federal Aviation Administration.
3. Fiscal year 2003 is the last year for which complete governmentwide data is available. FPDS is the federal government's central database on contracting and purchase card transactions. Additionally, we obtained

summary fiscal year 2003 contract action data from the Federal Aviation Administration, which is not required to report their procurement activities to the FPDS.

4. The current system contains known errors, as discussed in GAO (2003c). Although we have not fully assessed the extent of reporting errors, we have found sufficient problems to warrant concern about the current reliability of FPDS information. As we understand the design of an ongoing modernization of that system through FPDS-Next Generation, many of the sources of the errors in the current FPDS should be eliminated. In the short term, as the transition to FPDS-Next Generation occurs, we have made recommendations to improve data reliability.
5. Between 2000 and 2003, we studied procurement best practices of 11 companies—Bausch & Lomb; Brunswick Corporation; ChevronTexaco; Delta Air Lines; Dell; Dun & Bradstreet Corporation; Electronic Data Systems Corporation; Exxon Mobil Corporation; Hasbro, Inc; International Business Machines; and Merrill Lynch & Co., Inc. Our past work focused on how the companies used best practices to improve procurement of services where costs were increasing faster than for procurement of goods. However, the companies told us that they followed the same practices to procure goods. See GAO (2002a, 2003a).
6. A commodity is a category of products or services segmented by commonality of materials or service type. The term does not imply an expendable or noncomplex item. This grouping will allow volume and technical leveraging of organizational spending and the establishing of a network of commodity experts.
7. Companies use commodity teams to make sure they have the right mix of knowledge, technical expertise, and credibility. The teams can vary in size but generally include representatives from a company's procurement unit, internal clients or users of the product or service, and the budget or finance office. The teams analyze spending data, define internal needs and requirements, and conduct market research. This approach has helped companies to define their needs better and to identify, select, and manage suppliers and, in turn, helped ensure that users' needs were met at the lowest total costs to the companies.
8. According to Veterans Affairs, national contracts are used to leverage the agency's buying power on healthcare commodities identified as high usage. The agency develops the requirements for national contracts with clinician customer input and openly completes the requirements. The agency's national contracts are generally firm, fixed-price requirements-type contracts, with a base year and four one-year option periods. Veterans Affairs exercises options after market research reveals that the prices are fair and reasonable and the award is in the best interest of the government.
9. Although HHS intends to market the discount agreements to agency cardholders for small purchase card buys, HHS divisions with larger-dollar orders will also be able to buy the same discounted items through the agencywide agreements. However, the agreements are not mandatory sources of supply for either purchase card holders or other agency buys.
10. HHS anticipates awarding two more agreements in August 2004 for the office furniture and equipment categories.
11. HHS hired the consultant to provide spend analysis services and procedural, technical, and briefing support and collaboration with the agencywide workgroup to help implement various phases of the services acquisitions consolidation initiative. Workgroup members include representatives from the office of the secretary and all HHS divisions, such as the National Institutes of Health, Centers for Disease Control and Prevention, and the Food and Drug Administration.
12. For the spend analysis, Agriculture furnished the consultant fiscal year 2000 data files extracted from FPDS and the agency's Purchase Card Management System. The contractor analyzed about 473,000 contract transactions totaling about $1.6 billion and 2.3 million purchase card buys totaling $467 million. The contractor organized the spend data into 52 commodity categories of products and services, such as agricultural machinery, construction services, fleet maintenance, telecom equipment, and office supplies and paper.
13. Under the schedules program, the GSA negotiates to obtain discounted prices on a wide range of commercial goods and services on its contracts with multiple vendors.
14. Since 2002, Agriculture has carried out a cross-agency effort, with contractor technical and program management support, to develop, test, and phase-in the enterprise integrated acquisition system to

replace more than 40 different procurement systems in use across 11 agencies and administrative offices. Agriculture plans to have the replacement system fully operational by October 2006.

15. When fully operational, the data warehouse will automatically extract procurement data for all contract actions processed via the integrated acquisition system and extract procurement data on all purchase card buys captured in the agency's purchase card management system.
16. In 2002, the agency launched a unified financial management system program to replace six major accounting systems now in use with one agencywide system. Plans for the new system include integration of financial and acquisition management, assure access to timely information, and speed up business process and decision making. Justice hired a contractor in March 2004 to provide software for the new system and plans to replace legacy systems between fiscal years 2005 and 2009.
17. In fiscal year 2003, Justice had 12,842 purchase cardholders that accounted for over $588 million in small purchases of goods and services for $2500 or less. For more information, see GAO (2004a).
18. According to the deputy senior procurement executive director, the agency's architectural review board was expected to approve a charter and an enterprisewide IT procurement business process to guide the commodity councils' activities.
19. Since 1995, Transportation procurement activities have implemented this program as a major initiative to improve procurement performance. This program assists procurement managers in targeting areas for improvement based on the results of specified metrics chosen for their importance to the administration, agency management, or agency customers.
20. The general analysis did not include data for the Federal Aviation Administration or organizations transferred to the Department of Homeland Security (Coast Guard and Transportation Security Agency). Transportation's analysis used fiscal year 2003 FPDS data for contract actions in excess of $25,000. Dollars analyzed totaled $1.6 billion and were sorted by research and development (6 percent), other services (84 percent), and products (10 percent). Transportation did not analyze vendor or individual product and service details available in the FPDS records.
21. For more information on opportunities to improve Veterans Affairs' purchasing practices and increase savings, see GAO (2004c).

References

Government Accountability Office. 2001, May 25. *DOD and VA Pharmacy: Progress and Remaining Challenges in Jointly Buying and Mailing Out Drugs* (GAO-01-588). Washington, DC: Author.

Government Accountability Office. 2002a, January 18. *Best Practices: Taking a Strategic Approach Could Improve DOD's Acquisition of Services* (GAO-02-230). Washington, DC: Author.

Government Accountability Office. 2002b, July 22. *VA and DOD Health Care: Factors Contributing to Reduced Pharmacy Costs and Continuing Challenges* (GAO-02-969T). Washington, DC: Author.

Government Accountability Office. 2003a, June 9. *Best Practices: Improved Knowledge of DOD Service Contracts Could Reveal Significant Savings* (GAO-03-661). Washington, DC: Author.

Government Accountability Office. 2003b, September 10. *Contract Management: High-Level Attention Needed to Transform DOD Services Acquisition* (GAO-03-935). Washington, DC: Author.

Government Accountability Office. 2003c, December 30. *Reliability of Federal Procurement Data* (GAO-04-295R). Washington, DC: Author.

Government Accountability Office. 2004a, March 12. *Contract Management: Agencies Can Achieve Significant Savings on Purchase Card Buys* (GAO-04-430). Washington, DC: Author.

Government Accountability Office. 2004b, April 28. *Purchase Cards: Increased Management Oversight and Control Could Save Hundreds of Millions of Dollars* (GAO-04-717T). Washington, DC: Author.

Government Accountability Office. 2004c, June 22. *Contract Management: Further Efforts Needed to Sustain VA's Progress in Purchasing Medical Products and Services* (GAO-04-718). Washington, DC: Author.

Chapter 28

Contract Negotiations

Wendell C. Lawther

CONTENTS

28.1 Introduction

Negotiations are applied in a variety of settings and experiences. They are valued when agreement needs to be reached on issues where there is a divergence of opinion among affected parties. The goal of an effective or successful negotiation should always be a result that is fair, based on objective standards, and one that is concluded amicably and efficiently.

As public agencies enter into an increasing number of contracts with private and nonprofit organizations, negotiation skills have become increasingly important for procurement officials and program managers. For the purposes of this chapter, these skills include negotiation planning, creation of the negotiation team, and negotiation approach.

In addition, the advent of information technology (IT) has meant that public agencies are entering into contracts of increasing complexity and sophistication. This trend has had at least two profound impacts on contract negotiations: the complexity of negotiation content has increased and the opportunity for program managers and procurement officials to gain knowledge through negotiation has greatly expanded.

Government officials should have confidence that the contractor has the requisite skills and knowledge to produce the contractual identified product or service. For noncomplex items, this confidence can be based upon past work history, checking with other jurisdictions regarding past performance, and industry standards. For complex products, those based on IT technology, for example, it is expected that there will be a degree of customization[1] needed for any given contract. Negotiation can be a process in which the private contractor can educate and convince government officials that the final product will be acceptable.

For many purchases of services and complex goods, negotiation skills are required throughout the contact administration process. Traditionally, when making purchases that could be clearly specified, negotiation was only required during the pre-contract award process. After contracts were awarded, negotiation was required only when problems needed to be resolved.

Negotiations should take on different approaches depending on contract type, and depending on the amount and type of information readily available. Depending on several factors, including the amount of competition created in response to the invitation to bid (ITB) or request for proposal (RFP), the closeness of the ratings for the offeror's proposals, and the complexity of the final product or service, a government negotiating team will spend a wide range of time in preparation and in face-to-face negotiations.

The following discusses negotiation as it should be found in the public procurement cycle. Thai (2004b) views this cycle as consisting of three phases:

- Phase one: Strategic procurement planning
- Phase two: Solicitation development and supplier selection
- Phase three: Contract administration

For the purposes of this chapter, negotiation occurs primarily in the latter two phases. In phase two, it is anticipated that negotiations during supplier selection may alter solicitation and shape the final contract. Although negotiation needs and requirements differ in each phase, the extent to which there is a complete understanding of how solicitation development and supplier selection affects contract administration will greatly affect negotiation effectiveness for each phase.

To further illustrate the negotiation approach and process, two case studies are provided that provide some insights into how negotiation should occur throughout the public procurement process. The state of Florida master lease procurement process illustrates the impact of supplier selection negotiations on a contract administration phase characterized by a high degree of customization. The iFlorida conditions system procurement illustrates the need to negotiate rules, procedures, and policies during solicitation development/supplier selection that anticipate the need for highly complex negotiations during contract administration.

28.2 Negotiation during the Solicitation Development and Supplier Selection

Historically, there has been the expectation that both buyer and potential contractor will take an adversarial approach during supplier selection. Harney (1992, p. 118), in referring to service contracting, suggests that "A local government that accepts a proposal without negotiating will almost certainly pay too much for the service. And failing to challenge restrictive terms and conditions may mean that the local government is not an equal partner in the final contract."

The more complex the end product or service, the less this adversarial approach is appropriate (Ashford, 2004). Increasingly, as governments enter into partnerships with private and nonprofit organizations, it is recognized that negotiation should occur throughout the life of a given contract. Managing by relationship (Welch, 2003) involves accepting contractors as equals, and establishing a relationship that expects frequent interaction and communication concerning both the nature of the end products or deliverables as well as the delivery process.

28.2.1 Planning for Negotiation

Once responses to an RFP or other solicitation have been evaluated, the next step is to plan for negotiations that will occur with the top ranked offeror.[2] The issues that must be decided during this phase include the following:

- Identifying the key issues or questions that need to be resolved during negotiation
- Choosing the negotiation team
- Identifying whether negotiation training is required for any team members
- Identifying weaknesses in knowledge and understanding among team members and other key agency personnel, as well as ways by which this understanding can be increased before negotiation

Ideally, the solicitation document should contain goals and objectives that then become evaluation criteria during the offeror rating process. These same criteria should then furnish the basis for some of the items that appear on a negotiation agenda. For example, negotiation issues should appear from lower rated items and questions raised by members of the evaluation team that has rated all responses. There may be aspects of the highest rated offering that were given low marks. For example, if commitment to women minority enterprises in the offeror response is absent or unclear, and it was stated in the RFP that this would be a criteria that would be evaluated, then the negotiation team can gain assurances from the offeror that such a commitment will be present. Issues to be resolved during negotiation include the following.

28.2.1.1 Potential Changes in Key Management Personnel

If the contract is for operations, for example, and specific management personnel—complete with resumes—are discussed in each offeror response, the highest rated offeror may then state that one or more of these management personnel will not be able to work on the operations. Proposed replacement personnel must be reviewed.

28.2.1.2 Additional Discussion of How Key Contract Goals and Objectives Will Be Met

The RFP may specify that the winning contractor will have a specified amount of time (e.g., 90 days) to deliver drafts of specific policies (e.g., a procedures manual or training plan). Even though a brief description of these deliverables may be part of the responses, the negotiation team may have additional questions about what content is likely to appear in these deliverables.[3]

28.2.1.3 Quality Assurance

For contracts dealing with service delivery, the processes by which the winning contractor will ensure the highest quality of services should be discussed. Changes in these processes or in the required personnel may be negotiated.

28.2.1.4 Price/Cost

For the acquisition of products that can be clearly specified, analyses of the cost of similar products acquired by other government agencies may result in the need to negotiate the proposed cost as stated by the winning offeror. Specified aspects of costs, such as the overhead rate, profit margins, and administrative expenses may be analyzed (Karrass [1998] cited in Thai, 2004a).

Alternatively, there may be industry or marketplace standards. If an agency is negotiating a lease with a landlord, and remodeling existing space is required, a comparison of the charges for specific tasks to what other professionals may offer in the local labor market may lead to negotiations (Lawther, 2007).

Also, to the extent that Harney's statement is appropriate, the offeror may have artificially bid the cost too high, expecting that the government agency may wish to negotiate for a more reasonable cost (Dobler and Burt, 1996).

In contrast, however, it may be very difficult to negotiate price or cost in reference to other similar purchases or industry standards. To the extent that customization is required, for example, an IT-based service that is specific to an agency's needs, comparisons may be impossible. Also, a vendor may offer software that has been developed for other clients, and charge the agency less because the expertise gained by past efforts means the present response can be more efficient/cost less.

28.2.1.5 Terms and Conditions

Any changes to delivery timetables, service provision outcomes, or any other term and condition changes that are raised by the highest rated offeror obviously need to be negotiated. The negotiation team must decide whether there is flexibility in stated timetables or deliverables that allow differences from what is requested in the RFP. Measures that will judge the performance of the contractor during contract administration should be identified.

Overall, any aspect of the contract implementation that could cause potential problems during the contract administration phase should be negotiated before the contract award if possible.

28.2.2 Choosing the Negotiation Team

As indicated above, knowledge and understanding of the contract content is the key to determining the relative roles and responsibilities of the negotiation team as well as the negotiation content and strategy. Other factors include previous experience with other acquisitions, understanding of appropriate laws or government regulations, and organizational culture and role expectations.

The following roles are representative of who should constitute an ideal team. In many cases, consultants accompany public officials filling team roles as discussed below, or consultants can replace public officials in filling these roles.

28.2.2.1 Project Manager

A key member of the negotiation team is a representative from the user agency. Ideally, this individual also should be the agency employee in charge of postcontract award negotiations.[4] Of all the team members, he or she should be the most knowledgeable about the following:

- Service or system being purchased
- Needs of the agency personnel who will use the system
- Any postcontract deliverables and quality assurance processes
- Potential for change orders

28.2.2.2 Procurement Official

If the focus of contract negotiations is on one division of a large agency, the procurement official may be the one person on the team that understands what is in the overall best interest of the agency. If there is an agency business plan or strategic plan, for example, it is the responsibility of the procurement official to know how negotiations for a specific contract impact on achieving agency business plan goals and objectives. Furthermore, the procurement official has the ethical duty to ensure that all negotiations are transparent, fair, and in the public interest (Thai, 2004b).

In addition, to the extent that there are agencywide policies dealing with contractual issues such as timing, inspection, incentives/sanctions, etc., it is likely that the procurement official is the only member of the team that has such knowledge. The official has likely authored the instructions that accompanied the RFP, and therefore is the most appropriate person to judge whether these instructions have been followed (Adler, 2007). To the extent that the procurement official has received appropriate training or experienced past negotiations, he or she is the most appropriate person to orchestrate negotiation sessions with the contractor.

In terms of the team leader, if the contract is highly complex, the procurement official may not have sufficient expertise to understand fully all of the negotiation content. Under these conditions, the project manager along with the procurement official should co-lead negotiations.

28.2.2.3 Technical Experts

The more complex the contract, the more technical experts are needed as team members. They may be software engineers, for example, that have sufficient understanding to validly question some aspects of the technical proposal. They may play a role in designing a quality assurance program to adequately test the final product at various stages in the service delivery or product creation process. They may be able to identify potential implementation challenges and provide information to improve the project manager's ability to understand the full impact of the changes a new system may bring.

28.2.2.4 Financial Experts

If it wishes to negotiate price, the negotiating team must have information on which to base its negotiations. To some extent, this information can come from competing proposals.[5] Although specific competing proposals cannot be mentioned in the negotiation, prices mentioned in these proposals can provide some insights into whether the prices of the top-rated offeror are fair and reasonable. Information concerning market prices, however, may be best known by financial experts. If a government is negotiating leases for building space with landlords, for example, knowledge of the price per square foot in a given commercial market would best be conveyed during negotiations by financial experts, who should become negotiating team members.

28.2.2.5 Legal Experts

To the extent that there are legal issues that have not been thoroughly considered by specification writers or by offeror responses, a legal expert should be part of the negotiation team. At a minimum, this person can discuss potential legally based risks that may be present after the final product or service is delivered.

28.2.3 Negotiation Approach

The face-to-face negotiation process can be made more effective by choosing an appropriate approach and employing sound negotiation techniques. Several texts (Dobler and Burt, 1996; Thai, 2004b) present specific techniques that will not be discussed here. How the negotiating team approaches the negotiation is essential, however, to successfully reach an acceptable contract.

Principled negotiation, espoused by Fisher and Ury's now classic text (1991, p. 19; first edition in 1981), still offers valid insights relevant to negotiation approaches: "A working relationship where trust, understanding, respect and friendship are built up over time can make each new negotiation smoother and more efficient."

Developing a good working relationship with the top-rated offeror is essential, not only for the effectiveness of a given negotiation session, but also throughout the life of the contractual relationship. Two sides with reputations for being trustworthy will be better able to influence each other, thereby leading to a more favorable result (Hall, 1993).

There are at least three other reasons for public procurement officials to choose principled negotiation. First, it will be well received by media that often focuses on the process of achieving a goal rather than the end result. Second, it is an ethical practice whose usage improves the public officials' reputation for integrity. Finally, it would be a violation of the public trust to knowingly making artificial demands, a key characteristic of positional or adversarial negotiation (Bingham, 1996).

Each side will have differing perceptions concerning how the process will occur as well as what the other side's interests are. If there is the perception that the other side wishes to take a hard positional approach, then the success of the negotiation will depend on dispelling this perception. Seeking out interests that go beyond simply making more profit (private side) or reducing costs (government side) will be beneficial. To the extent that the contractor wishes to uphold and improve his or her reputation to deliver a high-quality product, the government team can discover the extent to which this motive is important.

It is likely there will be multiple interests in any given negotiation. State and local officials may wish to provide a service to their citizens, but if the project is funded in part by the federal government, satisfying its wishes/interests must be a concern as well. A private company will also wish to provide a high-quality product, and it also may wish to use a specific project to test and develop new ideas and as a training ground for new employees (Kelman, 1990). To the extent that all sides are clear in terms of expressing all of their interests, there will be greater focus on viewing the negotiation as a joint action, intended to solve a problem/deliver of a product or service.

A win–win outcome, in which some interests on both sides are completely met, is always much preferable to compromise, in which all interests are only partially met. A brainstorming session (Fisher and Ury, 1991, p. 63), in which alternatives to meeting a range of interests are identified, can help achieve this goal. If government officials insist on meeting an overall deadline, perhaps they can be flexible on other timetable issues, such as the quality assurance process, that can better meet the needs of the contractor.

Communication problems can be solved by ensuring that all can understand the subject or content of negotiation. This may not always be true, as project managers and procurement officials may not understand the technical aspects of a complex negotiation. Although it is not anticipated that everyone at a negotiating session should understand how to write software, for example, the issues regarding the proprietary nature of software code, the necessity for quality assurance efforts, and scope/results of the final product/service should be understood by all.

Ideally, both sides should make an effort to understand not only the other's positions and interests, but also to educate the other on the process of service or product creation and on the nature of the result. Government officials should research available products/services, and come prepared to ask content-related questions to improve understanding. Private sector representatives should research the uses and context in which the final product will be implemented, and come prepared to ask questions about scope and usage that may influence the nature of the final product.

If the contract is to create a complex service or product, there is greater need to establish a positive relationship that endures throughout the life of the contract. Even though the contract may not have been awarded yet, the approach taken by all sides should be to identify ways in which the contractual goal can be best accomplished. Taking hard and fast positions, from which the government is not willing to alter, may be counterproductive to postcontract award relationships. On the other hand, negotiations are a place to communicate top-rated priorities in terms of the life of the contract. If the government must have the final product by a certain date, for example, this information should be made aware during negotiation. To ease contractor concerns about reaching this goal, some flexibility regarding dates by which part of the product or service is established can be conveyed.

28.2.4 Power Relationships during Negotiation

From a public procurement viewpoint, it may seem as though government has more power in any negotiation because it is paying for a service or product. There is the assumption that if negotiations with one contractor are not resolved, there is always another to replace it. This assumption may not be accurate for a number of reasons. The result is that government officials must consider that they are not the most powerful in a given negotiation session for several reasons.

First, for some social services, for example, competition may not exist, and sole sourcing is the reality of a given situation (Van Slyke, 2003). More frequently, contractors who have been short-listed and rated second or third may not seem to offer anywhere close to the quality of the contractor rated first and chosen for negotiation: for example, providing the same product at a considerably higher price or suggesting a service delivery process that may be untested (Lawther, 2003). Finally, the greater the complexity of the end product or service, the less likely that government officials will understand the negotiation content enough to reach a settlement that is in the best interest of the public.

As a result, government officials may act in a manner that is too accommodating to the other side, feeling that they are under some pressure to reach a settlement. Fisher and Ury's (1991, p. 103) concept of BATNA (best alternative to a negotiated settlement) is invaluable in helping negotiations. They suggest that BATNA development consists of three steps:

(1) Listing actions/efforts that could be taken if there is no negotiated settlement
(2) Thinking through how practical the most attractive alternatives may be
(3) Selecting, tentatively, the one alternative that seems best

Common BATNA's for public procurement efforts would include issuing a new ITB or RFP. There would be costs to making this choice, as delays in implementing a service or in implementing a product or system would negate anticipated efficiency gains. Also, additional review time and the cost of issuance should be considered.

In many cases, the BATNA is choosing an alternative potential contractor and undergoing a new set of negotiations. If this is true, then the process of identifying a BATNA will be an essential part of the negotiation planning, as the criteria by which negotiations with the top-rated offeror are considered a failure should be developed.

28.3 Negotiation during the Contract Administration Phase

Negotiation during the contract administration phase greatly depends on the complexity of the product or service as well as the degree of customization required. If an ITB is issued, negotiation is not required. For services that are routine, such as waste management, negotiation is unlikely unless there are problems with service delivery.

If in contrast an agency is procuring an IT-based system, one that may require several years to create and implement, contract administration negotiation should be expected. The product is likely to have high degrees of complexity and customization. As such, both public and private managers may not have sufficient knowledge about the nature of the final product as well as the process needed to create it at the time of contract formation negotiations (Callendar et al., 2004).

Rapidly changing technology may mean that identifying appropriate design criteria, system requirements, and acceptance standards during contract formation may be difficult. Both the public negotiation team and the private contractor should realize that contract administration negotiation will occur. To the extent that changing technology will lead to a higher quality product, all parties should anticipate and plan for such negotiation. The risk is that increasing awareness of system capabilities may lead to requests for additional customization that increases the price above the cost of the initial contract. This phenomenon, known as scope creep, is likely to lead to cost overruns and implementation delays (Brown, 2001).

Ideally, the negotiation team that is created during contract formation still exists during contract administration, and can deal with issues that require contractual scope change as they arise. Alternatively, the project manager will involve technical, financial, or legal experts in any negotiation as needed.

For example, any software or IT-based system will face issues dealing system requirements and design, and implementation issues. An initial step is identifying system requirements specifications that would "describe the software architecture, the functional modules, and the high-level data flows between the functions" (FDOT, 2003, p. 10). To ensure that these specifications meet agency needs, the user agency could require a quality control (QC) program that would perform tasks such as clarifying ambiguous requirements and identify and prioritize missing requirements. Similarly, to the extent that customization requires that the final product interacts with agency legacy systems, it should be agreed that any potential delays and unanticipated technical challenges should be resolved within a specified time period.[6]

The existence and acceptance of a QC program as well as the resolution of implementation difficulties can be negotiated during contract formation, but the rules, procedures, and unanticipated changes that may occur as the system is being built must be negotiated and resolved during contract administration. This is true especially if proposed changes result in change orders and higher costs. The negotiation process can employ the same processes and approaches as are present in the contract formation phase, but there may be significant pressure to resolve differences in shorter time frames.

28.4 Case Studies Illustrating Negotiation Approaches and Processes

The two case studies discussed below illustrate the issues involved in negotiation during the solicitation development and supplier selection phase. In both instances, the issues raised in this phase are present in the contract administration phase. Successful negotiation during the former phase has produced a more effective outcome, characterized in part by greater clarity of issues to be resolved during the contract administration phase. In both cases, a principled approach was taken, as both public agencies and private contractors considered the needs of the other side, resulting in outcomes that increased the commitment to reach contract goals successfully.

The first case involves the leasing procurement process undertaken by the state of Florida since April 2004. This case illustrates the value of negotiating issues during supplier selection that maximized negotiating flexibility during contract administration. Industry standards, for example, refurbishing office space, do exist in negotiating leases, but there is a need to permit a high degree of customization during contract administration.

The second case involves the creation of the iFlorida conditions system, an IT-based system that provides a highly integrated view of traffic congestion for central Florida, integrating information from several sources. In this instance, the much greater complexity of the final product required the identification of policies and procedures during the solicitation development/supplier selection phase that would guide a much greater interaction among public and private personnel throughout the contract administration phase.

28.4.1 Florida Master Leasing Procurement Approach

Acquiring office space for state of Florida agencies consists of a process that involves the individual agency, the Florida Department of Management Services (DMS) and the Staubach Company, a private tenant broker firm. Before a rule change dated April 2004, state agencies were not allowed to negotiate with private landlords. This lack of negotiation most likely led to unneeded reconstruction and higher expense. In their response to an agency RFP, landlords provided an estimate of refurbishing costs based on exactly what agencies requested. Agencies were thus not given an opportunity to consider somewhat different needs, for example, office space of slightly different configuration, to save funds.

Also, quality of space was not taken into consideration, as much more weight was given to cost or price. With negotiation permitted, greater flexibility was provided to state agencies to assess space based on quality and discuss this issue during negotiations. During the supplier selection phase, negotiations focused on the amount of funds available for refurbishing and on the control over the distribution of these funds. During the contract administration phase, negotiation was decentralized, allowing specific issues to be negotiated between agency and landlord according to industry standards. This process also gives DMS greater discretion to act as a landlord for all state agencies, providing greater opportunity to colocate state agency personnel where possible (Marsiglio, 2004).

The solicitation development phase begins with agencies requesting additional space from DMS. If no unused space exists, then agencies are permitted to solicit responses from landlords. Staubach company representatives provide an initial market analysis of all responses, and participate as a member of the negotiating team after all responses are rated. The following provides a specific example of this master lease approach.

In July 2004, DMS announced an intent to consolidate 1.5 million square feet of space needs into government centers, areas containing a relatively short distance among all buildings housing state employees. After a lengthy solicitation and negotiation process, several leases were signed. One of the resulting leases, known as the Koger Center Master Lease, included over 570,000 square feet of office space in nineteen separate buildings for seven different state agencies.

Solicitation for this space resulted in responses from four landlords. As part of the evaluation process, an outside consultant rated all proposed building space using the BOMA (Building Owners and Managers Association) approach. Buildings were rated as A, B, C, or D. The ratings were based on a number of criteria, including the following:

- Physical inspection
- Buildings' age
- Assessment of original construction and any subsequent refurbishing
- Any perceived management issues, compared to the market
- Any amenities such as distance to restaurants, appearance of outside common areas, etc.

This information, along with Staubach provided market analysis, provided additional analysis for both the response rating and the concurrent negotiation process that occurred with these four landlords. These negotiations took place during September 27–30, 2004.

The goals discussed in the solicitation document constituted much of the response rating criteria, and served as the basis for negotiations during supplier selection. Issues regarding price described the intent of the state to include low-cost rental rates, more efficient planning and tenant improvement allowances, and creative mechanisms that will provide immediate financial relief to the state. Moving costs were also to be considered.

To some extent goals overlapped in their intent, further defining potential negotiation agenda items. Because one of the goals was to create government centers, the closeness of already existing government-occupied buildings to the proposed space was rated, as well as space that resulted in the least amount of disruption for state employees. Clearly moving costs would be higher for building space that was located further from existing occupied space.

The length of the proposed lease plus the existence of potential lease renewals are issues that serve the interests of both the public agencies and landlords. The longer the lease, the potentially lower the rental costs, as the landlord can expect a higher degree of occupancy over a longer time. Also, the renew option benefits both agencies and landlords. Past State of Florida experience with leases that did not contain renewal options resulted in less landlord attention paid to maintenance, for example, during the latter years of the lease. Finally, the longer the length of the lease, the more the chance that the state needs would change, requiring assurance that the landlord would be willing to adapt to space needs.

28.4.1.1 Negotiation Issues and Results: Cost

Cost issues included the following:

- Initial charge per square foot
- Rate of increase for each year of the leases
- Any rent payment waivers
- Amount of the tenant improvement fund
- Operating and maintenance costs
- Moving costs

Negotiations depended on the amounts for each category identified by each respondent, as well as how each issue impacted another. For example, during the negotiations with one offeror, the Staubach representative identified the market rate of rental increase in the region as approximately 3 percent per year, in contrast to the 4 percent identified by the offeror. The response from the offeror was a suggestion to lower the rental increase rate to 2 percent, but all increases in operating costs would be paid by the state. The public negotiating team was not willing to accept this offer, stating in fairness that all rate increases had to include operating costs, as this issue was identified in the solicitation document.

Three aspects of the tenant improvement funds proved important:

- Amount that depended on the perceived need for refurbishing as well as the amount of occupied space
- Control over the disbursement of these funds, that is, whether the landlord or agency personnel would decide when funds would be spent for what purpose
- Timing and the process by which these funds would be disbursed

In past leasing contracts, without negotiation, the landlord would determine the amount needed for refurbishing depending upon the agency request. Landlords would also determine when and how the funds would be spent, as long as agreed upon moving deadlines were met. However, if there were delays, state agencies were often placed in uncomfortable positions of adjusting plans, leading in some cases to lower service quality.

Results included the following. The time period of the lease was from November 1, 2004 to October 31, 2019. Up to two five-year renewal periods are allowed. The initial lease rate was $16.50 per square foot, an amount that rises 3.15 percent per year.

In addition, state agencies do not pay rent for the first 20 months of the lease. A tenant improvement program is funded by a payment of $11 million from the landlord to the state. This fund is placed into a tax bearing escrow account. Not only does the state gain interest, but it also has the flexibility to spend these funds in a variety of ways, not all of which must be relevant to renovation.

28.4.1.2 Negotiation Issues and Results: Space

State agencies may experience changing space needs, with agencies wishing to expand or contract the space that they occupy. Negotiations resulted in language that addresses the needs of both the state and the landlord. If space becomes vacant, two actions are possible. First, DMS promised to try to fill that space with employees from other state agencies. Second, the state of Florida can sublet space to private companies. If this occurs, any profit from this subletting is split evenly between the state and the landlord.

28.4.1.3 Negotiation Issues and Results: Repair and Maintenance

The relationship between the agency and the landlord during contract administration, after space has been refurbished and is occupied, is governed by a wide range of both specific and general language in the contract, as well as by standard industry practices and a desire to maintain a positive working relationship. A list of maintenance duties for the janitorial staff, for example, specifies how often cleaning tasks must be performed. This language is common to many leasing contracts, and allows agencies discretion to improve on industrywide standards if they wish.

In contrast, the responsibilities of the landlord include keeping major aspects of the buildings in good repair and working order, including structural elements of the building; all mechanical, electrical, and physical aspects; common areas; the roof; and interior surface. Although this language does not define these terms, there is the expectation that an agency employee who is designated the building manager will monitor building conditions and report to the landlord any aspects that are not acceptable. Because the lease length is considered long term, plus there are renewal options, there is the expectation that the landlord can reasonably expect the state agencies to remain a tenant, and therefore has an incentive to maintain building conditions to the satisfaction of the agency.

A much stronger commitment to negotiation, plus the willingness to consider longer term leases, resulted in a lease contract that contains several advantages to the state of Florida agency personnel. Greater control of refurbishing amounts and timetables should allow for more satisfactory outcomes and better service quality. Negotiations during the supplier selection phase have resulted in improved relationships during the contract administration phase, and allowed for maximum customization to occur.

28.4.2 iFlorida Conditions System

In March 2003, the U.S. Federal Highway Administration (FHWA) chose the Florida Department of Transportation (FDOT) to deploy the iFlorida conditions system for central Florida. The goal was to provide a Web-based system that was easily accessible by travelers.[7] This was a highly integrated system of information concerning traffic congestion that draws upon several sources, including the following:

- Cameras along the major interstate highway in central Florida (I-4)
- Transponders placed on vehicles that are part of the SunPass system
- Florida highway patrol computer-aided dispatch system
- Information from the toll road system under the jurisdiction of the Orlando Orange County Expressway Authority
- Specified local roadways from a multicounty area
- Transit information
- Weather data

The FDOT District Five, the district with responsibility for serving central Florida, issued a solicitation document on September 30, 2003 (Florida DOT, 2003a). The document contained a qualifications questionnaire, composed of questions that were designed to not only determine and evaluate offerors past performance and management and technical capabilities, but also served as criteria that influenced negotiations.

The total of 21 questions (Florida DOT, 2003b, p. 1) included the following:

- Has your firm been a developer or integrator of transportation systems and software systems of the level and complexity as described [in the appendices] for a period of time of no less than five years? If yes, how long... and describe the services. Also attach a list of software work references.
- What software languages and operating systems does your firm have expertise in?
- Please provide a proposed staffing chart and management plan for the project.
- Please describe the software development environment and facilities your firm uses to develop and manage software.
- Does your firm have a formal, documented process for configuration management of your products?
- Does your firm have a formal documented software quality assurance program?
- How will you test the subsystem software before final acceptance testing?

28.4.2.1 Negotiation Issues and Results

Seven offerors completed the questionnaire and returned it along with their technical and price proposals. A short list of three offerors was created, leading to negotiations with the top-rated offeror, Castle Rock Consultants (CRC), on December 8 and 9, 2003. The FDOT team, led by the general consultant for the project, reviewed the solicitation document and response section by section. The content of the negotiations raised several issues, allowing the FDOT team to prioritize and emphasize those topics that were of highest priority.

First, it was clearly stated that CRC was to build upon existing and newly developed agency Web sites in creating the iFlorida system, rather than creating an entirely new system. This meant that the contract administration phase would be characterized by extensive communications and potential negotiations among several data source representatives, for example, those from the Orlando Orange County Expressway Authority and from the Florida Highway Patrol.

Second, on several occasions, the FDOT team stressed the importance of meeting the stated May 1, 2005 deadline for final acceptance. FHWA representatives, contributing a significant share of project costs, insisted on this deadline.

More important, several discussions focused on the design and testing schedule for various components of the system. The key issues centered around the testing and acceptance of each component part and the subsequent acceptance of the entire system. CRC favored a more efficient approach, testing several functional requirements at once. The FDOT team insisted that each requirement must be tested singly, as one requirement may work in tandem with some of the others, but may not work when all the requirements are tested as a whole. This negotiation resulted CRC spending greater time and effort on testing than they had originally proposed.

It was agreed that CRC would test components before FDOT staff also testing the final version. This redundant testing process meant that CRC may have to adjust its internal testing schedule to ensure the final deadline was met. Also, it was recognized that creating interfaces to collect data from the various sources would vary in the amount of time required, as the legacy data systems varied widely in quality, and in some cases were being created concurrently with the iFlorida system.

Another key negotiated issue was the process of problem resolution. CRC agreed to create a log identifying when a problem occurred, when it was solved, and what methods were used to solve it. Periodically, public technical representatives would review this log, categorizing problems as high priority and low priority and assessing to what extent problems were solved. By implication, not only did this approach ensure a quality check, but it also allowed for negotiation that would lead to a satisfactory outcome for both CRC and public agency representatives.

Overall, negotiations conveyed a sense that public managers wished to work closely with CRC, understanding that some requirements may need to change as the project evolved. It was stated that as the condition interfaces were created, CRC should identify aspects of the functional requirements that would be difficult to meet. In response, the FDOT managers would have the opportunity to change or eliminate the requirement.

The negotiations were deemed a success by the public managers. On the second day of negotiations, CRC provided draft language involving changes that were agreed upon during the first day. A contract was awarded on January 12, 2004.

The complexity of the final product in this case meant that negotiations during the supplier selection process also to some extent changed the scope of the solicitation. Negotiations during this first phase identified some processes and procedures that were intended to govern future interactions and negotiations as more specific parts of the system were created. Although the final product could be adequately conceptualized by both public agencies and the private contractor before contract award, all recognized that many of the final details would not become apparent until actual system creation occurred.

28.5 Conclusion

In an era of increasing collaborative public management,[7] in which public agencies enter into inter-organizational relationships that help them better accomplish organizational goals, negotiation skills are becoming far more necessary than in the past. Many public–private partnerships are based on relationships that are framed by contracts (Klitgaard and Treverton, 2004). Choosing the best partner(s) entails using negotiation skills in ways that are applicable to all supplier selection processes. What is challenging for many public officials involved in procurement, however, is acting in ways that effectively represent the public interest while interacting with partners over a much longer period of time in creating a complex product or service.

The contract administration phase, in many cases, requires the same negotiation skills that for simple purchases only existed for solicitation development and supplier selection. Problem solving after a contract has been awarded often requires much more flexibility, as final product specifications are altered and timetables changed due to conditions and requirements that were unknown during solicitation development. The principled negotiation approach, in which trust, transparency, and strong adherence to the public trust, remains one that can lead to successful outcomes.

Notes

1. Customization can be defined as the degree to which the service or product must be altered to meet the unique needs of the client agency for purpose of increasing quality while decreasing price (Rothman, 2004).
2. In some cases, for example, in the state of Florida, using a concurrent form of negotiation means that more than one offeror may be negotiated within a proscribed timeframe. See Lawther (2003) for more discussion.
3. Even when employing performance-based contracting, there should be some discussion of process to assure agency personnel that contractors are capable.
4. This is especially true if the contract is among several public agencies, and one agency will be designated the lead agency: the one given the most responsibility for postcontract award management.
5. Of course, no auction bidding is permitted. This is in violation of FAR (Federal Acquisition Regulation) standards, and is viewed as an unethical practice.
6. See Lawther (2006) for more discussion.
7. The January 2007 issue of *Public Administration Review* contains further discussion of collaborative public management.

References

Adler, J. 2007. *Construction Contracting Methods*. Unpublished manuscript.

Ashford, S. 2004. Commercial negotiation skills. *Industrial and Commercial Training* 36(6): 229–233.

Bingham, L.B. 1996. Negotiating for the public good. In: J.L. Perry (Ed.), *Handbook of Public Administration*. San Francisco, CA: Jossey-Bass, pp. 647–664.

Brown, M.M. 2001. The benefit and costs of information technology innovations: An empirical assessment of a local government agency. *Public Performance & Management Review* 24(4): 351–366.

Callendar, G., Jamieson, D., and Vincent, K. 2004. Software costing analysis model for evaluating value for money. In: K.V. Thai, A. Araujo, R.Y. Carter, G. Callendar, D. Drabkin, R. Grimm, K. Jensen, R.E. Lloyd, C. McCue, and J. Telgen (Eds.), *Challenges in Public Procurement: An International Perspective*, Vol. 3. Boca Raton, FL: PRAcademics Press, pp. 81–103.

Dobler, D.W. and Burt, D.N. 1996. *Purchasing and Supply Management: Text and Cases*. New York: McGraw-Hill.

Fisher, R. and Ury, W. 1991. *Getting to Yes: Negotiating Agreement without Giving In*, 2nd ed. New York: Penguin Books.

Florida Department of Transportation, District Five (FDOT). 2003. *Appendix A: Scope of Work for iFlorida Conditions System*. Deland, FL: Author.

Hall, L. (Ed.). 1993. *Negotiation: Strategies for Mutual Gain*. Newbury Park, CA: SAGE Publications.

Harney, D.F. 1992. *Service Contracting: A Local Government Guide*. Washington, DC: International City/County Management Association.

Karrass, C.L. 1998. Tips for team negotiators. *Purchasing Magazine* 125(9): 24.

Kelman, S. 1990. *Procurement and Public Management: The Fear of Discretion and the Quality of Government Performance*. Washington, DC: The AEI Press.

Klitgaard, R. and Treverton, G.F. 2004. Assessing partnerships: New forms of collaboration. In: J.M. Kamensky and T.J. Burlin (Eds.), *Collaboration: Using Networks and Partnerships*. Lanham, MD: Rowman & Littlefield Publishers, Inc., pp. 21–60.

Lawther, W.C. 2003. Invitation to negotiate: Determining the boundaries of innovative source selection. *Journal of Public Procurement* 3(3): 301–319.
Lawther, W.C. 2006. The growing use of competitive negotiations to increase managerial capability: The acquisition of e-government services. *Public Performance Management and Review* 30(2): 204–221.
Lawther, W.C. 2007. Flexible procurement approaches that facilitate relationship change and negotiation: The use of the invitation to negotiate. *Journal of Public Procurement* 7(2): 173–193.
Marsiglio, C. 2004. ITN No. DMS 04/05–025 Procurement of "Government Center" Office Space in Leon County, Memorandum to Kaye Robertson, July 19.
Rothman, R. 2004. *Public Procurement in Florida*. http://dms.myflorida.com/dms/content/download/2591/10510/file. Last accessed February 25, 2007.
State of Florida, Department of Transportation, District Five (Florida DOT). 2003a. *Invitation to Negotiate iFlorida Conditions System*. Deland, FL: Author, IT–DOT-03/04–5002.
State of Florida, Department of Transportation, District Five (Florida DOT). 2003b. *Invitation to Negotiate iFlorida Conditions System Qualifications Questionnaire*. Deland, FL: Author, ITN–DOT-03/04–5002.
Thai, K.V. 2004a. *Developing and Managing Requests for Proposals in the Public Sector*. Herndon, VA: National Institute of Government Purchasing.
Thai, K.V. 2004b. *Introduction to Public Procurement*. Herndon, VA: National Institute of Government Purchasing.
Van Slyke, D.M. 2003. The myth of privatization in contracting for social services. *Public Administration Review* 63(3): 296–315.
Welch, B. 2003. Best Practices in Federal Acquisition. *The Public Manager* 32(3): 11–17.

Chapter 29

Controlling Service Process Performance with Statistical Process Control

Ralph G. Kauffman and Philip G. Lightfoot

CONTENTS

29.1 Introduction

In the public sector in general, the product that is produced or delivered to users or customers is a service and not a physically tangible product; for example, registration of a motor vehicle, collection of trash, delivery of mail, and maintenance of parks and public buildings. In every case, however, the users or customers of these services have expectations regarding the quality or performance level of the services, the consistency of performance quality, and, because tax money is used to pay the cost of the service in many cases, the efficiency of the provision of the service.

Control of the cost of public services is in most cases achieved by applying a budgeting process that compares actual cost to a budgeted amount. The budgeted amount can usually not be exceeded during a budget cycle (typically one year), and, if costs turn out to be greater than budgeted, the service may be terminated or curtailed for the part of the budget cycle after all the budgeted amount has been spent. Typically, there is no mechanism other than periodic budget reviews, to identify developing cost problems or trends that, if identified soon enough, may possibly be managed in a way to prevent termination or curtailment of the service.

Concerning service quality or performance level, there is often no means of control for the level of performance of the service or for the consistency of service performance (except perhaps to monitor the level of user or customer complaints of services that does not meet their expectations). There is also often no means of identifying developing service performance problems or trends.

This chapter discusses a tool that is most often associated with manufacturing industries but which can also be applied to service industries including the provision of services in the public sector. This tool, statistical process control (SPC), can be used to control and manage service performance and cost just as effectively as it is used in manufacturing industries to control quality level and consistency. In this chapter, the tool is explained by using the example of control of warehouse operations. Details are explained through a case study of an actual application of SPC to control and manage service levels of spare parts warehouses operated by a municipality. The principles behind SPC, and SPC itself however, can be applied to control and manage service quality and performance levels for any service process where performance level, performance quality, cost, and consistency are important.

29.2 Introduction to the Case Study

Warehouses serve several purposes or functions including, among others, protection of the goods stored, providing a location for just-in-time product completion or customization, product mixing or consolidation, and improving customer service by providing an assortment of products at a location close to, or that provides convenient access for, customers. This latter function is particularly important for warehouses that contain parts and supplies for maintenance, repair, and operation support (MRO items). This degree of importance is due to the short lead time often required by users or customers for MRO items.

For warehouses in general, and specifically for MRO warehouses, the two primary objectives or warehouse management are as follows: (1) maximize customer service and (2) minimize costs (Arnold and Chapman, 2004). A sub-objective of both of these is consistency of service level. Significant variation in warehouse operating costs is undesirable and significant variation in customer service is unacceptable because of its negative effect on customers' perception of the overall value proposition they are receiving from a supplier of a warehoused product.

To manage and control customer service and costs associated with operation of warehouses, basic budgeting approaches and tabular reports of actual activity and performance compared to budgeted norms can provide the necessary data. However, such approaches typically do not readily provide data with which to identify developing problem areas or trends of costs or performance. A management tool that does have the capability to identify developing performance problems and cost trends is SPC. This tool has been used mostly for manufacturing processes to control the quality level of manufactured parts and other products. However, it can be applied as a control tool to any process situation where consistency and adherence to standards or norms is desired. The following case study provides an example of the application of SPC to control warehouse cost and performance for the MRO warehouse facilities of a major municipality.

29.3 Case Study of Application of Statistical Process Methods to Service Activities

29.3.1 Case Summary

Agency management in the city of Houston, Texas, had a problem measuring and controlling MRO warehouse performance. This case study describes how better control can be achieved through application of SPC to certain activities. To develop the application, the agency viewed particular activities associated with warehousing as controllable processes. Historically, SPC has been applied mostly in a manufacturing or production environment as a means of maintaining an acceptable level of product quality. This case shows that SPC can be and is a useful tool for controlling and managing services in the public sector.

29.3.2 Introduction

To support maintenance activities, the city of Houston, Texas, operates ten MRO warehouses. The agency responsible for managing this inventory wanted a way to measure the performance of certain warehouse operations that would also alert them to developing and existing problem situations. After determining objectives and defining particular indicators to measure performance, the agency needed a way to track performance that would provide management reports of ongoing activity and exception reports usable to prevent and correct performance problems. Although basic tabular reports of activity and performance would provide the required data, it was determined that, to identify developing or ongoing problem areas for process operations, SPC methodology would be a more effective tool because of its graphical representation of trends and situations. Although SPC has most often been applied to manufacturing processes, it has been applied in other areas including improvement of inventory accuracy (Hart, 1998). Historically, SPC has been used to measure and control the quality of manufactured parts produced by a process. The resulting parts must be produced to a particular quality standard to achieve the required quality level. Certain aspects of the warehouse performance management problem faced by the city can also be viewed as controllable processes. Certain process tasks must be performed to deliver a service at a required level of quality. The only difference between the warehouse and a manufactured part is that the warehouse delivers a service and the manufacturing process produces a tangible part. This chapter describes the quality measures decided upon and the application of SPC as a means of controlling process aspects of warehouse performance to desired levels.

29.3.3 The Situation

The city of Houston, Texas, is the fourth largest in the United States with about two million residents and a city budget of $2.5 billion for 2002. The city encompasses about 640 square miles. Ten MRO warehouses serve a municipal maintenance operation for the Public Works and Engineering Department. Although the warehouses vary in size, number of items stocked, and personnel, all provide essentially identical services under the same set of operating procedures. An approach was desired to measure the efficiency and effectiveness of performance of all ten warehouses that would provide data with which to compare and control performance of the warehouses overall, to each other, and over time, and that would identify developing and existing performance problems to facilitate preventive or corrective action.

29.3.4 Objectives and Performance Measurements

The objectives of both inventory management and warehouse management can be stated as follows (Arnold and Chapman, 2004):

- Maximize customer service
- Minimize costs

The agency decided use the terms "efficiency of operations" to represent cost minimization, and "operational effectiveness" to represent customer service maximization.

Because it may be difficult to directly measure how well these objectives are being met, research indicated a number of possible performance measures that can be used for this purpose: possible measures of efficiency performance—inventory turnover, equipment utilization, personnel productivity, space utilization, and budget performance; and possible measures of effectiveness performance—on-time delivery of orders, completeness of orders, number of complaints received, avoidance of damage, and accuracy of order filling (Duncan, 1986; Ackerman, 1997). The following measures were selected for use.

29.3.4.1 Efficiency

Efficiency is measured by inventory turnover. Inventory turnover is an indication of how efficiently inventories are being used by relating inventory quantity to inventory usage. Because of different supply and demand characteristics, it was decided to use two turnover measures to indicate warehouse efficiency.

1. Turnover of commodity materials inventories, which is measured by dividing the value of warehouse issues of these materials by the average inventory of them
2. Turnover of spare parts inventories, which is measured by dividing the value of warehouse issues of spare parts by the average inventory of them

29.3.4.2 Effectiveness

Effectiveness is measured by using the following indicators of customer service and maintenance staff productivity:

- Service delivery performance, which is measured by completeness of orders (the number of line items issued as a percentage of the number of line items requisitioned)
- Service delivery time, which is measured by the time taken to locate, pick, and deliver to a requestor (the total person-time required to deliver an order to a requestor)
- Production downtime owing to stockouts, which is measured by the time equipment is out of service because of inventoried parts being out of stock
- Lost maintenance productivity owing to stockouts, which is measured by the time maintenance personnel are idle because of needed parts being out of stock

Turnover measures for efficiency are calculated from monthly summary data on average inventory and material issued. These are not process elements. Therefore, they were not included in the SPC application and are controlled by analysis of monthly summary data. The same is true for production downtime and lost maintenance productivity. The remaining two effectiveness measures, service delivery performance and service delivery time, are the core of the warehouse service process and the locus of application of SPC methodology.

29.3.5 SPC Methodology

SPC methodology is well established so only a brief summary is presented here. A more detailed discussion can be found in various references (e.g., Mitra, 1998; Summers, 2000; Evans and Lindsay, 2002). Every process, whether to produce a physical product or a service, has common ingredients of people, equipment, inputs, methods, and environment. All of these interact to produce an output. The intent of every process design is for the process to function identically each time it is executed to provide consistency of output. However, the natural variations that occur in materials, people, equipment, and environment, and in how they interact, introduce an element of variability of output. If the variability in a process is from such random causes and not from some specific cause affecting the process, over time the random variability often causes the frequency of occurrence of different amounts of variation to take on the characteristics of a normal distribution. If the production capability of the process is sufficiently centered on the target or desired value of the output, then the actual values over time will be symmetrical around the target value. Where these conditions exist, SPC is a method that can be used for monitoring the variability to ensure it does not exceed a tolerance required to produce an acceptable quality of output.

To use SPC, the process is monitored by taking periodic samples of output. The characteristics of the samples are measured and plotted to detect unacceptable output or trends toward exceeding acceptable tolerances. When such output or trends are found, corrective action can be taken to stop or prevent the production of defective units.

Various charts of performance can be used with SPC (Summers, 2000). For the warehouse application, the basic X-bar and R charts are used. These charts indicate the average value and the range of data, respectively, of samples taken from the process. For the X-bar chart, the average value of the measured service criterion is plotted, while for the R chart, the range of the criterion is plotted. The X-bar chart compares the current value to a desired value and the R chart indicates the current range of data compared to a desired range.

29.3.6 Application of SPC Methodology to Warehouse Control

To apply SPC, control limits must be set. These values indicate the range of acceptable process outcomes and values outside the limits or trending toward them indicate existing or developing nonrandom process problems (or, in SPC terminology, problems from assignable causes). For X-bar and R charts, it is common to set the control limits to achieve a particular objective probability that if the process is in control, the sample value will fall within the control limits. For example, using a commonly applied control objective of 99.7 percent, the control limits are set at ±3 standard deviations from the desired value. This is termed 3-sigma control. The result of this is, if the values are normally distributed and the process is in control, 99.7 percent of the sample average values will fall within the control limits.

For the city of Houston situation, it was determined from histogram analysis of samples of performance measurements that distributions of variation in the processes were approximately normal and means of the measurements were at acceptable levels of performance. Thus, the current processes over all warehouses were approximately centered on the desired performance levels, and the application of SPC to control warehouse performance was appropriate. Because current overall performance of all warehouses together was acceptable, the mean values of current performance were used as the target or desired performance values for all warehouses and overall. If current performance had not been acceptable, different target values could have been used with the data determining control limits from those values. To determine the variability and normality of distribution of the warehouse process results, samples of activity data were collected for sixteen days' operations for each of all ten warehouses. From this data, average performance values and ranges were obtained. Agency management determined that they wanted a 99.7 percent control objective, and therefore based control limits on ±3 standard deviations of the target performance value. For the X-bar charts, control limits for performance were determined using the widely accepted relationships:

$$\text{UCL} = \overline{X} + A_2\overline{R} \tag{29.1}$$

$$\text{LCL} = \overline{X} - A_2\overline{R} \tag{29.2}$$

where

UCL is the upper control limit
LCL is the lower control limit
$\overline{X}$ is the average (or desired) performance value
$\overline{R}$ is the average range of sample data
A_2 is a standard statistical factor

The A_2 factor is available in quality control texts and references. It varies with sample size and causes the A times R terms to be approximately equal to 3 standard deviations, or 3 sigma. Thus, the control limits are about 3 standard deviations above and below the desired value and result in the desired 99.7 percent control objective. In our situation with a sample size of 10, A_2 is 0.31 (Summers, 2000, Appendix 2).

For the R-bar charts, control limits were determined for the range of performance:

$$\text{UCL} = D_4\overline{R} \tag{29.3}$$

$$\text{LCL} = D_3\overline{R} \tag{29.4}$$

where

UCL is the upper control limit

LCL is the lower control limit

$\overline{R}$ is the average range of values of samples of the performance measure

D_3 and D_4 are the standard statistical factors

D_3 and D_4 are similar to the A_2 factor discussed above in Equations 29.1 and 29.2 for calculating control limits for performance. The D_3 and D_4 factors also vary with sample size and cause the D times R terms to be approximately equal to 3 standard deviations, or 3 sigma, to provide the desired 99.7 percent control objective as discussed previously. Using standard quality control tables (Summers, 2000, Appendix 2), D_3 is 0.22 and D_4 is 1.78.

To illustrate the application, we will discuss the control data across all warehouses. In practice, however, in addition to evaluating overall performance, each warehouse can be evaluated and controlled separately to enable identification of developing or existing problems specific to particular locations. In Section 29.3.7, some examples of individual warehouse performance data are discussed.

Service delivery performance was defined as the number of requested warehouse stock items issued as a percentage of the number of items requested. Service delivery time was defined as total person-time required to deliver an order to a requestor. For service delivery performance, the 16-day test period resulted in average performance (X-bar) of 96.3 percent and an average range (R-bar) of 15.2 percent (range was calculated by subtracting the lowest performance percentage from the highest percentage for each daily sample and taking the average of the resulting daily ranges). For service delivery time, we obtained an average performance (X-bar) of 42.4 person-minutes to deliver an order and an average range (R-bar) of 137.2 person-minutes (range was calculated in the same manner as for delivery performance). Using these values in Equations 29.1 through 29.4, we obtain the following:

1. Service delivery performance

$$\text{UCL} = 96.3 + 0.31 \times 15.2 = 101 \text{ percent} \quad (29.1\text{a})$$

(however, because 100 percent is the maximum performance possible, the upper control limit becomes 100 percent)

$$\text{LCL} = 96.3 - 0.31 \times 15.2 = 91.6 \text{ percent} \quad (29.2\text{a})$$

2. Service delivery performance range

$$\text{UCL} = 1.78 \times 15.2 = 27.1 \text{ percent} \quad (29.3\text{a})$$

$$\text{LCL} = 0.22 \times 15.2 = 3.3 \text{ percent} \quad (29.4\text{a})$$

3. Service delivery time performance

$$\text{UCL} = 42.4 + 0.31 \times 137.2 = 84.9 \text{ minutes} \quad (29.1\text{b})$$

$$\text{LCL} = 42.4 - 0.31 \times 137.2 = -0.1 \quad (29.2\text{b})$$

(however, because 0 is the minimum time possible, the lower control limit becomes 0)

4. Service delivery time range

$$\text{UCL} = 1.78 \times 137.2 = 244.2 \text{ minutes} \tag{29.3b}$$

$$\text{LCL} = 0.22 \times 137.2 = 30.2 \text{ minutes} \tag{29.4b}$$

If any changes are made to the process, variability should be reassessed and control limits recalculated using a test period. If different target performance values are desired, the control limits would also need to be recalculated.

After establishing control limits, the control process was implemented on a test basis. Testing and evaluation are continuing with final implementation pending completion of evaluation of

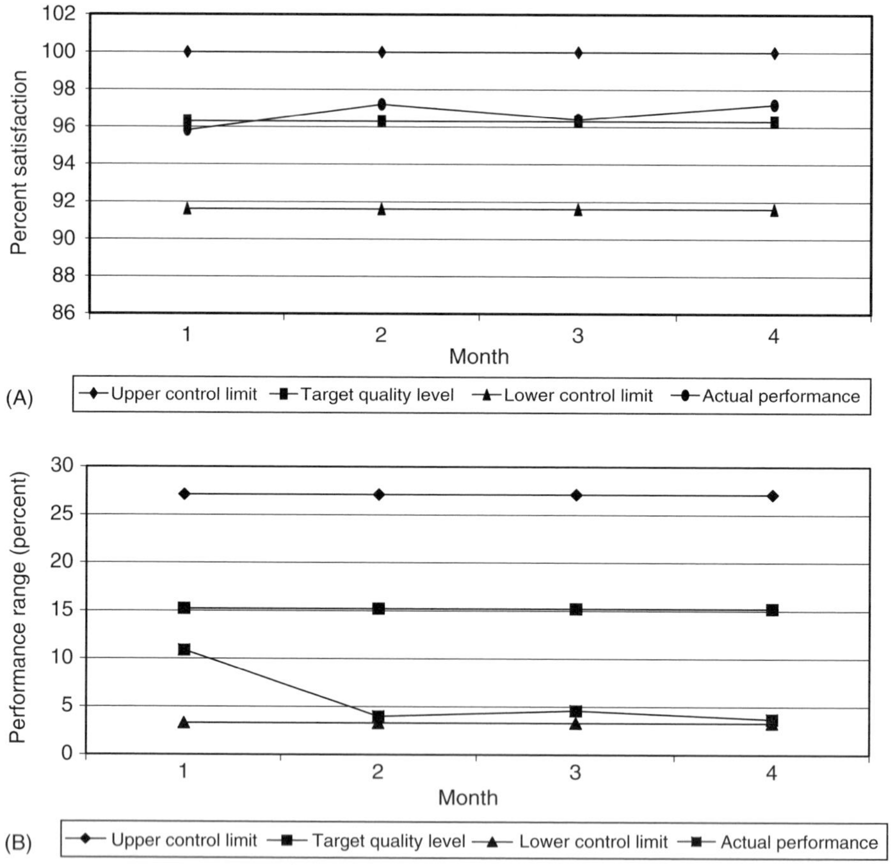

Figure 29.1 (A) Service delivery performance. Percent delivered: Month 1 = 95.8, Month 2 = 97.2, Month 3 = 96.4, Month 4 = 97.2; Upper control limit = 100, target quality level = 96.3, lower control limit = 91.6. (B) Range of service delivery performance. Range of percent delivered: Month 1 = 10.9, Month 2 = 4.0, Month 3 = 4.6, Month 4 = 3.7; Upper control limit = 27.1, target quality level = 15.2, lower control limit = 3.3.

test results. During the first four months of operation, the monthly averages of samples taken across all warehouses for service delivery performance and service delivery time are shown in Figures 29.1A and B and 29.2A and B. Table 29.1 contains individual warehouse data for a four-week period.

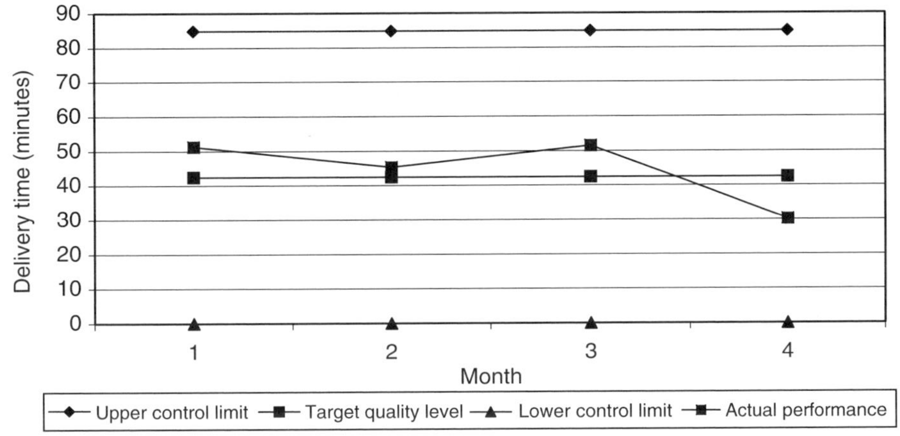

(A)

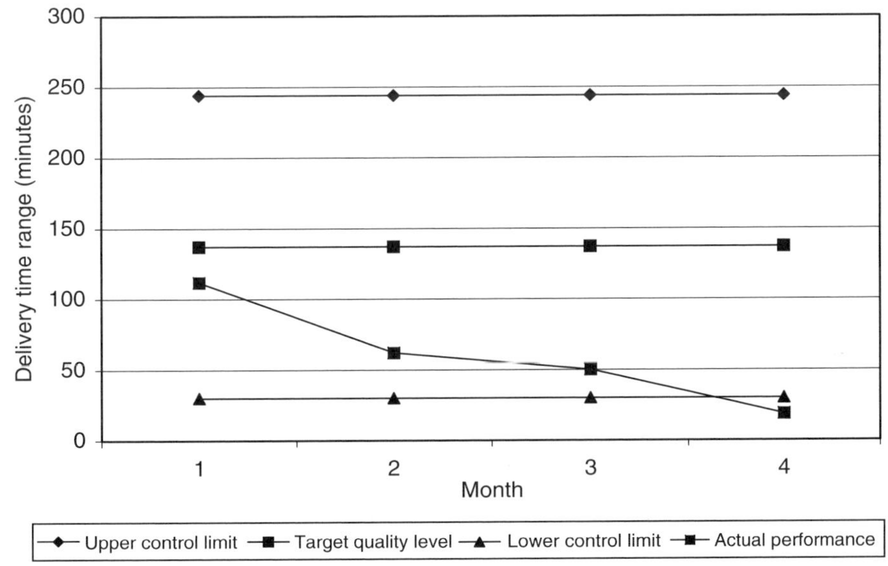

(B)

Figure 29.2 (A) Service delivery time. Delivery time in minutes: Month 1 = 51.3, Month 2 = 45.3, Month 3 = 51.5, Month 4 = 30.2; Upper control limit = 84.9, target quality level = 42.4, lower control limit = 0.0. (B) Range of service delivery time. Range of delivery time in minutes: Month 1 = 111.9, Month 2 = 62.1, Month 3 = 4.6, Month 4 = 3.7; Upper control limit = 244.2, target quality level = 137.2, lower control limit = 30.2.

Table 29.1 Weekly Warehouse Performance

Panel 1. Order Filling Percentage						
Warehouse	Week 1	Week 2	Week 3	Week 4	Average	Range
Alpha	100	96.6	94.4	95.2	96.55	5.6
Beta	100	100	100	98.4	99.60	1.6
Gamma	92.5	99.1	87.9	94.1	93.40	11.2
Delta	100	100	100	100	100	0
Epsilon	100	100	100	100	100	0
Zeta	94.2	91.8	95.8	93.7	93.88	4.0
Eta	85.6	93.6	95.9	88.6	90.93	10.3
Theta	98.0	99.1	99.5	98.5	98.78	1.2
Iota	100	100	100	97.2	99.30	2.8
Kappa	100	100	100	100	100	0
Panel 2. Transaction Service Time (in Minutes)						
Warehouse	Week 1	Week 2	Week 3	Week 4	Average	Range
Alpha	52.9	78.6	50.5	42.4	56.10	36.2
Beta	15.8	20.0	20.0	12.0	16.95	8.0
Gamma	29.7	22.1	34.1	28.9	28.70	12.0
Delta	14.3	14.7	12.9	13.8	13.93	1.8
Epsilon	24.1	15.9	20.6	17.3	19.48	8.2
Zeta	24.5	10.5	15.5	19.1	17.40	14.0
Eta	18.6	26.2	33.8	23.7	25.58	15.2
Theta	24.0	14.3	23.8	18.5	20.15	9.7
Iota	47.1	49.0	43.6	37.0	44.18	12.0
Kappa	102.1	32.7	49.0	56.1	59.98	69.4

29.3.7 Application of the Data to Improve Warehouse Management and Discussion of Results

29.3.7.1 Control Chart Results

Indications for all warehouses from Figure 29.1 are that overall the process is in control with no apparent developing trends and no out-of-control indications. We also see that the range of outcomes has narrowed over the time period included. From Figure 29.2, we can draw similar conclusions.

In both examples, the range measured dropped (narrowed) over the time period indicating less variability in performance as the time period progressed.

29.3.7.2 *Individual Warehouse Results*

Table 29.1 contains four weeks of data that we use to illustrate application of individual warehouse data to compare performance across all ten warehouse locations for that time period. This data can also be displayed with control charts for each warehouse, but to conserve space we use the tabular format and refer to overall control limits in Figures 29.1 and 29.2 in this analysis.

29.3.7.3 *Service Delivery Performance*

The top part of Table 29.1 indicates that for percent requisitioned line items filled completely (service delivery performance), warehouses Delta, Epsilon, and Kappa had 100 percent performance, well above the 96.3 percent target during this period, and all locations averaged over 90 percent performance. Although higher percentages are good because they indicate that more orders are more completely filled, consistent numbers in the vicinity of 100 percent may indicate excess inventory at particular locations. Our performance target is not 100 percent, it is 96.3 percent not only because management has determined that that is a satisfactory level of service, but also for the obvious additional reason that higher percentages will usually require higher inventories. Location Alpha's average performance was best of all locations by coming closest to the target value of 96.3 percent. We see that location Eta had two individual weeks, where performance was below the lower overall control limit of 91.6 percent for this criterion. Eta also had the second highest variability of performance as indicated by its data range. Location Gamma had the largest variability range and one week, where performance was below the lower control limit. Additional weeks or a trend of below-control performance would warrant investigation of the causes of these below-control performances. Warehouse Zeta came close to exceeding the lower control limit in Week 2 and is consistently below target for the other weeks. It may also merit investigation but, because it is within the control limits, it would rate a lower priority for investigation than Eta and perhaps Gamma.

29.3.7.4 *Service Delivery Time*

For transaction service time (service delivery time), less time is generally better, but consistently reported very short service times at particular warehouses could indicate reduced activity and possibly excess personnel at those locations. Location Iota had the best average performance by coming closest to the target of 42.4 minutes per delivery. During this period, warehouse Kappa had the worst average performance and also had one week, where its delivery time exceeded the upper control limit. Kappa also had the highest range of data. The combination of these two factors may warrant investigating the situation at that location to determine if any assignable causes exist or are developing.

In our situation, the process in use at all ten warehouse locations was identical. Therefore, to provide overall control, we use overall control limits calculated from performance data across all warehouses. To provide individual warehouse control, we use control limits calculated from individual warehouse data. However, if processes vary across locations, or if it is desired to test the variability of processes at different locations, overall controls may be misleading and only individual location data should be used. In such cases, samples of performance must be taken during test periods at individual locations and the resulting individual control limits calculated. It may also be determined that what were thought to be identical processes have differing variability by location and in fact some process element(s) may not be identical. The data can thus provide a basis for process investigation and improvement.

In general, data points that fall outside the control limits on the charts indicate that specific assignable causes likely existed at that time. These should be investigated to determine causes and action taken to prevent recurrence. Similarly, trends of sample values toward the control limits should also be investigated for underlying causes and corrective action taken before the control limits are exceeded. In the situation described here, current performance was acceptable overall and the technique functions mainly as a control mechanism. For certain locations, however, potential problems have been identified in the discussion of the data in Table 29.1. In situations where current performance is not acceptable, process changes can be made followed by a new test period to determine the variability and capability of the revised process and control limits for it. Acceptable performance targets and revised control limits from the new test period can then be used to control the revised process.

29.3.8 Case Conclusion

This case study shows how a warehouse performance management problem can be effectively improved by applying SPC to warehouse operations. It also demonstrates that warehouses and other service-type operations where SPC has not traditionally been applied can be managed and controlled by using SPC. SPC can also be used as a tool to evaluate and control revised and improved processes in service-type situations such as warehouse operations.

29.4 Other Applications of the SPC Tool to Management and Control of Services

Although this case illustrates the application of SPC to warehouse control and management, it should be evident that the SPC tool can be used to control any service process where performance, quality, and cost levels can be measured. For example, some possible applications of SPC could include the following: in the procurement area—response time to requests for items to be purchased, and performance of suppliers with regard to on-time delivery, consistency of delivery, consistency of in-stock for ordered items, and cost of items purchased; in the operations area—response time and costs of equipment maintenance and repair service, and response time and cost recovery for disposal of surplus materials.

References

Ackerman, K.B. 1997. *Practical Handbook of Warehousing*, 4th ed. New York: Chapman & Hall.

Arnold, J.R.T. and Chapman, S.N. 2004. *Introduction to Materials Management*, 5th ed. Upper Saddle River, NJ: Prentice Hall.

Duncan, A.J. 1986. *Quality Control and Industrial Statistics*, 5th ed. Homewood, IL: Richard D. Irwin.

Evans, J.R. and Lindsay, W.M. 2002. *The Management and Control of Quality*, 5th ed. Cincinnati, OH: South-Western.

Hart, M.K. 1998. Improving inventory accuracy using control charts. *Production and Inventory Management Journal* (Third Quarter): 44–48.

Mitra, A. 1998. *Fundamentals of Quality Control and Improvement*, 2nd ed. Upper Saddle River, NJ: Prentice Hall.

Summers, D.C.S. 2000. *Quality*, 2nd ed. Upper Saddle River, NJ, Prentice Hall.

Chapter 30

Fixed Asset Disposal: Methods and Strategies for Disposing of Personal Property in the Public Sector

Darin Matthews and Elizabeth Gibson

CONTENTS

30.1 Introduction

There are many opportunities for the public procurement professional to add value in the early stages of an acquisition. Market research of new products, supplier assessment, and specification development are all activities that take place early in the procurement process. However, often overlooked are the opportunities to add value after the purchase is made. The disposition of property at the end of its useful life cycle is actually the last step in the procurement cycle (NIGP, 1996), but it is often overlooked and underappreciated.

Just as there are many methods to acquire materials for the government (such as request for proposal, invitation to bid, and direct negotiation), there are also multiple ways to dispose of surplus property. These methods are discussed in this chapter, as there is no single approach that is best for all situations. Only by becoming aware of the tools available to them, can practitioners select the method that is most appropriate for a particular item. This chapter defines fixed assets and identifies the types that are commonly used within the public sector. All organizations need to address certain policy issues including who is responsible for management of the surplus program. Strategic planning will serve as a valuable tool within these programs.

Like other areas of procurement management, there are numerous fiscal and legal issues involved with fixed asset disposal. In addition to following all applicable laws and regulations, procurement professionals must also realize the importance of properly closing the books during the disposition process. The various methods of asset disposal are covered, including public bids and sales, donations, equipment trade-ins, recycling refurbishment, and redisposition. How an organization can measure performance is addressed, as this can greatly assist in assessing the effectiveness of a disposition program.

Recent years have seen the increased use of technology within fixed asset management and disposal. By utilizing these tools, organizations can increase their efficiency and effectiveness. Industry trends are explored, as well as various systems and programs that are readily available. Corporate social responsibility is a growing issue for organizations in all sectors, but frankly expectations are highest for public agencies. Opportunities exist for minimizing environmental impact with disposal methods, and also seeking out opportunities for community involvement. Finally, selected case studies highlight public agencies that employ best practices and operate effective disposition programs. Lessons can be learned from these examples, with the hope that these programs can provide guidance to other agencies that result in improved practices.

30.2 Fixed Assets

30.2.1 Types of Fixed Assets

There are many types of fixed assets in the public sector. It may be an item over a certain dollar threshold, or equipment that has a set amount of usable years. Besides the initial investment, which can be substantial, agencies must also consider what it takes to maintain, insure, and replace these assets. They can be found throughout an organization and are often movable items, such as building furniture or heavy equipment. Fixed assets are used up over time while they decline in value. These are referred to as depreciable assets. When they get to a point at the end of their useful life, they may even be considered a burden to an agency. Fixed assets are physical assets such as property, plant, and equipment (Figure 30.1). These assets can be also thought of as equipment owned by a public agency, something to which the agency holds title, or all the property is not considered real property. Land and buildings are considered real property (or real estate) and therefore not fixed asset. Real property is an example of an asset that increases in value over time, and is therefore considered appreciable.

Asset classifications

Property	Plant	Equipment
• Land and rights	• Shelving units	• Delivery vehicles
• Ground improvements	• Conveyor systems	• Forklifts and other lift equipment
• Utility systems	• Picking systems	• Computer hardware
• Buildings and structures		• Barcode readers

Figure 30.1 Asset classifications. (From ISM (2007); Christopher, M., *Logistics and Supply Chain Management*, Prentice Hall, London, United Kingdom, 1998. With permission.)

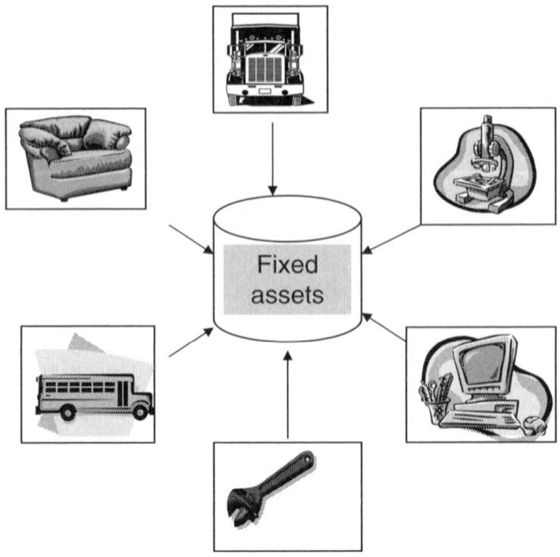

Figure 30.2 Fixed asset examples.

Specific examples of fixed assets an agency might possess and track include computer equipment and electronics, office furniture, fixtures, printers, scanners, file cabinets, tooling, supplies, and vehicles. Today, software applications and licenses used and tracked by nearly all organizations and are considered fixed assets. Items that are quickly used up and are often low cost, such as pencils, nuts and bolts, and fuel, are considered expendable items. Figure 30.2 depicts items commonly considered by the government as fixed assets.

The U.S. federal government establishes parameters for fixed assets, particularly as they relate to items purchased with federal grant dollars. The Office of Management and Budget (OMB) sets forth these standards to ensure uniformity and consistency among agencies. OMB Circular 110 defines equipment as tangible personal property having a useful life of more than one year and a purchase cost of at least $5000 (Brady, 2001). Smaller government entities such as state and local governments, however, often establish lower values for their own fixed assets.

Fixed assets can not only include standard items like medical test equipment or forklifts, but can also include customized equipment. For instance, if a company manufactures a mechanized picking system for a public warehouse, that would still be considered a fixed asset. According to Kieso and Weygandt (1995), there are three major characteristics of fixed assets:

1. Operational use. Fixed assets are acquired for use in operations and not for resale. Only assets used in normal business operations should be classified as fixed assets.
2. Long-term use. Fixed assets are long term in nature. Fixed assets yield services over a number of years.
3. Physical substance. Fixed assets are of physical substance. Fixed assets are characterized by physical existence or substance and thus are differentiated by intangible assets, such as patents and goodwill.

Property that is leased is also considered to be an asset, because it does hold value during the term of the lease. The two basic types of leases used by the government are operating and capital leases. An operating lease is much like a rental agreement, and is used primarily for shorter term needs.

They can include items like copiers or computers. A capital lease transfers nearly all of the benefits and risks of ownership to the public agency. This is used for longer term needs like acquiring heavy equipment. Often these leases contain a provision whereby ownership is transferred to the agency at the end of the lease, or is offered at a bargain purchase price (Brady, 2001).

30.2.2 Types of Surplus Property

Surplus property is best described as materials and assets that an organization no longer needs. This can include assets of all types and often fall under the control and authority of procurement. Property can become surplus for a variety of reasons, including spare parts that become outdated, furniture that has been replaced, and vehicles no longer used. Surplus assets generally fall within the following categories:

- Damaged stock is a property that has experienced neglect or damage and is not fit for the use intended. Defective manufacturing or improper packaging can be reasons for the damage.
- Scrap includes materials like metal or wood that have no use by an organization. It can come from left over special projects or material left over from normal production.
- Spoilage refers to assets that have no market value. It can include things like chemicals or rubber products that have a limited shelf life.
- Obsolete assets are items that can no longer serve their intended purpose because of operational or market charges. Advancements in technology can often render assets obsolete, such as electronic printing devices that are not network compatible.

30.2.3 Fixed Asset Management Cycle

As mentioned in Section 30.2.1, fixed assets have a useful life, which is also referred to as life cycle. The fixed management life cycle begins when the property is acquired and continues on until the end of its useful life. In the public sector, the acquisition step includes the specification, bidding, and purchase of the item. Once the equipment is received by the purchasing agency, it is verified as to its function and quality. Most agencies utilize electronic purchasing systems that include a receiving function (the use of technology is covered in Section 30.7). If the purchased item is in accordance with the specifications and requirements of the agency, then payment is the next step. According to the terms of the purchase order or contract, payment is made to the supplier within a certain time period.

The next step in the cycle is for the item to be identified as a fixed asset by tagging or other inventory method. A permanently attached asset tag can help identify and track the equipment throughout its useful life. Technology has advanced greatly in recent years to allow automated tracking of assets, which is discussed in Section 30.7.4. The longest step in the cycle is inventory, as the item will be accounted for and inventoried up until the time an agency disposes of it. Excess refers to a user declaring an asset unneeded. In these cases, it is common to transfer the asset to another department within the same agency. If the item continues to be used, the new owning department must continue to inventory the asset. The final state of the property management cycle is deeming the item as surplus. A surplus asset that is no longer needed or valued by an agency can be disposed of in a variety of ways. Once the item is disposed of, the agency no longer owns or accounts for the asset. The fixed asset management cycle is shown in Figure 30.3.

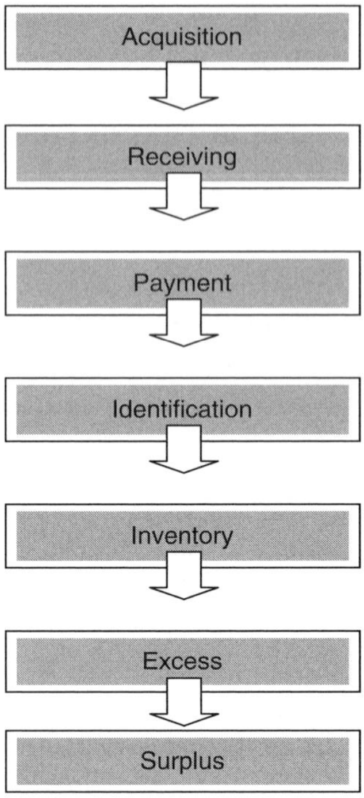

Figure 30.3 Fixed assets management cycle. (From Brady, W., *Managing Fixed Assets in the Public Sector*, Universal Publishers, USA, 2001.)

30.2.4 Return on Investment

Each asset that is acquired by an agency comes at a cost, or investment. It is only natural to seek the maximum return on that investment when it is disposed of. Although there are a number of methods available for disposal (discussed later in Section 30.5), the goal is to maximize the return to the agency (Brady, 2001). The higher the sale price for a surplus asset, the more an agency can offset the cost of the initial purchase. Organizational policies differ on how sale proceeds are receipted back into its coffers. It is quite common for the department that is parting with the surplus equipment to never see these proceeds. Rather than the funds going back into a specific department's operating budget, it is receipted into a general revenue account for the agency. Figure 30.4 is an example of such a policy from Cornell University. Even if the proceeds cannot come directly back into the using department's budget, it can still benefit the agency overall.

Many organizations have developed investment recovery groups to manage surplus assets. An example of this is Pacific Gas and Electric (PG&E), a natural gas and electric utility serving central and northern California. A division within its purchasing department is investment recovery (IR), which is responsible for the disposition of all surplus materials no longer useful to the organization. Everything from office equipment to fleet vehicles is sold on the open market by IR. Through the use of an online database, potential buyers can register for upcoming sales. PG&E partners with Nationwide Auction Company to conduct its public auctions and sealed bids (www.pge.com/suppliers_purchasing/).

Disposing of capital assets

Units must communicate plans for disposing of capital assets to inventory control before its final disposition. Items slated for disposal must be offered for sale to the university committee. Preference for purchases should be given as follows:

- Grants and contracts
- Other university units
- Employees for personal use
- Local charitable organizations
- General public

Once inventory control has received the detailed information requested, staff members will then post the surplus item to an electronic bulletin board. Units are responsible for contacting inventory control regarding updating and removing items from the bulletin board on a timely basis.

The notice must include the following: bar code number of item, brief description, condition of item, quantity, estimated market value, reason for disposal. The recommended method for removal from university can include sale, donation, trash, or use for parts.

NOTE: In general, items will be sold to the highest bidder. However, there may be occasions when a bid is given preference, even if it is lower than another.

Figure 30.4 Cornell University asset policy.

Nearly all property and surplus assets have some residual value at the end of its useful life. Some industries, such as automotive and trucking, have published resources to help determine value. Another way to determine asset value is to use the following guide (Figure 30.5). Although not an exact science, it can serve as a useful tool in value determination. In general, scrap value should only be considered if it results in the most revenue. There are times when the individual components of a piece of equipment can be worth more than the asset as a whole (Chandrashekar and Dougless, 1997). Yet another way to research prices is by going online to auction house sites that specialize in the type of equipment being researched. A site that is well developed and widely used is Go Industry.

Type	Condition	Factor
New	In original container	1.0
Excellent	Like new condition	0.90
Good	Solid working condition	0.85
Fair	Needs refurbishing	0.50
Poor	Needs complete rebuilding	0.40
Scrap	Appropriate for salvage	0.30

Figure 30.5 Value of surplus material. (From Chandrashekar and Dougless, 1997.)

Managing sales and auctions worldwide, they handle a wide range of surplus assets that can serve as a guide to public agencies (www.goindustry.com). By learning what similar items are selling for in a given industry, one can better determine the potential value of their surplus property. There are also times when it makes sense to cannibalize surplus technology assets to improve or refurbish other technology into producing assets. If an agency keeps surplus CPUs on hand, for instance, they may be able to rob parts from them for a computer repair and avoid purchasing new components.

30.2.5 Asset Recovery

The Institute for Supply Management defines asset recovery as the reemployment, reuse, recycling, or regeneration of value (property, equipment, goods, etc.) that is no longer needed for its original purpose (ISM, 2007). If an organization can find a new use for an asset, it can certainly reduce disposal costs and minimize impacts to the environment. Asset recovery is an important component of asset management, just as acquisition, tracking, reporting, and disposition are. When asset recovery is managed well, it can result in a positive impact on an organization's return on investment for a particular asset, capital spending, and cash flow. Organizations that operate world-class recover programs have several things in common:

- Accurate and up-to-date database reflecting all idle or surplus plant and equipment with detailed descriptions, asset history, and photos
- Access to the database for all internal users
- Responsible person at each major location who is designated the asset recovery point person and who functions within the internal network for asset management
- Professional who is responsible for overseeing the program, the database, and the network of internal contacts
- Internal policies that facilitate the fair value transfer of idle equipment among company locations
- Access to market expertise for used equipment or idle real estate through use of a master agreement with appropriate service provider
- Use of the master agreement service provider to determine fair value for internal transfers and to monetize the asset when no internal transfers are appropriate (Rudsk et al., 2006)

The term "asset investment recovery" refers to maximizing the financial return on the sale of surplus assets, while asset recover focuses on reuse and recycling. The Canadian province of British Columbia is among many places that use asset investment recovery in their surplus asset programs.

30.3 Organizational Issues

30.3.1 Organizational Placement

Asset management may reside in various parts of an organization. In many cases, the function is placed within the procurement and supply management department or division, particularly the disposal of surplus assets. Asset management also includes the tracking of assets, which may be done in conjunction with the finance or accounting department. Another option is to place asset management within a general services or facilities department. Technology-based assets, such as

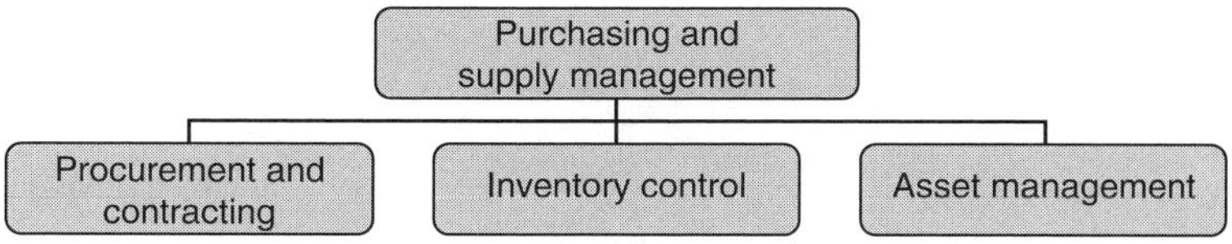

Figure 30.6 Typical organizational structure.

computer and printers, may be best handled by the information technology department. Possessing knowledge of advancing technologies and markets, they can secure competitive offers with online disposition programs. Wherever it resides, asset management needs to be clearly defined with regard to who handles what. If all departments are responsible for their own fixed assets, then confusion, inconsistent procedures, and poor reporting are likely to occur. Figure 30.6 depicts a common approach to the organizational placement of asset disposal.

30.3.2 Responsibility for Program Management

Once an organizational structure is determined, the next logical step is to assign program management responsibility. A large agency may have the luxury of assigning a full-time assets manager. This is certainly an ideal approach to managing assets. However, many small- and medium-sized agencies struggle with placing this additional responsibility on the shoulders of program managers with other significant duties. This can include procurement managers, warehouse managers, and facility professionals.

What are the primary duties of a fixed asset manager? This person plays an important role, as he or she is responsible for ensuring that assets are inventoried and accounted for, and that disposal of assets is done in accordance with applicable policies. He or she must also maintain a current listing of assets, identify the assets with some type of tagging system, ensure proper asset reporting is taking place, and serve as a resource to all levels of the agency in dealing with assets (Brady, 2001).

When determining the most appropriate placement of fixed asset management, an organization should definitely consider the procurement office. These individuals are familiar with asset disposal policies, often have financial backgrounds, and know best the commodity markets in their area. For instance, if an organization is looking to dispose of a dump truck, the procurement specialist who handles fleet acquisitions is likely a great resource for a list of potential buyers.

30.3.3 Importance of Planning

Like other activities in the public sector, asset management needs to include proper planning by the organization. Some may view asset management as elementary and therefore not give them the proper due, but a successful program does not happen by accident or without significant effort. Procurement managers must be diligent and thoughtful when dealing with asset management. Some questions that can serve an agency well include the following:

- Where is the organization currently with asset management?
- Where does the organization desire to be in the future?
- What resources are required to achieve desired outcomes?

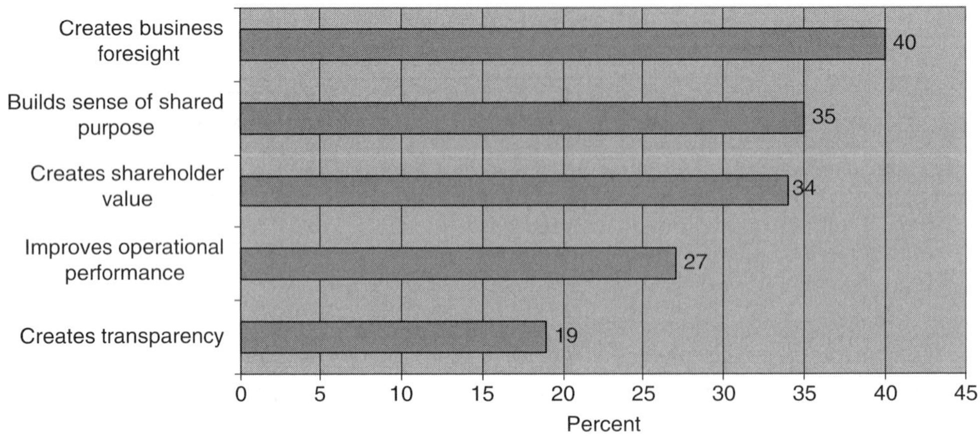

Figure 30.7 How do annual plans add value?

- What are best practices in public sector asset management?
- How does fixed asset management fit within agency's strategic plan?

A key concept for any organization to keep in mind is that planning is the act of thinking before acting. It is essential to setting a course and sticking to it, including within the field of asset management. Canada is realizing the value of planning with the Winter Olympic Games of 2010 in Vancouver, British Columbia. In stressing the importance of procurement planning for this event, Premier Campbell noted to the Vancouver Board of Trade all the assets that needed to be procured. Some 7,500 hockey pucks and 12,000 trash cans were among the assets that needed to be planned for and managed (Ward, 2003).

More and more, organizations are realizing the benefits of planning. Annual plans can be developed to guide strategic activities in many areas, including asset management and disposition. Figure 30.7 identifies the ways value can be added to an organization through the use of annual plans.

30.3.4 Policy Development

Policies are broad guidelines to business activities that lay the groundwork for specific operating procedures. Proper policy development is a component of sound asset management. Organizational policies must be created that are consistent with an agency's goals and strategies involving fixed assets. The fixed asset manager uses these policies to guide his or her decision making on a daily basis. For example, an agency's policy may be that all assets over a certain dollar value are inventoried on an annual basis. From there, operating procedures need to be put in place that ensures new items purchased by the agency are added to the asset inventory. How the inventory listing is maintained and reported are also procedural matters.

The following is an example from the University of Western Sydney (www.policies.uws.edu.au) on areas to be addressed in a policy manual for asset management:

- Authority to purchase assets
- Recording of assets

- Updating the asset register
- Asset management responsibility
- Acquisitions from consulting funds
- Acquisitions from research and trust funds
- Stocktaking
- Depreciation of assets
- Periodic valuations
- Assets on loan
- Disposal of assets

Clearly written policy manuals provide several benefits. They promote consistency and continuity in business operations, eliminate confusion about proper procedures, and discourage independent actions. They also demonstrate the asset management is operating in a businesslike manner, and is fully accountable.

30.4 Fiscal and Legal Issues

30.4.1 Fiscal Responsibility

Fiscal policy represents the government's spending plan including the expenditures they undertake to provide goods and services to the public, as well as how the assets obtained are managed and disposed of (ISM, 2007). Governments at all levels maintain a fiscal policy to preserve the public's trust. An example is the Department of National Defence (DND) in Canada, which ensures compliance with the Surplus Crown Assets Act when disposing of surplus aircraft. Offered on a competitive bid basis, the aircraft are only available to museums, legions, veterans' associations, and Canadian municipalities. Only if no interest is received by such groups will the aircraft be offered to other interested parties. Sale proceeds are used to offset the DND's demilitarization, storage, and handling costs (www.forces.gc.ca/admmat/dgiip/ddsal/Disposal_Policy_e.asp).

Regardless of the source of funding (taxes, user fees, municipal bonds, etc.), a public agency has an obligation to be wise stewards of the funds. Fiscal responsibility can be viewed as fiscal policy in action. Specific actions are taken by the agency, which demonstrate accountability and responsibility with the handling of public funds.

The University of Missouri bases their policies on fiscal responsibility on the tenet that the benefits of university expenditures must be readily apparent from supporting documentation (University of Missouri, 2000). This can include the purchase of assets as well as the disposition. A public asset has a life cycle and the responsibility for fiscal oversight continues throughout that life.

Also viewed as a component of fiscal responsibility, corporate governance refers to how the policies and functions of an organization are controlled and authorized. Ensuring that funds are spent properly, and assets are managed and controlled, are major concerns for most of the governance systems. Within the public sector, this concern is addressed within legislation and regulations that define processes and bestow authority (Dawson, 2003).

30.4.2 Legal Requirements

Because the purpose of asset management is to maintain control and accountability over organizational assets, it is logical that requirements must be set forth that designate proper responsibility and authority. This responsibility includes asset acquisition, identification, disposition, and reporting. Fixed asset management must have authority spelled out in resolution, charter, or legislation to properly operate within an organization (Brady, 2001). Ideally, the authorizing legislation is specific as to the authority of an agency or individual. This legislation should offer the minimum requisites to be met by public agency, and should provide a foundation for the establishment of rules and policies.

The Governmental Accounting Standards Board (GASB) describes accountability for public agencies. It requires that organizations supply accurate financial information to help users assess accountability and make proper decisions. GASB requires the agency to provide an explanation for all activities to the general public. In recent years, there has been an increased demand for improved accountability by government-funded fixed assets. When proper controls are in place and assets are managed properly, these needs for accountability are met.

Failure to properly dispose of surplus assets can have serious ramifications for public agencies. In 2002, two New York colleges were fined over $400,000 for improperly disposing of hazardous materials, which included a large quantity of computer monitors (Anonymous, 2005). Environmental considerations of asset disposition are further discussed in Section 30.8.1.

30.4.3 Closing the Books

The accounting procedures that take place at the end of an accounting period are referred to as closing the books. Adjusting entries are made and then the income and expense accounts are closed. The net profit (or loss) that results from this closing can then be transferred into the proper account. Closing the books is the last major step in the accounting process.

When assets are disposed of by an organization they must, of course, be accounted for. Assets are listed on the books at their purchased value, which is almost always more than what they will be sold for. For example, a piece of machinery may be listed in the inventory records at $900, but if it is deemed surplus and sold for only $350 the difference needs to be noted. The inventory records must document this $550 difference, which would be an example of a write-off.

30.5 Methods of Disposal

30.5.1 Sealed and Spot Bids

A bid is submitted by an interested offeror in response to an invitation. Normally in public procurement this is done to purchase an item. However, it is also a useful tool to dispose of surplus assets. When buying the item, the lowest price offer is most favorable, but logically when selling, the highest bid is sought. The principle in competitive bidding is to allow the open market to compete for a requirement in hopes that a fair price is established. This holds true with both buying and selling.

A sealed bid process is often utilized when an asset has substantial value and it warrants a formal process. Normally, buyers can inspect the item to be purchased, and then submit their bid price in a sealed envelope by a designated time. Once all bids are received, the agency representative opens and evaluates the offers and makes a determination on the best bid. When the sale occurs at the site of the good or equipment to be sold, it is referred to as a spot bid. Often items are offered in lots, with the winning bid being announced for each lot before the next item is sold. An advantage to spot bidding is that it can occur on an as-needed basis and prevents the agency from having to store the asset for a long period of time.

30.5.2 Trade-In

A trade-in occurs when older assets are transferred to a supplier at the same time new ones are purchased. Public agencies often use trade-in for vehicles, heavy trucks, and road maintenance equipment. By listing the surplus equipment to be replaced, and allowing bidders to submit trade-in value as well as new equipment prices, a public agency can use a single process to serve two purposes. In determining the lowest responsive bid for new equipment, an agency can deduct the value of the trade-in to determine the final cost. If a bidder offers a lower value for the trade-in than is acceptable, the public agency should always reserve the right to accept or reject the offer. If necessary, other disposal methods can be employed that bring a greater return.

30.5.3 Donation

When an agency offers a surplus asset to another organization at no cost, it is considered a donation. The recipients of these donations include other public agencies, nonprofits, and educational groups. Federal and state agencies often have qualified lists of donors that are eligible to receive surplus property donations. Donations can generate a great deal of goodwill in the community. Examples can include surplus computers donated to local schools or fire fighting equipment given to a rural fire district. The value of such cooperation and generosity can easily outweigh the revenue an agency misses out on by electing not to sell.

30.5.4 Auction

A public auction is a very common way for governments to dispose of their assets. These events are usually advertised locally and ran by a professional auctioneering firm, who are well versed in obtaining the highest possible bids for equipment. This method gives local citizens the opportunity to purchase the surplus items of a state or local agency they support as taxpayers. In recent years, the use of Internet auctions has increased dramatically. Potential buyers can review the available equipment on an agency Web site and submit offers electronically up to the time of bid closing. Because the Internet offers access to a broader geographical base, agencies often report higher sales revenue than traditional auctions.

30.5.5 Employee Sales

Employee sales should be carefully considered before being allowed by a public agency. Although offering surplus assets to employees on a first come, first served basis is common in the private sector, it is generally frowned upon in government. These sales can be perceived as giving public employees an unfair advantage that the general public is not getting. Even if a public employee pays a fair market price for an item, there is still a perception of favoritism, especially if the employee is doing so on agency time. There are simply more issues and risks to allowing public employee sales than are benefits. Coupled with public ethics laws and policies, employee sales can be a risky business. Now, as a member of the general public, an employee may very well attend a public auction on their own time and bid on surplus property from their agency. Again, even if they outbid others for the asset, the perception may be that they had inside knowledge that helped them. The best policy is to avoid public employee sales.

30.5.6 Market Knowledge

It is important for an organization to have a sound knowledge of the disposal marketplace. Depending on the type of asset to be disposed of, the procurement professional may have a number of options available to them. Utilizing outside industry experts can be of value to an organization. Often referred to as third party specialists, these firms are knowledgeable in a specific industry and assist with property disposition, although they are neither the buyer nor the seller. They can include brokers, dealers, and auctioneers. For example, a local agency with surplus tractors may decide to secure the services of an agricultural dealer to get the best price possible. Such a dealer has contacts within the industry, which can create a competitive environment for the equipment sale. Their professional fee is likely to be a good investment for the agency.

30.6 Performance Measurement

30.6.1 What to Measure

It has often been said, "What gets measured gets done," which refers to the need for an organization to identify key business areas for improvement. This will, in turn, allow it to concentrate on efforts to achieve the desired results. An organization's ability to measure its performance is certainly a key to its success. There are countless measurements that may be considered, so the challenge is to find those measurements that are meaningful and productive.

The University of Arizona (www.library.arizona.edu) has developed criteria for good performance measurements. They believe measurements must be as follows:

- Organizationally acceptable
- Timely
- Compatible
- Comparable
- Simple
- Responsibility linked
- Cost effective
- Balanced
- Customer focused
- Meaningful

An important concept to keep in mind is that performance measurements need to be aligned to an organization's strategic objectives. Purchasing and supply management professionals must ensure all their activities, including performance measurement, are consistent with these objectives.

30.6.2 Measuring Performance

Performance measurement is the process of assessing progress toward achieving predetermined goals. In some cases, these are related to outputs, such as resources transformed into goods, or they can be results of activities compared to intended results, or outcomes (Stanley and Matthews, 2007). Performance measures must also keep in mind the needs of the customer base. Within the public sector, this can include internal and external clients alike. Senior management, elected officials, and the general public should all be considered customers. It should also be mentioned that performance measures today are very likely to be replaced in the future. Just as organizations change and develop, so should their performance measures. Former Vice President Al Gore (1997) notes the following areas of focus for organizations when they consider performance measurements:

- Financial considerations
- Customer satisfaction
- Internal business operations
- Employee satisfaction
- Community and shareholder satisfaction

Stakeholders and participants need to agree on the type and number of measurements to be employed. The measurements will be far less effective in the long run if there is no agreement from the beginning. In addition to being meaningful, measurements should be easy to administer and leave little room for calibration error. It is also advisable to select just a few measurements, as too many can lead to little or no action. Finally, the cost of implementing and maintaining the measurements needs to be less than the tangible benefits received by the organization (Pilachowski, 1996).

30.6.3 Performance Tools

So what are some useful performance tools within asset management and disposition? Typical measurements for the acquisition or assets include the following: number of purchases and contracts issued, dollar value of expenditures, and reduction in purchasing cycle time. Although the measurements used in the disposal of assets will differ, they can still be just as valuable. The following are examples of performance measurements related to asset management:

- Assets owned. This factor indicates the total number of assets owned by an organization, as well as their value. As a relatively easy measurement to compile, it can be reported in three ways: number of assets owned, value of assets owned, or average value of assets.
- Disposal rate. The disposal rate refers to the number and dollar value of assets being disposed of for a set period of time.
- Redistribution rate. The rate of the number of assets and their dollar value that are redistributed within an organization is known as the redistribution rate. When its original department no longer needs an asset, it is usually in the best interest of the organization to transfer it to other departments in need.
- Inventory accuracy. The accuracy of the amount of physical inventory on hand compared to the actual inventory records can be a key measurement. This ratio is figured by dividing the number of errors by the number of inventory counts performed. A low ratio demonstrates an effective asset management program (Brady, 2001).

30.7 Utilizing Technology

30.7.1 Determining Appropriate Technology

There are countless more technologies available for today's procurement and supply professional. This includes the use of technology tools throughout the purchasing cycle, and certainly in the area of asset tracking and disposition. The challenge for the procurement professional is determining which technologies are appropriate for improving operational efficiency in managing surplus assets. According to Computer Systems Corporation (2001), more and more people expect to conduct business with the public sector through electronic means. They do so with private industry players in banking and retail, so naturally government should operate in a similar fashion. Between 2000 and 2001, the amount of external business done electronically in the public sector rose from 14 to 18 percent (CSC, 2001). This number will only continue to increase as public agencies deploy more and more technology applications.

30.7.2 Industry Trends

There are several trends merging within the asset management field. Like other key business areas (i.e., procurement, project management, financial reporting), information technologies tools are being used more than ever for managing public assets. Agencies at all levels are integrating their asset management programs within existing ERP (enterprise resource planning) systems. In many cases, asset management becomes an add-on module after implementation of areas like finance and human resources.

With the expectation to do more with less, public agencies are finding they must employ the use of technology tools to accomplish the necessary work with less staff. Budget cuts and staff reductions have only increased the need to better utilize technology. This is evident with the increased reliance on outside partners to handle online sales of surplus assets. Organizations like Public Surplus can manage the marketing and sales of an agency's assets with minimal time commitments from agency employees (www.publicsurplus.com). For a set percentage of sale proceeds, such a business partner can handle nearly all facets of surplus disposition while the agency provides the assets and receives the checks.

Another trend in the public sector is the development of agency Web sites dedicated to the management and disposition of surplus assets. Depending on the size of the agency, its available resources, and the amount of surplus assets it generates, this may be a viable means of asset disposition. Essentially, the government is doing the same types of things the private, for-profit industry is doing (online asset disposition), but avoiding the split of the sale proceeds.

30.7.3 Bar Coding

Bar codes are a series of parallel lines that translate into sequences of numbers and letters. These characters can identify a variety of information about a surplus item including description, model number, purchase date, original price, location, and manufacture. Bar codes have been around for many years and began extensive use within the retail grocery industry in the 1970s. Each industry has its own bar code standards and language, which can present a challenge to the organizations employing this technology (Stanley and Matthews, 2007).

Scanners are used in bar code systems to read the optical characters. These devices can be affixed permanently (i.e., airline ticket counter) or be made portable, which is more common when used with fixed asset programs. Handheld scanning devices are used by logistic personnel to monitor the use of fixed assets that are tagged with bar codes. Benefits of bar coding include the following: improved data accuracy, reduction in receiving time, reduction in data entry, and seamless data integration with inventory programs and databases. A sample bar code for asset tagging is depicted below in Figure 30.8.

Figure 30.8 Fixed asset tag.

30.7.4 Software Systems

Numerous software systems are on the market that can assist with asset disposition. These can include systems for tracking assets through their life cycle, as well as software that manages online property sales. Many feel that online auction systems are superior to traditional sealed bid or fixed price sales. Online systems allow sellers to set a minimum price and then, hopefully, watch the bid prices go up. With so many potential buyers having access to the Internet, online surplus sites have the tendency to inspire higher bids. The use of software systems to manage online surplus sale programs is likely to increase in the future.

Tracking software provides an efficient way to track fixed assets of all types, including appreciable and non-appreciable assets. These systems can track depreciation of capital equipment, computers, and furniture. Bar coding is used with these systems to store and retrieve data such as cost and purchase date. Many off-the-shelf applications are compatible with major operating systems, which include handheld reader devices, and are relatively inexpensive to purchase. They can also save photos of surplus assets to a database, which can be retrieved later to post on disposal Web sites.

Some key considerations for public agencies considering asset tracking software systems include the following:

- Functionality and features of system
- Hardware requirements
- Compatibility with existing systems
- Cost of system, implementation, and training
- Operating system requirements
- Reporting capabilities of software

30.7.5 Use of Internet Tools

Christopher (1998, p. 272) describes the Internet as “a perfect vehicle for the establishment of the virtual supply chain.” In the last decade, the use of the Internet has become commonplace for organizations in all sectors. Large organizations, small businesses, and consumers alike are utilizing the Internet on a daily basis. It is an ideal tool for the disposition of surplus public assets. This chapter discusses agencies that have developed in-house Web sites to manage surplus equipment sales, such as the state of Oregon and the Canadian government. Another effective approach to asset disposition is the use of service providers specializing in online sales. In each case, the public agency utilizes Internet technology to their advantage.

Intranets are commonly used by organizations to provide information to internal business units. These intranet sites can provide text-based documents on surplus disposal policies and procedures. When a portion of an organization's intranet is opened up to outside business partners, it is referred to as an extranet. This technology can assist public organizations in establishing external Web sites managed by third parties. These sites offer surplus property sales over the Internet that can benefit both the public agency and the third party seller. Internet is also a useful tool for researching other sale sites to help assist with property valuation. It can also be a resource for locating software companies that provide asset tracking systems and related services. Although significant advances have been made in the areas of technology and Internet applications, there are still opportunities for future improvements.

30.8 Social Responsibility

30.8.1 Environmental Considerations

A growing trend in both the public and private sectors is the advancement of corporate social responsibility (CSR), which is a concept that organizations have a duty to care for all stakeholders. CSR features decision making that includes traditional economic factors, as well as social and environmental impacts. It applies to all aspects of their operation and goes well beyond minimally meeting statutory obligations. Actions that provide support to the community encourage diversity within the workplace and by its suppliers, and the protection of international rights. Many are convinced that responsible business practices like these are just good business (Roberts, 2004).

Although CSR encompasses areas like minority supplier alliances and community involvement, a prime focus is on the environmental considerations. Business practices that minimize impact on the environment are being utilized more than ever. This includes the purchase of energy efficient equipment, environmental friendly cleaning products, and asset disposition. The latter is an area where organizations can implement like recycling and reuse of assets. An example of recycling would be the disposal of a surplus appliance at a metal recycler, while reuse would be transferring unneeded equipment to another department or agency.

Within the United Sates, the Resource Conservation and Recovery Act (RCRA) sets out the legal requirements and obligations for agencies disposing of surplus assets. A key component of RCRA is the fact that the organization that generates the waste is responsible for its disposition. This is sometimes referred to as "cradle to grave" responsibility. For instance, if a local agency donates surplus computers to a nonprofit organization, the agency can still be held liable if the computers end up in a landfill with their asset tag still attached. RCRA was recently updated to include guidelines for the disposal of surplus computers. The monitors are of particular concerns, because they can contain small amounts of lead, which is considered a hazardous waster. This has prompted many organizations to work closely with their suppliers when disposing of surplus computers. Many suppliers offer leasing programs that allow use of personal computers at a set monthly fee, and after a set period of time they are replaced with newer equipment. The supplier then takes the older computers back. Other suppliers, such as Dell and Hewlett Packard, have developed trade-in programs in recent years. When a customer purchases a new computer, the supplier credits them for the trade-in of their surplus computer, and ensures it is disposed of properly.

30.8.2 Expectations from General Public

More than ever the general public is holding governments accountable. This includes federal, state, and local agencies in all facets of their operations. What an agency purchases, how much they pay for it, and how they dispose of it all seem to be of high interest. Many public cases have surfaced in recent years that have resulted in skepticism from the general public. When government agencies do not conduct themselves in the manner expected, citizens are quick to judge. The U.S. government's response to Hurricane Katrina in the Gulf Coast left many questioning their business practices in the procurement arena.

The general public holds government to a high standard. It is expected that public agencies are transparent, accountable, and efficient. Goods and services should be obtained through an open, competitive bidding process, and surplus goods disposed of in a similar fashion. Public officials are not to use their position for personal gain, so any special deals in accessing surplus property cannot be tolerated. The disposal methods discussed in this chapter ensure open access to government surplus. Having the opportunity to purchase the surplus personally is an expectation (say through a public auction), but so is the government's obligation to seek maximum return on its investment. If an agency agrees to a trade-in value for a vehicle that is only half its market value, it will likely be seen as mismanagement of public funds.

30.8.3 Opportunities for Community Involvement

Public agencies are an important part of the communities they serve. The services they provide are essential, and the manner in which they interact with its citizens can be equally as important. There are numerous opportunities for procurement professionals handling asset disposition to demonstrate their value. Holding surplus sales open to the general public can demonstrate a great deal of goodwill. It offers the community an opportunity to personally interact with an agency, along with the chance to purchase surplus items of interest. Fiscal prudence in other areas of asset management can also instill confidence, such as tracking, storing, and accounting of fixed assets.

Other examples of community involvement include the donation of surplus equipment to other public agencies or nonprofit groups. A large city's fire department may elect to donate a surplus fire engine to a small, rural fire district, for instance. The donation of surplus office furniture from a state agency to a women's shelter is another great opportunity to give back to the community.

30.9 Case Studies

30.9.1 State of Oregon Surplus Program

Oregon's state surplus property program provides a central service to state and local agencies for surplus property management. The agency acts as a distribution conduit for surplus, seized, and recovered property of all types. The first priority for the program is to reutilize surplus property within the public sector, which can avoid purchasing new property unnecessarily. Oregon has received national recognition for its use of the Internet in disposing of surplus assets (www.oregon.gov).

Besides providing services to state and local agencies in Oregon, the surplus property program also supports federal and qualified nonprofit agencies. They also provide acquisition services to law enforcement agencies, including excess surplus personal property from the Department of Defense. Local police agencies are offered assistance in acquiring property at federal contract rates.

External sales are opened to the general public through the state's partnership with eBay, one of the most widely used online systems in the world. Property like heavy equipment, office furniture, and vehicles are sold at fair market prices. This sale arrangement is an example of a G2C (government to consumer) application that benefits the government, business, and the consumer.

30.9.2 Canadian Government Program

Public Works and Government Services Canada (PWGSC) is responsible for the disposal of surplus federal assets. Across Canada, there are six regional facilities known as Crown Assets Distribution Centres (CADC). This agency has provided disposition services to Canada for over 50 years. CADC also acts as an agent for foreign governments looking to dispose of surplus assets residing in Canada. Working arrangements with several European governments aide CADC with the disposal of military surplus assets located in Europe.

The surplus assets handled by CADC include office furniture, technology equipment, and even automobiles and boats. The agency employs a variety of methods for disposal including tenders (Canadian term for sealed bidding), public sales, and auctions.

Canada Online (www.crownassets.pwgsc.gc.ca), an electronic property management system, provides several value-added benefits to the general public, such as

- Posting of sale schedules by region
- Ability for public to search the surplus asset database for available merchandise
- Registering of interests buyers that allows for e-mail notification of future sales

Purchase of surplus items can also be made online. Once a buyer locates an item to be purchased, they can make an offer via fax to the appropriate distribution center. Winning bidders are promptly notified and can pay for their purchase via credit card, debit card, or certified check. Normally, the removal and transport of the purchased asset is the buyer's sole responsibility.

30.10 Conclusion

The proper management and disposition of surplus assets is an important part of the procurement cycle. Although much attention is given to upfront activities in the procurement process, it is just as important to focus on strategies aimed at IR. There are many types of surplus assets generated within the public sector. Each organization may have their own unique policies on disposition, but there are many common issues and practices. Whatever method is employed, the priority should be obtaining the highest sale price possible. Knowing the various methods of property disposition will help the public purchaser add value to their organization.

Purchasers must also be aware of all legal and fiscal issues related to asset management. Depending on the type and value of the asset, there may be various requirements for its sale. Measuring performance will allow the government to better monitor progress in surplus property management. The use of technology will continue to aid the public sector in its efforts to increase effectiveness and efficiency. Properly managing the assets the public has entrusted to an agency is all a part of social responsibility and accountability.

References

Anonymous. 2005. Computer disposal raises legal issues, *Financial Executive*, Morristown, October, Vol. 19, Issue 7.

Brady, W. 2001. *Managing Fixed Assets in the Public Sector: Managing for Service Excellence.* Boca Raton, Florida: Universal Publishers.

Chandrashekar, A. and Dougless, T. 1997. Asset recovery: New dynamics for purchasing organizations, *International Journal of Purchasing and Materials Management*, September 22.

Christopher, M. 1998. *Logistics and Supply Chain Management.* London, United Kingdom: Prentice Hall.

Computer Systems Corporation (CSC). 2001. *14th Annual Critical Issues of Information Systems Management Survey.* El Segundo, CA: CSC.

Dawson, J. 2003. The impact of corporate governance on procurement, Supply Chain Management: A Procurement Perspective, Melbourne, Australia: Hargreen Publishing.

Gore, A. 1997. *Serving the American Public: Best Practices in Performance Measurement.* National Performance Review, Benchmarking Study Report, June.

Institute for Supply Management (ISM). 2007. *Supply Management Glossary.* Tempe, AZ: ISM.

Kieso, D. and Weygandt, J. 1995. *Intermediate Accounting.* New York: John Wiley & Sons, Inc.

National Institute of Governmental Purchasing (NIGP). 1996. *Dictionary of Purchasing Terms.* Herndon, VA: NIGP.

Pilachowski, M. 1996. *Purchasing Performance Measurements: A Roadmap for Excellence.* West Palm Beach, FL: PT Publications, Inc.

Roberts, J. 2004. Responsible business equals good business. *Inside Supply Management*, May.

Rudski, R., Smock, D., Katzorke, M., and Stewart, S. 2006. *Straight to the Bottom Line.* Fort Lauderdale, FL: J. Ross Publishing.

Stanley, L. and Matthews, D. 2007. *Logistics and Transportation.* Herndon, VA: National Institute of Governmental Purchasing.

University of Missouri, Procurement Services, Asset Management Policies, www.pmm.missouri.edu/asset/amgmt.htm

Ward, G. 2003. Asset Management: part of the planning process, On the Level, UMA Group, Vancouver, BC, Fall 2003.

Chapter 31

Enhancing Use of Past Performance as a Source Selection Criterion

Keith F. Snider and Mark F. Walkner

CONTENTS

31.1 Introduction

The "Revolution in Business Affairs" in the Department of Defense (DoD), promoted by former Defense Secretary William Cohen, is based on the idea that government management operations, including procurement actions, should model those of leading private sector firms. Among the practices that the federal government seeks to emulate is the reliance of corporations, as they focus on their core functions, upon preferred suppliers as a way to reduce procurement risk. However, because of competition requirements, socioeconomic programs, and other concerns, government is often unable to follow the private sector's lead with respect to preferred suppliers.

One method federal procurement officials use to reduce procurement risk is to request, via the solicitation, information regarding a supplier's past performance and to use this information in source selection (Federal Acquisition Regulation (FAR) §42.1501).

> Past performance information is relevant information, for future source selection purposes, regarding a contractor's actions under previously awarded contracts. It includes, for example, the contractor's record of conforming to contract requirements and to standards of good workmanship... of forecasting and controlling costs... [of] adherence to contract schedules, including the administrative aspects of performance... of reasonable and cooperative behavior and commitment to customer satisfaction; and generally, the contractor's business-like concern for the interest of the customer.

Past performance differs from experience, in that experience reflects whether contractors have performed similar work before, while past performance reflects how well contractors have done the work (U.S. Department of Defense, 1999, p. 7). It also differs from the idea of contractor responsibility, which relates to the capability to perform work. When lowest price is not the driving factor in procurements, the FAR allows officials to make best value determinations—trade-offs between cost or price, technical merit, and past performance to ensure the best value to the government.

Although the FAR provides direction on the use of past performance as an evaluation criterion, it provides little guidance on how contracting officials are to evaluate past performance information (PPI). In the absence of standardized processes or norms, the possibility increases that errors or abuses may occur in evaluations and subsequent award decisions. According to Beausoleil (2000), less than 20 percent of the contracts that were completed in 1998 and 1999 were evaluated in a way that met the FAR requirements for PPI. He argues that current processes for postaward collection and evaluation of contractor performance are too cumbersome in today's acquisition environment. Solomon and Pfleger (2000) identified 1020 companies that were sued or prosecuted for fraud over the last five years of the 1990s. They found that 737 of these companies were still eligible in 2000 for future contracts and that several of these companies have subsequently won contract awards. They concluded that the federal procurement process places little value on an offeror's past performance.

Such findings indicate the need among public procurement officials and scholars to understand how supplier PPI may be more effectively incorporated in acquisition processes. This article contributes to such understanding through a synthesis of three major sources of information on past performance: (1) the FAR which, as mentioned above, gives directions and specifies procedures to be followed when using PPI as an evaluation criterion; (2) agency "best practice" guides, which reflect practical wisdom such as "rules of thumb" and lessons learned derived from experience; and (3) Government Accountability Office (formerly General Accounting Office [GAO]) cases of bid protests[1] involving past performance. These sources illuminate past performance as an evaluation criterion from three different aspects. Put simply, the FAR states the rules, the agency guides tell how the rules may be put into practice, and the GAO cases provide interpretations and judgments of practice. This chapter provides a coordinated discussion of these three frames and thereby integrates them to gain a more complete perspective of past performance, as well as new insights into its effective use.

Although the article presents policies, practices, and cases involving federal government procurements, mostly involving DoD, the implications and general conclusions of the discussion are applicable to public procurement officials at state and local levels as well.

The chapter begins with a sketch of the evolution of past performance policies in the federal government. Next, it elaborates on the problems, mentioned above, in the implementation of those policies as indicated by trends in GAO contract award protests involving use of PPI. It then identifies the top-10 past performance best practices based on a survey of selected agency guides and handbooks. The main body of the chapter then elaborates on each of these best practices with discussions of applicable FAR provisions and relevant GAO cases. It concludes with some brief remarks on development of public procurement theory.

31.2 The Challenge: Policies and Their Implementation

Office of Federal Procurement Policy (OFPP) Letter 92–5 (OFPP, 1992) provided the foundation for current past performance policies. It required that past performance be used as an evaluation factor in all competitively negotiated contracts exceeding $100,000, and that newly established firms could compete for contracts even though they lacked a history of past performance. In 1995, past performance became a mandatory evaluation factor for all solicitations with an estimated value of $1,000,000. The FAR now requires that PPI be evaluated in all source selections for negotiated competitive acquisitions expected to exceed $100,000 (unless the contracting officer documents the reasons why past performance is not an appropriate evaluation factor). Clearly, past performance is an area of significant policy interest, as indicated by the FAR's Statement of Guiding Principles (§1.102):

> The Federal Acquisition System will satisfy the needs of its customers in terms of cost, quality and timeliness by... using contractors who have a track record of successful past performance or who demonstrate a current superior ability to perform.

The intent of these policies notwithstanding, there is evidence of problems in their implementation. One problem concerns the collection of information during a contractor's period of performance so that it may be used in evaluating that contractor's subsequent proposals (Beausoleil, 2000). Another problem area—the focus of this chapter—is the use of PPI in source selection. Evidence of difficulties here may be seen in trends involving GAO protests of past contract awards. Table 31.1 depicts data[2] on protests, with emphasis on protests involving past performance as an evaluation criterion, for fiscal years (FYs) 1997–1999 and for the first three quarters of FY2000. This timeframe was chosen because it covers much of the implementation period for the policies mentioned above.

The data shows that, while the number of merit protests[3] declined, the number of past performance-related protests increased. In 1997, past performance protests constituted only 8 percent of all merit protests, and as of June 2000, that percentage has grown to 29 percent. An upward trend is also evident with the percentage of past performance protests as a percentage of sustained protest. In 1997, sustained past performance protests accounted for only 10 percent of the overall sustained protests, and by June of 2000, that percentage had risen to 30 percent.

It is ironic that, although the federal government attempted to follow the private sector's lead in adopting past performance as a criterion in selecting suppliers, industry responded with increasing protests. This points out difficulties that can arise when government attempts to emulate business.

Table 31.1 Government Accountability Office (GAO) Protests

	FY1997	*FY1998*	*FY1999*	*FY2000 (October–June)*
Merit protests	501	406	347	161
Protests sustained	61	63	74	44
Sustainment rate (percent)	12	16	21	27
Past performance protests	40	43	62	46
Protests sustained	6	13	15	13
Sustainment rate (percent)	15	30	24	28
Past performance protests as a percentage of merit protests	8	11	18	29
Sustained past performance protests as a percentage of sustained protests	10	21	20	30

The idea that "government is different" is a familiar theme in the field of public administration. As Paul Appleby (1945, p. 101) put it over half a century ago, "government administration differs from all other administrative work... by virtue of its public nature, the way in which it is subject to public scrutiny and public outcry... No other institution is so publicly accountable." These differences, and increasing numbers of protests, do not necessarily mean, of course, that the government is not receiving better quality products and services as a result of using PPI in source selections. The question of whether past performance policies are having their desired effects in terms of improved outcomes is open and requires further research.

This question aside, increasing numbers of protests should concern government procurement officials. Hart and Merle (2007) recently reported that the number of all protests had risen by 10 percent from 2002 to 2006, and the number of sustained protests had also risen by 30 percent. Even in protests that are denied, the settlement process consumes scarce agency resources. In certain cases, the agency may be required to withhold contract award and suspend performance for up to 90 days while the GAO's comptroller general completes the inquiry. Clearly, reducing numbers of protests is in the government's best interest.

One plausible explanation for increasing numbers of protests is simply that there is now one more criterion for evaluation in source selection, which increases the complexity of the process. A contract award based solely on cost or price is straightforward, but as additional criteria—technical, management, and so on—are added, the potential for errors and misunderstandings increases.

Another explanation is that, as past performance policies are relatively new, procurement agencies are struggling to institutionalize procedures for their implementation. Thus, firms protest more award decisions because they are not yet comfortable with the ways federal procurement agencies are using PPI. Businesses that deal with the federal government feel that the FAR allows too much latitude to evaluators, resulting in widely differing weighting and selection of evaluation factors among federal agencies (Clipsham, 1998). One senior DoD procurement official (S. Soloway, personal interview, August 31, 2000) agreed, stating that he was not surprised by these trends:

> Businesses want to be treated fairly. They want a level playing field, and they can't be guaranteed one with our current collection and tracking systems. With the increased emphasis on the collection and use of past performance information, it is understandable that businesses would challenge more of our evaluations and best value determinations... In the absence of a good collection and tracking system, there is always the possibility of mistakes in the collection and evaluation of past performance. These mistakes translate into more past performance protests that have substance.

This problematic situation is exacerbated by additional factors. First, when past performance is weighted heavily as a source selection factor, companies may increase the level of risk that they are willing to accept in today's competitive business environment by adjusting their pricing strategies to win the contract. With this added risk, companies may be more likely to file protests whenever it appears that reasonableness and consistency are lacking in the source selection process. Second, because past performance policies are relatively new, the body of "case law" from protests and contract disputes is still relatively immature (Phillips, 2000).

Businesses apparently have reason to be wary of government evaluations involving past performance. Table 31.2 summarizes the principal reasons given by the GAO in sustaining 41 past performance protests from FY1998 through the third quarter of FY2000.[2] It reveals that in the majority of sustained protests, acquisition officials failed to apply their own evaluation criteria consistently. Specifically, the evaluation of PPI was found either to be unreasonable or not consistent with the evaluation criteria contained in the solicitation.

High numbers of protests indicate the private sector's belief that procurement officials are acting and deciding improperly in source selections, and firms are using protests as a check on officials' discretion. The scholarly debate between Carl Friedrich and Herman Finer during the 1940s helps frame this issue. Friedrich and Finer were concerned with the question of how best to ensure administrative responsibility, or in other words, the accountability of public officials who exercised discretion in their positions. Finer (1941, p. 335) argued that external constraints, "arrangement[s]

Table 31.2 Sustained GAO Protests (October 1998–June 2000)

Reason for Sustainment	*Cases*
Evaluation not consistent with evaluation criteria	12
Unreasonable source evaluation	11
Source evaluation: inadequate documentation	8
Opportunity to respond to adverse information not provided	3
Past performance not similar in scope, magnitude, complexity	2
Offeror improperly penalized regarding disputes clauses	2
Prior past performance ignored	1
Awardee's negative information not reasonably considered	1
Source selection authority's decision not reasonable	1

of correction and punishment," were necessary, while Friedrich (1940, p. 19) maintained that responsibility "is not so much enforced as it is elicited" through internal checks such as an individual's sense of professionalism. Protests essentially act as an external check on the responsibility of public procurement officials. Fewer protests are likely to occur in the area of past performance unless firms have confidence that source selection processes are carried out properly. This confidence will spring from a corresponding confidence in the internal checks on officials' responsibility, that is, in their competent discretion.

Considering the difficulty in implementing past performance policies and industry's corresponding distrust of the government's use of PPI, it is critical that public procurement officials seek to increase their proficiency in this area. An understanding of how best to use PPI should result in fewer errors in source evaluations and contract awards, and private sector confidence in the government's use of PPI should follow.

31.3 Past Performance: Agency Best Practices

Several agencies have recognized that the problems described above stem at least in part from the relative novelty of past performance as an evaluation criterion and the corresponding lack of experience in and guidance available for its use. As a remedy, these agencies have published best practice guides for using PPI. The term "best practice" usually refers to a method that has been shown by experience to work successfully. Thus, one should be able to gain insights into effective PPI usage through an examination of these guides.

Neither the guides give detailed explanations as to how the best practices were obtained, nor have agencies made attempts to verify or validate them according to standards of positivist science. Rather, the identification and dissemination of best practices belie a more pragmatic epistemology of learning from practical experience (Dewey, 1998). Best practices may also be viewed as efforts on the parts of agencies to enable and facilitate organizational learning (Argyris and Schön, 1978; Lipshitz et al., 1996).

Five agency guides[4] were examined to identify the most important best practices. Numerous best practices appeared in more than one guide, which allowed a comprehensive top-10 list of commonly cited best practices to be developed. Table 31.3 groups these according to whether they occur during pre-solicitation or post-solicitation activities.

Clearly, most of these best practices have more general applicability than to past performance alone. For the purposes of this chapter, though, the discussions that follow emphasize past performance.

31.4 Best Practices Elaborated: The FAR and GAO Protest Cases

These best practices represent starting points for more in-depth discussions of past performance. In this section, the best practices are elaborated upon with accompanying summaries of applicable FAR provisions, as well as illustrations from GAO protest cases.[5] The GAO cases have an especially important role in these discussions. They are intended to have a function and benefit similar to cases used in law education. That is, the cases illustrate problematic aspects of practices involving past performance. They also provide interpretations and judgments for resolution, which contribute to insights into the effective use of PPI.

Table 31.3 "Top-10" Best Practices—Past Performance in Source Selection

Pre-solicitation Activities
1. Invest in command or program resources needed for a competent and well-documented best value source selection. Include the source selection authority (SSA) as an active participant. Train all the evaluators in best practices.
2. Tailor use and evaluation of PPI to fit the needs of the acquisition. Weight past performance to ensure that it is a valid discriminator. Limit subfactors to true discriminators (e.g., quality of performance, cost performance, schedule performance, and business relations).
3. Conduct pre-solicitation exchanges (e.g., draft solicitations and pre-solicitation conferences) with industry to explain approaches to be used to evaluate performance risk.
4. Structure the solicitation to communicate effectively to potential offerors. Evaluations may be properly made only on the basis of what is communicated via the solicitation.
Post-solicitation Activities
5. Use the most relevant, recent PPI available in making the source selection decision. PPI can come from federal, state, and local government databases, commercial contractors, references provided by the offeror, and quality certificates and awards.
6. Conduct reference checks and look for patterns or trends. Whenever possible, request two points of contact for each reference. Use questionnaires, face-to-face interviews, and telephone interviews.
7. Document strengths, weaknesses, and risks of each proposal to support the cost/past performance trade-off.
8. Justify price premiums with trade-off documentation regardless of the selected proposal's cost or past performance superiority.
9. Ensure that the source selection decision is consistent with the relative weights assigned to the evaluation factors in the solicitation.
10. Conduct a proper and timely debriefing to provide unsuccessful offerors with the opportunity to learn about their strengths and weaknesses and how to improve future proposals submitted to the government.

31.4.1 Pre-solicitation Activities

Best Practice 1. Invest in command or program resources needed for a competent and well-documented best value source selection. Include the SSA as an active participant. Train all the evaluators in best practices.

The FAR (§15.303 (b)) provides very limited direction that is related to this best practice, stating only that the SSA will

> ... establish an evaluation team, tailored for the particular acquisition, which includes appropriate contracting, legal, logistics, technical, and other expertise to ensure a comprehensive evaluation of offers [and] approve the source selection strategy or acquisition plan, if applicable, before solicitation release.

Such direction implies that the agency has the discretion to tailor the evaluation team, but that it also has the responsibility to ensure a comprehensive evaluation.

This duality of discretion and responsibility in source selection is illustrated in the protest of LB&B Associates (1999). Here the protester argued, among other points, that the contracting agency misevaluated its proposal, that it had more relevant experience than the awardee, and hence should have received a higher score in the "demonstrated success" category of the evaluation. The GAO's comptroller general ruled, however, that it was not its role to make independent determinations regarding merits of proposals. The protest was denied on the principle that "the evaluation of proposals is within the discretion of the procuring agency since it is responsible for defining its needs and the best method of accommodating them, and must bear the burden arising from a defective evaluation."

A presumed appropriate level of individual competence underlies this duality. Technical knowledge, sound judgment, and skill contribute to, but obviously cannot guarantee, procurement officials' abilities to exercise discretion in a responsible way. The FAR places the onus on the SSA to ensure an appropriate level of competence and, by implication, on the agency to provide for it. Best Practice 1 emphasizes the need for investment of resources to promote such competence.

Best Practice 2. Tailor the use and evaluation of PPI to fit the needs of the acquisition. Weight past performance to ensure that it is a valid discriminator. Limit subfactors to true discriminators (e.g., quality of performance, cost performance, schedule performance, and business relations).

This best practice follows very closely the FAR (§15.304).directions on evaluation factors:

> Evaluation factors and significant subfactors must represent the key areas of importance and emphasis to be considered in the source selection decision ... and support meaningful comparison and discrimination between and among competing proposals. The evaluation factors and significant subfactors ... and their relative importance, are within the broad discretion of agency acquisition officials ... [P]rice or cost ... shall be evaluated in every source selection, [and] quality shall be addressed through consideration of factors such as past performance, compliance with solicitation requirements, technical excellence, management capability, personnel qualifications, and prior experience.

As discussed earlier, the FAR now requires, in general, past performance as a mandatory evaluation factor in competitively negotiated procurements.

Best Practice 2 and the FAR stress that appropriate evaluation factors and weights should be selected to satisfy the requirements of the procurement, or in other words, to enable a best value solution to agency needs. But agency officials have wide flexibility in selecting factors and weights to accomplish this goal, especially with regard to PPI subfactors because they are not specified in the FAR. The discretion of public procurement officials in this area was affirmed in the protest of Borders Consulting, Inc. (1999). In this case, the protester asserted, generally, that the past performance criteria used in proposal evaluation were designed to favor the incumbent contractor. The comptroller general (ibid., pp. 1–2) denied the protest, finding essentially no problem with evaluation criteria that may actually "steer" an award to a particular firm, if the criteria directly relate to the statement of work.

> Agencies enjoy broad discretion in selecting evaluation criteria and [the Comptroller General] will not object to a solicitation's evaluation scheme so long as it reasonably relates to the agency's needs .... The fact that a solicitation's technical requirements or evaluation criteria may favor one offeror over another is unobjectionable, so long as they reflect the agency's actual needs, and the advantage enjoyed by a particular firm is not the result of improper government action.

Best Practice 3. Conduct pre-solicitation exchanges (e.g., draft solicitations and pre-solicitation conferences) with industry to explain approaches to evaluate performance risk.

The best practice guides overwhelmingly recommended conducting pre-solicitation exchanges of information with industry to provide the procuring agency with the opportunity to explain to potential offerors the proposed approach for the evaluation of past performance. These exchanges also facilitate a mutual understanding of government requirements and industry capabilities, thereby allowing potential offerors to judge whether or not they can satisfy the government's requirements, and the government to judge its ability to obtain quality supplies and services at reasonable prices. Pre-solicitation exchanges thus contribute to efficiency in proposal preparation, proposal evaluation, and contract award. The FAR (§15.201 (c)) encourages early exchanges with industry and provides a listing of recommended techniques for promoting early exchanges with industry. These include industry or small business conferences, public hearings, market research, one-on-one meetings with potential offerors, pre-solicitation notices, draft solicitations, pre-solicitation or pre-proposal conferences, and site visits.

Although pre-solicitation exchanges are encouraged, procurement officials must maintain the integrity of the process by not favoring one offeror over another (FAR §15.306 (e) (1)). In J.A. Jones Grupo de Servicios, SA (1999), the protester asserted, among other points, that the agency was indeed biased in favor of the awardee. A review of the source selection records found that the contracting officer had sent a message before the submission of initial offers, reminding the incumbent contractor to follow the solicitation's instructions for submitting information for evaluation, rather than rely upon the agency's familiarity with its capabilities. The comptroller general (ibid., p. 5) saw nothing improper in the exchange, finding it simply a "conscientious effort to enhance competition by ensuring that a significant competitor, the incumbent contractor, avoided a mistake often made by incumbents, which is failing to provide information needed for the evaluation, in the belief that the agency already has that information." The comptroller general (ibid., p. 5) found no basis to object to the contracting officer's gentle advice, apparently given for the purpose of enhancing competition, and it denied the protest, ruling that

> Where a protester alleges bias on the part of government officials, the protester must provide credible evidence clearly demonstrating a bias against the protester or for the awardee and showing that the agency's bias translated into action that unfairly affected the protester's competitive position.

This "presumption of good faith absent contrary evidence" grants procurement officials freedom to maximize use of pre-solicitation exchanges with industry. As long as exchanges are open and provide the same information to all potential offerors, officials may view them as valuable resources to enhance the quality of source selection.

Increasing the use of these exchanges could lead to varying outcomes regarding a firm's inclination to file a protest. If a firm's understanding of the evaluation scheme increases as a result of pre-solicitation exchanges, it may be either more or less inclined to protest, depending on its perception of how faithfully the scheme was executed.

Best Practice 4. Structure the solicitation to communicate effectively to potential offerors. Evaluations may be properly made only on the basis of what is communicated via the solicitation.

Solicitations communicate requirements to prospective offerors. The FAR (§15.305.2) describes the contents of the solicitation as it relates to past performance:

> The solicitation shall describe the approach for evaluating past performance, including evaluating offerors with no relevant performance history, and shall provide offerors an opportunity to identify past or current contracts (including federal, State, and local government and private) for efforts similar to the government requirement. The solicitation shall also authorize offerors to provide information on problems encountered on the identified contracts and the offeror's corrective actions.

Best Practice 4 focuses on the product of pre-solicitation activities. It indicates the central importance of the solicitation as the tangible basis for the entire source selection process. Although procurement officials may have wide discretion in crafting the past performance terms of a solicitation, their discretion will be constrained by these terms after its release.

The critical importance of the solicitation in resolving protests was affirmed in Enmax Corporation (1999). In this case, the protester argued that the agency's evaluation of the awardee's proposal was improper in two areas—the conclusion that the awardee's proposal was technically acceptable, and the decision that the awardee's proposal presented low performance risk. The comptroller general stated in the decision that, in considering a protest challenging an agency's evaluation of proposals, the record will be examined to determine whether the agency's judgment was fair, reasonable, and consistent with stated evaluation criteria in the solicitation. In this case, the comptroller general found that the agency's evaluators had failed to evaluate the awardee's proposal in accordance with the evaluation criteria contained in the solicitation. The protest was sustained, affirming the principle that the solicitation is "the touchstone for whether offerors have been treated fairly in an evaluation" (ibid., p. 5).

To summarize the discussion on this point, both the FAR and the comptroller general affirm the discretion of procurement officials in determining appropriate past performance schemes for particular procurements. This affirmation is grounded in the presumed competence of officials—in their presumed good faith actions, knowledge of agency needs, and expertise, which may be strengthened through investments in resources such as training. Officials are presumed to exercise competent discretion in the activities leading to preparation of the solicitation. The solicitation itself constrains officials' discretion once it is released, because they must evaluate proposals in strict accordance with its provisions.

31.4.2 Post-solicitation Activities

Best Practice 5. Use the most relevant, recent PPI available in making the source selection decision. PPI can come from federal, state, and local government databases, commercial contractors, references provided by the offeror, and quality certificates and awards.

Best Practice 6. Conduct reference checks and look for patterns or trends. Whenever possible, request two points of contact for each reference. Use questionnaires, face-to-face interviews, and telephone interviews.

These two best practices have to do mainly with sources of PPI to be used in evaluations. The FAR (§15.305 (a) (2)) provides specific guidance in this area:

> The currency and relevance of the information, source of the information, context of the data, and general trends in contractor's performance shall be considered… The evaluation should take into account past performance information regarding predecessor companies, key personnel who have relevant experience, or subcontractors that will perform major or critical aspects of the requirement…

Three recent protest cases illustrate some issues in considering PPI sources. First, in OMV Medical, Inc. and Saratoga Medical Center, Inc. (1999), the protesters contended that the agency arbitrarily neutralized past performance as an evaluation discriminator by according all offerors "low risk" performance ratings regardless of experience, which was allegedly prejudicial to the incumbent. The main purpose of the past performance evaluation was for the agency to identify and review relevant present and past performance to make an overall risk assessment of the offeror's ability to perform the requirement. To do so, the agency sent questionnaires to a minimum of two references provided by each offeror. On the basis of the responses received, the agency concluded that all offerors were capable of performing and, thus, all received a low performance risk rating. The protesters challenged the relevance of the references submitted by some offerors, but their protest was denied. The comptroller general (ibid., p. 4) found nothing unreasonable in the agency's approach to investigate the past performance history of the offerors and, based on that investigation, in concluding that all offerors presented a low risk of nonperformance.

> Where a solicitation requires the evaluation of offerors' past performance, an agency has discretion to determine the scope of the offerors' performance histories to be considered provided all proposals are evaluated on the same basis and consistent with the solicitation requirements.

The protest of Kellie W. Tipton Construction Company (1999) concerned a termination for convenience of a contract for the installation and replacement of water and sewer lines and the agency's decision to award a contract for these services to another offeror. The solicitation called for offerors to submit at least ten references; however, not all offerors did so. The agency determined that five past performance records were sufficient to evaluate an offeror. It reviewed three government project ratings and two customer performance surveys for both the awardee and the protester, who were rated as being equal under past performance. The protester alleged that the agency misevaluated proposals with respect to past performance. The comptroller general ruled, however, that the agency evaluation was reasonable and did not conflict with the solicitation evaluation criteria. Although the solicitation requested a minimum of ten references, it did not specify the number of references that the agency would contact for purposes of evaluation. The comptroller general denied the protest, holding that there is no requirement that an agency contacts all of an offeror's references, so long as offerors are evaluated consistently.

Finally, in Consolidated Engineering Services Inc. (1998), the protester argued that the agency improperly downgraded its proposal relative to the awardee's based on the awardee's more detailed description of the proposed maintenance subcontractor's experience. Although both offerors proposed the incumbent subcontractor, points were deducted from the protester's score—while the awardee received all points—for failure to adequately address the results achieved (e.g., quality of service, timeliness of performance, and cost control), by the subcontractor under prior contracts. The protester argued that, because the protester and the awardee proposed using the same subcontractor, they should have received the same score for the subcontractor's experience, and in any case, because the proposed subcontractor was the incumbent, the evaluators should have been aware of its performance and capabilities. The comptroller general sustained the protest, ruling that even if the agency was correct that the protester's proposal did not provide as much information as the awardee's regarding the subcontractor's experience, because both proposals offered the same subcontractor, the evaluation unreasonably accorded the two proposals different scores in this area. Once the agency became aware of the subcontractor's experience—whether from the awardee's proposal, personal knowledge, or otherwise—it could not have reasonably assigned the awardee's proposal a higher score than the protester's based on that experience. Thus, an agency may not ignore prior performance information of which it is aware.

From this portion of the discussion emerge themes like reasonableness, fairness, and consistency with the solicitation. The FAR provisions cited above indicate these themes in the use of wording such as "shall be considered" and "should take into account" without direction as to how, specifically, PPI should be considered and taken into account. Such direction being absent, procurement officials must judge their actions by standards of reasonableness and fairness to all offerors. They still exercise competent discretion, but only to the extent allowed by the terms of the solicitation.

Best Practice 7. Document strengths, weaknesses, and risks of each proposal to support the cost/past performance trade-off.

Best Practice 8. Justify price premiums with trade-off documentation regardless of the selected proposal's cost or past performance superiority.

Best Practice 9. Ensure that the source selection decision is consistent with the relative weights assigned to the evaluation factors in the solicitation.

These three best practices deal with proposal evaluation, with trade-offs among various evaluation factors, and with the need for adequate documentation of the evaluation and award decision. The FAR (§15.305) provides general direction in these areas:

> An agency shall evaluate competitive proposals and then assess their relative qualities solely on the factors and subfactors specified in the solicitation. Evaluations may be conducted using any rating method or combination of methods, including color or adjectival ratings, numerical weights, and ordinal rankings. The relative strengths, deficiencies, significant weaknesses, and risks supporting proposal evaluation shall be documented in the contract file.

In the final award determination—one of the last tasks before the contract is awarded—the offer or offers that represent the best value to the government are selected. In many cases, this is achieved through a trade-off process that reflects a willingness to accept a higher priced offer because the perceived benefits of that offer are in the best interests of the government. Though Best Practice 9 does not address documentation of the decision explicitly, the FAR (§15.308) provides clear direction:

> The source selection authority's (SSA) decision shall be based on a comparative assessment of the proposals against all source selection criteria in the solicitation. While the SSA may use reports and analyses prepared by others, the source selection decision

shall represent the SSA's independent judgment. The source selection decision shall be documented, and the documentation shall include the rationale for any business judgments and tradeoffs made or relied on by the SSA, including benefits associated with additional costs. Although the rationale for the selection decision must be documented, that documentation need not quantify the tradeoffs that led to the decision (FAR).

The use of PPI and trade-offs in best value source selections is illustrated in Marathon Watch Company Limited (1999). Here, the protester challenged the adequacy of a best value determination, which resulted in the agency's issuance of the purchase order to the another source. The comptroller general found, however, that the agency's selection of the awardee, a higher-priced vendor with excellent performance history, instead of the protester, a lower-priced vendor whose performance reflected delivery delinquencies, was reasonable and consistent with the solicitation. The solicitation advised that the best value determination would be based on a comparative assessment of prices and past performance, which were equally weighted. The past performance factor considered quality performance and delivery performance to be "of equal value." If the vendor with the best past performance history did not offer the lowest price, the agency would make the appropriate trade-off price for past performance, and list several considerations such as delivery schedule, inventory status, historical delivery, and quality problems that could affect the trade-off determination. The comptroller general (ibid., pp. 4,8) denied the protest, finding that

> Since [awardee] had the best past performance history..., but had not offered the lowest price, the contracting officer, as provided for by the [solicitation], determined that the appropriate tradeoff of price for past performance would include delivery schedule/inventory status and historical delivery problems. The contracting officer decided that, given these tradeoff considerations, Marathon's lower price was not worth the increased performance risk associated with its past delivery delinquencies, and that award to [awardee], with a slightly higher price but an excellent performance history, was justified to ensure timely delivery and represented the best value to the government. The contracting officer's conclusion was consistent with the [solicitation's] evaluation scheme and the discretion afforded the contracting officer in making the tradeoff decision.

Two other GAO protest cases illustrate issues in documenting source selection decisions involving past performance. In J&J Maintenance, Inc. (2000), the protester contended that the decision for the awardee on the basis of its higher-priced proposal was flawed because the agency unreasonably downgraded the protester's proposal and evaluated proposals unequally. The GAO's review found that minimal documentation had been kept, in part, because oral presentations had been used to streamline the source selection process. Oral presentations constituted the offerors' entire technical proposals, with the only written portions related to past performance. The record of the oral presentations and the evaluation was so sketchy that the comptroller general had no means to determine the reasonableness of the agency's selection. Although the comptroller general agreed that (1) the oral presentations are an effective means of streamlining the source selection process and enhancing an agency's understanding of an offeror's approach; (2) the FAR does not limit the flexibility afforded by their use; and (3) the FAR requires no particular method of establishing a record of what was said by offerors during oral presentations, the FAR does, however, establish an obligation to provide a reasonably adequate record of the presentations, the evaluation, and the cost/technical trade-offs. Such a record permits a meaningful review of the agency's decision. This protest was sustained.

In Support Services, Inc. (1999), the protester challenged the evaluation of past performance and relevant experience and argued that the award was based on a defective trade-off between price and past performance. The language in the source selection record suggested that one of the protester's past performance references was improperly not considered, and the comptroller general found that the written documentation provided by the agency lacked sufficient detail for a determination. Therefore, the comptroller general had to request clarifying statements from the contracting officer. In this case, the contracting officer's postprotest explanations were found to be generally consistent with the record and were sufficient to support the conclusion that all of the protester's submitted references were considered. The record as a whole indicated that all relevant references furnished by the protester were considered. The comptroller general (ibid., p. 4) denied the protest, stating that while it "will accord more weight to contemporaneous documents in determining whether an evaluation was reasonable, postprotest explanations that are credible and consistent" with the documentation will be considered.

This portion of the discussion has a more constrained tone in that the theme of procurement officials' discretion is not evidenced as strongly as in previous portions. Rather, consistency of the source selection evaluation and decision with the solicitation emerges as an overriding concern. Further, while tests of reasonableness still apply, and while the SSA exercises "independent judgment" in the award decision, the requirement for documentary evidence casts a shadow over these considerations. Although procurement officials are presumed to exercise competent discretion and to act reasonably and in good faith, a protest will in large part be decided on the basis of the content of an acquisition's documentation.

Best Practice 10. Conduct a proper and timely debriefing to provide unsuccessful offerors with the opportunity to learn about their strengths and weaknesses and how to improve future proposals submitted to the government.

The FAR (§15.505, 15.506) addresses debriefings to unsuccessful offerors. Debriefing information includes:

> The Government's evaluation of the significant weaknesses or deficiencies in the offeror's proposal ... The overall evaluated cost or price (including unit prices) and technical rating, if applicable, of the successful offeror and the debriefed offeror, and past performance information on the debriefed offeror ... The overall ranking of all offerors, when any ranking was developed by the agency ... A summary of the rationale for award ... [and] ... Reasonable responses to relevant questions about whether source selection procedures contained in the solicitation, applicable regulations, and other applicable authorities were followed.

As indicated by Best Practice 10, the purpose of these debriefings is to improve the quality of future proposals. However, as with pre-solicitation exchanges, these debriefings give unsuccessful offerors insights into the specifics of the agency's evaluation process. They may rely on information provided during debriefings to influence their decisions to file protests. Thus, they may be either more or less inclined to file a protest, depending on their perception of whether the process was fair, reasonable, and consistent with the solicitation. Certainly, in the absence of timely and productive briefings, unsuccessful offerors may be more likely to file protests as a way to determine if rationale for evaluations and trade-offs have been properly documented.

31.4.3 Summary

The GAO protest cases add substance and provide a real-world context to FAR provisions and agency best practices. They illustrate how some problematic past performance issues may be resolved as well as standards by which protests will be decided. Essentially, the comptroller general will be looking for reasonableness of action by procurement officials throughout the acquisition process, as well as for fair and impartial treatment for all businesses that compete for government contracts. An agency has discretion in crafting solicitations and evaluation schemes involving past performance, because it is responsible for defining its needs and the best method of accommodating them; it also bears any burden arising from a defective evaluation. When protests arise over past performance evaluation criteria or the use of best value trade-offs, the comptroller general will review source selection files to determine if the evaluation and selection were fair, reasonable, and consistent with the solicitation. The record must contain sufficient detail to allow review of the merits of the protest and to show that the evaluation was neither arbitrary nor in contravention with the solicitation.

Past performance-related protests should decrease in number as firms gain confidence in the competent discretion of public procurement professionals. Competent discretion in the use of PPI clearly must begin with a sound understanding of FAR provisions, and it may be further developed through training and experience. Best practice guides facilitate training by capturing and promulgating the experiences of agency members so that others may learn from them. To maximize their benefits, these guides should be reviewed and updated periodically to incorporate current experiences in an evolving procurement environment. The comptroller general's decisions on protests and rulings on other cases also facilitate training by providing interpretations of and resolutions to problematical cases. These cases also serve to illustrate and operationalize standards, such as reasonableness, fairness, and consistency, to which public procurement officials are held.

31.5 Initiatives in PPI Collection and Use

Two initiatives bear mention regarding collection and subsequent use of PPI. First, sample interview questions have been developed as a best practice to assist source selection officials in obtaining relevant qualitative PPI from contracting officers, contracting officer representatives, program management office representatives, and others who may have knowledge of an offeror's performance on prior contracts (U.S. Army, 2001). Second, in July 2002, OFPP announced that all available federal contractor PPI was being made available online for use by all agency contracting officials through the past performance information retrieval system (PPIRS) (OFPP, 2002). This initiative is intended to provide a central PPI retrieval system, which is to be fed by the various agencies' collection systems, thus unifying and simplifying PPI processes and eliminating collection redundancies. The memorandum also discouraged development of further agency-specific PPI systems in favor of this central federal system.

Assuming that PPI obtained through such initiatives is accurate and relevant to particular source selection actions, it should serve to increase offerors' confidence in the objectivity of the process. The more source selection officials rely on such useful information, the less discretion they will have to exercise.

In Section 31.1, it was noted that by using PPI, the government is seeking to emulate private industry's practice of relying upon preferred suppliers. In a study that compared public and private sector use of PPI, Lord (2005) noted that one of the major differences is the government's increasing reliance on large elaborate systems like PPIRS for collection and retrieval of PPI across all federal agencies. The government's incentives are twofold: to reduce the risk of selecting a less than satisfactorily performing offeror and to obtain objective data that will reduce risks of protests and their sustainment. Private industry collects vendor PPI only to achieve competitive advantage, and, thus, its PPI systems are much less complex (p. 27).

31.6 Conclusion: Procurement Theory

Readers might have noted that this chapter does not call for development or improvement of a body of knowledge or overarching theory of public procurement. Rather, its corrective emphasizes procurement practice as revealed in agency best practice guides and protest cases. A detailed explication of the pragmatic approach to theory development is not possible here but has been presented ably elsewhere (e.g., Miller and King, 1998). Grand theories or definitive bodies of knowledge are poor fits in contemporary professional fields like procurement for at least two reasons. First, procurement is a highly complex enterprise that entails the overlap and interplay of a variety of contexts—management, business, politics, and technology, to name a few. Second, each of these contexts is continually evolving in important ways. Under these conditions, the development of stable theories and bodies of knowledge becomes problematical. They become either too general to be useful or too specific to be interesting.

Pragmatic theories are practice based and, thus, have a local, situational, and tentative character. They are simply hypotheses about actions that might work to resolve problematic situations. Public procurement practice may always be marked by such situations. To the extent, then, that best practice guides and protest cases portray the constantly evolving state of public procurement practice, they provide resources for officials to reflect critically on practice (Miller and King, 1998, p. 58) and thus participate in the continual development of procurement theory.

Notes

1. Part 33 of the FAR describes procedures for protest if an offeror thinks a federal government contract may be or has been awarded unfairly. Protests are usually filed either against the terms of a solicitation or against a contract award, and they may be filed before or after submission of offers, as well as before or after contract award.

   Offerors have several routes for protests. They may file protests directly with the agency contracting officer. Offerors may also file protests with the GAO. Unless the protest is dismissed due to procedural or substantive defect, the contracting agency must submit to the GAO a report that responds to the protest, and which is also provided to the protester. During the protest process, the GAO's comptroller general may schedule meetings or conferences to resolve procedural matters and to obtain information pertaining to the disposition of the protest. Hearings may also be conducted to resolve factual and legal issues raised during the protest process.

   Within 100 days after the hearing, the comptroller general will issue a decision that either denies or sustains the protest. In the case of sustained protests, the comptroller general will recommend that the contracting agency implements an appropriate remedy.
2. Data was obtained from the GAO's Web site at http://www.gao.gov and the "Where in Federal Contracting?" Web site at http://www.wifcon.com.
3. Merit protests are those not dismissed due to procedural or substantive defects.
4. Office of Federal Procurement Policy (2000); U.S. Marine Corps (1997); U.S. Army (1998); U.S. Department of Defense (1999); U.S. Air Force (2000).
5. Cases were selected from the population of 151 past performance-related protests from FY1998 through June 2000.

References

Appleby, P. 1945. *Big Democracy*. New York: Knopf.

Argyris, C. and Schön, D. 1978. *Organizational Learning: A Theory of Action Perspective*. Reading, MA: Addison-Wesley.

Beausoleil, J. 2000. Past performance is not working. *Contract Management,* 40(7), 28–31.

Borders Consulting, Inc. March 10, 1999. *Comptroller General Decision B-281606*. Available at http://www.gao.gov (retrieved November 27, 2000).

Clipsham, N. 1998. Appraising performance appraisal systems. *The Military Engineer,* 591, 31–32.

Consolidated Engineering Services Inc. June 26, 1998. *Comptroller General Decision B-279565.2; B-279565.3*. Available at http://www.gao.gov (retrieved November 27, 2000).

Dewey, J. 1998. The development of American pragmatism. In L. Hickman and T.M. Alexander (Eds.), *The Essential Dewey,* volume 1, pp. 3–13. Bloomington, IN: Indiana University.

Enmax Corporation. May 12, 1999. *Comptroller General Decision B-281965*. Available at http://www.gao.gov (retrieved November 27, 2000).

Federal Acquisition Regulation. August 7, 2000. *Title 48, Code of Federal Regulations*. Washington, DC: Government Printing Office.

Finer, H. 1941. Administrative responsibility in democratic government. *Public Administration Review,* 1: 335.

Friedrich, C. 1940. Public policy and the nature of administrative responsibility. In C.J. Friedrich and E.S. Mason (Eds.), *Public Policy,* pp. 3–24. Cambridge. MA: Harvard University Press.

Hart, K. and Merle, R. February 27, 2007. As military contracts grow, so do protests. *Washington Post.*

J.A. Jones Grupo de Servicio, SA. October 25, 1999. *Comptroller General Decision B-283234*. Available at http://www.gao.gov (retrieved November 27, 2000).

J&J Maintenance, Inc. June 5, 2000. *Comptroller General Decision B-284708.2; B-284708.3*. Available at http://www.gao.gov (retrieved November 27, 2000).

Kellie, W. Tipton Construction Company. March 22, 1999. *Comptroller General Decision B-281331.3*. Washington, DC: General Accounting Office.

LB&B Associates. March 24, 1999. *Comptroller General Decision B-281706*. Available at http://www.gao.gov (retrieved November 27, 2000).

Lipshitz, R., Popper, M., and Oz, S. 1996. Building learning organizations: The design and implementation of organizational learning mechanisms. *Journal of Applied Behavioral Sciences,* 32(3): 292–305.

Lord, R. March 17, 2005. *Contractor Past Performance Information (PPI) in Source Selection: A Comparison Study of Public and Private Sector*. Technical Report NPS-CM-04-019. Monterey, CA: Naval Postgraduate School.

Marathon Watch Company Ltd. April 22, 1999. *Comptroller General Decision B-281876; B-281876.2*. Available at http://www.gao.gov (retrieved November 27, 2000).

Miller, H. and King, C. 1998. Practical theory. *American Review of Public Administration*, 28(1): 43–60.

Office of Federal Procurement Policy. December 1992. *Policy Letter 92–5*. Available at www/whitehouse/OMB.

Office of Federal Procurement Policy. May 2000. *Best Practices for Collecting and Using Current and Past Performance*. Available at www/whitehouse/OMB (retrieved November 27, 2000).

Office of Federal Procurement Policy. July, 2002. *Memorandum: Roll-out of the Past Performance Information Retrieval System*. Available at www/whitehouse/OMB (retrieved November 27, 2000).

OMV Medical, Inc.; Saratoga Medical Center, Inc. February 3, 1999. *Comptroller General Decision B-281387; B-281387.2; B-281387.3; B-281387.4*. Available at http://www.gao.gov (retrieved November 27, 2000).

Phillips, C.E. 2000. *Past Performance Revisited*. Available at http://www.wifcon.com (retrieved January 27, 2001).

Solomon, J. and Pfleger, K. July 24, 2000. Firms that defrauded the U.S. still getting government contracts. *Philadelphia Inquirer, A(4).*

Support Services, Inc. July 8, 1999. *Comptroller General Decision B-282407; B-282407.2*. Available at http://www.gao.gov (retrieved November 27, 2000).
U.S. Air Force. April 2000. Air Force Material Command. *Source Selection Activities Guide*. AFMC Pamphlet 64–113.
U.S. Army. January 1998. Contracting for best value: A best practices guide to source selection. *Army Material Command Pamphlet 715–3*.
U.S. Army. June 2001. Office of the Assistant Secretary of the Army: Acquisition, Logistics and Technology, *Army Source Selection Guide*. Available at www.arl.army.mil/contracts/library.htm
U.S. Department of Defense. May 1999. May. *Department of Defense Guide to Collection and Use of Past Performance Information*. Available at www.fedaccess.com/dod-03.htm
U.S. Marine Corps. June 1997. Marine Corps Systems Command. *Best Value Source Selection Handbook*. Available at www.akss.dau.mil/Documents/Policy/BestValue1.rtf

Chapter 32

Ban-on-Negotiations in Tender Procedures: Undermining the Best Value for Money

Kai Krüger

CONTENTS

32.1 Pre-Contractual Scenarios: Public and Private Sectors

Prudent commercial contracting involves thorough planning and visionary negotiations. Sometimes, stage-by-stage contracting is required in terms of a "letter of intent." This pre-contractual framework arrangement comprises the achievement of part consensus on matters with the need to avoid pitfalls through avenues for escape before the final selection of the successful candidate takes place. The private contract law on negotiations is tough. In principle, there are very few restrictions on the means and methods of making the ultimate of a strong bargaining position for the purchasing party, even when it comes to beating down the price, the extension of workload, or commanding contract milestones set with time penalties.[1]

The more complex the contract, the greater the necessity to spend time, expertise, resources, and efforts on details in negotiations. Long-term cooperative contracts in the planning procedure may fall outside the scope of legislative default regimes as well as of previous experiences gained by the negotiating parties. Thorough deliberations may prove essential to avoid litigation in infra-contract or post-contract disputes. Indeed, modern concepts of alternative dispute resolution (ADR) and contractual basis for renegotiations in unforeseen contingent incidents[2] may substitute litigation or arbitration proceedings. In that connection, there is a need for a waterproof, well-prepared extensive contract reflecting not only the main-stream prospects and expectations, but may also reflect both parties' visions, foresight, and imaginable ruling for the unexpected. Pre-contractual endeavors down to details of unexpected contingencies may prove to be cost-effective in the long run. All this is common ground in the commercial world of contracts.

In the world of public contracts, these observations seem to have limited bearing, at least under EU and European Economic Area (EEA) procurement law.[3] What is the reason for that? This question and certain aspects of restrictions on pre-contractual negotiations in public contracting is the subject of the following remarks.

32.2 Pre-Contractual Negotiations: A Legal Perspective

In public contracting, pre-contractual negotiations are often coming to a dead end because they turn out to be incompatible with mandatory statutory regimes, which require that any public[4] contract for suppliers, works, or services should in principle be awarded through the strictly regulated nonnegotiable tender procedures, equivalent to the U.S. Federal Acquisition Regulation (FAR) terminology "sealed bidding."[5]

To comply with principles of transparency and equal opportunities for suppliers, the regulated competitive procedure for the award of public (government and municipal) contracts normally assumes that the contracting entity invites the market to respond on a public call for competition, setting the object and specifications for the purchase as well as the contract terms to be applied. These pre-set "rules of the game" set the level playing field for the private parties in the subsequent procedure for selection of a winner to the contract. However, the current procurement regimes vary both on substance and in the procedural details.[5a]

The pan-European setting for the award of public contracts for supplies, works, and services is currently regulated in a comprehensive directives' regime originating from the early European Economic Community (EEC) in the 1970s, which was consolidated in the 1990s, and which later (1997–1998) got amended by incorporation of the WTO/GPA member states' commitments covering the European Union (EU).[6] EU Law on traditional public sector contracting requires the contracting authority[7] to strictly apply the competitive tender procedures, with very few exceptions.[8]

Following a comprehensive law reform initiated in the mid-1990s, the three directives were substituted by a present single Directive 2004/18 of the European Parliament and of the Council of March 31, 2004 on the coordination of procedures for the award of public works contracts, public supply contracts, and public service contracts—hereafter referred to as Dir 2004/18. A similar Directive 2004/17 on so-called utilities' contracts on water, energy, transport, and postal services was also part of the law reform. Deadline for implementation was set to January 31, 2006, but most of the EU/EEA states failed to legislate within this time limit.[9]

The EU regulated procurement law applies on contracts above certain threshold values set in euro, varying for supplies, services, and construction works contracts. Some member states have legislated also on subthreshold contracts, taking EU law as a guideline but with more liberal and flexible rules—national "procurement light" regulations.

Enforcement of EU/EEA procurement law is not dealt with in the new 2004/18 directive. Two separate remedies' directives on public and utilities' sectors, respectively deal with corrective mechanisms and damages to be awarded in case of violations.[10] The public sector remedies' Directive 1989/665 leaves enforcement to EU/EEA member states' regimes for court litigation or administrative bid protest arrangements similar to the U.S. Government Accountability Office. Many EU member states have established separate review bodies as complaint boards to deal with procurement disputes when a nonsuccessful contract candidate challenges the award decision. A recent EU law reform has tightened up the sanctions for procurement violations, Dir 2007/77 on review procedures, amending Dir 89/665 (public sector) and Dir 92/13. National court litigation and out-of-court bid protest disputes are supplementary to surveillance and judicial review through the EU Commission, the European Communities' Court of Justice (ECJ), and the EFTA Court (in EEA matters).

Separate from public contracting are the required procedures for contracts awarded within the excepted utilities' sector, which before 2004 implied water, energy, transport, and telecom governed by the Utility Dir 93/38/EC, permitting optional negotiated procedures as an accepted alternative to the formal tendering for contracts—Article 4 No. 1.[11] Contracts within the utilities' sectors will not be dealt with in this article.

Energy includes oil and gas industry contract awards, extending even to private multinational oil companies operating under public licenses in the industry. In the Norwegian offshore industry, the established practice before Norway's signing of the EEA agreement with (then) EEC was to combine traditional tender procedures for fabrication and service contracts with subsequent hard-core negotiations. The industry has always underlined that only strict cost-effective commercial criteria have ruled the selection of successful contract candidates, thus, the EU procedures were regarded to be unnecessary bureaucratic red tape. Arguments in favor of extensive post-tender negotiations before the contract award could be based on the partial need of the contracting entity to adapt joint design and project schemes to the subsequent contract commitment. A strict procurement regime prohibiting flexibility in this respect may mean that the adaptation must be done after conclusion of the contract—by variation orders (VOs) or worse: renegotiation of contents and scope of contract performance. In fact, in the early Norwegian oil and gas industry period of the 1970s, it would be fair to say that at the time of preparing tender documentation, neither the licensed operator issuing the tender invitation nor the bidders had anything but extremely sketchy ideas on what was actually to become the object of the contract. Subsequent to the utilities' directive, the so-called EC License Dir 94/33/EC on the conditions for granting and using authorizations for the prospection, exploration, and production of hydrocarbons establishes a regime for nondiscriminatory award of these licenses. This, in turn, led to a utilities' exception, Utilities' Dir 93/38 Article 3, now maintained in Dir 2004/17 Article 30 (3) with reference to Annex XI. North Sea oil and gas industry is consequently generally no longer ruled by the utilities' directive, but must, on the other hand, always honor treaty and EEA principles such as the EC Treaty Article 12 (to be renumbered as Article 18 according to the Lisbon 2008 Treaty on the Functioning of the European Union) prohibition against all discrimination on national grounds on the selection of contractors. Preferential contract awards to support domestic industries would be a blatant violation of these principles.

The 1994 UNCITRAL (United Nations Commission for International Trade Law) model law is strict on the procurement of goods or construction, stating in Article 18 (1) that except otherwise provided "a procuring entity engaging in procurement of goods or construction shall do so by means of tendering proceedings" (narrow exceptions from this in Article 18 (2)) while the procurement of services is made less rigid—Article 18 (3) with reference to Chapter IV provisions on methods for procurement of service and Article 43 on lawful selection procedures with simultaneous negotiations.

Other legal public contract regimes are generally less strict on the question of mandatory procedures for contract awards. The legal techniques in these regimes vary.

Some of these simply state that tendering for contracts may take place with or without negotiations, provided that the contract candidates are duly notified of the procedure to be followed. The WTO 1994 GPA Article IX Paragraph 2 leaves it to the entity's discretion whether the procedure will be a plain tendering procedure with or without the involvement of simultaneous negotiations. GPA Article XIV states (No. 1) that

A Party may provide for entities to conduct negotiations:

(a) In the context of procurements in which they have indicated such intent, namely in the notice referred to in paragraph 2 of Article IX (the invitation to suppliers to participate in the procedure for the proposed procurement) or
(b) When it appears from evaluation that no one tender is obviously the most advantageous in terms of the specific evaluation criteria set forth in the notices or tender documentation.

The NAFTA Part Four Chapter 10 on government procurement contains provisions basically similar to the WTO/GPA rules—cf. NAFTA Act 1010 No. 2 (b) and Article 1014 No. 1 (a).[12] The U.S. FAR[13] (Parts 14 and 15, cf.: "6.401 Sealed bidding and competitive proposals. Sealed bidding and competitive proposals, as described in Parts 14 and 15, are both acceptable procedures for use under Subparts 6.1, 6.2; and, when appropriate, under Subpart 6.3.") is applicable to all U.S. federal procurement.

The provision constitutes a preference for sealed bids in the situations envisaged in 6-401(a), but leaves wide discretion to the officer in charge of the purchase:

Contracting officers shall solicit sealed bidding if

(1) Time permits the solicitation, submission, and evaluation of sealed bids.
(2) Award will be made on the basis of price and other price-related factors.
(3) It is not necessary to conduct discussions with the responding offerors about their bids.
(4) There is a reasonable expectation of receiving more than one sealed bid."[14]

Sealed bidding resembles the EU/EEA tender procedure and involves a rather simple award procedure. After checking timeliness and the responsiveness of the bids, the lowest bidder in price will become the preferred contracting candidate. In this connection, the FAR regime differs from an EU tender procedure opening up for award to the most advantageous offer. Negotiations and modifications are forbidden. In the negotiated procedures, proposals from candidates can be handled with flexibility. An agency could set up a system that would rate the technical approach proposed by the offerors as unacceptable, marginal, fair, or outstanding, which would allow price/technical trade-offs. If proposal A is outstanding but high-priced, and proposal B is good and inexpensive, the agency might be allowed to select either A or B. The solicitation must indicate in advance whether the evaluation will be pass/fail (low price, technically acceptable) or will allow a cost/technical trade-off (best value). Negotiations are not mandatory and are often omitted, but whenever negotiations are initiated, the candidates having submitted proposals within competitive range should be invited for discussions. The U.S. trend has moved away from sealed bidding toward negotiated procedures, largely because the agencies like to be able to select a better, but more expensive item (which they cannot do under sealed bidding).

Chinese government procurement law is now regulated in Order No. 68 of the President of the People's Republic of China, adopted by the Ninth National People's Congress on June 19, 2002, effective as from January 1, 2003, supplemented (Article 4) by a separate law on bid invitation and bidding for government procurement of construction. Article 3 requires compliance with principles of openness and transparency, fair competition, impartiality, and good faith. Article 26 sets various methods to be adopted for government procurement: (1) public invitation, (2) invited bidding, (3) competitive negotiation, (4) single source procurement, (5) inquiry about quotations, and (6) other methods confirmed by the relevant authorities under State Council. Article 30 sets out the conditions for procurement of goods and services through competitive negotiations, apparently as exceptions from the more stricter main rule on nonnegotiable "public invitation" (Articles 26 and 27).

More restrictive regimes provide for tender bidding procedures without options or with very limited openings for negotiations. The World Bank (IBRD loans and IDA credits) Article 2.6 opens up for two-stage bidding, but assumes bid openings procedures of the traditional kind in Article 2.44. According to Article 2.46 (with limited exceptions),

> Except as otherwise provided in paragraphs 2.63 and 2.64 of these Guidelines, bidders shall not be requested or permitted to alter their bids after the deadline for receipt of bids. The Borrower shall ask bidders for clarification needed to evaluate their bids but shall not ask or permit bidders to change the substance or price of their bids after the

bids opening. Requests for clarification and the bidders' responses shall be made in writing, in hard copy or by an electronic system satisfactory to the Bank.

A third variant is the current EU/EEA module, which states (Dir 2004/18 Article 28) that a formal one and final offer "open or restricted procedure" is to be applied unless the provisions on "competitive dialogue" or "negotiated procedure" allow for exceptions. The EU/EEA mandatory "tender procedure" for contract awards is similar to the U.S. "sealed bidding," but applies both for low price and "most advantageous" tender bids (Article 53).

Alternatively, and as limited exceptions to the main rule on tender procedure, the directive allows for the so-called "negotiated procedure" to be performed simultaneously with all, or a fair and objective selection of contract candidates. The negotiated procedure is formally not seen as tendering at all even if the procedure starts with submittal of initial binding, but not final, offers. In the negotiated procedure, both price and contents of offers from the suppliers are subject to possible improvements in favor of the contracting authority. Pending prices as well as confidential details in the offers for consideration are not to be disclosed to other competitors. Different from private sector the negotiations are about the market response, not the concept for the actual purchase already published by the contracting authority prior to the opening of the negotiations. The "up-front" tender documentation is not subject to amendments or corrections to match any particular offeror. The "point of no return" for such amendments is set at the time limit for submittal of contract offers (leaving therefore the possibility to insert slight but not substantial amendments, for instance in response from potential contract candidates preparing their offers). Neither should the detailed "up-front" published indications on which subcriteria which will eventually decide the final award of the contract.[15] This protects the would-be candidates who may have abstained from participation in the competition for the contract, trusting that the published indications were to be conclusive for qualifications and final selection of the winner.

The 2004 EU law reform maintains the "negotiated procedure" exception and introduces certain clarifications,[16] but even more important: The new regime extends the area of acceptable negotiations to comprise also the fresh concept "competitive dialogue" applicable as a second exception from the tender procedure, provided that the award is about "particularly complex contracts." Member states' national legislators may provide for the procedure defined in Dir 2004/18/EC Article 29.

Because the EU/EEA tender procedure is mandatory in supplies, works, and service contract awards, one should not be surprised over the operators' pressure for liberal interpretation of the provisions on alternative negotiated procedures as well as for conducting communications and dialogues in the closed door tender procedure, both multilaterally (simultaneously) with competitive candidates and unilaterally with the apparent most preferential candidate, while attempting to impact on potential contract terms under the disguise of clarifications. The role of the parties changes as the process moves along. Before award decision is taken, all participating parties may press for latitude and discretion to win the beauty contest. Afterward, the litigant passed-over candidates and their attorneys will scrutinize the process to detect, identify, and invoke any potential violation of rules. Alleged unlawful negotiations are quite often invoked in national court cases or in cases put before national complaint boards. National courts and complaint boards will then police the regulations and administer remedies as provided for in the EU/EEA remedy directives.

The EU/EEA Public "Remedy" Dir 89/665/EC requires member states' to authorize review bodies on measures to have the procedure stopped, corrected, or reversed at least up until the conclusion of the contract, subject to explicit *option* for member states in Article 2 No. 6 to leave a concluded contract unaffected even in case of a procurement violation such as conducting negotiations where the directive orders the nonnegotiable tender procedure. The European Communities'

Court of Justice (ECJ) has repeatedly required national legislation on effective procedures whereby unsuccessful tenderers may challenge any award decision (cf., as an example, C-212/02 (June 24, 2004)). The important ECJ 1999 C-81/98 "*Alcatel*" case introduced a mandatory reasonable "standstill" period running from the award decision until the actual preclusive signing of the contract, now addressed explicitly in the (Dir 07/66) amended Dir 89/665 Article 2a. The forthcoming provision sets the statutory standstill period to at least 10 calendar days. And most important, if the contracting authority disregards the statutory standstill period and signs the infected contract, the amended remedies' directive requires the contract to be set aside as "ineffective"—amended Dir 89/665 Article 2d (1)(b). These amendments to the Dir 89/665 are to be transposed within EU/EEA at the latest by December 20, 2009.[16a]

The standstill period now made EU law will help a bid protester challenging a preliminary contract award decision invoking unlawful amendments in the winner's contract due to negotiations that should not have taken place. On the other hand, the amended Dir 89/665 will not in itself invalidate a contract because of procedural violations in general. The provision on ineffective contracts (inserted new Article 2d) only applies in the cases expressly listed, whereof direct purchase without a call for competition is the most serious besides disregarding the standstill period.

In contrast, the U.S. Government Accountability Office (GAO) regime is tougher. A successful bid protest may render the awarded contract invalid or revocable even after conclusion of the contract—cf. Bid Protests Regulations Section 21.6 on suspension of contract performance and Section 21.8 on remedies, including Section 21.8 (a)(2) on termination of the contract.

In the EU/EEA remedy regime, on the other hand, the call for remedies in damages is only dealt with in a sketchy way. Article 2 states that national law must provide "damages to persons harmed by an infringement." ECJ has not clarified the requirement of this provision, and national jurisdictions in cases of unlawful negotiations seem to vary. The Nordic approach has been to assume negative interest damages for all participating nonsuccessful tender bidders (costs and time spent in futile preparation of tender bids trusting that the contracting entity will not infect the procedure with preferential negotiations). Positive interest for loss of contract has been accepted in all Nordic jurisdictions, provided (1) serious inexcusable violations of rules and (2) a high degree of probability that the claimant would have acquired the contract if the infringement had not taken place (claimant's burden of proof). The Norwegian breakthrough for loss of contract was the Nucleus Supreme Court judgment August 30, 2001, which, inter alia, involved the unwarranted post-tender amendment of figures in the tender bid of the claimant that consequently did not win the contract.

In the U.S. GAO Bid Protests Regulations regime, questions on damages for negative interest or loss of contract are probably less practical, because an unauthorized award normally will invalidate the contract in favor of the bid protester. In protests before the U.S. GAO, money damages are usually limited to costs incurred in the protest litigation (Bid Protests Regulations Section 21.8 (d), (e), and (f)), although bid preparation costs are sometimes awarded. More often, though, a protester that is successful at GAO gets another chance to obtain the contract.

The (EU) European concept of a genuine tender procedure (similar to U.S. sealed bidding) assumes that a fully operative commercial contract may be established in the sequence of (1) soliciting, if necessary, of consultant resources for the project; (2) preparation of a documentation to be published, defining the concept and object of the contract, relevant technical information (specs), as well as the contents of contract terms to be applied; (3) the up-front call for competition invitation, open or restricted, to all or selected qualified potential candidates, published in appropriate means with indications on time limits for submission and on the procedure to be applied; (4) a potential intermediate clarification or necessary amendments of documentation subject to principles of equality preceding the submission of tender bids well within the set time limit; (5) opening of offers received by bidders; (6) the subsequent unilateral internally closed checking on part of the contracting authority for nonqualified or nonsuitable candidates, errors, miscalculations, and possible deviations from the initial contract documentation; and thereafter; (7) according to standard directives' formula common for supplies, works, and services Dir 04/18 Article 44 No. 1:[17]

> Contracts shall be awarded on the basis of the criteria laid down ... after the suitability of the economic operators not excluded ... has been checked ... in accordance with the criteria of economic and financial standing of professional and technical knowledge or ability referred to ...

The award decision and subsequent conclusion of the contract with the successful candidate end the process of a comparative unilateral handling of competing tender bids according to (1) qualifications and suitability and (2) criteria for the preferences, both of which are required to be published up front, similarly nonnegotiable and nonamendable in accordance with rules set by statute or by the contracting entity itself.

32.3 Concepts of Contract Award: Borderline Cases on Private Autonomy which Fall Outside the Scope of Procurement

Are all contracts about services to be provided or could there be public/private contracts that fall outside the scope of procurement law? Would these be undoubtedly based on autonomous engagement by participants and these admittedly serve private as well as public interests?

In the EU/EEA context, the scope provisions of the 2004 directive are legally decisive on the issue of this article. Contracting or quasi-contracting with private sector will come under the directives if the object is an award of a supplies, works, or service commitment on the part of the private party. On the other hand, the bona fide formation of companies with joint public and private shares would not come under the directives' regime, nor would the mere acceptance of public conditions for the award of licenses, grants, or permits.[18] This does not rule out EU/EEA law, especially in a transborder context where principles on nondiscrimination and transparency to secure subsequent judicial review might come into play. The point here is simply the ruling out of traditional procurement law in terms of mandatory procedures on tender bidding, the publishing of call for competitive negotiations, etc. There is a major difference in litigation strategies between law that only prohibits discrimination as opposed to mandatory law and that prescribes in procedural details how nondiscrimination and transparency are to be preserved.

Some procurement fringe scenarios have been dealt with in statute. The Dir 04/18/EC assumes in Article 5 Title III that the so-called works concession contracts as defined in Article 1 No. 3 (public works concession) are not subject to the extensive award procedure provided for. Similarly, service concessions are now explicitly excepted from the directive's procedures in Article 17. In both these cases, there is an element of contract autonomy, but the excluding element is that the holder of the concession will be remunerated through the third party (the general public) oriented exploitation of the permit or grant in question and not through pecuniary consideration by the public.

In this context, the point is that even the award of contract-based licenses, grants, or permits to operate concession facilities may be awarded irrespective of the strict EU/EEA procurement procedures, provided that EU/EEA principles of nondiscrimination are being honored.

32.4 Tender Bidding Procedure Ruling Out Post-Tender Negotiations Indispensable

Strangely enough, the EU procurement ban-on-negotiations rule applicable in tender procedures has never been expressed in any of the procurement directives themselves. Neither have other variants of the problem, such as the issue of amendments and modification of the bids, correction of mistakes in the bid, etc. Such issues have either been considered to have been evident, self-explanatory, or, more probably, left to interplay between EU/EEA law and national law.[19] There is, however, a scent of commission's hindsight in the EC Council separate statements published in 1989, 1990, and 1994 (see as for Dir 93/37/EC [1994] O J No. L 111/114), stating that

> in open and restricted procedures all negotiations with candidates or tender bidders on fundamental aspects of contracts variations in which are likely to distort competition, and in particular on prices, shall be ruled out

The statements can either be understood as an assertion that all negotiations on fundamental aspects of contracts will necessarily distort competition (and thus prevent both equal treatment and best value), or as a reference to those negotiations that in each particular case could be said to have a distorting effect. Because competition may also take place in conjunction with or in prolongation of tendering procedures, and is actually practiced in many markets that allow for negotiations, it is somewhat hard to accept that the implication of parallel negotiations with compatible contract candidates necessarily must distort competition; that is, if one assumes a loyal intention on the part of the entity to really go for the commercially best value such as the lowest price or the most advantageous offer in the current actual market.

The EU formula for tender procedure bans post-tender communication on contractual matters between the public entity and any of the candidates for the contract, even when the successful candidate appears to emerge during the process. This means a barrier to price adjustments as well as adaptations, modifications in scope, and definition of the object of the contract and ad hoc agreed amendments of any of the already published terms contained in the tender documentation published.[20] The up-front rule bars the entity from modifying the contract documentation in view of what now could seem to be a better means to achieve the object of the project.[21] Before time limit for bid, submittals, amendments, and modifications may be affected by a so-called technical dialogue initiated by the contract entity itself, its consultants, as well as by way of suggestions from any of the potential contractors. On the other hand, after time limit for submitting the bids, the ban-on-negotiations rule of the game closes the door and strikes down communications in a way as to allow only for minor clarification where the submitted bids are read to be ambiguous or truly questionable in their contents. Basically, neither the tender bid price nor the scope of commitments should be adjusted. Clarification of ambiguities or shortcomings of the tender documentations reflected in the tender bid do not fall under the narrow clarification rule.[22] Admittedly, however, the distinction between amending and clarification is ambiguous because the text in focus originates from the bidder and is not a result of joint deliberation involving the public entity.[23]

Strictness in the area of amendments and modifications serve first of all a need for transparent clear-cut commercial order open for efficient legal review (complaint or dispute bodies, court proceedings). As pointed out above, many regimes accept negotiations as an optional alternative to tender procedures (sealed bidding), but once the award is indicated to follow the nonnegotiable bidding formula, there seems to be general agreement on a "catholic" approach to later modifications. These are "rules of game" well established in jurisdictions that have applied tender procedures prior to or concurrently with the EU regime. The ban-on-negotiations provides a high degree of certainty and foreseeability—and it serves above all the principle of equal treatment of contract candidates. Historically, the EU regime facilitates inner market mobility for public contracting. The ban-on-discrimination on grounds of nationality may also be best served in excluding discussions between candidates individually or simultaneously. Add to this that the combat of bribery and corruption also assumes a high degree of transparency combined with a minimum of modifications and latitude in the pre-set framework for the award procedure.

Even if many stakeholders complain about the complexity of the EU regime, the ban-on-negotiations seems to be a rather clear-cut guideline and therefore not hard to overcome. But, admittedly, ban-on-negotiations prevents the contracting authority from achieving an even better "value for money" contract based on its normally strong bargaining position. The WTO/GPA and U.S. FAR regimes presented above are less rigid and prove that negotiated contract awards are not by themselves necessarily irreconcilable with proper procurement.

In the EU setting, however, the exceptional access to the negotiated procedure (and now the competitive dialogue) makes it clear that the mandatory tender procedure is meant to be conducted on the assumption that the tender bids should be prepared by the candidates as the final and conclusive offer not to be improved, neither by price reductions, increase of contract commitments, nor by *de facto* negotiating terms of the pre-published contract, whether such terms are the original terms drafted by the contracting entity or subsequent reservations inserted in the submitted candidates tender bid.

The ban-on-negotiations applies also in the standstill period after award decision has been taken until contract is actually signed (or otherwise concluded). Amendments and discussions with the preliminarily selected contract candidate should not take place as long as the tender procedure is not brought to an end.

After the signing of the contract and exit of procurement law, the parties are free to renegotiate terms in the same way as in otherwise applicable commercial contract law. The contracting entity under a construction contract may opt for variation (change) orders as long as such options are not amounting to a total change of the contract object, in which case there should be another call for competition. The contractor may even rightfully claim to perform the variations without market competition.

The "clarification" rule advocated in the 1994 EU Council statements assumes that purely obscure or ambiguous details in the tender bid may be discussed and corrected, either on request by the candidate or in course of the tender bid evaluation conducted by the contracting entity.

A typical case for clarification could be discrepancies in the tender bids when compared to the up-front tender documentation. The contracting entity could be expected to formally reject tender bids that have ambiguities of a kind that makes the comparison with competing bids impossible, but one could also have a situation where the bid contains a deliberate deviation from the tender documentation, in the form of alternative suggestions,[24] reservations on contract terms, etc.

Although clarifications assume communication with the tender bidder, errors and mistakes in tender bids create a different challenge. What should be done in cases where the checking of the tender bids reveals blatant errors and misunderstandings, varying from clear-cut miscalculation of figures to cases where there is a strong indication that the tender bidder must have made a mistake in the pricing of units, say in construction contract documentation? Or is the tender bid intended to be ambiguous and open to be interpreted in alternative ways, either being the lowest bid or, alternatively, a somewhat higher bid total than expected by the contracting entity in the evaluation of the bids, according to what suits the tenderer the best after opening of the bids and having seen the tendered price of all competitors?

Plain calculation errors may and should be corrected, provided that there is no doubt at all as to whether there is a mistake and how it should be corrected.[25] Failing to do so may result in a wrong award, and if it is apparent that the winner would have been the candidate affected by the error, possible positive damages in loss of contract might accrue.

In construction contract awards, the question often arises in connection with apparent mistakes in unit pricing. The item of sub-service unit offer may appear suspiciously high or low in comparison with the competing bids. This is an argument for applying the clarification rule to ascertain whether or not there is a mistake. The issue is not a simple one, for after the opening of the tender bids preceding the evaluation and checking of all bids, any of the candidates has knowledge of the submitted prices and could adapt to that by speculation in a strategic effort to increase the chances for winning the contract.[26] Injecting ambiguous price quotations in the bid might serve such purposes and should not be encouraged. Unilateral correction puts the contracting entity at great risk. If the correction rules out the candidate, he may come back asserting that there was no mistake, which might also happen if the contracting entity chooses to reject the bid for being ambiguous and therefore impossible to ascertain.[27]

Numerous U.S. GAO bid protests deal with the issue of mistakes in bids, cf. for illustration *Roy Anderson Corporation*, October 10, 2003, B-292555, 2003 CPD Paragraph 179:

> An agency may permit correction of a bid where clear and convincing evidence establishes both the existence of a mistake and the bid actually intended. Federal Acquisition Regulation §14.407-3(a). For upward correction of a low bid, work papers, including records of computer-generated software spreadsheets, may constitute clear and convincing evidence if they are in good order and indicate the intended bid price, and there is no contravening evidence (Alpha Constr. & Eng'g, Inc., B-261493, Oct. 5, 1995, 95-2 CPD ¶ 166 at 3; McInnis Bros. Constr., Inc., B-251138, Mar. 1, 1993, 93- 1 CPD ¶ 186 at 5). In addition, where the mistake has a calculable effect on the bid price and that effect can be determined by a formula evident from the bidder's work papers, the overall intended bid may be ascertained by taking into account the effects of the error on other bid calculations based on the mistaken entry (Continental Heller Corp., B-230559, June 14, 1988, 88–1 CPD ¶ 571 at 3). Moreover, correction may be allowed, even where the intended bid price cannot be determined exactly, provided there is clear and convincing evidence that the amount of the intended bid would fall within a narrow range of uncertainty and would remain low after correction (McInnis Bros. Constr., Inc., supra). Our Office treats the question of whether the evidence of the intended bid meets the clear and convincing standard as a question of fact, and we will not question an agency's decision in this regard unless it lacks a reasonable basis.

The European ban-on-negotiation on tender procedures has its parallel in a very blunt provision in UNCITRAL 1994 Model Law Article 34 (1)(a), simply statingon post-tender amendments the following: "No change…shall be sought, offered or permitted."

Similar restrictions are found in the World Bank publication "Guidelines on Procurement under IBRD Loans and IDA Credits" (May 2004) as Paragraph 2.46.

The WTO/GPA approach, on the other hand, is far more flexible and structured so that entity may choose a proposed procurement, in which case the entity decides by itself whether the procedure is to be open or selective and whether or not it will involve negotiations. Article XIV, cf. Article IX 6.b, sets out as alternatives:

1. A party may provide for entities to conduct negotiations:
   (a) In the context of procurements in which they have indicated such intent, namely in the notice referred to in paragraph 2 of Article IX (the invitation to suppliers to participate in the procedure for the proposed procurement)
   (b) When it appears from evaluation that no one tender is obviously the most advantageous in terms of the specific evaluation criteria set forth in the notices or tender documentation

The provision goes on to set standard procedures for alternative negotiations in Paragraphs 2–4 of the article.

Because the EU/EEA procurement directives have not dealt with negotiations during tender procedure, there seem to be no indications in the new 2004 regime on that matter. This is somewhat surprising, because unlawful negotiations both in tender procedures and by applying unwarranted negotiated procedures (as well as direct purchases with no competition at all) are a current scenario for procurement disputes and complaints. The inherent implications stated by the EU Council in the 1990s and widely accepted in national procurement law on the matter, remain in EU and EEA contract situations even under the joint EU/GPA regime. Because the GPA provisions do not prevent EU/EEA from legislating on more restrictive rules and practices, the mandatory tender procedure will even apply in the EU regime after the GPA public contract incorporation in 1997. The EU/GPA Dir 97/52/EC does not address the issue.

The relationship between GPA and EU/EEA directives with regard to negotiations seems to be that the more restrictive EU/EEA regime within its scope will prevail over the GPA negotiation principles expressed in Article XIV.

32.5 EU/EEA Negotiated Procedure: Still Limits for the Ambits and Scope of Negotiations

As demonstrated, the EU/EEA legal regime on cross-border public contracting is heavily based on the nonnegotiable tender bid scheme for contracting. The exceptions for alternative negotiating contracts have been kept within extremely narrow limits ever since the first directives on public sector issued in the 1970s. Whereas "open/restricted tender procedure" is not defined or expressly regulated in Dir 2004/18, the law reform has resulted in certain guidelines on how to conduct the negotiated procedure when the exceptions listed in Articles 30 and 31 apply. Article 30 No. 3 states that equal treatment of candidates should be observed and in particular:

> They shall not provide information in a discriminatory manner which may give some tenderers an advantage over others

cf. No. 4, which allows for negotiations in successive stages in order to reduce the number of tenders to be negotiated, by applying the award criteria in the contract notice or the specifications.[28]

The EU/EEA negotiated procedure deals only with adjustments in the candidates' offers. The contracting authority may not "negotiate" the initial contract documentation. So "negotiations" in this respect is very different from negotiating contracts in the private commercial sector.

The context of a negotiated procedure varies with the need and objectives of the parties concerned, except for one assumption: opening bids (in the U.S. FAR terminology proposals) may have been binding on the candidates, but the contracting entity must have displayed the intention to undertake discussions with the bidders on price, performance, and contents of contract obligations. Hence, unless the exceptions even from call for competition apply, such as where the negotiated procedure succeeds a tender procedure with no award,[29] there should normally be a regular call for competition. This should indicate that the offers to be submitted are not last shot tender bids of the classical kind, but opening offers (proposals) to be succeeded by further discussions with those of the candidates that are found to be commercially competitive.[30] For ascertaining the successful contract candidate, the public authority may seek to adapt the project, that is the contract documentation, to the information contained in the market offers. Negotiations may have cost-savings as their object, inducing candidates to cut prices or reduce elements of scope. In sophisticated projects, there might be a need to discuss major design to be prepared under progress of the work (options, formulas for VOs, or framework arrangements). In comparison to the tender procedure, the underlying principle of equal treatment of all competitive candidates becomes prerogative, although it must be accepted that the contracting entities gradually focus their attention on the fewer in the final lap, and may conclude the selective continued negotiations with only one of them, keeping the others at hand without having discarded them. For transparency purposes, prudent minutes recording the progress of negotiations may prove indispensable to substantiate that good practice has been applied.[31]

It seems to be a common feature that procurement regimes give very few answers on how to conduct the negotiated procedures, except for basic assumptions like overriding EU principles of nondiscrimination, equal treatment of candidates, foreseeability, transparency, and general code of conduct in line with good public governance (Trepte, 1993; Arrowsmith, 2005; Whiteford, 2003).[32] Inherent in this is the prudent management of apparent business trade secrets that are now in the possession of the public entity not to be revealed to competitors.[33]

32.6 Policy Considerations: Pro and Contra Pre-Contractual Ban-on-Negotiations

32.6.1 Argument for Pre-Contractual Ban-on-Negotiations

32.6.1.1 Securing EU/EEA Transparency for Cross-Border Award of Public Contracts

As already indicated, the EU Commission as initial legislator holds a restrictive position on two fundamental issues: (1) a main rule on mandatory tender procedure with narrowly drafted exceptions and (2) statement assumptions that tender procedure is incompatible with post-tender negotiations except for minor clarifications. The argument is apparent that a basically rule-oriented regime based on a maximum degree of transparency is necessary to conduct an efficient judicial review of all decision making on part of the contracting entity. Post-tender communication to bargain for a better price or at least adapt the intended purchase to what the market now can be seen to offer, might undeniably afford better value for money, but who will guarantee that potential negotiations in fact are not streamlined for a domestic contract candidate? The principle of equality in EU/EEA procurement law supports the call for transparency. Negotiations must necessarily imply parallel dialogues with several candidates, and even if negotiations should be recorded for subsequent supervision, the risk of discretionary preferences in the profiling and selection may not be ignored. ECJ has expressed strong criticism against discretionary overall assessments in the award of contract scenarios (C-513/99 *Concordia*, Judgment September 17, 2002).

32.6.1.2 Negotiations and Mal-Procurement

The competition for public contracts could operate as an arena for corruptive activities. One does not like to admit that this is a reality in the sophisticated Western world legal cultures for procurement practices. Such cases might rarely appear in disputes over tender bidding, but where there is profit to earn, there are rotten apples, and procurement—even on the EU public arena—cannot be taken as an evident exception.[34] In that context, there is another argument for pursuing a high degree of transparency, whereas cumulative competitive negotiations might undermine such objectives.

In the post-tender scenario, this becomes even more realistic: after opening of the bids, each candidate knows his position, and leniency in dealing with casual or even intended ambiguities inherent in the tender bid might under given circumstances foster attempts to exercise undue influence, which the actors may be able to hide from illuminated publicity. Accepting extras on scope would in situations like that be equal to amending the price.

32.6.1.3 Legal Certainty: Common Appreciation of the Rules of the Game and Considerations for Nonparticipating Potential Candidates

Mandatory tender procedures in public contracting combined with widespread market appreciation that a tender bid is the last and only shot for the contract could be said to support simplicity, foreseeability, and therefore a general good climate for competition. Some might add that contracts should be awarded on the merits of the offer, not on the talents for strategic bargaining. Small and medium sized entities (SME) may come out as losers in competition with major companies disposing vast expertise for combats involving legal, financial, and commercial resources.

Foreseeability has bearing on initial decisions on whether to compete for the contract or not. The up-front publication of the subject matter of the intended award, together with the contract terms and other information, might very well be decisive on the estimates to be made on the chances to be a competitive candidate. If the rules of the game are changed by negotiations, this may affect a candidate's assumptions in terms like "Had I known what I know now, I would certainly have made a shot to negotiate for this contract, either in price, in scope or in the initial concept indicated by the contracting entity in the tender documentation." In the EU/EEA regime, any interested party may file a bid protest, even candidates who were never invited to participate or candidates who could forward arguments as in the quotation above.[35]

32.6.2 Arguments against Pre-Contractual Ban-on-Negotiations

32.6.2.1 Public Entities Get Too Dependent on Pre-Tender Appreciation of Market: Alternative and Suggestive Bids

Nonamendable tender documentation in the post-tender stage means that the public entity, in given circumstances, may not adapt to what the market has to offer according to the submitted tender bids. This may not matter in simple supplies of commodities, but could have adverse consequences in sophisticated purchases where the entities' foresight at the end of the day proves insufficient to achieve the best buy.

The dependency addressed here is related to the role of the commissioned consultant assisting the contracting entity.[36] That consultant may or may not have the necessary insight and overview to prepare the optimal documentation. Such services often prove inadequate, forcing the public entity to settle for something short of best value. On the other hand, in a small market the only expert really able to evaluate the design of the purchase may have strong links to the potential market and therefore be disqualified on account of partiality (bias) (Treumer, 1999). This could be described as one *Scylla/Charybdis* scenario: the market expert may be commissioned to prepare the tender specifications but should not then participate in the competition. Or the expert may stand back to tender himself or assist others in the preparation for bids, but should not be on both sides of the fence, and therefore, valuable market expertise is not available for the contracting entity. This matter should have been dealt with in the EU/EA directives, but is only addressed in the Dir 97/52/EC under Preamble Recital No. 10,[37] assuming that contracting authorities may seek or accept advice for use in the preparation of specifications, "... provided that such advice does not have the effect of precluding competition."

What this means exactly is in total not clear, but European jurisdictions seem to read the preamble citations so that contracting entities should not hire anyone who might have an economical interest in the outcome of the tender procedure. The words "precluding competition" may not be read literally, however, the substantial risk for impeding competition should as a matter of policy suffice.[38]

32.6.2.2 Complex Purchases: IT Contracts, Major Composite Commitments, and Long-Term Framework Agreements

In certain contract schemes, the tender procedure might prove to be a literal straightjacket. As already mentioned, the various regimes requiring tender procedure allow exceptions when the tender procedure is manifestly inappropriate in view of the contract to be awarded. The UNCITRAL model law distinguishes between narrow exceptions available for goods and construction contracts (Article 18 (1) cf. Articles 19, 20, 21, and 22), whereas contracts for services in Article 43 allow for inter alia procedure with simultaneous negotiations. In the U.S. FAR regime, Article 6.401 states that both sealed bidding and competitive proposals (Parts 14 and 15) are acceptable procedures, and the provision leaves under (a) some discretion as to whether it is "necessary to conduct discussions with the responding offerors about their bids."[39] Restrictions on the modification and withdrawal of bids are stated in 14.303 and 14.304.

Under the previous EU/EEA regime, complex contracts were not explicitly dealt with.[40] The exceptions allowing for negotiated procedures were not meant to suit the complex nature of the contract, but rather to skip tender procedures in situations where this would seem unnecessarily bureaucratic, such as succeeding a tender procedure that has proved unsuccessful because none of the tender bids were acceptable.

The rules allowing for negotiations after termination of a previous futile tender procedure may tempt to abuse. One has experienced that municipalities have conducted quasi-tender procedures only to be cancelled and followed by negotiations with the ex-tender bidders, thus, circumventing the statutory rule on nonnegotiation. Under EU/EEA law, the protection for the bidders in a situation like this seems to be an ECJ-stated principle that a contracting authority must come up with valid documentation to substantiate a termination of a tender procedure without having awarded the contract. Termination of a procedure must be reasoned in writing subject to judicial review.

Pressed on these issues, EU Commission has conceded to the practical needs of the new single[41] 2004/18/EC public sector directive.[42] Article 29 opens up for a more flexible competitive dialogue, applicable in areas where the noncommunicative tender procedure is unsuitable for complex purchasing such as IT services or supplies of a similarly sophisticated technological nature. But the main rule on tender procedure is maintained, and many of the tender bidding characteristics are even preserved in the competitive dialogue, such as reverting to final post-dialogue tender bids before entity's final selection. The competitive dialogue is addressed below.

32.6.2.3 Cost Shortcomings of Rigid Nonnegotiated Contracts in the Construction/Works Contracts Area: Disputed and Undisputed Variation Orders May Undermine the Benefit of Lowest Price and Most Advantageous Offer

Construction contracts and similar contracts designed on the unit price formula present a special challenge in view of the post-tender ban-on-negotiations. In a turnkey contract, the contractor takes the risk of both design and execution, vicariously liable both for employees, consultant engineer (architect), and subcontractors. Unless the public authority has been specific on details of the work to be done, extras not anticipated in the design project meeting the tender documentation will be the risk of the contractor.

In other works contracts, the design and execution of the contract is divided between the contracting entity and the contractor. Preparing the tender bid means under these circumstances a meticulously detailed scrutiny of the contract documentation. The bottom total price sums up the added figures on each and every unit, work, or service listed in the documentation. Items, units, or services not listed for bidder's pricing will become extras, remunerable under standard schemes for the so-called variation or change orders. Whether the well-experienced contractor bidder has anticipated and therefore ascertained the necessity for such extras at this stage is generally irrelevant.

Design is a risk for the contracting entity. It is evident that a nonnegotiable scenario for such contracts may place a high risk on the contracting entity. Omissions and design errors become virtual boomerangs. A worst-case scenario may turn out to prove that very little has been gained in selecting the lowest bidder, as, in fact, the VOs may amount to figures well above the difference up to the second lowest nonsuccessful bidder.

Tactical bidding in a European context adds to this. Anticipating extras, which the contracting entity has failed to foresee and thus, opens up for speculation. Cutting the final price today may not turn out to be bad business. At the end of the day the inherent extras will pay the costs incurred in combating for the contract.

32.7 Competitive Dialogue

The competitive dialogue in Dir 2004/18/EC, Article 29 is the Commission's final response to the market discontent with the shortcomings of the 1990s directives in the area of nonnegotiable award scenarios. The setting is framed in the preamble recitals, especially Recital (31), which in turn should be seen in the context of the preparatory drafts in the late 1990s preceding the final text.

Contracting authorities that carry out particularly complex projects may, without this being due to any fault on their part, find it objectively impossible to define the means of satisfying their needs or of assessing what the market can offer in the way of technical solutions or financial/legal solutions. This situation may arise in particular with the implementation of important integrated transport infrastructure projects, large computer networks, or projects involving complex and structured financing the financial and legal makeup of which cannot be defined in advance. To the extent that use of open or restricted procedures does not allow the award of such contracts, a flexible procedure should be provided, which preserves not only competition between economic operators, but also the need for the contracting authorities to discuss all aspects of the contract with each candidate. However, this procedure must not be used in such a way as to restrict or distort competition, particularly by altering any fundamental aspects of the offers or by imposing substantial new requirements on the successful tenderer, or by involving any tenderer other than the one selected as the most economically advantageous.

The Article 29 procedure is not a substitution for the negotiated procedure still regulated as exceptions from tender procedure in the provisions succeeding Article 29, namely Articles 30 and 31.[43] The relationship between the two procedures is left somewhat in the open. Some have even advocated that the still vaguely regulated negotiated procedure leaves more and not less flexibility than the competitive dialogue does (Brown, 2004).

The text of the article is too long for complete citation in this article. To summarize, the main points are as follows:

1. Scope with reference to particularly complex contracts (Paragraph 1)[44]
2. Prior publication of the procedure to be applied (Paragraph 2)
3. Opening up of multilateral negotiations with candidates to identify and shortlist those within a competitive range of the needs of the contracting entity (Paragraph 3)
4. Two-stage procedure with distinction between stage one negotiations to achieve the preferred solution and stage two with more traditional tender procedure open for all participants of the dialogue
5. No limitations on the contents of such negotiations (Paragraph 3)
6. Observance of principle of equal treatment (Paragraph 3)
7. Confidential treatment of separate candidates' proposals for solutions (Paragraph 3)
8. Progressive focus on the solutions of actual relevance to the contracting entity to avoid cherry picking (Paragraph 4)[45]
9. Admissible additional specifications, clarifications, and fine-tuning of stage two tender bids (Paragraph 6)
10. Final award applying the criterion most economically advantageous tender, subject to additional clarification of aspect of the tender, confirmation of tender commitments short of modifying substantial aspects of the tender (Paragraph 7)

Whether the contracting authorities and the market will welcome the competitive dialogue remains to be seen.[46] The legal product is the output of a lengthy process that has been going on for the last decade, and some may have entertained expectations and later on, the market demands have not met entirely in the forthcoming regime. Regarding major infrastructure partnership, one should possibly not expect too much, but for genuinely complicated purchases, where the need for a thorough screening of market technological potentials to avoid hindsight surprises like the ones described above under Paragraph 1, the Article 29, could come in very handy.[47]

In the context of this article, the distinction between the dialogue preceding the tender bidding and the acceptance of continuing dialogue after that stage should be observed. Whereas, any and all aspects of the contract may be discussed before the bidding stage, the traditional ban-on-negotiations are assumed to apply after having submitted the tender bids. A novel provision in Article 29 (6) allows for further clarifications, specifications, and the so-called fine-tuning of the submitted bids, applicable at a stage before the identification of the most advantageous tender, after which additional discussions may take place. It is submitted that the protection against undue treatment of contract candidates in this post-tender stage is somewhat fragile, and possibly more likely than under the current directives. As correctly pointed out by Treumer (2004), " ... the possibilities for conducting illegal negotiations after the submission appears to be excellent and can be normally performed at a low risk."[48]

32.8 New Agenda for Public/Private Cooperation

The markets for public contracting are in the process of transition. Various public/private partnership (PPP) arrangements replace in many areas conventional purchasing of goods and services. Concepts and terms vary greatly in this area,[49] and so do the substance underlying contracted arrangements. There is already abundant literature on the issue, proving that new avenues for joining private and public resources in common interest are firmly placed on the agenda for contemporary public procurement law. In a Green Paper, European Union (EU) (2004) has now specifically addressed the PPP issues.

Not all innovative contract designing deserves legal approval. The circumvention of mandatory regimes invoking sophisticated legal architecture has been observed in many jurisdictions. The object of innovative more or less fragile legal constructions may have been to avoid red tape time-consuming tender procedures, and could also be applied to establish a negotiated contract with or without call for competition. The normal scenario for public contracting is a procedure initiated by the public entity, but one may also experience private initiatives, such as in major land schemes initiated by a private party or jointly in dialogue with landowners or agents entrusted to carry out private building schemes.

The ECJ *La Scala* preliminary judgment C-399/98 (Judgment July 12, 2001) is a state-of-the-art formula of considerable interest. The private party in this case operated with municipal permission to renovate and rebuild downtown areas in Milan, Italy, involving the erection of new theater facilities, commercial areas, housing, etc. Normally, an innovator would have to pay the municipality for infrastructural service. In this case, the private party was allowed to set off by way of undertaking such services by itself, thereby in a way performing partly its own project instead of having to pay for the public services. The court stated that the innovator's soliciting contractors for the infrastructural services would have to be considered a public works contract subject to the Dir 93/37/EC. On the other hand, the court assumes that the contractual relationship between the private party and the municipality was neither considered a works nor a service contract. In other words, that relationship fell outside the scope of the directives and could be negotiated without any call for competition. The most interesting part of the judgment is the Recital No. 52, dealing with the overriding principle of efficiency in EU procurement law:

> Since the existence of a "public works contract" is a condition for application of the Directive, Article 1(a) must be interpreted in such a way as to ensure that the Directive is given full effect. It is clear from the preamble to the Directive and from the second and tenth recitals, in particular, that the Directive aims to abolish restrictions on the freedom of establishment and on the freedom to provide services in respect of public works contracts in order to open up such contracts to genuine competition. As the tenth recital states, the development of such competition entails the publication at Community level of contract notices.

It might be expected that the quoted passage will afford considerable help in scenarios where the public party participates in joint venture arrangements that substantially have "as their object either the execution, or both the execution and design, of works ... " even though the formal arrangement may attempt to satisfy a more liberal scope definition, for instance, covert lease of land contracts for subsequent erection under a sale-and-lease-back arrangement that formally might be advocated to fall outside the scope of regulated procurement.[50]

It has been intended, and now expected, that the 2004 EU competitive dialogue might be suited to meet challenges within this area (Brown, 2004).[51] Before the 2004 law reform in the United Kingdom, it has been held that negotiations for the preferred private finance initiative (PFI) candidate may be held without conducting parallel negotiations with competitors (Brown, 2004).[52]

However, it might seem as if the two-stage procedure set forth in Dir 2004/18/EC Article 29 is not tailor-made to suit the establishment of multiyear atypical public/private arrangements that may be very different from the particularly complex technological commitments envisaged in the 2004 provision on competitive dialogue. It is not even a convincing argument that the preferred private partner should be expected to come up with a formal post-negotiation cost-effective tender bid to win the beauty contest for partnership. One could therefore ask the same questions as the one addressed to the current directives' regime: Are partnering contracts at all suited for the EU/EEA tender or quasi-tender procedure?

32.9 Two Infra-Contractual Implications

32.9.1 Lack of Negotiated Historical Context for the Contract: Subject to Sui Generic Rules on Interpretation?

Under common law outset, the parole evidence rule limits the incorporation of the pre-contractual context in the process of interpretation. Under continental and Nordic law, the rule seems to be different: The pre-contractual dialogue and mutual assumptions contribute substantially in the interpretative and gap-filling process when the true contents of the contract are to be ascertained.

The ban-on-negotiation mantra combined with the fact that the public contract has an up-front display of the buyer's demand would therefore create a somewhat sui generic climate for the contract interpretation in potential disputes.

The preference for individual terms above standard terms combined with the last shot rule[53] in contract interpretation would in this respect mean that the up-front tender documentation with its contract terms will prevail, but only as long as the tender bidder in his bid or the candidate forwarding an accepted proposal coincides. Open as well as intended or covert discrepancies between the accepted tender bid and the tender documentation would normally favor the bidder. Allegations on part of the contracting entity that the bidder has acted in bad faith would in a nonnegotiation situation like the ones envisaged in this article prove very hard to substantiate.

On the other hand, the contracting entity in the notoriously stronger position before the award procedure (having drafted the contract, defined the scope of contract, and issued the relevant specs) might come in a completely different position when doubts are tabled in disputes over ambiguities in the documentation. In some European contract law regimes, it is a well-established principle that the party having conducted the contents of the contract and having been in a bargaining position to dictate its terms and conditions, should bear the risk of any ambiguities inherent in the contract. The rule on ambiguity not only applies in consumer contracts, but is also applicable and relevant in commercial contracts. A very normal scenario would be the area of disputed VOs. The fact that the contract was not negotiated in a way that could have clarified otherwise inevitable pitfalls in terms of inconsistencies and ambiguities, may turn out to be a boomerang for the contracting entity. Money saved in going for the lowest bid may be consumed by extras well observed by the contractor when preparing the bid, but hitting totally unexpected the ignorant contracting entity trusting that the commissioned consultant (with his limited liability insurance) has done a good job.

32.9.2 Infra-Contractual Negotiations after Award: Extended Scope, Prolongation, and Options

Procurement law ends with the conclusion of the contract.[54] After this point, national contract law and principles for the interpretation of the contract take over. Negotiations that may have been ruled out in the pre-contractual stage, may be completely acceptable once the contract progresses. Simple contracts for immediate deliveries are short-termed and may not need any post-contractual attention. On the other hand, long-term contracts, framework agreements, and multi-annual contracts with options and terms on renewals and renegotiations, may have to be reviewed and monitored by the parties as time goes by. Traditional issues of unexpected contingencies could occur, in worst cases renegotiation in frustration scenarios:

1. EU law contains very few special rules applicable to commercial, let alone public contracts.[55] Private lex mercatoria schemes such as the Lando Commission Principles of European Contract Law (PECL) Parts I–III (2009–2003) have no official status. The commission's ambitious Green Paper, COM(2001)398 final, points in the direction of some kind of future approximation of European contract law, but no legislation is in place yet.
2. CISG 1980 on international sales of goods applies to public transborder purchases of goods, but within the area of works' and services' commitments no default legal regimes exist.
3. In short, public contract law in today's Europe is basically national law, partly codified (German Bürgerliches Gesetzbuch (BGB), French Code Civil, and others) partly case law (common law jurisdictions). Scandinavian commercial contract law outside the sales of goods area is generally case made law.
4. In the U.S. federal area, and different from EU/EEA, public contracts are dealt with specifically in USCA Title 41 "Public Contracts" (2000) with Chapter 9 on "Contracts Disputes."

All of this is not procurement law. But one issue is the long-term contracted exclusion of capable competitors in the market. The 2004 EU regime sets a time limit of four years for framework contracts to preserve market competition (Dir Article 32). This would in fact mean a ban-on-negotiations even for options and renegotiations to avoid the breaking up of good relationships established under a current contract regime.[56] Whether actual renegotiating or insertion of various options to be availed of fall under freedom of contract without initiating a new call for market competition is not explicitly dealt with in the EU legal regime. The magnitude of private investments in the project may be relevant, as well as the public entity's more or less legitimate needs for a stable and lasting uninterrupted relationship with a particular private partner.[57]

The regime of VOs in construction contracting may also prove counter to competition policies. Options for normal variations would not entitle competitors to invoke duty to open access for market competition. On the contrary, the contracting entity being discontent with its contractor may be precluded from calling for VOs in the form of reduction to import fresh competition. In the regime for construction contracts, it is generally accepted that the VO regime not only commits but also entitles the contractor to do all and any normal additional work on site (with subcontractors). On the other hand, if the contracting entity wishes to continue a once established contractual relationship for future engagements legally outside the commercial scope of an existing contract project, this might be a case for a successful competitor's challenge.

32.10 Concluding Remarks

Procurement law is a fascinating area of law, in crossroads between public administrative law, competition law, contract law, law of procedure, and tort law. The challenges connected with contracting procedures without or with very limited communication between the contracting entity and the contract candidates burning for a contract are no exceptions.

The article has discussed different approaches in legal regimes to balance the need for a pre-contractual dialogue in the act of selecting the winner of the award contest with general legal policies underlying restricted ban-on-negotiations rules of the game. Two main regimes seem to prevail. On the one hand, the strict EU/EEA call for tender procedures, ruling out such dialogues subject to limited statutory exceptions for a negotiated award as the European approach. On the other hand, there is the U.S. federal FAR that is a more lenient regime. It rules out negotiations in sealed bidding, but accepts options for negotiated contracts not applying sealed bidding.

Variations in WTO/GPA, NAFTA, UNCITRAL, and IBRD regimes have been addressed as examples of compromises between strict and liberal approaches to the procedures for public contracting.

New avenues for public/private interplay call for a new agenda and the EU 2004 scheme attempts to respond to the increased use of partnership arrangements in the shape of PPP, PFI, sale-and-lease-back of land, build-and-transfer (BOT), etc. The author believes that the new directive on public contracting facilitates a smooth approach to achieve optimal results in high-tech complicated contracts, but questions whether the competitive dialogue really can afford tailor-made solutions to cope with long-term PPP arrangements of the kind now spreading all over Europe.

Acknowledgment

The author is indebted to Dan Gordon, associate general counsel, U.S. GAO, for useful information offered on the U.S. government procurement regime relevant to the subject of this article.

Notes

1. Scandinavian and continental jurisdictions apply statutory or nonstatutory principles on culpa in contrahendo, requiring negotiating parties to honor good faith standards as well as duty to disclose certain information of relevance to the counter-negotiating party. The common law climate for such soft law principles seems to be tougher, corresponding to the estoppel doctrines on parole evidence, which, contrary to at least Scandinavian law, rules out the legal relevance of pre-contractual communication in the process of interpreting the contract.
2. On duty to renegotiate commercial contracts, cf. German major law reform 2002 on obligations Section 313 BGB and *Principles of European Contract Law 2000* (PECL) Article 5: 111.

3. EEA stands for the 1992 European Economical Area Agreement between the EU and the present remaining EFTA countries of Iceland, Liechtenstein, and Norway. Public and utilities procurement law is part of the EEA commitments, and consequently EEA law equals EU law on public and utilities' contracting. Switzerland is a remaining non-EU EFTA member country, but has not entered the EEA Agreement.

   Subsequent to this decade's extensions, the EU now totals 27 member states, including Baltic, Central, and Eastern European states.
4. Public contract in EU/EEA law extends beyond government procurement and includes regional and local municipal contracting, as well as contracting done by entities ruled by public law such as ex-public entities in a private market that operate under public ownership, funding or similar control.
5. U.S. FAR on government procurement rule the bid protest complaint regime under GAO implementing Title 4 Part 21 of the U.S. Code of Federal Regulations, a comprehensive set of bid protests regulations. On origins and present status of GAO, see Gordon (2004).

5a. (2006) 15 PPLR NA161-203 Articles: *Impact on Public Procurement Overview of the Current Work of Key International Institutions in the Field of Public Procurement*; authors: C. Nicolas, UNCITRAL; R. Anderson, WTO; J.-J. Verdaux, NA179, World Bank; J. Bertók, OECD.

6. Uruguay round commitments scheduled in the 1994 WTO Annex 4 (b) as well as in the GATS Annex 1 (b) Article XIII. EU accession for Member States took place with the issuing of Dir 97/52/EC and Dir 98/4/EC amendment directives, pursuant to Council decision December 22, 1994 (94/8000/EC). EEA (EFTA) states such as Norway adopted the WTO GPA regime separately. The Norwegian law reform took place in 1996. A number of non-EU states have adopted the GPA regime, such as the United States, Canada, Switzerland, Israel, and Japan. On interpretation, the stricter rule of EU or GPA regime will apply.
7. Public includes any entity governed by public law, including government entities, local municipalities, and even private entities under public governance—cf. Dir 04/18 Article 1 No. 9.
8. Dir 04/18 Article 28 No. 2 orders public contracts to be awarded "by applying the open or restricted procedure" as defined in Article 11 (a) and (b), where the distinction between "open" and "restricted" is drawn as to whether any interested economic operator may submit a tender or only those operators invited by the contracting authority. The directive has no further details on exactly how the tender procedure is to be conducted.
9. Lengthy revision had as its starting point a 1996 Green Paper (COM (96) 583), "Public Procurement in The European Union: Exploring the Way Forward," in 1998 succeeded by a White Paper (COM (1998) 143), "Public Procurement in the European Union." The EU law reform and the new concept competitive dialogue are dealt with comprehensively by Brown (2004) and Treumer (2004).
10. On corrective measures and on liability for mal-procedure, leaving details and procedures to national autonomy.
11. Law reform has also resulted in an updated directive for utilities' sector, where postal services substitute previous telecom services (Dir 2004/17/EC). Both directives are published in *Official Journal* (O.J.), No. L 134/1 and 114 (April 30, 2004).
12. On NAFTA in relation to the U.S. federal procurement regime, see Eyester (2002).
13. On comparison between U.S. and EU public procurement, see Verdeaux (2003).
14. Critical comments on the U.S. sealed bidding regime by Haberbush (2000).
15. Entities may in theory choose between lowest price and "economically most advantageous offer," but the informed contracting officer will opt for the latter since this affords more latitude in the selection than lowest price. Dir 2004/18/EC Article 53 "Contract award criteria" is exhaustive, but the provision accepts subcriteria under "most economically advantageous" and comprises even "aesthetic" and "environmental" characteristics, thus adopting the ruling of ECJ in the "Concordia" Judgment C-513/99 on municipal purchase of metropolitan buses in the Finnish capital Helsinki. The 2004 law reform has led to increased transparency on pre-published relative weighting to be applied in the evaluation of the submitted tender bids (Article 53 No. 2), to be completed by a specific justification of the award communication to all contract candidates (Article 41 No. 2).
16. It is somewhat unclear whether the 2004 regulated negotiated procedure, not falling under the competitive dialogue formula, has been changed in relation to intermediate negotiations in the negotiated

procedure. ECJ cases before the 2004 regime seem to have accepted some latitude in this respect C-337/98 *Rennes* (Judgment October 5, 2000).

16a. On the Dir 07/66 amendments to Dir 89/665, see further Williams (2006). On the tumbling down of contract sacrosanctity when signing a contract after procurement violations, see even the C-503/04 ECJ 2007 ruling on member states' duty (in casu Germany) to adopt necessary measures to comply with a previous ECJ judgment on procurement violation; that is, take necessary steps to terminate the contract under Treaty Article 228 (Lisboa Article 260). The Norwegian Supreme Court, however, in a 2005 judgment (Norsk Retstidende 2005, p. 1481), has ruled that even blatant unlawful negotiations inducing the contractor's to waive certain reservations on price indexing did not mean that the waiver was ineffective. In earlier cases, ECJ has occasionally ordered contracts to be suspended, cf. C-87/94 injunctive Court Order 1994-04-22 *"The Wallonian Buses"* (based on national Belgian law) and C-272/91 *"Lottomatica"* based on Treaty Article 243 (Lisboa Article 279). On ineffective contracts after EU procurement violations, see Treumer (2007) on latest development.

17. Replacing former Dir 93/36/EC Article 15 Dir 93/37/EC, and Dir 92/50/EC Services Article 23.
18. Note that the private party in the *La Scala* case C-399/98 apparently was selected without call for competition or mandatory tender bidding, while the infrastructure works solicited by that private party to fulfill the obligation toward the municipality (on behalf of the municipality?) was considered a works or service contract to be awarded according to the relevant directives.
19. Except for ex-communist jurisdictions now within EU, all European jurisdictions did operate more or less extensive and detailed legal regimes on government procurement, such as construction works, before the EU regime. Many also extended to local government municipal contracting from private sector. Thus, one must expect a considerable amount of continuous interplay between national law and case precedents and supranational EU secondary legislation.
20. In fact, the rigidity applies both ways: It is fundamental that the contracting entities' rules of the game cannot be modified or adapted in view of the information supplied in the bulk of tender bids. This aspect of nonnegotiations was clearly stated in one of the early ECJ cases in public procurement, the *Storebaelt* case C-243/389 (Judgment June 22, 1993). The only EFTA court judgment on pure tender bid amendments to the published documentation is the Case E-5/98 *Fagthun*, which, however, was not exactly to the point of the subject for this article. The Icelandic contracting entity inserted a buy-1 Icelandic provision in the tender documentation effective after the tender procedure and had thereby violated EEA Agreement Article 11 that bans quantitative trade restrictions.
21. In trivial day-to-day procurement dispute recordings, such as in the handling of procurement disputes, violation of the up-front rule is one of the most common failures to conduct a proper procedure: the directives require unbroken consistent shaping between the published contract for award, the tender documentation effective at the time of the submittal of tender bids, and the internal proposal for selection of the successful tenderer, ending up with the reasoned decision for the award of the contract.
22. In C-87/94 *The Wallonian Buses* (Court Order April 22, 1994), the contracting entity violated the rules for tender procedure by derogating unilaterally from its own specifications in allowing for a tenderer's amendment of tender bid without equal opportunities to the competitors.
23. How far the directives' clarification rule might go in allowing for adaptations is a debated issue. The stricter interpretation was advocated by Krüger (1998), later questioned by Arrowsmith (1998), arguing for more flexibility. But see Brown (2004, pp. 161–162) for comments on the relationship between current and 2004 directives. Previous statements in Arrowsmith (1996, pp. 247 and 520–521) now Arrowsmith (2005) pp. 540–552 are in the author's opinion far too liberal, especially as regard to negotiations with successful tender bidder to improve the bid favoring the contracting entity.
24. According to the ECJ C-421-01 *Traunfellner* (Judgment October 16, 2003), the contract documentation (and not only the national regulations) should state minimum standards to be met when allowing for alternative suggestive solutions, now revised provision in Dir 04/18 Article 24 No. 3.
25. An example from the author's experience in Norway: The tenderer summed up accumulate figures down each page, but at one point forgot to transfer the bottom figures to the top of the next page. The contract total offer was correctly amended to reflect the true unit price totals.
26. Certain items of the tender bid details may fall under trade secret protection such as most often the specified unit pricing in works contracts. The totals of the tender bids, however, must be open for access

for the participating tenderers, most often also for the public (such as media looking into the procedure for major public projects). See further McClure (2002).

27. A 2003-10-30 Norwegian Supreme Court decision supports the arguments in the text: The bidder who got the contract claimed for upgrading of a unit price quotation allegedly based on mistake. The Supreme Court rejected to do so and based the reasoning on the special scenario present in a noncommunication tender bid scenario. Interestingly, it seems that the very first filed 1924 U.S. GAO bid protest dealt with a similar issue (Gordon, 2004).
28. Equal treatment assumes that any invitation to improve the initial offer in price or workload should be made equally available to the competitors. Procedural decision-making in the progress of a negotiated procedure should be recorded in written records to enable efficient judicial review by national review bodies (transparency principle in Dir 04/18 Article 2). On the unauthorized use of the negotiated procedure challenged by the Commission before the ECJ, see for a Belgian case C-323/96 (Judgment September 17, 1998), a French case C-337/98 (Judgment 2000-10-05), a German case C-20/01 C-28/01 (Judgment April 10, 2003).
29. That applies generally to the No. 3 of the provisions of the preceding note (without prior publication of a tender notice).
30. For this reason, the contracting authority should make it clear that the initiation of negotiations should not be considered as a refusal of the offers, for instance, where negotiations lead to nothing and the entity may wish to settle for one of the first submitted offers. The rules of the game might then be different than in the more traditional exchange of offers and acceptances, where a declared intention to negotiate the offer might release the offeror, cf. CISG 1980 Part II Article 19.
31. Illustration from a Norwegian Complaint Board case where the conclusion of the written negotiation recordings of candidate A concluded with the consented option to come back with a revised offer while that item was left out in the minutes for the equally competitive candidate B. This was considered to be an infringement.
32. On recommendation of oral presentations in negotiated procurement, see Hannaway (2000). On commission's dealing with U.K. negotiated PFI cases, see furthermore Brown (2004) with comments also on a Greek case dealt with by the commission (*Thessaloniki* case 2003). Also see Brown and Golfinopolous (2003). As pointed out by Brown (2004, pp. 175–176), the uncertainty on understanding the current directives on negotiated procedures have been transported on to the 2004 regime, where the negotiated procedure is maintained as an alternative to the competitive dialogue.
33. Total figures in offers or tender bids would normally not be considered trade secrets, whereas unit prices in complex offers or bids for construction works should be viewed differently. On the issue, see McClure (2002).
34. On corruption in public procurement, see articles in Arrowsmith and Hartley (2002, Vol. I, Part III). N. Ehlermann-Cach (2006), K. Krüger (2007).
35. This is particularly true when the rules are violated by doing unauthorized direct purchase with no procedure at all, such as just buying or negotiating with the supplier with whom the contracting entity has already enjoyed a long-term pleasant business relationship, and therefore is reluctant to obey the required mandatory call for competition.
36. In the EU/EEA, the commissioning of consultants is in itself a service to be tendered for.
37. Preambles are standard introductory policy considerations in all EU directives, most often offering relevant indications on how the formal provisions are interpreted, but more seldom, as in this case, in a format that resembles a legally binding provision.
38. Norwegian Procurement Complaints Board (effective from 2003) stated in a local KOFA case 2003/36 that it was a violation of the national version of the EEA regulations to allow an agent for a particular manufacturer to assist in preparing the specifications for particular lock devices in the construction project. The question whether the actual contract candidate (the major Norwegian manufacturer for such products) should have been rejected from tender procedure participation was not the issue, but the board was doubtful as to whether there was legal basis for rejection.
39. On U.S. FAR negotiated procurement, see Whiteford (2003).
40. See as an example Dir 93/37/EC Article 7 No. 2 (a–c) and No. 3 (a–e), and similarly Dir 93/36/EC Article 6 No. 2 and No. 3, and Dir 92/50/EC Article 11 No. 2 and No. 3. Provisions allowing for negotiated procedures make a distinction between situations where such negotiations may be initiated with or without prior publication of contract notice.

41. Single directive comprises both contracts for supplies, works, and services, and is therefore a major practical simplification compared to the previous three separate directives with provisions partly identical, partly with minor technical nuances.
42. Advocated already in the 1998 commission's White Paper (1998), but in a premature form, see criticism voiced by Arrowsmith (2000), Boyle (2000), Brown (2004), and Treumer (2004).
43. Certain aspects on how to interpret the 2004 version of negotiated procedures not falling under Article 29 are addressed by Brown (2004) on comparison between the traditional and the maintained negotiated competitive procedures with the new competitive dialogue. On competitive dialogue challenges, see now special section on "The EC's New Competitive Dialogue Procedure" (2006) 15 PPLR Number 6 pp. 307–373 (articles by S. Treumer, C. Kennedy-Loest, S. Verschnur, A. Brown, McLean Sieverding, Catriona Munro, and J. Schwartz).
44. Some explanation on the notion of particularly complex is attempted in Article 1 (11) (c): "reference to the contracting authority's lack of ability to define the technical means ... or satisfying their needs or objectives." Whether this formulation is really of any help is open. Preamble (31) cited in the text gives additional guidance.
45. On this very practical restriction on the Article 29 scope of negotiations, see Treumer (2004, pp. 181–182), pointing to the question of whether a tender documentation may contain provisions that extend the authority of the contracting entity in this respect, answered in the affirmative, but in my opinion not entirely convincingly. Leniency in this may undermine the compromise character of the Article 29 provisions. Cherry picking would favor the contracting entity and a provision as suggested by Treumer (2004), could therefore be the rule and thus run counter to directives' policies.
46. Time limit for national implementation is by the end of January 2006 (Article 80). There are no express transitional provisions in the directive, but the immediate coming into effect of the directive would authorize member states to implement and apply the competitive dialogue long before the statutory time limit. It is expected that member states might launch law reforms even before 2006. Short of such national law amendments, the old regime will apply formally.
47. Criticism voiced by Brown (2004) is in the author's opinion relevant in the context of infrastructure partnering contract, but the positive impact on truly high-tech public purchases are somewhat underestimated.
48. Treumer (2004) argues over apparent lack of transparency on specifications in the stage after having conducted the competitive dialogue with individual candidates, to which this writer totally agrees.
49. Some currently applied: PFI is private finance initiative, PPP is public/private partnership, and BOT is build-and-transfer.
50. Such as the Danish National Complaint Board 2002 decisions on the *Farum Park* and *Farum Arena* cases dated January 29, 2002 and July 18, 2002, respectively, striking down a sale-and-lease-back arrangement for the construction of public works found to be clearly within the scope of works contract regulations' regime.
51. On the UNCITRAL model law adaptation to English PFI, see Arrowsmith (2003).
52. Overriding call for competition even in negotiated procedures is in other EU/EEA jurisdictions read to mean that generally more than one candidate should be allowed to participate for the final selection, and that a certain number of candidates should have equal possibilities to amend or modify prices, commitments, time schedules for performance, etc.
53. Battle of forms is equally familiar to U.S. continental and Nordic jurisdictions, although the approach may vary from one legal system to another. The point here is that the ranging of elements from the contracting entity with the tender or proposal elements from the contract candidate is a perfect example on just this set of problems.
54. Subsequent to the "Alcatel" standstill principle stated in C-81/98 (Judgment October 28, 1999), the ruling has established a distinction between the award decision and the subsequent actual entering into a binding contract with the successful candidate, closing the procurement remedies set forth in Dir 89/665. The "remedy" directive (Dir 89/665/EC) allows currently (Article 2 No. 6) member states to restrict corrective or injunctive legal actions to the stage prior to the actual conclusion of the contract. Consequently, the ban-on-negotiations will apply even after the decision to award has been taken, even though the contracting entity under national contract law may be restricted in its authority to terminate the infected contract. However, the recent Dir 07/66 amending remedies' Dir 89/665 will change this, as explained above. The inserted Article 2d will require that contracts awarded in disregard of the standstill

period are to be made "ineffective," although leaving it to national legislation to provide for either retroactive cancellation or limitation to obligations which still have to be performed. In the latter case, and generally where national statutory law allows for overriding reasons, the reviewing body shall impose a penalty, which (Article 2e (2)) could be either the imposition of fines or the shortening of the duration of the contract. Violation of ban-on-negotiations in tender procedures are not expressly dealt with in the new directive, but the contractual effect may follow if an improperly negotiated contract is signed before expiry of the future statutory standstill period.

55. In fact, only a handful of directives could be said to deal with commercial contracts: the Dir 86/653 on commercial agents, the Dir 2000/31 on electronic commerce, and the Dir 2000/36 on combating late payment in commercial transactions. Apart from this are regulations on jurisdiction and choice of proper law in contract disputes: EC Regulation 44/2001/EC and the EU convention on the law applicable to contractual obligations Rome June 19, 1980 (consumer and commercial). All of this might apply to public contracting in the EU or EEA.
56. Related question is whether amicable experiences gained with a particular supplier are legally relevant when another contract of a similar nature is published for award. It could be argued that both good will and bad will experiences acquired in a past contract relationship has a cost-effective dimension. On the other hand, the EU directives seem to focus on the cost figures apparent from the tender bids as such and apart from history, and a bidder not known to the public entity should be allowed to compete without having to prove that his good will potentials equal the ones of the former actually associated supplier. The issue seems to be somewhat in the open under present EU procurement law.
57. Norwegian 2003 Complaint Board's *Ementor* case is illustrative: A regional health institution in mid-Norway was considered to have violated the procurement mandatory call for competition through the conclusion of an eight to ten year contract for continuous IT supplies, comprising further options and clauses on renegotiations toward the end of the contract time axis. The board's criticism also involved the vague and discretionary price estimate on supplies and services so many years from the date of signing the contract.

List of Abbreviations

BOT	Build, operate, and transfer
C-	Case identification by number in the European Court of Justice
CISG	UN (UNCITRAL) Convention on Contracts for the International Sale of Goods (April 11 1980)
Dir	Directive addressed from EU to member states to legislate
Dir 2004/18	Directive 2004/18/EC of the European Parliament and of the Council of March 31 2004 on the coordination of procedures for the award of public works contracts, public supply contracts, and public service contracts
EC	European Communities
ECJ	European Communities' Court of Justice (Luxembourg)
EEA	European Economic Area Agreement (1992)
EFTA	European Free Trade Association
EU	European Union
FAR	Federal Acquisition Regulations (United States)
GAO	Government Accountability Office (United States)
GATS	General Agreement on Trade in Services (WTO)
GPA	Government Procurement Agreement (WTO)
IBRD	The International Bank for Reconstruction and Development
O.J.	EU official journal (legal acts, etc.)
PFI	Private finance initiative
PPP	Public–private partnership

PECL	Principles of European Contract Law I-III (Lando Commission 2000–2003)
PPLR	Public Procurement Law Review (ed. S. Arrowsmith, University of Nottingham)
UNCITRAL	United Nations Commission for International Trade
VO	Variation order (construction contracts)
WTO	World Trade Organization

References

Arrowsmith, S. 1996. *The Law of Public and Utilities Procurement*. London, United Kingdom: Sweet & Maxwell.

Arrowsmith, S. 1998. The problem of discussions with tenderers under the E.C.-procurement directives: The current law and the case for reform. *Public Procurement Law Review*, 7(3): 65–82.

Arrowsmith, S. 2000. The European Commission's proposals for new directives on public and utilities procurement. *Public Procurement Law Review*, 9(6): 125–137.

Arrowsmith, S. and Hartley, K. (Eds.). 2002. *Public Procurement*, Vol. I. Cheltenham, United Kingdom: Edward Elgar Publishing.

Arrowsmith, S. 2003. *New Development in UNCITRAL: Future Work on Public Procurement and New Model Provisions on Privately Financed Infrastructure Projects*, 12: PPLR NA131.

Arrowsmith, S. 2005. *The Law of Public and Utilities Procurement*, second edition, London, United Kingdom: Sweet & Maxwell.

Boyle, R. 2000. Critique of the commission's proposal for a new directive on the co-ordination of procedures for public contracts COM 175 final, as updated by the discussions in the working group. *Public Procurement Law Review*, 10(3): 65–74.

Brown, A. 2004. The impact of the new procurement directive on large public infrastructure projects: Competitive dialogue or better the devil you know? *Public Procurement Law Review*, 13(4): 160–177.

Brown, A. and Golfinopolous, C. 2003. The permissibility of post-selection modifications in a tendering procedure: Decision by the European Commission that the London underground public–private partnership does not involve state aid. *Public Procurement Law Review*, 12(3): 47–55.

Ehlermann-Cach, N. 2006. *Fighting Corruption in International Business Transaction*, 15: PPLR Number 6 NA195.

European Union (EU). April 30, 2004. *Public–Private Partnerships* (COM 327 final). Available at http://europa.eu.int.

Eyester, L. 2002. NAFTA and the barriers to federal procurement opportunities in the United States. *Public Contract Law Journal*, 31(4): 696–729.

Gordon, D. 2004. United States: The earliest bid protests filed with the US General Accounting Office. *Public Procurement Law Review*, 13(5): 147–164.

Haberbush, K.L. 2000. The government's exposure to bid rigging schemes: A critical look at the sealed bidding regime. *Public Contract Law Journal*, 30(1): 98–122.

Hannaway, S.M.P. 2000. Oral presentations in negotiated procurements: Panecea or Pandora's box. *Public Contract Law Journal*, 29(3): 455–509.

Hjelmborg, S.E. et al. 2006. *Public Procurement Law—the EU Directive on Public Contracts*, Copenhagen, Denmark: DJØF Publishing.

Krüger, K. 1998. The scope for post-tender negotiations in international tendering procedures. In: S. Arrowsmith and A. Davies (Eds.), *Public Procurement: Global Revolution*. London, United Kingdom: Kluwer Law International, pp. 181–198.

Krüger, K. 2007. *Paradise Lost. Is the Law Adequate in Combating Corruption in Public Procurement? A Norwegian Approach*, in T. Frantzen et al., Rett og toleranse. Festskrift til Helge Johan Thue, Oslo, Norway, Gyldendal akademisk.

McClure, G.H. 2002. The treatment of contract prices under the Trade Secrets Act and Freedom of Information Act Exemption 4: Are contract prices really trade secrets? *Public Contract Law Journal*, 31(2): 186–235.

Trepte, P.-A. 1993. *Public Procurement in the EC*. Oxfordshire, United Kingdom: CCH Limited.

Treumer, S. 1999. Technical dialogue prior to submission of tenders and the principle of equal treatment of tenderers. *Public Procurement Law Review*, 8(3): 147–160.

Treumer, S. 2004. Competitive dialogue. *Public Procurement Law Review*, 13(4): 178–186.

Treumer, S. 2007. *Towards an Obligation to Terminate Contracts Concluded in Breach of the EC Public Procurement Rules. The End of the Status of Concluded Contracts as Sacred Cows.*

Verdeaux, J.-J. 2003. Public procurement in the European Union and in the United States: A comparative study. *Public Contract Law Journal*, 32(4): 713–738.

Whiteford, D.A. 2003. Negotiated procurements: Squandering the benefit of the bargain. *Public Contract Law Journal*, 32(3): 509–562.

Williams, R. 2006. *The Commission's Proposal for a New Remedies Directive*, 15: PPLR NA141.

Chapter 33

Bid Protests: Theory and Practice[1]

Robert E. Lloyd

CONTENTS

33.1 Introduction

The dictionary defines the word "challenge" as "a call to engage in a contest or fight; a demand for an explanation; requirement for full use of one's abilities or resources" (Webster's II, 1994, 246). Nowhere in public procurement are the varieties of challenges more evident than when disappointed contractors lodge complaints against contracting officials. Dealing with such challenges is a major concern of public procurement officials in the United States, Canada, and elsewhere. In fact, this is now a global phenomenon, as a key requirement of the World Trade Organization's public procurement regime is a challenge procedure for companies seeking government contracts (Arrowsmith, 2003).

In the United States, the term "bid protest" is used to refer to challenges by the private sector against solicitations and contract awards by public sector buyers. In the United States, the modern bid protest system began in 1926 when the General Accounting Office (now known as the Government Accountability Office or GAO) heard its first protest by a disappointed company (GAO, 2006a). A previous study (Drabkin et al., 2004) described the mechanics of the protest mechanism, which may be invoked at all three domains of the federal government: the contracting office level (executive branch contracting officers), an arm of the legislative branch (GAO), or the judicial branch (federal courts). This chapter will focus primarily on U.S. federal bid protests, where GAO is the dominant forum.

The Federal Acquisition Regulation (FAR, Subpart 33.1) defines protest in simple terms, as a written objection by an interested party (normally, someone submitting an offer) regarding a solicitation, such as a request for proposals (or its cancellation), or award of a contract (or its termination). Before offers are due, companies may object to the terms of a solicitation, such as alleging that it restricts competition. After award is made, a company which submitted an offer may object to the selection of another firm. Usually, the protester will allege that some aspect of the U.S. government's voluminous contracting regulations in the FAR was not followed. Generally, there is a ten-day rule for bringing protests, and protests filed later are typically not required to be considered. No bond or monetary deposit is required to file a protest with GAO, and there is no penalty when a protester loses a protest (unless it violates the terms of a protective order concerning proprietary or source selection documents; FAR 33.104(a)(5)(iv)). A winning protester may be entitled to reimbursement of its costs in filing and pursuing a protest (FAR 33.104(h)). In response to the protest, the contracting officer must compile a detailed file and a formal written response, normally in conjunction with review and support from agency legal counsel. When GAO renders its decision, the head of the agency is advised of the results, and winning protesters are effectively able to compel agencies to take corrective action.

The GAO system is designed for ease of access, as the cost of a postage stamp is all that is required to lodge a protest. When a solicitation is protested, a contract award cannot be made, unless there is documentation approval of urgent and compelling circumstances (FAR 33.104(b)). Once a protest after contract award is received, the contracting officer normally must suspend performance of the contract (FAR 33.104(c)). Hence the colloquial term "39 cent injunction" is used to describe bid protests. GAO has 100 days to render a decision, or 65 days if the "express option" is used. Most observers share the view that this challenge system is designed in favor of equity rather than efficiency.

This sort of challenge mechanism is not unique to the United States. For example, Canada has established the Canadian International Trade Tribunal (CCITT), a quasi-judicial institution that conducts inquiries into complaints by disappointed potential contractors concerning procurement by federal agencies covered by the World Trade Organization's Agreement on Government Procurement (known as GPA) and two other trade agreements (CCITT, 2004). The CCITT follows rules similar to the GAO, with one major exception: CCITT can assess the government's costs of defending a protest against a losing protester. For example, in File No. PR-2003-030, Lemmex Group, Inc., CCITT determined that the challenge was not valid and awarded the government reasonable costs incurred in preparing and filing a response to the protest, to be paid by the protester.

Further, there is now a global underpinning of public procurement protests in WTO's GPA. Article XX of this agreement requires all member nations to "provide non-discriminatory, timely, transparent and effective procedures enabling suppliers to challenge alleged breaches of the agreement arising in the context of procurements in which they have, or have had, an interest" (World Trade

Organization, 1994). The WTO rules resemble the GAO approach by emphasizing written challenges, within established timelines, to be heard by a court or other impartial body able to offer relief in the form of correction of improper actions or compensation for loss, damages, and proposal or protest costs.

33.2 Protest Landscape

Public procurement is one of the few fields of government endeavor to have a highly developed system of nonjudicial challenges to actions by public officials. In addition to the normal litigation process that can be used in virtually any aspect of public administration, public procurement has more than one forum for hearing bid protests. The number of protests received by GAO, however, far surpasses that of any other forum (Drabkin et al., 2004), and for this reason will be central to the analysis here. GAO protest statistics over the past decade are shown in Table 33.1, along with the level of procurement volume in terms of dollars as well as number of procurement actions.

These statistics reveal the relative stability of protest volume. Despite the near doubling of funds obligated (awarded on contract) in U.S. public procurement and the wide variation in the quantity of procurement actions (awards of contracts, simplified acquisitions, etc.), the number of protests has remained relatively unchanged. The number of protests won by contractors is depicted in Table 33.2.

Table 33.1 Volume of U.S. Federal Procurement and Protests Filed

U.S. Government Fiscal Year	*Total U.S. Federal Government Procurement Dollars Obligated (in billions)*	*Total U.S. Federal Government Procurement Number of Actions (in millions)*	*Number of Protests Filed*
2006	—	—	1327
2005	378.4	5.9	1356
2004	341.4	10.4	1485
2003	305.5	11.5	1352
2002	250.8	8.7	1204
2001	234.9	11.4	1084
2000	218.8	9.8	1152
1999	198.7	10.5	1290

Sources: From GAO (2006b); Drabkin, D., Lloyd, R., and Thai, K., Bid Protests in the U.S. Federal Government: An Empirical Analysis. *IPSERA Conference Proceedings*, 2004; Federal Procurement Data System, Washington: U.S. General Services Administration. https://www.fpds.gov (accessed January 18, 2007), 2007. With permission.

Note: —Indicates statistics not available at time of publication.

Table 33.2 Volume and Win Rate for GAO Protests

U.S. Govervnment Fiscal Year	*Number of Protests Filed at GAO*	*Number of Protests Won (Sustained) by Protester*	*Win Rate (Percentage of Total Protests Won by Protester)*
2006	1327	72	5.4
2005	1356	71	5.2
2004	1485	75	5.1
2003	1352	50	3.7
2002	1204	41	3.6
2001	1084	66	6.1
2000	1152	63	5.5
1999	1290	74	5.7
1998	1427	63	4.4
1997	1852	61	3.3

Sources: From Drabkin, D., Lloyd, R., and Thai, K., Bid Protests in the U.S. Federal Government: An Empirical Analysis. *IPSERA Conference Proceedings*, 2004; GAO (2006b); Wifcon (Where in Federal Contracting?), *GAO Decisions: Description by Issue*. http://www.wifcon.com/pdbyissue.htm (accessed January 11, 2007), 2007. With permission.

The number of protests won by contractors is nearly as stable as the volume of protests filed. Although regression analysis might reveal further trends, it is clear that U.S. federal procurement officials as a group can expect to receive an average of 1353 protests to GAO each year, and, if past history holds true, they stand to lose an average of 64 GAO protests each year. Each loss typically involves a mandate from GAO for the buying agency to issue a revision of the solicitation or to give an opportunity to the winning protester to submit a revised proposal.

At the state government level in the United States, at least two states have published bid protest decisions available on the Internet. Alaska (2007) issued 20 decisions from 1997–2003, and South Carolina (2007) issued 11 decisions in 2006. Goldstein and Prieto (2000) discuss a wide variety of bid protest decisions from various fora in the state of Florida. They point out that the problem of suspending an ongoing procurement process has generated considerable controversy, and one Florida court clearly rejected the cause of efficiency as a basis for rejecting a “stay” of contract performance, siding with equity concerns above all. In any governmental agency, concern about public trust weighs heavily on the minds of both litigants and practitioners.

Canadian federal government bid protests are much fewer than in the United States. For example, in fiscal year 2003–2004, Table 33.3 shows the volume of activity at the CCITT.

Government contract dollars in Canada tend to be approximately one-tenth of that in the United States. Despite this ratio, one can attribute the paucity of protest to the fact that the advent of the challenge mechanism is relatively recent, and losing protesters may be required to pay the government’s costs.

Table 33.3 Number of Canadian Bid Protests

Number of Protests Filed	*Number of Protest Inquiries Conducted*[a]	*Number of Protests Decided for Protester*
83	34	15

Source: Canadian International Trade Tribunal (CCITT), *Determinations* [decisions on bid protests]. http://www.citt-tcce.gc.ca/procure/determin/prin2g_e.asp (accessed February 2, 2007), 2007. With permission.

[a] CCITT often denies requests for a formal inquiry process if the protest does not state a valid basis for challenge. (See, e.g., CCITT File Number PR-2003-060, Inland Technologies Canada, November 14, 2003.)

33.3 Theory: The Pros and Cons of Bid Protests

In a recent article, Gordon (2006) presents a useful framework for bid protest theory in terms of competing goals. He contrasts the urge to investigate complaints with the desire to move contracts forward. This goal conflict is a feature very much in the public administration tradition of exploring the trade-off between equity and efficiency and has recently been reemphasized as a major issue in public procurement (Brown et al., 2006). Gordon examines the rationale for bid protests from the viewpoint of the private sector as allowing a forum for private sector firms to petition the government for grievances and promoting integrity and open or transparent government. Another aspect of the "pro" bid protest standpoint is a stated concern for accountability in government, as well as an enhanced reputation for fairness that may be a particular concern in developing countries. This rationale echoes Goodsell's (2006, 633) emphasis on integrity and efficiency as key to a foundation of public trust in government in general. The opposing viewpoint, in Gordon's model, necessarily focuses on "cost to spend" and related efficiency concerns, including problems created by the disruptive nature of challenges to public procurement decisions. He notes the perils of frivolous protests as well.

Two leading authors in U.S. public procurement have staked out opposite positions on the merits of a bid protest system. Kelman (1990) was one of the early commentators to decry the ills of protests. In recent years, he has kept up the fight against the deleterious effects of bid protests for the public procurement profession, referring to the "scourge" of a "bid protest culture of winning business by litigation rather than customer satisfaction" (Kelman, 2004, 2005). While acknowledging that the rules allowing bid protests were designed to prevent abuse, Kelman (2001) points out that potential protests inhibit innovation in public procurement and create a tendency toward rule-bound behavior, due to the risk of receiving a challenge from losing firms. In testimony to Congress, Kelman (2003) referred to the abundance of protests that remains a critical feature of public procurement. He regards protests as leading to adversarial relations between the public and private sectors, as opposed to the sort of relationship based on trust that dominates commercial contracting. The "unintended negative consequences" cited by Kelman serve as the leading critique of big protests in general.

Schooner (2001) has responded to Kelman's position by positing the potential salutary effects that bid protests can have. Among these are deterrence against wrongdoing in public procurement and beneficial policing of the contract formation process. Schooner argues that the protest process helps preserve public trust in government and provides a measure of accountability that offers checks and balances against unfettered emphasis on efficiency in the administration of public procurement.

In previous works, this author has pointed out some additional concerns not highlighted by Schooner or Kelman (Lloyd, 1988, 1990). Specifically, the notion of allowing the private sector to control public sector procurement activities should be subject to considerable scrutiny from both positive and normative perspectives. The problem of economic rent-seeking and associated costs created by the protest system has been detailed in prior analyses, but this dilemma has largely been ignored in the United States, while Canada has adopted a more symmetrical system of dealing with protest costs, as noted above. Dysfunctional effects such as these bring into question the use of bid protest volume as a measure of the health of a public procurement system. To begin to deal with the problem of tactical or frivolous protests, some U.S. state and local governments are now moving closer to the symmetrical nature of the Canadian system by imposing filing fees on protesters (Miami-Dade County, 2005).

Firms can easily adopt protest filing as a tactical business tool, as Gordon (2006) acknowledges. In a similarly unproductive vein, public procurement officials can justifiably "hide behind the regulations" and devote their time to documenting files rather than proactively seeking creative contracting solutions. In directing their efforts to defensive measures intended to avoid protests, contracting officials may easily justify their actions or inactions as beneficial, safe in the assurance that any contract can easily be protested. U.S. federal officials work in an environment where there is virtually no penalty for contractors who make false allegations, even if they create additional costs. Such costs may encompass extensions of current contracts at higher rates than competitive successor contracts, litigation expenses incurred by federal officials, etc. These are some of the hidden costs of the bid protest system that need to be considered in the design of any public procurement challenge mechanism.

33.4 Practical Implications

Although the protest system is not the sole province of public procurement,[2] it tends to take on a more crucial role in influencing both contractors and government employees. Accordingly, the specific causes of protests are worthy of analysis. Practitioners ought to know why contractors challenge the procurement decisions of the public sector, recognize which bases most often lead to adverse decisions, and learn from the decisions rendered against fellow practitioners. Table 33.4 depicts the results of all published GAO bid protest decisions (44) for a recent six-month period (July 13, 2006 to January 17, 2007).

In a typical U.S. federal government procurement, the contracting officer requests two documents from each competitor: a price quotation and a technical proposal. As can be seen above, the relatively objective nature of pricing does not tend to generate very many protests. In contrast, technical features, particularly for service contracts, tend to be more subjective. The figures for technical evaluation listed above also include evaluation of past performance, which is another subjective area. It is important to note that the evaluation of technical proposals is nearly always conducted in a program office, not in the contracting office, by officials who manage projects (frequently engineers or similar nonprocurement professionals).

Protests concerning technical evaluations far surpass any other single basis for complaint. Furthermore, the percentage of protests citing improper technical evaluation is on the rise. The recent statistics in Table 33.4 are consistent with a study performed of GAO decisions from 2002 to 2004, which found that alleged improper technical evaluations accounted for 35 percent of protests filed

Table 33.4 Basis for Protests Filed and Won

Protest Basis[a]	*Frequency*	*Number Sustained*
Improper evaluation of technical proposal	24	3
Pricing errors	6	1
Lack of or unfair competition	6	1
Improper negotiations	5	
Small business program issues	4	1
Conflict of interest	2	
Improper price/technical trade-off analysis	2	
Unequal treatment in evaluation	2	
Contract administration	2	
Scope of multiple award contract	1	
Poor planning[b]	1	1
Improper specifications[b]	1	1
Cancellation of solicitation	1	
Legal authority	1	
Improper use of simplified procedures	1	
Bid responsiveness	1	1

Source: From GAO (2006).

[a] Of the 44 protests analyzed, one was dismissed as untimely and not included above. A given protest may cite more than one basis for complaint. The 43 protests decided as either sustained (won by the protesting contractor) or denied/dismissed (won by the government) cited 60 total bases for protest.

[b] One protest cited both reasons, and was sustained.

at GAO (Drabkin et al., 2004). In the sample above, nearly 55 percent of the protests were based on alleged improprieties in the evaluation of technical proposals. In other words, over a three-year period, the importance of technical evaluations in U.S. public procurement has substantially increased.

The situation in Canada is even more pointed. A random sample of 24 rulings of the CCITT from 2003 reveals the results shown in Table 33.5.

Canada thus exceeds the U.S. level of protests based on technical evaluation grounds (60 percent in Canada compared to 55 percent in the United States). As can be readily discerned, the primary cause of protests in both the United States and Canada is not defects in what most observers would consider typical activities of procurement professionals (soliciting and negotiating contracts). Instead, the quality of the evaluations of technical proposals performed by individuals working outside the contracting office tends to be the biggest source of complaint from the private sector.

Table 33.5 Basis for Protests Filed and Won

Protest Basis	*Frequency*	*Number Sustained*[a]
Improper evaluation of technical proposal	10	6
Biased/restrictive/unfair specifications	3	
Lack of competition	2	2
Undisclosed evaluation criteria	2	1
Pricing errors	2	1
Conflict of interest	1	1
Cancellation of solicitation	1	1
Improper negotiations	1	1
Insufficient time to submit bid	1	1
Improper bid rejection	1	

Source: CCITT, *Determinations* [decisions on bid protests]. http://www.citt-tcce.gc.ca/procure/determin/prin2g_e.asp (accessed February 2, 2007), 2007.

[a] CCITT uses the term "valid" for sustained, and "not valid" for denied.

If, as the cases analyzed above demonstrate, a prerequisite for sound, defensible public procurement decisions is a proper evaluation of technical proposals, then one would reasonably expect the technical evaluation process to be a prominent part of the training curriculum for U.S. government contracting. In fact, nothing could be further from the truth. Apart from the occasional internal agency guidelines on the subject, mentioned in passing in handbooks for project officers or contracting officer's representatives (U.S. Department of Health and Human Services, 2003; and other agency examples found in the appendices to Nash and Cibinic, 1993), the only published work dedicated entirely to this subject (Cole, 1995) is no longer in print.

The Federal Acquisition Institute (FAI), charged by law with developing training standards, competencies, and curricula for training the U.S. federal "acquisition workforce," including technical specialists who assist the contracting staff by evaluating technical proposals, has, in its published list of competencies for technical experts known as contracting officer's technical representatives, made little mention of skill in performing technical evaluations (FAI, 2007; SRA International, 2003). The subject is only briefly alluded to in a discussion of required technical competencies for contract specialists, in the skill "Apply non-price factors in evaluating quotations, proposals, and past performance" (FAI, 2003b, 15). One wonders how federal agencies can be expected to master public procurement if the management of the primary cause of bid protests is downplayed or simply not taught to practitioners.

If, however, there becomes a widespread recognition that improved technical evaluations are not likely to occur, due to resource/staffing constraints or similar reasons, then perhaps one solution might be to implement different procurement methods that do not rely on the evaluation of technical proposals for determining which firm should receive a contract. For example, if competitive negotiation is not a workable approach for certain contracts, due to incessant bid protests, then one might wish to consider removing the source of the problem by switching to a different contracting method. Sealed bidding is one approach that comes to mind, but this method has been often criticized for its rigidity. An alternative approach might be to adopt the Vickrey auction technique, in which sealed bidding is used but award is made to the second lowest bidder, thus reducing the powerful incentive on the part of competitors to offer unrealistically low prices (Lloyd, 1997). It is this sort of debate that should come to the forefront if public procurement officials intend to deal directly with the cause and effects of bid protests.

33.5 Protest Resolution: A Dying Art

Given the importance of bid protests and their potential impact on specific contracts as well as the acquisition workforce, one might expect considerable emphasis on protest handling and resolution skills to be part of the training curriculum for U.S. government contracting officials. In fact, the opposite is true. In the most recent compendium of competencies required in public procurement, the Federal Acquisition Institute in the U.S. (FAI, 2006) has downplayed protests. FAI's career model for public procurement catalogs nine core capabilities and fourteen technical competencies for contract specialists. These technical competencies fail to mention bid protests by name at all, instead using the more vague skill "Act to resolve acquisition complaints and concerns" (FAI, 2003b, 15). Even in FAI's more detailed underlying research reports on what competencies are most important for practitioners to have, protests are only mentioned in passing and could easily be ignored by those seeking to learn what drives public procurement at the federal level in the United States (FAI, 2003b: 22, 36; 2003c: 8, 28).

The treatment of bid protests is relegated to a single unit of instruction (Unit 48) out of a total of 71 included in FAI's *Contract Specialist Training Blueprints* (FAI, 2003a), and the guidance included is of a general nature. Just as the leading source of guidance on conducting technical evaluations in public procurement was a book published in the private sector, so is the best source of guidance a private sector resource. Wifcon (Where in Federal Contracting?), the public procurement Web site run by Robert Antonio, is a comprehensive Web site at http://www.wifcon.com featuring an indexed database of GAO decisions, sorted by contracting issue (ranging from advance planning to unbalanced pricing), providing summaries and links to those decisions (Wifcon, 2007). The Wifcon approach to learning about and resolving bid protests is more useful as an educational tool than FAI's minimal coverage of the topic.

There has been much discussion lately about the role and function of procurement officials in the public sector. One commonly advocated approach is to consider the public procurement practitioner as a "strategic business advisor" (Starinsky, 2007) who is knowledgeable about the marketplace, concentrates on exploring business arrangements, and applies his or her experience and business focus to achieving customer goals. This model employee is expected to possess nine core competencies defined by FAI, but as long as protest resolution is not listed as one of them, one can expect that protests will continue to pose a serious dilemma for public procurement staffs.

33.6 Note on Disputes during Contract Performance

This paper has discussed challenges to the solicitation and award of public procurement contracts. Disputes arising after contract performance has begun can likewise provide fertile ground for practical research. As is common in this field, pre-award activities tend to take precedence over post-award

Table 33.6 Post-Award Appeals

U.S. Government Fiscal Year	*Appeals Filed at ASBCA*	*Sustained Appeals (Percent)*[a]
2005	476	18
2004	461	23
2003	429	22
2002	435	23

Source: Schaengold, M. and Brams, R. Choice of Forum for Contract Claims: Court vs. Board/ Edition II. *Briefing Papers*. St. Paul: Thomson West (May issue), 2006.

[a] Number of decisions in favor of the contractor out of all decisions rendered; excludes withdrawn, untimely, or settled appeals.

contract administration. An equivalent form of challenge also occurs during the performance of contracts, commonly referred to as contract disputes. The public procurement profession would benefit from research and analysis similar to that described above for these disputes as well. Contrasting the causes and effects of disputes versus protests could prove illuminating, especially for practitioners.

The volume of contract disputes rivals that of bid protests in the U.S. federal government. For the Armed Services Board of Contract Appeals (ASBCA) alone (which governs defense contracts), Table 33.6 shows the number of appeals filed (Schaengold and Brams, 2006).

The causes of contract appeals could be subjected to the same sort of analysis shown above for bid protests. This analysis might guide contracting officers in promoting better and more harmonious performance by contractors.

A recent development in U.S. federal contract disputes is the creation in 2007 of the Civilian Board of Contract Appeals or CBCA (71 Federal Register 65825, November 9, 2006), which consolidates all nondefense contract appeals boards into one. The U.S. federal government now has only two administrative boards for hearing post-award disputes, the CBCA and the ASBCA. The inauguration of the new board provides a rare opportunity to perform the sort of analysis of appeals decisions that can, from the onset of this new year, provide useful lessons to practitioners.

33.7 Conclusion

Nearly any action taken by a public procurement practitioner is subject to immediate contest by disappointed parties. A recent conference referred to public procurement as being on a tightrope, but it is equally well described as being under a microscope. An example of the close scrutiny mandated for nearly all U.S. federal agency procurement transactions is the recent rule on use of brand-name specifications. If a program office requests any supplies or equipment on a brand-name basis, a written justification is required. In previous years, the justification would simply be a memorandum for the contracting officer to review and place in the contract file. A new policy issued by the Office of Federal Procurement Policy (2006) requires that this document be published on a public Web site (www.fedbizopps.gov) or the General Services Administration's "E-Buy" Web site for orders against GSA schedules. This effort at transparency also comes at a cost, however. One can expect that the more the internal decisions are subjected to public inspection, the greater the likelihood exists that a protest will be filed, for there will simply be more activities open to public scrutiny.

From a human resource management perspective, increased transparency creates yet another problem. Few officials would volunteer for this sort of public exposure to their office's internal operations. As a result of this and other aspects of contemporary public procurement, it has become increasingly difficult to recruit technical representatives to assist contracting officers in meeting their missions (SRA International, 2003). Not surprisingly, some large programs have selected contracting officials as their program managers (e.g., the U.S. VISIT program of the Department of Homeland Security).

At the outset, we observed that the word "challenge" has multiple meanings. The definition that focuses on maximizing one's abilities and resources is perhaps the most crucial for this chapter. The nature of public procurement as a field of government endeavor that requires a high level of openness to the public makes the existence of a protest system a natural development if public confidence is vital to success. At the same time, implementing these ideals comes at a cost. One can only hope that as transparency and trust in the system's integrity increase, the costs of these gains will not surpass their benefits.

Notes

1. Views expressed in this chapter are solely the author's and do not necessarily represent those of the U.S. Department of State or the U.S. government.
2. In the human resources area, for example, the Merit Systems Protection Board in the United States hears appeals of government employees who have complaints against improper personnel practices.

References

Alaska, Office of Tax Appeals and Administrative Hearings. 2007. *Procurement Hearing Decisions*. http://www.state.ak.us/local/akpages/ADMIN/ota/amdec.htm (accessed January 22, 2007).

Arrowsmith, S. 2003. *Government Procurement in the WTO*. The Hague: Kluwer.

Brown, T., Potoski, M., and Van Slyke, D. 2006. Managing Public Service Contracts: Aligning Values, Institutions, and Markets. *Public Administration Review*, 66(3): 323–331.

Canadian International Trade Tribunal. 2004. *Procurement Review Process: A Descriptive Guide*. http://www.citt-tcce.gc.ca/publicat/guide2004_e.asp (accessed June 9, 2004).

Canadian International Trade Tribunal (CCITT). 2007. *Determinations* [decisions on bid protests]. http://www.citt-tcce.gc.ca/procure/determin/prin2g_e.asp (accessed February 2, 2007).

Cole, P.S. 1995. *Technical Evaluations in Government Contracting: A Complete Guide*. Vienna, VA: Holbrook & Kellogg, Inc.

Drabkin, D., Lloyd, R., and Thai, K. 2004. Bid Protests in the U.S. Federal Government: An Empirical Analysis. 13th *IPSERA Conference Proceedings*, Cantana, Italy.

Federal Acquisition Institute (FAI). 2003a. *Contract Specialist Training Blueprints*. http://www.fai.gov/policies/contract.asp (accessed January 29, 2007).

Federal Acquisition Institute (FAI). 2003b. *Report on General Competencies for the Federal Acquisition Workforce*. http://www.fai.gov/policies/sturep.asp (accessed January 28, 2007).

Federal Acquisition Institute (FAI). 2003c. *Validation of Technical Competencies for the Federal Acquisition Workforce*. http://www.fai.gov/policies/sturep.asp (accessed January 28, 2007).

Federal Acquisition Institute (FAI). 2006. Competencies (Contracting and COTRs). http://www.fai.gov/worforce/compet.asp (accessed January 10, 2007).

Federal Acquisition Regulation (FAR). 2007. Washington: U.S. General Services Administration. http://acquisition.gov/far (accessed January 29, 2007).

Federal Procurement Data System. 2007. Washington: U.S. General Services Administration. https://www.fpds.gov (accessed January 18, 2007).

GAO. 2006a. *Bid Protests at GAO: A Descriptive Guide*. GAO-06–797SP.

GAO (U.S. Government Accountability Office). 2006b. *Bid Protest Statistics for Fiscal Years 2002–2006* (Report to Congress). B-158766, November 15, 2006.

Goldstein, J. and Prieto, V. 2000. A survey of Florida's recent district court of appeal and administrative decisions involving bid protests: Challenging the government's conduct regarding a public procurement. *Nova Law Review*, 25: 43–89 (accessible at http://www.wifcon.com).

Goodsell, C. 2006. A new vision for public administration. *Public Administration Review*, 66(4): 623–635.

Gordon, D.I. 2006. Constructing a bid protest process: Choices every procurement challenge system must make. *Public Contract Law Journal*, 35: 1–18.

Kelman, S. 1990. *Procurement and Public Management: Fear of Discretion and the Quality of Government Performance*. Washington, DC: AEI Press.

Kelman, S. 2001. *Remaking Federal Procurement*. John F. Kennedy School of Government: Visions of Governance in the 21st Century, Working Paper No. 3.

Kelman, S. 2003. Congressional Testimony on Services Acquisition Reform Act. *KSG on the Hill*, Kennedy School News & Communications. http://www.ksg.harvard.edu/news/onthehill/2003/kelman_043003.htm (accessed January 11, 2007).

Kelman, S. 2004. Perfecting performance. *Federal Computer Week*, May 31.

Kelman, S. 2005. Are we better off now? *Federal Computer Week*, June 6.

Lloyd, R.E. 1988. Alternative dispute resolution in federal contracts: The irony of process. *Policy Studies Journal*, 16(3): 543–561.

Lloyd, R.E. 1990. Efficiency, justice, and rent seeking in federal contract dispute resolution. In *Conflict Resolution and Public Policy*, ed. M. Mills, New York: Greenwood Press, 101–114.

Lloyd, R.E. 1997. Acquisition Reform using the Vickrey Auction Technique. *Proceedings of the 1997 Acquisition Research Symposium*. Ft. Belvoir: Defense Systems Management College and National Contract Management Association.

Miami-Dade County, Florida. 2005. *Administrative Order 3–21: Bid Protest Procedures*. http://www.miamidade.gov/dpm/policy-and-legislation.asp (accessed February 2, 2007).

Nash, R. and Cibinic, J. 1993. *Competitive Negotiation: The Source Selection Process*. Washington: George Washington University.

Office of Federal Procurement Policy. 2006. *Use of Brand Name Specifications*. Washington: Office of Management and Budget (memorandum of April 17 to Chief Acquisition Officers and Senior Procurement Executives).

Schaengold, M. and Brams, R. 2006. Choice of Forum for Contract Claims: Court vs. Board/Edition II. *Briefing Papers*. St. Paul: Thomson West (May issue).

Schooner, S.L. 2001. Fear of oversight: The fundamental failure of business-like government. *American University Law Review*, 50(3): 628–721.

South Carolina, Materials Management Office. 2007. *CPO Decisions for Goods and Services*. http://www.state.sc.us/mmo/legal/dec-spo.htm (accessed January 22, 2007).

SRA International. 2003. *Report on Competencies for the Contracting Officer's Technical Representative (COTR) Job Function*. Arlington, VA (submitted to FAI).

Starinsky, M. 2007. Rising to the Challenge with Strategic Business Advisors. *Acquisition Directions Advisory* (January) Virginia: Acquisition Solutions, Inc.

U.S. Department of Health and Human Services. 2003. *DHHS Project Officers' Contracting Handbook*. http://www.knownet.hhs.gov/acquisition/POHandbookSTD.doc (accessed January 30, 2007).

Webster's II. 1994. *New Riverside University Dictionary*. Boston: Houghton Mifflin.

Wifcon (Where in Federal Contracting?). 2007. *GAO Decisions: Description by Issue*. http://www.wifcon.com/pdbyissue.htm (accessed January 11, 2007).

World Trade Organization. 1994. *Agreement on Government Procurement*. http://www.wto.org/english/docs_e/legal_e/gpr-94_02_e.htm#articleXX (accessed January 30, 2007).

Chapter 34

Decision Technological Foundations of Public Procurement Processes

Csaba Csáki and Péter Gelléri

CONTENTS

34.1 Introduction

The field of public procurement has been evolving into a highly organized profession. This emergence is well indicated by the various international conferences held during the last three to four years (Thai and Piga, 2007) as well as by the international studies, surveys, and workshops spanning continents organized during the same period (Knight et al., 2003; Harland et al., 2005). Furthermore, the first issue of the *Journal of Public Procurement* was published in 2001.

The publication of this handbook fits well into this evolution. It covers all aspects of public procurement (PP) and intends to address an almost exhaustive list of topics, questions, and issues. Like most handbooks, it has a dual purpose:

- One is to offer elementary knowledge and avenues of basic learning and joining up for those less experienced in this field or even new to the field.
- The other is to offer capacity building for more experienced professionals who are looking for further improvement or new ideas.

Applying decision technologies (DTs) in the field of the PP profession is, in our opinion, a good way to contribute to the latter. In this chapter, we attempt to provide a fresh look at several of the topics covered in this handbook based on the principles and findings of decision theory and decision technological research concerning public procurement decision making (Csáki, 2006; Gelléri and Csáki, 2006). The goal of our approach is to provide examples of best-practice solutions for a few steps of the public procurement process by identifying key areas for improvement, defining the main expectations against these areas, and then offering potential improvement directions based on decision technologies already proved to be useful for capacity building.

34.1.1 Decision Technologies as Part of Public Procurement Capacity Building

Procurement is the process of acquiring goods, works, and services. Public procurement as a function of government includes decisions about the services that will be delivered to local authorities and the communities they serve (Hughes, 2005). It is not only utilized to secure goods and services required by public sector organizations for their missions and to support services provided to taxpayers but it is also used to implement national policies and to achieve social and other objectives (Thai, 2005). Therefore, public procurement is usually looked at as a set of tasks and decisions related to the processes of purchasing, logistics, project management, and their authorization. Related issues are mostly discussed in the context of public policy, political science, or economics.

Capacity building in public procurement relates to helping governments to plan, manage, and monitor their procurement processes effectively. It also aims at improving the accountability, integrity, and transparency of these processes thereby reducing the scope for corruption. This capacity building evidently requires the integrated use of domain, legal, and economic knowledge. We wish to emphasize the importance of a fourth type of knowledge—the expertise of decision support or decision technologies. This discipline is able to not only provide new insights on its own, but also, by its nature, to help the integration of all professions involved. Decision technologies could offer untapped resources by expanding and connecting the practice of public procurement to related areas—such as project management, logistics, knowledge management, group work,

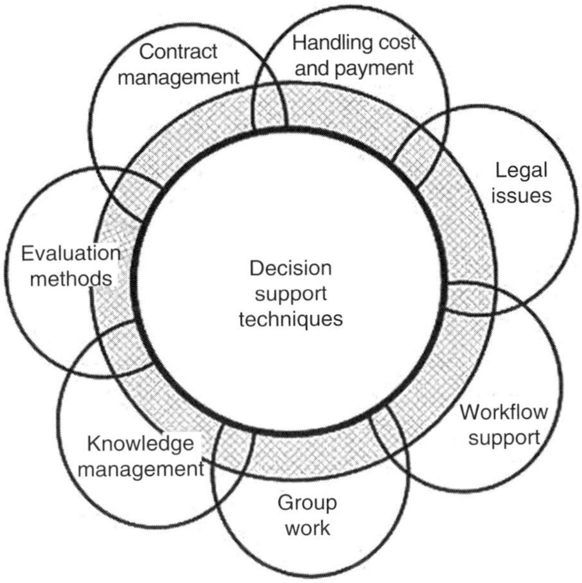

Figure 34.1 Decision support for an expanded public procurement practice.

contract management, evaluation methods, or workflow management—and by offering tools to handle problems associated with these and other areas (Figure 34.1).

Certain aspects of procurement decisions may be supported through decision technological solutions and decision support tools or various forms of decision aids. The available spectrum of decision support solutions is able to formalize the high-paced workflow and strengthen the performance of PP professionals—bringing benefits for both managers and PP experts. The key to potential advantages is that decision theory investigates each decision process as a whole—as a related set of decision points and tasks involving several players in various roles in a complex surrounding.

34.1.2 Expected Benefits of Applying Decision Technological Solutions in Public Procurement

Through enabling and supporting group work, decision technologies help to keep together and integrate expert knowledge of all areas involved (legal, financial, domain) and allow domain experts to express their (technical) interests better. As a result, running the PP process would be smoother with fewer issues to face. DT solutions lead to a more efficient workflow, save time, and ensure less "suffering." Various requirements, even very special ones may be handled in an integrated manner. There would be fewer legal challenges stemming from controversy or abuse of power. Application of decision technologies would reduce the risk of corruption charges regarding the selection and award-giving procedure and its result by ensuring compliance. PP professionals would receive positive feedback from upper management for a job well-done by reaching a good contract with the selected supplier. There could be other recognition from partners/experts involved, including increased respect of the profession due to a more professional image.

34.2 Field of Decision Technologies

34.2.1 Nature and View of Decision Technologies

The focus of DTs is to provide—find or develop—tools and methodologies to solve certain types of decision problems. However, it is essential to realize that there is no problem without a problem "owner," that is, without someone affected by the situation who either experiences it as a "problem" and wishes something were done about it or is told to do something about it. The owner of a problem may not necessarily be in a position of precisely defining the problem or identifying a solution though. Any solution is as good as much it is able to consider and handle the views, motivations, and interests of actual problem owners—and of other potentially related stakeholders. Therefore, in most cases, it is no use talking about a "general" solution. Instead, one may only talk about a solution tailored both to the specifics of the problem and to the goals of problem owners. Tools and methods used in solving decision problems should, therefore, not only fit the logic and structure of problems but also be able to capture and represent the preferences of decision makers. Decision technological solutions aim at the meeting point of problems, problem owners, and decision methodologies and tools that support problem owners to solve their problems (Figure 34.2).

DTs create decision aids and methodologies that could be tailored to and used in resolving specific decision situations. Problem types are typically independent of the domain or context within which the concrete problem occurs. One may look at decision technologies as a meta-methodology that offers generic solution approaches to typical problem types and these approaches can be transformed into actual processes and supporting tools in any given case. The final outcome is a closed process of a decision workflow typically supported by software tools and often facilitated by decision support experts.

34.2.2 Decision Technologies and Problem Solving

Decision theory differentiates three main types of problems as decision tasks: structured, semistructured, and unstructured (Simon, 1960). Structured problems usually have a well-defined set of input and a well-defined set of output, either theory or the decision maker may create a well-defined decision-making procedure and the task is routine and repetitive with standard solutions. This category is

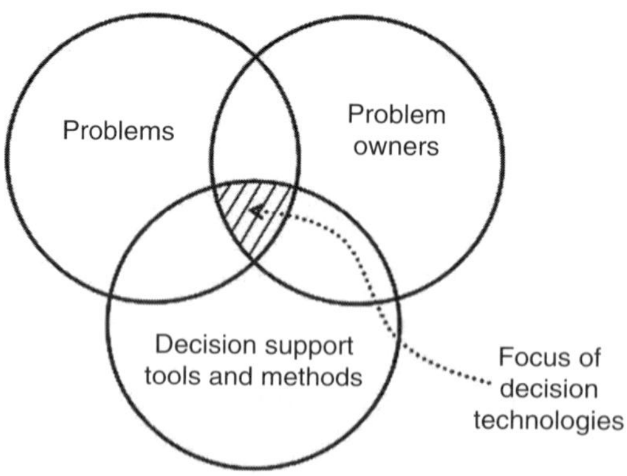

Figure 34.2 Focus of decision technologies.

also called programmable. Financial management or budget analysis are typical structured problems. Regarding the PP field, resource allocation and inventory forecasting are considered well structured and usually addressed by such research fields as operation research or decision analysis (Howard and Matheson, 1989). Similar types of issues are related to running auctions and are usually dealt with by economical mathematics (for PP applications see Soudry, 2004, for example).

In case of ill-structured (or unstructured) problems, all phases of the decision-making process are unstructured. They are also classified as nonprogrammable decisions. Typical unstructured problems are R & D planning, new technology development, and negotiating. Typical ill-structured PP tasks would be partnering, outsourcing, and single service company (SSC) decisions usually addressed by principles of "strategic decision-making" and organizational negotiation techniques.

Semistructured problems do have some structured aspect but some of the inputs or outputs or procedures are not well defined. They can be found somewhere between the two extreme cases of completely structured and unstructured decisions and they are, obviously, in a continuum between the programmable and nonprogrammable decisions. Problems that are typically considered semi-structured may include credit evaluation, new product planning, inventory planning, or inventory control. Planning, running, auditing, and monitoring individual PP procedures and managing the related contracts would also be typical semistructured decision-making problems.

One key observation of the decision support profession is that it is the easiest—has the most potential—to provide good support tools for those middle-management decision tasks, which have the same main characteristics irrespective of their actual content. These tasks, as shown by the framework in the seminal paper by Gorry and Scott Morton (1989), are typically recurring, semistructured, and have similar logic and structure, but their actual content changes from time to time. The goal is to develop support solutions that create a closed process and improve the outcome of decision making by standardizing the process and the workflow. In contrast, structured problems are typically handled by operational research, while ill-structured problems are addressed by the strategic stream of decision theory.

Knowledge and decision making are closely related concepts both in everyday life and in the area of science. To reach efficient decisions, it is necessary to ensure the availability of appropriate knowledge to the right people. Information and knowledge are the bread-and-butter of decision making. To meet the challenges of knowledge management, it is essential to learn about the actual organization and understand its decision processes in terms of who is involved and what types of expertise are required in solving issues. Decision aids consider the decision know-how of domain experts and their knowledge may be captured in software tools, which are also used in the integration of knowledge from various expert areas.

This immediately leads us to the group aspect of decision making. Decision theory investigates the players, roles, and situation of people involved as well as their cultures, behaviors, motivations, and preferences. It also investigates how people with their differing backgrounds, wide range of expertise, and various interests meet and collide in a problem-solving decision situation. Identifying the fact that there are indeed differing interests and they do collide is the cornerstone of providing effective support for groups to resolve their issues. There are techniques that are able to handle these differences and make it possible to resolve the conflict arising and find compromises through fostering cooperation.

One should not forget to analyze the environmental framework and how environmental factors influence decision making—especially in an organizational context. Investigating the application of tools and the way new solutions are implemented in an organization should be an integral part of understanding any organizational decision culture. In addition, most organizations have their own policies, workflows, and habits that determine how people identify problems, how they raise and tackle issues, and how members of the organization reach resolution through institutionalized decision making.

34.2.3 Role of the Decision Technology Expert

Solving organizational problems often involves or is led by a consultant. His or her task may span from working as an outside expert on one project to helping a full, unique implementation of a new practice, process, set of roles, or tools.

While exploring the task at hand (or a decision problem in general), decision consultants build up an understanding by identifying key decision points, roles, and players. They might collect and structure available domain knowledge from experts using knowledge capture techniques and may provide supporting software or develop dedicated support solutions. They will also help with the implementation of the selected decision aid and also ensure its integration into the organization by passing the related knowledge and application on to people to apply in their everyday practice. During this process, they need to handle environmental conditions, constraints, and various circumstances including the task of dealing with urgency or considering sensitivity. A decision support expert would help when interests collide (Gelléri and Csáki, 2006) by handling language, professional and cultural issues, or differences in logic and philosophies. By understanding the background of the various professions, the expert is able to help with the integration and application of knowledge represented by various organizational groups. A trained decision expert may offer help in case of outside pressure, challenge, or even attack on the decisions made.

Operational Definitions of a Few Key Decision Technological Categories

Decision technologies: On the basis of various decision support solutions, decision technologies create methodologies and closed processes that encapsulate a decision workflow supported by software tools and often facilitated by decision support experts.

Decision theory: On the basis of the results of mathematics, economics, and psychology, decision theory investigates how individuals, groups, and organizations make decisions and offers ways both normative and prescriptive ways to improve.

Decision support: A set of tools, decision aids, methodologies, and software systems used in solving various decision problems. It may also be provided through consulting.

Decision support system (DSS): Software tool designed to model decision problems. One system usually addresses one specific type of problem logic (and uses fitting mathematical constructs). Systems able to handle multiple users and model the opinion of several experts are called group decision support systems (GDSS).

Decision conferencing: A group decision-making technique, which consists of a series of intensive working meetings, where groups of people concerned about complex issues of their organization get together to resolve these issues with the guidance of one or more trained people.

Decision support expert/facilitator: Trained in decision theory and group dynamics, a decision expert maps the decision culture of organizations and offers decision technological solutions to unique or recurring decision problems.

Semistructured problem: Structured problems are routine and repetitive decision tasks with standard solutions, which usually have a well-defined set of input and a well-defined set of output, and may have a well-defined decision-making procedure, while in cases of ill-structured (or unstructured) problems, all phases of the decision-making process are unstructured. A problem is called semistructured if it is in between the two ends of the spectrum.

Problem owner(s): People, who are affected by a situation, experience it as a "problem" and wish something were done about it.

Criteria tree with weights (also called attribute tree): The set of attributes related to decision problem organized into a tree structure, where there are weights associated with each node expressing the importance of each criteria as viewed by the decision maker(s).

Utility functions: Probably the most important decision theoretical technique used for expressing individual preferences through associating a value with each state of an attribute.

Scoring mechanisms: The method in which scores from utility functions are integrated over the attribute tree taking weights into consideration. Two basic types are the additive and the multiplicative scoring.

34.3 Public Procurement Activities Supported by Decision Technologies

34.3.1 Public Procurement Areas That May Be Improved by Decision Support Solutions

The PP function exists in an organizational context. This setting implies complex managerial tasks, requires a wide range of expertise, and involves cooperation requirements for processes to work efficiently and effectively. As decisions related to public procurement have many intricate details, we may not address all of them. Our focus will be on showing how to support typical semistructured problems of the PP field, which meet certain requirements and provide considerable value if solved (to be worth the effort). As follows from what was said in Section 34.2.2, suitable problems would be those recurring tasks of middle management, which have reasonable potential loss or gain at "stake" and are typically riddled with organizational conflicts. There are both internal and external expectations concerning how this function should be executed. The latter is partly determined by its nature of spending public money, that is, the law, and partly by the needs of the recipients (constituencies, governmental agencies, and so on). Not only planning and strategic activities but also individual procedures need to be protected against the excessive scrutiny from external audits and control. Therefore, this is a great setting for the decision technologies to help by investigating the possibilities of accepted best-practice solutions and finding room for improvement. A good decision support solution would consider all stakeholder expectations and should offer ways to achieve these expectations or develop methodologies that offer additional advantages. When considering the application of a decision support solution or involvement of a decision expert, in our case a public procurement decision analyst, one needs to set goals of what is to be achieved and why it would be worthwhile to consider such an option.

Improving knowledge management aspects is a good cause. Public procurement problems are usually group decision processes in two senses: on the one hand, various organizational leaders (managers, officials, etc.) meet and their interests and preferences clash during the process, and on the other hand, making the proper decision usually calls for a wide range of expertise to be harnessed to make the decision. The decision-making workflow has to consider the workflow of the procurement process. Resolving negotiations and other issues among the stakeholders as well as among the experts is not a straightforward exercise and may require professional help. A decision support specialist may help to learn, understand, and handle organizational relationships including the catalysis of expert cooperation and determination of the various roles of participants.

In this sense, most problems related to individual procedures and contract management may be worth addressing. Decision technologies would treat the procedure in its entirety from the emergence of the need to the implementation including requirements, vendor selection, contracting, execution, control, and auditing.

34.3.2 Public Procurement Procedures as Decision-Making Processes

During individual public procurement procedures, there are a series of delicate moments that could be looked at as a series of more granular subdecisions leading to the complex decision of purchasing. Analyzing these procedures, the following typical steps may be recognized that each involves some decision making:

- Investigating the option of frame agreements
- Prequalification of potential suppliers (for restricted procedures)
- Raising, recognizing, and accepting the need (raising the need to relevant levels in the organization)
- Taking decisions about procurement (project initiation)
- Collecting and sorting market information
- Putting together the requirement specification
- Determining the number of procedures to run within the same procurement project (including the question of project management and subcontracting relationships)
- Choosing procedure types
- Setting vendor qualification requirements including validity, grounds for exclusion conditions, and criteria for suitability
- Creating technical specifications
- Determining the evaluation system
- Deciding about the content of the invitation documentation (CFP, CFT, RFI, RFQ, etc.)
- Evaluating proposals
- Short listing (in case of large number of applicants)
- Negotiations (could be price only or even content) if allowed
- Selecting the winning proposal/bid
- Finalizing and signing the contract
- Executing the contract, implementation
- Monitoring and feedback

The order of these steps does not necessarily indicate a fully sequential process, however. Instead, there are iterative elements and certain decision points that need to be considered in relation to each other. Furthermore, any particular PP decision process may or may not contain all of them. Out of the many tasks listed above we now investigate two examples that, according to our experience, can be supported with a good chance of success. These may be treated as representative examples.

We address some of the organizational and planning issues as well but only in the context of implementing decision technological solutions recommended for improving procurement procedures.

34.3.3 Complex Evaluation of Bids

The selection of potential candidates and evaluation of their proposals is one of the key tasks of running a procurement project. The difficulty does not relate to legal issues only. The source of complexity of running a procedure may be organizational, strategic, or domain-related or may come from the limitations of human ability. The issue here is threefold:

- It is not straightforward to determine who should be involved.
- There is the need to choose "the best" supplier; however, considering the various stakeholders, it is hard to agree upon what "best" means.
- Expectations from external parties usually concern the appropriateness of the outcome and legality of the process.

From the point of view of decision theory, a public procurement decision may be considered "good" if it is correct regarding the content of the purchase and it is accepted by all stakeholders. These stakeholders may involve the officials of the procuring organization, the suppliers (who submitted a bid), legal officials and authorities (judicial branch, appeal board, etc.), and—in case of grants, subsidies, or other forms of outside support—those who financed the project. Future recipients of the public supply, work or service, whose situation is to be improved, are considered to be the problem owners but they are represented by the procuring authority.

The goal of involving any form of decision support for bid evaluation is to help the effective and efficient creation of the tender document and the execution of the evaluation itself such that they serve the goals of the tender, the process leads to high-quality bids, and the result can be defended. Theoretically speaking, the solution of each decision problem requires a strategy, or to be more precise, one or more strategic goal(s). In case of PP, we may call this the procurement strategy, which means that it is the leading global principle that defines the high-level goals and expectations of the contracting authority. Examples of such procurement strategies may be to "find a good, known, reliable supplier," "price matters most," "it does not have to be cheap as long as the quality is high," and so on. Main factors that determine a procurement strategy are as follows:

- Market conditions (e.g., how many potential suppliers there are, what the average product/service quality is like)
- Expectations of the stakeholders against the supplier (i.e., the quality of the supply)

Knowledge of the market is also important in determining the expected costs and price of procurement projects. The resulting procurement strategy determines several components of the tendering solution and may also have effect on planning. It influences how resources are to be handled, how important deadlines are, how quality relates to price, as well as the number and type of procedures. From a modeling point of view, strategy is considered to be at the highest level of goals and is to be translated into specific criteria for subdecisions. However, the resultant outcome of subdecisions might not achieve the main goal set out by the strategy.

Experts are needed during both the development of the solicitation document (the specification) and the scoring and selection phase. The nature of these two tasks is different; therefore, unless it is required otherwise, the two groups of experts do not have to be the same. During the specification phase the decision support knowledge has more room, while during scoring, it might be advisable to involve independent domain experts (if allowed and affordable). It is important to make expert participants understand that they are responsible for the cause, the project, and not for interests.

To provide a goal for the group, the accountable authority should decide about the procurement strategy, which should be clearly communicated. In fact, to resolve the paradox of potentially losing control (as the details are in the hand of experts yet the responsibility is at the project leader), managers have the option to appoint reliable and trustworthy people. Furthermore, once the evaluation system (and solicitation document) is prepared, managers may review and approve it to make sure the result is in line with the strategy defined.

In the interpretation of decision technologies, the evaluation or the evaluation methodology is an organic part of a complex invitation, filtering, and selection process (as discussed above). The tender goals are achievable if the evaluation criteria are in line with other elements of the solicitation document (such as technical specifications, suitability criteria, grounds for exclusion, etc.) and the resulting documentation satisfies all of the technical, economic, and strategic expectations. The result should be protected both externally against official organizations and internally within the procuring entity. To acquire a high-quality bid, the documentation should not only be understandable for potential suppliers, but it should also point (or lead) them to the right direction.

One of the first key tasks during preparation of the evaluation system is to decide about the meaning of (overall) "best." The basic issue with defining evaluation criteria is threefold:

- It needs to be defined in advance and, therefore, the final winner is selected as a result of a set of evaluation rules instead of through deliberation or negotiation.
- Main goal is usually financial advantage, that is, cheaper purchasing; yet, details of technical superiority could also be important: finding a balance is at the heart of a "value for money" approach, for example.
- Process also needs balance among the various expert opinions involved.

One should apply criteria encompassing the most interests leading to a balance of technical quality/merits and financial conditions (prices and other financial constraints). To consider the most factors possible, as many people as possible should be involved, raise their voices, and contribute their expertise. This needs control, however, as the group aspect may be handled using decision conferencing (Phillips, 1990), while individual differences could be handled using voting power based on the competencies of participants (Gelléri and Martinez, 1987).

Decision conferencing using expert facilitation is a good vehicle to arrange the meeting of all stakeholders at the same time—instead of calling up participants step-by-step, one at a time. Facilitation not only stimulates their discussion but is also able to keep a firm hand on their divergent opinions and help them find a compromise. Although it is true that at the beginning, experts should discuss issues together and reach a consensus as a group, evaluation of bids is better done individually (representing personal opinion). Appropriate software tools should be able to store individual scores and calculate the overall group results according to the selected (or legally allowed) rules.

The first step of a PP decision conference is the discussion of the procurement strategy. Interpreting this strategy within the legal framework leads to the decision about the number of procedures to run (more complex public works purchases may require the integrated control of several procedures). Choosing the procedure type is done in relation to the potential suitability criteria and expected content of the evaluation criteria. This is followed by the detailed assembly of the evaluation system including selecting criteria and determining weights. The most important outcome of decision theoretical research is the technique to determine weights and the methods to create real utility functions actually reflecting the preferences of stakeholders and taking into consideration the nature of expert judgment. Using utility functions provide the ability to handle a richer set of criteria and evaluation models/methods. This way, the evaluation of a given criteria would go beyond a simple "yes" or "no" mark; and opinions may be handled in a more flexible way. The fine-tuning of the evaluation criteria system could be done through the application of sensitivity analysis, scenario analysis, or simulation techniques. These tools help experts to play around with options and scenarios and to investigate options and possibilities allowing an in-depth analysis of options and potential consequences.

Representative Case: Purchasing Passenger-Car Fleet for the Hungarian Government

During the late 1990s and early 2000s it was a recurring nagging issue at the Central Governmental Purchasing Unit of the PMO to refurbish the car fleet of various government offices. Every two to three years, many cars had to be replaced. However, each time the corresponding public procurement process was a nightmare: there was no procedure without legal challenges by lost bidders or corruption charges from the media. The process was watched closely by the public and there were always hints of the purchases being too expensive. As a result of appeals and legal challenges, many of the projects took longer than a year to come to a conclusion (instead of approximately four to five months).

Eventually, public procurement officers at the Central Governmental Purchasing Unit (CGPU) turned to the experts of the Decision Technologies Research Group of the Budapest University of Technology and Economics. The group had a decision support tool, named Tender-EXPERT, originally developed in the mid-1980s and used successfully for World Bank financed major procurement projects for the last decade. Experts at the group have run close to a hundred decision conferences of both public and private procurement projects—resulting in high-quality purchases with acceptable prices and no appeals.

The passenger-car fleet project run by the CGPU in 2002 consisted of nine procurement projects (in five car categories) with a total value of approximately 4 billion HUF ($20 million). Using procurement, decision consulting expertise allowed the CGPU to get many more people such as outside experts involved; yet, preparation of the invitations did not take longer than earlier. With the help of expert facilitation, the process led to a better structured, more detailed specification and a corresponding tight evaluation criteria system based on sophisticated utility functions.

The result surprised even the decision consultants themselves: although preparation costs some 0.1 percent of the full value more than the purchasing unit usually spent (it was the cost of the consultant and the experts involved), according to the calculations made by the project leader responsible for the whole program savings were up 10–40 percent compared to earlier results depending on car category. In addition, to breake a long-lasting "tradition" there was absolutely no appeal related to the evaluation schema or the selection process showing that even bidders have accepted the DSS-supported new solution.

34.3.4 Evaluating Service Supplier and Contractor Performance

Ensuring the fulfillment of service contracts and evaluating the performance of service providers is not an obvious task. There could be regular debates and one of the parties might even turn to the court.

It is even more difficult an issue if the service or operating agreement is a result of the public procurement procedures where the involvement of both public and private entities makes the situation even more complicated due to the legal environment created by public regulations. In cases of public–private partnership (PPP) and similar projects, for example, there are several players and groups involved or affected with differing or even contradicting interests.

Public regulations regularly require the service provider to cover the risk associated with the potential loss of service availability. Therefore, operation risk is usually carried by the private partner. On the other hand, it is crucial to protect the interest of the public institution against the service provider during the entire length of service contract period (potentially lasting 15–25 years). At the same time, the state side aims at achieving high-quality contract fulfillment and service delivery. It is also a typical policy requirement that the public partner should pay less in case of deficient service delivery. Executing the contract should lead to little dispute with the contractor/supplier: this means avoiding interruption, delay in delivery, or long-lasting resolution of problems. Within this typically contradicting set of interests, it is still essential to improve supplier relationships.

Turning to the details of the everyday managerial work, the expectation is that a proper performance evaluation should be objective, defendable (should not be legally challenged), and should be able to summarize overall performance and reflect actual quality. On top of this, it should even provide feedback based on lessons learned. The evaluation, therefore, should be built on facts instead of just "disputable" opinions, judgments, or "feeling" and "guesses." Preparation of such an evaluation solution needs also be integrated into the PP workflow as it is the invitation document and the resulting contract where all the rules may be laid out.

According to the approach of decision technologies, features of a proper solution follow from above expectations and from the interests of various stakeholders. The process should start with the identification of expectations against the performance, which then need to be turned into a criteria system. The idea is that it is worthwhile to build in a Service Level Agreement (SLA)-like monitoring solution of contractor performance into most private service delivery to a public entity. This is especially true for long-term operating contracts, such as PPPs. Such an agreement is to specify how evaluation of performance will be done and what the consequences of under-performance are. To be objective, a measurement is to be fact-based and built on the collection of utilities.

The recommended methodology uses decision conferencing process to compile a specific control-criteria system dedicated to the needs of service users of an institution. The criteria defined to control the completion of long-term service contracts including PPP are usually prepared in the form of contract extensions or fully built into the tender-contract. It does not focus on problems and flaws, instead, it only creates a system evaluating the level of achievement and includes potential bonuses. In fact, the form of the contract does not need to depend on the actual winner as it may be prepared in advance and could form part of the invitation (RFx) documentation. Having the evaluation rules set up in advance ensures a good base for a fruitful and painless relationship between the service provider and the building operator/owner. This way, the contract creates the way the relationship between the supplier and the purchaser is to be handled: it is in between the contractor and the contracting entity and becomes part of the contract. Then the contract defines what will be monitored and how, and what the consequences are, such as lowering fees, for example.

As a starting point, it is necessary to determine whether the given problem type (e.g., building and operating of a specific sports facility) is a good fit for a DSS solution. It is recommended to check the preparedness of an organization, including whether this particular organization is ready to engage in such an endeavor, for example, a PPP project. If the project is a go, all stakeholders are to be invited for a set of decision conference sessions. All user groups (e.g., students or management of a facility) could participate, bring their knowledge, represent their interests, and raise their issues. When has to identify functional roles needed to ensure smooth operation, these will be turned into access privileges to functions, reports, and data stored in the system.

The basic unit of the evaluation model is an event. All issues and consequences are to be listed in the form of either "if–then" or example-based scenarios of performance. Each potential issue has a weight. What is recorded is the location, scope, and severity of a problem, and, later, the length of time it took to respond and then resolve the issue. This data is processed by utility functions to determine problem points. The parameters to calculate the damage based on these events are fine-tuned and agreed upon by the representatives of both parties. It is here that the interest of players from the service provider side (investor, operator) may be taken into account. All events (e.g., issues) entered by users, or those with access, are doubly acknowledged as to whether it is true, acceptable, and how long repair should take (depending on the values of how many people are affected, the severity of the issue, etc.).

Accumulated problem points may be calculated for a given or a selected period of time or for a regular interval (e.g., month or for every quarter). It is also possible to create checklist type summaries indicating the status of given areas or issue types. Reports are generated on demand.

Representative Case: Controlling the PPP Operation of Educational Facilities

By 2005, state universities in Hungary had a major shortage of investment resources. Dormitory buildings were old, operating costs were running high, quality issues were frequent, and there was little money to invest into new facilities. PPP seemed to be a way to escape from this trap. Even the Ministry of Education was in favor of PPP plans, but there were plenty of problems to face and reservations galore. Committing resources for 15, 20, or even 25 years and calculating risks for such a long period are not straightforward. Officials were wary of loosing control of the contract and ending up with uncontrollable expenses.

Decision technology researchers at Winsdom Inc. investigated the nature and problems of long-term operating contracts and came up with a solution. The resulting decision support methodology and software, called Control-EXPERT, helps the control of long-term operating services of facilities built as a result of public procurement using PPP constructs. It guarantees legal compliance and high level of service.

The heart of the solution is a fact-based evaluation criteria system set up as part of the tender invitation and made part of the contract. Principles are accepted by both parties. Measured factors, maintenance events, and performance levels (severity, time, and scope of issues) are stored in a database. Utilities of performance indicators are agreed upon in advance and the resulting score is directly related to payment arrangements. Any decrease in service level leads to a lowering of service fees. Parameters may be adjusted during the course of the contract if necessary, and could be agreed upon by the parties involved. This way, the contracting institution can make sure that the service provider will cover the risk associated with availability of service for 15–20 years.

The solution was accepted and endorsed by the Ministry of Education. More than half a dozen university projects applied this DSS so far just within a year and a half—among them were four student dormitory renovation projects. Calculated return on investment for a typical project indicates that 6 percent of service level diminution of a 2 billion HUF ($10 million) controlled service value leads to a saving of approximately 80 million HUF ($400,000) with a guaranteed high level of service.

The solution does not only protect the owner but also brings a lot of advantages for the operator as well. Having access to all data stored in the database helps the understanding and improvement of the operating process. The service provider could identify recurring patterns and could make preemptive measures to protect the condition of the property or improve service delivery accordingly.

34.3.5 Additional Areas with Proven Results

As we mentioned at the beginning of the chapter, there are several potential areas to support and we could not cover them in detail. Yet, a few issues are worth a mention:

- Public procurement process audit: monitoring the whole process and the outcome of PP procedures is an organizational affair, not related to the contractor or contractors, neither is it about budgetary audit. Solutions similar to the one introduced in Section 34.3.4 may be used successfully. For each step—preparing the tender, choosing the procedure type, setting up the criteria system, how the choice was made, form and content of the contract including performance evaluation criteria, the final result—the focus of auditing should be correctness, and faults may be recorded, evaluated, and analyzed.
- Evaluating earlier (historical) supplier performance (to establish better suitability criteria for the future).
- Monitoring contract execution and handling issues arising by establishing guarantees of the quality of delivery.

34.4 Implementation and Experiences

Applying decision support solutions in the area of public procurement is similar to what happens in other areas. During our 20 years of consulting practice, we have identified three different ways how decision expertise is usually applied: (1) asking for individual consultant help, (2) *outsourcing* to well-prepared consulting firms with appropriate know-how, and (3) institutionalizing through the implementation of DSS software and methodology.

Individual consultants are best used for solving sensitive, rare, or occasional complicated problems. They may facilitate the search for a solution using decision conferencing where the key is to allow all stakeholders to raise their voice and to foster the cooperation of people involved. Regular, repetitive decision tasks may even be outsourced. As most decisions do have some level of sensitivity, it is crucial to keep some key control points, especially that the outsourcing authority is still legally responsible for all processes and outcomes. In the case of running PP procedures with regular outside consulting help, these may include setting the strategy, appointing key experts, or reviewing the documentation at given milestones. Introducing decision support software tools into an organizational procurement process might be justified by the volume of procedures to be run or the complexity of certain projects.

Implementing decision support solutions and making it part of the daily routine of an organization is not a straightforward exercise and requires careful preparation. Such an implementation assumes certain level of readiness by the organization (e.g., departments involved). This includes cultural acceptance and willingness of people to adopt. Obviously, such an endeavor would require changes in existing processes and modification of workflow. Out of the many possible implementation issues, let us address the three important areas from the point of view of decision making.

Regarding organizational problem-solving culture, it is of utmost importance that members of the project team need to be able to work together. It is not atypical for financial or legal department to only join the project when all domain-specific questions are answered and all technical documents are prepared. This, in our opinion, leads to unnecessary extra iterations and rework of the proposed solution. Even if it is otherwise not part of the culture of a given organization, we wish to emphasize that people from various departments involved need to be present at key meetings for an efficient problem resolution and progress. If necessary, facilitation could manage additional issues arising. Inability to make team members meet and work together could seriously question the effectiveness of any decision support solution. One root cause of segmented team work might be the low prestige of public procurement. Although this varies from sector to sector and from country to country, the status of the procurement function and its professionals on average is perceived to be lower compared to other public sector functions (when it is expressed through compensation and job attractiveness—see responses from the second International Research Study of Public Procurement reported by Harland et al., 2005). This potential problem area definitely needs to be investigated and addressed accordingly.

Another central question concerns the interest and attitude of high-level managers and their usual leadership behavior. This is a very sensitive point rarely discussed openly. On the basis of our experience of supporting PP decision processes we wish to clarify that proper application of decision technologies leads to a clean playing field ensuring the correctness of the process. As we have observed, it is not uncommon for managers wanting to have a lot of say, they might even wish to be sure that they know what is cert. However, DT solutions do not leave too much room for autocratic leadership, therefore managers relying on such a style might not be able to cope with or be willing to accept the resulting new mode of working. The implementation project would either fail or further organizational changes might be required.

The interest of outside control entities such as auditing authorities or financing organizations is another sensitive question as their influence might very well be an important factor. Our advise is to clarify whether they wish to represent their interests during individual procedures and how they intend to participate. Understanding their expectations is an essential component of success. We have observed that appropriate tools allow for follow-up analysis and leave room for a supervisory role similar to those exercised by steering committees without compromising decision power.

34.5 Concluding Comments

Public procurement is an organizational decision-making process strongly determined by the regulatory environment. Solutions offered by decision technologies are able to help public procurement professionals to face the complexities of their job and offer solutions to achieve their goals more effectively. Typical problems associated with PP procedures are not always of decisional nature but decision technologies may help to expand the reach of public procurement practitioners to handle these issues. Experienced consultants should be able to help the organization through most hurdles by investigating the motivation of management to cross to a new approach and readiness of interdisciplinary teams. The resulting advantages are manifold, most of which have been discussed already. In addition, using decision support software leads to more transparent procedures, standardized processes, and improved documentation as well as ability to store, review, and analyze historical data of procedures.

References

Csáki, Cs. 2006. Investigating the decision making practice of public procurement procedures. Paper presented at the 2nd International Public Procurement Conference held in Rome, Italy, September 21–23, 2006. (Proceedings available in CD format.)

Gelléri, P. and Csáki, Cs. 2006. Conditions and benefits of applying decision technological solutions as a tool to curb public procurement corruption. Special Edition on Public Procurement of the *European Journal of Purchasing and Supply Chain Management*, 11, 252–259.

Gelléri, P. and Martinez, F. 1987. How to handle differences in importance among participants with GDSS. In: R.M. Lee, A.M. McCosh, and P. Migliarese (Eds.), *Organizational Decision Support Systems*, Amsterdam, The Netherlands: North-Holland, pp. 117–128.

Gorry, G.S. and Scott Morton, M.S. 1989. A framework for management information Systems. *Sloan Management Review*, Spring, 30(3), 49–61.

Harland, C.M., Bakker, E.F., Caldwell, N.D., Phillips, W.E., and Walker, H.L. 2005. *The Changing Role of Public Procurement–Executive Report of the Second Workshop, International Research Study on Public Procurement.* Bath: Centre for Research in Strategic Purchasing and Supply, University of Bath School of Management.

Howard, R.A. and Matheson, J.E. (Eds.). 1989. *Readings on the Principles and Applications of Decision Analysis.* Vol. I–II. Menlo Park, CA: Strategic Decision Group.

Hughes, M. 2005. Evaluation of the Local Government Procurement Agenda—Baseline Survey Report. The Office of the Deputy Prime Minister, London. Available at www.odpm.gov.uk. (Last retrieved April 20, 2006.)

Knight, L., Caldwell, N.D., Harland, C., and Telgen, J. 2003. *Government Reform and Public Procurement—Report from the First International Research Study on Public Procurement.* Bath: Centre for Research in Strategic Purchasing and Supply, University of Bath.

Phillips, L. 1990. Decision Conferencing. White Paper. Available at http://www.catalyze.co.uk/search.html?/dcbody.htm. (Last downloaded: February 09, 2005.)

Simon, H.A. 1960. *The New Science of Management Decision*. New York: Harper & Row.

Soudry, O. 2004. Promoting economy: Electronic reverse auctions under the EC directives on public procurement. *Journal of Public Procurement*, 4(3), 340–374.

Thai, K.V. 2005. Challenges in public procurement. In: K.V. Thai, A. Araujo, R. Y. Carter, G. Callender, D. Drabkin, R. Grimm, K.R. Ejlskov Jensen, R.E. Lloyd, C.P. McCue, and J. Telgen (Eds.), *Challenges in Public Procurement: An International Perspective*, Boca Raton, FL: PrAcademics Press, pp. 1–20.

Thai, K.V. and Piga, G. (Eds.). 2007. *Advancing Public Procurement: Practices, Innovation and Knowledge Sharing.* Boca Raton, FL: PrAcademics Press.

Chapter 35

Pricing Strategies and Cost Analysis in Public Procurement

Rupert G. Rhodd

CONTENTS

35.1 Introduction

If the public sector wants to get the greatest bang for the buck, paying attention to the price that is paid to acquire resources is extremely important. Although the per capita income of Americans has increased over the years, the United States' increased involvement in international affairs, and unstable weather conditions in states like California, Florida, Louisiana, Mississippi, and Texas, have resulted in greater demand for public sector goods and services, and more public sector spending. Public spending has also increased in recent years because of inflation. Information obtained from the Bureau of Labor Statistics shows the inflation rate for the United States to be 2.7 percent in 1999, 3.4 percent in 2000, 3.3 percent in 2004, 3.4 percent in 2005, and 2.5 percent in 2006. In some categories, for example, energy commodities, the price increase was much higher at 29.5 percent in 1999 and 26.7 percent in 2004 (U.S. Department of Labor, 2007).

To purchase goods and services, procurement officials must respond to many proposals that are submitted by potential contractors. The proposals are then evaluated or analyzed to ensure that the final agreed-to price is fair and reasonable. Evaluation usually includes price and cost analysis. As reported in FAR (Federal Acquisition Regulation) 15, "price analysis shall be used when cost or pricing data are not required... and cost analysis shall be used to evaluate the reasonableness of individual cost elements when cost or pricing data are required." Whereas price analysis is used to determine if the overall price that is offered is fair and reasonable, cost analysis is used to evaluate information other than cost or pricing data to verify cost reasonableness.

Price analysis examines and evaluates the proposed price without evaluating the composition of cost and the resulting profit. Some examples of the various price analysis techniques and procedures used by procurement officials to ensure a fair and reasonable price include the following (FAR, 15.404-1):

1. Comparison of proposed prices received in response to the solicitation. Normally, adequate price competition establishes price reasonableness.
2. Comparison of previously proposed prices and previous government and commercial contract prices with current proposed prices for the same or similar items, if both the validity of the comparison and the reasonableness of the previous prices can be established.
3. Use of parametric estimating methods/application of rough yardsticks (such as dollars per pound or per horsepower, or other units) to highlight significant inconsistencies that warrant additional pricing inquiry.
4. Comparison with competitive published price lists, published market prices of commodities, similar indexes, and discount or rebate arrangements.
5. Comparison of proposed prices with independent government cost estimates.
6. Comparison of proposed prices with prices obtained through market research for the same or similar items.
7. Analysis of pricing information provided by the offeror.

Although (1) and (2) are most often used, the contracting officer may use any of the remaining techniques if it is determined that the information on the proposed prices or previous contract prices is not available or is insufficient to determine price reasonableness. Also, value analysis, which gives insight into the relative worth of a product, can be used in conjunction with the price analysis techniques listed above.

Cost analysis reviews and evaluates the separate cost elements and profit in the offeror's or contractor's proposal. These elements include cost or pricing data or information other than cost or pricing data. Cost analysis also includes "the application of judgment to determine how well the proposed costs represent what the cost of the contract should be, assuming reasonable economy and efficiency" (FAR, 15.404-1).

The cost analysis techniques and procedures used by the government to determine price reasonableness include the following (FAR, 15.404-1):

1. Verification of cost or pricing data and evaluation of cost elements, to determine the necessity for, and reasonableness of, proposed costs, including allowances for contingencies. The verification of cost and the evaluation of pricing elements also include the use of current and historical cost or pricing data to project cost trends, and the application of audited or negotiated indirect cost rates, labor rates, and cost of money or other factors.
2. Evaluating the effect of the offeror's current practices on future costs that includes a trend analysis of basic labor and materials, especially when complex equipment is being purchased.
3. Comparison of costs proposed by the offeror for individual cost elements with actual costs previously incurred by the same offeror, previous cost estimates from the offeror or from other offerors for the same or similar items, other cost estimates received in response to the government's request, independent government cost estimates by technical personnel, and with forecasts of planned expenditures.
4. Verification that the offeror's cost submissions are in accordance with the contract cost principles and procedures as laid out in the various federal government guidelines.
5. Review to determine the inaccuracy or incompleteness of cost or price because of data omission.

Cost analysis could also take the form of cost realism analysis in which specific elements of the offerror's proposed cost estimate are independently reviewed and evaluated to determine whether the estimated proposed cost elements are realistic for the work to be performed, and are consistent with the unique methods of performance and materials described in the offeror's technical proposal. Cost realism analyses are performed on cost-reimbursement contracts to determine the probable cost that may differ from the proposed cost, of performance for each offeror. The probable cost is the government's suggested cost or the government's best estimate of the cost from the offeror's proposal. The probable cost reflects adjustments in cost elements to realistic levels and is less than the offerror's proposed costs. Among the advantages of cost realism analyses is its use in competitive fixed-price-type contracts when new requirements may not be fully understood by competing offerors because of quality concerns, or when the past performance of contractors shows quality or service shortfalls.

Although price analysis is widely conducted by procurement officials, there is no standard form of analysis. This causes the evaluation process to be subjective as analysis by different procurement officials can arrive at different reasonable prices.

The public sector acquires goods mostly through negotiations, often resulting in long-term contracts. Negotiation, a subtopic of game theory, is concerned with the analysis of strategic interaction and uses the same players found in any market (buyers and sellers). Negotiation therefore "extends the analysis through which price is determined by including actual interaction such as asymmetric information and haggling over the price" (Rhodd, 2005). When public procurement officials negotiate to purchase a good, the primary pricing objective is to acquire goods and services from responsible sources at fair and reasonable prices. Based on the *Contract Pricing Reference Guides* of the Department of Defense Procurement and Acquisition Policy, "the contracting officer's primary objective in pricing a contract is to balance the contract type, cost, and profit or fee negotiated to achieve a total result: a price that is fair and reasonable to both the Government and the contractor" (Department of Defense, 2007). The obvious questions are what is fair and what is reasonable?

To execute an effective cost or price analysis, procurement agents must know the characteristics of the market in which they are operating and how prices are determined. The remainder of this chapter is outlined as follows: Section 32.2 presents an overview of different types of markets and market-based prices, Section 35.3 discusses prices based on cost, and Section 35.4 discusses cost analysis. A brief summary ends the chapter.

35.2 Types of Markets and Market-Based Pricing

Public procurement officials must be familiar with the characteristics of the market in which they operate. Markets are more competitive when the number of sellers increases, when there is freedom of entry into and exit from the industry, and when the commodity being traded is not easily differentiated.

The price of a good or service is determined in the market that is defined by the factors above. These factors cause markets to be classified into four broad categories. There is the "perfectly competitive" market in which there is a very large number of buyers and sellers of a homogeneous good. The perfectly competitive market also allows for freedom of entry and exit, and there is very little cost involved in obtaining information in this market. Firms operating under perfect competition are described as price takers, as individually, they have no influence over the market price and they take the industry price that is determined by total demand and total supply, as given. The market for agricultural produce is an example of a perfectly competitive market.

At the other end of the continuum is the market form in which there is only one seller of a good or a "monopolist." There are significant barriers to entry caused by factors such as resource control, economies of scale or the need to produce a large quantity to lower the average cost of production (utilities), and legal barriers. Unlike firms operating under perfect competition, the monopolist is a price maker. In between perfect competition and monopoly there are "imperfect or monopolistic competition" and "oligopoly." With imperfect competition, a large number of sellers offer a good that is differentiated by design, wrapping, or other factors. Firms operating under imperfect competition compete through price, quality, and marketing. Under imperfect competition, firms seek to make their already differentiated products more different and this causes advertising to play a major role. However, the increased product diversity has positive value to consumers as the need to make products in the market more different leads to a high level of product innovation.

In an oligopolistic market, there are a small number of sellers of goods that are either similar or differentiated. There is interdependence among competitors and the behavior of one firm affects the behavior of others in the market. If, for example, there is a dominant firm with a cost advantage, that firm essentially sets the price. If firms are equal in terms of market share, they could collude to fix output price. Then there could be the strategy in which firms do not match price increase of other firms, but they match price decrease. Although it is not permitted in the United States, some form of tacit collusion could take place in which agreements are implicit. Price setting under oligopoly often resembles a game with each firm anticipating the rivals' reaction and then engages in a complex series of strategic moves and reactive countermoves.

Knowing whether a market is competitive or monopolistic will give insight into how much negotiation can occur and could also help determine the length of the purchase contract. For example, in a less competitive market where suppliers have market power, it could be beneficial for procurement agents to opt for longer term contracts thus reducing the probability of higher prices in the short run. On the other hand, for a more competitive market, prices tend to be more stable as no supplier wants to take the lead to increase price for fear of losing their market share.

The types of markets outlined above and discussed in the following paragraphs have led to different price setting methods, collectively known as market-based pricing. If procurement officials have knowledge of the various methods used to set price, they are able to negotiate more skillfully.

35.2.1 Profit Maximization Pricing

Profit maximizing price is very popular in the marketplace as all firms seek to maximize profits. The profit maximizing position of a firm is achieved at the output level where the addition to cost from the last unit produced or what economists call marginal cost (MC) is equal to the addition to total revenue from that same last unit or marginal revenue (MR).

An example is provided in Table 35.1. If the total cost to produce the first unit is $30, and the total cost to produce two units is $45, the MC or the additional cost is $15. This is the cost to produce the second unit. If the first unit brings in total revenue of $25, and the first and second units bring in total revenue of $48, the MR or addition revenue from the second unit is $23. The second unit adds more to revenue than cost and this increases total profit. In the Table 35.1, the addition to cost is less than the addition to revenue up to the fourth unit and profit is maximized at that point.

When profit maximization pricing is used, it is assumed that the seller is aware of the buyer's sensitivity to price changes as MR depends on price sensitivity. By price sensitivity is meant, for example consumer demand increasing and decreasing more than proportionately when prices fall and rise, respectively. This means that total revenue will increase with a price decrease and decrease with a price increase. For a public procurement official, there is the ability to get a better deal in a price sensitive market by offering to buy more items as the seller is already aware that by reducing the price total revenue will increase.

The profit maximizing pricing strategy is most useful when price is an important factor affecting demand and when this relationship can be easily determined. Knowing that the public sector's

Table 35.1 Price and Output under Price Maximization Pricing Strategy

Quantity	*Total Revenue ($)*	*Total Cost ($)*	*Marginal Revenue ($)*	*Marginal Cost ($)*	*Price ($)*	*Profit ($)*
0	0	12				–12
1	25	30	25	18	25	–5
2	48	45	23	15	24	3
3	65	52	17	7	21.66667	13
4	79	64	14	12	19.75	15
5	90	77	11	13	18	13
6	100	95	10	10	16.666	5

ability to purchase is limited by the budget, the seller will be more willing to offer lower prices to secure patronage. In this position, there is no room for negotiation.

35.2.2 Market-Share Pricing

Market-share pricing, penetration pricing or predatory pricing, is the pricing strategy in which the prices of goods are set very low to eliminate competition and also to prevent potential competitors from entering the marketplace. The goal of market-share pricing strategy is to dominate the market through market penetration as it is assumed that the firm's profit is associated with its market share. Market-share pricing is most appropriate when demand is elastic or very responsive to price changes. This means that when price declines the quantity demanded and total revenue increase significantly. Furthermore, it is also assumed that as production increases the firm reaps economies of scale or advantages of large scale production, this resulting in a decline in average cost.

The disadvantage of this strategy is that there is a high probability of early losses as prices are reduced to eliminate competition and also because average cost tends to be higher with a smaller output. Knowing that this is happening, public procurement officials should seek to fix long-term contracts, getting the assurance of lower prices even after the price has risen in the future. This will force sellers to build efficient operations.

If the seller is successful in capturing a larger share of the market and becomes the dominant supplier, the seller also becomes the dominant price maker in the industry. Because there is a tendency to set the price high once the market is secured, public procurement specialists that are operating in a market where market-share or predatory pricing is practiced should seek to reduce the cost associated with purchasing supplies in this market. For example, they should encourage mass purchasing and reap the efficiencies from this type of transaction.

Caution must also be exercised when low prices are offered to win a contract and exclude others from the market. This could jeopardize contract performance especially if the contract price is not sufficient to cover costs.

35.2.3 Market Skimming Pricing

Market skimming pricing strategy entails the setting of prices to earn the highest profit on each unit of a product that is perceived to have a high value to the buyer. Market skimming pricing strategy seeks out buyers who are willing to pay the highest price for the product. To maximize overall sales and profit, different segments of the market are offered the product at different prices.

Market skimming pricing strategy is similar to demand differential pricing or what economists call discriminating monopoly, in which units of the good are sold at different prices for reasons that are not associated with difference in the cost of production. Higher prices are charged in different segments of the market and to those individuals that are less sensitive to price changes, and lower price are charged to those that are more sensitive to price changes. The emergence of the Internet and online transaction has increased the opportunities for market segmentation and price skimming. In some cases, it is also possible to modify the product slightly and this often results in price differentiation.

Public procurement officials should try to avoid firms that practice market skimming pricing strategy unless they are buying in a market that has many sellers, as the extent to which firms can charge high prices to extort the highest level of profit will be limited. With many sellers, there is a greater awareness of competition and firms will be less willing to charge high prices in one or two segments of the market.

A second reason why public procurement officials should avoid a market in which skimming is practiced is that very often the quality that is advertised to justify the higher price is difficult to determine and is also less. Even if the advertised quality is real, it could be more than the public sector needs. Again, a product that is advertised as the best may not be better than other products.

If procurement officials cannot avoid markets that practice price skimming, to be in a position to secure the best price they should be aware of what factors cause different prices to be charged in different market segments and should try and position their agencies to obtain the lowest price. For example, they should be aware that lower prices are usually charged to customers that have purchasing power, that is, customers that buy large quantities. Furthermore, public procurement officials should be aware that the location of the transaction affects the price of the product and that a lower price may be charged in markets that have adequate supply routes as shipping charges are generally lower.

35.2.4 Current-Revenue Pricing

In current-revenue pricing, the emphasis is on maximizing current revenue rather than profit or long-term revenue. The strategy is to determine the price/quantity combination that maximizes revenue. Because of uncertainty in the market and financial instability, some firms may choose to use current-revenue pricing strategy because to these firms, "a bird in the hand is worth two in the bushes" or a sure dollar today is much more important than the possibility of more dollars tomorrow (Department of Defense, 2007).

For public procurement officials, there must be an awareness of why this strategy is used: high risk. Firms that practice current-revenue pricing are unsure about their future. Although sellers practicing current-revenue pricing are likely to offer lower prices to ensure sale and to reduce sales and revenue fluctuations, public procurement officials must be aware of the nature of these firms as operating in this environment could make contractors more irresponsible. Generally, firms with limited financial resources tend to employ this strategy as for these firms there are no strong incentives to remain in the industry other than maximizing current revenue. There is no long-run planning horizon.

35.2.5 Promotional Pricing

In promotional pricing, products are priced to enhance the revenue and sale of the overall product line rather than to assure the profitability of each product. The seller usually considers whether selling one of the products in the group at a loss will increase the sale of related products and increase profit, or whether selling a product at a high (prestige) price will improve the product-line quality image and increase profit. The high-quality, high-priced item enhances the image of an entire product line and is used to attract buyers. In fact, some buyers are reluctant to buy from firms that do not charge enough as they associate the high price with high quality.

Because promotional pricing can be used for wide range of products, it is likely that public procurement administrators will encounter this strategy at some point. Public procurement officials must be aware of the "bait and switch" pricing strategy, which is a form of promotional pricing in which sellers entice and attract buyer with a low-priced item and then switches buyer to a better and higher priced item during the sale. If the public procurement officials fall for this strategy, the budget may be completely exhausted without securing an adequate amount of the product.

Some items complement each other and for these items promotional pricing strategy can be used to set a low price for one item and a high price for the complement. The low-priced attractive complement, often considered to be the loss-leader, is used to lock in the purchase of both goods it is of little or no use without the high-priced complement.

35.2.6 Market-Competition Pricing

Although many forms of competition are discussed in microeconomics, only in the oligopolistic model (few firms in the industry) is price setting based on the action or reaction of other firms in the market. As mentioned earlier, under oligopoly the number of sellers in the market is small enough for each seller to know what price the other seller is charging. Because of this, each firm is a price maker and will react to the pricing strategy of other firms in the market. Generally, an oligopolistic firm is not expected to follow other firms in the industry that have increased their price, unless there is tacit agreement to do so. However, when one firm lowers its price, others in an oligopolistic market will follow fearing a loss of market share. Price is therefore based on what other firms in the market are charging or are expected to charge.

35.3 Pricing Strategies Based on Cost

35.3.1 Cost-Plus Pricing

The method of cost-plus pricing is very simple and consists of a markup or a percentage added to the average total cost to produce the product. This yields the target return for the good or service produced.

$$\text{Market price} = \text{AC}(1 + x\%)$$

where

x is the targeted return
AC is the average cost

For example, if 500 units of a good are produced at \$15,000.00, the average cost of each good is \$30.00. If the manufacturer considers 30 percent to be a fair and reasonable profit margin, the selling price of the good is \$39.00.

$$\text{Market price} = \$30(1 + 0.30) = \$39.00$$

The obvious question is this: What is the basis for choosing the level of profit or the percentage markup on cost? Some suggest that the targeted return is based on the degree of competition as firms are more likely to charge a higher price and get a higher return and level of profit in a less competitive market. Others have suggested that the level of risk involved could determine the markup and the selling price (Wiley & Sons, 2007).

Although cost-plus pricing allows the producer to cover all direct cost involved in the production of a good or service, it does not take into account the price sensitivity in the market, and this could result in a loss of revenue if cost-plus pricing calls for a price increase when consumers are very sensitive to price changes.

For public sector procurement agents, knowing that a firm bases its price on cost and knowing the cost and markup could help in negotiating the purchase price. If the markup percentage is high, public procurement officials will be more successful in securing a more favorable price if they are purchasing a large amount and if the contract is for an extended period.

35.3.2 Markup Pricing

Markup pricing is similar to cost-plus pricing in which prices also depend on cost. There is, however, some flexibility regarding the base cost that is used in markup pricing. First, the markup can be based on direct cost which is a cost that is directly attributable to the manufacture of a good. Direct cost includes profit and overheard cost. Second, the markup can be based on total cost that is the sum of direct and indirect costs. Because direct cost is less than total cost, any firm that bases its markup on total or full costs is expected to have a lower markup rate than the firm that bases the markup on direct cost only.

The use of markup pricing varies by industry and product. In industries where negotiation is the accepted way to conduct business, markup pricing is common as it allows the seller the flexibility to set the profit high enough to provide room for compromise. Again, it is imperative that public procurement agents know the usual markup for the industry as this advantage will allow him to negotiate the best price.

With products, markup pricing is very common for unique items or services that are provided for a single customer or a small group of customers and generally the margin is based on the type of work and risk involved. The greater the risk and the more the work involved, the higher the markup.

To estimate the price based on markup pricing, the volume of sales in units and the unit cost are first estimated. After the markup rate is determined, the selling price is calculated as the unit cost multiplied by (1 + percentage markup). An example is given below.

$$\begin{aligned}
\text{Estimated sales volume} &= 50{,}000 \text{ units} \\
\text{Estimated unit cost} &= \$100 \\
\text{Markup rate} &= \text{Cost} + (\text{percentage markup} \times \text{cost}) \\
&= \$100 + (0.20 \times \$100) \\
&= \$100 + \$20 \\
&= \$120
\end{aligned}$$

In more technical formulation, markup pricing is expressed as a function of the elasticity of demand for the commodity in question and the MC. The MC of the commodity is the cost of the last unit produced. In this case, the optimal pricing rule as expressed below is a markup on the MC of the commodity. The optimal markup rule of thumb formula is given below: [For further reading see Brickley et al., 2004; and Samuelson and Marks, 2006]

$$P = \frac{\text{MC}}{1 - \frac{1}{\eta}}$$

where

P is the price

MC is the marginal cost

η is a measure of the elasticity of demand for the commodity, which is a measure of price sensitivity

The price elasticity of demand shows the sensitivity of demand to price changes. Generally, the higher the elasticity coefficient, the more responsive are consumers to changes in the price of the commodity. If various elasticities exceeding 1 are substituted in the formula above, the price declines as the elasticity coefficient increases.

Among the factors influencing the sensitivity of demand to price changes in any market are the number of substitutes and how close the substitutes are to the goods in question. Public procurement officials should note that the greater the number of substitutes in the market and the closer the substitutes, the closer the market price to the cost of the commodity. Public procurement officials should also be aware that with any form of markup or cost-plus pricing, profit is set using a markup rate that is simply a percentage of cost and that the rate depends on factors including competition. The greater the degree of competition in the market, the more substitutes are available and the lower the markup on the cost of the commodity. This leaves less wiggle room for public procurement officials and sellers to negotiate a lower price.

It should also be noted that although products that are similar are generally similarly priced, new and better products will command higher profit margins and hence higher markup on cost. Public procurement officials should be aware of relevant industry markup practices as this can be quite useful in negotiating reasonable prices, especially when buying in commercial markets.

35.3.3 Margin Pricing

Margin pricing is not new and is best used when there is small number of products and customers, and overhead costs are relatively small and unrelated to the products sold or customers served (Pryor, 2007). Many firms use margin pricing because it matches their accounting reports where costs and profits are reported as a percentage of sales.

As with markup pricing, margin pricing is based on the relationship between cost and profit. The dollar value difference between the selling price and total cost is the profit margin. If, for example, the selling price of a good is \$10.00 and the cost is \$6.00, the profit margin is \$4.00. The gross margin percent is profit margin as a percent of the selling price.

$$\begin{aligned}\text{Gross margin percent} &= (\text{selling price} - \text{total cost})/\text{selling price}\\ &= (\$10.00 - \$6.00)/\$10.00\\ &= \$4.00/\$10.00\\ &= 40 \text{ percent}\end{aligned}$$

The gross margin formula can be adjusted if the desired margin percentage is known. In this case, the selling price is calculated as expressed below.

$$\begin{aligned}\text{Selling price} &= \text{total cost}/(1-\text{margin})\\ &= \$6.00/(1-0.40)\\ &= \$10.00\end{aligned}$$

Procurement officials should be aware of production cost and the average margin for the industries with which they are dealing. Knowledge of cost and margins will help to determine if the markup charged by the seller in question exceeds the industry markup. This will give public procurements agents more flexibility in choosing the right vendor and negotiating a reasonable price for the contracted purchase.

35.3.4 Rate of Return Pricing

Rate of return pricing is generally used by industry leaders or monopolist with considerable degree of market power. Usually, a target rate of return is specified, maybe 20 percent of the capital invested or 30 percent of sales revenue, and the price structure is arranged to achieve the target rate of return. For example, if a firm invests $50 million to produce shirts and estimates the demand for shirt to be 1 million per year, then with the average total cost for each shirt being $50, the firms annual total cost of production is $50 million (1 million shirts at $50 each). If the target rate of return is 30 percent, the dollar value return on the amount invested is $15 million. Because the expected demand is 1 million shirts, the markup on the cost of each shirt based on the rate of return is $15.00. The selling price of each shirt will therefore be $65.00.

The formula for calculating the price based on the rate of returns on investment is given below.

$$\text{Price} = \frac{\text{TC}}{Q_\text{D}} + \frac{\text{ROI}^\text{T} \times I}{Q_\text{D}}$$

where

TC represents the total cost of production
QD is the estimated demand
ROI^T is the target rate of return on investment
I represents the initial investment

From the discussion above, it is obvious that the rate of return pricing method requires more information about the market than the other models discussed so far. In fact, profit is guaranteed only if the expectation about the market demand and cost is correct. If the firm wants to keep the target rate of return constant, the price must be changed whenever demand changes. Also, as the producer spreads cost over a larger output, because the original investment is fixed, the profit margin on each unit declines.

The rate of return pricing is similar to markup pricing as the dollar value target return is added to the estimated costs. Whereas with markup pricing, the markup is on the cost of labor and material required to provide the product, with rate of return pricing, profit is calculated based on the financial investment required to provide the product and the estimated sales volume. If public procurement officials are aware of the required investment to make different goods, they are in a better negotiating position. Understanding this pricing strategy requires specific knowledge and public procurement officials may need courses or training in finance. Armed with this additional knowledge and the ability to project demand for the product, public sector procurement officials will be able to determine if firms are charging more than that which should give them a reasonable return on investment.

35.4 Cost Analysis

Cost analysis is the evaluation or analysis of the overall cost and its components in relation to the price to determine the extent to which the contractor's offered price is realistic or practical. Cost analysis is undertaken to determine if the charges or proposed costs of the contract are in keeping with the work to be performed and if they are consistent with the methods of performance and materials described in the contractor's technical proposal. Apart from enabling the investigator to obtain and analyze cost or pricing data or information other than cost or pricing data, cost analysis helps to determine the reasonableness or allowability of costs and defines and evaluates the contractor's plan for accomplishing the work. Procurement officials that undertake cost analysis are able to identify contractors that are charging the lowest fee and this helps in the efficient allocation of the agency's budget.

With competing firms offering similar products, and with limited public sector funding, cost analysis is a necessary exercise for public procurement official, as it helps to determine the true cost of providing a given unit of service. Along with price analysis, cost analysis helps the procurement official prepare a negotiation position. This is done by recognizing alternatives and their effect on the contract price, by identifying and considering the effect of cost drivers, and by identifying key pricing elements in the prenegotiation objectives.

In negotiating a contract, the contract cost or the cost of the product to the contractor is generally lower than the contract price or the price at which the good is offered to the customer. The total cost of purchasing a good, also referred to as the contract cost, is the "sum of the allowable direct and indirect costs allocable to a particular contract, incurred or to be incurred, less any allocable credits, plus any allocable cost of money" (Department of Defense, 2007). Whereas direct cost is any identifiable costs that is specified by the contract, indirect cost is any cost that is not directly identified with a single, final cost objective like the contract cost. To complete a cost analysis, cost data should be accurate, complete, and current, and historical cost should be evaluated to determine it relevance. Assuming all relevant costs are included in the analysis, the difference between the contract cost and the contract price is the profit or fee of the contractor and the relationship between both is given below.

$$\text{Profit/fee} = \text{contract price} - \text{contract cost}$$

Cost analysis helps to determine the extent of the profit or fee the contractor is charging. Furthermore, cost analysis is able to provide insight into what it will cost the firm to complete the contract using some agreed upon method, and it must be used in conjunction with price analysis. This is so because cost analysis does not provide a picture of what the market is willing to pay for the product involved. Cost analysis is undertaken to determine the profit/fee charged by the contractor and in the end it also helps to determine if the proposed price is fair and reasonable.

As discussed in the introduction, the characteristics of particular markets in terms of the number of sellers in the industry and the ease with which potential sellers are able to enter the industry determine the degree of competition. A more competitive market will have more vendors and the implication for cost analysis is that the profit/fee tends to be lower.

Contract cost is affected by technical factors relating to the specific nature of the product, and the packaging requirements for safe shipping and survival of the product under extreme conditions. Technical factors could entice contractors to submit higher than usual price and this also increases the profit or fee. Because of the possibility that public procurement official can be charged a higher than usual price owing to circumstances beyond their control, for example, technical factors, there is the need to determine if the cost of higher prices are truly caused by technical factors and whether changes in these factors to minimize the price will still provide the product with the minimum specification. If the technical factors cannot be diluted, there is also the need to determine if the product is delivering a high value to the taxpayers.

Cost analysis is generally undertaken when cost or pricing data is submitted along with the offer voluntarily or when there is a requirement to submit cost information other than cost or pricing data to support the claim of price reasonableness. Furthermore the Truth in Negotiations Act (TINA) requires the purchaser or public procurement official to obtain cost or pricing data in specific contracting situations.

35.5 Summary

After knowing the various ways prices are determined in the market, a public procurement official must still decide on the price he or she is willing to pay for the commodity or service. Is the acceptable price that which is paid by the general public (the commercial price) for the product? Is there a published price list and is this list updated by the seller regularly, or is price the result of negotiation between the buyer and seller? Furthermore, the public procurement official needs to know whether prices are discriminatory, that is, whether larger buyers receive lower price through discounts than smaller buyers. And even with the above, the public procurement official must recognize that in addition to market conditions in which supply, demand, technology, and product design change, prices are also determined by geographic location and government unique requirements.

Public procurement officials are aware that there are laws that restrict the ability of firms to charge customers different prices unless the seller can justify the price through cost. There are also legal constraints that drive the firm's choice of pricing policies and public procurement officials must ensure that sellers are abiding by the rule of law.

Even with the research conducted by the procurement official, there are still many risk involved in purchasing a commodity: quality as it relates to price, and supply conditions that can change because of external factors. It has been suggested that public procurement officials "should start by estimating a 'should-pay' price when they begin acquisition planning, and that they should continue to refine their estimate as information is collected throughout the acquisition process" (Department of Defense, 2007). The should-pay price is generally the reasonable price for the commodity based on historical cost, price changes, and other factors in the market. This price is also the highest price the public procurement official is willing to accept based on the information available. With this strategy, there is less possibility of overcharging.

Other auxiliary techniques have been suggested to determine the reasonableness of prices. The U.S. Federal Government (2007) posits that a complete price analysis is possible when value analysis and visual analysis are used to supplement price comparisons. Whereas value analysis systematically and objectively evaluates the function of a product and its related costs, visual analysis requires inspecting the item to develop an approximate estimate of its value. Visual analysis is concerned with the external features of the product and value analysis is concerned with the functioning of the product. For value and visual analyses, knowledge of the product, its functions, and its use are essential.

The best the public procurement can do is to hope that in the end the agreed-upon price is reasonable both in term of comparison to other prices in the market and in terms of quality received for the price. To achieve this goal, here are some guidelines.

1. Commodities for which prices are being compared must have similar characteristics. Price analysis or comparison is easier when products are very similar. If the products are not very similar, the comparison may be subject and of little use.
2. Wherever possible, price comparison should be based on competitive prices. This will ensure that the analysis is based on the lowest set of prices and will result in more resources for the

public sector. Public procurement officials should always seek to get competitive offers from the best vendors in terms of integrity, price, and quality.
3. Use all the available information to ensure that in the end the most reasonable and fair price is achieved.

In the long run, the primary concern of procurement officials is to negotiate a contract that will be beneficial to the government while at the same time providing the contractor with the greatest incentive to produce the good or service efficiently.

References

Brickley, J., Smith, C., and Zimmerman, J. 2004. *Managerial Economics and Organizational Architecture.* McGraw-Hill, NY.

Department of Defense. 2007. Defense procurement and acquisition guide. *Contracting Price Reference Guide.* Retrieved from http://www.acq.osd.mil/dpap/contractpricing/vol1intro.htm#I.2.1 on February 15.

FAR, 15.404-1.

Pryor, T. 2007. *The Demise of Gross Margin Pricing.* Retrieved from http://www.icms.net/news-7.htm on February 15.

Rhodd, R. 2005. Acquiring resources through price negotiation: A public sector approach. *Encyclopedia of Public Administration & Public Policy.* Marcel Dekker, NY.

Samuelson, W. and Marks, S. 2006. *Managerial Economics.* Wiley.

U.S. Department of Labor. 2007. *Inflation and Consumer Spending,* Bureau of Labor Statistics. Retrieved from http://www.acq.osd.mil/dpap/contractpricing/vollintro.htm#1.2.1 on January 6.

U.S. Federal Government. 2007. *The Pricing Handbook.* Retrieved from http://fast.faa.gov/pricing/98–30-c5.htm#Auxiliary%20Techniques on March 23.

Wiley & Sons. 2007. Beyond cost-based pricing. *Book Corner.* Retrieved from http://www.pro2net.com/x48429.xml on February 2.

Chapter 36

Public–Private Partnerships

Lawrence L. Martin and Corey T. Stutte

CONTENTS

36.1 Introduction

Public–private partnerships (PPPs) have been described as one of the "dominating organizational ideas circulating at the beginning of the 21st Century" (Wettenhall, 2005, p. 22). PPPs are being used throughout the world to provide public infrastructure and services such as: roads, rail (light and heavy), water and wastewater, prisons, hospitals, schools, health, social welfare, and others (European Parliament, 2006).

PPPs constitute a new and unique challenge for public procurement because they transcend traditional contracting assumptions, policies, and procedures predicated upon the existence of a buyer/seller relationship. As the name implies, PPPs place governments not in the position of buyers of goods and services from the private sector, but rather in the position of partners with private sector organizations, both for-profit as well as nonprofit or third sector organizations. As such, PPPs represent a form of coproduction (Klijn and Teisman, 2005).

Although PPPs have many of the same characteristics as privatization and contracting (IMF, 2002), it can be argued that PPPs represent a new species of governance tool. Lawther and Martin (2005a, b) suggest that PPPs are really a synthesis of the direct government service delivery mode (the thesis) and market-based approaches (antithesis). PPPs attempt to combine the best aspects of both delivery approaches, while simultaneously minimizing the negative aspects. The European Commission (2005, p. ii) notes that PPPs can reduce life-cycle costs, provide for better resource allocation, enable the faster implementation of public works and services, improve service quality, and provide additional revenue streams.

The different types of actors (public, for-profit, and not-for-profit) involved in PPPs suggest different types of interactions between the partners. As Zarco-Jasso (2005) of the University of Navarra in Barcelona notes, the role of a public partner in a PPP is to "define and promote the achievement of the public purpose;" the role of a for-profit partner is to "produce goods and services" and the role of a not-for-profit partner is to meet "worthy social needs and allocate voluntary resources" (p. 24). PPPs then do not require an abandonment or change in the raison d'etre of sector partners, but rather involve the harnessing of their collective energies through cooperative interaction.

This chapter begins by placing PPPs in both their historical and modern contexts. Next, PPPs are defined and their common characteristics identified followed by a discussion of the major drivers of PPPs. A typology of PPPs is then presented based on a dichotomy of *infrastructure* PPPs and *functional* PPPs; case studies provide examples of each type. Next, the funding of PPPs is considered. The characteristics of successful PPPs are then discussed. Some initial evaluation results of PPPs are presented. Finally, the challenges of PPPs for public procurement are identified and discussed.

36.2 PPPs in Historical and Modern Contexts

PPPs are both a new and an old idea. Throughout history, governments have frequently looked to the private sector for assistance, particularly in times of crisis. Grame Hodge of Monash University in Australia and Carsten Greve of the University of Copenhagen (Hodge and Greve, 2005, p. 24–25.) remind us that the English government secured its great victory against the Spanish Armada in 1588 due in large measure to its use of PPPs. The English fleet at the time was undermanned and underresourced. In response to the crisis of the Spanish Armada, the English admiral Sir Francis Drake cobbled together a fleet consisting of some 197 vessels. The majority (163) of these vessels were "privateers" financed and outfitted by commercial interests. The spoils of war taken from the captured Spanish ships were distributed between the English Crown and its private sector partners making this a truly public–private partner-*ship*.

The principal difference between modern PPPs and those of the past is that the latter were essentially pragmatic responses to specific situations. Modern PPPs tend to be based on a priori government policy decisions to work in partnership with the private sector as a preferred way of conducting the public's business and addressing public policy goals (Klijn and Teisman, 2005). The modern world is much more complex, the pace of change is accelerating, and knowledge is no longer found exclusively (if it ever was) within the public sector. In the words of the Copenhagen Center (Schested, 2003, p. 89), "No individual actor today has the requisite skills, knowledge, capabilities and finances to address complex societal issues." Hence the need for the public sector to join forces with the private sector. Commenting on the modern approach to PPPs, Kettl (1993, p. 4), an American academic, points out that, every major public policy initiative launched by the U.S. federal government over the last 50 years, from highway infrastructure to healthcare delivery to social welfare support, has involved PPPs.

The renewed interest in PPPs today by governments around the world can be traced, at least partially, to the ideas of the "new public management" (e.g., Rhodes, 1996), the "governance" paradigm (e.g., Salamon, 2002), and the "reinventing government" movement (e.g., Osborne and Gaebler, 1992), all of which stress involvement of the private sector and the harnessing of private sector expertise and resources to assist in the accomplishment of public policy goals. Although the modern use of PPPs began in the so-called Anglo-Saxon countries (e.g., Australia, Canada, New Zealand, the United Kingdom, and the United States), the concept has migrated to the European Union and its member countries as well as other developed and developing countries. Even France, with its traditional "suspicion" of Anglo-Saxon ideas, has embraced PPPs (*The Economist*, 2007). The French company Caisse d'Epargne created continental Europe's first investment fund focusing exclusively on providing capital in support of French PPP initiatives (Hollinger, 2005).

36.3 What Are PPPs?

The concept of a "public–private partnership" might best be thought of as an "umbrella term" that encompasses a variety of approaches that have common features, but nevertheless vary significantly depending upon their focus, their construction, and their country of origin. Different governments in different countries utilize different types of PPPs to accomplish different public policy goals. Some countries (e.g., the United Kingdom) make extensive use of PPPs across a variety of policy areas, while other countries (e.g., Chile and Italy) make more targeted use of PPPs.

Because of their scope and breadth, as well as their country differences, there is no single consensus definition of a PPP. Some of the more instructive attempts at definition are:

- Organization for Economic Cooperation and Development (OECD) states that PPPs "refer to the private sector design, build, finance, maintain and operate (DBFMO) infrastructure assets traditionally provided by the public sector" (Blondal, 2005, p. 19).
- World Bank observes that, "The term 'public–private partnership' has taken on a very broad meaning. The key element, however, is the existence of a 'partnership' style approach to the provision of infrastructure as opposed to an arms length 'supplier' relationship…" (cited in Zarco-Jasso, 2005, p. 30).
- European Commission (2005) defines a PPP as "a contractual agreement between the public and private sectors, whereby the private operator commits to provide public services that have traditionally been supplied or financed by public institutions" (cited in Zarco-Jasso, 2005, p. 30).
- International Monetary Fund (IMF, 2004) states that, "Public–private partnerships refer to arrangements where the private sector supplies infrastructure assets and services that traditionally have been provided by the government" (p. 4).
- National Council for Public Private Partnerships (NCPPP, n.d.), a U.S.-based organization, defines a PPP as "… a contractual agreement between a public agency (federal, state, or local) and a private entity. Through this agreement, the skills and assets of each sector (public and private) are shared in delivering a service or facility for the use of the general public. In addition to the sharing of resources, each party shares in the risks and rewards potential in the delivery of the service and/or facility" (p. 1).
- U.K. Institute for Public Policy Research defines PPPs as:

> "a risk sharing relationship based upon an agreed aspiration between the public and private (including for-profit and not-for-profit) sectors to bring about a desired policy outcome. More often than not this takes the form of a long term flexible relationship, usually underpinned by contract, for the delivery of a publicly funded service" (cited in English and Skellern, 2005, p. 17).

The OECD and the World Bank definitions focus on *infrastructure* and reflect the origins of PPPs. The European Commission, the IMF, and the NCPPP definitions are broader in scope and include *services*. The definition supplied by the U.K. Institute for Public Policy Research is even more expansive stating that PPPs can be used to address any "desired policy outcome."

36.4 Common Characteristics of PPPs

Although obviously looking at the subject from different perspectives, the definitions highlighted in the previous section identify several characteristics that take PPPs out of the realm of traditional public procurement, competitive tendering, and government contracting: (1) sharing of skills and assets, (2) long-term flexible relations, (3) risk and reward sharing, and (4) joint decision making.

36.4.1 Sharing of Skills and Assets

Sharp (2005) states that the common thread in all PPPs is "... the public sector's efforts to take advantage of private-sector management skills, expertise, innovations, efficiencies ..." (p. 15). The sharing of skills and assets means that some form of joint decision making and dispute resolution, above and beyond that of traditional contracting relationships, is required.

36.4.2 Long-Term Relationships

PPPs frequently cover long time periods; partnership terms of 10, 20, or even 30 years are not unusual (e.g., Lawther, 2002; Quiggin, 2006). Some PPPs can have even longer time periods. Tollway PPPs in Australia routinely involve time periods in excess of 30 years (Forward, 2006, p. 267). Part of the rationale for the extended terms of PPPs is the need of private partners to recover and recapture their capital investments. The long-term nature of PPPs requires that they be flexible. It is doubtful that the PEST assumptions (e.g., political, economic, social, and technical) upon which any individual PPP is based will continue unchanged over a 10, 20, 30 year, or even longer time period. Thus, the idea of flexible PPPs flows logically from their long-term nature. The partners enter into PPPs with the understanding that the basic agreement will almost certainly need to change and evolve over time.

36.4.3 Risk and Reward Sharing

The entering into a PPP creates major risk exposure for both public and private partners. At least six major types of risk (see Table 36.1) can be identified: construction risk, financial risk, performance risk, demand risk, residual value risk, and political risk.

In managing the risk associated with PPPs, the general rule of thumb is that the risk should be assigned to the partner best positioned to manage it (Quiggin, 2006). Thus, a decision that confronts the public and private partners up front in the initial partnership understanding is which one will be assigned to manage each of the six types of risk. The political risk usually accrues to the public partner, while the financial risk is largely assigned to the private partner. The suggestion is made by some (e.g., Corner, 2005) that the financial risk should be largely born by the private partner as an incentive to hold costs down during implementation.

Table 36.1 Types of Risk in PPPs

Construction risk	Risk of poor partnership design, cost overruns, and late delivery of assets
Financial risk	Risk of partnership financing
Performance risk	Risk of poor performance on the part of either partner
Demand risk	Risk that the actual need for the service/assets will be less than the forecasted demand
Residual value risk	Risk that the residual value of partnership assets will be less than anticipated. This risk is particularly important when assets are to be transferred from the private to the public partner
Political risk	Risk that the partnership will not be brought to a successful conclusion leaving the public partner to deal with the negative political consequences

Sources: From European Parliament, *Public–Private Partnerships: Models and Trends in the European Union*, Brussels, Author, 2006; Lawther and Martin, 2005b, *J. Purchase Supply Manage.*, 11, 212); Lewis, M. (n.d.) *Risk Management in Public–Private Partnerships (monograph)*, University of South Australia; Hodge, G. and Greve, C., *The Challenge of Public–Private Partnerships: Learning from International Experience*, Edward Elgar, Cheltenham, U.K., 2005. With permission.

36.4.4 *Joint Decision Making*

Most government contracts are predicated on the existence of a buyer/seller relationship. As such, "principal/agent" theory and traditional legal and contracting principles are generally deemed to apply (Kettl, 2002). Under principal/agent theory, the government is the principal and the private sector contractor is the agent. It is the agent's duty to do the principal's bidding; the agent also has a fiduciary responsibility to make decisions which are in the best interest of the principal.

Because of the risks involved, the long-term nature of the relationships as well as the need to share skills and assets, it is questionable that principal/agent theory provides a satisfactory foundation for creating and managing PPPs (Klijn and Teisman, 2005). Instead, joint decision making is seen as a virtual necessity (Zarco-Jasso, 2005). It is hard to imagine a private sector organization that would be willing to commit its skills and assets to a long-term relationship with major attendant risk exposure without desiring, if not demanding, some role in partnership decision making.

36.5 Major Drivers of PPPs

The major drivers of PPPs are essentially twofold: (1) public infrastructure needs and (2) public budgetary constraints.

36.5.1 *Public Infrastructure Needs*

The most important driver of PPPs is the infrastructure needs of governments. Without this need, there would obviously be less interest worldwide in PPPs. Governments have significant amounts of aging infrastructure, much badly in need of repair and replacement; additionally governments have new unmet infrastructure needs. The use of PPPs, and in particular the private financing aspect, enables public infrastructure projects to be brought online much more expeditiously than via traditional public financing.

36.5.2 *Public Budgetary Constraints*

At the same time governments are facing increasing pressure to repair and replace old infrastructure as well as create new infrastructure, they also face budgetary constraints (Koppenjan, 2005). PPPs represent a method by which governments can address infrastructure needs while circumventing government laws and regulations concerning public borrowing (Commonwealth of Australia, Department of the Parliamentary Library, 2002. p. 8). The cost savings and cost deferrals to governments can be significant. For example, three recently completed road PPPs in Australia are estimated to be saving the government of New South Wales something on the order of $320 million in construction costs as well as $120 million annually in operating costs (Forward, 2006, p. 263). Without the use of PPPs, these Australian road projects would probably not have come online as rapidly as they did.

36.6 Types of PPPs

Just as there is no universally agreed upon definition, there is likewise no universally agreed upon taxonomy or classification system of PPPs. In general, PPPs are divided into two major classes: (1) infrastructure PPPs and (2) functional PPPs. Within these two broad classes, typologies and nomenclatures can vary significantly.

36.6.1 *Infrastructure PPPs*

Despite their differences, there is nevertheless considerable agreement among national and international organizations about the major types of infrastructure oriented PPPs (Evans and Bowman, 2005; Zarco-Jasso, 2005, European Parliament, 2006; World Bank, n.d.). What can be called a "meta-classification system" arranges infrastructure PPPs on a continuum based on the extent of private sector involvement and risk sharing (see Table 36.2). The continuum ranges from the relatively simple and less risky PPP where the private sector operates and maintains a public facility or asset (e.g., convention center, park, museum, etc.) to the complex and extremely risky build–own–operate (BOO) approach. Examples of the various types of PPPs are illustrated in the following sections.

36.6.1.1 Operations and Maintenance

Operations and maintenance (OM) PPPs involve the public partner retaining ownership and management of a facility or asset, while the private partner oversees the day-to-day OM. An example is provided by the OM PPP between the city of Washington, DC and the Lockheed Martin Corporation for parking meters. In 1996, more than half of the city's parking meters were out of service due to vandalism. The city's parking meter revenues had dropped from over $1 million per month to under $200,000 a month (DC Parking Meter Management, 1999). Under the OM PPPs that were created, Lockheed Martin agreed to repair, replace, and maintain the city's parking meters

Table 36.2 Taxonomy of Infrastructure PPPs

Infrastructure	*Approach*
Operations and maintenance	Private partner operates and maintains a public facility or asset; the public sector partner owns the facility or asset
Design–build	Private partner designs and builds a facility or asset; the public partner provides the funding, owns and operates the facility or asset
Design–build–operate	Private partner designs, builds, and operates a facility or asset; the public partner provides the funding and owns the facility or asset
Design–build–finance–operate	Private partner finances, designs, builds, owns, and operates (for a period of time, e.g., 30 years) a facility or asset; the public partner provides funding during the life of the facility or asset
Design–build–operate–transfer	Private partner designs, builds, and operates a facility or asset and transfers ownership to the public partner
Build–transfer–operate	Private partner builds a facility or asset and transfers title to the public partner. The public partner leases the facility or asset back to the private sector partner under a long-term lease
Build–own–operate–transfer	Private partner builds, owns, and operates a facility or asset for a period of time at which point ownership is transferred free of charge to the public partner
Build–own–operate	Private partner builds, owns, and operates a facility or asset in perpetuity and assumes all the risk that would have been born by the public partner (similar to privatization)

Sources: From European Parliament, *Public–Private Partnerships: Models and Trends in the European Union*, Author, Brussels, 2006; Zarco-Jasso, H., *Int. J. Public Policy*, 1(2), 22, 2005; Williams, T., Moving to Public–Private Partnerships: Lessons from Experience Around the World, IBM Center for the Business of Government, Washington, DC, 2003, http://www.businessofgovernment.org, January 15, 2007; United States General Accounting Office (GAO), *Public–Private Partnerships: Terms Related to Building and Facility Partnerships*, Author, Washington, DC, 1999. With permission.

as well as collect parking meter revenues. Lockheed Martin also agreed to provide the city with a guaranteed minimum revenue, keeping the excess as its share of partnerships income.

36.6.1.2 Design–Build

A design–build (DB) PPP is created when one private partner designs and constructs a project, which both saves time and reduces conflict between separate design and build contractors. The public partner provides for the operations of the facility, while maintaining ownership. An example is the

Hiawatha Light Rail project in Minnesota that connects downtown Minneapolis with the Minneapolis-St. Paul International Airport and the Mall of America. The Hiawatha Light Rail transit project accounts for 12 miles of track, 17 stations, and 26 light rail vehicles and cost a reported $674 million (Hiawatha Light Rail Transit, 2007). The private partner was Bombardier. The project opened in mid-2004 and has been operating since late 2004.

36.6.1.3 Design–Build–Operate

In a design–build–operate (DBO) PPP, the private partner designs, constructs, and operates the project. Having one private partner for all three phases expedites completion of the project because of cycle time reductions created by overlapping design and build phases. When the operations phase is added, there is a better possibility of private financing of the project, as they can see returns on their investments through user fees (Types of Public–Private Partnerships, 2007). A DBO PPP was utilized in Oak Ridge, Tennessee to dispose of radioactive waste.

In one DBO public–private partnership, the private partner (CDM, Inc., a private consulting firm) was tasked to design and build a facility to remove radioactive waste from underground tanks to safer aboveground tanks. "CDM configured, constructed, and operated a sluicing and pumping system to remove and transfer the waste from underground tanks to a newer, safer above ground storage facility for treatment and final disposition" (using Design–Build–Operate to Safely Remove Radioactive Waste for DOE, 2007). This DBO PPP earned the engineering excellence award from the Consulting Engineers Council of Metropolitan Washington as well as a national pollution prevention award from the U.S. Department of Energy.

36.6.1.4 Design–Build–Finance–Operate

In a design–build–finance–operate (DBFO) PPP, the private partner finances, designs, builds, and operates the facility or asset. Funding after construction is provided by the public partner and the facility or asset is eventually transferred to the public partner after some specified amount of time. An example of a DBFO PPP is provided by the Charles Jago Northern Sports Centre in Prince George, British Columbia, Canada.

The center is scheduled for completion by the end of 2007. The nearly $31 million facility will house a gym, a track, a field house, a weight room, as well as testing facilities. The Northern Sports Centre Consortium is the private partner and will operate the center for 25–30 years (PPP Project Tracker, 2007). The consortium provides everything necessary for creation of the center from financing to operation.

36.6.1.5 Design–Build–Operate–Transfer

Design–build–operate–transfer (DBOT) PPPs take place when the private partner handles the design, construction, and operation of a facility or asset. The ownership is transferred to the public partner when construction is complete. An example of DBOT PPPs is provided by the Makkah-Medina Rail Link (MMRL) in Saudi Arabia. The high speed rail link will connect Makkah and Medina. The contract for this DBOT PPP is expected to last between 30 and 50 years and is heavily focused on technology (Harmsen, 2006).

36.6.1.6 Build–Transfer–Operate

A build–transfer–operate (BTO) PPP involves a private partner building a facility or asset and then transferring ownership to the public partner. After transfer, the public partner leases the facility or asset back to the private partner. The Incheon Railway Express (IREX) in South Korea is an example of a BTO PPP. The private partner is Bechtel Corporation.

The IREX is a 61 km double track rail line scheduled for completion in 2009 at a cost of $4 billion (IREX [Incheon Railway Express], 2007). BTO PPPs have proven quite successful in the area of transportation infrastructure.

36.6.1.7 Build–Own–Operate–Transfer

A build–own–operate–transfer (BOOT) PPP is one in which a private partner builds, owns, and operates a facility or asset for a specified amount of time. The length of time involved in the concession is related to the need of the private partner to recapture its investment. At the end of the concession, the private partner transfers ownership of the facility or asset to the public partner at no cost. At the expiration of the concession, the public partner, at its discretion, can elect to operate the facility or asset itself, extend the concession with the original private partner, or select a new private sector partner. BOOT PPPs have been used successfully utilized in many countries. The Azito Power Project in Cote d'Ivoire, Africa, is one example.

The Azito Power Project PPP in Côte d'Ivoire is a 24 year BOOT. The private partner is Cinergy. The private partner built the $223 million facility with guaranteed financing from the International Development Association (IDA). Cinergy will operate the facility under a franchise agreement for a period of 24 years (Sub-Saharan Africa Benefits from the First IDA Guarantee for Azito, 1999).

36.6.1.8 Build–Own–Operate

In a BOO PPP, a private partner does exactly that. The private partner builds and operates a facility or asset, but does not transfer ownership to the public partner (United States General Accounting Office [GAO], 1999, p. 3). This type of PPP does not require a purchase by the public partner and thus it might qualify for tax exempt status if all requirements are fulfilled. This type of PPP is based on the private partner assuming all of the project risk. An example of a BOO PPP is the West Bangkok Project in Thailand.

The West Bangkok Project supplies drinking water to nearly 400,000 people (Thames Water—Bulk Water Supply—Bangkok). The project began when the Provincial Waterworks Authority of Thailand entered into a BOO PPP with the Thai Tap Water Supply Company which was formed to undertake and finance the project at a cost of $250 million. "The new treatment plant provides high-quality drinking water from the river source. It supports future domestic and commercial expansion in a significant growth area of Bangkok, raising health standards and economic prosperity in the area" (Thames Water—Bulk Water Supply—Bangkok).

36.6.1.9 Cross-National Overview of Infrastructure PPPs

A number of national and international organizations collect and report data and information on infrastructure PPPs. As Table 36.3 illustrates, PPPs are most frequently used for roads, bridges, tunnels, rail (both heavy and light), and water and wastewater. The other infrastructure areas show a more mixed pattern of use worldwide.

The United Kingdom makes significant use of PPPs in each of the identified infrastructure areas, with the exception of schools. The United Kingdom has perhaps the most highly developed PPP program of any country owing to its Private Finance Initiative created in 1992 (IMF, 2004).

Table 36.3 Infrastructure PPPs in Selected Countries

	Roads, Bridges, Tunnels	*Rail*	*Schools*	*Airports*	*Housing*	*Seaports*	*Prisons*	*Water and Wastewater*
Australia	X	X	X				X	X
Canada	X	X	X	X	X	X		X
Chile	X			X			X	
Cyprus				X				
Czech Republic								X
France	X	X						X
Germany	X	X	X	X				X
Greece	X			X				
Hungary	X							X
Hong Kong	X							
Ireland	X				X			
Italy	X	X						
Malta								
Netherlands	X	X	X					X
Poland								
Portugal	X	X						X

(continued)

Table 36.3 (continued) Infrastructure PPPs in Selected Countries

	Roads, Bridges, Tunnels	*Rail*	*Schools*	*Airports*	*Housing*	*Seaports*	*Prisons*	*Water and Wastewater*
Slovenia								X
Spain	X	X				X		X
Sweden								
United Kingdom	X	X	X	X	X	X	X	X
United States	X	X		X	X		X	X

Sources: From Blondal, J., *International Experience Using Outsourcing, Public–Private Partnerships, and Vouchers*, The IBM Center for the Business of Government, Washington, DC, 2005, http://www.businessofgovernment.org, January 27, 2007; Canadian Council for Public–Private Partnerships (CCPPP). (n.d.) *Canadian PPP Project Directory*, Author, Ottawa; International Monetary Fund (IMF), *Public–Private Partnerships*, Author, Washington, DC, 2002; Commonwealth of Australia, Department of the Parliamentary Library, *Public–Private Partnerships: An Introduction*, Author, Canberra, 2002; Williams, T., Moving to Public–Private Partnerships: Lessons from Experience Around the World, IBM Center for the Business of Government, Washington, DC, 2003, http://www.businessofgovernment.org, January 15, 2007; Koppenjan, J., *Public Adm.*, 83(1), 135, 2005; Boardmann, A., Poschmann, F., and Vining, A., *The Challenge of Public–Private Partnerships: Learning from International Experience*, Eds. G. Hodge and C. Greve, Edward Elgar, Cheltenham, U.K., 2005. With permission.

Note: This table is meant to be representative, not exhaustive. Many other types of PPPs are not shown (e.g., hospitals, healthcare, justice, recreation and culture, landfill, recycling, energy, and others). It should be noted that PPPs are created by both national and subnational governments.

PPPs in the United Kingdom today are estimated to account for some 14 percent of all public investment in infrastructure (IMF, 2002, p. 5). Canada, the United States, and to a lesser extent Australia also use PPPs in several infrastructure areas. Much of the PPP involvement in Canada and the United States is accomplished by subnational governments (Williams, 2003; Greenblatt, 2006). An example at the subnational level is provided by the Canadian province of Nova Scotia which used PPPs to construct some 41 public schools (Williams, 2003, p. 22).

The remaining countries identified in Table 36.3 appear to make more focused use of PPPs concentrating on one or a few functional areas. The patterns in Table 36.3 reinforce the notion that the use of PPP varies significantly from country to country.

36.6.2 Functional PPPs

Quantitative data on functional PPPs is difficult, if not impossible to collect, particularly on a cross-national basis. Nevertheless, some discussion of functional PPPs is necessary to present a complete picture of PPPs. In this section, functional PPPs are discussed using a case example approach. The functional areas reviewed include (1) health and human services, (2) conservancy management, (3) neighborhood revitalization and growth, and (4) recreation and culture.

36.6.2.1 Health and Human Services

In order for there to be a PPP in health and human services, the relationship must go beyond a simple collaborative relationship and the private entity must be willing to assume some of the risk, just as discussed above in regard to the definition of PPPs. Becker and Patterson believe that there are some common errors that occur when referring to health and human services. "The most common errors include (a) confusing traditional methods of privatization (primarily contracting) with establishing a partnership and (b) confusing collaboration with establishing a partnership" (Becker and Patterson, 2005, p. 132). Becker and Patterson also assert that government financial returns are low, so participation on its part is based on an increased level of service.

An interesting example of PPP can be seen in the United Kingdom. The U.K. Department of Health and the Independent Healthcare Association developed a PPP, which was at first controversial, but it has become clear that they have become one functioning entity (Agnew, 2005). At a conference, England's chief nursing officer posited, "there is now no place for the old 'I am the NHS—you are the independent sector' divide. 'It is about how we work together to provide the best service for patients.'" (Agnew, 2005, p. 14). This is precisely why the partnership was made. However, there is some resistance because of the fear of an overthrow by the private sector.

36.6.2.2 Conservancy Management

Becker and Patterson believe that PPPs play a role in conservancy management to "manage and conserve public lands and preserve and restore historic buildings" (Becker and Patterson, 2005, p. 133). They explain that in order for this to be a PPP, there is typically publicly owned land in which a private organization is usually charged with managing. This can be seen in many instances, such as nature conservation, where financial returns for both sides are generally very low. They also explain that it will be many years before we can see the impact that these PPPs have had on conservation, as many were started in the 1990s.

In 2004, the Conservation Fund, the Nature Conservancy, other conservation groups and the state of California developed a PPP that would preserve 24,000 acres of land.

> "This project is creating a model for landscape-scale forestland conservation across the northwest," said the Conservation Fund's president, Larry Selzer. "By balancing economic and environmental objectives, we are pioneering a unique brand of conservation that combats land fragmentation, preserves wildlife habitat and ensures the long-term restoration and management of these forests for future generations." (Thompson, 2004, p. #)

The Conservation Fund worked with its partners and governmental agencies to raise over $30 million to purchase the land. Working together, they also plan to develop a management strategy to protect the land and develop forestry practices that will last. Partnerships such as this have been successful around the world and it is only made possible through well-functioning PPP.

36.6.2.3 Neighborhood Revitalization and Growth

One of the more traditional areas of PPPs has been in housing and development. Typically, these are in lower-income neighborhoods and are "often justified in terms of economic development, but the programs' real purpose is the revitalization of neighborhoods to better social welfare or to mitigate for the past societal failures, such as racism" (Becker and Patterson, 2005, p. 134). A major difference that can be seen in PPPs in neighborhood revitalization is that what might be an economic failure, might be a social success.

With regards to economic development, many local governments are realizing that PPPs are an integral part of growth strategy. The problem with PPPs in regional economic development is that there is both high risk and high rewards, which can cause greater tension in the relationship. This should be worked around, however, and "the public partner should normally assume the role of a 'limited partner' by providing land, funds, legitimacy, or monopoly rights, whereas the private partner should be the 'general partner' in providing access to private investment and managerial expertise" (Becker and Patterson, 2005, p. 137).

"Downtown revitalization," according to Leinberger (2005), "requires a high degree of cooperation and is best achieved when a unique 'private/public' process is used" (p. 8). Although the local government might be the instigators of a revitalization project, the importance of private sector involvement is crucial. The private sector typically has the money and the time to make this a successful process (Leinberger, 2005, p. 8).

Leinberger states that it is very important for local politicians not to become involved and promote their own political worth. Politicians often have an agenda and the success or failure of any revitalization project can affect those involved. On the other hand, the public partner must be willing to do what it takes to promote success. This may be necessary in everything from parking and transportation to the changing of zoning laws to promote business development.

A great example of successful PPP in downtown revitalization can be seen in Franklin, Tennessee. After receiving designation as a National Main Street Town from the National Main Street Center, the city successfully revitalized its downtown and expanded economic growth. "Government officials have crafted plans that work together to preserve and enhance the city's downtown area, while establishing public–private partnerships with nonprofit groups and local residents" (O'Connell, 2005, p. 43). Franklin's growth and development is a real indicator of how successful PPPs can be. What was once becoming a suburb of Nashville, has now established itself as a unique town with character and economic prosperity.

36.6.2.4 Recreation and Culture

Sports facilities, art centers, and parks are all examples of PPPs. Normally, these pose little risk for either the private or public partner (Becker and Patterson, 2005, p. 139). Operations can be much the same as the above, but in regard to community recreation facilities, many are operated by public employees. Art centers and sports facilities are often a major source of conflict. Substantial capital, often tax dollars, is required to build these and that is a questionable move in some public opinion.

According to Herrick, "without the partnerships between public entities and the private sector, many of these sports facilities wouldn't exist" (Herrick, 2003). The author explains that many new facilities are being built and managed by PPP. An example given is the American Airlines center in Dallas, Texas. With a new arena coming to town and the Reunion Arena still being used, the developers and owners of the Dallas Mavericks and Stars formed the Arena Group. The city would have been unable to hire the staffing needed to keep both of these venues open, but due to partnerships, they were able to maximize their revenue.

After success with private management, the reunion is under public management. There were rumors of demolishing the arena, but the city has high hopes of making it an adjunct of the Dallas Convention Center (Herrick, 2003). With the partnerships between the city and private sectors, the reunion seems to have a future in Dallas. The partnerships and revenue created by both the American Airlines center and the Reunion Arena have given a great boost to the city economically and culturally.

36.7 Financing of PPPs

There are essentially two major types of financing utilized in most PPPs: (1) private sector financing and (2) user charges.

36.7.1 Private Sector Financing

Financing is crucial to any PPP and most commentators on PPPs suggest that the private partner should provide most if not all of the partnerships financing (Williams, 2003; Blondal, 2005). Private sector financing generally takes one or two forms: the creation of the so-called "special purpose vehicles" (SPVs) for a specific PPP, or institutions created by governments for the purposes of infrastructure development in general.

SPVs are typically formed by a group of banks or other financial institutions to coordinate capital and expertise for a specific PPP. *Infrastructure SpA* in Italy and the National Development Finance Agency in Ireland are examples of SPVs created by governments to finance PPPs (IMF, 2002, p. 9).

36.7.2 User Charges

User charges are tolls and other fees paid by those individuals who utilize facilities and assets involved in a PPP. Examples of user charges include road, bridge, and tunnel tolls as well as admission charges to museums, parks, and other public venues. There is a belief in at least some circles that private sector organizations have more latitude in increasing user charges than do governments.

In the best-case scenario, the utilization of user charges can make a facility or asset self-supporting. An example of the impact of user charges is provided by a road infrastructure PPP in France. As a result of the PPP and user charges, the French government's contributions to the national road system dropped from 56 to 22 percent while tolls increased from 32 to 56 percent (Williams, 2003, p. 20).

36.8 Characteristics of Successful PPPs

The U.S.-based NCPPP identifies six characteristics of successful PPP (http://www.ncppp.org.): (1) political leadership, (2) public sector involvement which we will term "partner accountability," (3) a well-thought-out plan, (4) a dedicated income stream, (5) communication with stakeholders, and (6) selecting the right partner.

36.8.1 Political Leadership

The use of political leadership in the development of a PPP is very important. Not only should political leaders be able to play a role in the development of the partnership through planning and any sort of statutory development, but they should also be advocates of the plan to the general public. By their participation and assurances to the public, it will make it much more likely that the citizens will support the partnership and its goals.

36.8.2 Partner Accountability

In the initial plan or contract, it should be stated what the involvement of the public agency will be. To reduce waste and provide results in a timely manner, the sort of accountability and monitoring standards that will be enacted to facilitate timely progress should be written into plans and contracts. Specificity of terms is extremely important and whether this monitoring is done on a daily, weekly, monthly, or quarterly basis (How Partnerships Work, 2006) should be noted as such. Even though the public agency and private entity enter into a partnership, it is still imperative that accountability and standards be in place, to facilitate a mutually beneficial relationship.

36.8.3 Well-Thought-Out Plan

Like anything in life, PPPs require a great deal of planning and development. Rushing into a partnership, without the right type of expertise and planning, could prove to be fatal for any blossoming partnership. Involvement by someone experienced in the field would be greatly beneficial for the plan. The plan itself should be incredibly detailed and indicate the specific responsibilities of individual partners and also lay out a clear method of conflict resolution, should one arise. As in any relationship, there is always a real possibility of disagreements between two parties and to avoid them or at least facilitate a quick resolution, every measure should be accounted for in a detailed plan.

36.8.4 Dedicated Income Stream

One of the most important factors in a partnership would be the repayment of loans or investments that were provided by the private partner. There are many options that can facilitate this revenue stream, but fees, taxes, and tolls are a few good examples of how this can be done. As with everything included in a partnership, this should be addressed in the contract, to ensure a consistent payment method for the life of the partnership. Because benefits and rewards are shared, it is important to ensure that financial obligations are taken into consideration during the planning phase of the partnership.

36.8.5 Communication with Stakeholders

Public perception, on all levels, is a very important consideration for any partnership. To build support for a partnership, it is important to inform community leaders and the general public of the partnership's intentions. Without the support of the public, a partnership is sure to run into many obstacles. Being open and creating an effective communication and marketing campaign is a key component to developing a partnership. Without the understanding of all of the stakeholders, a partnership will be in real danger of failure.

36.8.6 Selecting the Right Partner

Selection of the correct partner in a PPP should be one of the foremost considerations of the public agency. Although government is always looking for ways to cut costs, it should not be the only consideration in the selection of a partner. It is incredibly important to establish a relationship in which the private partner is experienced and trustworthy in the field of the partnership. This will allow the public agency to find a partner with the "best value" (How Partnerships Work, 2006), providing a high level of partnership for a cost that is justifiable.

These six drivers provide a very thorough guide to the development of a successful PPP. None of these six are necessarily more important than the other, but they will of course vary from partnership to partnership, as there is no cookie cutter or formulated way to develop a successful PPP.

36.9 Evaluating PPPs

In terms of an overall evaluation of PPPs, Hodge (2006) states that the "... performance of this governance tool is mixed" (p. 43). For example, the U.K. National Audit Office study of a sample of ten PPPs created under the Public Finance Initiative reported that the best deal was, ... "probably obtained in every case and good VFM (**V**alue **F**or **M**oney) was achieved in eight of ten cases" (cited in Hodge, 2006, p. 44). Another review of experiences in the United Kingdom (Shaoul, 2005) found a number of failed major PPPs as well as what she describes as a biased VFM methodology and a general lack of reliable data on which to make evaluative judgments (pp. 198–203).

In terms of increasing the funding available for public infrastructure, studies also present a mixed picture. For example, Quiggin (2006) comments that the notion that PPPs increase the amount of funding available for infrastructure has been "... refuted by economic analysis and disclaimed by government officials..." (p. 25).

The major lesson here may well be that there is no worldwide success/failure pattern to PPPs. The success or failure of an individual PPP may well be related to its nature (infrastructure/functional), its financing (private sector/user charges), it country of origin, the allocation of risk between the public and private partners, and other factors.

36.10 Challenges of PPPs for Public Procurement

PPPs present several challenges for public procurement including (1) the challenge of selecting the right type of solicitation and contract, (2) the challenge of dealing with risk and complexity, (3) the challenge of building and maintaining trust, and (4) the challenge of long-term contracts.

36.10.1 Challenge of Selecting the Right Type of Solicitation and Contract

Denhardt (2003, p. 6) describes the brave new world of PPPs as involving nonroutine contracts that start with many more unknowns and take unexpected turns during implementation. Increasingly, governments are coming to the realization that traditional procurement and contracting relationships are insufficiently flexible and can actually constitute an impediment in attracting private sector partners and creating PPPs.

A major government commenter on the European Commission's *Green Paper* on PPPs, suggested that procurement and contracting rules and regulations actually restrict the use of PPPs. The government commenter singled out for specific mention restrictions on the use of negotiation in lieu of competitive tendering (EU, 2005, p. 34).

Lawther (2002, p. 7) suggests that there are more and less appropriate contract types depending upon the level of complexity. For low complexity contracts, he suggests that traditional bidding is appropriate. For moderately complex situations, he suggests multistep procurement. However, for highly complex contracts like PPPs he suggests using "negotiated procurements" which correspond most closely to "requests for proposals" (RFPs) and "invitations to negotiate" (INTs).

The European Parliament (2006) suggests that, while still striving for a transparent and competitive procurement, when the quality of the service and even perhaps the very scope of the partnerships itself cannot be determined ex ante, a form of "competitive dialogue" may be the solution.

To facilitate the creation of PPPs, governments in Australia have moved to an alternative contracting model called "alliance or relationship contracting." Characteristics of alliance contracting include a commitment to resolve issues without resort to litigation; open and transparent transactions, books, and record; and shared decision making through leadership teams comprised of all partners based on consensus (Forward, 2006).

The U.S. federal government has gone so far as to create a new type of contractual arrangement that is calls a *cooperative agreement* to deal specifically with PPPs.*

36.10.2 Challenge of Dealing with Risk and Complexity

Complexity creates and vice versa. Because PPPs are more complex than traditional forms of government contracting, risk assessment is more difficult. Conversely, the difficulty of risk determination and management in PPPs makes them more complex.

How then can or should governments conduct risk assessments? The answer, according to Lawther and Martin (2005b, p. 215), is to combine:

* See the Federal Grant and Cooperative Agreement Act.

> … traditional risk assessment and risk management methods… with a new found appreciation for 'trust' as a moderating variable. *Can the partners trust each other to do the right thing and to act in the best interests of the partnership?*

Yet another risk and complexity challenge is determining how much risk can, and should be, transferred to the private sector partner (Corner, 2005). The corollary here is what type of compensation and incentives are necessary to induce the private partner to agree to this risk transfer.

The complexity of PPPs also makes them more risky in political terms. Elected officials, citizens, and other stakeholders are generally familiar with contracting, but not with PPPs (Hodge, 2006). In an era of governmental reform that prides itself on "transparency," the education of stakeholders about what PPPs are and are not is an important task.

36.10.3 Challenge of Building and Maintaining Trust

According to Lewis (n.d., p. 2), although a PPP "provides the basic architecture of the arrangement" it cannot cover all contingencies that may arise over the life of the partnership. A PPP is a high trust relationship.

Because of the risks inherent in PPPs, trust and trust assessment becomes an important consideration. How much trust can the public partner place in the private partner "to do the right thing" and vice versa.

36.10.4 Challenge of Dealing with Long-Term Contracts

As Kelman (1990) points out, short-term contractual relationships are a part of the government procurement and contracting culture. Managing long-term PPPs present unique challenges. For example, almost all Private Finance Initiatives in the U.K. have undergone contractual changes since first being implemented (Hodge and Greve, 2005). If a PPP goes wrong, the private partner can walk away from the project; for a variety of reasons including both economic and political, the public partner does not have the same luxury (Quiggin, 2006).

An additional consideration is who will be around in 20 years (the theoretical average life span of a PPP) who is familiar with the original goals and understandings of a PPP and can thus make informed decisions about changes and alternations? Some 15 years into a PPP and several years after one of the authors of this chapter had left his position with a government agency, he was contacted and asked specific questions about the original agreement. Apparently no one was still working for the government who had any knowledge about the PPP and much of the original documentation could not be located.

References

Agnew, T. 2005. Has the wall come down for ever? National Health Services, *Royal College of Nurses* 19 (46): 14(3).

Becker, F. and Patterson, V. 2005. Public–private partnerships: Balancing financial returns, risks and roles of the partners. *Public Performance & Management Review* 29(2): 125–144.

Blondal, J. 2005. *International Experience Using Outsourcing, Public–Private Partnerships, and Vouchers.* Washington, DC: The IBM Center for the Business of Government. http://www.businessofgovernment.org (01/27/07).

Boardmann, A., Poschmann, F., and Vining, A. 2005. North American infrastructure P3s: Examples and lessons learned. In *The Challenge of Public–Private Partnerships: Learning from International Experience.* Eds. G. Hodge and C. Greve, Cheltenham, U.K.: Edward Elgar, pp. 162–189.

Canadian Council for Public–Private Partnerships (CCPPP) (n.d.) *Canadian PPP Project Directory.* Ottawa: Author.

Center for Public Private Partnerships (n.d.) *How Partnerships Work.* Washington, DC: Author. http://www.ncppp.org/howpart/index.html#define (9/13/07).

Commonwealth of Australia, Department of the Parliamentary Library. 2002. *Public–Private Partnerships: An Introduction.* Canberra: Author.

Corner, D. 2005. The United Kingdom private finance initiative: The challenge of allocating risk. In *The Challenge of Public–Private Partnerships: Learning from International Experience.* Eds. G. Hodge and C. Greve, London: Edward Elgar, pp. 44–60.

Denhardt, K. 2003. *The Procurement Partnerships Model: Moving to a Team-Based Approach.* Arlington, VA: The IBM Center for the Business of Government.

DC Parking Meter Management. 1999. *Case Studies.* Retrieved February 1, 2007, from http://www.ncppp.org/cases/parking.shtml.

English, L. and Skellern, M. 2005. Editorial. *International Journal of Public Policy* (1/2): 1–21.

European Commission. 2005. *Report on the Public Consultation on the Green Paper on Public–Private Partnerships & Community Law on Public Contracts & Concessions.* Brussels: Author.

European Parliament. 2006. *Public–Private Partnerships: Models and Trends in the European Union.* Brussels: Author.

Evans, J. and Bowman, D. 2005. Getting the contract right. In *The Challenge of Public–Private Partnerships: Learning from International Experience.* Eds. G. Hodge and C. Greve. London: Edward Elgar, pp. 62–80.

Forward, P. 2006. Public–private partnership or conflict: Is it time for a new approach? *University of New South Wales Law Journal* 12 (2): 43–48.

Greenblatt, A. 2006. The sale goes on. *Governing* (February): 15–16.

Harmsen, N. 2006. Saudi Arabia is heading for the future: The Kingdom experiences boom in the construction sector. *WirtschaftsForum Nah-und Mittelost*, September/October, 11.

Herrick, J. 2003. Public assembly facilities benefit from unique public–private partnership. *Facility Manager*: 7.

Hiawatha Light Rail Transit. 2007. *PPP Case Studies.* Retrieved February 1, 2007, from http://www.fhwa.dot.gov/ppp/hiawatha.htm.

Hodge, G. 2006. Public private partnerships and legitimacy. *University of New South Wales Law Journal* 12 (2): 43–48.

Hodge, G. and Greve, C. 2005. *The Challenge of Public–Private Partnerships: Learning from International Experience.* Cheltenham, U.K.: Edward Elgar.

Hollinger, P. 2005. French bank launches public–private partnership fund. *Financial Times* (Thursday) December 1, p. 6.

How Partnerships Work 2006. [Website] [cited September 13, 2006]. Available from http://www.ncppp.org/howpart/index.html#define.

International Monetary Fund (IMF). 2002. *Public–Private Partnerships.* Washington, DC: Author.

IREX (Incheon Railway Express). 2007. Retrieved February 1, 2007, from http://www.sampyoenc.com/english/business/construction_02.asp.

Kelman, S. 1990. *Procurement & Public Management.* Washington, DC: The AEI Press.

Kettl, D. 1993. *Sharing Power. Public Governance and Private Markets.* Washington, DC: The Brookings Institution.

Kettl, D. 2002. Managing indirect government. In *The Tools of Government: A Guide to the New Governance.* Ed. L. Salamon. New York: Oxford University Press, pp. 490–510.

Klijn, E. and Teisman, G. 2005. Public–private partnerships as the management of co-production: Strategic and institutional obstacles in a difficult marriage. In *The Challenge of Public–Private Partnerships: Learning from International Experience*. Eds. G. Hodge and C. Greve, Cheltenham, U.K.: Edward Elgar, pp. 95–116.

Koppenjan, J. 2005. The formation of public–private partnerships: Lessons from nine transportation infrastructure projects in the Netherlands. *Public Administration* 83 (1): 135–157.

Lawther, W. 2002. *Contracting for the 21st Century*. Arlington, VA: The IBM Center for the Business of Government.

Lawther, W. and Martin, L.L. 2005a. Public–private partnerships: Innovation in public procurement. *International Government Contractor*. (2/3): 7–13.

Lawther, W. and Martin, L.L. 2005b. Innovative practices in public procurement partnerships: The case of the United States. *Journal of Purchasing & Supply Management* (11): 212–220.

Leinberger, C. 2005. *Turning Around Downtown: Twelve Steps to Revitalization* (*Research Brief*). Washington, D.C: Brookings Institution.

Lewis, M. (n.d.) *Risk Management in Public–Private Partnerships (monograph)*. University of South Australia.

National Council on Public Private Partnerships (NCPPPs) (n.d.) Public–Private Partnerships Defined. http://www.ncppp.org/howpart/index.shtml (02/06/07).

O'Connell, K.A. 2005. Core values. *American City and County*, 42–46.

Osborne, D. and Gaebler, T. 1992. *Reinventing Government*. Reading: Addison-Wesley.

PPP Project Tracker. 2007. Retrieved February 1, 2007, from http://www.pppcouncil.ca/pdf/tracker.pdf.

Quiggin, J. 2006. Public private partnerships: Options for improved risk allocation. *University of New South Wales Law Review* 29 (3): 25–27.

Rhodes, R. 1996. The new governance: Governing without government. *Policy Studies* (44): 652–667.

Salamon, L. 2002. *The Tools of Government: A Guide to the New Governance*. New York: Oxford University Press.

Schested, K. 2003. Cross sector partnerships as a new form of governance. In *Local Partnerships in Europe: An Action Research Project*. Ed. J. Kjaer. Copenhagen: The Copenhagen Center. http://www.copenhagencentre.org/sw204.asp (02/29/05).

Shaoul, K. 2005. The private finance initiative or the public funding of private profit? In *The Challenge of Public–Private Partnerships: Learning from International Experience*. Eds. G. Hodge and C. Greve. Cheltenham, U.K.: Edward Elgar, pp. 190–206.

Sharp, K. 2005. Public–private partnerships: Evolutions in the U.S. public procurement system and lessons learned from the UK and the EU. *International Government Contractor* 2 (3): 1–7.

Sub-Saharan Africa Benefits from the first IDA Guarantee for Azito. 1999. *Project Finance and Guarantees*. Retrieved February 1, 2007, from http://pages.stern.nyu.edu/~igiddy/cases/azito.pdf.

The Economist. 2007. Locking in the best price. January 27, pp. 60–61.

Thames Water—Bulk Water Supply—Bangkok. From http://www.ukwater.biz/content.aspx?TYPE=0&PID=6.

Thompson, J. 2004. Public Private Partnership Creates Model to Balance Nature Preserves and Sustainable Forestry: Groups Work to Create California's First Large-Scale Nonprofit-Owned Working Forest. *The Conservation Fund*.

Types of Public–Private Partnerships. 2007. *How Partnerships Work*. Retrieved January 20, 2007, from http://www.ncppp.org/howpart/ppptypes.shtml.

United States General Accounting Office (GAO). 1999. *Public–Private Partnerships: Terms Related to Building and Facility Partnerships*. Washington, DC: Author.

Using Design–Build–Operate to Safely Remove Radioactive Waste for DOE. 2007. *Case Studies*. Retrieved February 1, 2007, from http://www.cdm.com/knowledge_center/case_studies/oak_ridge_dbo_radioactive_waste_removal.htm.

Wettenhall, R. 2005. The public–private interface: Surveying the history. In *The Challenge of Public–Private Partnerships: Learning from International Experience.* Eds. G. Hodge and C. Greve. Cheltenham, U.K.: Edward Elgar, pp. 22–43.

Williams, T. 2003. Moving to Public–Private Partnerships: Lessons from Experience Around the World. Washington, DC: IBM Center for the Business of Government. http://www.businessofgovernment.org, January 15, 2007.

World Bank (n.d.) Private Participation in Infrastructure Database. http://ppi.worldbank.org/resources/ppi_glosasry.aspx, February 5, 2007.

Zarco-Jasso, H. 2005. Public–private partnerships: A multidimensional model for contracting. *International Journal of Public Policy* 1 (2): 22–40.

Chapter 37

Market's Response to Contract Award Announcements: Government versus Corporate Contracts

Stephen J. Larson and Armand Picou

CONTENTS

37.1 Introduction

The release of new information pursuant to a firm's prospects can result in a positive, negative, or immaterial reaction from the market. This study examines abnormal returns surrounding contract award announcements for successful grantees. Specifically, the reaction of stock prices in response to the announcement of contract awards is examined to determine if contract awards meet the criteria of the positive net present value (NPV) hypothesis or the fair contract hypothesis. Herein, the term "grantor" refers to a corporation or government body that grants a contract, and "grantee" refers to publicly traded corporations winning a contract.

Diltz (1990) studied the effect of government contract awards on the stock returns of successful grantees. He found some evidence that these contract awards were associated with positive abnormal returns. However, Diltz did not include contracts awarded by corporations in his sample. Therefore, he was unable to compare government contract awards to contracts awarded by corporations. The first contribution of this study is to make this comparison.

The second contribution of this study is the examination of government grantor subgroups. In a step beyond Diltz (1990), the sample of government contract awards is partitioned into four subsamples: federal government (nonmilitary), military, municipal, and foreign.

Although never before studied, some anecdotal claims even suggest contracts granted by foreign governments are more lucrative than contracts granted by other types of government or corporations. This is due in part to the complexity of cross-border contracts implying increased uncertainty and the assumed expediency of management's overpricing to cover the increased risks. For some discussion of perceptions of greater risk and management effort aversion, see Chaney (1989) and Woods and Randall (1989).

37.2 Research Hypotheses

Contract awards can be considered projects deemed acceptable by the management. The firm has agreed to perform actions in the future in exchange for a specified amount of revenue. Firms can obtain the required investment funds to fulfill contractual obligations by generating cash flow internally, by issuing debt, or by issuing new stock. The weighted average cost of these sources of capital is adjusted to reflect the specific risk characteristics of the contract. The result is the appropriate hurdle rate for the contract. For recent discussions of corporate cost of capital, see Fama and French (1999).

In this study, the objectives are to measure the market's response to contract award announcements, and to determine if government contract awards are perceived to be more lucrative than contract awards granted by corporations. The following equation is used to calculate the NPV of a project:

$$\text{NPV} = \sum_{t=1}^{N} \frac{\text{NCF}_t}{(1+\text{hr})^t} - I_0 \tag{37.1}$$

where

NCF is the net cash flow in time period t

N is the number of years of the contract's life

hr is the hurdle rate, which depends on the firm's weighted average cost of capital and the contract's specific risk characteristics

I_0 is the initial outlay of funds associated with performing the contract

A contract award will be associated with a positive NPV if the present value of its expected net cash inflows exceeds the initial outlay of funds. In this case, the contract's revenue exceeds the amount required to pay all expected expenses, including financing costs. The extra remuneration accrues to the firm's stockholders so the announcement of such a contract should be associated with an increase in stock price. The positive NPV hypothesis is stated formally below:

Positive NPV hypothesis: Contract award announcements will be followed by substantial increases in stock prices.

A fair contract is one where the revenue from the contract sufficiently covers all expected expenses, including the cost of financing. Such contracts generate just enough cash flow to cover all operating costs, and appropriately compensate security holders for the use of their funds. The announcement of these contracts should not be associated with increases in stock prices. The fair contract hypothesis, which is stated formally below, cannot be rejected if the positive NPV hypothesis is rejected.

Fair contract hypothesis: Contract award announcements will not be followed by substantial increases in stock prices.

A positive NPV contract indicates the grantor has agreed to pay more for the work performed than necessary to compensate the grantee for its costs, including paying a fair return to its security holders. It suggests the grantor possesses an agency problem as the agents agree to pay more than a fair price for products or services. If the grantor is another corporation, the agency problem exists between its management and its stockholders where the managers are the agents. If the grantor is a government body, the agency problem exists between public officials and constituents where the public officials are the agents.

It seems reasonable to assume that corporations are subject to more financial scrutiny than governments. Therefore, contracts granted by government bodies may be more lucrative than contracts granted by other corporations. Corporations must report financial dealings to stockholders who scrutinize the data. Moreover, many shares are typically owned by financial institutions, which are managed by professionals who closely monitor management decisions. In contrast, government bodies are not typically subject to this same level of financial scrutiny. In light of this argument, it is expected that contracts granted by governments will be more lucrative. The government contract hypothesis is stated formally below:

Government contract hypothesis: Contract award announcements will be associated with significantly higher increases in stock prices when the grantor is a government body.

37.2.1 Cross-Sectional Analysis

A cross-sectional analysis is conducted to test the government contract hypothesis while controlling for potentially confounding factors. The factors that could affect the market's response at the time the contract awards are announced are identified in Table 37.1 along with the hypothesized effect on the abnormal returns.

Contract award announcements include the revenue paid by the grantor, and the number of years over which the revenue will be paid out. A relatively large contract should produce more cash flow for stockholders so larger contracts should be associated with larger abnormal returns. Contracts that pay revenue over longer periods of time should be less lucrative because of the time value of money. Total assets pertain to the grantee. A certain contract award should have less impact on the stock price of a relatively large firm.

Table 37.1 Factors Affecting the Market's Response

Factor	*Description*	*Hypothesized Effect on the Abnormal Returns*
Contract size	Revenue specified in the contract	Positive
Years	Number of years over which the revenue is paid	Negative
Total assets	Grantee's total assets before contract award	Negative

37.3 Research Design

Contract award announcements are identified using Lexis/Nexis. The grantees trade on the New York Stock Exchange, the American Stock Exchange, or the NASDAQ. Three hundred and twenty-nine contract awards meet these requirements. Historical returns data is obtained from Dial Data's historical stock prices and the *Wall Street Journal.*

Following Mikkelson and Parch (1988), an event study method is used to measure the market's response to the contract award announcements. For each contract award, stock returns are calculated for the pre-event estimation period (day −240 to day −41), the examination period (day −3 to day +5), and the post-event estimation period (day +41 to day +240). Abnormal returns during the examination period are estimated using the following model:

$$\mathrm{AR}_{it} = R_{it} - (\alpha_i + \beta_i \times R_{\mathrm{m}t}) \tag{37.2}$$

where
R_{it} is the return of stock i on day t
$R_{\mathrm{m}t}$ is the return of the market on day t
α_i and β_i are the regression intercept and slope (β) coefficient estimates

The significance of the abnormal returns is determined by the following Z-statistic:

$$Z = \frac{1}{\sqrt{N}} \sum_{i=1}^{N} \left[\sum_{t=t_1}^{t_2} \mathrm{AR}_{it} \Bigg/ \sqrt{\mathrm{Var}\left(\sum_{t=t_1}^{t_2} \mathrm{AR}_{it} \right)} \right] \tag{37.3}$$

where
t_1 is the first day of the examination period window
t_2 is the last day of the examination period window
N is the number of observations
Denominator is the square root of the variance of the cumulated prediction error of firm i

This variance is defined to be as follows:

$$\text{Var}\left(\sum_{t=t_1}^{t_2} \text{AR}_{it}\right) = V_i^2 \left[T + \frac{T^2}{\text{ED}} + \frac{\left(\sum_{t=t_1}^{t_2} R_{mt} - T\bar{R}_m\right)^2}{\sum_{t=1}^{\text{ED}} \left(R_{mt} - \bar{R}_m\right)^2} \right] \tag{37.4}$$

where

V_i^2 is the residual variance of stock i's market model regression
T is the number of days in the examination period
ED is the number of days in the estimation period
R_{mt} is the market return on day t
$\bar{R}_m$ is the mean market return during the estimation period

Various event windows (day 0, days 0–1, and days 2–5) are used with the objective of analyzing the timing of any abnormal returns. If the abnormal returns in the event window are positive and statistically significant, the fair contract hypothesis will be rejected in favor of the positive NPV hypothesis.

37.3.1 Cross-Sectional Analysis

The following cross-sectional equation is employed to test for differences in abnormal returns across the contract types while controlling for potentially confounding factors. The potentially confounding factors are the size (revenue) of the contract, the number of years over which the revenue is paid, the grantee's size (total assets; Errunza and Senbet, 1984), the day of the week (Monday or Friday), and the change in the year (December and January). The dummy variables for day of the week and the change in the year represent recognized anomalies (French, 1980; Miller, 1988; Whyte and Picou, 1993).

$$\begin{aligned} \text{CAR}i(j, j+k) = {} & \alpha + \beta_1 \text{KSZ}i + \beta_2 \text{YRS}i + \beta_3 \text{TASST}i + \beta_4 \text{FED}i \\ & + \beta_5 \text{FORG}i + \beta_6 \text{MIL}i + \beta_7 \text{MUNI}i + \beta_8 \text{MON}i \\ & + \beta_9 \text{FRI}i + \beta_{10} \text{DEC}i + \beta_{11} \text{JAN}ii + \varepsilon i \end{aligned} \tag{37.5}$$

where

CAR$i(j,j+k)$ is the k-day cumulative abnormal return for security i commencing on day j
KSZ is the size (revenue) of the contract
YRS is the number of years of the contract's life
TASST is the total assets of the grantee for the previous fiscal year
FED is a dummy variable equal to 1 if the grantor is the U.S. federal government (nonmilitary)
FORG is a dummy variable equal to 1 if the grantor is a foreign government
MIL is a dummy variable equal to 1 if the grantor is the U.S. Military
MUNI is a dummy variable equal to 1 if the grantor is a municipal government
MON is a dummy variable equal to 1 if the contract announcement were on a Monday
FRI is a dummy variable equal to 1 if the contract announcement were on a Friday
DEC is a dummy variable equal to 1 if the contract announcement occurred in December
JAN is a dummy variable equal to 1 if the contract announcement occurred in January

The government contract hypothesis is not rejected if any of the following coefficients are positive and significant: FED, FORG, MIL, and MUNI. Four dummy variables representing the type of government are used to pinpoint which type of government, if any, grants contracts that are perceived to be more lucrative by the market.

37.4 Research Results

Descriptive statistics for the 329 contract awards are disclosed in Table 37.2; there are seven samples. The full sample is broken down into two main subsamples according to whether the grantor is a corporation or government. The government sample is then broken down according to the particular type of government awarding the contract: federal government (nonmilitary), military, municipal, and foreign. The first two rows inside the table disclose the number of contract awards and percentage of total contract awards for each sample. Rows three through five disclose the number of contract awards for each particular stock market, and the last three rows disclose the average size of the contracts, the average life of the contracts, and the average grantee size measured by total assets.

37.4.1 Abnormal Returns Surrounding the Contract Award Announcements

Table 37.3 presents the results from measuring the abnormal returns surrounding the contract award announcements. Panel 1 of the table discloses the results for the full sample of contract awards. The mean abnormal returns associated with the 329 contract awards are presented in the first row inside the table; each column pertains to a different event window. The mean abnormal returns over days −3, −2, and −1 are shown to determine whether there was any leakage of information before the contract award announcements. The hypotheses for the market's response to the contract awards are tested by assessing the mean abnormal returns for day 0, day 1, days 0–1, and days 2–5. These event windows are used to measure the timing of the market's response and to account for stock price drift and overreaction. The statistical significance of the mean abnormal return per event window is designated in the second and third rows.

Table 37.3 (Panel 1) pertains to all contract awards and shows there is a significant positive abnormal return on day 0 and day 1. The mean abnormal returns are positive and statistically significant on day 0, day 1, and days 0–1. The mean abnormal return for this two-day period is 2.33 percent, which is statistically significant. Thus, the fair contract hypothesis is rejected in favor of the positive NPV hypothesis for the full sample of contract awards. The cumulative abnormal return for days 2–5 is not statistically significant. This suggests the market fully assessed the contract award announcements on day 0 and day 1. Table 37.3 (Panel 2) pertains to contracts granted by other corporations. The mean abnormal returns for day 0, day 1, days 0–1, and days 2–5 are positive. For day 0 and days 0–1 these mean abnormal returns are statistically significant. The cumulative mean abnormal return for day 0 and day 1 is 1.88 percent. The results suggest the market fully assessed these contract awards on day 0 and day 1 as the mean abnormal return for days 2–5 is not statistically significant. The fair contract hypothesis is rejected in favor of the positive NPV hypothesis for this sample of contract awards. Table 37.3 (Panel 3) pertains to all government contracts. The mean abnormal return for day 0, day 1, days 0–1, and days 2–5 are positive. For day 0 and day 1 the mean abnormal returns sum to 2.52 percent and this cumulative mean abnormal return is statistically

Table 37.2 Descriptive Statistics for 329 Contract Award Announcements during the Period January 1990 to July 1998

	Type of Government						
	All	*Corporate*	*Government*	*Federal*	*Military*	*Municipal*	*Foreign*
Sample size	329	99	230	42	102	48	38
Percentage of total	100	30	70	13	31	15	11
No. of NYSE	91	25	66	17	30	7	12
No. of AMEX	37	18	19	3	13	1	2
No. of NASDAQ	201	56	145	22	59	40	24
Average contract size (in millions $)	39.05	17.41	48.36	37.77	68.99	36.29	19.95
Average contract life (in days)	2.17	1.87	2.29	2.61	2.79	1.79	1.27
Average total assets (grantee and in thousands $)	1930.3	1122.5	2278.1	2499.2	2354.9	1221.0	3162.6

Notes: NYSE, New York Stock Exchange; AMEX, American Stock Exchange; NASDAQ, National Association of Securities Dealers Automated Quotations.

Table 37.3 Abnormal Returns (Grantee) Pursuant to 329 Contract Awards during the Period January 1990 to July 1998

	Day −3	*Day −2*	*Day −1*	*Day 0*	*Day 1*	*Days 0–1*	*Days 2–5*
Panel 1: All Contracts (*n* = 329)							
Mean abnormal							
Return (in percent)	−0.19	0.11	**−0.29**	**1.38**	**0.95**	**2.33**	−0.02
Z-statistic	−0.67	0.82	−1.70	5.95	1.89	5.53	−0.37
Significance			*	***	*	***	
Panel 2: Corporate (*n* = 99)							
Mean abnormal							
Return (in percent)	−0.15	0.21	**−0.55**	**1.00**	0.88	**1.88**	0.19
Z-statistic	−0.52	0.85	−1.75	2.64	1.03	2.59	1.14
Significance			*	***		***	
Panel 3: All Government (*n* = 230)							
Mean abnormal							
Return (in percent)	−0.21	0.07	−0.17	**1.55**	0.98	**2.52**	0.19
Z-statistic	−0.46	0.42	−0.89	5.39	1.59	4.91	0.30
Significance				***		***	
3a. Federal Government—Nonmilitary (*n* = 42)							
Mean abnormal							
Return (in percent)	−0.31	−0.94	0.24	**1.56**	−0.97	0.59	−1.46
Z-statistic	−0.12	−1.26	0.46	2.75	−1.05	1.19	−1.26
Significance				***			
3b. Federal Government—Military (*n* = 102)							
Mean abnormal							
Return (in percent)	−0.01	0.33	0.30	**1.57**	**2.10**	**3.67**	−0.21
Z-statistic	−0.08	1.42	0.46	3.67	1.80	3.86	−0.56
Significance				***	*	***	
3c. Municipal Government (*n* = 48)							
Mean abnormal							
Return (in percent)	−0.44	1.02	−0.92	**1.18**	0.25	**1.44**	−0.32
Z-statistic	−0.32	1.29	−1.76	1.97	0.87	2.00	−0.45
Significance				**		**	

Table 37.3 (continued) Abnormal Returns (Grantee) Pursuant to 329 Contract Awards during the Period January 1990 to July 1998

	Day −3	*Day −2*	*Day −1*	*Day 0*	*Day 1*	*Days 0–1*	*Days 2–5*
3d. Foreign Government (*n* = 38)							
Mean abnormal							
Return (in percent)	−0.31	−0.75	−0.97	**1.92**	1.02	**2.94**	**3.74**
Z-statistic	−0.53	−1.42	−1.45	2.14	1.08	2.26	3.50
Significance				**		**	***

Notes: Bold type indicates statistical significance at the *** (0.01), ** (0.05), and * (0.10) levels. Results are materially the same when using post-event estimation period data.

significant. The fair contract hypothesis is rejected in favor of the positive NPV hypothesis for the full sample of government contract awards.

Four sections (3a, 3b, 3c, and 3d) under Panel 3 of Table 37.3 pertain to the different types of governments that awarded contracts to corporations. Panel 3a pertains to nonmilitary contracts awarded by the federal government. The mean abnormal return on day 0 is 1.56 percent, which is statistically significant. However, the mean abnormal returns on days 0–1 and days 2–5 are not statistically significant. This suggests the market initially (day 0) overreacted to the contract award announcements. Thus, the fair contract hypothesis is not rejected for this particular subsample of government contracts. Panel 3b pertains to U.S. Military contracts. The mean abnormal returns are positive and statistically significant for day 0, day 1, and days 0–1. The cumulative mean abnormal return for days 0–1 is 3.67 percent. The fair contract hypothesis is rejected in favor of the positive NPV hypothesis for military contracts. Panel 3c discloses the results for the mean abnormal returns for contract awards granted by municipal governments in the United States. The mean abnormal returns on day 0 and days 0–1 are positive and statistically significant. The fair contract award hypothesis is rejected in favor of the positive NPV hypothesis for this sample of contract award announcements. Panel 3d discloses the results for the mean abnormal returns for contract awards granted by foreign governments. The mean abnormal returns on day 0, days 0–1, and days 2–5 are positive and statistically significant. The mean abnormal return for days 0–5 is 6.68 percent suggesting these contracts are quite lucrative. The fair contract hypothesis is rejected in favor of the positive NPV hypothesis for this sample of contract awards. The positive and statistically significant cumulative abnormal return during days 2–5 suggests the market takes time to fully analyze these contract awards.

The fair contract hypothesis is rejected in favor of the positive NPV hypothesis for all contract awards except those granted by the federal government. These results also suggest contract awards granted by foreign governments may be more lucrative than contract awards granted by corporations or American governments. Finally, the market apparently takes longer (five days) to fully assess foreign government contracts.

37.4.2 Cross-Sectional Regression Results

Results for the cross-sectional analyses determine if the abnormal returns are conditioned on the grantor while controlling for potentially confounding factors, which are the size (revenue) of the contract, the number of years of the contract's life, the size (total assets) of the grantee, the day of the week (Monday or Friday), and the change in the year (December or January). Table 37.4 discloses cross-sectional results for three event windows: day 0, days 0–1, and days 2–5. These results should be interpreted with caution, as the *F*-statistics are insignificant.

The first two columns inside the table pertain to regressing the abnormal returns for day 0 on the independent variables. The sign on the coefficient estimate pursuant to total assets is negative and significant suggesting larger firm stock prices are affected by a lesser degree when contract awards are announced. The third and fourth columns of Table 37.4 pertain to regressing the cumulative

Table 37.4 Least Square Estimates of Cross-Sectional Regressions for 329 Contract Awards during the Period January 1990 to July 1998

	Dependent Variables					
Independent Variables	$CAR_{0,1}$ *(Day 0)* *Coefficient*	*t-Statistic*	$CAR_{0,2}$ *(Days 0–1)* *Coefficient*	*t-Statistic*	$CAR_{2,4}$ *(Days 2–5)* *Coefficient*	*t-Statistic*
KSZ	0.0000	0.03	–0.0000	–0.71	–0.0000	–0.55
YRS	–0.0030	–0.19	0.0028	1.03	–0.0000	–0.03
TASST	**–0.0001***	–1.65	**–0.0002***	–1.73	–0.0000	–0.49
FED	0.0060	0.61	–0.0140	–0.81	–0.0075	–0.47
FORG	0.0104	1.03	0.0122	0.68	**0.0436****	2.56
MIL	0.0072	0.93	0.0162	1.20	0.0054	0.43
MUNI	0.0026	0.28	–0.0025	–0.15	0.0018	0.12
MON	0.0059	0.73	0.0016	0.11	0.0094	0.72
FRI	0.0001	0.02	**0.0347****	2.08	–0.0071	–0.46
DEC	0.0012	0.10	–0.0028	–0.13	0.0185	0.96
JAN	–0.0049	–0.52	–0.0152	–0.92	0.0122	0.83
Adjacent R^2	0.0000		0.0067		0.0000	
F-statistic	0.47		1.18		0.98	

Notes: Bold type indicates statistical significance at the 0.01 (***), 0.05 (**), and 0.10 (*) levels. Adjusting for heteroskedasticity was not necessary. Results are materially the same when using post-event estimation period data. CAR is the cumulative abnormal return, KSZ is the size (revenue) of the contract, YRS is the number of years of the contract's life, TASST is the total assets of the grantee on the previous fiscal year, FED is a dummy variable equal to 1 if the grantor is the U.S. federal government (civil), FORG is a dummy variable equal to 1 if the grantor is a foreign government, MIL is a dummy variable equal to 1 if the grantor is the U.S. Military, MUNI is a dummy variable equal to 1 if the grantor is a municipal government, MON is a dummy variable equal to 1 if the contract announcement were on a Monday, FRI is a dummy variable equal to 1 if the contract announcement were on a Friday, DEC is a dummy variable equal to 1 if the contract announcement occurred in December, JAN is a dummy variable equal to 1 if the contract announcement occurred in January.

abnormal returns for days 0–1 on the independent variables. The sign on the coefficient estimate pursuant to total assets is negative and significant confirming that larger firm stock prices are affected to a lesser degree when contract awards are announced. The coefficient estimate on the dummy variable identifying the contract awards announced on Friday is positive and statistically significant indicating the market perceives contract awards as being more lucrative if announced on Friday. The last two columns of Table 37.4 pertain to regressing the days 2–5 cumulative abnormal returns on the independent variables. The coefficient estimate on the foreign government dummy variable is positive and statistically significant indicating the market perceives these contract awards as being more lucrative than contracts awarded by corporations or other types of government. Thus, the government contract award hypothesis is not rejected for this sample of government contract awards. It takes the market five days to fully assess contract awards granted by foreign governments.

37.5 Conclusion

For all contract awards except those issued by the federal government (nonmilitary), the results suggest the revenue from the contract is expected to exceed all of the costs (operating and financing) associated with fulfilling the contracts. For federal government (nonmilitary) contracts, the results indicate the revenue from the contract is expected to sufficiently cover all the costs (operating and financing) associated with fulfilling the contracts.

The returns pursuant to contracts granted by foreign governments are substantially higher than the returns pursuant to contracts granted by American governments or corporations. The cross-sectional analysis suggests the returns for these types of contract awards are significantly higher than the returns pursuant to contracts awarded by other grantors, even when controlling for potentially confounding factors. Apparently, foreign contract awards are particularly lucrative.

Finally, there is no evidence that American governments grant contracts that are more lucrative than those granted by American corporations. This finding is surprising and counter to subjective claims that U.S. government bodies grant particularly lucrative contracts.

Acknowledgment

We thank Robert Brian Larson for his valuable input.

References

Chaney, P.K. 1989, Summer. Moral hazard and capital budgeting. *The Journal of Financial Research*, 12(2): 113–118.

Diltz, J.D. 1990. Valuation effects of government contract awards. *Quarterly Journal of Business and Economics*, 29(3): 3–15.

Errunza, V.R. and Senbet, L.W. 1984. International corporate diversification, market valuation, and size-adjusted evidence/discussion. *Journal of Finance*, 39: 727–745.

Fama, E.F. and French, K.R. 1999. The corporate cost of capital and the return on corporate investment. *Journal of Finance*, 54(6): 1939–1967.

French, K.R. 1980. Stock returns and the weekend effect. *Journal of Financial Economics*, 8: 55–69.

Mikkelson, W.H. and Parch, M.M. 1988. Withdrawn security offerings. *Journal of Financial and Quantitative Analysis*, 23(2): 119–133 and errata.

Miller, E.M. 1988. Summer. Why a weekend effect? *Journal of Portfolio Management*, 14(4): 43–48.

Whyte, A.M. and Picou, A. 1993. Seasonality in industry specific indexes. *Journal of Economics and Finance*, 17(3): 57–69.

Woods, J.C. and Randall, M. 1989. The net present value of future investment opportunities. *Financial Management*, 18(2): 85–93.

Chapter 38

Economic Context of Public Procurement

Guy C. Callender and Darin Matthews

CONTENTS

38.1 Introduction

Using some diverse experiences in the United States, the United Kingdom, and Australia, this chapter illustrates the nature of some contractual challenges that can be expected to transform the sophistication of the procurement role in government to ensure the demands of public accountability continue to be met. Procurement has undergone a significant revolution in the past 20 years in identity, in practice, and in its professional focus. The principal procurement drivers of accountability, efficiency, and value for money have coincided with significant advances in information technology. New technology has made it possible to shift from the more mundane order processing and expediting era to a procurement management approach supported by E-business technology.

This shift, especially the focus on technology-based solutions, carried the risk that other areas of procurement, such as contract formation and management, the creation of effective strategic alliances, and the adoption of a strategic approach to procurement, might be neglected.

The essential features of contemporary procurement could be encapsulated in its definition as "a legally enforceable contract relationship containing the data management and product or service responsibility requirements for every activity arising from conception of a need for a product or service to the ultimate satisfaction of that need." Such a definition highlights the need for an organization to remain responsible for a component of all procurement transactions currently at risk in the drive toward technology-based solutions: *relationships*. A focus on relationships provides a framework for examining the scope and direction of government procurement, as practitioners attempt to meet contemporary and future goals, which include:

- Cost management
- Accountability and probity requirements
- Customer satisfaction
- Shift from goods procurement to services procurement
- Reduced time to satisfy client needs
- Outsourcing and contract optimization

The pursuit of these goals was assisted by the strong focus on organizational restructuring throughout the 1990s and early 2000s by enhancements in global technology and efforts by governments to increase efficiency through a range of cost-reduction strategies (Gore, 1993; Bell, 1997; Kuttner, 1997). With the operational advent of E-commerce and E-business strategies, valuable technological tools arrived to enhance the processing of government procurement activities. However, the underlying procurement strategies have created a number of policy and operating dilemmas at individual, supplier, and government levels. The scope of some of these dilemmas will be explored in this paper.

38.2 Cost Reduction as a Paradox

Global economic history since World War II reflects the economic ideology of two quite different eras. The first is generally regarded as the period between 1945 and 1972, when economic orthodoxy was significantly influenced by the outcomes of the Bretton–Woods Agreement and the dominance of the economic theories of John Maynard Keynes (around 1936–1964). The second began with the emerging failure of the Bretton–Woods Agreement to cope with currency instabilities and the inflationary cycles of the late 1960s and 1970s. As the Keynesian model of economic ideology faded, a more sharply focused market model emerged, pioneered by Milton Friedman and other economists of the, so-called, Chicago School (1962–1982). This new model represented a resurgence of the free-market approach that was widely accepted in the early 1980s by U.S. President Reagan and Prime Ministers Thatcher of the United Kingdom and Mulroney of Canada (Savoie, 1994). By the mid-1990s a large number of nations had begun to espouse these values and to enact policies leading in many cases to reduced taxation. An immediate consequence was a need to cut the cost of government, one of the paths being to change procurement policies and practice.

The adoption of one generalized, economic ideology supports the perception that economic theory represents a settled body of knowledge rather than the "technique of thinking" (Keynes, 1922). The market-focused model, representing a radical shift from the immediate past, was promoted by respected academics, such as Milton Friedman, John Muth, and Robert Lucus (Canterbery, 2001), and reaffirmed the dominant status of business and wealth generation in an economy. The market model suggested new possibilities to resolve intractable economic problems that emerged in the early 1970s and, arguably, also suggested to politicians that the demands of economic management were beginning to exceed their governments' willingness to remain a central part of economic management. The opportunity to implement significant change at the politico-economic level also matched the cultural inclinations of the first three major political proponents (the United States, the United Kingdom, and Canada). For example, "doing something," rather than "letting fate" influence the course of history, is an integral part of the dominant culture in each of these nations (Schneider and Barsoux, 2003). Although the nature of such changes varied from country to country, as each interpretation of the new public management (NPM) evolved (one of the titles given to this model of government reform) a number of common principles began to emerge.

The pursuit of the market model, the rapid enhancement of sophisticated electronic technology, and the shift from manufacturing to service-based economies have resulted in a number of fundamental changes in international economic and business behavior (Thurow, 1992; Hughes, 1994; Savoie, 1994; Bell, 1997; Canterbery, 2001; Giddens, 2001). Typical examples include wider support for floating exchange rates, the pursuit of low inflation, a lesser political priority placed on the achievement of full employment, the growth of private equity capital, the emergence of public–private partnerships (PPPs), a shift from government-managed fiscal policy to independent, central bank management of monetary policy, and a growing sense that economic cycles have smoothed (Chevallier, 2000).

The consequences of the changes are still emerging. There have been notes of caution as the economic policy pendulum swings back toward an almost total reliance on market mechanisms to provide the full range of economic management (Beddoes, 1999; Stiglitz, 2002). The caution has been expressed by Beddoes (1999, p. 9): "When tomorrow's historians look back at the recent financial crises and subsequent efforts to reform global finance, they will [note]… the grand rhetoric of creating a new global architecture yielded few concrete results." The positive view is expressed by Chevallier (2000, p. xxv) who suggests that the economic cycle can be seen, since the 1990s, as a long wave that reached the end of its down phase in 1997 in a world where economic depression is a myth and "the next ascending wave is not far."

A number of applications of the market-driven philosophy have had a significant impact on procurement managers, principally, the contracting out of "noncore" activities of public- and private-sector organizations, sale of government business enterprises in some jurisdictions, and the emergence of a culture of "doing more with less." The impact of these policies has varied, according to the nature of the economy segment affected. For example, program areas that have historically been performed by public employees are more commonly being "outsourced" or "privatized" by public entities of all types, with varying outcomes (Hodge, 1996). At the local government level, trade services, such as janitorial and landscaping, as well as professional services, including engineering and project management, are increasingly being contracted out by local government organizations seeking to reduce their operating budgets. Although critics suggest that such efforts result in depressed wages and hobbled labor unions (Kuttner, 1997), public agencies continue this organizational trend, with the responsibility of carrying out such decisions generally falling to the purchasing officer. According to the National League of Cities—a U.S. association that polled its members in 1997 regarding their intended future use of privatization—61 percent of the cities planned to employ privatized services at the same or an increased level (Kittower, 1998).

38.3 Privatization and Public Procurement Strategies

The nature of privatization itself, and, therefore, the impact of outsourcing, varies greatly between nations. For countries of the former Eastern bloc, such as the Czech Republic, privatization takes the form of "returning a property to [its] original owners or their heirs, sale of a property to domestic or foreign investors, [or] free transfer of a property to cities and municipalities" (Klvacova, 1993, p. 21). Conversely, in the United States, privatization does not involve "divestiture or load shedding" but, rather, aims to "subject government programs, wherever possible, to encourage competition and market discipline" (Seidman, 1990, p. 18). The effect has been not to sell government assets or operations in the United States but, instead, to maintain or increase the level of contracting out of government activities (Guttman, 2000). Recently, an apparently revised approach toward "privatization" within the United States was criticized as "merely contract reform under another name" (p. 875). Indeed, the tension between U.S. and international definitions of "privatization" can be traced to the historical relationship between the public and private sectors that emerged in the United States after the civil war. At that time, the policy became known as "laissez-faire... despite the anomalous fact that business continued to enjoy high subsidies and high protective tariffs. 'The peculiarly American version of laissez-faire,' Schlesinger dryly observed, meant 'aid from the state without interference from the state' " (Kuttner, 1997, p. 212).

In the United Kingdom, the rate of privatization, through the sale of government assets and undertakings, has been very substantial, followed closely by Australia and New Zealand. In these jurisdictions, there has been substantial adoption of outsourcing of government activities that have tended to provide new opportunities for the private sector (Callender and Johnston, 2001). This approach to privatization, involving substantial divestiture of the assets and undertakings of government, contrasts sharply with some European models of the NPM. For example, "privatization" may mean the transfer of a government department or business enterprise from the legal system governing the public sector to that governing privately owned institutions without a change of ownership (Hammerschmid et al., 2001) but, rather, a change in regulatory regime. The effect may be to reduce the transparency of government activities in organizations thus "privatized" and to remove them from budget scrutiny.

For government procurement, the existence of these varying models of privatization highlights the difficulties of drawing international comparisons between managing costs and making efficiency comparisons without substantial detailed research, particularly of the underlying legal and regulatory frameworks typical of public–private relationships. In spite of these limitations, it is apparent from Table 38.1 that most of the governments discussed in this article have achieved only limited reduction in government expenditure within the subject economies since 1975. Despite significant attention being given to government reform in many Anglo-American countries and those economies influenced by Anglo-American customs in relation to economic, social, and legal issues, the balance between public- and private-sector expenditures suggests an increasing share for government, when public policy rhetoric often suggests the reverse.

38.4 Cost Control and Government Procurement

Some aspects of procurement management, such as outsourcing, more sophisticated contracts management, the use of E-commerce, partnering and strategic alliances, have received growing practitioner and academic attention as awareness of the financial influence of this function develops. However, the potential for cost reduction created by these initiatives has not escaped

Table 38.1 Pattern of Changing Government Expenditures, Transfers, and Subsidies (as a Percentage of GDP) during the Late Twentieth Century

Country	*1980*	*1985*	*1990*	*1995*	*2000*	*2004*
Australia	34.0	34.7	33.0	35.6	35.3	36.1
Canada	40.5	45.1	44.2	44.4	38.5	36.2
France	46.1	50.9	45.7	58.2	62.5	55.1
Italy		49.9	46.1	49.4	44.4	46.0
New Zealand	47.0	41.5	48.7	31.7	35.5	34.7
United Kingdom	44.9	43.8	41.5	42.9	38.7	38.7
United States	33.7	34.0	33.5	33.0	30.2	30.8

Sources: Adapted from Gwartney, J., Lawson, R., and Samida, D., *Economic Freedom of the World 2000*, Fraser Institute, Vancouver, BC, 2000; Gwartney, J., Lawson, R., and Easterly, W., *Economic Freedom of the World 2006*, Fraser Institute, Vancouver, BC, 2006. With permission.

Note: Alphabetical order of entries follows the protocol of the report.

the attention of public sector policy makers, who have pursued this activity with vigor (Hodge, 1996). In more recent years, the so-called PPP has become an increasingly popular method for financing large infrastructure projects such as roads, hospitals, and other major undertakings. The formation of a PPP is designed to reduce costs (on the assumption that a private contractor is more cost efficient than a public agency) and minimize increases in public debt. In the United States, the United Kingdom, and Australia, the importance of improved supply management has been recognized in government reports (Gore, 1993; Commonwealth of Australia, 1994; Her Majesty's Government, 1999).

The focus on cost management is of particular interest to procurement professionals. Each iteration of government cost management that occurs, with a view to achieving greater supply chain efficiency, may reduce the income of other organizations in that supply chain. As the income of these "partners" falls, they too are forced to become more efficient, unless they find other ways of increasing their income. A much easier possibility is to reduce costs by applying technology-based solutions or, rightly or wrongly, by reducing labor costs (Abernathy et al., 1999). In an effort to reduce organizational costs with the letting of their contracts, procurement professionals are charged with selecting the most appropriate solicitation method. Even though the American Bar Association (1993) identifies the "lowest bid wins" philosophy, inherent to the invitation to bid as the predominant selection method, many governments are employing alternative procurement efforts to more efficiently manage and reduce costs. Value-based procurements, like the request for proposal process, that embody an evaluation of a supplier's experience, expertise, and past performance are quickly gaining ground as a contractor selection tool (Matthews, 1999).

The impact of critical issues, such as "cost" and "scarcity," on aspects of global economic performance appears to have been consistently overlooked in the rush by procurement and other supply chain managers to demonstrate the efficiency of their procurement function. The drive to manage costs may be contributing to a growth in income disparity (Stiglitz, 2002), when combined with the constant attempts to minimize average income growth and maintain control over inflation. The emerging evidence suggests that, although the wealthiest members of many economies appear to have benefited significantly from the policies accompanying economic rationalism, the majority of the population has seen its relative share of economic wealth decline (World Bank, 1997; Levy, 1999; Stiglitz, 2002).

For example, the major growth in employment in the U.S. and Australian economies has not occurred over recent years in high-paid, high-technology-based jobs. Instead, the growth tends to be in the lowest paid jobs in retail and accommodation services. Governments should not regard this as good news in terms of national discretionary income. For example, wages in the Australian retail industry were just 75 percent of average weekly earnings; and, in the accommodation and restaurant industry, it is just 73 percent (Australian Bureau of Statistics, 2000). For the United States, these figures were 68 and 69 percent , respectively (EMPSIT, 2001). Although it can be argued that these job categories employ many young or casual employees, there may not be better jobs for these employees. Keeping the pressure on cost management through wages may be having a significant impact by raising business income but it is also at the expense of individuals' earnings, which are constantly needed to generate and sustain demand (and ensure an adequate tax base for government revenue requirements).

As the real income of many workers falls under the effects of the free-market regime and the drive for buyer and supplier efficiency, the lessons of classical economic theory provide a reminder that "as income falls, fewer and fewer people save ... and consumption will equal income" (Lipsey, 1966, p. 626). It seems that current public- and private-sector policy makers have forgotten this history lesson in demand management. Some of the industrialists of the early twentieth century amassed their fortunes by supporting a consumer revolution that encouraged both the rich and the less rich to earn enough money to purchase their corporate products—Henry Ford in the United States (Lewis et al., 1983) and William Morris in the United Kingdom (Adeney, 1988).

The "cost-efficiency" and "better-service" models of managing suppliers seem to yield valuable commercial results for governments in the short term; but, in the longer term, this model may limit opportunities to enhance national economic performance. The increasing strength of trade blocs, such as NAFTA, APEC, and the European Union, suggests that many nations covertly feel that global free trade is risky and that greater economic security may be found within the more limited, free-trade boundaries of a formal trade group that extends national boundaries without creating a global marketplace (Bernstein, 1996; Kuttner, 1997).

38.5 Competitive Approach to Market Development: Some Cautionary, International Contracting Tales

In the United States, one of the driving forces of government reform has been the development of national markets, especially through the practice of contracting out (Guttman, 2000). A recent report, published by the Oregon Department of Transportation, demonstrates an example of this trend in the United States. During 2000 alone, a total of $170 million in public contracts was made available to private industry highway contractors (ODOT Transcripts, 2001). In Australia, also, the advent of the 1995 National Competition Policy (NCP) has emerged as a significant new force in reshaping the relationship between the public and private sectors. The nature of these activities shifts procurement responsibilities from a micro-single contract relating to the supply of specific goods or services to extensive long-term contracts, often associated with major infrastructure activities. This approach increases the mix of internal and external providers identified by Halachmi and Montgomery (2000), but the issues of risk management and accountability of private to the public sector (and civil society) remain unclear. The brief case studies that follow outline two areas in which government procurement policies and practices increasingly create dilemmas for practitioners:

- Situations where financial policies, especially cost-reduction policies, clash with government service and community service obligations
- Management of risk in the formulation and maintenance of contracts where government organizations and private businesses face a competitive market together

38.6 Case of Labor Issues in Oregon

Throughout the 1990s, the state of Oregon demonstrated a keen concern for its civilian labor force of approximately 1.8 million people. A 1996 ballot initiative passed by voters raised the state's minimum wage from $4.75 to $6.50 per hour, with the last increase occurring in 1999. This was a significant boost from Oregon's $2.30 wage of 1976, let alone the 1938 federal minimum wage of 25 cents signed into law by President Franklin Roosevelt. Supporters of the Oregon effort felt that the wage rate increase would reduce poverty for low-income workers, whose earnings had not kept up with inflation. Opposing positions included the belief that the increases would result in higher unemployment, as well as increased costs for both employers and consumers (Oregon Employment Department, 1998). Even with recent economic downturns, Oregonians continue to enjoy a relatively low unemployment rate of 5.6 percent (Anonymous, 2001), perhaps demonstrating the value of building the purchasing power of incomes across the community. If incomes have been eroded through inflation, then it is likely that demand patterns will also be eroded over time, especially for staple consumption items.

Along with some three-dozen public agencies across the United States, Multnomah County in Portland, Oregon, has established a living wage policy for a number of its contracts. For services, such as janitorial, building security, and food service, holders of county contracts are required to compensate their workers at a set level—currently at $9.28 per hour. This amount includes both wages and employee benefits and is significantly higher than the $6.50 per hour mandated by the Oregon Bureau of Labor and Industries (1998). Through a 1998 resolution passed unanimously by the board of commissioners, the county established this compensation threshold to combat poverty in the Portland metropolitan area. Supported by local community groups and labor unions, this effort highlighted the organization's commitment to the social and economic well-being of its citizens—in this case, a labor market where low wages were the norm.

With the slowing of Oregon's economy, demonstrated by several recent instances of private industry downsizing and layoffs, area governments were faced with revenue shortfalls and shrinking budgets (Hill, 2002). Both high technology and heavy trucking manufacturers in Portland have announced recent layoffs in significant numbers. What seemingly appeared to be a sound, and certainly socially correct, decision by the county is now being questioned in a time of financial crisis. The dilemma would appear to be: "How can the organization *reduce* costs when budget efficiency is imperative, while at the same time *increasing* contract costs through specific wage requirements imposed on its contractors?"

As discussed earlier in this chapter, public purchasing practitioners are groomed early in their careers to utilize the invitation for bid process to secure the lowest-priced contract. This fundamental and, according to many traditionalists, essential concept in government contracting has kept contract costs as low as the private market will permit. The dilemma for the purchasing practitioner is attempting to secure cost savings with a given procurement, while at the same time enforcing requirements that inevitably will increase the bid prices. Certainly, adjustments must be made by potential contract holders, who aim to secure the government's business. By calculating their offers based on increased wages and benefits to their workforce, they are, in a sense, forced to submit higher bid prices, which are ultimately absorbed by the entity and its citizenry.

Though challenged by the quandary of such social innovation, the procurement professional can certainly take some satisfaction from the achievement of the intended social goal—in this case, reduced poverty. Although not without its downfalls and limitations, living wage laws do appear to achieve at least a modest reduction in urban poverty, according to the National Bureau of Economic Research (Neumark and Adams, 2000).

38.7 Case of the Sydney Airport Rail Link

As noted earlier in the chapter, the creation of a PPP should include the requirement to conduct a procurement process at the outset of the project to prequalify potential bidders and to let the contract to the successful bidder. Unlike other types of public procurement, PPPs are usually let for an extended term, up to 30 years, at which point the PPP may be renewed or the assets and undertaking returned to government ownership. Although PPPs have become very popular in Australia, this enthusiasm is not shared internationally (Chong and Callender, 2007). In 1995, the federal and state governments of Australia agreed upon an NCP. The reform and privatization of public monopolies and the development of competitive markets, where government monopolies had previously existed, were a key part of the agreement between the national and subnational governments in Australia for the first five years of the NCP. In the case of railroads in Australia, the emphasis was on improving competitiveness and financial viability, problems that existed in the United States where rates and charges for railroad usage remains regulated (Baumol and Willig, 1999), and also in the United Kingdom (Knight, 1999).

At the subnational level—the locus of this case—the New South Wales (NSW) government split its single rail organization (the State Rail Authority [SRA]) into four smaller public corporations responsible for passenger services (SRA), freight (FreightCorp), track maintenance (Rail Services Authority), and the rail infrastructure owner (Rail Access Corporation). The reasons for the division were not entirely clear, although the government strategy was ostensibly aimed at improving the efficiency and competitiveness in the rail network, encouraging private-sector use of the railroad and, possibly, gaining further revenue from the sale of FreightCorp, which is a profitable institution (Australian Bureau of Statistics, 2000). However, there remains concern that the sale of FreightCorp to the private sector could lead to a "vertical integration of the freight business" at the national level (Hoyle, 2000, p. 6). Such integration may have negative implications for the viable operations of the existing road transport network, and, in effect, replace a transparent, publicly owned monopoly with a private, nontransparent monopoly.

When a proposed rail link between the city of Sydney and the nearby Sydney International Airport was announced, the NSW government pledged it would not cost taxpayers "one cent" (Morris and Coultan, 1994), despite the complexity of a contracting process that would require private- and public-sector cooperation. Indeed, the government (and its taxpayers) soon agreed to contribute $235 million toward the project after "being threatened with legal action by the private joint venturer" (p. 1). During the construction of the link, an annual report of the government-owned SRA claimed that, during construction and for the first 30 years of operation, the "majority of risks and benefits… [would] rest with the (contracting) company" (SRA, 1996, p. 55).

The NSW Audit Office, subsequently, challenged this view, finding that in the case of the Airport Rail Link (NSW Auditor General, 1996, p. 56):

> Private-sector equity of $US15m… is rarely at risk during the entire agreement term, whereas State Rail group may be liable for early termination of the agreement and to "maintain cashflows to ALC (Airport Link Company) so that ALC receives revenue… expected."

The Airport Link Company went into liquidation in November 2000. The causes cited included claims that state rail staff overestimated the likely passenger loadings expected to be around 48,000 per week, when, in fact, usage was only around 16,000 and, therefore, income projections were overoptimistic (Sandilands, 2001). The integration of multi-ownership into the rail network, which had been traditionally owned and operated by a government business enterprise, also affected the success of the airport link. Ticket prices were also felt to be too high given the short distance between the city and the airport—it being generally cheaper to travel by taxi if two or more people were traveling together. Furthermore, the rolling stock for the airport link was government-owned and -operated, and was not the most modern available in the urban network and was without any designated spaces for passenger luggage. Since its financial failure, the Airport Rail Link has been operated by the NSW government though plans exist to sell the railway, if a suitable buyer can be attracted. The criticisms that existed in 2000 still remain (Baker and Nixon, 2006).

The financial structure and operational of the Sydney Airport Link became inexorably linked to the NSW government's 1996 restructure of its railroads partly resembling a similar restructuring of rail services in the United Kingdom, which suffered a recurring pattern of system failures and accidents (Knight, 1999; Haigh, 2000; Harris, 2000). At the time NSW decided to corporatize its rail network, the U.K. government was well advanced in its privatization of rail services (Ford, 1995), including the now much-criticized sale of Railtrack (now Network Rail), the British railway infrastructure company (Knight, 1999). In the United Kingdom, as in NSW, a series of system failures and accidents have ensured that the benefits of privatization to the state and consumers are far from clear (Anonymous, 2000; Connolly, 2000; Rogers, 2000). If, as the British and NSW experiences suggest, government subsidies remain a feature of the rail network operations and the government continues to guarantee the debts of public and private operators, the basic advantages for the government of privatizing the rail network appear to be lost.

As a model for large-scale public procurement, the Sydney Airport Link experience leaves much to be desired for all the parties involved. The operating company is now in liquidation, involving a potential loss of income for shareholders and a long period of legal wrangling for the NSW government (Baker and Nixon, 2007). The service has been more effectively integrated into the government rail network, but poor rolling stock and station scheduling limit the potential of the service to achieve its objective of reducing automobile congestion and its associated delays at the airport. For taxpayers, the financial cost has been significant and has not ended. Curiously, the lessons available from this PPP (and others in NSW) have seemingly failed to generate a more robust approach to this type of contracting. A recently opened tunnel under the city of Sydney was established under a PPP arrangement, the tenders for which were called in 2001. The project was financed in a highly complex manner and the contractual arrangements supporting the PPP had implications for tunnel users, the public bus system, the city railways, and a host of other parties. This PPP collapsed in a blaze of publicity and cross-accusations, the legal consequences of which will be felt for many years. Access, price, low usage rates, and the implications for public policy were among the more serious weakness of this project. However, an underlying issue for PPPs—at least in this jurisdiction—remains: although the goals of public procurement include a requirement for transparent, accountable procurement processes, once a PPP is formed in conjunction with a public or private company, unless there are special requirements, the ability to scrutinize the continuing nature of a PPP becomes and remains limited.

38.8 Conclusion

The cases outlined in this chapter aim to provide examples of ways in which local and state governments may find themselves operating to manage the rapidly emerging economic pressures, while maintaining the professional integrity of the procurement process through minimizing costs and seeking to gain maximum benefit for the polity. As the Oregon experience shows, local government and its procurement practitioners have a critical role to play in balancing the issues of equity and economic responsibility. The NSW example, in a sense, demonstrates the potential difficulties that may emerge, when a large, long-term government procurement process fails to take into account the potential organizational, contract management, and operational problems that are likely to arise, when public- and private-sector institutions meet in a potentially competitive position.

Furthermore, this research suggests that, regardless of the economic principles or cost-management theories applied by governments, the procurement professional is ultimately called upon to implement these organizational policies in the contracting arena. Efforts to privatize specific business areas to reduce operational costs and also satisfy the equity issues that are important to the polity, will be laid at the door of the purchasing professional. Coupled with the ongoing focus on technological advances in the procurement field and a more uncertain economic and social environment in the near term, these expectations will continue to challenge the procurement professional.

References

Abernathy, F., Dunlop, J., Hammond, J., and Weil, D. 1999. *A Stitch in Time: Lean Retailing and the Transformation of Manufacturing—Lessons from the Apparel and Textiles Industries*. New York: Oxford University Press.

Adeney, M. 1988. *The Motor Makers: The Turbulent History of Britain's Car Industry*. London: Collins.

American Bar Association. 1993. *Model Procurement Code for State and Local Governments*. Washington, DC: ABA.

Anonymous. 2000, November 2. SRA Break-up led to Glenbrook deaths. *Daily Telegraph*. Available at www.dailytelegraph.com.au/0,3546,1373055%255E3163,00.

Anonymous. June 9, 2001. Oregon jobless rate climbs to 5.6 percent. *Register Guard*: 5B.

Australian Bureau of Statistics. 2000. *2000 Year Book Australia*. Canberra, Australia: Author.

Baker, J. and Nixon, S. March 11, 2006. For sale: Ghost train to Sydney airport. *Sydney Morning Herald*: 2.

Baumol, W. and Willig, R. 1999. Competitive rail regulation rules: Should price ceilings constrain final products or inputs? *Journal of Transport Economics and Policy*, 33(1): 43–53.

Beddoes, Z.M. 1999. From EMU to AMU. *Foreign Affairs*, 78(4): 8–13.

Bell, S. 1997. *Ungoverning the Economy*. New York: Oxford University Press.

Bernstein, P. 1996. *Against the Gods: The Remarkable Story of Risk*. New York: John Wiley.

Callender, G. and Johnston, J. 2001. Contracting between governments and the private sector: Private haven or public hell? In Farazmand, A. (Ed.), *Privatization and Public Enterprise Reform: Implications for Public Management*. Westport, CT: Greenwood Publishing Group, pp. 23–42.

Canterbery, E. 2001. *A Brief History of Economics: Artful Approaches to the Dismal Science*. Singapore: World Scientific Publishing.

Chevallier, F.-X. 2000. *Greenspan's Taming of the Wave or the Golden Age Revisited*. London: Kogan Page.

Chong, S. and Callender, G. 2007. One more time.... How to measure alliance success in conditions of public–private partnering. In Thai, K. and Pigo, G. (Eds.), *Advancing Public Procurement: Practices, Innovation and Knowledge-Sharing* (pp. 97–115). Boca Raton, FL: PrAcademics Press.

Commonwealth of Australia. 1994. *Australian Government Purchasing Policies, "Buying Our Future."* Canberra: Australian Government Publishing Service.

Connolly, E. 2000. Rail chief admits accidents rose when maintenance cut. *Sydney Morning Herald*. Available at www.smh.com.au/news/0011/10/national/national3.

EMPSIT. 2001. The Employment Situation: October 2001 (press release [on-line]) Washington, DC: Bureau of Labor Statistics. Available at www.bls.gov/news.release/pdf/empsit

Ford, R. 1995. The anatomy of average TOC Ltd. *Modern Railways*, 52(559): 6–7.

Giddens, A. (Ed.). 2001. *The Global Third Way Debate*. Cambridge, U.K.: Polity Press.

Gore, A. 1993. *Creating a Government That Works Better and Costs Less: The Report of the National Performance Review*. New York: Plume.

Guttman, D. 2000. Public purpose and private service: The twentieth century culture of contracting out and the evolving law of diffused sovereignty. *Administrative Law Review*, 52(3): 859–926.

Gwartney, J., Lawson, R., and Samida, D. 2000. *Economic Freedom of the World 2000*, Vancouver, BC: Fraser Institute.

Gwartney, J., Lawson, R., and Easterly, W. 2006. *Economic Freedom of the World 2006*, Vancouver, BC: Fraser Institute.

Haigh, P. 2000. Regulator's targets could cause crisis, says Railtrack. *Rail*, 393: 8.

Halachmi, A. and Montgomery, V. 2000. Best value and accountability: Issues and observations. *International Journal of Administrative Sciences*, 66(3): 393–414.

Hammerschmid, G., Meyer, R., Sandner, K., Callender, G., and Johnston, J. July, 2001. The Debate on Privatization and Corporatization of Employment Services in Austria and Australia. Paper presented at the EGOS Conference, Lyons, France.

Harris, N. 2000. The priority is 'why' and 'what next'—Not who's to blame. *Rail Digest*, 393: 3.

Her Majesty's Government. 1999. *Modernising Government* (The White Paper). London: Author. Available at www.official-documents.co.uk/document/cm43/4310/4310.

Hill, G. 2002. Prosperity lost: Oregon's economic hangover. *The Oregonian*, Oct. 20: 1

Hodge, G. 1996. *Contracting out Government Services: A Review of International Evidence*. Melbourne, Australia: Montech Polity Ltd.

Hoyle, J. 2000. NSW upper house holds FreightCorp inquiry review. *Railway Digest*, 38(12): 6.

Hughes, O. 1994. *Public Management and Administration*. London, U.K.: The Macmillan Press.

Keynes, J.M. 1922. Introduction. In Henderson, H. (Ed.), *Supply and Demand*. London, U.K.: Nisbet and Co., Ltd.

Kittower, D. 1998. Counting on competition. *Governing Magazine*, 63: 66–74.

Klvacova, E. 1993. The current situation of privatization in Czechoslovakia. *Quarterly Journal of Economic Theory and Policy*, 11(1): 21.

Knight, S. 1999. Public arguments between the railway industry must stop. *Rail*, 347: 10.

Kuttner, R. 1997. *Everything for Sale*. New York: Alfred A Knopf.

Levy, F. 1999. Rhetoric and reality: Making sense of the income gap debate. *Harvard Business Review*, 77(5): 163–170.

Lewis, D., McCarville, M., Poole, C., and Sorenson, L. 1983. *Ford: 1903 to 1984*. New York: Crown Publishers Inc.

Lipsey, R. 1966. *An Introduction to Positive Economics*. London: Weidenfeld and Nicholson.

Matthews, D. 1999. Selecting quality suppliers: Concepts and misconceptions about government purchasing. *Oregon Public Purchasing Association Newsletter*: 6.

Morris, L. and Coultan, M. August 1, 1994. Airport backflip: State government to fund rail link. *Sydney Morning Herald*: 4.

Neumark, D. and Adams, S. March, 2000. *Do Living Wage Ordinances Reduce Urban Poverty?* Cambridge, MA: National Bureau of Economic Research.

NSW Auditor-General. 1996. *NSW Auditor-General's Report for 1996*. Sydney, Australia: Author.

ODOT Transcripts, 2001. Lettings of Highway Construction Projects [on-line] Portland, OR. Available at www.oregon.gov/ODOT/HWY/ESTIMATING/docs/bid_item_prices/2000_list.pdf

Oregon Bureau of Labor and Industries. 1998. *Wage and Hour Laws*. Portland, OR: Author.

Oregon Employment Department. 1998. *Oregon Labor Trends*. Salem, OR: Author.

Rogers, D. 2000. Glenbrook inquiry targets structure of rail in NSW. *Railway Digest*, 38(1): 7, 15–16.

Sandilands, B. July 13, 2001. Connection turn into beaten track. *The Australian Financial Review*: 18.

Savoie, D. 1994. *Thatcher, Reagan and Mulroney*. Toronto, Canada: University of Toronto Press.

Schneider, S.C. and Barsoux, J.L. 2003. *Managing across Cultures* (2nd ed.). Harlow, England, U.K.: Pearson Education Limited.

Seidman, H. 1990. Public enterprise versus privatization in the United States. *International Journal of Administrative Sciences*, 56: 15–28.

State Rail Authority of New South Wales. 1996. *Annual Report, 1995–1996*. Sydney, Australia.

Stiglitz, J. 2002. *Globalization and Its Discontents*. London: Penguin Books Ltd.

Thurow, L. 1992. *Head to Head: The Coming Economic Battle among Japan, Europe and America*. New York: William Morrow and Company, Inc.

World Bank. 1997. *World Development Report: The State in a Changing World*. New York: Oxford University Press.

Chapter 39

Offset Policy Design in International Procurement

Travis K. Taylor

CONTENTS

39.1 Introduction

Consider the following ultimatum by the government procurement office of Malaysia. The government would only purchase locomotives from General Electric (GE) if the firm would sign a parallel agreement to purchase palm oil from a specified list of Malaysian exporters. If GE balked, the Malaysians would propose a similar arrangement with other multinational firms. GE accepted the terms of this contract and the $64.5 million deal was consummated (Balu and Norfadilah, 2002). This arrangement is similar to hundreds of other offset contracts that occur each year. Offsets are contracts that require the seller to transfer extra economic benefits to the buyer as a condition for the sale of goods and services. In many instances, governments prefer to realize these benefits in the form of in-kind transfer instead of bargaining for price discounts.

Although few other than those actually engaged in the practice of offsets are aware of this contractual arrangement, it has become a popular tool of government procurement. Common in exchanges involving aerospace goods and services, offsets permeate the market for defense systems and weapons. These arrangements also arise when governments purchase telecommunications equipment, computers, and a myriad of other goods that need not embody high technology.

The arrangement, at its most fundamental level, is straightforward: a purchasing government obliges a foreign seller to include extra benefits with the sale of the base good. The foreign firm may then sign individual offset contracts with local firms in the purchasing government's economy. Aside from this buyer–seller relationship, offsets vary considerably in form. Offset transactions may take—but are not limited to—any of the following forms: subcontracting, technology transfer, countertrade, foreign investment, marketing assistance, training, coproduction, and licensed production.

Although the international trade statistics of Organization of Economic Cooperation and Development (OECD) do not track offsets and other compensation agreements, studies show that the market is sizeable. For example, estimates of countertrade as a percentage of the world trade range from a conservative 8 percent to a high of 20 percent (Hammond, 1990). Countertrade that is a result of government procurement requirements qualifies as an offset, whereas an agreement between two companies does not. Most aerospace and defense goods sold to foreign governments include offsets ranging from approximately 10 to 150 percent of the sale price. In the U.S. defense industry alone, 42 U.S. companies signed 513 new offset arrangements between 1993 and 2004 valued at $55.1 billion (U.S. Department of Commerce, 2006). This data indicates that offsets accompanied the sale of 513 U.S. defense products during the period. The actual number of offset contracts is far greater than 513 because the seller typically agrees to provide offset work to a number of firms (not included in the base 513 figure) in the purchasing government's economy. The data also suggests that purchasing countries are negotiating harder bargains: compensation ratios—the percentage of the base sale that is returned to the buyer's economy via offsets—have increased to 71 percent.

According to Wood (1992), at least 130 countries maintain some form of an offset program. Countries with starkly different economies and institutions are equally likely to use offsets. Developing and industrialized nations both employ offsets, as do virtually all regions of the world.[1] The United States is one of the few large economies without an explicit offset policy. Offsets are neither an academic curiosity nor an exceptional contractual arrangement. Table 39.1 shows that between 1993 and 2004, U.S. defense firms alone accumulated approximately $55 billion in offset obligations to support $77 billion worth of exports.

Consider two representative government purchases involving offsets. In April 2003, the government of Poland announced the purchase of 48 F-16 jets valued at $3.5 billion from the U.S. company Lockheed Martin. In return, Lockheed Martin agreed to provide the Polish economy with a package of benefits including investment, technology, transfer, and job creation worth more than $6 billion over ten years. It was the attractiveness of the offset package that gave Lockheed Martin the edge over rivals from France and a British–Swedish consortium. (Lockheed Martin, 2003)

To win the bid to supply a telecommunications infrastructure for Saudi Arabia, AT&T also included offsets. In 1994, AT&T agreed to provide billions of dollars in new work and technology transfer for the Saudi economy (Matthews, 1996, p. 250). By 1998, AT&T had fulfilled most of its obligations by teaming with local Saudi businesses to form equal equity joint ventures. The joint ventures are now successfully supplying production inputs to AT&T and other export markets.

Table 39.1 Summary of U.S. Defense Offset Arrangements, 1993–2004 ($ Millions)

Year	*U.S. Companies*	*Agreements*	*Base Export Value[a] ($)*	*Offset Value ($)*	*Offset Ratio[b] (Percent)*	*Countries*
1993	17	28	13,935	4,784.4	34.3	16
1994	18	49	4,792.4	2,048.7	42.7	20
1995	20	47	7,529.9	6,102.6	81.0	18
1996	16	53	3,119.7	2,431.6	77.9	19
1997	15	60	5,925.5	3,825.5	64.6	20
1998	12	41	3,029.2	1,768.2	58.4	17
1999	10	45	5,656.6	3,456.9	61.1	11
2000	10	43	6,576.2	5,704.8	86.7	16
2001	11	34	7,017.3	5,460.9	77.8	13
2002	12	41	7,406.2	6,094.8	82.3	17
2003	11	32	7,293.1	9,110.4	124.9	13
2004	14	40	4,927.5	4,329.7	87.9	18
Year total	42	513	77,208.6	55,118.5	71.4	41

Source: From U.S. Department of Commerce, in *Offsets in Defense Trade: Annual Report to Congress*, U.S. Government Printing Office, Washington, D.C., 2006, p. 33.

Notes: Other areas include all countries outside of Europe.
Time refers to the average time (in months) allowed for fulfillment of the offset obligation.

[a] Base export value is the summation of U.S. sales to countries that require offsets.
[b] Offset ratio percent is the compensation ratio defined as the (offset value/base export value).

Notwithstanding the reported success of many offset arrangements (particularly from the buyer's perspective), economists are understandably cautious of any policy that diminishes the role of prices in market exchange. Instead of competing in terms of price and quality, offsets encourage sellers to focus on benefits packages that may have no relevance to the procurement good. In most settings, the exchange of goods for money in markets is more efficient than barter.

Furthermore, the World Trade Organization (WTO) has ruled that many types of offset arrangements are illegal. In its Agreement on Government Procurement (WTO, 1996), Article XVI states that "Entities shall not, in the qualification and selection of suppliers, products or services, or in the evaluation of tenders and award of contracts, impose, seek or consider offsets." The second part of article XVI, and also articles V and XXIII, however, allow for numerous exceptions. For example, offsets are legal for any of the following transactions: national security interests, public morals, order or safety, health or intellectual property. In effect, nearly all of the transactions involved in the defense industry, and some in the telecommunications and information technology industries, are open to offset bidding. It should also be noted that as a plurilateral agreement, not all member countries are bound by the agreement. Presently, developing countries are permitted to use offsets, as long as it is not a determining factor in the awarding of contracts.

Why then, do governments often accept in-kind offsets instead of price discounts for the procured good? Even if we acknowledge a role for government intervention when markets fail to transfer goods and services efficiently, it is not at all clear that the expected net benefits of offsets exceed those of other policy tools. Indeed, offsets may be helpful to an economy in some circumstances, and quite damaging in other settings. Commenting on the state of policy art, Udis and Maskus (1991, p. 163) "recommend a serious effort to develop a criteria to distinguish between beneficial offsets and detrimental offsets before attempts at international control of the phenomenon are mounted."

This chapter develops a criterion to determine when the offset is an appropriate policy instrument for government procurement. A policy matrix is presented that offers some general guidelines to government officials considering offsets as part of a broader procurement strategy. Using transaction cost theory complemented by the capabilities view of the firm,[2] I explain how the welfare effect of offsets hinges on the exchange setting and the institutions of the purchasing economy. The main finding of the chapter is that any attempt to use a mandatory offset policy for all government procurement limits the dimensions of the negotiation and may suffer from diseconomies of scale and scope. A more flexible variable offset policy, which uses offsets for a particular class of goods and relies on markets in other cases, is preferable in most settings.

The organization of the chapter is as follows. Section 39.2 differentiates offsets from other government policies. Before advocating any sort of offset policy, it is necessary to specify the circumstances in which offsets are preferable to other instruments. Section 39.3 develops a prescriptive model to assist procurement officers (and ministries of finance/development) in the selection of an optimal policy instrument. A conclusion follows in Section 39.4.

39.2 Offset Policy Design

The offset is a flexible policy instrument that can serve multiple objectives. Depending on the objectives of the purchasing government, an offset can be designed to support any of the following: generation of jobs, technology transfer, increased workloads, promotion of joint ventures, labor training, management services, and safeguarding the base exchange.

There are numerous ways of promoting the economic objectives listed above. Tax incentives, subsidies, tariffs, local content protection, export promotion, and investment are commonplace in the government intervention lexicon. All of these policies can—to varying degrees of success—achieve a number of objectives. On the other hand, these policies can be dreadfully inefficient. In competitive markets where information transfers seamlessly and contracts are complete, such intervention techniques hamper economic growth. The market is remarkably well suited to induce competition, transfer technology, lower costs, and foster the benefits therein.

The same can be said about offsets. By leaving the price margin of monetary exchange, offsets can introduce inefficiencies to the economy similar to those endemic in the policies listed above. However, if the offset is designed properly in a procurement setting marked by imperfect competition, poor information transfer, and incomplete contracts, it can actually be welfare enhancing.

The fact that the offset policy is merely an attachment to an international procurement is what differentiates it from other government policies. When procuring goods in imperfectly competitive markets, the price is typically set above the cost. Governments can use their bargaining power (as a large buyer) to extract some of this surplus from sellers. The extraction can yield savings from a

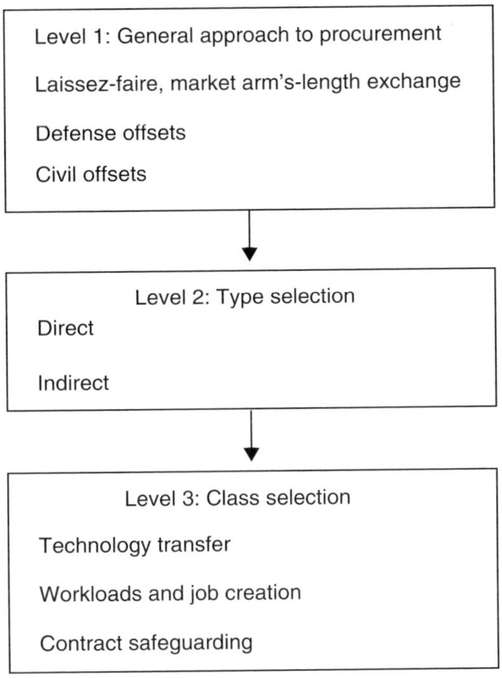

Figure 39.1 Offset policy design by a purchasing government.

discounted price; alternatively, the government can opt for a package of benefits in the form of an offset. We will return to this critical decision in Section 39.3 with the policy matrix.

As shown in Figure 39.1, after selecting an offset in conjunction with a civil or defense purchase, the procurement officer must decide between a direct and an indirect offset (level 2).

Direct offsets require the seller to transfer benefits to the purchasing government's economy, which are related to the base procurement. For example, when Boeing sells its airplanes to other countries, the company often provides subcontracting work to firms in the purchasing government's economy. Airplane tires, wings, and subsystems production would all qualify as direct subcontracting work. A direct offset is ideal for countries wishing to generate workloads, employment, and technology transfer for an established industry.

Indirect offsets are more flexible. The benefits package need not be related to the base procurement. Indeed, developing countries often employ indirect offsets as part of a broader economic growth strategy. Indirect offsets worth several billion dollars were an integral part of British Aerospace's (BAe) bid to supply the Kingdom of Saudi Arabia with a massive defense program. The indirect offsets included investment, joint ventures, and technology transfer to multiple industries.

Level 3 of offset policy design further delineates the benefits package. Here, the procurement officer matches the offset (direct or indirect) to the targeted objective. The officer will frequently match the seller with a particular industry or firm to foster the employment gains, workloads, and technology transfer. Level 3 safeguarding is sufficiently esoteric to save its discussion for another time.

39.3 Policy Selection Model[3]

We can make some general recommendations for procurement policy by varying the parameters of the matrix: the degree of exchange hazards, $Z(Z \in [0,1])$, and the expected benefit to the offset recipient of interaction with the seller (B is low or high). Consider the matrix in Figure 39.2.

Six distinct policy instruments are advisable for the six economic settings (cells in the matrix). An offset policy is advisable in only two of the six cases. Perhaps, most importantly, a mandatory offset program is appropriate if and only if exchange hazards are high (approach the index value of 1) and the expected benefit index, B, is high. Let us examine the policy prescription for each economic setting.

39.3.1 Arm's-Length Exchange

In the absence of impediments to the transaction, markets are the most efficient means of exchange. This economic setting comprises atomistic and largely anonymous sellers. The high-powered incentives of market competition, teamed with nominal transaction costs, make this form of procurement policy plausible for governments—irrespective of market power. If the government does in fact boast some degree of market power, it can bargain for price discounts of the procurement good.

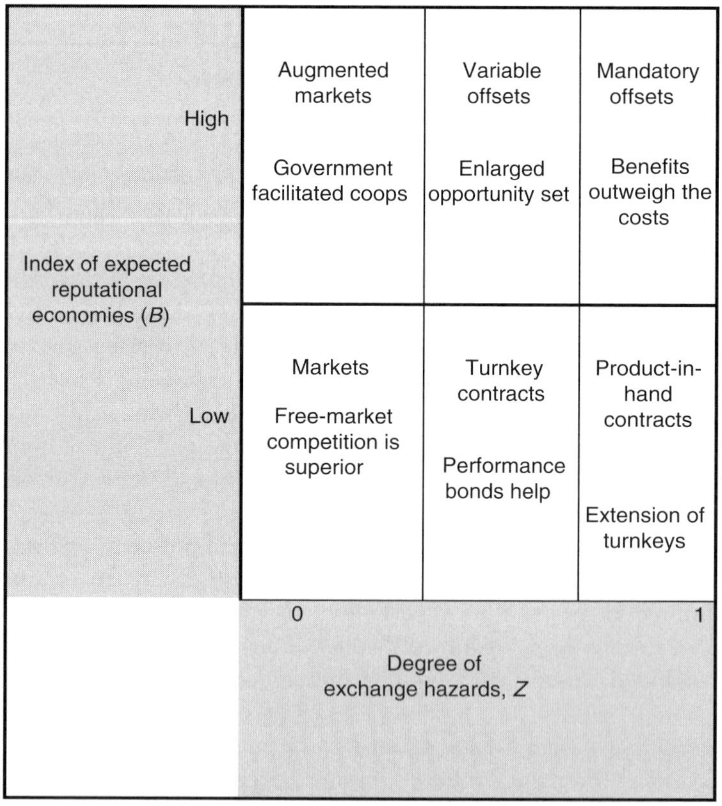

Figure 39.2 Procurement policy matrix.

There is no a priori reason to leave the price margin in this economic setting. This policy prescription holds irrespective of the government's overarching development strategy. Employing offsets in a perfectly functioning market tends to reduce welfare for three reasons: (1) sellers are already pricing at cost (hence no opportunity for further rent extraction by the government), (2) technology is already transferring efficiently, and (3) offsets incur an administrative burden.[4] Examples of procurement in this category include food, paper clips, ball bearings, and so forth.

39.3.2 Augmented Markets: Markets with Alliances

Consider a scenario where markets function efficiently (z approaches zero), and B is positive. This scenario is common for the procurement of goods that embody medium technology in production. The medium technology category of industries, which includes goods such as scientific equipment, petroleum refining, shipbuilding, and motor vehicles, is suitable for the augmented markets scenario. Although we can expect markets to perform well, a nascent industry in the purchasing government's economy may benefit from a strategic alliance with an incumbent.

The procurement team opts for markets but also encourages collaborative projects. Markets are preferable because information problems are nonexistent, which greatly reduces the probability of opportunistic behavior in the exchange. However, if buyers generally display an allegiance to brand name capital, a strategic alliance may prove beneficial to the domestic firms. The government can use its bargaining power to encourage collaborative agreements without formally requiring them (e.g., an offset), thereby avoiding extra administrative costs.

Importantly, the market is still the driving force behind the collaboration opportunity. Only domestic firms that possess the requisite capabilities can submit bids under this procurement program. The seller selects domestic firms based entirely on price and quality competition. Therefore, the high-powered incentives of market competition remain largely intact. The administrative burden of the augmented market policy exceeds that of pure markets (scenario 1), but not by a sizeable amount.

Governments are already experimenting with the augmented markets procurement policy. Mathews (1996, p. 234) finds that "a number of countries such as Greece and Spain are now encouraging the creation of long term business partnerships within their [procurement] programs." The most popular collaborative instruments include joint ventures, licensed production, coproduction, and direct foreign investment.

The Australian Partnerships for Development (PfD) is an example of a successful augmented markets policy. Created in 1990, the PfD encourages foreign companies to undertake long-term investment in research and development (R&D) and augment the industrial technological base. The program waives "offsets requirements for foreign companies which agree to enter into strategic alliances with Australian companies in the information and telecommunications industries" (Capling, 1994, p. 12).

The program maintains a competitive bidding process for domestic firms wishing to participate, while using its market power to increase the stock of reputational capital in these industries. The PfD program is especially beneficial to Australian software manufacturers, "who have developed world class products but have not had sufficient resources to devote to worldwide marketing" (Capling, 1994, p. 12). By 1993, 21 multinational enterprises had signed agreements with the Australian government to participate in the PfD program (Capling, 1994, p. 12). This augmented markets policy is well conceived and appropriate for an environment with low exchange hazards and a positive reputation/future interaction variable.

39.3.3 Turnkey Contracts

In a procurement setting exposed to moderate exchange hazards, combined with little or no expected reputational economies from the seller, a turnkey contract supported by a performance bond is a sound policy choice. Turnkey contracts lower exchange hazards by shifting risk from the buyer to the seller. The seller signs a contract to build an operational factory (or other good) for the buyer. By signing a detailed contract, the seller is legally responsible for the initial feasibility study, the design, engineering, and construction of the plant. In addition, the seller does not receive full payment until several production runs are complete.[5] Table 39.2 lists the advantages and disadvantages of turnkey contracts.

Turnkey contracts improve the integrity of the exchange, but they do not eradicate seller opportunism entirely. Occasionally, the output of the initial production trials is acceptable, but local workers trained under the supervision of the technical staff fail to replicate the outcome.[6] This is not surprising: production in a sterile environment under the direction of the seller's technical staff is in stark contrast to real-time production by local workers. Profitability of a firm depends, to a large degree, on how it can adapt to economic change. Detailed instructions and the transfer of ancillary capabilities in a sterile environment frequently do not prepare the firm for exogenous shocks. The seller has incentive to perform its duties in an overly perfunctory manner with the foreign staff to minimize cost, and more importantly, to guard core competences. Algeria's problems with turnkey contracts have been well documented in this regard (see Oman, 1984, pp. 48–50).

Information asymmetries and other imperfections render market exchange hazardous and inefficient as the technological intensity of production increases. The government can use its buying power to negotiate a more efficient mode of exchange with the turnkey contract, which places the onus on the seller. Because the primary objective in this setting is to improve the integrity of the transaction, the procurement officer's relevant choice is between turnkey and offset arrangements.

Table 39.2 Turnkey Contracts in Procurement

Advantages	*Disadvantages*
Ownership and control in the post-contract stage is retained by the owner/purchaser	Higher price and fewer bids
Single, legally responsible seller reduces transaction costs for the buyer	Plant facility (or other contracted good) is constructed with little participation by the buyer and employees; less learning-by-doing
Single seller generally ensures shorter time-to-completion for project[a]	Although ancillary competences transfer easily, local employees may not gain the crucial tacit knowledge
Less risk for the buyer	
Useful for the construction of complete plants	

Source: Adopted from United Nations, in *Features and Issues in Turnkey Contracts in Developing Countries: A Technical Paper*, United Nations Press, New York, 1983, pp. 10–11.

[a] Because responsibility for the multiple stages of design and production resides with one entity, one can expect better coordination between the stages and fewer disputes.

Generally, if the objective is to obtain an end-use good like a functioning chemical plant, the turnkey contract is a good choice. In this case, the buyer's primary interest is to improve the incentives of the exchange to minimize the transaction hazards. If, however, the government intends to develop the capabilities of the good for other applications, the choice between offsets and turnkeys is not so obvious. Officials can design the offset to acquire capabilities while also increasing the integrity of the exchange.

39.3.4 Variable Offset Policy

The variable offset policy is suitable for exchange environments characterized by moderate hazards and high-expected benefits from interaction with the seller. This policy gives procurement officers the choice of attaching an offset to the government purchase, or negotiating price discounts in markets. It offers more flexibility than strict mandatory offset schemes. Negotiators can compare the net benefits of a price margin exchange with an offset for the particular economic setting. This increases the dimensions of the exchange and reduces the probability of the buyer accepting an offset proposal that results in production diseconomies.

With more flexibility in contract negotiations, however, comes added responsibility for procurement officers. Governments using variable programs require bureaucrats to compare the complex intertemporal costs and benefits associated with offsets to the price changes from market exchange. Governments without highly skilled professionals in procurement may be better off using a mandatory scheme or markets—not both embedded in a variable offset policy.

Of the various nonstandard contracts, the variable offset policy offers the most dimensions for mutually beneficial exchange. Procurement officers can adjust the terms of the exchange to support a development strategy that is appropriate for the particular economic environment. After experimenting with mandatory offsets during the 1970s and part of the 1980s, Australia switched to a variable offset policy. The consensus in Australia is that the policy has fulfilled its objectives (namely, technology transfer), while not handcuffing negotiators to non-price margin schemes (Capling, 1994; Hall and Markowski, 1994). Nevertheless, today most governments opt for mandatory offsets in procurement.

39.3.5 Mandatory Offsets

Mandatory offsets are ideal for procurement that is subject to severe exchange hazards and high-expected benefits from interaction with the seller. A mandatory offset policy requires offsets for government procurement (of specified goods and services) from a foreign seller above a threshold dollar value. This policy encourages competition based on content rather than price. Mandatory offsets are easier to administer than the challenging variable scheme because bureaucrats are solving an optimization problem over fewer variables.[7]

Another benefit of the mandatory policy is its impact on rent-seeking behavior. All types of government intervention in the marketplace attract some degree of rent-seeking behavior by economic agents, firms, interest groups, and government officials. Rent-seeking behavior is inimical to societal welfare because agents expend real resources to capture rents without producing new output. Buchanan et al. (1980, p. 10) argue persuasively that "once markets are not allowed to work [on the price margin], or once they are interfered with in their allocative functioning, politics must enter. And political allocation, like market allocation, involves profit seeking as a dynamic activating force… the rents secured reflect a diversion of value from consumers generally to the favored rent seeker, with a net loss of value in the process."

Variable offsets are susceptible to higher levels of rent seeking than the mandatory policy because procurement officials have free reign to choose between prices (markets) and content modifications (offsets). Price changes directly affect government expenditures, and offsets impact domestic industry. The variable policy, therefore, attracts rent seekers internally (including the offset agency itself) and externally (interest groups).

The mandatory policy attracts less rent-seeking because of the strict directive for offsets whenever government makes a purchase above a threshold dollar value. The key is to design the policy such that government procurement of a selected list of goods automatically triggers a mandatory scheme. High technological intensity goods can support a mandatory scheme. Government procurement of aerospace, information technology, and telecommunications equipment, for example, occupies this category.

The conclusions drawn from the model allow one to argue strongly against the use of mandatory offsets outside of high technology procurement. If exchange hazards are less severe and government still employs a mandatory offset policy, the buyer is implicitly rejecting price margin contracts that are potentially superior to the offset.

We can make a simple analogy to offsets using the housing market.[8] Suppose you could purchase either a completely furnished house that boasts extras (a bundle) like a swimming pool and a deck for a given price, or another house that includes no additional amenities. Not surprisingly, the unfurnished house has the lower price. Nontrivially, after performing the cost accounting you find that the price differential is far greater than the total cost of purchasing the extras as components. If transaction costs are low, the buyer may benefit from purchasing the unfurnished home, depending on the consumer's utility function. However, if you announce to the housing market that you will only consider bids that include bundled extras, real estate agents will act accordingly and reduce the size of the market. This is the pitfall of a mandatory offset policy applied indiscriminately.

Some countries are, in fact, following the selective mandatory policy outlined above. Israel, for instance, maintains a sophisticated program that mandates offsets for procurement of high-tech military hardware, hospital equipment, computer hardware, and civilian aircraft (Harben, 1984, p. 33). These goods qualify as potentially severe exchange hazards, and the expected benefit from the seller's reputational capital is high.

Conversely, many West European governments require 100 percent mandatory offsets for most large-scale defense procurement. At first glance, this policy appears to fulfill the necessary conditions for optimality put forth in the model. However, defense industry procurement encompasses an incredibly wide range of goods and services, many of which are of low technology. Defense procurement includes generic ammunition and other ordnance, tires, clothing, and ball bearings, for example. The rigid mandatory policy is detrimental to West European welfare because the opportunity cost of imposing offsets for goods that do not present an exchange hazard is price margin savings.

After observing the dissatisfactory results of a mandatory policy in the 1980s, Malaysia switched to a variable program in the 1990s.[9] Australia had a similar experience. The objective of the mandatory policy of the 1980s was to increase the level of technological capabilities in strategic industries. Government officials believed an across the board, mandatory offset policy would generate high rates of technology transfer. The policy was a failure. Sellers inundated procurement officials with thousands of offset proposals.

Clearly, requiring atomistic firms to include offsets in the sale simply raises the output price with almost no reputational effect for the purchasing economy. Liesch (1991) finds that Australian procurement officials used workload and job creation data to determine the efficacy of an offset proposal, often failing to evaluate the quality of technology transfer. According to Liesch (1991, p. 121), "government mandated countertrade [offsets] programs seem particularly prone to this outcome."

39.3.6 Product-in-Hand Contracts

The sixth economic setting of the policy matrix combines severe exchange hazards with little or no expected benefit from interaction with the seller. In this setting, it is critical to build safeguards into the contractual arrangement, but offsets would be an inefficient way of doing so. Because strategic alliances and other interaction with the seller are unlikely to bear fruit, the cost of the offset burden will likely exceed any benefits. Instead, government may find it advantageous to employ a variant of the turnkey, known as the product-in-hand contract.

This arrangement requires the seller to set up an operational system, akin to the turnkey contract. In contrast to the turnkey, however, the seller's staff remains on-site after the trial runs to teach local employees how to maintain and troubleshoot the system. Only after local personnel demonstrate competency during multiple production runs does the seller receive full payment. This contract greatly reduces the probability of seller opportunism.

With risk transferring almost entirely to the seller, the output price of product-in-hand contracts rises drastically.[10] Moreover, the strict conditions of the contract attract a much smaller pool of bids than the turnkey arrangement. For these reasons, governments seldom employ product-in-hand contracts in procurement. The purchase of an entire chemical plant that includes numerous specific assets in the production process is an example.

39.4 Conclusion

This chapter enumerated the pros and cons of several policy instruments used in government purchasing, with a focus on offset arrangements. The offset is an attractive option for procurement officers, mainly because its benefits are visible and can double as an economic development strategy, while its costs are masked. However, care must be taken to determine whether it is in fact the most cost-effective policy to achieve the stated aims of the government. Indeed, among the thousands of products that governments purchase annually, only a small minority would be suitable for an offset. Several points are worth emphasizing.

First, procurement officers should conduct a benefit–cost estimate to determine whether the offset is superior to other instruments. For example, is bargaining for price discounts on the base good and then using these proceeds to purchase new technology on the open market preferable to the offset? Alternatively, perhaps government could provide a subsidy to a targeted industry and foster growth more effectively in the domestic economy compared to the offset.

Second, when an offset is selected as an attachment to the transaction, the government should construct a well-defined contract. The contract should specify (1) a list of products or firms in the domestic economy that the seller can partner with to fulfill the offset obligation, (2) a schedule for fulfillment of various stages of the offset obligation, and (3) a penalty clause for noncompliance. Research has shown that such specification is desirable.[11]

Third, governments should build databases to allow for formal accounting of the offset programs. Like other government policies, offsets involve massive amounts of public funds. The performance of these funds ought to be accounted for by an offset audit team. Then and only then, argues Brauer (2002, p. 13), can the "public-at-large decide whether the losses or profits are worth the original objective."

Notes

1. As of 2006, the African continent is an exception. A majority of the governments in this region did not have an official offset policy. This is largely due to the small government budgets and the associated limits placed on procurement of defense and information technology. South Africa, however, uses offsets and, in fact, held a contentious public debate during 2003–2004. Offsets are on the rise in South America, with middle-income countries like Brazil, Chile, and Colombia leading the way with explicit offset requirements in 2006.
2. Transaction cost economics explores the costs of using markets, outside of the firm's production function. Economic capabilities, generally speaking, are the skills and competences that labor possesses. The capabilities view of the firm considers the firm to be a pool of core and ancillary competences that become "routinized" over time to perform production activities.
3. Portions of this section originated in Taylor (2004).
4. See Taylor (2001) for a discussion of how offsets alter the marginal, average, total, and transaction costs of the seller.
5. The seller receives partial payment during the initial stages of the project, and the remainder upon successful completion of the trial runs. There are notable variations to this sort of compensation scheme. For highly technical projects, the seller receives payments according to the percentage of the project that is complete. In the extreme case, a buyer may not release full payment for one or two years after the trial production runs. Such compensation schemes are rare, however, because sellers are unwilling to assume this level of risk, and also because the output price rises significantly.
6. Some trial periods last only 24–48 hours.
7. The relevant comparison for the bureaucrat is between bundled packages offered by different sellers. The bureaucrat does not need to calculate the offset's shadow price equivalent to make an accurate comparison with price margin offers.
8. I attribute this analogy to discussions with Stefan Markowski, Department of Economics and Management, Australian Defence Force Academy.
9. Interview with Mr. Ahmed Khalili, director of the Malaysian Offset Program, June 2, 1998.
10. Hennart (1989) reports that product-in-hand contracts are 50–100 percent more expensive, on average, than turnkey contracts.
11. See Hall and Markowski (1996) and Markowski and Hall (1998) for analysis of offset performance in Australia. In general, offset contracts that included a penalty clause raised the average rate of compliance.

References

Balu, N. and Norfadilah, 2002. Countertrade: The Malaysian experience. *Oil Palm Industry Economic Journal*, 2(1), 45–49.

Brauer, J. 2002. Economic Aspects of Arms Trade Offsets (Unpublished manuscript). Augusta, GA: Augusta State University.

Buchanan, J., Tollison, R., and Tullock, G. (Eds.). 1980. *Toward a Theory of the Rent-Seeking Society*. College Station, TX: Texas A&M University Press.

Capling, A. 1994. Bargaining for competitive advantage: Government purchasing and the changing relationship between the state and multinational enterprises in Australia. *Journal of Industry Studies*, 1(2), 1–22.

Hall, P. and Markowski, S. 1994. On the normality and abnormality of offset obligations. *Defence and Peace Economics*, 5, 173–188.

Hall, P. and Markowski, S. 1996. Some lessons from the Australian defense offsets experience. *Defense Analysis*, 12(3), 289–314.

Hammond, G. 1990. *Countertrade, Offsets and Barter in International Political Economy*. New York: St. Martin's Press.

Harben, P. 1984. Offset overview. *Countertrade and Barter Quarterly*, 3, 29–37.
Hennart, J.-F. 1989. The transaction cost rationale for countertrade. *Journal of Law, Economics and Organization*, 5, 127–153.
Liesch, P. 1991. *Government Mandated Countertrade*. Aldershot, England: Avebury.
Lockheed Martin. 2003. Lockheed Martin and Poland Sign Offset Agreement Valued at More than $6 Billion. (Press Release) Available at www.lockheedmartin.com/news/articles/041803_1.
Markowski, S. and Hall, P. 1998. Challenges of defence procurement. *Defence and Peace Economics*, 9, 3–37.
Matthews, R. 1996. Saudi Arabia's defense offsets programmes: Policy and performance. *Defence and Peace Economics*, 7, 233–251.
Oman, C. 1984. *New Forms of International Investment in Developing Countries*. Paris: OECD.
Taylor, T.K. 2001. A New Institutional Economic Analysis of Offset Arrangements in Government Procurement. (Unpublished Doctoral Dissertation). Storrs, CT: University of Connecticut.
Taylor, T.K. 2004. Using procurement offsets as an economic development strategy. In Brauer and Dunne (Eds.), *Arms Trade and Economic Development*. New York: Routledge.
Udis, B. and Maskus, K. 1991. Offsets as industrial policy: Lessons from aerospace. *Defence Economics*, 2, 151–164.
United Nations. 1983. *Features and Issues in Turnkey Contracts in Developing Countries: A Technical Paper*. New York: United Nations Press.
U.S. Department of Commerce. 2006. *Offsets in Defense Trade: Annual Report to Congress*. Washington, D.C.: U.S. Government Printing Office.
Wood, D. 1992. *Australian Defence Offsets Program*. Proceedings of the Defence Offsets Seminar. Canberra, Australia: Department of Defence.
World Trade Organization. 1996. *Agreement on Government Procurement: Uruguay Round*. Available at http://www.wto.org/english/docs_e/legal_e/gpr-94_01_e.htm.

Chapter 40

Regression Approach for Estimating Procurement Cost

Gary W. Moore and Edward D. White III

CONTENTS

40.1 Introduction

An ongoing problem for over three decades, cost growth during the acquisition of major weapon systems concerns not only those who work in the acquisition environment, but also the members of the Congress and the general public. According to reports by the Government Accountability Office (GAO), RAND, and the Institute for Defense Analysis, the average cost growth in major defense acquisition programs ranges anywhere from 20 to 50 percent (Calcutt, 1993: i). This fiscal escalation in major acquisition programs adversely impacts the defense department, the defense industry, and the nation.

The Department of Defense (DoD) coined the phrase "realistic costing" for the current reform being undertaken in the defense acquisition community. "Under the new costing approach, the Pentagon will adopt program estimates developed by the Cost Analysis Improvement Group (CAIG)[1] in conjunction with a service estimate" (Grossman, 2002: 2). Realistic costing utilizes the CAIG's cost estimating expertise to provide higher quality estimates. DoD's dedication to realistic costing contributed significantly to the cancellation of the Navy area missile defense program, sending a strong message to the acquisition community. If managers overrun their budget and breach the Nunn–McCurdy law, their program will be terminated (ibid).

For managers to understand and to contain cost growth, they must identify and control the root causes of cost growth. Program managers often resort to a process known as "buffering" to increase the accuracy of the baseline estimate and to limit the program's likelihood of incurring cost overruns. Buffering of an estimate entails assigning a cost estimate (dollar value) to each of the cost risks, e.g., additional engineering effort because of a new weapon system, avionics package, or stealth technology. If/when the risk comes to fruition, the plan is to have sufficient funds available so that the program does not have to request additional funding. In the past, costs have been assigned to these risks; however, they have been shown to be sometimes underestimated. According to McCrillis (2003), who presented the conclusions of a ten-year study by OSD CAIG, procurement cost growth has occurred primarily because of optimistic learning curves.

An example of a current acquisition program struggling to keep costs under control is that of the F/A-22. The production quantity of the Air Force's newest air-to-air fighter has fluctuated considerably over the past decade in the attempt to maintain some modicum of control over increased cost growth. Because of rising program costs, the F/A-22 program has reduced the number of initial desired aircraft from 750 to 658 in 1991 to a more recently lowered number of 276 in 2002. In 1997 and 2001, the DoD conducted reviews of the F/A-22 Raptor program. During these reviews, the Air Force attributed estimated production cost growth to increased labor, airframe, and engine costs. These factors totaled almost 70 percent of the overall cost growth (GAO, 2003).

Although some aspects of cost growth will always be hard to control or even to predict (e.g., the political arena), the real challenge remains to be accurately estimating the amount of costs to assign to risks. This process necessitates that the manager accurately identify risks related to potential cost growth in program estimates and assign appropriate dollar values to these risks. Although ultimately responsible for their programs, managers rely on the cost estimating community, comprising engineers, mathematicians, financial analysts, and acquisition personnel (procurement specialists), to assign accurate dollar values to specific risk factors and include these dollar amounts into the cost estimate.

Cost estimators determine and assign dollar amounts to risk factors by utilizing a vast assortment of tools. Cost estimators oftentimes use subjective means, such as expert opinions, for making these dollar assignments. When available, the estimator may utilize more objective methods, such as gathering historical data and comparing analogous systems. If possible, the analyst should group historical cost growth data into different categories and then analyze these categories to determine if different types of cost growth have different and distinct predictors. Statistical regression techniques prove useful for determining such relationships provided they are based upon sound framework and past research.

One such historical encapsulation is by Sipple et al. (2004) who conducted an exhaustive review of all cost growth studies performed during the past ten years. From this review, they gained valuable insight into the root causes of cost growth, which consists of funding increases in research and development, procurement, or operating and support (O&S). They also found extensive amounts of research devoted to establishing predictive relationships and determining predictor variables. For example, their consolidated review revealed that the average production cost growth is 19 percent; that the urgency of the program, difficulty of technology, and degree of testing affects cost growth; and that there exists a relationship between the cost growth and the schedule growth in both the development and the production phases. That is, if there is cost growth in one aspect, there is a likelihood of the other also realizing an increased growth.

From this foundational framework, White et al. (2004) assembled an extensive database with over 70 predictor variables from a collection of data gathered from the selected acquisition reports (SARs) on 115 major acquisition programs spanning from 1990 to 2000. From this database, they constructed regression models aimed at predicting engineering and manufacturing development (EMD)[2] cost growth directly related to engineering changes.[3] They found that combining logistic and multiple regression techniques most accurately represented the projected cost growth without violating the underlying regression assumptions.

Additionally, White et al. (2004) suggested that the usefulness of this two-step approach might extrapolate beyond predicting engineering cost growth during the EMD phase of the acquisition life cycle. That is, can this methodology be extended to other cost areas? While they focused on engineering cost growth, we investigate the feasibility of this joint approach in modeling procurement cost growth during EMD. Much of the performed research that we annotate in this chapter mirrors the efforts carried forth in White et al. (2004), although we do allow for more complicated regression models via interactions of predictors, which we discuss in detail later.

40.2 Methods

We use the SAR database as the sole source for cost variances and other information included in this analysis as in White et al. (2004). This database contains historical, schedule, cost, budget, and performance information for major acquisition programs from all military services. Therefore, the programs listed in the SAR consistently represent programs with high-level government interest.[4] The SARs provide cost variance data in both base year and then year dollars. We use base year dollars and then convert to 2002 dollars for analysis, making comparison across programs more feasible. Although, SARs record cost variances in seven different categories, we focus exclusively on total procurement cost variance during the EMD phase, as most dramatic program changes occur during this phase, and not specifically on one targeted cost category as most cost estimators are only concerned with overall cost growth.

White et al. (2004) constructed a database that contains SAR data from 1990 through the summer of 2000. Because this research effort follows theirs, we had access to their established database. We verified the existing information by checking past SARs and then updated the newest/most recent data by program in the SAR database to capture recent trends. Specifically, the latest SARs at our disposal at the time of this research were from December 2001. Thus, our data collection efforts begin with those SARs and work backward through the summer of 2000. These reports are then incorporated into the previous database, resulting in it now spanning from 1990 through 2001.

We use the same predictor variables as in White et al. (2004). A complete list of these predictors can be found in the Appendix along with a description of each. The continuous variable classification denotes a quantitative measurement variable, while a binary classification is reserved for the typical, dummy categorical variable. Similar to what White et al. (2004) encountered, we learn that when we incorporate into our model the EMD maturity variables[5] that use initial operational capability (IOC) or first unit equipped (FUE) computations, we face a scarcity of data points. Unfortunately, FUE dates are not mandatory SAR requirements (DoD, 2001). Additionally, FUE is primarily an Army term and is not present in Air Force programs other than joint ventures (DAU, 1999). Consequently, this limits the potential use of these as predictors, but does not necessarily limit their potency in incorporating within predictive regression models. In fact, we demonstrate that one of these variables is highly predictive of procurement cost growth[6] in the EMD phase of a weapon system.

We concern ourselves with two different response variables: one that indicates if procurement cost growth occurs and another that expresses the degree to which procurement cost growth occurs. The first of the two, we express as a binary variable where the value "1" means that we estimate a program will have cost growth in procurement dollars, while the value "0" means that it will not. We call this variable "procurement cost growth." To construct the most useful model possible, we decide that the second response variable should be the percentage of procurement cost growth rather than just relative cost growth. This format applies equally well to programs with both large and small acquisition costs. We call this second response variable "procurement cost growth percent," and we define it as the difference between the current estimate and development estimate, divided by the development estimate. (Note: the current estimate may or not may be the same as the initial contract award. The current estimate may have been revised/rebaselined since the program's inception.)

To determine if our data falls in line with the discovery of White et al. (2004), we preliminarily investigated our response variable, which could consist of positive, negative, or even no cost growth. We soon discovered that a discrete point mass, representing approximately 20 percent of the data, lay at zero. A basic assumption of ordinary least squares (OLS) regression requires that the response variable be from a reasonably continuous distribution without such "spikes" of point probability. As such, our findings mirrored what White et al. (2004) realized. Hence, our methodology and subsequent analysis follow precisely what they established. Therefore, we duplicate those said procedures, which we now briefly review.

Before initiating any regression analysis, we randomly set aside approximately 20 percent of our data (25 out of a total of 122 programs) for model validation and to ensure that we construct a robust statistical model. Later, we "split" the remaining 80 percent data into two pieces. Our first cut involves coding the data into 1's and 0's. We code each program that incurs cost growth with a 1 and each program that has either no cost or negative cost growth with a 0. Because an estimator would not realistically assess negative cost growth in an estimate, we do not consider negative cost growth in our model. As with White et al. (2004), we then utilize logistic regression to analyze this discrete distribution as this particular type of regression is appropriate to model binary outcomes, i.e., those usually coded 0 and 1 (Neter et al., 1996: 567). Logistic regression has become the standard method for regression analysis of dichotomous data in many fields, especially in the health sciences (Hosmer and Lemeshow, 2000: vii). The reader is referred there for further background, if needed.

Our second, and last cut so to speak of the data, involves grouping just those programs that have positive cost growth. The idea is to have available a model that will predict the percentage amount of cost growth given the logistic model's cue suggesting the likelihood of procurement cost growth. This resultant second pool of data is relatively continuous and hence OLS regression becomes the standard analysis to employ. Our multiple regression efforts focus not only on individual variables but also include logical interactions between variables that may enhance their predictive relationships. In explaining interactions, we present the following scenario depicted in

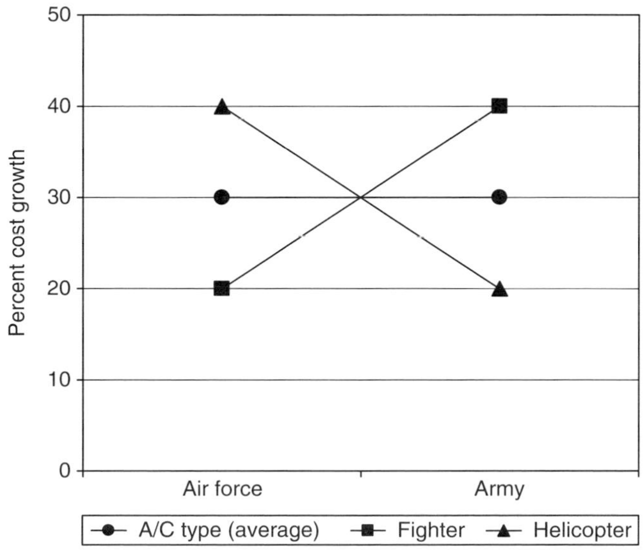

Figure 40.1 Statistical interaction between two model variables.

Figure 40.1. If the interactions are not considered, then the centerline shows the amount of cost growth (30 percent) associated with aircraft type across Air Force and Army. When we consider interactions, we find that the cost growth varies depending on both the aircraft type and the lead service involved (i.e., 40 percent for Air Force helicopters).

40.3 Results

40.3.1 Logistic Regression

The immense number of possible predictor variable combinations makes finding a true "best" logistic model an unattainable goal. So, we set out to produce the most predictive model possible within our resource constraints. Given the enormity of exploring all of the possible combinations, we narrow our predictor combinations to only those that show the most promise as we progress from simple to more complicated models. We begin by regressing all one-variable models and recording the results. From these findings, we select the ten best one-variable models and regress all possible two-variable models that stem from each of those models. Next, we select the nine models that appear most significant from the two-variable results and regress all possible three-variable models that stem from each of those models. We continue, bearing in mind not to violate the suggested 10:1 data point to variable ratio as admonished by Neter et al. (1996: 437).

After many analyses, we pick the model shown in Table 40.1 as our best logistic regression model. This three-variable model's overall p value is less than 0.0001, making us 99.99 percent confident that the presented statistical model is highly predictive. The listed $R^2(U)$ that JMP® uses is the mathematical difference of the negative log likelihood of the fitted model minus the negative log likelihood of the reduced model divided by the negative log likelihood of the reduced model. In other words, this $R^2(U)$ statistic "is the proportion of the total uncertainty that is

Table 40.1 Logistic Regression Results

Model Characteristics		
Overall model *p*-value	<0.0001	
$R^2(U)$	0.831	
Data point/variable ratio	11.67	
Area under ROC curve	0.993	
Predictor Variables		
Variable	*Estimate*	*p-Value*
Intercept	21.61	0.0349
X_1: Class-S	–9.53	0.0689
X_2: Length of prod in funding years	–1.10	0.0390
X_3: FUE-based maturity of EMD percent	–8.58	0.0594

attributed to the model fit (JMP 5.0, 2002: Help)." As with OLS, a value of 0 indicates a weak model and that the explanatory variables have no predictive effect, while an $R^2(U)$ of 1 indicates a perfect fit.

As for the other model characteristics, we do not violate the 10:1 data point to variable ratio. The number of data points a model utilizes is particularly important for two reasons. First, the larger the sample size, the more of our population we capture in our sample. Second, the greater the number of data points, the more predictor variables we can add before the model becomes invalid statistically. According to Neter et al., a model should have at least six to ten data points for every predictor used (Neter et al., 1996: 437). Lastly, we consider the area under the receiver operating characteristic (ROC) curve. According to JMP, the ROC curve maps out the proportion of the true positives out of all actual positives versus the proportion of false positives out of actual negatives, both calculated across all possible calibrations of the model. We classify a true positive as a program incurring cost growth when the model predicts that cost growth will occur. Further, we define a false positive when the model predicts that cost growth will occur, but the program does not incur cost growth. The area under the ROC curve, then, gives an idea of the probability associated with ability of the model to accurately predict whether a program will have cost growth, based on results from the fitted values (Goodman, 1998: Appendix A).

To test the robustness of our logistic model, we use the 25 data points that we randomly selected from the original 122-point data set. Of these 25 data points, however, 21 data points have missing values for some of the variables, overwhelmingly because of FUE-based maturity percent. This leaves only four data points for validation, clearly too small a number. So, we pursue more extensive measures, namely by looking at all the viable data points in our database. Again, the FUE-based variable is a limiter, as mentioned earlier in this chapter. This limitation narrows our "usable" validation pool to 39. The validation process entails saving the functionally predicted values (1 or 0, cost growth or no cost growth) in JMP for each of the validation data points and comparing those predicted values to the actual values. We find the model to be accurate for 37 out of the 39 useable data points (i.e., a 95 percent success rate), establishing that this model has a high degree of predictive ability.

In terms of the actual model's mathematical structure and of a form a user can directly use and incorporate in, perhaps, Microsoft Excel, it takes the following form:

$$\text{Estimated probability of cost growth} = \frac{\exp(XB)}{1+\exp(XB)} \tag{40.1}$$

where

XB would consequently come from the parameter estimates in Table 40.1 and would be represented as, $21.61 - 9.53X_1 - 1.10X_2 - 8.58X_3$

exp refers to the natural exponent function

40.3.2 Ordinary Least Squares Regression

Turning to multiple OLS regression, we build this model for those occasions where a decision maker believes a program will have cost growth and wants to predict the amount of incurred cost growth. We begin model construction with our randomly selected 97 data points and exclude programs that have negative or no cost growth, leaving us with 55 data points. Focusing our efforts on only these points increases the models prediction accuracy, because it prevents data points outside the range of interest from skewing the results. We utilize the same 78 predictor variables as in logistic regression and we consider all possible interactions between variables. For the response variable, Y, we use procurement cost growth percent, which measures the percent increase of procurement cost growth from the development estimate.

Because of what White et al. (2004) discovered before their OLS model building effort, we perform a preliminary analysis of the response variable to ensure that it is continuous in nature. From the results (Figure 40.2), we determine that the Y variable exhibits a lognormal distribution, suggesting

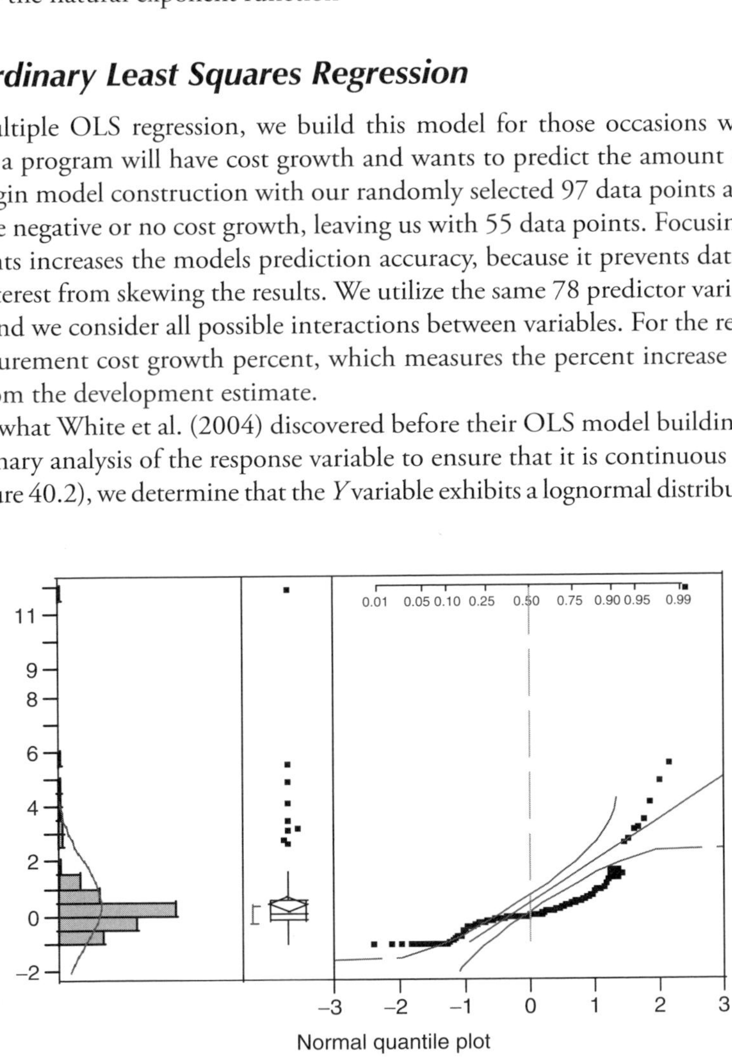

Figure 40.2 Histogram, boxplot, and quantile plot of procurement cost growth (in percent).

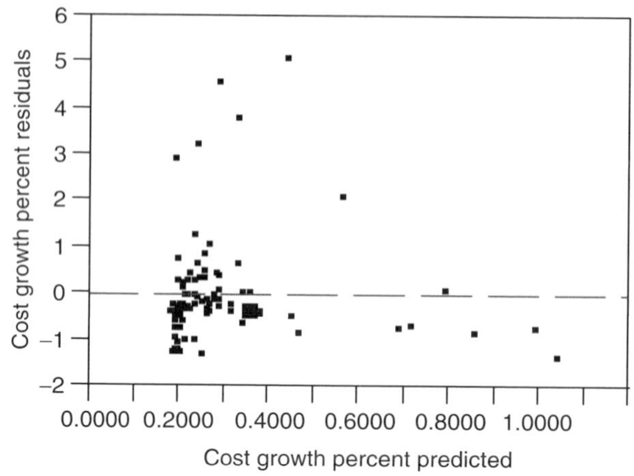

Figure 40.3 Plot of residuals where *Y* = procurement cost growth (in percent).

that it might suffer the same nonconstancy of model residuals alluded to by White et al. (ibid.). We perform a few test regressions and analyze the resulting residual plots (Figure 40.3). The plots fail to pass the visual inspection for constant variance as well as the Breusch–Pagan test (Neter et al., 1996: 112) at an alpha level of 0.05. On the basis of on these findings, we transform the *Y* variable by taking the natural logarithm. This transformation successfully removes the heteroskedasticity (Figure 40.4) previously found and results in a distribution shape that is approximately normal (Figure 40.5). The distribution easily passes the Shapiro–Wilk test for normality at an alpha level of 0.05 considering its *p*-value as 0.85.

We utilize the automated stepwise regression found in JMP to aid us in narrowing the number of possible predictor variable combinations. Because we start with only 55 data points, we limit the number of predictors to six in order to prevent the predictor to data point ratio from going too far

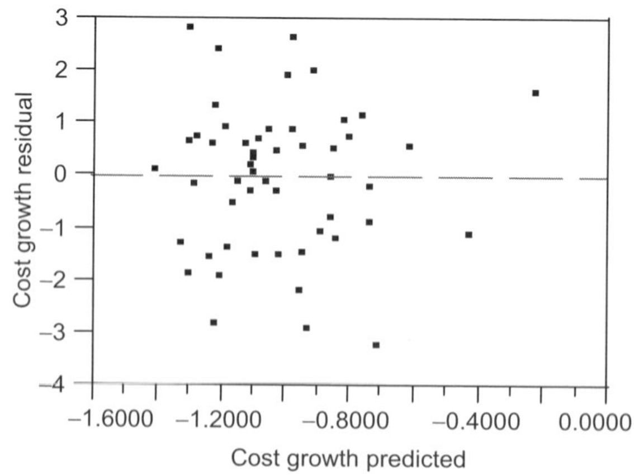

Figure 40.4 Plot of residuals where *Y* = natural logarithm of procurement cost growth.

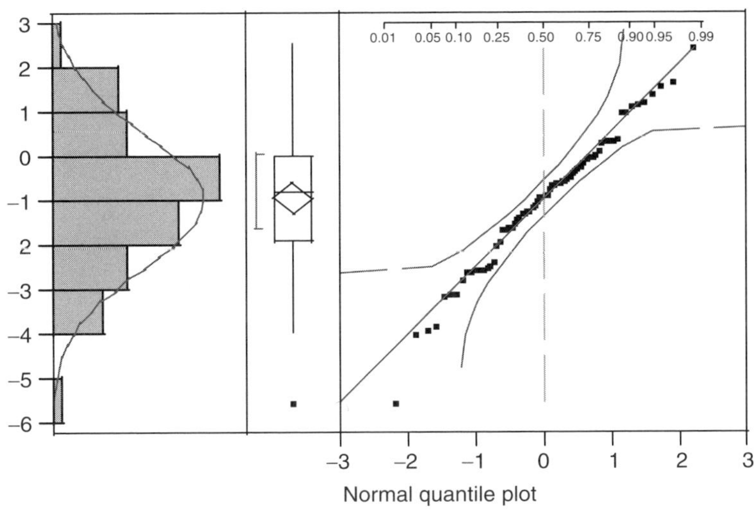

Figure 40.5 Histogram, boxplot, and quantile plot of the natural logarithm of procurement cost growth (in percent).

below ten to one (Neter et al., 1996: 437). Additionally, because we consider all variable interactions, we further constrain all models to contain at least three variables. We then analyze a multitude of regression models for each number of predictors, just as we do for logistic regression, choosing the model that appears to provide the best prediction capability without violating any underlying statistical assumptions. Table 40.2 summarizes the details of our best OLS model.

Table 40.2 Multiple Regression Results

Model Characteristics		
Overall model *p*-value	0.0001	
Adjusted $R^2(U)$	0.595	
Data point/variable ratio	7.33	
Predictor Variables		
Variable	*Estimate*	*p-Value*
Intercept	0.892	0.0967
X_1: FUE-based length of EMD	0.001	0.7787
X_2: Service = army	−0.098	0.8030
X_3: FUE-based length of EMD × (service = army)	0.058	0.0002
X_4: Electronic	−0.569	0.2262
X_5: FUE-based length of EMD × electronic	0.032	0.0189

Although we dip below the desirable 10:1 data point/variable ratio, we still remain above the minimum requirement cutoff of 6:1.

In terms of the actual model's mathematical structure and in a form a user can readily incorporate in an estimating role, again perhaps in Microsoft Excel, it takes the following form:

$$\text{Estimated percent of cost growth} = \exp(XB) \tag{40.2}$$

where XB would consequently come from the parameter estimates in Table 40.2 and would be represented as $-0.892 + 0.001X_1 - 0.098X_2 + 0.058X_3 - 0.569X_4 + 0.032X_5$.

We analyze the resultant model to ensure compliance with the underlying assumptions of constant variance, normality, and independence. We find the model's residuals meet the required assumptions of normality and constant variance at an alpha level of 0.05. Furthermore, we removed all dependent programs during our initial data scrubbing and we find no obvious serial correlation present. Consequently, we assume independence within the data set. As an additional precaution, we investigate all predictors for multicollinearity (i.e., linear redundancy) by ensuring all variance inflation factors as calculated by JMP are less than ten (Neter et al., 1996: 387).

We choose the adjusted R^2 to measure the model's predictive ability over the standard R^2 because of its conservative nature. The customary R^2 value is subject to artificial inflation from simply adding additional independent variables to the model. Adjusted R^2 penalizes the model builder for adding variables that do not significantly increase the models predictive ability. Thus, by utilizing adjusted R^2, we ensure that the variables within our model are significant, and not just used to "pad" the model's apparent predictive ability. The p-values of the individual predictor variables are influenced by the interactions used in the models, and thus are not proper to address individually. However, all of the interaction predictors significantly add to the model at an alpha level of 0.05.

For validation, we use the same candidate data as for logistic regression. Only 17 of the original 25 validation data points have cost growth; the other 8 do not. The 17 represent approximately 25 percent of the programs within the data that contain cost growth. Therefore, we feel reasonably confident in the validation results. During model validation, we realize that only 4 of the 17 data points are usable because of missing data for some of the predictor variables, specifically, FUE-based length of EMD. These results are not surprising as they mirror the results from logistic regression. Thus, we feel confident proceeding with the amalgamated validation process. That is, to further ensure the validity of the results, we perform validation on 100 percent of the data set just as with the logistic regression model.

We create an upper bound for validation as opposed to a prediction interval for practicality reasons. In the cost-estimating environment very few decision makers are concerned with having too much money. Consequently, our goal is to accurately predict the amount of cost growth while ensuring that the program is not underestimated. We consider an 80 percent upper prediction bound. For an 80 percent upper bound, we expect to see approximately 80 percent of the validation data points fall under the bound. From the results of our validation, we determine that for the validation data, our model is 100 percent accurate at a prediction bound of 80 percent. As with the logistic regression, we are confident of our proposed model.

40.4 Conclusion

Defense spending has undergone great change in the last 20 years—large increases during the Reagan administration of the 1980s, and record setting reductions under the Clinton administration of the 1990s. The threat to the security of the United States, however, has not declined; it has merely changed form. This puts the defense acquisition community in the position of having to find ways to do more with less. For this reason, elected representatives, as well as higher ranking members of the DoD, pay close attention to the cost performance of major defense acquisition programs.

In this vein, cost estimators need viable tools to produce better cost estimates. A previous cost growth research by White et al. (2004) established a statistically valid methodology for predicting engineering cost growth in the research and development dollars for the engineering manufacturing development (EMD) phase. In that article, they mention their two-step approach of multiple and logistic regression may crossover to other cost areas. We investigated the plausibility of that with respect to predicting total procurement cost growth during the EMD phase of development and discovered that this methodology works well. In that end, we supplemented the SAR database first constructed by White et al. (2004). From this database, we then constructed, analyzed, and validated cost estimating relationships (CERs) for use by the cost estimating community.

Overall, our presented logistic and multiple regression models perform reasonably well in determining whether a program will have cost growth and, if so, how much expected cost growth (in percent) a program manager might observe. We find that the EMD maturity measure "first unit equipped-based variable" is the proverbial 600-lb gorilla in the statistical models. We also learn that this information is infrequently recorded in the SAR database, perhaps because estimators are unaware of the importance of their contributions to CERs. However, when these variables are present, they appear to be significant predictors of procurement cost growth. As with any on-going research, we do not pretend that our models are the absolute best. However, they do display good predictive capability of procurement cost growth. This ability should allow the program manager to budget dwindling resources with greater confidence, thereby promoting greater credibility of the DoD acquisition community to the American public.

Appendix

Program Size Variables

Total cost CY $M 2002—continuous variable which indicates the total cost of the program in CY $M 2002

Total quantity—continuous variable that indicates the total quantity of the program at the time of the SAR date; if no quantity is specified, we assume a quantity of one (or another appropriate number) unless the program was terminated

Prog acq unit cost—continuous variable that equals the quotient of the total cost and total quantity variables above

Qty during PE—continuous variable that indicates the quantity that was estimated in the planning estimate

Qty planned for R&D—continuous variable that indicates the quantity in the baseline estimate

Physical Type of Program

Domain of Operation Variables

Air—binary variable: 1 for yes and 0 for no; includes programs that primarily operate in the air; includes air-launched tactical missiles and strategic ground-launched or ship-launched missiles

Land—binary variable: 1 for yes and 0 for no; includes tactical ground-launched missiles; does not include strategic ground-launched missiles

Space—binary variable: 1 for yes and 0 for no; includes satellite programs and launch vehicle programs
Sea—binary variable: 1 for yes and 0 for no; includes ships and ship-borne systems other than aircraft and strategic missiles

Function Variables

Electronic—binary variable: 1 for yes and 0 for no; includes all computer programs, communication programs, and electronic warfare programs that do not fit into the other categories
Helo—binary variable: 1 for yes and 0 for no; helicopters; includes V-22 Osprey
Missile—binary variable: 1 for yes and 0 for no; includes all missiles
Aircraft—binary variable: 1 for yes and 0 for no; does not include helicopters
Munition—binary variable: 1 for yes and 0 for no
Land vehicle—binary variable: 1 for yes and 0 for no
Ship—binary variable: 1 for yes and 0 for no; includes all watercraft
Other—binary variable: 1 for yes and 0 for no; any program that does not fit into one of the other function variables

Management Characteristics

Military Service Management

Svs > 1—binary variable: 1 for yes and 0 for no; number of services involved at the date of the SAR
Svs > 2—binary variable: 1 for yes and 0 for no; number of services involved at the date of the SAR
Svs > 3—binary variable: 1 for yes and 0 for no; number of services involved at the date of the SAR
Service = Navy only—binary variable: 1 for yes and 0 for no
Service = Joint—binary variable: 1 for yes and 0 for no
Service = Army only—binary variable: 1 for yes and 0 for no
Service = Air Force only—binary variable: 1 for yes and 0 for no
Lead Svc = Army—binary variable: 1 for yes and 0 for no
Lead Svc = Navy—binary variable: 1 for yes and 0 for no
Lead Svc = DoD—binary variable: 1 for yes and 0 for no
Lead Svc = Air Force—binary variable: 1 for yes and 0 for no
Air Force involvement—binary variable: 1 for yes and 0 for no
Navy involvement—binary variable: 1 for yes and 0 for no
Marine corps involvement—binary variable: 1 for yes and 0 for no
Army involvement—binary variable: 1 for yes and 0 for no

Contractor Characteristics

Lockheed-Martin—binary variable: 1 for yes and 0 for no
Northrop Grumman—binary variable: 1 for yes and 0 for no
Boeing—binary variable: 1 for yes and 0 for no
Raytheon—binary variable: 1 for yes and 0 for no

Litton—binary variable: 1 for yes and 0 for no
General dynamics—binary variable: 1 for yes and 0 for no
No major defense KTR—binary variable: 1 for yes and 0 for no; a program that does not use one of the contractors mentioned immediately above = 1
More than 1 major defense KTR—binary variable: 1 for yes and 0 for no; a program that includes more than one of the contractors listed above = 1
Fixed-price EMD contract—binary variable: 1 for yes and 0 for no

Schedule Characteristics

RDT&E and Procurement Maturity Measures

Maturity (funding years complete)—continuous variable, which indicates the total number of years completed for which the program had RDT&E or procurement funding budgeted
Funding year total program length—continuous variable, which indicates the total number of years for which the program has either RDT&E funding or procurement funding budgeted
Funding years of R&D completed—continuous variable, which indicates the number of years completed for which the program had RDT&E funding budgeted
Funding years of prod completed—continuous variable, which indicates the number of years completed for which the program had procurement funding budgeted
Length of prod in funding years—continuous variable which indicates the number of years for which the program has procurement funding budgeted
Length of R&D in funding years—continuous variable which indicates the number of years for which the program has RDT&E funding budgeted
R&D funding year maturity percent—continuous variable which equals funding years of R&D completed divided by length of R&D in funding years
Proc funding year maturity percent—continuous variable which equals funding years of R&D completed divided by length of prod in funding years
Total funding year maturity percent—continuous variable which equals maturity (funding years complete) divided by funding year total program length

EMD Maturity Measures

Maturity from MS II in mos—continuous variable calculated by subtracting the earliest MS II date indicated from the date of the SAR
Actual length of EMD (MS III-MS II in mos)—continuous variable calculated by subtracting the earliest MS II date from the latest MS III date indicated
MS III-based maturity of EMD percent—continuous variable calculated by dividing maturity from MS II in mos by actual length of EMD (MS III-MS II in mos)
Actual length of EMD using IOC-MS II in mos—continuous variable calculated by subtracting the earliest MS II date from the IOC date
IOC-based maturity of EMD percent—continuous variable calculated by dividing maturity from MS II in mos by Actual Length of EMD using IOC-MS II in mos
Actual length of EMD using FUE-MS II in mos—continuous variable calculated by subtracting the earliest MS II date from the FUE date
FUE-based maturity of EMD percent—continuous variable calculated by dividing maturity from MS II in mos by actual length of EMD using FUE-MS II in mos

Concurrency Indicators

MS III complete—binary variable: 1 for yes and 0 for no

Proc started based on funding years—binary variable: 1 for yes and 0 for no; if procurement funding is budgeted in the year of the SAR or before, then = 1

Proc funding before MS III—binary variable: 1 for yes and 0 for no

Concurrency measure interval—continuous variable which measures the amount of testing still occurring during the production phase in months; actual IOT&E completion minus MS IIIA (Jarvaise et al., 1996: 26)

Concurrency measure percent—continuous variable which measures the percent of testing still occurring during the production phase; (MS IIIA minus actual IOT&E completion) divided by (actual minus planned IOT&E dates) (Jarvaise et al., 1996: 26)

Other Characteristics

product variants in this SAR—continuous variable which indicates the number of versions included in the EMD effort that the current SAR addresses

Class-S—binary variable: 1 for yes and 0 for no; security classification secret

Class-C—binary variable: 1 for yes and 0 for no; security classification confidential

Class-U—binary variable: 1 for yes and 0 for no; security classification unclassified

Class at least S—binary variable: 1 for yes and 0 for no; security classification is secret or higher

Risk mitigation—binary variable: 1 for yes and 0 for no; indicates whether there was a version previous to SAR or significant pre-EMD activities

Versions previous to SAR—binary variable: 1 for yes and 0 for no; indicates whether there was a significant, relevant effort before the DE; a pre-EMD prototype or a previous version of the system would apply

Modification—binary variable: 1 for yes and 0 for no; indicates whether the program is a modification of a previous program

Prototype—binary variable: 1 for yes and 0 for no; indicates whether the program had a prototyping effort

Dem/Val prototype—binary variable: 1 for yes and 0 for no; indicates whether the prototyping effort occurred in the PDRR phase

EMD prototype—binary variable: 1 for yes and 0 for no; indicates whether the prototyping effort occurred in the EMD phase

Did it have a PE—binary variable: 1 for yes and 0 for no; indicates whether the program had a planning estimate

Significant pre-EMD activity immediately before the current version—binary variable: 1 for yes and 0 for no; indicates whether the program had activities in the schedule at least six months before the MSII decision

Did it have an MS I—binary variable: 1 for yes and 0 for no

Terminated—binary variable: 1 for yes and 0 for no; indicates if the program was terminated

Notes

1. Created in 1972, the Office of Secretary of Defense Cost Analysis Improvement Group (OSD CAIG) serves as an advisor to the Armed Services and Congress. Their role is to form an independent cost estimate/assessment for major acquisition programs in addition to that developed by the service program

office governing the acquisition. The CAIG is comprised of OSD cost analysts and senior OSD officials and normally involves key members from the program that is under review.

2. In terms of the government acquisition timeline, the standard order is EMD, Production, and O&S. EMD is normally the riskiest stage of the acquisition process. This is where the program goes through dramatic changes. The item being built goes from drawing/concept to an actual physical product (normally a prototype). Also, it is not uncommon for the initial design to undergo configuration changes either due to user changes or possibly just because of engineering constraints (e.g., cutting-edge technology).
3. Engineering changes are more commonly referred to as engineering change orders (ECOs) and normally equate to approximately 5% of a program's total cost. These changes can result from a shift in the user's requirements (e.g., longer range, more speed, greater load capacity, change in the political arena (i.e., the fall of the Soviet Union for the F/A-22), etc.). More commonly, these changes result from a shortfall in the original system's design or from some advancement in technology. Therefore, changes (ECOs) are required to fulfill the system's operational requirements.
4. These are the largest DoD acquisition programs, and are also known as Major Defense Acquisition Programs (MDAP). To achieve this level of designation, a program must exceed $365 million in research and development funding or exceed $2.190 billion in procurement funding. The Air Force's F/A-22 Raptor and the Marine's V-22 Osprey are two examples of an MDAP.
5. EMD maturity variables are utilized to determine how far a program has progressed into the development stage and how quickly it achieved certain milestones. IOC is the point at which the system in development first achieves operational capability. First unit equipped (FUE) is when the first operational unit is provided to the customer. To calculate a system's maturity, you would determine how far a program was into development when it reached one of these milestones and then divide that by the total length of EMD.
6. Procurement cost growth refers to any growth (schedule slips, estimates changes, engineering changes, etc.) that has affected procurement dollars. This is a categorization of cost growth based on the "color" of money that experiences cost growth. The government uses this saying to designate specific areas where certain portions of funds are designated for specific expenditures. For example, research and development dollars cannot be used to offset procurement expenditures and vice versa. They are deemed to have different "colors" of money.

References

Calcutt, H.M. 1993. Cost growth in DoD major programs: A historical perspective. Executive Research Project. The Industrial College of the Armed Forces, National Defense University, Fort McNair, Washington, D.C.

DAU. 1999. AT&L knowledge sharing system. *Defense Acquisition University*. http://akss.dau.mil/askaprof-akss/normal/qdetail2.asp?cgiSubjectAreaID=9&cgiQuestionID=4171.

DoD. 2001. *Mandatory Procedures for Major Defense Acquisition Programs and Major Automated Information System Acquisition Programs*. DoD 5000.2-R. Washington, D.C.: USD(AT&L).

General Accounting Office (GAO). 2003. TACTICAL AIRCRAFT: DoD Needs to Better Inform Congress about Implications of Continuing F/A-22 Cost Growth, GAO-03-280.

Goodman, C.S. 1998. TA101: Introduction to health care technology assessment. A Presentation Prepared for Health Care Professionals by the Lewin Group. Bethesda, MD: US National Library of Medicine. http://www.nlm.nih.gov/nichsr/ta101/ta101_c1.htm.

Grossman, E. 2002, February 7. Defense Budgets Include $7.4 Billion Boost For Realistic Costing. Early Bird Article. Inside the Pentagon. https://www.asc.wpafb.af.mil/news/earlybird.

Hosmer, D.W. and Lemeshow, S. 2000. *Applied Logistic Regression*, 2nd edn. New York: Wiley & Sons.

Jarvaise, J.M., Drezner, J.A., and Norton, D. 1996. *The Defense System Cost Performance Database: Cost Growth Analysis Using Selected Acquisition Reports*. Santa Monica, CA: RAND (MR-625-OSD).

JMP®. 2002. Version 5.0, (Academic), CD-ROM. Computer software. SAS Institute Inc., Cary, NC.

McCrillis, J. 2003. Cost Growth of Major Defense Programs. Briefing at the 36th Annual DoD Cost Analysis Symposium. Williamsburg, VA.

Neter, J., Kutner, M.H., Nachtsheim, C.J., and Wasserman, W. 1996. *Applied Linear Statistical Models*, 4th edn. Boston, MA: McGraw-Hill.

Sipple, V.P., White, E.D., and Greiner, M.A. 2004. Surveying cost growth, *Defense Acquisition Review Journal*, 11(1), 78–91.

White, E.D., Sipple, V.P., and Greiner, M.A. 2004. Using logistic and multiple regression to estimate engineering costs, *Journal of Cost Analysis and Management*, Summer, 67–79.

Chapter 41

Procurement Design: Lessons from Economic Theory and Illustrations from the Dutch Procurement of Welfare-to-Work Projects[1]

Sander Onderstal and Flóra Felsö

CONTENTS

41.1 Introduction

When a public institution intends to procure a project, it faces the difficult task of finding the procurement mechanism that is most likely to satisfy the institution's goals. The set of potential mechanisms is a priori unbounded, and not sufficiently restricted by legal requirements to make the choice of the optimal mechanism an easy one. For instance, in the European Union, public procurement is subject to community rules, which require public bodies "to follow transparent open procedures ensuring fair conditions of competition for suppliers" (European Commission, 2007). Indeed, there is a large range of transparent, open, and fair allocation mechanisms, and some will be better suited to contribute to the public institution's targets than others. Imagine, for instance, a lottery in which all parties that show interest in completing the project have an equal chance of winning. This mechanism is transparent (the rules are simple and well defined), open (anybody can participate), and fair (all have the same probability to win), but it is very unlikely that it will select the bidder that is best able to finish the project.

For many practical instances, it is well known that in procurement design, the devil is in the details: the success or failure of procurement may depend crucially on the subtleties of its design. In other words, procurement design is not a trivial exercise. In addition, a failure of procurement may fuel arguments in favor of in-house provision, also for projects for which procurement may work very well, if not better. Therefore, the following question begs for an answer: How (not) to design public procurement?

In practice, this question is a very relevant one. In 2002, total expenses on public procurement in the European Union amounted to roughly €1500 billion, i.e., 16 percent of GDP (European Commission, 2007). Similar figures apply to many other developed countries. Of course, the other chapters in this handbook are centered around the same research question as the one above. In the current chapter, we aim to answer it on the basis of lessons from economic theory, in particular auction theory and mechanism design.[2]

We focus on procurement in which the public institution invites several bidders to compete with each other to complete a project. There is a large range of procurement mechanisms, including auctions and beauty contests. In an auction, for instance, the institution could allocate a project to the bidder having the cheapest offer, who could be paid his or her bid once he or she has finished the project. A typical example of a beauty contest is competition on the basis of prototypes. The bidder with the best prototype wins. Other procurement mechanisms are lotteries (the government selects the winner at random among all bidders that show interest in the project), grandfathering (the government directly assigns the project to a preferred supplier), and benchmarking (the government selects a supplier among a set of several on the basis of performance in past projects). We answer the following sub-questions in this chapter:

- Which allocation mechanism is most likely to fulfill the public institution's goals, given the circumstances?
- If the institution decides to use a particular allocation mechanism, what kind of practical things does it have to bear in mind?

We answer these questions in Sections 41.2 and 41.3, respectively. In Section 41.4, we illustrate the main lessons using an example from the Dutch practice, namely procurement of welfare-to-work programs. In the conclusion in Section 41.5, we summarize the main lessons. In addition, we argue that the theory remains silent about many practically important questions. This allows us to finish with several interesting avenues for future research.

41.2 Optimal Procurement Mechanism

In Section 41.1, we mentioned five procurement mechanisms: auctions, beauty contests, benchmarking, grandfathering, and lotteries. Which mechanism is optimal? To answer this question, we need to be more precise about the objective of the government. Hereunder, we assume that the government wishes to select a "supplier" from a set of "bidders" to complete a "project" to maximize "social welfare."[3] Social welfare is higher when (1) the winning bidder delivers a higher quality, (2) the winner requires lesser compensation for completing the project, (3) spin-offs from the project are richer, (4) the government is able to maintain its reputation as a trustworthy party, (5) the organizational costs are lower, (6) the cost of participation is lower, (7) the winning bidder is the most cost efficient, and so forth. Some of these dimensions may be in conflict with each other, so the government faces the difficult task of finding a procurement mechanism that is most likely to result in high social welfare.

As discussed in Section 41.1, there are a large range of mechanisms the government can apply. However, lotteries, grandfathering, and benchmarking will hardly ever be optimal. In the remainder of this chapter, we only focus on auctions and beauty contests. In contrast to lotteries and grandfathering, auctions and beauty contests let several suppliers compete for the project, which forces them to offer high quality for a sharp price. Although competition is present in benchmarking, we believe that auctions and beauty contests perform better because (1) benchmarking could encourage bidders to put socially suboptimal excessive effort in earlier projects, (2) the performance of bidders in different projects is difficult to compare, (3) the possibilities to expropriate the surplus of the supplier are limited, and (4) benchmarking limits the entry of new firms.

The difference between auctions and beauty contests is that in an auction, the winning supplier is selected on the basis of a well-defined rule, whereas in a beauty contest, the selection decision has at least some degree of subjectivity. A typical example of an auction is procurement in which the government selects the winner on the basis of the lowest price to complete the project. A typical beauty contest is a competition in which the most creative, innovative, or imaginative proposal is being selected based on a subjective evaluation of several proposals. This implies that during the evaluation process, there are no well-defined evaluation criteria. Note that a request for bids (RFB) is an auction, and a request for proposals (RFP) a beauty contest.

Note that both an auction and a beauty contest could be multidimensional. Suppose that the government selects that bidder with the highest score $S = wQ - P$, where Q is a quality dimension, P the price the supplier wishes to receive once the project is finished, and w is the weight the government assigns to quality.[10] By calculating wQ, we assign a monetary value to quality level Q. This auction is referred to as the scoring auction. For instance, for the construction of a road, the government could ask a bid on price and the delivery date, where quality is higher the earlier the delivery date.

Also a beauty contest can incorporate multiple criteria including objective ones, such as the price. However, as long as there is at least one criterion that is based subjectively, we refer to these mechanisms as a beauty contest. Cabizza and De Fraja (1998) report on procurement for television franchises, where the seller of the license is concerned with the quality of broadcast program. The contest was organized as a sealed-bid auction, but the seller reserved the right to make a subjective judgment on the quality. In our terminology, this is a beauty contest. Indeed, governments usually turn out to use beauty contests for public procurement.

This observation is remarkable as it seems that economic literature strongly advocates auctions over beauty contests. For instance, Binmore and Klemperer (2002) argue that "the difficulty of specifying and evaluating criteria for a beauty contest makes this a time-consuming and opaque process that leads to political and legal controversy, and the perception, if not reality, of favouritism and corruption. [...] [Moreover], an auction can raise staggering sums of money to support the public finances. [...] A beauty contest, by contrast, can give away valuable assets at a fraction of what they are worth."

However, Binmore and Klemperer's reasoning does not seem to be complete. First, they presume that a monetary bid cannot be part of a beauty contest, whereas clearly it can. Second, in some cases, it is hard to imagine that the government uses an auction because a priori it is simply impossible to define a sensible objective allocation rule. A good example is a research contest in which academics compete for grants on the basis of research proposals. It is difficult to imagine an objective allocation rule which allows the research funding institution to select the most promising proposal.

Indeed, there are good reasons for preferring beauty contests that boil down to the following simple rule:

Lesson 1: Use an auction if all relevant quality dimensions can be defined ex ante. Otherwise, a beauty contest is preferable. Benchmarking, grandfathering, and lotteries are seldom optimal.

This rule does give some credit to researchers who advocate auctions over beauty contests. The starting point is that auctions are the best choice: only if the government cannot specify a well-defined rule by which it can evaluate bids on all relevant quality dimensions, it should use a beauty contest (Dykstra and van der Windt, 2004). There are two motivations for this bias in favor of auctions (Asker and Cantillon, 2008). The first one is that an auction does not have an inherent commitment problem. The first-best mechanism may require that the government employs a minimum value that it wishes to obtain for the project. In an auction, the government may communicate a minimum score to the bidders, because, by definition, the bidders know the scoring rule ex ante. This is, again by definition, impossible in a beauty contest. So, if the scores on all bids turn out to be below the minimum score the government has in mind, it may be very tempting to still assign the project. The second reason why auctions are preferable over beauty contest is that by publishing the scoring rule, the government reveals its preferences over price/quality combinations. In a beauty contest, the bidders have to guess the preference. Asker and Cantillon (2008) show that the winning offer in a beauty contest will turn out to be less favorable than the winning offer in an auction.

41.3 Auction and Beauty Contest Design

Once the government has decided on the selection mechanism, it should fill in the details of the mechanism. In this section, we discuss several lessons from economic theory that relate to the design of auctions and beauty contests. Section 41.3.1 includes lessons that apply to both auctions and beauty contests while Sections 41.3.2 and 41.3.3 focus on lessons that are specific for auctions and beauty contests, respectively.

41.3.1 Auctions and Beauty Contests

Let us first summarize the main lessons from the literature that apply to both auctions and beauty contests.

Lesson 2: There is no one-size-fits-all design

The first lesson is a negative one. Different procurement situations may require different mechanisms (Klemperer, 2002). Two commonly used auction types to select the winner on the basis of price alone are the lowest-price sealed-bid auction and the descending auction. In the lowest-price sealed-bid auction, all bidders independently submit a bid. The lowest bidder wins the project, and receives his or her bid from the government.[4] The descending auction starts with a high price, which is decreased until only one bidder is left. This bidder wins, and the government compensates him with the price at which the runner-up left.[5] The lowest-price sealed-bid auction is usually preferable over the descending auction if competition is "weak" (there are only a few potential bidders, or one bidder has a clear advantage over others). The reason is that in the lowest-price sealed-bid auction, weak bidders have a positive probability to beat a strong bidder, because the latter finds it attractive to bid high, so that he or she may lose against a competitive offer by a weak bidder. By contrast, in a descending auction, the strong bidder will observe the weak bidders' bids, and can always overbid them, so that a weak bidder has zero probability of winning. In symmetric situations with ample competition between strong bidders, the descending auction performs better than the lowest-price sealed-bid one, because it is the former more likely to select the most efficient supplier (Klemperer, 2002).

Lesson 3: The devil is in the details

Details in the procurement environment may highly influence the success of procurement. For instance, the governments of the United Kingdom and the Netherlands employed the same auction type to allocate UMTS[6] licenses. The British auction was considered a huge success: it attracted a new bidder to the market for mobile telecommunications, and raised a staggering £30 billion, or €650 per capita. The auction in the Netherlands was much less successful: the only potential entrant that entered the auction left the auction after threats by one of the incumbents. The auction ended soon after that, at a much lower price than the one in the United Kingdom: €170 per capita. Most economists agree that the key difference between these auctions was the number of bidders with an existing network on the mobile telecommunications markets: there were four bidders in the United Kingdom, and five bidders in the Netherlands. The following lessons will help the designer fill in some of the details that may render procurement a success or a failure.

Lesson 4: Prescreen

An obvious contribution to the success of procurement is that the project, once assigned to a bidder, is completed. In other words, a procurement procedure can be hardly considered successful if the winning bidder defaults on his obligations. However, firms that are on the edge of bankruptcy may find it attractive to enter the contest for the following two reasons. First, they bid for "options on prizes" rather than on "prizes." If the project turns out to be cheaper than expected, they make a nice profit. But if it turns out to be more expensive, the firms will default, which they probably would have done in any case if they had not participated in the contest (Klemperer, 2002). Second, they have an advantage relative to financially healthy firms, because the latter have to take the downward risks of the project into account, and are therefore willing to bid less aggressively than underfinanced firms (Klemperer, 2002). In other words, it is advisable to prescreen the bidders on the basis of their financial position. Nevertheless, it is a good idea to restrict requirements on financial situation to the minimum that is necessary. If the requirement on the minimal annual revenue of the supplier for building an identical road is twice as high in one town than another (a situation that is not uncommon in the Netherlands), then this is a sign that preselection rules are applied in a rather arbitrary manner.

A different type of prescreening is based on bidders' experience or reputation. Although experience and reputation are good signals of capability of carrying out a project, the procurement agency should be careful about the requirements being too restricting. We advocate against using experience or reputation for the same reasons that we have advocated against selection on the basis of benchmarking (see Section 41.2). Still, it could be advisable to exclude a blacklist of bidders who performed extremely poorly in past projects.

Lesson 5: Keep the cost of entering the procurement as low as possible

Usually, participation in procurement is not without costs for the bidders. They have to gather information on the project, prepare a bidding strategy, and submit bids. The government may affect each of these. It may reveal information about the project, apply simple or complex auction rules, and require a bid that is just a single number (e.g., the price) or a business plan consisting of several pages. Because the driving force behind the success of procurement is competition between bidders, the more bidders enter the contest, the more likely the end result is satisfactory for the government. Therefore, it makes sense for the government to keep the entry costs as low as possible (Milgrom, 2004). Still, sometimes it is better to exclude some bidders, particularly those who are close to bankruptcy (see Lesson 4), or to only let a limited number of preferred suppliers compete in a beauty contest (see Lesson 14). However, high entry costs are unlikely to select just those bidders the government wishes to enter.

Lesson 6: Avoid collusion

The key idea behind using either an auction or a beauty contest is that competition between bidders results in high quality for a sharp price. These benefits may be easily lost if bidders manage to form a cartel, and make agreements to keep the price high, or quality low (Klemperer, 2002; Salmon, 2004). Although collusion is a violation of the competition law, the literature offers many examples of successful cartels in procurement. For instance, Pesendorfer (2000) describes collusion among bidders for school milk contracts, and Boone et al. (2006) report on a large-scale cartel in Dutch construction procurement. Motta (2004) argues that "it is better to create an environment that discourages collusion in the first place than trying to prove unlawful behaviour afterwards." This is especially relevant in public procurement where the main target of the procurement agency is to get the project done and promoting competition is just a means of achieving that in the most efficient way. Therefore, the procurement agency suspecting anticompetitive behavior is inclined not to report unlawful behavior because of the possibility that the procurement is being stopped by the competition authority.

How to prevent collusive behavior? We see later that the government may impose a sharp maximum price or minimum score to prevent collusion. Moreover, Robinson (1985) argues that the lowest-price sealed-bid auction is less conducive to collusion than the descending auction. The reason is that in the latter, the "designated winner" can still react if a cartel member deviates from the agreement by submitting a bid below the agreed price by bidding an even lower price. This is not possible in the sealed-bid auction, because each bid is "once and for all."

Lesson 7: Reveal all relevant information

There are at least three reasons that the government may reveal information that is relevant for the bidders when preparing a bid on the project (Klemperer, 2002; Milgrom, 2004). First, this information may reduce uncertainty about the costs to complete the project, which reduces the risk premium that has to be paid to the winner. Second, the revealed information reduces the risk on the winner's curse, i.e., the winner finding out after the auction that his bid was too optimistic. If the government is hesitant in publishing relevant information, bidders will take into account that they may fall prey to the winner's curse, and may be cautious in bidding. Third, all information revealed about the rules of the auction (scoring rule, maximum bid) strengthen the government's commitment to the rules. Suppose that the government has a maximum price in mind above which the project will not be assigned. If the government does not announce the maximum price, it may feel tempted to accept a bid just above this price if it does not receive lower bids. The bidders will take this into account, and will bid less aggressively (see also Lesson 11).

In practice, some procurement agencies apply communication rules that ensure that each bidder has the same information. For instance, bidders are allowed to ask questions on the project and they are being answered extensively. All competitors are informed of the questions and the answers. The disclosure of information on the maximum price could, however, lead to a problem. A procurement agency announcing a maximum price should bear in mind that the announced maximum price could easily become the focal price, inducing each competitor to charge the same price and competition being restricted to the other dimensions of the auction or beauty contest.

Lesson 8: In the case of asymmetries, give weak bidders an advantage

In many procurement situations, one bidder (usually the incumbent party) has a clear advantage over other bidders. Because weak bidders may judge it unlikely to beat the strong bidder, they may refrain from bidding at all, so that the incumbent party faces little competition in the contest. The government may stir up competition by giving an advantage to weak bidders. One way of doing this is giving bidding credits to weak bidders (Myerson, 1981). For instance, if a weak (strong) bidder wins, he receives 120 percent (100 percent) of the price that he offered.

However, such bidding credits could be in conflict with EU state aid law (Maasland et al., 2004). Whether or not this is the case depends on the standard with which the "(potential) distortion of competition" criterion is applied: although economists have stressed the importance of using a "total welfare standard" for testing whether there is a distortion of competition, in the practice of state aid cases it is often the "(negative) effect on rivals standard" that is used.[7] Such problems do not arise outside the EU, as other countries are not concerned of interstate trade and state aid to this degree.

If the government is restricted to nondiscriminatory rules, the lowest-price sealed-bid auction may attract more bidders than the descending auction. The reason is that the lowest-price sealed-bid auction is more likely to allocate the project to a weak bidder than the descending auction (as we argued in our motivation to Lesson 2). Another way to attract weak bidders to the contest, and (hence) encourage competition is to give a premium to the runner-up for driving down the price (Goeree and Offerman, 2004; Milgrom, 2004).

Lesson 9: Provide ex-post incentives

The government should give the winning supplier incentives to complete the project as satisfactorily as possible. For instance, if the government cares about the time of completion of the project, the supplier should be rewarded (or punished) if he completes the project before (or after) the deadline. Moreover, to avoid overly optimistic bids, the government should force the winning bidder to fulfill the promises he makes in the contest. If not, bidders are tempted to promise the sky, so that the bids amount to cheap talk and in turn lose discriminatory power (see also Lesson 10). Of course, the government should announce before the contest that these incentives will be provided (cf. Lesson 7).

Lesson 10: Fix the winning bid in a contract

To avoid "cheap talk bids," the winning bid should be fixed in a contract. Consequently, no decision should be based on criteria that are not ex post contractible (Janssen, 2004). If the desired quality is not contractible (perhaps because it is not measurable), then one should not base the decision on that criterion.

Lesson 11: Commit to the rules

Sometimes, the government may be tempted to change the rules during or after the contest. For instance, if a bidder violates the rules, the government may be reluctant to exclude this bidder from the auction, especially if it results in a less favorable outcome of the auction. Moreover, in the case of a bidding cap (see Lesson 13), the project may remain unassigned if none of the bidders beats the cap. It may be tempting to organize a new contest with a looser bidding cap. However, the government's reputation in future contests may be at stake if it breaks its own rules. So, for its future credibility, commitment to the rules is of the highest importance (Klemperer, 2002; van Damme, 2002).

41.3.2 Auctions

The following lessons apply to auctions alone (and not necessarily to beauty contests).

Lesson 12: Attract as many bidders as possible

The starting point of any auction (or procurement mechanism in general) is to attract bidders, because "an auction can hardly be considered optimal if no bidders choose to participate" (Milgrom, 2004). So each auction should start with a marketing campaign to attract bidders. Generally, the more bidders the better.[8] Many issues are automatically resolved if many bidders participate in the auction. For instance, it is much harder to collude with many bidders than with a few (see Lesson 6). Moreover, it is less important for the seller to impose a tight bidding cap (Lesson 13), because competition between bidders will encourage them to bid aggressively in any case. In addition, if many strong bidders enter the auction, it is not necessary to favor the weak ones (Lesson 8). Next to a marketing campaign that informs potential bidders that the government will organize an auction, the government can make entering the auction attractive by keeping bidding costs low (Lesson 5) and using transparent and fair rules (Milgrom, 2004).

Lesson 13: Impose a bidding cap

Imposing a bidding cap in the sense of a maximum price or minimum score is a good policy for at least three reasons. First, for any project, there is a maximum price the government is willing to pay for the project to be completed. Bids above this price should not be accepted. Second, the government may impose an even lower maximum price to discourage collusion (see Lesson 6). The lower the maximum price, the less attractive is the collusion, because the lower are the spoils that the cartel members can divide among themselves. Third, a tight bidding cap stirs up competition, so that the government may expect a better offer for the project. Note, however, that the government faces the risk of not assigning the project if it imposes a tight bidding cap. Politically, it may be difficult to sell that a welfare-enhancing project is not started. Moreover, the government may feel tempted to organize a new contest with a looser bidding cap, which may destroy its reputation in future contests (see also Lesson 11).

41.3.3 Beauty Contests

Before we discuss some specific lessons for beauty contest design, let us classify beauty contests along the following two dimensions. The first one is open versus closed. In an open beauty contest, anybody is allowed to participate while in a closed beauty contest only a small set of preselected bidders can participate. The second dimension is weighted versus unweighted. In a weighted beauty contest, bidders know in advance the criteria on which their proposal will be assessed and what weights will be assigned to the different criteria, whereas in unweighted beauty contest, the bidders do not know the criteria in advance. EU tenders on research are a good example of open weighted beauty contests. The call for proposal contains a detailed list of criteria and specifies extensively how the criteria are defined and weighted.

Lesson 14: Use a closed beauty contest if the effort that is invested in the bid has a positive effect on ex-post quality, and an open one otherwise

If the awarding authority wants contestants to put effort in their proposals, it does well restricting the number of contestants. Classic examples of these beauty contests are architectural design contests, competition for research grants, and high-technology defense equipment. In the restricted tender, there is a prequalification phase where the awarding authority determines who is entitled to participate. Knowing that there are only a limited number of competitors, contestants "run harder" and submit higher quality proposals. The other way around, if there are many contestants, the chances of winning the contest are low, so contestants could be reluctant to put a lot of effort in the proposal. Che and Gale (2003) show that it may be optimal to invite as few as two bidders. Indeed, for the procurement of the Joint Strike Fighter, only two prototypes were invited.

In contrast, if bidders sell products or services that are standardized within their firm, an open contest is preferable. The arguments are the same as in why the government should attract many bidders in an auction (see Lesson 12). For example, a firm supplying telephone interview services can complete an offer for a telephone survey of 500 households in an hour's time. Each firm supplying telephone interview services have standardized offers. In this case, there is no need to restrict the number of bidders.

Lesson 15: Make the rules as simple and transparent as possible

The rules of a beauty contest should be simple and transparent. Simple and transparent rules (1) induce a high probability that the government selects the best offer, (2) result in low bidding costs (cf. Lesson 5), (3) result in a quick and easy selection process when the government evaluates the bids, (4) render it unlikely that bidders make mistakes, (5) keep the probability on a lawsuit after the auction low, and (6) discipline the awarding authority to commit to the rules (cf. Lesson 11). In contrast to this lesson, sometimes procurement agencies require pages-long bid-books from the bidders, contributing neither to the simplicity nor to the transparency of the contest. The above lesson implies that weighted beauty contests are a priori better than unweighted ones, because the former are more transparent. However, the question is to what extent can one determine the weights ex ante. A procurement agency organizes a beauty contest because it wants to invite creativity. The bidders are often better informed than the awarding authority, so that the awarding authority needs to learn from the bids. So, it is often easier to compare the proposals or the prototypes rather than try to devise rules and weights ex ante.

41.4 Case Study: Procurement of Welfare-to-Work Projects in the Netherlands

In this section, we discuss procurement of welfare-to-work projects in the Netherlands to illustrate several lessons from the previous two sections. In several countries, governments use procurement to allocate welfare-to-work projects.[9] The bidders in these contests are employment service providers. A welfare-to-work project encompasses all sorts of trainings and coaching that improve the employability skills of unemployed people. Welfare-to-work projects typically consist of many unemployed people, and the winning provider is rewarded on the basis of the number of these people who find a job within a specified period. The success of a welfare-to-work project depends on (1) the number of people who find a job, (2) the costs incurred by the employment service provider, (3) the reduction in unemployment benefits, and (4) the payments made from the government to the employment service provider. The latter two are important as they imply that the government raises less distortionary taxes.

In reaching these targets, governments may be confronted with two types of economic problems: adverse selection and moral hazard. Adverse selection occurs when the procurement does not select the best employment provider, i.e., the provider that, relative to all other providers, is able to help the unemployed people back to work in the most cost-efficient way. There might be a moral hazard as the winner of the procurement has no incentive to put much effort in the welfare-to-work project. An additional target may be a cheap procurement process.

Most governments that procure welfare-to-work projects use a beauty contest. Table 41.1 shows a typical scoring slide that we have modeled after the procurement rules that were employed by the

Table 41.1 Fictitious Scoring Card for Welfare-to-Work Procurement by Dutch Public Institution UWV

Evaluation Criteria	*Scores*			
Experience (target group and region)	None = 5	Some = 10	Sufficient = 15	Ample = 20
Experience (region)	None = 4	Some = 6	Sufficient = 8	Ample = 10
Reward per placement (in €100)	>39 = 0	34–39 = 10	27–33 = 20	<27 = 30
Placement fraction after six months	30–35 percent = 0	36–40 percent = 5	41–45 percent = 10	>45 percent = 15
Placement fraction after 12 months	60–65 percent = 5	65–70 percent = 10	71–75 percent = 20	>75 percent = 25

Dutch social security agency, UWV, around 2002. The rules are as follows. Employment service providers submit an offer that contains a bid on several prespecified dimensions (five in this example). On each dimension, a bidder obtains a score. The sum of the scores on each dimension results in the total score. The bidder with the highest total score wins the project.

Let us discuss the five dimensions of the scoring card in Table 41.1. The first refers to experience with the target group. UWV subdivided all unemployed people who were eligible to participate in a welfare-to-work program in groups on the basis of age, profession, type of handicap (if applicable), and so forth. The score on the dimension "experience with the target group" depends on how well the bidder dealt with similar groups in the past, if at all. Similarly, "experience with the region" refers to how well the bidder dealt with unemployed people in the region in which the people in the current project live. The next dimension, "reward per placement," is the amount the bidder wishes to receive for each person in his project who finds a job in a prespecified period. The final two dimensions are related to the minimum fraction of people in the project whom the bidder promises to find a job for in six and twelve months, respectively.

There are several reasons why this beauty contest is unlikely to yield satisfactory results. In particular, UWV did not seem to have taken several of the lessons discussed in Sections 41.2 and 41.3 into account. Let us start with Lesson 1 (use an auction if all relevant quality dimensions can be defined ex ante). Quality in the context of welfare-to-work projects can be defined as, for instance, the number of people who find a job or the reduction in unemployment benefits during the time of the project. Both can easily define ex ante, so that an auction is preferable over a beauty contest. This reasoning implies that the first two dimensions should not be part of the selection procedure, because they are subjective.

The design also violates Lessons 5 (keep the entry costs low) and 15 (the mechanism should be as simple and transparent as possible). A bid typically consisted of 40 pages in which the bidder motivated how he gained experience with the target group and in the region. So, for a bidder it was costly and time consuming to enter the contest, whereas for UWV it was not easy to identify the best bidder. Once again, the conclusion is that the first two subjective dimensions should be left out of the contest.

Then consider Lesson 7 (reveal all relevant information). To avoid strategic bidding, UWV did not announce a priori how it mapped bids into scores. It only communicated the dimensions to the bidders, and the maximum score they could obtain on each dimension. Given the design, UWV's reason for doing so is not surprising; because the scores make jumps at certain thresholds, revealing the scoring rule would have resulted in bids at exactly these thresholds. However, being unclear about how bids will map into a final score, bidders have to guess where these thresholds are, which reduces the probability that the best bidder wins. Not using steps but a continuous mapping, and communicating the rules to the bidders would have substantially improved UWV's design.

Finally, let us consider Lessons 9 (provide ex-post incentives) and 10 (fix the winning bid in a contract). At first sight, the winner obtains ex-post incentives in the sense that for each placement, he will be rewarded the amount that he bid on the third dimension in Table 41.1. However, it does not seem to be a good idea to let bidders bid on this dimension. Why not? Suppose that the reward is the only dimension. Then the lowest bidder wins. This gives rise to a "race to the bottom," resulting in a low price, which hardly provides incentives to find a job for the unemployed in the project. Relatedly, the final two dimensions amount to cheap talk because UWV did not punish (reward) the winner if its placement rate was below (above) the threshold that he bid. In other words, bidders had an incentive to promise the sky on these dimensions, so that it lost its discriminatory power.

Indeed, UWV's procurement was not considered extremely successful. Bidders complained that it was costly and time consuming to prepare a bid, while ex post, it was not always clear why a certain bid had won. UWV, in turn, was frustrated because some bidders made unrealistic promises and beat other bidders that seemed more capable of doing the job. Winning bidders had little incentives to fulfill their promises, because they had been engaged in a race to the bottom on the reward per placement dimension.

OECD (2001) proposes "the constant-reward auction" as an alternative to UWV's beauty contest. This auction follows the following rules. UWV sells the project to the highest bidder and pays the winner a fixed reward for each person in the project who finds a job within a prespecified period. Onderstal (2006) shows that the constant-reward auction solves the adverse selection problem because the winner is always the most efficient provider. Moreover, the moral hazard problem is almost absent because the winning provider's output approximates the output in the socially optimal mechanism. Finally, the constant-reward auction is easy to implement in practice, in contrast to the optimal mechanism.

41.5 Conclusion

In this chapter, we discussed several valuable lessons from economic theory for the design of procurement mechanisms. We summarized these lessons in Table 41.2. Our case study shows that if the public institution does not take these lessons into account, procurement may lead to unsatisfactory results, from both the institution's and the bidders' point of view.

Although these lessons can be extremely useful for procurement design in practice, several practically important questions remain unanswered. Let us mention three of these questions. First, how to define the optimal scoring rule in an auction? It is often the case that the procurement agency has little information on what the right minimal or optimal quality should be, or equivalently what the "right" trade-off between quality and price should be. These are aspects a procurement agency should be very clear about as it should be unambiguous on what project suppliers are bidding for. Bounded rationality models in which the government is, to some extent, unaware of its preference before it obtains the bids may be useful in answering the above question.

Table 41.2 Main Lessons for Procurement Design

Scope	*Lesson*
Optimal procurement mechanism	1. Use an auction if all relevant quality dimensions can be defined ex ante. Otherwise a beauty contest is preferable. Benchmarking, grandfathering, and lotteries are seldom optimal
Lessons for both auctions and beauty contests	2. There is no one-size-fits-all design 3. Devil is in the details 4. Prescreen 5. Keep the cost of entering the procurement as low as possible 6. Avoid collusion 7. Reveal all relevant information 8. In the case of asymmetries, give weak bidders an advantage 9. Provide ex-post incentives 10. Fix the winning bid in a contract 11. Commit to the rules
Specific lessons for auctions	12. Attract as many bidders as possible 13. Impose a bidding cap
Specific lessons for beauty contests	14. Use a closed beauty contest if the effort that is invested in the bid has a positive effect on ex-post quality, and an open one otherwise 15. Make the rules as simple and transparent as possible

Second, which criteria to use in a beauty contest and how to evaluate them? Apart from the above, rather general lessons, the literature remains silent about this question. Indeed, most of the theoretical literature focuses on auctions rather than beauty contests. This question opens an interesting avenue for future theoretical research, which could supplement the many practical issues on beauty contest design that are raised in the other chapters in this handbook.

Third, how to allocate multiple projects? So far, we have only looked at cases where the government assigns a single project. In the case of multiple projects, procurement design may be even more challenging. In practice, the government often wishes to assign several related projects. Collusion may become an increasingly serious problem, because this allows bidders to "divide the market" and to punish a cartel member in later contests if he deviates from the cartel agreement in an earlier one. Moreover, synergies between projects may call for combinatorial bids. In the past few years, the focus in auction theory has switched from mainly single-object auctions to multiple-object ones, so the lessons from this branch of the literature could be very relevant for procurement design as well (Krishna, 2002; Milgrom, 2004).

Before these, and other, questions are answered, designing good procurement mechanisms remains an area for expert economists. In the past decade, being advisors in spectrum auctions in the United States and in Europe, economists have become increasingly experienced in designing tailor-made allocation mechanisms. Let us, therefore, conclude with the words of Wilson (2002) in his article Architecture of Power Markets:

> The normative tone [of this article] reflects the increased role of economics as an engineering discipline capable of providing guidance on details of market design. This role grew as game theory and derivative theories of incentives and information expanded economists' tools to include methodologies for predicting how procedural aspects influence participants' strategies and affect overall performance. Part of this toolkit pertains to the standard concerns of economic policy such as productive and allocative efficiency and mitigation of market power; another part is like law in its concern for closing loopholes in procedural rules and avoiding "screwups;" and another concerns experimental testing ex ante and empirical analysis ex post. I intend my title to convey its double meaning-*architecture* as a description of the main structural features of a market, and *architecture* as the professional discipline that designs those features using a body of theory and practical skills.

Notes

1. We wish to thank Emiel Maasland and Koert van Buiren for useful comments on an earlier version of this chapter.
2. For excellent overviews of auction theory and its role in auction design see Krishna (2002), Klemperer (2004), and Milgrom (2004).
3. Note that we restrict our attention to situations where the government allocates a single project. In the conclusion, we shortly discuss practical issues that may arise if the government wishes to outsource several projects.
4. This auction is equivalent to the first-price sealed-bid auction in the case that an auctioneer sells an object.
5. This auction is equivalent to the ascending or English auction in the case that an auctioneer sells an object.
6. Universal Mobile Telecommunication Services: a third-generation mobile telecommunications standard.
7. In addition to a "distortion of competition" and "affecting trade between member states," for being incompatible with the common market, the state aid measure should also be selective, financed through state resources (in any form whatsoever). A selective bidding credit is by definition selective and as we focus on public procurement, it is financed from state resources.
8. An exception is a project with a strong risk on the winner's curse. Increased competition may result in less attractive bids (Bulow and Klemperer, 2002).
9. See OECD (2001) and Productivity Commission (2002) for Australia, and OECD (2003) for the Netherlands. Bruttel (2004) and SEO and TNO (2004) provide a comparison of welfare-to-work procurements in Australia, the Netherlands, and the United Kingdom. In addition, SEO and TNO (2004) examine the procurements in Denmark, Sweden, and the United States.
10. By calculating wQ. (Q is a measure for the offered quality, let's say a number between 0 and 10. w is a measure for the monetary value per quality unit. So, if Q=7 and w=\$10,000, wQ=\$70,000. If P=\$60,000, the bidder's score $S=wQ-P$=\$10,000.)

References

Asker, J. and E. Cantillon 2008. Properties of scoring auctions, *The RAND Journal of Economics*, forthcoming.

Binmore, K. and P. Klemperer 2002. The biggest auction ever: The sale of the British 3G Telecom Licences, *Economic Journal* 112, C74–C96.

Boone, J., R. Chen, J.K. Goeree, and A. Polydoro 2006. Risky procurement with an insider bidder, working paper, California Institute of Technology.

Bruttel, O. 2004. Contracting-out the public employment service and the consequence for hard-to-place jobseekers: Experiences from Australia, the Netherlands and the UK. Paper presented at the Second Annual ESPAnet Conference, University of Oxford.

Bulow, J.I. and P.D. Klemperer 2002. Prices and the winner's curse, *The RAND Journal of Economics* 33, 1–21.

Cabizza, M.M. and G. De Fraja 1998. Quality considerations in auctions for television franchises, *Information Economics and Policy* 10, 9–22.

Che, Y.-K. and I. Gale 2003. Optimal design of research contests, *American Economic Review* 93, 646–671.

Dykstra, M. and N. van der Windt 2004. Beauty contest design, in M.C.W. Janssen (Ed.), *Auctioning Public Assets: Analysis and Alternatives*. Cambridge: Cambridge University Press.

European Commission 2007. Public procurement. Downloaded on February 20, 2007 from http://ec.europa.eu/internal_market/publicprocurement/index_en.htm.

Goeree, J.K. and T. Offerman 2004. The Amsterdam auction, *Econometrica* 72, 281–294.

Janssen, M.C.W. 2004. Introduction, in M.C.W. Janssen (Ed.), *Auctioning Public Assets: Analysis and Alternatives*. Cambridge: Cambridge University Press.

Klemperer, P. 2002. What really matters in auction design, *Journal of Economic Perspectives* 16, 169–190.

Klemperer, P. 2004. *Auctions: Theory and Practice*. Princeton New Jersey: Princeton University Press.

Krishna, V. 2002. *Auction Theory*. San Diego: Academic Press.

Maasland, E., Y. Montangie, and R. van den Bergh 2004. Levelling the playing field in auctions and the prohibition of state aid, in M.C.W. Janssen (Ed.), *Auctioning Public Assets: Analysis and Alternatives*. Cambridge: Cambridge University Press.

Milgrom, P. 2004. *Putting Auction Theory to Work*. Cambridge: Cambridge University Press.

Motta, M. 2004. *Competition Policy—Theory and Practice*. New York: Cambridge University Press.

OECD 2001. *Innovations in Labour Market Policies: The Australian Way*. Paris, France: OECD.

OECD 2003. The competitive market for employment services in the Netherlands. OECD Social, Employment and Migration Working Papers 13, Paris, France.

Onderstal, S. 2006. Bidding for the unemployed: An application of mechanism design to welfare-to-work programs. Mimeo, University of Amsterdam.

Pesendorfer, M. 2000. A study of collusion in first-price auctions. *Review of Economic Studies* 67, 381–411.

Productivity Commission 2002. Independent Review of Job Network, Report Nr. 21, Canberra, Australia.

Robinson, M.S. 1985. Collusion and the choice of auction. *RAND Journal of Economics* 16, 141–145.

Salmon, T. 2004. Preventing collusion between firms in auctions, in M.C.W. Janssen (Ed.), *Auctioning Public Assets: Analysis and Alternatives*. Cambridge: Cambridge University Press.

SEO and TNO 2004, *Buitenlandse Ervaringen met de Aanbesteding van Reïntegratiediensten* (*Foreign Experiences with Welfare-to-Work Procurement*, in Dutch). Amsterdam: SEO Economisch Onderzoek.

van Damme, E. 2002. The European UMTS-auctions, *European Economic Review* 46, 846–869.

Wilson, R. 2002. Architecture of power markets, *Econometrica* 70, 1299–1340.

Index

C

D

M

N

O

P

Q

R

S

T

U

V

W